# Disability Rights Handbook

43rd Edition
April 2018 – April 2019

by Ian Greaves

# Disability Rights UK

## About Disability Rights UK

We are disabled people leading change, working for equal participation for all. Disability Rights UK is led by people with diverse experiences of disability and health conditions from different communities. We work with allies committed to equal participation for all. Together we can be stronger.

It has never been more important to have a strong organisation that stands up for disabled people's rights and support. We enable disabled people to have voice and influence. We 'show, not tell' how participation can be made real, working with other disabled people's organisations to showcase approaches to social, economic and public participation. We campaign to strengthen and protect disabled people's rights, influencing national and local decision makers.

Our priorities for 2016-19 are:
- independent living – getting a life;
- career opportunities – getting work, education and skills;
- influencing public attitudes and behaviours – seeking a sea change in perceptions of disability and tackling hostility, bullying and hate crime.

We produce user-friendly guides to benefits and independent living and publish the *Disability Rights Handbook* annually. Our website contains a wealth of information about benefit entitlement, independent living and careers, with downloadable factsheets, as well as more detailed information for professional advisers – including briefings and policy reports on the issues that matter most to disabled people.

## Membership of Disability Rights UK

We encourage individuals and all organisations – whether statutory, voluntary or corporate – to support our work by becoming members of Disability Rights UK.

## Acknowledgements

We would like to thank the contributors to this edition of the handbook for their valuable work. Thanks also to colleagues at Disability Rights UK for their work on sales administration and distribution and to the production team for their professional support and high-quality work. Special acknowledgements go to Judith Paterson, who wrote the *Disability Rights Handbook* from the 19th through to the 26th edition, and to her predecessor Sally Robertson.

This edition is dedicated to the memory of Peter Townsend, Disability Alliance's founder and President, without whom the *Disability Rights Handbook* would not exist. Peter spent his life working tirelessly to highlight the unacceptable levels of poverty experienced by disabled people and their families, and he is sorely missed by all those striving to maintain his impressive legacy.

## Disclaimer

We do our best to ensure the information in the handbook is correct. However, changes in the law after April 2018 might affect the accuracy of some of the information. Where this could be important to you, you should check the details with a local advice centre or the Department for Work and Pensions.

If you think anything in this handbook is incorrect, please write and tell us. Thanks to all those who wrote to us this year with comments; your contributions are always very welcome.

**Editor**
Ian Greaves

**Contributors**
Jane Booth
Mike Ellison
Richard Forrest
Carlos Hagi
Daphne Hall
Sandie Lock
Simon Robinson
Desmond Rutledge
Fiona Seymour
Kate Smith
Tony Stevens
Victoria Todd
Joanne Walker
Rebecca Walker
Sharron West
Helen Winfield

**Index checkers**
Ben Kersey and
Michael Paul
(Disability Rights UK)

**Sales administration and distribution**
Chelsey French
Jason Jaspal
Steve Newsham
Michael White

**Production**
Copyediting:
Mary Snell
Design/production management:
Deb Kamofsky,
Anderson Fraser
Typesetting:
Humphrey Weightman

**Disability Rights Handbook**
43rd Edition
April 2018 - April 2019
ISBN: 978-1-903335-78-9
£33.99 (£18.50 concessions)

Donations, sponsorship and advertising help fund our work. Acceptance of advertising, sponsorship or editorial reference should not be interpreted as an endorsement of the commercial firms involved. If you are interested in sponsoring one of our publications or placing an advertisement, please get in touch.

**Published by**
Disability Rights UK © 2018
Registered Charity No 1138585

Disability Rights UK
Plexal
14 East Bay Lane
Here East
Queen Elizabeth Olympic Park
Stratford
London E20 3BS
Telephone 0330 995 0400
www.disabilityrightsuk.org

# Contents

| Reference | | Benefit rates | Inside front cover |
|---|---|---|---|
| | | Benefits checklist | 4-5 |
| | | Legal references | 6-7 |
| | | Abbreviations | 8 |

| Section | A | Overview | |
|---|---|---|---|
| Chapters | 1 | Introduction | 9 |
| | 2 | The benefits system | 9 |
| | 3 | Your right to equal treatment | 11 |

| Section | B | Care and mobility | |
|---|---|---|---|
| Chapters | 4 | Disability living allowance | 16 |
| | 5 | Personal independence payment | 30 |
| | 6 | Attendance allowance | 46 |
| | 7 | Help with mobility | 55 |

| Section | C | Help for carers | |
|---|---|---|---|
| Chapters | 8 | Carer's allowance | 58 |
| | 9 | Other help for carers | 62 |

| Section | D | Not in work? | |
|---|---|---|---|
| Chapters | 10 | Statutory sick pay | 64 |
| | 11 | Employment and support allowance | 68 |
| | 12 | The work capability assessment | 82 |
| | 13 | Jobseeker's allowance | 97 |

| Section | E | Universal credit | |
|---|---|---|---|
| Chapters | 14 | Universal credit | 106 |
| | 15 | Your responsibilities | 110 |
| | 16 | Calculating universal credit | 121 |
| | 17 | Earnings, income and capital | 126 |

| Section | F | Means-tested benefits (pre-universal credit) | |
|---|---|---|---|
| Chapters | 18 | Income-related ESA | 132 |
| | 19 | Income support | 134 |
| | 20 | Income-based jobseeker's allowance | 138 |
| | 21 | Premiums | 139 |
| | 22 | Income and capital | 143 |
| | 23 | Tax credits | 154 |

| Section | G | Help with housing costs | |
|---|---|---|---|
| Chapters | 24 | Universal credit housing costs amount | 165 |
| | 25 | Housing benefit | 175 |
| | 26 | Support for mortgage interest loans | 190 |
| | 27 | Housing costs | 196 |
| | 28 | Council tax | 198 |

| Section | H | Grants and loans | |
|---|---|---|---|
| Chapters | 29 | The social fund | 203 |
| | 30 | Housing grants | 205 |
| | 31 | Other loans and grants | 209 |

| Section | I | Education and work | |
|---|---|---|---|
| Chapters | 32 | Financing studies | 212 |
| | 33 | Benefits and work | 218 |
| | 34 | Employment and training | 223 |
| | 35 | Income tax | 226 |

| Section | J | Care and support | |
|---|---|---|---|
| Chapters | 36 | Care and support services | 229 |
| | 37 | Paying for care and support | 241 |
| | 38 | Benefits in care homes | 250 |

| Section | K | Children and young people | |
|---|---|---|---|
| Chapters | 39 | Maternity and parental rights | 254 |
| | 40 | Disabled children | 256 |
| | 41 | Child benefit | 259 |
| | 42 | Young disabled people | 261 |

| Section | L | Retirement | |
|---|---|---|---|
| Chapters | 43 | Benefits in retirement | 262 |
| | 44 | Pension credit | 263 |
| | 45 | State pension | 267 |

| Section | M | Compensation schemes | |
|---|---|---|---|
| Chapters | 46 | Industrial Injuries scheme | 273 |
| | 47 | Armed Forces Compensation scheme | 281 |
| | 48 | Criminal injuries compensation | 285 |
| | 49 | Vaccine damage payments | 287 |
| | 50 | Compensation recovery | 288 |

| Section | N | Other matters | |
|---|---|---|---|
| Chapters | 51 | After a death | 290 |
| | 52 | Health benefits | 292 |

| Section | O | Common rules to benefits | |
|---|---|---|---|
| Chapters | 53 | Coming to the UK | 295 |
| | 54 | Leaving the UK | 300 |
| | 55 | Benefits in hospital | 303 |
| | 56 | Claims and payments | 307 |
| | 57 | Challenging decisions | 313 |

| Section | P | Help and information | |
|---|---|---|---|
| Chapters | 58 | Getting advice | 324 |
| | 59 | Making a complaint | 324 |
| | 60 | Useful publications | 326 |
| | 61 | Government addresses | 327 |

| Reference | | Index | 328 |
|---|---|---|---|

# Benefits checklist

| Circumstance | Benefit | Chapter |
|---|---|---|
| **Problems with walking** | | |
| ■ disabled child (aged under 16) | disability living allowance (DLA) mobility component | **4** |
| ■ aged 16 to 64 (inclusive) at the time you claim | personal independence payment (PIP) mobility component | **5** |
| ■ lease a car using the higher rate of DLA or enhanced rate of PIP mobility component | Motability | **7** |
| ■ if you get DLA (higher rate) or PIP mobility component | Vehicle tax exemption/reduction | **7** |
| ■ parking concessions | Blue Badge scheme | **7** |
| **Need help with personal care** | | |
| ■ aged under 16 when you claim | DLA care component | **4** |
| ■ aged 16 to 64 (inclusive) when you claim | PIP daily living component | **5** |
| ■ aged 65 or over when you claim | attendance allowance | **6** |
| **Practical help at home** | | |
| ■ practical help if you are disabled | care and support services | **36** |
| **Caring** | | |
| ■ you care for a disabled person for at least 35 hours a week | carer's allowance | **8** |
| ■ you or your partner get carer's allowance or would do but for an overlapping benefit | carer premium with means-tested benefits | **21** |
| | carer amount with universal credit | **16** |
| **Limited capability for work** | | |
| ■ employed | statutory sick pay (SSP) | **10** |
| ■ not employed or SSP has run out | employment and support allowance (ESA) | **11 & 18** |
| **Unemployed or working less than 16 hours a week** | | |
| ■ payable for 26 weeks if you've paid enough NI contributions | contribution-based jobseeker's allowance (JSA) | **13** |
| ■ if you've not paid enough NI contributions, or your contribution-based JSA has run out or is not enough to live on | income-based JSA* | **20** |
| ■ if you don't have to sign on for work (eg you are a carer or a lone parent with a young child) and your income and savings are low | income support* | **19** |
| **Working at least 16 hours a week** | | |
| ■ you have a child, or you have a disability and get a qualifying disability benefit or recently got a qualifying incapacity benefit, or you are aged 60+, or you are aged 25 or over and working at least 30 hours a week | working tax credit* | **23** |
| **You do not have enough to live on** | | |
| ■ limited capability for work | income-related employment and support allowance* | **18** |
| ■ not working, or working less than 16 hours a week, and you do not have to sign on for work (eg you are a carer) | income support* | **19** |
| ■ if you have to sign on for work | income-based jobseeker's allowance* | **20** |
| ■ from pension credit qualifying age | pension credit | **44** |
| ■ working at least 16 hours a week (see above) | working tax credit* | **23** |
| ■ responsible for a child (see below) | child tax credit* | **23** |
| ■ paying rent for your home | housing benefit* | **25** |
| **You have needs difficult to meet out of regular income** | | |
| ■ if you have received income-related ESA, income support, income-based JSA or pension credit for at least 26 weeks | budgeting loan | **31** |
| ■ if you get universal credit and have received a qualifying benefit for at least 26 weeks | budgeting advance | **31** |
| ■ you have a low income | local welfare assistance schemes | **31** |
| **Need help with NHS costs, glasses, hospital fares** | health benefits | **52** |

This brief guide can help you see which benefits you might be entitled to. More than one of the circumstances may apply to you and you may qualify for more than one benefit. Box A.1 in Chapter 1 tells you which benefits depend on your national insurance (NI) record and which are affected by other income. The benefits marked with an asterisk (*) will be replaced with universal credit over time; see Box E.1 in Chapter 14 for details.

| Circumstance | Benefit | Chapter |
|---|---|---|
| **Housing problems** | | |
| ■ repairs, adaptations, improvements | housing grants | 30 |
| ■ help with the mortgage interest if you are entitled to income support, income-related ESA, income-based JSA, pension credit (guarantee credit) or universal credit (if you are not working) | support for mortgage interest loans | 26 |
| ■ help with rent | housing benefit* | 25 |
| ■ help with council tax | council tax reduction, disability reduction or discount schemes | 28 |
| **You are pregnant or have recently had a baby** | | |
| ■ employed | statutory maternity pay (SMP) | 39 |
| | statutory paternity pay | 39 |
| | statutory shared parental pay | 39 |
| ■ recently self-employed, or employed but not entitled to SMP | maternity allowance | 39 |
| ■ limited capability for work | employment and support allowance | 11 & 18 |
| ■ if income and savings are low | income support* | 19 |
| ■ help with maternity expenses for first child | Sure Start maternity grant | 29 |
| ■ vouchers for milk, fruit and vegetables | Healthy Start | 52 |
| **Responsibility for children** | | |
| ■ employed (responsible for adopted child) | statutory adoption pay | 39 |
| ■ responsible for a child aged under 16, or aged 16-19 in full-time non-advanced education or approved unwaged training | child benefit | 41 |
| | child tax credit* | 23 |
| ■ responsible for an orphan | guardian's allowance | 41 |
| ■ disabled child | disability living allowance | 4 |
| | Family Fund | 40 |
| ■ vouchers for milk, fruit and vegetables | Healthy Start | 52 |
| **Injured or contracted disease in work** | | |
| ■ disabled through an industrial accident or prescribed disease | industrial injuries disablement benefit | 46 |
| ■ the industrial accident or disease occurred before 1.10.90 and your earnings capacity is reduced | reduced earnings allowance | 46 |
| ■ replaces reduced earnings allowance when you give up regular employment after state pension age | retirement allowance | 46 |
| **War disablement** | | |
| ■ injured because of service in the armed forces (before 6.4.05), or a civilian disabled due to World War 2 | war pension | 47 |
| ■ your spouse or civil partner died because of the war, or because of service in the armed forces | war widow's or widower's pension and survivor's benefits | 47 |
| ■ injured because of service in the armed forces on or after 6.4.05 | Armed Forces Compensation scheme | 47 |
| **Disabled due to vaccine damage** | vaccine damage payment | 49 |
| **Injured due to violent crime** | criminal injuries compensation | 48 |
| **Retirement** | | |
| ■ from state pension age | state pension | 45 |
| ■ from pension credit qualifying age and income and savings are low | pension credit | 44 |
| **Death** | | |
| ■ widow, widower or surviving civil partner | bereavement support payment | 51 |
| ■ help with the cost of a funeral | social fund funeral payment | 29 |

# Legal references

The footnotes in this handbook are references to Acts and Regulations, case law and official guidance. Each footnote applies to the block of text above it. If there are several paragraphs in a block, with just one footnote at the bottom, the footnote applies to all text within the block. If text contains several footnotes, each one refers to the text directly above it, up to the previous footnote. Text that provides tactical advice or discussion on specific points is not generally footnoted.'

## Acts and Regulations

Acts of Parliament (also known as statutes) contain the basic rules for social security benefits, tax credits and care and support administration. Regulations flesh out the law and provide the detail that determines procedure for the rules as laid down in the Acts. These are also known as statutory instruments (SIs) and can be amended at any time using other SIs.

## Finding Acts and Regulations

You can find Acts and Regulations on the National Archives website (www.legislation.gov.uk).

Most regulations are updated over time with further amending regulations. The consequent consolidated and updated legislation is set out in:
■ *The Law Relating to Social Security* (The Blue Volumes), available via our website: www.disabilityrightsuk.org/links-government-departments (listed under 'department for work and pensions').

Consolidated and updated legislation is also available in:
■ *Social Security: Legislation 2017/18 Volumes I, II, III* and *IV* (Sweet & Maxwell). These have detailed footnotes explaining the legislation and highlighting relevant case law. They are used by members of appeal tribunals (see Chapter 57).

## Case law

Case law is created through decisions or judgments made on points of law by the Upper Tribunal, the Court of Appeal (or Court of Session in Scotland) or the Supreme Court (before 1.10.09 this was the jurisdiction of the House of Lords).

These decisions clarify any doubt about the meaning of the law or its application to individual cases. When case law sets up a general principle, it also creates a precedent to be followed in similar cases.

The Upper Tribunal (previously the Social Security Commissioners) hears appeals against appeal tribunal decisions (see Box O.10 in Chapter 57), the Court of Appeal (or Court of Session in Scotland) against decisions of the Upper Tribunal, and the Supreme Court against Court of Appeal or Court of Session judgments.

## Finding case law

Commissioners/Upper Tribunal decisions are available on the website (http://administrativeappeals.decisions.tribunals.gov.uk//Aspx/default.aspx), where reported decisions from 1991 and selected unreported decisions deemed to be of interest from 2002 are published.

**Case law summaries** – Disability Rights UK produces up-to-date case law summaries covering the principle disability benefits. These are available at: www.disabilityrightsuk.org/how-we-can-help/benefits-information/law-pages/case-law-summaries.

Our factsheet *Finding the Law* helps you find the law relevant to disability benefits (www.disabilityrightsuk.org/finding-law).

## Official guidance

See www.disabilityrightsuk.org/links-government-departments for the following:
■ *Decision Makers Guide* and *Advice for Decision Making* – Covering all benefits administered by the Department for Work and Pensions (DWP)
■ *Medical guidance for DLA decision makers (child cases): staff guide* – To help decide disability living allowance for children (see Chapter 4(22))
■ *Medical guidance for DLA and AA decision makers (adult cases): staff guide* – To help decide disability living allowance and attendance allowance (see Chapter 6(17))

See also the boxes entitled 'For more information' in various chapters of this handbook (and Box J.3 in Chapter 36 for Section J).

### Acts

| | |
|---|---|
| **CA** | Care Act 2014 |
| **CCH(S)A** | Community Care and Health (Scotland) Act 2002 |
| **HGCRA** | Housing Grants, Construction and Regeneration Act 1996 |
| **HSA** | Housing (Scotland) Act 2006 |
| **JSA** | Jobseekers Act 1995 |
| **LGFA** | Local Government Finance Act 1992 |
| **PA** | Pensions Act 2007 |
| **SPCA** | State Pension Credit Act 2002 |
| **SSA** | Social Security Act 1998 |
| **SSAA** | Social Security Administration Act 1992 |
| **SSCBA** | Social Security Contributions and Benefits Act 1992 |
| **SSWB(W)A** | Social Services and Well-being (Wales) Act 2014 |
| **TCA** | Tax Credits Act 2002 |
| **TCEA** | Tribunals, Courts and Enforcement Act 2007 |
| **VDPA** | Vaccine Damage Payments Act 1979 |
| **WRA 2007** | Welfare Reform Act 2007 |
| **WRA 2012** | Welfare Reform Act 2012 |

### Regulations

| | |
|---|---|
| **AA Regs** | Social Security (Attendance Allowance) Regulations 1991 (SI 1991/2740) |
| **ARF(CS) Order** | Armed Forces and Reserve Forces (Compensation Scheme) Order 2011 (SI 2011/517) |
| **CB Regs** | Child Benefit (General) Regulations 2006 (SI 2006/223) |
| **CE Regs** | Social Security Benefit (Computation of Earnings) Regulations 1996 (SI 1996/2745) |
| **Cont. Regs** | Social Security (Contributions) Regulations 2001 (SI 2001/1004) |

| | |
|---|---|
| **C&P Regs** | Social Security (Claims and Payments) Regulations 1987 (SI 1987/1968) |
| **Credit Regs** | Social Security (Credits) Regulations 1975 (SI 1975/556) |
| **CS(CAR) Regs** | Care and Support (Charging and Assessment of Resources) Regulations 2014 (SI 2014/2672) |
| **CTC Regs** | Child Tax Credit Regulations 2002 (SI 2002/2007) |
| **D&A Regs** | Social Security and Child Support (Decisions and Appeals) Regulations 1999 (SI 1999/991) |
| **DLA Regs** | Social Security (Disability Living Allowance) Regulations 1991 (SI 1991/2890) |
| **DP(BMV) Regs** | Disabled Persons (Badges for Motor Vehicles) (England) Regulations 2000 (SI 2000/682) |
| **ESA Regs** | Employment and Support Allowance Regulations 2008 (SI 2008/794) |
| **ESA Regs 2013** | Employment and Support Allowance Regulations 2013 (SI 2013/379) |
| **ESA(WRA) Regs** | Employment and Support Allowance (Work-Related Activity) Regulations 2011 (SI 2011/1349) |
| **GB Regs** | Social Security (General Benefit) Regulations 1982 (SI 1982/1408) |
| **HB Regs** | Housing Benefit Regulations 2006 (SI 2006/213) |
| **HB(SPC) Regs** | Housing Benefit (Persons who have Attained the Qualifying Age for State Pension Credit) Regulations 2006 (SI 2006/214) |
| **HB&CTB (D&A) Regs** | Housing Benefit and Council Tax Benefit (Decisions and Appeals) Regulations 2001 (SI 2001/1002) |
| **HCA Regs** | Social Security (Housing Costs Amendments) Regulations 2015 (SI 2015/1647) |
| **HCSA(A&M) Regs** | Social Security (Housing Costs Special Arrangements)(Amendment and Modification) Regulations 2008 (SI 2008/3195) |
| **HR Regs** | Social Security Pensions (Home Responsibilities) Regulations 1994 (SI 1994/704) |
| **HRG Regs** | Housing Renewal Grants Regulations 1996 (SI 1996/2890) |
| **ICA Regs** | Social Security (Carer's Allowance) Regulations 1976 (SI 1976/409) |
| **IIPD Regs** | Social Security (Industrial Injuries)(Prescribed Diseases) Regulations 1985 (SI 1985/967) |
| **IS Regs** | Income Support (General) Regulations 1987 (SI 1987/1967) |
| **IW Regs** | Social Security (Incapacity for Work)(General) Regulations 1995 (SI 1995/311) |
| **JPI Regs** | Social Security (Jobcentre Plus Interviews) Regulations 2002 (SI 2002/1703) |
| **JSA Regs** | Jobseeker's Allowance Regulations 1996 (SI 1996/207) |
| **JSA Regs 2013** | Jobseeker's Allowance Regulations 2013 (SI 2013/378) |
| **LATO(EDP) Regs** | Local Authorities' Traffic Orders (Exemptions for Disabled Persons)(England) Regulations 2000 (SI 2000/683) |
| **LMIR Regs** | Loans for Mortgage Interest Regulations 2017 (SI 2017/725) |
| **NHS(CDA) Regs** | National Health Service (Charges for Drugs and Appliances) Regulations 2000 (SI 2000/620) |
| **NHS(TERC) Regs** | National Health Service (Travel Expenses and Remission of Charges) Regulations 2003 (SI 2003/2382) |
| **OB Regs** | Social Security (Overlapping Benefits) Regulations 1979 (SI 1979/597) |
| **O&R Regs** | Social Security (Overpayments and Recovery) Regulations 2013 (SI 2013/384) |
| **PA Regs** | Social Security Benefit (Persons Abroad) Regulations 1975 (SI 1975/563) |
| **PAB Regs** | Social Security (Payments on Account of Benefit) Regulations 2013 (SI 2013/383) |
| **PAOR Regs** | Social Security (Payments on Account, Overpayments and Recovery) Regulations 1988 (SI 1988/664) |
| **PIP Regs** | Social Security (Personal Independence Payment) Regulations 2013 (SI 2013/377) |
| **PIP(TP) Regs** | Personal Independence Payment (Transitional Provisions) Regulations 2013 (SI 2013/387) |
| **SFM&FE Regs** | Social Fund Maternity and Funeral Expenses (General) Regulations 2005 (SI 2005/3061) |
| **SMP Regs** | Statutory Maternity Pay (General) Regulations 1986 (SI 1986/1960) |
| **SP Regs** | State Pension Regulations 2015 (SI 2015/173) |
| **SPC Regs** | State Pension Credit Regulations 2002 (SI 2002/1792) |
| **SSP Regs** | Statutory Sick Pay (General) Regulations 1982 (SI 1982/894) |
| **TC(C&N) Regs** | Tax Credits (Claims and Notifications) Regulations 2002 (SI 2002/2014) |
| **TC(DCI) Regs** | Tax Credits (Definition and Calculation of Income) Regulations 2002 (SI 2002/2006) |
| **TC(I) Regs** | Tax Credits (Immigration) Regulations 2003 (SI 2003/653) |
| **TC(IT&DR) Regs** | Tax Credits (Income Thresholds and Determination of Rates) Regulations 2002 (SI 2002/2008) |
| **TC(R) Regs** | Tax Credits (Residence) Regulations 2003 (SI 2003/654) |
| **TPEA Regs** | Employment and Support Allowance (Transitional Provisions, Housing Benefit and Council Tax Benefit)(Existing Awards)(No.2) Regulations 2010 (SI 2010/1907) |
| **TP(FTT)SEC Rules** | Tribunal Procedure (First-tier Tribunal) (Social Entitlement Chamber) Rules 2008 (SI 2008/2685) |
| **TP(UT) Rules** | Tribunal Procedure (Upper Tribunal) Rules 2008 (SI 2008/2698) |
| **UC Regs** | Universal Credit Regulations 2013 (SI 2013/376) |
| **UCPIP(C&P) Regs** | Universal Credit, Personal Independence Payment, Jobseeker's Allowance and Employment and Support Allowance (Claims and Payments) Regulations 2013 (SI 2013/380) |
| **UCPIP(D&A) Regs** | Universal Credit, Personal Independence Payment, Jobseeker's Allowance and Employment and Support Allowance (Decisions and Appeals) Regulations 2013 (SI 2013/381) |
| **VDP Regs** | Vaccine Damage Payments Regulations 1979 (SI 1979/432) |
| **WBRP Regs** | Social Security (Widow's Benefit and Retirement Pensions) Regulations 1979 (SI 1979/642) |
| **WTC(E&MR) Regs** | Working Tax Credit (Entitlement and Maximum Rate) Regulations 2002 (SI 2002/2005) |

# Abbreviations

Most abbreviations used in this handbook are explained here. If you come across one that isn't listed, you will usually find it explained towards the beginning of the chapter, towards the beginning of the subsection in a chapter, or in a box headed 'For more information'.

| | | | |
|---|---|---|---|
| **AFCS** | Armed Forces Compensation scheme | **JSA** | jobseeker's allowance |
| **AFIP** | armed forces independence payment | **LAC** | Local Authority Circular |
| **AFPS** | Armed Forces Pension scheme | **LHA** | local housing allowance |
| **art** | article | **MDC** | Metropolitan District Council |
| **CC** | county council | **MP** | Member of Parliament |
| **CCD** | Community Care Circular | **NHS** | National Health Service |
| **CCLR** | Community Care Law Reports | **NI** | national insurance |
| **CEL** | Chief Executive Letter | **NVQ** | national vocational qualification |
| **CoA** | Court of Appeal | **p./para** | paragraph in a schedule to an Act or set of Regulations, or in a Guidance Manual |
| **CoSLA** | Convention of Scottish Local Authorities | | |
| **CRAG** | Charging for Residential Accommodation Guide | **PAYE** | Pay As You Earn |
| **CRU** | Compensation Recovery Unit | **PEA** | personal expenses allowance |
| **CTC** | child tax credit | **PIP** | personal independence payment |
| **DCS** | Disability & Carers Service (Northern Ireland) | **PSIC** | person subject to immigration control |
| **DEA** | disability employment adviser | **RA** | rating appeals |
| **DHP** | discretionary housing payment | **REA** | reduced earnings allowance |
| **DIAL** | Disability Information and Advice Line | **Reg** | regulation in a set of Regulations |
| **DLA** | disability living allowance | **S.** | section of an Act of Parliament |
| **DMG** | Decision Makers' Guide | **S2P** | state second pension |
| **DRE** | disability-related expenditure | **SAAS** | Student Awards Agency for Scotland |
| **DSA** | disabled students' allowance | **SAP** | statutory adoption pay |
| **DVLA** | Driver and Vehicle Licensing Agency | **SC** | Supreme Court |
| **DWP** | Department for Work and Pensions | **Sch** | schedule, at the end of an Act or a set of Regulations |
| **ECJ** | European Court of Justice | | |
| **EEA** | European Economic Area | **SDA** | severe disablement allowance |
| **EHRC** | Equality and Human Rights Commission | **SDP** | severe disability premium |
| **ESA** | employment and support allowance | **SERPS** | state earnings-related pension scheme |
| **EU** | European Union | **SMP** | statutory maternity pay |
| **EWCA** | Court of Appeal (England and Wales) | **SPP** | statutory paternity pay |
| **EWHC** | High Court (England and Wales) | **SSP** | statutory sick pay |
| **GB** | Great Britain (England, Scotland and Wales) | **SSPP** | statutory shared parental pay |
| **GIP** | guaranteed income payment | **UK** | United Kingdom (England, Northern Ireland, Scotland, Wales) |
| **GP** | general practitioner | | |
| **HMCTS** | HM Courts & Tribunals Service | **UKEAT** | UK Employment Appeal Tribunal |
| **HMRC** | HM Revenue & Customs | **VTE** | Valuation Tribunal for England |
| **HRP** | home responsibilities protection | **WCA** | work capability assessment |
| **HRT** | habitual residence test | **WPA** | widowed parent's allowance |
| **IAP** | individual assistance payment | **WTC** | working tax credit |
| **IIDB** | industrial injuries disablement benefit | | |

This section of the handbook looks at:

| | |
|---|---|
| Introduction | Chapter **1** |
| The benefits system | Chapter **2** |
| Your right to equal treatment | Chapter **3** |

# Overview

# 1 Introduction

| | | |
|---|---|---|
| 1 | What does the handbook include? | 9 |
| 2 | What's new in this edition? | 9 |
| 3 | Disability and benefits | 9 |
| | Types of benefit – Box A.1 | 10 |

## 1. What does the handbook include?

This handbook is a comprehensive guide to social security and related benefits for disabled people, their families and their carers and the many professionals who work with them. It is aimed at disabled people, whether their impairment is physical, mental or sensory. You may find it helpful to start by looking at the benefits checklist on pages 4 and 5.

In addition to social security benefits and tax credits, the handbook covers practical help and services and other essential matters including care and support services, income tax, council tax, housing grants and equality legislation.

## 2. What's new in this edition?

Perhaps the most important issue this coming year is what has not changed. Most benefits for those of working age have been frozen again. This includes some types of support for disabled people, such as the basic allowance of employment and support allowance (ESA) and the lower rate of the universal credit disabled child addition. The three-year freeze actually started in April 2016, but now that inflation has hit a six-year high, the effects of the freeze are really starting to bite. Compounded with the cuts to benefits over the last two years, many disabled people and their families, already struggling, are facing a gloomy prospect.

The key change to the benefit system in April 2018 was the removal of the support in means-tested benefits (such as income-related ESA and pension credit) towards the interest on mortgages and eligible home improvement loans. This support has been replaced by a repayable loans scheme: 'support for mortgage interest loans'. We cover this in Chapter 26.

**Other changes** – If you are claiming ESA or universal credit (and have a limited capability for work), you will need to attend work-capability re-assessments from time to time, to assess your continued eligibility for the benefit. You may now no longer need to attend such re-assessments in some circumstances (see Chapter 12(21)).

If you are claiming universal credit, the 'waiting days' (seven days at the beginning of your claim when you could not be paid) have been abolished. See Chapters 14 to 17 for more on universal credit.

## 3. Disability and benefits

Few of your rights depend on what your condition is called. In most cases, your entitlement to a benefit or service depends on the effect of the disability on your life. In addition to the disability tests and definitions listed below, there may be other conditions you must meet to get a particular benefit or service.

### What is disability?

Within the benefits and tax credits systems there are several different tests of disability:

- **limited capability for work** – used for employment and support allowance and the work capability amount of universal credit;
- **incapacity for work** – used for statutory sick pay, incapacity benefit, severe disablement allowance, income support and the unemployability supplement under the Industrial Injuries and War Disablement schemes. The tests of incapacity differ, depending on the benefit you claim;
- **degree of disablement** – used for industrial injuries disablement benefit, war disablement pension and vaccine damage payments;
- **at a disadvantage in getting a job** – used for the disabled worker element of working tax credit.

Disability living allowance, personal independence payment and attendance allowance each have their own tests of disability – see Chapters 4(9), 4(14), 5(10), 5(12) and 6(8).

Two further definitions are in use:

- **substantially and permanently disabled** – used for getting a disability reduction in your council tax;
- **physical or mental impairment that has a substantial and long-term adverse effect on your ability to carry out normal day-to-day activities** – used to define those people covered by the disability sections of the Equality Act 2010.

### The different categories of benefits

Benefits can be divided into three broad categories:

- those that are intended to replace earnings;
- those that compensate for extra costs; *and*
- those that help alleviate poverty.

The first category includes benefits that compensate you if you are unable to work because of sickness, disability, unemployment, pregnancy or caring responsibilities. In general, these benefits are not subject to a means test, but some will depend on your national insurance contribution record (see Box A.1).

Benefits intended to contribute towards the extra costs of disability are not means tested and do not depend on national insurance contributions.

Benefits intended to alleviate poverty by providing a basic income or topping up a low income are means tested.

# 2 The benefits system

| | | |
|---|---|---|
| 1 | Department for Work and Pensions | 9 |
| | Contacting the DWP – Box A.2 | 10 |
| 2 | Scotland and Northern Ireland | 10 |
| 3 | Who's who in the benefits system | 11 |
| 4 | HM Revenue & Customs | 11 |
| 5 | Ministry of Justice | 11 |

## 1. Department for Work and Pensions

The Department for Work and Pensions (DWP) is responsible for most of the financial help available for disabled people. It administers disability living allowance, personal independence payment, attendance allowance, carer's allowance and vaccine

## A.1 Types of benefit

Entitlement to benefits depends on your circumstances and may be affected by your income, savings and national insurance (NI) contribution record.

### Means-tested benefits
The following 'means-tested' or income-related benefits are affected by most other types of income and by the amount of savings you have. However, child tax credit and working tax credit are affected only by income from your savings, not by your actual level of savings. Your NI contribution record does not matter.
- ❏ Child tax credit
- ❏ Housing benefit
- ❏ Income-related employment and support allowance
- ❏ Income-based jobseeker's allowance
- ❏ Income support
- ❏ Pension credit
- ❏ Social fund
- ❏ Universal credit
- ❏ Working tax credit

### Non-means-tested benefits
The following non-means-tested benefits are not usually affected by other money you have, but some are dependent on you earning a certain amount, whereas others can be reduced if you have earnings or an occupational or private pension. There are two types of non-means-tested benefits: non-contributory and contributory.

### Non-contributory benefits
For these benefits, your NI record does not matter. Those marked (*) are dependent on you earning a certain amount. Carer's allowance can be affected by your earnings or your occupational or private pension. Child benefit can be affected by your income. See relevant chapters for details.
- ❏ Armed forces independence payment
- ❏ Attendance allowance
- ❏ Carer's allowance
- ❏ Child benefit
- ❏ Disability living allowance
- ❏ Guardian's allowance
- ❏ Guaranteed income payment (Armed Forces Compensation scheme)
- ❏ Industrial injuries benefits
- ❏ Maternity allowance*
- ❏ Personal independence payment
- ❏ State pension (Category D)
- ❏ Statutory adoption pay*
- ❏ Statutory maternity pay*
- ❏ Statutory paternity pay*
- ❏ Statutory shared parental pay*
- ❏ Statutory sick pay*
- ❏ War disablement pensions

### Contributory benefits
For these benefits you (or in some cases your partner) must have paid enough NI contributions. See relevant chapters for details. Those marked (**) can be affected by your earnings or your occupational or private pension.
- ❏ Bereavement support payment
- ❏ Contribution-based jobseeker's allowance**
- ❏ Contributory employment and support allowance**
- ❏ State pension (Categories A & B) and new state pension

damage payments. The offices responsible for these benefits are listed in Chapter 61(2).

The DWP administers some benefits for people of working age through its Jobcentre Plus arm, and benefits for pensioners through the Pension Service (see below). The DWP contracts out some of its functions to private companies; eg Independent Assessment Services (previously Atos Healthcare), Capita and Maximus are contracted to provide medical advice and assessments.

Tax credits, child benefit and guardian's allowance are administered by HM Revenue & Customs (see 4 below).

**Jobcentre Plus** – Jobcentre Plus provides services to people of working age, administering most of the benefits they can claim through a network of local Jobcentre Plus offices. The benefits it administers include employment and support allowance, jobseeker's allowance and universal credit.

**The Pension Service** – The Pension Service provides services for pensioners and people planning for retirement. It administers the state pension, pension credit and winter fuel payments, through largely telephone-based pension centres.

## 2. Scotland and Northern Ireland
**Scotland** – Responsibility for substantial parts of the social security system in Scotland has been devolved to the Scottish government. Benefits being transferred to the Scottish government include those paid because of ill health and disability, including disability living allowance, personal independence payment (PIP), attendance allowance and industrial injuries disablement benefit. Other benefits to be transferred include carer's allowance, Sure Start maternity grants, funeral payments and winter fuel payments. In each of the devolved areas, the Scottish government has the right to create new benefits. Universal credit, state pension and pension credit are to remain the responsibility of the UK government, although the Scottish government can top these benefits up.

At time of writing, systems have generally not yet been set in place to put the devolved powers into effect, so most of those benefits to be transferred continue to be administered by the DWP for the time being.

**Northern Ireland** – The Department for Communities is responsible for social security matters. Northern Ireland has its own legislation, and the structure and organisation of the benefits system are different from that of Great Britain (GB). However, for most of the time Northern Ireland legislation mirrors GB legislation and the rates of benefits and their qualifying conditions are correspondingly similar. In some cases, extra payments are available in Northern Ireland to

## A.2 Contacting the DWP

### England, Scotland and Wales
Details of how to contact Jobcentre Plus are on the website (www.gov.uk/contact-jobcentre-plus). Claims for benefits administered by Jobcentre Plus can be made by contacting the claim-line (0800 055 6688; textphone 0800 023 4888).

For details of pension centres, contact the Pension Service (0800 731 0469; textphone 0800 731 0464; www.gov.uk/find-pension-centre).

Contact details for DWP offices dealing with specific benefits are listed in Chapter 61.

### Northern Ireland
To find your local Jobs & Benefits or Social Security Office, look in the phone book under 'Social Security' or on the website (www.nidirect.gov.uk/contacts/jobs-benefits-offices-jobcentres-and-social-security-offices).

mitigate the effects of welfare reform; see Box B.6 in Chapter 5 for such payments in relation to the introduction of PIP.

### 3. Who's who in the benefits system

The services are organised in slightly different ways. What follows is an outline – you'll find further details in the chapters on the individual benefits. The rules about claims and payments are in Chapter 56 and those on challenging decisions are in Chapter 57.

In all cases, you have the right to expect a good standard of service. If you want to complain about something or have suggestions about how services could be improved, see Chapter 59.

**Administrative staff** – The people you talk to when you ring or visit a local office are not always legally responsible for making a decision on your claim. They will do the support and maintenance work for claims and may handle many routine claims, particularly for means-tested benefits, but decisions must, in law, be made by a decision maker authorised by the Secretary of State.

**The Secretary of State** – The Secretary of State for Work and Pensions is responsible for decisions on your social security benefit entitlement. In practice, this responsibility is delegated to decision makers who are officers acting under the Secretary of State's authority. In a few cases, the Secretary of State delegates decision-making responsibility to officers of HM Revenue & Customs (eg for some national insurance credits decisions).

**Decision makers** – Decision makers are officers acting under the authority of the Secretary of State. They make decisions on your entitlement to benefits. If you are not satisfied with a decision, you can ask for it to be revised or reconsidered. In many cases, you can appeal to an independent tribunal if you are not happy with a decision after it has been reconsidered. The letter giving you the decision must always explain what you can do next. See Chapter 57 for more on challenging decisions.

### 4. HM Revenue & Customs

HM Revenue & Customs (HMRC) is responsible for decisions on tax credits, child benefit and guardian's allowance, and these are made by officers based in the Tax Credit Office and the Child Benefit Office. HMRC is also responsible for decisions on national insurance contributions and employer-paid benefits (such as statutory sick pay). Appeals on HMRC decisions are heard by First-tier Tribunals (see 5 below).

### 5. Ministry of Justice

The Ministry of Justice has responsibility for running the appeals system. It does this through the HM Courts and Tribunals Service, which provides common administrative support to the main central government tribunals: the First-tier Tribunals and the Upper Tribunals.

**First-tier Tribunals** – In addition to hearing appeals on decisions made by the Secretary of State for Work and Pensions (on benefits such as employment and support allowance, universal credit and personal independence payment), First-tier Tribunals also hear appeals against local authority decisions on housing benefit and HMRC decisions on tax credits, national insurance contributions and employer-paid benefits. First-tier Tribunals cover a range of other areas, including mental health reviews, care standards and criminal injuries compensation. The role and powers of the First-tier Tribunals are explained in Chapter 57.

**Upper Tribunals** – Upper Tribunals hear appeals against decisions of the First-tier Tribunals. Their decisions set precedents and form case law. Chapter 57(18) explains more about appealing to the Upper Tribunal.

# **3** Your right to equal treatment

| 1 | What protection is there and who is covered? | 11 |
|---|---|---|
| 2 | Disability | 11 |
| 3 | Prohibited conduct | 12 |
| 4 | Employment rights | 13 |
| 5 | Access to goods and services | 13 |
| 6 | Housing | 14 |
| 7 | Education | 14 |
| 8 | Transport | 14 |
| 9 | Private clubs and political parties | 15 |
| 10 | Enforcing your rights | 15 |
| | For more information – Box A.3 | 15 |

## 1. What protection is there and who is covered?

The Equality Act 2010 brought together and replaced previous discrimination laws, including the Disability Discrimination Act (DDA). The Equality Act prohibits discrimination against disabled people, as well as discrimination on the grounds of age, gender, gender-reassignment, marriage or civil partnership, race, religion or belief, or sexual orientation. It applies to Great Britain only; the DDA remains the law in Northern Ireland. The Equality Commission for Northern Ireland website has information on the DDA (see Box A.3).

The Equality Act treats disability discrimination in distinctive ways, in particular by requiring *'reasonable adjustments'*. The Act makes it unlawful to discriminate against anyone who has, or has had, a disability; it is unlawful to discriminate in connection with employment, education, the provision of services, the exercise of public functions, and premises.

*Note:* The UN Convention on the Rights of Persons with Disabilities, ratified by the UK, does not have direct legal effect but is increasingly referred to by the courts and tribunals.

## 2. Disability

Disability is defined as *'a physical or mental impairment which has a substantial and long-term adverse effect on [your] ability to carry out normal day-to-day activities'*. If you can show that you meet this definition, you will have the protection of the disability provisions of the Equality Act. If you have had a disability (as defined) you are still protected from discrimination even if you no longer have the disability.

**Impairment** – This includes sensory impairments (sight or hearing loss), learning disabilities, mental health conditions and long-term health conditions such as heart disease or type 1 diabetes. Any steps taken to treat or correct your disability (eg a hearing aid, artificial limb or medication) are ignored; it is the effect the impairment would have without the treatment that is relevant. But if you wear glasses or contact lenses, it is the effect on your vision with the lenses that is considered.

**Substantial** – This means *'more than minor or trivial'*. Progressive conditions are treated as having a substantial adverse impact as soon as they have any adverse impact, provided this is likely to become substantial. These include: motor neurone disease, lupus and many types of dementia.

**Long term** – This means effects that have lasted at least 12 months, or are likely to last at least 12 months or for the rest of your life (if that is less than 12 months). Conditions likely to recur, eg epilepsy, will be considered as long term if it is more likely than not that their substantial adverse effects will recur beyond 12 months. If, without medication or other treatment, the effects would be long term, the impairment may amount to a disability, eg untreated depression.

Equality Act 2010, S.6 & Sch 1 and Guidance on matters to be taken into account in determining questions relating to the definition of disability: www.gov.uk/government/publications/equality-act-guidance

## Special provision

Some conditions, namely cancer, multiple sclerosis and HIV infection, count as a disability effectively from your date of diagnosis. Others are covered as soon as they affect your ability to carry out normal activities. Severe disfigurements are covered, even if they do not affect your ability to carry out normal activities. You automatically meet the disability definition if a consultant ophthalmologist has certified you as blind, severely sight impaired, sight impaired or partially sighted.

Equality Act 2010 Regulations, reg 7

## Wider protections

**Discrimination by association** – The Act gives you the right not to be subjected to direct discrimination or harassment on the grounds of your association with a disabled person (eg if you care for a disabled child).

**Discrimination by perception** – The Act protects people from direct discrimination or harassment because they are perceived (whether correctly or not) to be a disabled person.

Jv DLA Piper LLP [2010] IRLR 936 *Chief Constable of Norfolk v Coffey* [EAT December 2017]

## 3. Prohibited conduct

*'Prohibited conduct'* is a key concept of equality: it is what employers, service providers and others may not do. There are four types:

■ discrimination;

■ failure to comply with the duty to make *'reasonable adjustments'*;

■ harassment; *and*

■ victimisation.

The Equality Act considers whether, in relation to any specific area (work, services, education, etc), there has been prohibited conduct linked to a *'protected characteristic'*. For example, a woman who is registered blind applies for a job but does not get it because of her sight loss. The specific area in this case is work, the protected characteristic is her disability and the prohibited conduct is direct discrimination.

## Discrimination

There are three types of discrimination:

❑ **Direct discrimination** – occurs where, because of your disability, you are treated less favourably (that is, you receive worse treatment) than someone without that particular disability. This means you need another person to compare yourself with.

❑ **Discrimination arising from disability** – occurs where you are treated unfavourably because of something connected to your disability. This is interpreted in a normal or common-sense manner. It only applies if employers or service providers know, or could reasonably be expected to know, that you are a disabled person.

❑ **Indirect discrimination** – occurs when there is a rule, policy or practice that applies to everyone but particularly disadvantages disabled people compared to others.

Equality Act 2010, Ss.13, 15 & 19

**Justification** – Only discrimination arising from disability and indirect discrimination can be *'justified'*. It applies in all areas covered by the Act. These types of discrimination can be justified if the treatment is a *'proportionate means of achieving a legitimate aim'*. This requires striking a balance between the needs of the potential discriminator and those of the disabled person; the more serious the effect on the disabled person, the more substantial the reason for the treatment must be. The key point is whether the treatment is *'proportionate'*.

Buchanan v Commissioner of Police of the Metropolis (2016 UKEAT/0112/16/RN)

Justification must be considered after reasonable adjustments have been made.

## Reasonable adjustments

The duty to make reasonable adjustments applies across the Equality Act. There are three *'requirements'* to this duty:

❑ **Changing the way things are done** – This involves taking steps to overcome barriers that present substantial disadvantage to disabled people which are caused by the way an organisation does things: *'provision, criterion or practice'*. This does not have to apply to anyone other than the disabled person and must anyway be neutral (Pulman v Merthyr Tydfil College Ltd (2017 UKEAT/0309/16/JOJ)).

❑ **Making changes to physical features** – This involves making changes to overcome barriers that present substantial disadvantage to disabled people which are created by the physical features of premises.

❑ **Providing extra equipment or services** – This involves providing extra equipment (*'auxiliary aids'*) or an additional service (an *'auxiliary service'*). It includes ensuring that information is provided in an accessible format.

The duty applies to disabled people only. There is no duty to make adjustments for someone who is associated with a disabled person, such as the parents of a disabled child (Hainsworth v Ministry of Defence [2014] EWCA Civ 763).

**Reasonable** – What is *'reasonable'* depends on different factors, including: the effectiveness of the adjustment, how practical it is to make it, and the cost of making it. The Equality and Human Rights Commission's codes of practice and technical guidance give details (see Box A.3).

**Paying for reasonable adjustments** – The person or organisation that must comply with the duty to make reasonable adjustments cannot require a disabled person to pay for them.

Equality Act 2010, S.20

**Failure to comply** – A failure to comply with the requirements is a failure to comply with the duty to make reasonable adjustments.

Equality Act 2010, S.21

## Harassment

Harassment occurs if an employer or service provider, or someone working for them, engages in unwanted behaviour:

■ that is related to the protected characteristic of disability; *and*

■ which has the purpose or effect of violating your dignity, or creating an intimidating, hostile, degrading, humiliating or offensive environment.

Harassment can never be justified. However, if an employer or organisation can show it did all it could to stop the person from acting in that way, your harassment claim would not be successful, although you could sue the harasser.

Harassment also applies in education settings, eg harassment of students or pupils by staff. The Act does not protect them from harassment by other students or pupils, but the education establishment has obligations to take steps to deal with harassment.

Equality Act 2010, S.26

## Victimisation

Victimisation has a specific meaning. It means you are subjected to a *'detriment'* (ie anything that you might reasonably consider has changed your position for the worse or put you at a disadvantage) because you have made a complaint or taken a legal case under the Equality Act, or because you have supported someone to make their own complaint or take a case under the Act. The 'detriment' must be linked to the Equality Act. Being treated badly on its own is not victimisation.

Equality Act 2010, S.27; EHRC Code of Practice on Employment, para 9.8

## 4. Employment rights

It is unlawful for an employer to discriminate. The Equality Act covers almost all employment, except the armed forces. It covers temporary, contract and permanent staff and all employment matters, including recruitment, training, promotion, dismissal and redundancy, and discrimination against former employees. Volunteers are not covered unless the volunteering agreement has the same level of obligation towards, and control by, the organisation as an employment contract.

Employers are legally responsible for the actions of their employees and agents (eg a company is responsible if a manager discriminates against a disabled worker). You do not need to be employed for a minimum period of time to bring a discrimination claim, and compensation is unlimited.

Equality Act 2010, Part 5

### Reasonable adjustments

Employers have to make *'reasonable adjustments'* to the workplace and to employment arrangements, including recruitment. The duty only applies if an employer knows, or could reasonably be expected to know, that an employee needs an adjustment. Reasonable adjustments include:

- changes to working practices (eg allowing flexible working hours or providing additional training). This can include protecting pay if an employee acquires a disability and is reassigned to a lower-paid job (G4S Cash Solutions (UK) Ltd v Powell (2016 UKEAT/0243/15/RN));
- changes to the physical environment (eg widening a doorway for wheelchair access or allocating a parking space for a disabled person); *and*
- providing auxiliary aids and services (eg buying specialised equipment or providing communication support).

Equality Act 2010, Sch 8

**Rented premises** – If your employer rents premises, the landlord cannot unreasonably refuse permission for the premises to be altered to accommodate you, although they may attach reasonable conditions to their permission (eg the premises must be returned to their original condition when vacated). If your employer does not make a reasonable adjustment because the landlord unreasonably refuses permission, you could take your employer to the Employment Tribunal, and you or your employer could ask the Tribunal to make the landlord a party to the case. The landlord would then have to go to the Tribunal.

### Pre-employment questions

The Equality Act makes it unlawful for employers to enquire about your health or disability before making a job offer. Sole exceptions are to:

- ask if you need reasonable adjustments to take part in an interview;
- conduct anonymous diversity monitoring;
- ask questions relating to your ability to carry out specific job functions, with reasonable adjustments if need be; *and*
- conduct positive action.

Employers can ask for medical information after offering the job. However, if the employer withdraws the job offer because of this information, it must show that doing so is non-discriminatory, including that they have considered reasonable adjustments.

If you think an employer has asked questions about health or disability that are not permitted, you can complain to the Equality and Human Rights Commission (EHRC), which can take enforcement action. Disabled people themselves can take action in Employment Tribunals if an employer has asked prohibited health or disability questions and used the information to discriminate against them. More information is available from the government website and the EHRC (see Box A.3).

Equality Act 2010, S.60

### Specific provisions

There are specific provisions that prohibit discrimination in relation to:

- occupational pension schemes and insurance obtained through employers (eg health insurance);
- work experience done as part of vocational training (eg an NVQ in plumbing);
- occupations such as police officer, barrister, partnerships and office holders (eg members of non-departmental public bodies);
- membership of trade organisations;
- employment services (eg careers guidance services); *and*
- qualifying bodies that regulate entry into a profession (eg the Nursing and Midwifery Council).

## 5. Access to goods and services

It is unlawful for organisations that provide goods, facilities or services directly to the public to discriminate against disabled people. It does not matter whether the services are free or paid for, or whether they are provided by the public or private sector or by charities. Service providers include: shops, hotels, banks, cinemas, restaurants, courts and solicitors, private education and training providers, schools, colleges and universities (in relation to non-education activities, eg parents' evenings), students' unions, telecommunication companies, libraries, leisure facilities, healthcare, social/housing services, government offices and voluntary services. Airports, stations and booking facilities are covered. Insurance companies are covered but special rules apply. The Act can apply in some circumstances to services provided outside of the UK – eg reasonable adjustments to holidays.

Service providers are legally responsible for any discriminatory actions committed by their employees or anyone else (eg contractors) who works as part of their business (eg door staff who refuse to allow a disabled person into a pub/club). Not only is it prohibited to refuse to provide a service, it is also prohibited to provide service of a lower standard or in a worse manner (eg a cafe tells someone with a facial disfigurement to sit apart from others) or to provide a service on worse terms (eg a travel agent asks a disabled person for a larger deposit because they think the person is more likely to cancel due to their disability).

The Equality Act does not cover the manufacture and design of products.

Equality Act 2010, Part 3

### Reasonable adjustments

Examples of how the duty applies to services include:

- changing the service's 'provision, criterion or practice' (see 3 above) – eg changing a 'no dogs' policy to allow for assistance dogs;
- changing/altering physical features: lowering counters, removing heavy doors, improving lighting;
- providing a reasonable means of avoiding physical features: eg conducting interviews in an accessible room or without a glass screen to help lip-readers;
- providing the service in an alternative way: eg offering home visits if the provider's premises are inaccessible;
- providing an additional aid or service if it would help disabled people to access the service: eg communication support.

The duty is *anticipatory*: service providers must plan ahead to meet these duties, and must comply even if they do not know that someone is disabled.

Equality Act 2010, Sch 2

### Use of transport

The use and provision of transport vehicles such as buses, taxis, minicabs, trains, trams, car hire and breakdown services are covered by the Equality Act. Disabled people have protection against less favourable treatment and rights to reasonable adjustments to help them use services. These duties do not cover changes to physical features (see 8 below for the accessibility requirements for public transport vehicles) except in respect of rental vehicles and breakdown recovery vehicles (the latter must overcome physical features that present barriers to disabled people by providing the service in a reasonable alternative way).

Ships and aircraft remain exempt from the Equality Act, although the European Union gives disabled people (and those with reduced mobility) rights to special assistance when travelling. Since 1.12.14, the Civil Aviation Authority has full legal authority to ensure airlines or airports comply with European regulations.

*European Council Regulation 1107/2006; Civil Aviation (Access to Air Travel for Disabled Persons & Persons with Reduced Mobility) Regs 2014*

To require that a wheelchair space be vacated by a person without a disability, the duty to make reasonable adjustments implies a policy of *'require and pressurise'*, under which a bus driver should go as far as they believe is reasonable in the circumstances.

*First Group plc v Paulley [2017] UKSC 4 (SC)*

See Box A.3 for details of the code of practice on transport.

## 6. Housing

It is unlawful for anyone letting, selling or managing rented property (namely, houses, flats or offices) to discriminate against disabled people. The same three types of discrimination apply (see 3 above – although the reasonable adjustment requirements are narrower). For example, not granting a tenancy to a disabled person because of their disability could be direct discrimination. Disabled tenants also have protection against eviction if the eviction is linked to their disability. The protection provided by the Act is stronger and more targeted than the general protection provided by Article 8 of the European Convention on Human Rights.

*Akerman-Livingstone v Aster Communities Ltd [2015] UKSC 15*

The rules apply to most agencies involved in letting, selling or managing rented property, including local authorities, housing associations, private landlords, estate agents, accommodation agencies, banks, building societies, property developers and owner-occupiers.

Landlords who let rooms in their own homes to six or fewer people are exempted. There is no obligation on anyone selling or letting property to alter the premises to make them accessible. The law does not cover sales arranged without an estate agent.

Managing agents of rented accommodation or leasehold property are prohibited from harassing disabled tenants and may not victimise them.

**Reasonable adjustments** – Landlords and management companies must make reasonable adjustments to policies and procedures, and take reasonable steps to provide additional aids and services. The duty does not apply to physical features. However, some features do not count as 'physical features' (eg signs, adapted doorbells/entry phones and changes to taps/door handles) and are covered by the duty.

Landlords cannot refuse, unreasonably, to allow tenants to make changes because of a disability. But you must pay for the alterations (or seek a grant) and must ask permission first. The Act also applies this right to 'common parts', eg hallways or stairs. However, there is no indication when, if ever, this will actually be implemented. In Scotland, the right already applies to common parts, but other tenants and the landlord need to agree to the changes.

For more information, see the Equality and Human Rights Commission code of practice on services, public functions and associations (see Box A.3).

*Equality Act 2010, Part 4 & S.190 & Sch 4*

## 7. Education

It is unlawful for education providers to discriminate against or harass disabled students. This applies to admissions, education and related services and exclusions.

### Schools

Schools must ensure that disabled pupils are not treated less favourably. However, discrimination is not unlawful if it complies with a permitted form of selection, eg academic ability. Schools must make reasonable adjustments to provisions, criteria and practices and provide auxiliary aids/services. There is no right to reasonable adjustments to premises, as these are covered by 'accessibility plans'.

The duties apply to all schools, including publicly funded, independent and mainstream schools, special schools, pupil referral units, 'free schools', local authority-maintained nursery schools and classes, and nursery provision at independent and grant-aided schools. Private, voluntary and statutory providers of nursery education not constituted as schools are covered by the services provisions (see 5 above).

Bodies that provide general qualifications such as GCSEs, A and AS levels and other non-vocational exams (including the Scottish and Welsh equivalents) must not discriminate against disabled people. Such bodies must make reasonable adjustments for disabled candidates, eg by providing extra time or exam materials in alternative formats (for guidance, see Box A.3).

Local authorities and schools must, respectively, publish accessibility strategies and plans to improve access to school education for disabled pupils, and these are monitored by Ofsted (England) and ESTYN (Wales). Similar duties exist under Scottish education law.

*Equality Act 2010, Part 6 & Sch 13*

### Post-16 education

This includes further, higher, adult and community education and the statutory youth service. It is unlawful to discriminate against or harass disabled students. Post-16 education providers must comply with all three requirements of the reasonable adjustments duty (see 3 above).

Examination bodies and education providers must make reasonable adjustments to exams and other assessments. However, there is no duty to make an adjustment to a 'competence standard' (this is an academic, medical or other standard used to determine if someone has a particular level of competence).

Services provided by student unions and institutions of further/higher education to members of the public other than students are covered by the services provisions, as are private/voluntary sector education providers (see 5 above).

*Equality Act 2010, Part 6 & Sch 13*

## 8. Transport

The Equality Act gives the government power to make accessibility regulations for public transport vehicles. New buses, coaches and trains must comply with specified accessibility standards, eg width of doors or colour contrast. All buses had to comply with the regulations by 2017, and coaches must comply by 2020. All trains must comply by 2020 at the latest.

The government has not yet published regulations on taxi accessibility. However, licensed taxis and minicabs cannot refuse to carry and cannot charge more for a disabled person accompanied by an assistance dog – doing this is a criminal offence punishable by a fine. Drivers can ask to be exempt from this duty on medical grounds, but must provide independent medical evidence.

Taxis and private hire vehicles must carry wheelchair users, without an additional charge, and provide users with assistance to get in and out of the vehicle, including with

luggage; the driver commits an offence if they fail to do this. The licensing authorities can grant exemptions and must maintain lists of accessible vehicles.
Equality Act 2010, Part 12

## 9. Private clubs and political parties
Private clubs and political parties with 25 or more members cannot discriminate against, and have duties to make reasonable adjustments for, current and potential disabled members, associates and guests.
Equality Act 2010, Part 7

## 10. Enforcing your rights
You should always try to get advice. In the first instance, look at the Equality and Human Rights Commission website or the Citizens Advice website, or contact the Equality Advisory and Support Service (see Box A.3). Be aware of time limits: if you want to bring a legal case for discrimination, you must do so within the specific time period (see below). If you go beyond this date, you cannot start the claim unless the court or tribunal gives you permission.

**Employment** – If you think you have been discriminated against under the employment provisions, you can make a complaint to an Employment Tribunal. The complaint must be registered with the Tribunal within three months of the date of the discriminatory act, eg the date you were dismissed.

If you wish to start an Employment Tribunal case, you must first contact ACAS (Advisory, Conciliation and Arbitration Service). This is so that ACAS can explore whether 'Early Conciliation' could resolve the dispute. This service is free. You must contact ACAS to explore conciliation within the 3-month time limit. If you do not, you cannot start your claim in the Tribunal.

The previous system of employment tribunal fees has been withdrawn. See www.gov.uk/employment-tribunals/make-a-claim.

**Goods and services** – You can enforce your rights under the goods and services and post-16 education provisions through the County Court (or the Sheriff Court in Scotland). You must take the case to court within six months of the discriminatory act, eg the date you were refused service. The courts charge fees to start a case, as well as for later stages, such as the final hearing. People on certain state benefits or low incomes can apply for exemptions.

You can make a complaint to the Pensions Ombudsman if you think the managers of a pension scheme have discriminated against you (see Box L.3, Chapter 45).

**Education** – Rights under the education provisions that apply to schools are enforceable in England through the First-tier Tribunal and in Wales through the Special Educational Needs Tribunal for Wales. There are similar tribunals in Northern Ireland.

Claims of unlawful discrimination in respect of a refusal to admit to, and permanent exclusions from, maintained schools and city academies are heard by admissions appeal panels or independent appeals panels. Disability discrimination claims against schools in Scotland are heard in the Additional Support Needs Tribunal for Scotland. You must take a case to court or the tribunal within six months of the date of the discriminatory act.
Equality Act 2010, Part 9

**What you can expect**
If you are successful in a tribunal or court, you can obtain damages for financial loss or hurt feelings. The tribunals and Sheriff Court cannot award financial compensation in claims against schools, but can make other orders including: that staff receive training or guidance; policy changes; insisting on school admissions; and demanding apologies.

Courts can order service providers to make adjustments in some circumstances, and tribunals can recommend that an employer makes an adjustment. Tribunals can recommend action that benefits the wider workforce as well as the individual claimant. Courts and tribunals can make a public declaration that you were discriminated against because of your disability.

**Other remedies**
As an alternative to legal action, you can use a mediation service in all types of situations. The courts expect parties to try to resolve disputes in this way and only to start court cases if there is no other option. Mediation can be quicker and more cost effective than going to court or tribunal.

ACAS provides a free conciliation service, as does the Labour Relations Agency for Northern Ireland. There are also specialist workplace mediators available.

For education cases, local authorities in England and Wales must provide independent resolution services to deal with disagreements or disputes between parents and schools (and in Wales between pupils and schools) and must tell parents about these services.

## A.3 **For more information**

For publications containing information on the Equality Act – see Chapter 60. Other useful resources include:

❑ The Equality Advisory and Support Service provides free advice, information and guidance to individuals on equality and human rights issues (helpline: 0808 800 0082; textphone 0808 800 0084; www.equalityadvisoryservice.com).

❑ Information and advice on equality and human rights issues are available on the Citizens Advice website (www.citizensadvice.org.uk).

❑ Codes of practice and technical guidance are on the Equality and Human Rights Commission website (www.equalityhumanrights.com/en/advice-and-guidance/equality-act-codes-practice) and the government website (www.gov.uk/government/publications/equality-act-guidance).

❑ The Equality Commission for Northern Ireland publishes codes of practice, guidance and advisory leaflets (Equality House, 7-9 Shaftesbury Square, Belfast BT2 7DP; 028 9050 0600; textphone 028 9050 0589; www.equalityni.org).

❑ The regulator Ofqual provides guidance on reasonable adjustments in qualifications for England: *Specifications in Relation to the Reasonable Adjustment of General Qualifications* (www.gov.uk/government/publications/specifications-in-relation-to-the-reasonable-adjustment-of-general-qualifications). For similar guidance in Wales, go to gov.wales/docs/dcells/publications/120430specreasonablequalen.pdf Also see *Access Arrangements, Reasonable Adjustments and Special Consideration* by the Joint Council for Qualifications (www.jcq.org.uk/exams-office/access-arrangements-and-special-consideration).

❑ Information about the Equality Act transport provisions is available from the Equality and Human Rights Commission website (www.equalityhumanrights.com).

❑ Information about making a claim to an Employment Tribunal is available from: www.gov.uk/employment-tribunals.

❑ Information about general employment issues and Early Conciliation is available from the Advisory, Conciliation and Arbitration Service (ACAS) (www.acas.org.uk).

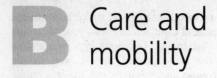

# Care and mobility

This section of the handbook looks at:

| | |
|---|---|
| Disability living allowance | Chapter **4** |
| Personal independence payment | Chapter **5** |
| Attendance allowance | Chapter **6** |
| Help with mobility | Chapter **7** |

# 4 Disability living allowance

| **A** | **General points** | |
|---|---|---|
| 1 | What is disability living allowance? | 16 |
| 2 | Does your child qualify for DLA? | 16 |
| 3 | Age limits | 16 |
| 4 | Qualifying periods | 17 |
| 5 | How much is DLA? | 17 |
| 6 | Does anything affect payment? | 17 |
| | DLA and other help – Box B.1 | 17 |
| 7 | If your child goes into hospital | 17 |
| 8 | If your child goes into a care home | 18 |
| **B** | **The mobility component** | |
| 9 | The disability tests | 18 |
| 10 | Other factors | 19 |
| 11 | 'Virtually unable to walk' | 19 |
| 12 | Severe mental impairment | 20 |
| | Learning disabilities – Box B.2 | 21 |
| 13 | The lower rate | 20 |
| **C** | **The care component** | |
| 14 | The disability tests | 22 |
| 15 | Extra care or supervision needs | 23 |
| 16 | Infants (children under 1 year old) | 23 |
| 17 | Older infants and young children | 23 |
| 18 | Older children | 24 |
| 19 | Renal dialysis | 24 |
| **D** | **Claims, payments & appeals** | |
| 20 | How do you claim? | 24 |
| | Completing the DLA claim-form – Box B.3 | 26 |
| 21 | Keeping a diary | 24 |
| | One-day diary – Box B.4 | 28 |
| 22 | How the claim is assessed | 24 |
| 23 | The award | 25 |
| 24 | If you are not happy with the decision | 25 |
| 25 | How is DLA paid? | 25 |
| 26 | What if your child's condition changes? | 25 |
| **E** | **DLA for adults** | |
| 27 | How is DLA different for adults? | 28 |
| | The cooking test – Box B.5 | 28 |

## A. GENERAL POINTS

### 1. What is disability living allowance?

Disability living allowance (DLA) provides help towards the extra costs of bringing up a disabled child. It is paid in addition to other social security benefits and can give you access to other types of help (see Box B.1).

DLA has two parts:
- **a mobility component** – for children with walking difficulties, paid at two rates. See 9 to 13 below.
- **a care component** – for children needing extra personal care, supervision or watching over because of a disability. It is paid at three different rates. See 14 to 19 below.

Your child can be eligible for either the care component or the mobility component on its own, or both components at the same time.

**Adults claiming DLA** – DLA is normally for children under the age of 16. From age 16, a young person can claim personal independence payment (PIP) instead (see 3 below). Before PIP was introduced in 2013 (or June 2016 in Northern Ireland), disabled adults under the age of 65 could also claim DLA.

If you still get DLA as an adult, you will be re-assessed for PIP at some point. For details of the re-assessment, see Box B.6 in Chapter 5. If you were aged 65 or over on 8.4.13, you are not affected and your DLA continues as normal (however, it is now administered by the same unit as attendance allowance – see Chapter 61(2)). While DLA for adults is the same as for children in most respects, there are significant differences, explained in 27 below.

### 2. Does your child qualify for DLA?

To qualify for DLA, your child must:
- pass at least one of the disability tests (see 9 and 14 below); *and*
- be within the age limits (see 3 below); *and*
- meet the qualifying periods conditions (see 4 below); *and*
- not be subject to immigration control (see Chapter 53(2)); *and*
- pass the residence and presence tests (see Chapter 53(3)).

A claim for DLA must be made (see 20 below). If your child meets all these conditions, they are entitled to DLA. They keep their underlying entitlement to DLA even if other rules mean it cannot actually be paid (see 6 below).

### 3. Age limits

**Lower age limit** – There is no lower age limit for the DLA care component. However, as there is a 3-month qualifying period (see 4 below), the DLA care component cannot be paid until your child is 3 months old. For example, if your baby has severe feeding problems from birth, the qualifying period means payment can only start from the day they reach 3 months. If your child is terminally ill (see Box B.8 in Chapter 5 for the definition) there is no qualifying period, and the care component can be paid from birth.

The higher rate mobility component can start from when your child reaches the age of 3 and the lower rate from the age of 5. Claims for the mobility component can be made earlier, but payment will not start until they have reached the appropriate age.

SSCBA, S.73(1A)

**Upper age limit** – You can claim DLA for a child up until their 16th birthday. If the young person you care for has reached their 16th birthday and is not already entitled to DLA, they need to claim personal independence payment instead (PIP; see Chapter 5).

If your child is getting DLA when they are approaching their 16th birthday, the DWP will write to you to explain about claiming PIP. The letter will also ask whether your child will need an appointee to act on their behalf (see Chapter 56(4)). Shortly after your child turns 16, the DWP will write to them (or their appointee) inviting them to claim PIP (unless they are terminally ill – see Box B.6 in Chapter 5). Contact the PIP helpline (see Chapter 61(2)) if your child (or their appointee) does not receive this letter. It is very important to make the claim by the date given in the letter so that DLA can continue until the PIP claim is decided.

## 4. Qualifying periods
### Backwards condition
To qualify for DLA, your child must pass the disability test(s) (see 9 and 14 below) throughout the three months before their claim. The claim can be made during this 3-month period, but payment will not start until the qualifying period has been served.
SSCBA, Ss.72(2)(a) & 73(9)(a)

**Renal dialysis** – If your child passed the dialysis test (see 19 below) during the three months before their claim, they will have served the qualifying period. Spells dialysing at least twice a week in hospital or as an outpatient with help from hospital staff count for this qualifying period.
DLA Regs, reg 7(3)

**Linked claims** – If your child re-claims DLA within two years of the end of a previous award, the claims are linked. This means if they have a relapse they don't have to re-serve the qualifying period. They can get DLA as soon as they re-claim, but only at the previous rate and component. If they qualify for a different amount, they will have to serve the qualifying period before it is paid.
DLA Regs, Regs 6(1) & 11

### Forwards condition
Your child must be likely to satisfy the disability test(s) throughout the six months after their claim.
SSCBA, Ss.72(2)(b) & 73(9)(b)

### Terminal illness
There is no qualifying period if your child is awarded DLA because they are terminally ill (see Box B.8 in Chapter 5). They automatically get the highest rate care component. To get the mobility component, they must pass one of the disability tests (see 9 below) from the date of claim.
SSCBA, Ss.72(5) & 73(12)

## 5. How much is DLA?
Your child can get one of the three rates of care component and one of the two rates of mobility component. They will receive the highest rate to which they are entitled. Payment of DLA is affected by some situations (see 6 below).

| Mobility component | per week |
|---|---|
| Lower rate | £22.65 |
| Higher rate | £59.75 |

| Care component | per week |
|---|---|
| Lowest rate | £22.65 |
| Middle rate | £57.30 |
| Highest rate | £85.60 |

The disability tests for the mobility component are explained in 9 to 13 below. The disability tests for the care component are explained in 14 to 19.

## 6. Does anything affect payment?
### Other benefits or help
DLA can usually be paid in full in addition to other social security benefits and tax credits. DLA is ignored as income for means-tested benefits and tax credits. If your child is awarded DLA, check to see if you then qualify for housing benefit or child tax credit, or higher amounts of either of these benefits. See Box B.1 for how an award of DLA to your child may help you qualify for other types of help.

The care component may be taken into account in non-social security means tests, such as in charging for care and support services (see Chapter 37(6)). However, the mobility component can only be taken into account if the law (not policy or practice) governing a means test specifically states that the mobility component should count.
SSCBA, S.73(14)

### If your child goes abroad
See Chapter 54(2) for details.

### If your child goes into hospital or a care home
See 7 and 8 below.

## 7. If your child goes into hospital
If your child goes into hospital, they should continue to receive DLA indefinitely, as long as they continue to meet the other qualifying conditions (see 2 above).

## B.1  DLA and other help

DLA acts as a gateway to other types of help. Listed below are the rates and components of DLA that entitle you to further help, provided you meet all the other conditions for that help.

If your child gets the middle or highest rate of the DLA care component, your family is also eligible for the help available if your child receives only the lowest rate. Similarly, if your child gets higher rate mobility component, your family is also eligible for the help available if your child receives only the lower rate.

'Premiums' are included in the assessments of housing benefit (HB) and health benefits. 'Elements' are included in child tax credit (CTC). 'Amounts' are included in universal credit (UC).

### Care component
❑ **Lowest rate**
■ Child amount, disabled child addition, lower rate (UC) – see Chapter 16(4)
■ Benefit cap exemption (HB and UC) – see Chapter 16(12) and Box G.6, Chapter 25
■ Disabled child element, disabled child rate (CTC) – see Chapter 23(4)
■ Disabled child premium (HB) – see Chapter 21(8)
❑ **Middle or highest rate**
■ Carer's allowance: carer test – see Chapter 8(2)
■ National insurance carer's credit – see Box D.3, Chapter 11
■ Income support: carer's eligibility – see Box F.1, Chapter 19
❑ **Highest rate**
■ Child amount, disabled child addition, higher rate (UC) – see Chapter 16(4)
■ Disabled child element, severely disabled child rate (CTC) – see Chapter 23(4)
■ Enhanced disability premium: child (HB) – see Chapter 21(4)

### Mobility component
❑ **Lower rate**
■ Child amount, disabled child addition, lower rate (UC) – see Chapter 16(4)
■ Benefit cap exemption (HB and UC) – see Chapter 16(12) and Box G.6, Chapter 25
■ Disabled child element, disabled child rate (CTC) – see Chapter 23(4)
■ Disabled child premium (HB) – see Chapter 21(8)
❑ **Higher rate**
■ Exemption from vehicle tax – see Chapter 7(2)
■ Blue Badge – see Chapter 7(1)
■ Motability – see Box B.16, Chapter 7

## 8. If your child goes into a care home

Normally, your child cannot get the care component if they live in a care home but you should apply for it anyway. Once you establish that your child passes the disability tests, they can get the care component for any day they stay in your home, including the day they leave and the day they return. For example, if they spend a weekend at home with you, coming home on Friday and returning on Sunday, they will get the care component for those three days.

What counts as a *'care home'* is explained in Chapter 6(7) and usually includes a residential school.

The mobility component is not affected by a stay in a care home.

**The care component in care homes** – Your child can get the care component if:

■ they are terminally ill and in a hospice;

DLA Regs, reg 10(6)

■ a local authority has placed them with someone in a private dwelling and they are under 16 and being looked after by the authority, or are under 18 and getting support from the authority because of their disability or health;

DLA Regs, reg 9(4)(a)&(b)&(5)

■ they are living outside the UK and being funded under the Education Act (such as at the Peto Institute in Hungary).

DLA Regs, reg 9(4)(c)

### The 28-day concession

If your child has been awarded the care component before they go into a care home, it can continue for up to 28 days. Payment may stop sooner if they have been in a care home within the previous 28 days. In this case, the different periods are added together and treated as one stay, and their care component will stop after a total of 28 days.

DLA Regs, reg 10(1)&(5)

You count a stay in a care home from the day after they enter to the day before they leave. Box B.13 in Chapter 6 shows how you can plan a pattern of respite care that allows them to keep their care component.

DLA Regs, reg 9(7)

## B. THE MOBILITY COMPONENT

## 9. The disability tests

### Higher rate

To qualify for the £59.75 higher rate mobility component, your child must be aged 3 or over and satisfy one of the seven tests listed below. For tests 1, 2 or 3, they must be *'suffering from physical disablement'* (but if they have severe learning disabilities that have a physical cause, they may also qualify). Their *'physical condition as a whole'* must be such that:

No. 1 they are unable to walk (see below); *or*

No. 2 they are virtually unable to walk (see 11 below); *or*

No. 3 the *'exertion required to walk would constitute a danger to [their] life or would be likely to lead to a serious deterioration in [their] health'* (see below); *or*

SSCBA, S.73(1)(a); DLA Regs, reg 12(1)(a)

No. 4 they have no legs or feet (from birth or through amputation) (see 10 below); *or*

SSCBA, S.73(1)(a); DLA Regs, reg 12(1)(b)

No. 5 they have a severe visual impairment (see below); *or*

SSCBA, Ss.73(1)(ab)&(1AB); DLA Regs, reg 12(1A)

No. 6 they are both deaf and blind (see below); *or*

SSCBA, Ss.73(1)(b)&(2); DLA Regs, reg 12(2)&(3)

No. 7 they are entitled to the highest rate care component and are severely mentally impaired with extremely disruptive and dangerous behavioural problems (see 12 below).

SSCBA, S.73(1)(c)&(3); DLA Regs, reg 12(5)&(6)

### Lower rate

To qualify for the £22.65 lower rate mobility component your child must be aged 5 or over. It doesn't matter if they are able to walk but they must be *'so severely disabled physically or mentally that, disregarding any ability [they] may have to use routes which are familiar to [them] on [their] own, [they] cannot take advantage of the faculty out of doors without guidance or supervision from another person most of the time'* (see 13 below).

SSCBA, S.73(1)(d)

They must also show that either:

■ they require *'substantially more guidance or supervision from another person than persons of [their] age in normal physical and mental health would require'*; or

■ people of their age *'in normal physical and mental health would not require such guidance or supervision'*.

SSCBA, S.73(4A)

### Unable to walk?

*'Unable to walk'* means not being able to take a step by putting one foot in front of the other. If your child has one artificial leg, their walking ability is considered when using it; they are unlikely to count as being unable to walk but they may qualify on the basis that they are virtually unable to walk (see 11 below).

### Effects of exertion

For the third disability test for the higher rate it is the exertion needed to walk that must cause the serious problem. Children with serious lung, chest or heart conditions may qualify in this way.

The *'danger'* or *'serious'* deterioration does not have to be immediate (CM/23/1985). Although any deterioration in your child's health would not have to be permanent, their recovery would need to take a significant length of time or need some kind of medical intervention (eg oxygen or drugs) (R(M)1/98). If they would get better without medical intervention after a few days rest, they won't qualify. Danger from other causes besides the effort needed to walk (eg being run over) cannot be taken into account.

### Severe visual impairment

Your child will be considered to have a severe visual impairment if their visual acuity (measured on an eye test chart called the Snellen scale) with appropriate corrective lenses if necessary, is:

■ less than 3/60; *or*

■ less than 6/60 and they have both a complete loss of peripheral vision and severely restricted central vision of no more than 10 degrees.

They must be certified by a consultant ophthalmologist as severely sight impaired or blind. If you have a CVI (certificate of visual impairment) for your child, this may provide enough information but if not, or if you tell the DWP that your child's eyesight has worsened, they may be referred for a sight test. If your child doesn't qualify for the higher rate on this basis, they may qualify for the lower rate (see 13 below).

### Deaf and blind

Your child may qualify for the higher rate if they are blind and also profoundly deaf. It must be the case that because of those conditions in combination with each other, your child is *'unable, without the assistance of another person, to walk to any intended or required destination while out of doors'*. Blind is defined as 100% disablement resulting from loss of vision (with respect to an adult, this means loss of vision such that they are unable to do any work for which eyesight is essential). Deaf is defined as 80% disablement resulting from loss of hearing (where 100% is absolute deafness). An average hearing loss at 1, 2 and 3 kHz of at least 87dB in each ear counts as 80% disablement. Your child will be referred to a DWP healthcare professional to assess their hearing loss and loss of vision.

DLA Regs, reg 12(2)-(3); R(DLA)3/95; GB Regs, Sch 2; IIPD Regs, Sch 3, Part II

## 10. Other factors

### In a coma

If your child's condition is such that they cannot *'benefit from enhanced facilities for locomotion'*, they won't be entitled to the mobility component. This generally only excludes children who are in a coma or whose medical condition means it is not safe to move them. If they can get out from time to time, they are not excluded from the mobility component.

SSCBA, S.73(8); R(M)2/83; CDLA/544/2009

### The locality

The first three disability tests for the higher rate ignore the effect of where your child lives on their mobility. Therefore, it is irrelevant if they live on a steep hill or far from the nearest bus stop.

DLA Regs, reg 12(1)(a)

### Artificial aids and medical treatment

Your child will automatically qualify under the fourth disability test if they have no legs or feet, regardless of their ability when using prostheses. However, the first three disability tests for the higher rate do take into account your child's walking abilities when using an artificial aid (such as a built-up shoe) or a prosthesis. If there is an aid or prosthesis that is *'suitable in [their] case'*, and they wouldn't be unable or virtually unable to walk if they used it, they will fail the test.

DLA Regs, reg 12(4)

If your child uses crutches and can only swing through them, rather than use them to walk with each leg able to bear their weight, then they are unable to walk.

R(M)2/89; CDLA/97/2001; [2010] EWCA Civ 962 (CoA 'Sandhu')

Painkillers do not count as an artificial aid. What counts is your child's walking ability after taking any painkillers or other medication they normally use, if it is reasonable to expect them to take it. For example, it may not be reasonable to expect a bulky nebuliser to be carried around, even though it helps when your child gets breathless (CDLA/3188/02). If you have refused treatment that might have improved your child's condition, that cannot be held against them: it is their ability to walk as they are that counts (R(M)1/95).

### Terminal illness

If your child is terminally ill, although they are treated as passing the qualifying period for the mobility component (see 4 above), they must actually pass one of the disability tests to be paid the mobility component from the time that it is claimed.

## 11. 'Virtually unable to walk'

There are four factors to be taken into account in deciding whether your child is *'virtually unable to walk'*; the test is whether their *'ability to walk out of doors is so limited, as regards:*

- *the distance over which, or*
- *the speed at which, or*
- *the length of time for which, or*
- *the manner in which*

*[they] can make progress on foot without severe discomfort, that [they are] virtually unable to walk'.*

DLA Regs, reg 12(1)(a)(ii)

### Physical cause

The test of being *'virtually unable to walk'* looks only at physical factors that limit your child's walking and only at factors that restrict their walking outdoors on a flat surface

and level ground, rather than, for example, where or when they walk outdoors.

If your child has a severe learning disability but does not meet the test described in 12 below, they may still qualify for the higher rate as virtually unable to walk if the interruptions to their walking ability can be shown to be physical in origin (see Box B.2). If your child can walk but is often unable or afraid to do so, for example because of mental illness, they may qualify for the lower rate instead (see 13 below).

If your child's walking is limited by pain or dizziness or some other symptom but their doctors do not know what is causing it or say there is no physical reason for it, it may be difficult for them to get the higher rate. However, a medical diagnosis is not necessary, and decision makers should not assume that your child's disability must be psychological because no physical cause has been identified. They should consider all the evidence. However, to get the higher rate, your child's pain, dizziness or other symptoms must have some kind of physical cause. If it is entirely psychological, they will not qualify. On the other hand, the physical cause only needs to contribute a little (ie to an appreciable extent) towards their walking difficulty. So they could qualify even if the pain is made much worse by, for example, depression.

R(DLA)4/06; R(DLA)3/06

### Severe discomfort

From the point your child starts to suffer severe discomfort walking outdoors, any extra distance they walk should be ignored (R(M)1/81). For example, they may be able to walk about 20 metres without too much pain or breathlessness, but this discomfort begins to get worse until eventually they are forced to stop. By the time they stop, they may be in agony. The first question is: at what point do they start to suffer what can be called *'severe discomfort'*? If it is at, say, 40 metres, then any extra walking should be discounted. The second question is whether or not the 40 metres they are capable of walking *'without severe discomfort'* is *'so limited... that [they are] virtually unable to walk'*.

*'Severe discomfort'* is subjective; different people have different pain thresholds and will show pain in different ways. Severe discomfort does not mean severe pain or distress; severe discomfort is less than severe pain and is far from excruciating agony, which would cause the most stoic person to stop walking.

R(M)2/92 (CoA: 'Cassinelli')

Severe discomfort includes *'pain'* or *'breathlessness'* – factors brought on by the act of walking (R(M)1/83). It does not include the screaming fits of an autistic child or other factors brought on by resistance to the idea of walking. Normally, severe discomfort has to be brought on by walking, not just by being outside (so that, for example, a child whose skin blisters badly on exposure to sunlight does not qualify). However, this does not mean any pain your child suffers must increase when they walk; if they are already in severe discomfort when they start walking, they can still qualify (R(DLA)4/04).

### Distance, speed, time and manner

These four factors affect the ability to walk outdoors and will often be closely interrelated. There is no set walking distance to mark the difference between success and failure. The decision maker must look at the speed, time and manner of walking as well as the question of severe discomfort. For example, if your child has to stop, but then after a rest they can walk again without severe discomfort, that extra distance counts, but so does the extra time it takes (R(DLA)4/03).

### Intermittent walking ability

If your child's walking ability varies from day to day, they may have difficulty showing that they are virtually unable to walk (including during the two qualifying periods).

It may help to keep a diary of their walking ability over a period of time. The fact that your child can walk on some days might not disqualify them. The question is whether or not the evidence about their walking abilities would allow a decision maker to consider that, looking at your child's physical condition as a whole, it would be true to say they are virtually unable to walk (including for the duration of the two qualifying periods).

## 12. Severe mental impairment

This way of qualifying for the higher rate mobility component is aimed at children with severe learning disabilities. If your child doesn't pass this test, they may pass the virtual inability to walk test. Box B.2 looks at how that test applies to children with learning disabilities. If your child fails both tests, they will probably pass the disability test for the lower rate (see 13 below).

To be entitled to the higher rate mobility component on the basis of severe mental impairment, your child must meet all the following conditions:

■ they must be entitled to the highest rate care component, even if it cannot be paid, for example because they live in a care home. (This rules out children who receive only the middle rate care component because they sleep soundly and safely all night. If your child is in this situation, see Box B.2.); *and*

SSCBA, S.73(3)(c)

■ they suffer from *'a state of arrested development or incomplete physical development of the brain, which results in severe impairment of intelligence and social functioning'; and*

■ they *'exhibit disruptive behaviour'* that *'is extreme'; and*

■ they *'regularly require another person to intervene and physically restrain [them] to prevent [them] causing physical injury to [themselves] or another, or damage to property'; and*

■ their behaviour *'is so unpredictable that [they require] another person to be present and watching over [them] whenever [they are] awake'.*

DLA Regs, reg 12(5)&(6)

The DWP will normally obtain a specialist's opinion before awarding the higher rate on the basis of severe mental impairment.

*'Arrested development'* refers to restricted development of the brain. *'Incomplete physical development of the brain'* must take place before the brain is fully developed. However, the brain may still be developing into the 30s or 40s, so your child's brain should be accepted as still developing.

CDLA/1079/2012

An IQ of 55 or less is generally taken to be *'severe impairment of intelligence'*. However, an IQ test is not the only measure of impaired intelligence. Some children, such as those with autism, may do well in abstract intelligence tests but cannot apply their intelligence in a useful way in the real world. For them, an IQ test can give a misleading impression of useful intelligence. Therefore, if IQ is above 55 or there is no IQ test, the decision maker must consider other evidence, including evidence of impairment of social functioning if that has an effect on useful intelligence. For example, having no sense of danger may indicate a severe impairment of intelligence (CDLA/3215/01).

R(DLA)1/00 (CoA: 'M')

Your child's level of *'social functioning'* includes their language skills and should be considered not only in a protected school or home environment but also on the street or out of doors. It should also consider their ability to interact with strangers, not just people they know well.

CDLA/1034/2014

For a younger child, the *'physical restraint'* they need to prevent them causing injury or damage can include most types of physical contact, including just a hand on the arm. However, you may have to show that an older child requires more restraint than this. In all cases, you will need to show that your child needs restraining *'regularly'*, taking into account their needs indoors as well as outdoors.

CDLA/943/2011

Your child must need watching over whenever they are awake due to their disruptive behaviour being so unpredictable. But they might have trouble passing the test if their home or school life is structured so that their behaviour is no longer disruptive, or they can be safely left alone behind closed doors. Emphasise the way in which their behaviour is disruptive despite such a structured environment. If they cannot be left alone anywhere while awake, but regularly need active intervention only in some places but not others, they can still pass the test (CDLA/943/2011 and CDLA/2955/2008).

If you think your child satisfies each part of this disability test but is turned down, consider challenging the decision (see 24 below).

## 13. The lower rate

The lower rate mobility component is for children who can walk but who generally need someone with them to guide or supervise them on unfamiliar routes. It is particularly aimed at children with learning disabilities or those with a visual impairment not severe enough to qualify for the higher rate. However, other children can qualify, eg a hearing-impaired child may need such guidance or supervision.

You must be able to show that your child needs *'substantially more'* guidance or supervision than a child of the same age would need, or that a non-disabled child of the same age would not need such guidance or supervision. Because most young children need guidance or supervision in unfamiliar places, what matters is the nature and extent of your child's needs compared with another child of the same age.

SSCBA, S.73(4A); CDLA/3048/2013

Examples of where there may be a need for guidance or supervision beyond that normally required include: if a child lacks awareness of danger from traffic and other outdoor hazards, or could not give their name and address if they got lost, or would become more disoriented or distressed than a child of the same age without a disability. A deaf child might need someone within reach watching out for them because they can't hear warnings or dangers (CDLA/2268/99). A non-disabled child may not need such close supervision.

**Guidance**
This means directing or leading. It can be physical (eg holding your child's elbow or putting a hand on their arm) or it can be verbal (eg telling them which turning to take or helping them avoid obstacles). It can also include persuasion or encouragement if they are feeling panicked and too afraid to continue (CDLA/42/94). If your child is deaf and cannot read enough to follow road maps or signs and cannot easily understand by lip reading, they may need someone with them to ask for directions or tell them which turnings to take (R(DLA)4/01).

**Supervision**
This means at least monitoring your child or the route for signs of a need to intervene, but can be more active than this (CDLA/42/94). If your child gets the middle rate care

## B.2  Learning disabilities

If your child does not qualify for the higher rate mobility component on the basis of 'severe mental impairment' (see 12 in this chapter), they are likely to pass the test for the lower rate (see 13). However, some children who are autistic or have a learning disability may qualify for the higher rate due to being 'virtually unable to walk' (see also 11).

### 'Virtually unable to walk'?
The *'virtually unable to walk'* test considers the physical limitations on your child's ability to put one foot in front of the other and continue to make progress on foot. These physical limitations can include behavioural problems if they are a reaction to or result of your child's physical disablement (eg genetic damage in the case of Down's syndrome, or brain damage). The need for help to get from one point to another and the purpose of walking are not relevant to the test.

The test looks at interruptions in the ability to make progress on foot. The interruptions must be accepted as physical in origin and part of your child's accepted physical disablement rather than, for example, being under their direct conscious control. Thus, being able to put one foot in front of the other does not stop your child passing the test. But you must be able to show that:

- their behavioural problems, which might sometimes include a failure to exercise their powers of walking, stem from a physical disability; *and*
- their walking difficulties, including interruptions in their ability to make progress on foot, happen often enough that their walking is *'so limited... that [they are] virtually unable to walk'*.

Case law establishes two parts to the 'virtually unable to walk' test:

❑ The decision maker should consider separately the distance, speed, length of time, and manner in which your child can make progress on foot (see 11). Any walking achieved only with severe discomfort must be discounted.

❑ If your child is 'virtually unable to walk', the decision maker must then decide whether that inability results from a physical impairment (such as brain damage) or from a *'physical disability which prevents the co-ordination of mind and body'*.
*R(M)3/86*

If your child has had a history of behavioural problems since birth, the decision maker *'should provide very clear reasons for attributing the behavioural problems in question to something other than brain damage'* [or Down's syndrome, etc].
*CM/98/89*

### What can you do?
Provide evidence (from a GP, consultant, etc) to show that:

- the learning disabilities have a physical cause (eg brain damage);

- all the behavioural problems that interrupt outdoor walking stem directly from that physical cause; *and*
- there is no deliberate and self-conscious choice not to walk. The interruptions are reactions to various stimuli and are the result of the brain damage or genetic damage that caused the learning disabilities and interfere with the normal co-ordination of mind and body.

You need to give the decision maker a clear picture of your child's normal walking difficulties and the frequency of interruptions in their ability to make independent progress on foot. The idea is to present an objective picture of how they normally make, or don't make, progress on foot outdoors without active help from another person.

### A walking test
In order to get a clear picture of your child's normal walking difficulties, we suggest you carry out a short outdoor walking test. Ensure the surface is reasonably flat. Choose a period of time that you consider long enough to get a good impression of your child's walking difficulties, be it one minute or ten minutes. Ask someone else to take notes if necessary.

For each test:

❑ Describe the place where you carry out the test. Mark the starting point. Note the time.

❑ Let your child loose. Don't actively intervene to help them walk. A gentle hand on the shoulder or words to help them go in the right direction is OK (for example, to help overcome any fear if they cannot see where they are going). But don't give any physical support or restraint you wouldn't routinely expect to give to a non-disabled child of the same age (so you'll need to be sure the place you do the test is safe).

❑ Describe exactly what happens. Do they move at all? If yes, how do they walk? Note what size steps they take; how they lift their legs; the speed of walking; changes in speed and in direction; their balance; and the effect of distractions. This all relates to the manner in which they walk, and the speed at which they walk.

❑ For each stop or interruption in their walking, note the time, mark the place and measure the distance from the starting point or the previous stop.

❑ Describe exactly what happened. Why do you think they stopped? Note the time they start to move on again. What made them move on, or why do you think they moved on? Give all your reasons.

❑ At the end of the period, mark the place they have reached and note the time. How far, in a straight line, is it from their starting point? If they didn't move in a straight line, measure how far they walked or ran.

*Note:* If your child's walking ability is also limited by severe discomfort, do not continue with the test. As soon as they start to suffer what they, or you, consider to be severe discomfort, note the time and mark the place. Describe the severe discomfort that made them stop. Are there any physical changes in their appearance from when they started walking? Any breathing problems? Any outward and visible signs of discomfort?

component for continual supervision to avoid danger, they could get the lower rate mobility component because of the same problems, but this is by no means automatic: you need to explain what supervision they need outdoors and how this enables them to get about (R(DLA)4/01). They may need supervision when out walking to avoid danger but this need not be the reason for supervision or guidance. What is important is that guidance or supervision enables them to overcome their mobility problems, whatever they are, and to take advantage of their ability to walk, which they would not otherwise be able to do.

### Mental or physical disability

Your child's mobility problems must be due to physical or mental disability. If fear or anxiety prevents them from walking on unfamiliar routes, it must be a symptom of a mental disability.

If your child's anxiety is connected to a physical condition, but could nevertheless be described as a symptom of mental disability, they may still qualify. For example, a deaf child needing your reassurance to overcome anxiety about being on an unfamiliar route may qualify if their anxiety is accepted as a separate mental disability.

DLA Regs, reg 12(7)&(8)

## C. THE CARE COMPONENT

### 14. The disability tests

To qualify for the DLA care component, your child's care needs must ultimately stem from disability; both physical and mental disabilities may help them qualify. They must need care, supervision or watching over from another person because of their disabilities.

Five different conditions apply to the care component. Your child must be *'so severely disabled physically or mentally that ... they require [from another person]'*:

**during the day**

No. 1 *'frequent attention throughout the day in connection with [their] bodily functions'* or

No. 2 *'continual supervision throughout the day in order to avoid substantial danger to [themselves] or others'* or

**at night**

No. 3 *'prolonged or repeated attention in connection with [their] bodily functions'* or

No. 4 *'in order to avoid substantial danger to [themselves] or others [they require] another person to be awake for a prolonged period or at frequent intervals for the purpose of watching over [them]'* or

**part-time day care**

No. 5 *'[they require] in connection with [their] bodily functions attention from another person for a significant portion of the day (whether during a single period or a number of periods)'*.

SSCBA, S.72(1)

In each case they must show that *either*:

■ their needs are *'substantially in excess of the normal requirements of persons [their] age'*; or

■ they have *'substantial'* care, supervision or watching-over needs *'which younger persons in normal physical or mental health may also have but which persons of [their] age and in normal physical and mental health would not have'*.

SSCBA, S.72(1A)

Words and phrases used here are defined below.

### Which rate will they get?

**Highest rate care component** – Your child passes the disability test for the £85.60 highest rate if they meet:

■ either (or both) No. 1 or No. 2 daytime conditions; *and*

■ either (or both) No. 3 or No. 4 night-time conditions.

Basically, their care or supervision needs must be spread throughout both the day and the night. If your child is terminally ill, they qualify automatically for the highest rate (see Box B.8 in Chapter 5 for details).

**Middle rate care component** – Your child passes the disability test for the £57.30 middle rate if they meet:

■ either (or both) No. 1 or No. 2 daytime conditions; *or*

■ either (or both) No. 3 or No. 4 night-time conditions.

Basically, their care or supervision needs can be spread throughout either the day or the night.

If your child is undergoing dialysis two or more times a week and normally needs some help with the dialysis, they may qualify automatically for the middle rate (see 19 below).

**Lowest rate care component** – Your child passes the disability test for the £22.65 lowest rate if they meet the No. 5 part-time day care condition.

### Definitions

Brief definitions are provided here. More detailed definitions are provided in Chapter 6; the information applies to DLA for children and to attendance allowance.

**Attention** – This means any active help from another person that your child needs to do the personal things they cannot do for themselves. To count as 'attention', the help they need because of their disability must be in connection with their *'bodily functions'*.

**Bodily functions** – These are personal actions such as breathing, hearing, seeing, eating, drinking, walking, sitting, sleeping, getting in or out of bed, dressing and undressing, going to the toilet, getting in or out of the bath, washing, communicating, speech practice, help with medication or treatment, etc. Anything to do with the body and how it works can count. See Chapter 6(9) for more on 'attention' and 'bodily functions'.

R(A)2/80

**Continual supervision** – 'Supervision' means there is a need for someone to be around to prevent accident or injury. 'Continual supervision' means frequent or regular, but not non-stop; your child does not need to be supervised every single minute; see Chapter 6(10) for details. Supervision and attention tend to overlap; generally speaking, however, attention tends to be active help while supervision is more passive; see Chapter 6(11) for details.

**Frequent** – This means *'several times – not once or twice'*.

R(A)2/80

**Prolonged** – This is generally accepted as being at least 20 minutes.

**Repeated** – This means needed two times or more.

R(DLA)5/05

**Significant portion of the day** – This has been interpreted as being at least an hour, though not necessarily all at once.

CDLA/58/93

Less than one hour's care may still count as a significant portion of the day. In deciding this, your position as carer may be taken into account. If your own life is disrupted by the need to give attention for short periods of time on a considerable number of occasions during the day, then those periods of providing attention taken together may be significant, even though individually they may be relatively insignificant. Periods of intense, concentrated activity may be more significant than more routine tasks.

CSDLA/29/94; R(DLA)2/03 (CoA: 'Ramsden')

**Substantial danger** – This must be real, not just a remote possibility. But the fact that an incident may be isolated or infrequent does not rule it out. As well as looking at the chances of the incident happening, the decision maker must look at the likely consequences if it does. If the consequences could be dire, then the frequency with which it is likely to happen becomes less relevant.

R(A)1/83

**Watching over** – This has its ordinary English language meaning, so it includes when you need to be awake and listening, as well as getting up and checking how your child is. See Chapter 6(12) for details.

## 15. Extra care or supervision needs
Your child's needs must also be *'substantially in excess'* of what is normally required by a child of the same age, or your child must have substantial needs that non-disabled children of the same age would not have. The needs can be additional to those of an average child the same age, or different to those of a child the same age but perhaps similar to the needs of a younger child.
SSCBA, S.72(1A); CDLA/3048/2013

The point of comparing a child's needs in this way is to ensure the DLA award is based on needs arising from disability rather than the usual care or supervision that children get. Such needs might be 'in excess' of the care and supervision needed by a non-disabled child because they are more frequent or take longer to attend to, or your child might need a greater quality or degree of attention or supervision. For example, a child who needs to be fed has needs in excess of a non-disabled child of the same age who just needs food cut up, even though both might need attention for the same length of time at meal times. Another example is a child with disabilities who needs someone watching them, whereas a non-disabled child of the same age might need someone around but it would be enough if they were in another room.

The extra condition involves a comparison between your child and non-disabled children of the same age. Children's needs vary greatly, so comparison is made with an 'average' child. Your child's needs are 'substantially' greater if they are outside the range of attention or supervision normally needed by the 'average' child, even though a particularly needy or difficult child might need similar attention or supervision. You might find it useful to compare your child's needs with those of school friends or brothers and sisters at that age.
CA/92/92

This extra condition does not apply to children who are terminally ill.
SSCBA, S.72(5)

## 16. Infants (children under 1 year old)
DWP guidance, the *Medical guidance for DLA decision makers (child cases): staff guide* (see 22 below), states that because of the amount of care and supervision all infants need, the amount needed by an infant with disabilities may not be much greater than that needed by a healthy infant, but may differ in kind. For example, instead of being handled in an ordinary manner, an infant with disabilities may need more specific stimulation or physiotherapy to develop muscle tone in their limbs, but the amount of care or supervision they need may not be greater than that given to a healthy infant.
This guidance arguably runs counter to CA/92/92 and CDLA/3048/2013 in 15 above

The guidance lists those infants who will need considerable amounts of stimulation, care or supervision in addition to the normal care routine, including infants with:
- frequent loss of consciousness usually associated with severe fits secondary to birth asphyxia or rare forms of congenital metabolic disease;
- severe impairment of vision and/or hearing;
- severe multiple disabilities;
- severe feeding problems due to physical reasons such as malformations of the mouth (eg cleft palate) or cerebral palsy; *and*
- some infants with developmental delay or learning disabilities who take longer to get enough food when feeding.
The guidance states that other infants with disabilities may

well need extra care, eg infants with renal failure, cystic fibrosis, asthma or cerebral palsy and survivors of extremely pre-term birth.

**From birth**
The guidance accepts that infants with disabilities who need the following technical procedures will have attention or supervision needs from birth that may be greatly in excess of the needs of a healthy infant:
- regular mechanical suction because they have a tracheostomy or other upper airway problem;
- regular administration of oxygen;
- tube feeding into the stomach or vein; *or*
- dealing with a gastrostomy, ileostomy, jejunostomy, colostomy or nephrostomy.

## 17. Older infants and young children
The *Medical guidance for DLA decision makers* (see 22 below) clarifies that with older infants and young children (usually 9-15 months), the gap between the care needs of a healthy child and a child with disabilities may have widened to the extent that the needs of the child with disabilities are now significantly in excess of those of a healthy child of the same age. A child with disabilities may have continued attention needs no longer needed by a healthy child of the same age. Alternatively, a child with disabilities may now need extra attention to develop new skills such as crawling, standing or walking.

The guidance lists some groups of children with needs at a level greater than is normal for their age. The list includes:
- children with brittle bones, haemophilia and other severe bleeding disorders at risk of fractures or haemorrhage from bumps and falls;
- mobile children with hearing or visual problems who cannot respond to a warning shout or see a potential danger;
- children with cerebral palsy whose mobility is impeded who need to have their position changed frequently in order to reduce the risk of postural deformity;
- children with severe learning disabilities who need extra stimulation to maximise their potential, or who eat undesirable substances or mutilate themselves; *and*
- children in whom developmental delay may first become evident because of their need for a continuing level of attention appropriate for a much younger baby.
The guidance does not provide exhaustive advice and children with other needs may qualify. For example, it mentions the care needs created by severe eczema but not those created by ichthyosiform erythroderma and similar skin conditions, which can also involve a substantial amount of extra care – eg frequent bathing, nappy changing, applying preparations and dressings, and comforting a child whose sleep is disturbed.

**Night needs in infants and young children**
The *Medical guidance for DLA decision makers* points out that specific, regular attention at night in excess of normal levels may be needed by some children with disabilities whose medical condition requires parental intervention in the form of turning, nebuliser or oxygen therapy, suction, intubation, and care during fits, etc.

It states that where such attention is not needed and suitable precautions are taken (such as the child being safely placed in a cot), there may be few conditions requiring watching over that is substantially in excess of that needed by a healthy child of the same age. However, the guidance accepts that children with severe learning difficulties may have an abnormal tendency to develop a persistent habit of night wakening, in which case extra attention may be needed at night. Explain carefully on the claim-form why the attention that your child needs during the night is in excess of that normally needed by other children of the same age.

## 18. Older children

As children develop, both physically and mentally, there may be a reduction in their care needs; on the other hand, some care needs may increase.

For example, a child with a physical disability may get better at using aids to move independently. Increasing maturity may mean children with chronic illnesses, such as diabetes, can take responsibility for the care of their condition (and so need less supervision). Specialist education may help to reduce the needs of children with sensory impairments.

On the other hand, physical development may increase care or supervision needs. A child with a learning disability may need more supervision as they get older and become more mobile. Adolescents with disabilities may have to cope with their care or mobility needs while undergoing rapid changes to their bodies. This may exacerbate the non-conforming or rebellious behaviour common among this age group.

## 19. Renal dialysis

If your child undergoes renal dialysis, special rules can help them to qualify for the middle rate care component. Depending on when and where they dialyse, they will be treated as satisfying the disability tests for the day or the night. The conditions are that:

■ they undergo renal dialysis two or more times a week; *and*
■ the dialysis is of a type that normally requires the attendance or supervision of another person during the period of the dialysis; *or*
■ because of their particular circumstances (eg their age) during the period of dialysis they need someone to supervise them in order to avoid substantial danger to themselves, or to give them some help with their bodily functions.

DLA Regs, reg 7

For more details, see Chapter 6(14); the rules are the same for DLA.

## D. CLAIMS, PAYMENTS & APPEALS

## 20. How do you claim?

**Starting the claim** – To get a DLA claim-form (the *DLA1A Child*) ring 0800 121 4600 (textphone 0800 121 4523) or download it from the website (www.gov.uk/disability-living-allowance-children/how-to-claim). To get a DLA claim-form in Northern Ireland ring 0800 587 0912 (textphone 028 9031 1092) or download it from the website (www.nidirect.gov.uk/publications/disability-living-allowance-dla-child-claim-form-and-guidance-notes-dla-1a). For advice on how to complete the claim-form, see Box B.3.

**The date of claim** – If you phone for a claim-form, your child's DLA can be backdated to the date of your call. A claim-form issued by the DWP will be date stamped and come with a postage-paid envelope. If you return the completed claim-form within six weeks, the date you asked for it is your date of claim. If you take longer than six weeks to return the completed form, explain why on the form. If the delay is reasonable, the time limit can be extended. If not, your date of claim is the day the completed claim-form reaches the Disability Benefits Centre.

If you download a claim-form from the website, your date of claim is the day the completed form reaches the Disability Benefits Centre.

## 21. Keeping a diary

If you are claiming DLA for your child, keeping a diary of their day-to-day needs can improve their chances of success. It can also be important when trying to explain needs that fluctuate either during a single day or over a longer period.

**One-day diary** – The simplest form of diary would be an account of your child's needs over a typical day. Start from the time your child gets up in the morning, through a 24-hour period, ending with the time they get up the following morning. Try to list all the times when they need help from someone else and how it is different to the help needed by other children of the same age. When you write something down, try to answer the following questions:

■ what help do they need?
■ why do they need the help?
■ at what time do they need help? *and*
■ how long do they need the help for?

The information booklet that comes with the DLA claim-form gives an example of such a diary; see Box B.4 for another example.

If your child's needs vary from day to day, it would be worthwhile keeping the diary over a few days to get a clearer picture of their needs.

**Long-term diary** – Long-term diaries can be useful when explaining more sporadic problems caused by your child's condition, such as falls or fits. If your child needs continual supervision or watching-over, such a diary can show exactly what happened or what could have happened if someone had not been there to stop it. See Box B.15 in Chapter 6 for an example of a long-term diary.

### Making use of the diary

Once you have finished the diary, put your child's name and child reference number at the top and make several copies of it. Attach a copy to the claim-form and keep a copy for yourself. If you ask someone to complete the 'Statement from someone who knows the child' on the form, give them a copy. Finally, you should send copies of the diary to anyone else you have listed on the claim-form, such as the paediatrician, GP or specialist nurse.

## 22. How the claim is assessed

Decisions are made by DWP decision makers, not by healthcare professionals. To help make decisions, the DWP uses online guidance: the *Medical guidance for DLA decision makers (child cases): staff guide*, which outlines the main care and mobility needs likely to arise from different illnesses and disabling conditions. It is available via our website (www.disabilityrightsuk.org/links-government-departments).

The completed claim-form and this guidance may give the decision maker enough information to make a decision. If not, they may request a short report from your child's paediatrician, GP or specialist nurse (or any other person you mentioned on the claim-form who is involved in your child's treatment or care). If your child is at school, the decision maker may request a copy of an education, health and care plan or a statement of special education needs from the school.

If these do not give a complete picture, the decision maker can arrange for a DWP-approved healthcare professional to assess your child (normally in your home) in order to prepare a report. An assessment can also be arranged instead of getting in touch with the paediatrician, GP, nurse, etc.

### The assessment

Before the assessment, read through the information booklet that came with the claim-form and the copy you made of the completed form.

During the assessment, the healthcare professional should ask questions relating to each of the areas covered on the claim-form (see Box B.3).

In the case of an infant or young child, the healthcare professional will put the questions to you. They may address an older child directly, depending on the nature of their impairment; you can add to what your child has to say in terms of the care you provide.

Ensure that the healthcare professional knows about any pain or tiredness your child feels when carrying out each task. If you need to encourage or prompt your child to start or complete a task properly, make sure you tell the healthcare professional about this. Let them know about any variation in your child's condition and about both good and bad days. Show them any medical evidence you have confirming your child's problems.

The healthcare professional might carry out a brief physical examination of your child.

After completing their report, the healthcare professional sends it to the decision maker, who decides whether or not to award DLA and, if it is awarded, at what rate.

### Delays

The DWP aims to give you a decision within 40 working days (ie not including weekends or public holidays) of the day they receive the DLA claim for your child. If your child is terminally ill and the claim is made under the 'special rules' (see Box B.8 in Chapter 5), you should get a decision within eight working days. Compensation may be payable for long delays (see Chapter 59(2) for details).

In any case, if the claim is taking too long, complain to the Disability Benefits Centre dealing with the claim.

### 23. The award

Once the claim for your child is decided, you are sent notice of the decision. Any award made will be for a fixed period. This could be for just one year, or for a longer period if it is clear that the condition(s) giving rise to a need for help are likely to continue. The DWP will invite you to make a renewal claim about four months before the end of the award, unless your child is approaching 16, in which case they normally have to claim personal independence payment instead once they reach that age (see 3 above).

**Backdating** – DLA cannot be backdated to earlier than the date of claim (see 20 above). There are only limited situations in which an earlier date can be treated as the date of claim, which are:

❏ If industrial action has caused postal disruption, the day the claim would have been delivered to a Disability Benefits Centre is treated as the date of claim.

C&P regs, reg 6(5)

❏ If a decision maker uses their discretion to treat anything written as being sufficient to count as a valid claim, the date that earlier document was received is treated as the date of claim.

### 24. If you are not happy with the decision

If you are not happy with the decision on your child's claim, you can ask for a *'mandatory reconsideration'* of the decision within one calendar month of the date the DWP sends it to you. When the decision maker reconsiders the decision, they can confirm the initial decision, or increase or reduce the rate of the award, or the length of the award. You have a further month to appeal to an independent tribunal if you are not happy with the reconsidered decision. The 1-month time limit to ask for a mandatory reconsideration can be extended only if there are special reasons for the delay. Otherwise, if the decision was notified to you more than one month ago, see below.

**Asking for a mandatory reconsideration** – If you want to challenge the decision, it will help to know why it was made. You must also get your reconsideration in on time. Write to the address (or ring the number) on the decision letter and do the following:

■ request a mandatory reconsideration of the decision. State your grounds simply at this stage; for example, *'I believe you have underestimated how my child's disability affects her and how much care and supervision she needs'*;

■ ask them to send you copies of all the evidence they used to make the decision; *and*

■ ask them not to take any further action until you have had the chance to respond to that evidence.

If you phone, put your request in writing as well; keep a copy for yourself. If you have not received the evidence after two weeks, ring again to remind them to send it. When you do receive the evidence, you should have a better idea of why the decision was made.

Advice Now has created a tool you can use to generate a detailed mandatory reconsideration letter: www.advicenow. org.uk/dla-tool.

### Building a case

Sometimes the only evidence used will be the information you gave on the claim-form. However, there may be a report as well. This could be a short one from your child's paediatrician, GP or specialist nurse, etc, or a longer one from the healthcare professional who examined your child for the DWP. Compare the report with the claim-form. Try to find where a difference of opinion arises.

For example, you may have written on the claim-form that your child could not feed themselves or wash and bathe themselves without support, but the healthcare professional's report said they considered that your child could manage these tasks unassisted. Now try to get evidence that shows that what you said on the claim-form is correct, for example a letter from your child's paediatrician confirming the difficulties that your child has with washing, bathing and feeding and why you need to provide them with help doing these things.

Once you have obtained some supportive evidence, make a copy of it and send it to the address on the decision letter. If it could take a while to obtain the evidence, you should tell the DWP how long it is likely to take, so they do not make a decision straight away.

A decision maker will look at any further evidence that you send in. They will then either revise the decision in your child's favour or write back explaining that they have been unable to change the decision. Either way, if you are not satisfied with the result, you now have a month from the date of the reconsidered decision to appeal to an independent tribunal. For more on appeals, see Chapter 57.

### If the decision was notified more than one month ago

To challenge a decision notified more than one month ago (or if there has been a change of circumstances), you need to show there are specific grounds, eg:

■ there has been a change of circumstances since the decision was made – eg your child's care needs have increased; *or*

■ the decision maker didn't know about a relevant fact – eg you missed out some aspect of your child's care needs or mobility difficulties when you filled in the claim-form.

See Box O.8, Chapter 57 for details.

### 25. How is DLA paid?

DLA is usually paid every four weeks in arrears, on a Wednesday, into your bank, building society or Post Office card account. If your child is terminally ill, DLA can be paid weekly if you ask.

### 26. What if your child's condition changes?

**If your child's condition gets worse** – If your child already receives DLA, give the DWP details of the change (0800 121 4600; textphone 0800 121 4523; or write to Disability Benefit Centre 4, Post Handling Site B, Wolverhampton, WV99 1BY). If you live in Northern Ireland, contact the Disability & Carers Service (DCS: 0800 587 0912; textphone 028 9031 1092; or write to Castle Court, Royal Avenue, Belfast, BT1 1HR). The DWP or DCS will usually send you a claim-form to complete, similar to that used for new claims (see Box B.3).

## B.3 Completing the DLA claim-form

Most of the DLA claim-form consists of a series of questions relating to your child's mobility and their care and supervision needs. These questions have a tick-box format – there is a list of statements and you are asked to tick the box next to each statement that applies to your child. There is space to give more detail of your child's difficulties.

Read the information booklet that comes with the claim-form before answering the questions, as it gives an idea of what to say and provides examples of answers. We focus below on some of the questions in more detail.

### Mobility questions

#### Do they have physical difficulties walking?

This question relates to the higher rate of the mobility component for children aged 3 or over. Read 9 and 11 in this chapter before answering.

You are asked to tick the boxes that best describe how far your child can walk without severe discomfort, how long it takes them, what their walking speed is and the way they walk. You are also asked whether the effort of walking would seriously affect their health.

**A walking test** – If you are not sure which boxes to tick, you can do a test of your child's walking ability outdoors. Ensure the surface is reasonably flat. Focus on the distance they can walk, their speed, the time it takes them and the way they walk.

Ask your child to walk until they feel they can no longer continue (if it is safe for them to do so). Write down what happens and when in terms of distance and time (the information booklet that comes with the claim-form has tips for estimating distances correctly). Include things like pain, dizziness, coughing, spasms, uncontrollable actions or reflexes, breathlessness or asthma attacks. Note how long it takes them to recover before they can walk again. Transfer your findings to the claim-form.

**Severe learning difficulties** – If your child has severe learning difficulties and behavioural problems, they may qualify for the higher rate of the mobility component (the conditions are set out in 12 in this chapter). Use this part of the claim-form to describe your child's behaviour when they are walking outdoors and how this limits their walking. You could carry out the walking test described in Box B.2.

#### Do they need guidance or supervision most of the time when they walk outdoors?

This question relates to the lower rate of the mobility component for children aged 5 or over. Read 13 in this chapter before answering. You must be able to show that the help your child needs is more than the help other children of the same age need. Try to give examples, eg: *"I have to hold her hand all the time because I never know what she's going to do next – my friend's 6-year old can run ahead and knows to wait at the next road."*

If your child has severe learning difficulties, then you should answer the question even if they are under 5, as this information is relevant to whether they qualify for the higher rate as well (see above).

You are asked if your child falls due to their disability. A long-term diary may help to show how often your child has fallen recently and what happened when they fell. You can attach a copy of the diary to the claim-form. See Box B.15 in Chapter 6 for an example of a long-term diary.

### Care questions

These questions relate to the care component and are for children of all ages. If your child is a baby, read 16 in this chapter before completing the questions; if they are a young child, read 17; if they are an older child, read 18. Also read the information booklet that comes with the claim-form; this explains what is relevant for each question and provides examples of answers.

The first questions relate to different daily tasks. Each question has a box where you can give more detail, such as why your child needs the help and how their needs vary. Think about all the help your child needs and compare this to the help a non-disabled child of the same age would need. For instance, if you have older children, what were they like at that age? Or, compare to a friend's child or others at nursery or school. Write down if things take longer with your child or you have to do different things to help them.

If your child's condition is variable, do not focus just on good days. You need to explain what help your child needs regularly. Try to focus on an average day and list the problems your child faces more often than not. Also, explain what your child is like on their worst days and how often these occur. A diary could help with this (see 21 in this chapter).

#### Do they have difficulty seeing/hearing?

Two questions focus on seeing and hearing difficulties. If you have a certificate of visual impairment or an audiology test report for your child, attach a copy of it to the claim-form. Because there may be so many different things you need to do for your child if they have sight or hearing problems, it may be easier to write a 1-day diary to list them (see Box B.4). If your child has difficulty communicating due to sight or hearing problems, explain these in the question *'Do they have difficulty and need help communicating?'*.

#### Do they have difficulty speaking?

Your child may have limited speech, perhaps because of hearing problems or a learning disability. They may have an odd tone of voice or speed of talking, unusual vocabulary, or limited or no body language that make it difficult to understand them. In the next question you can give more details of how their speech problems affect their ability to communicate.

#### Do they have difficulty and need help communicating?

This question is about difficulties your child has communicating. Here we look at three types of problem.

**Understanding others** – If your child has hearing problems, they may have difficulty understanding others who do not sign or they may not be able to lip-read people they do not know well. Children with learning disabilities may rely on non-verbal communication and find strangers difficult to understand. They may misread the body language of others, eg they may not be able to tell when someone is angry or upset. If your child is confused by figures of speech (eg *"I'm fed up to the back teeth"*) or finds long or complex sentences difficult, write this down.

Your child may need someone to interpret what another person is saying, or for them to repeat it several times or re-phrase it into simpler language. Try to give an idea of how much longer it takes your child to understand something compared to other children, eg *"David finds lip-reading strangers really tough – they always have to repeat themselves four or five times and even then he only gets about half of what's said – he's always doing the wrong thing because he hasn't understood properly."*

**Being understood** – Explain the difficulties your child has being understood and how it affects them, for example if they get very frustrated. What do you do to help them be understood and deal with the frustration? For example, you may interpret for them, or encourage them to say things in different ways or speak more clearly. Your child may communicate by signing or other non-verbal communication and need someone to interpret what they are saying.

**Unwilling to communicate** – Does your child live in their own world and show little desire to communicate? Do they find it easier to talk to adults and only about their own limited topics of conversation? Would they like to talk to other children but lack the skills or confidence, or do they get frustrated or angry when trying to communicate?

Write down the help they need. For example, you may encourage your child to talk about different things or help them in conversations with other children to build their skills and confidence. You may do exercises or games at home designed to build their communication skills.

### Do they have fits, blackouts, seizures, or something similar?

You could keep a diary over a period of time to show how often your child has fits or blackouts and what happens when these occur. Attach a copy of the diary to the claim-form. Box B.15 in Chapter 6 has an example of a long-term diary.

### Do they need to be supervised during the day to keep safe?

This question looks at the supervision that your child needs; read 14 in this chapter and Chapter 6(10) before answering it.

All children need some supervision, particularly very young children, so you need to show that your child needs more supervision; see 15 in this chapter. Write down examples of incidents such as falls, fits or asthma attacks. Was your child injured? Was anything broken? Or did your intervention prevent such occurrences? You could keep a long-term diary of such incidents and attach a copy to the claim-form.

You may have to monitor your child's diet more closely because of diabetes, a severe food allergy or an eating disorder. If your child has a skin condition, they may need monitoring to stop them scratching.

With conditions such as diabetes, older children might be expected to monitor themselves. However, they can sometimes refuse to accept the reality of their condition, leading to rebellious behaviour that requires more supervision.

### Do they need extra help with their development?

This question is about what you do to help your child understand the world around them and react to it appropriately. Here we look at four areas of development.

**Physical or sensory skills** – List any difficulties your child has moving around (eg sitting, standing, running, walking or crawling) and any problems with co-ordination and manipulation (eg holding a pen or cutlery, picking things up, throwing or kicking). Write down if they need help with exercises to develop these skills, how long they take and how often they need to be done.

If your child has sight problems, it may be more difficult for them to learn about the world around them; you may have to spend more time making physical contact with them and speaking to them to ensure they get enough stimulation. Or, if they have hearing problems, you may have to teach them sign language and make extra efforts to communicate (eg by ensuring you are in the same room, facing them, and that they can see you clearly).

**Learning skills** – Write down if your child has difficulty learning everyday skills, such as dressing and washing, learning to read and write, or if they find it difficult to understand or follow instructions. Or maybe they can learn skills, but have difficulty applying them to other appropriate situations, eg; *"He knows how to ask at the newsagents for his comic and to pay for it, but if I ask him to go to the shop and get something else, he can't do it, he can't see that it's the same thing."* Explain

what sort of extra help they need; this may be physical help or verbal encouragement. Say how long it takes and how your child reacts.

**Social skills** – If your child has difficulty in social situations, write this down. For example, they may spend time on their own and avoid others, their behaviour might be aggressive or inappropriate, they may lack empathy or the ability to read body language, or they may interrupt people and not understand the rules of turn-taking. You might encourage them to respond to people when asked a question and to maintain eye contact, or read 'social stories' with them to help them understand people's responses. Explain that it is important for your child to learn these skills to prevent isolation or bullying in the future.

**Play** – Does your child find it difficult to play with other children or can they be aggressive; do they need adult involvement when they play; do they have physical difficulty holding toys or seeing where they are; do they lack imagination or have a tendency to be obsessional; do they have difficulty maintaining an interest in any activity? Explain the help they need. For example, you may encourage them to stay interested in a particular game, show them different parts of a toy and help them hold or feel it, ask questions to develop their imagination, or intervene to prevent them hurting themselves or someone else. Do you have special games to play with them to develop certain skills, eg social, manipulative or language skills?

Two questions follow: *'Do they need encouragement, prompting or physical help at school or nursery?'* and *'Do they need encouragement, prompting or physical help to take part in hobbies, interests, social and religious activities?'* (see the information booklet that comes with the claim-form for a good list of hobbies, etc). Try to give as much information as you can. You may need to use extra paper; if you do, put your child's name and child reference number on each sheet. You may want to cross-refer to what you have already written for other questions (particularly the one on development – see above).

### Do they wake and need help at night, or need someone to be awake to watch over them at night?

Read 14 in this chapter and the information booklet that comes with the claim-form before answering this question. If your child needs help at night with things they also need help with during the day (eg using the toilet), you can cross-refer to the questions you have already answered.

If you need to make extra checks on your child in the night, say why. Do they get up and wander? What sort of things do they do – could they hurt themselves or others? Are they liable to have fits, seizures or breathing problems at night? Do you need to check medical equipment? Write down how often you need to check on your child, or if you sleep in the same room to keep an eye on them, explain why this is necessary.

### Statement from someone who knows the child

The claim-form includes an optional part to be completed by someone who knows your child; this could be their paediatrician or specialist nurse. However, if a lot of your child's problems are related to learning, a teacher or specialist support worker would be equally appropriate. If possible, make an appointment with them so you can discuss the matter. The Child Poverty Action Group has a useful factsheet listing the points that should be covered in the statement (www.cpag.org.uk/content/dla-statements-guidance-education-staff).

## B.4 One-day diary

**This is a diary for Ayesha, a 10-year-old girl with cerebral palsy**

*6.30-6.40am* Wake Ayesha up – doesn't want to get up but we have to get up early to have time to do her physio before school – watch over her as she gets out of bed – just needs a hand to steady her as she gets up and gets her sticks.

*6.48am* Breakfast – Ayesha pours the cereal into her bowl – bit spilt but not too bad today – I do the milk.

*7.15-7.45am* Help her get cleaned up after breakfast – she always gets dressed after as can be a bit messy. Bit of trouble getting the toothpaste out – too much – help her clear it up. She gets a bit frustrated getting her clothes on – takes a few attempts – I chat to her to keep her calm and encourage her. She wants me to do it but I encourage her to do what she can. I give her a hand with the buttons on her school shirt and her socks.

*7.55-8.20am* Help Ayesha with physio – she's not keen but I do it alongside her and put on her favourite song to try to make it more fun.

*8.45-8.55am* Off to school – needs help climbing into the car. Drive up – have to park in the teacher's car park, help her out and see her into school. Most of her friends walk up or get dropped at the gate but that's too far for her. She tries to lean on me as we go in but I encourage her to use her sticks.

*9.00am-3.30pm* At school. Ayesha has a support worker for two hours a day – she helps her with PE and getting dressed and undressed, speech, and handwriting as she has difficulty with fine motor control. She also helps her keep focused – because Ayesha gets tired easily she has difficulty concentrating.

*3.30-3.45pm* Pick up Ayesha and her friend – help her into car and out again when we get home.

*3.50pm* Girls watching TV while I make the tea – Ayesha gets really tired at school and finds it hard to do much when she gets in.

*5.00-5.25pm* Tea – I cut up Ayesha's food for her – she feeds herself but gets a bit frustrated when she keeps dropping it – also she gets embarrassed in front of her friend – I chat away to them both to help the moment pass.

*5.40-6.30pm* Ayesha's friend goes home and we have to do physio again – she's tired but I push her – by the end she's very tearful so we cut it short – sit and have a cuddle instead.

*6.40-7.55pm* Homework – writing takes a lot longer for Ayesha and she gets very tired with the concentration needed – it takes a long time as it's a big effort and she needs lots of encouragement and praise. Do what we can but don't manage to finish it.

*7.55-8.00pm* Help Ayesha feed her pet axolotl. She cannot get the top off the food jar without spilling it.

*8.00-8.30pm* Watch Eastenders.

*8.35-8.55pm* Bath – help Ayesha in – leave her to it and she shouts when she's ready to get out. Help her out of the bath. Give her a hand getting dried – she can do it but it takes a lot longer and she's getting cold. Give her a hand with pyjamas – she's getting tired now.

*9.05pm* Make her bedtime drink.

*9.20pm* Ayesha goes up to bed – listens to a story download – she likes to read but turning the pages of a book is difficult when she's tired.

*2.20am* Ayesha calls out – needs toilet – go to help her out of bed and get to the toilet and then back again – she's too sleepy to manage with her sticks.

Your child's existing award may be superseded to include a higher rate or a new component (from three months after their needs increased). A top-up claim for the component they do not already have does not count as a new claim, but rather as a change to their existing award.

**If your child's condition improves** – If your child's care or mobility needs lessen, this may mean the rate of their DLA should drop. Contact the DWP or DCS (see above) to give them details. A decision maker will usually supersede their award.

If your child's rate of DLA drops (or ends) but they have a relapse within two years, they can get back their former rate of benefit in a linked claim without having to serve the qualifying period (see 4 above) again.

DLA Regs, regs 6(1) & 11

## E. DLA FOR ADULTS

### 27. How is DLA different for adults?

The DLA rules for people aged 16 or over are broadly the same as for children but with some differences.

First, the comparison of your needs with children of the same age, described in 15 above, no longer applies once you reach the age of 16.

Second, if you are aged 16 or over, there is an extra way of

## B.5 The cooking test

Once you turn 16, you can qualify for the lowest rate of the DLA care component on the basis of the *'cooking test'*. The upper age limit for passing the test for the first time is the day before you turn 65. But if you claimed before turning 65, the lowest rate can be maintained and renewed.

To satisfy the cooking test you must be *'so severely disabled physically or mentally that... [you] cannot prepare a cooked main meal for [yourself] if [you have] the ingredients'*.

SSCBA, S.72(1)(a)(ii)

The cooking test is a hypothetical test of your level of disability rather than your cooking ability. It tests whether you can carry out all the activities necessary to prepare a cooked main meal without help from someone else.

### What does the cooking test involve?

There are a number of issues involved in the cooking test. The *'cooked main meal'* that you must show you *'cannot prepare'* for yourself is a labour-intensive, reasonable, main meal, freshly cooked on a traditional cooker. This is a standard meal for just one person, not for the rest of the household. The use of the word 'prepare' in the law emphasises your ability to prepare all the ingredients ready for cooking. It is not a meal made up of ready-prepared convenience foods, such as pies and frozen vegetables.

You *'cannot prepare a cooked main meal for [yourself]'* if you can only do so with some help. Any type of help counts – it doesn't have to involve any substantial effort. But it must be crucial in enabling you to start or carry on with tasks you are otherwise capable of doing by yourself. The cooking test also covers you if your disability means you cannot cook at all, even if you had help.

As the test is hypothetical, it is not relevant if you don't want to or can't afford to cook a traditional main meal. Nor is it relevant that you prepare, cook and freeze several meals on the days someone is there to help you (and then defrost and heat them up in the microwave on the other days). The test depends on what you cannot do, without help, if you tried to do it on each day.

R(DLA)2/95

qualifying for the lowest rate of the care component. This is if *'[you] cannot prepare a cooked main meal for [yourself] if [you have] the ingredients'*. Details of the 'cooking test' are in Box B.5.
SSCBA, S.72(1)(a)(ii)

Third, if you are aged 18 or over, you cannot be paid DLA once you have been in hospital for more than 28 days; the rules are the same as for personal independence payment (see Chapter 5(7)).

There are further differences if you are aged 65 or over, when the rules for DLA are similar to those for attendance allowance (see Chapter 6). Attendance allowance has no equivalent to the mobility component or the lowest rate care component. There is a 6-month qualifying period (rather than a 3-month qualifying period; see 4 above). The differences have implications for renewal and top-up claims for DLA.

## Renewal and top-up claims from age 65
If your DLA award ends and you were 65 or over on 8.4.13, you can make a renewal claim, or a linked claim within one year of your previous award ending. If you leave it longer than a year, you must claim attendance allowance instead. If you had not yet reached 65 on 8.4.13, you will need to claim personal independence payment instead (see Box B.6 in Chapter 5).

**Care component** – You can maintain or renew the lowest rate if you qualified for it before reaching 65. If your care needs lessen after 65, you cannot drop to the lowest rate – you will lose the care component altogether. You can, however, regain the lowest rate if you re-claim it within 12 months of your earlier award ending. If your care needs change after you reach 65, you can switch between the middle and highest rates or move up from the lowest rate, but you must meet the 6-month qualifying period.
DLA Regs, Sch 1, para 3(2)&(3)

There is an exception that allows the DWP to drop you to the lowest rate even if you pass the disability test after the age of 65. This applies if the DWP decides you were not entitled to the rate you were getting before you reached 65 because the original decision maker did not know about, or made a mistake about, a fact in your case (rather than because your circumstances have changed).
DLA Regs, Sch 1, para 1; CDLA/301/2005

If you receive the mobility component, a change in your care needs after you reach 65 enables your DLA award to be superseded. This means you can claim the care component (at the middle or highest rate) rather than attendance allowance, even if you are aged, say, 70. You can still claim the lowest rate care component after age 65 if you met the qualifying conditions before you turned 65 and have a

---

If you would be limited to cooking a very narrow range of main meals, you should pass the test.
*CDLA/17329/96*

### Intermittent disability
You don't have to show you cannot cook on every day of the three months before your claim and are likely to be unable to cook on every day of the next six months. The test is rather about what is normal for you over a period of time. Taking the ordinary meaning of the words, and the effects of your disability, is it true to say that (over the 9-month qualifying period) you *'cannot prepare a cooked main meal...'*?
*R(A)2/74; R(DLA)7/03 (HoL: 'Moyna')*

The ability to cook a main meal on four out of seven days each week does not mean that you must fail the test. All depends on the pattern of what you cannot do over the whole qualifying period. You may still have difficulties on your good days that can tip the balance your way. You should explain fully what you can't do on both your good and bad days. In practice, if you say on the DLA claim-form that you need help only on one to three days, your chances of success are much lower.

### Reasonableness
The test is whether you cannot reasonably be expected to prepare a cooked main meal for yourself. Things like safety, tiredness, pain, nausea, breathing difficulties in a hot, steamy kitchen or the time it takes you to do everything may mean that it is not reasonable to expect you to do so (R(DLA)1/97).

If you can't stand for long enough, it may be suggested that you could use a stool. This might be reasonable if all you had to do was wait for a pan to boil, but you might not be able to stir or check food, move pans about on the cooker, or chop vegetables from a sitting position (R(DLA)8/02 and CDLA/1714/2005). Whether it is reasonable for you to use a stool also depends on the size and layout of your kitchen (CDLA/972/2012). It might not be reasonable if you would have to move the stool while cooking and don't have the strength to do so.

### Special equipment
The cooking test doesn't depend on the type of facilities or equipment you have. The test is satisfied if you can't perform the tasks necessary to prepare a meal using normal facilities and devices (R(DLA)2/95). Whether you could manage by specially adapting your kitchen is irrelevant. Being able to heat convenience food in a microwave is not relevant. However, if you use a microwave to cook main meals with ingredients you prepare yourself, you might not pass the test. If you use a microwave in this way, explain any drawbacks, eg can you only cook a narrow range of meals?

### Practice and process
To produce an edible cooked main meal you must be able to carry out, alone, all the physical and mental actions, tasks and stages involved. If there is any part of the process you are (or would be) unable to carry out alone, you pass the test – even if you cope (or would cope) well with the rest.

If you have a mental disability and cannot plan ahead or complete complex tasks, you will pass the cooking test. If lack of motivation is caused by, or is a symptom of, a mental disability, so that you cannot prepare a meal, you could pass the test (CSDLA/80/96).

The process of preparing a cooked main meal includes:
- planning what to prepare – eg choosing each ingredient and the quantity required. It is assumed you have the ingredients for the meal ready, so preparation may not include getting them out;
- carrying out all the stages in the correct order and at the right time;
- washing and chopping ingredients;
- using taps – eg to fill a pan;
- using a cooker – eg lighting and adjusting the gas, opening and closing an oven door;
- putting food into pans, stirring, tasting, checking it is properly cooked;
- lifting and moving full pans (you are usually expected to use a slotted spoon to drain vegetables);
- bending to lift pans from the oven (explain why it is reasonable for you to use the oven – eg to prepare a reasonable variety of meals, or to use a low-level grill); *and*
- serving your meal.

current mobility award made before you turned 65.
DLA Regs, Sch 1, para 7; CSDLA/388/00

**Mobility component** – Once you reach the age of 65, you can only stay on the rate you got before you were 65. You cannot move up or down a rate. There is an exception to this rule: you can switch to the higher rate after age 65 if you can show that you met the conditions for it before you turned 65.

If you have a current award of the care component made before you were 65, you can claim the mobility component after your 65th birthday if your mobility difficulties began before you were 65. If you begin to satisfy the disability test for the mobility component only after you turn 65, you cannot get it.
DLA Regs, Sch 1, paras 1, 5 & 6; CSDLA/388/00

# 5 Personal independence payment

## A General points

| | | |
|---|---|---|
| 1 | What is personal independence payment? | 30 |
| | Re-assessment of existing DLA claimants – Box B.6 | 31 |
| | PIP and other help – Box B.7 | 32 |
| 2 | Do you qualify? | 30 |
| 3 | Age limits | 30 |
| 4 | The required period condition | 32 |
| | Terminal illness – Box B.8 | 34 |
| 5 | How much do you get? | 32 |
| 6 | Does anything affect what you get? | 33 |
| 7 | If you go into hospital | 33 |
| 8 | If you go into a care home | 33 |

## B The PIP assessment

| | | |
|---|---|---|
| 9 | What is the PIP assessment? | 35 |
| 10 | The daily living component | 36 |
| 11 | What are daily living activities? | 36 |
| | Daily living activities – Box B.9 | 38 |
| 12 | The mobility component | 40 |
| 13 | What are mobility activities? | 40 |
| | Mobility activities – Box B.10 | 40 |

## C Claims, payments & appeals

| | | |
|---|---|---|
| 14 | How do you claim? | 41 |
| | Completing the form | |
| | *How your disability affects you* – Box B.11 | 42 |
| 15 | How your claim is assessed | 44 |
| 16 | The decision | 44 |
| 17 | If you are not happy with the decision | 44 |
| 18 | How are you paid? | 45 |
| 19 | What if your condition changes? | 45 |
| 20 | Reviewing your claim | 45 |
| 21 | What happens when your award is due to end? | 45 |

## A. GENERAL POINTS

### 1. What is personal independence payment?

Personal independence payment (PIP) is a benefit for people who have a physical or mental disability and need help taking part in everyday life or find it difficult to get around. It replaced disability living allowance (DLA) for people aged 16 or over. People who still get DLA will normally be asked to claim PIP instead at some stage (Box B.6 explains how and when this will happen). However, if you had reached the age of 65 by 8.4.13, you can keep and renew your DLA award and won't be asked to claim PIP instead.

PIP is tax free, is not means tested and you do not need to have paid national insurance contributions to get it. It is not affected by earnings or other income. It is almost always paid in addition to other social security benefits or tax credits. PIP has two parts:

■ **a daily living component** – for help taking part in everyday life; *and*
■ **a mobility component** – for help with getting around.
You can be paid either the daily living component or the mobility component on its own, or both components at the same time.
WRA 2012, S.77(2)

Each component is paid at two different levels: a *'standard rate'* and an *'enhanced rate'*.

PIP is for you, not for a carer. You can qualify for PIP whether or not you have someone helping you; what matters is the effects of your disability or health condition and the help you need, not whether you already get that help. You can spend your PIP on anything you like. PIP acts as a 'passport' for other types of help (see Box B.7).

### 2. Do you qualify?
To qualify for PIP, you must:
■ claim PIP (see 14 below); *and*
■ pass the PIP assessment (see 9 below); *and*
■ be within the age limits (see 3 below); *and*
■ meet the required period condition (see 4 below); *and*
■ not be subject to immigration control (see Chapter 53(2)); *and*
■ pass the residence and presence tests (see Chapter 53(3)).
If you meet all these conditions, you are entitled to PIP. You keep your underlying entitlement to PIP even if other rules mean that payment has been suspended (see 6, 7 and 8 below). If you are already receiving disability living allowance, you cannot get PIP at the same time; see Box B.6 for details of the re-assessment process.

### 3. Age limits
**Lower age limit** – The lower age limit for claiming PIP is 16. Children aged under 16 who have either care needs or mobility problems may be able to claim disability living allowance. See Chapter 4 for details.
PIP(TP) Regs, reg 5

**Upper age limit** – PIP can continue to be paid after you reach the age of 65, but you must establish your entitlement by making a successful claim before you reach that age. You do not need to meet the 3-month qualifying period condition (see 4 below) but you must meet all the other qualifying conditions before your 65th birthday. If you have reached 65, you cannot claim PIP for the first time (except, in limited circumstances, if you already get disability living allowance – see Box B.6). Instead of PIP, you should consider claiming attendance allowance; see Chapter 6 for details.
WRA 2012, S.83; PIP Regs, reg 25

**Top-up claims and switching rates from age 65**
**Daily living component** – From the age of 65, if you are not already entitled to the daily living component, you can still claim it, as long as you are already entitled to the mobility component.

If your care needs change after you reach 65, you can switch between the standard and enhanced rates of the daily living component.
**Mobility component** – From the age of 65, if you are not already entitled to the mobility component, you cannot claim it, even if you are already entitled to the daily living component (unless you are re-claiming the benefit within one year of a previous award of the mobility component ending – see below).

Once you reach 65, if your mobility needs increase, you cannot move up from the standard to the enhanced rate.
PIP Regs, reg 27

### Re-claiming PIP from age 65

If a PIP award ends after you reach 65, you can re-claim the benefit within one year of your previous award ending, as long as your new claim relates to substantially the same physical or mental condition(s) (or a new condition which developed as a result of the one for which the previous award was made). You do not have to meet the 3-month qualifying period condition (see 4 below). If you leave it longer than a year or your claim relates to a different condition or conditions, you need to claim attendance allowance instead.

**The mobility component** – In the case of the mobility component, there is an additional restriction. You can only receive an award of the enhanced rate in the new claim if you were receiving that rate in the previous award. If you were receiving the standard rate in the previous award, you

## B.6 Re-assessment of existing DLA claimants

Personal independence payment (PIP) is gradually being introduced for existing disability living allowance (DLA) claimants throughout the UK.

### When will you be re-assessed?

If any of the three circumstances listed below apply to you, you will be invited to claim PIP. You will not have the choice to stay on DLA.

❑ Your fixed-period award of DLA is ending.

❑ The DWP receives information about a change in your care or mobility needs (including where you inform them of such a change).

❑ You reach the age of 16 (see below).

**Random transfer** – Other existing claimants are also being invited to claim PIP, chosen at random by the DWP.

### Who will not be re-assessed?

**Aged 65 or over** – If you get DLA and on 8.4.13 (or 20.6.16 in Northern Ireland) you were aged 65 or over, you will not be re-assessed for PIP and cannot choose to claim it. Your DLA continues and can be renewed as normal. For details of how DLA applies to people aged 65 or over, see Chapter 4(27).

*PIP(TP) Regs, reg 4(a)*

If you get DLA and were under 65 on 8.4.13 (or 20.6.16 in Northern Ireland) but have since reached 65, you will be re-assessed for PIP in the same way as other DLA claimants, including being able to claim both the daily living and mobility components. If your PIP claim is turned down, the DWP should check to see if you are entitled to attendance allowance instead (see Chapter 6).

**Under 16** – Children claim DLA until they reach the age of 16. At age 16, they will normally be re-assessed for PIP. However, a child turning 16 who gets DLA under the special rules for terminal illness (see Box B.8) will not be re-assessed for PIP until their DLA award ends or during the random transfer.

### Can you choose to claim PIP?

If you currently get DLA, you can choose to claim PIP instead of waiting to be re-assessed. However, you should consider this carefully. Many people who currently get DLA will not qualify for PIP at all, or will qualify only for a lower rate, because the entitlement conditions are different. Once you have made a claim for PIP, your DLA will subsequently be stopped even if you change your mind.

If you are waiting for a DLA appeal to be heard, claiming PIP means that any DLA award you get if your appeal is successful can only run until the date of your PIP claim, whether you are awarded PIP or not.

### What happens when you are re-assessed for PIP?

**Making the claim** – You will get a letter telling you to start your claim for PIP. You have four weeks to make your claim. You don't have the choice to stay on DLA. As long as you claim PIP by the date given on the letter, your DLA continues while you are assessed for PIP. The DWP can extend the time for claiming, so if you do need more time, contact them and explain why.

*PIP(TP) Regs, regs 3, 7 & 8(4)(b)*

If you do not claim PIP by the date given on the letter, your DLA will be suspended. The DWP must write to tell you that the DLA is suspended and will give you another four weeks to claim PIP. As long as you claim PIP by the date given, DLA payments start again. If you do not claim PIP during this period, DLA entitlement ends. You can still make a claim for PIP after this, but you will not be paid DLA in the meantime. More information on the process for claiming PIP is in Chapter 5(14).

*PIP(TP) Regs, regs 9, 10 & 11*

**The assessment** – For how PIP is assessed, see Chapter 5(15). During the process, you may be asked to complete a form and attend a face-to-face consultation. If you fail to do either, your PIP claim is disallowed. If this happens, DLA entitlement ends 14 days after your next DLA pay day.

*PIP(TP) Regs, reg 13(1)(b)*

You can challenge the PIP decision, see Chapter 5(17).

**Date of award** – If you get a decision to award PIP, entitlement to DLA ends four weeks after the next DLA pay day and the PIP award will begin on the following day. So if the decision is just after your pay day, the PIP award may not start for almost eight weeks. Unfortunately, this will be the case even if the PIP award has resulted in an increase in your entitlement (unless you asked for your claim to be re-assessed under the special rules for terminal illness – see Box B.8).

If your PIP claim is turned down, DLA entitlement will still run on for four weeks after your next DLA pay day.

*PIP(TP) Regs, reg 17*

### Northern Ireland: supplementary payments

*'Supplementary payments'* are available in Northern Ireland to temporarily compensate people who are worse off as a result of being re-assessed for PIP. There are three types of supplementary payment; you can only receive one type at a time. You are eligible for a supplementary payment after the re-assessment in the following circumstances:

❑ You do not qualify for PIP and you appeal. A supplementary payment may be made, equal to your DLA payment, until your appeal is heard and a decision made (this can be up to the level of the Northern Ireland Commissioners).

❑ You do not qualify for PIP but can show that your disability or illness (whether physical or psychological) results from a violent incident in the Northern Ireland conflict. You must have been awarded at least 4 points for daily living activities (see Box B.9) or for mobility activities (see Box B.10). The supplementary payment will be equal to the standard rate of the PIP component for which you received the points. It is payable for up to a year.

❑ You qualify for PIP, but at a reduced rate, and your weekly loss is more than £10. The supplementary payment will be equal to 75% of the difference between your DLA and PIP awards. It is payable for up to a year.

Supplementary payments will be available up to 31.3.20.

*Welfare Supplementary Payment (Loss of Disability Living Allowance) Regs thern Ireland) 2016*

can only be awarded that rate in the new claim, even if your mobility needs have increased.
WRA 2012, S.83(3); PIP Regs, regs 15 & 26

## 4. The required period condition
### The 3-month qualifying period
To qualify for either component of PIP, you must pass the relevant part of the PIP assessment (see 9 to 13 below) throughout the three months before your claim. You can, however, claim (or ask for the award to be superseded) before the three months are up.
WRA 2012, S.81(1)(a); PIP Regs, regs 12(1)(a)&(2)(a) and 13(1)(a)&(2)(a)

**Linked claims** – If you re-claim PIP within two years of the end of a previous award for substantially the same physical or mental condition(s) (or a new condition that developed as a result of the one for which the previous award was made), the claims are linked. This means if you have a relapse, you do not have to re-serve the 3-month qualifying period. You can get PIP as soon as you re-claim, but only at the previous rate and component; if you qualify for a higher amount, you will need to serve the 3-month qualifying period before it is paid.

There is no such linking of claims if your claim relates to a different condition or conditions; so you will need to serve the 3-month qualifying period on the new claim before it is paid.
WRA 2012, S.81(4); PIP Regs, reg 15

If you are aged 65 or over, claims can be linked in this way if the gap between them is no more than one year.
PIP Regs, reg 26(2)(b)

If you are a disability living allowance (DLA) claimant undergoing the PIP re-assessment (see Box B.6), you do not have to serve the 3-month qualifying period. Nor do you have to serve the qualifying period if you claim PIP within two years of the end of an award of DLA (or one year, if you are aged 65 or over).
PIP(TP) Regs, reg 23

### The 9-month prospective period
To qualify for either component of PIP, you must show you are likely to satisfy the relevant part of the PIP assessment (see 9 to 13 below) throughout the nine months after your claim.
WRA 2012, S.81(1)(b); PIP Regs, regs 12(1)(b)&(2)(b) and 13(1)(b)&(2)(b)

Once PIP has been awarded, the award can only continue if you remain likely to satisfy the relevant part of the PIP assessment for the next nine months.
PIP Regs, regs 14(b)

### Terminal illness
If you are terminally ill and have claimed PIP on this basis (see Box B.8), you do not have to meet the required period condition. You automatically get the enhanced rate of the daily living component. To get the mobility component, you must still meet the conditions outlined in 12 below (with the exception of the required period condition).
WRA 2012, S.82

## 5. How much do you get?
Each component of PIP has two rates, a *'standard rate'* and

---

## B.7  PIP and other help

PIP acts as a gateway to other types of help. The rates and components of PIP that entitle you to further help (if you meet all the other conditions for that help) are listed below. If you get the enhanced rate of either component, you are also eligible for the help available to people receiving only the standard rate.

'Premiums' are included in income support (IS), income-based jobseeker's allowance (JSA), income-related employment and support allowance (ESA), housing benefit (HB) and health benefits.

'Elements' are included in child tax credit (CTC) and working tax credit (WTC). 'Amounts' are included in universal credit (UC).

### Mobility component
❏ **Standard rate**
- 50% discount on vehicle tax – see Chapter 7(2)
- Benefit cap exemption (HB and UC) – see Chapter 16(12) and Box G.6, Chapter 25
- Childcare costs earnings disregard (HB) – see Chapter 22(6)
- Childcare element (WTC) – see Chapter 23(7)
- Child amount, disabled child addition, lower rate (UC) – see Chapter 16(4)
- Disabled child element, disabled child rate (CTC) – see Chapter 23(4)
- Disabled child premium (HB) – see Chapter 21(8)
- Disabled worker element (WTC) – see Chapter 23(8)
- Disability premium – see Chapter 21(2)
- 16-19 Bursary Fund – see Chapter 32(1)
- Student eligibility for income-related ESA and UC – see Chapters 18(4) and 32(2)
❏ **Enhanced rate**
- Exemption from vehicle tax – see Chapter 7(2)
- Motability – see Box B.16, Chapter 7
- Driving licence at age 16

### Daily living component
❏ **Standard rate**
- Additional amount for severe disability (guarantee credit of pension credit) – see Chapter 44(3)
- Benefit cap exemption (HB and UC) – see Chapter 16(12) and Box G.6, Chapter 25
- Carer's allowance: carer test – see Chapter 8(2)
- Childcare costs earnings disregard (HB) – see Chapter 22(6)
- Childcare element (WTC) – see Chapter 23(7)
- Child amount, disabled child addition, lower rate (UC) – see Chapter 16(4)
- Disabled child element, disabled child rate (CTC) – see Chapter 23(4)
- Disabled child premium (HB) – see Chapter 21(8)
- Disabled worker element (WTC) – see Chapter 23(8)
- Disability premium – see Chapter 21(2)
- Income support: carer's eligibility – see Box F.1, Chapter 19
- National insurance carer's credit – see Box D.3, Chapter 11
- No non-dependant deductions (HB, ESA/IS/JSA/UC housing costs and support for mortgage interest loans) – see Chapters 24(10), 25(21) and 26(12)
- Severe disability premium – see Chapter 21(3)
- 16-19 Bursary Fund – see Chapter 32(1)
- Student eligibility for income-related ESA and UC – see Chapters 18(4) and 32(2)
❏ **Enhanced rate**
- Child amount, disabled child addition, higher rate (UC) – see Chapter 16(4)
- Disabled child element, severely disabled child rate (CTC) – see Chapter 23(4)
- Enhanced disability premium – see Chapter 21(4)
- Severe disability element (WTC) – see Chapter 23(7)

an *'enhanced rate'*. You get the highest rate to which you are entitled. Payment of PIP is affected by some situations (see 6, 7 and 8 below).

| Daily living component | per week |
| --- | --- |
| Standard rate | £57.30 |
| Enhanced rate | £85.60 |

| Mobility component | per week |
| --- | --- |
| Standard rate | £22.65 |
| Enhanced rate | £59.75 |

PIP Regs, reg 24

## 6. Does anything affect what you get?
### Earnings
PIP is not affected by earnings. It is payable whether you work or not, and no matter how much you earn. You don't need to tell the DWP if you start work, unless your daily living needs or mobility problems have changed.

### Other benefits or help
PIP can usually be paid in full in addition to other social security benefits or tax credits. There are exceptions. Constant attendance allowance (as part of industrial injuries disablement benefit or war pension) overlaps with the daily living component; you will be paid the higher of the two. War pensioners' mobility supplement overlaps with the mobility component, so you will get the supplement instead. Armed forces independence payment (see Chapter 47(8)) overlaps with both components, so you will get that payment instead.

OB Regs, Sch 1, paras 5 & 5a

PIP is ignored as income for means-tested benefits, universal credit and tax credits and may trigger extra benefit or tax credits. If you are awarded PIP, check to see if you now qualify for income support, income-based jobseeker's allowance, income-related employment and support allowance, pension credit, housing benefit, working tax credit, child tax credit or universal credit, or higher amounts of any of these benefits. See Box B.7 for how getting PIP may help you qualify for other types of help in cash or kind.

### If you go abroad
See Chapter 54(2) for details.

### If you go into prison
Payment of PIP stops once you have been in prison or legal custody for 28 days. This applies whether you have been convicted or are on remand. Payment may stop sooner if you have been in prison or legal custody within the previous year, or in hospital (see 7 below) or a care home (see 8 below) within the last 28 days. In these cases, the different periods are added together, and your PIP will stop after a total of 28 days in prison, legal custody, hospital or a care home.

If you claim PIP while in prison, it cannot be paid until you are released. Suspended payments are not refunded, regardless of the outcome of the proceedings against you.

WRA 2012, S.87; PIP Regs, regs 31 & 32

## 7. If you go into hospital
Usually, if you are aged 18 or over on the day you enter, neither component of PIP is payable while you are an inpatient of a hospital (or similar institution) in which any of the costs of your treatment, accommodation or related services are met out of public funds. The term *'similar institution'* is not defined in legislation, although you must receive inpatient medical treatment or professional nursing care in the home under specified NHS legislation. What matters is not so much the nature of the accommodation, but whether your assessed needs for care are such that the NHS is under a duty to fund the accommodation free of charge, in which case you will still be treated as an inpatient.

WRA 2012, S.86; R(DLA)2/06

PIP can generally be paid, however, for the first 28 days of a hospital stay (or indefinitely if you are under 18); see Chapter 55(4) for details.

### Private patients
If you are a private patient paying the whole cost of accommodation and non-medical services in hospital, PIP can still be paid.

## 8. If you go into a care home
The daily living component is not normally payable while you are staying in a care home in which any of the costs of your accommodation, board, personal care or other services are met out of public or local funds. The mobility component is not usually affected by a stay in a care home (but see Chapter 38(2)).

WRA 2012, S.85; PIP Regs, reg 28(1)

Even though the daily living component is not normally payable while you are in a care home, you should apply for it anyway. Once you establish that you are entitled, you can get the daily living component for any day you are not in the care home, including the day you leave and the day you return. For example, if you spend a weekend at home with relatives, going home on Friday and returning on Sunday, you will be paid the daily living component for those three days.

PIP Regs, reg 32(2)

### What is a care home?
A care home is defined as an *'establishment that provides accommodation together with nursing or personal care'*.

The daily living component is not normally payable if any of the costs of your accommodation, board or personal care are met out of public or local funds under any of the following legislation:
- Part III of the National Assistance Act 1948 (local authority services);
- section 57 of the Health and Social Care Act 2001;
- dgement 59 and 59A of the Social Work (Scotland) Act 1968;
- Part 4 of the Social Services and Well-being (Wales) Act 2014;
- Mental Health Act 1983;
- Community Care and Health (Scotland) Act 2002;
- Mental Health (Care and Treatment) (Scotland) Act 2003;
- Part 1 of the Care Act 2014 (care and support); *or*
- any other legislation *'relating to persons under a disability'* or to young people or to education or training (with specific exceptions, such as grants in aid of educational services or research).

WRA 2012, S.85(3); PIP Regs, reg 28(2)

### People entitled to the daily living component in care homes
You can receive the daily living component if:
- you are terminally ill (see Box B.8) and in a hospice;

PIP Regs, reg 30(3)

- you are under the age of 18 and a local authority has placed you with someone in a private dwelling because of your health or disability; *or*
- you are living outside the UK and being funded under the Education Act (such as at the Peto Institute in Hungary).

PIP Regs, reg 28(3)&(4)

**Paying your own fees** – If you are paying your own care home fees, you are a self-funder and can receive the daily living component as long as you:
- do not get any funding from the local authority; *or*

■ are only getting funding on an interim basis from the local authority and will be paying it back in full – ie you are a 'retrospective self-funder'. This is most likely to apply if you are in the process of selling your home and/or you have a 'deferred payment agreement' with the local authority (see Chapter 37(12)).

See Chapter 38(2) for details.

PIP Regs, reg 30(5)

**The 28-day concession**

If you already have an award of the daily living component before you move into a care home, it can continue for up to 28 days of your stay. Payment may stop sooner if you have been in a care home within the previous 28 days. In this case, the different periods are added together and treated as one stay, and your daily living component will stop after a total of 28 days. You count a stay in a care home from the day after

## B.8  Terminal illness

### Automatic awards

If you are considered to be terminally ill, *'special rules'* are applied to your claim for disability living allowance (DLA), personal independence payment (PIP) or attendance allowance, to ensure it is dealt with swiftly. The test for terminal illness is described below. Depending on which benefit you claim, if you pass this test, you will qualify automatically for the following:

■ the highest rate of the DLA care component;

■ the enhanced rate of the PIP daily living component; *or*

■ the higher rate of attendance allowance.

This will be the case even if at the time of the claim you don't need help from another person. Furthermore, if you pass the terminal illness test, you won't have to serve the 3-month qualifying period to get DLA or PIP or the 6-month qualifying period for attendance allowance.

SSCBA, Ss.66 & 72(5); WRA 2012, S.82

Living with a terminal illness, particularly with the shock on first diagnosis, is distressing. Claiming benefits and sorting out any financial problems may be the last thing on your mind. In part, claiming DLA, PIP or attendance allowance is an acknowledgement, if not acceptance, of what is happening to you: and you may not be ready to face up to that. Unfortunately, these benefits cannot be backdated to a date before you claimed them, and there is no extension of the time limit for claiming. All we can advise is to claim as soon as you feel able. It is possible for someone else to put in the claim on your behalf (see below).

Note that even if you have a terminal illness, you will fail the terminal illness test if, at the time you claim, your death cannot reasonably be expected within the next six months.

Talk to your doctor, consultant or Macmillan nurse to ensure a claim is submitted quickly. If you are turned down, challenge the decision (see below) or make a fresh claim when your situation changes.

**The mobility component** – The mobility component payable with DLA or PIP is not paid automatically. Consequently, to be entitled to it, you must meet the conditions outlined in Chapters 4(9) or 5(12), apart from the qualifying period.

SSCBA, S.73(12); WRA 2012, S.82(3)

If you are claiming PIP under the special rules, you will be asked questions about your mobility during the phone call you make to start the claim. This should speed up the decision on the mobility component (as well as ensuring you do not have to complete a further form or attend a face-to-face consultation).

### How do you claim?

Claim in the normal way (see the appropriate chapter for details). If you are claiming under the special rules, you will be asked to send a factual statement (a DS1500 report) from your doctor or consultant to the DWP when you make the claim. Doctors, consultants and Macmillan nurses should have a supply of DS1500 forms. For PIP claims in England and Scotland, electronic versions can be emailed to the DWP.

The person who is terminally ill does not have to make the claim. Another person, including their doctor or Macmillan nurse, can claim the benefit on their behalf, for example if the terminally ill person is not up to dealing with the claim process, or has not yet been told the full nature of their condition. In this box we refer to the terminally ill person as the 'claimant' even though they may not physically make the claim. They should be informed that the benefit claim is being made, but it is not necessary to tell them it is being made under the special rules. Payment will be made direct to the claimant.

**Hospital** – If you are aged 18 or over and in hospital when you first claim DLA, PIP or attendance allowance, it cannot be paid until you leave hospital.

### What happens once you claim?

Once you have claimed the benefit under the special rules, a decision maker decides if you satisfy the test of terminal illness. They will base their decision on advice provided by the healthcare professional assigned to your case. The healthcare professional will consider the evidence on your clinical condition, diagnosis and treatment, which your doctor or consultant gives in the DS1500 report. The report does not ask about prognosis (ie about your life expectancy). The healthcare professional may phone your doctor or consultant to clarify matters.

If the decision maker decides that you satisfy the terminal illness test, you will be awarded the appropriate component (listed above). Awards are usually made for three years so they can be looked at again if you live longer than originally expected.

If the decision maker considers that you do not satisfy the terminal illness test, they will consider your claim under the ordinary assessment for the benefit (see the relevant chapter for details).

### What if you already get the benefit?

If you are already getting DLA, PIP or attendance allowance (but not at one of the three higher rates listed above), you don't have to make a separate claim under the terminal illness rules. Instead, contact the DLA, PIP or attendance allowance helpline (see Chapter 61 for contact details) or write to the address on your award letter and ask for the award to be superseded on the basis that you are now terminally ill. However, if you get DLA, are 16 or over and were under 65 on 8.4.13 (or 20.6.16 in Northern Ireland), you will be invited to claim PIP instead and won't have the choice to stay on DLA (see Box B.6).

You don't have to send a DS1500 report (see above) immediately, but it will speed up the decision if you do.

If you are successful, the new higher rate of the benefit should normally be backdated to the date you first counted as terminally ill if you told the DWP within one month, whether through one of the above helplines or in writing. If it has been longer than one month, the higher rate can still be fully backdated if special circumstances caused the delay (see Chapter 57(5)), so when you first contact the DWP, explain why it has taken you longer – eg you were too ill or distressed to cope.

If you get DLA and must now claim PIP because you are terminally ill, you can qualify for a higher rate of benefit from the day after the DLA payment period has ended or from the first Tuesday after the PIP decision (whichever is earlier).

you enter to the day before you leave. Box B.13 in Chapter 6 shows how to plan a pattern of respite care that allows you to keep your daily living component.

PIP Regs, regs 30(1)&(2) and 32(4)

**Linked spells in a care home, hospital or prison** – For the daily living component, spells in a care home, hospital (if you are aged 18 or over), prison or legal custody are linked if the gap between them is no more than 28 days (or one year in the case of periods between spells in prison or legal custody). The daily living component stops being paid after a total of 28 days in a care home, hospital, prison or legal custody, or a combination of these if you've moved from one to another with a gap of 28 days (or one year in the case of periods between spells in prison or legal custody) or less in between.

PIP Regs, reg 32(4)&(5)

## B. THE PIP ASSESSMENT

### 9. What is the PIP assessment?

The PIP assessment is a points-related assessment of your physical and mental condition and cognitive functions considered within a range of 12 different types of activity. Under each activity heading is a list of *'descriptors'* with different scores. The descriptors explain related tasks of varying degrees of difficulty and different types of help you need to complete each task. You score points when you are not able to complete a described task safely, to an acceptable standard, repeatedly and in a reasonable time (see below).

The different types of activity are grouped under two broad categories: 'daily living activities' and 'mobility activities', which relate to the daily living component and mobility component respectively. Details of the assessment as it relates to each of these components are described in 10 and 11 below (for the daily living component) and 12 and 13 below (for the mobility component). However, there are common definitions that apply to both parts of the assessment (see below).

**Who carries out the assessment?** – The assessment is carried out by two private sector 'provider' organisations: Capita and Independent Assessment Services (previously Atos Healthcare). Each provides the service across different parts of the UK: Capita across central England, Wales and Northern Ireland, and Independent Assessment Services across the rest of the UK. There are differences in the way that each of these organisations provides the service, but the framework of the assessment is the same across the UK.

**Common definitions**

**Assistance** – This means physical intervention by another person. It does not include speech. The person intervening needs to be in your presence and has to help with some or all of the activity in question. It is not necessary for them to help with the whole activity; as long as they need to help with part of the activity, you will count as needing assistance.

**Prompting** – This is where someone needs to remind or encourage you to undertake or complete an activity or explain to you how it is done. This can be done in your presence or over the phone. It does not have to be done by an adult; children can also provide the prompting (CPIP/2354/2017). If you only need prompting with part of an activity, it still counts.

**Supervision** – This means someone needs to be continuously with you to ensure your safety. If you are being supervised with others, one-to-one supervision is not required as long as your safety can be maintained by the level of supervision given (CPIP/1823/2017). A risk that gives rise to a need for supervision need not be specific to the activity in question; a general risk will be enough (CPIP/1671/2015).

**Unaided** – You can perform an activity unaided if you do not use any aids or appliances (see below) or need assistance, prompting or supervision from another person.

PIP Regs, Sch 1, Part 1

**Aids or appliances**

*'Aid or appliance'* means any device that improves, provides or replaces your impaired physical or mental function, including a prosthesis (eg an artificial leg). It could include non-specialist aids, such as electric tin openers or long-handled sponges.

---

### The terminal illness test

**The legal definition** – You count as being terminally ill at any time *'if at that time [you suffer] from a progressive disease and [your] death in consequence of that disease can reasonably be expected within 6 months'.*

SSCBA, Ss.66(2)(a) & 72(5); WRA 2012, S.82(4)

**Diagnosis** – The diagnosis question should be straightforward. Do you have a progressive disease? Is the disease one which, by its nature, develops and gets worse, perhaps in identifiable stages?

**Prognosis** – What is crucial for qualifying for benefit automatically is the question of prognosis – that your *'death in consequence of that disease can reasonably be expected within 6 months'*. The prognosis test looks forwards, not backwards. It may be that, given your progressive disease alone, your death could not reasonably be expected within six months: but your age or general physical condition may, for example, make respiratory infections more likely. You may be more prone to complications associated with, but not part of, your progressive disease. As long as the progressive disease plays the key role in whether your death can reasonably be expected within six months, you should succeed in your claim for an automatic award.

This test does not put an upper limit on life expectancy: it is not a matter of what is the longest period you can reasonably be expected to live. Clearly, no one can predict death six months ahead to the day, nor even to the month. It is quite possible that your death could reasonably be expected at any time within a period of five to 10 months ahead. In that case, the upper limit of your reasonable life expectancy would be 10 months ahead, with death at that stage fairly certain, while five months ahead would be the start of the period during which your death could reasonably be expected, rather than just being a possibility.

### Challenging the decision

Decisions on whether or not you satisfy the terminal illness test can be reconsidered and appealed in the normal way (see Chapter 57). An existing award under the special rules can also be superseded if your prognosis changes so that you no longer count as terminally ill. If your benefit has been paid under the special rules for over two years, you may be sent an enquiry form asking for up-to-date information on your condition.

**Harmful medical information** – On appeal, if the claimant has not been told about specific medical evidence or advice about their condition or prognosis, and the tribunal considers that disclosure of that evidence or advice *'would be likely to cause [her or him] serious harm'*, it won't be included in any papers sent to the claimant. If you consider that such evidence or advice should be kept from the claimant, you should say in your appeal letter why you think it would be harmful.

TP(FTT)SEC Rules, rule 14

In assessing your ability to carry out an activity, you will be assessed as if wearing or using any aid or appliance that you would normally wear or use, or which you could reasonably be expected to wear or use if you do not currently do so. It should not be considered reasonable for you to wear or use an aid or appliance if it is too expensive, difficult to obtain, or culturally inappropriate for you.

PIP Regs, regs 2 & 4(2)

## Variable and fluctuating conditions

In the assessment, a descriptor will apply to you if it reflects your ability for the majority of days (ie on over 50% of days). This is considered over a 12-month period – three months looking backwards and nine months forwards (in line with the required period condition; see 4 above).

If one descriptor is satisfied on over half of the days of the period, that descriptor will apply. If two or more descriptors are satisfied on over half the days of the period, the descriptor that scores the highest number of points will apply.

If no single descriptor is satisfied on over half the days of the period, but two or more descriptors* (when the days on which you satisfy each are added together) are, the descriptor that is satisfied for the longest period will apply. If both or all these descriptors apply for the same number of days, the descriptor that scores the highest number of points will apply.

Unlike disability living allowance, PIP does not separate your needs into daytime and night-time needs. Instead, a descriptor can apply to you if your condition affects your ability to complete a task, at some stage of the day, on over half of the days of the period. In determining this, the timing of the task should be considered, and whether you can carry out the task when you need to do it. For instance, if you can only wash and toilet yourself after taking pain-killing medication that takes a long time to take effect, you cannot be said to undertake these tasks as often as is reasonably required (CPIP/2054/2015).

If you are waiting for medical treatment (such as an operation), the result of which is difficult to predict, descriptor choices should be based on your continued condition as if the treatment were not taking place.

PIP Regs, reg 7; PIP Assessment Guide, Part Two, paras 2.1.7-2.1.12 (www.gov.uk/government/publications/personal-independence-payment-assessment-guide-for-assessment-providers)

\* other than one that scores zero points

## Safely, to an acceptable standard, repeatedly and in a reasonable time period

A descriptor will only apply to you, if you can complete the task concerned at the level required safely, to an acceptable standard, repeatedly and within a reasonable time period.

PIP Regs, reg 4(2A)

**Safely** – *'Safely'* means in a manner that is unlikely to cause harm to you or anyone else, either during or after the completion of the task. For example, if you have epilepsy and don't get enough warning of a fit to make yourself safe, you may score points for a particular task because you need someone with you when carrying out the task to ensure your safety.

Before 9.3.17, the DWP considered that a serious adverse event must have been 'likely to occur' rather than 'may occur' for it to count. Following an Upper Tribunal decision, the DWP changed the guidance: in assessing whether you can carry out a task safely, the DWP must now consider whether there is a real possibility of harm occurring that cannot be ignored, having regard to the nature and gravity of the harm in question. If the severity of harm is very high then an activity might be considered unsafe, even if the frequency of the adverse event is quite low. The DWP is contacting all those claimants adversely affected by the earlier guidance, making payments (where appropriate) back to 9.3.17.

PIP Regs, reg 4(4)(a); CPIP/1599/2016; ADM Memo 29/17

**To an acceptable standard** – An acceptable standard is one which is *'good enough'*; ie of a standard that most people would normally expect to achieve.

PIP Assessment Guide, Part 2, para 2.2.13

An example of you not completing a task to an acceptable standard would be if you wash yourself inadequately and do not realise you are still not clean after you have finished.

**Repeatedly** – *'Repeatedly'* means being able to repeat the task as often as is reasonably required. Consideration should be given to the cumulative effects of symptoms such as pain and fatigue, and whether you can only manage to complete the task at some times during the day. The DWP should take into account the fact that the effort of completing a task can adversely affect your ability to repeat it or to undertake other activities.

For instance, if you are able to prepare breakfast unaided, but the exhaustion from doing this would mean that you could not prepare another meal that day, you should be treated as being unable to prepare a meal unaided as it is reasonable to expect someone to be able to prepare more than one meal a day. Consideration should also be given as to whether you can repeat the task on subsequent days.

PIP Regs, reg 4(4)(b); PIP Assessment Guide, Part 2, paras 2.2.17 & 2.2.18; CPIP/2054/2015

**A reasonable time period** – You can do something in *'a reasonable time period'* if you do not take more than twice the maximum time normally taken by someone without a disability.

PIP Regs, reg 4(4)(c)

## 10. The daily living component

You are entitled to the daily living component at the standard rate if:

■ your ability to carry out daily living activities is limited by your physical or mental condition; *and*

■ you meet the required period condition (see 4 above).

You are entitled to the daily living component at the enhanced rate if:

■ your ability to carry out daily living activities is severely limited by your physical or mental condition; *and*

■ you meet the required period condition (see 4 above).

WRA 2012, S.78(1)-(2); PIP Regs, reg 12

## 11. What are daily living activities?

Your ability to carry out daily living activities is assessed by focusing on a range of tasks under 10 different activity headings:

■ preparing food;

■ taking nutrition;

■ managing therapy or monitoring a health condition;

■ washing and bathing;

■ managing toilet needs or incontinence;

■ dressing and undressing;

■ communicating verbally;

■ reading and understanding signs, symbols and words;

■ engaging with other people face to face; *and*

■ making budgeting decisions.

**Scoring** – Under each activity heading is a list of descriptors with scores ranging from 0 to 12 points. The descriptors explain related tasks of varying degrees of difficulty and different types of help you need to complete each task. You score points for the descriptor that best describes the level at which you can complete the task safely, to an acceptable standard, repeatedly and in a reasonable time period (see 9 above). If more than one descriptor applies to you under an activity heading, you only include the score from the one with the highest points.

To be entitled to the standard rate of the daily living component, you need to score at least 8 points; to be entitled to the enhanced rate, you need to score at least 12 points.

These points can be scored from just one activity heading or from any of the activity headings added together. The descriptors and the points assigned to each one are listed in Box B.9. We now look at each activity heading in more detail.
PIP Regs, reg 5

## Preparing food
This activity focuses on your ability to prepare and cook a simple meal. Any problems you have must be due to your physical or mental condition, rather than a basic inability to cook (eg because you have never been taught how to).

A *'simple meal'* is a cooked, one-course meal for one person using fresh ingredients. It is not intended to be a meal made up of convenience foods, such as pies or frozen vegetables, that involve no real preparation. *'Preparing'* food means making the food ready for cooking or eating. This could include opening packaging (including opening tins with a tin opener), checking the food is not out of date, peeling and chopping the food and serving the meal. *'Cooking'* food means heating food safely at or above waist height (eg using a cooker hob or a microwave oven); the activity does not consider any difficulties you may have in bending down to use an oven (CSPIP/40/2015).

When considering whether or not you need an aid or appliance to prepare and cook a meal, the sort of things that could count include: perching stools (UK/4056/2014), lightweight pots and pans, easy-grip handles on utensils, single-lever arm taps (CPIP/1695/2015) and spiked chopping boards. Pre-chopped vegetables are not considered an aid or appliance. However, if you can only prepare a meal using them, this suggests that you would need an aid or appliance or assistance from someone else to prepare food.

If you have fits or blackouts, when considering whether you need supervision to cook, the risk that you might suffer burns or scalds if you lost consciousness when carrying hot food unsupervised is particularly relevant (CPIP/3573/2015).
PIP Regs, Sch 1, Part 1; PIP Assessment Guide, Part 2, para 2.3 (Activity 1)

## Taking nutrition
This looks at your ability to eat and drink. *'Taking nutrition'* means:
■ cutting food into pieces;
■ conveying food or drink to your mouth;
■ chewing and swallowing food or drink; *or*
■ taking nutrition by using a therapeutic source (ie parenteral or enteral tube feeding, using a rate limiting device such as a delivery system or feed pump).
PIP Regs, Sch 1, Part 1

When considering whether you need supervision to take nutrition, what matters most is whether there is a real risk of you choking when eating or drinking.

If you spill food, this should be taken into account, particularly if you do so regularly and need to change your clothes after meals.
PIP Assessment Guide, Part 2, para 2.3 (Activity 2)

## Managing therapy or monitoring a health condition
This activity focuses on your ability to manage your medication or therapy or monitor a health condition.
**Managing medication** – *'Managing medication'* means taking medication (in the right way and at the right time), where a failure to do so is likely to result in a deterioration in your health. The medication must have been prescribed or recommended by a registered doctor, nurse or pharmacist and could include tablets, inhalers and creams. It needs to be taken at home.

Aids or appliances to manage medication could include a tablet organiser box or an alarm if you would otherwise have problems taking the medication in the right dose or at the right time (eg because of memory problems). However, syringes,

inhalers and nebulisers are not treated as relevant aids or appliances, as they are used to deliver medication rather than manage it (CPIP/1206/2015 and CPIP/2916/2016).
**Managing therapy** – *'Managing therapy'* means undertaking therapy, where a failure to do so is likely to result in a deterioration in your health. The activity considers the amount of time each week that you need support from another person to be able to manage the therapy (but excludes any therapy time where you do not need such support – CPIP/1679/2015). In adding up the hours of support you need each week, it does not matter if you only need such support on a minority of days.

The therapy needs to be undertaken at home and needs to have been prescribed or recommended by a registered doctor, nurse or pharmacist or a health professional regulated by the Health and Care Professions Council. It could include home oxygen supply, home dialysis, exercise regimes designed to prevent your condition getting worse (eg stretching exercises to prevent muscle contraction) and the fitting and removal of a TENS machine (CSPIP/40/2015). It does not include taking or administering medication or anything related to the monitoring of your health condition.
**Monitoring a health condition** – This means:
■ detecting significant changes in your health condition which are likely to lead to a deterioration in your health; *and*
■ taking action advised by a registered doctor, registered nurse or a health professional who is regulated by the Health and Care Professions Council, without which your health is likely to deteriorate.
This would include, for example, monitoring your blood-sugar levels if you have insulin-dependent diabetes. It could also include the support you need if you are at risk of accidental or deliberate overdose or deliberate self-harm.
PIP Regs, Sch 1, Part 1; PIP Assessment Guide, Part 2, para 2.3 (Activity 3)

## Washing and bathing
Washing means cleaning your whole body. It does not include shaving. *'Bathing'* includes getting into or out of an un-adapted bath or shower. You would still satisfy the descriptor *'Needs assistance to be able to get in or out of a bath or shower'* if you could not manage to get in or out of the bath unaided, but could manage with the shower, or vice versa (CPIP/2094/2015).
PIP Regs, Sch 1, Part 1; PIP Assessment Guide, Part 2, para 2.3 (Activity 4)

## Managing toilet needs or incontinence
In this activity *'toilet needs'* are defined as:
■ getting on and off an un-adapted toilet;
■ evacuating your bladder and bowel; *and*
■ cleaning yourself afterwards.
You only need to have problems with one of these to have toilet needs (CPIP/1787/2015).

*'Managing incontinence'* means managing involuntary evacuation of your bowel or bladder, including using a collecting device (such as a bottle or bucket) or self-catheterisation, and cleaning yourself afterwards.

Aids or appliances could include colostomy bags (UK/5352/2014), incontinence pads (including on a precautionary basis, as long as they are reasonably required: CPIP/387/2017), grab rails (CPIP/3872/2016) and commodes (CPIP/449/2016). DWP guidance advises that if you use a commode because you have reduced mobility (and do not have problems with your bladder or bowels), you will be considered to be able to manage your toilet needs unaided. However, if you use a commode because of a condition that causes urgency (such that you do not reach the toilet in time), the commode could be accepted as an aid. You could argue this should include urgency caused by medication.
PIP Regs, Sch 1, Part 1; PIP Assessment Guide, Part 2, para 2.3 (Activity 5)

### Dressing and undressing

*'Dressing and undressing'* looks at your ability to select, put on, and take off un-adapted clothing (which could include fastenings such as zips or buttons). It includes putting on and taking off socks and shoes. The activity also looks at your ability to select clothing that is appropriate (eg in the right order and suitable for the weather and time of day). The clothing should also be culturally appropriate for you. You should not be expected to limit yourself to the minimum clothing necessary for warmth and decency (UK/5338/2014).

*'Select appropriate clothing'* can include the ability to make decisions about the selection of newly washed or adequately clean clothing (CPIP/3730/2016). If you take longer to select clothing than most people, this can be taken into account if your hesitation or indecision is caused by your condition (CPIP/3760/2016).

PIP Regs Sch 1, Part 1; PIP Assessment Guide, Part 2, para 2.3 (Activity 6);

### Communicating verbally

This activity focuses on your ability to convey and understand information verbally. It is only concerned with oral communication (CPIP/2306/2015). Two types of information are covered in the descriptors: basic and complex. *'Basic verbal information'* means information in your own language conveyed verbally in a single sentence (such as asking for a drink of water). *'Complex verbal information'* means information in your own language conveyed verbally in either more than one sentence or one complicated sentence. In either

---

## B.9  Daily living activities

Add together the highest score from each activity heading that applies to you. To be entitled to the standard rate of the daily living component, you need to score at least 8 points; to be entitled to the enhanced rate, you need to score at least 12 points. These points can be scored from just one activity heading or from any of the headings added together.

| Activity | Points |
|---|---|

**1. Preparing food**

| | | |
|---|---|---|
| a | Can prepare and cook a simple meal unaided | 0 |
| b | Needs to use an aid or appliance to be able to either prepare or cook a simple meal. | 2 |
| c | Cannot cook a simple meal using a conventional cooker but is able to do so using a microwave. | 2 |
| d | Needs prompting to be able to either prepare or cook a simple meal. | 2 |
| e | Needs supervision or assistance to either prepare or cook a simple meal. | 4 |
| f | Cannot prepare and cook food. | 8 |

**2. Taking nutrition**

| | | |
|---|---|---|
| a | Can take nutrition unaided. | 0 |
| b | Needs – | |
| | (i) to use an aid or appliance to be able to take nutrition; *or* | |
| | (ii) supervision to be able to take nutrition; *or* | |
| | (iii) assistance to be able to cut up food. | 2 |
| c | Needs a therapeutic source to be able to take nutrition. | 2 |
| d | Needs prompting to be able to take nutrition. | 4 |
| e | Needs assistance to be able to manage a therapeutic source to take nutrition. | 6 |
| f | Cannot convey food and drink to their mouth and needs another person to do so. | 10 |

**3. Managing therapy or monitoring a health condition**

| | | |
|---|---|---|
| a | Either – | |
| | (i) does not receive medication or therapy or need to monitor a health condition; *or* | |
| | (ii) can manage medication or therapy or monitor a health condition unaided. | 0 |
| b | Needs any one or more of the following – | |
| | (i) to use an aid or appliance to be able to manage medication; | |
| | (ii) supervision, prompting or assistance to be able to manage medication; | |
| | (iii) supervision, prompting or assistance to be able to monitor a health condition. | 1 |
| c | Needs supervision, prompting or assistance to be able to manage therapy that takes no more than 3.5 hours a week. | 2 |
| d | Needs supervision, prompting or assistance to be able to manage therapy that takes more than 3.5 but no more than 7 hours a week. | 4 |
| e | Needs supervision, prompting or assistance to be able to manage therapy that takes more than 7 but no more than 14 hours a week. | 6 |
| f | Needs supervision, prompting or assistance to be able to manage therapy that takes more than 14 hours a week. | 8 |

**4. Washing and bathing**

| | | |
|---|---|---|
| a | Can wash and bathe unaided. | 0 |
| b | Needs to use an aid or appliance to be able to wash or bathe. | 2 |
| c | Needs supervision or prompting to be able to wash or bathe. | 2 |
| d | Needs assistance to be able to wash either their hair or body below the waist. | 2 |
| e | Needs assistance to be able to get in or out of a bath or shower. | 3 |
| f | Needs assistance to be able to wash their body between the shoulders and waist. | 4 |
| g | Cannot wash and bathe at all and needs another person to wash their entire body. | 8 |

**5. Managing toilet needs or incontinence**

| | | |
|---|---|---|
| a | Can manage toilet needs or incontinence unaided. | 0 |
| b | Needs to use an aid or appliance to be able to manage toilet needs or incontinence. | 2 |
| c | Needs supervision or prompting to be able to manage toilet needs. | 2 |
| d | Needs assistance to be able to manage toilet needs. | 4 |
| e | Needs assistance to be able to manage incontinence of either bladder or bowel. | 6 |
| f | Needs assistance to be able to manage incontinence of both bladder and bowel. | 8 |

**6. Dressing and undressing**

| | | |
|---|---|---|
| a | Can dress and undress unaided. | 0 |
| b | Needs to use an aid or appliance to be able to dress or undress. | 2 |
| c | Needs either: | |
| | (i) prompting to be able to dress, undress or determine appropriate circumstances for remaining clothed; *or* | |
| | (ii) prompting or assistance to be able to select appropriate clothing. | 2 |
| d | Needs assistance to be able to dress or undress their lower body. | 2 |
| e | Needs assistance to be able to dress or undress their upper body. | 4 |
| f | Cannot dress or undress at all. | 8 |

case, a lack of understanding of English, if this is not your first language, is not relevant.

Three of the descriptors refer to *'communication support'*. This is support from a person trained or experienced in communicating with people with specific communication needs, including interpreting verbal information into a non-verbal form and vice versa (eg using sign language). The *'experienced'* person could potentially include a family member or close friend (CPIP/1534/2016). It does not matter if you currently do not have such support, as long as you can show that you have a need for it.

An aid could include a hearing aid or an electrolarynx.

*PIP Regs, Sch 1, Part 1; PIP Assessment Guide, Part 2, para 2.3 (Activity 7)*

### 7. Communicating verbally

| | | |
|---|---|---|
| a | Can express and understand verbal information unaided. | 0 |
| b | Needs to use an aid or appliance to be able to speak or hear. | 2 |
| c | Needs communication support to be able to express or understand complex verbal information. | 4 |
| d | Needs communication support to be able to express or understand basic verbal information. | 8 |
| e | Cannot express or understand verbal information at all even with communication support. | 12 |

### 8. Reading and understanding signs, symbols and words

| | | |
|---|---|---|
| a | Can read and understand basic and complex written information either unaided or using spectacles or contact lenses. | 0 |
| b | Needs to use an aid or appliance, other than spectacles or contact lenses, to be able to read or understand either basic or complex written information. | 2 |
| c | Needs prompting to be able to read or understand complex written information. | 2 |
| d | Needs prompting to be able to read or understand basic written information. | 4 |
| e | Cannot read or understand signs, symbols or words at all. | 8 |

### 9. Engaging with other people face to face

| | | |
|---|---|---|
| a | Can engage with other people unaided. | 0 |
| b | Needs prompting to be able to engage with other people. | 2 |
| c | Needs social support to be able to engage with other people. | 4 |
| d | Cannot engage with other people due to such engagement causing either – (i) overwhelming psychological distress to the claimant; *or* (ii) the claimant to exhibit behaviour which would result in a substantial risk of harm to the claimant or another person. | 8 |

### 10. Making budgeting decisions

| | | |
|---|---|---|
| a | Can manage complex budgeting decisions unaided. | 0 |
| b | Needs prompting or assistance to be able to make complex budgeting decisions. | 2 |
| c | Needs prompting or assistance to be able to make simple budgeting decisions. | 4 |
| d | Cannot make any budgeting decisions at all. | 6 |

*PIP Regs, Sch 1, Part 2*

### Reading and understanding signs, symbols and words

This activity focuses on your ability to read and understand written or printed information in your own language. Two types of written information are covered in the descriptors: basic and complex. *'Basic written information'* means signs, symbols and dates of written or printed standard-sized text in your own language. *'Complex written information'* means more than one sentence of written or printed standard-sized text in your own language, eg a gas bill or bank statement. In either case, a lack of understanding of English, if this is not your first language, is not relevant.

*'Reading'* in the context of this activity includes reading signs, symbols and words but does not include reading Braille (so if you cannot read signs, symbols or words at all but can read Braille, you should satisfy the descriptor giving you the maximum 8 points). Your ability to read information should be considered both indoors and outdoors. If you can read at some times of the day, but cannot at others, you should still score points (CPIP/2054/2015). If you are illiterate, this will only be taken into account if it results from a physical or mental condition (CPIP/1769/2016).

*PIP Regs, Sch 1, Part 1; PIP Assessment Guide, Part 2, para 2.3 (Activity 8)*

### Engaging with other people face to face

This activity considers your ability to engage socially, which means to interact with others in a contextually and socially appropriate manner, understand body language and establish relationships. It should consider your ability to engage with people generally, not just with people you know well or with your own age group (CPIP/2034/2017). It should consider your ability to engage one to one or with a small group, rather than with a crowd (CPIP/2983/2016). Your inability to engage socially must be due to your condition, rather than to shyness. *'Establishing a relationship'* is more than just the ability to 'reciprocate exchanges', such as a brief chat about the weather (CPIP/1127/2017).

One descriptor deals with whether or not you need social support to be able to engage with other people. *'Social support'* means support from someone trained or experienced in assisting people to engage in social situations. The *'experienced'* person could potentially include a family member or close friend (CPIP/3603/2015). It does not matter if you currently do not have such support or if the support is not available all the time, as long as you can show that you need it to engage with other people (CPIP/1984/2015).

Another descriptor refers to an inability to engage with other people due to such engagement causing *'overwhelming psychological distress'*. This is defined as distress related to an enduring mental health condition or an intellectual or cognitive impairment. This condition may have a physical root cause.

If you have a visual impairment, you may need prompting if you cannot read body language or facial expressions, or identify whether someone is talking to you or to someone else (CPIP/3707/2016).

*PIP Regs, Sch 1, Part 1; PIP Assessment Guide, Part 2, para 2.3 (Activity 9)*

### Making budgeting decisions

This activity looks at your ability to spend and manage your money. Two types of decision are considered: simple and complex. *'Simple budgeting decisions'* involve calculating the cost of goods and calculating the change needed after a purchase. *'Complex budgeting decisions'* are those that involve calculating household and personal budgets, managing and paying bills, and planning future purchases. Impulsive spending can be considered under complex budgeting decisions if this is as a result of a health condition, such as ADHD (CPIP/3730/2016).

*PIP Regs, Sch 1, Part 1*

## 12. The mobility component

You are entitled to the mobility component at the standard rate if:

■ your ability to carry out mobility activities is limited by your physical or mental condition; *and*

■ you meet the required period condition (see 4 above).

You are entitled to the mobility component at the enhanced rate if:

■ your ability to carry out mobility activities is severely limited by your physical or mental condition; *and*

■ you meet the required period condition (see 4 above).

WRA 2012, S.79(1)-(2); PIP Regs, reg 13

## 13. What are mobility activities?

Your ability to carry out mobility activities is assessed by focusing on tasks under two activity headings:

■ planning and following journeys; *and*

■ moving around.

**Scoring** – Under each activity heading is a list of descriptors with scores ranging from 0 to 12 points. The descriptors explain related tasks of varying degrees of difficulty. You score points for the descriptor that best describes the level at which you can complete the task safely, to an acceptable standard, repeatedly and in a reasonable time period (see 9

---

### B.10 Mobility activities

Add together the highest score from each activity heading that applies to you. To be entitled to the standard rate of the mobility component, you need to score at least 8 points; to be entitled to the enhanced rate, you need to score at least 12 points.

| Activity | Points |
|---|---|
| **1. Planning and following journeys** | |
| a Can plan and follow the route of a journey unaided. | 0 |
| b Needs prompting to be able to undertake any journey to avoid overwhelming psychological distress to the claimant. | 4 |
| c Cannot plan the route of a journey. | 8 |
| d Cannot follow the route of an unfamiliar journey without another person, assistance dog or orientation aid. | 10 |
| e Cannot undertake any journey because it would cause overwhelming psychological distress to the claimant. | 10 |
| f Cannot follow the route of a familiar journey without another person, an assistance dog or an orientation aid. | 12 |
| **2. Moving around** | |
| a Can stand and then move more than 200 metres, either aided or unaided. | 0 |
| b Can stand and then move more than 50 metres but no more than 200 metres, either aided or unaided. | 4 |
| c Can stand and then move unaided more than 20 metres but no more than 50 metres. | 8 |
| d Can stand and then move using an aid or appliance more than 20 metres but no more than 50 metres. | 10 |
| e Can stand and then move more than 1 metre but no more than 20 metres, either aided or unaided. | 12 |
| f Cannot, either aided or unaided, – (i) stand; *or* (ii) move more than 1 metre. | 12 |

*PIP Regs, Sch 1, Part 3*

---

above). If more than one descriptor applies to you under an activity heading, you only include the score from the one with the highest points.

To be entitled to the standard rate of the mobility component, you need to score at least 8 points; to be entitled to the enhanced rate, you need to score at least 12 points. These points can be scored from just one activity heading or from both headings added together.

The descriptors and the points assigned to each one are listed in Box B.10. We now look at each activity heading in more detail.

PIP Regs, reg 6

### Planning and following journeys

This activity assesses your ability to work out and follow a route safely and reliably. Two types of route are considered: familiar and unfamiliar. You should only be considered able to journey to an unfamiliar destination if you are able to use public transport such as a bus or train. Your ability to deal with small disruptions or changes along the journey (such as roadworks or changed bus stops) should be taken into account.

Two descriptors consider whether or not you need an assistance dog or an orientation aid. An *'assistance dog'* is one trained to guide or assist someone with a sensory impairment. An *'orientation aid'* is a specialist aid designed to assist disabled people to follow a route safely (such as a long cane). A standard SatNav is not considered to be an orientation aid, but one that has been specially designed for disabled people might be (CPIP/239/2016 and CPIP/3759/2016).

**Psychological distress** – Two of the descriptors refer to *'overwhelming psychological distress'*. This is defined as distress related to an enduring mental health condition or an intellectual or cognitive impairment. The mental health condition may have a physical root cause (eg if you have an anxiety about making journeys that stems from unmanageable incontinence).

PIP Regs, Sch 1, Part 1; PIP Assessment Guide, Part 2, para 2.4 (Activity 11)

On 16.3.17, the government introduced restrictions to descriptors 1c, 1d and 1f (in response to an Upper Tribunal decision) to ensure that the descriptors did not apply when the reason someone was unable to plan or follow the route of a journey was because of psychological distress. The restrictions were overturned in a High Court judgment on 21.12.17.

Consequently, the government is going through all cases where someone has a PIP award and also all decisions (including decisions for those who scored zero points in the PIP assessment) made since the Upper Tribunal decision (28.11.16), to identify anyone who may be entitled to more PIP.

If you are affected, the DWP will contact you directly; any extra benefit due will be backdated to the date of claim, or to 28.11.16, whichever is later. There will be no face-to-face consultations in this process; if the DWP needs more information, they will contact you or your GP directly.

*MH v Secretary of State for Work and Pensions* [2016] UKUT 0531 (AAC); *RF v SSWP & Ors* [2017] EWHC 3375 (Admin)

### Moving around

This activity focuses on your physical ability to stand and then move around without severe discomfort (such as breathlessness, pain or fatigue). *'Stand'* means stand upright *'with at least one biological foot on the ground'* (therefore if you have had both your legs or feet amputated, you are considered unable to stand, even if you can do so with prosthetic limbs). The words *'... and then move'* mean that you need to be able to move independently while remaining upright. So if you could only cover, say, 20 metres by standing, transferring to a wheelchair and then completing the journey, you will not be considered capable of moving that distance.

A number of different distances are covered by the descriptors. However, unless you also score points under the previous activity heading, you would only get the 12 points needed for the enhanced rate of mobility component if you:

- cannot, either aided or unaided, stand or move more than 1 metre; *or*
- can stand and then move more than 1 metre but no more than 20 metres, either aided or unaided.

Your ability to move around should be judged in relation to the type of surface normally expected out of doors, such as pavements, roads and kerbs, but not flights of steps or steep slopes (CPIP/139/2016). Where you live cannot be taken into account; therefore, it is irrelevant if you live on a steep hill or far from the nearest bus stop.

You must also be able to move the distance concerned safely, to an acceptable standard, repeatedly and in a reasonable time period (see 9 above). Factors such as pain, breathlessness, abnormalities of gait and fatigue should be taken into account. If you can only move a certain distance in a state of excessive fatigue, you should be regarded as unable to move that distance.

If you need to keep stopping (eg to get your breath back), this does not mean that you cannot move the distance 'to an acceptable standard' (CPIP/193/2016) but the stops should be taken into account when assessing whether you can cover the distance 'in a reasonable time period'.

When considering whether you can move safely, only the actual act of moving around is relevant; any dangers posed by traffic, etc are considered in the previous activity.
PIP Regs, Sch 1, Part 1; PIP Assessment Guide, Part 2, para 2.4 (Activity 12)

**Aids and appliances** – The use of aids or appliances that you normally use to support your physical mobility without assistance (eg walking sticks or frames, crutches and prostheses) is considered.
PIP Regs 4(2)

If you can move more than 50 metres with an aid but less than this unaided, either descriptor 2a or descriptor 2b will apply to you, depending on the distance you can manage, rather than 2c. This is an exception to the usual rule that where more than one descriptor applies to you under an activity heading, the one that scores the highest points is used.
UK/694/2015 & CPIP/3352/2015 (although these conflict with a more generous interpretation in CPIP/4572/2014)

## C. CLAIMS, PAYMENTS & APPEALS

## 14. How do you claim?
### Starting your claim
You can start your PIP claim by ringing 0800 917 2222 (textphone 0800 917 7777), or in Northern Ireland 0800 012 1573 (textphone 0800 012 1574). The lines are open 8am to 6pm Monday to Friday. Someone else can make the call on your behalf (eg a support worker), but you need to be with them when they do so. During this call, which should last about 15 minutes, basic details will be obtained from you, including:

- your personal and contact details and national insurance number;
- information about your nationality (see Chapter 53(2)) and whether you have been abroad for any periods over the last three years (see Chapters 53(3) and 54(2));
- whether you are in hospital, a hospice or a care home or have been in one of these over the last 28 days (see 7 and 8 above);
- which healthcare professional supporting you would be the best to contact. It would help if this person is aware of your day-to-day problems; if you have kept a diary (see below) provide them with a copy of it;

- details of your bank or building society;
- questions relating to the special rules, if you are claiming under these (see Box B.8); these will include questions on your mobility (see 12 and 13 above); *and*
- whether you find it difficult to return forms because of a mental health or behavioural condition, learning disability, developmental disorder or memory problems.

It will speed things up if you have all this information ready when you make the call.

**Your date of claim** – The date of your claim will be the date of this phone call, as long as you provide the information needed.
UCPIP(C&P) Regs, reg 12(1)(b)

**Paper claims** – You can ask for a paper claim-form instead if you are unable to start the claim by phone. To request the form, write to: Personal Independence Payment New Claims, Post Handling Site B, Wolverhampton WV99 1AH (or in Northern Ireland: Personal Independence Payment Centre, Castle Court, Royal Avenue, Belfast BT1 1HR). You will have one month from the date your request is received in which to return the completed form. If you do so, the date your request was received is treated as your date of claim.
UCPIP(C&P) Regs, reg 12(1)(c)

### The *How your disability affects you* form
If it is clear from the information you have provided above that you do not meet the basic qualifying conditions for PIP, the DWP will send you a letter stating that your claim has been disallowed. Otherwise, you will then normally be sent a form to complete: *How your disability affects you*. This form aims to give you the chance of describing how your condition affects your daily life. For advice on completing this form, see Box B.11. You will not need to complete the form if you are terminally ill and your claim is accepted under the special rules (see Box B.8).

**Returning the form** – You must return the form within one calendar month of the date it was sent out. If you need more time, phone the PIP helpline and ask for it (see Chapter 61). If you do not return the form within the month without good reason (taking into account your state of health and the nature of any disability) your claim will normally be disallowed. However, if the DWP knows that you need additional support (ie you have a mental health or behavioural condition, learning disability, developmental disorder or memory problems), they can arrange for an assessment, usually through a face-to-face consultation (see 15 below), even if you have not managed to return the form.
PIP Regs, regs 8 & 10; PIP Assessment Guide, Part 1, para 1.3.9

**What to do next** – Once you have completed the form, make a copy of it for future reference, and send it in the freepost envelope provided with the form.

### Keeping a diary
If your condition varies from day to day, you may wish to keep a diary over a few days, focusing on the tasks described in 11 and 13 above. This can help give a picture of what your abilities are like over time. For instance, in a diary over a typical week, you may note down that you need help managing your toilet needs over four days, and can manage your toilet needs unaided on the other three days. This will help you correctly answer the questions on managing toilet needs in the form *How your disability affects you*.

Long-term diaries can be useful when explaining more sporadic problems that result from your condition, such as stumbles, falls or fits. If your condition is getting slowly worse, such a diary can help pinpoint the date that you start to satisfy the appropriate disability test (see 10 and 12 above). See Box B.15 in Chapter 6 for an example of a long-term diary.

## B.11 Completing the form
### *How your disability affects you*

### Question 1

The first question asks for details of the professional(s) who are best placed to provide advice on how your disability or health condition affects you. Examples are given, which include social workers, counsellors and support workers, as well as medical professionals, such as your GP. If possible, make an appointment with the professionals that you list to discuss the claim with them. They will need to know about your daily living needs and any mobility problems you have. If you have written a diary (see 14 in this chapter), give them a copy of it.

### Question 2

The second question asks about your health conditions or disabilities and approximately when each of these started. You do not need to go into detail about how they affect you; there is space further down the form for that. You are asked to list any tablets or other medication you are taking or treatments you are having; if you have a printed prescription list, you can attach that. If you have any side effects from the medication, you should list these.

### Questions 3 to 12

The next 10 questions relate to the daily living component activities. When you are completing each question, you should refer to 11 in this chapter for the definitions relevant to each activity. Note that the wording in the form is sometimes different from that in 11 (and Box B.9 in this chapter), where we use the exact wording of the law.

Each question introduces the activity and explains what is relevant, then has a tick-box section (with a similar format for questions 3 to 10).

❏ First, you are asked if you need to use an aid or appliance to complete the activity. If it is accepted that you do, you will get at least 2 points under that activity, except with 'managing treatments' where you just get 1 point.

❏ Second, you are asked if you need help from another person with that activity. If it is accepted that you do need help, you will get between 1 and 10 points under the activity, depending on the activity concerned and the nature of the help that you need (from just supervision or prompting to physical assistance).

In each case, you can tick: 'yes', 'no' or 'sometimes', the last being helpful if your condition is variable.

**Extra information** –The 'extra information' box for each question provides space for you to explain the difficulties you face with each activity. The examples given above the box and in the information booklet that comes with the form are useful.

The descriptors relating to each activity and the points that apply to each descriptor are not given on the form, so you should check these in Box B.9 in this chapter. You should write down in the extra information box which descriptor applies to you and explain why it applies. In each case, you need to consider whether or not you can do the activity safely, to an acceptable standard, as often as you need to and in a reasonable time (see 9 in this chapter).

If your condition varies, write down how many days each week you would be able to complete the activity, and how many you would not.

### 3 Preparing food

Write down if there is any aspect of preparing or cooking a simple meal that is a risk to you. List any incidents that have happened in the past. Have you cut yourself mishandling knives or burnt yourself on hot pans? Write down if you are not able to read or understand use-by dates or cooking instructions on packets. If you use any aids or appliances to cook, do you need some help even when you use them? Write down if you have difficulty timing the cooking correctly. Let them know if you are so exhausted after cooking a meal that you could not do it again that day.

### 4 Eating and drinking

This activity is called *'Taking nutrition'* in 11 in this chapter. Write down if you need someone to encourage you to eat the right portion sizes or to help you cut up tougher items, such as meat. Let them know whether anything is spilled, or would be if you did not have help. Write down if you use any aid to help you eat or drink (such as adapted cutlery). If you need an appliance such as a feed pump to eat, write down if you need any help to use it properly.

### 5 Managing treatments

This activity is called *'Managing therapy or monitoring a health condition'* in 11 in this chapter. Write down if there have been any times in the past when you have forgotten to take your medication, or have taken too much. Let them know if you have taken a deliberate overdose, or if you self-harm. Write down if you need someone to keep an eye on you because you are not aware that your condition is getting worse; sometimes this is the case with conditions such as diabetes or epilepsy.

If you need supervision, prompting or assistance to be able to manage your therapy, write down how many hours on average each week you need it. The more hours of help you need, the more points you get (which are listed in Box B.9 in this chapter). You may find it helpful to keep a diary over a typical week to answer this correctly (see 14 in this chapter).

### 6 Washing and bathing

Write down any aids or adaptations you use to wash or bathe yourself. These could include a long-handled sponge, shower seat or bath rail. Write down if there are any parts of your body that you cannot reach even using such aids (eg if you could not wash your back properly).

### 7 Managing toilet needs

This activity is called *'Managing toilet needs or incontinence'* in 11 in this chapter. Write down if you need to use any aids, such as a commode, raised toilet seat, bottom wiper or bidet. Write down if you need help even when you use an aid. If there is an aid that could help, but which you do not use, explain why. For instance, you may not use a commode during the day because there is no private space on the level where you spend the day.

### 8 Dressing and undressing

List any aids you use to dress, such as modified buttons, zips, front-fastening bras, Velcro fastenings and shoe aids. Write down if you still need assistance, despite using such aids. Let them know if you need someone to choose clean and appropriate clothing (eg if you have a visual impairment and cannot see stains or marks on clothing).

### 9 Communicating

This activity is called *'Communicating verbally'* in 11 in this chapter. Write down if you cannot hear or understand what people are saying to you. If you use a hearing aid and still cannot hear what people are saying to you properly, write this down. Let them know if other people find it difficult to understand your speech. Write down if you have a support worker (such as a sign language interpreter) who helps you to communicate or if a family member or friend helps you. If you have no one to help you, write down what difference such help would make.

### 10 Reading
This activity is called *'Reading and understanding signs, symbols and words'* in 11 in this chapter. Write down if you need to use aids to help you read, eg a large magnifier or magnifying glass. Let them know if you can manage indoors, but cannot adequately read signs or notices outdoors. Let them know if you have more problems with reading in poor light, and how you manage with this.

### 11 Mixing with other people
This activity is called *'Engaging with other people face to face'* in 11 in this chapter. If you avoid mixing with other people because you have no one to help you, write this down. How would you feel mixing with others without any support? Write down how you would feel; would you get panicky, angry or paranoid, or do you have difficulty understanding the way that people behave towards you?

### 12 Making decisions about money
This activity is called *'Making budgeting decisions'* in 11 in this chapter. Write down if you would have problems in buying a few items from your local shop. Would you be able to give the shop assistant the right amount of money for the items? Would you know if the change was correct?

If going to the local shop would pose no problems, but you would have problems with more complex budgeting decisions, such as working out the household budget for the month or sorting out a gas bill, write this down. Let them know if you can do most of the job by yourself, but would still need some support to finish it properly.

### Questions 13 and 14
The next two questions relate to the mobility component activities. When you are answering each question, you should refer to 13 in this chapter for the definitions relevant to each activity. Note that the wording in the form is sometimes different from that in 13 (and Box B.10 in this chapter), where we use the exact wording of the law.

Each question first introduces the activity and explains what is relevant, then has a tick-box section.

The 'extra information' box for each question gives you space to explain the difficulties you face with each activity. Examples are provided above the box and in the information booklet that comes with the form. When you fill in each box, look at Box B.10 in this chapter, which lists the descriptors that apply to each activity and the points that apply to each descriptor.

You should write down in the extra information box which descriptor applies to you and explain why it applies. In each case, you need to consider whether or not you can do the activity safely, to an acceptable standard, as often as you need to and in a reasonable time (see 9 in this chapter).

### 13 Going out
This activity is called *'Planning and following journeys'* in 13 in this chapter.

Write down if you are unable to plan a route, or if you need help to do so. Write down if you are unable to use public transport due to stress or anxiety – eg if you get claustrophobic on buses or trains.

Write down if you need to have someone with you to get somewhere, or if you would need an assistance dog or aid

(such as a long cane). Would you need such support only on unfamiliar routes, or would you also need it in places you know well? If you need to have someone with you, explain why: is it because you get very anxious or distressed, or would you get lost? Could you cross a busy road safely without support? Let them know if you would find small disruptions or unexpected changes difficult to deal with – eg roadworks where you normally cross the road or if your bus stop has been moved.

### 14 Moving around
In the tick-box section for this question, you are asked how far you can walk, using, if necessary, aids such as a walking stick, crutches or a prosthesis. It is your ability to move without severe discomfort such as pain, breathlessness or fatigue that matters. What counts is not just how far you can walk once, but how far you can walk repeatedly, as often as you need to. For example, if you walk 100 metres but by the time you stop the discomfort is such that for the next few hours you can only walk a few steps, you should not be treated as capable of walking 100 metres. Your walking must also be safe (eg whether you might fall matters), *'to an acceptable standard'* (ie how you walk matters) and *'within a reasonable time period'* (ie taking into account rest stops, whether it would take you more than twice as long to cover the distance as someone without a disability).

Only tick the *'It varies'* box if none of the other boxes apply for at least half the time. If you do tick the 'It varies' box, explain why in the 'extra information' box on the next page (eg *"In an average week, for three days I can manage to walk about 40 metres before I can go no further; for another three days this distance is 20 metres, and on one day I cannot walk at all because of the pain."*). A diary kept over a week, identifying your walking limit on each day, may help clarify matters.

List any symptoms that you feel on walking, such as pain, fatigue or breathlessness. Once the symptoms come on, how long do they take to subside? Write down if you are at risk of falling; give examples of falls you have had in the past outdoors. Were you injured? Were you able to get up again? Describe how you walk (eg any unsteadiness), and give an idea of your speed; if you walk slowly, and were to cover 20 metres, what distance would someone without a disability or health condition cover in that time?

If you are not sure how limited your mobility is, you can do an outdoor walking test (see Box B.3 in Chapter 4 for an example).

### Question 15
### Additional information
The box provides more space to explain your problems. If you run out of space here, you can use extra sheets of paper, which you need to write your name and national insurance number on.

### Declaration
Once you are satisfied that what you have written on the form is a true and accurate reflection of your situation, sign the declaration. Attach to the form any evidence you may have, such as a letter from your consultant outlining your condition, a report from an occupational therapist or a certificate of visual impairment. If you have written a diary (see 14 in this chapter), attach a copy of it.

You should make a copy of the form before posting it.

Once you have completed the diary, make a copy of it, which you can attach to the form *How your disability affects you* before posting it.

## 15. How your claim is assessed

Decisions on PIP entitlement are made by DWP decision makers (referred to as *'case managers'*). However, the assessment itself will be carried out by one of two *'provider'* companies: Capita or Independent Assessment Services (see 9 above). When the DWP receives your completed form *How your disability affects you*, they will refer your case to the provider that deals with assessments in your part of the UK.

Once the provider receives your case, they will allocate it to one of the healthcare professionals working for them. This healthcare professional may initially contact your GP, consultant or other medically qualified person treating you for further information. They may ring them or they may ask them to produce a report. The healthcare professionals are advised to seek such information where they consider that *'the claimant lacks insight into their condition'*. They may also ring you for further information. In most cases, the healthcare professional will arrange to see you at a face-to-face consultation (see below).

PIP Assessment Guide, Part 1, para 1.4.1

**Delays** – There are no set time limits for deciding claims. If your case is taking too long, you can make a complaint to the DWP and to whichever provider is carrying out the face-to-face consultation. See Chapter 59 for information about making a complaint.

### The face-to-face consultation

The face-to-face consultation will be carried out by the healthcare professional assigned to your case. It will usually take place in an assessment centre. If you are not able to attend an assessment centre and need the consultation to take place in your home, you should inform the office arranging the consultation as soon as possible, explaining why you cannot attend the centre.

You must be given at least seven days' notice of the time and place for the consultation, unless you agree to accept a shorter notice period. If you cannot attend, you should inform the office arranging the consultation as soon as possible.

PIP Regs, reg 9

**If you fail to attend or take part** – If you do not attend or take part in the consultation without good reason (taking into account your state of health and the nature of any disability) your claim will be disallowed. You should be contacted and asked to explain your reasons. If, due to your condition, the consultation was not suitable in the first place, this could be accepted as good reason ((CPIP/1567/2017). If the case manager refuses to accept that you had good reason, you can challenge the decision, with the right of appeal. For details on challenging decisions, see Chapter 57.

PIP Regs, regs 9(2) & 10

### At the face-to-face consultation

At the face-to-face consultation, the healthcare professional will identify which descriptors they consider apply to you with respect to the PIP assessment (see 9 to 13 above). To do this, they will ask questions about your day-to-day life, your home, how you manage at work if you have a job, and about any social or leisure activities that you take part in (or have had to give up). They will often ask you to describe a 'typical day' in your life.

When answering the healthcare professional, explain your abilities as fully as you can. You should tell them about any pain or tiredness you feel, or would feel, while carrying out tasks, both on the day of the consultation and over time. Consider how you would feel if you had to do the same task repeatedly. Tell them if you need reminding or encouraging

to do the tasks. Try not to overestimate your ability to do things. If your condition varies, let them know about the variability and what you are like on bad days as well as good days. The healthcare professional's opinion should not be based on a snapshot of your condition on the day of the consultation; they should consider the effects of your condition over time.

At the consultation the healthcare professional will be able to observe your ability to stand, sit and move around. They may watch you getting on and off the examination couch or your settee and bending down to pick up your belongings. They will check whether you have any aids or appliances, and the extent to which you use them. They will also be able to assess your levels of concentration and your ability to understand them and express yourself, if these matters are at issue.

The healthcare professional may carry out a brief physical examination.

Once the healthcare professional has completed their report, they will send it to the case manager who will decide whether or not to award you PIP and, if it is awarded, at what rate and for how long.

**Support** – If you have a carer, you could ask them to attend the consultation with you. Your carer will not be able to answer questions on your behalf (unless the healthcare professional cannot understand your speech or you cannot understand their questions), but they will be able to add to what you have to say, particularly with respect to their role as carer.

## 16. The decision
### If your claim is disallowed

If a decision is made to disallow or reduce your claim, the DWP will send you a notification of that decision. The letter will tell you which descriptors they think apply to you and give their reasons for choosing them.

If you are unhappy with the decision, you can ask for a mandatory reconsideration of it; see 17 below.

### If you are awarded PIP

If a decision is made to award you PIP, you will be sent a notification of that decision. You will usually be awarded PIP for a fixed term. This may be for a short period, such as one or two years, if changes in your needs are reasonably expected. Alternatively, a longer award of five or 10 years may be made if changes in your needs are less likely but still possible. An ongoing award (ie one that does not have a fixed term) would only be considered if improvements in your condition (either over time or in response to treatment) or rehabilitation are unlikely and your needs are likely to remain broadly the same. You can challenge a decision (see 17 below) if you do not agree with the level of the award or the period for which it has been granted, including if you have been granted a fixed-term award and you consider that you should have been granted an ongoing award (UK/5459/2014).

WRA 2012, S.88(2)-(3)

## 17. If you are not happy with the decision
### Mandatory reconsiderations

If your claim for PIP is disallowed, you have one calendar month from the date of the decision in which to ask the DWP for a *'mandatory reconsideration'* of the decision. You can also ask for a mandatory reconsideration if you are unhappy with the level of the benefit that has been awarded (eg if you are awarded the standard rate of the daily living component but you believe you are entitled to the enhanced rate) or the period for which it has been granted. Be careful, however, because when you ask for a mandatory reconsideration, they will look at the whole award and can take away the rate already granted. If you are in any doubt, seek advice.

**Asking for a mandatory reconsideration** – To ask for a mandatory reconsideration, write to the address (or ring the number) on the decision letter and do the following:

■ request a mandatory reconsideration of the decision. State your grounds simply at this stage, such as, *'I believe that you have underestimated the degree of my disability and consequently underestimated the extent of my mobility problems and/or the difficulties I have in carrying out daily living activities'*;

■ ask them to send you copies of all the evidence they used to make the decision; *and*

■ ask them not to take any further action until you have had the chance to respond to that evidence.

If you phone, put your request in writing as well; keep a copy for yourself. If you have not received the evidence after two weeks, ring them again to remind them to send it. When you do receive the evidence, you should have a better idea of why the decision was made.

### Building a case

Sometimes the only evidence used will be the information you gave on the form *How your disability affects you* (see 14 above). However, there will usually also be a report produced by the healthcare professional at the face-to-face consultation (see 15 above). Compare the report with your account on the form *How your disability affects you*. Try to find where a difference of opinion arises. For example, you may have written on the form that you could not get on and off the toilet without support, but the healthcare professional noted in their report that they thought you could manage by yourself. Now try to get medical evidence showing that what you said on the form was correct – eg a letter from your GP or consultant confirming the difficulties and risks you have getting on and off the toilet unassisted.

Once you have obtained evidence to support your case, send it to the address on the decision letter. If it could take a while to obtain the evidence, you should inform them how long it is likely to take, so that they do not make a decision straight away.

A case manager will look at any further evidence you send. They will then either revise the decision in your favour or write back explaining that they have been unable to change the decision. Either way, if you are not satisfied with the result, you now have a month from the date of the reconsidered decision to appeal to an independent tribunal. For more on appeals, see Chapter 57.

### If the decision was notified more than one month ago

To challenge a decision notified more than one month ago in relation to an award of PIP, you need to show there are specific grounds, eg:

■ there has been a change of circumstances since the decision was made – eg your condition has deteriorated and your mobility has reduced;

■ the case manager didn't know about some relevant fact – eg you missed out some aspect of your daily living needs or mobility difficulties when you filled in the form *How your disability affects you*.

See Box O.8, Chapter 57 for more details.

### 18. How are you paid?

PIP is usually paid every four weeks in arrears into your bank, building society or Post Office card account. However, if you are awarded PIP under the special rules for terminal illness (see Box B.8), it can be paid weekly in advance.
UCPIP(C&P) Regs, reg 48(1)-(2)

**Appointees** – If you cannot manage your own affairs, the DWP can appoint another person to act on your behalf (see Chapter 56(4)). But PIP is your benefit, not your appointee's benefit. If you don't want someone else formally appointed to act for you, but cannot collect your PIP yourself, you can arrange with the bank, building society or Post Office for someone to do this for you.

### 19. What if your condition changes?

Whether you have been awarded PIP for a fixed period or the award is ongoing, you must continue to meet all the qualifying rules throughout the award. Although the DWP tells you the main changes in circumstances that you must report, it is up to you to let the DWP know if *anything* changes that might affect your existing award, such as your condition getting better or worse.

**If your condition gets worse** – If you already receive PIP, ring the PIP helpline to give details of the change (see Chapter 61 for contact details) or write to the address at the top of your award letter. Following a re-assessment (which will be similar to the assessment for new claims – see 15 above), your existing award may be superseded to include a higher rate or a new component. (A top-up claim for the component you do not already have does not count as a new claim, but rather as a change to your existing award.)

**If your condition improves** – If your need for assistance or your mobility difficulties lessen, this could mean your rate of PIP should drop or your PIP entitlement should cease. Contact the PIP helpline to give them details. The case manager will usually supersede your award once they have re-assessed it (again, the re-assessment will be similar to the assessment for new claims – see 15 above).

### 20. Reviewing your claim

Most PIP awards are for a fixed period and will be reviewed at regular intervals. How often reviews happen will depend on the timescale over which any changes in your condition (or your ability to manage) are likely to occur. If you have an ongoing award, even though this means the DWP considers that your condition is likely to stay much the same, your award will still be reviewed periodically.

For the review, you will be sent a shortened version of the *How your disability affects you* form (see 14 above). This goes through the daily living and mobility activity headings (listed in Boxes B.9 and B.10), asking you in each case whether things have got easier, harder or have not changed.

It is important that you return this form by the deadline given. If you do not, your entitlement may be ended. However, you can ask for more time if you need it. When the DWP case manager receives your completed form, they will see if they have enough information to make a decision straightaway. Otherwise, the assessment process is similar to that of new claims (see 15 above).

When the case manager reviews your award, they can alter the rate at which it is paid, award a new component or remove one already in payment, or reduce or extend the fixed period of the award. You can challenge the decision in the usual way (see Chapter 57).
PIP Regs, reg 11

### 21. What happens when your award is due to end?

If your PIP award is for a fixed period, it will normally be reviewed (see 20 above) about a year before it is due to end. At this review, the case manager can extend the fixed period of the award.
Advice for Decision Making, Chapter P2, para P2067

If your award is not reviewed in this way, or if the review does not lead to an extension of the award period, you can make a renewal claim up to six months before the current award is due to end. The claim and assessment process for renewal claims is similar to that of new claims (see 14 and 15 above).
UCPIP(C&P) Regs, reg 33(2)

If you put in the renewal claim at the earliest opportunity (ie six months before the current award is due to end), this can minimise the risk of a gap in payment between the awards if there are delays in assessing the renewal claim. On the downside, if you put in the claim early and, from the evidence of the re-assessment, the DWP considers that your needs have reduced, they can reduce (or even terminate) your current award before the fixed period has come to an end. If you are in any doubt as to whether you should put in your renewal claim early, seek advice.

# 6 Attendance allowance

| A | **General points** | |
|---|---|---|
| 1 | What is attendance allowance? | 46 |
| | Attendance allowance and other help – Box B.12 | 47 |
| 2 | Do you qualify? | 46 |
| 3 | Qualifying period | 46 |
| 4 | How much do you get? | 46 |
| 5 | Does anything affect what you get? | 46 |
| 6 | If you go into hospital | 47 |
| 7 | If you go into a care home | 47 |
| | Respite care – Box B.13 | 48 |
| B | **The disability test** | |
| 8 | The disability test | 49 |
| 9 | What is 'attention'? | 49 |
| 10 | What is 'continual supervision'? | 50 |
| 11 | Attention or supervision? | 51 |
| 12 | What is 'watching over'? | 51 |
| 13 | Simpler methods | 51 |
| 14 | Renal dialysis | 51 |
| C | **Claims, payments & appeals** | |
| 15 | How do you claim? | 51 |
| | Completing the attendance allowance claim-form – Box B.14 | 52 |
| 16 | Keeping a diary | 52 |
| | Long-term diary – Box B.15 | 54 |
| 17 | How your claim is assessed | 53 |
| 18 | The award | 54 |
| 19 | If you are not happy with the decision | 54 |
| 20 | How are you paid? | 55 |
| 21 | What if your condition changes? | 55 |

## A. GENERAL POINTS

### 1. What is attendance allowance?
Attendance allowance is a tax-free benefit you can get if you are aged 65 or over, are physically or mentally disabled and need help with personal care or supervision to remain safe. You do not actually have to be getting any help; it is the help you need that is relevant. You can get attendance allowance even if you live alone; you do not need to have a carer. Attendance allowance is not means tested, there are no national insurance contribution tests, and it is paid in addition to other money in most cases (see 5 below).

Attendance allowance acts as a 'passport' to other types of help (see Box B.12).

Attendance allowance is not affected by the introduction of personal independence payment (see Chapter 5).

### 2. Do you qualify?
To qualify for attendance allowance, you must:
■ claim attendance allowance (see 15 below); *and*
■ satisfy the disability test (see 8 below); *and*
■ be aged 65 or over (if you have not yet reached your 65th birthday, you should claim personal independence payment instead – see Chapter 5); *and*
■ meet the qualifying period condition (see 3 below); *and*

■ not be subject to immigration control (see Chapter 53(2)); *and*
■ pass the residence and presence tests (see Chapter 53(3)).
If you meet all these conditions, you are entitled to attendance allowance. You keep your underlying entitlement to attendance allowance even if other rules mean it cannot be paid (see 5 below).

### 3. Qualifying period
You must have been in need of care for six months before your award can begin, but you can make your claim during that 6-month period. It does not matter if during that time you could not receive attendance allowance in any case – eg if you were in hospital.
SSCBA, S.65(1)(b)&(6)

If you already have lower rate attendance allowance, you can qualify for the higher rate after you have needed the greater level of attention or supervision for six months. You can put in your request for the higher rate before the six months have passed.
SSCBA, S.65(3)

**Renal dialysis** – If you have passed the dialysis test (see 14 below) during the six months before your claim, you have served the qualifying period. Spells dialysing at least twice a week in hospital or as an outpatient getting help from hospital staff count for this qualifying period.
AA Regs, reg 5(4)

**Linked claims** – If you previously received attendance allowance (or have dropped to the lower rate) and have a relapse no more than two years from the end of that award, you do not have to serve the qualifying period to get back your former rate. You still need to claim (or ask for your current award to be superseded), but you do not have to have needed the level of help for six months to be paid.

For example, you used to get the higher rate but this was reduced to the lower rate because your condition improved. You have a relapse within two years, and ask for your award to be superseded to move back to the higher rate. The higher rate can be paid from the date you make the request, or from the date of the relapse if you tell the DWP within one month.
SSCBA, S.65(1)(b) & AA Regs, reg 3

**Terminal illness**
There is no qualifying period if you are awarded attendance allowance because you are terminally ill (see Box B.8 in Chapter 5). You automatically get higher rate attendance allowance.
SSCBA, S.66

### 4. How much do you get?
Attendance allowance has two rates, lower and higher. The lower rate is £57.30 a week, the higher rate is £85.60. The rate you are awarded is decided by the disability test described in 8 below. Payment of attendance allowance is affected by some situations (see 5 below).

### 5. Does anything affect what you get?
Attendance allowance can be paid in addition to almost any other benefit – eg state pension or pension credit. It is not affected by earnings. It is payable whether you work or not, and no matter how much you earn.

Attendance allowance is ignored as income for means-tested benefits, so does not reduce the amount of any pension credit or housing benefit you get. It may, however, be taken into account in the local authority's means test for care and support services (see Chapter 37(6)).

You cannot get attendance allowance if you are entitled to disability living allowance or personal independence payment. If you get constant attendance allowance with industrial

injuries disablement benefit or war pension, this overlaps with attendance allowance and you are paid whichever is higher. If you have been in the armed forces, you may be able to get armed forces independence payment instead of attendance allowance (see Chapter 47(8)).
SSCBA, S.64(1)&(1A); OB Regs, Sch 1, paras 5 & 5a

**Check your benefits** – Getting attendance allowance can trigger extra help with means-tested benefits. You might qualify for a severe disability premium in your housing benefit, or an additional amount for severe disability in your pension credit guarantee credit. If you could not get these benefits previously because your income was too high, you may qualify now. Contact the Pension Service and your local authority to make sure they know you are getting attendance allowance.

### If you go abroad
See Chapter 54(2) for details.

### If you go into hospital or a care home
See 6 and 7 below.

### If you go into prison
Payment of attendance allowance is suspended if you go into prison on remand to await trial. If you do not receive a custodial or suspended sentence, you will be paid arrears of attendance allowance for the time you spent on remand.
SSCBA, S.113(1)(b); GB Regs, reg 3

## 6. If you go into hospital
Generally, payment of attendance allowance stops after you've been in hospital for 28 days. Payment starts again from the day that you leave hospital. If you leave hospital temporarily and expect to return within 28 days, you can be paid attendance allowance for each day out of hospital (see Chapter 55(6)).

If you first claim attendance allowance when you are already in hospital, you cannot be paid until you leave. But you can then be paid for the full 28 days if you return to hospital, even if you do so within 28 days.

**Back to hospital within 28 days?** – If you are readmitted to hospital, having been at home for 28 days or less since you were last in hospital (or a care home – see 7 below), the number of days during each stay are added together and payment of attendance allowance stops after a total of 28 days.

You count days in hospital from the day after you are admitted to the day before you go home. Neither the day you go in nor the day you leave count as days in hospital.
AA Regs, regs 6 & 8

**Private patients** – If you are a private patient and meeting the whole cost of accommodation and non-medical services in hospital, attendance allowance can still be paid.

**Hospice patients** – If you are terminally ill and in a hospice, attendance allowance may still be paid in some circumstances (see 7 below).

## 7. If you go into a care home
Normally, you cannot be paid attendance allowance if you live in a care home, but you should apply for it anyway. Once you establish your entitlement, you can be paid attendance allowance for any day you are not in a care home, including the day you leave and the day you return. For example, if you spend a weekend at home with relatives, going home on Friday and returning on Sunday, you are paid attendance allowance for those three days.

### What is a care home?
A care home is defined as an *'establishment that provides accommodation together with nursing or personal care'.*

Attendance allowance is not normally payable if any of the costs of your accommodation, board or personal care are met out of public or local funds under any of the following legislation:
- Part III of the National Assistance Act 1948;
- section 57 of the Health and Social Care Act 2001;
- sections 59 and 59A of the Social Work (Scotland) Act 1968;
- Part 4 of the Social Services and Well-being (Wales) Act 2014;
- Mental Health (Care and Treatment) (Scotland) Act 2003;
- Community Care and Health (Scotland) Act 2002;
- Mental Health Act 1983;
- Part 1 of the Care Act 2014 (care and support); *or*
- any other legislation *'relating to persons under disability'.*

SSCBA, s.67(2)-(4); AA Regs, reg 7(1)&(2)

**People entitled to attendance allowance in care homes**
See Chapter 38(2) for details, but, in brief, you can receive attendance allowance while in a care home if:
- you are terminally ill (see Box B.8 in Chapter 5) and in a hospice, defined as *'a hospital or other institution whose primary function is to provide palliative care for persons... suffering from a progressive disease in its final stages'* (but not an NHS hospital);

AA Regs, reg 8(4)&(5)
- you are living in a care home and paying the fees for accommodation, board and personal care in full (with or without the help of benefits such as pension credit). In Scotland, if you are 65 or over and get free personal

---

## B.12 Attendance allowance and other help

Attendance allowance acts as a gateway to other types of help. Listed below are the rates of attendance allowance that can entitle you to further help (if you meet all the other conditions for that help).

If you get higher rate attendance allowance, you are also eligible for the help available to people receiving only the lower rate.

'Premiums' are included in the assessments of housing benefit (HB) and health benefits. 'Elements' are included in working tax credit (WTC).

### Lower rate
- Benefit cap exemption (HB and universal credit (UC)) – see Chapter 16(12) and Box G.6, Chapter 25
- Additional amount for severe disability (guarantee credit of pension credit) – see Chapter 44(3)
- Carer's allowance: carer test – see Chapter 8(2)
- Childcare costs earnings disregard (HB) – see Chapter 22(6)
- Childcare element (WTC) – see Chapter 23(7)
- Disabled worker element (WTC) – see Chapter 23(8)
- Disability premium – see Chapter 21(2)
- Income support: carer's eligibility – see Box F.1, Chapter 19
- National insurance carer's credit – see Box D.3, Chapter 11
- No non-dependant deductions (HB, UC/guarantee credit of pension credit housing costs and support for mortgage interest loans) – see Chapters 24(10), 25(21) and 26(12)
- Severe disability premium – see Chapter 21(3)

### Higher rate
- Severe disability element (WTC) – see Chapter 23(7)

care payments from the local authority, you are not paid attendance allowance in a care home even if you are otherwise self-funding. If you are self-funding except for nursing care payments, you can be paid attendance allowance. Using direct payments to pay fees means you are not self-funding;

AA Regs, reg 8(6)

■ the local authority is paying your fees only until you are able to repay them in full (eg once you sell your house) – see Chapter 37(12).

### The 28-day concession

If you have been awarded attendance allowance before you go into a care home, it can continue for up to 28 days. Payment may stop sooner if you have been in a care home (or hospital – see below) within the previous 28 days. In this case, the different periods are added together and treated as one stay, and your attendance allowance will stop after a total of 28 days. You count a stay in a care home from the day after you enter to the day before you leave. Box B.13 shows how you can plan a pattern of respite care that allows you to keep your benefit.

AA Regs, reg 8(1)&(2)

**Linked spells in hospital and a care home** – Spells in hospital and a care home are linked if the gap between them is no more than 28 days. Attendance allowance stops being paid after a total of 28 days in hospital or a care home, or both if you've moved from one to the other with a gap of 28 days or less in between.

---

## B.13 Respite care

This box explains how disability living allowance (DLA), personal independence payment (PIP) and attendance allowance are affected if you go in and out of hospital or a care home more than once and how you could keep your benefit if you plan a pattern of respite care.

### The linking rule

Generally, payment of DLA, PIP or attendance allowance stops after you've been in hospital for 28 days (unless you are aged under 18). If you go back into hospital after being at home for 28 days or less, the two (or more) hospital stays are linked. Adding together the number of days in hospital in each linked stay, benefit stops after a total of 28 days. You are still paid for days at home.

Similarly, payment of the DLA care component, the PIP daily living component or attendance allowance stops after you've been in a care home for a total of 28 days (adults and children) in one stay, or in linked stays where the gaps at home are 28 days or less.

If you are aged 18 or over and go into hospital then into a care home, or the other way round, payment of DLA care component, the PIP daily living component or attendance allowance stops after 28 days, adding together days spent in hospital and in the care home. Stays in hospital and a care home are linked if they follow on from each other or if you spend 28 days or less at home in between.

You count a stay in hospital or a care home from the day after you enter to the day before you leave.

### Careful counting

If you keep a careful count of the days you are in hospital or a care home (or a care home in the case of anyone aged under 18), you can establish a pattern of respite care that will allow you to keep the benefit. But even if you can't keep your benefit for all the days in respite care, you can be paid for days at home.

*Example:* If you have two full days of respite care every weekend, you can continue like this for 14 weeks (2 x 14 = 28 days). For 14 weekends, you can go into respite care on a Friday and return home on a Monday. Only Saturday and Sunday count as days in hospital or a care home – the day you enter and the day you leave count as days at home.

If your respite care is provided in a care home, the DLA care component, the PIP daily living component or attendance allowance will not be paid for days of respite care (Saturday and Sunday) after the 14 weeks unless you break the link (see below) – although you can be paid for days at home (Monday to Friday). The DLA or PIP mobility component is not affected by a stay in a care home so continues to be paid as usual.

If you are aged 18 or over and your respite care is provided in hospital, DLA, PIP or attendance allowance will not be paid for days of respite care after the 14 weeks unless you break the link. You will continue to be paid benefit for days at home.

### Break the link

If you spend 29 days in your own home, you will break the link between respite care stays. The next time you go into respite care in a care home, your DLA care component, PIP daily living component or attendance allowance can be paid for another 28 days, in one stay or in linked stays. Similarly, the next time you go into respite care in hospital, your DLA, PIP or attendance allowance can be paid for another 28 days.

A pattern of respite care interrupted by spells of at least 29 days in your own home will allow you to keep the benefit. Direct payments of benefit into a bank or other account will continue, but you must give the DWP details of all dates you enter or leave respite care.

In the example above, you can break the link and at the same time continue to have some respite care. For the next four weekends, instead of going into respite care on a Friday and leaving on a Monday, you go in on the Saturday morning and return home on the Sunday evening. Because the day you enter and the day you leave hospital or a care home count as days at home, you'll have spent more than 28 days in a row at home and so you'll have broken the link. For the next 14 weekends, you can return to your main Friday to Monday pattern of respite care.

### Informing the DWP

When you first go into respite care, contact the DLA, PIP or attendance allowance helpline (see Chapter 61) or write to the address on your award letter, giving the name and address of the home or hospital you are going to, the date you will be entering it and the date you will be leaving to return to your own home. If you have planned a specific pattern of respite care in advance, let the DWP have details. If there are any changes from your planned pattern of care, contact the DWP and let them know.

Arranging or keeping to a pattern of respite care that allows you to keep your benefit (by breaking the link every 28 days) will not always be possible. Until that link is broken, you will not be entitled to the DLA care component, the PIP daily living component or attendance allowance (and the DLA or PIP mobility component in the case of hospital stays) for any further days spent in respite care from the 29th day onwards. However, you will be entitled for the days spent in your own home. When you inform the DWP of the dates you will be entering and leaving care, they adjust each payment to your bank or other account as necessary.

# B. THE DISABILITY TEST

## 8. The disability test

To pass the disability test, you must meet at least one of these four conditions. You must be *'so severely disabled physically or mentally that... [you require] from another person'*

**during the day**
- *'frequent attention throughout the day in connection with [your] bodily functions, or*
- *continual supervision throughout the day in order to avoid substantial danger to [yourself] or others' or*

**during the night**
- *'[you require] from another person prolonged or repeated attention in connection with [your] bodily functions, or*
- *in order to avoid substantial danger to [yourself] or others [you require] another person to be awake for a prolonged period or at frequent intervals for the purpose of watching over [you]'.*

SSCBA, S.64(2)&(3)

The meanings of the words and phrases used here are explained in 9 to 12 below.

**Kidney patients** – There are special rules that may help you qualify for attendance allowance at the lower rate if you are undergoing renal dialysis (see 14 below).

### Lower or higher rate

The higher rate is for people who need help day and night. If you meet one of the daytime conditions and one of the night-time conditions, you get the higher rate. The lower rate is for people who need help only during the day or only at night. If you meet one of the daytime conditions or one of the night-time conditions, you get the lower rate.

### The starting point

The starting point for your attention, care, supervision and/or watching-over needs must be that you are *'so severely disabled physically or mentally that [you require]...'*. In most cases this poses no problem.

If you do not have a specific diagnosis of your condition, your needs can still be taken into account. What matters is that you have a disability (ie some impairment in your ability to perform activities) and it affects your ability to care for yourself.

If you have a mental or physical disability (eg depression or cirrhosis) because of alcohol or drug misuse, your care needs should be taken into account even if you could control your habit. If you *choose* to drink alcohol, the short-term effects of intoxication (eg incontinence) are ignored. If, however, you are dependent on alcohol, these effects can count, although you should try to provide evidence that rehabilitation programmes do not cure your dependence or are not suitable for you.

R(DLA)6/06

## 9. What is 'attention'?

*'Attention'* means active help from another person to do the personal things you cannot do for yourself. It does not matter whether you actually get help; what counts is the help you need. It must also be help that would need to be given in your presence, not, for example, over the telephone.

To count as 'attention', the help you need because of your disability must be both in connection with your 'bodily functions' and 'reasonably required' (see below).

### Help with bodily functions

*'Bodily functions'* are personal actions such as breathing, hearing, seeing, eating, drinking, walking, sitting, sleeping, getting in or out of bed, dressing and undressing, going to the toilet, getting in or out of the bath, washing, shaving, communicating, speech practice, help with medication or treatment, etc. Anything to do with your body and how it works can count.

R(A)2/80

Indirect or ancillary attention counts but is often forgotten. Think about the beginnings and ends of particular activities. If there are other tasks involved during the course of helping you with a bodily function, these can count if they are done on the spot. For example, if you need help to change bedding because of incontinence, then rinsing out the bedclothes counts if done straight away, as does soothing you back to sleep. If you need help with eating, then cleaning up spills may also count.

R(A)2/98 (HoL: 'Cockburn'); R(A)2/74; R(DLA)2/03 (CoA: 'Ramsden')

If you need help with part of an activity (and could not complete the activity without it) that also counts. For example, you may be able to dress yourself, but you cannot get your clothes, or you need to be prompted to dress. It is irrelevant that you can manage most of the activity by yourself. If it takes you a long time to do something, eg getting dressed, you may reasonably require help even though you persevere and eventually manage by yourself.

Help to overcome problems communicating or interacting with others may count if, for example, you have a learning disability. This is because brain function also counts as a bodily function. This help can include someone prompting you or keeping you motivated if your concentration is impaired (R(DLA)1/07).

**Deafness** – If you are deaf, the help of an interpreter to communicate counts (including translating into another language to allow you to lip-read – CDLA/36/2009), as does assistance in developing communication skills. Extra effort attracting your attention may count (R(DLA)1/02). The extra effort involved in two-way communication if one of you is not adequately skilled in sign language may also be included as 'attention' (R(DLA)3/02).

### Domestic duties and other kinds of help

You might need help with things that don't seem like bodily functions, such as reading, guiding, shopping, cooking, housework, etc. However, if your disability means that there is one bodily function that is 'primarily impaired', then whatever activities you need help with in connection with that bodily function can count (as long as they are *'reasonably required'*). For example, if you are blind, the 'primarily impaired' function is seeing. So help reading correspondence or labels can count; the help would be attention in connection with the bodily function of seeing, not reading (which is not a bodily function). Similarly, if you are deaf or paralysed, the primarily impaired function is hearing or movement. Once you have identified the impaired bodily function, think of all the help you need from other people to do things that you could manage if you did not have that disability. For example, if you use a wheelchair but need someone to push it for you, they are giving attention in connection with your bodily function of walking, whether you need help inside or outside your house (CA/209/2015). You don't actually have to be getting help, it is enough that the help is *'reasonably required'* (see below).

R(A)3/94 (HoL: 'Mallinson')

In each case, the help you need must be carried out in your presence and involve personal contact with you – this can be physical contact, talking or signing. Generally, this rules out domestic tasks like cooking, shopping and cleaning – they are not bodily functions and do not normally need to be carried out in your presence. However, while it would not count if someone cooked a meal for you, if someone helps you to do the cooking *for yourself*, eg reading labels and recipes, checking cooker settings, this can count if it is reasonably required (see below). You can argue it is reasonable for you to develop or maintain a level of independence; try to link the help you need to the bodily function that is impaired – and be prepared to appeal.

CDLA/3711/95, CDLA/12381/96 & CDLA/8167/95, although there are conflicting decisions: CSDLA/281/1996 & CSDLA/314/1997; see also CDLA/3376/05

### 'Reasonably required'

The attention you need must be *'reasonably required'* rather than medically required.

R(A)3/86

You may reasonably require more attention than you actually get. For example, if the only help you get is over the telephone, perhaps to encourage you to dress or eat or to check on you, you could argue that your needs would be more reasonably met by direct help in your presence, or more direct help than is currently available to you. If you are deaf, communication might be easier if you had an interpreter (R(DLA)3/02). Think about activities you manage only very slowly, with difficulty or in an unsafe way, even if you don't actually get help from another person.

The test is whether *'the attention is reasonably required to enable [you] as far as reasonably possible to live a normal life'*. This includes social, recreational and cultural activities – what is reasonable depends on your age, interests and other circumstances.

R(A)2/98 (HoL: 'Fairey')

### Refusing medical treatment

If you refuse medical treatment that would reduce the help you need from others, you may find this help is consequently not taken into account. You should explain why your refusal is reasonable. You cannot be expected to undergo invasive surgery, and it should not count against you if treatment would have unwanted side effects or if a psychiatric condition leads you to avoid treatment (R(DLA)10/02).

### During the day

You must need *'frequent attention throughout the day'*, ie during the middle of the day, as well as in the morning and evening. The fact that you can manage most of your bodily functions without help does not mean you fail this test; it depends on the pattern of your accepted care needs. *'Frequent'* means *'several times – not once or twice'* (R(A)2/80), and the pattern of help must be such that, looking at all the facts about your accepted care needs as a whole, it is true to say you need *'frequent attention throughout the day'*.

If your care needs vary because your condition fluctuates, give an idea of the pattern of those needs over, say, a month or whatever period of time accurately reflects your circumstances; it may help to keep a diary (see 16 below). The decision maker must then focus on what care you need and the pattern of those needs, rather than the length of time it takes to meet your needs and the gaps between the attention.

R(A)4/78, CA/140/85, CDLA/4825/2014

### During the night

During the night, the help you need must be *'prolonged'* (normally at least 20 minutes) or *'repeated'* (needed two times or more).

R(DLA)5/05

There is no fixed time for the start of the night. It depends on when your household closes down for the night. It normally starts when your carer goes to bed and ends when they get up in the morning. On the other hand, if a carer stays up late or gets up early to help you, that should count as night-time attention. If you live alone and keep unusual hours, like getting up at 4.30am, your care needs may count as night-time care between the more usual bedtime hours of 11pm to 7am.

R(A)4/74, CDLA/2852/02, CDLA/997/03, R(A)1/04 & CDLA/3242/03

## 10. What is 'continual supervision'?

Supervision means you need someone around to prevent accidents to yourself or other people. The words used are *'continual supervision'*. This means frequent or regular, but not non-stop; you don't have to show you need supervision every single minute. The supervision doesn't have to prevent the danger completely, but it must be needed *'in order to effect a real reduction in the risk of harm'* to you (R(A)3/92).

The supervision must be *'reasonably required'*, rather than medically required (R(A)3/86). For example, you may be mentally alert and know what you shouldn't do without someone there to help. Medically speaking, you could supervise yourself. But the question is whether or not you reasonably require supervision from someone else. In practice, supervising yourself might mean that to avoid the risk of danger you would have to do nothing but stay in bed or an armchair. If you would have to restrict your lifestyle in order to keep safe without needing help, the question is whether or not those restrictions are reasonable. Do they allow you to have anything approaching a normal life? If the restrictions on your lifestyle are not reasonable, then you reasonably require help from another person to live a normal life (CA/40/1988).

The next question is whether you satisfy the rest of the continual supervision test, which has four parts.

❏ You must show that your medical condition is such that it may (not will) give rise to substantial danger to yourself or to others. The danger to you could arise from your own actions or from the actions of other people. The danger to others could be wholly unintended (eg if you are unable to care for a young child safely).

❏ The substantial danger must not be too remote a possibility. The fact that an incident may be isolated or infrequent does not rule this out. As well as looking at the chances of the incident happening, the decision maker must look at the likely consequences if it does. If the consequences could be dire, then the frequency with which it is likely to happen becomes less relevant.

❏ You must need supervision from someone else to avoid the substantial danger.

❏ The supervision must be continual, but the person providing the supervision need not always be alert, awake and active. Standby supervision, and being ready to intervene and help, can also count.

R(A)1/83

If you have epilepsy and your seizures are unpredictable, without enough warning for help to arrive or for you to put yourself in a place of safety, you may qualify for attendance allowance, certainly at the lower rate for your daytime supervision needs. The same applies to others whose needs for supervision and attention are unpredictable, and if the consequences of an unsupervised attack would be grave, including those who are mentally alert and can supervise themselves between attacks but not during attacks.

R(A)1/88 (CoA: 'Moran')

### Supervision and falls

If you are mentally alert and sensible, it is sometimes said you could supervise yourself and so avoid the risk of falling without help from another person. But it is not enough just to say you are sensible (R(A)3/89 and R(A)5/90); decision makers must identify precautions you could take and/or activities you should not do to avoid the risk of falls without help from someone else. It is only if it is *'possible to isolate one or two activities which alone might give rise to a fall, and which could be avoided except for one or two occasions during the course of the day, and [you would] still be left to enjoy a more or less normal life, [that] it would be justifiable to say that continual supervision was not required. Everything will depend upon the facts of the case'* (CA/127/88, para 8).

However, there is a close overlap between supervision and attention. Even if your need for help to avoid the risk of falls does not amount to continual supervision, it is possible that particular help could count as attention (see below).

## 11. Attention or supervision?

Attention tends to be active help, while supervision is more passive. Sometimes both can be given at the same time; for example, if you are deaf and have poor traffic sense, someone walking beside you could be supervising you (ready to stop you walking) and giving attention in connection with hearing (informing you of what you need to know to continue walking in safety).

Similarly, if you are unsteady on your feet and liable to fall, you might need both supervision and attention when walking. The supervision could involve looking out for any unexpected obstacles or uneven surfaces, and being there to catch you if you fell. The attention might involve telling you what is in front of you, or putting a hand on your arm to steady you.

There are many other situations where the help you need can amount to both attention and supervision. Keeping a 24-hour diary, listing all your needs throughout a typical day, may help you think about the types of help that could count as both (see 16 below).

If the decision maker does not look at the same needs under both the attention and supervision conditions, you may fail to meet either. A long gap during the middle of the day might mean the pattern of help you need does not amount to *'frequent... throughout the day'*. Under the supervision condition, the risk of danger and the situations of potential danger may not be great or frequent enough to warrant continual supervision. But if some of the needs considered under the supervision condition were also considered under the attention condition, the combination of needs could then amount to frequent attention throughout the day. This argument only works if some of the supervision you need also amounts to active attention in connection with a bodily function.

Use the attendance allowance claim-form to explain all your care needs. If you are unsuccessful, you can challenge the decision (see 19 below). When doing so, ask that all your needs are considered under both conditions. If you can, list those needs that could count as both attention and supervision.

## 12. What is 'watching over'?

*'Watching over'* has its ordinary meaning, so it includes needing to have someone else being awake and listening, as well as getting up and checking how you are.
Decision Makers Guide, Vol 10, Chap 61, para 61161

You do not need to show that you need watching over every night of the week. It depends on the normal pattern of your needs – three or four nights a week may be sufficient, perhaps less if the dangers would be very grave.

A *'prolonged period'* is normally at least 20 minutes.
Decision Makers Guide, Vol 10, Chap 61, para 61165

*'Frequent intervals'* means at least three times.

The test is based on what you reasonably require, not on what is actually done for you. If you have had a fair number of accidents or incidents at night (or even just one bad accident), that might suggest you need more watching over than you've been getting. If you've had few accidents, etc, the chances are that the watching over you get is the watching over you need.

## 13. Simpler methods

It may be suggested that you would need less attention or supervision from another person if you used certain aids or tried simpler methods. A typical simpler method is the use of a commode or portable urinal. If you could use one without help, it is usually concluded that you do not reasonably require help with trips to the toilet.

Sometimes an assumption is made that you can use a commode, but all the practical issues involved (eg privacy, hand washing, etc) have not been considered, nor the effect on your morale or general health if trips to the toilet are your only regular exercise. In any case, you might actually need help using the commode. Emptying and cleaning the commode can count as attention if it needs to be done right away (as it generally would be during the day if not necessarily at night) (CSDLA/44/02).

## 14. Renal dialysis

If you are a kidney patient undergoing renal dialysis, special rules may help you to qualify for the lower rate of attendance allowance. Depending on when and where you dialyse, you can be treated as satisfying the disability test for the day or the night. You must show that:

■ you undergo renal dialysis two or more times a week; *and*
■ the dialysis is of a type which normally requires the attendance or supervision of another person during the period of the dialysis; *or*
■ because of your particular circumstances (eg age, visual impairment or loss of manual dexterity) during the period of dialysis you need someone to supervise you to avoid substantial danger to yourself, or to give you some help with your bodily functions.

AA regs, reg 5

### Dialysis in hospital

If you are dialysing as an outpatient and getting help from hospital staff, you won't automatically satisfy the disability test, but it does help you to serve the qualifying period (see 3 above). This is helpful if you alternate between outpatient dialysis and dialysis at home. You will be treated as satisfying the disability test for the period you dialyse at home (if this is at least twice a week and you need assistance as above) even if it is only for a short period. If the help you get as an outpatient is from someone who doesn't work for the hospital, you pass the disability test. Inpatient dialysis counts for both the qualifying period and the disability test, but payment of attendance allowance is affected by a spell in hospital (see 6 above).

### Other types of dialysis

Continuous ambulatory peritoneal dialysis (CAPD) and automated peritoneal dialysis (APD) are designed to be done without help. You are only covered by the above rules if your disabilities or frailty mean you need help. If you are fully independent in dialysing you are not covered. But if you need even a small amount of help (eg to change the bag) you should pass the day or night disability test. You do not need to show that the attention needed is frequent or that the supervision required is continual.

## C. CLAIMS, PAYMENTS & APPEALS

## 15. How do you claim?

### Starting your claim

To get the attendance allowance claim-form (the *AA1*) ring the Attendance Allowance Helpline (0800 731 0122; textphone 0800 731 0317) or download it from the website (www.gov.uk/attendance-allowance/how-to-claim). To get a claim-form in Northern Ireland, ring the Disability & Carers Service (0800 587 0912; textphone 028 9031 1092) or download it from the website (www.nidirect.gov.uk/articles/attendance-allowance). For advice on how to complete the claim-form, see Box B.14.

### Your date of claim

If you phone for a claim-form, attendance allowance can be backdated to the date of your call. A claim-form issued by the DWP will be date stamped and will come with a postage-paid envelope. If you return the completed claim-form within six weeks, the date you asked for it is your date of claim. If you take longer than six weeks to return the completed form, explain why on the form. If the delay is reasonable, the time limit can be extended. If not, your date of claim is the day the completed claim-form reaches the Attendance Allowance Unit.

If you download a claim-form from the website, your date of claim is the day the completed form reaches the Attendance Allowance Unit.

### 16. Keeping a diary

Writing a short diary of your day-to-day needs can lend support to your attendance allowance claim. The diary can be

## B.14 Completing the attendance allowance claim-form

Most of the claim-form consists of a series of questions relating to your care and supervision needs. The questions have a tick-box format. Each question looks at a different area of day-to-day life. They generally follow a similar pattern. You are first asked to tick 'yes' or 'no' to confirm whether or not you have difficulties or need help with that area of day-to-day life; read the whole page before answering this. You are then asked more specific questions on each subject, including how often you need help.

Some questions ask if you have difficulty concentrating or motivating yourself and therefore need encouragement to carry out a task. You might need such encouragement because of a mental health problem (such as depression) or a condition affecting your mental capacity (such as dementia).

At the end of each question there is space to provide details of your difficulties. You may live alone and manage because you have no choice, but it is important to describe what would help you if someone was there to help. You might be managing by yourself at the moment, but some of the tasks may be difficult (eg painful, time consuming or risky) without help from someone else. Make sure you write down how much longer things take you than they used to or what dangers you face. Try to be specific.

Your condition may be variable. Many people claiming attendance allowance focus on good days. But you need to explain what help you need on a regular basis. Try to focus on an average day and list the problems you face more often than not. Explain what you are like on your worst days and how often such days occur. A diary may help you explain this (see 16 in this chapter).

In each case, if you have tried an aid or simpler method that has not helped (see 13 in this chapter), explain why it wasn't practical or reasonable for you. We now look at some of the questions in more detail.

### Help with your care needs during the day
**Do you usually have difficulty or do you need help with your toilet needs?**
This is one of the most difficult subjects to write about, because the questions are of such a personal nature. Try to include as much information as you can; the claim-forms are treated with strict confidentiality.

If you have difficulty walking, the most difficult part of toileting may be getting to and from the toilet, especially if there are stairs involved. If this is the case, explain on the form why using a commode would not be easier; for instance, there may be no private space for one on the floor you live on.

Mention any difficulties you have using the toilet, including sitting down or getting back up from it, wiping yourself, adjusting your clothing and washing afterwards. If you need to visit the toilet more often than is usual, explain why; it might be due to the medication you are on. If you are incontinent, you may need help changing your clothes and washing yourself.

**Do you fall or stumble because of your illnesses or disabilities?**
You may fall or stumble because of poor co-ordination or weakness in your legs, or because your ankle, knee or hip joints give way. The falls could be a result of dizzy spells, perhaps brought on by the medication you take, or you could fall during a fit or blackout. You may stumble into things because of a visual impairment. Whatever the reason, write down why you fall and what happens when you fall. Can you get up without help? Have you ever been stuck on the floor unable to get up; if so, for how long? Have you hurt yourself; if so, have the injuries needed treatment? How often do you fall or stumble? Is it happening more frequently? These questions may be easier to answer if you keep a long-term diary of your falls and stumbles – see Box B.15 for an example. Also see 'Supervision and falls' in 10 in this chapter.

**Do you usually need help from another person to communicate with other people?**
You may have difficulties communicating with people if you have hearing or speech problems. If you have a mental health problem or a learning disability, you may have difficulty concentrating during conversations or remembering what has been said. If you hear voices, this may make it more difficult to have a conversation. If any of these apply to you, list examples of the help you need either understanding or being understood during a conversation. This could be if someone comes to the door or calls on the telephone or when you need to communicate in shops, buses or taxis, etc. Write down what help you need even if there is no one to help you with this.

If you have a visual impairment, list all the situations where you need someone to read things to you. These could include checking labels on medication and use-by dates on food, reading your post, dealing with official letters, or reading radio and TV listings or a newspaper.

If you are deaf, write down if you need help from an interpreter to communicate, or if you need help developing your communication skills.

**Do you usually need someone to keep an eye on you?**
This question relates to any need you may have for *'continual supervision'* (defined in 10 in this chapter). You may need such supervision because you get confused. Confusion can arise from a mental health problem, learning disability, dementia or memory loss. It can also arise as a side effect of some types of medication. List examples of potential dangers that could result from the confusion, such as turning on the gas and not lighting it, or allowing strangers to come into the house without checking who they are. Write down if such incidents have already occurred.

If your condition is likely to deteriorate or relapse, you may not be able to recognise the symptoms or take any action once they have come on. Write down if you need someone to keep an eye on you to make sure you get help quickly to stem the deterioration or prevent too bad a relapse.

You might be at risk of hurting yourself or someone else. List any occasions when this has happened. Try to remember what brought on the incidents. Write down if you have any phobias that affect your daily life, for example claustrophobia a reminder of the help you need, which you might otherwise forget because it is so much a part of your everyday life. It can also be important when trying to explain needs that fluctuate either during a single day or over a longer period. The simplest form of diary would be an account of your needs over a typical day.

or agoraphobia. Mention if you get anxious or panicky and need someone to calm you down.

If you have fits or seizures, write down whether you get any warning. Could anyone else see warning signs and take steps to ensure you are safe? List times you have fallen in the past during a fit or seizure. Give examples of any injuries you got and treatment you received as a result. Write down how long it takes for you to recover from the fit or seizure and what other people could do to keep you safe in the meantime. If you keep a long-term diary before completing the claim-form (see 16 in this chapter and Box B.15), these points might be easier to answer.

### Help with your care needs during the night
**Do you usually need someone to watch over you?**
This question relates to any need you may have for 'watching over' (defined in 12 in this chapter). You need to show how your disability or medical condition is such that it may give rise to substantial danger. Outline the nature of the danger(s). Explain the basis for your fears of danger; refer to anything that supports your fears – eg the previous pattern and course of seizures, wandering at night, falls, etc. Explain why you cannot avoid the danger without help from another person – eg because of a mental disorder or an inability to administer medication, oxygen, etc during an attack of breathlessness. Relate the danger(s) to the need to have someone awake and watching over you. Do the dangers mean you need someone watching over you for 20 minutes or longer, waking up to listen out for you or getting up to check on you two, three or more times in the night? On how many nights a week?

Think about simpler methods (see 13 in this chapter) that may bypass the need to have someone watching over you. Explain fully how and why they do not or would not work. Are they reasonable in your circumstances?

If you need any active help at night (eg soothing back to sleep, rearranging bedding), write down that your night-time care needs are both attention and supervision – you might pass the attention test more easily than the watching over test.

### Statement from someone who knows you
The claim-form includes an optional section to be completed by someone who knows you; this could be your doctor or another professional involved in your care. The best person to complete this section is the one most involved with your treatment or care. It is better if that person is medically qualified, for example your GP, consultant or specialist nurse. If possible, make an appointment with them to discuss the matter. They will need to know about your care or supervision needs. If you have written a diary (see 16 in this chapter), give them a copy of it.

### What to do next
Once you have completed the claim-form make a copy of it, which you should keep. If you have kept a diary of your care needs (see 16 in this chapter), attach a copy of that to the claim-form. Also attach copies of a prescription list, if you have one, and any other medical evidence that could support the claim. Then send the claim-form in the envelope that came with it.

### One-day diary
Start from the time you get up in the morning, through a 24-hour period, ending with the time you get up the following morning. List all the times when you need help from someone or you have difficulties doing something because there is no one around to help. When you write something down, try to answer the following questions:
- what help do you need?
- why do you need the help?
- at what time do you need help? *and*
- how long do you need the help for?
If your needs vary from day to day, keep the diary over a few days to get a clearer picture of your needs. See Box B.4 in Chapter 4 for an example of a 1-day diary (in this case, for a child).

### Long-term diary
Long-term diaries can be useful when explaining more sporadic problems caused by your condition, such as stumbles, falls or fits. If you need continual supervision or watching over, such a diary can show exactly what happened, or what could have happened, if someone had not been there to intervene. If your condition is slowly worsening, a long-term diary can help pinpoint the date that you start to satisfy the disability test (see 8 above). See Box B.15 for an example of a long-term diary.

### Making use of the diary
Once you have finished the diary, write your name and national insurance number on it and make several copies of it. Attach a copy to the claim-form and keep a copy for yourself. If you ask someone to complete the 'Statement from someone who knows you' on the attendance allowance claim-form, give them a copy. You should send copies of the diary to anyone else who you have listed on the claim-form, such as your GP, consultant or specialist nurse.

### 17. How your claim is assessed
Your attendance allowance claim is decided by a DWP decision maker, not a healthcare professional. To help make decisions, the DWP produces online guidance called the *Medical guidance for DLA and AA decision makers (adult cases): staff guide* available via our website (www.disabilityrightsuk.org/links-government-departments). The guidance outlines the main care and supervision needs likely to arise from a number of different illnesses and disabling conditions.

The completed claim-form and this guidance may give the decision maker enough information to make a decision. If not, they may request a short report from your GP or another medical person you named on the claim-form. If that does not give a complete picture, the decision maker can arrange for a DWP-approved healthcare professional to assess you (normally in your home) in order to prepare a report. An assessment can also be arranged instead of getting in touch with your GP, consultant or nurse, etc.

**Refusing to take part in the assessment** – If you refuse to take part in the assessment, the claim will be decided against you unless you have 'good cause' for your refusal.
SSA, S.19

### The assessment
If you have a carer, you can ask them to attend the assessment. Your carer will not be able to answer questions on your behalf (unless the healthcare professional cannot understand your speech or you cannot understand their questions), but they can add to what you have to say, particularly with respect to their role as carer. Before the assessment, read through the copy that you made of your attendance allowance claim-form.

During the assessment, the healthcare professional should ask questions relating to each of the areas covered on the claim-form. You should tell the healthcare professional about any pain or tiredness you feel when carrying out each task. Let them know about any variation in your condition and about both good and bad days. Show them any medical evidence you have confirming your problems. Try to make sure that what you tell the healthcare professional is consistent with what you put on the claim-form, unless of course there has been a significant change in your condition.

The healthcare professional may then carry out a brief physical examination.

Once the healthcare professional has completed their report, they send it to the decision maker, who decides whether or not to award you attendance allowance and, if it is awarded, at what rate.

### Delays
It usually takes up to 40 working days (ie not including weekends or public holidays) to deal with your claim. If you are terminally ill (see Box B.8 in Chapter 5) you should get a decision within eight working days. Compensation may be payable for long delays (see Chapter 59(2) for details).

In any case, if your claim is taking too long, complain to the office that is dealing with your claim.

### 18. The award
Attendance allowance may be awarded for a fixed period or indefinitely. If your award is for a fixed period, the Attendance Allowance Unit will invite you to make a renewal claim about four months before the end of your current award.

**Backdating** – Attendance allowance cannot be backdated to earlier than your date of claim (see 15 above). There are only limited situations in which an earlier date can be treated as your date of claim. These are:
❑ If industrial action has caused postal disruption, the day your claim would have been delivered to the Attendance Allowance Unit is treated as your date of claim.

C&P regs, reg 6(5)

---

### B.15 Long-term diary

**This is a diary kept over a 3-month period by a 73-year-old man with rheumatoid arthritis**

*04/02/18* Fell in the front room. My left ankle gave way. (I use a frame to walk, which helps me to steady myself, but when my ankles or knees give way I cannot bear my weight as my arms are weak at the elbow and I usually end up on the floor.) I bruised my left hip. It took me five minutes to get up.

*17/02/18* Tripped in the hall. My left ankle again. This time fell against the cupboard. There was no injury or damage.

*26/02/18* Stumbled on patio, carrying small plant pot. My right knee gave way. Banged my head on the door. Small cut above left eyebrow.

*12/03/18* Fell in shower. Early in the morning – just due to general stiffness and weakness. Badly bruised right shoulder. Took 10 minutes to get out. Scalded my right thigh. I rang my GP, who sent nurse round to look at the injuries. Not too serious; could have been much worse. She dressed the scald.

*24/03/18* Stumbled in hall. Right knee again. Didn't hurt myself, but trod on the cat.

*13/04/18* Fell on the patio again, left ankle this time. My son was there. Badly sprained my right ankle. My son suspected I might have broken something and took me to casualty, where the ankle was cold-compressed and dressed.

---

❑ If a decision maker uses their discretion to treat anything written as being sufficient to count as a valid claim, the date that earlier document was received is treated as your date of claim.

### 19. If you are not happy with the decision
If you are not happy with the decision on your claim, you can ask for a *'mandatory reconsideration'* of the decision within one calendar month of the date the DWP sent it to you. When the decision maker reconsiders the decision, they can confirm the initial decision, or increase or reduce the rate of the award, or the length of the award. You have a further month to appeal to an independent tribunal if you are not happy with the reconsidered decision. The one-month time limit to ask for a mandatory reconsideration can be extended only if there are special reasons for the delay. Otherwise, if the decision was notified to you more than one month ago, see below.

### Asking for a mandatory reconsideration
If you want to challenge the decision, it will help to know why it was made. You must also get your reconsideration in on time. Write to the address (or ring the number) on the decision letter and do the following:
■ request a mandatory reconsideration of the decision. State your grounds simply at this stage, eg, *'You have underestimated how my disability affects me and how much care and supervision I need'*;
■ ask them to send you copies of all the evidence they used to make the decision; *and*
■ ask them not to take any further action until you have had a chance to respond to that evidence.

If you phone, put your request in writing as well; keep a copy for yourself. If you have not received the evidence after two weeks, ring them again to remind them to send it. When you do receive the evidence, you should have a better idea of why the decision was made.

### Building a case
Sometimes the only evidence used will be the information you gave on the claim-form. However, there may be a report as well. This will be either a short report from your GP, consultant or nurse, etc, or a longer one from the healthcare professional who assessed you for the DWP. Compare the report with the claim-form. Try to find where a difference of opinion arises.

For example, you may have written on the claim-form that you could not get up and down the stairs without support, but the healthcare professional's report said that they considered you could manage by yourself. Now try to get medical evidence showing that what you said on the claim-form is correct: eg a letter from your GP, consultant or nurse, etc, confirming the difficulties and risks you face in getting up and down stairs, detailing any falls you have had that they are aware of.

While good medical evidence is usually the most effective, a letter from someone who knows the help you need, such as a carer, can also be useful.

Once you have evidence to support your case, send it to the address on the decision letter. If it could take a while to get the evidence, you should let the DWP know how long it is likely to take, so they do not make a decision straight away.

A decision maker will look at any further evidence you send in. They will then either revise the decision or write back to you explaining that they have been unable to change the decision. Either way, if you are not satisfied with the result, you now have a month from the date of the reconsidered decision to appeal to an independent tribunal. For more on appeals, see Chapter 57.

### If the decision was notified more than one month ago

To challenge a decision notified more than one month ago (or if there has been a change of circumstances), you need to show there are specific grounds, for example:

■ there has been a change of circumstances since the decision was made – eg your care needs have increased; *or*

■ the decision maker didn't know about a relevant fact – eg you missed out some aspect of your care needs when you filled in the claim-form.

See Box O.8, Chapter 57 for more details

### 20. How are you paid?

Attendance allowance is paid to you, not to a carer, to spend as you wish. It is usually paid on a Monday, every four weeks in arrears, into your bank, building society or Post Office card account or paid with your state pension.

### Appointees

If you cannot manage your own affairs, the DWP can appoint another person to act on your behalf (see Chapter 56(4)). But attendance allowance is your benefit, not your appointee's benefit. If you don't want someone else formally appointed to act for you, but cannot collect your attendance allowance yourself, you can arrange with the bank, building society or Post Office for someone to do it for you.

### 21. What if your condition changes?

**If your condition gets worse** – If you already receive attendance allowance at the lower rate, give the DWP details of the change (0800 731 0122, textphone 0800 731 0317; or write to Attendance Allowance Unit, Mail Handling Site A, Wolverhampton WV98 2AD). If you live in Northern Ireland, contact the Disability & Carers Service (DCS: 0800 587 0912; textphone 028 9031 1092; or write to Castle Court, Royal Avenue, Belfast, BT1 1HR). The DWP or DCS will usually send you a claim-form to complete, similar to that used for new claims (see Box B.14).

Your existing award may be superseded to award the higher rate. You can qualify for the higher rate from six months after your needs increased. You can put in your request for the higher rate before the six months have passed.

SSCBA, S.65(3)

**If your condition improves** – If your need for help lessens, this could mean your rate of attendance allowance should drop. Contact the Attendance Allowance Unit or DCS (see above) to give them details. The decision maker will usually supersede your award.

If your rate of attendance allowance drops (or ends) but you have a relapse within two years, you can get back your former rate of benefit in a linked claim without having to serve the qualifying period (see 3 above) again.

AA regs, reg 3

# 7 Help with mobility

| | | |
|---|---|---|
| 1 | Blue Badge scheme | 55 |
| | Mobility checklist – Box B.16 | 56 |
| 2 | Exemption from vehicle tax | 57 |

## 1. Blue Badge scheme

The Blue Badge scheme allows people with severe mobility problems, registered blind people, and people with severe disabilities in both arms to park close to places they wish to visit.

You should not be wheel-clamped or towed away if you are displaying a valid badge, although your vehicle may be moved if it is causing an obstruction. The badge does not apply to parking on private roads and land. The badge does not automatically give you exemption from car park charges.

The entire side of the badge showing the hologram must be visible from outside the vehicle; displaying the wrong side (the photo) can result in a parking fine or penalty charge notice.

DP(BMV) Regs, regs 11 & 12

It is an offence not to allow a police officer, traffic warden, parking attendant or civil enforcement officer to fully examine a badge.

For more information about the Blue Badge in England, ring 0343 100 1000.

### Where can you park?

The scheme allows you to park:

■ without charge or time limit at on-street parking meters and in Pay and Display bays, unless signs show a time limit for badge holders;

■ without time limit in streets where otherwise waiting is allowed for only limited periods;

■ for up to three hours in England, Northern Ireland and Wales, or without any time limit in Scotland, on single or double yellow lines.

In England and Wales, a parking clock must also be displayed showing the time of arrival if you are parked on yellow lines or in a reserved parking place for badge holders that has a time limit. If you are visiting England or Wales from Northern Ireland or Scotland, ask your local authority for a parking clock. The time limit only applies during the operating hours of the restriction.

It is required that:

■ the badge holder is in the vehicle when it arrives at or when it leaves the parking place;

■ the vehicle is not parked in a bus or cycle lane during the lane's hours of operation;

■ the vehicle is not parked where there is a ban on loading or unloading; *and*

■ all other parking rules are met.

LATO(EDP) Regs, regs 7-9

Red routes are subject to special controls on stopping, but there are usually parking bays for badge holders.

### Where does the scheme apply?

The scheme applies throughout the UK, but there are major differences in the scheme's operation in certain London boroughs (City of London, Kensington and Chelsea, Westminster, and part of Camden). Contact the local authority for details. The scheme does not apply in security zones, eg at airports.

LATO(EDP) Regs, reg 5(2)

### Qualification: automatic

You qualify automatically for a Blue Badge if you are aged 2 or over *and*:

■ receive the higher rate mobility component of disability living allowance (DLA); *or*

■ (in Scotland) previously received an indefinite or lifetime award of the higher rate mobility component of DLA, which has been terminated following a personal independence payment (PIP) re-assessment (see Box B.6, Chapter 5); *or*

■ (in England and Northern Ireland) have been awarded 8 points or more in the 'moving around' activity of PIP or (in Scotland and Wales) have been awarded 8 points or more in the 'moving around' activity or 12 points in the 'planning and following journeys' activity (see Box B.10, Chapter 5); *or*

■ (in Scotland) previously received a fixed-term award of the higher rate mobility component of DLA, have not been awarded the appropriate points at a PIP re-assessment (as in the above bullet) and you have requested a mandatory reconsideration of the decision within the last year; *or*

- receive war pensioners' mobility supplement; *or*
- are registered blind; *or*
- have received a lump sum payment from the Armed Forces Compensation scheme (within tariff levels 1-8) and have been certified as having a permanent and substantial disability that causes inability to walk or very considerable difficulty in walking; *or*
- (in Wales) have received a lump sum payment from the Armed Forces Compensation scheme due to a permanent mental disorder (tariff level 6).

### Qualification: the 'assessed route'

You may also qualify through the *'assessed route'* if you are aged 2 or over *and*:

- have a *'permanent and substantial disability which causes inability to walk or very considerable difficulty in walking'*; or

- drive regularly, have a severe disability in both arms and are unable to operate, or have considerable difficulty in operating, all or some types of parking meter; *or*
- (in Scotland) are unable to walk or virtually unable to walk because of a temporary but substantial disability which is likely to last for a period of at least 12 months but less than three years; *or*
- (in Scotland) lack an awareness of the danger from traffic, either for a temporary period of at least 12 months or permanently; *or*
- (in Wales) as a result of a severe cognitive impairment are unable to follow the route of any journey without the help of someone else; *or*
- (in Wales) have a terminal illness that seriously limits your mobility.

In these cases, you may be assessed by your local authority. In Wales, you can apply for a temporary 12-month badge if

---

## B.16  Mobility checklist

### Motability

Motability is an independent charity set up to help people with disabilities use one of the following *'qualifying benefits'* to improve their mobility:

- higher rate mobility component of disability living allowance (DLA);
- enhanced rate mobility component of personal independence payment (PIP);
- armed forces independence payment; *or*
- war pensioner's mobility supplement.

The scheme offers cars on lease (including cars adapted to carry a driver or passenger seated in their wheelchair), powered wheelchairs and mobility scooters. Many of the costs of adapting a car can be included.

To use the Motability scheme, your qualifying benefit must usually have at least 12 months still to run. The DWP (or Veterans UK) will make payments direct to Motability.

You cannot start or renew a Motability car agreement if you are in hospital.

Motability can sometimes help towards the cost of driving lessons if you receive a qualifying benefit.

You can get details of the scheme from www.motability. co.uk or by ringing 0300 456 4566

**PIP re-assessments** – If you are re-assessed for PIP (see Box B.6, Chapter 5) and are not awarded the enhanced rate of the PIP mobility component, you will no longer be eligible to use the Motability scheme. In these circumstances, the DLA mobility component can continue for up to four weeks after the DLA payday following the re-assessment decision. After that, Motability will allow you to keep the vehicle for a further eight weeks from the date the mobility component payments stop. This will provide you with some time to challenge the decision and make alternative arrangements.

If you lose your Motability vehicle following a PIP re-assessment and you were on the Motability scheme before January 2013, you may be entitled to a £2,000 lump sum payment from Motability to enable you to buy a used vehicle. If you lose your Motability vehicle following a PIP re-assessment and you joined the Motability scheme in 2013, you may be eligible for a £1,000 lump sum payment. In either case, you should be given the opportunity of buying the vehicle you are currently leasing from Motability.

If you are eligible for a lump sum payment and challenge the PIP decision, you can keep your Motability vehicle for up to six months during the reconsideration and appeal process instead of receiving the full lump sum payment. If you do this, you will also be eligible for a reduced lump sum payment of £500, or £250 if you joined the Motability scheme in 2013.

### Concessions on cars and wheelchairs

The NHS can supply and maintain wheelchairs free of charge in some circumstances, and may provide a voucher towards the cost of a more expensive wheelchair of your choice.

If you are working, you may be able to get help with travel costs through Access to Work (see Chapter 34(5)).

You can get a wheelchair or scooter on the Motability scheme instead of a car if you receive a qualifying benefit (see Motability above).

### Concessions on public transport

A Disabled Person's Railcard (£20 for one year or £54 for three years) gives you and a companion one-third off the cost of most train journeys. Check the claim-form or website for a full list of the disabilities that are covered by the scheme. You can get details from www. disabledpersons-railcard.co.uk or by ringing 0345 605 0525 (textphone 0345 601 0132).

In England, people who have reached the qualifying age for pension credit (see Chapter 44(2)) and eligible disabled people are entitled to free off-peak travel on all local buses anywhere in England. Application forms are available from local authorities. In Wales, there is a similar concession for any time of day.

In Scotland, older and disabled people are entitled to free Scotland-wide bus travel on most services. You need to apply for a National Entitlement Card; application forms are available from local authorities.

For travel concessions in Northern Ireland, enquire at Translink bus and rail stations or ring 028 9066 6630.

Concessions are available on some ferry routes and Eurotunnel for disabled people travelling with a car. Contact Disabled Motoring UK (01508 489 449; www. disabledmotoring.org).

**Help with travel to work** – See Chapter 34(5).

### Assessment services and information

It is important to choose the car and adaptations that are best suited to you. A network of accredited mobility centres (which are members of Driving Mobility) offers professional assessment, advice and recommendations for drivers and passengers with mobility needs. To be put through to the accredited centre in your region, ring 0800 559 3636. Advice, information and contact details for mobility centres can also be found on the website (www.drivingmobility.org.uk).

you are recovering from, or awaiting treatment for, a serious illness or injury; in this case you will also be assessed by your local authority.

In Scotland, carers and relatives of people who pose a risk to themselves or others in traffic can apply for a badge.

### Qualification: children
Special rules allow children under the age of 3 to qualify for a Blue Badge if they have a specific medical condition which means they:
- must always be accompanied by bulky medical equipment that cannot be carried around with the child without great difficulty; *and/or*
- need to be kept near a vehicle at all times so that they can, if necessary, be treated in the vehicle or quickly driven to a place where they can be treated.

*'Bulky medical equipment'* includes, in particular, any of the following:
- ventilators;
- suction machines;
- feed pumps;
- parenteral equipment;
- syringe drivers;
- oxygen administration equipment;
- continual oxygen saturation monitoring equipment; *and*
- casts and associated medical equipment for the correction of hip dysplasia.

DP(BMV) Regs, reg 4

### Applications
Applications are processed by local authorities or by the Blue Badge Unit in Northern Ireland (0300 200 7818). In England, you may be charged a maximum fee of £10; in Scotland, up to £20; in Northern Ireland the fee is £10; in Wales it is free of charge. The badge lasts up to three years. You can apply online at www.gov.uk/apply-blue-badge if you live in England or Wales, or at www.mygov.scot/apply-blue-badge if you live in Scotland.

DP(BMV) Regs, reg 6

### Appeals
If your local authority refuses to issue you with a Blue Badge, you have no formal right of appeal. However, many authorities have internal procedures for dealing with reviews, so it is worth writing to ask for a review.

In Scotland, there is a formal review process. If a local authority decides that you do not qualify, you can ask for a review of the decision within 28 days of receiving it.

### Congestion charging exemption
Exemption from congestion charging in central London is available to Blue Badge holders for an initial £10 administration fee if they apply to the Congestion Charge Office (for an application form ring 0343 222 2222 or apply online at https://tfl.gov.uk/modes/driving/cc-blue-badge-before-you-begin-29758). This exemption can be used on any two vehicles. Vehicles taxed in the 'Disabled' class are automatically exempt if appropriately registered at DVLA, Swansea.

### European concessions
Blue Badge holders visiting European Union countries that provide disabled parking concessions can take advantage of these by displaying their badge. Concessions vary. Details can be found in the European Commission booklet *Parking card for people with disabilities in the European Union* (ec.europa. eu/justice/discrimination/files/parking_card_leaflet_en.pdf).

### For more information
The *Blue Badge Guide for London* contains information on how the scheme operates in London (£6.99, PIE Mapping 020 7952 0450; www.thepieguide.com).

## 2. Exemption from vehicle tax
### Who can get exemption?
Exemption from vehicle tax (including the first registration fee) for one car is given to some disabled people. If you receive one of the following *'qualifying benefits'*:
- higher rate mobility component of disability living allowance (DLA);
- enhanced rate mobility component of personal independence payment (PIP);
- armed forces independence payment (AFIP); *or*
- war pensioners' mobility supplement,

you (or your appointee or someone you choose to nominate in your place) can apply for exemption from vehicle tax.

If you receive the standard rate mobility component of PIP, you will be entitled to a 50% discount off your vehicle tax.

A vehicle is exempt *'when it is being used, or kept for use, by or for the purposes of a disabled person.'* What exactly this means has never been defined. The use of an exempt car for purposes totally unconnected with the disabled person is unlawful.

Vehicle Excise & Registration Act 1994, Sch 2, para 19

When you are awarded DLA higher rate or PIP enhanced rate mobility component, you should receive a re-usable *'Certificate of Entitlement'* that lasts for the duration of your mobility award. You will need to show this certificate the first time you apply for vehicle tax; when you renew the tax, you just need the serial number of the certificate. If your circumstances change (eg you change your vehicle), you will need to apply for a new certificate. If you have not been sent the certificate (or want guidance on it), contact the specific benefit office (see Chapter 61(2)).

If you receive war pensioners' mobility supplement or the AFIP, you need to apply for an exemption certificate: WPA0442. To do this, contact Veterans UK (0800 169 2277; textphone: 0800 169 3458).

Motability customers enjoy the same exemptions, but the process is handled by Motability.

### Nominating another person's vehicle
If you receive a qualifying benefit, you can nominate another person's vehicle to be exempt from vehicle tax. This may also apply to a company car registered in the name of the company; the person receiving the qualifying benefit should nominate the company for exemption. In order to qualify for exemption, the vehicle should be used *'by or for the purposes of'* the disabled person. The named person who gets the exemption may be changed at any time. For example, if you have nominated someone else for exemption and then get your own car, the exemption can be returned to you.

### If you are refused exemption
Even if you have a Certificate of Entitlement from the DWP, the DVLA can refuse to grant exemption from vehicle tax if they think the vehicle will not be used *'solely by or for the purposes of'* the disabled person. They are unlikely to do this unless your intended use of the vehicle would blatantly breach this condition. If you are refused exemption, there is no formal procedure for appealing. However, you can write, giving full details of why you think you qualify for exemption, the purposes for which the vehicle will be used, etc to: Specialist Casework, DVLA Swansea SA99 1ZZ (0300 790 6802).

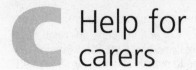

# Help for carers

This section of the handbook looks at:

| | |
|---|---|
| Carer's allowance | Chapter **8** |
| Other help for carers | Chapter **9** |

# 8 Carer's allowance

| | | |
|---|---|---|
| 1 | What is carer's allowance? | 58 |
| 2 | Do you qualify? | 58 |
| 3 | How much do you get? | 59 |
| 4 | How do you claim? | 59 |
| 5 | How do earnings affect carer's allowance? | 59 |
| 6 | How do other benefits affect carer's allowance? | 60 |
| 7 | Carer's allowance and income support | 61 |
| 8 | Carer's allowance and state pension | 61 |
| 9 | Carer's allowance and universal credit | 61 |
| 10 | Why claim carer's allowance? | 61 |
| 11 | Time off from caring | 61 |
| | Caring away from your home – Box C.1 | 60 |

## 1. What is carer's allowance?

Carer's allowance is a benefit for people who regularly spend at least 35 hours a week caring for a severely disabled person. You do not have to be related to, or live with, the disabled person. You can get carer's allowance even if you have never worked. You are not prevented from getting carer's allowance if you are disabled yourself and also need care. If you are entitled to carer's allowance, a *'carer premium'* is included in the award of any means-tested benefit you receive; a similar *'carer amount'* is included in universal credit (see 10 below).

Carer's allowance is not means tested and does not depend on national insurance (NI) contributions. It is taxable and counts as income for tax credits and universal credit. Carer's allowance gives you Class 1 NI contribution credits (see Box D.3, Chapter 11).

**The severe disability premium** – If you are paid carer's allowance, the person you care for cannot get the *'severe disability premium'* included in the award of any means-tested benefit they receive (or the equivalent amount in pension credit). Because of this, it is not always advantageous to claim carer's allowance even if you are eligible. See Chapter 21(3). The person you care for will not lose the severe disability premium (or the pension credit equivalent) if you are entitled to carer's allowance but cannot be paid it because of the overlapping benefits rule (see 6 below).

**The benefit cap** – If you are entitled to carer's allowance, your household will be exempt from the 'benefit cap', which limits the total weekly benefits that can be claimed. See Chapter 16(12) and Box G.6 in Chapter 25 for details.

## 2. Do you qualify?

❑ You must regularly spend at least 35 hours a week (see below) caring for a person who receives one of the following *'qualifying benefits'*:
  – disability living allowance (DLA) care component (at the middle or highest rate only); *or*
  – attendance allowance (at either rate); *or*
  – personal independence payment (PIP) daily living component (at either rate); *or*
  – constant attendance allowance (of £69.90 or more) paid with the Industrial Injuries/War Pensions schemes; *or*
  – armed forces independence payment.
❑ You must be aged 16 or over.

❑ You must not be in full-time education (see below).
❑ If you work, you must not earn more than £120 a week (see 5 below).
❑ You must not be subject to immigration control (see Chapter 53(2)) and must pass the UK residence and presence tests (see Chapter 53(3)).
SSCBA, S.70 & ICA Regs, regs 3, 4(1), 5, 8 & 9

Carer's allowance can continue for up to eight weeks after the person you look after dies. You must continue to meet all the qualifying conditions other than those related to the care of a disabled person or that person's receipt of a qualifying benefit.
SSCBA, S.70(1A)

If someone else gets carer's allowance (or the universal credit carer amount) to look after the same person you look after, you cannot also get carer's allowance to look after them. You can get national insurance credits (see Box D.3, Chapter 11) to help protect your entitlement to a state pension and you may get income support as a carer (but not the carer premium). You and the other carer can decide who should claim carer's allowance (or the carer amount). You can only get one award of carer's allowance, even if you care for more than one person.
SSCBA, S.70(7)-(7A)

If you were aged 65 or over and entitled to carer's allowance on 27.10.02 (then called invalid care allowance), you can continue to get carer's allowance even if you stop caring for 35 hours a week or if the qualifying benefit of the person you look after stops or if you start full-time work. You must, however, continue to meet the other carer's allowance qualifying conditions.
Regulatory Reform (Carer's Allowance) Order 2002, art 4

**Northern Ireland: supplementary payments** – *'Supplementary payments'* are available in Northern Ireland to temporarily compensate you if you lose your carer's allowance as a result of the person you care for losing their qualifying benefit at a PIP re-assessment (see Box B.6 in Chapter 5). The supplementary payment makes up for the loss of carer's allowance (less any overlapping benefit that may be payable – see 6 below) and can be paid for up to one year.
Welfare Supplementary Payment (Loss of Carer Payments) Regs (Northern Ireland) 2016

**Caring for 35 hours a week**

If you are caring for more than one person, you cannot add together the time you spend caring for each of them. You have to show that for at least 35 hours each week you are caring for one person. If you meet the 35-hours test during part of the year (eg in school holidays), you may qualify for carer's allowance during that period. The carer's allowance benefit week runs from the start of Sunday to the end of the following Saturday.
ICA Regs, reg 4(1)-(1A); SSCBA, S.122

The hours of caring in any given week must total at least 35: you cannot average the hours over a number of weeks. If, for example, you provide care on alternate weekends, it may be difficult to show you provide care for 35 hours in any given benefit week, as the care you provide on Saturday will fall within one benefit week and Sunday's care will fall into the next. The time you spend caring includes preparing for the visit of the person you care for on the day they arrive, clearing up after they leave, and collecting them from or taking them back to the place where they usually live (CG/6/1990).

### Full-time education

You are generally treated as being in full-time education if your course is described as such by your educational establishment, although there can be exceptions, eg you have been granted exemptions from parts of your course or your course is not a traditional university-type course. Even if your course is not described as full time, you will be treated as in full-time education if the course involves supervised study of 21 hours a week or more.

If you have deferred your studies to care for someone, and have the agreement from your educational establishment to do so, you may be considered to be no longer actively pursuing a full-time course of study, in which case you can be entitled to carer's allowance. Relevant factors that are considered here include: the length of your break, whether or not you can still access funding for your studies, and whether you can access learning materials.

ICA Regs, reg 5; CG/838/2015; DMG Memo 2/17

## 3. How much do you get?

| Carer's allowance | per week |
| --- | --- |
| For yourself | £64.60 |
| For an adult dependant* | £38.00 |
| For dependent children   extra for the oldest child** | £8.00 |
| extra for each other child** | £11.35 |

\* available only on claims made before 6.4.10
\*\* available only on claims made before 6.4.03

## 4. How do you claim?

Claim on form DS700, or on DS700(SP) if you get a state pension. These forms are available from the Carer's Allowance Unit (0800 731 0297; textphone 0800 731 0317) or the Disability & Carers Service in Northern Ireland (0800 587 0912; textphone 028 9031 1092). They can be downloaded from: www.gov.uk/government/publications/carers-allowance-claim-form. You can also apply online at: www.gov.uk/carers-allowance/how-to-claim.

The claim-form includes a statement to be signed by the cared-for person. This asks them to confirm that they know a claim for carer's allowance is being made, that the carer provides them with at least 35 hours of care a week and that they are aware their own benefits could be affected by the claim (ie if they receive the severe disability premium or pension credit equivalent – see Chapter 21(3)). If the cared-for person is incapable of signing the statement themselves, it can be done by someone acting on their behalf.

Once you claim carer's allowance, you may be offered the option of attending a voluntary interview to discuss work prospects. However, if you are also claiming certain other benefits, eg income support, you may be obliged to attend an interview as a condition of receiving that other benefit (see Box O.4, Chapter 56).

### Backdating

If you were entitled to carer's allowance before claiming it, you can ask for it to be backdated for up to three months. If you have been waiting for the person you are caring for to be awarded a qualifying benefit (see 2 above), and you claim carer's allowance within three months of the date of a decision to award the qualifying benefit, your claim for carer's allowance can be treated as having been made on the first day of the benefit week in which the qualifying benefit became payable. Thus carer's allowance can be fully backdated to that

time if you met the other qualifying conditions throughout that period.

C&P Regs, reg 6(33) & 19(2)-(3)

If entitlement to carer's allowance means you could start receiving a benefit such as income support because of the award of a carer premium, you should claim the benefit at the same time as claiming carer's allowance to ensure it is also backdated.

### What happens next?

You will be sent a written decision on your claim. If you disagree with the decision, you have one month to ask for a mandatory reconsideration of it. If you are not happy with the outcome of the reconsideration, you have a further month to appeal. See Chapter 57 for more on challenging decisions.

## 5. How do earnings affect carer's allowance?

You cannot get carer's allowance if your net earnings are more than £120 a week – the *'earnings limit'*. See below for the way in which earnings are calculated.

ICA Regs, reg 8

Your partner's earnings do not affect your basic benefit but can affect any addition(s) for a dependent adult or children. If you are entitled to an adult dependant's addition, it will not be paid if your partner earns more than £38 a week. If you are still entitled to any child dependant's addition(s) and your partner earns £235 or more a week, you will lose an addition for one child. For each extra £31 earned, you lose another child dependant's addition.

Occupational and personal pensions count as earnings for adult and child dependants' additions, but not for the basic rate of carer's allowance.

Social Security Benefit (Dependency) Regs 1977, Sch 2, paras 2A-2B, 7 & 9(1)

Earnings of £120 a week or less do not affect carer's allowance, but any means-tested benefit you also receive may be reduced (see Chapters 17(1)-(6) and 22(4)-(6)).

### Calculating earnings

In working out how much of your earnings are taken into account, certain deductions and disregards can be made from gross earnings. Count any payment from your employer as earnings (eg bonus, commission, retainer).

If you stop work and then claim carer's allowance, most payments made at the end of your job are disregarded, eg pay in lieu of notice or holiday pay.

If you are self-employed, the rules on working out net profit follow the rules for means-tested benefits (see Chapter 22(5)).

From your gross weekly earnings (or net profit) deduct:
- income tax, national insurance contributions (Class 1, 2 or 4) and half of any contribution you make to an occupational or personal pension;
- expenses *wholly, exclusively and necessarily incurred in the performance of the duties of the employment'*, eg equipment, special clothing, travel between workplaces (but not travel between home and work);
- advance of earnings or a loan from your employer;
- fostering allowances (for official arrangements only);
- payments from a local authority, health body or voluntary organisation for providing someone with temporary care;
- the first £20 a week of rent paid to you by a subtenant(s);
- the first £20 a week plus half the rest of the income from a boarder;
- the whole of any contribution towards living and accommodation costs from someone living in your home (other than boarders and subtenants);
- earnings from employment payable abroad if transfer to the UK is prohibited;
- charges for currency conversion;
- income tax refunds;

■ annual bounty paid to part-time members of the fire brigade or lifeboat service, or to auxiliary coastguards or members of the reserve forces;

■ payments for expenses for taking part in a public body service-user consultation.

CE Regs, regs 9 & 10 & Sch 1

If your earnings in one week are over the limit, you lose carer's allowance the following week. Monthly earnings are worked out on a weekly basis and affect benefit for the month ahead. If earnings fluctuate, they may be averaged over a recognisable cycle of work or over five weeks, but this is discretionary. One-off payments that are not for any specific period are divided by the relevant weekly earnings limit to work out the number of weeks your benefit will be affected.

CE Regs, reg 8

## Care costs

In working out how much of your earnings are taken into account, certain childcare costs can be deducted. There are different rules for basic carer's allowance and for dependant additions.

**Basic carer's allowance** – For basic carer's allowance, if, because of your work, you pay someone other than a close relative to look after the person you care for or to look after a child aged under 16, these payments are deducted from your earnings. A maximum of half your net earnings can be disregarded in this way. A *'close relative'* is the parent, son, daughter, brother, sister or partner of either yourself or the disabled person you care for.

CE Regs, regs 10(3)(b) & 13(3)(b) and Sch 3

**Dependant additions** – For dependant additions in carer's allowance, or for calculating earnings in other non-means-tested benefits, more restrictive rules apply. Childcare costs of up to £60 a week can be deducted from earnings for the care of children aged under 11.

You must be paying a registered childminder or other registered childcare provider (or paying for childcare provided on Crown premises or by schools, hospitals, etc where childcare is exempt from registration) or paying an out-of-school-hours scheme (run on school premises or provided by a local authority and offering childcare to children aged 8 or over but under 11).

Childcare costs can only be counted if you are a lone parent, or you are one of a couple and *either* both of you are working *or* one of you is working and the other is incapacitated.

CE Regs, regs 10(2)(b) & 13(2)(b) and Sch 2

You are treated as *'incapacitated'* if you get:

■ disability living allowance, personal independence payment or attendance allowance (or the equivalents in the War Pensions or Industrial Injuries schemes);

■ armed forces independence payment;

■ long-term incapacity benefit or severe disablement allowance; *or*

■ housing benefit and either childcare costs have been allowed under the rules for this benefit (see Chapter 22(6)) or a disability premium or higher pensioner premium has been awarded based on your (not your partner's) disability.

CE Regs, Sch 2, para 8

## 6. How do other benefits affect carer's allowance?

You can receive carer's allowance at the same time as disability living allowance, attendance allowance or personal independence payment.

If the person you look after has the severe disability premium included in the award of a means-tested benefit, it will stop once you get carer's allowance. If you cannot be

---

## C.1 Caring away from your home

### Seek legal advice

If you have to leave your own home to care for a disabled or elderly relative or friend, seek advice before you go (see Chapter 58). Consider what you will do if the need for that care stops, if your relationship with the cared-for person deteriorates, or if they die, go into a care home or become mentally incapable of looking after their own affairs.

### Housing costs

If you leave your main home temporarily, you remain liable for housing costs, including the rent or mortgage. If you are getting help towards these, how long you continue to receive this will depend on whether you are getting universal credit or one of the pre-universal credit means-tested benefits (income-related employment and support allowance, income support, income-based jobseeker's allowance and housing benefit) or pension credit.

**Universal credit** – If you receive universal credit, help with rent through the housing costs amount (see Chapter 24) or help with your mortgage through *'support for mortgage interest loans'* (see Chapter 26) will normally stop if your absence from home exceeds, or is expected to exceed, six months. See Box G.2, Chapter 24 for details.

**Pre-universal credit means-tested benefits and pension credit** – If the absence is for up to 13 weeks, you can continue to get help with your rent from housing benefit (see Chapter 25(6)) or help with your mortgage through support for mortgage interest loans (see Chapter 26). That help continues for up to 52 weeks if the care

you provide is medically approved. If you think your absence might be for longer than 13 weeks, ask a doctor or other medical professional (eg a nurse) involved in the disabled person's treatment to write a letter approving the care you provide.

Housing benefit and support for mortgage interest loans stop after a continuous absence of 13 or 52 weeks, as just explained. However, if you return home (perhaps with the disabled person) for even a very short stay, a new period of absence should then start, allowing you to continue getting help beyond those initial limits. Tell the office dealing with your claim of each visit to your home and keep a record of the dates of the visits. If you leave your home permanently, help with housing costs will stop immediately.

### Council tax

If you have left your home empty to live elsewhere to care for someone, your former home may be exempt from council tax. The person you care for must need that care because they are elderly, ill or disabled, have a mental illness or disorder, or have a drug or alcohol problem. For the exemption to apply, the empty property must have ceased to be your sole or main residence. See Box G.10 in Chapter 28.

If the home of the person you care for becomes your sole or main residence, you may be treated as living there. However, your presence in their home will be disregarded if:

■ they are not your child under 18 or your partner;

■ they are entitled to a 'qualifying benefit' (see Chapter 8(2)); *and*

■ you spend at least 35 hours a week on average caring for them.

This means council tax for the home will be the same as if you were not living there. See Chapter 28(9).

paid carer's allowance because of the overlapping benefits rule (see below), the person you care for will not lose the severe disability premium, even if you get a carer premium. See Chapter 21(3) for details.

### The overlapping benefits rule

You cannot be paid carer's allowance while you are receiving the same amount or more from:

- state pension;
- maternity allowance;
- incapacity benefit or unemployability supplement;
- contributory employment and support allowance;
- contribution-based jobseeker's allowance;
- widows' benefits and widowed parent's allowance; *or*
- a government training allowance.

This is known as the *'overlapping benefits'* rule. If you get less than the basic rate of carer's allowance from one of the above benefits, that benefit is paid and topped up with carer's allowance to the amount you would get from carer's allowance alone. Only the basic rate of these benefits overlaps with carer's allowance. Carer's allowance can be paid in addition to any earnings-related or age-related addition to the other benefit.

If your partner is entitled to a dependant's addition for you with one of these benefits, the addition cannot be paid if you get the same amount or more from carer's allowance. If carer's allowance is less than the addition, you will receive carer's allowance and your partner will get the difference between carer's allowance and the standard rate of the addition. If you receive an adult dependant's addition with your carer's allowance, it will stop if your dependant gets an overlapping benefit of £38 a week or more.

OB Regs, regs 4, 6, 9 & 10

**Severe disablement allowance (SDA)** – SDA and carer's allowance also overlap. Normally, carer's allowance is paid in full, topped up with any balance of SDA. However, if the amount of your SDA is the same as or more than carer's allowance, you can ask for your SDA to be paid in full. The person you care for is then not excluded from the severe disability premium and you can still claim a carer premium.

## 7. Carer's allowance and income support

You may be entitled to both carer's allowance and income support (see Box F.1, Chapter 19). Because income support is means tested, it is reduced by the amount of your carer's allowance (although any additional carer's allowance paid for a dependent child is disregarded if you also receive child tax credit). The advantages of claiming carer's allowance are outlined in 10 below.

If you are paid carer's allowance and the person you care for is receiving income support, they will not qualify for the severe disability premium (see Chapter 21(3)).

## 8. Carer's allowance and state pension

If you begin receiving a state pension that is more than carer's allowance (not including age- or earnings-related additions), payment of carer's allowance will stop due to the overlapping benefits rule (see 6 above). If your state pension is less than carer's allowance, state pension is paid and topped up with carer's allowance to the basic weekly rate of carer's allowance.

If all that prevents payment of carer's allowance is your state pension, an *'additional amount for carers'* (£36) is included in the award of your pension credit (see Chapter 44(3)), and a *'carer premium'* (£36) is included in the award of housing benefit (see Chapter 21(6)).

If you defer claiming your state pension (see Chapter 45(8)), you will not receive increased pension payments for any period in which you get carer's allowance instead.

## 9. Carer's allowance and universal credit

Universal credit is replacing means-tested benefits for people of working age (see Box E.1 in Chapter 14). If you claim universal credit, your award will be reduced by the amount of carer's allowance you get. However, you will get an extra amount, the *'carer amount'* (£156.45 a month), in your award (see Chapter 16(7)).

If you get carer's allowance, you will not need to look for work, be available for work or attend work-focused interviews, as you will be accepted as having 'regular and substantial caring responsibilities for a severely disabled person' (see Box E.3, Chapter 15).

## 10. Why claim carer's allowance?

Your household income might not appear to be higher after you claim carer's allowance, since it overlaps with other benefits. However, if you are entitled to carer's allowance, even if it cannot be paid because of other benefits, you might receive:

- a *'carer premium'* included in your income-related employment and support allowance, income support, income-based jobseeker's allowance, housing benefit or health benefits. The premium is included if you get carer's allowance or have an underlying entitlement to carer's allowance but get an overlapping benefit instead (see 6 above). An additional amount equivalent to the carer premium can be included in an award of pension credit. See Chapter 21(6);
- a *'carer amount'* included in your universal credit award (see Chapter 16(7));
- Class 1 national insurance contribution credits (see Box D.3, Chapter 11) or help towards meeting the national insurance contribution conditions for contributory employment and support allowance (see Chapter 11(24)) and jobseeker's allowance (see Chapter 13(17));
- in Scotland, a *'carer's allowance supplement'* of £221 every six months from the Scottish government. This is disregarded in the calculations of means-tested benefits and universal credit.

## 11. Time off from caring

You are allowed breaks in care. Carer's allowance is payable for up to four weeks in any 26-week period for temporary breaks in care – eg a holiday or short-term stay in a care home for the person you look after. This can be in one spell or a series of short breaks. The period can be extended to up to 12 weeks in any 26-week period, as long as you or the person you look after spend at least eight of these weeks in hospital (but see below). After this, you cannot be paid carer's allowance for any week in which you do not provide care for at least 35 hours.

**New carers** – In order to be paid carer's allowance for breaks in care, new carers must have been caring for the disabled person for at least 35 hours a week for an initial period of at least 22 weeks and the disabled person must also have been getting a qualifying benefit (see 2 above). However, it is not necessary for the carer to have actually been getting carer's allowance during this initial period. You can include up to eight weeks of hospital stays in those 22 weeks if you would have cared for the disabled person had they (or you) not been in hospital.

ICA Regs, reg 4(2)

### Going into hospital

If you are in hospital, your carer's allowance will stop after 12 weeks. It may stop sooner if you have been in hospital or had a break in care within the previous 26 weeks.

If the person you look after goes into hospital, the 12-weeks-off rule still applies, but in practice your carer's allowance may stop sooner. Your carer's allowance depends on the disabled person receiving a *'qualifying benefit'* (see 2 above). If they are aged 18 or over and go into hospital, and the stay is arranged by the NHS, payment of the qualifying benefit stops after 28 days. Your carer's allowance will stop when their qualifying benefit stops. If the person can arrange a pattern of respite care that allows them to keep their qualifying benefit, carer's allowance may continue to be paid (see Box B.13, Chapter 6).

### Arranging care breaks
A week off is a week in which you care for the disabled person for less than 35 hours, so odd days or weekends away are unlikely to affect your carer's allowance entitlement. A weekend straddles two carer's allowance weeks: the carer's allowance week runs from Sunday to Saturday. This means that if you arrange respite care from midweek to midweek, you may still care for the required 35 hours both in the week the disabled person goes into respite care and the week they come home. Those weeks will not count as weeks off and carer's allowance will be paid even though you've had a full week of respite care.

### Reporting changes
Report any of these changes in writing to the Carer's Allowance Unit or the Disability & Carers Service as soon as possible to avoid having to repay overpaid benefit.

# 9 Other help for carers

| 1 | Introduction | 62 |
|---|---|---|
| 2 | Giving up work | 62 |
| 3 | Working part time or full time | 63 |
| 4 | Limited capability for work | 63 |
| 5 | Over state pension age | 63 |
| 6 | National insurance credits | 63 |
| 7 | Practical help | 63 |
| 8 | If the person you care for dies | 63 |

## 1. Introduction
This chapter covers some of the financial and practical help available for carers. Parents of disabled children should also look at Chapter 40. Some of the help depends on you getting carer's allowance (see Chapter 8). See Chapter 28(9) for details of the council tax discount scheme as it affects carers caring in their own home. Other help depends on your circumstances – eg whether you have given up work, have a low income or have a disability yourself. See the benefits checklist (pages 4-5) for other benefits you may be able to claim.

## 2. Giving up work
You may be entitled to carer's allowance if you spend at least 35 hours a week caring for someone who gets a qualifying disability benefit (see Chapter 8(2)). You are eligible for carer's allowance even if you have a partner who is working.

If your income and savings are low and you are under pension credit qualifying age, you may be able to claim income support (see below). If you have other income or savings, you may be better off claiming contribution-based jobseeker's allowance for the first six months (see below). If you have a limited capability for work, you may be able to claim employment and support allowance (see 4 below). If you have reached pension credit qualifying age, you may be able to claim pension credit (see Chapter 44). If you have dependent children, claim child tax credit (see Chapter 23). You may be eligible for housing benefit (see Chapter 25) and help with NHS costs (Chapter 52).

Means-tested benefits and tax credits for people of working age are being replaced by universal credit (see Box E.1, Chapter 14 and below).

### Income support
Income support is a means-tested benefit for people under pension credit qualifying age. It can be paid on its own if you (and your partner, if you have one) have no other income, or it can top up your carer's allowance or other income. You normally cannot get income support if you have capital over £16,000 or a partner who works for 24 hours a week or more. See Chapter 19 for details.

You are eligible for income support if you get carer's allowance. You are also eligible for income support if you are *regularly and substantially engaged in caring for a disabled person* who gets a qualifying benefit (see Chapter 8(2)); it is possible to be eligible under this rule even if you provide less than 35 hours of care a week. If you stop being treated as a carer for income support, you continue to be eligible for income support for a further eight weeks if you meet all of the other qualifying conditions. You are eligible for income support as a carer for up to 26 weeks while you are waiting for a claim for a qualifying benefit to be processed (plus the further eight weeks just mentioned, making 34 weeks in total).

**Carer premium** – If you or your partner get carer's allowance, a carer premium of £36 a week is included in the award of income support and other means-tested benefits (see Chapter 21(6)). You can still get this premium if all that prevents the payment of carer's allowance is the overlapping benefits rule (see Chapter 8(6)).

### Jobseeker's allowance
Contribution-based jobseeker's allowance (JSA) of up to £73.10 a week (less if you are aged under 25) is payable for up to six months if you have paid enough national insurance contributions. You are eligible even if you have a partner who works. The amount may be reduced if you have earnings or an occupational or personal pension. It is not affected by other income or savings. You might be better off claiming JSA instead of income support for the first six months if you have other household income or savings.

Carer's allowance overlaps with contribution-based JSA – if you claim both, you will be paid JSA, perhaps topped up with carer's allowance if that is higher (see Chapter 8(6)).

**Work-related responsibilities** – JSA is for people who are available and actively looking for work. Usually, you are expected to look for a full-time job even if you have given up work to be a carer. However, if you care for a person who is a close relative or member of your household, you can restrict the hours you are available for work. Carers are also allowed to ask for one week's notice before taking up a job offer and 48 hours' notice to attend other employment opportunities (eg an interview). If you have caring responsibilities for a child aged under 16, these notice periods can be extended in certain circumstances. See Chapter 13(8) for details.

**Sanctions** – JSA is not payable for a fixed sanction period if you leave your job voluntarily without 'good reason'. You should not be sanctioned in this way if your caring responsibilities meant it was no longer reasonable for you to continue working, although you are expected to look for alternatives before giving up work. See Chapter 13(14) for details.

### Universal credit
Means-tested benefits for people of working age are being replaced by universal credit (see Box E.1, Chapter 14). If you meet the qualifying conditions for carer's allowance (see Chapter 8(2)), or you would meet them but for the fact that your earnings are too high, a *carer amount* of £156.45 a month is included in your universal credit award (see Chapter 16(7)). You do not need to claim carer's allowance to get the amount included.

In addition, you will not have to look for work, be available for work or attend regular work-focused interviews, as you will be accepted as having 'regular and substantial caring responsibilities for a severely disabled person' that exempt you from such requirements (see Box E.3, Chapter 15).

If you provide at least 35 hours of care each week to one or more severely disabled people but do not meet the qualifying conditions for carer's allowance (eg because someone else is claiming this already), you may be allowed to claim universal credit without having to meet any work-related requirements – but only if the DWP agrees this is reasonable. Otherwise, you are likely to be expected to look for work and be available for work, although you may be able to restrict your work search and availability because of your caring responsibilities (see Chapter 15(5)-(6)).

## 3. Working part time or full time

**Income support** – If you are eligible for income support as a carer, you can work without any limit on your weekly hours. However, you can only keep £20 a week of your net earnings (or of joint net earnings if your partner also works); anything over that reduces your income support penny for penny (see Chapter 22(6)). You cannot get income support if your partner works 24 hours or more a week.

**Carer's allowance** – Your carer's allowance will stop if your earnings after allowable deductions are more than £120 a week (see Chapter 8(5)). If your earnings are at or below £120 a week, the amount you receive is unaffected.

**Universal credit** – If your earnings are too high to qualify for carer's allowance, you can still get a 'carer amount' included in your universal credit award (see Chapter 16(7)) as long as you meet all the other qualifying conditions for carer's allowance (see Chapter 8(2)). See Chapter 17(1)-(6) for how earnings are treated in the universal credit calculation.

## 4. Limited capability for work

**Employment and support allowance** – If you have a limited capability for work due to disability or ill health and are under state pension age, you may be able to claim employment and support allowance (ESA – see Chapter 11). Payment of carer's allowance usually stops when you get contributory ESA because these benefits overlap, but you keep an underlying entitlement. This means the 'carer premium' continues to be included in any income-related ESA award (see Chapter 21(6)). Because carer's allowance is not actually paid, the person you care for may still get the 'severe disability premium' included in the award of any means-tested benefit they receive (see Chapter 21(3)).

**Universal credit** – If you have caring responsibilities and a limited capability for work, a 'carer amount' cannot be included in your universal credit award at the same time as a 'work capability amount'; only the highest paid amount is included. See Chapter 16(7) for details.

## 5. Over state pension age

If you have not paid enough national insurance contributions to get a state pension of at least £64.60, it can be topped up to that figure with carer's allowance. If you were 65 or over and entitled to invalid care allowance on 27.10.02, you can continue to qualify for carer's allowance even if you cease to care for at least 35 hours a week, or the person you care for stops getting a qualifying benefit (see Chapter 8(2)).

Pension credit is a means-tested benefit for older people (see Chapter 44). If you claim carer's allowance and it cannot be paid because your state pension is higher, an 'additional amount for carers' is still included in your pension credit award.

If you are disabled, you may be eligible for attendance allowance or personal independence payment (PIP) even though you are caring for another person (see Chapters 5 and 6). If you and your partner get attendance allowance, middle or highest rate disability living allowance care component or PIP daily living component, or you live alone and get one of these benefits, an 'additional amount for severe disability' may be included in your pension credit award.

## 6. National insurance credits

For each week that you are entitled to carer's allowance, you get a Class 1 national insurance contribution credit (as long as you have lost, given up or never had the right to pay reduced-rate contributions). Each tax year in which you have 52 Class 1 credits is a qualifying year for state pension and new state pension (see Box L.1, Chapter 45).

**Carer's credit** – From 1978 to April 2010, home responsibilities protection could protect your state pension record if you were caring for someone but did not receive carer's allowance. In April 2010 this was replaced by 'carer's credit'. See Box D.3 in Chapter 11 and Box L.2 in Chapter 45 for details.

## 7. Practical help

The person you care for is entitled to an assessment from the local authority social care department (or social work department in Scotland) to determine their need for services. If you ask them to do so, social care must also assess your support needs as a carer and look at your continuing ability to provide care (see Chapter 36(3) and Boxes J.5 and J.6). Contact your social care department for information about short breaks and other practical help.

There might be a local carers' support group where you can share information with other carers. Contact Carers UK for details (0808 808 7777; www.carersuk.org).

## 8. If the person you care for dies

Your benefit entitlement may depend on the benefits received by the person you care for. This is the case if you receive carer's allowance or income support as a carer.

Carer's allowance can continue for up to eight weeks following the death of the person you cared for. Throughout those eight weeks you must continue to meet all of the qualifying conditions for carer's allowance not related to caring or payment of a qualifying benefit to the person you cared for (see Chapter 8(2)). If you were 65 or over and entitled to invalid care allowance on 27.10.02, you may continue to qualify for carer's allowance indefinitely after the person you cared for has died.

You continue to be eligible for income support with a 'carer premium' and/or to claim income support as a carer for eight weeks after the death. You continue to be eligible for the 'additional amount for carers' in pension credit for eight weeks after the death, or indefinitely if you were 65 or over and entitled to invalid care allowance on 27.10.02.

If you are under pension credit qualifying age, you may be expected to claim jobseeker's allowance from eight weeks after the death. If you gave up work to be a carer, you may qualify for contribution-based jobseeker's allowance based on national insurance contributions paid when you were working (see Chapter 13(17)). Check first to see if you might be eligible for income support (see Box F.1, Chapter 19) or employment and support allowance (see Chapter 11). Even if you had not claimed income support before the death, you may be able to claim it now, either as a carer for up to eight weeks following the death, or on other grounds after the 8-week period has ended.

If you receive universal credit, the carer amount can continue to be included in your award for the remainder of the monthly assessment period in which the person you cared for died and for the following two assessment periods.

You may be eligible for bereavement support payment if it was your spouse or civil partner who died (see Chapter 51(3)).

# Not in work?

This section of the handbook looks at:

| | |
|---|---|
| Statutory sick pay | Chapter **10** |
| Employment and support allowance | Chapter **11** |
| The work capability assessment | Chapter **12** |
| Jobseeker's allowance | Chapter **13** |

# 10 Statutory sick pay

| | | |
|---|---|---|
| 1 | What is statutory sick pay? | 64 |
| 2 | Do you qualify? | 64 |
| 3 | Period of incapacity for work | 64 |
| 4 | Period of entitlement | 64 |
| | Who cannot get SSP? – Box D.1 | 65 |
| 5 | Qualifying days | 65 |
| 6 | How much do you get? | 65 |
| 7 | Does anything affect what you get? | 66 |
| 8 | How do you get SSP? | 66 |
| 9 | Supporting evidence | 66 |
| | Lengthy or frequent absences – Box D.2 | 67 |
| 10 | Challenging a decision | 66 |
| 11 | Enforcing a decision | 67 |
| 12 | What information will the DWP provide? | 67 |
| 13 | What happens when SSP ends? | 67 |
| 14 | What if your job ends? | 67 |

## 1. What is statutory sick pay?

Statutory sick pay (SSP) is paid to employees by their employers for up to 28 weeks in any period of sickness lasting for four or more days. You do not need to have paid national insurance contributions to be entitled to it. You can work full time or part time but must earn at least £116 a week. SSP is taxable. There are no additions for dependants.

SSP is primarily the responsibility of employers. The scheme is run by HMRC. Online guidance for both employees and employers is available at www.gov.uk/government/collections/statutory-pay.

You can get SSP as an agency worker if you meet the qualifying conditions. You cannot get SSP if you are unemployed or self-employed, but you may be able to claim employment and support allowance instead (see Chapter 11).

SSP may be topped up by income support if your income is low (see Chapter 19). If you do not get income support, you may still get housing benefit because SSP is treated more generously in the calculation of that benefit (see Chapters 22(7) and 25).

---

## Disability Rights UK services

### Welfare Rights Advice Service

Available to advisers from member organisations only, this service focuses on tax credits and social security issues. We aim to enable organisations to develop their workforce skills and to provide expert guidance for those using their services. Unfortunately we do not have the resources to answer queries from individuals.

Telephone 0203 687 0779
Monday to Friday 10am-12noon and 2-4pm
or email ken.butler@disabilityrightsuk.org

To find out more, visit
**www.disabilityrightsuk.org/how-we-can-help**

---

## 2. Do you qualify?

Three terms are used when deciding whether you qualify for SSP:
- SSP period of incapacity for work;
- period of entitlement; *and*
- qualifying days.

You can be paid SSP only if you are sick on a qualifying day and your days of sickness form part of an SSP period of incapacity for work that comes within a period of entitlement. The three qualifying conditions are explained in 3 to 5 below.

## 3. Period of incapacity for work

The first qualifying condition for SSP is that there must be an SSP *'period of incapacity for work'* (PIW): you must be incapable of doing the job you are employed to do because of sickness or disability. This period must last for at least four days in a row. Weekends and public holidays count – therefore, every day of the week can count towards a PIW, including days when you would not have worked even if you had been fit. PIWs separated by eight weeks or less are linked and count as one PIW. Further spells of sickness must be at least four or more days in a row to link with a previous SSP PIW.
SSCBA, S.152

There are some situations when you will qualify even if you are not actually sick on a particular day. You can be treated as incapable of work for days when you are under medical care for some specific disease or bodily or mental disablement and a doctor has advised you not to work for precautionary or convalescent reasons, provided you do not work on those days. You are also treated as incapable of work if you are prevented from working (having received the due notice in writing) because you have, are suspected of having or have been in contact with an infection, disease or contamination listed under public health law (including certain types of food poisoning).
SSP Regs, reg 2

## 4. Period of entitlement

The second qualifying condition for SSP is that there must be a *'period of entitlement'*, meaning the actual period of time when you are entitled to SSP. It begins with the start of the SSP period of incapacity for work (PIW) and ends when your employer is no longer liable to pay you SSP.

Your employer's liability to pay SSP ends if:
- you are no longer sick; *or*
- you have had 28 weeks of SSP, either in one go or linked periods; *or*
- your contract of employment comes to an end (unless your employer has dismissed you solely or mainly to avoid paying you SSP); *or*
- for pregnant women, you are at the start of the *'disqualifying period'*, which is the 39 weeks during which you are entitled to statutory maternity pay or maternity allowance (unless this is the reduced rate maternity allowance paid because you are helping out in your spouse or civil partner's business). If you are entitled to neither (or only the reduced rate maternity allowance just mentioned), there are two possibilities, depending on whether or not you are already getting SSP:

- if you are already getting SSP, it cannot be paid from the day your baby is born or, if earlier, from the first day you are off work sick with a pregnancy-related illness on or after the start of the 4th week before the week your baby is due;
- if you are not already getting SSP, it cannot be paid for a period of 18 weeks, which starts from the earlier of either the start of the week your baby is born or the start of the week you are first off sick with a pregnancy-related illness if this is after the start of the 4th week before the week your baby is due; *or*

■ you are taken into legal custody; *or*

■ your linked SSP PIW has spanned three years.

SSCBA, Ss.153(2)&(12); SSP Regs, reg 3(1) & (3)-(6)

SSP will also end if your employer no longer considers you to be incapable of work. In this case, you can challenge the decision (see 10 below).

**People who cannot get SSP** – In some circumstances, you won't be entitled to SSP at all (so no period of entitlement can start). These circumstances are listed in Box D.1 – but they must apply on the first day of an SSP PIW for you to be excluded from SSP altogether.

## 5. Qualifying days

SSP is paid only for *'qualifying days'*. These are normally the days you would have been expected to work if you had not been sick – but they don't have to be.

If your working pattern varies from one week to another, you and your employer can come to some other arrangement as to which days will be qualifying days. If you and your employer reach agreement, you have a free choice of qualifying days – as long as they are not fixed by reference to the actual days you are off sick and there is at least one qualifying day in each week.

If you cannot reach agreement with your employer, the qualifying days are the days your contract would have required you to work if you had not fallen sick. If it is not clear which days would be working days in a particular week, every day of that week except days you and your employer agree are rest days should be qualifying days.

If you would not normally have worked in a particular week and do not have an agreement on qualifying days with your employer, the Wednesday of that week will be a qualifying day regardless.

If there are any doubts about qualifying days, it is important to sort this out with your employer.

SSCBA, S.154 & SSP Regs, reg 5

**Waiting days** – SSP is not paid for the first three qualifying days of an SSP period of incapacity for work – the *'waiting days'*. However, you do not need to wait another three days if you re-claim SSP and your second spell of sickness (which must last for at least four days) starts no more than eight weeks after the end of the first period of incapacity for work.

SSCBA, Ss.152(3) & 155(1)

## 6. How much do you get?

SSP is £92.05 a week. There are no additions for dependants. If you are due SSP for a part-week, your employer will work out the daily rate by dividing the weekly rate by the number of qualifying days in that week. To qualify, your average weekly earnings must be at least the level of the lower earnings limit (£116 from April 2018). You can qualify even if you are on a short-term contract, provided your earnings are sufficient. To get an average weekly figure, gross earnings are averaged over the eight weeks ending with the last pay day before the start of the SSP period of incapacity for work.

SSCBA, S.157 & Sch 11, para 2(c); SSP Regs, reg 19

SSP is subject to deductions for income tax and national insurance (NI) contributions. However, no NI deductions are due if SSP is the only payment you receive because SSP is below the primary threshold for NI contributions (but you can get credits – see Chapter 11(22)). Other normal deductions, eg union subs, can be made from SSP. It is important to make sure your payslip shows details of SSP payments you have received, together with deductions made by your employer, so that you can check it is correct.

SSCBA, S.151(3)

**Payment of SSP** – You should normally be paid SSP at the same time and in the same way as you would have been paid wages for the same period. SSP cannot be paid in kind or as board and lodging or through a service.

If there has been some disagreement with your employer about your entitlement to SSP, and HMRC states you are entitled to it (provided you meet all the other conditions), your employer must pay SSP within a certain time limit. In certain circumstances, if your employer defaults on payment of SSP or becomes insolvent, liability for any outstanding SSP transfers to HMRC (see 11 below).

SSP Regs, regs 8, 9 & 9A

**Occupational sick pay** – If your employer has an occupational sick pay scheme, any sick pay you get under that scheme will count towards your SSP entitlement for a particular day. Similarly, SSP paid by your employer will count towards any pay due to you for a particular day. But if the occupational scheme pays less than your full SSP, your employer must make up the balance so that you get all the SSP you are due. Employers are not obliged to operate the SSP scheme rules, provided they pay wages or occupational sick pay at or above

---

## D.1  Who cannot get SSP?

You are not entitled to SSP if, on the first day of your SSP period of incapacity for work (PIW), any of the following apply.

❏ You are not treated as an employee.

❏ Your average earnings are less than £116 a week. The first day of the first linked PIW should be used when working out your average earnings. If a new tax year starts while you are receiving SSP, this makes no difference (but you will get any increase in payment).

❏ You were entitled to employment and support allowance (ESA) within the previous 85 days, or incapacity benefit or severe disablement allowance (SDA) within the previous 57 days.*

❏ There is a strike where you work, unless you can prove you have no direct interest in the dispute.

❏ You have received SSP from your employer for 28 weeks in the same PIW.

❏ You are pregnant and into the 'disqualifying period' (see 4 in this chapter).

❏ You are employed in another country; however, you may be entitled if your employer is liable for Class 1 contributions in the UK for you, or would be if your earnings were high enough.

❏ You are in legal custody.

❏ You have not yet done any work for your employer. PIWs with the same employer that are separated by eight weeks or less count as one continuous PIW (ie they are linked together).

Once you have been off sick for four days in a row and your employer decides you cannot get SSP, they must give you form SSP1 so you can claim ESA (see 13 in this chapter).

* If you were previously entitled to incapacity benefit or SDA you will not be able to return to that benefit. You will need to claim ESA instead.

SSCBA, S.153(3), 155(2)-(4) & Sch 11 and SSP Regs, reg 3 & 16(2)(a)

the SSP rate. Employees retain an underlying right to SSP. If your employer has their own sick pay scheme, they may have different rules, which you must keep to get payment.
SSCBA, Sch 12, para 2

## 7. Does anything affect what you get?
**Other benefits** – You cannot get SSP while you are receiving employment and support allowance, incapacity benefit, severe disablement allowance, contribution-based jobseeker's allowance, statutory maternity pay, maternity allowance, statutory paternity pay, statutory shared parental pay or statutory adoption pay. Other benefits do not affect your entitlement to SSP. See Box D.1 for other circumstances in which you cannot get SSP.

**Earnings from another job** – If your employer accepts you are incapable of doing the work they employ you to do, you can earn money from a different type of work while receiving SSP. There is no limit on what you can earn from a different job while receiving SSP. However, doing other work may lead an employer to doubt you are genuinely incapable of doing your usual job.

**Going into hospital** – This will not affect entitlement to SSP.

## 8. How do you get SSP?
To get SSP, you must notify your employer that you are off sick. Your employer can decide how and when you do this, and must inform you of the process. They cannot demand that you notify them of your sickness before the end of the first qualifying day of a period of incapacity for work. They must be willing to accept notification from someone else on your behalf.

If you post your notification, your employer should treat it as having been given on the day it was posted. If your employer has not given you a time limit, they must still accept notification of sickness, if it is given in writing within seven days of the first qualifying day. See 9 below for what sort of evidence of sickness you need to give your employer.
SSP Regs, reg 7

If you also get occupational sick pay, you will have to keep to the rules of that scheme to safeguard those payments.

### Late notification
If you are late notifying your employer that you are sick (according to their rules, as long as these comply with the law) they do not need to pay you SSP for any day notified late. But SSP can be paid if your employer accepts you have 'good cause' for late notification, provided it is given within one month of the normal time limit. This can be extended to 91 days from the first qualifying day if the employer accepts that it was not reasonably practicable for you to contact them within the month. After that time, your employer need not pay SSP for that day even if you have good cause for late notification. If your employer withholds SSP because they do not accept there is good cause for late notification, you can challenge the decision (see 10 below).
SSP Regs, reg 7(2)

## 9. Supporting evidence
For your first seven days of sickness, employers can either use their own self-certificates as evidence of incapacity or accept confirmation from you, either verbally or in writing. It is important that you agree what type of evidence will be acceptable. You can get a self-certificate SC2 from your GP or at www.gov.uk/government/publications/statutory-sick-pay-employees-statement-of-sickness-sc2.
Statutory Sick Pay (Medical Evidence) Regs 1985, reg 2(2)

After your first seven days of sickness, your employer can ask for supporting medical evidence. DWP advice confirms that a GP's certificate (or fit note – see below) is *'strong evidence of incapacity and should normally be accepted as conclusive, unless there is evidence to the contrary'.*
Questions and answers about certification and medical reports – for healthcare practitioners

Medical evidence may be accepted from someone who is not a registered medical practitioner – eg an osteopath, acupuncturist or herbalist.
Statutory Sick Pay (Medical Evidence) Regs 1985, reg 2(1)(b)

It is up to your employer to decide whether to accept the evidence that you are not fit for work. If they do not accept it, SSP can be withheld. You can challenge this decision (see 10 below).

If your employer wants more medical evidence, they must arrange and pay for it – unless HMRC agrees to provide advice (see Box D.2).

**The fit note** – The GP's certificate is called the 'statement of fitness for work' or *'fit note'*. On this, your GP can indicate that either you are not fit for work or you may be fit for work after taking into account certain advice, eg a phased return to work, altered hours or duties, or workplace adaptations.

## 10. Challenging a decision
If your employer does not accept that you are incapable of work (or they do not pay SSP for some other reason), you have the right to ask them for a written statement setting out the reasons for this and the dates you will not receive SSP.
SSAA, S.14(3)

You also have the right to apply to HMRC for a decision. You can appeal against this decision.

### Applying for a decision
You should apply for a decision using form SSP14, available from the HMRC Statutory Payments Disputes Team (0300 056 0630; National Insurance Contributions and Employer Office, HMRC, BX9 1AN). They will expect you to have discussed the matter with your employer, if it is reasonable to do so, and to have gone through the agreed grievance procedure, if there is one where you work.

Both you and your employer may be asked to send comments in writing to HMRC. You can provide other evidence – eg further medical statements. A copy of the decision will be sent to you and your employer. If the decision says you are incapable of work, your employer must pay you the correct amount of SSP within fixed time limits, providing that you meet the other qualifying conditions for SSP.

### Appealing a decision
Both you and your employer have the right to appeal against the HMRC decision to a First-tier Tribunal (Tax). If your employer appeals, they do not have to pay SSP until a final decision has been given.

You must appeal in writing, giving the reasons why you wish to appeal, and send this, along with any further supporting evidence, to the HMRC Statutory Payments Disputes Team (see above). You have 30 days from the date of the HMRC decision in which to do this.

On receiving your appeal, HMRC may be in a position to change the decision straightaway; they will write to inform you of the result. If they cannot change the decision straightaway, they will write to ask if you want them to review the decision or if you would like to lodge an appeal directly to a First-tier Tribunal. If you agree to have the decision reviewed and you do not agree with the result of the review, you can then lodge an appeal directly to the First-tier Tribunal; you have 30 days from the date of the review decision in which to do this.

You can appeal to the First-tier Tribunal online or download the 'Notice of Appeal' form T240 at: www.gov.uk/tax-tribunal/appeal-to-tribunal. You can also get the T240 by ringing 0300 123 1024.
Taxes Management Act 1970, Ss.49A-H

## 11. Enforcing a decision

If HMRC has issued a decision that you are entitled to SSP, and your employer doesn't pay it within the time laid down by law and has not appealed, inform the HMRC Statutory Payments Disputes Team (see 10 above). In this situation, responsibility for paying SSP transfers to HMRC, who will pay any SSP to which you are entitled.

SSP Regs, reg 9A

## 12. What information will the DWP provide?

To decide if you are entitled to SSP, your employer can ask the DWP for limited information about you. Before disclosing it, the DWP should be satisfied that the enquiry comes from your employer and no one else. Employers are told that detailed personal information about employees will not be disclosed.

## 13. What happens when SSP ends?

If you are still sick at the start of the 23rd week of your period of entitlement to SSP and likely to remain sick beyond the 28th week, you will need to claim employment and support allowance (ESA; see Chapter 11). Your employer must complete and send you form SSP1. On the form, your employer must state why SSP is ending and the last day it will be paid. You will need this form to support your claim for ESA. If your employer delays issuing it, you should register your claim for ESA so you do not lose benefit.

The employer must issue the SSP1 if you are not entitled to SSP or whenever they stop paying it. The form should be issued within seven days of your request for it or, if this is impracticable, by the next pay day.

If your employer is holding any of your GP's fit notes covering days beyond the last day of your SSP entitlement, these should be returned to you with form SSP1. You will need these to support your claim for ESA.

SSP Regs, reg 15(1A),(3)&(4)

## 14. What if your job ends?

If your job ends before you have had 28 weeks' SSP from your last employer and you are still incapable of work, you can claim employment and support allowance (ESA) – see Chapter 11. You will need to send form SSP1 (see 13 above) to support your claim.

But if your employer is found to have dismissed you solely or mainly to avoid paying SSP, they remain liable to pay it until liability ends for some other reason. Whatever the reason for your dismissal, you should claim ESA. Seek advice if you have difficulties or would not qualify for ESA.

SSP Regs, reg 4

---

## D.2  Lengthy or frequent absences

If you are off work for a long time or have had repeated short absences from work, your employer can ask HMRC for advice on your continuing incapacity for work. However, your employer is expected to try to resolve the matter themselves before asking HMRC for advice, eg by using a company doctor. HMRC will only provide advice if you give your consent and they consider that you have been:

■ off work for an unduly long period of time;
■ repeatedly off sick for four to seven days in a relatively short period; *or*
■ sick for four or more short periods in a 12-month period.

If HMRC agrees to provide advice, they will refer your case to their medical services provider. The medical services provider will contact your own doctor for an opinion or arrange for you to attend an examination by one of their doctors. The medical services provider will then produce a report that considers your continuing incapacity for work.

The report is not sent to your employer, who is only told whether or not you are considered to be capable of work or if there are reasonable grounds for you having frequent absences from work. This is not a decision; its purpose is only to help your employer decide whether payment of SSP should continue. If your employer stops SSP and you disagree, see 10 in this chapter.

The table below is the HMRC guide on the more common and less serious illnesses (www.gov.uk/statutory-sick-pay-employee-fitness-to-work). It suggests review periods after which your employer may consider asking HMRC for advice.

| Illness or diagnosis | Review period (weeks) |
|---|---|
| Addiction (drugs or alcohol) | 10 |
| Anaemia (other than in pregnancy) | 4 |
| Anorexia | 10 |
| Arthritis (unspecified) | 10 |
| Back and spinal disorders – prolapsed intervertebral disc, sciatica, spondylitis | 10 |
| Concussion | 4 |
| Debility – cardiac, nervous, post-op, post-partum | 10 |
| Fainting | 4 |
| Fractures of lower limbs | 10 |
| Fractures of upper limbs | 10 |
| Gastro-enteritis, gastritis, diarrhoea and vomiting | 4 |
| Giddiness | 4 |
| Haemorrhage | 4 |
| Headache, migraine | 4 |
| Hernia (strangulated) | 10 |
| Inflammation and swelling | 4 |
| Insomnia | 10 |
| Joint disorders, other than arthritis and rheumatism | 10 |
| Kidney and bladder disorders, cystitis, urinary tract infection | 4 |
| Menstrual disorders, menorrhagia, dilation and curettage | 10 |
| Mouth and throat disorders | 4 |
| No abnormality detected | Immediate |
| Nervous illnesses | 10 |
| Obesity | Immediate |
| Observation | 4 |
| Post-natal conditions | 10 |
| Respiratory illness | |
| – asthma | 10 |
| – bronchitis, cold, coryza, influenza, upper respiratory tract infection | 4 |
| Skin conditions, dermatitis, eczema | 10 |
| Sprains, strains, bruises | 4 |
| Tachycardia | 10 |
| Ulcers | |
| – corneal, peptic, gastric, duodenal | 4 |
| – perforated | 10 |
| Varicose veins | 10 |
| Wounds, cuts, lacerations, abrasions, burns, blisters, splinters, foreign bodies | 4 |

## Fit for Work

The *'Fit for Work'* scheme provides that if you have been off work, or are likely to be off work, for at least four weeks, your GP or employer can, with your consent, refer you for a telephone assessment by an occupational health professional. This health professional will look at the issues that may be preventing your return to work. A *'return to work'* plan will be drawn up, which will include recommendations on how you can get back to work more quickly and information on the support available to you.

# **11** Employment and support allowance

**A   General conditions**
1   What is employment and support allowance?   68
2   Assessment phase   68
3   Work capability assessment   68
4   Work-related activity group   69
5   Support group   69
6   ESA rates   69
7   Do you qualify?   69
8   Making a claim   70
   ESA: Claim route   71
9   Date of claim   70
10   Payments   72
11   Linking rule   72
**B   Your responsibilities**
12   Introduction   72
13   Work-focused interviews   72
14   Work-related activity   73
15   Sanctions   73
16   Hardship payments   74
17   Disqualification   74
**C   Contributory ESA**
18   What is contributory ESA?   75
19   Do you qualify?   75
20   Time limits   75
21   National insurance contributions   75
22   Contribution credits   76
   Contribution credits – Box D.3   78
23   Contribution conditions   76
24   First condition: paid contributions   76
25   Second condition: paid or credited contributions   77
26   How much do you get?   77
27   Does anything affect what you get?   77
**D   Existing incapacity claimants**
28   What will happen to existing claimants of incapacity benefits?   80
   Incapacity benefit – Box D.4   81
   Severe disablement allowance – Box D.5   81
29   Work capability assessment   80
30   Moving onto ESA   80
31   If you are found not to have a limited capability for work   81
   Transferred from invalidity benefit – Box D.6   82
32   Housing benefit   82

## A. GENERAL CONDITIONS

### 1. What is employment and support allowance?

Employment and support allowance (ESA) is a benefit paid to you if your ability to work is limited by either ill health or disability. Your eligibility for the benefit is tested under a *'work capability assessment'*.

ESA has two elements: contributory ESA and income-related ESA. You may receive either of these elements or both together, depending on your circumstances.

**Universal credit** – If you are eligible to claim universal credit (see Box E.1 in Chapter 14), you will not be able to make a new claim for income-related ESA and will need to claim universal credit instead (see Chapter 14). If you are claiming contributory ESA, some of the rules are different under the universal credit system; we point out when this is the case. Under the universal credit system, contributory ESA is known as *'new style'* ESA.

**The benefit cap** – ESA is included in the list of benefits to which the 'benefit cap' applies. This cap, which limits the total weekly benefits that can be claimed, will not apply if you have been placed in the 'support group' (see

5 below). See Chapter 16(10) and Box G.6 in Chapter 25 for details.

**Contributory ESA**

Contributory ESA is linked to your national insurance contribution record. To be entitled, you must have paid national insurance contributions over a certain number of years. Some awards of contributory ESA are limited to 12 months. For details, see 18 to 27 below.

**Income-related ESA**

Income-related ESA is the means-tested element of ESA. It provides for your basic living expenses (and those of your partner, if you have one). It can be paid on its own or as a top-up to contributory ESA. Income-related ESA can help you access support for mortgage interest loans (see Chapter 26) and helps with other housing costs directly (see Chapter 27). For more on income-related ESA, see Chapter 18.

### 2. Assessment phase

A 13-week assessment phase applies to all new ESA claimants. During this phase, you are normally paid just a basic allowance of ESA (see 6 below for exceptions); if you are under 25, this is paid at a lower rate.

During the assessment phase you should undergo the work capability assessment (see 3 below). The assessment phase can be extended beyond 13 weeks if there is a delay in completing this assessment. Such delays are currently the norm and can last for several months. The assessment phase can also be extended if you appeal over a decision that you do not have a limited capability for work and claim ESA in the meantime; the assessment phase will continue until the appeal has been dealt with by a First-tier Tribunal.

The assessment phase will be reduced by any time that you have spent on a jobseeker's allowance 'extended period of sickness' immediately before moving onto ESA (see Chapter 13(4)).

ESA Regs, regs 4 & 147A(2); ESA Regs 2013, regs 5 & 87(2)

**Linked awards** – If your ESA claim links to an earlier ESA award (see 11 below) during which the assessment phase was completed, you will be treated as having served the assessment phase on the new claim. If you were part-way through the 13 weeks when your last award ended, you will only need to serve the remaining weeks of the assessment phase on your new claim.

ESA Regs, reg 5; ESA Regs 2013, reg 6

### 3. Work capability assessment

There are two parts to the work capability assessment (WCA):
**Limited capability for work assessment** – The first part looks at whether you have a *'limited capability for work'*. You are not entitled to ESA unless you have (or can be treated as having) a limited capability for work.
**Limited capability for work-related activity assessment** – The second part looks at whether you have a *'limited capability for work-related activity'*. It determines which of two different groups you are placed in: the *'work-related activity group'* or the *'support group'* (see 4 and 5 below). The group you are placed in determines the amount of ESA you receive, the responsibilities you must meet to retain the benefit in full and whether or not your ESA award may be time limited.

See Chapter 12 for details of the WCA.
**When will the WCA take place?** – The first WCA should take place during the assessment phase that follows your initial claim (see 2 above). Once it has taken place, and your entitlement to ESA has been established, you may have to attend further WCAs at intervals in the future to determine whether you are still entitled to ESA and, if so, whether you should remain in the same group.

If you have successfully appealed against a WCA decision, the DWP should not normally apply a new WCA within eight months of the appeal, or a longer period if recommended by the First-tier Tribunal, unless they have good grounds for believing that an earlier review is needed (eg there is evidence that your condition has improved).

Decision Makers Guide, Vol 8, Chap 42, para 42297-301

In some circumstances, you will not need to attend any further WCAs (see Chapter 12(21)).

## 4. Work-related activity group

If you are found not to have a limited capability for work-related activity, you are placed in the work-related activity group. In this group, you must meet work-related conditions, including attending work-focused interviews (see 13 below) and possibly doing work-related activity (see 14 below). If you fail to meet the conditions, a sanction may be applied (see 15 below).

If you are placed in the work-related activity group, you receive a lower level of ESA than if placed in the support group. Furthermore, if you are entitled to contributory ESA, the award of it will be limited to just 12 months (see 20 below), although you may be able to claim income-related ESA instead once the award has come to an end (see Chapter 18).

## 5. Support group

If you are found to have a limited capability for work-related activity, you are placed in the support group. In this group, you do not have to take part in work-related activities, although you can volunteer to do so.

If you are placed in the support group, you receive a higher rate of ESA than if placed in the work-related activity group. If you are entitled to contributory ESA, your award may continue for as long as you continue to meet the qualifying conditions and remain in the support group; it will not be limited to 12 months.

## 6. ESA rates

ESA is paid at different rates depending on your circumstances. You may be entitled to contributory ESA or income-related ESA, or a combination of the two. The levels of payment for these two elements are detailed in 26 below and Chapter 18(5)-(8) respectively.

The level of ESA you receive (whether contributory or income-related) may also be determined by whether you are in the *'assessment phase'* or the *'main phase'* of your claim.
**Assessment phase** – During the 13-week assessment phase (see 2 above), you are paid the *'basic allowance'* of ESA. If you are aged under 25, you are paid a lower rate of the basic allowance.

ESA can be paid at the 'main phase' rate (which may include an additional component – see below) during the assessment phase in the following circumstances:

■ you are terminally ill and claiming ESA (or have asked for the award to be superseded or revised) for that reason;
■ your claim links to an earlier ESA award (see 11 below) in which you were already receiving one of the additional components or were placed in the work-related activity group (as long as your previous award was not terminated because you were found not to have a limited capability for work);
■ your claim links to an earlier ESA award that was terminated because you were found not to have a limited capability for work (or before such a finding could be made), that award was at least 13 weeks long and you have been assessed as having a limited capability for work in relation to the new claim;
■ your claim links to an earlier ESA award that was terminated because you were found not to have a limited

capability for work, you were already receiving one of the additional components in that earlier award or had been placed in the work-related activity group and you have been assessed as having a limited capability for work in relation to the new claim;
■ you are a lone parent previously on income support with a disability premium and within the last 12 weeks you have been moved off income support because of the age of your youngest child; *or*
■ you re-qualify for contributory ESA following its termination at the end of the 12-month payment period because you have moved into the support group (see 20 below).

ESA Regs, reg 7; ESA Regs 2013, reg 7

**Main phase** – After the assessment phase, you may receive an additional component on top of the basic allowance (see below).

If you are aged under 25, you will remain on the lower rate of the basic allowance unless you are placed in the support group (see 5 above), in which case you will be paid the same rate as someone aged 25 or over.

If there is a delay in completing the work capability assessment (WCA) and the assessment phase is extended beyond 13 weeks, you will continue receiving just the basic allowance. However, once the WCA has taken place, as long as you are found to have a limited capability for work, then any additional component that you may be entitled to can be backdated to the beginning of the 14th week of your claim.

D&A Regs, reg 7(38); UCPIP(D&A) Regs, reg 35(7)

### The additional components

**The support component** – The *'support component'* is included in your award once you are in the main phase if you are placed in the support group (see 5 above).

WRA 2007, Ss.2(2) & 4(4)

**The work-related activity component** – The *'work-related activity component'* has been abolished for new claims from 3.4.17. It could be included in your award if you were placed in the work-related activity group (see 4 above). The work-related activity component can still be included in your award in the following circumstances:

■ you were already claiming ESA by 3.4.17;
■ your claim links to an ESA award made before 3.4.17 – see 11 below;
■ you are moved onto ESA from an incapacity benefit – see 28 below;
■ you claimed ESA on or after 3.4.17, but it is backdated to before this date;
■ you claimed ESA on or after 3.4.17, but the assessment phase is deemed to have started before this date; *or*
■ you claimed ESA within 12 weeks of the date your maternity allowance ended, and immediately before the maternity allowance award you were entitled to ESA. The earlier ESA award must have begun before 3.4.17.

The Employment & Support Allowance & Universal Credit (Miscellaneous Amendments & Transitional & Savings Provisions) Regs, Sch 2

## 7. Do you qualify?

To be entitled to either element of ESA, you need to meet all the following basic qualifying conditions. You must:

■ have a limited capability for work – see Chapter 12(2);
■ have accepted a claimant commitment, if required to do so – see 12 below;
■ be aged 16 or over;
■ be under state pension age – see Chapter 45(2);
■ be in Great Britain (GB) – see below;
■ not be in work – see below;
■ not be entitled to income support;
■ not be entitled to jobseeker's allowance (and not one of a couple entitled to joint-claim jobseeker's allowance); *and*

■ not be within a period of entitlement to statutory sick pay – see Chapter 10(4).

WRA 2007, Ss.1(3) & 20(1); ESA Regs, reg 40(1); ESA Regs 2013, reg 37(1)

You must also meet:

■ the national insurance contribution conditions – see 23 below; *or*
■ the qualifying conditions for income-related ESA – see Chapter 18(2).

WRA 2007, S.1(2)

You can be entitled to both contributory ESA and income-related ESA at the same time (see Chapter 18(5)).

### Work

You are generally not entitled to ESA in any week in which you work. This means any work you do, whether or not you expect to be paid for it.

ESA Regs, reg 40(1)&(7); ESA Regs 2013, reg 37(1)&(8)

**Work you can do** – There are certain types of work that you can do and still be entitled to ESA. For details, see Chapter 33(2).

### Presence in Great Britain

To be entitled to ESA, you must be in GB, which means England, Scotland and Wales. You can, however, continue to be entitled to ESA during a temporary absence from GB in the circumstances described in Chapter 54(5).

### 8. Making a claim

If you are eligible to claim universal credit (see Box E.1 in Chapter 14), call 0800 328 5644 (textphone: 0800 328 1344) to claim ESA. Otherwise, call the ESA contact centre on 0800 055 6688 (textphone 0800 023 4888), or in Northern Ireland call the ESA centre on 0800 085 6318 (textphone 0800 328 3419). You should have the following available when you start:

■ your (and your partner's, if you have one) national insurance number;
■ your medical certificate – see below;
■ your GP's address and telephone number;
■ details of your bank or building society account (if you have one);
■ details of your mortgage or landlord (if you have either);
■ your council tax bill;
■ details of any income, savings or capital you (or your partner) have;
■ if you have (or recently have had) an employer, their address and telephone number and the dates of your employment (or the last day you worked);
■ details of any earnings you (or your partner) receive; *and*
■ details of any other benefits you (or your partner) receive.

However, do not delay claiming if you cannot get all this information straight away. The contact centre will confirm your identity, then ask if you want to claim under the 'special rules' that apply to terminally ill claimants (see below). The contact centre then takes the details of your claim over the telephone. Once they have finished, a *'customer statement'* is sent to you confirming the details so you can check they are correct. The contact centre may ring back for additional information if you do not have it to hand.

Alternatively, you can ask for a paper claim-form, ESA1, to make a written claim. You can also download an ESA1 from: www.gov.uk/employment-support-allowance/how-to-claim (or in Northern Ireland from: www.nidirect.gov.uk/publications/employment-and-support-allowance-claim-form-esa1).

**Health and work conversation** – Once you have made the claim, you may need to attend a work-focused interview within the first four weeks: the *'health and work conversation'* (see 13 below).

### Who should claim?

If you are one of a couple and both of you could claim income-related ESA, you must decide which of you will make the claim. If one of you would be more likely to be assessed as having a limited capability for work (and thus remain entitled to ESA) or having a limited capability for work-related activity (and thus be placed in the support group, where a higher level of ESA will be payable), it would be sensible if they were the claimant.

For anyone who cannot claim for themselves because of mental incapacity, the DWP can appoint someone to act on their behalf (see Chapter 56(4)).

### Medical certificates

For the first seven days of any period of limited capability for work, you do not need a medical certificate (the 'fit note' – see Chapter 10(9)). Once you have had a limited capability for work for more than seven days, you must forward a fit note from your doctor to the office dealing with your ESA claim; Jobcentre Plus should send you an envelope to do this when you first claim.

Social Security (Medical Evidence) Regs 1976, regs 2 & 5 & Sch 1

If you work for an employer and do not get statutory sick pay (or it is ending), you will also need to send in form SSP1, which you get from your employer, as well as a fit note from the first day of your claim.

C&P Regs, reg 10(1A)-(2); UCPIP(C&P) Regs, reg 17

It is important to keep your fit notes up to date; ask your doctor for a new fit note well before the old one runs out. If you are not covered by a fit note for each day of your claim, benefit could be withheld. Until you are assessed as having (or treated as having) a limited capability for work (see 3 above), you must carry on sending in fit notes. The DWP will let you know if this is no longer required.

### No claim necessary

If you are appealing against a decision that you do not have a limited capability for work, you do not need to make a new claim to continue getting ESA while your appeal is being dealt with. However, if you have claimed jobseeker's allowance while your mandatory reconsideration request was being dealt with, you will need to ask for your ESA to be reinstated. See Chapter 12(18) for details.

C&P Regs, reg 3(1)(j); UCPIP(C&P) Regs, reg 7

### Special rules

If you are terminally ill, your claim can be dealt with under the *'special rules'*. You count as terminally ill if you are *'suffering from a progressive disease and [your] death in consequence of that disease can reasonably be expected within 6 months'*. Under the special rules, your ESA claim will be fast-tracked. Once you have made the claim, the DWP will normally contact your GP, consultant or specialist nurse to confirm that you are terminally ill. Once the DWP receives such confirmation, they will automatically treat you as having a limited capability for work (thus entitling you to ESA) and a limited capability for work-related activity (thus putting you in the support group – see 5 above). If your GP, consultant or specialist nurse has given you a DS1500 form, you should give it to the DWP, as they may be able to deal with your claim immediately.

When a claim is made on the grounds of terminal illness, you do not have to serve the 13-week assessment phase before being put in the support group, and the support component (see 6 above) can be paid from the beginning of your award.

ESA Regs, regs 2 & 7(1)(a); ESA Regs 2013, regs 2 & 7(1)(a)

### 9. Date of claim

For telephone claims, your date of claim is the date of the initial telephone call to the claim-line, as long as you provide the required information during that call or within a month of the call (or longer if the decision maker considers it reasonable) and you approve the customer statement (see 8 above).

For written claims, your date of claim is the date you inform the DWP of your intention to claim, as long as they receive a properly completed claim-form from you within a month of your first contact (or longer if the decision maker considers it reasonable). The same time limit applies if you are making an ESA claim at the housing benefit office.

C&P Regs, reg 6(1F); UCPIP(C&P) Regs, regs 14 & 16

**Advance awards** – A decision maker can make an advance award of income-related ESA when you have income that exceeds your applicable amount (see Chapter 18(6)) and the decision maker considers that you would only become entitled to ESA once the additional component (see 6 above) becomes payable.

WRA 2007, S.5(1); ESA Regs, reg 146

**Advance claims** – If you are receiving statutory sick pay (SSP) you cannot claim ESA, but you can claim income support (see Chapter 19). However, if you know your SSP will be running out, you can make an advance claim for ESA up to three months before your SSP expires. This can help to ensure minimal delays in receiving any ESA to which you may be entitled.

C&P Regs, reg 13(1); UCPIP(C&P) Regs, reg 34

**Late claims**

Your award of ESA can be backdated for up to three months before the date of your claim if you claim for that earlier period and would have met all the qualifying conditions during it. You will need to ask your doctor to confirm on the fit note that you were not fit for work during that earlier period.

C&P Regs, Sch 4, para 16; UCPIP(C&P) Regs, reg 28

## ESA: Claim route

**On the basis of information provided with the claim, if the DWP is satisfied that you have a limited capability for work-related activity, you will be placed in the support group.**

**A** **CLAIMING ESA**
Start by calling the appropriate contact centre (see Chapter 11(8)). You will need to answer some questions and may be asked to send further information. The assessment phase begins.
You may be asked to attend a 'health and work conversation' (see Chapter 11(13)).

**B** **WORK CAPABILITY ASSESSMENT (WCA)**
During the assessment phase, the WCA will be applied. First you will be sent a capability for work questionnaire to complete and return. You may then be asked to attend a face-to-face assessment.

The WCA is made up of two parts:

**1** **Limited capability for work?**
This part of the assessment looks at whether you have a limited capability for work and are therefore eligible for ESA.

No → Claim jobseeker's allowance or challenge the decision – see Chapter 12(16)-(18)

**2** **Limited capability for work-related activity?**
This part of the assessment looks at whether you could do work-related activity.

This determines whether you are placed in:
■ the support group; *or*
■ the work-related activity group.

Yes →

No → **Work-related activity group**
You do not have a limited capability for work-related activity.

You must attend the work-focused interviews. Failure to take part may result in your ESA being sanctioned.

Claimants in this group receive a lower rate of ESA than those in the support group.

If you receive contributory ESA, this will be limited to 12 months.

**Support group**
You have a limited capability for work-related activity.

You do not have to do work-related activity unless you volunteer to do so.

Claimants in this group receive a higher rate of ESA than those in the work-related activity group.

**C** **WORK-FOCUSED INTERVIEWS**
If you are in the work-related activity group, you will be expected to take part in a series of work-focused interviews with a work coach. These will usually be monthly. See Chapter 11(13).

You may be required to do work-related activity. This will be detailed in an 'action plan'. See Chapter 11(14).

## 10. Payments

**Waiting days** – You are not normally entitled to ESA for the first seven days of your claim (these are called *'waiting days'*), unless:

■ your claim links to an earlier ESA award (see 11 below); *or*
■ you claim expressly on the grounds that you are terminally ill; *or*
■ your entitlement to ESA begins within 12 weeks of a previous entitlement to carer's allowance, income support, jobseeker's allowance, maternity allowance, pension credit or statutory sick pay; *or*
■ you are a one of a couple, your partner was already getting income-related ESA (having already served the waiting days) and you have decided to become the claimant instead; *or*
■ you have been discharged from the armed forces and for at least three days immediately before discharge were absent from duty through sickness; *or*
■ your contributory ESA has been terminated at the end of the 12-month payment period, your condition has deteriorated so that you can now be placed in the support group and consequently you become entitled to contributory ESA again (see 20 below).

ESA Regs, reg 144; ESA Regs 2013, reg 85

**How you are paid** – ESA is paid fortnightly in arrears, but if this causes you problems, the DWP can consider a different arrangement. If your ESA payment is less than £1 a week, it may be paid at 13-week intervals in arrears. The minimum payment of ESA is 10p a week; an entitlement of less than 10p a week is not payable.

C&P Regs, reg 26C; UCPIP(C&P) Regs, reg 51

Your benefit is normally paid into a bank, building society, credit union or Post Office card account (see Chapter 56(5)).

## 11. Linking rule

Any two periods of limited capability for work (ie days in which you have a limited capability for work) that are separated by no more than 12 weeks are treated as a single period. Therefore, if you have to reclaim ESA within 12 weeks of a previous award, you will not have to serve any waiting days (see 10 above).

Additionally, if you had already served the 13-week assessment phase (see 2 above) in the previous award, you can go back onto the rate of payment of the earlier ESA award straightaway (as long as your previous award was not terminated because you were found not to have a limited capability for work). If you had served part of the 13-week assessment phase in the previous award, you only have to serve the remaining weeks before you can move into the main phase (see 6 above).

ESA Regs, reg 145; ESA Regs 2013, reg 86

## B. YOUR RESPONSIBILITIES

## 12. Introduction

If you have been placed in the work-related activity group (see 4 above), to continue receiving ESA at the full rate you must meet work-related conditions, including attending work-focused interviews (see 13 below) and possibly doing work-related activity (see 14 below). If you fail to meet the conditions, a sanction may be applied to your ESA (see 15 below). If your ESA is sanctioned, you may be entitled to a hardship payment (see 16 below).

ESA Regs, regs 54-64D

**Claiming under the universal credit system**
If you are claiming ESA under the universal credit system (see 1 above), the rules match those of universal credit instead. These are described in Chapter 15. You will need to accept a claimant commitment (see Chapter 15(2)), and may need to take part in work-focused interviews (see Chapter 15(3)) and work preparation (see Chapter 15(4)). Box E.3 in Chapter 15 clarifies which requirements you need to meet, depending on your circumstances. If you fail to meet those requirements, sanctions may be applied at either the lowest level (see Chapter 15(9)) or the low level (see Chapter 15(10)). In each case, payment of ESA will normally cease for the sanction period.

ESA Regs 2013, regs 41-61

## 13. Work-focused interviews
### The health and work conversation

The *'health and work conversation'* is a mandatory work-focused interview that you may need to attend if you are making a new claim for ESA. It will normally take place in around the fourth week of your claim. If you do not attend or take part in the interview without good cause, your benefit can be sanctioned (see 15 below).

At the interview, you will discuss with a *'work coach'* what actions you can take to build your confidence and motivation. Any agreed actions will be voluntary; you cannot be sanctioned if you do not agree to take them.

The exemption for claimants in the support group does not apply to the health and work conversation; in most cases the conversation will take place before the work capability assessment anyway. You will be exempt from the conversation, however, if you:

■ meet one of the conditions where you can be treated as having a limited capability for work (see Chapter 12(3) – though the last three bullets under the 'Additional circumstances: ESA' do not apply here);
■ provide care for a severely disabled person for at least 35 hours a week. A person is considered to be severely disabled if they get a 'qualifying benefit' (see Chapter 8(2)) or are waiting for a claim for one to be processed;
■ are a disabled student in full-time education (see Chapter 18(4));
■ are a young person without parental support (see Chapter 14(4)) and are in full-time non-advanced education (up to A-level or equivalent). This can apply until you are aged 21, or the end of the academic year in which you reach that age (or the end of the course, if earlier);
■ have reached pension credit qualifying age (see Chapter 44(2)) and are entitled to attendance allowance, the highest rate of the disability living allowance care component or the enhanced rate of the personal independence payment daily living component;
■ are a lone parent responsible for a child under the age of 1;
■ have adopted a child within the last 12 months and are their main carer; *or*
■ are only entitled to limited capability for work national insurance credits (see Box D.3).

This list is not set in law. You may need to inform the DWP that you are in an exempt group.

### Work-focused interviews

If you are placed in the work-related activity group, you will need to attend one or more *'work-focused interviews'* with a work coach. At the first work-focused interview, the work coach will be an officer from the DWP. At follow-up interviews, the work coach may be from a private or voluntary sector organisation contracted to do this work.

A work-focused interview has the following functions:

■ to assess your prospects and assist or encourage you to remain in or get work;
■ to identify activities, training, education or rehabilitation you could do to improve your job prospects; *and*
■ to identify current or future work opportunities (including self-employment) relevant to your needs and abilities.

ESA Regs, reg 55; ESA Regs 2013, reg 46

If you do not attend or take part in a work-focused interview as required, your benefit can be sanctioned (see below).

**Who does not need to take part**
You do not need to take part in a work-focused interview if you:
- have been placed in the support group (see 5 above); *or*
- have reached pension credit qualifying age (see Chapter 44(2)); *or*
- are a lone parent responsible for a child under the age of 1; *or*
- are only entitled to limited capability for work national insurance credits (see Box D.3).

ESA Regs, reg 54

The need to take part can be waived altogether in limited circumstances or deferred to a later date at the discretion of the work coach. If the work coach declines your request to defer or waive the interview, you cannot appeal against that decision (although you can appeal against any benefit sanction applied as a result).

D&A Regs, Sch 2, para 26

**Attendance is waived** – The work coach can waive the need to take part in an interview if they believe the interview would not be of assistance to you because you are likely to be starting or returning to work soon.

ESA Regs, reg 60

**Attendance is deferred** – The need to take part can be deferred if the work coach believes it would not be of assistance or appropriate in the circumstances at that particular time. A decision to defer can be backdated if the date of the work-focused interview has already passed, at the discretion of the work coach. If the interview is deferred, the work coach will arrange with you another date for the interview.

ESA Regs, reg 59

**At the interview**
The DWP (or the private or voluntary sector contractor) will usually phone you to arrange the date, time and location of the interview. If they are not able to do this, they will write to you with details of the appointment.

If they are persuaded that attending a work-focused interview elsewhere would cause you undue inconvenience or endanger your health, they can arrange for it to take place in your own home. In practice, they are more likely to carry it out over the phone.

ESA Regs, reg 56

**Taking part in the interview** – You must not only attend the interview at the right time and place, but also must 'take part' in it. Taking part involves participating in discussions with the work coach on:
- any activity you are willing to do to improve your job prospects;
- any such activity that you may have done previously;
- any progress you may have made towards remaining in or getting work; *and*
- your opinion on the extent to which your condition restricts your ability to remain in or get work.

ESA Regs, reg 57(3)

**What are you asked at the interview?** – When taking part in the interview, you are expected to answer questions about any of the following:
- your educational qualifications and vocational training;
- your work history;
- any paid or unpaid work you are doing;
- your aspirations for future work;
- your work-related skills and abilities; *and*
- any caring or childcare responsibilities you may have.

ESA Regs, 57(2)

**What if you do not take part in the interview?**
If you fail to take part in a work-focused interview, your ESA may be sanctioned (see 15 below). You should be notified of your failure. The sanction will not take place if you can show *'good cause'* for the failure; you have five working days to do this. If the notification is sent by post, the 5-day period is counted from the second working day after posting.

ESA Regs, reg 61 & 65

If the failure was due to your condition (eg you did not attend an interview because you were unwell), you may wish to obtain medical evidence (eg a letter from your GP or specialist nurse) to back up your case.

## 14. Work-related activity
If you need to take part in a work-focused interview, you may also be expected to do *'work-related activity'*. This is defined as: *'activity which makes it more likely that [you] will obtain or remain in work or be able to do so'*. What this actually entails is left to the work coach. It can include voluntary work experience. However, you cannot be required to:
- apply for a job or do work; *or*
- undergo medical treatment.

WRA 2007, S.13; ESA(WRA) Regs, reg 3(4)(b)

**Who does not need to do work-related activity**
You do not need to do work-related activity if you are:
- a lone parent and responsible for a child aged under 3;
- entitled to carer's allowance or a carer premium; *or*
- in the support group (see 5 above).

If you are a lone parent and responsible for a child aged under 13, you only need to do work-related activity during your child's normal school hours.

ESA(WRA) Regs, reg 3

**The action plan**
When you are notified that you need to do work-related activity, you should be provided with a written *'action plan'*. This will specify what work-related activity you are expected to do. You can ask for an existing action plan to be reconsidered if you think that it is out of date.

ESA(WRA) Regs, regs 5 & 7

**What if you fail to do work-related activity?**
If you fail to do work-related activity, your ESA may be sanctioned (see 15 below). This sanction will not take place if you can show *'good cause'* for your failure within five working days of having been notified of it. You may be able to show good cause if the particular work-related activity was not properly identified in your action plan. Your ESA cannot be sanctioned if you fail to take part in work experience, as this is voluntary.

ESA(WRA) Regs, regs 5 & 8

## 15. Sanctions
A sanction will be applied to your ESA if you fail to meet a *'compliance condition'*. Two of these conditions relate to work-focused interviews. These are, that you fail to:
- take part in a work-focused interview; *or*
- agree with your work coach to take part in a work-focused interview at a later date.

Three of the conditions relate to work-related activity. These are, that you fail to:
- do activity specified in your action plan (see 14 above); *or*
- do an alternative activity notified by your work coach; *or*
- agree with your work coach to do such activity at a later date.

ESA Regs, regs 63(11)

### How much is the sanction?

When a sanction is applied, your ESA is reduced by £73.10 a week.

ESA Regs, regs 63(2)

If you are entitled to both contributory and income-related ESA (see Chapter 18(5)), this reduction will first be applied to contributory ESA. The reduction is only applied to income-related ESA if the reduction has resulted in the complete removal of contributory ESA and there is still some reduction outstanding.

ESA Regs, reg 63(4)

A sanction will never result in the complete removal of ESA; you will always be left with at least 10p a week. This allows claimants receiving income-related ESA to retain their entitlement to ESA while the sanction is in place, thus preserving their rights to benefits such as free prescriptions and housing benefit.

ESA Regs, reg 63(3)(a)

If a sanction is applied, you may be able to claim a hardship payment in some circumstances (see 16 below).

### How long will the sanction be imposed?

The period over which the sanction is imposed is made up of two parts: one open ended, one fixed. The open-ended sanction will apply until the compliance condition has been met (eg you take part in a work-focused interview). This will be followed by a fixed-period sanction, which will apply as follows:

- one week, if this is your first failure to meet a compliance condition;
- two weeks, if this is your second failure, having already received a 1-week fixed-period sanction within the last year;* *and*
- four weeks, if this is your third or subsequent failure, having already received a 2- or 4-week fixed-period sanction within the last year.*

If you fail to meet a compliance condition for a period of less than one week, only the fixed-period sanction will apply.

ESA Regs, reg 63(6)-(10)

A sanction will end if you move into one of the groups of people who do not have to do work-related activity, for example, if you are placed in the support group.

ESA Regs, reg 64

* but not within two weeks of the current failure; where a failure takes place within two weeks of an earlier failure, the sanction period will be the same as that of the earlier failure

### Safeguards

DWP internal guidance advises that their staff will try to visit you before applying a sanction if you have a mental health condition, learning disability or condition affecting communication or cognition (such as a stroke, autistic spectrum disorder or drug or alcohol addiction). This will be to ensure that you understood what you needed to do, and to find out whether you had good cause for your failure to meet the compliance condition.

A home visit should take place each time you fail to meet a compliance condition. At least two attempts must be made to visit you at home. If it fails in its attempts to visit you, the DWP should notify a third-party agency (such as your social worker) before applying a sanction. A decision to apply a sanction should be revised if the safeguards have not been followed.

ESA Guidance for Jobcentres (unpublished)

### Challenging decisions

If a sanction is imposed, you can challenge the decision through the normal reconsiderations and appeals process (see Chapter 57). There is no time limit for asking for a sanction to be lifted; a sanction decision can be revised at any time (see 'Ground 10' in Box O.8 in Chapter 57). You can appeal against a decision that you failed to take part in a work-focused interview and against one that you failed to do the work-related activity agreed in your action plan. In either case, you can also appeal against a decision that you did not show good cause for your failure within the 5-day time limit. In each case, a request for a mandatory reconsideration must be made first. For more on challenging decisions, see Chapter 57.

### 16. Hardship payments

If your ESA is sanctioned following a failure to meet a compliance condition, you may be able to claim a reduced-rate hardship payment for the duration of the sanction. Payment is not automatic; you must be able to show that you or your family will suffer hardship unless a hardship payment is made. You must also be entitled to income-related ESA (see Chapter 18). The rate of the hardship payment is set at £43.85 a week, or £58.50 a week if you are not getting the work-related activity component and you (or a member of your family) are pregnant or seriously ill. You must complete an application for a hardship payment.

**What is 'hardship'?** – In deciding whether or not you will suffer hardship if no payment is made, the decision maker must take into account any resources likely to be available to you (excluding child benefit and child tax credit). They must look at whether there is a substantial risk that you will have much-reduced amounts of, or lose altogether, essential items such as food, clothing, heating or accommodation. The length of time that any such risk will apply will be relevant. It is also relevant whether a severe disability premium, enhanced disability premium or disabled child element of child tax credit is payable. The decision maker may take other factors into account.

ESA Regs, regs 64A-64D

### 17. Disqualification

You can be disqualified from receiving ESA for up to six weeks if you:

- have a limited capability for work through your own misconduct (but not if it is due to pregnancy or a sexually transmitted disease). Misconduct is a wilful act, eg recklessly and knowingly breaking accepted safety rules;
- do not accept medical or other treatment (not including vaccination, inoculation or major surgery) recommended by a doctor or hospital that is treating you – but only if the treatment would be likely to remove the limitation on your capability for work and you do not have good cause for refusing;
- behave in a way that will slow down your recovery, without having good cause; *or*
- are away from home without leaving word where you can be found, without having good cause.

A disqualification will not apply if you are considered to be a *person in hardship*. In that case your ESA will be reduced instead. A 20% reduction will be imposed on your basic allowance (if you get contributory ESA) or your personal allowance (if you get income-related ESA).

ESA Regs, reg 157 & Sch 5, para 14, ESA Regs 2013, regs 63(2) & 93

**Hardship** – You are considered to be a person in hardship if:

- you or a member of your immediate family are pregnant; *or*
- you are under 18 (or if you have a partner, you are both under 18).

You will also be considered to be a person in hardship if you or your partner:

- are responsible for a child or young person who lives with you (unless you are claiming under the universal credit system);
- have been awarded attendance allowance, disability living allowance (DLA) care component, armed forces

independence payment (AFIP) or personal independence payment (PIP) daily living component (or have claimed one of these benefits in the last 26 weeks and are waiting for a decision);

■ devote considerable time each week to caring for another person who has been awarded attendance allowance, DLA care component, AFIP or PIP daily living component (or has claimed one of these benefits in the last 26 weeks and is waiting for a decision); *or*

■ have reached pension credit qualifying age (see Chapter 44(2)).

Even if none of the above grounds are met, you can still be considered to be a person in hardship if a decision maker is satisfied that unless ESA is paid, you or a member of your family will suffer hardship. The decision maker must take into account any resources likely to be available to you. They must also look at whether there is a substantial risk that you will have much-reduced amounts of, or lose altogether, essential items such as food, clothing and heating, and, if so, for how long.

If you have been disqualified from receiving ESA and you believe one of the above categories applies to you, you must tell the DWP which one applies.

ESA Regs, reg 158; ESA Regs 2013, reg 94

## C. CONTRIBUTORY ESA

### 18. What is contributory ESA?

You can qualify for contributory ESA if you have paid sufficient national insurance contributions. Contributory ESA is not affected by savings or most other income, except for occupational or personal pensions (see 27 below). It is taxable.

You should claim contributory ESA if you cannot get statutory sick pay (SSP) because, for example, you are not in employment, you are self-employed or your SSP entitlement has run out. You cannot normally work and receive contributory ESA; for exceptions, see Chapter 33(2).

### 19. Do you qualify?

To be entitled to contributory ESA, you must meet the national insurance contribution conditions (see 23 below) as well as the basic qualifying conditions listed in 7 above.

WRA 2007, S.1(2)(a)

**Contributory ESA in youth** – Before 1.5.12, the requirement to meet the contribution conditions could be waived if your limited capability for work began before the age of 20 (or 25 in some cases). This would enable you to receive 'contributory ESA in youth' (CESA(Y)). For details, see *Disability Rights Handbook* 36th edition, page 63.

If you were already receiving CESA(Y) by 1.5.12 and had been placed in the support group (see 5 above) at that date, you can continue to receive it for as long as you continue to meet the qualifying conditions and remain in the support group. If in future you are moved from the support group to the work-related activity group (following a new work capability assessment), the 12-month time limit will be imposed (see 20 below).

### 20. Time limits

Since 1.5.12 contributory ESA is payable for a maximum of 12 months if you are placed in the work-related activity group (see 4 above). The 12 months can be in one spell, or in separate 'linked' periods of limited capability for work (see 11 above). The 13-week assessment phase (see 2 above) will form part of the 12-month payment period unless you are subsequently placed in the support group (see 5 above).

If you are placed in the support group, the time limit does not apply and you will continue to receive contributory ESA for as long as you meet the qualifying conditions. If in future you are moved from the support group to the work-related activity group (following a new work capability assessment), the time limit will be imposed. The time you spent in the support group will not form part of the 12-month payment period.

Once your 12-month payment period is exhausted, unless your condition gets worse (see below) you can only re-qualify for contributory ESA when you begin a new period of limited capability for work (which must be separated from the earlier period of limited capability for work by more than 12 weeks) and your new claim is based on different tax years (see 23 below).

WRA 2007, S.1A

### If your condition gets worse

If your contributory ESA is terminated at the end of the 12-month payment period, you should ask the DWP to continue to assess you as having a limited capability for work. This will allow you to be credited with national insurance contributions (see 22 below). More importantly, if your condition deteriorates in the future, it is possible that you could be placed in the support group (see 5 above), in which case you should make a new claim for ESA. You will probably be referred for a work capability assessment (see Chapter 12). If it is accepted at this assessment that you have a limited capability for work-related activity (and can thus be placed in the support group), and provided that you continued to have (or can be treated as having) a limited capability for work from the time that the first ESA award was terminated, you can be awarded contributory ESA once more. You will not have to serve the waiting days (see 10 above) or undergo the assessment phase (see 2 above).

This route back onto the benefit applies in a similar manner to awards of 'contributory ESA in youth' (see 19 above).

WRA 2007, S.1B

### Income-related ESA

The time limit does not apply to income-related ESA. If you are receiving only time-limited contributory ESA, the DWP should contact you before the benefit ends to ask if you want to be considered for income-related ESA. If your contributory ESA is due to end, you want to be considered for income-related ESA and you have not heard from the DWP, contact them directly (0800 169 0310; textphone: 0800 169 0314). See Chapter 18 for details of income-related ESA.

### 21. National insurance contributions

There are six different classes of national insurance (NI) contributions, but only Classes 1 and 2 count towards contributory ESA. Voluntary Class 3 contributions only count towards the new state pension. Classes 1A and 1B are paid by employers only and do not count towards benefit entitlement. Class 4 contributions are normally paid by self-employed people on profits or gains above a certain level.

### Class 1 contributions

Class 1 contributions are paid by employees and employers. You pay these, and hence build up entitlement to contributory ESA, on any earnings above the *'primary threshold'* of £162 a week (for the tax year 2018/19).

Your contribution will be 12% on earnings between £162.01 and £892 a week. The contribution on earnings over £892 a week, the *'upper earnings limit'*, is just 2%.

If you earn less than the primary threshold, but more than the *'lower earnings limit'* of £116 a week (for the tax year 2018/19), you will be treated as having paid Class 1 contributions even though you do not actually have to pay any contributions.

SSCBA, Ss.6(1), 6A & 8(1)-(2)

| Earnings per week | level of NI contribution |
|---|---|
| Below £116 | Nil |
| From £116 to £162 | Nil (but treated as paid) |
| From £162.01 to £892 | 12% |
| £892.01 and above | 2% |

**Reduced rate for married women** – If you are a married woman or widow and have kept your right to pay reduced-rate contributions and you earn over £162 a week, you will pay Class 1 contributions of 5.85% on your earnings between £162.01 and £892 and 2% on earnings above £892. These do not count towards contributory ESA, so you should consider giving up your right to pay reduced-rate contributions.
SSCBA, S.19(4) & Cont. Regs, regs 127(1)(a) & 131

### Class 2 contributions

Class 2 contributions are flat-rate contributions of £2.95 a week (2018/19) paid by self-employed people. Liability for these arises at the end of the tax year. If your net profits or gains are below the *'small profits threshold'* (£6,205 for 2018/19), you should not be liable for the contributions. In this case, you can pay Class 2 contributions voluntarily to protect your contribution record for contributory ESA and new state pension. If you have low earnings from self-employment and want to pay contributions voluntarily, it is sensible to pay Class 2 rather than Class 3 contributions.
SSCBA, S.11

A married woman or widow who has kept her reduced-rate election does not have to pay Class 2 contributions. But if her taxable profits from self-employment are £8,424 a year or more, she will be liable to pay Class 4 contributions.
Cont. Regs, reg 127(1)(b)

**Future changes** – The government intends to abolish Class 2 contributions from April 2019 and use a reformed system of Class 4 contributions for self-employed people to build up entitlement to contributory benefits.

### Class 3 contributions

Class 3 contributions are voluntary, flat-rate contributions. In the 2018/19 tax year they are £14.65 a week. You may want to pay them if the other contributions you have paid (or been credited with) in a tax year are not enough to make that year count as a 'qualifying year' for new state pension (see Box L.1, Chapter 45).
SSCBA, S.13

### 22. Contribution credits

There are situations when you are not in a position to pay national insurance (NI) contributions but are awarded NI *'credits'* instead. These only count towards the second contribution condition for contributory ESA (see 25 below). There are different ways of receiving such credits. For instance, you are awarded a Class 1 credit for each week you receive jobseeker's allowance or are entitled to carer's allowance. If you are awarded a Class 1 credit, you are treated as if you had earnings equal to the lower earnings limit for that week. If you are a married woman and have kept your right to pay reduced-rate NI contributions, you cannot get Class 1 credits (except bereavement credits).

The different ways that you can be awarded NI credits are listed in Box D.3.

### 23. Contribution conditions

There are two national insurance (NI) contribution conditions, both of which you must meet to be entitled to contributory ESA. The first condition depends on the NI contributions that you have actually paid in the relevant tax year (see 24 below). For the second condition, credited NI contributions, as well as paid NI contributions, count (see 25 below). In both cases,

there is a relationship between 'tax years' and 'benefit years', so it is important to know the difference between them.
**Tax years** – A tax year runs from 6 April to 5 April the following year.
**Benefit years** – Benefit years start on the first Sunday in January and end on the Saturday before the first Sunday in January the following year. The 2018 benefit year started on Sunday 7.1.18 and will end on Saturday 5.1.19.
SSCBA, S.21(6)

The *'relevant benefit year'* is usually the year that includes the start of your *'period of limited capability for work'*.
WRA 2007, Sch 1, para 3(1)(f)

However, if you have already made a claim for contributory ESA which was unsuccessful because you did not meet the contribution conditions at that time and you re-claim in a subsequent year, then that year can be treated as the relevant benefit year if it would now enable you to meet the contribution conditions.
ESA Regs, reg 13; ESA Regs 2013, reg 14

**Period of limited capability for work** – This is the period throughout which you have, or are treated as having, a limited capability for work. It usually begins once you have made a claim for ESA. There is a linking rule which means that, in some circumstances, your period of limited capability for work begins before you actually claim.

**The linking rule** – Any two periods of limited capability for work separated by no more than 12 weeks are treated as one single period. This is important because it is the beginning of the period of limited capability for work that determines which tax years are relevant.
ESA Regs, reg 145; ESA Regs 2013, reg 86

### 24. First condition: paid contributions

You must have paid, or be treated as having paid, at least 26 weeks of Class 1 or Class 2 national insurance (NI) contributions on earnings at the lower earnings limit in one of the last two complete tax years before the start of the relevant benefit year. For instance, if you make your ESA claim in the 2018 benefit year, you need to have paid 26 weeks' contributions in one of the following tax years: 2015/16 or 2016/17 (unless one of the exceptions listed below applies).
WRA 2007, Sch 1, para 1; ESA Regs, reg 7A; ESA Regs 2013, reg 8

**Lower earnings limits** – These are uprated each year. For the last nine years they were:

| | | |
|---|---|---|
| 2010/11: **£97** | 2013/14: **£109** | 2016/17: **£112** |
| 2011/12: **£102** | 2014/15: **£111** | 2017/18: **£113** |
| 2012/13: **£107** | 2015/16: **£112** | 2018/19: **£116** |

*Example:* If you claim ESA in the 2018 benefit year, you meet the first condition if you earned at least £112 a week for 26 weeks between April 2015 and April 2016 or between April 2016 and April 2017.

### Exceptions

There are exceptions for some people whose circumstances may have prevented them from working or paying enough contributions in the usual 2-year period. If you are in one of the following groups, you will meet the first contribution condition if you have paid, or can be treated as having paid, at least 26 weeks of Class 1 or Class 2 NI contributions on earnings at the lower earnings limit in *any* complete tax year:

❑ **Carers** – You were entitled to carer's allowance for at least one week in the last complete tax year before the relevant benefit year. For example, if you claim ESA in the 2018 benefit year and you were getting carer's allowance at any time between 6.4.16 and 5.4.17, you can meet the first condition based on contributions paid in any tax year.

❑ **Low-paid disabled workers** – You were working and entitled to the disabled worker element or severe disability element of working tax credit. You must have been working for at least two years immediately before the first day of your period of limited capability for work. This helps you claim contributory ESA when your earnings were below the limit for NI contributions.

❑ **Spouses and civil partners of members of HM armed forces** – You were entitled to an NI credit to cover a period of assignment outside the UK (see Box D.3) for at least one week in the last complete tax year before the relevant benefit year.

❑ **In prison or detention but conviction or offence quashed** – You were entitled to an NI credit for a period in prison or detention, or would be if you applied, for at least one week in any tax year before the relevant benefit year.
ESA Regs, reg 8; ESA Regs 2013, reg 9

## 25. Second condition: paid or credited contributions

You must have paid or been credited with Class 1 or Class 2 national insurance contributions on earnings 50 times the lower earnings limit in each of the last two complete tax years before the start of the relevant benefit year. For example, if your benefit year is 2018, you meet this condition if you paid contributions on earnings of £5,600 in the 2015/16 and 2016/17 tax years.
WRA 2007, Sch 1, para 2

## 26. How much do you get?

For the first 13 weeks of your claim, you are paid the basic allowance, which depends on your age.

| Contributory ESA (assessment phase) | per week |
| --- | --- |
| Aged under 25 years | £57.90 |
| Aged 25 years or over | £73.10 |

Following the 13-week assessment phase, the basic allowance may be topped up with an additional component (see 6 above).

| Contributory ESA (main phase) | per week |
| --- | --- |
| Basic allowance (lower rate)* | £57.90 |
| Basic allowance (standard rate) | £73.10 |
| Work-related activity component** | £29.05 |
| Support component | £37.65 |

ESA Regs, reg 67(2)-(3) & Sch 4, paragraph 1(1) & Part 4; ESA Regs 2013, reg 62
* lower rate applies if you are under 25 and are placed in the work-related activity group unless you are still entitled to the work-related activity component; otherwise standard rate applies
** normally available only on claims made before 3.4.17

## 27. Does anything affect what you get?
### Other benefits

To be entitled to ESA, you must not be entitled to either income support or jobseeker's allowance. Additionally, you cannot receive contributory ESA as well as state pension, maternity allowance, carer's allowance, widows' benefits, widowed parent's allowance or unemployability supplement, as these are 'overlapping benefits'. If you are entitled to more than one of these benefits, you are paid the one that is worth most.
WRA 2007, S.1(3)(e)-(f) & OB Regs, reg 4

You can receive other benefits such as disability living allowance, personal independence payment and industrial injuries disablement benefit without contributory ESA being affected. You may also be entitled to income-related ESA to top up contributory ESA if you are on a low income (see Chapter 18(5)).

### Employer-paid benefits

Statutory maternity pay, statutory adoption pay and statutory shared parental pay also 'overlap' with contributory ESA. Consequently, if you are entitled to contributory ESA and claim one of these employer-paid benefits, you will receive whichever is the higher (which will usually be the employer-paid benefit).
ESA Regs, regs 80-82A; ESA Regs 2013, regs 73-75A

### Occupational and personal pensions

If you receive an occupational or personal pension (including permanent health insurance payments, Pension Protection Fund periodic payments and Financial Assistance Scheme payments – but see below) that pays more than £85 a week, then your contributory ESA payment is reduced by half of the amount over this limit. For example, if you receive £105 a week before tax from a personal pension, your ESA is reduced by £10 a week, ie half of the excess figure of £20. If you receive more than one pension, they are added together for this calculation.

Some payments are ignored for this purpose, ie:
■ payments you receive because of the death of the pension scheme member;
■ any pension paid because of death due to military or war service;
■ any shortfall, if a full pension cannot be paid because the pension scheme is in deficit or has insufficient funds;
■ guaranteed income payments made under the Armed Forces Compensation scheme; *and*
■ a permanent health insurance payment if you paid more than 50% of the premium.
ESA Regs, regs 72, 72A, 74 & 75; ESA Regs 2013, regs 64, 65, 67 & 68

**Existing incapacity claimants** – If you have been claiming incapacity benefit or severe disablement allowance since 2001, your occupational or personal pension will still be fully disregarded. If you are 'migrated' onto ESA (see 28 below), the full disregard will be protected, ie the above £85 limit will not be applied to you.

### Sick pay

Any contractual sick pay paid by your employer will not affect your entitlement to contributory ESA.
ESA Regs, reg 95(2)(b); ESA Regs 2013, reg 80(2)(b)

### Hospital and care homes

You can continue to receive contributory ESA while in hospital or a care home.

### Prison

You are generally disqualified from receiving contributory ESA for any period during which you are in prison or legal custody.
WRA 2007, S.18(4)(b)

Payment of contributory ESA is suspended if you are on remand awaiting trial or sentencing. Full arrears of benefit are payable if you do not receive a penalty (such as a fine or imprisonment) at the end of proceedings. No arrears are payable if you do receive a penalty.

If you are detained in a hospital or similar institution following a criminal conviction as a person 'suffering from a mental disorder', contributory ESA is payable for the length of the sentence unless you are detained under s.45A or s.47 of the Mental Health Act 1983 (or equivalent Scottish legislation).
ESA Regs, regs 160 & 161; ESA Regs 2013, regs 96 & 97

### Councillor's allowance

If you receive a councillor's allowance of more than £125.50 a week (excluding expenses), the excess will be deducted from your contributory ESA.
ESA Regs, reg 76; ESA Regs 2013, reg 69

## D.3 Contribution credits

In the following circumstances you can be credited with national insurance (NI) contributions. Depending on which circumstance applies, you will be credited with Class 1 contributions or Class 3 contributions (see 21 in this chapter). In each case, we state how this will benefit you. References to state pension in this box include the new state pension and the earlier basic state pension (see Chapter 45).

**Applying for the credits** – Most of the credits are awarded automatically. In some cases, however, you will need to apply for them. You must normally do this before the end of the benefit year after the tax year in which the week(s) to which the credit applies fall (see 23 in this chapter). To apply for credits, you should normally write to: National Insurance Contributions and Employer Office, HMRC, BX9 1AN. Include your NI number and say when the credits are for and why you are eligible.

### Credits for limited capability or incapacity for work

You get a Class 1 credit for each complete week you have a limited capability for work.

If your contributory employment and support allowance (ESA) is terminated because of the 12-month time limit (see 20 in this chapter) and you are not entitled to income-related ESA, you can protect your NI contribution record by continuing to claim *'credits for limited capability for work'*. You will get a credit for each week in which you meet the basic ESA qualifying conditions (other than the specific contributory or income-related conditions for receipt of the benefit) – see 7 in this chapter.

You get a Class 1 credit for each complete week of incapacity for work – ie on each day of the week you are entitled to incapacity benefit, statutory sick pay (SSP), severe disablement allowance (SDA), income support on the grounds of incapacity or maternity allowance.

The rules for assessing limited capability for work are described in Chapter 12(2); the rules for assessing incapacity for work are described in Chapter 13, *Disability Rights Handbook*, 35th edition.

If you were getting SSP, you will have paid, or been treated as having paid, Class 1 contributions if your employer also had an occupational sick pay scheme that brought your total sick pay up to the lower earnings limit. But if you only got SSP, and therefore did not earn enough to pay, or be treated as paying, contributions and your contribution record is deficient, you should apply for credits.

You get a Class 1 credit for each week for any part of which you receive a war pensions or industrial injuries unemployability supplement.

You will not get a credit for limited capability or incapacity for work for any week in which you are entitled to universal credit for any part of the week, unless you are also entitled to incapacity benefit, SDA, maternity allowance, ESA or SSP.

A week for NI contribution purposes begins on a Sunday and ends on a Saturday.

Incapacity and limited capability for work credits can help meet the contribution conditions for any contributory benefit.

*Credit Regs, reg 8B; SP Regs, regs 26 & 29*

### Credits for unemployment

You get a Class 1 credit for each complete week you are paid jobseeker's allowance (JSA).

If you cannot be paid JSA (eg because your 6-month award of contribution-based JSA has come to an end), you can protect your NI contribution record by signing on at the Jobcentre Plus office for credits only. You will get a credit for each week in which you meet the basic JSA qualifying conditions (other than the specific contribution-based or income-based conditions for receipt of the benefit) – see Chapter 13(2). If you have a limited capability for work or are incapable of work for part of the week, you are still entitled to a credit for unemployment.

However, you will not get a credit for any week in which:

- your JSA is not paid (or joint-claim JSA reduced) because of a sanction;
- you get JSA hardship payments or severe hardship payments;
- you are not entitled to JSA because you are on strike; *or*
- you are entitled to universal credit for any part of the week.

If, consequently, there is a gap in your contribution record, you can protect your state pension entitlement by paying voluntary Class 3 contributions (see 21 in this chapter).

Credits for unemployment help meet the contribution conditions for any contributory benefit.

*Credit Regs, reg 8A; SP Regs, regs 26 & 29*

### Credits for caring
#### Carer's allowance credits

You get a Class 1 credit for each week in which you are paid carer's allowance, or in which you would be paid carer's allowance were you not receiving widowed parent's allowance, widow's pension or widowed mother's allowance instead. Carer's allowance credits help meet the contribution conditions for any contributory benefit.

*Credit Regs, reg 7A; SP Regs, regs 26 & 29*

#### Carer's credit

From 6.4.10, to help meet the contribution conditions for state pension and widowed parent's allowance, you get a Class 3 credit for each week in which you:

- are caring for one or more disabled people for at least 20 hours a week and *either* they get a qualifying benefit (see Chapter 8(2)) *or* a health or social care professional has certified that the care you provide is needed. The credits can continue for a period of 12 weeks after you cease to meet these conditions for any reason; *or*
- are entitled to income support as a carer (see Box F.1, Chapter 19).

You also get these credits to cover the 12-week period before or after an award of carer's allowance.

Before 6.4.10, 'home responsibilities protection' gave similar cover (see Box L.2, Chapter 45).

You will usually need to apply for these credits; ring 0800 731 0297 (textphone 0800 731 0317) or go to: www.gov.uk/government/publications/carers-credit-application-form for a CC1 claim-form.

*SSCBA, S.23A(2)-(3); Social Security (Contributions Credits for Parents & Carers) Regs 2010; SP Regs, regs 27, 37 & 38*

### Credits for caring for children
#### Credits for parents and foster parents

From 6.4.10 to help meet the contribution conditions for state pension and widowed parent's allowance, you get a Class 3 credit for each week in which you:

- (or your partner, if they have already met the contribution conditions for state pension that tax year) are awarded child benefit for a child under the age of 12; *or*
- are an approved foster parent or carer (or a kinship carer in Scotland).

Before 6.4.10, 'home responsibilities protection' gave similar cover (see Box L.2, Chapter 45).

You will usually need to apply for these credits; ring 0300 200 3500 or go to: www.gov.uk/government/publications/national-insurance-credits-for-parents-and-carers-cf411a for a CF411A.

*SSCBA, S.23A(2)-(3); Social Security (Contributions Credits for Parents & Carers) Regs 2010; SP Regs, regs 27, 34 & 36*

### Credits for family members who care for a child

From 6.4.11, to help meet the contribution conditions for state pension and widowed parent's allowance, you can get a Class 3 credit for each week in which you provide familial care for a child under the age of 12. These credits may apply if you are the child's parent, (great- or great-great-) grandparent, brother, sister, aunt, uncle, nephew or niece (or partner or former partner of any of these).

The credits will apply only if you are not entitled to 'credits for parents and foster parents' (as above) and someone else is getting child benefit for the child (and they have already met the contribution conditions for state pension that tax year).

You will usually need to apply for these credits; ring 0300 200 3500 or go to: www.gov.uk/government/publications/national-insurance-application-for-specified-adult-childcare-credits-ca9176 for a CA9176. The person getting child benefit will need to agree to your application.

*Credit Regs, reg 9F & Sch; SP Regs, regs 26 & 35*

### Credits for tax credits

You get a Class 1 credit for each week in which you receive the disabled worker element or severe disability element of working tax credit (WTC). These credits count for any contributory benefit. You may also get a Class 3 credit, which counts for state pension and widowed parent's allowance, for any week you receive WTC. If you are a couple, the credit is awarded to the one who is earning; if both of you are earning, it is awarded to the one being paid WTC. In each case, you must be either:

- employed and earning less than the lower earnings limit for that year; *or*
- self-employed and not liable to pay Class 2 contributions (see 21 in this chapter).

*Credit Regs, regs 7B & 7C; SP Regs, regs 26, 29 & 30*

### Credits for universal credit

To help meet the contribution conditions for state pension and widowed parent's allowance, you get a Class 3 credit for each week in which you are entitled to universal credit for any part of the week.

*Credit Regs, reg 8G; SP Regs, regs 26 & 31*

### Training and education credits

**Termination of full-time education/training credits** – To help meet the contribution conditions for contribution-based JSA or contributory ESA only, you can get Class 1 credits for one of the two tax years before your benefit year if in that tax year you were aged 18 or over and in full-time education or on a full-time training course (or a part-time course of at least 15 hours a week if you are disabled) or in an apprenticeship, and the course or apprenticeship, which must have begun before you became 21, has now ended. In the other year, you must have met the contribution conditions in a different way. You will need to apply for the credits if Jobcentre Plus has not arranged to send you on the course or apprenticeship.

*Credit Regs, reg 8*

**Approved training credits** – To help meet the contribution conditions for any contributory benefit, you can get a Class 1 credit for each week you are on an approved training course. You must not be entitled to universal credit. The course must be full time, or at least 15 hours a week if you are disabled, or

be an introductory course. It must not be part of your job. It must be intended to run for no longer than one year (unless a longer period is reasonable because of your disability). You must have reached the age of 18 before the start of the tax year for which you need the credits. You will need to apply for the credits if Jobcentre Plus has not arranged to send you on the course.

*Credit Regs, reg 7; SP Regs, regs 26 & 29*

### Others

**Maternity, shared parental and adoption pay period credits** – If you receive statutory maternity pay (SMP), statutory shared parental pay (SSPP) or statutory adoption pay (SAP) and do not earn enough to pay or be treated as paying contributions on your SMP, SSPP or SAP, you can apply for Class 1 credits. These credits count for any contributory benefit.

*Credit Regs, reg 9C; SP Regs, regs 26 & 29*

**Jury service credits** – If you are on jury service for all or part of any week, you can apply for Class 1 credits (unless you are self-employed). These credits count for any contributory benefit.

*Credit Regs, reg 9B; SP Regs, regs 26 & 29*

**Spouses and civil partners of members of HM armed forces** – From 6.4.10, if you were accompanying (or treated as accompanying) your spouse or civil partner who is a member of HM armed forces on an assignment outside the UK, you can apply for Class 1 credits to cover the period of the assignment using form MODCA1 (www.gov.uk/government/publications/national-insurance-application-for-national-insurance-credits-modca1). These credits count for any contributory benefit.

*Credit Regs, reg 9E; SP Regs, regs 26 & 29*

**Starting credits** – To help meet the contribution conditions for Category A or B state pension and widowed parent's allowance, you can get Class 3 credits for the tax year in which you reached the age of 16 and for the two following years (for tax years between 6.4.75 and 5.4.10).

*Credit Regs, reg 4*

**Credits for men approaching state pension age** – Men can get Class 1 credits automatically for the tax year in which they reach pension credit qualifying age (see Chapter 44(2)) and for the following tax years up to the year they reach the age of 65, provided they are not out of the UK for six months or longer in the year. These credits cover gaps in your NI record for these years and count for all contributory benefits.

*Credit Regs, reg 9A*

**Bereavement credits** – To help meet the contribution conditions for contribution-based JSA or contributory ESA when your bereavement benefit ends, you can get Class 1 credits for each year up to (and including) the year in which the bereavement benefit ends, except where it ends because of remarriage, forming a civil partnership or cohabitation. Women who were getting widow's allowance or widowed mother's allowance can similarly get credits to help meet the contribution conditions for contributory ESA (again, except where the benefit ends because of remarriage, etc).

*Credit Regs, reg 8C; The Social Security (Benefit) (Married Women & Widows Special Provisions) Regs 1974, reg 3(1)(b)*

**Credits for periods in prison** – You can apply for Class 1 credits for any weeks in which you were imprisoned or detained in legal custody for convictions or offences which were subsequently quashed by the courts, provided there were no other reasons for you being in prison or custody at that time. These credits count for all contributory benefits.

*Credit Regs, reg 9D; SP Regs, regs 26 & 29*

## D. EXISTING INCAPACITY CLAIMANTS

### 28. What will happen to existing claimants of incapacity benefits?

The following benefits are being phased out:

- incapacity benefit (see Box D.4);
- severe disablement allowance (SDA) for those under state pension age (see Box D.5); *and*
- income support paid on the grounds of incapacity (see Chapter 19).

If you are receiving one of these benefits, at some point you will be asked to take part in a work capability assessment (see 29 below). If you are found to have a limited capability for work in this re-assessment, you will be moved (or 'migrated') onto ESA.

### 29. Work capability assessment

**First contact** – The DWP will write to inform you of the changes and that you are to be re-assessed. Shortly afterwards, they should ring to check that you have received the letter and understand what is going to happen.
TPEA Regs, reg 4

**The assessment** – You will then be sent a *Capability for work questionnaire* to complete. This is the first stage of the work capability assessment, which is covered in Chapter 12. The process for claimants undergoing the re-assessment will be similar to that of new ESA claimants. Read Chapter 12(9)-(12) carefully before completing the questionnaire. Your completed questionnaire will be assessed by a DWP-approved healthcare professional. They may request further information from your GP, or they may ask you to attend a face-to-face assessment (see Chapter 12(14)).

If you fail to send back the questionnaire or attend the face-to-face assessment without good cause (see Chapter 12(13)), a decision will be made that you do not have a limited capability for work and that your existing award of benefit does not therefore qualify for conversion to ESA. The existing award will be terminated. If you think you had good cause for not sending back the questionnaire or not attending the assessment, you can challenge the decision through the mandatory reconsideration and appeals process (see Chapter 57).
TPEA Regs, Sch 2, para 7; ESA Regs, regs 22(1), 23(2) & 24

### 30. Moving onto ESA

Following the work capability assessment, if you are found to have (or can be treated as having) a limited capability for work, you will be moved onto ESA.

If you were previously getting incapacity benefit or severe disablement allowance (SDA), it will be converted into contributory ESA (see 18-27 above). Payment of this may be limited to 12 months (see below).

If you were previously getting income support, it will be converted into income-related ESA (see Chapter 18).

If you were previously getting incapacity benefit or SDA topped up with income support, it will be converted into a single award of ESA, consisting of both the contributory and income-related elements.

You will not need to make a claim for ESA, nor will you need to serve any waiting days (see 10 above) or the 13-week assessment phase (see 2 above).
TPEA Regs, regs 5(1)-(2)(a), 7 & 8(1)

The DWP will notify you of your ESA award and provide you with details of the benefit. They will let you know if you are entitled to contributory ESA, income-related ESA or both together. They will also let you know if you have been placed in the work-related activity group (see 4 above) or the support group (see 5 above).
TPEA Regs, regs 5(3)&(5)

**ESA underpayments** – In a substantial number of cases, the DWP has incorrectly converted awards of incapacity benefit or SDA (in each case, where income support was not also in payment) to contributory ESA only, where income-related ESA should also have been awarded. Following an Upper Tribunal decision, the DWP is now contacting all those who may be affected in order to correct the underpayments (although any backdated benefit will be restricted to 21.10.14, the date of the Upper Tribunal decision).
CE/4181/2013

### Contributory ESA time limit

Since 1.5.12 contributory ESA has been payable for a maximum of 12 months for anyone placed in the work-related activity group. This time limit will be applied to the claims of those moved onto ESA from incapacity benefit or SDA. The 12-month period will run from the point that the previous benefit is converted into ESA. For details of how the time limit is applied, see 20 above.

### What if ESA is paid at a higher rate?

If the level of ESA you are entitled to is greater than that of your previous benefit, the amount you receive will be increased as soon as you are migrated onto ESA.

### What if ESA is paid at a lower rate?

**Transitional addition** – If the level of ESA you are entitled to is lower than that of your previous benefit, your ESA will be topped-up by a *'transitional addition'* to the rate of your previous benefit and frozen at that level.
TPEA Regs, regs 9-12

If there is a substantial difference between the level of ESA you are entitled to and that of your previous benefit, you may find that the level of your ESA is effectively frozen for several years (unless there is a change of circumstances). Once the level of ESA you are actually entitled to has reached the same level as your previous benefit (eg through annual upratings), your ESA can start to be increased with each uprating. The transitional addition will not extend beyond 5.4.20.
TPEA Regs, regs 18-21

If there is a break in your ESA claim of up to 12 weeks, your transitional addition is protected and can be included in your new claim (as long as your previous award was not terminated because you were found not to have a limited capability for work).
TPEA Regs, regs 21(4)-(5); ESA Regs, reg 145

### National insurance credits only

If you are entitled only to national insurance (NI) credits (see 22 above), ie you are incapable of work but not entitled to incapacity benefit, SDA or income support, you will be moved onto NI credits for limited capability for work (see Box D.3). This will help towards your entitlement to the new state pension. You will not be expected to take part in work-focused interviews to remain entitled to these credits.
ESA Regs, reg 54(2)(d)

### If you have children

ESA does not include extra money for any children or young people you are responsible for. If you are responsible for a child or young person and you have previously been getting extra for them in your income support, the DWP should send your details to HMRC, who will assess you for child tax credit. You do not need to make a claim for child tax credit, but the DWP will try to contact you by phone to seek your agreement to the move. The process should take place before your migration onto ESA to ensure there is minimal disruption to your payments. See Chapter 23 for more on tax credits.

**Tax credits**

If you were previously receiving SDA or your incapacity benefit included an invalidity allowance (see Box D.6), these will have been disregarded as income in the tax credit calculation. If you are transferred onto contributory ESA from one of these benefits, the contributory ESA will now be taken into account in the tax credit calculation, thus reducing the amount of tax credit payable. You should notify HMRC of the change of circumstances.

## D.4 Incapacity benefit

Incapacity benefit was abolished for most new claims from 27.10.08 and replaced by contributory employment and support allowance (ESA) – see 18 to 27 in this chapter.

### Staying on incapacity benefit

If you are still receiving incapacity benefit, you may remain on it for the time being if you continue to meet the qualifying conditions. However, at some point you will be re-assessed under the work capability assessment (see Chapter 12). If you are found to have a limited capability for work under this assessment, you will be moved onto ESA. For details, see 28 to 32 in this chapter.

### How much do you get?

| Incapacity benefit | | per week |
|---|---|---|
| Long-term basic rate | | £109.60 |
| Adult dependant | | £63.65 |
| Child dependant | first child | £8.00 |
| | each other child | £11.35 |
| Age addition | under 35 | £11.60 |
| | 35-44 | £6.45 |

*SSCBA, S.30B & Sch 4 (Parts I & IV)*

You can qualify for an increase for an adult dependant only if you were already receiving the increase on 6.4.10, and for a dependent child or young person only if you were already receiving the increase on 5.4.03.

**Work and earnings** – Generally, if you do any work you are treated as capable of work and cannot get incapacity benefit. But some work is exempt from this rule (see Chapter 33(2)). Your partner's earnings do not affect your basic benefit, but can affect increases for children and dependent adults.

**Other benefits** – You cannot get incapacity benefit as well as maternity allowance, carer's allowance, widows' benefits, widowed parent's allowance and unemployability supplement, as these benefits overlap. If you are entitled to more than one of these benefits, you are paid the one that is worth most. State pension and jobseeker's allowance cannot be paid at the same time as incapacity benefit.

Other benefits can be paid in addition to incapacity benefit, including disability living allowance, personal independence payment, attendance allowance and industrial injuries disablement benefit. Working tax credit can be paid on top, but incapacity benefit is taken into account in the tax credit assessment (unless you previously got invalidity benefit and are still in the same period of incapacity for work).

**The benefit cap** – Incapacity benefit is a benefit to which the benefit cap applies (see Box G.6, Chapter 25).

**Occupational and personal pensions** – Occupational and personal pensions affect your incapacity benefit in a similar way to contributory ESA (see 27 in this chapter).

**Other incapacity benefit rules** – More information about incapacity benefit can be found in Chapter 14, *Disability Rights Handbook*, 33rd edition. If you don't have a copy, send us an A4-sized, stamped addressed envelope and we'll send a photocopy.

## 31. If you are found not to have a limited capability for work

Following the work capability assessment (WCA), if you are found not to have a limited capability for work and are therefore not entitled to ESA, your incapacity benefit, income support or severe disablement allowance will be terminated (along with any award of national insurance credits you were getting on account of your illness or incapacity). You should receive a phone call informing you of the decision and asking if you want to claim jobseeker's allowance (see Chapter 13).

The phone call will be followed by a decision letter informing you of the outcome of the WCA, that your existing award of benefit has not qualified for conversion to ESA, and of the date from which your existing award will be terminated.
*TPEA Regs, regs 5(1)&(2)(b) & 15*

## D.5 Severe disablement allowance

Severe disablement allowance (SDA) was abolished for new claims on 6.4.01. If you are still receiving SDA, you may remain on it for the time being if you continue to meet the qualifying conditions. However, at some point you will be re-assessed under the work capability assessment (see Chapter 12), unless you reached state pension age before 6.4.14. If you are found to have a limited capability for work under this assessment, you will be moved onto employment and support allowance; for details, see 28 to 32 in this chapter.

### How much do you get?

| SDA rates | | per week |
|---|---|---|
| For yourself | | £77.65 |
| Age addition | higher rate | £11.60 |
| | middle rate | £6.45 |
| | lower rate | £6.45 |
| Adult dependant | | £38.20 |
| Child dependant | first child | £8.00 |
| | each other child | £11.35 |

**Earnings** – Your partner's earnings do not affect your basic benefit but can affect entitlement to dependants' additions. The rules are the same as for incapacity benefit (for details, see *Disability Rights Handbook*, 33rd edition, page 87). SDA is not affected by any wages, sick pay or occupational or personal pension you get. However, it is only possible to do limited work and still be counted as incapable of work for SDA (see Chapter 33(2)).

**Other benefits** – If you get SDA, you may get a disability premium included in income support or housing benefit. SDA overlaps with other benefits such as carer's allowance, maternity allowance, state pension, widows' benefits, widowed parent's allowance and unemployability supplement. If you are entitled to more than one, you are paid the one that is worth most.

**The benefit cap** – SDA is included in the list of benefits to which the benefit cap applies (see Box G.6, Chapter 25).

**Other SDA rules** – There is more information about SDA in Chapter 15, *Disability Rights Handbook*, 25th edition. If you don't have a copy, send us an A4-sized, stamped addressed envelope and we'll send you a photocopy.

The way that you can challenge a decision that you are not entitled to ESA is covered in Chapter 12(16) and (18). See Box D.10 in Chapter 12 for appeal tactics on the limited capability for work assessment. For general information on appeals, see Chapter 57.

### Staying on income support

If you were getting income support paid on the grounds of incapacity and have been found not to have a limited capability for work, you may be able to remain on income support if you are eligible in another way. You may be eligible for income support if you:

■ are a lone parent and your youngest child is under 5; *or*
■ are caring for someone and either you get carer's allowance or they get a qualifying benefit (see Chapter 8(2)).

IS Regs, Sch 1B, paras 1 & 4

The full list of categories is shown in Box F.1 in Chapter 19. The DWP should already have enough information to make a decision on your continued eligibility for income support. If they do, they will inform you of the decision in writing. Contact the DWP if your income support is terminated following a WCA and you believe you meet one of the other eligibility grounds which they have not taken into account.

**Disability premium** – Even if you are eligible for income support through another route, the amount may be substantially reduced if the disability premium (see Chapter 21(2)) is removed. The disability premium is £33.55 for a single person and £47.80 for a couple. You will lose the premium if you only qualified for it on the basis that you were considered incapable of work. You will not lose the premium if you still qualify for it another way, eg if you receive personal independence payment. If you continue to get income support but lose the disability premium, you may wish to challenge the ESA decision (see Chapter 12(16) and (18)).

### 32. Housing benefit

Your housing benefit may be recalculated when you are migrated onto ESA. In some circumstances, your entitlement to housing benefit may be reduced. This could be the case if:

■ your housing benefit included a disability premium (see Chapter 21(2)) before re-assessment; *and*
■ following the work capability assessment you are placed in the work-related activity group (see 4 above); *and*
■ you are entitled to contributory ESA but not income-related ESA.

If you are moved from income support onto income-related

---

ESA, your housing benefit award should remain unchanged. **Transitional addition** – If your housing benefit entitlement is reduced, you may be awarded a 'transitional addition', which will restore your housing benefit to the level it was before the re-assessment. This transitional addition will be eroded when benefits are uprated, until it is reduced to nothing. Consequently, the level of your housing benefit may be effectively frozen for a number of years (unless there is a change of circumstances).

HB Regs, Sch 3, paras 27-31

# 12 The work capability assessment

| | | |
|---|---|---|
| 1 | What is the work capability assessment? | 82 |
| 2 | Limited capability for work assessment | 83 |
| | Limited capability for work assessment – physical disabilities – Box D.7 | 84 |
| | Limited capability for work assessment – mental, cognitive and intellectual functions – Box D.8 | 86 |
| 3 | Treated as having a limited capability for work | 83 |
| 4 | Treated as not having a limited capability for work | 85 |
| 5 | Limited capability for work-related activity assessment | 87 |
| | Limited capability for work-related activity assessment – Box D.9 | 88 |
| 6 | Treated as having a limited capability for work-related activity | 87 |
| 7 | Treated as not having a limited capability for work-related activity | 87 |
| 8 | How is the WCA applied? | 88 |
| 9 | The capability for work questionnaire | 88 |
| 10 | Completing the questionnaire – physical disabilities | 88 |
| 11 | Completing the questionnaire – mental, cognitive and intellectual functions | 91 |
| 12 | Completing the questionnaire – eating and drinking | 92 |
| 13 | Returning the questionnaire | 93 |
| 14 | Face-to-face assessment | 93 |
| 15 | Exceptional circumstances | 93 |
| 16 | Challenging the decision: mandatory reconsiderations | 94 |
| 17 | Challenging the decision: appeals | 94 |
| | Appeal tactics – limited capability for work assessment – Box D.10 | 95 |
| 18 | Appeals on the limited capability for work assessment | 94 |
| 19 | Appeals on the limited capability for work-related activity assessment | 96 |
| 20 | If your condition deteriorates | 96 |
| 21 | Re-assessments | 96 |

### 1. What is the work capability assessment?

The *'work capability assessment'* (WCA) looks at the extent to which your disability or health condition affects your ability to work.

If you are claiming employment and support allowance (ESA), the WCA determines whether or not you can remain on the benefit and, if you can, which of two groups you are then placed in: the *'work-related activity group'* (see Chapter 11(4)) or the *'support group'* (see Chapter 11(5)). The group you are placed in determines the level of ESA you receive, the responsibilities you must meet to retain the benefit in full and whether or not your ESA award may be time limited.

If you are claiming universal credit, the WCA determines whether the 'work capability amount' is payable (see Chapter 16(6)) and the requirements you must meet to retain the benefit in full (see Box E.3 in Chapter 15).

The WCA has two parts: the *'limited capability for work assessment'* (see 2 below) and the *'limited capability for work-related activity assessment'* (see 5 below).

---

### D.6 Transferred from invalidity benefit

Invalidity benefit was abolished on 13.4.95 and replaced by incapacity benefit (itself now replaced by employment and support allowance). If you were entitled to invalidity benefit on 12.4.95, the amount of your benefit is protected (your award is a 'transitional award').

*Social Security (Incapacity Benefit)(Transitional) Regs 1995, reg 17(1)*

| Amounts for 2018/19 | | per week |
|---|---|---|
| Long-term incapacity benefit | | £109.60 |
| Invalidity allowance | higher rate | £11.60 |
| | middle rate | £6.45 |
| | lower rate | £6.45 |
| Dependant's addition | | £63.65 |
| Additional pension (SERPS) – the amount is based on your contribution record and frozen at your 1994/95 level. | | |

## 2. Limited capability for work assessment

The first part of the WCA looks at whether you have a *'limited capability for work'*. You are not entitled to ESA unless you have (or can be treated as having) a limited capability for work. If you are claiming universal credit, you will be expected to search for work and be available for work unless you have (or can be treated as having) a limited capability for work.

This part of the WCA is a points-related assessment of your physical, mental, cognitive and intellectual functions considered within a range of activities. Points are awarded on the basis of any limitations you have for each activity and then totalled up. If the total reaches 15 points or more, you have a limited capability for work.

ESA Regs, reg 19(3); ESA Regs 2013, reg 15(3); UC Regs, reg 39(3)

**Some 'specific' disease or disablement** – In the assessment, it must be clear that an inability to do an activity arises:

- from a specific bodily disease or disablement (in the case of the physical disabilities activities listed in Box D.7);
- from a specific mental illness or disablement (in the case of the mental, cognitive and intellectual functions activities listed in Box D.8); *or*
- as a direct result of treatment provided by a registered medical practitioner for such a disease, illness or disablement.

ESA Regs, reg 19(5); ESA Regs 2013, reg 15(5); UC Regs, reg 39(4)

*'Specific'* is not the same as 'specified', so it may not be essential that the cause of the disease or disablement is identified (CS/7/82). For example, you may suffer pain, the cause of which has not yet been diagnosed. A normal pregnancy does not count as a disease or disablement, but conditions such as high blood pressure arising because of pregnancy do count.

### Physical disabilities

The limited capability for work assessment has 10 activity headings relating to physical disabilities (abbreviated here):

- mobilising;
- standing and sitting;
- reaching;
- picking up and moving things;
- manual dexterity (using your hands);
- making yourself understood;
- understanding communication;
- navigation and maintaining safety;
- absence or loss of control ... of the bowel or bladder; *and*
- consciousness.

Under each activity heading is a list of *'descriptors'* with scores ranging from 0 to 15 points. The descriptors explain related tasks of varying degrees of difficulty. You score points when you are not able to complete a task described safely, to an acceptable standard, as often as you need to and in a reasonable time. The highest points you score under each activity heading are added together.

ESA Regs, reg 19(6); ESA Regs 2013, reg 15(6); UC Regs, reg 39(5)

If you score 15 points or more, you have a limited capability for work. These points can be scored under just one activity heading or from any of the activity headings (in both the physical and the mental parts of the assessment) added together.

ESA Regs, reg 19(3); ESA Regs 2013, reg 15(3); UC Regs, reg 39(3)

The descriptors and the points assigned to each one are listed in Box D.7.

### Mental, cognitive and intellectual functions

There are seven activity headings relating to mental, cognitive and intellectual functions (abbreviated here):

- learning tasks;
- awareness of everyday hazards;
- initiating and completing personal action;
- coping with change;
- getting about;
- coping with social engagement; *and*
- appropriateness of behaviour with other people.

As with the physical disabilities, there is a list of descriptors under each activity heading and the scoring follows the same pattern. You score points when you are not able to complete a task described safely, to an acceptable standard, as often as you need to and in a reasonable time. The highest points you score under each activity heading are added together. If you score 15 points or more, you have a limited capability for work. These points can be scored under just one activity heading or from any of the activity headings (in both the physical and the mental parts of the assessment) added together.

ESA Regs, reg 19(3)&(6); ESA Regs 2013, reg 15(3)&(6); UC Regs, reg 39(3)&(5)

The descriptors and the points assigned to each one are listed in Box D.8.

## 3. Treated as having a limited capability for work

You can automatically be treated as having a limited capability for work, without having to score 15 points, in the following circumstances:

- you are terminally ill. This is defined as *'a progressive disease and death in consequence of that disease can reasonably be expected within six months'*;
- you are receiving chemotherapy or radiotherapy for cancer (or are likely to receive it within six months), or you are recovering from that treatment and the DWP is satisfied that you should be treated as having a limited capability for work;
- you have been given official notice not to work because you have been in contact with an infectious disease or contamination; *or*
- you are pregnant and there would be a serious risk to the health of you or your child if you did not refrain from work.

ESA Regs, reg 20(a)-(d); ESA Regs 2013, reg 16(1)(a)-(d); UC Regs, Sch 8, para 3 & Sch 9, paras 1-3

### Hospital inpatients

You are treated as having a limited capability for work on any day you are being treated in a hospital or similar institution (including residential rehabilitation for treatment of drug or alcohol addiction), having been medically advised to stay there for at least 24 hours. The DWP may also treat you as having a limited capability for work on any day you are recovering from such treatment.

ESA Regs, reg 25; ESA Regs 2013, reg 21; UC Regs, Sch 8, para 2

### Renal failure and certain other regular treatments

You are treated as having a limited capability for work during any week in which you are receiving:

- regular weekly haemodialysis for chronic renal failure;
- plasmapheresis; *or*
- regular weekly total parenteral nutrition for gross impairment of enteric function.

The DWP may also treat you as having a limited capability for work during any week in which you have a day of recovery from such treatment.

However, for employment and support allowance (ESA) you are only treated as having a limited capability for work from the first week in which at least two days of that week are days of treatment or recovery. The two days need not be consecutive. Thereafter, you can continue to be treated as having a limited capability for work if there is only one day of treatment or recovery a week.

ESA Regs, reg 26; ESA Regs 2013, reg 22; UC Regs, Sch 8, para 1

### Additional circumstances: ESA

For ESA, you will be treated as having a limited capability for work if you:

■ are pregnant or have recently given birth, are entitled to maternity allowance and are within the maternity allowance payment period;

■ are pregnant or have recently given birth but are not entitled to maternity allowance or statutory maternity pay, from six weeks before the baby is due to two weeks after the birth;

■ satisfy either descriptor 15 (conveying food or drink to the mouth) or 16 (chewing or swallowing food or drink) in the 'limited capability for work-related activity assessment' (see Box D.9);

■ (for income-related ESA only) are a student in full-time education (and not a 'qualifying young person' for child benefit purposes) entitled to income-related ESA because you receive disability living allowance, personal independence payment or armed forces independence payment; *or*

■ (for contributory ESA only) are entitled to universal credit and have already been found to have a limited capability

for work under that benefit.

ESA Regs, reg 20(e)-(g) & 33(2); ESA Regs 2013, reg 16(1)(e)-(h)

As long as you provide the required fit notes (see Chapter 10(9)), you will be treated as having a limited capability for work during the assessment phase (see Chapter 11(2)) while waiting for the WCA to be carried out. This will not apply, however, if you have previously failed the assessment (unless you have a different condition or your condition has significantly worsened since the decision). Neither will it apply if you have been treated as having failed the assessment within the last six months because you did not return the capability for work questionnaire (see 13 below) or attend the face-to-face assessment (see 14 below) without good cause (unless you have a different condition or your condition has significantly worsened since the decision).

ESA Regs, reg 30; ESA Regs 2013, reg 26

### Additional circumstances: universal credit

For universal credit, you will be treated as having a limited capability for work if you:

■ have some specific illness, disease or disablement, and

---

## D.7  Limited capability for work assessment – physical disabilities

Activities 1 to 10 cover physical disabilities and must arise from a physical condition. To be assessed as having a limited capability for work, you need to score 15 points or more. Add together the highest score from each activity heading that applies to you. The scores from these activity headings can be added to those in the mental, cognitive and intellectual function activities (see Box D.8). If any task highlighted in *italics* applies (see activities 1, 2, 3, 4, 5, 6, and 7) you will also satisfy the 'limited capability for work-related activity assessment' (see Box D.9).

| Activity | Points |
|---|---|

**1. Mobilising unaided by another person with or without a walking stick, manual wheelchair or other aid if such aid is normally or could reasonably be worn or used**

A *Cannot, unaided by another person, either:*
   *(i) mobilise more than 50 metres on level ground without stopping in order to avoid significant discomfort or exhaustion; or*
   *(ii) repeatedly mobilise 50 metres within a reasonable timescale because of significant discomfort or exhaustion.*  **15**

B Cannot, unaided by another person, mount or descend two steps even with the support of a handrail.  **9**

C Cannot, unaided by another person, either:
   (i) mobilise more than 100 metres on level ground without stopping in order to avoid significant discomfort or exhaustion; *or*
   (ii) repeatedly mobilise 100 metres within a reasonable timescale because of significant discomfort or exhaustion.  **9**

D Cannot, unaided by another person, either:
   (i) mobilise more than 200 metres on level ground without stopping in order to avoid significant discomfort or exhaustion; *or*
   (ii) repeatedly mobilise 200 metres within a reasonable timescale because of significant discomfort or exhaustion.  **6**

E None of the above applies.  **0**

**2. Standing and sitting**

A *Cannot move between one seated position and another seated position which are located next to one another without receiving physical assistance from another person.*  **15**

B Cannot, for the majority of the time, remain at a work station:
   (i) standing unassisted by another person (even if free to move around);
   (ii) sitting (even in an adjustable chair); *or*
   (iii) a combination of paragraphs (i) and (ii) for more than 30 minutes, before needing to move away in order to avoid significant discomfort or exhaustion.  **9**

C Cannot, for the majority of the time, remain at a work station:
   (i) standing unassisted by another person (even if free to move around);
   (ii) sitting (even in an adjustable chair); *or*
   (iii) a combination of paragraphs (i) and (ii) for more than an hour before needing to move away in order to avoid significant discomfort or exhaustion.  **6**

D None of the above applies.  **0**

**3. Reaching**

A *Cannot raise either arm as if to put something in the top pocket of a coat or jacket.*  **15**

B Cannot raise either arm to top of head as if to put on a hat.  **9**

C Cannot raise either arm above head height as if to reach for something.  **6**

D None of the above applies.  **0**

**4. Picking up and moving or transferring by the use of the upper body and arms**

A *Cannot pick up and move a 0.5 litre carton full of liquid.*  **15**

B Cannot pick up and move a one litre carton full of liquid.  **9**

C Cannot transfer a light but bulky object such as an empty cardboard box.  **6**

D None of the above applies.  **0**

because of that there would be a substantial risk to any person's mental or physical health if you were found not to have a limited capability for work. This will not apply to you if the risk could be significantly reduced by making reasonable adjustments in your workplace or by you taking medication as prescribed;*

■ are suffering from a life-threatening disease for which there is medical evidence that it is uncontrollable or uncontrolled by a recognised therapeutic procedure (and, in the latter case, there is a reasonable cause for this);* *or*

■ have reached pension credit qualifying age (see Chapter 44(2)) and are entitled to either disability living allowance or personal independence payment.

\* There are equivalent rules for ESA under the 'exceptional circumstances' (see 15 below).

UC Regs, Sch 8, paras 4-6

If you have been found to have a limited capability for work for ESA, you will also have a limited capability for work for universal credit and will not need to undergo two separate assessments.

UC Regs, reg 39(1)(a)

## 4. Treated as not having a limited capability for work

For ESA, you will be treated as not having a limited capability for work, even if you have been assessed as having a limited capability for work, in the following circumstances:

■ you are, or were, a member of the armed forces and are absent from duty through sickness;

■ you attend a training course that day for which you are paid a government training allowance or premium (unless this is only paid to cover travelling or meals expenses);

■ within the six months before your ESA claim you had been found not to have a limited capability for work in a claim for universal credit. The DWP must be satisfied that the universal credit decision was not based on an incorrect fact (see 'Ground 6' in Box O.8 in Chapter 57) and your physical or mental condition has not changed since then;

■ you have failed to provide a 'fit note' (see Chapter 10(9)) within six weeks of being asked to provide one (or within six weeks of the last one running out, if that is later);

■ you are treated as not entitled to ESA because you have done work in that week; *or*

■ you have been disqualified from receiving contributory

---

### 5. Manual dexterity

A *Cannot press a button (such as a telephone keypad) with either hand or cannot turn the pages of a book with either hand.*   15

B Cannot pick up a £1 coin or equivalent with either hand.   15

C Cannot use a pen or pencil to make a meaningful mark with either hand.   9

D Cannot single-handedly use a suitable keyboard or mouse.   9

E None of the above applies.   0

### 6. Making self understood through speaking, writing, typing, or other means which are normally or could reasonably be used, unaided by another person

A *Cannot convey a simple message, such as the presence of a hazard.*   15

B Has significant difficulty conveying a simple message to strangers.   15

C Has some difficulty conveying a simple message to strangers.   6

D None of the above applies.   0

### 7. Understanding communication by:
### (i) verbal means (such as hearing or lip reading) alone;
### (ii) non-verbal means (such as reading 16-point print or Braille) alone; *or*
### (iii) a combination of sub-paragraphs (i) and (ii), using any aid that is normally or could reasonably be used, unaided by another person

A *Cannot understand a simple message, such as the location of a fire escape, due to sensory impairment.*   15

B Has significant difficulty understanding a simple message from a stranger due to sensory impairment.   15

C Has some difficulty understanding a simple message from a stranger due to sensory impairment.   6

D None of the above applies.   0

### 8. Navigation and maintaining safety using a guide dog or other aid if either or both are normally used or could reasonably be used

A Unable to navigate around familiar surroundings, without being accompanied by another person, due to sensory impairment.   15

B Cannot safely complete a potentially hazardous task such as crossing the road, without being accompanied by another person, due to sensory impairment.   15

C Unable to navigate around unfamiliar surroundings, without being accompanied by another person, due to sensory impairment.   9

D None of the above applies.   0

### 9. Absence or loss of control whilst conscious leading to extensive evacuation of the bowel and/or bladder, other than enuresis (bed-wetting), despite the wearing or use of any aids or adaptations which are normally or could reasonably be worn or used

A At least once a month experiences:
(i) loss of control leading to extensive evacuation of the bowel and/or voiding of the bladder; *or*
(ii) substantial leakage of the contents of a collecting device, sufficient to require cleaning and a change in clothing.   15

B The majority of the time is at risk of loss of control leading to extensive evacuation of the bowel and/or voiding of the bladder, sufficient to require cleaning and a change in clothing, if not able to reach a toilet quickly.   6

C Neither of the above applies.   0

### 10. Consciousness during waking moments

A At least once a week, has an involuntary episode of lost or altered consciousness resulting in significantly disrupted awareness or concentration.   15

B At least once a month, has an involuntary episode of lost or altered consciousness resulting in significantly disrupted awareness or concentration.   6

C Neither of the above applies.   0

*ESA Regs 2013, Sch 2, part 1; UC Regs, Sch 6, part 1*
*(ESA Regs, Sch 2, part 1 is similar, with minor differences, mostly in punctuation)*

ESA for at least six weeks during a period of imprisonment or detention.

ESA Regs, regs 32, 32A, 44 & 159; ESA Regs 2013, regs 27, 28, 38 & 95

For universal credit, you will be treated as not having a limited capability for work if you have previously been found not to have a limited capability for work in a claim for universal credit or ESA under the universal credit system. The DWP will not re-assess you unless there is evidence to suggest that the earlier decision was based on an incorrect fact (see 'Ground 6' in Box O.8 in Chapter 57) or that your physical or mental condition has changed since then.

UC Regs, reg 41(4)

## D.8 Limited capability for work assessment – mental, cognitive and intellectual functions

Activities 11 to 17 cover mental, cognitive and intellectual functions and must arise from a mental illness or disablement (although this, in turn, could arise from an underlying physical cause). To be assessed as having a limited capability for work, you need to score 15 points or more. Add together the highest score from each activity heading that applies to you. The scores from these activity headings can be added to those in the physical disability activities (see Box D.7). If any task highlighted in *italics* applies (see activities 11, 12, 13, 14, 16 and 17) you will also satisfy the 'limited capability for work-related activity assessment' (see Box D.9).

| Activity | Points |
|---|---|

### 11. Learning tasks

A *Cannot learn how to complete a simple task, such as setting an alarm clock.* — 15

B Cannot learn anything beyond a simple task, such as setting an alarm clock. — 9

C Cannot learn anything beyond a moderately complex task, such as the steps involved in operating a washing machine to clean clothes. — 6

D None of the above applies. — 0

### 12. Awareness of everyday hazards (such as boiling water or sharp objects)

A *Reduced awareness of everyday hazards leads to a significant risk of:*
*(i) injury to self or others; or*
*(ii) damage to property or possessions*
*such that the claimant requires supervision for the majority of the time to maintain safety.* — 15

B Reduced awareness of everyday hazards leads to a significant risk of:
(i) injury to self or others; *or*
(ii) damage to property or possessions
such that the claimant frequently requires supervision to maintain safety. — 9

C Reduced awareness of everyday hazards leads to a significant risk of:
(i) injury to self or others; *or*
(ii) damage to property or possessions
such that the claimant occasionally requires supervision to maintain safety. — 6

D None of the above applies. — 0

### 13. Initiating and completing personal action (which means planning, organisation, problem solving, prioritising or switching tasks)

A *Cannot, due to impaired mental function, reliably initiate or complete at least two sequential personal actions.* — 15

B Cannot, due to impaired mental function, reliably initiate or complete at least two sequential personal actions for the majority of the time. — 9

C Frequently cannot, due to impaired mental function, reliably initiate or complete at least two sequential personal actions. — 6

D None of the above applies. — 0

### 14. Coping with change

A *Cannot cope with any change to the extent that day-to-day life cannot be managed.* — 15

B Cannot cope with minor planned change (such as a pre-arranged change to the routine time scheduled for a lunch break), to the extent that, overall, day-to-day life is made significantly more difficult. — 9

C Cannot cope with minor unplanned change (such as the timing of an appointment on the day it is due to occur), to the extent that, overall, day-to-day life is made significantly more difficult. — 6

D None of the above applies. — 0

### 15. Getting about

A Cannot get to any place outside the claimant's home with which the claimant is familiar. — 15

B Is unable to get to a specified place with which the claimant is familiar, without being accompanied by another person. — 9

C Is unable to get to a specified place with which the claimant is unfamiliar without being accompanied by another person. — 6

D None of the above applies. — 0

### 16. Coping with social engagement due to cognitive impairment or mental disorder

A *Engagement in social contact is always precluded due to difficulty relating to others or significant distress experienced by the claimant.* — 15

B Engagement in social contact with someone unfamiliar to the claimant is always precluded due to difficulty relating to others or significant distress experienced by the claimant. — 9

C Engagement in social contact with someone unfamiliar to the claimant is not possible for the majority of the time due to difficulty relating to others or significant distress experienced by the claimant. — 6

D None of the above applies. — 0

### 17. Appropriateness of behaviour with other people, due to cognitive impairment or mental disorder

A *Has, on a daily basis, uncontrollable episodes of aggressive or disinhibited behaviour that would be unreasonable in any workplace.* — 15

B Frequently has uncontrollable episodes of aggressive or disinhibited behaviour that would be unreasonable in any workplace. — 15

C Occasionally has uncontrollable episodes of aggressive or disinhibited behaviour that would be unreasonable in any workplace. — 9

D None of the above applies. — 0

*ESA Regs 2013, Sch 2, part 2; UC Regs, Sch 6, part 2*
*ESA Regs, Sch 2, part 2 is similar, with minor differences, mostly in punctuation)*

## 5. Limited capability for work-related activity assessment

The second part of the WCA considers whether you have a *'limited capability for work-related activity'*.

**ESA** – This assessment determines whether you are placed in the work-related activity group (see Chapter 11(4)) or the support group (see Chapter 11(5)). The group you are placed in determines the level of ESA you receive, the responsibilities you must meet to retain the benefit in full and whether or not your ESA award may be time limited.

**Universal credit** – This assessment determines whether the work capability amount is payable (see Chapter 16(6)) and the requirements you must meet to retain universal credit in full (see Box E.3 in Chapter 15).

### The descriptors

The assessment has a list of *'descriptors'* relating to both physical and mental/cognitive functions.

For ESA, if you meet at least one of these descriptors, you will be placed in the support group, in which case your ESA can be paid at a higher level, you will not need to take part in work-related activities and any contributory ESA awarded will not be limited to 12 months.

For universal credit, if you meet at least one of these descriptors, you will receive the work capability amount (see Chapter 16(6)) and none of the work-related requirements will apply to you (see Box E.3 in Chapter 15).

The descriptors are grouped together under the following 16 activity headings (abbreviated here):
■ mobilising;
■ transferring from one seated position to another;
■ reaching;
■ picking up and moving things;
■ manual dexterity;
■ making yourself understood;
■ understanding communication;
■ absence or loss of control … of the bowel or bladder;
■ learning tasks;
■ awareness of hazard;
■ initiating and completing personal action;
■ coping with change;
■ coping with social engagement;
■ appropriateness of behaviour with other people;
■ conveying food or drink to the mouth;
■ chewing or swallowing food or drink.
The descriptors are listed in Box D.9.

### Some 'specific' disease or disablement

In the assessment, it must be clear that an inability to do an activity arises:
■ from a specific bodily disease or disablement, in the case of descriptors 1 to 8, 15A-B and 16A-B;
■ from a specific mental illness or disablement, in the case of descriptors 9 to 14, 15C-D and 16C-D; *or*
■ as a direct result of treatment provided by a registered medical practitioner for such a disease, illness or disablement.
ESA Regs, reg 34(6); ESA Regs 2013, reg 30(6); UC Regs, reg 40(3)

## 6. Treated as having a limited capability for work-related activity

You can automatically be treated as having a limited capability for work-related activity if you:
■ have a terminal illness, which is defined as *'a progressive disease and death in consequence of that disease can reasonably be expected within six months'*;
■ are receiving chemotherapy or radiotherapy for cancer (or are likely to receive it within six months) or you are recovering from that treatment, and the DWP is satisfied that you should be treated as having a limited capability for work-related activity;

■ are pregnant and there would be a serious risk to the health of you or your child if you did not refrain from work-related activity;
■ (for contributory ESA) are entitled to universal credit and have already been found to have a limited capability for work-related activity under that benefit;
■ have a specific disease or bodily or mental disablement and consequently there would be a *'substantial risk'* to the mental or physical health of any person if you were found not to have a limited capability for work-related activity (see below); *or*
■ (for universal credit) have reached pension credit qualifying age (see Chapter 44(2)) and are entitled to:
  – attendance allowance;
  – the highest rate of the care component of disability living allowance; *or*
  – the enhanced rate of the daily living component of personal independence payment.
ESA Regs, reg 35; ESA Regs 2013, reg 31(1)-(2); UC Regs, Sch 9

### Substantial risk

DWP advice suggests that a risk is substantial where the harm or damage to your health would be serious, and could not be prevented or mitigated. Decision makers are encouraged to consider the following:
■ the nature, severity and duration of your health condition;
■ whether or not your condition has been stable;
■ any previous deterioration or improvement in your condition, what caused deteriorations in the past and whether work-related activity is likely to engage any of these triggers;
■ whether there are several conditions that might interact with each other;
■ the nature and strength of any medication; *and*
■ whether any risk can be mitigated.
DMG Memo 01/18

In assessing whether or not there would be a substantial risk, the DWP needs to obtain evidence as to what work-related activity is available in your area, including examples of the least and most demanding types, and therefore what you might be expected to do.
CE/3453/2013 & CE/4887/2014

The risk can arise from the journey to and from the place where work-related activity is undertaken, as well as from the activity itself; consideration should be given here as to whether the risk could be reduced if you were to have someone with you on the journey, and whether such a person would reasonably be available.
CE/5625/2014

This category can be applied even if you do not need to take part in work-related activity for some other reason (eg you are entitled to carer's allowance – see Chapter 11(14)). This will then allow you to be placed in the support group.
CE/1767/2013

## 7. Treated as not having a limited capability for work-related activity

For ESA, you are treated as not having a limited capability for work-related activity if in the six months before your ESA claim you had been found not to have a limited capability for work-related activity in a claim for universal credit. The DWP must be satisfied that:
■ the universal credit decision was not based on an incorrect fact (see 'Ground 6' in Box O.8 in Chapter 57); *and*
■ your physical or mental condition has not changed since then.
ESA Regs 2013, reg 31(3)

## 8. How is the WCA applied?

A DWP decision maker looks at the information you have provided with your claim for ESA or universal credit to see, without having to make further enquiries, if there is evidence that you have a limited capability for work and for work-related activity. They should also see if there is evidence that you can be treated as having a limited capability for work and for work-related activity (see 3 and 6 above). If the decision maker considers they do not have such evidence, they will send you a questionnaire to complete: the *'capability for work questionnaire'*.

## 9. The capability for work questionnaire

The questionnaire begins by asking for general personal details (your name, address, etc). If you are returning the questionnaire late, there is a box where you can explain the reasons for the delay.

You are asked to provide details of your GP and the professional, carer, friend or relative who knows most about your disability or health condition. You are asked if you have cancer and are having, waiting for or recovering from chemotherapy or radiotherapy (in which case, you will not have complete all the questions in the questionnaire).

You are then asked about your disability or condition and the medication you are receiving (including side effects). There are also questions relating to any hospital, clinical or other special treatment you are receiving or that is planned.

Next, there is an assessment of how your conditions affect you. This makes up the bulk of the questionnaire and is divided into three parts. The first part asks about your physical disabilities (see 10 below), the second about your mental, cognitive and intellectual functions (see 11 below) and the third about any problems you have eating or drinking (see 12 below).

You are then asked for any times or dates you would not be able to attend a face-to-face assessment (see 14 below) and any help you would need to attend.

Once you are satisfied that what you have written on the questionnaire is a true reflection of your situation, sign the declaration that follows.

If you are having, waiting for, or recovering from cancer treatment, there is a page at the end of the questionnaire to be completed by the health professional treating you. This could be your GP, consultant or Macmillan nurse. If they are able to complete the page, it should speed up the decision on your claim.

Before you post the questionnaire, photocopy it for future reference.

## 10. Completing the questionnaire – physical disabilities

Part 1 of the questionnaire is divided into 10 activity headings. These headings relate to the activities listed in Box D.7. Note that the wording in the questionnaire is sometimes different from the wording in Box D.7 (in which we use the exact wording of the law).

Under each heading, you are first asked whether you can do that particular activity without difficulty. Read all the text relating to the activity before ticking the box, as you will find out more about what is meant by having difficulty with that activity.

You are then usually asked about specific tasks related to each activity. In each case, you are usually offered one of three boxes to tick: *'no'*, *'yes'* or *'it varies'*, the last being helpful if your condition is variable. When deciding which box to tick, bear in mind that the question is whether you reasonably can or cannot do the particular task safely, to an acceptable standard, as often as you need to and in a reasonable time. Things like tiredness, pain and discomfort may mean that it is not reasonable to expect you to do a task or, although you could do it occasionally, you could not repeat it with reasonable regularity.

There is a box in each section where you can give extra information on the difficulties you have with each task. Use the box to give details of how you are affected if you attempt to complete a task. Are there any risks involved in attempting the task? Have you previously had any injuries or accidents attempting it? Explain how often you would need to rest and whether you take painkillers. Explain the cumulative effects of exhaustion or pain on your ability to complete the task. If you take pain-killing medication, say whether it affects your ability to complete the task effectively. If your condition varies, try to give an idea of how many days each week you would be able to complete the task and how many you would not.

This is a points-related test. To see how many points your answers in this part can potentially score, see Box D.7. We look at each activity heading in more detail below.

**Risk** – When a certain task would be a risk to your health, enough to put off any reasonable person from doing it, you

---

## D.9 Limited capability for work-related activity assessment

If one or more of the following descriptors applies to you, you will be assessed as having a limited capability for work-related activity. For ESA, this will place you in the support group of claimants (see Chapter 11(5)). For universal credit, it will entitle you to the work capability amount (see Chapter 16(6)). In each case, you will be exempt from having to meet work-related conditions in order to keep receiving the benefit in full.

**1. Mobilising unaided by another person with or without a walking stick, manual wheelchair or other aid if such aid is normally or could reasonably be worn or used**
Cannot either:
A mobilise more than 50 metres on level ground without stopping in order to avoid significant discomfort or exhaustion; *or*
B repeatedly mobilise 50 metres within a reasonable timescale because of significant discomfort or exhaustion.

**2. Transferring from one seated position to another**
Cannot move between one seated position and another seated position located next to one another without receiving physical assistance from another person.

**3. Reaching**
Cannot raise either arm as if to put something in the top pocket of a coat or jacket.

**4. Picking up and moving or transferring by the use of the upper body and arms (excluding standing, sitting, bending or kneeling and all other activities specified in this Schedule [ie this box])**
Cannot pick up and move a 0.5 litre carton full of liquid.

**5. Manual dexterity**
Cannot press a button (such as a telephone keypad) with either hand or cannot turn the pages of a book with either hand.

**6. Making self understood through speaking, writing, typing, or other means which are normally, or could reasonably be, used unaided by another person**
Cannot convey a simple message, such as the presence of a hazard.

should be treated as not able to do it. If you have been advised by a doctor, physiotherapist or other health professional to avoid an activity, be sure to note this in the box.
CSIB/12/96

**Pain and fatigue** – Pain, tiredness, stiffness, breathlessness, nausea, dizziness or balance problems might affect how difficult you find it to do things. If doing a particular task causes you too much pain or discomfort, you should be treated as not able to do it.
CIB/14587/96

Similarly, if you find it so tiring or painful to do a particular task that you could not repeat it within a reasonable time, or could only do it so slowly that you could not effectively complete the task, you should be treated as unable to do it.

## Artificial aids
In each case, you are assessed as if you were:
■ fitted with or wearing any prosthesis with which you are normally fitted or normally wear; *or*

■ wearing or using any aid or appliance which is normally, or could reasonably be expected to be, used or worn (eg a walking stick or glasses).
ESA Regs, regs 19(4) & 34(3); ESA Regs 2013, regs 15(4) & 30(3); UC Regs, reg 42(2)

If an aid or appliance has been prescribed or recommended to you by a suitable expert, you will be assessed as if you were using it, unless it would be unreasonable for you to do so. If an aid or appliance has not been prescribed or recommended in your case, you may still be assessed as if using one, if it would normally be used by someone in your circumstances and it would be reasonable for you to do so.
CE/1217/2011

The decision maker needs to consider whether your physical or mental condition would mean that you are unable to make use of the aid or appliance (eg you could not use a walking stick to improve your mobility because of arthritis in your elbows). They also need to take into account how long your condition is likely to last; that is, would it be reasonable

---

### 7. Understanding communication by:
**(i) verbal means (such as hearing or lip reading) alone;**
**(ii) non-verbal means (such as reading 16-point print or Braille) alone; *or***
**(iii) a combination of sub-paragraphs (i) and (ii) using any aid that is normally, or could reasonably be, used unaided by another person**
Cannot understand a simple message, such as the location of a fire escape, due to sensory impairment.

---

### 8. Absence or loss of control whilst conscious leading to extensive evacuation of the bowel and/or voiding of the bladder, other than enuresis (bed-wetting), despite the wearing or use of any aids or adaptations which are normally or could reasonably be worn or used
At least once a week experiences:
A loss of control leading to extensive evacuation of the bowel and/or voiding of the bladder; *or*
B substantial leakage of the contents of a collecting device, sufficient to require the individual to clean themselves and change clothing.

---

### 9. Learning tasks
Cannot learn how to complete a simple task, such as setting an alarm clock, due to cognitive impairment or mental disorder.

---

### 10. Awareness of hazard
Reduced awareness of everyday hazards, due to cognitive impairment or mental disorder, leads to a significant risk of:
A injury to self or others; *or*
B damage to property or possessions,
such that the claimant requires supervision for the majority of the time to maintain safety.

---

### 11. Initiating and completing personal action (which means planning, organisation, problem solving, prioritising or switching tasks)
Cannot, due to impaired mental function, reliably initiate or complete at least two sequential personal actions.

---

### 12. Coping with change
Cannot cope with any change, due to cognitive impairment or mental disorder, to the extent that day-to-day life cannot be managed.

---

### 13. Coping with social engagement, due to cognitive impairment or mental disorder
Engagement in social contact is always precluded due to difficulty relating to others or significant distress experienced by the claimant.

---

### 14. Appropriateness of behaviour with other people, due to cognitive impairment or mental disorder
Has, on a daily basis, uncontrollable episodes of aggressive or disinhibited behaviour that would be unreasonable in any workplace.

---

### 15. Conveying food or drink to the mouth
A Cannot convey food or drink to the claimant's own mouth without receiving physical assistance from someone else;
B Cannot convey food or drink to the claimant's own mouth without repeatedly stopping or experiencing breathlessness or severe discomfort;
C Cannot convey food or drink to the claimant's own mouth without receiving regular prompting given by someone else in the claimant's presence; *or*
D Owing to a severe disorder of mood or behaviour, fails to convey food or drink to the claimant's own mouth without receiving:
(i) physical assistance from someone else; *or*
(ii) regular prompting given by someone else in the claimant's presence.

---

### 16. Chewing or swallowing food or drink
A Cannot chew or swallow food or drink;
B Cannot chew or swallow food or drink without repeatedly stopping, experiencing breathlessness or severe discomfort;
C Cannot chew or swallow food or drink without repeatedly receiving regular prompting given by someone else in the claimant's presence; *or*
D Owing to a severe disorder of mood or behaviour, fails to:
(i) chew or swallow food or drink; *or*
(ii) chew or swallow food or drink without regular prompting given by someone else in the claimant's presence.

*ESA Regs 2013, Sch 3; UC Regs, Sch 7*
*(ESA Regs, Sch 3 is similar, with minor differences, mostly in punctuation)*

to expect you to buy an aid if your condition is unlikely to last long.

Decision Makers Guide, Vol 8, Chap 42, para 42239

### Moving around and using steps

Two tasks are considered under this heading (activity 1 in Box D.7; the heading is differently worded).

First, you are asked how far you can move safely and repeatedly on level ground without needing to stop (with choices of 50 metres, 100 metres, 200 metres or more, or 'it varies'). 'Moving' in this case includes using aids such as crutches, a walking stick or a manual wheelchair (but not an electric wheelchair) without help from another person; it is not simply about walking. If you have difficulty walking, but do not use a manual wheelchair because it would not make getting around any easier for you, explain why. For instance, you may lack the arm strength to be able to manoeuvre the chair properly.

Think carefully before ticking the boxes. Only tick the 'it varies' box if none of the other boxes apply for at least half the time. If you are unsure how far you can move before you need to stop, then you should test yourself on an average day. It would help if you had someone with you to measure the distance in paces; one pace of an average healthy male adult is about three-quarters of a metre. Time how long it takes you to cover the distance.

Second, you are asked whether or not you can go up or down two steps without help from another person if there is a rail to hold onto. Even if you can do this once, if fatigue, pain or co-ordination or balance difficulties prevent you from being able to do it repeatedly (after reasonable rest periods), you should state that you are incapable of doing it. If you have fallen when trying to negotiate steps in the past, write down what happened.

WCA Handbook, para 3.2.2

### Standing and sitting

Two tasks are considered under this heading (activity 2 in Box D.7). First, you are asked if you can move from one seat to another right next to it without help from someone else. This will be relevant if you are a wheelchair user and are unable to transfer from the wheelchair without help. Simple aids such as a transfer board will be taken into account, but the use of more elaborate apparatus, such as a hoist, will be ignored. Write down if you have problems with similar activities, such as getting on and off the toilet or getting in and out of a car.

WCA Handbook, para 2.3.1.2

Second, you are asked how long you can stay in one place (defined in Box D.7 as a 'work station'), either standing or sitting, or a combination of the two, without help from another person, without pain. You are not expected to remain still, and you can change position. With standing, you would be expected to use aids such as a walking stick, if they help. However, if you can only stand using two sticks, you will be treated as unable to stand because this would severely limit the sort of work you could do while standing (such as using the phone).

WCA Handbook, para 3.2.3

Although you are expected to alternate between sitting and standing if this would help you to stay in one place, there may be situations in which you have to alternate so much between the two positions that you cannot 'remain at a work station' in any meaningful way (CE/1516/2012). Let them know if this is the case.

### Reaching

This activity (activity 3 in Box D.7) focuses on your ability to raise your arms above waist height. It is about reaching upwards, not about manual dexterity (which is covered later). To get points, you must have problems with both arms.

When answering whether you can or cannot do the task described, you need to consider whether you can do it repeatedly, not just once.

If you cannot raise either arm to the top of your head as if to put on a hat, you should write this down. Such a limitation would provide you with 9 points in the assessment, but the questionnaire does not ask you this question.

WCA Handbook, para 3.2.4

### Picking up and moving things – using your upper body and either arm

This activity (activity 4 in Box D.7) focuses on your ability to pick up and move light objects (specifically: a half-litre carton of liquid, a litre carton of liquid and an empty but bulky cardboard box). You are not asked if you can pick up the objects from the ground, so it is assumed that you are moving the object at waist level; neither are you asked if you can do each task with just one hand.

WCA Handbook, para 3.2.5

Remember to focus on whether or not you can do the task described repeatedly (after a reasonable rest period in each case), not whether you can do it just once.

If you have dropped objects of a similar size in the past when trying to move them, write down what happened. In this way, you may be able to show that you cannot perform the task in question *'reliably'*.

### Manual dexterity (using your hands)

This activity (activity 5 in Box D.7) focuses on your ability to use your hands and wrists in relation to the kind of things you would be expected to do at work. A number of different tasks are dealt with here, including using a pen or pencil and a suitable keyboard or mouse. It is the problems you have in being able to press, turn, pick up or manipulate the object in question that matters here, not whether you are literate or understand how to use a computer.

WCA Handbook, para 3.2.6

You are asked if you can manage the tasks with either hand. So, if you can manage to do something effectively with one hand, but not the other, you will not pick up any points for that task. Bear in mind that it is your ability to perform each task repeatedly and reliably that matters.

It has yet to be agreed in case law if the phrase *'cannot single-handedly use a suitable keyboard or mouse'*, means you have to be unable to perform both tasks to pick up points.

CE/3466/2012 & CE/3650/2012 provide conflicting conclusions

A *'meaningful mark'* could be as simple as a tick or a cross.

CE/1982/2017

### Communicating – speaking, writing and typing

This activity (activity 6 in Box D.7) looks at your ability to express yourself, by talking or by other methods. It may be relevant if your condition affects your speech and you also have difficulty writing or typing because of reduced dexterity. It is assumed you are using the same spoken language as the person you are communicating with and that they can understand your accent or dialect.

WCA Handbook, para 3.2.8

You are asked if you can communicate a simple message to other people (such as the presence of something dangerous) by speaking, writing, etc but without the help of another person (with the usual answers of 'yes', 'no' and 'it varies').

You would get 15 points if you cannot convey a simple message by speaking, writing, etc. You could also get 15 points if you have *'significant difficulty'* conveying a simple message to strangers and 6 points if you have *'some difficulty'* doing so. If any of these apply, you should make that clear on the questionnaire. You will also need to explain why you cannot write or type the message; if you have dexterity problems, you can cross-refer to the previous activity.

## Communicating – hearing and reading

This activity (activity 7 in Box D.7) is relevant if you have hearing or visual problems. You are asked two questions. First, whether or not you can understand simple messages (such as the location of a fire escape) from other people by hearing or lip-reading without the help of another person. Second, whether or not you can understand simple messages from other people by reading large-size print or using Braille.

You would get 15 points if you cannot understand either a simple spoken message or a simple written message due to sensory impairment. You could also get 15 points if you have *'significant difficulty'* understanding a simple message from a stranger due to sensory impairment and 6 points if you have *'some difficulty'* doing so. If any of these apply, you should make this clear on the questionnaire.

Note that in each case you can score points if you are unable to understand or have difficulty understanding either a spoken message *or* a written message. So, if you have visual problems and cannot read large-size print or use Braille, but would have no problem hearing a simple message, descriptor 7A *'cannot understand a simple message, such as the location of a fire escape, due to sensory impairment'* would apply and you would score 15 points.

CE/3086/2014; WCA Handbook, para 3.2.9

## Getting around safely

This activity (activity 8 in Box D.7) focuses on your ability to navigate and get around safely. It may apply if you have visual problems.

If your vision has only recently deteriorated, this may have affected your confidence and should be taken into account. If your vision varies from day to day, describe what you are like on both bad days and good days and how frequently the former occur.

Give details of any situations that have occurred when you have tried to get around without someone with you, for example bumping into things or people, getting lost, or incidents with traffic. Write down if your driving licence has been withdrawn because of your visual problems.

If you are unable to get around a *'familiar'* place without someone else (due to sensory impairment), you would get 15 points. If you cannot safely cross the road (or deal with a similar hazard) without someone else, you could also get 15 points. You would get 9 points if you are unable to get around an *'unfamiliar'* place without someone else (due to sensory impairment).

WCA Handbook, para 3.2.7

If your ability to get around safely is caused by balance problems (eg from Ménière's disease), this can be accepted as a sensory impairment and can therefore be taken into account. CE/3273/2016

## Controlling your bowel and bladder and using a collecting device

This activity (activity 9 in Box D.7) concerns your ability to control your bowel or bladder (or use a collecting device, such as stoma bag or catheter, without leakage). This is one of the most difficult parts of the questionnaire to complete because the questions are of such a personal nature. Try to put as much information down as you can; the questionnaire is treated with strict confidentiality.

Bladder incontinence that occurs when you are asleep will be ignored, as will minor leakage that can be contained by the use of pads.

If you have mobility problems that mean you are not able to get to the toilet in time, these should be taken into account (CE/1695/2013).

You would get 15 points if the loss of control of your bowel or bladder leads to an extensive evacuation or voiding at least once a month. You could also get 15 points if at least once a month there is substantial leakage of a collecting device which means you need to clean yourself and change your clothing.

If there is an extensive evacuation, voiding or substantial leakage once a week, you will also satisfy the 'limited capability for work-related activity assessment' (see Box D.9).

If, for the majority of the time, you risk the loss of control of your bowel or bladder (leading to an extensive evacuation or voiding where you need to clean yourself and change your clothing) if you are not able to reach a toilet quickly, you would get 6 points.

If any of these apply to you, make this clear on the questionnaire. Explain what precautions you have tried to take and why these may not always work.

WCA Handbook, para 3.2.10

## Staying conscious when awake

This activity (activity 10 in Box D.7) covers fits, seizures or absences. It should cover *'any involuntary loss or alteration of consciousness resulting in significantly disrupted awareness or concentration'* that occurs during the hours when you are normally awake. The DWP describes *'altered consciousness'* as *'... a definite clouding of mental faculties resulting in loss of control of thoughts and actions'*. The DWP does not consider giddiness, dizziness or vertigo (in the absence of an epileptic or similar seizure) to be states of altered consciousness. Neither does it consider that migraine symptoms would result in a significant loss of consciousness in most cases (basilar-type migraine is potentially an exception).

WCA Handbook, para 3.2.11

Drowsiness caused by medication could be considered to be an involuntary loss or alteration of consciousness, if severe enough.

CE/578/2013

## 11. Completing the questionnaire – mental, cognitive and intellectual functions

Part 2 of the questionnaire relates to a number of different conditions, including mental illness, learning difficulties, the effects of head injuries, and autistic spectrum disorders. You are asked broad questions about how your disability or health condition affects your daily life. The questions are grouped into seven headings relating to the activities listed in Box D.8. Note that the wording in the questionnaire is sometimes different from the wording in Box D.8 (in which we use the exact wording of the law).

Under each heading, you are first asked if you can manage with that particular area of daily life; read all the text relating to the activity before ticking the box. Each section is usually broken down into two or three further questions. You are given a number of options in each case, such as *'no'*, *'yes'* and *'it varies'*. There is a box within each section where you can give extra information on the difficulties you have with each area of daily life.

This is a points-related test. To see how many points your answers in this part can potentially score, see Box D.8. We now look at each activity heading in more detail.

## Learning how to do tasks

This activity (activity 11 in Box D.8) focuses on your ability to learn (and remember) how to do things. If you can learn a task one day, but have forgotten how to do it the next day, you will not be considered to have learnt it.

Two types of task are considered: *'simple'* and *'moderately complex'*. A simple task is one involving one or two steps; the example given is the setting of an alarm clock. A moderately complex task may involve three or four steps; the example given is the operating of a washing machine. Other moderately complex tasks could include playing

CDs on a stereo, using a microwave oven or using a games console (at a fairly basic level).

If you are able to learn a moderately complex task, but cannot learn anything more complex than this (a task involving five or more steps – such as setting up a DVD player and programming the channels), you should make this clear on the questionnaire. If you are not able to learn anything *'beyond'* a moderately complex task, you would get 6 points. Write down examples of the kind of tasks you would have problems learning, perhaps ones you tried to learn recently but did not succeed in doing so.
WCA Handbook, para 3.5.2

### Awareness of hazards or danger

This activity (activity 12 in Box D.8) may be relevant if your condition (or the medication you take for it) has affected your concentration such that your awareness of the risks posed by common hazards has been reduced. It may also be relevant if you have a learning disability or a brain injury, or if depressive illness or a psychotic disorder has affected your attention or concentration.

If you consequently need supervising to keep you safe for the *'majority of the time'* (ie you need daily supervision, according to the DWP), you would get 15 points. If you *'frequently'* need supervision (ie several times a week) you would get 9 points. If you *'occasionally'* need supervision, you would get 6 points. Mention any accidents you have had because you were not aware of a danger and list any injuries you, or anyone else, sustained as a result.
WCA Handbook, para 3.5.3

### Starting and finishing tasks

This activity (activity 13 in Box D.8) looks at your ability to start and complete *'personal actions'* without needing prompting from someone else. To be relevant, the problems must stem from an *'impaired mental function'* (such as autism or severe depression), rather than from any physical symptoms you may have. Examples of personal actions could include: making travel arrangements; sorting out the laundry and using a washing machine; writing shopping lists; and dealing with finances. Habitual tasks, such as washing and brushing teeth, should not be considered in isolation here (CE/2966/2014). In each case, your ability to complete the task reliably and repeatedly must be considered.

If you are unable to complete two such actions following on from each other, you would get 15 points. If you are unable to complete two such actions *'for the majority of the time'* you would get 9 points. If you *'frequently'* are unable to do so, you would get 6 points. Provide examples of the kind of things you are no longer able to finish because of your mental condition.
WCA Handbook, para 3.5.4

### Coping with changes

This activity (activity 14 in Box D.8) focuses on your ability to cope with minor changes to your daily routine. Two types of change are considered: *'planned'* and *'unplanned'*. The activity may be relevant if you have a moderate or severe learning disability, an autistic spectrum disorder, a brain injury, an obsessive compulsive disorder, severe anxiety or a psychotic illness.

The activity is not intended to reflect a simple dislike of changes to your routine, but rather your inability to cope with them. If you are unable to cope with any change, such that your day-to-day life would grind to a halt, you would get 15 points. If a minor planned change made your life *'significantly more difficult'*, you would get 9 points; if a minor unplanned change had the same effect, you would get 6 points.
WCA Handbook, para 3.5.5

### Going out

This activity (activity 15 in Box D.8) considers your ability to go out on your own. It is concerned with the problems posed by disorientation or agoraphobia (rather than by visual problems, which are dealt with by activity 8 in Part 1 of the questionnaire; see 10 above). This activity may also be relevant if you have a learning disability.

If you would be unable to get to a place you know well even if you had someone with you, you would get 15 points. If you need to be accompanied to get to a place you know well, you would get 9 points. If you need to be accompanied to get to a place that is unfamiliar to you, you would get 6 points. In each case, the way that you arrive at the destination is not relevant (eg if you cannot use public transport, but could manage to get there by another means unaccompanied, you would not score points).

If you become disoriented or agoraphobic outdoors, explain on the questionnaire what is likely to happen to you were you to go out alone. Provide details of any incidents that have occurred (and what you felt like) if you have attempted to go somewhere alone in the past.
WCA Handbook, para 3.5.6

### Coping with social situations

This activity (activity 16 in Box D.8) focuses on problems you may have in meeting people because of a *'significant lack of self-confidence'* rather than mere shyness or reticence. Meeting people in a workplace setting, as well for pleasure and leisure, is considered. If you have severe anxiety or autism, suffer panic attacks or have agoraphobia, this heading may apply.
WCA Handbook, para 3.5.7; CE/3183/2013

If you are always precluded from meeting with people (whether you know them or not) because of difficulty relating to them or because of significant distress, you would get 15 points. If you are always precluded from meeting with strangers (for the same reason), you would get 9 points. If you are sometimes able to meet with strangers, but for the majority of the time are unable to do so, you would get 6 points.

*'Always'* in this context, has been defined as 'repeatedly', 'persistent' or 'often', rather than on every single occasion, but at a greater frequency than 'the majority of the time'.
CE/4125/2012; CSE/22/2013

### Behaving appropriately

This activity (activity 17 in Box D.8) focuses on the way you behave socially, whether or not you have episodes of *'aggressive or disinhibited behaviour'* that you are unable to control and, if so, how often these occur. It may be relevant if you have a psychotic illness, an autistic spectrum disorder, or a drug or alcohol dependency. It particularly looks at whether behaviour would be unreasonable *'in any work place'*, where expectations may be higher than in general.
WCA Handbook, para 3.5.8

## 12. Completing the questionnaire – eating and drinking

Part 3 of the questionnaire covers two activities in the 'limited capability for work-related activity assessment' (activities 15 and 16 in Box D.9):

- conveying food or drink to the mouth; *and*
- chewing or swallowing food or drink.

Write down on the questionnaire if:

- you cannot get food or drink to your mouth without help from another person;
- you can manage without help, but need to stop repeatedly because of, for instance, poor coordination or poor grip, spasm, shaking or weakness;
- getting food or drink to your mouth would cause breathlessness or severe discomfort;

- you need regular prompting to get food or drink to your mouth, or if you need physical assistance to do so because you have a severe mood or behaviour disorder;
- you cannot chew or swallow food or drink, or cannot do so without stopping, feeling breathless or feeling severe discomfort; *or*
- you cannot chew or swallow food or drink without repeatedly receiving regular prompting, or if you fail to do so (or need regular prompting to do so) because you have a severe mood or behaviour disorder.

## 13. Returning the questionnaire

If you have not returned the questionnaire within three weeks, you should be sent a reminder. If you do not return the questionnaire within a week of receiving the reminder, you will be treated as not having a limited capability for work (and thus not entitled to ESA) unless you can show you had *'good cause'* for failing to return it (or in the case of universal credit, an undefined *'good reason'*).

ESA Regs, regs 22 & 37; ESA Regs 2013, regs 18 & 34; UC Regs, reg 43(3)-(4)

**Good cause** – When deciding whether you had good cause for failing to complete and send back the questionnaire, the DWP must take into account your health, your disability and whether you were outside Great Britain. However, other reasons could be valid. You have a right of appeal against a decision that you failed to send back a completed questionnaire, but you cannot be paid the basic allowance of ESA pending an appeal on this matter (see 18 below).

ESA Regs, regs 24 & 39; ESA Regs 2013, regs 20 & 36

**What happens next?** – Your completed questionnaire is assessed by a DWP-approved healthcare professional. The healthcare professional considers all the evidence on your claim and may request further information from your GP (or any other professional treating you) and/or ask that you attend a face-to-face assessment.

## 14. Face-to-face assessment

The face-to-face assessment will take place at an assessment centre and will be carried out by a healthcare professional working for the Health Assessment Advisory Service. This is operated by Maximus, the organisation carrying out the WCA on behalf of the DWP.

You must be given at least seven days' notice of the date, time and place for the assessment, unless you agree to accept a shorter notice period. This may be arranged over the phone. If you cannot attend, you should inform the office arranging the assessment as soon as possible.

ESA Regs, regs 23(3) & 38(3); ESA Regs 2013, regs 19(3) & 35(3); UC Regs, reg 44(3)

### If you fail to attend

If you do not attend the face-to-face assessment, you will be treated as not having a limited capability for work, unless you can show you had 'good cause' for not attending (see 13 above) or in the case of universal credit, an undefined *'good reason'*. You have a right of appeal against a decision that you failed to attend the assessment.

ESA Regs, regs 23(2) & 24; ESA Regs 2013, regs 19(2) & 20; UC Regs, reg 44(2)

**Payment of ESA** – You cannot be paid the basic allowance of ESA pending an appeal on this matter. You should make a new claim for ESA in case your appeal is unsuccessful, although ESA will not be paid until you have attended a face-to-face assessment.

### At the assessment

When the healthcare professional is ready to see you, they will come to the waiting area to take you into the assessment room. This gives them a chance to watch how you manage to rise from a chair, walk and sit down again or how you manage with a wheelchair.

During the assessment, the healthcare professional will identify the descriptors that they consider apply to you with respect to both the limited capability for work assessment and the limited capability for work-related activity assessment. To do this, they will ask questions about your daily activities, including hobbies or leisure activities. They will observe how you manage during the assessment itself and may give you a clinical examination.

**Physical disabilities** – When answering the healthcare professional, explain your abilities as fully as you can. Tell them about any pain or tiredness you feel, or would feel, while carrying out each task, both on the day of the assessment and over time. Consider how you would feel if you had to do the same task repeatedly. Are you able to complete the task to a reasonable standard? Let them know if there would be any risk if you tried to undertake the task or if it would take you a long time to complete it.

If your condition varies, let them know about the variability and what you are like on both bad days and good days. The healthcare professional's opinion should not be based on a snapshot of your condition on the day of the assessment; they should consider the effects of your condition over time.

**Mental, cognitive and intellectual functions** – The healthcare professional needs to consider a number of different disabilities and conditions that may apply to you, including mental health conditions, learning disabilities and autistic spectrum disorders. To do this, they should ask you how your condition affects your day-to-day abilities (eg going to the shops, cooking food and travelling on your own), whether you can understand and remember things, whether you can concentrate on tasks, how you cope with change and unexpected situations, and how you get on with other people.

When you explain how your condition affects your day-to-day abilities, tell the healthcare professional how you are on an average day. If your condition varies over time or from day to day, tell them how often it varies and for how long at a time. Let them know how you are on bad days, and how often these occur. Answer the questions as honestly and fully as you can. If you do not understand a question, ask the healthcare professional to explain what they mean or to repeat the question.

You may find it helpful to have someone with you at the assessment. This could be a relative, friend or care worker. They can help to fill in any gaps in what you tell the healthcare professional.

### Who makes the decisions?

The decisions (technically called *'determinations'*) on whether or not you have a limited capability for work or a limited capability for work-related activity are not made by the healthcare professional. They will produce a report of the assessment and send it to a DWP decision maker, who will make the decisions. The decision maker may ring you before making the decisions, to ensure they have all the available evidence. They will then write to you, informing you of their decisions.

## 15. Exceptional circumstances

For ESA, if the decision maker decides you do not meet the limited capability for work assessment, they can still treat you as having a limited capability for work if one of the following *'exceptional circumstances'* applies, that is, you are suffering from either:

- a life-threatening disease for which there is medical evidence that it is uncontrollable or uncontrolled by a recognised therapeutic procedure (and, in the latter case, there is a reasonable cause for this); *or*
- some specific disease or bodily or mental disablement, and because of that there would be a substantial risk to

any person's mental or physical health if you were found not to have a limited capability for work. The risk should be linked to the work, and any work considered should be work you could realistically do according to your education or skills (R(IB)2/09). This circumstance will not apply to you if the risk could be significantly reduced by making reasonable adjustments to your workplace or by you taking medication as prescribed.

ESA Regs, reg 29; ESA Regs 2013, reg 25

For universal credit, see 3 above for a similar rule.

**Decisions on exceptional circumstances** – The decision maker decides if any of the exceptional circumstances apply, based on the report from the healthcare professional who examined you. If there is medical evidence from your own doctor, they must consider this as well and decide on the basis of *'the most reliable evidence available'*. You can appeal against the decision made (after requesting a mandatory reconsideration – see below).

ESA Regs, reg 29(4); ESA Regs 2013, reg 25(4)

## 16. Challenging the decision: mandatory reconsiderations

You cannot appeal straight away. You must first ask the decision maker to reconsider the decision, which you can do within one calendar month of the date of the decision letter. This is called a *'mandatory reconsideration'*. You can ask for this over the phone, but you should confirm your request in writing and keep a copy of your letter. See Chapter 57(3) for more on mandatory reconsiderations.

### Reconsidering decisions on limited capability for work

If it is decided that you do not have a limited capability for work and none of the exceptional circumstances apply (see 15 above), you will not be entitled to ESA. If you are claiming universal credit, you will be expected to search for work and be available for work. In either case, you will be sent a decision letter explaining this.

Attached to the decision letter will be a summary of the healthcare professional's report, telling you how many points you scored and from which activities you scored them. For lists of descriptors and points, see Boxes D.7 and D.8. If you have kept a copy of the *'capability for work questionnaire'* that you completed (see 9 to 12 above), you can compare the points you think you should have scored with the points actually awarded. When you ask for the mandatory reconsideration, you need to make it clear which descriptors you believe should apply to you. For instance, someone with severe arthritis in their arms may explain: *"In Activity 3, I cannot raise either arm to the top of my head as if to put on a hat (which would give me 9 points), and in Activity 4, I cannot transfer a light but bulky object such as an empty cardboard box (which would give me 6 points)."*

**ESA entitlement while the reconsideration is being dealt with** – You will not be entitled to ESA while your request for a mandatory reconsideration is being dealt with. You may be able to claim jobseeker's allowance (JSA) instead; see Chapter 13.

If you claim JSA, this will not have a bearing on the reconsideration decision. However, to qualify for JSA you will need to be available for work. You can restrict your availability in any way, providing the restrictions are reasonable given your physical or mental condition (see Chapter 13(8)). In addition, you must be actively seeking work (see Chapter 13(9)) and sign up to the claimant commitment (see Chapter 13(10)).

Once the decision has been reconsidered, the decision maker will send you two copies of the *'mandatory reconsideration notice'* to let you know the outcome. Once you have received this notice and put in an appeal, you can normally receive ESA (see 18 below).

If you obtain medical evidence to support your case (see Box D.10), it is usually best from a tactical point of view to wait until the appeal stage to send it in. This is because the decision maker will often seek advice when they receive such evidence, which will delay the reconsideration and lengthen the period of time during which you have to stay on JSA.

If you can show that your condition has worsened or you have a new condition, you could re-claim ESA (see 20 below).

### Reconsidering decisions on limited capability for work-related activity

**ESA** – If it is decided that you do not have a limited capability for work-related activity, you will be placed in the work-related activity group (see Chapter 11(4)). In that case, you receive a lower level of ESA than if placed in the support group and, if you are entitled to contributory ESA, your award of it will be limited to 12 months.

If you think at least one of the descriptors listed in Box D.9 applies to you, or that one of the circumstances where you can be treated as having a limited capability for work-related activity applies to you (see 6 above), you may wish to ask for a mandatory reconsideration. When you ask for this, you need to make it clear which of the descriptors (or circumstances) applies to you.

**Universal credit** – If it is decided that you do not have a limited capability for work-related activity, you will not normally receive the work capability amount (see Chapter 16(6)), and the 'work-focused interview' and 'work preparation' requirements will be imposed on you (see Box E.3 in Chapter 15).

If you think at least one of the descriptors listed in Box D.9 applies to you, or that one of the circumstances where you can be treated as having a limited capability for work-related activity applies to you (see 6 above), you may wish to ask for a mandatory reconsideration. When you ask for this, you need to make it clear which of the descriptors (or circumstances) applies to you.

## 17. Challenging the decision: appeals

You can appeal against most decisions made during the WCA. You can appeal against a decision:

- that you do not have a limited capability for work (see 2 above);
- that you do not have a limited capability for work-related activity (see 5 above);
- that you do not have good cause (see 13 above) for failing to send back the capability for work questionnaire or attend the face-to-face assessment;
- on exceptional circumstances (see 15 above).

The appeals process is described in Chapter 57.

## 18. Appeals on the limited capability for work assessment

If the mandatory reconsideration notice (see 16 above) confirms that you are not considered to have a limited capability for work, you can now appeal. The appeal tactics you can use in such cases are described in Box D.10.

### Claiming ESA while you are appealing

While you are appealing against a decision on your limited capability for work, you can normally receive the basic allowance of ESA (see Chapter 11(6)), and any appropriate premiums (see Chapter 21) and housing costs (see Chapter 27) in the case of income-related ESA; but see below for exceptions.

ESA Regs, regs 5(4) & 30(1)&(3); ESA Regs 2013, regs 6(5) & 26(1)&(3)

If you have not claimed jobseeker's allowance (JSA) during the mandatory reconsideration, then as soon as the DWP receives your appeal, the ESA basic allowance (and appropriate premiums and housing costs for income-related

ESA) will be put back into payment automatically. The basic allowance (and any premiums/housing costs) can be backdated to when it stopped, provided that either you have sent in fit notes (see Chapter 10(9)) to cover the period or you send backdated fit notes later.

ESA Regs, reg 30(2)(a); ESA Regs 2013, reg 26(2)(a)

If you have claimed JSA during the mandatory reconsideration, you will remain on this unless you specifically ask for your ESA to be re-instated.

In either case, you will need to send in fit notes until the appeal is heard or otherwise dealt with.

If your appeal is successful, you will receive full arrears for any additional component that has not been paid.

**Exceptions** – You cannot receive ESA pending the appeal if you have had two consecutive decisions that you do not have (and cannot be treated as having) a limited capability for work. This will not apply however, if, at the time of the second decision, you can show that you have a different condition or your condition has significantly worsened. If you cannot receive ESA pending the appeal, you can claim JSA instead (see Chapter 13).

ESA Regs, reg 30; ESA Regs 2013, reg 26

You cannot automatically receive ESA pending the appeal if you are appealing against a decision that you do not have good cause for failing to send back the capability for work questionnaire or attend the face-to-face assessment. In these situations, you will need to submit a new claim pending your appeal; payment of ESA may be suspended until you return a capability for work questionnaire or attend a face-to-face assessment. Alternatively, you can claim JSA pending the appeal.

## D.10 Appeal tactics – limited capability for work assessment

This box explains ways to maximise your chance of success with appeals over the limited capability for work assessment. Note that before your appeal can be accepted, you must have first asked for a mandatory reconsideration of the decision (see 16 in this chapter). You have one calendar month from the date the mandatory reconsideration notice was sent to you to appeal. Your appeal will be heard by a First-tier Tribunal, the members of which are independent of the DWP. Details of the appeal process are covered in Chapter 57.

### Opt for a hearing
Your chance of success is much higher if you go in person to the appeal hearing. You can take someone with you and it is a good idea to do so. When you complete the appeal form, make sure you opt for a hearing.

### Prepare your case
Seek advice from Citizens Advice, DIAL or other advice centre. They may be able to help you prepare your case.
Here are some general guidelines to start with:
❑ Use Box D.7 and/or Box D.8 to see which descriptors apply to you and add up the points. Remember to consider your ability to complete each task safely, to an acceptable standard, as often as you need to and in a reasonable time, and the effects of pain, fatigue, etc. You can use this information to gather good medical evidence (see below) and to help you clarify to the tribunal exactly where in the assessment you should score points.
❑ If you think one of the circumstances applies in which you can be treated as having a limited capability for work (see 3 in this chapter) seek medical evidence to confirm which one applies.
❑ If your medication affects your ability to complete tasks, or your physical condition affects your alertness, check whether this has been properly assessed under the mental, cognitive and intellectual functions assessment. Perhaps you have a mental health problem that has not been taken into account. For example, you may suffer from depression or anxiety but have not seen your GP about it. If so, you will stand more chance of having this taken into account if you have evidence, preferably medical evidence, to back you up.

### Get medical or other supportive evidence
Seek medical evidence in advance of the hearing. An advice centre may be able to help you with this. Note that your doctor may want to charge a fee for providing evidence.

Ask your doctor, consultant, physiotherapist, etc to comment on the practical and functional problems you have regarding each descriptor that is at issue in your appeal.
❑ Where there is a dispute, what descriptors do they think should apply?
❑ Is your assessment of your limitations consistent with their understanding of your condition?
❑ Do any of the circumstances apply in which you can be treated as having a limited capability for work?
It is important that your evidence focuses on these things, not simply on what condition you have and the treatment you receive.

If you have recently been awarded disability living allowance or personal independence payment (PIP), the medical evidence obtained in the course of that award may be helpful. This may be the case, for instance, if you are disputing the points awarded in activity 1 (mobilising) and you have recently been awarded the PIP mobility component; although the eligibility criteria differ between the benefits, the medical evidence could well be valid for both. The tribunal should not ignore such evidence (CE/3441/2013 and CE/54/2014).

If your condition has changed since the decision that you are appealing against was made, the tribunal cannot take that into account. So make sure that your evidence is about your condition as it was at the time of the decision.

You know your abilities better than anyone. The DWP healthcare professional will only have seen you briefly so cannot know everything about you. What you say will count as evidence as long as it is not self-contradictory or implausible (R(I)2/51, R(SB)33/85). Your statements will, however, carry more weight when supported by medical evidence.

If you cannot get medical evidence, check whether you could get evidence from any other professional (eg a support worker). Alternatively, you can ask for a copy of your medical records/letters and should only be charged a fee for photocopying.

Once you have obtained evidence, make a copy and send it to HM Courts and Tribunal Service.

### At the tribunal hearing
The tribunal should be conducted in an informal manner and should consider all the medical and other evidence in making its decision, and reach its own conclusions on each descriptor that is at issue in the appeal, not simply adopt the report of the DWP healthcare professional (CIB/14722/96). If you think you need more evidence from your own doctor, ask for an adjournment. However, you do not have an automatic right to an adjournment for this reason, so it is best to get all of your medical evidence ready before the hearing.

### If you get worse before the appeal is heard

A tribunal can look at your situation only as it was at the time of the decision you are appealing against. If your condition has deteriorated since then, or you have a new condition, the tribunal cannot take this into account.

To make sure you do not lose out while your appeal is pending, you should inform the DWP that your condition has deteriorated or that you have a new condition and you would like them to review the decision. If you have medical evidence to support your request, forward it to them. A fresh WCA would normally then be arranged.

If, following the new WCA, it is decided that you still do not have a limited capability for work, you should ask for a mandatory reconsideration of the decision (see 16 above). If the decision is not changed on reconsideration, you should appeal. You can request that an appeal tribunal hears both appeals together.

## 19. Appeals on the limited capability for work-related activity assessment

If the mandatory reconsideration notice (see 16 above) confirms that you are not considered to have a limited capability for work-related activity, you can now appeal. The appeal tactics you can use in such cases are described below.

### Claiming ESA while you are appealing

If you appeal against the decision to place you in the work-related activity group, you will continue to be paid the lower level of ESA for claimants placed in that group. If the appeal tribunal decides that you do have a limited capability for work-related activity, you can be placed in the support group and will become entitled to the higher level of ESA. The difference between the two levels of benefit can be backdated to the time that the additional component for the support group would have become payable (which would normally be once the ESA assessment phase was completed – see Chapter 11(2)).

### Appeal tactics

The general advice provided in Box D.10, which applies to appeals on the limited capability for work assessment, also applies to appeals on the limited capability for work-related activity assessment. Any medical evidence you obtain should focus on confirming which Box D.9 descriptor(s) apply to you or which circumstance where you can be treated as having a limited capability for work-related activity applies (see 6 above). In the former case, you could ask your doctor, consultant or physiotherapist, etc to comment on the practical and functional problems you have with respect to the descriptor(s) in question.

## 20. If your condition deteriorates

### After a decision on limited capability for work

**ESA** – If you re-claim ESA at some point in the future after it has been decided that you do not have (and cannot be treated as having) a limited capability for work, fit notes from your doctor (see Chapter 10(9)) will be sufficient evidence of your limited capability until you are assessed under a WCA, provided:

■ you have a different condition; *or*
■ your condition has significantly worsened since the decision.

It would be helpful if your fit notes clearly showed this was the case. This allows benefit to be paid pending a new decision under the WCA.

ESA Regs, reg 30(2)&(4)(a)-(b); ESA Regs 2013, reg 26(2)&(4)(a)-(b)

If you re-claim ESA for the same condition and it has not significantly worsened, you will not get paid while waiting to be assessed.

**Universal credit** – If it has been decided that you do not have (and cannot be treated as having) a limited capability for work, and your condition has deteriorated or you have a new condition, you should inform the DWP. You should try to obtain evidence of the new condition or the deterioration (eg a letter from your doctor, consultant or specialist nurse) and forward a copy of this to the DWP. The DWP can arrange for a new WCA to be carried out as long as they accept there is evidence to suggest that there has been a relevant change of circumstances in relation to your physical or mental condition.
UC Regs, reg 41(4)

### After a decision on limited capability for work-related activity

**ESA** – If you have been placed in the work-related activity group and your condition has recently got worse, it is possible you will now satisfy one (or more) of the descriptors that will allow you to be placed in the support group (see Box D.9).

If you are still getting ESA, you will need to contact the DWP, explain that your condition has recently got worse and tell them which of the descriptors in Box D.9 now apply to you. If you do this by phone, follow it with a letter to the office confirming your request. If you can, get medical evidence to back up your case, eg a letter from your doctor, consultant or specialist nurse confirming the descriptors that apply to you. Attach a copy of the evidence to your request.

If you are not getting ESA because your 12-month contributory ESA has ended, you will need to make a new claim for ESA. See Chapter 11(20) for details.

**Universal credit** – If you are assessed as having a limited capability for work and your condition has recently got worse, it is possible you will now satisfy one (or more) of the descriptors in Box D.9 that will entitle you to the work capability amount (see Chapter 16(6)). You will need to contact the DWP, explain that your condition has recently got worse and tell them which of the descriptors in Box D.9 now apply to you. If you do this by phone, follow it with a letter to the office confirming your request. If you can, get medical evidence to back up your case, eg a letter from your doctor, consultant or specialist nurse confirming the descriptors that apply to you. Attach a copy of this evidence to your request.

## 21. Re-assessments

Once the first WCA has taken place, you will normally need to attend further WCAs at intervals in the future. The healthcare professional who assesses you as part of the WCA (see 14 above) will provide advice on when you should next be re-assessed. However, you may not need to attend such re-assessments if you:

■ are placed in the ESA support group (see Chapter 11(5)); *or*
■ have a limited capability for work-related activity for universal credit (see 5 above); *and*
■ have a severe, lifelong disability, illness or health condition (see below); *and*
■ are unlikely to be able to work again.

The healthcare professional will consider whether you meet these conditions. If they consider that you do, they will advise that no further assessments will be needed (unless there is a change of circumstances). A DWP decision maker will decide on the matter, based on the advice provided by the healthcare professional.

If you do not need to be re-assessed, you will be informed of this. If you consider that the conditions above apply to you but you have not been exempted from re-assessments, you do not have the right of appeal. You can, however, ask the decision maker to look at the matter again.

### Severe, lifelong disability, illness or health condition

There is no definitive list of conditions which meet these criteria. DWP advice states that your level of function would always need to meet the limited capability for work-related activity assessment (see Box D.9). Conditions that might satisfy this include:

- motor neurone disease;
- severe and progressive forms of MS;
- Parkinson's;
- all dementias;
- all chromosomal conditions;
- Huntingdon's;
- severe irreversible cardiorespiratory failure; *and*
- severe acquired brain injury.

The condition must be lifelong, once diagnosed, and there should be no realistic prospect of your level of function improving. Conditions that might be cured by surgery or improved through rehabilitation will not be covered. The decisions on these matters should be based on treatment currently available on the NHS and not on the prospect of a cure being discovered in the future. Finally, a recognised diagnosis must have been made, so symptoms that have not been formally diagnosed or are still undergoing investigation will not be covered.

DWP Severe Conditions Guidance

# 13 Jobseeker's allowance

**A General conditions**
1 What is jobseeker's allowance? 97
2 Qualifying conditions 97
3 Working full time or part time 98
4 Limited capability for work 98
5 How do you claim? 98
**B Your responsibilities**
6 Introduction 99
7 Signing on and in-depth interviews 99
8 Available for work 99
9 Actively seeking work 101
10 The claimant commitment 101
11 Sanctions 102
12 Lower-level sanctions 102
13 Intermediate-level sanctions 102
14 Higher-level sanctions 103
15 Hardship payments 103
**C Contribution-based JSA**
16 Do you qualify? 104
17 National insurance contribution conditions 104
18 How much do you get? 105
19 Does anything affect what you get? 105
20 How long does contribution-based JSA last? 105

## A. GENERAL CONDITIONS

### 1. What is jobseeker's allowance?

Jobseeker's allowance (JSA) is for people who are unemployed or working less than 16 hours a week and who are seeking work. People with a limited capability for work due to illness or disability should claim employment and support allowance instead (see Chapter 11). Others who do not have to sign on for work (eg carers or lone parents with responsibility for young children) should claim income support instead (see Chapter 19). There are two forms of JSA.

- **Contribution-based JSA**: This is a flat-rate personal allowance based on your national insurance contribution record; it is payable for up to six months and is taxable. For details, see 16 to 20 below.
- **Income-based JSA:** This is means tested, taxable and payable if you have no income or a low income and no more than £16,000 in savings. If you have a partner, they cannot work 24 hours a week or more. For details, see Chapter 20.

One set of jobseeking conditions applies to JSA as a whole, so you must be available for work, taking active steps to look for work, and have a current claimant commitment. For details, see 6 to 15 below.

**Universal credit** – If you are eligible to claim universal credit (see Box E.1 in Chapter 14), you will not be able to make a new claim for income-based JSA and will need to claim universal credit instead (see Chapter 14). If you are claiming contribution-based JSA, some of the rules are different under the universal credit system; we point out when this is the case. Under the universal credit system, contribution-based JSA is known as *'new style'* JSA.

**The benefit cap** – JSA is included in the list of benefits to which the 'benefit cap' applies. This cap limits the total weekly benefits that can be claimed. See Chapter 16(10) and Box G.6 in Chapter 25 for details (including exemptions).

### 2. Qualifying conditions

To be entitled to JSA, you must meet all the following conditions.

- You are not working 16 hours or more a week (see 3 below).
- You do not have a limited capability for work (see 4 below).
- You meet the labour market conditions (see 6 below).
- You are under state pension age (see Chapter 45(2)).
- You are not in full-time education (see Chapter 32(4) for exceptions).
- You are in Great Britain (GB) (see Chapter 54(6) for exceptions).

For contribution-based JSA, you must also meet the contribution conditions (see 17 below) and for income-based JSA, you must meet the income-related conditions (see Chapter 20(2)).

You may be entitled to contribution-based JSA topped up with income-based JSA if you meet the conditions for both (see Chapter 20(5)).

JSA, S.1(1)-(2B)

### Couples

You are considered to be one of a couple if you are married, in a civil partnership, or cohabiting (with someone of the opposite or the same sex). For contribution-based JSA, both members of a couple can claim separately based on their own national insurance contribution records. For income-based JSA, unless you are in a joint-claim couple, one of you must claim for both partners. The person who claims must sign on as available for work and meet all the other qualifying conditions for the benefit.

**Joint-claim couples** – Some couples must make a joint claim for income-based JSA. This applies to couples without dependent children (or 'qualifying young people' – see Chapter 41(1)), where one or both members of the couple are aged at least 18. If you are one of a joint-claim couple, both you and your partner must meet the JSA labour market conditions (see 6 below), unless one of you is 'excused' – see below. You and your partner need to decide which one of you receives payment of JSA.

If one of you does not meet all the labour market conditions, JSA is paid at the single person rate. But if one of you would be eligible for income support (see Box F.1, Chapter 19) or employment and support allowance (ESA – see Chapter 11(7)) instead, that person is excused from meeting the JSA labour market conditions. In this case, there is a choice: the eligible partner can claim income support or income-related ESA for both of you (and the other can sign on voluntarily for national insurance credits), or you claim JSA jointly and get paid the full couple rate but only one of you needs to meet the JSA labour market conditions.

JSA Regs, regs 3A, 3D & Sch A1

There are a few further circumstances in which only one of a joint-claim couple is expected to meet all the JSA qualifying conditions, including if one of you is not habitually resident in GB (in which case you may be paid income-based JSA, but at the same rate as a single person) or is working at least 16 hours but less than 24 hours a week (in which case the normal rate for a couple is payable).

JSA Regs, reg 3E

## 3. Working full time or part time

You cannot claim JSA if you are in *'remunerative work'* of (on average) 16 hours or more a week. Work counts if you are paid or if you work *'in expectation of payment'*. The rules closely follow the income support rules and provide for specific circumstances in which work can be ignored or, conversely, in which you can be treated as working even when you are not (see Chapter 19(3)).

You are not treated as working if you are on certain government employment schemes. If you do not come under the universal credit system (see 1 above), these schemes include: the New Enterprise Allowance, the sector-based work academy, traineeships and the Work Experience programme. If you come under the universal credit system, you are not treated as working if you are on the Work Experience programme.

If you stop work because of a trade dispute at your workplace, you cannot claim JSA; your partner could claim income-based JSA or you could claim income support, but payment would be at a reduced rate.

JSA, S.14; JSA Regs, regs 51, 52 & 53; JSA 2013 Regs, regs 42, 43 & 44

**Partners** – For contribution-based JSA it makes no difference to your entitlement whether or not your partner works or how much they earn. For income-based JSA, see Chapter 20(3).

## 4. Limited capability for work

Generally, you only need to state that you do not have a limited capability for work, which is sufficient to meet the qualifying condition.

**If you are disabled or ill** – If you have a limited capability for work through ill health or disability, you are generally not entitled to JSA, but you may be able to claim employment and support allowance (ESA) (see Chapter 11). Two exceptions apply that allow you to stay on JSA for short periods of sickness (see below).

JSA, S.1(2)(f)

**Up to two weeks of sickness** – If you fall ill, you may choose to stay on JSA for up to two weeks: you must fill in a form (JSA28) to declare that you are unfit for work and for how long.

You may only do this twice* in each 'jobseeking period' (ie period of entitlement to JSA – see 17 below) or, if you are entitled to JSA for over a year (ignoring breaks in entitlement of 12 weeks or less) you may only do this twice* a year. If you fall ill a third time, you may still be able to stay on JSA if it is for an extended period of sickness (see below).

If you fall ill within eight weeks of getting statutory sick pay, you cannot stay on JSA but need to claim ESA instead.
* a 2-week period of sickness that is converted into an extended period is not counted

JSA Regs, reg 55; JSA Regs 2013, reg 46

**Extended period of sickness** – If your illness is expected to last for more than two weeks, but no more than 13 weeks, you may choose to stay on JSA for a continuous period of up to 13 weeks. You need to provide the DWP with evidence of the illness and its likely duration, such as a fit note (see Chapter 10(9)).

You can do this once in any rolling 12-month period. You can also use this option if you have already had two 2-week periods of sickness within the last year (or jobseeking period).

During this 13-week period you will be treated as available for work (see 8 below). You can also be treated as actively seeking work (see 9 below), although your work coach (see 5 below) can require you to take reasonable steps to seek work, depending on the nature of your condition. This reduced conditionality should be reflected in your claimant commitment (see 10 below), which can be revised accordingly for the duration of this period.

If you are still sick after 13 weeks, you cannot stay on JSA but need to claim ESA instead.

JSA Regs, regs 19(1)(lzl) & 55ZA; JSA Regs 2013, reg 46A

## 5. How do you claim?

On the first day you become unemployed, you should claim JSA. Do not delay, otherwise you will lose benefit unless you can show there are 'special reasons' for the delay (see Chapter 56(3)).

JSA is administered by Jobcentre Plus, the arm of the DWP that administers benefits for people of working age. Most contact will be with a *'work coach'* at the local office where you sign on. Decisions on your claim will normally be made at a processing centre, which you can contact by phone.

**Waiting days**

The first seven days of your claim are *'waiting days'*, during which you cannot usually be paid either type of JSA. You do not have to serve waiting days if:

■ your claim is linked to a previous 'jobseeking period' (see 17 below), including that of your partner in the case of a joint claim (see 2 above);

■ a decision maker moves you onto JSA from income support or employment and support allowance; *or*

■ you claim within 12 weeks of being entitled (or your partner being entitled, in the case of a joint claim) to employment and support allowance, incapacity benefit, income support or carer's allowance.

JSA, Sch 1, para 4; JSA Regs, reg 46; D&A Regs 14A(4); JSA Regs 2013, reg 36 & UCPIP(D&A) Regs, reg 48(5)

**Starting your claim**

**England, Scotland and Wales** – The way that you start your claim for JSA will depend on whether or not you are eligible to claim universal credit (see Box E.1 in Chapter 14).

If you are eligible to claim universal credit, call 0800 328 9344 (textphone: 0800 328 1344) or claim online (www.gov. uk/jobseekers-allowance/how-to-claim).

If you are not eligible to claim universal credit, claim JSA online (www.gov.uk/jobseekers-allowance/how-to-claim) or ring the national claim number (0800 055 6688; textphone 0800 023 4888). If you apply online, you should get a text or phone call to arrange for you to see a work coach at a work-focused interview (see below). If you ring the national claim number, call centre staff will take your details and arrange for you to attend the work-focused interview. If you find it hard to claim online or use the phone, you can ask for a paper claim-pack to be sent to you; seek advice if you are refused this option.

**Northern Ireland** – To claim in Northern Ireland, contact your local Jobs & Benefits or Social Security Office.

**The work-focused interview**

The work-focused interview will take place at your local Jobcentre Plus office. You will need to take along documents that prove your identity (eg your passport or driving licence), your date of birth (eg your birth certificate) and your address (eg an energy bill).

At the interview, the work coach will discuss your benefit entitlement and confirm the information you provided online or over the phone. They will ask questions to check whether you are capable of and available for work and what you intend to do to look for work (the 'labour market conditions'; see 6 below). You will also be asked to discuss, agree and sign the claimant commitment (see 10 below).

Once it has been established that you meet the labour market conditions for JSA, your claim will be assessed for both contribution-based JSA and (unless you are under the universal credit system – see 1 above) income-based JSA.

### Payment
JSA is paid every two weeks in arrears, usually into a bank or building society account (see Chapter 56(5)).

## B. YOUR RESPONSIBILITIES

### 6. Introduction
To be entitled to JSA, you must meet the following *'labour market conditions'*. You must:
■ be available for work (see 8 below);
■ be actively seeking work (see 9 below); *and*
■ have entered into a claimant commitment that remains in force (see 10 below).
If you fail to meet the conditions, your JSA may be sanctioned (see 11 to 14 below). If your JSA is sanctioned, you may be able to claim hardship payments (see 15 below).

#### Claiming under the universal credit system
If you are claiming JSA under the universal credit system (see 1 above), the rules match those of universal credit instead. These are described in Chapter 15. You normally have to meet all the following work-related requirements:
■ the work-focused interview requirement (see Chapter 15(3));
■ the work preparation requirement (see Chapter 15(4));
■ the work search requirement (see Chapter 15(5)); *and*
■ the work availability requirement (see Chapter 15(6)).
Box E.3 in Chapter 15 clarifies the requirements you need to meet, depending on your circumstances. If you fail to meet these requirements, sanctions may be applied; either at the low level (see Chapter 15(10)), medium level (see Chapter 15(11) or higher level (see Chapter 15(12)). In each case, payment of JSA will normally cease for the sanction period. You also need to accept a claimant commitment, which is a record of the requirements you are expected to meet (see 10 below).
JSA Regs 2013, regs 4-30

### 7. Signing on and in-depth interviews
#### Signing on
You will normally have to sign on at a Jobcentre Plus office every fortnight (although sometimes you may be required to do so more frequently). If you fail to attend your signing-on day, your benefit entitlement will stop, unless you can show within five working days that you had a good reason for not attending.
JSA, S.8 & JSA Regs, regs 24(6), 25(1)(c) & 27

Each time you sign on, you will be asked to explain what you have done to look for work or improve your prospects of finding work. Keep a record of what you have done in this respect (including any use of the internet and email) so you can show that you are 'actively seeking work' (see 9 below).

#### In-depth interviews
There will also be more in-depth interviews at regular intervals where your claimant commitment will be reviewed and updated if necessary. These interviews can take place over the phone, online or at a Jobcentre Plus office. If you do not take part or are late (having previously been warned, in writing, about lateness) your benefit entitlement will stop, unless you can show within five working days that you had a good reason for failing to take part or for being late. If you contact the DWP within five days but are unable to show

good reason for your failure, a sanction will be applied (see 12 below).
JSA Regs, regs 23, 25(1)(a)-(b) & 70A(2)(b)-(4)

If you are under the universal credit system, you will need to take part in similar *'work-focused interviews'* (see Chapter 15(3)). A sanction will be applied if you do not take part in such an interview (see Chapter 15(10)).
JSA Regs 2013, reg 10

#### Jobseeker's direction
At an in-depth interview, your work coach may issue a *'jobseeker's direction'* requiring you to take a specific step to improve your job prospects. For example, you could be directed to attend a course or to improve the way you present yourself to employers. If you don't comply with a jobseeker's direction that is reasonable in your circumstances, a sanction will be applied unless you have a good reason (see 12 below).
JSA, Ss.17A & 19A(2)(c)

### 8. Available for work
You must be willing and able to take up immediately any paid work of at least 40 hours a week (see below for restrictions you are allowed to make).
JSA, S.6 & JSA Regs, reg 6

**Treated as unavailable for work** – You are not regarded as available for work and therefore not entitled to JSA if you:
■ get maternity allowance or statutory maternity pay; *or*
■ are on paternity, shared parental or adoption leave; *or*
■ are a full-time student – there are limited exceptions (see Chapter 32(4)); *or*
■ are a prisoner on temporary release.
JSA Regs, reg 15

**The permitted period** – For a *'permitted period'* of up to 13 weeks from the beginning of your claim (the length is at the discretion of the DWP), you may be allowed to restrict your availability and jobseeking to your usual occupation and/or to your usual pay. After this, you must be prepared to widen your availability for work and job searching activity.
JSA Regs, reg 16

#### Can you restrict the hours you are available for work?
**The 40-hours rule** – You must be prepared to take up employment of at least 40 hours a week, or less than 40 if required to do so. In most cases, you do not have to accept a job of less than 24 hours a week unless it has been agreed that you may restrict the hours you are available for work to less than 24 hours a week (eg due to caring responsibilities; see below).

JSA is a 7-day benefit, so you must meet the qualifying conditions on each day of the week. This does not mean you must be prepared to work seven days a week. You can restrict the times in the week you are available to take up work (eg Monday to Saturday, 9am to 6pm) provided your *'pattern of availability'* would give you *'reasonable prospects of securing employment'* (see below), your job prospects are not considerably less than they would be if you were available at all times, and your available hours are at least 40 a week.
JSA Regs, regs 6 & 7

You can restrict the hours you are available for work to less than 40 hours a week if that is reasonable in the following situations:
**Carers** – If you care for a child, an elderly person or someone needing care because of their physical or mental condition who is a close relative or a member of your household, you may restrict the hours you are available for work to less than 40 hours, but not less than 16 hours, a week. A *'close relative'* means a partner, parent, parent-in-law, step-parent, son, daughter, son/daughter-in-law, stepson/daughter, grandparent, grandchild, brother or sister, or the partner of any of those.

You must be available for as many hours and at the times

that your caring responsibilities allow, taking into account: the times you spend caring; whether the caring is shared; and the age and physical and mental condition of the person you care for.

You must normally show you have *'reasonable prospects of securing employment'* (see below). However, if you care for a child, the DWP may accept that you do not need to have reasonable prospects of securing employment in light of the type and number of job vacancies within daily travelling distance of your home.
JSA Regs, regs 4 & 13(4)-(7)

**Lone parents** – If you are a lone parent responsible for a child under the age of 13, you can restrict your availability for employment to the child's normal school hours.
JSA Regs, reg 13A

**Laid off or short-time working** – For the first 13 weeks you are treated as available for work, provided you are available to take on casual employment to top up any hours you actually work to at least 40 a week, and you are prepared to resume immediately the work you were laid off from, or return full time to the job in which you are being kept on short time. After 13 weeks, you must show you have reasonable prospects of employment if you want to continue to restrict the hours you are available for work.
JSA Regs, reg 17

**Disability** – You can restrict your hours of availability if it is reasonable given your physical or mental condition (see 'Disability-related restrictions' below).
JSA Regs, reg 13(3)

## Can you put any other restrictions on the type of work you'll accept?

Provided you can show you have 'reasonable prospects of securing employment' (see below), you can restrict:
■ the nature of the employment (eg due to sincerely held religious or conscientious objections);
■ the terms and conditions of employment;
■ the rate of pay – but only for the first six months of your claim (after six months you can't insist on a rate of pay higher than the relevant national living/minimum wage); *and*
■ the areas you will work in – generally, you are expected to be prepared to travel for up to 1½ hours both to and from work.
JSA Regs, regs 8, 9 & 13(2)

**Disability-related restrictions** – You can restrict your availability in any way (eg pay, hours, travel time, type of work), providing the restrictions are reasonable given your physical or mental condition. It is not relevant whether the restrictions affect your employment prospects, providing you do not also put non-disability-related restrictions on your availability. If you do, you will have to show you have reasonable employment prospects given all the restrictions. If you restrict the rate of pay you are prepared to accept, this is not subject to the general 6-month limit, but applies for as long as the restriction is reasonable given your physical or mental condition.

If you refuse a job offer where the hours of work or other conditions of the job are beyond your agreed restrictions, you won't generally be sanctioned for this (see 11 below for more on sanctions).
JSA Regs, reg 13(3)

## Reasonable prospects of employment

If you put any restrictions on your availability, unless these are solely disability-related, you must show you have reasonable prospects of securing employment. The decision maker must consider all the evidence, and in particular:
■ your skills, qualifications and experience;
■ the type and number of vacancies within daily travelling

distance;
■ how long you have been unemployed;
■ your job applications and their outcome; *and*
■ if the restrictions are on the nature of the work, whether you are prepared to move home to take up work.
It is important to think carefully before you put restrictions on your availability. If you can't show you have reasonable employment prospects, your benefit could be disallowed.
JSA Regs, reg 10

## Can you delay taking up an offer of employment?

Generally, you must be able to take up employment immediately. However, if you are a carer (see above) or a volunteer, you must be able to take up employment given one week's notice and attend any employment opportunity interview given 48 hours' notice.

If you care for a child, you can be given up to 28 days' notice to take up employment and seven days' notice to attend an interview, as long as you can show this is reasonable.

If you are providing a service (paid or unpaid) you must be able to take up work given 24 hours' notice. If you are employed for less than 16 hours a week, you must be able to take up work immediately after the statutory minimum notice period (rather than any contractual notice) that your employer is entitled to – usually one week.
JSA Regs, reg 5

## Absences, emergencies and other circumstances

You may be treated as available for work in the following situations. You are also treated as actively seeking work for the week if the situation applies to you for at least three days in the week (unless marked *).
❑ **Absences from home**
■ you are at a work camp – for up to two weeks, once in 12 months;
■ you are on a Venture Trust programme – for up to four weeks, once in 12 months;
■ you are on an Open University residential course – for up to one week per course;
■ you are absent from Great Britain (GB) to attend a job interview (up to one week) or for a child's medical treatment (up to eight weeks) or your partner has reached pension credit qualifying age or is disabled and you are both abroad (up to four weeks) – see Chapter 54(6).
❑ **Emergencies**
■ you need time to deal with: the death, serious illness or funeral of a close relative or close friend; a domestic emergency affecting you, a close relative or close friend; or the death of the person you have been caring for – for up to one week, no more than four times in 12 months (or, if you care for a child, in the case of a death, serious illness or domestic emergency, up to eight weeks once every 12 months);
■ you have recently become homeless, as long as you are taking reasonable steps to find accommodation;
■ you are working as a part-time firefighter or helping to run or launch a lifeboat;
■ you are part of a group of people organised to respond to an emergency – eg part of a search for a missing person.
❑ **Other circumstances**
■ you are sick for a short while and treated as not having a limited capability for work (see 4 above);
■ you are a full-time student on an employment-related course and have prior approval from the DWP – for up to two weeks, once in 12 months;
■ you are taking part in a traineeship;
■ you are looking after your child while your partner is temporarily absent from the UK – for up to eight weeks;
■ you are temporarily looking after a child because the usual carer is ill, temporarily away from home, or looking after

a member of the family who is ill – for up to eight weeks;
■ you are looking after your child during the child's school holidays (or similar vacations) and it would be unreasonable to make other care arrangements;*
■ you are looking after your child who has been excluded from school and it would be unreasonable to make other care arrangements;*
■ you are a party to court or tribunal proceedings and have prior approval from the DWP – for up to eight weeks;
■ you are taking part in annual continuous training as a member of a reserve force for up to 15 days in any calendar year (or 43 days in your first year of training);
■ you are temporarily detained in police custody – for up to 96 hours;
■ you have been discharged from prison, remand centre or youth custody and have not been told to take part in a scheme to help you get employment – for one week from the date of release;
■ you have been threatened with, or subjected to, domestic violence (see below) during the previous 26 weeks by a partner, former partner or a family member (or their partner) – for up to four weeks after you have notified the DWP of the situation, which can be extended to 13 weeks if you are able to provide evidence from someone acting in an official capacity (see below) of the violence or threats. For this to apply, you must no longer be living with the person who inflicted or threatened the violence. It can only apply once during any 12-month period.

JSA Regs, regs 14 & 14A

**Domestic violence** – *'Domestic violence'* is any incident(s) of controlling behaviour, coercive behaviour, violence or abuse, including (but not limited to): psychological abuse, physical abuse, sexual abuse, emotional abuse or financial abuse, regardless of your gender or sexuality.

*'Controlling behaviour'* is an act designed to make you subordinate or dependent by isolating you from sources of support, exploiting your resources and capacities for personal gain, taking away your means of independence, resistance or escape, or regulating your everyday behaviour.

*'Coercive behaviour'* is an act of assault, humiliation or intimidation or other abuse that is used to harm, punish or frighten you.

**Acting in an official capacity** – Someone *'acting in an official capacity'* means a healthcare professional, a police officer, a registered social worker, your employer, a representative of your trade union, or any public, voluntary or charitable body which has had direct contact with you in connection with domestic violence.

JSA Regs, reg 14A(10)

**Holidays** – If you are on holiday in GB, you must still be available for work (although you might not have to be actively seeking work – see 9 below). Contact the DWP before you go. You must show you can be contacted regularly while away and be willing to return at once to start work. If you go abroad on holiday, you are not usually entitled to JSA (see Chapter 54(6)).

## 9. Actively seeking work

As well as being available for work, you are expected to take such steps, usually at least three a week, as you can *'reasonably be expected to have to take'* to have the best prospects of getting employment, eg:
■ applying for jobs;
■ looking for vacancies, including via the internet;
■ registering with an employment agency;
■ on referral from the DWP, seeking specialist advice on improving your prospects with regard to your particular needs or disability;
■ drawing up a CV or getting a reference;
■ drawing up a list of relevant employers and seeking

information from them; *and*
■ seeking information on an occupation.
Even if you've taken reasonable steps to look for work, they can be disregarded if you acted in a violent or abusive way, spoiled a job application or if your behaviour or appearance undermined your prospects of getting a job. But it can't be held against you if the circumstances were beyond your control (eg because of mental health problems).

JSA, S.7(1) & JSA Regs, reg 18

### Absences, emergencies and other circumstances

In some circumstances, for a limited time, you can be treated as actively seeking work. The circumstances in which you are treated as both actively seeking work and available for work are listed in 8 above, under 'Absences, emergencies and other circumstances'. There are other times when you are not expected to take any steps to look for work, although you must still be available to take up work.

JSA Regs, reg 19

**If you are absent from home** – In any 12-month period, you may be treated as actively seeking work for a maximum of:
■ two weeks for any reason (eg a holiday); *or*
■ six weeks if you are blind: the six weeks consists of a maximum of four weeks during which you are attending, for at least three days a week, a training course in using a guide dog, and a further two weeks for any reason; *or*
■ three weeks if you are attending an Outward Bound course for at least three days a week.

In each case, you must give notice (in writing if necessary) that you intend to stay away from home for at least one day in each week and that you do not intend to actively seek work in that week.

The weeks don't have to be consecutive. You can't use more than one provision in any one 12-month period.

For the 2-week 'any reason' provision, once you've notified your intention, you'll be treated as actively seeking work. If you change your mind and don't go anywhere, you must give written notice withdrawing your intention before the start of the week you were due to be away to make sure you don't use up a week unnecessarily.

JSA Regs, reg 19(1)(p)&(2)

**Training** – You are treated as actively seeking work in any week in which you spend at least three days on a government employment or training programme (other than the Work Experience programme) for which a training allowance is not payable.

JSA Regs, reg 19(1)(q)

**Becoming self-employed** – You are treated as actively seeking work for up to eight weeks during which you are taking steps to establish yourself in self-employment, starting with the week you are accepted onto a government scheme for helping people into self-employment.

JSA Regs, reg 19(1)(r)

You are treated as actively seeking work while you are taking part in the New Enterprise Allowance scheme.

Jobseeker's Allowance (Schemes for Assisting persons to Obtain Employment) Regulations 2013, reg 7(1)

## 10. The claimant commitment

The claimant commitment is a record of the work-related requirements you are expected to meet to continue receiving JSA. You have to accept the commitment to remain entitled to JSA. The claimant commitment is normally developed through a face-to-face meeting with the DWP work coach assigned to you. It must include:
■ a record of the work-related requirements that you must meet; *and*
■ details of the consequences if you fail to meet any of them.
If you do not agree with the proposed commitment, you have the right to ask the work coach to refer it to a decision

maker, who will decide whether it is reasonable for you to act in accordance with the commitment. They should make the decision *'so far as practicable'* within 14 days. The decision maker may decide to backdate the claimant commitment, but not necessarily back to your date of claim. Consequently, it would probably be safer to accept the claimant commitment to start off with and then ask for it to be varied (see below).

**Varying an existing claimant commitment** – The claimant commitment can be *'varied'*, ie reviewed and updated, at any time by the DWP. You must be notified of any variation to the claimant commitment before it is varied.

You can also ask that the claimant commitment be varied. However, a claimant commitment will not be varied unless you will continue to be available for work and actively seeking work if you adhere to the new version.

If you do not agree with the proposed variation, you have the right to ask the work coach to refer it to a decision maker, who will decide whether it is reasonable for you to act in accordance with the new claimant commitment. Your JSA will continue to be paid while the decision maker considers the variation, as long as you continue to adhere to the existing claimant commitment. The decision maker should make a decision *'so far as practicable'* within 14 days.

JSA, Ss.9 & 10 (for JSA under the universal credit system, as amended by WRA 2012, S.44)

## 11. Sanctions

Sanctions can be applied if you fail to meet the JSA labour market conditions. These failures are known as *'sanctionable failures'*. Three levels of sanctions apply: lower, intermediate and higher. In each case, payment of JSA will normally cease for a fixed sanction period of between four and 156 weeks. In the case of intermediate-level sanctions, your JSA claim may also be disallowed. See 12 to 14 below.

If a sanction is applied, you may be able to claim hardship payments (see 15 below).

For a joint-claim couple (see 2 above), if just one of you is subject to a sanction, JSA is reduced to the single person rate (a lower reduction will be made if you get hardship payments).

If JSA is already being reduced due to the application of one of these sanctions, and you commit another sanctionable failure, a further reduction is not imposed.

JSA, Ss.19(7), 19A(10) & 19B(8); JSA Regs, reg 70

If a sanction has been imposed, you come off JSA before the sanction period has ended and then re-claim it at a later date, the outstanding sanction period will be applied to the new claim. However, since the sanction period starts from the date of failure, any time spent off JSA is treated as time served and deducted from the sanction period.

Any outstanding sanction period will not be applied in this way if you have been in employment for at least 26 weeks in the intervening period (in one or several spells).

JSA Regs, reg 70C

You can challenge a decision to impose a sanction (see Chapter 57). There is no time limit for asking for a sanction to be lifted; a sanction decision can be revised at any time (see 'Ground 10' in Box O.8 in Chapter 57).

### Good reason

In several of the circumstances that could lead to a sanction, you can avoid one if you can show there was a *'good reason'* for your action or failure to act. This is not defined in law. Decision makers are under guidance to establish three points when deciding whether or not you had a good reason:
■ what would it be reasonable to expect someone to do in the particular circumstances (ie was the action or failure to act preventable);
■ what did you do or fail to do that was different from the expected action; *and*

■ what were the reasons for your action or failure to act.

Decision Makers' Guide, Vol 6, Chap 34, para 34221

Examples of circumstances that should be treated as contributing to good reason for an action or failure to act include where you:
■ are a victim of domestic violence;
■ have a mental health condition or disorder;
■ are the victim of bullying or harassment;
■ are homeless; *or*
■ lose or leave a work experience opportunity or placement other than for reasons of gross misconduct.

Decision Makers' Guide, Vol 6, Chap 34, paras 34226

## 12. Lower-level sanctions

Lower-level sanctions relate to failures to meet conditions attached to employment programmes, training schemes and jobseeker's directions. They can be applied in the following circumstances:
❏ You fail to take part in an interview with your work coach (see 7 above).
❏ You fail to take part in a particular employment programme (such as the Work and Health Programme – see Chapter 34(2)).
❏ You do not comply with a reasonable jobseeker's direction (see 7 above).
❏ You do not take the opportunity of a place on a training scheme or employment programme.
❏ You refuse or fail to apply for, or accept if offered, a place on a training scheme or employment programme that your work coach notifies you of.
❏ You give up, fail to attend or lose through misconduct, a place on a training scheme or employment programme.

In any case other than misconduct, a sanction will not be applied if you can show you had good reason for your action or failure to act (see 11 above). If a failure could result in both a lower and a higher-level sanction, only the higher-level sanction will apply (see 14 below).

JSA, S.19A

### How long is the sanction applied?

In the case of a first sanctionable failure, the sanction will apply for a fixed period of four weeks. However, if this is the second sanctionable failure within 52 weeks (but not within the first two weeks*) and the previous failure resulted in a 4-week sanction, the sanction period will be 13 weeks. In the case of joint-claim couples (see 2 above), both failures must have been by the same claimant for the longer sanction period to apply. Any subsequent failure that occurs within 52 weeks of a previous failure will also result in a 13-week sanction.

If JSA is already in payment, the sanction period runs from the beginning of the benefit week following the one for which you were last paid JSA. If JSA is not already in payment, the sanction period runs from the beginning of the week in which the sanctionable failure took place.

* If the second sanctionable failure takes place within two weeks of the first, the sanction period will be four weeks instead.

JSA Regs, reg 69A

## 13. Intermediate-level sanctions

Intermediate-level sanctions relate only to failures to meet the JSA jobseeking conditions. JSA is disallowed (or paid at a single person's rate if one member of a joint-claim couple fails to meet the conditions – see 2 above) if:
■ you are not available for work (see 8 above); *or*
■ you do not actively seek work (see 9 above).

If you reclaim JSA following such a failure, a sanction of four weeks may apply to your new JSA award if this is your first sanctionable failure. However, if this is the second sanctionable failure within 52 weeks (but not within the first two weeks\*) and the previous failure resulted in a 4-week sanction, your new JSA award may have a sanction applied for 13 weeks. Any subsequent failure that occurs within 52 weeks of a previous failure will also result in a 13-week sanction.

The sanction period runs from the date of claim for the new JSA award. However, the 4- or 13-week sanction period will be reduced by the period of time starting from the day after the end of the benefit week in which you were last paid JSA and ending with the day before the date of claim for the new JSA award.

If you were previously treated as being available for work or actively seeking work (see 8 and 9 above under 'Absences, emergencies and other circumstances') and your failure is a result of this status coming to an end, the DWP can choose not to apply the sanction.

\* If the second sanctionable failure takes place within two weeks of the first, the sanction period will be four weeks instead.

JSA, S.19B; JSA Regs, reg 69B

## 14. Higher-level sanctions

Higher-level sanctions relate to failures to meet conditions regarding employment. They can be applied in the following circumstances:

❏ You lose your job through misconduct (see below).
❏ You voluntarily leave your job (see below).
❏ You refuse or fail to apply for a vacancy or accept a job offer that your work coach notifies you of.
❏ You do not take up a reasonable job opportunity.

JSA, S.19

In any case other than misconduct, a sanction will not be applied if you can show you had good reason for your action or failure to act (see 11 above). In the last two cases above, if your reason for not applying or accepting the offer (or taking up the opportunity) relates to the travel time to and from work, it won't count as a good reason if the travel time is normally less than 1½ hours each way, unless the time is unreasonable due to your health or caring responsibilities.

JSA Regs, reg 72

A sanction will not be applied if you refuse or fail to apply for a job offering a zero-hours contract, nor if you leave such a job voluntarily or lose it through misconduct.

### How long is the sanction applied?

In the case of a first sanctionable failure, the sanction will apply for a fixed period of 13 weeks. However, if this is the second sanctionable failure within 52 weeks (but not within the first two weeks\*) and the previous failure resulted in a 13-week sanction, the sanction period will be 26 weeks. In the case of joint-claim couples (see 2 above), both failures must have been by the same claimant for the longer sanction period to apply. During the sanction period you will still technically be entitled to JSA; since entitlement to contribution-based JSA lasts for a maximum of 26 weeks, you could be left with no payment at all if the 26-week sanction is applied.

For a third (and any subsequent) sanctionable failure within 52 weeks of a previous failure (but not within the first two weeks\*), the sanction period will be set at 156 weeks.

If JSA is already in payment, the sanction period runs from the beginning of the benefit week following the one for which you were last paid JSA. If JSA is not already in payment, the sanction period runs from the beginning of the week in which the sanctionable failure took place.

\* If a sanctionable failure takes place within two weeks of an earlier sanctionable failure, the sanction period will be the same as that of the earlier failure.

**Pre-claim failures** – If your sanctionable failure was due to your voluntarily leaving a job, losing your job through misconduct or failing to take up a job opportunity, and the failure took place before you claimed JSA, the sanction period (as fixed above) will be reduced to take account of any period in which you did not claim JSA. In this case, the sanction period will be reduced by the number of days starting from the day after the sanctionable failure to the day before your JSA claim.

Where the sanctionable pre-claim failure relates to work that was due to end anyway, and the period you were expected to remain in work was less than the sanction period (as fixed above), the sanction period will be based on the period between the day after the sanctionable failure and the day on which your job was due to end. From this figure, any days in which you did not claim JSA will be deducted (as above). Effectively this means that if you claim JSA only after the job was due to have finished anyway, the sanction will not apply.

Pre-claim failures will also be disregarded when working out the sanction periods for later sanctionable failures.

JSA Regs, regs 69 & 70A(1)

### If you lose your job through misconduct

Being dismissed does not necessarily lead to a benefit sanction. When you claim JSA, you will be asked for details of the dismissal at the work-focused interview (see 5 above). It is important to give as much detail as you can, and take along any evidence that could help your argument (such as a letter from your GP or consultant if your condition may have a bearing on the case).

The DWP will contact your former employer to get their side of the story. You can ask the DWP to provide you with a copy of the employer's account. Once you have read this, you may wish to respond to it. Do this in writing, and send the response to the DWP.

You may also be making a claim of unfair dismissal to an Employment Tribunal. If someone is helping with this (eg your union representative) you should ask them for advice. If a sanction is applied, you can challenge the decision (see Chapter 57).

### If you leave your job voluntarily

The decision maker must show that you left your job voluntarily. If they do this, you must show you had a good reason for leaving if you want to avoid a sanction. If you can, show that handing in your notice was the only thing you could do given all the circumstances, including your attempts to resolve the problems. This may enable you to avoid a sanction. You should therefore try to resolve work-related problems (using the firm's grievance procedures, if they have any) before handing in your notice. You should also look for other work before leaving, or find out if you can be transferred to lighter work. If possible, discuss your personal or domestic difficulties with your employer to see if you can resolve the difficulty without handing in your notice.

You should not normally be sanctioned for taking voluntary redundancy, as you are not regarded as having left your job voluntarily.

JSA, S.19(3); JSA Regs, reg 71

### Employment on Trial

This allows you to leave a job and still claim JSA without the risk of being sanctioned if you were in the job at least four weeks and one day, and left within 12 weeks. You must have worked at least 16 hours in each complete week. In the 13 weeks before you took on the job, you must not have worked (including self-employment) or been a full-time student. Dismissal or leaving the job through misconduct could still lead to sanctions. The DWP can provide more details.

JSA, S. 20(3) & JSA Regs, reg 74

## 15. Hardship payments

If your benefit is sanctioned, suspended or disallowed, or there is a delay in making a decision on your claim, you may be entitled to reduced-rate hardship payments of income-based JSA. Payment is not automatic, and in most cases you must show that you or your family will suffer hardship unless benefit is paid. Unless you fall into a particular vulnerable group, no benefit will be paid for the first two weeks.

The applicable amount is calculated as normal (see Chapter 20(6)) but is then reduced by 40% of the appropriate single person's personal allowance. If you, your partner or your child are seriously ill or pregnant, the reduction is just 20%. If your partner is entitled to income support, they can claim it for both of you; it will not be subject to the reduction.
JSA Regs, regs 145 & 146G

You may be entitled to hardship payments if you have no JSA in payment for one of the following reasons.
❏ There is a delay in the decision on your claim because of a question about whether you meet the labour market conditions (see 6 above).
❏ Your benefit has been sanctioned.
❏ Your benefit has been suspended because of a doubt about whether you meet the labour market conditions.
❏ You do not meet the labour market conditions. In this case, you must be considered to be vulnerable (see below) even after the first two weeks. This reason will not apply if you are 'treated' as unavailable for work (see 8 above).
JSA Regs, regs 141 & 146C

### For the first two weeks
Hardship payments are not payable for the first two weeks unless you or your partner are considered to be *'vulnerable'*, ie:
■ are responsible for a child or qualifying young person (see Chapter 41(1)), in which case you must be able to show that the child or qualifying young person will suffer hardship unless payments are made; *or*
■ are pregnant;* *or*
■ are a carer looking after someone who gets a qualifying benefit (see Chapter 8(2)) or has claimed a qualifying benefit in the last 26 weeks and is waiting for a decision or payment, and you cannot continue to care for them unless payments are made; *or*
■ qualify for a disability premium;* *or*
■ are suffering from a *'chronic medical condition which results in functional capacity being limited or restricted by physical or mental impairment'* that has lasted, or is likely to last, for at least 26 weeks, and during the first two weeks your (or their) health would probably decline more than that of a healthy person unless payments are made;* *or*
■ are under 18 and eligible for income-based JSA at that age (see Chapter 20(4));* *or*
■ are under 21 and have recently left local authority care; *or*
■ are homeless.
* In these cases, you must satisfy the decision maker that the vulnerable person will suffer hardship unless payments are made.
JSA Regs, regs 140(1) & 146A(1)

### After two weeks
If you are not considered 'vulnerable', you are eligible for hardship payments only after the first two weeks after the sanction has been applied, or suspension made, etc. You must show that you or your partner will suffer hardship unless payments are made.
JSA Regs, regs 142 & 146D

### What is hardship?
You must complete form JSA/ESA10JP, setting out your grounds for applying for a hardship payment. In deciding whether or not you will suffer hardship if no payment is made, the decision maker must take into account any resources likely to be available to you. They must also look at whether

there is a substantial risk that you will have much-reduced amounts of, or lose altogether, essential items such as food, clothing, heating and accommodation. It is also relevant if a disability premium, or disabled child element of child tax credit, are payable. The decision maker may take other factors into account.
JSA Regs, regs 140(5) & 146A(6)

## C. CONTRIBUTION-BASED JSA

### 16. Do you qualify
To qualify for contribution-based JSA, you must meet the national insurance contribution conditions (see 17 below). You must also meet the qualifying conditions for JSA (see 2 above).

Contribution-based JSA is a personal flat-rate benefit payable for a maximum of six months (182 days). If you don't meet the national insurance conditions, you may be entitled to income-based JSA instead. You may also be entitled to income-based JSA to top up your contribution-based JSA (eg if you have a dependent partner). See Chapter 20 for more on income-based JSA.

### 17. National insurance contribution conditions
There are two national insurance (NI) contribution conditions, both of which you must meet to be entitled to contribution-based JSA. The first condition depends on NI contributions you have actually paid in the relevant tax year. For the second condition, credited NI contributions, as well as paid NI contributions, count. The different classes of NI contribution are covered in Chapter 11(21). Credited contributions are covered in Chapter 11(22).

With both conditions, there is a relationship between 'tax years' and 'benefit years', so it is important to know the difference between them.
**Tax years** – Tax years run from 6 April to 5 April the following year.
**Benefit years** – Benefit years start on the first Sunday in January and end on the Saturday before the first Sunday in January the following year. The 2018 benefit year started on Sunday 7.1.18 and will end on Saturday 5.1.19.
SSCBA, S.21(6)

The *'relevant benefit year'* is usually the benefit year that includes the start of your 'jobseeking period' (see below).
JSA, S.2(4)(b)

### The first condition – paid contributions
You must have paid, or be treated as having paid, at least 26 weeks of Class 1 NI contributions on earnings at the lower earnings limit (see Chapter 11(24)) in one of the last two complete tax years before the start of the relevant benefit year. For instance, if you claim JSA in the 2018 benefit year, you need to have paid 26 weeks' contributions in one of the following tax years: 2015/16 or 2016/17.
JSA, S.2(1)(a), (2) & (4)

If you are the spouse or civil partner of a member of HM forces, you will meet the first condition with sufficient NI contributions paid in *any* complete tax year if you were entitled to an NI credit to cover a period of assignment outside the UK (see Box D.3, Chapter 11) for at least one week in the last complete tax year before the start of the relevant benefit year.
JSA Regs, reg 45(B); JSA Regs 2013, reg 35

### The second condition – paid or credited contributions
You must have paid or been credited with Class 1 NI contributions on earnings 50 times the lower earnings limit (see Chapter 11(24)) in each of the last two complete tax years before the start of the relevant benefit year. For example, if you claim JSA in the 2018 benefit year, you meet this

condition if you paid, or had been credited with, contributions on earnings of £5,600 in the 2015/16 or the 2016/17 tax years. A credited contribution counts as having earnings at the amount of the lower earnings limit for that tax year. You can combine credits and paid contributions.

JSA, S.2(1)(b), (3), (3A) & (4)

### Jobseeking period and linking rules

**The jobseeking period** – This is any period for which you:

- claim and meet the qualifying conditions for JSA – see 2 above;
- are signing on to protect your NI contribution record; *or*
- (unless you are claiming JSA under the universal credit system) get a hardship payment – see 15 above.

The following are not included in the jobseeking period:

- any period in which you lose entitlement because of a failure to sign on or take part in an interview (unless you are claiming JSA under the universal credit system); *or*
- any period in which you are not entitled to JSA because you are involved in a trade dispute.

JSA Regs, reg 47; JSA Regs 2013, reg 37

**Linking rules** – Two jobseeking periods link together and are treated as one single jobseeking period if they are separated by:

- 12 weeks or less; *or*
- one or more linked periods – periods when you are (or treated as) incapable of, or have a limited capability for, work, or entitled to maternity allowance, or training and getting a training allowance; *or*
- a period on jury service.

Gaps of 12 weeks or less between jobseeking periods and linked periods, or between linked periods, are ignored.

JSA Regs, reg 48; JSA Regs 2013, reg 39

For JSA, the beginning of the jobseeking period or any linked period is used to decide the tax years for which you must meet the contribution conditions. For example, if your employment and support allowance (ESA) ends and you sign on for JSA instead, and you claim JSA within 12 weeks of the end of your ESA award, the relevant tax years for your JSA claim will be the same as the ones used for your earlier ESA claim.

**Carers** – Another linking rule helps people who give up work to care for someone to qualify for JSA on the basis of the contributions they paid when they were working. If you were getting carer's allowance and this ended within 12 weeks of the beginning of your jobseeking period (or linked period), the period of carer's allowance entitlement also links to the jobseeking period, if this would help you meet the contribution conditions for JSA. So your benefit year would be the year in which your carer's allowance entitlement began.

JSA Regs, reg 48(2)(a)&(3); JSA Regs 2013, reg 39(2)(a)&(4)

### 18. How much do you get?

| Contribution-based JSA | per week |
| --- | --- |
| Aged under 25 | £57.90 |
| Aged 25 or over | £73.10 |

JSA Regs, reg 79; JSA Regs 2013, reg 49

### 19. Does anything affect what you get?

The amount you get may be affected by earnings or by an occupational or personal pension. Only your earnings (not those of your partner or other family members) are taken into account. Payment is not affected by other income or savings you have.

If one or more of these sources of money mean you are not paid benefit, you will still remain 'entitled' (unless your earnings exceed your 'prescribed amount' – see below). Any day for which you are entitled but not paid will count towards your 182 days of entitlement (see 20 below).

### Earnings

Your weekly earnings from employment or self-employment are deducted in full from the amount of benefit due, apart from an earnings disregard of £5 (or £20 if you are working as a part-time firefighter, auxiliary coastguard, lifeboat operator or member of the reserve forces).

If you receive earnings from any annual continuous training as a member of the reserve forces for a maximum of 15 days in any calendar year (or 43 days in your first year of training), an earnings disregard ensures that you are still entitled to at least 10 pence contribution-based JSA after the earnings have been taken into account. This is to ensure that a new claim for benefit is not necessary after the training has been completed.

In other respects, the assessment of earnings is broadly the same as for means-tested benefits – see Chapter 22(4)-(5).

JSA Regs, regs 98-102 & Sch 6; JSA Regs 2013, regs 58-62 & Sch

**The prescribed amount** – On days in any week when your earnings exceed your *'prescribed amount'* (which is the amount of contribution-based JSA payable for your age plus your earnings disregard minus one pence) you are not entitled to contribution-based JSA and these days do not count towards your 182 days of entitlement (see 20 below).

JSA, S.2(1)(c); JSA Regs, reg 56; JSA Regs 2013, reg 48

### Occupational or personal pensions

Income of over £50 a week from an occupational or personal pension, the Pension Protection Fund or the Financial Assistance Scheme is deducted from the amount of benefit due – eg, if your pension is £55 a week, £5 is deducted from your benefit. Days when no contribution-based JSA is payable because the level of your pension reduces it to nil count towards your 182 days of entitlement. A one-off lump-sum payment does not affect your benefit.

JSA Regs, reg 81(1); JSA Regs 2013, reg 51(1)

### Other benefits

You cannot get more than one contributory benefit at the same time, nor can you get income support or income-related employment and support allowance (ESA) while claiming contribution-based JSA, although you may be entitled to income-based JSA paid as a top-up. However, if you have a partner, they may be able to claim income support (if they come within one of the groups listed in Box F.1, Chapter 19) or income-related ESA (if they have a limited capability for work) for both of you, provided you only get contribution-based JSA. If this applies, you should check whether you will be better off if you claim income-based JSA or if your partner claims income support or ESA.

### 20. How long does contribution-based JSA last?

Entitlement to JSA lasts for a total of six months (182 days). This can be one spell of unemployment lasting for six months or more than one spell of unemployment where you make shorter claims for JSA but your entitlement in each of those claims is based on the same two tax years. Once your 182 days are exhausted, you can only re-qualify when you begin a new 'jobseeking period' (see 17 above) and your new JSA claim is based on different tax years. See 17 above for details of the tax years on which your claim is based.

JSA, S.5

# Universal credit

This section of the handbook looks at:

| | |
|---|---|
| Universal credit | Chapter **14** |
| Your responsibilities | Chapter **15** |
| Calculating universal credit | Chapter **16** |
| Earnings, income and capital | Chapter **17** |

# 14 Universal credit

| | | |
|---|---|---|
| 1 | What is universal credit? | 106 |
| | Universal credit roll-out – Box E.1 | 107 |
| 2 | Do you qualify? | 106 |
| 3 | Joint claims | 106 |
| 4 | Aged 16 or 17 | 107 |
| 5 | How do you claim? | 107 |
| | Claim not required: change in status – Box E.2 | 108 |
| 6 | Date of claim | 108 |
| 7 | Late claims and backpayments | 108 |
| 8 | The decision | 108 |
| 9 | How are you paid? | 108 |
| 10 | Alternative payments | 109 |
| 11 | Change of circumstances | 109 |
| 12 | Care homes and hospitals | 109 |
| 13 | Prisoners | 109 |

## 1. What is universal credit?

*'Universal credit'* is a means-tested benefit paid to people of working age who are on a low income. It does not depend on your national insurance contributions and is not taxable. You can claim it if you are looking for work, if you are unable to work through sickness or disability, if you are a lone parent, if you are caring for someone or if you are working and your wages are low. You can claim it to cover just your needs if you are a single person, or those of your partner and/or children if you have a family.

Universal credit replaces the following benefits:
- child tax credit;
- housing benefit;
- income-related employment and support allowance;
- income-based jobseeker's allowance;
- income support; *and*
- working tax credit

Universal credit is being introduced over several years. The timetable for this is described in Box E.1.

To qualify for universal credit, you must normally meet certain work-related conditions, which vary according to your circumstances. These are described in Chapter 15.

### How is universal credit worked out?

Universal credit is worked out by comparing your basic financial needs with your financial resources. It is worked out on a monthly basis. See Chapter 16 for the calculation.

Your financial resources include your earnings, income, capital and savings. How these are treated in your universal credit calculation is described in Chapter 17.

Your universal credit award may include an amount to cover rent and certain other housing costs: the *'housing costs amount'*. This is explained in Chapter 24.

### Passported benefits

Getting universal credit may entitle you to:
- support for mortgage interest loans (Chapter 26);
- budgeting advances (Chapter 31(3));
- free prescriptions and dental treatment (Chapter 52);
- housing grants (Chapter 30);
- free school meals (Chapter 40(1)); *and*
- help with hospital travel fares (Chapter 55(2)).

## 2. Do you qualify?

**The basic conditions** – To qualify for universal credit, you (and your partner, if you are making a 'joint claim' – see 3 below) must meet the following *'basic conditions'*. You must:
- be aged 18 or over (or aged 16 or 17 in certain cases – see 4 below);
- be under pension credit qualifying age (see Chapter 44(2));
- be in Great Britain (see Chapters 53(3) and 54(7));
- not be subject to immigration control (see Chapter 53(2));
- not be in education (see Chapter 32(2)); *and*
- have accepted a claimant commitment (see Chapter 15(2)).

WRA 2012, S.4(1)

You are not entitled to universal credit if you are a member of a religious order that financially supports you or if you are a prisoner (see 13 below).

UC Regs, reg 19

**The financial conditions** – You must also meet both the *'financial conditions'*:
- you (and your partner if you are making a 'joint claim' – see 3 below) must not have capital of more than £16,000 (see Chapter 17(16)); *and*
- your (and your partner's) earnings (see Chapter 17(1)) or other income (see Chapter 17(7)) are not too high for universal credit to be paid. See Chapter 16 for the calculation.

WRA 2012, S.5; UC Regs, regs 17 & 18

## 3. Joint claims

If you are one of a couple (see below), you must normally make a *'joint claim'* for universal credit. In a joint claim, you and your partner must usually each meet the basic conditions and, jointly, the financial conditions set out in 2 above. However, you and your partner may still be entitled to universal credit as joint claimants if just one of you:
- has reached pension credit qualifying age; *or*
- is in education,

as long as you both meet all the other basic and financial conditions.

WRA 2012, S.3; UC Regs, reg 3(2)

**What is a 'couple'?** – You are considered to be one of a couple if you are married (including in a same-sex marriage), in a civil partnership, or cohabiting (whether with someone of the opposite or the same sex).

WRA 2012, S.39

### Claiming as a single person

If you are one of a couple, you may claim universal credit as a single person if your partner:
- has not reached the age of 18 (and does not qualify for universal credit as a 16- or 17-year-old – see 4 below);
- is not in Great Britain (see Chapters 53(3) and 54(7));
- is a prisoner (see 13 below);
- is a member of a religious order that financially supports them; *or*
- is subject to immigration control (see Chapter 53(2)).

If you are one of a couple but claiming as a single person,

in the calculation of your universal credit the 'standard allowance' that applies in your case (see Chapter 16(3)) will be that of a single person, but your combined capital, earnings and income will be taken into account.
UC Regs, reg 3(3)

### If your partner is away
If you are one of a couple, and your partner is temporarily away from home, you will be treated as a single person if their absence is expected to exceed (or does exceed) six months.
UC Regs, reg 3(6)

## 4. Aged 16 or 17
If you are aged 16 or 17, you may qualify for universal credit if one of the following applies:
❏ You have a limited capability for work (see Chapter 12(2)).
❏ You have a 'fit note' (see Chapter 10(9)) and are waiting for a work capability assessment (see Chapter 12).
❏ You have regular and substantial caring responsibilities for a severely disabled person (see Chapter 16(7)).*
❏ You are responsible for a child aged under 16.
❏ You have a partner who is responsible for a child or qualifying young person (see Chapter 16(4)) and they meet the other basic conditions (see 2 above).
❏ You are pregnant and it is 11 weeks or less before the week in which your baby is due.*
❏ You have had a baby within the last 15 weeks.*
❏ You do not have parental support (see below).*
* These do not apply if you have left local authority care.
UC Regs, reg 8(1)&(2)

### No parental support
You are considered to have no parental support if you are not being looked after by a local authority and you:
■ have no parent* (ie you are an orphan);
■ cannot live with your parents* because;
– you are estranged from them; or
– there is a serious risk to your physical or mental health, or you would suffer significant harm, if you lived with them; or
■ are living away from your parents,* and they are not able to support you financially because they;
– have a physical or mental impairment;
– are in custody; or
– are prohibited from coming to Great Britain.
* or anyone acting in their place
UC Regs, reg 8(3)

## 5. How do you claim?
You must normally claim universal credit online at www.gov.uk/apply-universal-credit. If you need help, you can ring the universal credit helpline (0800 328 9344; textphone: 0800 328 1344); unfortunately this is currently difficult to get through to. A claim may also be made by telephone if the DWP has provided you with a number to do so.
UCPIP(C&P) Regs, reg 8(1)-(2)

You do not need to make a claim for universal credit in the circumstances listed in Box E.2.
**What information do you need?** – You should have the following ready when you start:
■ your postcode;
■ your (and your partner's, if you have one) national insurance number(s);
■ details of your bank, building society or credit union account (if you have one);
■ if you pay rent, your rent agreement and landlord's contact details;
■ details of your (and your partner's) income, savings or capital;
■ details of your (and your partner's) earnings;
■ if you have children, their child benefit reference numbers;
■ if you pay for childcare, how much you pay; and
■ details of any other benefits you (or your partner) receive.
**Appointees** – If a person is unable to act for themselves and therefore cannot make the claim for themselves, an appointee can do so on their behalf; see Chapter 56(4)).

---

## E.1 Universal credit roll-out

### Timetable for introduction
Universal credit has now been rolled out to all Jobcentre Plus areas across England, Scotland and Wales. The introduction was delayed in Northern Ireland; the rollout there started on 27.9.17.

### Live service areas
Before 1.1.18, in some parts of GB, 'live service areas', universal credit was available, but only to certain groups of claimants. The live service has now finished, so if you live in one of these areas and are making a fresh claim for benefit, you will need to claim one or more of the existing means-tested benefits that universal credit is due to replace (see (1) in this chapter). If you live in one of these areas and are already claiming universal credit, you will remain in the universal credit system.

### Full service areas
In 'full service' areas, all new claimants will come under the universal credit system – unless they are responsible for three or more children or qualifying young people (see Chapter 16(4)) at the date of claim. Even if you are responsible for three or more children, you may still come under the universal credit system if:
■ you have had an earlier award of universal credit in the last six months and are re-claiming it; or
■ you are making a new claim as a single person within a month of a joint claim ending because you have split up from your partner.
In a full service area, you will also need to claim universal credit if you have an ongoing award of an existing means-tested benefit (see (1) in this chapter) and you have a change of circumstances that would have previously involved claiming a different means-tested benefit.

For instance, if you are currently receiving working tax credit and you become too ill to work, you will not be able to claim income-related employment and support allowance, but will need to claim universal credit instead. Similarly, if you move home to another local authority area that is full service, you will not be able to claim housing benefit to cover your rent, but will need to claim universal credit.

Any other existing means-tested benefit you are receiving will stop once you are moved onto universal credit. See Box F.2 in Chapter 23, for how tax credit awards are treated in such circumstances.

### Eligibility
To check whether you are eligible to claim universal credit (based on your circumstances and the area you live in), go to www.gov.uk/guidance/jobcentres-where-you-can-claim-universal-credit or use the tool produced by Lasa and the Low Incomes Tax Reform Group: http://universalcreditinfo.net.

If you cannot claim universal credit, you will need to claim one of the existing means-tested benefits. These are described in Chapters 18 to 23.

## Interviews

Once you have made the claim, you will be asked to attend an interview at your local Jobcentre Plus office to confirm the information you have already provided online or over the phone. You will need to take to the interview documents that prove your identity (eg your passport or driving licence), your date of birth (eg your birth certificate) and your address (eg an energy bill), as well as any documents relating to the information listed above. If you are unfit for work, you will also need to take the relevant supporting evidence for this (a self-certificate for the first seven days and a 'fit note' thereafter – see Chapter 10(8)-(9)). All these documents are needed to complete your claim. A further interview will then be arranged: the *'work search interview'*. This may take place following the first interview, or on another day.

**The work search interview** – At the work search interview, you will see a DWP adviser called a *'work coach'*. The work coach will discuss your work prospects and the support you need. A *'claimant commitment'* will be drawn up. This is a record of any work-related conditions (or 'requirements') you must meet to continue receiving universal credit in full. For details, see Chapter 15(2).

If you are required to search for work, you will need to attend further interviews: 'work search reviews'. See Chapter 15(5) for details.

**Attending the interviews** – If you have a carer or an appointee (see above), you can ask them to attend the interviews with you.

If you are not able to get to the Jobcentre Plus office and need the interviews to take place in your home, you should inform the office arranging them as soon as possible.

If you do not attend the interviews, your universal credit claim will be cancelled. If you cannot attend for any reason, get in touch with the office arranging the interviews as soon as possible to explain the reason and re-arrange them.
WRA 2012, S.23

## 6. Date of claim

If you claim online, your date of claim is normally the date on which the claim is received by the DWP. However, if you receive help from the DWP to claim online, your date of claim will be the date that you first asked for such help.

For telephone claims, your date of claim is the date of your initial call to the claim-line, as long as you provide the DWP with all the information they need during that call or, where this is not possible, within one month of that date.

**Defective claims** – If your claim is not completed according to the DWP instructions, it is *'defective'*. You should be informed of this. As long as you complete the claim properly within one month, your claim must be treated as though the original claim had been properly made. Therefore, the date of claim would be the date that the original defective claim was received or made. The 1-month time limit can be extended if the DWP considers this reasonable.
UCPIP(C&P) Regs, regs 8(3)-(6) & 10

## 7. Late claims and backpayments

Claims for universal credit cannot normally be backdated to before the date the claim was made (see 6 above). However, a claim can be backdated for up to one month if any one or more of the following circumstances applies to you (and your partner in the case of a joint claim – see 3 above), as a result of which you could not reasonably be expected to have made the claim any earlier:

■ you were previously receiving an award of either jobseeker's allowance or employment and support allowance and you were not informed that this was due to end before it did so;
■ you have a disability;
■ you had an illness that prevented you making the claim and you have provided the DWP with evidence of this, which they are satisfied with;
■ you were unable to claim online because the system was not working (and you made the claim as soon as it was working);
■ (unless you are claiming in a full service area – see Box E.1) your universal credit award has been terminated because you have separated from your partner, you are the first to let the DWP know about the separation and you claim universal credit as a single person; *or*
■ a joint claim has been refused or terminated because your former partner did not accept a claimant commitment, you have separated from them and you have now claimed universal credit as a single person.
UCPIP(C&P) Regs, reg 26

## 8. The decision

Once a decision on your claim has been made, you will be informed how your universal credit has been calculated and when it will be paid each month. A breakdown of the calculation will be given, which will include a list of the amounts that you are eligible for (see Chapter 16(2)) and how your earnings, income or capital have affected the award (see Chapter 17).

If you are unhappy with the decision, the different ways you can challenge it are explained in Chapter 57.

## 9. How are you paid?

Universal credit is normally paid once every calendar month in arrears. You should get your first payment within seven days of the end of your first monthly 'assessment period' (see Chapter 16(1)) or, if this is not possible, as soon as reasonably practicable after that. This means that you will effectively have to wait around five weeks from the date of claim to receive any payment. In the meantime, you may be able to get help from universal credit advances (see below).

Universal credit is normally paid into a bank, building society, Post Office card account or current account with a credit union (see Chapter 56(5)). A single payment is made to the household. If you are claiming jointly (see 3 above), you and your partner can choose the bank or other account into which the benefit will be paid. If the DWP considers it in the interests of you, your partner, your child or a severely disabled person you receive the carer amount for (see Chapter 16(7)),

---

### E.2 Claim not required: change in status

You do not need to make a claim for universal credit if:

■ you were claiming universal credit jointly with your partner (see 3 in this chapter), that award is terminated because you have split up* and your former partner has already informed the DWP of the separation;

■ you and your new partner were claiming universal credit as two single people, those awards are terminated because you have formed a couple* and universal credit may now be awarded as a joint claim;

■ you were claiming universal credit as a single person, that award is terminated because you have formed a couple (your new partner was not previously claiming universal credit) and universal credit may now be awarded as a joint claim; *or*

■ you were claiming universal credit jointly with your partner and that award is terminated because your partner has died.

* You may be required to provide the DWP with evidence of this.

*UCPIP(C&P) Regs, reg 9(6)-(10)*

they can arrange for the payment to be made to just you or your partner or they can divide it between you.
UCPIP(C&P) Regs, regs 46 & 47

If you are eligible for the housing costs amount (see Chapter 24), it will normally be included in your universal credit payment; it will only be paid direct to your landlord in exceptional cases (see 10 below).

Many claimants will face difficulties in moving from the weekly or fortnightly payments of earlier benefits onto the monthly payment system of universal credit. If you are having difficulty managing your money or paying your bills on time as you transfer onto universal credit, you should be offered personal budgeting support. This may be in the form of money advice (through the Money Advice Service: 0800 138 7777; www.moneyadviceservice.org.uk) or alternative payments (see 10 below).

**Housing benefit transitional payment** – If you are claiming housing benefit and are moved onto universal credit, your housing benefit award can continue for two weeks beyond the day you are first entitled to universal credit. If you claim universal credit because you have moved home, housing benefit can be paid directly to you for two weeks from the day you are first entitled to universal credit.
The Universal Credit (Transitional Provisions) Regs 2014, regs 8(2A) & 8A

**Universal credit advances** – You may be able to claim a short-term advance payment of universal credit to tide you over until you receive the first regular payment – see Chapter 56(6).

## 10. Alternative payments

Alternative payments will only be made if it is considered that you genuinely cannot manage with a single monthly payment and as a result there would be a risk of financial harm to you or your family. Alternative payments could include:

- more frequent payments, eg bi-monthly;
- payments split between partners (rather than a single payment); *and/or*
- rent being paid direct to the landlord.

Alternative payments are designed to be time limited, with support put in place to help you transfer to monthly budgeting.

If you are refused alternative payments, there is no right of appeal but you can ask the DWP to look at the decision again.

### Scotland

If you are claiming universal credit in Scotland, the payment system is more flexible. You can ask the DWP to pay your universal credit twice a month in arrears, rather than once a month. If you get the housing costs amount for renters, you can ask for this to be paid direct to your landlord. In either case, the DWP can only refuse your request where it would be unreasonable to set up such an arrangement. These flexible arrangements will only apply, however, if you claim universal credit in a full service area; they do not apply if you are being transferred from a live service area (see Box E.1).
The Universal Credit (Claims & Payments)(Scotland) Regs 2017

## 11. Change of circumstances

If your circumstances change and this could affect your entitlement to universal credit, you must let the DWP know as soon as you can. If you have a universal credit online account, you should be able to report the change online; otherwise, you can do it in writing or by phone (0800 328 9344; textphone: 0800 328 1344). If you do it in writing, keep a copy of the letter.

The effective date of a change of circumstances will normally be the start of the monthly assessment period (see Chapter 16(1)) in which it occurs. However, if the change is one that will increase your award and you report it late, it will normally only apply from the beginning of the assessment period in which you do report it, unless special

circumstances apply (see Chapter 57(5)). In the case of an award of a 'qualifying benefit', further backdating is possible (see 'Ground 5' in Box O.8, Chapter 57).
UCPIP(D&A) Regs, Sch 1, paras 20 & 21

If the change of circumstances could lead to an increase in your award and the DWP asks for further information or evidence, you will have just 14 days to supply this (unless the DWP allows you more time).
UCPIP(D&A) Regs, reg 33(4)

If the change of circumstances results in a significant increase in your benefit entitlement, you may be able to claim a universal credit advance to tide you over until you receive the increased payment – see Chapter 56(6).

For more on how changes of circumstance relate to universal credit, see Chapter 57(5).

**Earnings** – If you are working for an employer, you will not need to report a change in your earnings if these are reported automatically through the new *'real time information'* (RTI) system. Under the RTI system, your employer sends information directly to HMRC as soon as you have been paid. If you are in any doubt as to whether an RTI system has been set up with your employer, you should contact the DWP to inform them of the change of earnings.

## 12. Care homes and hospitals

You can continue to receive universal credit while you are in a care home or hospital. See Chapters 38(5) and 55(3) for details.

## 13. Prisoners

You are normally not entitled to universal credit if you are a prisoner (whether in prison, a remand centre or a young offender's institution). You are still considered to be a prisoner if you are in custody awaiting trial or sentencing or if you are on temporary release. However, you can receive just the housing costs amount of universal credit (see Chapter 24) for up to six months if:

- you were entitled to universal credit immediately before becoming a prisoner;
- your award of universal credit included the housing costs amount; *and*
- your sentence is not expected to last longer than six months.

You are not entitled to universal credit if you are serving a prison sentence in hospital under s.45A or s.47 of the Mental Health Act 1983. However, if you are detained in hospital after your sentence has come to an end, the normal rules for hospital inpatients will apply to you (see Chapter 55(3)). You are not entitled to universal credit if you are serving a prison sentence in hospital under certain Scottish legislation.
UC Regs, regs 2 & 19

**Advance claims** – The DWP may allow you to make a claim for universal credit up to one month before you are released. Your award will only start once you have been released.
UCPIP(C&P) Regs, reg 32

---

**Disability Rights UK training**

**Welfare Rights and Benefits Overview**
Developed for professionals who work in advice or advocacy, this course is designed to provide a basic overview of the current welfare benefits and social security system. It's ideal for advice workers, social workers, support workers and anyone else supporting clients with social security issues.

To find out more, visit
**www.disabilityrightsuk.org/how-we-can-help**

# 15 Your responsibilities

**A  Work-related requirements**
1   Introduction                                                      110
    Which work-related requirements apply to you?
    – Box E.3                                                         112
2   The claimant commitment                                          110
3   Work-focused interview requirement                               110
4   Work preparation requirement                                     111
5   Work search requirement                                          111
6   Work availability requirement                                    114
**B  Sanctions**
7   Introduction                                                     114
8   The sanction period                                              115
    Sanction periods – Box E.4                                       116
9   Lowest-level sanctions                                           115
10  Low-level sanctions                                              115
11  Medium-level sanctions                                           116
12  Higher-level sanctions                                           116
13  Voluntarily leaving your job or losing pay                       117
14  Misconduct                                                       117
15  Good reason                                                      118
16  How is the sanction calculated?                                  118
**C  Hardship payments**
17  Introduction                                                     119
18  What is hardship?                                                120
19  How much do you get?                                             120
20  How do you claim?                                                120
21  Recovering hardship payments                                     120
22  Challenging decisions                                            120

## A. WORK-RELATED REQUIREMENTS

### 1. Introduction

To qualify for universal credit, you have to meet certain work-related conditions, known as *'requirements'*. These are recorded in a *'claimant commitment'* (see 2 below).

There are four sets of requirements:
■ work-focused interview requirement (see 3 below);
■ work preparation requirement (see 4 below);
■ work search requirement (see 5 below); *and*
■ work availability requirement (see 6 below).

Your benefit is likely to be sanctioned if you fail to meet a work-related requirement (see 7 to 16 below), though hardship payments may be available (see 17 to 22 below).
WRA 2012, S.13(1)-(2)

The circumstances in which each requirement (or a combination) applies to you are listed in Box E.3.

### 2. The claimant commitment

To be entitled to universal credit, you need to have accepted a *'claimant commitment'*. If you are claiming jointly with your partner (see Chapter 14(3)), you both need to have accepted a commitment.
WRA 2012, S.4(1)(e)

---

## Join Disability Rights UK

### Help get our voice heard

Become a member and add your voice to ours. You will receive regular e-bulletins, *Handbook Updater*, and our bi-monthly newsletter including disability and welfare rights news. Membership is open to individuals (from £7.50 a year) and organisations (from £52 a year).

To join, email members@disabilityrightsuk.org or visit **www.disabilityrightsuk.org/membership**

---

**What is a claimant commitment?** – The claimant commitment is a record of the requirements that you must meet to continue receiving universal credit in full. The DWP decides the way in which you can accept the commitment – eg online, by phone or in writing.
WRA 2012, S.14; UC Regs, reg 15(4)

### When you do not have to accept a commitment

The DWP can decide that you do not need to accept a commitment if:
■ you lack the capacity to do so (see below); *or*
■ exceptional circumstances apply in which it would be unreasonable to expect you to accept a commitment (see below).
UC Regs, reg 16

**Lacking capacity** – This primarily relates to claimants who have an appointee acting for them (see Chapter 56(4)). However, such an appointment is not essential and the DWP can accept other evidence showing that a claimant lacks capacity.
Advice for Decision Making, Chapter J1, para J1022

**Exceptional circumstances** – DWP guidance provides examples of when exceptional circumstances may apply, for example:
■ you are in hospital and likely to be there for weeks;
■ the Jobcentre Plus office is closed due to an emergency; *or*
■ there is a domestic emergency preventing you from accepting the commitment.
Once the exceptional circumstances have passed, you would then be required to accept the commitment.
Advice for Decision Making, Chapter J1, para J1026

### Accepting the commitment

The claimant commitment is normally developed through a *'work search interview'* with a *'work coach'* (see Chapter 14(5)). While you are waiting for the work search interview to take place, you will be treated as having accepted the commitment so that universal credit can remain in payment. If you need to consider the commitment before accepting it, the DWP can allow you a *'cooling off'* period of up to a week to consider matters.
UC Regs, reg 15(1)-(2); Advice for Decision Making, Chapter J1, para J1010

**Extending the period** – The period of time within which you have to accept the commitment (or an updated commitment – see below) can be extended if you ask the DWP to review:
■ any action proposed as a work search requirement (see 5 below) or a work availability requirement (see 6 below); *or*
■ whether any limitation should apply to either of these requirements,
as long as the DWP considers the request reasonable.
UC Regs, reg 15(3)

### Reviewing the commitment

The commitment can be reviewed and updated at any time by the DWP (eg when your work-related requirements change). If the commitment is reviewed, you must accept it in order to remain entitled to universal credit.
WRA 2012, S.14(2)

### 3. Work-focused interview requirement

The *'work-focused interview'* requirement is a requirement that you take part in one or more work-focused interviews.
WRA 2012, S.15

A work-focused interview is set up to:
■ assess your prospects and assist or encourage you to obtain or stay in work;
■ identify activities you could do or training, educational or rehabilitation opportunities which might make it more likely that you could obtain or stay in work;

- identify current or future work opportunities relevant to your needs and abilities; *and*
- find out whether you are in gainful self-employment or are in the start-up period of such employment (see Chapter 17(5)).

UC Regs, reg 93

**Work** – This is *'paid work'* – that is work done for payment or in expectation of payment. It does not include work done for a charitable or voluntary organisation or as a volunteer where the only payment you receive is towards expenses. It can include more paid work or better paid work if you already have a part-time or low-paid job.

UC Regs, regs 2 & 87

## 4. Work preparation requirement

The *'work preparation requirement'* is a requirement that you take action to improve your chances of getting work (see 3 above). This can include:

- attending a skills assessment;
- improving your personal presentation;
- taking part in training or an employment programme;
- undertaking work experience or a work placement; *or*
- developing a business plan.

WRA 2012, S.16

## 5. Work search requirement

The *'work search requirement'* is a requirement that you take all reasonable action, and *'any particular action'* specified by the DWP, to obtain work (see 3 above). This can include:

- searching for work;
- making job applications;
- creating and maintaining an online profile;
- registering with an employment agency; *and*
- seeking references.

WRA 2012, S.17

If you are offered a job interview and do not take part in it, you will be treated as not having met the work search requirement.

UC Regs, reg 94

**Work search reviews** – If the work search requirement applies to you, you will need to attend regular *'work search reviews'*. These are designed to check your progress and ensure you are meeting your requirements.

WRA 2012, S.23

### How long do you need to spend searching for work?

You must normally spend a minimum amount of time each week searching for work. This will usually be the number of hours that you are expected to work (see below), less any time that the DWP agrees you can spend:

- carrying out paid work*;
- carrying out voluntary work* (which can only be taken into account for up to 50% of the agreed time – see below);
- carrying out work preparation* – whether as part of the work preparation requirement (see 4 above) or in a voluntary capacity; *or*
- dealing with temporary childcare responsibilities, a domestic emergency, funeral arrangements or other temporary circumstances.

If you have not spent the agreed number of hours a week searching for work, the DWP can still treat you as having met the work search requirement if they are satisfied that you have taken *'all reasonable action'* to obtain work.

* including, in each case, the travel time it takes to get to and from the place where you do this

UC Regs, reg 95; Advice for Decision Making, Chapter J3, para J3065

**Volunteering** – If you are working as a volunteer, the time you spend doing voluntary work can reduce by up to 50% the number of hours that you are required to search for work. This does not mean there is a limit on how much voluntary work you can do. For example, if you are volunteering for 35 hours a week and you would normally be required to search for work for 35 hours a week, this requirement can be reduced by 50% to 17.5 hours.

### How many hours are you expected to work?

You are normally expected to work for at least 35 hours a week. You may restrict your search to work of fewer hours, if you have caring responsibilities or a physical or mental impairment (see below).

UC Regs, regs 88(1)

**Caring responsibilities** – If you are a carer, the DWP will agree to a reduced number of hours that it considers compatible with your caring responsibilities. You must:

- be the *'responsible carer'* of a child aged under 16 (see below);
- be the parent of a child, with caring responsibilities for them, but not the responsible carer;
- have caring responsibilities for someone who has a *'physical or mental impairment'* (see below); *or*
- be a *'responsible foster parent'* (the definition is similar to that of the 'responsible carer' given below).

UC Regs, regs 85 & 88(2)(a)

The DWP must be satisfied that you have reasonable prospects of getting work given those reduced hours. In considering this, the DWP should take into account:

- the type and number of vacancies within 90 minutes of your home;
- your skills, qualifications and experience;
- how long it is since you last worked; *and*
- the job applications you have made and what the outcomes were.

Advice for Decision Making, Chapter J3, para J3056

If you are the 'responsible carer' (see below) of a child under the age of 13, the DWP will agree to a reduced number of hours that it considers compatible with your child's normal school hours (including the time it takes them to travel to and from school). If you are the responsible carer of a child who has not reached school age, the DWP will agree to a reduced number of hours that it considers compatible with your caring responsibilities.

UC Regs, reg 88(2)(aa)&(b)

**Physical or mental impairment** – If you have a physical or mental impairment, the DWP will agree to a reduced number of hours that it considers reasonable in the light of your impairment. It is not relevant whether the restriction affects your job prospects, but you must show the limitation is reasonable and directly connected with your physical or mental impairment.

UC Regs, reg 88(2)(c); Advice for Decision Making, Chapter J3, para J3062

### Responsible carer

You are a *'responsible carer'* if you are:

- a lone parent; *or*
- in a couple who are responsible for a child(ren), and have agreed between you that you are to be nominated as the responsible carer (ie the lead carer) of the child(ren).

**Responsible carer nominations** – Only one of you can be nominated in this way; ie if you have two children, you cannot each be nominated as the responsible carer for one child. You can ask the DWP to change the nomination if you think that the nomination should apply to the other partner. However, if it is less than 12 months since the last decision on nomination, you will need to persuade the DWP that there has been a change of circumstances that is relevant to the nomination.

WRA 2012, S.19(6); UC Regs, reg 86

### Limitations to the work search requirement

**Travel to work** – You do not have to search for work that is more than 90 minutes travel from your home each way.

UC Regs, reg 97(3)

**Previous job** – If you have been in another job recently, for an agreed period (the *'permitted period'*) you can limit your work search to work of a similar nature and rate of pay as the previous job. You can do this for up to three months (at the discretion of the DWP; they can choose a shorter period), starting from:

■ the date of your claim for universal credit; *or*
■ the date on which you finished the previous job, if that is later (ie you were already receiving universal credit when working previously but were exempt from work-related requirements).

This will only apply if the DWP is satisfied that you have reasonable prospects of getting work despite the limitation.
UC Regs, reg 97(4)-(5)

**Disability** – If your *'physical or mental impairment has a substantial adverse effect'* on your ability to carry out work of a particular nature or in a particular place, you cannot be expected to search for such work or in such a place. If you have medical

## E.3 Which work-related requirements apply to you?

There are four types of work-related requirement that apply to universal credit:

■ work-focused interview requirement;
■ work preparation requirement;
■ work search requirement; *and*
■ work availability requirement.

Which, if any, apply to you depends on your circumstances.

### None of the work-related requirements apply

In some circumstances, none of the work-related requirements will apply to you. This may be because of your disability or health condition, your caring responsibilities or because you are already working enough hours. The circumstances in which none of the work-related requirements apply to you are as follows:

### Disability or health condition

❑ As a consequence of a *'specific disease or disablement'* (whether physical or mental), you have a *'limited capability for work-related activity'* (see Chapter 12(5)).
WRA 2012, S.19(2)(a)

### Caring responsibilities

❑ You have *'regular and substantial caring responsibilities for a severely disabled person'* (see Chapter 16(7)).
❑ You have caring responsibilities for at least one severely disabled person for 35 hours a week or more but are not entitled to carer's allowance, and the DWP is satisfied that it would be unreasonable for you to meet the work search and work availability requirements. A *'severely disabled person'* is someone who gets:
 – armed forces independence payment;
 – attendance allowance;
 – disability living allowance middle or highest rate care component;
 – constant attendance allowance (under the Armed Forces or Industrial Injuries schemes); *or*
 – personal independence payment daily living component.
WRA 2012, S.19(2)(b); UC Regs, reg 89(1)(b)&(2)

### Education and training

❑ You are on a full-time non-advanced course of study or training, are aged under 21 (or are 21 and reached that age while on the course) and are without parental support (see Chapter 14(4)).
❑ You are a student who is entitled to universal credit and you have student income for your course that is taken into account in your universal credit calculation (see Chapter 32(3)).
UC Regs, reg 89(1)(e)

### Pregnancy and maternity

❑ You are pregnant and it is 11 weeks or less before the week your baby is due.
❑ You have had a baby within the last 15 weeks (including if your baby was stillborn).
UC Regs, reg 89(1)(c)

### Childcare responsibilities

❑ You are the *'responsible carer'* of a child under 1 (see 5 in this chapter).
❑ You are an *'adopter'* and it is 12 months or less since your child was placed with you; in this case you can ask that this 12-month period starts in the 14 days before the placement. You are an adopter if you have been matched with a child (who is not a close relative or your foster child) for adoption and you are, or will be, their responsible carer.
❑ You are the *'responsible foster parent'* (the definition is similar to that of the responsible carer) of a child under 1.
WRA 2012, S.19(2)(c) & (6); UC Regs, reg 89(1)(d)&(f) & (3)

### Already working

❑ You are working (whether employed or self-employed) and your monthly earnings are at least at your *'individual threshold'* if you are single, or your combined earnings are at least at your *'earnings threshold for a couple'* if you are one of a couple. It is your gross earnings that count, ie before any income tax, national insurance contributions or pension contributions are paid, rounded down to the nearest £1.
❑ You are self-employed and a *'minimum income floor'* has been applied (see Chapter 17(5)).

**Individual threshold** – To obtain your *'individual threshold'*, the hourly rate of the national living/minimum wage that applies in your case (see Box I.5 in Chapter 33) is multiplied by the number of hours you are expected to work each week. This figure is converted to a monthly amount by multiplying by 52 and dividing by 12.

You are normally expected to work 35 hours a week (or 30 hours if you are an apprentice), although the DWP can agree to reduce this if you have caring responsibilities or a physical or mental impairment; the rules are the same as for the 'work search requirement' – see 5 in this chapter for details.

However, if you would otherwise only have to meet the 'work-focused interview requirement' and/or the 'work preparation requirement', you will be expected to work just 16 hours a week.

**Earnings threshold for a couple** – This will normally be the sum of your individual thresholds (as above). If you are one of a couple but claiming as a single person (see Chapter 14(3)), your earnings threshold will be your individual threshold added to the amount someone would be paid working for 35 hours a week at the national living/minimum wage, again converted to a monthly amount.
UC Regs, reg 90

### Age

❑ You have reached pension credit qualifying age (see Chapter 44(2)).
UC Regs, reg 89(1)(a)

evidence (such as a letter from your GP) confirming that you cannot carry out certain work or work in certain places, you should provide the DWP with a copy of that evidence.
UC Regs, reg 97(6)

## When does the work search requirement not apply?
A work search requirement will not apply to you if:
■ you are attending a court or tribunal as a party to the proceedings or as a witness;

■ you are in prison;
■ you are temporarily away from GB for medical treatment or medically approved convalescence or care, or are accompanying your partner, child or qualifying young person (see Chapter 16(4)) for such treatment, convalescence or care (for up to six months);
■ your partner or child (or qualifying young person) has died within the past six months;
■ you are receiving and taking part in a structured alcohol

### Domestic violence
❏ No work-related requirement will apply to you for a period of 13 consecutive weeks in the following circumstances:
■ you notify the DWP that you have suffered, or been threatened with, domestic violence (see below) by your partner, former partner or a family member (see below) within the last six months;
■ on the date that you notify the DWP, you are not living with the person who inflicted or threatened the violence; *and*
■ within one month of the notification, you provide evidence from someone acting in an official capacity (see below) which confirms that your circumstances are consistent with someone who has suffered domestic violence or the threat of domestic violence within the last six months, and that you have contacted them in connection with the incident.
The 13-week period will not be applied if one has already been applied in the 12 months before you notify the DWP of the incident.

*'Domestic violence'* is any incident(s) of controlling behaviour, coercive behaviour, violence or abuse, including (but not limited to): psychological abuse, physical abuse, sexual abuse, emotional abuse or financial abuse, regardless of your gender or sexuality.

*'Controlling behaviour'* is an act designed to make you subordinate or dependent by isolating you from sources of support, exploiting your resources and capacities for personal gain, taking away your means of independence, resistance or escape or regulating your everyday behaviour.

*'Coercive behaviour'* is an act of assault, humiliation or intimidation or other abuse that is used to harm, punish or frighten you.

A *'family member'* is a grandparent, grandchild, parent, step-parent, parent-in-law, son, stepson, son-in-law, daughter, stepdaughter, daughter-in-law, brother, stepbrother, brother-in-law, sister, stepsister, sister-in-law (or partner of any of these).

Someone *'acting in an official capacity'* means a healthcare professional, a police officer, a registered social worker, your employer, a representative of your trade union, or any public, voluntary or charitable body which has had direct contact with you in connection with domestic violence.
UC Regs, reg 98

### Only the work-focused interview requirement applies
#### Childcare responsibilities
In some circumstances, it is accepted that due to your childcare responsibilities it would be inappropriate for you to prepare for work, search for work or be available for work. The circumstances in which only the work-focused interview requirement will apply to you are as follows:
❏ You are the responsible carer (see 5 in this chapter) of a child aged 1.
❏ You are the *'responsible foster parent'* (the definition is similar to that of the responsible carer) of a child aged at least 1 but under 16.
❏ You are the responsible foster parent of a *'qualifying young person'* (see Chapter 16(4)) and the DWP is satisfied that the young person has care needs which would make it unreasonable for you to meet a work search requirement or a work availability requirement.

❏ You are a foster parent (but not the responsible foster parent as above) of a child or qualifying young person and the DWP is satisfied that the child or young person has care needs which would make it unreasonable for you to meet a work search requirement or a work availability requirement.
❏ You have been a foster parent (falling within one of the above three cases) in the past eight weeks, you currently do not have a child or qualifying young person placed with you, but you expect to resume being a foster parent.
❏ You are the responsible carer of a child under 16 who is not your child or stepchild (eg you are their grandparent), who you have started to care for in the past 12 months because:
  – they are an orphan;
  – their parents are unable to look after them; *or*
  – it is likely that they would otherwise have to go into local authority care because of concerns over their welfare.
WRA 2012, S.20(1)(a); UC Regs, reg 91

### Only the work-focused interview and work preparation requirements apply
#### Disability or health condition
You will not be expected to search for work or be available for work if you have a *'specific disease or disablement'* (whether physical or mental), as a consequence of which you have a *'limited capability for work'* (see Chapter 12(2)). In this case, only the work-focused interview and work preparation requirements will apply to you. (If you have a *'limited capability for work-related activity'* none of the work-related requirements will apply to you – see above.)
WRA 2012, S.21

#### Childcare responsibilities
You will not be expected to search for work or be available for work if you are the responsible carer (see 5 in this chapter) of a child aged 2.
WRA 2012, S.21(1)(aa)

**Domestic violence** – You will not be expected to search for work or be available for work for a period of 13 weeks if:
■ you have been the victim of domestic violence (see above);
■ you are the responsible carer of a child;
■ you were previously subject to all the work-related requirements; *and*
■ the 13-week period in which no work-related requirements applied due to the domestic violence has just come to an end (see above).
UC Regs, reg 98(1A)

### All the work-related requirements apply
If none of the above circumstances are relevant to you, all four work-related requirements will apply to you. However, their application may sometimes be limited; see 5 and 6 in this chapter for details.

or drug dependency treatment programme (for up to six months);

■ you are under a witness protection programme (for up to three months);

■ you are taking part in a public duty approved by the DWP;

■ your monthly earnings are at least £338 if you are single (or, if you are one of a couple, your combined monthly earnings are at least £541); *or*

■ you are unfit for work, for up to 14 consecutive days after you have provided the relevant supporting evidence for this (a self-certificate for the first seven days and a 'fit note' for the second – see Chapter 10(8)-(9)), and on no more than two periods in any 12 months.

**A work search requirement would be unreasonable** – A work search requirement will not apply to you if the DWP is satisfied that it would be unreasonable for you to meet one because you:

■ are carrying out work preparation – whether as part of the work preparation requirement (see 4 above) or in a voluntary capacity;

■ have temporary childcare responsibilities, or are dealing with a domestic emergency, funeral arrangements or other temporary circumstances; *or*

■ are unfit for work for periods longer than those listed in the final bullet above.

**Disruption to your childcare responsibilities** – A work search requirement will not apply to you if you are the responsible carer of a child (see above) and within the last two years one of the following events has resulted in significant disruption to your normal childcare responsibilities:

■ the child's parent, brother, sister, the person who was previously their responsible carer or anyone else who lived with the child (and was not liable to make payments on a commercial basis for the accommodation) has died; *or*

■ the child has been the victim of, or witness to, an incident of violence or abuse (and you were not the perpetrator).

This exemption can apply for one period of a month in each of the four consecutive periods of six months following the event.

UC Regs, regs 6(1A) & 99

### 6. Work availability requirement

The *'work availability requirement'* is a requirement that you are available for work. To be available for work, you need to be able and willing to take up work (see 3 above) immediately. You must also be able and willing to attend a job interview immediately.

WRA 2012, S.18; UC Reg 96(1)

#### Does the requirement always apply immediately?

You must generally be available for work immediately. However, in the circumstances below you can be treated as available for work even if you are not able to take up work immediately.

UC Regs, reg 96(2)

**Carers** – The DWP can allow you up to one month to take up work, and up to 48 hours to attend a job interview, so that you can make alternative care arrangements if:

■ you are the *'responsible carer'* of a child aged under 16 (see 5 above);

■ you are the parent of a child, with caring responsibilities for them, but are not the responsible carer; *or*

■ you have caring responsibilities for someone who has a *'physical or mental impairment'*.

In each case, you must be able and willing to take up the work or attend the interview on being given notice for the agreed period.

UC Regs, regs 85 & 96(3)

**Volunteers** – The DWP can allow you up to one week to take up work, and up to 48 hours to attend a job interview, if you are doing voluntary work. You must be able and willing to take up the work or attend the interview on being given notice for the agreed period.

UC Regs, reg 96(4)

**Working through a notice period** – If you are leaving a job and have to give your employer notice, the DWP can treat you as available for work until the notice period has ended. You must be able and willing to:

■ take up work once the notice period has ended; *and*

■ attend an interview on being given 48 hours' notice.

UC Regs, reg 96(5)

**The work search requirement does not apply** – If the work search requirement does not apply to you in the circumstances listed in 5 above, you will normally be treated as available for work if you are able to take up work or attend a job interview immediately once the circumstances that exempt you from the requirement no longer apply. An exception applies in those three cases where a work search requirement would be unreasonable; in these cases the DWP can require you to attend an interview before the circumstances no longer apply.

UC Regs, reg 99(1)(b), (2B), (2C), (5A) & (5B)

### Limitations to the work availability requirement

The limitations to the work availability requirement, including the hours' restrictions that apply if you have caring responsibilities or a physical or mental impairment, are the same as for the work search requirement. See 5 above for details.

## B. SANCTIONS

### 7. Introduction

You can be given a sanction if you fail to meet any of the work-related requirements that apply in your case (see Box E.3). These failures are called *'sanctionable failures'*. There are four types of sanction:

■ lowest-level sanctions (see 9 below);

■ low-level sanctions (see 10 below);

■ medium-level sanctions (see 11 below); *and*

■ higher-level sanctions (see 12 below).

In each case, your universal credit can be reduced over varying lengths of time: the *'sanction period'* (see 8 below). How the reduction affects your universal credit award is explained in 16 below.

You can challenge a sanction decision through the normal reconsiderations and appeals process (see Chapter 57). There is no time limit for asking for a sanction to be lifted; a sanction decision can be revised at any time (see Ground 10 in Box O.8 in Chapter 57).

If a sanction is applied, you may be eligible for hardship payments (see 17 to 22 below).

**Sanctions from other benefits** – If you already have an employment and support allowance (ESA) or jobseeker's allowance (JSA) sanction when you become entitled to universal credit, that sanction will be applied to your universal

credit award. The sanction reduction will be made under universal credit rules (see 16 below). The sanction period will be that which applied to the ESA or JSA sanction, less any time that you already spent on the sanction while receiving either of those benefits. Any period for which you did not claim universal credit after the ESA or JSA award ended will count towards your serving the sanction period.

UC Regs, reg 112 & Sch 11, paras 1 & 2; The Universal Credit (Transitional Provisions) Regs 2014, regs 30 & 32

## 8. The sanction period

In the case of medium-level and higher-level sanctions, the sanction period will be a fixed period, which can range from one week to three years. In the case of lowest-level sanctions, the sanction period is open ended (ie it will last until you meet the requirement in question). In the case of low-level sanctions, the sanction period will consist of an open-ended period, followed by a fixed period. See Box E.4 for a simplified table of the sanction periods and 9 to 12 below for more details.

### Start of the sanction period

The sanction period will normally start on the first day of the monthly assessment period (see Chapter 16(1)) in which the DWP decides to apply the sanction. However, if your award is already under a sanction, the new sanction period will begin once the existing sanction period ends.

If your award of universal credit ended before a decision is made to apply a sanction, but after the decision is made you have become entitled to a new award of universal credit, the decision will be treated as having been made on the day before your earlier award ended. Consequently, the days between the two awards can count as part of the sanction period.

UC Regs, reg 106 & 107(2)

### Continuation of the sanction period

If your universal credit award ends and there is still some sanction period outstanding, the sanction period will continue, even though universal credit is not in payment. If you then become entitled to universal credit again, the sanction will be re-applied until the sanction period has run its course.

UC Regs, reg 107(1)

If you are subject to more than one sanction, the sanction periods run consecutively (ie one after the other). However, when this happens, the total outstanding sanction period will be limited to three years.

UC Regs, reg 101

### Suspension of the sanction period

If a fraud penalty has been applied to your universal credit, the sanction will be suspended. It will begin again once the fraud penalty has been lifted.

UC Regs, reg 108

### Termination of the sanction period

The sanction period can be terminated (even if there is some of it left to run) if you have been in one or more spells of paid work for a total of at least six months since the date of the most recent sanctionable failure. For this to apply, your earnings during that period (or periods) must have been at or above:

■ your individual threshold (see Box E.3); *or*
■ (if the individual threshold does not apply to you) the amount you would be paid for 16 hours' work at the national living/minimum wage that applies in your case, converted to a monthly amount by multiplying by 52 and dividing by 12.

If you are self-employed and a minimum income floor has been applied (see Chapter 17(5)), you will be treated as having earnings equal to your individual threshold.

UC Regs, reg 109

## 9. Lowest-level sanctions

You can be given a lowest-level sanction if only the work-focused interview requirement applies to you (see 3 above) and you do not take part in a work-focused interview without good reason (see 15 below). This can include a pre-arranged telephone interview.

**How long is the sanction period?** – The sanction period will start on the day of the sanctionable failure and will last until the day before the day you do take part in a work-focused interview. The sanction period will end sooner than this if your circumstances change so that none of the work-related requirements apply to you (see Box E.3). The sanction period will also end if your universal credit award is terminated (unless it is terminated because you cease to be, or become, one of a couple).

WRA 2012, S.27; UC Regs, reg 105

## 10. Low-level sanctions

You can be given a low-level sanction if all the work-related requirements apply to you (see Box E.3), or only the work-focused interview and/or work preparation requirements apply, and you fail to meet:

■ a work-focused interview requirement (see 3 above);
■ a work preparation requirement (see 4 above);
■ a work search requirement to take any particular action (see 5 above); *or*
■ a connected requirement (see below),

without good reason (see 15 below).

WRA 2012, S.27; UC Regs, reg 104(1)

### Connected requirements

In connection with any work-related requirement, the DWP may ask you to:

■ take part in an interview to confirm that you have met the requirement or to help you meet it (eg the work search review – see 5 above);
■ provide information and evidence to confirm that you have met the requirement; *or*
■ report any changes in your circumstances relevant to the requirement.

WRA 2012, S.23

### How long is the sanction period?

The sanction period will consist of an open-ended period, followed by a fixed period.

The open-ended period will start on the day of the sanctionable failure and will last until the day before the day you meet the requirement in question. The period will end sooner than this if your circumstances change so that the work-related requirements no longer apply to you (see Box E.3). The period will also end if your universal credit award is terminated (unless it is terminated because you cease to be, or become, one of a couple).

UC Regs, reg 104(2)(a)&(3)(a)

The length of the fixed period will depend on your age when the sanctionable failure took place and whether any previous sanctionable failures can be taken into account. In the latter case, an employment and support allowance or lower-level jobseeker's allowance sanctionable failure will be counted as a low-level universal credit sanctionable failure.

UC Regs, reg 112 & Sch 11, para 3

**Aged 18 or over** – If you were aged 18 or over on the date that the sanctionable failure took place, the fixed period will be seven days. However, if this is the second sanctionable failure within one year* giving rise to a low-level sanction, the fixed period will be 14 days. For a third sanctionable failure (and any subsequent failures) within one year* of a previous failure, the fixed period will be 28 days (four weeks).

UC Regs, reg 104(2)(b)

**Aged 16 or 17** – If you were aged 16 or 17 on the date that the sanctionable failure took place, a fixed period of seven days will apply only if this is the second (or subsequent) sanctionable failure within one year (but not within 14 days of the current failure) giving rise to a low-level sanction.

UC Regs, reg 104(3)(b)

\* but not within 14 days of the current failure; where a sanctionable failure has taken place within 14 days of a previous one, the sanction period will be the same length as the earlier sanction period

## 11. Medium-level sanctions

You can be given a medium-level sanction if you fail to search for work (see 5 above) or to be available for work (see 6 above), as required, without good reason (see 15 below).

WRA 2012, S.27; UC Regs, reg 103(1)

### How long is the sanction period?

The length of the sanction period will depend on your age when the sanctionable failure took place and whether any previous sanctionable failures can be taken into account. In the latter case, an intermediate-level jobseeker's allowance sanctionable failure will be counted as a medium-level universal credit sanctionable failure.

UC Regs, reg 112 & Sch 11, para 3

**Aged 18 or over** – If you were aged 18 or over on the date that the sanctionable failure took place, the sanction period will be a fixed period of 28 days (four weeks). However, if this is the second sanctionable failure (or a subsequent failure) within one year\* giving rise to a medium-level sanction, the sanction period will be 91 days (13 weeks).

---

### E.4 Sanction periods

| Sanction | Reduction period |
| --- | --- |
| **Lowest-level sanction** (see 9) | Open-ended period |
| **Low-level sanction** (see 10)<br>Plus fixed period: | Open-ended period |
| ■ **Aged 18 or over** | |
| First sanctionable failure | 7 days |
| Second sanctionable failure | 14 days |
| Third or subsequent failure | 4 weeks |
| ■ **Aged 16 or 17** | |
| First sanctionable failure | no sanction |
| Second or subsequent failure | 7 days |
| **Medium-level sanction** (see 11) | |
| ■ **Aged 18 or over** | |
| First sanctionable failure | 4 weeks |
| Second or subsequent failure | 13 weeks |
| ■ **Aged 16 or 17** | |
| First sanctionable failure | 7 days |
| Second or subsequent failure | 14 days |
| **Higher-level sanction** (see 12) | |
| ■ **Aged 18 or over** | |
| First sanctionable failure | *13 weeks |
| Second sanctionable failure | *26 weeks |
| Third or subsequent failure | *3 years |
| ■ **Aged 16 or 17** | |
| First sanctionable failure | *14 days |
| Second or subsequent failure | *4 weeks |

\* These may be reduced in the case of 'pre-claim' failures; see 12 in this chapter.

*UC Regs, regs 102-105*

---

**Aged 16 or 17** – If you were aged 16 or 17 on the date that the sanctionable failure took place, the sanction period will be a fixed period of seven days. However, if this is the second sanctionable failure (or a subsequent failure) within one year\* giving rise to a medium-level sanction, the sanction period will be 14 days.

UC Regs, reg 103(2)

\* but not within 14 days of the current failure; where a sanctionable failure has taken place within 14 days of a previous one, the sanction period will be the same length as the earlier sanction period

## 12. Higher-level sanctions

You can be given a higher-level sanction if you fail, without good reason (see 15 below), to:

■ apply for a particular vacancy for work (see below);
■ take up an offer of work (see below);\* *or*
■ undertake a work placement under a work preparation requirement (see 4 above).

You can also be given a higher-level sanction if you:

■ voluntarily leave your job or lose pay for no good reason (see 13 below);\* *or*
■ lose your job or pay through misconduct (see 14 below).\*

\* In these cases, you can be given a sanction if the sanctionable failure took place before you claimed universal credit (eg you lose your job through misconduct and then claim universal credit; a sanction may be applied to the new universal credit award).

WRA 2012, S.26(2)&(4)

### Failure to apply for or take up work

You can be given a higher-level sanction if you fail, without good reason, to apply for a particular vacancy for work under a work search requirement (see 5 above) or take up an offer of work under a work availability requirement (see 6 above). You can also be given a higher-level sanction if you behave in such a way that you lose your chance of getting the vacancy, for instance if you:

■ arrive at a job interview late, or go to the wrong place, through your own negligence;
■ impose unreasonable restrictions, so that the prospective employer withdraws the job offer; *or*
■ make statements designed to put the employer off.

Advice for Decision Making, Chapter K3, para K3057

**Zero-hours contracts** – You can be given a sanction for refusing or failing to apply for a job with a zero-hours contract without good reason. However, you will not be given a sanction for refusing to accept a zero-hours contract with an exclusivity clause (ie one that would not allow you to work elsewhere).

Advice for Decision Making, Chapter K3, paras K3271-3275

### When you cannot be given a sanction

You cannot be given a higher-level sanction if:

■ you fail to apply for a vacancy or take up an offer of work if the vacancy is due to a strike; *or*
■ your sanctionable failure was due to your voluntarily leaving a job (or losing pay) or losing your job or pay through misconduct, but even after leaving the job (or losing pay) your pay (or combined pay if you are one of a couple) is still above the level where the DWP is satisfied that you do not need to meet a work search or work availability requirement at the present time.

UC Regs, reg 113(1)(a)&(g)

### How long is the sanction period?

The length of the sanction period will depend on your age when the sanctionable failure took place and whether any previous sanctionable failures can be taken into account. In the latter case, a higher-level jobseeker's allowance sanctionable failure will be counted as a higher-level universal credit sanctionable failure. However, a pre-claim failure (see below) will be disregarded.

UC Regs, regs 102(3) & 112 and Sch 11, para 3

**Aged 18 or over** – If you were aged 18 or over on the date that the sanctionable failure took place, the sanction period will be a fixed period of 91 days (13 weeks). However, if this is the second sanctionable failure within one year* giving rise to a higher-level sanction, the sanction period will be 182 days (26 weeks). For a third sanctionable failure (and any subsequent failures) within one year* of a previous failure, the sanction period will be set at 1,095 days (three years).

UC Regs, reg 102(2)(a)

**Aged 16 or 17** – If you were aged 16 or 17 on the date that the sanctionable failure took place, the sanction period will be a fixed period of 14 days. However, if this is the second sanctionable failure (or a subsequent failure) within one year* giving rise to a higher-level sanction, the sanction period will be set at 28 days (four weeks).

UC Regs, reg 102(2)(b)

* but not within 14 days of the current failure; where a sanctionable failure has taken place within 14 days of a previous one, the sanction period will be the same length as the earlier sanction period

**Pre-claim failures** – If your sanctionable failure was due to your voluntarily leaving a job or losing pay, losing your job or pay through misconduct or failing to take up an offer of work, and the failure took place before you claimed universal credit, the sanction period (as fixed above) will be reduced to take account of any period in which you did not claim universal credit. In this case, the sanction period will normally be reduced by the number of days starting from the day after the sanctionable failure to the day before your universal credit claim.

However, where the sanctionable pre-claim failure relates to work that was due to end anyway, and the period you were expected to remain in work was less than the sanction period (as fixed above), the sanction period will be based on the period between the day after the sanctionable failure and the day on which your job was due to end. From this figure, any days in which you did not claim universal credit will be deducted (as above). Effectively this means that if you claim universal credit only after the job was due to have finished anyway, the sanction will not apply.

Pre-claim failures will also be disregarded when working out the sanction periods for later sanctionable failures.

WRA 2012, S.26(4); UC Regs, regs 102(3)-(5) & 113(1)(e)

## 13. Voluntarily leaving your job or losing pay
### If you leave your job voluntarily
Before giving you a higher-level sanction, the DWP has to show that you left your job voluntarily. If they do this, you must show that you had a good reason for leaving if you want to avoid a sanction. If you can, show that handing in your notice was the only thing you could do given all the circumstances, including your attempts to resolve the problems. This may enable you to avoid a sanction. You should therefore try to resolve work-related problems (using the firm's grievance procedures if they have any) before handing in your notice. You should also look for other work before leaving, or find out if you can be transferred to lighter work. If possible, discuss your personal or domestic difficulties with your employer to see if you can resolve the difficulty without handing in your notice.

### Voluntary redundancy
If there is a redundancy situation at your workplace, you should not be given a sanction for taking voluntary redundancy. You will not be given a sanction if you have volunteered or agreed to be made redundant and you are *either*:

- dismissed by your employer; *or*
- not dismissed but leave on a date agreed with your employer following a voluntary redundancy agreement.

You should not be given a sanction if you have been laid off or are on short-time working (ie you receive less than half the weekly pay that you usually get) for four consecutive weeks, or six weeks out of 13, and you have asked your employer for a redundancy payment.

UC Regs, reg 113(1)(f); Advice for Decision Making, Chapter K3, paras K3251 & K3255

### Trial period
If it is agreed that you may restrict your search for work to a reduced number of hours' work (see 5 above) and you take up a job (or increase your hours) so that the subsequent hours you work are greater than the agreed limitation, you will not be given a higher-level sanction if you voluntarily finish the job (or reduce your hours or pay) within a trial period. This 'trial period' will be 56 days (eight weeks) beginning on the 29th day after you took up the job (or increased your hours) and ending on the 84th day.

UC Regs, reg 113(1)(b); Advice for Decision Making, Chapter K3, para K3213

Some employers offer 4-week paid work trials through a work experience placement. If you leave such a work trial within the first four weeks, you will be treated as having a good reason for leaving if both you and the employer agree that the job is not suitable for you (unless you lose the place through misconduct).

Advice for Decision Making, Chapter K3, para K3216

### Minimum wage
You should not be given a sanction if you left your job because your employer paid less than the national living/minimum wage, action was planned or undertaken (such as your employer being prosecuted) and your employer consequently treated you in a detrimental way.

Advice for Decision Making, Chapter K3, paras K3242 & K3243

### Other cases when you cannot be given a sanction
You cannot be given a higher-level sanction if you voluntarily leave your job or lose pay:

- because of a strike; *or*
- as a member of the regular or reserve forces.

UC Regs, reg 113(1)(c)&(d)

## 14. Misconduct
You can be given a higher-level sanction if you lose your job or lose pay through misconduct. DWP guidance lists some of the points that should be taken into account when deciding whether or not misconduct applies in your case.

- ❑ You are guilty of misconduct only if your actions or omissions are *'blameworthy'*. This does not mean that the DWP needs to show that you did anything dishonest or deliberately wrong; serious carelessness or negligence may be enough.
- ❑ It is accepted that everyone makes mistakes or is inefficient from time to time. Consequently, if you are a naturally slow worker who, despite making every effort, could not meet the output required by your employer, you are not guilty of misconduct even if they have dismissed you for poor performance.
- ❑ The misconduct has to have some connection with your job. It does not have to take place during working hours to count as misconduct. However, the DWP cannot impose a sanction if the actions or omissions took place before your job started (such as giving inaccurate information about yourself in your job application).
- ❑ Some behaviour is clearly misconduct, eg dishonesty (whether or not connected with work) if it causes your employer to dismiss you because they no longer trust you.

❑ Bad timekeeping and failing to report in time that you are sick might amount to misconduct (eg if, on a number of occasions, you failed to report you were sick).

❑ A refusal to carry out a reasonable instruction by an employer is not misconduct if you had a good reason for refusing or your refusal was due to a genuine misunderstanding.

❑ Breaking rules covering personal conduct might be misconduct, depending on the seriousness of the breach. A breach of a trivial rule might not be misconduct.

❑ A refusal to work overtime is misconduct if you were under a duty to work overtime when required and the request to do it was reasonable.

The DWP should not give you a sanction for misconduct if there is medical evidence that at the time of the alleged misconduct you were suffering from a mental illness and not responsible for your actions.

*Advice for Decision Making, Chapter K3, paras K3072 & K3073*

### How is a decision made on misconduct?

If the DWP considers that misconduct may apply in your case, they will normally get a statement from your former employer describing your alleged acts or omissions. You should then be given the opportunity of replying to the employer's allegations. The DWP should not give you a sanction for misconduct unless they are satisfied that you have been given an adequate chance to comment on all the statements made against you.

*Advice for Decision Making, Chapter K3, paras K3083 & K3086*

### Employment tribunals

You may also be making a claim of unfair dismissal to an Employment Tribunal. If someone is helping with this (eg your union representative) you should ask them for advice. If you get a sanction, you can challenge the decision (see Chapter 57).

### 15. Good reason

With the exception of higher-level sanction misconduct cases, you can avoid a sanction if you can show that there was a *'good reason'* for what you did or did not do. Good reason is not defined in law. DWP guidance lists three points that need to be looked at when deciding whether or not you had a good reason.

❑ What would it be reasonable to expect someone to do in the particular circumstances (ie was the action or failure to act preventable)?

❑ What did you do or fail to do that was different from the expected action?

❑ What were your reasons for your action or failure to act?

If you have a record of previous failures, the DWP will take this into account when making their decision.

*Advice for Decision Making, Chapter K2, paras K2022 & 2041*

Examples of circumstances that may be treated as contributing to good reason for an action or failure to act include where you:

■ are a victim of domestic violence;

■ have a mental health condition or disorder (see below);

■ are the victim of bullying or harassment;

■ are disadvantaged – eg you are homeless, have a disability (see below) or learning difficulties;

■ have a domestic emergency;

■ have a sincere religious or conscientious objection;

■ have caring responsibilities (see below),

■ have a child who has been affected by death or violence,

*or where:*

■ there will be:

– significant harm to your health (see below);

– unreasonable physical or mental stress; *or*

– a risk to the health and safety of you or others.

*Advice for Decision Making, Chapter K2, para K2051*

### Mental health

You should not be given a higher-level sanction if you leave your job either voluntarily or through alleged misconduct because of your poor mental health and its effect on workplace relationships.

Even if you do not have a diagnosed condition, the DWP should still consider whether or not you are temporarily distressed by particular circumstances that could set off or worsen your condition.

*Advice for Decision Making, Chapter K2, paras K2073 & K2074*

### Disability

DWP guidance states that disability in itself should not be a good reason for failing to carry out work-related requirements. However, related factors should be considered, such as:

■ the level of support available to help you meet the work-related requirements (eg if you are living alone, you may find it more difficult to meet the requirements than someone living with others who could provide support); *and*

■ the reasonable adjustments that may be needed if you are newly disabled and need support in coming to terms with your disability.

*Advice for Decision Making, Chapter K2, para K2101*

### Significant harm to your health

If a particular type of employment is likely to cause significant harm to your health, you should try to get evidence of this from your doctor (or anyone else who is treating you) and give a copy of it to the DWP. But even without such evidence, the DWP can still decide you have good reason if the job itself or the workplace would clearly have worsened your condition (eg if you have asthma and are offered a job working in a dusty atmosphere).

If you have pneumoconiosis and/or tuberculosis, you may already have a certificate of suspension or letter of advice issued by the Pneumoconiosis Medical Board. The DWP should accept that you have good reason for refusing employment of a type listed in such a certificate or letter.

*Advice for Decision Making, Chapter K2, paras K2117-2121*

### Caring responsibilities

If you are the responsible carer (see 5 above) of a child aged between 5 and 13, you will have good reason if you:

■ do not accept a job that is not compatible with your child's normal school hours (including the time it takes your child to travel to and from school); *or*

■ leave work or lose pay because your working hours are incompatible with your caring responsibilities.

In other circumstances, your caring responsibilities must make it unreasonable for you to take the job; for example, you care for a teenager with health problems and the hours of the job are too long or inconvenient for you to care properly.

*Advice for Decision Making, Chapter K2, paras K2140 & K2141*

### Employment expenses

When deciding if good reason applies, the DWP should take into account any employment-related expenses that would be an unreasonably high proportion of the expected pay. Such expenses could include:

■ travelling expenses to and from the workplace; *and*

■ the cost of tools, equipment and protective clothing that you have to provide.

The DWP should separately take into account any childcare expenses which have to be paid for you to stay in work.

*Advice for Decision Making, Chapter K2, paras K2157-K2163*

### 16. How is the sanction calculated?

If you are given a sanction, your universal credit is reduced in each monthly assessment period (see Chapter 16(1)) until the sanction period (see 8 above) has ended. The sanction reduction for each assessment period is worked out as follows:

**Step 1:** The number of days of the assessment period* (or, if lower, the number of days remaining of the sanction period) is multiplied by the *'daily reduction rate'* (see below).

**Step 2:** The result of Step 1 is compared with the standard allowance that applies in your case (see Chapter 16(3)), or 50% of the 'standard allowance for joint claimants' if you are claiming jointly with your partner and only one of you has received a sanction. If the standard allowance figure (in either case) is lower, the standard allowance figure is used instead.

**Step 3:** The figure from Step 1 (or Step 2 if the standard allowance figure is lower) is deducted from your universal credit award for the assessment period (as calculated in Chapter 16) after any deduction has been made due to the benefit cap (see Chapter 16(10)).

* If the sanction has been suspended because you have been given a fraud penalty, the days of the suspension are deducted from the number of days in the assessment period.

UC Regs, reg 110

***Example:*** Peter has been given a medium-level sanction of 28 days. He is single and 27 years old. Before the sanction, he received a universal credit award of £443.93 for each monthly assessment period. The reduction is applied to the current assessment period as follows:

**Step 1:** The sanction period is 28 days. His 'daily reduction rate' is £10.40 (see below). Multiplying 28 by £10.40 gives £291.20.

**Step 2:** Compare the result of Step 1, £291.20, with the standard allowance that applies in his case (£317.82). The result from Step 1 is lower, so use this figure in Step 3.

**Step 3:** Deduct £291.20 from Peter's universal credit award of £443.93, leaving £152.73. This will be his universal credit award for the current assessment period.

**The daily reduction rate**

The daily reduction rate is normally calculated by taking the standard allowance that applies in your case (see Chapter 16(3)), multiplying this figure by 12 and dividing the result by 365. If you are claiming jointly with your partner, you will be treated individually in the calculation (all the amounts will be divided by two). The result of the calculation is rounded down to the nearest 10p. Consequently, the daily reduction rates are normally as follows:

| Daily reduction rate | | Amount |
|---|---|---|
| Single claimant | aged under 25 | £8.20 |
| | aged 25 or over | £10.40 |
| Joint claimant | both aged under 25 | £6.40 |
| | either aged 25 or over | £8.20 |

The daily reduction rates will be 40% of the amounts calculated above if, at the end of the assessment period:

■ you are aged 16 or 17;

■ you do not need to meet any of the work-related requirements because you:
  – are the responsible carer or responsible foster parent of a child under one (see 5 above);
  – are pregnant and it is 11 weeks or less before the week your baby is due;
  – have had a baby within the last 15 weeks (including if your baby was stillborn);
  – are an adopter and it is 12 months or less since your child was placed with you (see Box E.3); *or*

■ due to your childcare responsibilities, you only need to meet the work-focused interview requirement (see Box E.3).

In these cases, the daily reduction rates will be:

| Daily reduction rate | | Amount |
|---|---|---|
| Single claimant | aged under 25 | £3.30 |
| | aged 25 or over | £4.10 |
| Joint claimant | both aged under 25 | £2.50 |
| | either aged 25 or over | £3.20 |

The daily reduction rate will be zero if, at the end of the assessment period, you have a limited capability for work-related activity (see Chapter 12(5)).

UC Regs, reg 111

## C. HARDSHIP PAYMENTS

### 17. Introduction

If you have been given a sanction, the DWP may grant you a recoverable *'hardship payment'*. Such a payment can only be made if you:

■ are aged 18 or over;

■ (and your partner if you are claiming jointly) have met any compliance condition specified by the DWP if you have been given a low-level sanction (such as attending a work-focused interview);

■ apply in the correct way and provide evidence and information to support the claim if asked; *and*

■ (and your partner if you are claiming jointly) accept that any hardship payments are recoverable.

In addition, the DWP must be satisfied that you (and your partner if you are claiming jointly) have met all the work-related requirements that you must have met in the seven days before you applied for the hardship payment and that you are in *'hardship'* (see 18 below).

You will not be able to receive a hardship payment if the sanction is applied at the 40% reduced rate (see 16 above).

UC Regs, reg 116(1)&(2)(a)(i)

**What period will it cover?**

A hardship payment will normally cover the period which begins on the date on which you meet all the conditions listed above and ends the day before the next universal credit payday. This is the *'hardship period'*.

At the end of this period, if a reduction still applies and you are still in hardship, you will normally need to make another application (unless the hardship period is for seven days or less).

UC Regs, reg 117

---

### Disability Rights UK services

**Helplines**
Our helplines provide expert information on a variety of issues. All carry Advice Quality Standard accreditation.

**Disabled Students Helpline**
Information and advice for disabled students and the professionals working with them, covering further education, higher education and apprenticeships.

**Personal Budgets Helpline**
Provides advice on direct payments, including information on personal budgets and employing personal assistants.

**Welfare Rights Advice Service**
Advises Disability Rights UK member organisations, on social security benefits and tax credit issues.

To find out more, visit
**www.disabilityrightsuk.org/how-we-can-help**

## 18. What is hardship?

You (and your partner if you are claiming jointly) can only be considered to be in hardship if you:

■ cannot meet your immediate (see below) and most basic and essential needs of accommodation, heating, food and hygiene (or those of a child or qualifying young person (see Chapter 16(4)) you or your partner are responsible for) only because of the sanction;

■ have made every effort to get alternative sources of support (see below) to help meet those needs; *and*

■ have made every effort to stop spending money on anything that does not relate to those needs (see below).

UC Regs, reg 116(2)&(3)

DWP guidance advises that you are more likely to suffer hardship if you:

■ have children in your family;

■ have health problems;

■ have caring responsibilities or are pregnant;

■ have disabilities; *or*

■ are seriously or chronically ill,

and therefore may have *'more complex and more expensive'* needs.

Advice for Decision Making, Chapter L1, para L1051

### Immediate

The DWP interprets this as meaning you cannot meet your household's basic and essential needs at the time you apply for the hardship payment. If you have children, *'immediate'* means within a week of the application.

Advice for Decision Making, Chapter L1, para L1047

### Alternative sources of support

DWP guidance suggests this could include asking your family for help (but not if they have their own difficulties, the request would put a strain on relationships or risk violence or they live too far away), asking your employer for an increase in hours, or contacting local charities or support groups. However, it would not be considered reasonable to expect you to:

■ sell or pawn items you own;

■ find cheaper housing;

■ increase your debts by seeking credit; *or*

■ rely on charities (ie you may contact a charity for support but cannot be denied a hardship payment if you don't).

Advice for Decision Making, Chapter L1, paras L1086-1093

### Spending money on anything else

You need to have made every effort to stop spending money on anything that does not relate to basic and essential needs. DWP guidance states it would not be reasonable to expect you to stop spending:

■ on anything needed to meet your work-search requirements (eg on a mobile phone contract or internet broadband);

■ to maintain your children's access to education;

■ to cover continuing medical costs or wellbeing needs not covered by free prescriptions; *or*

■ on service charges for supported accommodation not covered by universal credit.

Advice for Decision Making, Chapter L1, paras L1099-L1103

## 19. How much do you get?

Your hardship payment is worked out as follows:

**Step 1:** The sanction reduction for the monthly assessment period before the one in which you apply for the hardship payment is calculated (see 16 above). This figure is then multiplied by 12 and divided by 365 to get a daily rate.

**Step 2:** 60% of the result of Step 1 is worked out.

**Step 3:** The result of Step 2 is multiplied by the number of days in the hardship period (see 17 above).

UC Regs, reg 118

*Example:* In Peter's case (from 16 above), the sanction reduction in his last assessment period was £291.20. He applies for a hardship payment on 9.5.18; his next universal credit payday is 6.6.18.

**Step 1:** Peter's sanction reduction was £291.20. Multiplying £291.20 by 12 and dividing the result by 365 gives a figure of £9.57 a day.

**Step 2:** 60% of the result of Step 1 is £5.74 a day.

**Step 3:** Peter has a 'hardship period' of 28 days. (This is the number of days between the date he applied for the hardship payment (9.5.18) and the day before his next universal credit payday (6.6.18).) Multiply the result of Step 2 by 28 to give a total of £160.72. This is Peter's hardship payment, which will be paid on top of his reduced payment of universal credit.

## 20. How do you claim?

To apply for a hardship payment, ring the universal credit helpline (see Chapter 14(5)) or call in to your local Jobcentre Plus office. In either case, an appointment will normally be arranged at the Jobcentre Plus office for you to provide the information and evidence needed to support your claim (eg evidence that you cannot meet your heating or fuel bills).

## 21. Recovering hardship payments

Once the recoverable hardship payments end and the sanction(s) no longer applies, the total amount paid to you will be recoverable.

**Suspending recovery** – The recovery of hardship payments can be suspended in certain circumstances when you move into work.

The recovery of hardship payments will be suspended during any period in which you (and/or your partner if you are claiming jointly) do not have to meet any of the work-related requirements because your monthly earnings (or combined monthly earnings) are at least at the relevant threshold (see Box E.3).

If you are single and do not have to meet the work-related requirements for some other reason (eg due to your caring responsibilities) but choose to work anyway, the recovery of hardship payments will be suspended during any period where your earnings are at least the amount you would be paid for 16 hour's work at the national living/minimum wage that applies in your case*.

If you have a partner and one or both of you do not have to meet the work-related requirements but choose to work anyway, the recovery of hardship payments will be suspended during any period where your combined earnings are at least the amount that the younger of you would be paid for 16 hour's work at the national living/minimum wage*.

* converted to a monthly amount by multiplying by 52 and dividing by 12

**Writing off hardship payments** – If hardship payments are suspended as above for a total of six months (whether in one spell or several) the remaining un-recovered balance of hardship payments is written off.

UC Regs, reg 119

## 22. Challenging decisions

You can ask for a mandatory reconsideration of the decision not to pay a hardship payment (that has been made on the basis that you are not considered to be in hardship). You can appeal against a decision that has not been revised following such a reconsideration. You cannot appeal about the amount of hardship payment payable. See Chapter 57 for more on challenging decisions.

# 16 Calculating universal credit

| | | |
|---|---|---|
| 1 | How is universal credit worked out? | 121 |
| 2 | The maximum amount | 122 |
| | Universal credit rates – Box E.5 | 121 |
| 3 | The standard allowance | 122 |
| 4 | Child amounts | 122 |
| 5 | Housing costs amount | 123 |
| 6 | Work capability amount | 123 |
| 7 | Carer amount | 123 |
| 8 | Childcare costs amount | 124 |
| 9 | The work allowance | 124 |
| 10 | The benefit cap | 125 |
| 11 | How is the cap applied? | 125 |
| 12 | When the cap does not apply | 125 |

## 1. How is universal credit worked out?

The amount of universal credit you are paid depends on your circumstances. It is worked out by comparing your basic financial needs with your financial resources for each monthly *'assessment period'* (see below). If you are single, only your needs and resources are relevant. If you are claiming jointly with your partner, the needs and resources of both of you are relevant.

Set amounts for different financial needs are added together to arrive at a figure called your *'maximum amount'* (see 2 below). This is the basic amount the law says you need to live on each month. From this figure amounts are deducted for any earnings (some of which may be disregarded using a *'work allowance'* – see 9 below) and other income you receive over the assessment period. The resulting amount will be your universal credit (rounded up or down to the nearest 1p, where necessary). The calculation is as follows:

**Step 1: Work out your maximum amount** – See 2 below.

**Step 2: Add up your earnings during the assessment period** – Add up your total earnings (whether from employment or self-employment) during the assessment period and deduct any allowable expenses (see Chapter 17(A) for how earnings are assessed).

**Step 3: If you are entitled to a work allowance, deduct this from your earnings** – Deduct the work allowance that applies to you (see 9 below) from the result of Step 2. If your work allowance is greater than your earnings, all your earnings are disregarded (and the result of this step will be zero).

**Step 4: Add up your other income during the assessment period** – See Chapter 17(B) for how income other than earnings is assessed. See Chapter 17(17) for how your capital or savings can be treated as generating income for you.

**Step 5: Apply earnings and income deductions to your maximum amount** – From the result of Step 1, deduct 63%* of the result of Step 3 and all of the result of Step 4. The resulting figure will be your universal credit for the assessment period.

WRA 2012, S.8; UC Regs, regs 6 & 22(1)&(3)

* This 63% figure is a 'taper'. As your earnings rise, your universal credit is reduced at a constant rate of 63p in the £1. So for each extra £10 earned, you keep £3.70 and £6.30 will be taken off your universal credit.

*Example:* John is a lone parent aged 43. He has one daughter aged 9. He has a part-time job at a bookshop. He has no childcare costs. He also has a small occupational pension from a previous employer. During this monthly assessment period, John earns £490 in his job (after allowable deductions

have been made, such as income tax and national insurance contributions) and receives £42 from the occupational pension. He lives in a flat that he owns, and has paid off the mortgage on it. Using the steps above, the calculation of John's universal credit is as follows:

**Step 1:** His maximum amount is £594.90 (this is the standard allowance of £317.82 for a single claimant aged 25 or over and the child amount of £277.08 – see 2, 3 and 4 below).

**Step 2:** His earnings during the assessment period are £490.

**Step 3:** The work allowance that applies in his case is £409 (see 9 below). Deduct this figure from the result of Step 2: £490 less £409 equals £81.

**Step 4:** His other income during the assessment period is the occupational pension of £42.

**Step 5:** From the result of Step 1 (£594.90), deduct 63% of the result of Step 3 (63% of £81 = £51.03) and all of the result of Step 4 (£42): £594.90 less £51.03, and less £42, equals £501.87. John will therefore be entitled to universal credit of £501.87 for this assessment period.

### Assessment periods

Universal credit is worked out on a calendar monthly basis. It is calculated for each monthly *'assessment period'*. The first assessment period will normally be the month beginning with the first day that you are entitled to universal credit; subsequent monthly assessment periods will follow for as long as you remain entitled to universal credit. Therefore all the figures given in this chapter will be monthly amounts.

UC Regs, reg 21(1)

---

## E.5 Universal credit rates

| Amount | | per month |
|---|---|---|
| **Standard allowance** | | |
| Single claimant | aged under 25 | £251.77 |
| | aged 25 or over | £317.82 |
| Joint claimants | both aged under 25 | £395.20 |
| | either is aged 25 or over | £498.89 |
| **Child amount** | | |
| Higher rate: only/eldest child* | | £277.08 |
| Standard rate: other child** | | £231.67 |
| **Disabled child addition** | | |
| Higher rate | | £383.86 |
| Lower rate | | £126.11 |
| **Work capability amounts** | | |
| Higher rate | | £328.32 |
| Lower rate*** | | £126.11 |
| **Carer amount** | | £156.45 |
| **Childcare costs amount** | | |
| Maximum amount for one child | | £646.35 |
| Maximum amount for two or more children | | £1,108.04 |

\* only if your eldest child or qualifying young person was already included in your award on 6.4.17, otherwise standard rate will apply – see 4 in this chapter
\*\* and any subsequent child or qualifying young person already included in your award on 6.4.17 – see 4 in this chapter
\*\*\* normally only on claims made before 3.4.17 – see 6 in this chapter

*UC Regs, reg 36*

## 2. The maximum amount

The *'maximum amount'* is made up of a *'standard allowance'* (see 3 below) and *'amounts'*, paid to cover different needs. The amounts are:

■ child amount (see 4 below);
■ housing costs amount (see 5 below);
■ work capability amount (see 6 below);
■ carer amount (see 7 below); *and*
■ childcare costs amount (see 8 below).

WRA 2012, S.8(2)

The rates for these (except the housing costs amount) are listed in Box E.5.

***Example:*** Debbie and Nicole are claiming universal credit jointly. They are both over 25. Nicole has rheumatoid arthritis; Debbie receives carer's allowance for caring for her. Nicole has recently had a work capability assessment and been found to have a limited capability for work-related activity. They live in a local authority 1-bedroom flat, for which the rent is £250 a month. Their maximum amount for one assessment period is calculated as follows:

| | |
|---|---:|
| Standard allowance | |
| (for joint claimants, either aged 25 or over) | £498.89 |
| Housing costs amount | |
| (covering all their rent – see Chapter 24) | £250.00 |
| Work capability amount* | £328.32 |
| Carer amount* | £156.45 |
| *Total: the maximum amount* | *£1,233.66* |

* Both amounts are included in this case, as they do not apply to the same person; see 7 below.

## 3. The standard allowance

The *'standard allowance'* is always included in your award. It is the basic amount to cover essential living costs for you, and for your partner if you are claiming jointly (see Chapter 14(3)). Lower amounts are paid if you (and your partner if you are claiming jointly) are under the age of 25. The rates of the standard allowance are as follows:

| Standard allowance | | per month |
|---|---|---:|
| Single claimant | aged under 25 | £251.77 |
| | aged 25 or over | £317.82 |
| Joint claimants | both aged under 25 | £395.20 |
| | either aged 25 or over | £498.89 |

UC Regs, reg 36

**If your partner dies** – If your partner dies, the standard allowance for a joint claim can continue for the remainder of the monthly assessment period (see 1 above) in which they died and for the following two assessment periods.

UC Regs, reg 37(a)

## 4. Child amounts

A *'child amount'* of £231.67 a month may be included in your award for each child or *'qualifying young person'* (see below) you are responsible for (see below). However, a two-child limit was introduced on 6.4.17; you can only get a child amount for a third or subsequent child (or qualifying young person) if they were already included in your universal credit award on 6.4.17. Exceptions apply, which reflect those for child tax credit (see Chapter 23(4)).

The child amount is paid at a higher rate of £277.08 a month for your eldest child or qualifying young person if they were already included in your universal credit award on 6.4.17; otherwise the standard rate of £231.67 will apply.

**Disabled child additions** – An additional amount is included for each child or qualifying young person who is disabled. The additional amount is set at two different levels:

■ a higher rate of £383.86 a month for a child/young person who is:
  – entitled to disability living allowance (DLA – see Chapter 4) highest rate care component;
  – entitled to personal independence payment (PIP – see Chapter 5) enhanced rate daily living component; *or*
  – certified by a consultant ophthalmologist as severely sight impaired or blind; *and*

■ a lower rate of £126.11 for a child/young person who is entitled to any other rate of DLA or PIP.

UC Regs, reg 24

### Qualifying young person

Once your child has reached the age of 16, they can be treated as a *'qualifying young person'* up until (but not including) the 1 September following their 16th birthday. This period can be extended up until (but not including) the 1 September following their 19th birthday if they are enrolled on (or have been accepted for) approved training or a course of full-time non-advanced education.

A course is considered to be full time if at least 12 hours a week during term time are spent receiving tuition, engaging in practical work or supervised study, or taking exams. The education or training must not be provided under a contract of employment. Nineteen-year-olds can only be included if they started such education or approved training (or were accepted or enrolled to undertake it) before their 19th birthday.

If the young person receives employment and support allowance, jobseeker's allowance or universal credit in their own right, they will not be classed as a qualifying young person.

UC Regs, reg 5

### Responsible for a child or qualifying young person

You are considered to be responsible for a child or qualifying young person if they normally live with you. Where a child or qualifying young person lives with both you and someone who is not your partner (eg you are separated), only one of you can be treated as responsible for them and that will be the person who has the main responsibility. You can agree between you who has the main responsibility; if you fail to do so, the DWP will decide.

You are not treated as responsible for a child or qualifying young person for any period during which they are being looked after by a local authority. This will not apply, however, in the case of planned short-term respite care breaks. Nor will it apply if the child is under the care of the local authority but has been placed to live with you (or continues to live with you) and you are the parent or have parental responsibility for them. (Parental responsibility means you have all the powers, responsibilities and authority of a parent; it does not include a foster parent or, in Scotland, a kinship carer.)

You are not treated as responsible for a child or qualifying young person for any period during which they are a prisoner.

You are not considered to be responsible for a qualifying young person if you are living with that person as a couple.

If the child or qualifying young person is temporarily absent from your household, you can be treated as still responsible for them for up to six months as long as their absence is not expected to be longer than this. If they are absent from Great Britain, see Chapter 54(7).

UC Regs, regs 4 & 4A

### If the child or young person dies

If the child or young person you are responsible for dies, the child amount can continue to be included in your award for the remainder of the monthly assessment period (see 1 above) in which their death occurred and for the following two assessment periods.

UC Regs, reg 37(b)

## 5. Housing costs amount

A *'housing costs amount'* may be included in your award if you pay rent or are an owner-occupier. The following is a brief outline; for details, see Chapter 24.

**Amount for renters** – If you are renting (whether privately, from a local authority or from a housing association) you may get an amount to cover your eligible rent. The amount is normally based on the number of rooms you are deemed to need, although there are exceptions. Deductions may be made if you have any *'non-dependants'* living with you, eg an adult son or daughter.

UC Regs, regs 25-26 & Sch 4

If you are in certain types of supported or temporary accommodation, your housing support is still met through housing benefit rather than through the universal credit housing costs amount.

**Amount for owner-occupiers** – If you are buying your home, you may get an amount to cover certain service charges. There is normally a 9-month qualifying period before you can be paid this amount. You cannot be paid the amount if you, or your partner, have any earnings (irrespective of the number of hours you work or how much you are paid). You are not subject to deductions because you have non-dependants living with you.

UC Regs, regs 25-26 & Sch 5

You may also be eligible for support for mortgage interest loans (see Chapter 26).

## 6. Work capability amount

If you have a *'limited capability for work-related activity'* (see Chapter 12(5)), a *'work capability amount'* of £328.32 a month (the higher rate) is included in your award. This is tested under the *'work capability assessment'* (see Chapter 12). Before 3.4.17, if you were only found to have a limited capability for work at this assessment (and not a limited capability for work-related activity), a lower rate of the work capability amount of £126.11 could be included in your award. The lower rate does not normally apply to new claims for universal credit (but see below).

If you are claiming universal credit jointly (see Chapter 14(3)), and both you and your partner meet the condition for the work capability amount, only one such amount is included.

UC Regs, reg 27

If you have a limited capability for work-related activity and you have caring responsibilities, a carer amount cannot be included in your award at the same time as a work capability amount; only the latter is included. See 7 below for details.

UC Regs, reg 29(4)

### The waiting period

A work capability amount cannot always be included in your award immediately; a *'waiting period'* of three months usually applies first of all. This will normally begin when you provide the DWP with a fit note (see Chapter 10(9)). If the waiting period is applied, the amount can only be included in your award in the monthly assessment period following on from the waiting period. During the waiting period, you should undergo the work capability assessment (see Chapter 12).

**Exceptions** – The waiting period will not apply (and the work capability amount can be included in your award immediately) in the following circumstances:

■ you are terminally ill (ie you have a progressive disease and your death from this can reasonably be expected within six months);

■ you are entitled to contributory employment and support allowance (ESA) under the universal credit system that includes the work-related activity component (or would be entitled but for the fact that your 12-month payment period is exhausted – see Chapter 11(20)) or support component;

■ your award already includes the lower work capability amount and a decision is made to include the higher work capability amount instead; *or*

■ you were previously entitled to universal credit which included a work capability amount *and*
  – your previous award ended immediately before your current award because you became, or ceased to be, one of a couple; *or*
  – your previous award ended in the six months before your current award because your income was too high.

If the last bullet point applies and you were still serving the waiting period when your previous universal credit award ceased, the waiting period will be treated as having continued without break.

UC Regs, reg 28

If you are being transferred from ESA (or limited capability for work national insurance credits) onto universal credit, and have already been through the work capability assessment, the appropriate work capability amount can be included in your award from the first assessment period. If you were part-way through the assessment phase when transferred to universal credit, the time you served on the assessment phase for ESA or national insurance credits will also count towards serving the universal credit waiting period.

The waiting period will be reduced by any time that you have spent on a jobseeker's allowance 'extended period of sickness' before moving onto ESA (see Chapter 13(4)).

The Universal Credit (Transitional Provisions) Regs 2014, regs 19-21

### The lower rate

The lower rate can still be included in your award in the following circumstances:

■ the lower rate was already included in your award by 3.4.17 (or would have been but for the waiting period – see above);

■ the higher rate was already included in your award by 3.4.17 and you are subsequently moved onto the lower rate following a work capability assessment;

■ you provided a fit note (see Chapter 10(9)) by 3.4.17 but the decision that you have a limited capability for work was not made until after this date (which may be through a mandatory reconsideration or appeal);

■ you have been entitled to ESA, or limited capability for work national insurance credits, continuously from 2.4.17 to the date of your universal credit claim;

■ your award is revised to include the lower rate, following the successful outcome of a mandatory reconsideration or appeal of a decision not to award ESA, where the ESA claim was made before 3.4.17; *or*

■ you are moved onto universal credit from an incapacity benefit (listed in Chapter 11(28)).

If any of the above circumstances apply, you can continue to be entitled to the lower rate, as long as you continue to be entitled to universal credit and have a limited capability for work. Your entitlement to the lower rate is protected if your universal credit award is terminated and a further award made because you cease to be, or become, one of a couple and if you come off universal credit for up to six months because your income (or joint income) is too high.

The Employment & Support Allowance & Universal Credit (Miscellaneous Amendments & Transitional & Savings Provisions) Regs

## 7. Carer amount

A *'carer amount'* of £156.45 a month is included in your award if you have *'regular and substantial caring responsibilities'* for a severely disabled person. You are considered to have such responsibilities if you meet the qualifying conditions for carer's allowance (see Chapter 8(2)) or would do so but for the fact that your earnings are too high. You do not need to have made a claim for carer's allowance to have the amount included. You are not entitled to a carer amount if you receive any earnings for your caring responsibilities.

If you and someone else both care for the same person, only one of you can qualify for a carer amount; you can jointly decide which of you it will apply to.

If you are claiming universal credit jointly (see Chapter 14(3)), and both you and your partner have caring responsibilities, two carer amounts can be included in your award if you each care for a different person.

If you have caring responsibilities and a limited capability for work or a limited capability for work-related activity, a carer amount cannot be included in your award at the same time as a work capability amount (see 6 above); only the highest paid amount is included. However, if you have a partner who has a limited capability for work or a limited capability for work-related activity and you have the caring responsibilities, both the work capability amount and the carer amount can be included in your award.

UC Regs, regs 29-30

**If the person you care for dies** – If the person you care for dies, the carer amount can continue to be included in your award for the remainder of the monthly assessment period (see 1 above) in which they died and for the following two assessment periods.

UC Regs, reg 37(c)

## 8. Childcare costs amount

A *'childcare costs amount'* is included in your award if you pay for certain types of childcare to stay in work; see below for what types are relevant. For the amount to be included, the *'work condition'* and the *'childcare costs condition'* must apply during each assessment period (see below).

UC Regs, reg 31

**How much do you get?** – For each monthly assessment period (see 1 above), 85% of the relevant childcare costs can be met up to a maximum amount of £646.35 for one child, or £1,108.04 for two or more children. In determining the amount to be paid, the DWP can ignore any costs they consider to be excessive in relation to the amount of work you actually do. They can also ignore costs met by your employer or paid for you when you take part in work-related activity or training.

UC Regs, reg 34

### The work condition

You must be in paid work or have been offered paid work that is due to start before the end of the next monthly assessment period. *'Paid work'* means work done for payment or in expectation of payment. It does not include work done for a charitable or voluntary organisation, or as a volunteer, where the only payment you receive is towards expenses. There is no set number of hours you need to work.

If you are one of a couple, your partner must also be in paid work, unless they are unable to look after the child because they:

- have a limited capability for work (see Chapter 12(2));
- have regular and substantial caring responsibilities for a severely disabled person (see 7 above); *or*
- are temporarily away from home (ie are in prison, hospital or a care home).

**If you have just left your job** – You continue to be treated as being in paid work if you have just left your job within this or the previous assessment period (or the month before the beginning of your universal credit award, if this is a new claim). This is to allow you a short time to look for a new job without losing the childcare place.

**Employer-paid benefits** – You are also treated as being in paid work if you are receiving statutory sick pay, statutory maternity pay, statutory paternity pay, statutory shared parental pay, statutory adoption pay or maternity allowance.

UC Regs, regs 2 & 32

### The childcare costs condition

You must be paying charges for the childcare of a child or young person you are responsible for (up until the 1 September following their 16th birthday). The charges must be for childcare arrangements that enable you to take up paid work or continue in paid work (including a charge for a deposit, advance or retaining fee). You continue to be covered if you have recently left your job for the period described above.

You must let the DWP know the level of the charges and the childcare provider's registration number by the end of the monthly assessment period following the assessment period in which you pay them.

UC Regs, reg 33; Advice for Decision Making, Chapter F7, paras F7020 & F7042

### Relevant childcare

Generally, the childcare must be provided by someone who is registered for childcare or an equivalent. The childcare does not count if it is provided by a close relative of the child (see below) wholly or mainly in the child's home. Nor does it count if it is provided by a foster parent.

In England, the childcare must be provided by a childcare provider (registered under Part 3 of the Childcare Act 2006), a school (as part of the school's activities: out of school hours if the child has reached compulsory school age, or at any time if they have not reached that age) or a domiciliary care provider (registered with the Care Quality Commission).

In Scotland, the childcare must be provided by a registered childminder or daycare provider, a childcare agency or a local authority. In each case, the registration or services must come under the relevant part of the Public Services Reform (Scotland) Act 2010.

In Wales, various types of registered childcare or daycare provision are covered, as are certain domiciliary care workers and out-of-school hours provision (by a school on school premises or by a local authority).

Childcare provided outside Great Britain has to be by an accredited organisation.

**Close relative** – A *'close relative'* means parent, parent-in-law, son, son-in-law, daughter, daughter-in-law, step-parent, stepson, stepdaughter, brother or sister (or partner of any of these).

UC Regs, regs 2 & 35

### If the child or young person dies

If the child or young person you are responsible for dies, the childcare costs amount can continue to be included in your award for the remainder of the monthly assessment period (see 1 above) in which they died and for the following two assessment periods.

UC Regs, reg 37(b)

## 9. The work allowance

When you are calculating your earnings (see 1 above), you may be able to disregard some of them by applying a *'work allowance'*. This will only apply if you or your partner:

- are responsible for one or more children or qualifying young people (see 4 above); *or*
- have a limited capability for work (see Chapter 12(2)).

There are two different rates:

- a *'lower work allowance'* of £198; *and*
- a *'higher work allowance'* of £409.

The lower work allowance will apply if a housing costs amount is included in your award (see 5 above) or, if you are in temporary accommodation (see Chapter 24(7)), you receive housing benefit. If a housing costs amount is not included in your award (and you do not receive housing benefit for temporary accommodation), the higher work allowance will apply instead. In each case, the same rate will apply whether you are a single claimant or claiming jointly with your partner.

UC Regs, reg 22; The Universal Credit (Transitional Provisions) Regs 2014, reg 5A

## 10. The benefit cap

There is a cap on the total amount of universal credit and other benefits that you can claim. For each monthly assessment period (see 1 above) it is set at the following rates:

- £1,916.67 for couples (with or without children) and single parents in Greater London;
- £1,284.17 for single people in Greater London;
- £1,666.67 for couples (with or without children) and single parents outside Greater London; *and*
- £1,116.67 for single people outside Greater London;

In some circumstances, the cap is not applied (see 12 below).

UC Regs, regs 79(1) & 80A

### Which benefits are taken into account?

The benefits that are taken into account when calculating the cap are:

- bereavement allowance;
- child benefit;
- child tax credit;
- employment and support allowance (ESA);
- housing benefit;
- incapacity benefit;
- income support;
- jobseeker's allowance;
- maternity allowance;
- severe disablement allowance;
- universal credit;
- widowed mother's allowance;
- widowed parent's allowance; *and*
- widow's pension.

If any of these benefits are reduced or not paid due to the overlapping benefits rule (see Chapter 8(6)), only the amount actually paid is taken into account.

If a sanction has been applied to your universal credit (see Chapter 15(7)), the amount of universal credit paid before the sanction was applied is taken into account.

If you have been disqualified from receiving ESA (see Chapter 11(17)), that benefit will not be taken into account.

If a benefit is awarded for a period other than a month, a monthly equivalent will be calculated (see Chapter 17(8)).

WRA 2012, S.96(10); UC Regs, reg 80

## 11. How is the cap applied?

When a benefit cap is applied, the following steps are taken:

**Step 1:** The *'excess figure'* is calculated: this is the difference between the total amount of benefits taken into account in the monthly assessment period (listed in 10 above) and the cap figure that applies in your case (see 10 above).

**Step 2:** Any childcare costs amount (see 8 above) is deducted from the result of Step 1. (If the childcare costs amount is the same as or greater than the result of Step 1, the cap will not apply.)

**Step 3:** Your universal credit for the monthly assessment period (as worked out in 1 above) is reduced by the result of Step 2.

UC Regs, reg 81

*Example:* Walter and Skyler have three children. They live in Manchester. Walter receives employment and support allowance (ESA). Skyler works part time and pays for a childminder to look after their youngest child. This month they receive child benefit of £208.43 and ESA of £442.65; their universal credit has been calculated at £1,508.40. The universal credit award includes a childcare costs amount of £215. The cap for the current assessment period will be applied as follows:

**Step 1:** Their total benefit is: £208.43 plus £442.65 plus £1,508.40 giving £2,159.48. The benefit cap that applies to them is £1,666.67 (see 10 above). Deducting £1,666.67 from £2,159.48 gives £492.81.

**Step 2:** Their childcare costs amount is £215. Deduct this figure from the result of Step 1: £492.81 less £215 gives £277.81.

**Step 3:** Their universal credit of £1,508.40 is reduced by the result of Step 2: £1,508.40 less £277.81 gives £1,230.59.

Their universal credit award after the cap has been applied will therefore be £1,230.59.

## 12. When the cap does not apply
### Earnings

The benefit cap does not apply if your net earnings (or combined earnings, if you are one of a couple) in a monthly assessment period (see 1 above) are at or above the *'earnings exemption threshold'* (see below). Your earnings do not include earnings that you are assumed to have because of the 'minimum income floor' (see Chapter 17(5)).

**Earnings exemption threshold** – This figure is calculated by taking the amount someone would be paid for working 16 hours at the national living wage (see Box I.5 in Chapter 33) and converting this into a monthly amount by multiplying by 52 and dividing by 12 (rounded down to the nearest £1). It is currently £542. Before 1.4.17 it was set at a fixed rate of £430.

**Grace period** – If you do not have monthly earnings (or combined earnings, if you are one of a couple) at or above the earnings exemption threshold, the benefit cap does not apply during a *'grace period'*. This is a period of nine consecutive months, which begins on *either:*

- the first day of the assessment period during your current universal credit award in which your earnings (or combined earnings) are less than the earnings exemption threshold that applied at that time; *or*
- the day after the day on which you ceased paid work prior to your current universal credit award,

whichever is most recent. In each of the 12 months before the first day of your grace period, your earnings (or combined earnings) must have been at or above the earnings exemption threshold that applied at that time. Earnings when you were working abroad or when you were covered by zero-hours contracts can count here.

UC Regs, reg 82; HB Bulletin G1/2017

### Lone parents

A recent Court of Appeal judgment has overturned a High Court decision that it is discriminatory to apply the benefit cap to lone parents with a child aged under 2. The families concerned have now appealed to the Supreme Court. There is also a separate test case waiting to be heard in relation to the application of the cap for all lone parents, regardless of the age of their children. Seek specialist advice if you are in either position.

[2018] EWCA Civ 504

### Disability benefits

The benefit cap does not apply if:

- the carer amount (see 7 above) or the higher rate of the work capability amount (see 6 above) is included in your universal credit award;
- you (or your partner if you are claiming jointly – see Chapter 14(3)) are receiving:
  - attendance allowance, constant attendance allowance, exceptionally severe disablement allowance or armed forces independence payment;
  - the support component of employment and support allowance;

 – a guaranteed income payment or survivor's guaranteed income payment under the Armed Forces Compensation scheme;
 – guardian's allowance;
 – an industrial injuries benefit (including industrial injuries disablement benefit, reduced earnings allowance, retirement allowance and industrial death benefit); *or*
 – a war pension (including a war disablement pension, a war widow/widower's pension and similar payments made by countries outside the UK);

■ you, your partner (if you are claiming jointly) or a child or qualifying young person you are responsible for (see 4 above) are receiving:
 – carer's allowance;
 – disability living allowance;
 – personal independence payment; *or*

■ you, your partner or child or qualifying young person are entitled to one of the above benefits but it is not being paid because of hospitalisation or residence in a care home.

UC Regs, reg 83

# 17 Earnings, income and capital

| A | Earnings | |
|---|---|---|
| 1 | Earnings | 126 |
| 2 | Earnings from employment | 126 |
| 3 | Earnings from self-employment | 126 |
| 4 | Permitted expenses from self-employment | 127 |
| 5 | Minimum income floor | 127 |
| 6 | Notional earnings | 128 |
| B | Income other than earnings | |
| 7 | Income | 128 |
| 8 | How income is calculated | 128 |
| 9 | Benefits | 128 |
| 10 | Pension income | 129 |
| 11 | Payments for your home | 129 |
| 12 | Employment and training schemes | 129 |
| 13 | Compensation schemes | 129 |
| 14 | Miscellaneous income | 129 |
| 15 | Notional income | 129 |
| C | Capital | |
| 16 | Capital limits | 129 |
| 17 | Assumed income from capital | 130 |
| 18 | What is included as capital? | 130 |
| 19 | How is capital valued? | 130 |
| 20 | Your home | 130 |
| 21 | Personal possessions | 131 |
| 22 | Compensation schemes | 131 |
| 23 | Right to receive income or payment in future | 131 |
| 24 | Benefit arrears | 131 |
| 25 | Business assets | 131 |
| 26 | Other capital | 131 |
| 27 | Notional capital | 131 |

## A. EARNINGS

### 1. Earnings

Income that comes from earnings (whether from employment or self-employment) is defined as *'earned income'* in the universal credit regulations. However, we will simply refer to it in this chapter as 'earnings'.

**How do earnings affect universal credit?** – You may be allowed to keep some of your earnings up to a certain limit before your universal credit is affected. This is called the *'work allowance'* and is set at two different rates, depending on your circumstances. If a work allowance is applied, earnings* in excess of the allowance will reduce your universal credit by 63p in the £1. If you are not eligible for a work allowance, all your earnings* will reduce your universal credit by 63p in the £1. See Chapter 16(1) and (9) for details.

* after the appropriate deductions have been made – see 2 below

**Your partner's earnings** – If you are claiming universal credit jointly with your partner (see Chapter 14(3)), your combined earnings are taken into account in the calculation.

UC Regs, reg 22

### 2. Earnings from employment

Earnings include any salary, wages or fees paid to you, either as an employee (under a contract of service) or as an office-holder. Earnings include bonuses, commission, holiday pay and overtime.

From your earnings, deduct any amount that is *'incurred wholly, exclusively and necessarily in the performance of the duties of the employment'*. If you are taking part in a service user consultation, deduct any expenses arising from this.

Deduct from your earnings income tax, Class 1 national insurance (NI) contributions and any contributions you make towards an occupational or personal pension scheme. Also deduct charitable donations made under a payroll donation scheme (PAYE).

Any refund of income tax or NI contributions from HMRC is normally treated as earnings.

**Employer-paid benefits** – The following benefits are treated as earnings:
■ statutory sick pay;
■ statutory maternity pay;
■ statutory paternity pay;
■ statutory shared parental pay; *and*
■ statutory adoption pay.

Any sick pay, maternity pay, paternity pay or adoption pay from your employer is also treated as earnings.

**On strike** – If you are on strike, your earnings will be assumed to be at the same level as if you had continued working. However, this will not apply if your employer terminates your contract.

UC Regs, regs 55 & 56

### Reporting your earnings

You are responsible for informing the DWP of your earnings, unless these are reported automatically under the *'real time information'* system (see Chapter 14(11)).

UC Regs, reg 61

### 3. Earnings from self-employment

Work out your earnings from self-employment as follows:

**Step 1:** Add up your gross profits. This is all the money you receive from your business over the monthly assessment period. This can include payments in kind and any refund or repayment of income tax, VAT or national insurance contributions for the business. Certain expenses can be deducted (see 4 below). The resulting figure is your gross profits for the period.

**Step 2:** From your gross profits (or, if you are in a partnership, your share of those profits) deduct any of the following that you pay over the monthly assessment period:
■ income tax – related to your appropriate personal tax allowances (see Chapter 35(3));
■ national insurance contributions; *and*
■ any contribution you make to an occupational or personal pension scheme.

UC Regs, reg 57

If your earnings are below a set minimum, you may be treated as earning a higher amount. See 5 below.

## 4. Permitted expenses from self-employment

To work out your gross profits from self-employment, you can deduct any expenses that have been *'wholly and exclusively incurred'* for the purpose of the business during the monthly assessment period, including:

■ regular costs such as rent or wages;
■ stock purchase;
■ utilities, phone and travel costs (but see below);
■ the purchase or hire of equipment and tools; *and*
■ VAT.

Advice for Decision Making, Chapter H4, para H4202

Where expenses have been run up for more than one purpose (eg they have also been used for personal reasons), if it is possible to identify a specific amount that was used only for your business, then that amount can be deducted.

No deduction can be made for the following:

■ expenditure on non-depreciating assets (including property, shares and investments);
■ payments to cover any loss for a previous assessment period;
■ payments to cover capital on a loan used for the business;
■ expenses for business entertainment; *and*
■ any expenses that have been unreasonably run up (ie they are considered inappropriate or unnecessary to the business or are excessive).

A deduction for a repayment of interest on a business loan cannot exceed £41.

UC Regs, reg 58

If you sell a business asset (eg a laptop) that has previously been deducted as an allowable expense, then the proceeds of the sale will be included in your gross profits. Similarly, if you stop using the asset in your business, the amount that you would be able to make from its sale will be included in your gross profits.

UC Regs, reg 57(5)

### Standard deductions

Standard flat-rate deductions can be made for:

■ car, van or other vehicle (other than motorcycle) usage for business purposes: 45p per mile for the first 833 miles during the assessment period and 25p per mile after that (for a van or other vehicle only; if your actual expenses are higher, you can use that figure instead);
■ motorcycle usage, 24p per mile; *and*
■ expenses related to the use of your home for business (eg if you prepare your accounts at home): if it used for business for at least 25 hours but no more than 50 hours during the monthly assessment period, £10; if used for more than 50 hours but no more than 100 hours, £18; and for more than 100 hours, £26.

If you live at your business property (for instance, if you run a bed and breakfast), you calculate your business expenses normally, as if you did not live there, but you then need to apply a flat-rate reduction to this figure, depending on how many people you live with:

■ £350 if you live alone;
■ £500 if you live with one other person; *and*
■ £650 if you live with two or more other people.

UC Regs, reg 59

## 5. Minimum income floor

If your earnings from self-employment (plus any earnings from other employment) in any monthly assessment period are lower than a set amount, the *'minimum income floor'*, your universal credit may be worked out using this figure instead. This will only apply if you:

■ are in gainful self-employment (see below); *and*
■ need to meet all of the work-related requirements (see Box E.3 in Chapter 15).

The minimum income floor will not be applied during a 12-month start-up period (see below).

The minimum income floor that applies in your case will be based on your *'individual threshold'* or the *'earnings threshold for a couple'* if you are claiming jointly. See Box E.3 in Chapter 15 for how the thresholds are calculated. From the threshold figure a deduction is made to take account of income tax and national insurance contributions you would have needed to pay if you had earned this amount. If you are single, the resultant figure is your minimum income floor. If you are claiming as a couple, the calculation is more complicated (see below).

You can challenge a decision to impose a minimum income floor (see Chapter 57). You may wish to do this if you think that you are not 'gainfully self-employed' (see below).

UC Regs, reg 62

### Couples

If you are claiming jointly as a couple, the minimum income floor will only apply to you if your earnings are less than your individual threshold and your combined earnings are less than the earnings threshold for a couple. The minimum income floor is then worked out as follows:

**Step 1:** Add your individual threshold (with appropriate deductions – see above) to your partner's earnings during the monthly assessment period.
**Step 2:** Subtract the earnings threshold for a couple (with appropriate deductions) from the result of Step 1.
**Step 3:** Subtract the result of Step 2 from your individual threshold. The resulting figure will be the amount of earnings you are treated as having.
**Step 4:** Add the result of Step 3 to your partner's earnings. The resulting figure will be your minimum income floor.

*Example:* Simon and Patricia are both self-employed. For this monthly assessment period, Simon earns £470 and Patricia earns £1,200. The DWP has calculated that Simon's individual threshold for the month is £1,187.55* and the earnings threshold for the couple is £2,375.10*.
**Step 1:** Simon's individual threshold is added to Patricia's earnings: £1,187.55 plus £1,200 gives £2,387.55.
**Step 2:** Subtracting the earnings threshold for a couple (£2,375.10) from the result of Step 1 (£2,387.55) gives £12.45.
**Step 3:** Subtracting the result of Step 2 (£12.45) from Simon's individual threshold (£1,187.55) gives £1,175.10.
**Step 4:** Adding the result of Step 3 (£1,175.10) to Patricia's earnings (£1,200) gives £2,375.10. This is their minimum income floor.
* For the sake of simplicity, we have omitted the deductions for income tax and national insurance contributions – these will result in lower figures being used.

### Gainful self-employment

You are treated as being in *'gainful self-employment'* if the DWP considers that:

■ you are carrying on with a trade, profession or vocation as your main employment;
■ this is organised, developed, regular and carried on in expectation of profit; *and*
■ the earnings you receive are self-employed earnings.

If you are also working for an employer and spend more time in that job, you should not be treated as being in gainful self-employment. You will be asked at the work search interview (see Chapter 14(5)) about the hours you work and the earnings you receive in your business. If you are also in some other form of employment, you will be asked which you consider to be your main employment. From the information that you provide, the DWP will decide whether or not you are in gainful self-employment.

UC Regs, reg 64

### The start-up period

During a *'start-up period'* your universal credit is worked out on your actual earnings, even if these are less than the minimum income floor that applies in your case.

The start-up period applies from the beginning of the monthly assessment period (see Chapter 16(1)) in which the DWP decides you are in gainful self-employment, as long as you began the self-employment within the previous 12 months.

The start-up period will last for up to 12 months, as long as you are taking active steps to increase your earnings up to the level of your individual threshold (see above) throughout that period. During the start-up period, you will need to attend interviews so that you can provide evidence that you are trying to increase your earnings.

Once you have had a start-up period, you cannot have another one unless:

■ it is more than five years since the last start-up period began; *and*

■ you are now carrying on a different trade, profession or vocation.

UC Regs, reg 63

## 6. Notional earnings

If you have reduced your earnings (or your employer has done so for you) specifically so that you can claim, or get more, universal credit, you will be treated as still having those earnings. This is called *'notional earned income'*.

This will also apply if you work for nothing, or less than would be expected. In this case, you will be treated as having the earnings that are reasonable for the work you are doing, as long as your employer has the means to pay. This will not apply, however, when you:

■ work for a charitable or voluntary organisation and the DWP is satisfied that it is reasonable for you to work for nothing or at a reduced rate;

■ take part in a service user consultation; *or*

■ take part in a government-approved employment or training programme.

UC Regs, reg 60

## B. INCOME OTHER THAN EARNINGS

## 7. Income

Income that does not come from earnings is defined as *'unearned income'* in the universal credit regulations. However, we simply refer to it in this chapter as 'income'. Some types of income are taken fully into account in the universal credit calculation, other types are disregarded. We list which types of income are taken into account and which are disregarded in 9 to 14 below.

The income that is taken fully into account reduces your universal credit £1-for-£1 (eg an income of £15 will reduce your universal credit by £15).

The universal credit regulations specifically list those items of income that are to be taken into account in the calculation; if they are not listed, they will be disregarded and so will not affect the amount of universal credit you receive.

In some cases, you can be treated as possessing income that you do not actually have – this is called *'notional income'* (see 15 below).

### Your partner's income

If you are claiming universal credit jointly with your partner (see Chapter 14(3)), your combined income is taken into account. Any income that your children have is disregarded.

UC Regs, reg 22(1)(a)

## 8. How income is calculated

In calculating universal credit, your income is worked out on a month-by-month basis for each assessment period. If you receive regular income payments that are not made on a monthly basis, they are calculated as follows:

■ weekly payments are multiplied by 52 and divided by 12;

■ 4-weekly payments are multiplied by 13 and divided by 12;

■ 3-monthly payments are multiplied by 4 and divided by 12; *and*

■ annual payments are divided by 12.

If your income fluctuates, the monthly equivalent is calculated over an identifiable cycle, if there is one. If there is no identifiable cycle, the monthly equivalent is calculated over three months (or any other period, if that would give a more accurate figure).

For the way that student income is calculated, see Chapter 32(3).

UC Regs, reg 73

## 9. Benefits

The following benefits are taken fully into account as income:

■ carer's allowance;

■ employment and support allowance;

■ incapacity benefit;

■ industrial injuries benefits (excluding constant attendance allowance and exceptionally severe disablement allowance);

■ jobseeker's allowance;

■ maternity allowance;

■ severe disablement allowance;

■ widowed mother's allowance;

■ widowed parent's allowance; *and*

■ widow's pension.

Any benefit paid by a foreign country which is similar to one of the above benefits is also taken fully into account.

UC Regs, reg 66(1)(b)-(c); Universal Credit (Transitional Provisions) Regs, reg 25(1)

**Disregarded benefits** – The following benefits are not listed in the universal credit regulations and can therefore be disregarded:

■ armed forces independence payment;

■ attendance allowance;

■ bereavement support payment;

■ child benefit;

■ constant attendance allowance and exceptionally severe disablement allowance payable under the War Pensions or Industrial Injuries schemes;

■ disability living allowance;

■ guaranteed income payment and survivor's guaranteed income payment under the Armed Forces Compensation scheme;

■ guardian's allowance;

■ personal independence payment;

■ war pension;

■ war pensioner's mobility supplement; *and*

■ war widow's and widower's pension.

## 10. Pension income

Retirement pension income is taken fully into account. This includes:

- income from an occupational pension, personal pension or retirement annuity contract;
- income from an overseas pension;
- civil list pension;
- payments made by your former employer due to your early retirement on health or disability grounds (unless ordered by a court or made in settlement of a claim);
- regular payments under an equity release scheme;
- payments made under the Financial Assistance scheme;
- state pension (including a state pension from abroad); *and*
- Pension Protection Fund periodic payments.

UC Regs, reg 66(1)(a),(da)&(la) and 67

## 11. Payments for your home

Any payment from a scheme set up or approved by the government to support someone with a disability to live independently is disregarded.

UC Regs, reg 76(1)(b)&(2)

**Income from tenants and lodgers** – Payments you receive from tenants if you have sub-let part of your home, or from lodgers if you provide board and lodging in your home, are disregarded. However, any such payments you receive for property that you do not live in are treated as capital.

UC Regs, reg 72(3)

## 12. Employment and training schemes

Payments under a government training programme or employment scheme made as a substitute for universal credit or for living expenses (see 14 below) are taken fully into account.

UC Regs, reg 66(1)(f)

Other types of payment are disregarded, including payments to cover childcare and travel expenses.

## 13. Compensation schemes

**Compensation for personal injury** – If you have been awarded compensation because of a personal injury, any regular payments from it are disregarded. If the compensation has been used to buy an annuity, payments under the annuity are disregarded. If the compensation is held in a trust, any income from the trust is disregarded. If the compensation is administered by the court on your behalf or can be used only by direction of the court, regular payments from it are disregarded.

UC Regs, reg 75

**Special compensation schemes** – Any payment from a scheme set up or approved by the government (or from a trust set up with funds from such a scheme) is disregarded if it compensates for:

- your having been diagnosed with variant Creutzfeldt-Jakob disease or infected from contaminated blood products (eg the Macfarlane and Eileen Trusts and the Skipton Fund);
- the London and Manchester terrorist attacks of 2005 and 2017; *or*
- your having been interned or suffered forced labour, injury, property loss or loss of a child during the Second World War.

UC Regs, reg 76

## 14. Miscellaneous income

The following types of income are taken fully into account:

- maintenance payments made by your spouse or civil partner, or former spouse or civil partner, under a court order or maintenance agreement (however, maintenance payments for a child are disregarded);
- Sports Council National Lottery awards, where the payment is for living expenses (see below);
- payments received under an insurance policy to insure against the risk of losing income due to illness, accident or redundancy;
- income from an annuity, unless the annuity has been bought using personal injury compensation (see 13 above);
- income from a trust, unless the trust has been set up using personal injury compensation or with funds from one of the special compensation schemes listed in 13 above; *and*
- any other income that is taxable under Part 5 of the 2005 Income Tax (Trading and Other Income) Act.

UC Regs, reg 66(1)(d)(g)(h)(i)(j)&(m)

**Living expenses** – These are the costs of:

- food;
- ordinary clothing or footwear; *or*
- household fuel, rent or other housing costs – including council tax,

for you, your partner or any child or qualifying young person (see Chapter 16(4)) you are responsible for.

UC Regs, reg 66(2)

### Disregarded income

The following types of income are not listed in the universal credit regulations and can therefore be disregarded:

- adoption and fostering allowances;
- child arrangements order allowances;
- special guardianship order allowances;
- payments in kind (eg a bus pass, food or petrol);
- payments to third parties (eg if someone pays a garage for your car to be repaired); *or*
- regular charitable or voluntary payments.

## 15. Notional income

If income would be available to you on application, you are treating as having that income, whether or not you apply for it. This is called *'notional'* income. However, this rule does not apply to the list of benefits in 9 above.

Once you reach pension credit qualifying age (see Chapter 44(2)), you will be treated as having any retirement pension income that may be available to you on application, whether or not you apply for it. The main types of retirement pension income are listed in 10 above.

UC Regs, reg 74

## C. CAPITAL

## 16. Capital limits

There is a *'lower capital limit'* and an *'upper capital limit'*. You cannot get universal credit if your capital is above the upper limit of £16,000. This figure applies whether you are claiming as a single claimant or as a couple. If your capital is at or below the lower limit of £6,000, universal credit is unaffected. If your capital is between the lower and upper limits, it is treated as generating a monthly income (see 17 below).

Some types of capital are disregarded for these capital limits (see 20 to 26 below). You can also be treated as having capital that you may not actually possess: this is called 'notional capital' (see 27 below).

**Whose capital is included?** – If you are one of a couple (see Chapter 14(3)), your partner's capital is added to yours. Otherwise, only your own capital is taken into account. Capital belonging to dependent children is disregarded.

WRA 2012, S.5(1)(a)&(2)(a); UC Regs, reg 18 & 72(1)

## 17. Assumed income from capital

If your capital is between the lower and upper limits, it is treated as generating a monthly income, *'assumed income'*, of £4.35 for each £250 (or part of £250) above the lower limit of £6,000. For instance, if you have capital of £6,300, it is treated as generating a monthly income of £8.70. Each time your capital moves into the next block of £250 (even by as little as one penny) an additional £4.35 a month is added to the assumed income. This is then added to your other income when calculating your universal credit award.

If assumed income is included in your assessment, let the DWP know if the amount of your capital changes. If your capital drops to the next assumed income block and you have not told the DWP, you will be getting too little universal credit. If your capital increases to the next assumed income block and you have not told the DWP, you will have been overpaid universal credit. Watch out for the 'notional capital' rule (see 27 below). Keep records and all receipts to show how and why you spent your capital.

If your capital is treated as generating income, any actual income you get from that capital (eg rent from property you own) is also treated as part of your capital from the day it is due to be paid to you.

**Annuities and trusts** – The assumed income rule does not apply to capital held as an annuity or in a trust. In this case, the actual income from the annuity or trust is usually treated as income. See 14 above for details.

UC Regs, reg 72

## 18. What is included as capital?

Capital includes savings, investments, some lump-sum payments and the value of property and land (but if you own the home you live in, the value of your home, garden, garage and outbuildings is not taken into account). Certain types of capital can be disregarded; these are listed in 20 to 26 below.

**Capital treated as income** – Sometimes capital can be treated as income, in which case it is disregarded as capital. Sums paid regularly and for a specific period (eg payments under an annuity) are treated as income. If capital is payable by instalments, each payment of an instalment is treated as income if the total of all your capital, including the outstanding instalments, exceeds the £16,000 upper capital limit. If your total capital is less than or equal to £16,000, each instalment is treated as a payment of capital.

UC Regs, reg 46

## 19. How is capital valued?

Capital is calculated at its current market or surrender value, less 10% if there would be costs involved in selling and less any mortgage or debt secured on it.

If the capital is held abroad while transfer to the UK is prohibited, its market value will be considered to be the amount it would raise if sold in the UK to a willing buyer.

If capital is not held in sterling, any banking charge or commission payable for converting it is deducted.

UC Regs, reg 49

**Jointly owned capital** – If you own a capital asset jointly with one or more others so that each person has an interest in the whole asset with no separate or distinct shares, then you are treated as though you own an equal share. Thus, if four people jointly own a capital asset, each will be treated as possessing 25% of that capital.

UC Regs, reg 47

The DWP must establish the market value or price that a willing buyer would pay to a willing seller for your share of the asset. The market value could be low or even nil if other joint owners would not be prepared to sell the asset as a whole or to buy your share of it.

## 20. Your home

The value of the following is disregarded:

■ your own home as long as you occupy it;
■ property occupied by a close relative (see below) as their home, if they have a limited capability for work (see Chapter 12(2)) or have reached pension credit qualifying age (see Chapter 44(2));
■ property occupied by your former partner as their home, if you are not estranged but have to live apart (eg if you have had to move into a care home);
■ property you have acquired in the past six months* but not yet moved into;
■ property you intend to occupy as your home if you are taking steps to own of it. You must have first sought legal advice or started proceedings in the past six months;*
■ property you intend to occupy as your home once essential repairs or alterations make it fit to live in, if these have been started in the past six months;* *and*
■ your former home for up to six months* after you left it because you separated from your partner. If the former partner is a lone parent, the value is disregarded for as long as they continue to occupy your former home.

In all the above cases, only one property may be treated as your home.

You can disregard for six months* the value of property that you are taking reasonable steps to sell from the date on which you first took such steps.

UC Regs, Sch 10, paras 1-6

Any payment from a scheme set up or approved by the government to support someone with a disability to live independently is disregarded.

UC Regs, reg 76(1)(b)&(2)

* the DWP can allow more time if that is reasonable in the circumstances to enable you to conclude the matter

UC Regs, reg 48(2)

**Close relative** – A *'close relative'* means parent, parent-in-law, son, son-in-law, daughter, daughter-in-law, step-parent, stepson, stepdaughter, brother or sister (or partner of any of these).

UC Regs, reg 2

### Money set aside

The following sums earmarked for special purposes are also disregarded:

■ a sum deposited with a housing association as a condition of occupying the home. If you have removed that deposit and intend to use it to buy another home, it can be disregarded for six months;*
■ the proceeds of the sale of your former home if you intend to use this to buy another home within six months* of receiving the money;
■ a grant you have received in the past six months* to be used for the sole purpose of purchasing a home;
■ an amount you have received under an insurance policy in the past six months* paid to you because of damage to, or loss of, the home; *and*
■ an amount you have received (whether by grant, loan or otherwise) in the past six months* to be used for making essential repairs or alterations to your home.

UC Regs, Sch 10, paras 12-15

* the DWP can allow more time if that is reasonable in the circumstances to enable you to conclude the matter
UC Regs, reg 48(2)

## 21. Personal possessions
The value of personal possessions is disregarded, except those bought to reduce your capital in order to get more universal credit. A payment from an insurance policy to cover the loss of, or damage to, personal possessions is disregarded for six months, or longer if that is reasonable in the circumstances.
UC Regs, reg 46(2) & Sch 10, para 14

## 22. Compensation schemes
**Compensation for personal injury** – If you have been awarded compensation because of a personal injury and it is held in a trust, its value is disregarded indefinitely. If the compensation is administered by the court on your behalf or can be used only by direction of the court, it is also disregarded. If you have been awarded compensation but it has not been put into a trust or used to buy an annuity (or other such arrangement), it can be disregarded for up to 12 months from the date you receive it, to allow you time to set up a trust or buy an annuity.
UC Regs, reg 75

**Special compensation schemes** – Any payment from a scheme set up or approved by the government (or from a trust set up with funds from such a scheme) is disregarded if it compensates for:
■ your having been diagnosed with variant Creutzfeldt-Jakob disease or infected from contaminated blood products (eg the Macfarlane and Eileen Trusts and the Skipton Fund);
■ the London and Manchester terrorist attacks of 2005 and 2017; or
■ your having been interned or suffered forced labour, injury, property loss or loss of a child during the Second World War.
UC Regs, reg 76

## 23. Right to receive income or payment in future
Certain forms of capital can be released at some stage to provide you with income or payment in the future. The following types are disregarded:
■ the full surrender value of a life insurance policy;
■ the value of the right to receive a pension under an occupational or personal pension scheme (or any other registered pension scheme); and
■ the value of a funeral plan contract.
UC Regs, Sch 10, paras 9-11

## 24. Benefit arrears
Any payment you have received in the past 12 months to cover arrears (or compensation for the late payment) of the following benefits is disregarded:
■ universal credit;
■ income-based jobseeker's allowance;
■ income-related employment and support allowance;
■ income support;
■ housing benefit;
■ council tax benefit;
■ child tax credit;
■ working tax credit; or
■ any UK social security benefit not listed as taken fully into account as income in 9 above.
UC Regs, Sch 10, para 18

## 25. Business assets
If you are self-employed, any assets used wholly or mainly for your business are disregarded. If you have stopped such work in the past six months (or longer if the DWP considers it reasonable in the circumstances), the assets can be disregarded if:
■ you are taking reasonable steps to sell them; or
■ you have stopped work because of incapacity and can reasonably be expected to restart when you recover.
UC Regs, reg 48(2) & Sch 10, paras 7 & 8

## 26. Other capital
The following payments made in the past 12 months are disregarded:
■ social fund payments;
■ the initial larger payment of bereavement support payment;
■ discretionary payments from social care or social work departments to help children in need or to provide help to young care leavers; or
■ other statutory payments made to you to meet your welfare needs related to your old age or disability, other than for living expenses (see 14 above).
Victoria Cross and George Cross payments are disregarded indefinitely.
UC Regs, Sch 10, paras 16, 17, 19 & 20

If you have an online account under the new Tax-Free Childcare scheme, 80% of that is taken into account as capital; the remaining 20% is disregarded.
Advice for Decision Makers Memo 26/16

## 27. Notional capital
If you have spent or given away some capital in order to get, or increase the amount of, universal credit, you will be treated as still having that capital. This is called *'notional'* capital. In some cases, the amount of notional capital along with any actual capital will exclude you from universal credit. Or, you may still be entitled to universal credit, but at a reduced rate because your notional capital puts you into to a higher assumed income block than your actual capital warrants (see 17 above).

You will not be treated as having notional capital if you used it for:
■ reducing or paying off a debt; or
■ buying goods or services if the expenditure was reasonable in your circumstances.
If you are treated as having notional capital, you won't be excluded from universal credit (or placed in a higher assumed income block) permanently. Your notional capital will be reduced over time. How this is done depends on the level of your notional capital.

**If your notional capital exceeds £16,000** – Following a decision to treat you as having notional capital that is greater than the upper capital limit of £16,000 (thus excluding you from universal credit), for each subsequent month the amount of notional capital you are treated as having is reduced by the amount of universal credit which the DWP considers you would have been entitled to were it not for the notional capital. Once your notional capital has been reduced in this way to less than £16,000, you may become entitled to universal credit and the following paragraph will now apply.

**If your notional capital exceeds £6,000 but not £16,000** – Following a decision to treat you as having notional capital that lies between the capital limits (thus reducing the rate of universal credit to which you are entitled), for each subsequent monthly assessment period (see Chapter 16(1)) the amount of notional capital that you are treated as having is reduced by the amount of assumed income (see 17 above) that applies in your case.
UC Regs, reg 50

# Means-tested benefits
## (pre-universal credit)

This section of the handbook looks at:

| | |
|---|---|
| Income-related ESA | Chapter **18** |
| Income support | Chapter **19** |
| Income-based jobseeker's allowance | Chapter **20** |
| Premiums | Chapter **21** |
| Income and capital | Chapter **22** |
| Tax credits | Chapter **23** |

# **18** Income-related ESA

| | | |
|---|---|---|
| 1 | What is income-related ESA? | 132 |
| 2 | Do you qualify? | 132 |
| 3 | Full-time or part-time work | 132 |
| 4 | Full-time education | 132 |
| 5 | How is income-related ESA worked out? | 132 |
| 6 | What is your applicable amount? | 133 |
| 7 | Personal allowances and additional components | 133 |
| 8 | Premiums | 133 |
| 9 | Passporting to other benefits | 134 |
| 10 | Other matters | 134 |

## 1. What is income-related ESA?

Income-related employment and support allowance (ESA) is the means-tested element of ESA, the benefit paid to people whose ability to work is limited by either ill health or disability (see Chapter 11). Income-related ESA provides for basic living expenses for you and your partner, if you have one. It does not depend on your national insurance contributions. It can be paid on its own if you have no other income, or it can top up contributory ESA (see 5 below and Chapter 11(18)-(27)).

Income-related ESA only covers the needs of you and your partner. If you have dependent children, you can claim child tax credit to cover their needs (see Chapter 23).

If you are eligible to claim universal credit (see Box E.1 in Chapter 14), you cannot make a new claim for income-related ESA and should claim universal credit instead (see Chapter 14).

**Making a claim** – See Chapter 11(8).

## 2. Do you qualify?

To be entitled to income-related ESA, you must meet the basic qualifying conditions listed in Chapter 11(7) as well as all of the following conditions.

❏ You must have no income, or your income is below your 'applicable amount' (a set amount that depends on your circumstances) – see 6 below.
❏ You must not have more than £16,000 in savings or capital (see Chapter 22(24)).
❏ You must not be entitled to pension credit.
❏ If you are one of a couple, your partner must not be claiming income-related ESA, pension credit, income support or income-based jobseeker's allowance.
❏ You must not be in remunerative work (see 3 below).
❏ If you are one of a couple, your partner must not be working for 24 hours or more a week (see 3 below).
❏ You must not be in full-time education (see 4 below).

WRA 2007, Sch 1, para 6(1)

You must not be subject to immigration control (see Chapter 53(2)) and must satisfy the habitual residence test (see Chapter 53(4)).

### Couples

You are considered to be one of a couple if you are married, in a civil partnership, or cohabiting with someone of the opposite or the same sex.

ESA Regs, reg 2

## 3. Full-time or part-time work

You cannot get income-related ESA if you or your partner are in *'remunerative work'*, which is work done for payment or in expectation of payment. You are not entitled to income-related ESA if you, the claimant, do any such work (except in some limited circumstances – see Chapter 33(2)). If you have a partner, you are not entitled to income-related ESA if they work for 24 hours or more a week, unless one of the exceptions listed in Chapter 19(3) applies to them (the rules that apply to income support also apply to income-related ESA). If one of these exceptions does apply, earnings are taken into account in the usual way (see Chapter 22(4)-(6)).

ESA Regs, regs 41(1) & 42(1)

## 4. Full-time education

You cannot usually study full time and receive income-related ESA. However, you can do so if you get disability living allowance, personal independence payment or armed forces independence payment.

You are treated as receiving full-time education if you are a 'qualifying young person' (see Chapter 41(1)). Otherwise, whether your course is classed as full time or part time usually depends on the academic institution you attend.

If you are on a government-funded further education course in England or Wales, it is full time if it involves more than 16 hours of guided learning a week.

If you are on a government-funded further education course in Scotland that is not a course of higher education, it is full time if it involves more than 16 hours a week of classroom-based or workshop-based programmed learning under the direct guidance of a teacher. Hours including structured learning packages supported by teaching staff can be included, if the total adds up to more than 21 hours a week.

ESA Regs, regs 14, 15 & 18

### Under 19

If you are aged under 19 (but not a qualifying young person – see Chapter 41(1)), you are treated as being in full-time education if the course of study is:

■ a course leading to a first degree or postgraduate degree (or comparable qualifications), a higher education or higher national diploma; *or*
■ any other course of a standard above advanced GNVQ or equivalent.

ESA Regs, reg 16

Any student grants, loans or bursaries you receive while in education can be taken into account as income when working out your income-related ESA. See Chapter 32(3) for details.

## 5. How is income-related ESA worked out?

Income-related ESA is worked out by comparing your needs with your resources (ie any income or capital you have). If you are a single person, only your needs and resources are relevant. If you are one of a couple (see 2 above), the needs and resources of both of you are relevant.

Set amounts for different needs are added together to reach the total amount the law says you need to live on. This is called your *'applicable amount'*. Your income (worked out under set rules) is deducted from your applicable amount, which leaves the amount of income-related ESA you are entitled to. The calculation is as follows:

**Step 1: Add up your total capital resources** – See Chapter 22(22)-(37). You will not be entitled to income-related ESA if your capital, and any capital belonging to your partner, is more than £16,000.

**Step 2: Work out your applicable amount** – See 6 below.

**Step 3: Add up your total income resources** – See Chapter 22(2)-(21). Include tariff income (see Chapter 22(25)) if you have capital over £6,000, or £10,000 if you live permanently in a care home.

**Step 4: Deduct your income from your applicable amount** – If your income is less than your applicable amount, income-related ESA makes up the difference in full, provided you meet the other qualifying conditions (see 2 above and Chapter 11(7)).

WRA 2007, S.4, ESA Regs, reg 67

**Example:** Iain is 57 years old. He lives by himself and receives the daily living component of personal independence payment (PIP) at the standard rate (which entitles him to the severe disability premium; see Chapter 21(3)). He owns his flat and has no housing costs. He has no savings. He receives a pension from a previous employer of £25 a week. He has been on ESA for 18 months and has been placed in the support group (entitling him to the 'support component' – see Chapter 11(6) – and enhanced disability premium; see Chapter 21(4)).

His applicable amount is:

| | |
|---|---|
| Personal allowance (see 7 below) | £73.10 |
| Severe disability premium (see 8 below) | £64.30 |
| Enhanced disability premium (see 8 below) | £16.40 |
| Support component (see 7 below) | £37.65 |
| *Applicable amount* | *£191.45* |

His income is:

| | |
|---|---|
| The occupational pension | *£25.00* |
| (his PIP is disregarded – see Chapter 22(7)) | |

| | |
|---|---|
| Applicable amount | £191.45 |
| Less income | £25.00 |
| *Income-related ESA entitlement* | *£166.45* |

### If you are also entitled to contributory ESA

If you have no other income that should be taken into account, the amount of ESA you get will be whichever is the higher: contributory ESA or the applicable amount (see 6 below).

If you do have income that should be taken into account, the amount of ESA you get will be whichever is the higher: contributory ESA or the amount by which your applicable amount exceeds your income (the result of Step 4 above).

In each case, if ESA is payable at a rate greater than the contributory ESA rate, your ESA payment will consist of two combined elements: contributory ESA and a top-up of income-related ESA.

WRA, S.6

If your contributory ESA ends once the 12-month payment period is completed (see Chapter 11(20)), your income-related ESA should be adjusted to take this into account. The income-related ESA can then continue for as long as you meet the qualifying conditions.

## 6. What is your applicable amount?

Your applicable amount is the amount of money the law says you need to live on. It consists of:
■ a personal allowance – for either a single claimant or a couple (see 7 below);
■ an additional component – normally, only if you are placed in the support group (see 7 below);
■ premiums – flat-rate extra amounts if you meet certain

conditions (see 8 below);
■ certain housing costs (see Chapter 27).

ESA Regs, reg 67

## 7. Personal allowances and additional components
### Personal allowances

The personal allowance is part of your applicable amount. The rate that applies to you depends on your age and whether or not you are one of a couple. There are lower rates of the personal allowance for people aged under 25, although these no longer apply following the 13-week assessment phase (see Chapter 11(2)) if you are placed in the support group (see Chapter 11(5)), in which case the standard rate will apply instead. If you are under 25 and still entitled to the work-related activity component (see Chapter 11(6)), the standard rate will also apply.

| Personal allowance | | per week |
|---|---|---|
| Single person | 25 or over | £73.10 |
| | under 25 (lower rate) | £57.90 |
| | under 25 (standard rate) | £73.10 |
| Lone parent | 18 or over | £73.10 |
| | under 18 (lower rate) | £57.90 |
| | under 18 (standard rate) | £73.10 |
| Couple | both 18 or over[1] | £114.85 |
| | both under 18 (lower rate)[2] | £87.50 |
| | both under 18 (standard rate)[2] | £114.85 |
| | one 25 or over[3] | £73.10 |
| | one 18-24 (lower rate)[3] | £57.90 |
| | one 18-24 (standard rate)[3] | £73.10 |

ESA Regs, Sch 4, Part 1

**Couples (where one partner is aged under 18)** – In the table of rates above, the reference numbers mean:
1: includes couples where one is aged under 18 but would be eligible for either income-related ESA or income support if they were single, or is eligible for income-based jobseeker's allowance (JSA) or severe hardship payments;
2: only if one is responsible for a child, or each would be eligible for income-related ESA if they were single, or the claimant's partner would be eligible for income support if they were single or is eligible for income-based JSA or severe hardship payments. If none of these conditions are met, the single person's amount will apply (lower rate: £57.90; standard rate: £73.10);
3: only if the other is aged under 18 and would not be eligible for either income-related ESA or income support (even if they were single), income-based JSA or severe hardship payments.

### The additional component

Following the 13-week assessment phase, you may be paid an additional component (see Chapter 11(6)).

| Components | per week |
|---|---|
| Work-related activity component* | £29.05 |
| Support component | £37.65 |

ESA Regs, Sch 4, Part 4

* available on claims made before 3.4.17

## 8. Premiums

There are four different premiums, each with specific qualifying conditions, as detailed in Chapter 21. The premiums are part of your applicable amount (see 6 above). Unless otherwise specified in Chapter 21, each premium you are entitled to is added to the total of your applicable amount. The rates of the pensioner premium vary according to whether you are entitled to the support component, the work-related activity component or neither (see Chapter 11(6)).

| Premiums | | per week |
|---|---|---|
| Severe disability | single | £64.30 |
| | couple (one qualifies) | £64.30 |
| | couple (both qualify) | £128.60 |
| Enhanced disability | single | £16.40 |
| | couple | £23.55 |
| Pensioner (single) | work-related activity component | £60.85 |
| | support component | £52.25 |
| | neither component | £89.90 |
| Pensioner (couple) | work-related activity component | £104.90 |
| | support component | £96.30 |
| | neither component | £133.95 |
| Carer | | £36.00 |

ESA Regs, Sch 4, Part 3

## 9. Passporting to other benefits

Income-related ESA can help towards certain housing costs (see Chapter 27). If you get income-related ESA, you may be eligible for housing benefit and will not have to go through a separate means test (see Chapter 25(20)).

Getting income-related ESA may entitle you to other types of benefit, eg:

- support for mortgage interest loans (Chapter 26);
- free prescriptions and dental treatment (Chapter 52);
- housing grants (Chapter 30);
- help from the social fund (Chapter 29) and budgeting loans (Chapter 31(2));
- free school meals (Chapter 40(1)); *and*
- help with hospital travel fares (Chapter 55(2)).

## 10. Other matters

**Care homes** – For how income-related ESA is calculated for care home residents, see Chapter 38(4).

**Hospital** – For how income-related ESA is affected by a stay in hospital, see Box O.2, Chapter 55.

**Going into prison** – You are generally disqualified from receiving income-related ESA for any period during which you are in prison or legal custody. However, if you are detained in custody awaiting trial or sentence, you can continue to receive an amount of income-related ESA to cover housing costs.

ESA Regs, Sch 5, Part 1, para 3

# 19 Income support

| | | |
|---|---|---|
| 1 | What is income support? | 134 |
| | Who can claim income support? – Box F.1 | 135 |
| 2 | Do you qualify? | 134 |
| 3 | Full-time or part-time work | 134 |
| 4 | Aged 16 or over | 136 |
| 5 | Full-time education | 136 |
| 6 | How is income support worked out? | 136 |
| 7 | What is your applicable amount? | 137 |
| 8 | Personal allowances | 137 |
| 9 | Premiums | 137 |
| 10 | How do you claim? | 137 |
| 11 | Who should make the claim? | 137 |
| 12 | How are you paid? | 138 |
| 13 | Your responsibilities | 138 |
| 14 | Passporting to other benefits | 138 |

## 1. What is income support?

Income support is a means-tested or income-related benefit intended to provide for basic living expenses for you (and your partner, if you have one). It does not depend on your national insurance contributions. It can be paid on its own if you have no other income, or it can top up other benefits or earnings from part-time work. If you have children, their basic living expenses can be met by child tax credit (see Chapter 23).

Income support is available only to limited groups of people; Box F.1 lists the eligible groups. If you are not in one of these groups, you should consider claiming an equivalent means-tested benefit instead. If you have a limited capability for work, claim income-related employment and support allowance (see Chapter 18). If you are looking for work, claim income-based jobseeker's allowance (see Chapter 20). If you have reached the qualifying age for pension credit, that will be the equivalent benefit (see Chapter 44).

If you are eligible to claim universal credit (see Box E.1 in Chapter 14), you will not be able to make a new claim for income support and will need to claim universal credit instead (see Chapter 14).

For how income support is calculated for care home residents, see Chapter 38(4).

For how income support is affected by a stay in hospital, see Box O.2, Chapter 55.

**The benefit cap** – Income support is included in the list of benefits to which the 'benefit cap' applies. This cap limits the total weekly benefits that can be claimed. See Box G.6 in Chapter 25 for details (including exemptions).

## 2. Do you qualify?

In order to be entitled to income support you must meet all the following qualifying conditions.

- ❑ You must normally be in Great Britain (GB); however income support can be paid for the first four or eight weeks of a temporary absence from GB (see Chapter 54(8)).
- ❑ You must be aged 16 or over (see 4 below).
- ❑ You must be under pension credit qualifying age (see Chapter 44(2)); once you have reached this age, claim pension credit instead. If your partner receives pension credit, you are not entitled to income support.
- ❑ You must not be claiming either jobseeker's allowance (JSA) or employment and support allowance (ESA). If you have a partner, they must not be claiming income-based JSA or income-related ESA. (You can switch claims if you find you have made the wrong choice – see 11 below.)
- ❑ You must not be working 16 or more hours a week (see 3 below).
- ❑ If you have a partner, they must not be working 24 or more hours a week (see 3 below).
- ❑ You must not be in full-time education, though there are exceptions (see 4 and 5 below).
- ❑ You must have no income, or your income is below your 'applicable amount' (see 7 below).
- ❑ Your savings or capital (and any belonging to a partner, but not to a dependent child) must be no more than £16,000 (see Chapter 22(24)).
- ❑ You must be in one of the categories of people who can claim income support (see Box F.1).

SSCBA, Ss.124(1) & 134

You must not be subject to immigration control (see Chapter 53(2)) and must satisfy the habitual residence test (see Chapter 53(4)).

For the rules for people in care homes, see Chapter 38(4).

## 3. Full-time or part-time work

You cannot get income support if you or your partner are in *'remunerative work'*. This means you are not entitled to income support if you, the claimant, work for 16 hours or more a week or if your partner works for 24 hours or more a week. But there are exceptions (see below).

To count as 'remunerative' it must be work *'for which payment is made or which is done in expectation of payment'*.

Lunch breaks, if you are paid for them, count towards the 16 or 24 hours.

Some people may be treated as being in full-time work, eg if they are off work because of a holiday. But if you are off work because you are ill or on maternity leave, you are not treated as being in remunerative work, even if you are getting sick pay or maternity pay from your employer. You are also not treated as being in remunerative work if you are off work because you are on paternity, shared parental or adoption leave.

**Fluctuating hours** – If your hours fluctuate from week to week, an average is worked out. If you have a pattern of

## F.1  Who can claim income support?

You can claim income support only if one of the categories below applies to you. You are eligible for the whole benefit week if the category applies for at least one day. You must also meet the qualifying conditions listed in (2) in this chapter.

The categories marked with an asterisk*, which allowed income support claims to be made on the grounds of disability, do not apply to new claims from 27.10.08.

### Disability
❑ You are entitled to statutory sick pay.
❑ You are incapable (or treated as incapable) of work.* If you are treated as incapable of work because you are receiving the highest rate of the disability living allowance care component, you can remain in this category if you are moved onto the enhanced rate of the personal independence payment (PIP) daily living component following a PIP re-assessment. If you are claiming income support in this category, at some stage you will be asked to take part in the 'work capability assessment'. If you are found to have a limited capability for work in this re-assessment, you will be moved onto income-related employment and support allowance (see Chapter 11(28)-(32) for details).
❑ You are registered (or, in Scotland, certified) as blind, or it is less than 28 weeks since you were taken off the register (on regaining your sight).*
*IS Regs, Sch 1B, paras 7 & 13*

### Education and training
❑ You are on a full-time course and eligible for income support as a disabled or deaf student (see Chapter 32(2)).*
❑ You are a 'qualifying young person' (see Chapter 41(1)) and in one of the categories not excluded from income support (see 5 in this chapter).
❑ You are aged under 22, are an orphan or living away from your parents (see 5 in this chapter) and are taking part in a full-time non-advanced course that you started before your 21st birthday.
❑ You are a refugee and attending an English course for over 15 hours a week during your first year in Great Britain (to help you obtain work); you are eligible this way for up to nine months only.
❑ You are not a 'qualifying young person' (see Chapter 41(1)), are under 25, and are taking part in training provided by the DWP, the Welsh government or, in Scotland, a local enterprise company.
*IS Regs, Sch 1B, paras 10-12, 15, 15A, 18 & 28*

### Pregnancy
❑ You are pregnant and incapable of work because of your pregnancy.
❑ You are pregnant and due to have your baby in the next 11 weeks.
❑ You have had a baby in the last 15 weeks.
*IS Regs, Sch 1B, para 14*

### Caring
❑ You are looking after your partner or a child or qualifying young person (see Chapter 41(1)) you are responsible for who is 'temporarily ill'.
❑ You are 'regularly and substantially engaged in caring for another person' and either you are receiving carer's allowance or the person you are caring for gets a 'qualifying benefit' (see Chapter 8(2)). If carer's allowance entitlement stops, or the person you are looking after stops getting the qualifying benefit, you continue to be eligible for income support for an 8-week run-on period. If the person you are looking after has claimed a qualifying benefit, you will be eligible for income support for up to 26 weeks while you are waiting for their claim to be processed (plus the additional eight weeks' run-on mentioned previously, making 34 weeks in total). You are also eligible if they have an advance award of a qualifying benefit but are still in the qualifying period.
❑ If you would have been eligible for income support as a carer had you made a claim for income support, then you are eligible for income support for eight weeks from the date your carer's allowance and/or the disabled person's qualifying benefit stops.
*IS Regs, Sch 1B, paras 3(b), 4-5 & 6*

### Childcare responsibility
❑ You are a lone parent and responsible for a child aged under 5 who lives with you.
❑ You are a lone parent under the age of 18.
❑ You are single or a lone parent and are fostering a child aged under 16 through a local authority or voluntary organisation or are looking after a child placed with you by an adoption agency prior to adoption.
❑ You are looking after a child aged under 16 because the child's parent, or the person who usually looks after the child, is temporarily ill or away from their home.
*IS Regs, Sch 1B, paras 1, 2-2A & 3(a)*
❑ You are taking unpaid parental leave to look after a child who lives with you. You must have been entitled to housing benefit, working tax credit or child tax credit (payable at a higher rate than the family element) on the day before your leave began.
❑ You are taking paternity leave and you do not receive statutory paternity pay or any payment from your employer, and/or you were entitled to housing benefit, working tax credit or child tax credit (payable at a higher rate than the family element) on the day before your leave began.
❑ Your partner is temporarily outside the UK and you are responsible for a child aged under 16 who lives with you.
*IS Regs, Sch 1B, paras 14A, 14B & 23*

### Other
❑ You have started work and are eligible for housing costs run-on (see Chapter 33(4)).
❑ You need to attend a court or tribunal as a JP, juror, witness, defendant or plaintiff.
❑ You are involved in a trade dispute.
❑ You are remanded or committed in custody for trial or sentencing (but you can only get income support to cover housing costs – see Chapter 27).
*IS Regs, Sch 1B, paras 9A, 19, 20 & 22*

working some weeks on, some weeks off, your hours may be worked out over your working cycle: that average is then also taken into account in your off weeks. Otherwise, hours are averaged over a period of five weeks, or another period if that would give a more accurate calculation.

Exceptionally, if you work in a school, college or university (or otherwise work on a similar basis) and you have a recognisable pattern of employment over the year that includes periods when you do not work, the average is worked out based only on the weeks in which you are working. This can mean that if you are in remunerative work during term time, you will also be treated as in remunerative work during holiday periods, and are therefore excluded from income support during these.
IS Regs, reg 5

### Exceptions to the 16-hour/24-hour rule

If you come within one of the exceptions listed below, you can qualify for income support even if you are working for 16 hours or more a week. If your partner is working 24 hours or more a week, they must come within one of these exceptions.

Although you are not excluded from income support in these cases, any earnings are taken into account in the usual way (see Chapter 22(4)-(6)).

Unless you are a carer (see below), if you have an additional job that is not in one of these exceptions, the hours you work in that job count towards the 16-hour or 24-hour limit.

You are not treated as being in remunerative work in the following circumstances.

❏ **Volunteering** – You are a volunteer or working for a charity or voluntary organisation, and the only payment you receive, or expect to receive, is just to cover your expenses. If you are paid anything else, even if it is below your earnings disregard, all your hours of work count. If your average hours are 16 or more a week, you cannot get income support. If the decision maker is not *'satisfied that it is reasonable for [you] to provide [your] service free of charge'*, they may treat you as having 'notional' earnings (see Chapter 22(21)).

❏ **Caring** – You are eligible for income support because you are caring for a person who gets a 'qualifying benefit' or you get carer's allowance (see Box F.1). If this exception applies, you are not excluded from income support even if you have another job. For example, if you care for your mother during the day and she gets attendance allowance, and you also work 20 hours a week in a supermarket in the evenings, because you are a carer none of your hours count, not even the 20 hours' evening work.

❏ **Continuing care (Scotland only)** – You are caring for a young person who is leaving local authority care and you are receiving payments under the continuing care arrangements.

❏ **Foster or respite care** – You are a foster carer or you are paid by a health body, local authority or voluntary organisation to provide respite care in your own home for someone who does not normally live with you.

❏ **Childminding** – You are working as a childminder in your home.

❏ **Other** – You are not treated as being in remunerative work if you are:
- on a training scheme and you get an allowance for it;
- on a government scheme for helping people into self-employment;
- starting work and eligible for housing costs run-on (see Chapter 33(4));
- working as councillor;
- working as a part-time firefighter, auxiliary coastguard or lifeboat person, or a member of the reserve forces;
- in a trade dispute (but not during the first seven days after the day you stopped work);

- engaged in an activity for which a sports award has been, or is to be, made and no other payment is expected.
IS Regs, reg 6

## 4. Aged 16 or over

If you are aged under 16, you cannot get income support in your own right in any circumstances.

If you are aged under 20 and still at school or doing a non-advanced course at college or certain types of approved unwaged training, you are usually excluded from income support (see 5 below for exceptions); your parents can claim child benefit and child tax credit for you instead.

If you are aged under 20 and on a full-time advanced course, see Chapter 32(2) for details of income support entitlement.

Once you have left school, you can claim income support from the 'terminal date' (see Chapter 41(1)) if you fit into one of the groups listed in Box F.1. If you don't fit into one of these groups, claim employment and support allowance (if you have a limited capability for work) or jobseeker's allowance (JSA) instead. There are additional conditions for 16-17-year-olds claiming income-based JSA (see Chapter 20(4)).

**Care leavers** – If you are a care leaver, your local authority has a duty to support you until your 18th birthday. Generally, you would be excluded from income support but this does not apply if you are a lone parent or single foster carer.
Children (Leaving Care) Social Security Benefits Regs 2001, reg 2

## 5. Full-time education

You are normally excluded from income support if you are aged 16-19 and are at school or doing a non-advanced course at college for more than 12 hours a week or taking part in approved unwaged training (and thus treated as a 'qualifying young person' – see Chapter 41(1)).
IS Regs, reg 12

However, you won't be excluded from income support in this way if you:
- are a parent and your child is living with you; *or*
- are a refugee on an English course (see Box F.1); *or*
- are an orphan and no one is acting in place of your parents; *or*
- are living away from your parents (and anyone acting in their place) and they cannot financially support you as they are chronically sick or disabled (mentally or physically), in custody, or prohibited from coming into Great Britain; *or*
- have to live away from your parents (and anyone acting in their place) because:
  - you are estranged from them; *or*
  - you are in physical or moral danger; *or*
  - there is a serious risk to your physical or mental health; *or*
- have left local authority care and have to live away from your parents (and anyone acting in their place).
IS Regs, reg 13

If you are aged 20 or over and on a full-time course, you will be treated as a student whether your course is advanced or non-advanced. Chapter 32(2) explains which students are entitled to income support.

## 6. How is income support worked out?

Income support is worked out by comparing your needs with your resources (ie any income or capital you may have). If you are a single person, only your needs and resources are relevant. If you are one of a couple (see 11 below), the needs and resources of both of you are relevant.

If you have dependent children living with you, their needs and resources will be ignored, unless your claim for income support began before April 2004 and you continue to receive support for your children through income support rather than child tax credit.

Set amounts for different needs are added together to reach the total amount the law says you need to live on. This is called your *'applicable amount'*. Any income you have (worked out under set rules) is deducted from your applicable amount. This leaves the amount of income support you are entitled to. The calculation is as follows:

**Step 1: Add up your total capital resources** – See Chapter 22(22)-(37). You will not be entitled to income support if your capital, and any capital belonging to your partner, is more than £16,000.

**Step 2: Work out your applicable amount** – See 7 below.

**Step 3: Add up your total income resources** – See Chapter 22(2)-(21). Include the tariff income (see Chapter 22(25)) if you have capital over £6,000, or £10,000 if you live permanently in a care home.

**Step 4: Deduct your income from your applicable amount** – If your income is less than your applicable amount, income support makes up the difference in full, provided you meet the other qualifying conditions (see 2 above).

## 7. What is your applicable amount?

The *'applicable amount'* is the amount of money the law says you need to live on. It consists of:

■ a personal allowance – for a single claimant or for a couple (see 8 below);

■ premiums – flat-rate extra amounts if you meet certain conditions (see 9 below);

■ certain housing costs (see Chapter 27).

IS Regs, reg 17

## 8. Personal allowances

The personal allowance is part of your applicable amount (see 7 above). The rate that applies to you depends on your age and whether you are one of a couple.

| Personal allowances | | per week |
|---|---|---|
| Single person | aged 25 or over | £73.10 |
| | aged under 25 | £57.90 |
| Lone parent | aged 18 or over | £73.10 |
| | aged under 18 | £57.90 |
| Couple | both aged 18 or over [1] | £114.85 |
| | both under 18 [2] | £87.50 |
| | one aged 25 or over [3] | £73.10 |
| | one aged 18-24 [3] | £57.90 |

**Couples** (where one partner is aged under 18) – In the table of rates above, the reference numbers mean:

1: includes couples where one is aged under 18 but is: eligible for income support or income-related employment and support allowance (ESA), or would be if they were single; or eligible for income-based jobseeker's allowance (JSA) or severe hardship payments;

2: only if one is responsible for a child, or each would be eligible for income support or income-related ESA if they were single, or the claimant's partner is eligible for income-based JSA or severe hardship payments. If only one of the couple is eligible for income support, etc, the single person's allowance of £57.90 would apply;

3: only if the other is aged under 18 and would not be eligible for income support or income-related ESA (even if they were single), income-based JSA or severe hardship payments.

IS Regs, Sch 2, Part I

## 9. Premiums

There are five premiums, each with specific qualifying conditions. These are detailed in Chapter 21. The premiums are part of your applicable amount (see 7 above). Unless otherwise specified in Chapter 21, each premium you are entitled to is added to the total of your applicable amount.

| Premiums | | per week |
|---|---|---|
| Disability | single | £33.55 |
| | couple | £47.80 |
| Enhanced disability | single | £16.40 |
| | couple | £23.55 |
| Severe disability | single | £64.30 |
| | couple (one qualifies) | £64.30 |
| | couple (both qualify) | £128.60 |
| Pensioner | couple | £133.95 |
| Carer | | £36.00 |

IS Regs, Sch 2, Parts III & IV

## 10. How do you claim?

You start your claim for income support by ringing the Jobcentre Plus claim-line (0800 055 6688; textphone 0800 023 4888). The claim-line will put you through to a regional Jobcentre Plus contact centre. The contact centre will take your details and go through your claim over the phone. In some cases, they may need to ring you back for additional information. They may also arrange a date for you to attend a Jobcentre Plus interview with a work coach about job prospects (see Box O.4, Chapter 56).

If an interview is not arranged, you will be sent a statement containing the information you provided over the phone. You need to sign to confirm the statement is correct and return it in the envelope provided. You may be asked to provide supporting documents, such as payslips or proof of savings, with the statement; these will be necessary for your claim to be accepted as properly made. If you do this within one month of the date you first notified Jobcentre Plus of your intention to claim, your date of claim will be the date of that first contact. If you have problems getting the necessary information or evidence within one month, tell Jobcentre Plus straightaway and send the statement anyway. If your difficulty is for certain specified reasons, your claim can still be treated as made on the date of your first contact. For details, see Chapter 56(2).

C&P Regs, reg 6(1A)

If you are not able (or it is inappropriate for you) to use the telephone, a claim can be made on a paper form – the A1, which you can get from your local Jobcentre Plus office or from: www.gov.uk/government/publications/income-support-claim-form.

To claim in Northern Ireland, contact your local Jobs & Benefits office or Social Security office.

**Backdating**

If you think you were entitled to income support before you put in your claim, ask, in writing, for your claim to be backdated. Income support can be backdated for up to three months if there are 'special reasons' why you couldn't reasonably have been expected to claim earlier. Income support can backdated for longer than three months if you have been waiting for a decision on another 'qualifying' benefit. See Chapter 56(3) for details.

## 11. Who should make the claim?

You should normally make the claim yourself. If you are unable to act for yourself, a decision maker can appoint someone else (eg a parent, carer or close friend) to take over the management of your claim (see Chapter 56(4)).

**Couples**

You are considered to be one of a couple if you are married, in a civil partnership, or cohabiting (whether with someone of the opposite or the same sex).

**If one is eligible for income support** – If you are eligible for income support but your partner would need to sign on for jobseeker's allowance (JSA), you can choose which of you should make a claim. Either you claim income support or your partner claims JSA. However, if you are in the joint-claim age group for JSA (see Chapter 13(2)), either you claim income support or you both claim JSA jointly. You can't get income support and JSA at the same time unless your partner is only claiming contribution-based JSA. In this case, you can claim income support to top up the JSA.

Whether you claim income support or JSA, the amount of benefit is usually the same. However, income support is tax free (whereas JSA is taxable) and JSA carries a greater risk of sanctions (see Chapter 13(11)). If you claim income support, your partner can sign on voluntarily at the Jobcentre Plus office to secure national insurance credits.

If you find you've made the wrong choice, simply put in a claim for income support. The DWP will stop the JSA award if your income support claim is successful.

If you are eligible for income support and your partner is eligible for employment and support allowance (ESA), you can choose which of you should make the claim – either you claim income support or your partner claims income-related ESA. If a disability premium is payable with the income support (which, for instance, would be the case if your partner receives personal independence payment – see Chapter 21(2)), you will usually be better off claiming income support. If a disability premium is not payable with the income support, you will probably be better off if your partner claims income-related ESA.

**If both are eligible for income support** – You can choose which of you should make the claim. You can switch roles at any time. Your partner just has to put in a claim for income support with your agreement that they should make the claim, or vice versa.

C&P Regs, reg 4(3) & (4)

## 12. How are you paid?

Income support is paid fortnightly in arrears. If your income support payment is less than £1 a week, it may be paid at 13-week intervals in arrears. The minimum payment is 10p a week; entitlement of less than 10p a week is not payable unless it can be paid with another benefit.

C&P Regs, reg 26(4) & Sch 7, paras 1&5

Your benefit is normally paid into a bank, building society, credit union or Post Office card account (see Chapter 56(5)).

## 13. Your responsibilities

### Jobcentre Plus interviews

You (or your partner) may be asked to attend a work-focused interview with a work coach. If you fail to attend or take part without good cause, your income support will be paid at a reduced rate. See Box O.4 in Chapter 56.

### Work-related activity

If you are entitled to income support solely on the basis of being a lone parent and your youngest child is aged 3 or 4, you may need to take part in mandatory work-related activity. This is *'activity which makes it more likely that [you] will obtain or remain in work or be able to do so'*. What this actually entails is left to the work coach. The requirement must be reasonable, having regard to your circumstances. You cannot be required to apply for a job or do paid work. Details of the work-related activity will be given to you in a written 'action plan'.

If you fail to take part in the work-related activity, a deduction of £14.62 a week is made from your income support. The deduction will continue to be made until you do take part in work-related activity or no longer need to do so (eg you have become eligible for income support in a different way; see Box F.1). The deduction will not be made if you can show good cause for your failure within five working days of having been notified of it.

You may restrict the hours you need to take part in work-related activity, but cannot exclude:
■ your child's normal school hours; *or*
■ any periods in which you entrust temporary supervision of your child to someone over the age of 18 (unless it is for their healthcare).

SSAA, S.2D(9)(d); Income Support (Work-related Activity) and Miscellaneous Amendments Regs 2014

## 14. Passporting to other benefits

Income support can help towards certain housing costs (see Chapter 27). If you get income support, you may be eligible for housing benefit to help with rent and will not have to go through a separate means test (see Chapter 25(20)). Getting income support may entitle you to other types of benefit, eg:
■ support for mortgage interest loans (Chapter 26);
■ free prescriptions and dental treatment (Chapter 52);
■ housing grants (Chapter 30);
■ help from the social fund (Chapter 29) and budgeting loans (Chapter 31(2));
■ free school meals (Chapter 40(1)); *and*
■ help with hospital travel fares (Chapter 55(2)).

# 20 Income-based jobseeker's allowance

| | | |
|---|---|---|
| 1 | What is income-based jobseeker's allowance? | 138 |
| 2 | Do you qualify? | 138 |
| 3 | If your partner is working | 139 |
| 4 | If you are aged 16 or 17 | 139 |
| 5 | How is income-based JSA worked out? | 139 |
| 6 | What is your applicable amount? | 139 |
| 7 | Passporting to other benefits | 139 |

## 1. What is income-based jobseeker's allowance?

Income-based jobseeker's allowance (JSA) is the means-tested component of JSA, the benefit for people who are unemployed (or working less than 16 hours a week) and seeking work (see Chapter 13). Income-based JSA provides for basic living expenses for you (and your partner, if you have one). It does not depend on your national insurance contributions. It is taxable.

You claim for yourself and your partner, if you have one. If you are one of a couple, you can choose who should make the claim. The one who claims must sign on and meet all the basic qualifying conditions. (If you are one of a 'joint-claim couple', see Chapter 13(2).) Income-based JSA can be paid in addition to contribution-based JSA.

For how to claim JSA, see Chapter 13(5).

If you are eligible to claim universal credit (see Box E.1 in Chapter 14), you will not be able to make a new claim for income-based JSA and will need to claim universal credit instead (see Chapter 14).

## 2. Do you qualify?

To qualify for income-based JSA, you must meet the basic qualifying conditions for JSA set out in Chapter 13(2). In addition, you must meet the following conditions.
❑ You must have no income, or your income is below your 'applicable amount' (see 6 below).
❑ You (and your partner) must not be claiming income support, income-related employment and support allowance or pension credit.
❑ You cannot have more than £16,000 in savings or capital (see Chapter 22(24)).

❏ If you have a partner, they must not be working for 24 or more hours a week (see 3 below).
❏ You must be aged 18 or over; or aged 16 or 17 and pass other tests (see 4 below).

JSA, Ss.3, 3A & 13

You must not be subject to immigration control (see Chapter 53(2)) and must satisfy the habitual residence test (see Chapter 53(4)).

## 3. If your partner is working

You are not entitled to income-based JSA if your partner is in *'remunerative work'* of (on average) 24 or more hours a week. Work counts if it is paid or done *'in expectation of payment'*. The rules closely follow the income support rules (see Chapter 19(3)) and provide for specific circumstances in which work can be ignored or, conversely, in which your partner can be treated as working even when they're not. If your partner's work does not exclude you from entitlement, their earnings are taken into account in the assessment of your benefit (see Chapter 22(4)-(6)).

JSA Regs, regs 51(1)(b) & (2)-(3), 52 & 53

## 4. If you are aged 16 or 17

If you are aged 16 or 17, you are eligible for JSA only if you are in a certain specified group (see below). You must register for work and training as directed and meet the basic qualifying conditions for JSA (see Chapter 13(2)), including being available to take up work and taking active steps to look for work and training. Provided you are not subject to a JSA sanction, you can restrict your availability to jobs where the employer is providing suitable training – ie you can turn down a job if no such training is offered.

JSA Regs, regs 62 & 64

**Who is eligible?** – You are eligible for income-based JSA while aged 16-17 if you fall into one of the specified groups of people who are eligible for income support (see Box F.1, Chapter 19) or employment and support allowance (see Chapter 11(7)), but you choose to claim JSA instead. You are also eligible if you are one of a couple and responsible for a child who lives with you, or if you are laid off or on short-time working (up to a maximum of 13 weeks).

JSA Regs, reg 61

**Severe hardship payments** – If you don't fit into any of the circumstances outlined above in which JSA can be paid to people aged 16-17, you can be paid JSA on a discretionary basis if you would otherwise suffer severe hardship. Such payments will only be made for a temporary period (usually eight weeks). You must also meet the basic qualifying conditions for JSA (see Chapter 13(2)).

Factors such as your training and job prospects, health, vulnerability and risk of homelessness should be taken into account. In some situations (eg if you fail to complete a training course without good reason), the amount you get is reduced for the first two weeks by 40% of the personal allowance (or 20% if you are seriously ill or pregnant).

JSA, Ss.16 & 17 and JSA Regs, reg 63

## 5. How is income-based JSA worked out?

Income-based JSA is worked out by comparing your needs with your resources (ie any income or capital you have). If you are a single person, only your needs and resources are relevant. If you are one of a couple, the needs and resources of both of you are relevant.

Set amounts for different needs are added together to reach the total amount the law says you need to live on. This is called your *'applicable amount'*. Any income you have (worked out under set rules) is deducted from your applicable amount. This leaves the amount of income-based JSA you are entitled to.

The calculation is as follows:

**Step 1: Add up your total capital resources** – See Chapter 22(22)-(37). You will not be entitled to income-based JSA if your capital, and any capital belonging to your partner, is more than £16,000.

**Step 2: Work out your applicable amount** – See 6 below.

**Step 3: Add up your total income resources** – See Chapter 22(2)-(21). Include the tariff income (see Chapter 22(25)) if you have capital over £6,000, or £10,000 if you live permanently in a care home.

**Step 4: Deduct your income from your applicable amount** – If your income is less than your applicable amount, income-based JSA makes up the difference in full, provided you meet the other JSA qualifying conditions (see Chapter 13(2)).

### If you meet the contribution-based conditions

You are paid contribution-based JSA if you meet the contribution conditions (see Chapter 13(17)). Your income-based JSA is also worked out and if this exceeds the contribution-based JSA, the extra is paid as a top-up.

## 6. What is your applicable amount?

The applicable amount is the amount of money the law says you need to live on. It consists of:

■ a personal allowance – for a single claimant or for a couple (these are the same as those for income support – see Chapter 19(8));
■ premiums – see below;
■ certain housing costs – see Chapter 27.

JSA Regs, reg 83, Sch 1 & Sch 2

**Premiums** – There are five premiums, each one with specific qualifying conditions. These are the same as for income support (see Chapter 19(9)), but there is an additional pensioner premium for a single person of £89.90.

JSA Regs, Sch 1, Parts III & IV

## 7. Passporting to other benefits

Income-based JSA can help towards certain housing costs (see Chapter 27). If you get income-based JSA, you may be eligible for housing benefit and won't have to go through a separate means test (see Chapter 25(20)).

Getting income-based JSA may entitle you to:

■ support for mortgage interest loans (Chapter 26);
■ free prescriptions and dental treatment (Chapter 52);
■ housing grants (Chapter 30);
■ help from the social fund (Chapter 29) and budgeting loans (Chapter 31(2));
■ free school meals (Chapter 40(1)); *and*
■ help with hospital travel fares (Chapter 55(2)).

# 21 Premiums

| 1 | Introduction | 139 |
|---|---|---|
| 2 | Disability premium | 140 |
| 3 | Severe disability premium | 141 |
| 4 | Enhanced disability premium | 142 |
| 5 | Pensioner premium | 142 |
| 6 | Carer premium | 143 |
| 7 | Family premium | 143 |
| 8 | Disabled child premium | 143 |

## 1. Introduction

The premiums described in this chapter apply to the following means-tested benefits:

■ income-related employment and support allowance (ESA);
■ income support;
■ income-based jobseeker's allowance (JSA);
■ housing benefit; *and*
■ pension credit.

In each case, they make up part of the *'applicable amount'* (or for pension credit, the *'appropriate minimum guarantee'*) of the benefit, which is the amount of money the law says you need to live on.

### The premiums

There are seven types of premium:
- disability premium;
- severe disability premium;
- enhanced disability premium;
- pensioner premium;
- carer premium;
- family premium; *and*
- disabled child premium.

You are entitled to these premiums if you meet certain conditions, detailed in 2 to 8 below. The qualifying rules for these premiums are generally the same for each benefit; where there are differences, we will point this out. However, not all the premiums apply to each means-tested benefit.

The family premium, disabled child premium and enhanced disability premium (for a child) usually only apply to housing benefit. They can only apply to income support or income-based JSA if your claim for either of these benefits began before April 2004 and you continue to receive support for your children through that benefit rather than through child tax credit.

The disability premium does not apply to income-related ESA and only applies to housing benefit in limited circumstances.

Only the severe disability premium and carer premium apply to pension credit (and are called 'additional amounts' rather than premiums, although the qualifying rules are similar).

For the sake of simplicity, we generally confine the legal references to those that apply to income-related ESA and income support.

**Northern Ireland: supplementary payments** – *'Supplementary payments'* are available in Northern Ireland to temporarily compensate people who lose their disability-related premium(s) in income support, income-related ESA or income-based JSA as a result of being re-assessed for personal independence payment (PIP). The disability-related premiums are: the disability premium, severe disability premium and enhanced disability premium. The supplementary payments make up for the loss of the premium(s) in full and can be paid for up to one year. There is similar provision for the pension credit additional amount for severe disability. For details of the PIP re-assessment, see Box B.6 in Chapter 5.

Welfare Supplementary Payment (Loss of Disability-Related Premiums) Regs (Northern Ireland) 2016

## 2. Disability premium

The disability premium does not apply to either income-related employment and support allowance (ESA) or pension credit. Nor does it apply to housing benefit if you are the claimant and have (or can be treated as having) a limited capability for work for an ESA award (see Chapter 12(2)-(3)).

HB Regs, Sch 3, para 13(9)

For a single claimant aged 16 or over, the disability premium is £33.55 a week. For a couple, the disability premium is £47.80 a week, whether one or both of the couple count as disabled.

The disability premium can be awarded in addition to any enhanced disability premium, carer premium or severe disability premium that is payable. The disability premium is payable only while the person who qualifies is under pension credit qualifying age (see Chapter 44(2)).

There are three ways of qualifying for the premium:
- you (or your partner) meet at least one of the disability conditions; *or*

- the person who is, or becomes, the claimant meets the incapacity condition; *or*
- for joint claims of jobseeker's allowance (JSA) only, you or your partner meet the limited capability for work condition.

IS Regs, Sch 2, paras 11-12; JSA Regs, Sch 1, paras 20G & 20H

### The disability conditions (claimant or partner)

You (or your partner) must be:
- certified by a consultant ophthalmologist as severely sight impaired or blind, or have ceased to be so certified in the past 28 weeks; *or*
- receiving one of the following *'qualifying benefits'*:
  - attendance allowance;
  - disability living allowance (DLA);
  - personal independence payment (PIP);
  - long-term incapacity benefit;*
  - severe disablement allowance (SDA);*
  - the disabled worker element or severe disability element of working tax credit;
  - war pensioner's mobility supplement;
  - constant attendance allowance; *or*
  - armed forces independence payment.

* In the case of income support or housing benefit, you must be receiving this qualifying benefit; in the case of income-based JSA, your partner must be receiving it (and in the case of a joint claim, either of you can be receiving it).

IS Regs, Sch 2, paras 12(1)(a)&(2) and 14B; JSA Regs, Sch 1, paras 14 & 19

If your attendance allowance, DLA or PIP stops when you are in hospital, you won't lose the disability premium – it can continue for up to 52 weeks of your hospital stay.

IS Regs, Sch 2, para 12(1)(d)

The premium will not be withdrawn if the overlapping benefits rule (see Chapter 8(6)) means you cannot be paid long-term incapacity benefit or SDA.

IS Regs, Sch 2, paras 7(1)(a)

As mentioned above, the disability premium does not apply to housing benefit if you are the claimant and you have (or can be treated as having) a limited capability for work for an ESA award. However, if you are the ESA claimant and you have a partner who claims housing benefit instead, and one of you gets a qualifying benefit (eg DLA), then the disability premium could be awarded.

**Backdating the premium** – If you get one of these qualifying benefits backdated, you should ask for the disability premium to be backdated to either the start of your means-tested benefit award or the start of your qualifying benefit award, whichever is the later.

### The incapacity condition (claimant only)

This is only relevant if your incapacity for work started before 27.10.08. To qualify, you must have been (or treated as having been) incapable of work or entitled to statutory sick pay during the qualifying period of 52 weeks (or 28 weeks if you are terminally ill) and still be incapable of work.

IS Regs, Sch 2, para 12(1)(b)

### The limited capability for work condition

This applies only to joint claims for JSA (see Chapter 13(2)). To qualify, you or your partner must:
- have had (or been treated as having had) a limited capability for work during the qualifying period of 52 weeks (or 28 weeks if you are terminally ill); *and*
- still have a limited capability for work.

Gaps of up to 12 weeks in your periods of limited capability for work (for any reason) are ignored. See Chapter 12(2) for details of the limited capability for work assessment.

JSA Regs, Sch 1, para 20H(1)(ee)

## 3. Severe disability premium

The severe disability premium (SDP) can be awarded in addition to any other premium that may be payable. It is £64.30 a week for each person who qualifies. To qualify:

■ you must receive a *'qualifying benefit'*. These are:
  – attendance allowance (or constant attendance allowance paid with industrial injuries disablement benefit or war pension);
  – disability living allowance care component at the middle or highest rate;
  – personal independence payment daily living component; *or*
  – armed forces independence payment; *and*
■ no one gets carer's allowance* for looking after you; *and*
■ you technically count as living alone (see below).

**Couples** – You can qualify for the SDP if:

■ both you and your partner get a qualifying benefit; *and*
■ you technically count as living alone (see below); *and either*
■ no one gets carer's allowance* for looking after either of you; *or*
■ someone gets carer's allowance* for looking after just one of you.

If your partner is certified by a consultant ophthalmologist as severely sight impaired or blind (or has ceased to be so certified in the past 28 weeks), you can still qualify for the SDP even if they do not get a qualifying benefit. You are treated as if you were a single person.

If you both get a qualifying benefit and no one gets carer's allowance* for looking after either you or your partner, your SDP will be £128.60.

If you both get a qualifying benefit, and one person gets carer's allowance* for looking after you (or your partner), your SDP will be £64.30.

If two people get carer's allowance* for looking after you and your partner, you won't qualify for any SDP.

* or the universal credit carer amount

ESA Regs, Sch 4, paras 6 & 11(2); IS Regs, Sch 2, para 13 & 15(5)

### Is someone caring for you?

If someone gets carer's allowance for looking after you, you cannot qualify for the SDP. If carer's allowance is not actually paid to your carer, for whatever reason, you can qualify for the SDP. For example, if carer's allowance cannot be paid to your carer because they get another non-means-tested benefit that cancels out carer's allowance under the *'overlapping benefits'* rule (which restricts you to getting paid just one type of non-means-tested benefit when you may be entitled to more than one), you may be entitled to the SDP. In this example, your carer may also qualify for a carer premium (see 6 below).

If your carer stops being paid carer's allowance, but it is some time before the office administering your means-tested benefit becomes aware of that fact, arrears of the SDP can be paid from the date that the carer's allowance stopped.

D&A Regs, reg 7(2)(bc)

Your carer cannot be forced to claim carer's allowance. The DWP will ask if anyone is caring for you, and may send you the carer's allowance claim-form to give to your carer, but nothing should happen if a non-resident carer decides not to claim. If your carer does claim carer's allowance, they will need you to confirm on the claim-form that they are caring for you for at least 35 hours a week.

*Note:* The deprivation of income and notional income rules apply also to carer's allowance (see Chapter 22(21)). Seek advice if you or your carer fall foul of these rules (see also *Decision Makers Guide*, Vol 5, Chap 28, para 28608).

**Couples** – It is possible for you and your partner to each get carer's allowance for looking after each other. Normally, this would disqualify you both from getting the SDP. However, when carer's allowance cannot actually be paid because of the overlapping benefits rule, the SDP would not be affected. If you both have overlapping benefits, such that neither of you are paid carer's allowance, you could get the higher SDP of £128.60, and also get two carer premiums (see 6 below).

**Arrears of carer's allowance** – Your premium is only affected once carer's allowance* is actually awarded. Arrears of carer's allowance* for any period before the date of the award will not affect your SDP.

* or the universal credit carer amount

ESA Regs, Sch 4, para 6(6); IS Regs, Sch 2, para 13(3ZA)

### Living alone?

You cannot qualify for the SDP if you have a partner who is not also getting a qualifying benefit (see above) unless your partner is certified as severely sight impaired or blind. Nor can you qualify if you have anyone living with you who is classed as a *'non-dependant'*, eg an adult son or daughter, friend or relative. The following are not classed as non-dependants and their presence in your home is ignored:

■ anyone aged under 18;
■ anyone aged 18 or 19 who is part of your family and is a 'qualifying young person' (see Chapter 41(1));
■ any person (and their partner) who is not a *'close relative'* (see below) of you or your partner and *'jointly occupies'* your dwelling as a co-owner or is sharing legal liability to make 'rent' payments – a joint occupier, eg a joint tenant, cannot count as a non-dependant. If a co-owner or joint tenant is a close relative of you (or your partner), they will count as a non-dependant (and so exclude you from the SDP) unless the co-ownership or joint liability began:
  – before 11.4.88;* *or*
  – after 11.4.88 but began *'on or before the date upon which [you or your] partner first occupied the dwelling in question'*;*
■ any person (and member of their household) who is not a close relative of you (or your partner) and who is your resident landlord sharing living accommodation with you, to whom you or your partner are *'liable to make payments on a commercial basis in respect of [your] occupation of [his or her] dwelling'*;
■ any person (and member of their household) who is not a close relative of you (or your partner) and who shares living accommodation with you and is *'liable to make payments on a commercial basis to [you or your partner] in respect of [his or her] occupation of [your] dwelling'*. A licensee, tenant or sub-tenant cannot count as a non-dependant;
■ a live-in helper (and their partner*) who has been placed with you by a charitable or voluntary body (not by a public or local authority), where the organisation (not the helper) charges you for that help. The charge need only be nominal.

ESA Regs, reg 71, IS Regs, reg 3

The presence of the following are also ignored:

■ someone who gets a qualifying benefit (see above);
■ anyone who is certified by a consultant ophthalmologist as severely sight impaired or blind (or has ceased to be so certified in the past 28 weeks).

ESA Regs, Sch 4, para 6(4)(a)&(c) & (9); IS Regs, Sch 2, para 13(3)(a)&(d)

If someone does not *'normally'* reside with you because they normally live elsewhere, they cannot count as a non-dependant (there is no definition of 'normally resides' in terms of time, frequency or anything else – see CSIS/100/93 and CIS/14850/96).

If you are already getting the SDP and someone joins your household for the first time to care for you or your partner, the SDP can continue for up to 12 weeks.* This is to give them time to claim carer's allowance. Once carer's allowance is awarded, the SDP stops.

ESA Regs, Sch 4, para 6(4)(b) & (7); IS Regs, Sch 2, para 13(3)(c) & (4)

* for income-related employment and support allowance,

income support, income-based jobseeker's allowance and pension credit only

### Close relatives and living arrangements
A *'close relative'* is a parent, parent-in-law, son, daughter, son-in-law or daughter-in-law, step-parent, stepson or stepdaughter, brother, sister or partner of any of those.
ESA Regs, reg 2; IS Regs, reg 2

If you have a licence or tenancy agreement with a relative who is not a close relative, you (or they) would be excluded from the SDP only while you were residing with them if your occupancy agreement was not on a commercial basis.
**Living independently?** – If you have entirely separate living accommodation, you cannot be said to *'normally reside'* with other people living under the same roof (eg if you live in a separate 'granny flat', your right to the SDP is not affected, even if a close relative lives under the same roof).

If you are living under the same roof as other people, with a separate bedroom, kitchen and living room, you won't count as residing with those other people so you can qualify for the SDP. It makes no difference if you share a bathroom, lavatory or communal area (which does not include any communal rooms, unless you are living in sheltered accommodation).
**Separate liability** – If you share a living room or kitchen with other people but are *'separately liable to make payments in respect of [your] occupation of the dwelling to the landlord'*, you won't count as residing with those other people even if they are close relatives. This would typically cover someone in supported lodgings.
ESA Regs, reg 71(6)-(7); IS Regs, reg 3(4)-(5)

### Protecting pre-21.10.91 SDP
If you are a co-owner or joint tenant with a close relative and had an award of income support, including an SDP, in the week before 21.10.91, your position is protected. Protection will survive changes in the type of agreement or the parties to the agreement, and even a move of home. It cannot survive a carer getting carer's allowance or a non-dependant joining your home. If you have a break off income support, you can regain your protected SDP if:
■ the break is no more than eight weeks (for any reason); *or*
■ the break is no more than 12 weeks (covered by the work 'trial period' provisions); *or*
■ you have just finished employment training or an employment rehabilitation course and you reclaim income support immediately.
Income Support (General) Amdt No.6 Regs 1991, regs 4-6

### Hospital
If you enter hospital, the SDP will be withdrawn once your qualifying benefit is withdrawn – usually once you've been in hospital for 28 days.

For couples, if you each receive a qualifying benefit, and one or both of you enter hospital, you will still get the SDP even after the qualifying benefit is withdrawn, but it will only be paid at the rate of £64.30 a week.
ESA Regs, Sch 4, paras 6(5) & 11(2)(b)(i); IS Regs, Sch 2, paras 13(3A) & 15(5)(b)(i)

If your carer enters hospital and their carer's allowance is withdrawn, you may get the SDP while they are in hospital.

### 4. Enhanced disability premium
The enhanced disability premium does not apply to pension credit. It is £16.40 a week for a single person and £23.55 for a couple where one or both qualify. You or your partner qualify for this premium if you or they:
■ are paid a qualifying benefit – see below;
■ (for housing benefit only) have, or can be treated as having, a limited capability for work-related activity – see Chapter 12(5)-(6); *or*
■ (for employment and support allowance only) are in the

support group – see Chapter 11(5).
The *'qualifying benefits'* are:
■ disability living allowance (DLA) highest rate care component;
■ personal independence payment (PIP) enhanced rate daily living component; *and*
■ armed forces independence payment.
The enhanced disability premium can be awarded in addition to any disability premium or severe disability premium that may be payable. It is payable only while the person who qualifies is under pension credit qualifying age (see Chapter 44(2)).

If your DLA or PIP is withdrawn while you are in hospital, you won't lose the enhanced disability premium. It can continue for up to 52 weeks of the hospital stay.
ESA Regs, Sch 4, para 7; IS Regs, Sch 2, para 13A

**Enhanced disability premium (child)** – This premium generally applies only to housing benefit. It can, however, be paid with income support or income-based jobseeker's allowance if your claim began before April 2004 and you continue to receive support for your children through one of those benefits rather than through child tax credit. The enhanced disability premium is paid at the rate of £25.48 for each child who qualifies.

A child qualifies for the enhanced disability premium if they are paid a qualifying benefit (see above). The enhanced disability premium can be awarded in addition to a disabled child premium. If a child is in hospital, you keep the enhanced disability premium for as long as the child is treated as a member of your family.
HB Regs, Sch 3, para 15

### 5. Pensioner premium
The pensioner premium does not apply to pension credit or housing benefit. It is paid if you or your partner have reached pension credit qualifying age (see Chapter 44(2)). It can be awarded in addition to any severe disability premium or carer premium that may be payable.

There are only limited circumstances in which the pensioner premium will be relevant to an income support claim. It is payable only when the income support claimant is under pension credit qualifying age and their partner reaches that age first and chooses not to claim pension credit instead. Since pension credit has a number of features that make it more attractive than income support (particularly with respect to the way in which capital and savings are treated), this is not likely to occur very often.

The pensioner premium is normally £89.90 a week for a single person and £133.95 for a couple. For income-related employment and support allowance, however, these figures are then reduced by any additional component that may be payable (this ensures that your applicable amount, before any other premiums are added on, is equivalent to the pension credit 'standard minimum guarantee' – see Chapter 44(3)).
ESA Regs, Sch 4, paras 5 & 11(1)

**Enhanced and higher pensioner premiums** – For income support and income-based jobseeker's allowance, the pensioner premium was originally paid at three different levels: the pensioner, enhanced and higher pensioner premiums. Although these separate premiums still technically exist, they are now all paid at the same rate. The difference occasionally becomes important (we point out elsewhere in this handbook when it does).

❏ **Pensioner premium** – You qualify for this if you or your partner have reached pension credit qualifying age but are still aged under 75.
❏ **Enhanced pensioner premium** – You qualify for this if you or your partner are aged 75-79 (inclusive).
❏ **Higher pensioner premium** – You qualify for this if you or your partner:

- are aged 80 or over; *or*
- have reached pension credit qualifying age and also meet a 'disability condition' for the disability premium (see 2 above).
  There are other ways to qualify. For details, see *Disability Rights Handbook* 25th edition, page 20.

IS Regs, Sch 2, paras 9-10

## 6. Carer premium

The carer premium can be awarded in addition to any of the other premiums covered in this chapter. It is £36 a week for each person who qualifies.

You qualify for a carer premium if you or your partner:
- are actually paid carer's allowance; *or*
- have an underlying entitlement to carer's allowance, ie you are entitled to carer's allowance but it cannot be paid because of the overlapping benefits rule (see Chapter 8(6)).

**Eight-week extension** – The carer premium can continue for eight weeks after you stop getting carer's allowance or lose an underlying entitlement to it. Your caring role can have ended temporarily or permanently and for any reason, with one exception: if the person you are caring for dies. In that case, since carer's allowance can also be extended for eight weeks, the carer premium can continue during the same period and is limited to that period. Thus, it must stop being paid eight weeks after the death of the person being cared for.

ESA Regs, Sch 4, para 8; IS Regs, Sch 2, para 14ZA

## 7. Family premium

This premium generally applies only to housing benefit, income support and income-based jobseeker's allowance (JSA) in limited circumstances. It can apply to housing benefit if your claim began before 1.5.16 and you were already responsible for a child or 'qualifying young person' (see Chapter 41(1)) at that date. It can apply to income support or income-based JSA if your claim began before April 2004 and you continue to receive support for your children through one of those benefits rather than through child tax credit.

You only get one family premium, regardless of the number of children you have. The ordinary rate of £17.45 a week applies if you are one of a couple or a lone parent, unless you have transitional protection for the housing benefit higher lone parent rate of £22.20 (see below). The ordinary rate can be awarded in addition to any other premium.

**Protected lone parent rate** – The lone parent rate was abolished on 6.4.98 but existing housing benefit claimants can continue to get it. You must:
- have been a lone parent continuously entitled (or treated as entitled) to housing benefit since 5.4.98;
- not cease to be or become entitled to income support, income-based JSA or income-related employment and support allowance (ESA), although you can switch between these three benefits; *and*
- not be entitled to a disability premium or an ESA additional component (see Chapter 11(6)).

HB Regs, Sch 3, para 3

## 8. Disabled child premium

This premium generally applies only to housing benefit. It can, however, be paid with income support or income-based jobseeker's allowance (JSA) if your claim began before April 2004 and you continue to receive support for your children through one of those benefits rather than through child tax credit. The disabled child premium can be awarded in addition to any of the other premiums. The disabled child premium is £62.86 a week for each child who lives with you and counts as disabled. Your child counts as disabled if they:
- are certified by a consultant ophthalmologist as severely sight impaired or blind or have ceased to be so certified in the past 28 weeks; *or*

- receive disability living allowance, personal independence payment or armed forces independence payment.

HB Regs, Sch 3, para 16

For income support and income-based JSA, the premium cannot be awarded for a child or young person if they have more than £3,000 in capital or have been in hospital for more than 52 weeks.

IS Regs, Sch 2, para 14; JSA Regs, Sch 1, para 16

# 22 Income and capital

| | | |
|---|---|---|
| 1 | Introduction | 143 |
| **A** | **Income** | |
| 2 | Whose income is included? | 144 |
| 3 | Disregarded income | 144 |
| 4 | Earnings from employment | 144 |
| 5 | Earnings from self-employment | 144 |
| 6 | Earnings disregards | 145 |
| 7 | Income from benefits, tax credits and pensions | 146 |
| 8 | Charitable, voluntary and personal injury payments | 147 |
| 9 | Maintenance payments | 147 |
| 10 | Payments to third parties | 148 |
| 11 | Payments in kind | 148 |
| 12 | Training and employment schemes | 148 |
| 13 | Payments towards education | 148 |
| 14 | Payments for your home | 148 |
| 15 | Income from tenants and lodgers | 149 |
| 16 | Payments for care homes | 149 |
| 17 | Payments for children | 149 |
| 18 | Income generated from capital | 149 |
| 19 | Capital treated as income | 149 |
| 20 | Miscellaneous income | 149 |
| 21 | Notional income | 150 |
| **B** | **Capital** | |
| 22 | Introduction | 150 |
| 23 | Whose capital is included? | 150 |
| 24 | Capital limits | 150 |
| 25 | Tariff income | 151 |
| 26 | How is capital valued? | 151 |
| 27 | Benefits | 151 |
| 28 | Personal possessions | 151 |
| 29 | Trust funds and personal injury payments | 151 |
| 30 | Training and employment | 152 |
| 31 | Your home | 152 |
| 32 | Right to receive income or payment in future | 152 |
| 33 | Other capital | 152 |
| 34 | Loans | 153 |
| 35 | Income treated as capital | 153 |
| 36 | Notional capital | 153 |
| 37 | Diminishing notional capital rule | 153 |

## 1. Introduction

In this chapter we look at how your income and capital are treated when the pre-universal credit means-tested benefits are being calculated. The rules in this chapter apply to the following benefits:
- income-related employment and support allowance;
- income support;
- income-based jobseeker's allowance; *and*
- housing benefit – as long as you (and your partner) are under pension credit qualifying age or you (or your partner) are receiving one of the three benefits above; if not, the rules are similar to pension credit.

Where there are significant differences in the way income or capital are treated for different benefits, we say so. As income and capital are treated in a substantially different way for pension credit, we describe these separately in Chapter 44(5) and 44(6).

For the sake of simplicity, we generally confine the legal references to those that apply to income-related employment and support allowance and income support.

**Income or capital?** – Generally, it will be clear whether a particular resource is income or capital, although the distinction is not defined in the regulations. Where it is unclear, the general principle (developed in case law) is that payments of income recur periodically and do not include ad hoc payments, whereas capital payments are one-off and not linked to a particular period (although capital may be paid in instalments). In some cases, the rules treat capital as income (see 19 below) and vice versa (see 35 below).

## A. INCOME

## 2. Whose income is included?

If you are one of a couple (married or living together as a married couple or in a civil partnership), your partner's income is added to yours. Otherwise, only your own income is taken into account; income belonging to dependent children is disregarded (unless you have a claim for income support or income-based jobseeker's allowance that began before April 2004 and you still receive support for your children through one of those benefits rather than through child tax credit – see *Disability Rights Handbook* 28th edition, page 25).

ESA Regs, reg 83; IS Regs, reg 23

## 3. Disregarded income

All income is considered, including earnings, benefits and pensions. However, some income may then be disregarded, partially or fully. In 4 to 6 below, we outline how earnings are assessed and how much is disregarded; in 7 to 20, we describe how other income is treated.

In some cases you can be treated as possessing income that you don't actually have (see 21 below).

## 4. Earnings from employment
### How earnings from employment are assessed

The income assessment is normally related to your actual earnings for a particular week. If you are paid monthly, that month's pay is multiplied by 12 and then divided by 52 to give a weekly amount. If your income varies from week to week, your average earnings may be worked out over a more representative period. If you have a pattern of working some weeks on, some weeks off, your average weekly earnings may be worked out over your working cycle: that average is then also taken into account in your off weeks. Otherwise, earnings are averaged over a period of five weeks, or over another period if that would be more accurate.

ESA Regs, reg 94(1)&(6); IS Regs, reg 32(1)&(6)

If you are not being paid, or are underpaid for a service, 'notional' earnings may be taken into account (see 21 below).

**Final earnings** – If you have just retired, or your job has ended or been interrupted for some other reason (but not if you have been suspended), your last normal earnings as an employee will usually be disregarded. This includes pay in lieu of notice, holiday pay (payable within four weeks of the employment ending or being interrupted) and pay in lieu

of wages (but not periodic redundancy payments). These disregards only apply when the job ends or is interrupted before the first day of entitlement to the means-tested benefit. Retainer payments and employment protection payments will be taken into account.

ESA Regs, Sch 7, para 1; IS Regs, Sch 8, para 1

**Housing benefit** – Your average weekly earnings are estimated over the five weeks before your housing benefit claim if you are paid weekly, or the two months before your claim if you are paid monthly. Your local authority can average them over another period if that would give a more accurate estimate.

HB Regs, reg 29

### Working out net earnings

Do not count any payment in kind (see 11 below) or any payment for *'expenses wholly, exclusively and necessarily incurred in the performance of the duties of the employment'*. Occupational pensions are not treated as earnings, but are normally taken into account in full as income, less tax payable (see 7 below).

ESA Regs, Sch 8, para 3; IS Regs, Sch 9, para 3

For income support, income-based jobseeker's allowance and income-related employment and support allowance, do not count as earnings any of the following payments from your employer: sick pay, maternity pay, paternity pay, adoption pay, statutory sick pay (SSP), statutory maternity pay (SMP), statutory paternity pay (SPP), statutory shared parental pay (SSPP) or statutory adoption pay (SAP). Instead, these are counted in full as income, less tax, national insurance contributions and half of any contributions you make towards an occupational or personal pension scheme.

ESA Regs, regs 95(2)(b) & Sch 8, paras 1&4; IS Regs, reg 35(2)(b) & Sch 9, paras 1&4

For housing benefit, the following are counted as earnings: sick pay, maternity pay, paternity pay or adoption pay from your employer, SSP, SMP, SPP, SSPP and SAP.

HB Regs, reg 35(1)(i)-(j)

An advance of earnings or a loan made by your employer counts as capital.

ESA Regs, reg 112(5) & IS Regs, reg 48(5)

Count any other payment from your employer as earnings: eg bonuses, commission, payments towards travel expenses between your home and workplace or towards childminding fees and retainers. Also count pay in lieu of notice and holiday pay, unless your job has ended or been interrupted for some other reason – see 'Final earnings' above. Most non-cash vouchers, but not childcare vouchers, count as earnings.

ESA Regs, reg 95(1)&(3); IS Regs, regs 35(1)&(2A)

Deduct from your earnings income tax, national insurance contributions and half of any contribution you make towards an occupational or personal pension scheme.

ESA Regs, reg 96; IS Regs, reg 36

## 5. Earnings from self-employment

There are specific rules for working out income from self-employment related to the net profit of your business or your share of the business. If you get royalties or copyright payments, seek advice from an organisation supporting artists in your field (eg The Writers' Guild).

### Step 1: Take full gross receipts of the business

This is the money you receive from the business over a specific trading period. This is normally one year, but if you have recently started self-employment or there has been a change that is likely to affect the normal pattern of business, the DWP can pick a more representative period.

ESA Regs, reg 92; IS Regs, reg 30

For housing benefit, earnings are usually assessed over the period covered by your last year's trading accounts. A different period can be used if appropriate, as long as it is no longer than one year.

HB Regs, reg 30

---

## Disability Rights UK

### Visit our website

Our website contains a wealth of information about benefits, news about our current campaigns and updates on the projects we run across the whole of the UK.

To find out more about what we do, visit
**www.disabilityrightsuk.org**

## Step 2: Deduct the following expenses:

■ '*any expenses wholly and exclusively defrayed* [ie actually paid] *in that period for the purposes of that employment*': this is subject to some exceptions and extra rules, eg the expenses must be 'reasonably incurred'; business entertainment is specifically excluded. Expenses can be apportioned between business and personal use (see R(FC)1/91 and R(IS)13/91);

■ a repayment of capital on any loan used for replacing equipment or machinery, or for repairing existing business assets (less any insurance payments);

■ the excess of any VAT paid over VAT received;

■ expenditure out of income to repair an existing business asset (less any insurance payment);

■ interest (but not capital) payments on a loan taken out for the purposes of the employment.

However, if you work as a childminder, simply deduct two-thirds of those earnings.

ESA Regs, reg 98(3)(a) & (5)-(9); IS Regs, reg 38(3)(a) & (5)-(9)

## Step 3: To calculate your net profit, deduct:

■ income tax – this is related to your appropriate personal tax allowances, on a pro rata basis if necessary (see Chapter 35(3));

■ Class 2 and Class 4 national insurance contributions;

■ half of any contribution to a personal pension scheme (including annuity contracts or trust schemes approved under tax law).

ESA Regs, regs 98(3)(b)-(c) & 99; IS Regs, regs 38(3)(b)-(c) & 39

## Step 4: See which earnings disregards apply

Check to see which, if any, earnings disregards apply (see 6 below).

## 6. Earnings disregards

After working out your total earnings, as above, deduct the appropriate '*earnings disregard*'. This applies to the earnings of employees and the self-employed. The level of the disregard will depend on which benefit you are claiming.

### Employment and support allowance (ESA)

If you are doing 'permitted work' (see Chapter 33(3)), earnings from this work up to the permitted work earnings limit that applies in your case will be disregarded.

Up to £20 can normally be disregarded if you are doing any other kind of work that is allowed (see Chapter 33(2)).

If your earnings from permitted work are less than the limit that applies in your case, and you are undertaking duties as the disability member of a First-tier Tribunal, up to £20 a week of earnings from that work can also be disregarded until the permitted work earnings limit is reached. If your earnings from permitted work are less than the limit and you have a partner who is doing other work, up to £20 of their earnings can be similarly disregarded to make up the shortfall.

ESA Regs, Sch 7, paras 5-7

### Other means-tested benefits

For housing benefit, if you are claiming contributory ESA, incapacity benefit or severe disablement allowance and are doing permitted work (see Chapter 33(3)), all your earnings up to the permitted work earnings limit that applies in your case will be disregarded. If your earnings from permitted work are less than this limit, earnings from other work that is allowed can also be disregarded until the limit is reached. If your earnings from permitted work are less than the limit and you have a partner who is doing other work, up to £20 of their earnings can be similarly disregarded to make up the shortfall.

The same disregard applies to housing benefit if you are only claiming national insurance credits (for incapacity or limited capability for work) and are doing permitted work.

For income support, income-based jobseeker's allowance (JSA) and, if a permitted work disregard does not apply, housing benefit, disregard £20 a week of your earnings (or joint earnings with your partner) if any of the following apply.

❑ You qualify for a disability premium or, for housing benefit, a severe disability premium, the support component or you (or your partner) are in the work-related activity group (see Chapter 11(4)).

❑ You qualify for a carer premium. The disregard applies to the carer's earnings; if you are the carer and your earnings are less than £20, up to £5 (or £10 for housing benefit) can be disregarded from your partner's earnings, subject to the overall £20 maximum.

❑ You are a lone parent. For housing benefit only, the disregard for lone parents is £25.

❑ For income support and income-based JSA only, you qualify for the higher pensioner premium – but only if you or your partner were working part time immediately before reaching pension credit qualifying age and were then entitled to the £20 disability premium earnings disregard. Since then, you or your partner must have continued in part-time employment, although breaks of up to eight weeks when you were not getting the means-tested benefit are ignored.

❑ For income support and income-based JSA only, you are one of a couple and the benefit would include a disability premium but for the fact that the higher pensioner premium applies instead. Either you or your partner must be under pension credit qualifying age with either one of you in part-time employment.

❑ If you are working as a part-time firefighter, an auxiliary coastguard on coast rescue activities, a part-time member of a lifeboat crew or a member of the reserve forces, up to £20 of those earnings are disregarded. If you are one of a couple and you are both doing one of those jobs, you are still restricted to the joint earnings disregard of £20. If you are doing one of those jobs, your earnings are less than £20 and either you or your partner are also doing an ordinary part-time job, up to £5 (or £10 for housing benefit) can be disregarded from the earnings of the ordinary job, subject to the overall £20 maximum.

If you do not qualify for the £20 earnings disregard, disregard £5 from earnings if you are single. Disregard £10 from joint earnings if you are one of a couple, whether one or both of you are working.

IS Regs, Sch 8, paras 4-9; HB Regs, Sch 4, paras 3-10A

For housing benefit there are two extra disregards: the 'childcare costs' disregard and the 'additional earnings' disregard.

### Childcare costs earnings disregard in housing benefit

For housing benefit only, you may get an extra earnings disregard for childcare costs.

❑ You must be:

■ a lone parent working at least 16 hours a week; *or*

■ one of a couple and you both work at least 16 hours a week; *or*

■ one of a couple and one of you works at least 16 hours a week and the other is incapacitated (see below), a hospital inpatient or in prison.

In each of these three categories you are still treated as working for up to 28 weeks when you are off sick and claiming statutory sick pay, ESA or income support or national insurance credits on the grounds of incapacity or limited capability for work. You are also still treated as working when you are on maternity, paternity, shared parental or adoption leave, as long as you are entitled to statutory maternity, paternity, shared parental or adoption pay, maternity allowance or income support while on paternity leave. In each case, you must have previously been working for at least 16 hours a week.

❏ Your child must be aged 15 or under, or aged 16 or under if they are eligible for a disabled child premium (see Chapter 21(8)). The disregard is available until the day before the first Monday in September after their 15th or 16th birthday.

❏ The childcare must meet certain requirements. You must be paying an approved or registered childcare provider, which can include out-of-school-hours schemes run on school property or childcare provided by local authorities. If a relative of the child is providing the care, it needs to be done away from your home.

Disregard from your earnings childcare payments up to a maximum of £175 weekly for one child, or £300 weekly for two or more children.

HB Regs, regs 27(1)(c)&(3) and 28

If you get working tax credit or child tax credit and your earnings, once other earnings disregards have been taken off, are less than the disregard for childcare costs, then the disregard is made from the total of your earnings and your tax credits added together.

HB Regs, reg 27(1)(c)&(2)

**Incapacitated** – You count as *'incapacitated'* if:

■ you get main-phase ESA, long-term incapacity benefit or severe disablement allowance; *or*

■ you get attendance allowance, disability living allowance, personal independence payment, armed forces independence payment or constant attendance allowance (or payment has stopped because you are an inpatient); *or*

■ your housing benefit includes the disability premium (on account of your incapacity) or the support component (on account of your limited capability for work-related activity) or you are in the work-related activity group (see Chapter 11(4)); *or*

■ you are the claimant and have been incapable of work for at least 28 weeks (ignoring gaps of eight weeks or less) or have had a limited capability for work for at least 28 weeks (ignoring gaps of 12 weeks or less).

### Additional earnings disregard in housing benefit

There is an additional earnings disregard, only in housing benefit, for certain groups of people who work on average either 16 or 30 hours or more a week. Disregard an extra £17.10 from earnings if you (or your partner):

■ receive the 30-hour element in your working tax credit – see Chapter 23(7); *or*

■ are aged at least 25 and work at least 30 hours a week; *or*

■ work at least 16 hours a week; *and*

– you are one of a couple and are responsible for a child or young person; *or*

– you are a lone parent; *or*

– your housing benefit includes the disability premium or the support component (see Chapter 25(24)) or you (or your partner) are in the work-related activity group (see Chapter 11(4)). If you are the one eligible for the premium or component or you are in the work-related activity group, then you must be the one who is working for at least 16 hours a week.

Only one such disregard can be made from earnings or from a couple's joint earnings. If your earnings are less than the sum of all the relevant earnings and childcare costs disregards, then £17.10 can be disregarded from any working tax credit that is awarded instead.

HB Regs, Sch 4, para 17

### Earnings from reserve forces training

If you or your partner receive earnings from any annual continuous training as a member of the reserve forces for a maximum of 15 days in any calendar year (or 43 days in your first year of training), an earnings disregard ensures that you are still entitled to at least 10p in income support or income-based JSA after the earnings have been taken into account.

This is to protect entitlement to passported benefits in cases where the earnings are paid at a higher level than income support or income-based JSA and to ensure that a new benefit claim is not necessary after the training is completed. Similar rules apply to income-related ESA if your partner receives earnings for such training.

ESA Regs, Sch 7, para 11A; IS Regs, Sch 8, para 15A

## 7. Income from benefits, tax credits and pensions

Most benefits are taken into account in full (less income tax payable) but some are completely or partly disregarded.

### Benefits that are completely disregarded

The following benefits are completely disregarded:

■ guardian's allowance;

■ child benefit (unless you have a claim for income support or income-based jobseeker's allowance (JSA) that began before April 2004 and you continue to receive support for your children through one of those benefits rather than through child tax credit);

■ child dependants' additions to non-means-tested benefits (for income-related employment and support allowance (ESA), income support and income-based JSA; but with the latter two benefits, only if child tax credit has been awarded);

ESA Regs, Sch 8, paras 6 & 7(2)-(3); IS Regs, Sch 9, paras 5A & 5B(2)-(3)

■ disability living allowance, personal independence payment and attendance allowance;

■ war pensioners' mobility supplement;

■ constant attendance allowance, severe disablement occupational allowance and exceptionally severe disablement allowance (payable under the War Pensions or Industrial Injuries schemes);

■ ex-gratia payments made to compensate for non-payment of income-related ESA, income support, income-based JSA, universal credit or any of the benefits listed in the above three bullet points;

ESA Regs, Sch 8, paras 8-11; IS Regs, Sch 9, paras 6-9

■ social fund or local welfare assistance payments;

■ Christmas bonus;

■ payment or repayment of health benefits, and payment made instead of Healthy Start vouchers or vitamins;

ESA Regs, Sch 8, paras 35, 35A, 37 & 45-46; IS Regs, Sch 9, paras 31, 31A, 33 & 48-49

■ certain supplementary payments or pensions for war widows, widowers or surviving civil partners;

■ dependants' additions to non-means-tested benefits if the dependant is not a member of your family;

ESA Regs, Sch 8, paras 49-52; IS Regs, Sch 9, paras 53-56

■ housing benefit;

■ armed forces independence payment; *and*

■ bereavement support payment (unless this is disregarded as capital – see 27 below).

ESA Regs, Sch 8, paras 64, 66 & 68; IS Regs, Sch 9, paras 5, 76A & 80

**If you save your benefit** – Although these benefits are disregarded as income in the assessment, if there is money left at the end of the period for which the benefit is paid, it will be treated as capital and, in most cases, will count with any other capital you have. For example, if you save your mobility component towards a wheelchair, the savings will count as capital. This will only affect your benefit if it takes your capital above the lower limit for tariff income (see 25 below). Benefit can be disregarded as capital in limited cases – see 27 below.

### Benefits that are partly disregarded

For income-related ESA, income support and income-based JSA, disregard up to £10 of:

■ widowed parent's or widowed mother's allowance;

■ a war disablement pension;

- a guaranteed income payment (GIP) or survivor's GIP made under the Armed Forces Compensation scheme (if another pension reduces the GIP to less than £10, the remaining disregard can be made from that pension instead);
- war widow's or widower's pension;
- pensions comparable to the above, paid by another country; *and*
- pensions paid by governments to victims of Nazi persecution.

ESA Regs, Sch 8, para 17; IS Regs, Sch 9, para 16

**Housing benefit** – For housing benefit, the rule is the same except that £15 is disregarded from the widowed parent's or widowed mother's allowance. Local authorities can choose to run a local scheme under which they disregard more than £10 of a war pension or GIP. Your local authority can tell you if it runs a scheme and how much it disregards.

HB Regs, Sch 5, paras 15 & 16

### Tax credits

Working tax credit (WTC) is taken into account in full for income-related ESA, income support and income-based JSA. Child tax credit (CTC) is disregarded.

ESA Regs, Sch 8, para 7(1); IS Regs, Sch 9, para 5B(1)

For housing benefit, both WTC and CTC are taken into account in full. They will be reduced, however, by any deduction being made to recover an overpayment of tax credit that arose in a previous tax year.

HB Regs, reg 40(6)

Additionally, if your earnings are less than the sum of all the relevant earnings and childcare costs disregards, the WTC taken into account can be reduced by the £17.10 additional earnings disregard (see 6 above).

### Employer-paid benefits

**ESA/income support/JSA** – Statutory sick pay (SSP), statutory maternity pay (SMP), statutory paternity pay (SPP) statutory shared parental pay (SSPP) and statutory adoption pay (SAP) are taken into account in full for income-related ESA, income support and income-based JSA, less Class 1 national insurance contributions, tax and half of any contributions you make towards an occupational or personal pension scheme.

ESA Regs, reg 95(2)(b) & Sch 8, paras 1 & 4; IS Regs, reg 35(2)(b) & Sch 9, paras 1 & 4

**Housing benefit** – SSP, SMP, SPP, SSPP and SAP are counted as earnings for housing benefit. So when you go on sick leave, maternity leave, paternity leave, shared parental leave or adoption leave, your SSP, SMP, SPP, SSPP or SAP are added to any actual earnings you continue to receive. All the rules on assessing earnings then apply. In particular, you get an 'earnings disregard' (see 6 above) even if you receive only SSP, SMP, SPP, SSPP or SAP.

HB Regs, reg 35(1)(i)

### Occupational and personal pensions

Occupational, personal and state pensions are normally taken into account in full, less any tax payable. If you have reached pension credit qualifying age (see Chapter 44(2)), income from an occupational or personal pension or the Pension Protection Fund that would be available to you on application, or from a pension fund or pot that could be turned into an annuity, may be taken into account as 'notional income' (see 21 below). The same applies to your partner.

ESA Regs, reg 104(8); IS Regs, reg 40(4)

### ESA sanctions

For income support and income-based JSA, if your partner is receiving contributory ESA and a sanction has been applied to it (see Chapter 11(15)), then the contributory ESA will be taken into account in full as if it had not been sanctioned.

The same rule applies to housing benefit if either you or your partner receive a contributory ESA sanction.

IS Regs, reg 40(6)

## 8. Charitable, voluntary and personal injury payments

**Regular payments** – Regular charitable and voluntary payments are usually disregarded. Charitable payments are payments made by a charitable trust at the trustees' discretion. Voluntary payments are similar, but not usually made from charitable trusts; they are payments that have a benevolent purpose and are given without anything being given in return (R(IS)4/94). Regular payments are those paid or due to be paid at recurring intervals, such as weekly, monthly, annually or following some other pattern. For income support and income-based jobseeker's allowance, the disregard does not apply to such payments made to strikers.

For maintenance payments, see 9 below.

ESA Regs, Sch 8, para 16; IS Regs, Sch 9, para 15

**Irregular payments** – Charitable or voluntary payments that are not paid to you at regular intervals are treated as capital. Irregular gifts in kind from a charity are disregarded. See 10 below for how payments made to third parties are treated.

ESA Regs, reg 112(7); IS Regs, reg 48(9)

### Payments from specific trusts

Payments in kind or cash made by the Macfarlane Trusts, the Fund, the Eileen Trust, MFET Ltd, the Skipton Fund, the Caxton Foundation, the Scottish Infected Blood Support scheme, an approved blood scheme or the Independent Living Fund are disregarded.

Payments made by or on behalf of a person with haemophilia, HIV or hepatitis C (or their partner) who received money from any of the trusts or funds above are disregarded in full if they originate from that trust or fund. To qualify for the disregard, the payment must be made to (or for the benefit of) the partner or former partner of the person who is making the payment (unless you are separated), or to dependent children or young people (if they are a member of the donor's family, or were, but are now a member of the claimant's family). If the person making the payment has no partner or dependent children, a payment (including a payment from their estate if they have died) to their parent, step-parent or guardian is disregarded for a period of two years after their death, as long as the payment originates from any of these trusts. Payments deriving from the London Bombings Relief Charitable Fund, the London Emergencies Trust and the WeLoveManchester Emergency Fund are treated in the same way.

ESA Regs, Sch 8, para 41; IS Regs, Sch 9, para 39

### Personal injury payments

Payments made or due to be made at regular intervals are disregarded as long as they are:

- from a trust set up from an award made because of any personal injury to you;
- under an annuity bought from funds derived from an award made because of any personal injury to you; *or*
- received under an agreement or court order to pay you because of any personal injury to you.

Personal injury payments include vaccine damage payments (Chapter 49) and criminal injuries compensation payments (Chapter 48), as well as payments from insurance companies and damages awards by the courts.

ESA Regs, Sch 8, para 16(3); IS Regs, Sch 9, para 15(5A)

## 9. Maintenance payments

Payments made (including those made voluntarily) by *'liable relatives'* towards the maintenance of children or young people who live with you are disregarded. A liable relative will normally be a former spouse or civil partner or a non-resident parent of the child or young person.

ESA Regs, Sch 8, para 60; IS Regs, Sch 9, para 73

Other maintenance payments (eg spousal maintenance) are taken fully into account, unless, for housing benefit, you are responsible for a child or young person, in which case £15 will be disregarded. If more than one payment is made in any week, they will be added together and treated as a single payment, so only one disregard can apply.

HB Regs, Sch 5, para 47

If you pay maintenance, there is no disregard for your payments.

## 10. Payments to third parties

A payment of income made to a third party for the benefit of you or your partner can be taken into account but only to the extent that it is used for everyday living expenses (see below). If it is used for something else (eg paying a garage for your car to be repaired or adapted), it will be disregarded. If the payments are used to provide benefits in kind, see 11 below.

A payment made to a third party towards the cost of your care home is treated as your income. This may be partly disregarded under other rules (see 16 below).

A payment to a third party from an occupational or personal pension or the Pension Protection Fund is normally taken into account even if it is not used for everyday living expenses.

ESA Regs, reg 107(3); IS Regs, reg 42(4)

**Everyday living expenses** – These are defined as: food, ordinary clothing or footwear, household fuel, council tax, water charges, rent (for which housing benefit is payable) or any housing costs (which are met by employment and support allowance, income support or jobseeker's allowance). Ordinary clothing or footwear includes items for normal daily use, but does not include school uniforms, or clothing or footwear used solely for sporting activities.

ESA Regs, regs 2(1) & 107(3)(c); IS Regs, reg 42(4)(a)(ii)&(9)

## 11. Payments in kind

Payments in kind, eg a bus pass, food, petrol, etc, are disregarded unless (for income support and income-based jobseeker's allowance) you are involved in a trade dispute. However, payments made to third parties that are used to provide benefits in kind to you are treated as your income.

ESA Regs, Sch 8, para 22; IS Regs, Sch 9, para 21

Non-cash vouchers from an employer that are liable for Class 1 national insurance contributions are not treated as payments in kind but as earnings. Vouchers not liable for contributions are treated as payments in kind (eg certain charitable vouchers) and are thus disregarded.

ESA Regs, reg 95(3); IS Regs, reg 35(2A)

## 12. Training and employment schemes

If you are on a government training programme or employment scheme (under either s.2 (but not s.2(3)) of the Employment and Training Act 1973 or s.2 (but not s.2(5)) of the Enterprise and New Towns (Scotland) Act 1990) any payment is disregarded unless it is:

- made as a substitute for employment and support allowance, incapacity benefit, income support, jobseeker's allowance or severe disablement allowance;
- to cover the cost of everyday living expenses (see 10 above) while you are taking part in the programme or scheme; *or*
- to cover the cost of living away from home, if the payment is to cover rent charged for the accommodation where you are staying, for which housing benefit is payable.

ESA Regs, Sch 8, para 15; IS Regs, Sch 9, para 13

The following are also disregarded:

- payments to cover travel and other expenses while you are taking part in any of the jobseeker's allowance schemes for helping people into work (eg the New Enterprise Allowance or the Work and Health Programme) or doing work-related activity; *and*
- payments to help a disabled person get or keep work, made under the Disabled Persons (Employment) Act 1944 – eg Access to Work payments – but not if it is a government training allowance.

ESA Regs, Sch 8, paras 1A, 15A & 48; IS Regs, Sch 9, paras 1A & 51

## 13. Payments towards education

The following are disregarded:

- education maintenance allowance and 16-19 bursary fund payments;
- repayments of student loans to certain newly qualified teachers;
- maintenance payments to the school or college for a dependent child or young person made by someone outside your family (income-related employment and support allowance, income support and income-based jobseeker's allowance only);

ESA Regs, Sch 8, paras 13, 14 & 27; IS Regs, Sch 9, paras 11, 11A & 25A

- if you make assessed parental contributions to a student son or daughter, the amount you pay is disregarded from your income – unless the student is under 25, is in advanced education and receives only a discretionary grant or gets no grant or loan, in which case the disregard is limited to £57.90 a week, less the amount of any discretionary grant payable (housing benefit only).

HB Regs, Sch 5, paras 19 & 20

Certain amounts of a student grant or loan and other support to students can be disregarded (see Box I.2, Chapter 32).

## 14. Payments for your home

**Employment and support allowance (ESA), income support, jobseeker's allowance (JSA)** – For income-related ESA, income support and income-based JSA, the following payments related to your home are disregarded:

- payments under a mortgage protection policy used to meet repayments on a mortgage or on a loan for eligible repairs and improvements;
- payments (from any source) made to you that are intended and used towards:
  - payments due on a loan secured on your home that are not covered by support for mortgage interest loans – see Chapter 26;
  - interest payments not met by support for mortgage interest loans when you are otherwise receiving such support (eg when a ceiling is applied – see Chapter 26(9));
  - housing costs covered by income-related ESA, income support or income-based JSA but not met in your applicable amount;
  - capital repayments on loans covered by support for mortgage interest loans;
  - premiums on a policy taken out to meet any of the above costs or for buildings insurance;
  - any rent not met by housing benefit;
  (unless these are already covered by an insurance policy).

ESA Regs, Sch 8, paras 31 & 32; IS Regs, Sch 9, paras 29 & 30

**Housing benefit** – For housing benefit, disregard payments under an insurance policy taken out against the risk of being unable to maintain repayments on a loan secured on your home, and used to maintain repayments and premiums on that policy and any premiums for buildings insurance if this is a requirement of the loan. Unless the payments are made under the continuing care arrangements in Scotland, you must be aged 18 or over.

HB Regs, Sch 5, para 29

## 15. Income from tenants and lodgers

Disregard the following income from tenants and lodgers:

■ contributions towards living and accommodation costs made to you by someone living as a member of your household (but not if they are a commercial boarder or a sub-tenant);

■ if you have sub-let part of your home (under a formal contract), a maximum of £20 from the weekly payment received from each sub-tenant;

■ if you provide board and lodging in your home, £20 and half of the remainder of the weekly charge paid by each person provided with such accommodation (even if that person lodges with you for just one night).

ESA Regs, Sch 8, paras 19-21; IS Regs, Sch 9, paras 18-20

## 16. Payments for care homes

Some payments towards the cost of your care are disregarded for income-related employment and support allowance, income support and income-based jobseeker's allowance. See also Chapter 38(4).

**If the local authority arranged your care** – Payments made by the local authority towards the care home charges are fully disregarded.

ESA Regs, Sch 8, para 56; IS Regs, Sch 9, para 66

**If the local authority did not arrange your care** – Any payment intended for and used to meet the care home charge is partly disregarded (unless it is a regular charitable or voluntary payment, when it is fully disregarded – see 8 above). The amount disregarded is the weekly accommodation charge less your applicable amount.

ESA Regs, Sch 8, para 34; IS Regs, Sch 9, para 30A

## 17. Payments for children

The following payments for children or young people in your care are disregarded:

■ adoption allowances, child arrangements order allowances and special guardianship payments. However, for income support and income-based jobseeker's allowance, if your claim began before April 2004 and you continue to receive support for your children through one of those benefits rather than child tax credit, only the amount of allowance or payment that exceeds the child's personal allowance and disabled child premium is disregarded;

■ fostering allowances (for official arrangements only);

■ kinship care assistance payments (Scotland);

■ discretionary payments from social care or social work departments to help children in need or to provide help to young care leavers;

■ any direct payment towards a personal budget made under an education, health and care plan.

ESA Regs, Sch 8, paras 26, 28, 29A, 30 & 67; IS Regs, Sch 9, paras 25, 26, 27A, 28 & 79

## 18. Income generated from capital

Income generated from capital is generally not treated as income but as capital (from the day you receive it). However, income generated from the following items of disregarded capital (see 29 to 31 below) is treated as income:

■ your home;

■ property you have bought to live in, but have not yet been able to move in to;

■ property occupied by a partner or relative who has reached pension credit qualifying age or is incapacitated, or a former partner if you are not estranged but are living apart by force of circumstances (eg if you have had to move into a care home);

■ your former home if you have separated from your partner;

■ property you are taking reasonable steps to sell;

■ property you intend to occupy and are taking legal steps to own;

■ property you intend to occupy but which needs essential repairs or alterations;

■ business assets;

■ a trust fund from compensation for personal injury;

■ capital administered by the courts from damages awarded for personal injury or, for under-18s, compensation for the loss of a parent.

ESA Regs, reg 112(4); IS Regs, reg 48(4)

During the period in which you receive income from any of the property listed above (other than the home you live in), any mortgage payments made, or council tax or water charges paid, for the disregarded property can be offset against that income. The amount above this is taken into account as income.

ESA Regs, Sch 8, para 23(2); IS Regs, Sch 9, para 22(2)

If you let out your property and it is not covered under one of the disregards above, rent is treated as capital not income. The full amount is taken into account as capital without any deductions for mortgage payments, etc.

## 19. Capital treated as income

If any capital is payable by instalments, each instalment outstanding when your claim is decided (or on the first day for which the means-tested benefit is paid if this is earlier), or at a later supersession, is treated as income if your total capital, including the outstanding instalments, adds up to more than £16,000. If your total capital is less than or equal to £16,000, each instalment is treated as a payment of capital.

The following are also treated as income:

■ periodic personal injury payments made to you under an agreement or court order (see 8 above for when these can be disregarded);

■ Career Development Loans (but as these loans are payments under s.2 of the Employment and Training Act 1973, disregards apply – see 12 above);

■ payments from an annuity; *and*

ESA Regs, reg 105; IS Regs, reg 41

■ payments made to compensate you for past pay inequalities (single status payments).

CJSA/0475/2009 (CoA 'Minter')

Any capital treated as income is disregarded as capital.

ESA Regs, Sch 9, para 25; IS Regs, Sch 10, para 20

## 20. Miscellaneous income

The following types of income are disregarded:

■ expenses paid to you as a volunteer, including advance payments to cover expenses – but only if you are paid nothing else by the charity or organisation and are not treated as having 'notional' earnings (see 21 below);

■ expenses paid if you are taking part in a service user consultation;

■ Victoria Cross/George Cross annuities and similar payments;

■ income abroad while transfer to the UK is prohibited;

■ charges for currency conversion if income is not paid in sterling;

ESA Regs, Sch 8, paras 2, 2A, 12, 24 & 25; IS Regs, Sch 9, paras 2, 2A, 10, 23 & 24

■ payments you receive for someone temporarily in your care, made by a health body, voluntary organisation or local authority (or by the person placed with you by the local authority). This covers respite care payments for overnight (or longer) stays or for just a few hours in the day. It does not cover any direct payments of housing benefit made to you;

ESA Regs, Sch 8, para 29; IS Regs, Sch 9, para 27

■ payments under an insurance policy taken out against the risk of being unable to maintain repayments under a credit agreement, hire purchase or conditional sale agreement, up to the amount used to maintain the repayments and pay

premiums on that policy;
- payments for your attendance at court as a juror or witness (but not if they are to compensate for loss of earnings or loss of benefit);
- payments under the Assisted Prison Visits scheme;

ESA Regs, Sch 8, paras 33, 43 & 47; IS Regs, Sch 9, paras 30ZA, 43 & 50

- community care or NHS direct payments (unless you use them to pay your partner for the care they give you, in which case the direct payment paid to your partner will be treated as their earnings and taken into account – see 5 above for the way self-employed earnings are treated);
- Sports Council National Lottery award, except for amounts awarded for everyday living expenses (see 10 above, although 'food' in this case does not include vitamins, minerals or other special dietary supplements intended to enhance performance);
- discretionary housing payments from a local authority;
- payments from a local authority under the Supporting People scheme.

ESA Regs, Sch 8, paras 53, 57, 62 & 63; IS Regs, Sch 9, paras 58, 69, 75 & 76

## 21. Notional income

Income that you do not actually have may be taken into account in some circumstances.

❑ **Deprivation of income** – You are treated as having any income you have deprived yourself of in order to get a means-tested benefit or increase it (the issue is similar to that of deprivation of capital – see 36 below).

ESA Regs, reg 106(1), IS Regs, reg 42(1)

❑ **Income available if applied for** – You are treated as having income from the date that you could expect to receive it. This also applies to most social security benefits, but only up until the time you put in a claim (CIS/16271/1996). The rule does not apply to the following types of income:

- employment and support allowance (ESA; for ESA only);
- jobseeker's allowance (for income support and income-related ESA only);
- working tax credit and child tax credit;
- payments from a discretionary trust or a personal injury compensation trust;
- compensation administered by the courts for personal injury;
- employment rehabilitation allowances;
- income from a personal pension scheme (including an annuity contract or trust scheme approved under tax law), occupational pension scheme or the Pension Protection Fund (PPF), as long as you are under pension credit qualifying age (see Chapter 44(2)). For income-related ESA, income support and income-based jobseeker's allowance (JSA), once you reach pension credit qualifying age, if you defer or fail to draw an income from the pension or PPF, you are assumed to have notional income; income that could be obtained from money purchase benefits or 'pension pot' under an occupational or personal pension scheme is treated in the same way;

ESA Regs, reg 106(2)-(9); IS Regs, reg 42(2)-(2CA)

- any Category A or B state pension, additional state pension or graduated retirement benefit that has been deferred – see Chapter 45(8) (for housing benefit only).

HB(SPC) Regs, reg 41(2)-(3)

❑ **Notional earnings** – If you are a volunteer, or engaged by a charitable or voluntary organisation, notional earnings cannot be assumed if it is reasonable for you to provide your services free of charge. (A carer may count as a 'volunteer' – see CIS/93/91, but see CIS/701/94 for exceptions.) If it is reasonable to expect you to charge for your services, or you are performing a service for someone else in some other capacity, you are treated as having *'such earnings (if any) as is reasonable for that employment unless* [you] *satisfy* [the decision maker] *that the means of that person are insufficient for him to pay, or to pay more, for the service'*. Decision makers are advised to assume earnings of at least the relevant national living/minimum wage. If notional earnings are assumed, seek advice.

ESA Regs, reg 108(3)&(4)(a); IS Regs, reg 42(6)&(6A)(a); Decision Makers Guide, Vol 5, Chap 26, para 26180

❑ **Income owed** – For income-related ESA, income support and income-based JSA, you are treated as having any income owing to you, but there are exceptions (eg income from a discretionary or personal injury trust, or delays in social security benefits).

ESA Regs, reg 107(1); IS Regs, reg 42(3)

❑ **Care homes** – Payments made towards the cost of your care home are treated as your income, but some of them may be disregarded (see 16 above).

ESA Regs, reg 107(6); IS Regs, reg 42(4A)

## B. CAPITAL

## 22. Introduction

Your capital can affect your entitlement to means-tested benefits when it is above certain set limits (see 24 below). Capital includes savings, investments, some lump-sum payments and the value of property and land (but if you own the home you live in, the value of your home, garden, garage and outbuildings is disregarded). Certain types of capital can be disregarded (see 27 to 33 below). Sometimes capital can be treated as income (see 19 above) and vice versa (see 35 below). In some cases you can be treated as possessing capital that you don't actually have (see 36 below).

## 23. Whose capital is included?

If you are one of a couple (married or living together as a married couple or in a civil partnership), your partner's capital is added to yours. Otherwise, only your capital is taken into account; capital belonging to dependent children is disregarded (unless you have a claim for income support or income-based jobseeker's allowance that began before April 2004 and you still receive support for your children through one of those benefits rather than through child tax credit – see *Disability Rights Handbook* 28th edition, page 25).

ESA Regs, reg 83; IS Regs, reg 23

## 24. Capital limits

There is a *'lower capital limit'* and an *'upper capital limit'*. You cannot get any of the means-tested benefits listed in 1 above if your capital is above the upper limit of £16,000.

WRA 2007, Sch 1, para 6(1)(b); ESA Regs, reg 110; SSCBA, S.134(1); IS Regs, reg 45

If your capital is at or below the lower limit of £6,000, your means-tested benefit is unaffected. If you move permanently into a care home, an Abbeyfield Home or an independent hospital, this lower limit goes up to £10,000. If your stay is only temporary, the £6,000 limit still applies. For housing benefit, the lower limit is also set at £10,000 if you or your partner are over pension credit qualifying age (and not claiming income-related employment and support allowance, income support or income-based jobseeker's allowance).

If your capital is between the lower and upper limits, an amount of 'tariff income' is assumed (see below).

## 25. Tariff income

If your capital is between the lower and upper limits, a *'tariff income'* is assumed, ie your capital is treated as if it were generating income. Normally, £1 a week for every £250 (or part of £250) above the lower limit is included as income in this way (but see below for an exception). For instance, if you have capital of £6,300, £2 a week is included as income. Each time capital moves into the next block of £250 (even by as little as 1p) an additional £1 a week is included as income. This tariff income is then added to your other income when calculating entitlement to the means-tested benefit.

ESA Regs, reg 118; IS Regs, reg 53

For housing benefit, if you or your partner are over pension credit qualifying age (and not claiming income-related employment and support allowance, income support or income-based jobseeker's allowance), the assumed tariff income is £1 for every £500 (or part of £500) above the lower limit.

HB(SPC) Regs, reg 29(2)

If tariff income is included in your assessment, let the DWP know if the amount of your capital changes. If your savings drop to the next lower tariff income band and you have not told the DWP, you will be getting too little of the means-tested benefit. If your savings have increased to the next higher tariff income band and you have not told the DWP, you will have been overpaid benefit. Watch out for the 'notional capital' rule (see 36 below). Keep records and all receipts to show how and why you spent your capital.

## 26. How is capital valued?

Capital is calculated at its current market or surrender value, less 10% if there would be costs involved in selling and less any mortgage or debt secured on it.

ESA Regs, reg 113; IS Regs, reg 49

**Joint capital** – If you own property or other capital jointly with anyone else, so that each person owns the whole asset jointly with no separate or distinct shares, then you are treated as though you own an equal share. For example, if four people jointly own £1,000, each is treated as owning a quarter of it: £250.

ESA Regs, reg 117; IS Regs, reg 52

However, if you share the property as tenants-in-common rather than as joint tenants, the share you are treated as owning should reflect the actual split.

R(IS)4/03

The decision maker must establish the market value or price that a willing buyer would pay to a willing seller for your share. The market value could be low or even nil if other joint owners would not be prepared to sell the property as a whole or to buy your share of it.

## 27. Benefits

Arrears (or an ex-gratia payment) of the following benefits are disregarded for 52 weeks after you get them:
■ attendance allowance, disability living allowance and personal independence payment (or the equivalents under the Industrial Injuries and War Pensions schemes);
■ bereavement support payment;
■ housing benefit and council tax benefit;
■ discretionary housing payments;
■ income-related employment and support allowance;
■ income support;
■ income-based jobseeker's allowance;
■ universal credit; *and*
■ child tax credit and working tax credit.

If arrears made to compensate for an official error are £5,000 or more, they can be disregarded until the end of your award of the means-tested benefit.

ESA Regs, Sch 9, para 11; IS Regs, Sch 10, para 7

Social fund and local welfare assistance payments are disregarded. Payments or repayments to cover prescription charges, dental charges or hospital travelling expenses are disregarded for 52 weeks after you receive the money. Payments made instead of Healthy Start vouchers or free vitamins are disregarded for 52 weeks after receipt. The initial larger payment of bereavement support payment is disregarded for 52 weeks after you receive it.

ESA Regs, Sch 9, paras 23, 23A, 37, 38 & 60; IS Regs, Sch 10, paras 18, 18A, 38, 39 & 72

## 28. Personal possessions

The value of personal possessions is disregarded, except those bought to reduce capital in order to get more benefit. A compensation payment for loss of or damage to personal possessions that is to be used for repair or replacements is disregarded for 26 weeks, or longer if reasonable.

ESA Regs, Sch 9, paras 14 & 12(a); IS Regs, Sch 10, paras 10 & 8(a)

## 29. Trust funds and personal injury payments
### Personal injury payments

When a trust fund is created from payments for a personal injury to you or your partner, the value of the fund is disregarded indefinitely. 'Personal injury' includes a disease or an injury suffered as a result of a disease (R(SB)2/89).

Trusts created from vaccine damage payments and criminal injuries compensation payments are covered, as may a trust of funds collected for a person because of their personal injuries. Payments from a trust fund for a personal injury can count in full as capital, but may be disregarded as income (see 8 above).

If a lump-sum payment for a personal injury to you or your partner has not been put into a trust, it can be disregarded for up to 52 weeks from the date you receive it (to allow you time to set up a trust). However, this applies only to the first payment; subsequent lump-sum payments made for the same injury count in full as capital until they are put into a trust.

ESA Regs, Sch 9, paras 16 & 17; IS Regs, Sch 10, paras 12 & 12A

If capital is administered by the courts, damages awarded for personal injury and, for under-18-year-olds, compensation for the loss of a parent are disregarded.

ESA Regs, Sch 9, paras 43 & 44; IS Regs, Sch 10, paras 44 & 45

### Life interest

The value of the right to receive any income under a life interest or from a life rent (this is a type of trust in Scotland) is disregarded. Actual income received counts in full as income.

ESA Regs, Sch 9, para 18; IS Regs, Sch 10, para 13

### Specific trusts

Payments from the Macfarlane Trusts, the Fund, the Eileen Trust, the Skipton Fund, the Caxton Foundation, the Scottish Infected Blood Support scheme, an approved blood scheme, the London Bombings Relief Charitable Fund, the London Emergencies Trust, the WeLoveManchester Emergency Fund, MFET Ltd or the Independent Living Fund are disregarded.

Payments made by or on behalf of a person with haemophilia, HIV or hepatitis C may be disregarded under the same rules as income (see 8 above).

ESA Regs, Sch 9, para 27; IS Regs, Sch 10, para 22

A payment from the government-funded trust for people with variant Creutzfeldt-Jakob disease (vCJD) paid to a person with vCJD or their partner is disregarded for life. If the trust payment is made to a parent or child of a person with

vCJD (including payment from the estate if they have died), it is disregarded for two years from the date it is paid or until the child reaches age 20 or leaves full-time education, whichever is the latest.
ESA Regs, Sch 9, para 53; IS Regs, Sch 10, para 64

## 30. Training and employment
Disregard the following:
- business assets while you are self-employed. If sickness or disability means you cannot work, the assets will be disregarded for 26 weeks from your date of claim, or longer if reasonable in the circumstances. You must intend to start or resume work in your business as soon as you are able to or as soon as you recover. If the self-employment ends, the assets will be disregarded for as long as is reasonable in the circumstances to allow you to sell them;
ESA Regs, Sch 9, para 10; IS Regs, Sch 10, para 6
- payments (but not a government training allowance) made under the Disabled Persons (Employment) Act 1944 to help a disabled person get or keep work;
- start-up capital under the Blind Homeworkers' scheme.
ESA Regs, Sch 9, paras 41 & 42; IS Regs, Sch 10, paras 42 & 43
Disregard for 52 weeks from the date you receive them:
- payments to cover travel and other expenses while you are taking part in any of the jobseeker's allowance schemes for helping people into work (eg the New Enterprise Allowance or the Work and Health Programme) or undertaking work-related activity;
- any payment from a government training programme or employment scheme (under either s.2 of the Employment and Training Act 1973 or s.2 of the Enterprise and New Towns (Scotland) Act 1990);
- any discretionary payment or arrears of subsistence allowance from an Employment Zone contractor.
ESA Regs, Sch 9, paras 1A, 32, 32A & (48 & 49); IS Regs, Sch 10, paras 1A, 30 & (58 & 59)

## 31. Your home
The following items are disregarded:
- the value of your own home;
- the value of property you have bought, if you intend to move in within 26 weeks of the date of purchase;*
- the proceeds of the sale of your home, if you intend to use it to buy another home within 26 weeks of the sale;*
ESA Regs, Sch 9, paras 1, 2 & 3; IS Regs, Sch 10, paras 1, 2 & 3
- the value of property occupied by your partner or by a relative if they have reached pension credit qualifying age or are incapacitated; or by a former partner if you are not estranged but are living apart by force of circumstances (eg if you have had to move into a care home);
- the value of your former home for 26 weeks after you left it because you have separated from your partner. If your former partner is a lone parent, the value is disregarded for as long as they continue to live there;
- the value of property that you are taking reasonable steps to sell, for 26 weeks from the date on which you first took such steps;*
ESA Regs, Sch 9, paras 4, 5 & 6; IS Regs, Sch 10, paras 4, 25 & 26
- the value of property you intend to occupy as your home if you have either sought legal advice or started legal proceedings to own it. The value is disregarded for 26 weeks from the date on which you first sought such advice or started proceedings (whichever is earlier);*
- the value of property you intend to occupy as your home once 'essential repairs or alterations' make it fit to live in, for 26 weeks from the date on which you first took steps to get the property repaired or altered.* This can help if you are adapting your property using a disabled facilities grant;
ESA Regs, Sch 9, paras 7 & 8; IS Regs, Sch 10, paras 27 & 28
- any sum paid to you because of damage to, or loss of,

the home or any personal possession and intended for its repair or replacement, or any sum given or loaned to you expressly for essential repairs or improvements to the home, will be disregarded for 26 weeks if you are going to use that sum for its intended purpose;*
- any sum deposited with a housing association as a condition of occupying the home. If you have removed that deposit and intend to use it to buy another home, it can be disregarded for 26 weeks;*
ESA Regs, Sch 9, paras 12 & 13; IS Regs, Sch 10, paras 8 & 9
- any grant made by a local authority (if you are one of its tenants) to buy property you intend to live in as your home, or to do repairs or alterations needed to make the property fit to live in. The grant is disregarded for 26 weeks;*
- arrears of discretionary housing payments from a local authority for 52 weeks from the date received.
ESA Regs, Sch 9, paras 36 & 11(1)(c) ; IS Regs, Sch 10, paras 37 & 7(d)
* In each case more time is allowed if reasonable in the circumstances to enable you to conclude the matter.

### Help to Buy ISAs
The government's contributions to a Help to Buy ISA (intended to help first-time homebuyers with a deposit) are disregarded for housing benefit. The rest of the capital in the Help to Buy ISA counts in full.
HB Bulletin G9/2015

## 32. Right to receive income or payment in future
Certain forms of capital can be released at some stage to provide you with income or payment in the future. The value of the right to receive any of the following is disregarded:
- income under an annuity, and the surrender value of an annuity;
- income that is disregarded because it is frozen abroad;
- an occupational or personal pension, and the value of funds held under a personal pension scheme (including annuity contracts and trust schemes approved under tax law);
- any rent, except where you have a future interest in the property.
ESA Regs, Sch 9, paras 15, 19, (28 & 29) & 30; IS Regs, Sch 10, paras 11, 14, (23 & 23A) & 24
The following are also disregarded:
- any future interest in property other than land or property that have been let by you;
- the full surrender value of a life insurance policy.
ESA Regs, Sch 9, paras 9 & 20; IS Regs, Sch 10, paras 5 & 15

## 33. Other capital
The following types of capital are disregarded:
- where capital is payable by instalments, the value of the right to receive any outstanding instalments (see also 19 above);
- discretionary payments from social care or social work departments to help children in need or to provide help to young care leavers;
- a refund of tax deducted on loan interest if that loan was taken out to buy the home or carry out repairs or improvements to the home;
ESA Regs, Sch 9, paras 21, 22 & 24; IS Regs, Sch 10, paras 16, 17 & 19
- any charge for currency conversion if your capital is not held in sterling;
- payments in kind made by a charity, the Macfarlane Trusts, the Fund, the Eileen Trust (for income-related ESA), MFET Ltd, the Skipton Fund, the Caxton Foundation, the Scottish Infected Blood Support scheme, an approved blood scheme or the Independent Living Fund;
- payments for your attendance at court as a juror or witness (but not if it was to compensate for loss of earnings or loss of benefit);
ESA Regs, Sch 9, paras 26, 31 & 34; IS Regs, Sch 10, paras 21, 29 & 34

- Victoria Cross/George Cross payments;
- a Sports Council National Lottery award, less everyday living expenses (see 10 above), although 'food' in this case does not include vitamins, minerals or other special dietary supplements intended to enhance performance, for 26 weeks after you receive the award;
- £10,000 special payment made to you or your partner (or for a deceased spouse/civil partner or partner's deceased spouse/civil partner) because of internment by the Japanese during the Second World War;

ESA Regs, Sch 9, paras 45, 47 & 50; IS Regs, Sch 10, paras 46, 56 & 61

- education maintenance allowance and 16-19 bursary fund payments;
- payments made to you or your partner (or for a deceased spouse/civil partner or partner's deceased spouse/civil partner) to compensate for being a slave labourer or a forced labourer, suffering property loss or personal injury or being the parent of a child who had died, during the Second World War;
- payments from local authorities under the Supporting People scheme;
- community care or NHS direct payments;

ESA Regs, Sch 9, paras 52, 54, 55 & 56; IS Regs, Sch 10, paras 63, 65, 66 & 67

- a payment made under s.2(6)(b), 3 or 4 of the Adoption and Children Act 2002;
- a special guardianship payment;
- any direct payment towards a personal budget made under an education, health and care plan;
- any payment from an approved Thalidomide relief and assistance trust;
- kinship care assistance payments (Scotland);

ESA Regs, Sch 9, paras 57, 58, 59, 61 & 62; IS Regs, Sch 10, paras 68, 68A, 71, 73 & 74

Disregard the following for 52 weeks after you receive them:
- payments made under the Assisted Prison Visits scheme;
- arrears of supplementary pensions to war widows, widowers and surviving civil partners.

ESA Regs,Sch 9, paras 39 & 40; IS Regs, Sch 10, paras 40 & 41

## 34. Loans
If you borrow money, it will almost always count as money you possess (generally as capital if it is a one-off loan or, in some cases, as income if it is part of a series of payments). You may be able to argue that a loan should not count as capital if the money was given to you for a specific purpose and on condition that it be repaid if it is not used in that particular way.

## 35. Income treated as capital
The following payments of income are treated as capital:
- income derived from capital (but see 18 above);
- income tax refunds;*
- irregular charitable or voluntary payments (other than payments made from the Macfarlane Trusts, the Fund, the Eileen Trust, MFET Ltd, the Skipton Fund, the Caxton Foundation, the Scottish Infected Blood Support scheme, an approved blood scheme or the Independent Living Fund);*
- holiday pay payable more than four weeks after the employment ends or is interrupted;
- advance of earnings or a loan from an employer;*
- payment for a discharged prisoner (for income-related employment and support allowance, income support and income-based jobseeker's allowance (JSA));
- lump-sum payment of arrears of Employment Zone subsistence allowance;
- a bounty paid no more than once a year to a part-time firefighter, for coast rescue duties or running a lifeboat, or to a member of the reserve forces.
* except for those involved in a trade dispute (for income

support/income-based JSA)

ESA Regs, reg 112; IS Regs, reg 48

In addition to the above, arrears of child tax credit and working tax credit are treated as capital for housing benefit.

HB Regs, reg 46

## 36. Notional capital
If you are held to have deprived yourself of some capital in order to get or increase a means-tested benefit, you will be treated as if you still had it. This is called 'notional' capital. This can include money that you spend, transfer or give away from your pension pot. In some cases, the amount of notional capital along with your actual capital will exclude you from the benefit. Or, you may be entitled to the benefit, but because of your notional capital the assessment is related to a higher tariff income than your actual capital warrants (see 25 above).

If there were good reasons for spending your capital, and getting the means-tested benefit (or more of it) wasn't a significant motive for spending part of your savings, you should not be affected. It is worth appealing if capital you no longer have is taken into account, but seek expert advice.

If you are held to have notional capital on this basis, you won't be excluded from the means-tested benefit permanently, nor will a tariff income be related permanently to the higher amount of notional capital. The DWP will apply the 'diminishing notional capital rule', which reduces the amount of notional capital over time (see below).

ESA Regs, reg 115; IS Regs, reg 51

## 37. Diminishing notional capital rule
Your notional capital is treated as having been reduced by the amount of the means-tested benefit 'lost' over a set period. If you are held to have deprived yourself of an amount of capital, the DWP will work out:
- how much benefit you would have been entitled to in the normal way if you had no notional capital – (A);
- how much benefit, if any, you are entitled to on the basis of your notional capital (as well as any actual capital) – (B);
- (A) minus (B) = the benefit you have lost – (LB).

If you have also lost any of the other means-tested benefits, the DWP (or the local authority) will add on those amounts of lost benefit, eg LB 1 (income support) + LB 2 (housing benefit) = total lost benefit (TLB).

Your notional capital is treated as being reduced each week by your total lost benefit.

The decision on your claim for a means-tested benefit will include the amount of that benefit you have lost because of notional capital. Keep that decision letter. You may need to produce it if you claim another means-tested benefit and you are held to have deprived yourself of some capital in order to get that benefit as well. For example, if you are excluded from income support because of notional capital and you are also held to have deprived yourself of some capital to get housing benefit, you will need to show the income support decision letter to the local authority department dealing with your housing benefit claim. It is possible to receive different decisions on deprivation of capital, and different amounts of notional capital, for each benefit.

ESA Regs, reg 116; IS Regs, reg 51A

**If the notional capital rule reduces your entitlement to the means-tested benefit**

Each time your notional capital goes below another tariff income step, you will be entitled to more benefit. A change of circumstances may also increase or reduce your benefit. Both (A) and (B) will be re-calculated, giving you a new amount of lost benefit (LB(2)). For other means-tested benefits, the amount of lost benefit may also change, so you will add these on (LB 1(2) + LB 2(2), etc). Your notional capital will now be treated as being reduced by your current total lost benefit (TLB(2)).

**If the notional capital rule means you are no longer entitled to the means-tested benefit**

Once your total lost benefit is worked out, it cannot be reduced. It can only be increased to enable your notional capital to diminish faster, eg if there is a change of circumstances that would increase the amount of your benefit. However, whenever the amount of notional capital you are deemed to have changes, the new amount is fixed for a period of 26 weeks. The onus is on you to make a fresh claim for each benefit affected by the deprivation of capital rule and to produce the decision letters showing the amount(s) of the other lost benefit(s).

**More deprivation?**

If you have actual capital as well as notional capital, you should still be careful about how you spend it. Obviously, you will have to draw on actual capital to supplement your income and cover expenses not met by benefit. But the deprivation of capital rule can be re-applied to the actual capital spent.

# 23 Tax credits

| A | Tax credits | |
|---|---|---|
| 1 | What are tax credits? | 154 |
| | Moving from tax credits to universal credit – Box F.2 | 155 |
| 2 | Do you qualify for CTC? | 154 |
| 3 | Responsible for a child or qualifying young person | 155 |
| 4 | CTC elements | 155 |
| 5 | Do you qualify for WTC? | 156 |
| 6 | What does and does not count as work? | 156 |
| 7 | WTC elements | 157 |
| 8 | WTC disabled worker element | 158 |
| | The 'disability' test – Box F.3 | 159 |
| 9 | Income and savings | 159 |
| 10 | Claiming tax credits | 160 |
| 11 | Payment of tax credits | 161 |
| 12 | Penalties | 161 |
| 13 | Challenging decisions and complaints | 161 |
| B | Calculating tax credits | |
| 14 | Introduction | 161 |
| 15 | Rates of CTC and WTC | 162 |
| 16 | Steps in the tax credit calculation | 162 |
| | Calculating tax credits – Box F.4 | 163 |
| 17 | Changes in your circumstances | 162 |
| | Change of circumstances calculation – Box F.5 | 163 |
| 18 | The £2,500 disregard if your income rises | 162 |
| 19 | The £2,500 disregard if your income falls | 163 |
| 20 | Overpayment or underpayment of tax credit | 164 |
| 21 | Overpayments | 164 |
| 22 | Underpayments | 164 |

## A. TAX CREDITS

### 1. What are tax credits?

Tax credits are means-tested or income-related tax-free payments administered by HMRC at the Tax Credit Office.

There are two types, child tax credit and working tax credit. Each consists of one or more elements (see 4 and 7 below). All the elements you are eligible for are added together. The total is compared to your income (see 9 below) and any reduction due to this income is calculated (as explained in 16 below). The resulting amount, if any, is your total tax credit award.

**Child tax credit** (CTC) – CTC is for people, whether working or not, who are responsible for children.

**Working tax credit** (WTC) – WTC is for those in low-paid work, whether or not they are responsible for children.

**The benefit cap**

CTC is one of the benefits subject to the 'benefit cap', which limits the total weekly benefits that you can claim. The benefit cap will not apply if you qualify for WTC. See Box G.6 in Chapter 25 for details.

**Universal credit**

The government is replacing tax credits with universal credit. In some areas, it is no longer possible in most cases to make a new claim for tax credits. The timetable for the introduction is outlined in Box E.1 in Chapter 14. Universal credit is described in Chapters 14 to 17. Box F.2 in this chapter explains briefly how existing claimants of tax credits will be moved onto universal credit.

**Will you be better off going back to work?**

Going back to work usually means some benefits will stop (eg employment and support allowance (ESA)), some will carry on as normal (eg personal independence payment) and others will continue at a reduced rate depending on income (eg housing benefit). Box I.5 in Chapter 33 outlines benefits and other help available when you start work. To work out whether you might be better off on tax credits, note the following points.

❑ You may be able to earn up to £125.50 a week from 'permitted work' on top of ESA, incapacity benefit or severe disablement allowance. You may be better off doing this (see Chapter 33(3)).

❑ Income-related ESA, income-based jobseeker's allowance (JSA) and income support may allow you to access support for mortgage interest loans (see Chapter 26), while tax credits do not.

❑ Depending on your level of tax credits, you may be entitled to free prescriptions and other health benefits (see Chapter 52), free legal help (see Chapter 58(2)) and disabled facilities grants (see Chapter 30).

❑ Some tax credit awards (WTC that includes a disabled worker element or severe disability element, or CTC that includes a child element or disabled child element) give access to the Sure Start maternity grant and social fund funeral payment (see Chapter 29).

❑ Income-related ESA, income-based JSA and income support entitle your children to free school meals, and to vouchers for milk, fruit and vegetables under the Healthy Start scheme if they are aged under 4 (see Chapter 52(6)). You are generally not entitled to these if you receive tax credits, but you may be entitled if you get CTC *without any* WTC and have annual taxable income of £16,190 or less (or £16,105 in Scotland).

### 2. Do you qualify for CTC?

You can get CTC if you meet all the following conditions when you make your claim:

■ you are at least 16 years of age;

■ you (or your partner) are responsible for a child or qualifying young person who normally lives with you (see 3 below);

■ you meet the residence and presence conditions and are not subject to immigration control (see Chapter 53); *and*

■ your income (see 9 below) is low enough for CTC to be paid. See 14 to 22 below for the calculation.

**Joint claims** – If you are one of a couple (see below), you claim jointly and your claim is called a *'joint claim'*. Otherwise, you claim as a single person. Your entitlement will end immediately if you are one of a couple who separate or your partner dies, or if you are a single claimant who becomes one of a couple. Your entitlement will also usually end if you stop being responsible for any children or qualifying young people (see 3 below).

See 21 below if you have been overpaid because you delayed reporting a change in status (going from a joint to a single claim or the other way round).

**Couples** – A *'couple'* is defined as: a married couple or civil partners (unless separated under a court order or separation is likely to be permanent), or two people living together as though they were a married couple.

TCA, Ss.3, 8 & 42

### 3. Responsible for a child or qualifying young person

A child is someone aged under 16. Between their 16th birthday and the following 31 August, they will be treated as a *'qualifying young person'* without the need to be in education or training. To continue to be treated as a qualifying young person after that date, they must be aged under 20 and in full-time, non-advanced education or approved, unwaged training. They must not be receiving the education through their employment and the training must not be provided under a contract of employment. If they are aged 19, they must have been accepted or enrolled onto the education or training course *before* they turned 19. Non-advanced education includes anything up to A-level or equivalent.

Following their 16th birthday, young people will no longer count for tax credit purposes once they:

■ cease full-time education or approved training and start paid work of at least 24 hours a week; *or*

■ claim income-related employment and support allowance (ESA), income-based jobseeker's allowance, income support or universal credit in their own right.

Young people can continue to count for tax credit purposes for the first 20 weeks after they leave the education or training if they are aged under 18 and registered for work or training with a 'qualifying body' (ie the Careers or Connexions Service, the Ministry of Defence or in Northern Ireland, the Department for Employment and Learning or an Education and Library Board).

TCA, S.8; CTC Regs, regs 2, 4 & 5

If two or more households make a claim for the same child (eg the child of separated parents spends time with both), the two households can agree who will receive CTC for that child. If they cannot agree, HMRC will decide for them.

You do not count as responsible for a child or young person who:

■ has been placed by a local authority in certain types of care accommodation;

■ has been placed for adoption with you by a local authority that is making specific payments for their accommodation or maintenance;

■ is serving a custodial sentence of more than four months;

■ is aged 16 or older and claiming CTC for their own child, WTC or contributory ESA; *or*

■ is living with a partner (opposite or same sex) who is not in full-time education or approved training.

CTC is not payable if you are the partner of the young person and you live together.

CTC Regs, reg 3

If a child or young person dies during the period of an award, CTC will normally continue for eight weeks following their death.

CTC Regs, reg 6

### 4. CTC elements

CTC is made up of a number of elements.

#### Family element

One element per family, as long as the claim includes a child or qualifying young person (see 3 above) born before 6.4.17, otherwise no family element is included.

TCA, S.9(2)(a); CTC Regs, reg 7(2)(a)

#### Child elements

Before 6.4.17, you could receive one *'child element'* for each child or qualifying young person (see 3 above) in the family. The child element was payable at three rates: the standard rate, disabled child rate and severely disabled child rate. From 6.4.17, the child element has only one rate (but see below for the new 'disabled child element').

---

## F.2 Moving from tax credits to universal credit

Universal credit is replacing working tax credit and child tax credit. In some areas, you can no longer claim tax credits and will have to claim universal credit instead (unless you have three or more children at the date of claim and certain exceptions do not apply – see Box E.1 in Chapter 14). Universal credit is described in Chapters 14 to 17.

If you are already claiming tax credits, you will not be affected by universal credit yet unless you:

■ choose to claim universal credit – get advice if you are thinking about doing this;

■ have a change in circumstances that ends your tax credits award (eg you move in with a partner who is already getting universal credit); *or*

■ need to claim another benefit that has been replaced by universal credit.

Otherwise, you will not be affected until July 2019 at the earliest.

It is not possible to claim universal credit and tax credits at the same time, therefore when you move onto universal credit, your tax credit entitlement will cease. HMRC will then *'finalise'* the tax credit award at the point where your entitlement ceases (rather than, as is usual, after the end of the tax year). This is called *'in-year finalisation'*. To do this, HMRC will send you an *'award review pack'* for you to confirm your circumstances and income during the tax credit award period. You should read the notes that come with this review pack carefully because the way your income for this period is calculated may be different to the way it has previously been done, especially if you are employed or self-employed. The way income is calculated for in-year finalisation may lead to an overpayment or underpayment of tax credits.

*The Universal Credit (Transitional Provisions) Regs 2014, regs 5(1), 7, 8 & 12A*

**Payment** – As tax credits may be paid on a weekly basis, but universal credit is paid once every calendar month, there is often a gap between payments. If this is the case you may be able to claim a universal credit advance to bridge this gap; see Chapter 56(6) for details.

**Overpayments** – If you have an overpayment of tax credit outstanding when you are moved onto universal credit, it will be passed over to the DWP. Deductions can then be made from your universal credit award to clear the debt; your consent will not be needed for this. Even if you stop claiming universal credit later, the debt to the DWP will remain and you will need to arrange with them directly to pay it back.

*The Universal Credit (Transitional Provisions) Regs 2014, reg 12*

You will get one child element for each child or qualifying young person born before 6.4.17. A two-child limit was introduced on 6.4.17. If your child was born on or after 6.4.17, you will normally only get the child element for them if they are an only child or you are claiming for just one other child. However, exceptions apply (see below).

Even if you will not receive the child element for a child or qualifying young person, you should still tell HMRC when they become part of your household, so their details can be added to the system. The two-child limit does not affect child benefit or the childcare element of WTC.
CTC Regs, reg 7(2)(b),(2A)&(4)

**Exceptions** – You can receive a child element for a third, or subsequent, child born on or after 6.4.17 if:
- they were part of a multiple birth, and were not the first-born;
- it is likely they were born as a result of rape or a domestic abuse situation involving coercion or control. Unless there has been a conviction or compensation award for the rape or abuse, you must provide evidence from an appropriate official (eg a police officer or registered social worker) who you have been in contact with in connection with the rape or abuse;
- they are living with you and you are a *'friend or family carer'* of the child or you are also responsible for a child or young person who is the parent of the child. This can include if there is a child arrangements order in place, you are a special guardian or kinship carer of the child or if you receive guardian's allowance for them. Even if there is not an official arrangement in place, you will still be treated as a friend or family carer if the child would otherwise be likely to go into local authority care; *or*
- they have been adopted by you from a local authority.
CTC Regs, reg 9-14

### Disabled child elements
The *'disabled child element'* is payable at two different rates: the 'severely disabled child rate' and the 'disabled child rate'. Even if the two-child limit applies, so that you do not qualify for the child element for your child (see above), you will still get the disabled child element for them if they meet the qualifying conditions for it.
**Severely disabled child rate** – This higher rate is payable if any child or qualifying young person (see 3 above) receives disability living allowance (DLA) highest rate care component, personal independence payment (PIP) enhanced rate daily living component or armed forces independence payment (AFIP).
**Disabled child rate** – This rate is payable if any child or qualifying young person:
- receives any other payment of DLA or PIP; *or*
- is certified by a consultant ophthalmologist as severely sight impaired or blind, or has ceased to be so certified within 28 weeks of the claim for CTC being made.
CTC Regs, reg 7(2)(c) & 8

### Backdating
If you have been waiting for a child or young person to be awarded DLA, PIP or AFIP, as long as you inform HMRC within one month of the date it is awarded, the disabled child element can be backdated to the date that DLA, PIP or AFIP became payable (or to the date of the CTC claim, if that is later).
TC(C&N) Regs, regs 26A

### 5. Do you qualify for WTC?
You can get WTC if you are at least 16 years old and either you or your partner are working for 16 or more hours a week, provided that at least one of the following conditions apply:

- you are a single parent responsible for a child or qualifying young person (see 3 above); *or*
- you are a couple, one or both of you are responsible for a child or qualifying young person, one of you works at least 16 hours a week and you work at least 24 hours a week between you; *or*
- you are a couple, one or both of you are responsible for a child or qualifying young person and one of you works at least 16 hours a week where the other partner is:
  - in hospital; *or*
  - in prison; *or*
  - entitled to carer's allowance; *or*
  - 'incapacitated' (see 7 below under 'Childcare element' for the definition); *or*
- you or your partner (whichever of you is working) qualify for the disabled worker element (see 8 below); *or*
- you are aged 60 or over.
Otherwise, you can only qualify if you are aged 25 or over and work at least 30 hours a week.
TCA, S.10 & WTC(E&MR) Regs, reg 4(1)

You cannot generally qualify for WTC if you are subject to immigration control, unless you are the partner of someone who is not subject to immigration control (see Chapter 53(2)). You must meet the residence and presence conditions (see Chapter 53(3)). Your income (see 9 below) must be low enough for WTC to be paid. See 14 to 22 below for the calculation.

**Joint claims** – If you are one of a couple, you claim WTC jointly and your claim is called a joint claim. Otherwise you claim as a single person. Your entitlement will end immediately if you are one of a couple who separate or your partner dies, or you are a single claimant who becomes one of a couple. See 21 below if you have been overpaid because you delayed reporting a change in status (going from a joint to single claim or the other way round). WTC will also usually end if you cease working the right number of hours to qualify (see above and 6 below).
TCA, Ss.3 & 42

### 6. What does and does not count as work?
To be treated as being in *'qualifying remunerative work'* you must be employed or self-employed and *either*:
- be working at the date of your claim, and the work must be expected to continue for at least four weeks after you claim; *or*
- have an offer of work which you are expected to start within seven days of making your claim, and the work must be expected to last for at least four weeks.
*'Work'* means work done for, or in expectation of, payment.

If you are an employee, the number of hours that count are the number of hours you normally work each week, including any regular overtime. In calculating the number of hours you work, time spent on unpaid meal breaks or periods of customary or paid holiday is disregarded. Exceptionally, if you work in a school, college or university (or otherwise work on a similar basis) and you have a recognisable pattern of employment over the year which includes periods when you do not work, the school holidays or other holiday periods can be disregarded. This rule benefits people like school dinner staff who might otherwise be found not to be working enough hours to qualify.

If you are self-employed, the employment needs to be on a commercial basis with a view to the realisation of profits and it must be organised and regular. If your income from self-employment falls below the hours you declare that you work, multiplied by the national living/minimum wage that applies in your case (see Box I.5 in Chapter 33), then you may be asked for evidence that you meet this test. The number of hours that count are those you work in your self-employed capacity, including time spent on *'activities*

*necessary to'* your self-employed activity, eg bookkeeping or distributing advertising flyers.
WTC(E&MR) Regs, regs 4 & 7

## When you are not treated as being in work
Some kinds of work do not count:
■ work as a volunteer if you are only paid expenses;
■ work on a training scheme where you are paid a training allowance (unless taxable as trade profit);
■ work while you are in prison;
■ activities where you receive a sports award and no other payment; *and*
■ caring for someone who is temporarily living with you if the only payment you get is from a local authority, health authority, voluntary organisation or the cared-for person, and this is disregarded for tax credit purposes. However, foster carers, adult placement carers and other shared-lives carers are able to claim WTC for their care work.
WTC(E&MR) Regs, reg 4(2)&(2A)

## When you are treated as being in work
You can qualify for WTC during certain interruptions or after you have stopped working, provided you were in qualifying remunerative work immediately beforehand. Your working hours will be treated as being the same as before in the following circumstances.

❑ You are not working because you are sick. You continue to be treated as being in work for up to 28 weeks while you receive statutory sick pay (SSP), employment and support allowance or national insurance credits due to limited capability for work. If you are self-employed and off sick, you will be treated as being in work if you would have got SSP but for the fact that self-employed people are not entitled to it.
WTC(E&MR) Regs, reg 6

❑ You are off work and getting maternity allowance, statutory maternity pay (SMP) or statutory adoption pay (SAP), or you are on the first 39 weeks of maternity or adoption leave. If you are self-employed and off work due to birth or adoption, you will be treated as being in work if you would have met these rules but for the fact that self-employed people are not entitled to SMP/SAP or maternity/adoption leave. If you worked less than 30 hours and only meet the remunerative work rule after the birth or adoption of your first child, you are treated as being in qualifying remunerative work during such leave from the date of the birth or adoption.

❑ You are off work and getting statutory paternity pay or statutory shared parental pay (SSPP), or you are on paternity leave or shared parental leave (providing, in the latter case, that you would have been paid SSPP if you had met the qualifying conditions).
WTC(E&MR) Regs, regs 5 & 5A

❑ You are temporarily suspended from work while complaints or allegations against you are being investigated.
WTC(E&MR) Regs, reg 7B

❑ You are on strike, but only for a period of up to ten consecutive days on which you would normally work.
WTC(E&MR) Regs, reg 7A

**Working tax credit run-on** – If you have recently finished working (or started to work for less than the required hours each week), you may be treated as being in qualifying remunerative work for a further four weeks.
WTC(E&MR) Regs, reg 7D

## 7. WTC elements
WTC is made up of a number of elements. If you are a couple and qualify for more than one disabled worker element or severe disability element they will all be included in the calculation.

**Basic element** – This is included in the calculation for all who qualify for WTC.
TCA, S.11(2)

**Couple element** – This is included if you are one of a couple (see 2 above). If you are not responsible for a child or qualifying young person (see 3 above), this element is not included where one partner is subject to immigration control or is in prison.
WTC(E&MR) Regs, reg 11

**Lone parent element** – This is included if you are single and responsible for a child or qualifying young person.
WTC(E&MR) Regs, reg 12

**30-hour element** – This is included if you:
■ work at least 30 hours a week; *or*
■ are one of a couple and:
  – you are responsible for a child or qualifying young person; *and*
  – between you, you work at least 30 hours a week; *and*
  – at least one of you works at least 16 hours a week.
*Note:* You can only get one 30-hour element, even if you are a couple who both work at least 30 hours a week.
WTC(E&MR) Regs, reg 10

**Disabled worker element** – See 8 below.
**Severe disability element** – This is included if you get:
■ attendance allowance higher rate;*
■ disability living allowance highest rate care component;*
■ personal independence payment enhanced rate daily living component;* *or*
■ armed forces independence payment.
* or would but for the fact that you are in hospital
If you are one of a couple and one of you meets this condition, you get one severe disability element. If both of you meet this condition, you get two. The person who meets this condition does not have to be the person who is working.
WTC(E&MR) Regs, reg 17

*'Supplementary payments'* are available in Northern Ireland to temporarily compensate people who lose their severe disability element as a result of being re-assessed for personal independence payment (PIP). The payment makes up for the loss of the element in full and can be paid for up to one year. For details of the PIP re-assessment, see Box B.6 in Chapter 5.
Welfare Supplementary Payment (Loss of Disability-Related Premiums) Regs (Northern Ireland) 2016, regs 27-32

## Childcare element
This is 70% of the cost of 'relevant childcare' (see below), up to a maximum of £175 a week for one child and £300 a week for two or more children. Therefore, the highest childcare element you can get is £122.50 a week for one child or £210 for two or more children.

The childcare element is included if you are:
■ a lone parent working at least 16 hours a week; *or*
■ one of a couple and you both work at least 16 hours a week; *or*
■ one of a couple and one of you works at least 16 hours a week and the other is 'incapacitated' (see below), entitled to carer's allowance, in hospital or in prison.
If you are on maternity, paternity, shared parental or adoption leave, you may be treated as being in work and may get help with childcare costs for a new child (see 6 above).

In order for you to qualify, your child(ren) must be aged 15 or younger, or aged 16 or younger if they meet the conditions for the disabled child element (see 4 above). You can claim a childcare element up to the last day of the week containing the 1 September following their 15th birthday, or following their 16th birthday if they are disabled. The childcare element is not affected by the two-child limit in CTC (see 4 above).

Childcare counts as *'relevant childcare'* if the provider is registered by Ofsted in England or by the equivalent body in Scotland or Wales. It includes out-of-school-hours childcare provided by schools.

If you have arranged the childcare but it hasn't started by the time you make your claim, the amount is based on an estimate provided by the childcare provider.

If your childcare costs vary (eg you pay more during school holidays), your childcare element is based on your *average* weekly costs. If you pay childcare only for a short period (eg the 6-week summer holiday) you can choose to average the costs over that period. If there is a change while you are getting WTC and your average weekly childcare charges go down by £10 a week or more, or stop, you must report this promptly (see 17 below). Your WTC will then be recalculated.

WTC(E&MR) Regs, regs 13-16; see also booklet WTC5, available from: www.gov. uk/government/publications/working-tax-credit-help-with-the-costs-of-childcare-wtc5

**Incapacitated** – You count as *'incapacitated'* if you receive housing benefit that includes a disability premium or higher pensioner premium, or if you have already been counted as 'incapacitated' for housing benefit childcare costs (see Chapter 22(6)). You also count as incapacitated if you receive one of the following benefits:

- incapacity benefit;
- severe disablement allowance;
- contributory employment and support allowance (ESA), providing you have been entitled to it for at least 28 weeks – including linked periods and periods on statutory sick pay when you otherwise met the contribution conditions;
- national insurance credits due to limited capability for work (if your contributory ESA has been terminated at the end of the 12-month payment period);
- attendance allowance;
- disability living allowance;
- personal independence payment;
- constant attendance allowance (payable with the Industrial Injuries or War Pensions schemes);
- war pensions mobility supplement;
- armed forces independence payment; *or*
- a benefit similar to any of the above paid by another EEA state or Switzerland,

or would get one of these benefits but for the fact that you are a hospital inpatient.

WTC(E&MR) Regs, reg 13(5)-(7)

## 8. WTC disabled worker element

This element is a significant one for disabled people. In addition to working at least 16 hours a week, you have to meet two other tests, one relating to your disability and one to your receipt (or recent receipt) of a qualifying benefit. For couples, the partner who works must meet the disability and qualifying benefit tests. So, if you are working and not disabled, but have a disabled partner who is not working, you will not receive the disabled worker element. You may, however, receive the severe disability element (see 7 above). Conversely, if both you and your partner meet the rules about working and the disability and qualifying benefit tests, you can receive two disabled worker elements.

### The 'disability' test

To get the disabled worker element, you must have a *'physical or mental disability which puts [you] at a disadvantage in getting a job'*. How this is assessed depends on whether you are making an initial claim or a renewal claim.

**Initial claims** – If you are claiming WTC for the first time, you need to meet the rules set out in *either* Part 1 *or* Part 2 of Box F.3.

**Renewal claims** – When making a WTC renewal claim, you need to meet the rules set out in Part 1 of Box F.3.
WTC(E&MR) Regs, reg 9(1)(b)

### The 'qualifying benefit' test

To get the disabled worker element, you must also meet *one* of the following conditions.

- ❑ **Condition A** – At any time in the last 26 weeks before your claim, you were getting: employment and support allowance (ESA) or national insurance credits due to limited capability for work if your contributory ESA has been terminated at the end of the 12-month payment period (provided that you had been entitled to ESA or the credits for at least 28 weeks, including linked periods and periods on statutory sick pay (SSP)) or incapacity benefit or severe disablement allowance (SDA).
- ❑ **Condition B** – At any time in the last 26 weeks before your claim, you were getting the disability premium or higher pensioner premium in income support, income-based jobseeker's allowance or housing benefit.
- ❑ **Condition C** – You get disability living allowance (DLA – either component, any rate) or personal independence payment (PIP – either component, either rate) or attendance allowance (or an Industrial Injuries or War Pensions scheme equivalent) or armed forces independence payment. You must meet this condition throughout the period of your claim, not just at the start of it (R(TC)1/06).
- ❑ **Condition D** – On the date of your claim, and throughout your claim (R(TC)1/06), you have a Motability car.
- ❑ **Condition E** – This route to the disabled worker element is referred to as the *'Fast Track'* because it allows some people who have been off work for a while to return to work without having either to have been off sick for a prolonged period or to meet the qualifying conditions for DLA, PIP, etc (as in Conditions A to D). At the date of claim:
- you have a disability likely to last at least six months (or for the rest of your life if your death is expected within six months); *and*
- your gross earnings are less than they were before your disability began, by at least 20% or £15 a week, whichever is greater; *and*
- at any time in the last eight weeks before you claim, you had been getting, for at least 20 weeks: ESA, SSP, occupational sick pay, incapacity benefit, income support paid on the basis of incapacity, or national insurance credits on the basis that you were incapable of work or had a limited capability for work.
- ❑ **Condition F** – At any time in the last eight weeks before you claim, you:
- had been taking part in training for work (which means certain government training courses or a course of 16 hours or more a week learning occupational or vocational skills); *and*
- within the eight weeks before the start of the training course, had been getting one of the benefits or credits listed under Condition A.
- ❑ **Condition G** – You will be treated as qualifying for the disabled worker element if, within the eight weeks before your claim (including renewal claims), you were entitled to the disabled worker element by virtue of Condition A, B, E or F. This means if you were getting a qualifying benefit, such as ESA, you can continue to get the disabled worker element long after you stopped receiving that benefit (CTC/2165/2017). If you got the disabled worker element because you met Condition C or D, as you were getting, for example, DLA or PIP, you must be currently receiving that benefit.
WTC(E&MR) Regs, regs 9 & 9B

## 9. Income and savings
CTC and WTC have no 'capital limits', that is, there is no upper limit on savings above which they are not payable. However, income from savings is taken into account in the calculation (see below).

The rules on what income is taken into account for tax credits are largely based on income tax legislation. The general rule is that taxable income is taken into account and other income is disregarded, although there are some exceptions.

For people who move from tax credits onto universal credit, the calculation of income may be different because HMRC use an in-year finalisation process to finalise the tax credit award shortly after the universal credit claim is accepted (see Box F.2).

*TC(DCI) Regs*

### Income that has the first £300 disregarded
The following are included in the calculation, but the first £300 a year of the total is disregarded:
- pension income, but excluding war disablement pensions, war pensioners' mobility supplement and certain other war service pensions that are exempt from income tax;
- Armed Forces Compensation scheme survivor's guaranteed income payment and child payments;
- investment income;
- property income;
- most foreign income, although some foreign income is disregarded entirely, eg payments to victims of Nazi persecution; *and*
- notional income; the rules are similar but not identical to those for means-tested benefits – see Chapter 22(21).

*TC(DCI) Regs, regs 5, 10, 11, 12 & 13-17*

### Employment income
All taxable income from employment is usually taken into account. In contrast to means-tested benefits, income from employment is taken into account gross, that is, before income tax and national insurance contributions have been deducted. Such income includes:
- earnings from employment, including pay, holiday pay, bonus and commission;
- payment for expenses not *'wholly, exclusively and necessarily incurred'* in your job;
- cash vouchers, non-cash vouchers or credit tokens (but not if for eligible childcare – see 'Disregarded employment income' below);
- the value of a car for private use and the fuel (but not if you are a disabled employee with an adapted or automatic company car);
- goods or assets your employer gave you that you could sell for cash (eg gifts of food) or payments made by your employer that you should have paid yourself (eg if they paid your rent or gas bill);
- redundancy payments to the extent that they are subject to income tax;
- statutory sick pay;
- statutory maternity, paternity, shared parental or adoption pay – but only the amount in excess of £100 a week;
- certain retainer fees;
- armed forces' accommodation allowance;
- strike pay; *and*
- taxable gains from security options (eg company shares, bonds, government gilts) acquired as a result of your employment.

*TC(DCI) Regs, reg 4(1)*

## F.3  The 'disability' test

### Disability that puts you at a disadvantage in getting a job
You will pass the disability test for working tax credit if:
- on an initial claim, any one (or more) of the conditions in Parts 1 or 2 apply to you;
- on a renewal claim, any one (or more) of the conditions in Part 1 apply to you.

#### Part 1
- When standing you cannot keep your balance unless you continually hold on to something.
- Using any crutches, walking frame, walking stick, prosthesis or similar walking aid which you habitually use, you cannot walk a continuous distance of 100 metres along level ground without stopping or without suffering severe pain.
- You can use neither of your hands behind your back as in the process of putting on a jacket or of tucking a shirt into trousers.
- You can extend neither of your arms in front of you so as to shake hands with another person without difficulty.
- You can put neither of your hands up to your head without difficulty so as to put on a hat.
- Due to lack of manual dexterity you cannot, with one hand, pick up a coin which is not more than 2.5 centimetres in diameter.
- You are not able to use your hands or arms to pick up a full jug of one-litre capacity and pour from it into a cup, without difficulty.
- You can turn neither of your hands sideways through 180 degrees.
- You are certified by a consultant ophthalmologist as severely sight impaired or blind.
- You cannot see to read 16-point print at a distance greater than 20 centimetres, if appropriate, wearing the glasses you normally use.
- You cannot hear a telephone ring when you are in the same room as the telephone, if appropriate, using a hearing aid you normally use.
- In a quiet room you have difficulty hearing what someone talking in a loud voice at a distance of 2 metres says, if appropriate, using a hearing aid you normally use.
- People who know you well have difficulty understanding what you say.
- When a person you know well speaks to you, you have difficulty understanding what that person says.
- At least once a year during waking hours you are in a coma or have a fit in which you lose consciousness.
- You have a mental illness for which you receive regular treatment under the supervision of a medically qualified person.
- Due to mental disability you are often confused or forgetful.
- You cannot do the simplest addition and subtraction.
- Due to mental disability you strike people or damage property or are unable to form normal social relationships.
- You cannot normally sustain an 8-hour working day or a 5-day working week due to a medical condition or intermittent or continuous severe pain.

#### Part 2
- As a result of an illness or accident you are undergoing a period of habilation or rehabilitation.

*WTC(E&MR) Regs, Sch 1*

### Disregarded employment income

Some payments are disregarded as income, including:

■ payments for expenses *'wholly, exclusively and necessarily incurred'* in your job;

■ travelling expenses, if exempt from income tax;

■ the provision of transport to a disabled employee, if it is exempt from income tax;

■ car parking at work;

■ certain overnight expenses or removal expenses;

■ vouchers for 'relevant childcare' costs (see 7 above, and note that your WTC childcare element will apply only to costs that have not been covered by the vouchers);

■ meal vouchers received as an employee;

■ certain allowances paid to members of HM armed forces; *and*

■ the provision of one mobile phone to an employee, if it is exempt from income tax.

TC(DCI) Regs, reg 4(4)&(5)

### Self-employment income

Your taxable profit for income tax purposes, as a sole trader or a partner in a business, is taken into account. The following items can be deducted from your taxable profit:

■ gross contributions to a pension scheme or retirement annuity (as long as these have not already been deducted from any other income); *and*

■ current year trading losses can be offset against your other income or your partner's income. Any surplus losses can be carried forward and offset against profits of the same trade in future years (see HMRC working sheet TC825).

If your business made a loss, contact HMRC (see 10 below), as there are special rules dealing with losses.

Any income covered by the new 'trading and property allowance' (introduced by HMRC from 6.4.17) is not counted as income for tax credit purposes.

TC(DCI) Regs, regs 3(1)[Step 4] & (7)(c) and 6

### Benefit income

All benefit income is taken into account in full as income, except:

■ armed forces independence payment;

■ attendance allowance;

■ bereavement support payment;

■ carer's allowance supplement (Scotland);

■ child benefit;

■ Christmas bonus;

■ council tax reduction;

■ disability living allowance;

■ guardian's allowance;

■ housing benefit and discretionary housing payments;

■ incapacity benefit for people previously receiving invalidity benefit and still in the same period of incapacity for work;

■ income-based jobseeker's allowance (JSA);

■ income-related employment and support allowance;

■ income support, except to strikers;

■ industrial injuries benefits (except industrial death benefit);

■ maternity allowance;

■ pension credit;

■ personal independence payment;

■ severe disablement allowance;

■ social fund payments;

■ certain compensation payments, including compensation payments for the non-payment of income support, JSA or housing benefit; *and*

■ payments in lieu of milk tokens or vitamins.

TC(DCI) Regs, regs 7 & 19 (Table 6, para 17)

### Student grants

Student grants and loans are disregarded (except grants for adult dependants and lone parents).

TC(DCI) Regs, regs 8 & 9

### Other income

Most other forms of taxable income are counted for tax credits. The following are disregarded:

■ mandatory top-up payments (and discretionary payments to help meet special needs) to those taking part in certain training or employment programmes;

■ payments made to disabled people to help them obtain or retain employment;

■ education maintenance allowance;

■ expenses paid to you as a volunteer, but only if you are paid nothing else by the charity or organisation and you are not treated as having 'notional earnings' (the rules are similar but not identical to those for means-tested benefits – see Chapter 22(21));

■ adoption allowances and special guardianship payments;

■ fostering allowances and allowances paid to adult placement carers and other shared-lives carers (up to certain tax-exempt limits);

■ maintenance payments;

■ community care direct payments;

■ payments of NHS travelling expenses; *and*

■ payments from a local authority under the Supporting People scheme.

This is not an exhaustive list.

TC(DCI) Regs, reg 19 (Tables 6 & 7)

The gross amount of pension contributions to an approved pension scheme and of authorised Gift Aid payments should be deducted from the gross income figure.

## 10. Claiming tax credits

Claims for CTC or WTC are made on claim-form TC600, available from HMRC (0345 300 3900 or textphone 0345 300 3909). When you make the call, you may be asked to provide some basic information before the claim-form is sent out, including:

■ your national insurance number (if you have one);

■ your income for the last tax year;

■ details of any benefits you get;

■ details of any childcare payments you make; *and*

■ if you work, the number of hours you work per week.

You must provide a valid national insurance number, or information or evidence to enable one to be traced or allocated. If you are unable to make a claim on your own behalf, it can be done by your appointee or someone empowered to act on your behalf.

Online claims are not available at the time of writing, but you can order a claim-form online (www.gov.uk/claim-tax-credits).

TC(C&N) Regs, regs 5, 17 & 18

**Backdating claims** – If you meet the qualifying conditions, tax credits can be backdated for up to 31 days – or longer if entitlement to WTC is dependent on a disabled worker element being included in the calculation. If you claim WTC within 31 days of the decision to award a qualifying benefit for this element, the claim can be backdated to the date on which the qualifying benefit became payable or, if later, the first day on which your eligibility for WTC was dependent on receipt of the qualifying benefit. You must meet all the other qualifying conditions for WTC throughout this backdated period.

The Tax-Free Childcare (TFC) scheme was rolled-out from 21.4.17. You cannot normally claim tax credits and TFC at the same time. Therefore backdating of your tax credit claim may be limited if you were in a live TFC entitlement period in the 31 days before the claim, unless an exception applies.
TC(C&N) Regs, regs 7 & 8

**Renewal claims** – If you got tax credits in 2017/18, HMRC will send a renewal pack early in the 2018/19 tax year. In most cases, you can also renew online at www.gov.uk/manage-your-tax-credits.

The renewal process involves establishing your final entitlement for 2017/18 by establishing your actual income and circumstances in that year. Your 2017/18 income and current circumstances are used as the basis for your initial award in 2018/19.

If you are required to complete and return the forms, you must do so by 31.7.18. If you have difficulty giving final income details for 2017/18 (eg because you were self-employed and your accounts are not yet available), you must still provide an estimate by 31.7.18 and provide the actual figure by 31.1.19. If you miss the deadline, but renew within 30 days of the notice stating that your payments have ceased, your renewal is treated as if made on time. Alternatively, HMRC may allow you until 31.1.19 to renew if you can show you had good cause for not renewing on time. Otherwise, you may have to make a new claim*, which can be backdated by 31 days only.

You can withdraw from the tax credit system by finalising your previous year's income and responding to the final notice stating that you no longer wish to claim tax credits for the new tax year. However, it is important to act quickly, as you may have to pay back any provisional payments you receive between 6.4.18 and the withdrawal date. Either partner of a couple who separate during the renewal period will be able to complete the renewal process by responding to the final notice, but each partner will need to make their own fresh claim* if they want to continue receiving tax credits.
TC(C&N) Regs, regs 11 & 12

* in some areas, it is no longer possible to make a new claim for tax credits and you will need to claim universal credit instead (see Box E.1 in Chapter 14)

## 11. Payment of tax credits

In the case of couples, CTC and help with childcare costs are normally paid to the main carer, while WTC, apart from help with childcare costs, is normally paid to the worker.

Payments are normally made by credit transfer to a bank account or similar account. Payments into your account will be made weekly or 4-weekly; this is generally your choice, but HMRC has the power to change it.
Tax Credits (Payments by the Commissioners) Regulations 2002

## 12. Penalties

Tax credits contain a system of financial penalties, but the £50 'civil penalty' (see Chapter 56(8)) does not apply to tax credits.

A penalty of up to £3,000 can be imposed if you *'fraudulently or negligently'* make an incorrect statement or declaration or give incorrect information or evidence either in your claim or on a change of circumstances. If you claim as a couple, the penalty can be imposed on either of you unless one of you can show you were not aware and could not *'reasonably have been expected'* to be aware that your partner was making a false statement or providing incorrect information or evidence about your claim. You can also be subject to this penalty if you make a false statement when you are acting for someone else.

A penalty of up to £300 can be imposed if you fail to provide information or evidence that HMRC has asked you to provide in connection with your claim, or if you fail to notify HMRC of a change of circumstances which you must report (see 17 below).
TCA, Ss.31 & 32

## 13. Challenging decisions and complaints

HMRC can end or amend your tax credit award at any time. They can do so if you have told them of a change of circumstances (see 17 below) or if they have *'reasonable grounds'* for believing you should be getting a different amount or nothing at all. If there has been an official error by HMRC or the DWP, HMRC can revise a decision in your favour up to five years after the date of the original decision.
TCA, Ss.16(1) & 21

The rules on challenging decisions are similar but not identical to those for other social security benefits. Chapter 57 gives details of how to challenge a decision. Some specific differences are:

❑ You must request a mandatory reconsideration within 30 days of the decision you disagree with. You can request a mandatory reconsideration using form WTC/AP (www.gov.uk/government/publications/child-tax-credit-and-working-tax-credit-appeal-form). Appeals are made direct to HM Courts & Tribunals Service and must be made within one calendar month of the date on the mandatory reconsideration notice.

❑ Appeals and mandatory reconsiderations up to 13 months from the date of the decision may be allowed in some cases. It will be up to HMRC whether to accept a late mandatory reconsideration request and up to the tribunal whether to accept a late appeal.

❑ Your notice of appeal must state your grounds of appeal. The tribunal may allow you to put forward grounds that were not specified in your notice if they think the omission was *'not wilful or unreasonable'*.

❑ There is no right of appeal against a decision to recover an overpayment, so arguments about *'failure to disclose'* or *'misrepresentation'* are irrelevant. However, you may be able to appeal against the underlying decision(s) that led HMRC to believe they overpaid you.

Sometimes, HMRC may contact you by phone to settle with you if you submit a valid appeal. You may persist with your appeal if you do not wish to negotiate in this way.
TCA, Ss.38, 39 & 39A; The Tax Credits (Settlement of Appeals) Regs 2014

**Complaints** – The HMRC complaints procedure is set out in the factsheet *Complaints* (www.gov.uk/government/publications/putting-things-right-how-to-complain-factsheet-cfs). HMRC have a customer charter called 'Your Charter' which may be helpful to refer to in a complaint (www.gov.uk/government/publications/your-charter/your-charter). If you are not satisfied with the internal HMRC process, you can refer the matter to the Adjudicator's Office (www.adjudicatorsoffice.gov.uk; 0300 057 1111). Beyond the Adjudicator, you can approach the Parliamentary and Health Service Ombudsman (see Chapter 59(5)) through your MP, but the Ombudsman will normally expect you to have exhausted all other routes, including the Adjudicator, before considering your complaint.

## B. CALCULATING TAX CREDITS

## 14. Introduction

Child tax credit (CTC) and working tax credit (WTC) calculations are based on the maximum annual amount that you could receive in the tax year (6 April to the following 5 April). Entitlement is based on daily, not annual, rates. You can be entitled to tax credits at different rates for different periods (known as *'relevant periods'*) during the tax year, in which case entitlement is calculated separately for the number of days in each relevant period.

Initially, the income taken into account is your income in the previous tax year. So, if you are awarded WTC/CTC in 2018/19, it is initially based on your income in 2017/18. Your award can be based on current tax year income instead if your income has gone up or down by more than £2,500 since the previous tax year (see 18 and 19 below).

The final decision on your entitlement is made after the end of the tax year and is normally based on your actual income for that year or that of the previous year, whichever is lower, subject to the 'disregards' at 18 and 19 below.

## 15. Rates of CTC and WTC
The elements described in 4 and 7 above are:

| CTC elements 2018/19 | yearly amount |
| --- | --- |
| Family element | £545 |
| Child element | £2,780 |
| Disabled child element | |
| – disabled child rate | £3,275 |
| – severely disabled child rate | £4,600 |

| WTC elements 2018/19 | yearly amount |
| --- | --- |
| Basic element | £1,960 |
| Couple element | £2,010 |
| Lone parent element | £2,010 |
| 30-hour element | £810 |
| Severe disability element | £1,330 |
| Disabled worker element | £3,090 |
| Childcare element* | (weekly amount) |
| – maximum eligible cost for one child | £175 |
| – maximum eligible cost for two or more children | £300 |

* Childcare element is paid at 70% of actual childcare costs. The maximum you can receive is therefore £122.50 for one child or £210 for two or more children.

CTC Regs, reg 7; WTC(E&MR) Regs, reg 20 & Sch 2

## 16. Steps in the tax credit calculation
To work out your tax credits for a whole tax year, use the steps below and see the example in Box F.4. To work out your tax credits for part of a tax year, calculate the 'relevant period' amounts at each step and see the example in Box F.5.

**Step 1: Work out maximum tax credits for you and your family** – This is the sum of the CTC and WTC elements that apply to you and your family (see 15 above).

**Step 2: Work out your income** (see 9 above) – The income taken into account is normally your income in the previous tax year but it can be current tax year income instead: see 14 above and the 'disregards' at 18 and 19 below. There is no income calculation for periods when you are receiving income-related employment and support allowance, income-based jobseeker's allowance, income support or pension credit. Getting one of these benefits automatically entitles you to an award of your maximum tax credits. The exception to this is where you receive one of these benefits during the 4-week run-on of WTC (see 6 above), in which case the calculation is done as normal.

**Step 3: Find the appropriate income threshold** (see below).

**Step 4: Compare your income to the threshold** – If your income is below or the same as the threshold, you will get maximum tax credits. If your income is above the threshold, deduct the threshold from your income, to work out the 'excess income'. Then apply the 41% taper (see below) to your excess income.

**Step 5: Deduct the result at Step 4 from your maximum tax credits at Step 1** – The amount you are left with is your tax credit entitlement.

*Note:* This calculation gives only a provisional entitlement figure, as your actual entitlement is based on a comparison of your actual income in the year of the award and your income in the previous tax year. This will not be known until after the year has ended. See 14 above.

TC(IT&DR) Regs, regs 7 & 8

### Income thresholds and the taper
**Income thresholds** – There are two thresholds for 2018/19 and they depend on whether you qualify for either CTC or WTC or both:
- WTC and CTC £6,420;
- WTC only £6,420;
- CTC only £16,105.

**The taper** – The taper is 41%. HMRC must apply the taper in the following order: first to the WTC adult elements, then to the WTC childcare element, then to the CTC child elements and finally (if this is still included) to the CTC family element. The effect of this on a couple is that payments made to the partner who is working (the non-childcare elements of WTC) are reduced before those made to the main carer (CTC and the childcare element of WTC).

TC(IT&DR) Regs, reg 8(3)

## 17. Changes in your circumstances
CTC and WTC awards normally run to the end of the tax year but if you stop meeting the qualifying conditions, your entitlement ends and you should tell HMRC immediately. On the other hand, if your income goes up or down, even substantially, you don't usually need to tell HMRC right away, although it may sometimes be in your interest to do so (see 'When you should ask for a re-assessment', under 18 and 19 below).

You *must* tell HMRC within one month if:
- you change your status from single person to couple, or the other way round;
- you cease to meet the residence conditions (eg you move abroad);
- your childcare costs end, or your average childcare costs go down by £10 a week or more;
- your work hours change and you no longer meet a 16-, 24- or 30-hours a week qualifying rule: see 5 above;
- you cease to be entitled to the 30-hour element;
- you stop being responsible for a child or qualifying young person, or one you are responsible for dies, or a qualifying young person stops counting as such (eg because they leave college and start work).

If you don't report the change within one month of becoming aware of it, you may face a penalty (see 12 above). Changes can be reported online (www.gov.uk/manage-your-tax-credits), by phoning the tax credits helpline (0345 300 3900; textphone 0345 300 3909) or by writing to the Tax Credit Office (see Chapter 61(2)).

TC(C&N) Regs, Reg 21

A change of circumstances that increases your maximum tax credits (such as the birth of a child) should be reported within one month to allow full backdating.

## 18. The £2,500 disregard if your income rises
For 2018/19, your income can increase by up to £2,500 a year, compared to the previous year, before it affects your tax credit entitlement for the current year. (The annual disregard was £2,500 until April 2006, then £25,000 until April 2011, then £10,000 for 2011/12, then £5,000 until April 2016.)

The £2,500 disregard is applied in the following way.
- If current year income is greater than the previous year income by £2,500 or less, the lower previous year income is used to work out current year entitlement.
- If current year income is greater than the previous year income by more than £2,500, current year income less £2,500 is used.

TCA, S.7(3)(a)&(b); TC(IT&DR) Regs, reg 5(a)

**Example 1:** If your income last year was £10,000 but this year is £12,000, your award this year will be based on last year's income of £10,000.

**Example 2:** If your income last year was £10,000 but this year is £14,000, your award this year will be based on your income of £14,000 less the disregard of £2,500, ie £11,500.

### When you should ask for a re-assessment

If your current year income is likely to be higher than last year's by more than £2,500 (eg if you get a better-paying job), you should ask for a re-assessment right away so that your award is based on your estimated current year income. This will avoid you building up a recoverable overpayment. The second example above illustrates this: HMRC will base your initial award on last year's income of £10,000 and will only use the actual £11,500 figure after the year end. Unless you ask for a re-assessment sooner, you will be overpaid.

Following the re-assessment, HMRC will stop payment of tax credits if they have calculated that you have already received your full entitlement for the current year.

### 19. The £2,500 disregard if your income falls

Normally, income disregards work in your favour: you can receive a higher award because less income is taken into account. This disregard, on the other hand, can work against you. If your current year income is less than your previous year's, the first £2,500 of the decrease is disregarded. Where the fall is less than £2,500, the higher previous year figure will apply. If the fall is more than £2,500, the figure used is the lower current year figure plus £2,500.

TCA, S.7(3)(c)&(d); TC(IT&DR) Regs, reg 5(b)

**Example 1:** If your income last year was £13,000 and your estimated income for this year is £12,000, your award will be based on last year's income of £13,000. Although your income has gone down, the disregard of £2,500 means the fall is ignored.

**Example 2:** If your income last year was £13,000 and your estimated income for this year is £10,000, your award will be based on income of £12,500. Although your income has gone down by £3,000, the disregard of £2,500 means that only £500 of the fall is counted.

---

## F.4 Calculating tax credits

Shirley is a lone parent with two children aged 4 and 10. She works 20 hours a week and her gross annual income is £9,000. She gets disability living allowance highest rate care component for one child. Childcare costs are £160 a week (£8,320 a year).

**Step 1: work out maximum tax credits**

| | |
|---|---|
| WTC basic element | £1,960.00 |
| WTC lone parent element | £2,010.00 |
| WTC childcare (£8,320 x 70%) | £5,824.00 |
| CTC disabled child element | |
| – severely disabled child rate | £4,600.00 |
| CTC child elements (£2,780 x 2) | £5,560.00 |
| CTC family element | £545.00 |
| *Maximum tax credits* | *£20,499.00* |

**Step 2: annual income**

| | |
|---|---|
| Annual income | £9,000.00 |

**Step 3: find income threshold**

| | |
|---|---|
| Income threshold (WTC) | £6,420.00 |

**Step 4: compare income to threshold**

| | |
|---|---|
| Excess income | |
| (Step 2 result less Step 3 result) | £2,580.00 |
| *Tapered at 41%* | *£1,057.80* |

**Step 5: Step 1 result less Step 4 result**

| | |
|---|---|
| £20,499 less £1,057.80 | |
| *Tax credit entitlement* | *£19,441.20* |

*Note:* For simplicity, this example is based on annual, not daily, rates. HMRC uses daily rates for each element, calculated by dividing the annual rates by 365 and rounding up to the nearest penny. HMRC also uses daily rates for income and threshold figures, with the resulting income figure rounded down and the threshold figure rounded up to the nearest penny. After rounding, the claimant's actual entitlement will be slightly higher than shown in this example. The discrepancy is more marked when there are more 'relevant periods' and more rounding. See the example in Box F.5.

---

## F.5 Change of circumstances calculation

Farouk is single, 35, works 30 hours a week and has a disability. His salary is £11,700 a year. At the start of the year he does not meet the conditions for the WTC disabled worker element, but after 150 days (about five months) he is awarded personal independence payment mobility component. He is not entitled to the WTC disabled worker element for the first relevant period, but is for the second.

**First relevant period (150 days)**
**Step 1: work out maximum tax credits at daily rates**

| | |
|---|---|
| WTC basic element: £5.37* x 150 | £805.50 |
| WTC 30-hour element: £2.22* x 150 | £333.00 |
| *Maximum tax credits* | *£1,138.50* |

**Step 2: income**

| | |
|---|---|
| Income: £11,700 x 150/365 | **£4,808.21 |

**Step 3: income threshold**

| | |
|---|---|
| Income threshold (WTC) £6,420 x 150/365 | *£2,638.36 |

**Step 4: compare income to threshold**

| | |
|---|---|
| Excess income (Step 2 result less Step 3 result) | £2,169.85 |
| Taper excess income by 41% | **£889.63 |

**Step 5: Step 1 result less Step 4 result**

| | |
|---|---|
| £1,138.50 less £889.63 | |
| *Tax credit entitlement for first period* | *£248.87* |

**Second relevant period (215 days)**
**Step 1: work out maximum tax credits at daily rates**

| | |
|---|---|
| WTC basic element: £5.37* x 215 | £1,154.55 |
| WTC disabled worker element: £8.47* x 215 | £1,821.05 |
| WTC 30-hour element: £2.22* x 215 | £477.30 |
| *Maximum award* | *£3,452.90* |

**Step 2: income**

| | |
|---|---|
| Income: £11,700 x 215/365 | **£6,891.78 |

**Step 3: income threshold**

| | |
|---|---|
| Income threshold (WTC) £6,420 x 215/365 | *£3,781.65 |

**Step 4: compare income to threshold**

| | |
|---|---|
| Excess income (Step 2 result less Step 3 result) | £3,110.13 |
| Taper excess income by 41% | **£1,275.15 |

**Step 5: Step 1 result less Step 4 result**

| | |
|---|---|
| £3,452.90 less £1,275.15 | |
| *Tax credit entitlement for second period* | *£2,177.75* |

**Actual tax credits payable for both relevant periods**

| | |
|---|---|
| First relevant period | £248.87 |
| Second relevant period | £2,177.75 |
| *Total* | *£2,426.62* |

\* Figures rounded up to nearest penny
(see note in Box F.4)
\*\* Figures rounded down to the nearest penny

### When you should ask for a re-assessment

As with other changes of income, you don't have a duty to tell HMRC about these changes right away. If you do, however, you may get an increase in your ongoing payments, which may be better than waiting for a lump-sum of underpaid tax credits after the end of the tax year. If you are claiming other benefits, such as housing benefit, you should get advice about how changes to tax credits might affect those benefits.

## 20. Overpayment or underpayment of tax credit

Because tax credits are assessed by reference to the tax year and are provisional in nature, being paid throughout the year but not finalised until the year-end, overpayments or underpayments sometimes arise. Also, as the system is designed to be flexible and respond to changes in household circumstances, a change in circumstances that affects the tax credits to which you are entitled is bound to give rise, even if only for a limited period, to 'in-year' overpayments or underpayments. Finally, errors – whether they are yours or official ones (ie by HMRC or another government department) – can lead to too much or too little tax credit being paid.

## 21. Overpayments

An overpayment arises when the amount of tax credit paid to you for a tax year is more than you are or were entitled to. For the reasons given in 20 above, it is not until after the end of a tax year that your award(s) for that year can be seen to be under or over the right amount.

If it appears to HMRC during a tax year that you are likely to be overpaid, they may adjust your ongoing award to reduce or avoid the overpayment. This is generally a computer-generated operation, triggered by you reporting a change of circumstances that reduces entitlement.

TCA, S.28(1)&(5)

### Methods of recovery

The two usual methods of recovery are by:
- direct recovery; *or*
- deduction from payments under future awards.

TCA, S.29(1),(3)&(4)

Under the second method, the rate at which payments can be reduced varies according to the type of award. Your payments are usually reduced by:
- 10% if you receive maximum tax credits;
- 25% if you receive less than the maximum award but more than the family element of CTC and your household income is no more than £20,000 a year;
- 50% if you receive more than the family element of CTC and your household income is more than £20,000 a year; *and*
- 100% if you receive only the family element of CTC.

From October 2018, HMRC may pass tax credit debts over to the DWP to recover even if you are not receiving any DWP benefits. This means that the DWP may use their recovery powers, including an attachment of earnings order requiring your employer to deduct money from your pay.

Tax Credits (Payments by the Commissioners) Regulations 2002, reg 12A

If you do not have an ongoing award because you no longer qualify for tax credits or you have to make a new claim because your household makeup has changed, HMRC will seek repayment in monthly instalments for one year or, if you have little disposable income, for up to 10 years (called a 'time to pay' arrangement). In cases of hardship, it is possible for overpayments to be remitted (this means that HMRC will not ask you for the money, but may do so in future if your circumstances improve). HMRC may also recover the overpayment by adjusting your tax code in your employment.

If you are already paying back an overpayment on an ongoing award and are asked to pay back another overpayment by direct recovery, you should ask HMRC to suspend the direct recovery until the ongoing recovery is finished. You must ask HMRC for this as it is not an automatic process.

Where HMRC is recovering an overpayment from a couple who have split up, each partner has 'joint and several' liability, which means HMRC can pursue either one for the whole amount. However, in practice HMRC will recover only 50% from each one (unless a different split is agreed by the couple); you must ask HMRC for this as it is not an automatic process.

TCA, S.28(4)

If you move from tax credits onto universal credit, see Box F.2 for how the debt is handled.

### When will an overpayment not be recovered?

**Official error** – HMRC has discretion whether or not to recover an overpayment in whole or in part and they generally opt for recovery. There is no right of appeal against a decision to recover an overpayment, but there is a right of appeal against an award notice showing an overpayment (eg whether it has been calculated incorrectly). HMRC practice on recovery is set out in code of practice COP26 (available at www.gov.uk/government/publications/tax-credits-what-happens-if-youve-been-paid-too-much-cop26). If you meet all your responsibilities as listed in COP26, but HMRC has not met theirs, overpayments generated by official error are generally written off.

While you cannot generally avoid HMRC recovering an overpayment from you, you can try to avoid overpayments arising by:
- comparing the payment schedules on your award notice with your bank statements and raising any queries within 30 days of the award notice being issued; *and*
- reporting changes of circumstances (see 17, 18 and 19 above) as soon as they happen.

If you dispute recovery of an overpayment on the grounds of official error, you must do so in writing, preferably on form TC846 (available at www.gov.uk/government/publications/tax-credits-overpayment-tc846). On receiving your written dispute, HMRC will consider your case but they will not stop recovery of the debt. It is important that you negotiate repayment with them. If your dispute is successful, any repayments made will be paid back to you.

Since most dealings with HMRC are by phone (see 10 above), keep detailed notes of calls, including the date and time, who you spoke to and what was said.

**Hardship** – If repaying the overpayment would cause hardship to you or your family, you can ask HMRC to reduce it or write it off.

**Change of status** – If you delay reporting a change of status (going from joint to single claim or the other way round) and there is an overpayment, you may be able to have the overpayment reduced by the amount you would have received had you made a fresh claim at the correct time. This is called notional entitlement or *'offsetting'*. You must make a new claim under the correct status and ask HMRC for the offsetting, as it is not an automatic process.

## 22. Underpayments

If you are underpaid tax credit (eg because your income goes down) and the underpayment comes to light during that tax year, the award can be changed to reflect your new circumstances, but any accrued underpayment may be held back until the end of the year. If the underpayment comes to light after the end of the year, the award will be corrected to reflect your circumstances: if there are no outstanding overpayments, you will get a lump sum to make good the underpayment.

This section of the handbook looks at:

| | |
|---|---|
| Universal credit housing costs amount | Chapter **24** |
| Housing benefit | Chapter **25** |
| Support for mortgage interest loans | Chapter **26** |
| Housing costs | Chapter **27** |
| Council tax | Chapter **28** |

# Help with housing costs

# **24** Universal credit housing costs amount

| A | **Common rules** | |
|---|---|---|
| 1 | Introduction | 165 |
| 2 | When can the amount be included in your award? | 165 |
| 3 | The payment condition | 166 |
| 4 | The liability condition | 167 |
| | Who cannot get the housing costs amount? – Box G.1 | 166 |
| 5 | The occupation condition | 167 |
| | Treated as occupying accommodation – Box G.2 | 168 |
| 6 | Service charge payments | 167 |
| | Service charge payment categories – Box G.3 | 170 |
| B | **Housing costs amount for renters** | |
| 7 | Rent | 169 |
| 8 | Periods of payment | 169 |
| 9 | The size criteria | 169 |
| | The size criteria: absences from home – Box G.4 | 171 |
| 10 | Non-dependant deductions | 171 |
| 11 | Calculations involving two homes | 172 |
| 12 | Calculating the amount: private sector | 172 |
| 13 | Core rent | 172 |
| 14 | Cap rent | 173 |
| | Exceptions to the shared accommodation rule – Box G.5 | 173 |
| 15 | Calculating the amount: social rented sector | 174 |
| 16 | The calculation: joint tenants | 174 |
| 17 | Excessive payments | 174 |
| C | **Housing costs amount for owner occupiers** | |
| 18 | What are owner-occupier payments? | 174 |
| 19 | When you cannot get the housing costs amount | 175 |

## A. COMMON RULES

### 1. Introduction

Your universal credit award may include a *'housing costs amount'* to cover rent and some service charges. A housing costs amount can only be included in your award when your home:
■ is in Great Britain; *and*
■ is residential accommodation.
It does not matter whether the accommodation consists of the whole or part of a building and whether or not it is made up of separate and self-contained premises.
WRA 2012, S.11(2)

Two types of payment are covered by the housing costs amount:
■ the housing costs amount for renters (see 7 to 17 below); *and*
■ the housing costs amount for owner-occupiers (see 18 and 19 below).
**Care leavers** – The housing costs amount for renters cannot be paid to anyone who is aged 16 or 17 years and has left local authority care.
UC Regs, Sch 4, para 4

**Aged 18 to 21** – The government has announced that the tight restrictions to the housing costs amount for renters in this age group are to be lifted.

### 2. When can the amount be included in your award?

The housing costs amount can be included in your universal credit award if you meet:
■ the payment condition (see 3 below);
■ the liability condition (see 4 below); *and*
■ the occupation condition (see 5 below).
UC Regs, reg 25(1)&(5)

If you meet all three conditions and are liable to pay rent, you will be eligible for the housing costs amount for renters (see 7 to 17 below). This will still be the case if you are also liable to pay service charges (see 6 below).

If you meet the three conditions and are only liable to pay service charges, you will be eligible for the housing costs amount for owner-occupiers (see 18 and 19 below).
UC Regs, reg 26(1)-(3)

### 3. The payment condition

You meet the *'payment condition'* if the payments that you make for the accommodation are:
■ rent payments (see 7 below); *or*
■ service charge payments (see 6 below).
UC Regs, reg 25(2)

### 4. The liability condition

You meet the *'liability condition'* if you (or your partner) are liable to make the above payments on a commercial basis or are treated as having a liability to make them (see below). In some circumstances you (or your partner) can be treated as not being liable to make the payments, even if you actually are. These circumstances are listed in Box G.1.
UC Regs, reg 25(3)

**What does 'liable' mean?** – A liability to make payments imposes conditions on both parties to the agreement which can be legally enforced. If either party breaks the agreement, the other party can take them to court.

**What does 'commercial' mean?** – A commercial agreement must include terms that are legally enforceable. If the parties do not intend the agreement to be legally enforceable, it cannot be commercial. Just because a rent is low does not mean it is not commercial.
Advice for Decision Making, Chapter F2, paras F2081-F2083

## Treated as liable to make payments
**Another person is liable** – You will be treated as liable to make payments if the person who is actually liable is:
- a child or qualifying young person (see Chapter 16(4)) you are responsible for; *or*
- your partner, where you are a one of a couple but claiming as a single person (see Chapter 14(3)).

UC Regs, Sch 2, para 1

**If you take over paying someone else's payments** – If the person liable to make payments on your home stops making them, you can be treated as liable to make them in the following circumstances:
- you have to make the payments to continue living in your home;
- it would be unreasonable to expect you to make other arrangements; *and*
- it is reasonable to treat you as liable to make the payments. In the case of owner-occupier payments, the DWP will take into account the fact that the arrangement may benefit the person normally liable to make them.

UC Regs, Sch 2, para 2

**Repairs to your home** – If the payments on your home are waived (eg by your landlord waiving your rent) in return for you doing reasonable repairs or redecoration to your home, you can be treated as liable to pay them.

UC Regs, Sch 2, para 3

**Rent-free periods** – You will be treated as still liable to pay rent and service charges during any rent-free periods set out in your rental agreement.

UC Regs, Sch 2, para 4

## 5. The occupation condition
You meet the *'occupation condition'* if you are treated as occupying the accommodation as your home.

UC Regs, reg 25(4)

You cannot generally be treated as occupying accommodation made up of more than one dwelling. If you do occupy more than one dwelling, the decision as to which dwelling you should be treated as occupying should be made taking all the circumstances into account, including any people living with you in each dwelling. The circumstances in which you can be treated as occupying more than one dwelling, or treated as occupying a dwelling that you are not currently living in, are listed in Box G.2.

UC Regs, Sch 3, para 1

**Croft land** – If your home is on a croft, the croft land used for your home is treated as part of your accommodation.

UC Regs, Sch 3, para 2

---

### G.1 Who cannot get the housing costs amount?

To get the housing costs amount in your universal credit award, you must be 'liable' to pay your accommodation costs. In the following circumstances, you can be considered not 'liable', even though you do actually pay them.

**Liability to pay rent or service charges:**
**To a close relative**
You are treated as not liable to pay rent or service charges if you are liable to pay them to someone who lives in the accommodation and who is:
- your partner;
- a child or qualifying young person (see Chapter 16(4)) you (or your partner) are responsible for; *or*
- a close relative (see below) of you, your partner or your child/qualifying young person.

*UC Regs, Sch 2, para 5*

**Close relative**
A *'close relative'* means parent, parent-in-law, son, son-in-law, daughter, daughter-in-law, step-parent, stepson, stepdaughter, brother or sister (or partner of any of these).

*UC Regs, reg 2*

**To a company or trust**
**Rent** – You are treated as not liable to pay rent if you are liable to pay it to a company or trust and the owners or directors of the company, or the trustees or beneficiaries of the trust, include:
- you;
- your partner;
- a qualifying young person (see Chapter 16(4)) you (or your partner) are responsible for; *or*
- a close relative (see above) of any of the above who lives with you.

**Service charges** – If you are liable to pay service charges to the same company or trust as above (or to another company or trust of which the owners, directors, trustees or beneficiaries include any of the people listed above), you will be treated as not liable to pay them.

*UC Regs, Sch 2, paras 6 & 7*

**Liability to pay service charges as an owner-occupier:**
**To a member of your household**
You are treated as not liable to pay service charges if you are liable to pay them to anyone living in your household.

*UC Regs, Sch 2, para 8*

**Household** – While the term *'household'* is not defined in legislation, it should be given its normal everyday meaning, ie a domestic establishment containing the essentials of home life.

*R(SB)4/83*

'Household' should not be confused with 'dwelling'. A single dwelling or property may have several different households within it, each containing independent living arrangements.

**Arrears of payment**
You are treated as not liable to make any payment that is more than you usually pay, which has been set up to cover:
- outstanding arrears of any payment or charge for your current or previous accommodation; *or*
- any other unpaid liabilities to make a payment or charge.

*UC Regs, Sch 2, para 9*

**Contrived liability**
Even if none of the above paragraphs apply, you can still be treated as not liable to make payments if the DWP considers that the liability was contrived in order to secure the housing costs amount (or an increase in the amount).

*UC Regs, Sch 2, para 10*

The contrivance can be on your part, the person to whom payments are made, or both of you acting together. There must be something about the liability arrangements that indicates it was set up to take advantage of the housing costs amount. The DWP must therefore establish the facts and determine the main purpose of the arrangement before it can decide to treat you as not liable to make the payments.

*Advice for Decision Making, Chapter F2, para F2142*

## 6. Service charge payments
*'Service charge payments'* are payments which are, in whole or in part:
- to help cover the cost of (or charges for) providing services or facilities that the people in your home can use or benefit from; *or*
- fairly attributable to such costs or charges connected with your accommodation.

It does not matter whether or not the service charges are separately identified as such. Nor does it matter whether or not they are made in addition to, or as part of, any other payment (such as rent) or made under the same or a different agreement as that relating to your home.

If you are living in the social rented sector or are an owner-occupier, additional conditions apply (see below).

**Excluded payments** – The following are not treated as service charge payments:
- a loan that was secured on your home taken out to cover service charge payments; *or*
- payments for services or facilities provided if you occupy:
  - a tent;
  - a probation or bail hostel;
  - a care home (see 7 below); *or*
  - supported accommodation (see Chapter 25(11)).

UC Regs, Sch 1, para 7

### Additional conditions
If you are living in the social rented sector or are an owner-occupier, four additional conditions must be met before a service charge payment can be included in your housing costs amount:

**Condition 1:** Your right to occupy the accommodation must depend on you paying the service charges.

**Condition 2:** The payments must fall in at least one of four categories, which are listed in Box G.3.

**Condition 3:** The costs and charges must be reasonable and relate to services or facilities that are reasonable to provide.

**Condition 4:** No service charge payments will be included in your housing costs amount if:
- public funding is available from some other source to meet the payments (regardless of whether or not you are entitled to such help);
- you acquire an interest in an asset when you pay a service charge for it (eg you will end up owning a piece of furniture); *or*
- they are to cover food, medical services or personal services (including personal care).

**Owner-occupier and rent payments** – Any service charge payment not eligible to be included in your housing costs amount because one of these four conditions is not met cannot be treated as either an owner-occupier payment (see 18 below) or a rent payment (see 7 below).

UC Regs, Sch 1, para 8

### Ineligible service charge payments
DWP guidance lists the following as examples of service charge payments that cannot be included in the housing costs amount. These are charges to cover:
- living expenses (eg heating, lighting, hot water or meals);
- personal services (eg a laundry or cleaning service);
- nursing or personal care services (help with personal hygiene, eating, dressing, etc);
- the provision of an emergency alarm system;
- counselling, medical or support services;
- medical expenses (including those covering counselling);
- transport;
- licences or permits;
- maintenance of un-adopted roads;
- installation, maintenance or repair of any special equipment or adaptations to the property for disability or illness;
- individual emergency alarm systems;
- subscription or fee-based television;
- communal social recreational areas (eg gyms, bars or shops);
- gardening for individuals' gardens;
- intensive housing management;
- water, sewerage and utility charges relating to anything other than communal areas; *or*
- buildings insurance.

Advice for Decision Making, Chapter F2, para F2077

## B. HOUSING COSTS AMOUNT FOR RENTERS

## 7. Rent
### What is rent?
The following are considered to be *'rent payments'* and therefore may be met by the housing costs amount:
- payments of rent;
- payments for a licence (or other permission to occupy the accommodation);
- houseboat mooring charges;
- site fees for a caravan or mobile home; *or*
- payments to a charitable almshouse (provided by a housing association) towards the cost of maintenance and essential services.

UC Regs, Sch 1, para 2

### What is not rent?
The following are not considered to be *'rent payments'* and therefore cannot be met by the housing costs amount:
- ground rent;
- payments for a tent and the site it is pitched on;
- payments for probation and bail hostels;
- payments for a care home (see below);
- payments for specified accommodation (see below); *or*
- payments for temporary accommodation (see below).

UC Regs, Sch 1, para 3

---

## G.2 Treated as occupying accommodation

The housing costs amount can normally only be included in your universal credit award to cover payments you are liable to make for the accommodation you occupy as your home. Normally, you can only be treated as occupying one dwelling. However, there are exceptions. This box lists the circumstances in which you can be treated as occupying more than one dwelling, or treated as occupying a dwelling that you are not currently living in.

### Housing costs amount for two homes

In the following circumstances you can be treated as occupying two dwellings, in which case you may be eligible for the housing costs amount for both.

### Your new home is being adapted

You can be treated as occupying both your new home and your old home for up to one month if:

- you have moved into a new home and immediately before the move you were liable to pay for the new home; *and*
- there was a delay in moving to enable the new home to be adapted to meet the needs of a disabled person (see below); *and*
- immediately before the move, you were entitled to the housing costs amount for the old home; *and*
- the delay was reasonable.

**Who counts as a disabled person?** – This can be you, your partner, or any child or qualifying young person (see Chapter 16(4)) you are responsible for, if you (or they) receive:

- the care component of disability living allowance at the middle or highest rate;
- attendance allowance, constant attendance allowance or exceptionally severe disablement allowance;
- the daily living component of personal independence payment; *or*
- armed forces independence payment.

*UC Regs, Sch 3, para 5*

### You are living elsewhere because of fear of violence

You can be treated as normally occupying both your normal home and other accommodation for up to 12 months if you had to move into the other accommodation because of a reasonable fear of violence.

This will apply if:

- you are occupying accommodation other than your normal home; *and*
- you are liable to make payments for both your normal home and the other accommodation; *and*
- it is unreasonable to expect you to return to your normal home because of your reasonable fear of violence in the home, or by your former partner, against:
  - you; *or*
  - any child or qualifying young person (see Chapter 16(4)) you are responsible for; *and*
- you intend to return to your normal home; *and*
- it is reasonable for the housing costs amount to cover both your normal home and the other accommodation.

If you are liable to make payments for just one of the homes, you can be treated as normally occupying that home as long as it is reasonable for the housing costs amount to cover it.

*UC Regs, Sch 3, para 6*

### You have a large family

If you have been housed in two homes by a provider of social housing (such as a local authority or housing association), these will be treated as a single home if you:

have been housed in the two homes because of the number of children or qualifying young people (see Chapter 16(4)) living with you; *and*

- normally occupy both homes with the children or qualifying young people; *and*
- are liable to make payments for both homes (the liability need not be to the same person).

*UC Regs, Sch 3, para 4*

### Moving home
#### Moving is delayed by adaptations

If you have moved into a property, you can be treated as having occupied it as your home for up to one month before the date you actually moved in if:

- you have since moved in and immediately beforehand you were liable to make payments for it; *and*
- there was a delay in moving in to enable the home to be adapted to meet the needs of a disabled person (see above); *and*
- it was reasonable to delay moving in.

*UC Regs, Sch 3, para 7*

### Moving into accommodation following a stay in hospital or care home

If you have moved into a property, you can be treated as having occupied it as your home for up to one month before the date you actually moved in if:

- you have since moved in and immediately beforehand you were liable to make payments for it; *and*
- the liability to make payments arose while you were a hospital inpatient or living in a care home (or in the case of a joint claim, you were both patients or in a care home).

*UC Regs, Sch 3, para 8*

### Temporary absences

If you are temporarily absent from your home, you can be treated as occupying it for up to six months. Once that absence exceeds or is expected to exceed six months, you will no longer be treated as occupying your home, and are therefore not eligible for the housing costs amount for that home.

Any re-occupation of the home (other than by a prisoner on temporary release) will break the period of absence – a stay of 24 hours is usually enough, although the DWP has to be satisfied that the stay at home was genuine.

The 6-month time limit will not apply if you have to live away from your home while essential repairs are carried out on it (see below).

A 12-month time limit will apply instead if you are living away from your home because of fear of violence (see above).

*UC Regs, Sch 3, para 9*

### You are living elsewhere during essential repairs

If you have to move into other accommodation so that essential repairs can be carried out to your home and you:

- intend to return to your home following the repairs; *and*
- are liable to pay for only one home,

you can be treated as normally living in that home, and may therefore be eligible for the housing costs amount for that home. If you are liable to pay for both homes, the decision maker will decide which one you normally occupy as your home, and you will be eligible for the housing costs amount only for that one.

*UC Regs, Sch 3, para 3*

**Essential repairs** – The DWP defines these as *'necessary and not a luxury'*.

*Advice for Decision Making, Chapter F2, para F2173*

Rent payments do not include mesne profits (or violent profits in Scotland), that is, payments made by a former tenant who remains in occupation unlawfully.
Advice for Decision Making, Chapter F2, paras F2032 & F2043

### Care homes
In England and Wales, a care home is defined as somewhere that provides accommodation, together with nursing or personal care, for people who:
- are (or have been) ill;
- have (or have had) a mental disorder;
- are disabled or infirm; *or*
- are (or have been) dependent on alcohol or drugs.

It is not a care home if it is an NHS hospital,* independent clinic or children's home.

In Scotland, a care home is defined as a 'care home service' that provides accommodation, together with nursing, personal care or personal support, for people due to their vulnerability or need. It is not a care home if it is an NHS hospital* or a public, independent or grant-aided school.
* An independent hospital can, however, be included in the definition of a care home.
UC Regs, Sch 1, para 1

### Specified accommodation
*'Specified accommodation'* is:
- 'supported accommodation' (see Chapter 25(11));
- a local authority hostel or accommodation provided by a relevant body,* in which you receive care, support or supervision; *or*
- accommodation in a refuge provided by a local authority or relevant body* because you have left home as a result of domestic violence.

Such accommodation will continue to be met through housing benefit, rather than universal credit. See Chapter 25.
* a housing association, registered charity, voluntary organisation or English county council
UC Regs, Sch 1, para 3A

### Temporary accommodation
*'Temporary accommodation'* is defined as accommodation where:
- you pay rent to a local authority (or other provider of social housing); *and*
- they have provided you with the accommodation because you are homeless (or to prevent you becoming homeless); *and*
- it is not supported accommodation (see Chapter 25(11)).

Such accommodation will continue to be met through housing benefit, rather than universal credit. See Chapter 25.
UC Regs, Sch 1, para 3B

## 8. Periods of payment
All rent payments are calculated as a monthly amount. If your rent is due for a period other than calendar monthly, the amount is calculated as a monthly equivalent:
- weekly payments are multiplied by 52 and divided by 12;
- 2-weekly payments are multiplied by 26 and divided by 12;
- 4-weekly payments are multiplied by 13 and divided by 12;
- 3-monthly payments are multiplied by 4 and divided by 12; *and*
- annual payments are divided by 12.

If you have rent-free periods, obtain the monthly average by adding up all the rent payments due over a 12-month period and dividing the result by 12.
UC Regs, Sch 4, para 7

## 9. The size criteria
In calculating your housing costs amount, the DWP will take into account the type of accommodation the law considers it reasonable for you to live in: the *'size criteria'*. The size criteria focuses on the number of bedrooms your household (or 'extended benefit unit' as the regulations define it) is deemed to need, taking into account the number of people in your household, their ages, disabilities and genders.
UC Regs, Sch 4, para 8

**Your household** – The following people make up your household:
- you and your partner, if you have one;
- any child or qualifying young person (see Chapter 16(4)) you or your partner are responsible for; *and*
- anyone who is a *'non-dependant'* (see 10 below).
UC Regs, Sch 4, para 9(1)

### How many bedrooms are you allowed?
You are allowed one bedroom for each of the following people in your household:
- you (and your partner, unless it is inappropriate for you to share a room because of disability – see below);
- a qualifying young person (see Chapter 16(4)) you or your partner are responsible for;
- a non-dependant (see 10 below) aged 16 or over;
- two children aged under 10 (unless it is inappropriate for them to share a room because of disability – see below);
- two children aged under 16 of the same sex (unless it is inappropriate for them to share a room because of disability – see below); *and*
- any other child aged under 16.
UC Regs, Sch 4, para 10(1)

If you have a larger family that allows for a number of different bedroom arrangements, the one that needs the fewest number of rooms will apply.

You are allowed an additional bedroom if you, your partner, your child or an adult non-dependant need overnight care. You are also allowed an additional bedroom if you are a foster parent or adopter. See below for details.

## G.3 Service charge payment categories

If you are living in the social rented sector or are an owner-occupier, four additional conditions must be met before a service charge payment can be included in your housing costs amount (see 6 in this chapter). The second of these conditions lists the types of service charge payment that can be covered: they are listed below.

### Payments to maintain the general standard of the accommodation

These payments are for:
- the external cleaning of the upper-floor windows of a multi-storey building; *or*
- other internal or external maintenance or repair of the accommodation, but only where the payments are separately identifiable as such. You must be in a shared ownership tenancy or be an owner-occupier.

### Payments for the general upkeep of communal areas

These payments are for:
- the ongoing maintenance or cleaning of internal and external areas; *and*
- the supply of water, fuel or any other commodity relating to those areas.

This could include:
- ground maintenance (eg lawn mowing, litter removal and lighting costs for access areas);
- tenant parking (but not the staffing of car parks for security);
- laundry rooms;
- upkeep of internal common use areas (eg hallways and corridors); *and*
- children's play areas.

### Payments for basic communal services

These payments are for provision, ongoing maintenance, cleaning or repair in connection with basic services generally available to everyone living in the accommodation. This could include:
- refuse collection;
- a communal telephone (but not the cost of calls);
- communal lifts;
- secure building access (eg key cards and keypad door locking mechanism);
- radio or television aerials to receive a service free of charge; *and*
- CCTV for communal areas.

### Specific charges for the accommodation

These payments are limited to those for the use of essential items in your accommodation that are specific to that accommodation. This will include furniture or domestic appliances. It will not apply if the items in question could remain as your property when you move out.

*UC Regs, Sch 1, para 8(4); Advice for Decision Making, Chapter F2, paras F2072 & F2073*

If any members of your household are temporarily absent from your home, they can still be included in the above assessment in the circumstances listed in Box G.4.
*UC Regs, Sch 4, para 10(2)&(3)*

Each bedroom must be one that can be used as a bedroom by the actual occupants (as listed above).
*CH/1987/2016*

***Example:*** Robert and Anna have three children: two boys aged 14 and 7 and one girl who is 6. They would be allowed three bedrooms: one for Robert and Anna, and two for their children (the two youngest or the two boys would be expected to share).

### Disability

**Couples** – If you are not reasonably able to share a bedroom with your partner because of your (or their) disability, you will be allowed an additional bedroom. You (or your partner) must also be receiving a qualifying disability benefit (see below).
*UC Regs, Sch 4, para 12(1)(d)&(6A); MA & Others, A and Rutherford v SSWP [2016] SC*

**Disabled children** – If you have a child who is not reasonably able to share a bedroom because of their disability, you will be allowed an additional bedroom for them. They must also be receiving the care component of disability living allowance (DLA) at the middle or highest rate.

In such a case, the DWP must consider the nature and frequency of the care your child needs during the night, and the extent and regularity of the disturbance to the sleep of the child who would normally have to share the bedroom with them.
*UC Regs, Sch 4, para 12(1)(c)&(6); Burnip, Trengove, Gorry v SSWP [2012] EWCA Civ 629*

### Overnight care required

You are allowed one additional bedroom for a carer or carers to sleep in if you, your partner, your child (including a foster or adopted child – as below) or an adult non-dependant (see 10 below) need overnight care and receive a qualifying disability benefit (see below) or attendance allowance at the lower rate. The carer(s), who must not be living with you, must be engaged to provide the overnight care and must need to stay overnight at your home on a regular basis.

Only one additional bedroom is allowed, even if more than one carer is needed.
*UC Regs, Sch 4, para 12(A1)&(3); MA & Others, A and Rutherford v SSWP [2016] SC*

### Qualifying disability benefits

The following are *'qualifying disability benefits'*:
- the care component of DLA at the middle or highest rate;
- attendance allowance at the higher rate;
- the daily living component of personal independence payment; *or*
- armed forces independence payment.
*UC Regs, Sch 4, para 12(6A)*

### Foster parents and adopters

You are allowed one additional bedroom if you (or your partner) are:
- a foster parent; *or*
- an adopter and a child has been placed with you for adoption.

You can still be treated as a foster parent for up to 12 months if you have been approved as a foster parent but do not currently have a child placed with you. A recent Upper Tribunal decision (CH/3471/15) has held that this also applies if you are an approved carer for a person under an adult placement scheme.
*UC Regs, Sch 4, para 12(1)(b),(4)&(5)*

**Discretionary Housing Payments (DHPs)**
If you cannot afford the shortfall between your housing costs amount and your actual housing costs because of the application of the size criteria, you can request a DHP from your local authority to make up the difference. The government has advised local authorities to give priority to cases involving disability, eg if you cannot move to smaller accommodation because your property has been adapted or you need to be close to a support network. However, DHPs are cash-limited and there is no guarantee that you will receive one. For more on DHPs, see Chapter 25(16).

**10. Non-dependant deductions**
In calculating the housing costs amount, a deduction of £72.16 is made for each non-dependant (see below) living in your home. The deduction is referred to in law as a *'housing cost contribution'*. It is assumed that the non-dependant will contribute towards your housing costs, whether they do or not. However, there are circumstances when no deduction can be made (see below).

Deductions for non-dependants are made only after all the other steps in the calculation of your housing costs amount have been made. If the deduction is greater than your housing costs amount, as calculated so far, the result will be set at nil, which means you will not end up with a negative housing costs amount that eats into the rest of your universal credit award.
*UC Regs, Sch 4, paras 13 & 14*

**Who is a non-dependant?**
A *'non-dependant'* is someone who normally lives in your home on a non-commercial basis – usually an adult son, daughter, friend or relative. The following people do not count as your non-dependants:
- your partner;
- any child or qualifying young person (see Chapter 16(4));
- a foster child you (or your partner) are responsible for;
- anyone liable to make payments to you, your partner or another person on a commercial basis for the accommodation that you live in: a tenant, sub-tenant or joint tenant cannot count as a non-dependant;
- any person (or member of their household) you are liable to pay rent or service charges to: a resident landlord cannot count as a non-dependant; *and*
- anyone who has already been treated as a non-dependant in another person's claim for universal credit, if that person is liable to pay rent or service charges for the accommodation that you live in.
*UC Regs, Sch 4, para 9(2)&(3)*

**No non-dependant deduction: your (or your partner's) circumstances**
There is no deduction for your non-dependants (no matter how many you have) if you or your partner are certified by a consultant ophthalmologist as severely sight impaired or blind, or if you or your partner receive:
- the care component of disability living allowance (DLA) at the middle or highest rate;
- attendance allowance, constant attendance allowance or

---

## G.4 The size criteria: absences from home

If any member of your household is temporarily absent from your home, they will still be included in the assessment of the number of bedrooms you are allowed (see 9 in this chapter) in the following circumstances.

### You (or your partner)
You (or your partner) are still included in the assessment of the number of bedrooms you are allowed:
- if you (or your partner) are temporarily absent from Great Britain (GB) in the circumstances listed in Chapter 54(7); *or*
- for the first six months that you (or your partner) are a prisoner, as long as the term of custody is not expected to last longer than that and immediately before becoming a prisoner you (or your partner) were receiving the housing costs amount.
*UC Regs, Sch 4, para 11(3)*

### Children and young people
**Local authority care and prison**
A child or qualifying young person (see Chapter 16(4)) is included in the assessment of the number of bedrooms you are allowed for the first six months of their absence if:
- they are being looked after by a local authority; *or*
- they are a prisoner,
as long as immediately before they went into local authority care or into custody they were part of your household and you were receiving the housing costs amount. If they are a prisoner, they must not have been sentenced to a term of custody that is expected to last longer than six months.
*UC Regs, Sch 4, para 11(2)(a)&(b)*

### Other temporary absences
If your child or qualifying young person is temporarily absent, but you (or your partner) are treated as still being responsible for them because:
- their absence is not expected to, and does not, exceed six months; *or*
- they are absent from GB and their absence is not expected to, and does not, exceed one month (or longer in limited circumstances – see Chapter 54(7)),
they will be included in the assessment of the number of bedrooms you are allowed.
*UC Regs, Sch 4, para 11(2)(c)*

### Non-dependants
A non-dependant (see 10 in this chapter) is included in the assessment of the number of bedrooms you are allowed:
- for the first month of their temporary absence from GB (and a further month if the absence is in connection with the death of a close relative – see Chapter 54(7));
- for the first six months of their temporary absence from GB if the absence is solely in connection with medically approved care, convalescence or treatment (see Chapter 54(7)); *or*
- for the first six months that they are a prisoner, as long as their term of custody is not expected to last longer than that,
as long as immediately before the absence they were part of your household and you were receiving the housing costs amount.

If the non-dependant is the son, daughter, stepson or stepdaughter of you or your partner, they are included in the assessment for any period that they are a member of the armed forces and away on operations.

In any other case, the non-dependant is included in the assessment if their absence is not expected to, and does not, exceed six months.
*UC Regs, Sch 4, para 11(4)-(6)*

exceptionally severe disablement allowance;
■ the daily living component of personal independence payment (PIP); *or*
■ armed forces independence payment,
or would get one of the above benefits but for being a hospital inpatient.
UC Regs, Sch 4, para 15

### No non-dependant deduction: your non-dependant's circumstances

There is no deduction for a non-dependant if they are:
■ aged under 21;
■ in prison; *or*
■ responsible for a child aged under 5.
**Benefits** – There is no deduction for a non-dependant if they receive one of the following benefits:
■ pension credit;
■ the care component of DLA at the middle or highest rate;*
■ attendance allowance, constant attendance allowance or exceptionally severe disablement allowance;*
■ the daily living component of PIP;* *or*
■ carer's allowance.
* or would get one of these benefits but for being a hospital inpatient
**Armed forces** – A deduction is not made for a non-dependant if they are a member of the armed forces away on operations who:
■ is the (step)son or (step)daughter of you or your partner;
■ lived with you immediately before going on operations; *and*
■ intends to return to live with you at the end of operations.
UC Regs, Sch 4, para 16

### 11. Calculations involving two homes
**You have a large family**
If you have a large family, and a provider of social housing (such as a local authority) has housed you in two houses that are treated as a single home (see Box G.2), your housing costs amount is worked out using a single calculation for both homes. The calculation will include the rent and any service charges for both homes. In assessing the type of accommodation it is deemed reasonable for you to occupy (see 9 above), the total number of bedrooms in both homes is counted.

If you are liable to make payments for both homes to a provider of social housing, your housing costs amount is worked out as in 15 below. In any other case, your housing costs amount is worked out as in 12 below.
UC Regs, Sch 4, para 17

**Your new home is being adapted**
If you are treated as occupying both your new home and your old home while waiting for your new home to be adapted to meet the needs of a disabled person (see Box G.2), your housing costs amount is worked out by calculating the housing costs amount for each home (see 12 and 15 below) and adding these together. Any non-dependant deduction applicable (see 10 above) is only made to the housing costs amount of your old home.
UC Regs, Sch 4, para 18

**You are living elsewhere because of fear of violence**
If you are treated as occupying both your normal home and other accommodation because you have to move into the other accommodation because of reasonable fear of violence (see Box G.2), your housing costs amount is worked out by calculating the housing costs amount for each home (see 12 and 15 below) and adding these together. Any non-dependant deduction applicable (see 10 above) is only made to the housing costs amount of the accommodation you are staying in.
UC Regs, Sch 4, para 19

### 12. Calculating the amount: private sector
If you are a private tenant, your housing costs amount is worked out as follows:
**Step 1: Work out your 'core rent'** – See 13 below.
**Step 2: Work out your 'cap rent'** – See 14 below. Compare your core rent with your cap rent and take the lower amount (if both amounts are the same, take that amount).
**Step 3: Apply any non-dependant deductions** – If you have non-dependants living in your home, subtract any non-dependant deductions (see 10 above) from the result of Step 2. The result is your housing costs amount.
UC Regs, Sch 4, para 22

If the non-dependant deductions are greater than the result of Step 2, the result will be set at nil. This way, you will not have a negative housing costs amount that eats into the rest of your universal credit award.
UC Regs, Sch 4, para 14(3)

*Example:* Greg and Jamila are a couple renting a 2-bedroom private flat. Their 23-year-old son lives with them. They pay £635 rent a month. There is no service charge. A rent officer has determined that their cap rent is £610 a month (based on the 'local housing allowance' in their area for 2-bedroom accommodation – see 14 below).
**Step 1:** Greg and Jamila's eligible rent payments are £635 a month. That is their core rent.
**Step 2:** Their cap rent is £610 a month. As this is lower than their core rent figure, it will be used in the next step.
**Step 3:** Their son is treated as a non-dependant; a deduction of £72.16 will be made for him (see 10 above); £610 minus £72.16 gives £537.84. This is their housing costs amount.

### 13. Core rent
Unless you are a joint tenant (see below), your *'core rent'* is worked out by adding up all the eligible rent payments (see 7 above) and any eligible service charge payments (see 6 above) that you are liable to pay. If the payments are not made on a monthly basis, a monthly equivalent is worked out (see 8 above for the calculation). The result is your core rent.
UC Regs, Sch 4, para 23

**Joint tenants**
If you are liable to make the payments with other joint tenants, your core rent is worked out as follows:
**Step 1:** All the eligible rent payments (see 7 above) and any eligible service charge payments (see 6 above) that you and the other joint tenants are liable to pay are added up. If the payments are not made on a monthly basis, a monthly

equivalent is worked out (see 8 above for the calculation).

**Step 2:** If the only people liable to make payments are members of your family (ie you, your partner or a child or qualifying young person (see Chapter 16(4)) you or your partner are responsible for), the core rent will be the result from Step 1.

If other people are also liable to make payments, the result of Step 1 is divided by the total number of people (including family members) liable to make payments. The resulting figure is then multiplied by the number of family members liable to make payments. The result will be your core rent.*

UC Regs, Sch 4, para 24

*Example:* Stefan and Carla are a couple who live with their friend Derek. They are all liable for the payments on the house they live in: rent of £600 a month and eligible service charges of £24 a month.

**Step 1:** The eligible payment total is £600 plus £24, resulting in £624.

**Step 2:** The result from Step 1, £624, is divided by 3 (the number of people liable to make payments) and multiplied by 2 (the number of family members: Stefan and Carla) giving £416. This will be Stefan and Carla's core rent.

* If the DWP considers it unreasonable to allocate your core rent in this way, they can allocate it differently, taking into consideration the number of people liable to make payments and the actual proportion each person is liable for.

### 14. Cap rent

Your cap rent is normally the *'local housing allowance'* that applies to the type of accommodation you are allowed under the *'size criteria'*.

UC Regs, Sch 4, para 25(1)

#### The local housing allowance

The local housing allowance is based on a determination made by a local authority rent officer according to the *'broad rental market area'* where your home is situated and the type of accommodation you are allowed under the size criteria (see below). The rates are based on:

■ rents at the 30th percentile for properties of the relevant size within the broad rental market area (ie three in 10 properties in the area would be cheaper, the rest more expensive); *or*

■ the local housing allowance rate that applied on 30.1.15, if that would be lower.

**Broad rental market area** – This is an area within which you could reasonably be expected to live, having regard to both facilities and services (including health, education, recreation, personal banking and shopping). The distance of travel, by public and private transport, to and from those facilities and services needs to be taken into account.

The broad rental market area must include various types of accommodation and tenancy and enough privately rented properties to ensure that the local housing allowance is representative of the rents that a landlord might reasonably be expected to obtain in that area.

UC Regs, Sch 4, para 25(2); The Rent Officers (Universal Credit Functions) Order 2013

#### The size criteria

The *'size criteria'* is used to determine the type of accommodation which the law considers it reasonable for you to live in. It focuses on the number of bedrooms that your household is deemed to need. For instance, you may be allowed 1-bedroom shared accommodation, 1-bedroom self-contained accommodation, 2-bedroom accommodation, etc, depending on who is sharing your household. See 9 above for the general rules on size criteria. The following additional size criteria also apply to the private rented sector:

**4-bedroom limit** – You are not allowed more than four bedrooms.

UC Regs, Sch 4, para 26

**One-bedroom shared accommodation only** – The local housing allowance for 1-bedroom shared accommodation will apply to you if you:

■ are a single person (or one of a couple claiming as a single person);

■ are under the age of 35 and none of the exceptions in Box G.5 apply;

■ are not responsible for a child or qualifying young person (see Chapter 16(4)); *and*

■ do not have a non-dependant living with you (see 10 above).

UC Regs, Sch 4, paras 27 & 28

### Two homes

If you have a large family and have been housed by a provider of social housing (such as a local authority) in two houses that are treated as a single home (see Box G.2), and the cap rents for the two homes are different, the cap rent that will apply to you will be the lower of the two cap rents at the time that the housing costs amount was first calculated. This cap rent will apply until you are re-housed.

UC Regs, Sch 4, para 25(3)&(4)

---

## G.5 Exceptions to the shared accommodation rule

If you are a single person under the age of 35, are not responsible for a child or qualifying young person (see Chapter 16(4)) and do not have a non-dependant living with you (see 10 in this chapter), the local housing allowance that will apply to you will be that for 1-bedroom shared accommodation. This limit will not apply to you (even if you do live in 1-bedroom shared accommodation) in the following circumstances.

### Disability benefits

You are receiving:

■ the care component of disability living allowance at the middle or highest rate;

■ constant attendance allowance or exceptionally severe disablement allowance;

■ the daily living component of personal independence payment; *or*

■ armed forces independence payment.

### Previously in a homeless hostel

You are aged at least 25 and have lived in one or more hostels for homeless people for a total of at least three months (in one or more spells), where you accepted rehabilitation and community resettlement support services.

### Previously in care

You are aged at least 18 but under 22, were being looked after by the local authority before you were 18 and were provided with accommodation by the authority under specified legislation.

### Under risk management arrangements

You are subject to active multiple-agency risk management arrangements set up for assessing and managing risks posed by certain offenders.

UC Regs, Sch 4, para 29

## 15. Calculating the amount: social rented sector

Unless you are a joint tenant (see 16 below), if you rent from a provider of social housing (see below), your housing costs amount is worked out as follows:

**Step 1: Work out your eligible payments** – All the eligible rent payments (see 7 above) and eligible service charge payments (see 6 above) that you are liable to pay for your home are added up (excluding payments towards commodities such as water or fuel). If these are deemed excessive, lower figures may be used instead (see 17 below). If the payments are not made on a monthly basis, a monthly equivalent is worked out (see 8 above for the calculation).

**Step 2: Apply any deduction for under-occupancy** – If you are deemed to be under-occupying your property, a deduction is applied (the so-called 'bedroom tax'*). This is worked out by using the 'size criteria', which defines the number of bedrooms your household is deemed to need (see 9 above). If the actual number of bedrooms in your home is greater than the number you are deemed to need, a deduction is made to the result from Step 1: this will be 14% for one spare bedroom or 25% for two or more spare bedrooms. Such a deduction is not made if you have a shared ownership tenancy.

**Step 3: Apply non-dependant deductions** – If you have any non-dependants living in your home, subtract any non-dependant deductions (see 10 above) from the result of Step 2 (or Step 1 if Step 2 does not apply). The result is your housing costs amount.

UC Regs, Sch 4, paras 31, 33, 34 & 36

If the non-dependant deductions are greater than the result of Steps 1 or 2, the result will be set at nil. This way, you will not have a negative housing costs amount that eats into the rest of your universal credit award.

UC Regs, Sch 4, para 14(3)

* Although the bedroom tax also applies in Scotland, the Scottish government has allowed for an extension of discretionary housing payments (see Chapter 25(16)) to cover tenants who would otherwise lose out. You need to apply for a discretionary housing payment to receive this support. Similar measures are likely to be in place in Northern Ireland until at least 2020.

*Example:* Ewan and Grace are a couple who live in a 2-bedroom housing association flat. Their rent is £360 a month.
**Step 1:** Their eligible rent is £360.
**Step 2:** Applying the 'size criteria' (see 9 above), Ewan and Grace are allowed one bedroom, so they are deemed to have one spare bedroom. Consequently, the result from Step 1 is reduced by 14%, giving £309.60.
**Step 3:** They do not have any non-dependants living in their home, so a non-dependant deduction will not apply. Their housing costs amount will therefore be £309.60

### Provider of social housing

A *'provider of social housing'* means:
■ a local authority;
■ a non-profit-making registered social housing provider;
■ a profit-making registered social housing provider; *or*
■ a registered social landlord.

UC Regs, Sch 4, para 2

**Tenant Incentive scheme** – Any reduction in your rent or service charges that has been applied by a provider of social housing under the Tenant Incentive scheme is disregarded in the calculation.

UC Regs, Sch 4, para 32A

## 16. The calculation: joint tenants

If you are liable to make the payments with other joint tenants, your housing costs amount is worked out as follows:
**Step 1:** All the eligible rent payments (see 7 above) and eligible service charge payments (see 6 above) that you and

the other joint tenants are liable to pay are added up (excluding payments towards commodities such as water or fuel). If these are deemed excessive, lower figures may be used instead (see 17 below). If the payments are not made on a monthly basis, a monthly equivalent is worked out (see 8 above for the calculation).

**Step 2:** If the only people liable to make payments are members of your family (ie you, your partner or a child or qualifying young person (see Chapter 16(4)) you or your partner are responsible for), apply any deduction for under-occupancy to the result of Step 1 (as in Step 2 in 15 above).

If other people are also liable to make payments, the result of Step 1 is divided by the total number of people (including family members) liable to make payments. The resulting figure is then multiplied by the number of family members liable to make payments.*

**Step 3:** If you have any non-dependants living in your home, subtract any non-dependant deductions (see 10 above) from the result of Step 2. The result is your housing costs amount.

UC Regs, Sch 4, paras 31, 33, 35 & 36

If the non-dependant deductions are greater than the result of Step 2, the result will be set at nil, which means you will not have a negative housing costs amount that eats into the rest of your universal credit award.

UC Regs, Sch 4, para 14(3)

*Example:* Natalie and Jim are a couple who live with their friend Stephen. They are all liable for the payments on the housing association house they live in: rent of £400 a month and eligible service charges of £50 a month. Natalie and Jim's housing costs amount is worked out as follows:
**Step 1:** The eligible payment total is £400 plus £50, resulting in £450.
**Step 2:** The result from Step 1, £450, is divided by 3 (the number of people liable to make payments) and multiplied by 2 (the number of family members: Natalie and Jim) giving £300.
**Step 3:** Stephen is not treated as a non-dependant (see 10 above), so a non-dependant deduction will not apply. Therefore Natalie and Jim's housing costs amount will be £300.

* If the DWP considers it unreasonable to make the calculation in this way, they can work it out differently, taking into consideration the number of people liable to make payments and the actual proportion each person is liable for.

## 17. Excessive payments

If the DWP considers that a rent payment or service charge is excessive, they can apply for a rent officer to determine what they consider to be reasonable. Where the rent officer determines that the rent or service charge should be a lower amount, that amount will be used in your housing costs amount calculation, unless the DWP is satisfied that it would be inappropriate to do so.

UC Regs, Sch 4, para 32

Factors that should be taken into account include whether the rent or service charge is unreasonably high compared to the area you live in and what would be paid in the private sector. However, other circumstances that apply only to you should be taken into account, such as whether or not your property includes adaptations to enable you to live there.

Advice for Decision Making, Chapter F3, para F3253

## C. HOUSING COSTS AMOUNT FOR OWNER OCCUPIERS

## 18. What are owner-occupier payments?

If you are an owner-occupier and liable to make eligible service charge payments (see 6 above), these may be met by the housing costs amount. From 6.4.18, the housing costs amount can no longer cover the interest on mortgages and eligible home improvement loans; these costs may now be met by repayable *'support for mortgage interest'* loans (see Chapter 26 for details).

To work out how much the housing costs amount can cover, add up each of the service charge payments that are due that month. If the payments are not made on a monthly basis, the amount is calculated as a monthly equivalent (see 8 above). If you have service charge-free periods, obtain the monthly average by adding up the service charge payments due over a 12-month period and dividing the result by 12.

UC Regs, reg 26(3)(b)(ii) & Sch 5, para 13

If you have a shared ownership tenancy, service charge payments will be calculated under the rules for renters (see 7 to 17 above).

UC Regs, reg 26(5)

### 19. When you cannot get the housing costs amount
**You have earnings**
A housing costs amount for owner-occupiers cannot be included in your universal credit award during any monthly assessment period (see Chapter 16(1)) in which you (or your partner) have any earnings. This is irrespective of the nature of the work, how much you earn or how long you work for. If you have a shared-ownership tenancy, you can still get a housing costs amount towards rent and service charge payments.

UC Regs, Sch 5, para 4

**The qualifying period**
A housing costs amount for owner-occupiers cannot be included in your universal credit award during a *'qualifying period'*.

In the case of a new award for universal credit, the qualifying period will last for the first nine consecutive monthly assessment periods in which you receive universal credit and, were it not for the qualifying period, would qualify for the housing costs amount.

In a case where a housing costs amount has ceased to be included in your universal credit award for any reason (eg you started work), the qualifying period will last for nine consecutive assessment periods starting from the date on which, were it not for the qualifying period, you would re-qualify for the amount (eg you finish work).

If you cease to qualify for the housing costs amount before the end of the qualifying period, the qualifying period will stop running. A new qualifying period will only start once you re-qualify for the amount.

Once you have served the qualifying period, the housing costs amount can be included in the next assessment period.

UC Regs, Sch 5, para 5

**Exceptions to the qualifying period**
**Previously receiving JSA or ESA** – If you were previously receiving jobseeker's allowance (JSA) or employment and support allowance (ESA) (under the universal credit system) immediately before the start of your universal credit award, any days when you were receiving JSA or ESA will count towards the qualifying period.

UC Regs, Sch 5, para 6

**Ceasing to be a couple** – If your universal credit award as a joint owner-occupier is terminated because you are no longer a couple, a further award is made to you and you continue to occupy the same home (see 5 above), then:

■ if you had already served the qualifying period on your earlier award, you will not have to serve it again; *and*

■ if you were part-way through the qualifying period on your earlier award, the days already served in that period will count towards the new qualifying period.

The same rule will apply to your former partner.

UC Regs, Sch 5, para 7

**Transition from income-related ESA, income-based JSA or income support** – If you claim universal credit within one month of your (or your partner's) income-related ESA, income-based JSA or income support ending and housing costs were included in the previous award, you do not have to serve the qualifying period again. If you were part-way through the qualifying period on your earlier award, the days already served in that period will count towards the new qualifying period (added to any days between the two awards).

Universal Credit (Transitional Provisions) Regs 2014, reg 29

# 25 Housing benefit

**A  General conditions**
| | | |
|---|---|---|
| 1 | What is housing benefit? | 175 |
| | The benefit cap – Box G.6 | 176 |
| 2 | Who can get housing benefit? | 176 |
| | Who cannot get housing benefit? – Box G.7 | 178 |
| 3 | What is rent? | 177 |
| 4 | Housing costs that housing benefit cannot meet | 177 |
| 5 | Liability for rent on your normal home | 177 |
| 6 | Temporary absence | 177 |
| 7 | Moving home and getting housing benefit on two homes | 179 |

**B  Rent restrictions**
| | | |
|---|---|---|
| 8 | Introduction | 179 |
| | Why housing benefit may not cover all your rent – Box G.8 | 180 |
| 9 | Local housing allowance | 180 |
| | The 'bedroom tax' – Box G.9 | 180 |
| 10 | Rent officers' determinations | 182 |
| 11 | Exceptions to rent restrictions | 182 |
| 12 | Ineligible charges | 183 |

**C  Claims, payments & appeals**
| | | |
|---|---|---|
| 13 | How to claim housing benefit | 184 |
| 14 | When housing benefit starts, changes and ends | 184 |
| 15 | How housing benefit is paid | 184 |
| 16 | Getting more benefit | 185 |
| 17 | Underpayments | 185 |
| 18 | Overpayments | 185 |
| 19 | Challenging decisions | 186 |

**D  Calculating housing benefit**
| | | |
|---|---|---|
| 20 | How much do you get? | 187 |
| 21 | Non-dependants | 187 |
| 22 | Capital | 189 |
| 23 | Income | 189 |
| 24 | Applicable amounts | 189 |
| 25 | Rules for people who have reached pension credit qualifying age | 190 |

## A. GENERAL CONDITIONS

### 1. What is housing benefit?
Housing benefit helps people pay their rent. It can also be known as rent rebate or rent allowance. In nearly all areas, local authorities run the housing benefit scheme. But in a few areas, other organisations run the scheme and some authorities have contracted out part of the administration to private firms.

In Northern Ireland, the Northern Ireland Housing Executive administers the scheme.

**The benefit cap** – The *'benefit cap'* limits the total amount of weekly benefits that can be paid. If the cap applies to you, your housing benefit will be reduced to ensure that the total amount of benefit you receive is not greater than the cap level. The cap applies to people of working age. See Box G.6 for details.

**Universal credit** – The government is replacing housing benefit (as well as other means-tested benefits) with universal credit. If you are eligible to claim universal credit (see Box E.1 in Chapter 14), support towards your rent payments will be made through that benefit, not housing benefit (unless you are in 'specified' or temporary accommodation – see Chapter 24(7)). See Chapters 14 to 17 for more on universal credit and Chapter 24 for the support for housing costs you can get through that benefit.

## 2. Who can get housing benefit?

You can get housing benefit if you meet all the following conditions:

- you are not excluded from getting housing benefit (see below and Box G.7);
- you are liable to pay rent on your normal home (see 5 below);
- with the exception of some people who have reached

---

## G.6 The benefit cap

There is a cap on the total amount you can receive from the main out-of-work benefits and children's benefits. If your total income from the relevant benefits is greater than the cap level, your housing benefit will be reduced so that your total benefit does not exceed the cap. There are exemptions (see below). You can ring the government helpline for further details (0800 169 0145; textphone 0800 169 0314). A similar cap applies to universal credit (see Chapter 16(10)).

### Which benefits are taken into account?

The 'relevant' benefits that are taken into account when calculating the cap are:
- bereavement allowance;
- child benefit;
- child tax credit;
- employment and support allowance (ESA; you will be exempt from the cap if you or your partner receive the support component);
- housing benefit (this is not included in the cap calculation if you are in 'specified accommodation'; see below);
- incapacity benefit;
- income support;
- jobseeker's allowance (JSA);
- maternity allowance;
- severe disablement allowance;
- widowed mother's allowance;
- widowed parent's allowance; and
- widow's pension.

All other benefits are ignored when calculating the cap.

*HB Regs, reg 75G*

**Specified accommodation** – 'Specified accommodation' is:
- 'supported accommodation' (see 11 in this chapter);
- accommodation provided by a relevant body* or a local authority hostel, in which you receive care, support or supervision; or
- accommodation in a refuge provided by a local authority or relevant body* because you have left home as a result of domestic violence.

* a housing association, registered charity, voluntary organisation or English county council

*HB Reg, regs 75C(2)(a) & 75H*

### How much is the benefit cap?

The weekly amount of the cap is:
- £442.31 for couples (with or without children) and single parents in Greater London;
- £296.35 for single people in Greater London;
- £384.62 for couples (with or without children) and single parents outside Greater London; and
- £257.69 for single people outside Greater London.

*HB Regs, reg 75G*

### Who is exempt?

You are exempt from the benefit cap if you, your partner or your child (or qualifying young person – see Chapter 41(1)) receive any of the following:

- Armed Forces Compensation scheme guaranteed income payment;
- armed forces independence payment;
- attendance allowance;
- carer's allowance;
- disability living allowance;
- ESA support component;
- guardian's allowance;
- industrial injuries benefits;
- personal independence payment;
- war pension;
- war widow's or widower's pension; or
- working tax credit (the government has said this will still apply if you work enough hours to qualify for working tax credit but are not paid it because your income is too high),

or would get one of these benefits if you (or they) were not in hospital or a care home.

*HB Regs, regs 75E(2) & 75F*

The benefit cap will not be applied during a 'grace period' if you or your partner were working for 50 out of the 52 weeks immediately before your last day of work, as long as you were not claiming income support, ESA or JSA while you were working. Periods of work abroad and periods covered by zero hours contracts count as work here. The grace period lasts for 39 weeks from the date the job ends.

*HB Regs, reg 75E*

The cap will not be applied if you have reached pension credit qualifying age (see Chapter 44(2)), unless you or your partner are continuing to claim income support, income-related ESA or income-based JSA.

A recent Court of Appeal judgment has overturned a High Court decision that it is discriminatory to apply the benefit cap to lone parents with a child aged under 2. The families concerned have now appealed to the Supreme Court. There is also a separate test case waiting to be heard in relation to the application of the cap for all lone parents, regardless of the age of their children. Seek specialist advice if you are in either position.

*[2018] EWCA Civ 504*

### How does the cap work?

If your total income from the relevant benefits is above the cap, your housing benefit will be reduced until this income equals the cap. However, you will always be left with at least 50p of housing benefit; this means you will remain eligible for discretionary housing payments (see 16 in this chapter) and passported benefits. An online calculator can be found at www.gov.uk/benefit-cap-calculator.

*HB Regs, regs 75 & 75D*

**Example:** John and Mary are a couple with children in Greater London. Their income from the relevant benefits is £550 a week, including £240 housing benefit. As a couple in Greater London, the benefit cap that applies to them is £442.31 a week. Their housing benefit will be reduced by £107.69 to £132.31 a week. Their total relevant benefit income will now be £442.31.

pension credit qualifying age, you do not have capital of more than £16,000 (see 22 below);

■ you are on income-related employment and support allowance, income-based jobseeker's allowance, income support or the guarantee credit of pension credit, or you have a fairly low income (see 20 and 23 below); *and*

■ you claim and provide the information requested (see 13 below).

SSCBA, S.130

## People who cannot get housing benefit

If you are in any of the groups below, you cannot get housing benefit.

❑ **16-17-year-olds who have recently left local authority care** – This is because social care will usually remain responsible for providing support with accommodation (there are exceptions: seek further advice if you are in this situation). In Scotland, this also applies to care leavers aged under 21 receiving 'continuing care'.

❑ **People in care homes** – There are rare exceptions (see Chapter 38(3)).

❑ **'Persons from abroad' or 'subject to immigration control'** – This does not cover every non-UK national, and can cover some UK nationals who do not habitually reside in the UK. See Chapter 53 for details.

❑ **Many full-time students** – Full-time students cannot get housing benefit unless they fall within certain groups – eg disabled students (see Chapter 32(2)). If you are one of a couple and only one of you is a full-time student, the other one can get housing benefit for both of you.

❑ **Members of religious orders** – If you are maintained by the order, you cannot get housing benefit.

See Box G.7 for details of other people who cannot get housing benefit.

## 3. What is rent?

You can get housing benefit towards almost any kind of rent, whether paid to a local authority (including a health authority), the Northern Ireland Housing Executive, a housing association, a co-op, a hostel, a bed and breakfast hotel, a private company or a private individual (including a resident landlord – but see Box G.7). This is the case whether your letting is a 'tenancy' or 'licence', whether your payments are for 'rent', 'use and occupation of the dwelling', 'mesne profits' or 'violent profits', or whether you have a written or a verbal letting agreement. If you are buying a share of your home through a shared ownership scheme but still pay rent, you can get housing benefit towards the rent (and you may also get support for mortgage interest loans – see Chapter 26). You can also get housing benefit towards the following, which count as 'rent' for housing benefit purposes:

■ mooring charges and/or berthing fees for a houseboat (as well as your rent, if you do not own it);

■ site fees for a caravan or mobile home (as well as your rent, if you do not own it);

■ payments to a charitable almshouse;

■ payments under a 'rental purchase' agreement; *and*

■ payments (in Scotland) on a croft or croft land.

HB Regs, reg 12(1)

**Tenant Incentive schemes** – If you rent from a provider of social housing and the rent is reduced under a Tenant Incentive scheme, for housing benefit purposes your rent will be treated as if the reduction had not been made.

HB Regs, reg 12(2A)-(2B)

## 4. Housing costs that housing benefit cannot meet

You cannot get housing benefit towards any of the following costs, but some may be met by support for mortgage interest loans (see Chapter 26):

■ payments you make on your home if you own it or have a long tenancy (over 21 years or a life tenancy created in writing), except for a shared ownership lease;

■ payments you make in a co-ownership scheme where, if you left, you would be entitled to a sum based on the value of your home;

■ rent if you are a Crown tenant (there is a separate scheme for Crown tenants), although tenants of the Crown Estate Commissioners and the Duchies of Cornwall and Lancaster can get housing benefit;

■ hire purchase or credit sale agreements;

■ conditional sale agreements (unless for land); *and*

■ payments for a dwelling owned by your partner.

HB Regs, reg 12(2)

## 5. Liability for rent on your normal home

To get housing benefit, the general rule is that you must be personally liable to pay the rent on your home. You can usually get housing benefit on only one home at a time, which is the dwelling *'normally occupied'* by you and members of your family. (Seek advice if you live in more than one dwelling due to the size of your family.) However, there are exceptions to these rules, as described in the next few paragraphs.

**Couples** – Either one of you can get housing benefit towards the rent on your normal home. Even if the letting agreement is in one name only, the other person is treated as liable to make payments. If one of you is excluded from housing benefit (see 2 above), the other partner should make the claim.

HB Regs, Reg 8(1)(b)

**If you take over paying someone else's rent** – If the person liable for the rent on your home stops paying it and you take over the payments to continue living there, you can get housing benefit even though you are not legally liable for the rent. This applies if the liable person is your former partner, and in any other reasonable case.

HB Regs, Reg 8(1)(c)

**Repairs to your home** – If your landlord agrees to forego rent while you do repairs to your home, you can carry on getting housing benefit for the first eight weeks. After that, you cannot get housing benefit until you start paying rent again.

HB Regs, Reg 8(1)(d)

If you have to move into temporary accommodation while essential repairs are carried out to your normal home, you can get housing benefit on the property for which you are liable to make payments – but only if you are not liable for payments (of either rent or mortgage interest) on the other home.

HB Regs, Reg 7(4)

**Joint occupiers** – *'Joint occupiers'* means two or more people (other than a couple) who are jointly liable to pay rent on their home. If you are a joint occupier and not subject to the local housing allowance (see 9 below), you can get housing benefit towards your share of the rent. This share is assessed by taking into account the number of joint occupiers, how much each of you pays and how many rooms you each occupy.

If the local housing allowance rules apply, rent is not apportioned in this way. However, joint tenants are not usually included in the size criteria (unless they are members of your household).

HB Regs, reg 12B(4); CH107/2010

**Bail or probation hostels** – If you have to reside in a bail or probation hostel, you will not be treated as occupying that dwelling as your home, and so will be unable to claim housing benefit for any rent charged.

HB Regs, reg 7(5)

## 6. Temporary absence

You can continue to get housing benefit while you are temporarily absent from your normal home in the circumstances described below.

## The 13-week rule

You can get housing benefit for up to 13 weeks during a temporary absence from your normal home if:

- you intend to return to occupy it as your home;
- the part you normally occupy has not been let or sub-let; *and*
- your absence is unlikely to exceed 13 continuous weeks.

However, if you leave Great Britain, it is likely that your housing benefit will be limited to four weeks, although there are exceptions – see Chapter 54(10).

Calculation of the length of a prison sentence should include periods of temporary release, but should be reduced by any remission allowable for good behaviour.

HB Regs, reg 7(13)-(15)

## The 52-week rule

You can get housing benefit for up to 52 weeks during a temporary absence from your normal home if:

- you intend to return to occupy it as your home;
- the part you normally occupy has not been let or sub-let;
- your absence is unlikely to exceed 52 weeks or, in exceptional circumstances, is unlikely to substantially exceed 52 weeks; *and*
- your absence is for any of the reasons listed below.

However, if you leave Great Britain, it is likely that your housing benefit will be limited to either four or 26 weeks – see

Chapter 54(10).

You can get housing benefit under this rule if you are:

- a patient in a hospital or similar institution;
- receiving medical treatment or medically approved care or convalescence (other than in a care home);
- accompanying your child or partner who is receiving medical treatment or medically approved convalescence (other than in a care home);
- providing care to a child whose parent or guardian is absent from home because they are receiving medically approved care or medical treatment;
- providing medically approved care to anyone;
- receiving care in a care home (but not for a trial period – see below);
- on an approved training course;
- on remand awaiting trial or sentencing or required to reside in a hostel or property other than your home as a condition of bail;
- a student who is eligible for housing benefit and not covered by the 'two homes' rule (see Chapter 32(2)); *or*
- in fear of violence but only if you are not liable for rent on your other home (the conditions are the same as in the rule for getting housing benefit on two homes in such cases – see 7 below).

HB Regs, reg 7(16) & (17)

---

# G.7 Who cannot get housing benefit?

The rules in this box apply in addition to those in the main text (see 2 in this chapter). If you have difficulty getting housing benefit because of these rules, seek advice.

**Your letting is not on a commercial basis** – You cannot get housing benefit if your letting is not on a commercial basis. This rule applies whether you live with your landlord or somewhere else. Factors to be considered when deciding this include: the relationship and agreement between the parties; the living arrangements; the amount of rent; and whether the agreement contains terms enforceable by law.

**You live with your landlord who is a close relative of you or your partner** – You cannot get housing benefit if you live with your landlord and they are a close relative. Sharing just a bathroom, toilet, hallway, stairs or passageways does not count as living with your landlord, but sharing other rooms might. A *'close relative'* means only a parent, parent-in-law, step-parent, son, daughter, son/daughter-in-law, stepson/daughter, sister, brother or the partner of any of those.

**Your landlord is an ex-partner** – You cannot get housing benefit if you rent your home from:

- your ex-partner, and you used to live there with that ex-partner; *or*
- your (current) partner's ex-partner, and you (current) partner used to live there with that ex-partner.

**Your landlord is the parent of your child** – You cannot get housing benefit if you or your partner are responsible for a child whose father or mother is your landlord. You (or your partner) count as 'responsible' for any child who is included in your housing benefit award.

**Your landlord is a company or a trust connected with you** – You cannot get housing benefit if your landlord is a company or a trust of which any director or employee (of the company), or any trustee or beneficiary (of the trust) is:

- you or your partner, or an ex-partner of either of you; *or*
- a person who lives with you and who is a 'close relative' of you or your partner (see above).

This rule does not apply if your letting agreement was created for a genuine reason (rather than to take advantage of the housing benefit scheme). What counts as 'taking advantage of the housing benefit scheme' can be open to argument.

**Your landlord is a trust connected with your child** – You cannot get housing benefit if your landlord is a trust of which your or your partner's child is a beneficiary. For this rule, you cannot get housing benefit even if your letting agreement was created for a genuine reason.

**You used to be a non-dependant** – You cannot get housing benefit if:

- you lived in your home before you began renting it; *and*
- at that time you were a non-dependant (see 21 in this chapter) of a person who then lived in your home; *and*
- that person still lives in your home.

This rule does not apply if your letting agreement was created for a genuine reason (rather than to take advantage of the housing benefit scheme). What counts as 'taking advantage of the housing benefit scheme' can be open to argument.

**You used to own or have a long tenancy of the home you rent** – You cannot get housing benefit if you or your partner used to own or have a long tenancy of the home you are now renting. However, this rule only applies if you owned the home or had a long tenancy of it within the past five years and have lived there continuously since you owned or had a long tenancy of it. It does not apply if you or your partner would have to have left your home if it was not sold or the tenancy given up. For example, this rule should not apply if you are renting your home under a 'mortgage rescue scheme' after exploring all other options.

**Tied accommodation** – You cannot get housing benefit if you or your partner are employed by your landlord and have to live in your home as a condition of that employment.

**Contrived lettings** – In addition to all the above rules, you cannot get housing benefit if your or your landlord's principal or dominant purpose in creating your letting agreement was to take advantage of the housing benefit scheme. The motives and intentions of landlord and tenant may be considered in order to determine this.

HB Regs, reg 9

## Your period of absence

If your absence is likely to exceed 13 or 52 continuous weeks, you cannot get housing benefit for any of the time you are away. If you are not able to give an estimate of the length of the absence, you are unlikely to get housing benefit during any of it, so give the local authority an estimate if possible. Your intention to return must be a realistic possibility.

Any re-occupation of the home (other than a prisoner's temporary release) will break the period of absence – a stay of 24 hours is usually enough, although the authority has to be satisfied that your stay at home was genuine.

As soon as it becomes likely that the absence will exceed the 13- or 52-week limit, your housing benefit entitlement will stop.

## Trial periods in care homes

You can get housing benefit for up to 13 weeks during an absence from your normal home if:

- you are trying out a care home to see whether it suits your needs;
- when you enter the care home, you intend to return to your normal home if the care home does not suit your needs; *and*
- the part of your home that you normally occupy has not been let or sub-let.

You can have further trial periods so long as the total absence does not exceed 52 weeks.

HB Regs, reg 7(11) & (12)

## 7. Moving home and getting housing benefit on two homes

### The general rule

When you move from one rented home to another, you can get housing benefit on both homes for up to four weeks if you have moved into the new home but the local authority agrees you could not reasonably have avoided liability for rent on both the new and the old home (eg because you had to accept the new tenancy and move quickly and had to give notice on your old home). This general rule applies only if you have actually moved into the new home. Exactly what it means to *'move in'* can be interpreted in different ways. It could be enough if you have moved some furniture and personal possessions into the property (R(H)9/05). This 4-week rule also applies if you move to a new home where you are not liable for rent but continue to have a rental liability on your old property.

HB Regs, reg 7(6)(d) & (7)

Different rules apply in the cases below.

### Fear of violence

This rule applies if you move because of fear that violence may occur in your old home (regardless of who might cause the violence) or in the locality (in which case, only if the violence would be caused by a former member of your family). In either case, you can get housing benefit on both homes for up to 52 weeks as long as you intend to return to your old home at some point and the local authority agrees it is reasonable to pay housing benefit on both. You do not have to say exactly when you intend to return: it should be sufficient if you intend to return when it is safe to do so. If you do not intend to return, you continue to get housing benefit on your former property for up to four weeks if the continuing liability was unavoidable.

HB Regs, reg 7(6)(a) & (10)

### Delays in moving into your new home

**Waiting for your new home to be adapted** – If you do not move into a new rented home straight away because it is being adapted to meet your disablement needs or those of a member of your family, and the local authority agrees the delay is reasonable, you can get housing benefit for up to four weeks before you move in. If you are liable for rent on your old home, you can get housing benefit on both during those four weeks.

HB Regs, reg 7(6)(e) & (8)(c)(i)

**Waiting for a loan or grant before moving** – If you do not move into a new rented home straight away because you have asked for a budgeting loan or local welfare assistance to help with the move or with setting up home, and the local authority agrees the delay is reasonable, you can get housing benefit for up to four weeks before you move in. However, this will only apply if:

- there is a child under the age of 6 in your family; *or*
- you or your partner have reached pension credit qualifying age (see Chapter 44(2)); *or*
- you qualify for one of the housing benefit disability, severe disability or disabled child premiums (see Chapter 21(2), (3) and (8)); *or*
- you qualify for an employment and support allowance additional component (see 24 below) or have been placed in the work-related activity group (see Chapter 11(4)).

Under this rule you cannot get housing benefit on your old home at the same time.

HB Regs, reg 7(8)(c)(ii)

**When you leave hospital or a care home** – If you do not move into a new rented home straight away because you are waiting to leave hospital or a care home, and the local authority agrees the delay is reasonable, you can get housing benefit for up to four weeks before you actually move in.

HB Regs, reg 7(8)(c)(iii)

**Claiming on time** – In the above three cases, you must claim straight away; do not wait until you have moved in. If the authority rejects the claim, but you re-apply within four weeks of moving in, the rejected claim must be reconsidered. If you move within a local authority area, you will qualify if you notify the authority of the new tenancy before the move.

HB Regs 7(8)(a)&(b)

### Large families and students

If your local authority has arranged for you to be housed in two homes, you can get housing benefit on both.

Some students with partners who have to maintain two homes can get housing benefit on both (if they are eligible for housing benefit in the first place) – see Chapter 32(2).

HB Regs, Reg 7(6)(b)&(c)

## B. RENT RESTRICTIONS

### 8. Introduction

The housing benefit calculation is based on your weekly *'eligible rent'*, which may be less than your actual rent if a restriction applies. Whether or not a restriction applies, and the nature of the restriction, depends on whether you rent from the local authority, a housing association or any other landlord (including a private landlord).

### If you rent from the local authority

The authority will administer your housing benefit claim. Ineligible charges (see 12 below) will be deducted from your contractual rent to arrive at a figure for your eligible rent. If it is considered that you have spare bedrooms, your eligible rent may be reduced (see Box G.9).

If you rent from any other authority (such as a non-metropolitan county council), all the rules about renting from a private landlord will apply to you (see below).

The government originally announced that local authority rents would be capped at local housing allowance levels (see 9 below) from April 2019. However, they have now confirmed that this will no longer happen.

### If you rent from a housing association

If you rent from a registered housing association or private registered provider of social housing, ineligible charges (see 12 below) will be deducted from your contractual rent to arrive at a figure for your eligible rent. Your eligible rent may be reduced if it is considered that you have spare bedrooms (see Box G.9), or if the local authority considers the rent unreasonably high or the accommodation unreasonably large; if this happens, the authority will refer your case to the rent officer.

If you rent from an unregistered housing association or private provider of social housing, all the rules about renting from a private landlord will apply to you (see below).

The government originally announced that housing association rents would be capped at local housing allowance levels (see 9 below) from April 2019. However, they have now confirmed that this will no longer happen.

### If you rent from any other landlord, including a private landlord

Your eligible rent is restricted to a figure called your *'maximum rent'*, unless a delay is applied (see 9 below) or you fall within certain protected groups (see 11 below). If you moved or started to claim housing benefit on or after 7.4.08, your maximum rent will be set at a standard rate: the local housing allowance (see 9 below). Before 7.4.08, maximum rents were set at rates that followed determinations by rent officers (see 10 below).

*Note:* Check whether any exceptions to the rent restriction rules apply to you (see 11 below).

### Eligible rent – no restrictions

If a restriction does not apply, your eligible rent will be:
- the actual rent on your home;
- plus in some cases the rent on a garage;
- minus amounts for water, fuel, meals and certain other services (see 12 below).

To convert monthly rent to a weekly figure, multiply by 12 then divide by 52. If you jointly occupy your home with others, see 5 above.

### 9. Local housing allowance

If you moved or started to claim housing benefit on or after 7.4.08, your *'maximum rent'* will be set at a standard rate, the *'local housing allowance'* (LHA). The LHA is a standard amount of maximum housing benefit, set according to where you live and who is in your household, including non-dependants (see 'Rate of LHA' below). The figure is used whatever the amount of your rent. The amount is restricted to the 'cap' rent (your contractual rent), so it can never be more than the rent you pay. This means your housing benefit may

be less than your rent, even if you are entitled to maximum benefit. Claimants are expected to make up any shortfall or seek cheaper accommodation.

HB Regs, regs 12D & 13D

The LHA rules apply to most private sector tenancies. However, they may not apply to you if:
- you have been claiming housing benefit at the same property without a break since before 7.4.08; *or*
- your tenancy is exempt (see below); *or*
- there is a delay in place before the rules are applied and your LHA would be less than your eligible rent (see 'Delaying the restriction' below).

---

## G.9  The 'bedroom tax'

Your housing benefit is reduced if you are a working-age tenant of a local authority or housing association and are considered to have one or more spare bedrooms. This rule has been dubbed the *'bedroom tax'*. At the time of writing, it applies in England and Wales.

The bedroom tax also applies in Scotland, but the Scottish government has allowed for an extension of discretionary housing payments (see below) to cover tenants who would otherwise lose out. You need to apply for a discretionary housing payment to receive this support. Similar measures are likely to be in place in Northern Ireland until at least 2020.

### How does it apply?

Your eligible rent will be reduced by 14% if you have one spare bedroom, or by 25% if you have two or more spare bedrooms.

One bedroom is allowed for:
- every adult couple (unless it is inappropriate for you to share a room because of disability – see below);
- any other adult aged 16 or over;*
- two children aged under 10 (unless it is inappropriate for them to share a room because of disability – see below);
- two children aged under 16 of the same sex (unless it is inappropriate for them to share a room because of disability – see below);
- any other child; *and*
- a non-resident carer(s) who regularly provides overnight care for you, your partner, your child or an adult non-dependant – see below.

A further bedroom is allowed if you:
- have a child or qualifying young person (see Chapter 41(1)) placed with you for adoption; *or*
- are a foster parent; *or*
- (for a period of up to 52 weeks only), have been approved as a foster parent but do not currently have a child/qualifying young person placed with you. A recent Upper Tribunal decision (CH/3471/15) has held that this also applies if you are an approved carer for a person under an adult placement scheme.

* This can include a son, daughter, stepson or stepdaughter of you or your partner who was living with you as a non-dependant (see 21 in this chapter) and is now serving away on operations as a member of the armed forces, who intends to move back in with you when they return.

HB Regs, reg B13

---

## G.8  Why housing benefit may not cover all your rent

Your housing benefit may not cover all of your rent if:
- your housing benefit is restricted (eg because a local housing allowance or 'maximum rent' applies) (see 8-11 in this chapter);
- the level of your income means you do not qualify for the whole of your rent to be met (see 20);
- your rent includes service charges or other ineligible charges that must be deducted in the calculation of housing benefit (see 12);
- you have one or more non-dependant(s) in your home and a deduction must be made because of this (see 21); *or*
- a benefit cap has been applied (see Box G.6).

## Exempt tenancies

These are:

■ registered social landlord tenancies (eg local authority or housing association);

■ protected cases – such as supported housing provided by certain local authorities, housing associations, registered charities or voluntary organisations;

■ protected tenancies with a registered fair rent;

■ exceptional cases (eg caravans, houseboats and hostels); *and*

■ board and attendance cases if the rent officer judges that a substantial part of the rent is for board and attendance.

HB Regs, reg 13C(5)

See 11 below for details of other tenancies that are exempt from both the LHA and rent officer rules.

## Rate of LHA

If the LHA applies, the amount of eligible rent is the standard LHA, initially determined by a local authority rent officer according to the *'broad rental market area'* where your home is situated, the size of your household and the number of bedrooms you are deemed to need (the 'size criteria' – see below). These rates are adjusted annually.

HB Regs, reg 13D(1)

**Broad rental market area** – This is an area within which you could reasonably be expected to live, having regard to facilities

## Couples

If you are not reasonably able to share a room with your partner because of your, or their, disability and you, or they, receive a qualifying disability benefit (see below), you will be allowed an additional bedroom.

HB Regs, reg B13(5)(za)&(zb); MA & Others, A and Rutherford v SSWP [2016] SC

## Disabled children

If you have a child who is not reasonably able to share a room because of their disability and they receive the care component of disability living allowance (DLA) at the middle or highest rate, you will be allowed an additional bedroom for them. In such a case, the DWP must consider the nature and frequency of the care your child needs during the night, and the extent and regularity of the disturbance to the sleep of the child who would normally have to share the bedroom with them.

HB Regs, reg B13(5)(ba); Burnip, Trengove, Gorry v SSWP [2012] EWCA Civ 629

## Overnight care required

You are allowed one additional bedroom for a carer or carers to sleep in if you, your partner, your child or an adult non-dependant (see 21 in this chapter) need overnight care and receive a qualifying disability benefit* (see below) or attendance allowance at the lower rate. The carer(s), who must not be living with you, must be engaged to provide the overnight care and must need to stay overnight at your home on a regular basis. Only one additional bedroom is allowed, even if more than one carer is needed.

* even if a qualifying disability benefit is not in payment, the local authority can accept alternative evidence that overnight care is needed – eg a letter from your GP

HB Regs, reg B13(6)(a)&(ab); MA & Others, A and Rutherford v SSWP [2016] SC

## Qualifying disability benefits

The following are *'qualifying disability benefits'*:

■ the care component of DLA at the middle or highest rate;

■ attendance allowance at the higher rate;

■ the daily living component of personal independence payment; *or*

■ armed forces independence payment.

HB Regs, reg 2(1)

## What is a 'bedroom'?

The regulations do not set out definitions of what is meant by a *'bedroom'* nor do they state a minimum bedroom size. Factors to be considered when deciding if a room is a bedroom include: size; access; natural and electric light; ventilation and privacy. It does not matter that the room may be used as something other than a bedroom; what matters is whether, given the above factors, it could be used as a bedroom.

CSH/41/14

The room must be one that can be used as a bedroom by the actual occupants (as listed above in 'How does it apply?').

CH/1987/2016

## Protection for certain people

Your local authority cannot apply the reduction if:

■ you (or your partner) have reached pension credit qualifying age (see Chapter 44(2));

■ you and/or any member of your household (see 9 in this chapter) could afford the financial commitments of your home when you first entered into them, and you (and your partner) have not received housing benefit during the 52 weeks before your current claim – the authority cannot apply the reduction for the first 13 weeks of your claim; *or*

■ a member of your household has died, and you have not moved since then. The authority cannot apply the reduction until a year after the date of their death (unless there was already a reduction that applied before their death, in which case that continues).

HB Regs, regs 12BA & A13(2)(d)

## Exempt accommodation

Your local authority cannot apply the reduction to:

■ a shared ownership tenancy;

■ mooring charges for houseboats and payments for a caravan or mobile home site; *or*

■ temporary accommodation provided by the local authority or a registered housing association to homeless people.

If you are paid housing benefit as a rent allowance, rather than as a rent rebate, and your landlord is not a registered housing association, the local authority cannot apply the reduction to:

■ a pre-January 1989 tenancy (see 11 in this chapter);

■ a tenancy regulated under the 1977 Rent Act (and similar listed rent controls);

■ a bail or probation hostel tenancy; *or*

■ a housing action trust tenancy.

HB Regs, regs A13(2)-(4)

Your local authority cannot apply the reduction if you are living in supported accommodation (see 11 in this chapter).

## Discretionary Housing Payments (DHPs)

If you cannot afford the shortfall between your housing benefit and your rent as a result of a reduction, you can request a DHP from your local authority to make up the difference. The government has advised local authorities to give priority to cases involving disability, eg if you cannot move to smaller accommodation because your property has been adapted or you need to be close to a support network. However, DHPs are cash-limited and there is no guarantee that you will receive one. For more on DHPs, see 16 in this chapter.

and services, and including a range of accommodation and tenancy types.

**Maximum amounts** – LHA rates are usually based on:

- the 30th percentile of rents for properties of the relevant size within the broad rental market area (ie three in 10 properties in the area would be cheaper, the rest more expensive); *or*
- the LHA rate that applied on 30.1.15, if that would be lower.

The Rent Officers (Housing Benefit Functions) Order 1997, Sch 3B, para 2(3)

From January 2017, LHA rates in 'high rent' areas of the country were increased by 3%.

### Getting information before you sign up to a letting

LHA rates for each size category of property should be available from every local authority. These rates can help you find out how much housing benefit you would receive if you moved to a new address. Details of the LHA rates for any area are at lha-direct.voa.gov.uk/search.aspx.

HB Regs, reg 13E

### Size criteria

The *'size criteria'* focuses on the number of bedrooms your household is deemed to need, taking into account the number of people in your household, their ages, disabilities and genders. See Box G.9 for the way this is calculated: the 'bedroom tax' rules also apply to LHA. However, under the LHA you are restricted to a maximum of four bedrooms. Further restrictions apply to single claimants aged under 35 and those in shared accommodation (see below).

HB Regs, regs 2(1) and 13D(2)(c), (3)-(3B) & (12)

### Young people

Single claimants aged under 35 without children have an LHA based on one bedroom in shared accommodation. This does not apply if they qualify for a severe disability premium or are a care leaver aged under 22. Nor does it apply to those aged 25 or over who have been in a hostel for the homeless for three months and received support to resettle in the community, or to some recent offenders who are deemed a risk to the public.

HB Regs, regs 2(1)&(1A)-(1C) and 13D(2)(a)

### Shared accommodation

Single claimants aged 35 or over and all couples without children are allowed the normal 1-bedroom rate unless they live in shared accommodation, in which case the 1-bedroom rate in shared accommodation is used. Accommodation is defined as 'shared' if the claimant does not have exclusive use of at least two rooms, or the exclusive use of one room, a bathroom and toilet and a kitchen or facilities for cooking.

HB Regs, reg 13D(2)(b)

### Delaying the restriction

Local authorities may not use the maximum rent figure described above in the following two cases. (For how eligible rent is calculated in cases where there are no restrictions, see 8 above.)

- ❏ If you and/or any member of your household could afford the financial commitments of your home when you first entered into them, and you (and your partner) have not received housing benefit during the 52 weeks before your current claim, the authority may not use the maximum rent figure for the first 13 weeks of your claim.
- ❏ If a member of your household has died, and you have not moved since then, the authority may not use the maximum rent figure until a year after the date of their death (unless there was already a maximum rent figure that applied before their death, in which case that continues).

However, if your LHA rate would be higher than your 'protected' rate, you can receive the LHA rate instead.

Although your local authority may not use the maximum rent figure in the above two cases, it can restrict your eligible rent if it considers it is unreasonable in all the circumstances of your case. If this happens, seek advice.

**Your household** – The following count as members of your household:

- each member of your family: you, your partner, children aged under 16 and young people aged 16-19 for whom child benefit is payable; *and*
- any other relative of yours (or your partner) who lives with you but does not have an independent right to do so. A *'relative'* means a parent, parent-in-law, step-parent, son, daughter, son- or daughter-in-law, stepson or stepdaughter, sister, brother or the (married or unmarried) partner of any of those, grandparent, grandchild, uncle, aunt, niece or nephew.

HB Regs, regs 12D & 2(1)

## 10. Rent officers' determinations

Before 7.4.08, maximum eligible rents were set at rates that followed determinations by rent officers. Rent officers are independent of the local authority; they look at your rent and various other factors before providing the authority with various figures that are used to calculate your maximum rent. Once your maximum rent has been set at a rate following such a determination, it will continue to be based on this determination until it is referred back to the rent officer because:

- there has been a relevant change of circumstances; *or*
- 52 weeks have passed since the last referral.

For details on this type of rent restriction, see *Disability Rights Handbook* 32nd edition, page 41.

The Rent Officers (Housing Benefit Functions) Order 1997, Sch 1

## 11. Exceptions to rent restrictions

If one of the following exceptions applies to you, neither the local housing allowance nor the rent officer rules will apply. If you fall within more than one exception, just look at the first one that applies to you.

The exceptions can be complicated in some cases and it is often worth seeking advice. Also check the points under 'Delaying the restriction' in 9 above.

**Pre-January 1989 tenancies** – This applies if your letting began before 15.1.89 in England and Wales or 2.1.89 in Scotland. In these cases, it is very unlikely that the local authority will restrict your eligible rent.

HB Regs, Sch 2, para 4

**Supported accommodation** – This applies if:

- your home is provided by a non-metropolitan county council, housing association, registered social landlord, registered charity, non-profit-making voluntary organisation or certain similar bodies; *and*
- your landlord provides you with 'care, support or supervision' or has arranged for it to be provided to you (for this to apply there must be some contractual obligation between the landlord and care provider).

This exception also applies to you if your home is a resettlement hostel.

In these cases, your local authority can only restrict your eligible rent if it has evidence that your rent is unreasonably high or your home unreasonably large.

There are further rules that give protection to certain vulnerable people. If you have difficulties, seek advice.

HB & CTB (Consequential Provisions) Regs 2006, Sch 3, para 4(1)(b) & (10)

**If you have been on housing benefit since 1.1.96** – This applies if you:

- were getting housing benefit on 1.1.96 (in Northern Ireland on 1.4.96); *and*
- have been on housing benefit continuously since that date,

ignoring gaps of no more than four weeks; *and*
■ have not moved since that date (unless as a result of a fire, flood, explosion or natural catastrophe).

If your partner or another member of your household previously met these conditions, you may be able to take advantage of these rules. Seek further advice.

In the above cases, the local authority can only restrict your eligible rent if it has evidence that your rent is unreasonably high or your home unreasonably large.

HB & CTB (Consequential Provisions) Regs 2006, Sch 3, para 4(1)(a), (2) & (3)

**People who pay caravan/mobile home site rent or mooring fees** – This applies if you:
■ pay a county council for the rent of a caravan or mobile home or its site for Gypsies and Travellers; *or*
■ pay a housing authority for the rent of a site for a caravan or mobile home or for houseboat mooring charges, and housing benefit is payable as a 'rent allowance'.

These tenancies should only be referred to the rent officer if the accommodation is considered to be unreasonably large or expensive.

HB Regs, Sch 2, para 3

## 12. Ineligible charges

The following apply only to tenancies exempt from the local housing allowance (see 9 above) and those housing benefit awards not subject to the local housing allowance.

### Garages

If you rent a garage, it is included as part of the rent on your home only if you were obliged to rent the garage from the beginning of your letting agreement, or you are making (or have made) all reasonable efforts to stop renting it.

HB Regs, reg 2(4)(a)

### Water charges and council tax included in your rent

If your rent includes water or sewerage charges, the actual amount of the charge for your home (or if your water is metered, an estimate) is deducted, unless you are separately liable to pay the charge. If your rent includes a contribution towards the council tax because your landlord pays it, this is included as part of your eligible rent.

HB Regs, reg 12B(2)(a) & (5)

### Service charges: general conditions

The rules for several types of service charge are given below, indicating whether they can be taken into account as part of your eligible rent. But even if they can, there are two further conditions.
❑ The amount of the charge must be reasonable for the service provided. If it is not, the unreasonable part is deducted.
❑ Payment of the charge must be a condition of occupying your home, whether from the beginning of your letting agreement or from later on. If it is not a condition, the whole charge is deducted.

HB Regs, reg 12(1)(e); Sch 1, para 4

**Exception** – If the rent officer fixes a maximum rent for your home (see 10 above), they also fix a value for some services.

### Fuel and related charges

If your rent includes fuel of any kind, the fuel charge is deducted if there is evidence of the amount (eg in your rent book or letting agreement). If there is no evidence of the amount, flat-rate amounts are deducted for various fuel costs; the amounts are given below.

Whenever your local authority makes flat-rate deductions, it must write inviting you to provide evidence of the actual amount. If you can provide reasonable evidence (which need not be from your landlord), the authority must estimate the actual amount and deduct that instead of the flat rates.

**Exceptions** – A fuel charge for a communal area (including communal rooms in sheltered accommodation) is included as part of your eligible rent if it is separately specified in your rent book or letting agreement. The same is true for a separately specified charge for providing a heating system.

**Flat-rate deductions** – If you rent more than one room (not counting any shared accommodation), these are:

| Deductions | per week |
| --- | --- |
| Heating | £30.30 |
| Hot water | £3.50 |
| Lighting | £2.40 |
| Cooking | £3.50 |

If you rent only one room (not counting a shared kitchen, bathroom or toilet), the flat-rate deduction for heating is £18.10. If you get a flat-rate deduction for heating, there is no further deduction for hot water or lighting, but the figure for cooking is as above.

HB Regs, Sch 1, paras 5 & 6

### Meal charges

If your rent includes meals (the preparation or provision of food) a flat-rate amount is deducted for these. The flat rate is always used, regardless of how much you are actually charged. One flat-rate deduction is made for each person (even if not a member of your family) whose meals are included in your rent.

| Weekly deductions per person | Aged 16+ | under 16 |
| --- | --- | --- |
| For at least 3 meals every day | £27.90 | £14.15 |
| For breakfast only | £3.45 | £3.45 |
| For any other arrangement | £18.60 | £9.35 |

For these purposes, a person counts as aged 16+ from the first Monday in the September following their 16th birthday.

HB Regs, Sch 1, paras 1(a)(i) & 2

### Other services

**Cleaning and window cleaning** – A charge for cleaning and window cleaning of communal areas is included in your eligible rent; so is a charge for exterior window cleaning if neither you nor anyone in your household can do it. A charge (estimated if necessary) is deducted for any other cleaning and window cleaning.

**Furniture and household equipment** – A charge for these is included in your eligible rent unless your landlord has agreed they will become your personal property.

**Medical, nursing and personal care** – A charge for any of these (estimated if necessary) is deducted.

**Communal or accommodation-related services** – Most charges for these are included in your eligible rent. Examples are: TV/radio aerial and relay, refuse removal, lifts, communal telephones, entry phones, children's play areas, garden maintenance necessary for the provision of adequate accommodation and communal laundry facilities.

**Day-to-day living expenses, etc** – Charges for these (estimated if necessary) are deducted. Examples are: TV subscription and licence fees, laundering (ie if washing is done for you), transport, sports facilities, leisure items and any other service not related to the provision of adequate accommodation.

**Staffing and administration charges** – These are covered only if they are connected to the provision of adequate accommodation. To determine this, it is necessary to look at the number of hours a week that employees spend on providing accommodation-related services.

HB Regs, Sch 1, para 1(g)

# C. CLAIMS, PAYMENTS & APPEALS

## 13. How to claim housing benefit

### Telephone claims

You can claim housing benefit over the phone at the same time that you claim employment and support allowance (ESA), income support, jobseeker's allowance (JSA) or pension credit. The relevant DWP office will take your details over the phone. They may send you a statement of your circumstances to sign and return to them; they will then forward the details to your local authority.

Claims for housing benefit can be made by phone, direct to the local authority, if it has a number for this purpose. However, authorities are not required to do so and must continue to accept paper claims.

### Paper claims

If you are not claiming one of the above benefits, ring your local authority for a housing benefit claim-form, complete it and send it back within one month. Make a copy of the claim before sending it off.

**What you need to send with your claim-form** – The claim-form asks you to provide various documents (eg your rent book). If you do not have all the information or documents requested, send the form back as soon as possible, and write on it that you will send the further information or documents as soon as you can. Explain any reasons for the delay. Sometimes the authority writes with further questions. Always ensure your reply reaches them within one month of when they sent the letter.

If you do not keep to the one-month time limit for sending information to your local authority, they can agree a delay of whatever period is *'reasonable'*. This will mean you are treated as having claimed within the time limits (see below).
HB Regs, reg 86(1)

### E-claims

Some local authorities have introduced email or online claiming. However, they are not required to do so and must continue to accept paper claims.

### Date of claim

If you make a claim for a means-tested benefit (income-related ESA, income support, income-based JSA or the guarantee credit of pension credit) that is successful, and your housing benefit claim is received within one month of this claim, your housing benefit will start from the same date as the means-tested benefit.

If you notify the housing benefit or DWP office of your intention to claim housing benefit, your date of claim will be the date on which you notify them if you return the claim-form within one month. The 1-month time limit can be extended if the housing benefit office thinks it is 'reasonable'.

If you have separated from your partner or your partner has died, and they were receiving housing benefit, your claim for housing benefit will start from the date of the separation or death as long as you claim within one month.

In all other cases, your claim begins on the day your claim-form is received by the housing benefit office. However, it may be possible for your claim to be backdated (see 16 below).
HB Regs, reg 83(5)

### Appointees

If you are unable to manage your affairs, an *'appointee'* can take over the responsibilities of claiming for you and dealing with further matters relating to your claim. That person (who must be aged 18 or over) should write to your local authority to request approval to act as your appointee. Permission should not be withheld unreasonably.

## 14. When housing benefit starts, changes and ends

**Your first day of entitlement** – Housing benefit usually starts on the Monday after the date of your claim (see 13 above). Even if that date was itself a Monday, housing benefit starts the following Monday.

The exception is if the date of your housing benefit claim is in the same benefit week (Monday to Sunday) as you moved into your home (or first became liable for rent for any other reason). In that case, your housing benefit starts on the day your rent liability began (whether your rent is due daily, weekly or monthly).
HB Regs, reg 76

**When housing benefit ends** – You cease to be entitled if a change in your circumstances means you no longer qualify.

### Change of circumstances

You have a duty to notify your local authority about any change in circumstances that may affect your entitlement. The authority should advise you of changes you should notify.
HB Regs, reg 88(1)

If a change in circumstances means you qualify for more housing benefit, write to the authority promptly. If you take more than one calendar month and you have no good reason for the delay, you will lose money because the increase will only be given to you from the Monday following the day your letter reaches them. If you have a good reason for delaying more than a month, explain this in your letter, as otherwise it may not be taken into account. In all cases, 13 months is the absolute limit for notifying changes.
HB&CTB(D&A) Regs, regs 8(3) & 9

If a change in circumstances means you qualify for less housing benefit, write to the authority promptly, or you will probably be asked to repay any overpayment (see 18 below).

You normally need to let the local authority know of a change of circumstances in writing, but some authorities give a telephone number to use instead. Jobcentre Plus offices often give you a number to contact if you find work. If you or your partner have been receiving income support or jobseeker's allowance (JSA) and it ends because you have started work (or contribution-based JSA becomes payable at a reduced rate because you have started work) and you ring the number that Jobcentre Plus gave you, you will have discharged your duty to inform of the change of circumstances.
HB Regs, reg 88(6)

## 15. How housing benefit is paid

### If you pay rent to the local authority

Housing benefit is awarded as a rebate towards your rent account, which is why it is also called a 'rent rebate'. In other words, the rent you have to pay will be reduced. This also applies if you pay rent to the Northern Ireland Housing Executive.

### Payment for everyone else

Housing benefit is usually paid into your bank account, although it can be paid by cheque, which is why it is also called a 'rent allowance'. The local authority must take into account your *'reasonable needs and convenience'* in choosing the method of payment, so should not insist on paying you into a bank account if you do not have one.
HB Regs, regs 91(1)(b)

**Payments on account** – The local authority should make your first payment within 14 days of receiving your properly completed claim-form or, if that is not reasonably practicable, as soon as possible after that. That payment must be either the correct amount of your award or, if that is not yet known, an estimated amount, known as a *'payment on account'*, which will be adjusted when the correct amount is known. You should not have to ask the authority for a payment on account, but if you do not get one, contact them and remind them of their duties. Authorities do not, however, have to make a payment on account if you have not given them the information and documents they have asked for, unless you can show that your failure to do so is reasonable (eg if the delay in providing these is outside your control).

HB Regs, regs 91(3) & 93

**Payment to your landlord** – Housing benefit is paid direct to your landlord if:

■ you request or consent to it; *or*

■ it is in your or your family's best interests; *or*

■ you have left the dwelling with rent arrears (but payment will only be made up to the level of rent owing); *or*

■ an amount of income support, jobseeker's allowance, employment and support allowance or pension credit is being paid direct to the landlord to cover rent arrears; *or*

■ you have at least eight weeks of rent arrears (six weeks in Northern Ireland) unless it is in your overriding interest not to make direct payment to the landlord.

In the first three cases, the authority does not have to agree. In the fourth and fifth cases, they must pay the landlord unless the landlord is deemed not to be a 'fit and proper' person to receive payment. The authority can also choose to pay your first payment of housing benefit to your landlord (regardless of whether you agree) if they consider it appropriate.

HB Regs, regs 95 & 96(1)-(2)

**Local housing allowance (LHA) payments** – These are normally made to you, but can be made to the landlord if:

■ the authority believes you are likely to have difficulty managing your affairs; *or*

■ the authority considers it improbable that you will pay your rent; *or*

■ for eight weeks, if the authority suspects that either of the above may apply and is considering this; *or*

■ the authority has previously had to pay the landlord; *or*

■ you have left the property and there are rent arrears (but payment will only be made up to the level of rent owing); *or*

■ the authority considers that it will assist you in securing or retaining a tenancy.

The local authority must pay LHA direct to the landlord if you have rent arrears of at least eight weeks (unless it is in your overriding interest not to make payments direct to the landlord) or when an amount of a means-tested benefit is being paid to the landlord to cover rent arrears.

HB Regs, regs 95 & 96(1)(c), (3A) & (3B)

## 16. Getting more benefit
### Discretionary housing payments

Discretionary housing payments (DHPs) are technically not a kind of housing benefit, but are administered by the same authorities and can only be given to people who qualify for at least some housing benefit.

The local authority can give you a DHP if you *'appear to [the] authority to require some further financial assistance… in order to meet housing costs'*. DHPs are discretionary (no one has a right to one) – as is the amount of DHP and the period for which it is granted. The combined amount of your housing benefit and DHP in any one week cannot usually exceed your 'eligible rent' (see 8 above). However, a DHP can exceed the current amount of eligible rent in some circumstances, eg if you have rent arrears and the DHP covers the past period.

DHPs cannot be used if benefit has been reduced or suspended (eg for failure to attend a work-focused interview), or for ineligible service charges (see 12 above) or water and sewage charges.

**How to apply** – Most local authorities have a form on which to request a DHP; if your authority does not, write a letter instead. The authority may ask for detailed information about your circumstances and those of your household. Explain these fully, in particular your disability needs, as otherwise

the authority could take into account the fact that you receive state benefits, such as disability living allowance, when deciding on your DHP request (even if the housing benefit rules would normally disregard these). DHPs are cash-limited and there is no guarantee you will receive one. The housing benefit appeals system does not apply to DHPs, but you have the right to ask the authority to look again at its decision if you are dissatisfied. It is your duty to report changes in your circumstances that could affect the payment of a DHP.

The Discretionary Financial Assistance Regs

### Getting your benefit backdated

If you are under pension credit qualifying age (see Chapter 44(2)), housing benefit can be backdated for up to one month if you have continuous *'good cause'* for the delay in claiming. If you have reached pension credit qualifying age (and neither you nor your partner are on income support, income-based jobseeker's allowance, income-related employment and support allowance or universal credit), housing benefit can be backdated for up to three months without you having to show good cause.

HB Regs, reg 83(12)&(12A), HB(SPC) Regs, reg 64(1)

**Good cause** – This means some fact or facts which *'having regard to all the circumstances (including the claimant's state of health and the information which he had received and that which he might have obtained) would probably have caused a reasonable person of his age and experience to act (or fail to act) as the claimant did'*.

R(S)2/63(T)

For example, you may have good cause if you are ill and have no one to help you make the claim, or if you are unable to manage your affairs and don't have an appointee. Ignorance of the law is not normally good cause unless there are exceptional circumstances (eg mental health or learning disabilities, educational limitations, youthfulness, language difficulties, or a combination of these and other factors). Generally, you are expected to make reasonable enquiries about your right to benefit. You will normally be able to show good cause if you ask the DWP or local authority for advice and act on the basis of their wrong or misleading advice or if you reasonably misunderstood the advice.

**Ex-gratia payments** – If your claim was delayed for over one or three months and the delay was the local authority's fault, you can ask for an ex-gratia compensation payment to cover the period remaining after the maximum 3- or 1-month backdate.

### 17. Underpayments

If your local authority has awarded you less housing benefit than they should have, due to official error, they must make up the difference. An *'official error'* means a mistake by the local authority, DWP or HMRC. There is no limit to the period for which arrears may be paid in these cases. However, if you were awarded less housing benefit because you failed to tell the authority something, see 14 above.

HB&CTB(D&A) Regs, reg 4(2)(a)

### 18. Overpayments

Overpayments are amounts of housing benefit you were awarded but which you weren't entitled to – perhaps because you did not tell the local authority something you should have, because the authority or DWP made a mistake, or for some unavoidable reason. Different rules apply to different types of overpayment, as follows.

**Overpayments of payments on account** – If you were granted a payment on account (see 15 above) and it turned out to be greater than your actual entitlement to housing benefit, the overpayment will be recovered from your future housing benefit entitlement.

HB Regs, reg 93(3)

**Overpayments due to official error** – An *'official error'* means a mistake, to which you did not contribute, by your local authority, the DWP or HMRC.

If the DWP does not tell your local authority that you have come off income support, income-based jobseeker's allowance or income-related employment and support allowance (or started receiving any other benefit), this may count as an official error. However, because the law says it is your duty to tell the authority about changes in your circumstances, the DWP will not be deemed as having caused the overpayment and it will be recoverable from you.

Your local authority must not recover an overpayment due to official error unless you (or someone acting for you, or the person who received the payment, eg your landlord if your housing benefit is paid to them) could *'reasonably have been expected to realise that it was an overpayment'* at the time the payment, or any notification about it, was received. The authority should take into account what you (or the other person) personally could have been expected to realise.
HB Regs, reg 100(2)-(3)

**Overpayments due to a mistake about capital** – An overpayment of more than 13 weeks of housing benefit due to a mistake about capital may not be recoverable in full. There are 'diminution of capital' rules that treat the capital as gradually reducing (see Chapter 56(7)).
HB Regs, reg 103

**All other overpayments** – Any overpayment of housing benefit not mentioned above may be recovered by your local authority. This includes overpayments due to a failure or mistake by you, and even overpayments that were unavoidable (such as overpayments due to a backdated pay rise or a backdated social security benefit).
HB Regs, reg 100(1)

## How much is the overpayment?

If you qualified for at least some housing benefit during the period for which you were overpaid, the local authority should allow you to keep it (even if you didn't claim it or tell them everything you should have at the time). It should normally only recover the difference between what you were paid and what you should have been paid. If the authority does not do this, seek advice.
HB Regs, reg 104

## How are overpayments recovered?

An overpayment can be recovered from you or your partner (but where recovery is by deductions from ongoing housing benefit, only if you were a couple at the time of both the overpayment and the recovery). In most cases, an overpayment can also be recovered from the person who received the payment (eg your landlord) or the person who caused the overpayment. It can be recovered as follows:

■ by reducing your future housing benefit entitlement (including entitlement on a new address when you move within the same local authority area). The most the authority can recover in this way is £11.10 a week, or £18.50 a week if the overpayment was caused by fraud. These amounts can be increased in certain cases if you are working or receive a war widow's or war disablement pension; *or*

■ if the above method is not possible, by making deductions from almost any other social security benefit you receive; *or*

■ if housing benefit was paid direct to your landlord, by deduction from another tenant's (or the landlord's own) housing benefit.
HB Regs, regs 101-102 & 104A

In all cases, you can negotiate with the authority over how to re-pay the overpayment. As a last resort, the authority can take action in the courts to recover an overpayment.

If an overpayment is recovered from your housing benefit paid to your landlord, then (unless you rent your home from the local authority or Northern Ireland Housing Executive) the landlord is legally allowed to treat the amount repaid as rent arrears due from you (but seek housing advice about possible rent arrears).

If the local authority suspects that you have committed fraud, see Chapter 56(8).

**Discretion and hardship** – Even if an overpayment is recoverable, the local authority can exercise its discretion not to recover it (eg if you can show that you would otherwise suffer hardship).
SSAA, S.75(1)

**Notifications and appeals** – In all cases, if the authority decides to recover an overpayment, it must write notifying you of the details and your appeal rights. You can use the appeal procedure if you are dissatisfied with its decision.

## 19. Challenging decisions

The following rules apply to housing benefit. For more on challenging decisions, see Chapter 57.

### Notice of decisions

Your local authority has a duty to send you a written notice about the decision it makes on your housing benefit claim. If you do not qualify, the notice will say why not. If the authority makes further decisions during the course of your award (eg about a change of circumstances or an overpayment), it must send you a written notice about each one. In each case, it will also explain your right to get more information and to appeal.

**Written statement** – If you want more information about how your entitlement (or lack of it) to housing benefit was worked out, write to the authority and ask for a written statement. You must do this within one month of notification of the decision. You can ask about specific things or for full details of how your claim was assessed. The authority should reply in writing within 14 days, or as soon as possible after that.
HB Regs, reg 90

**Exceptions** – In certain circumstances, the authority does not have to make a decision, and the tribunal does not have to deal with an appeal. This is called 'staying' a decision or appeal. It arises when a test case is pending, the result of which could affect your case (see Chapter 57(6)).

### Asking the authority to revise its decision

You have the right to ask your local authority to revise its decision on almost any matter relating to a housing benefit claim (eg how much you qualify for, whether you should have to repay an overpayment, etc). If your request is made within the 'dispute period' (see below), the authority must reconsider its decision, taking account of what you say. It should give you a written notice saying whether it is revising or sticking to its original decision, and giving the reasons.
HB&CTB(D&A) Regs, reg 4

### Appeals to a tribunal

Either instead of, or after, asking your local authority to revise a decision (see above), you can appeal to an independent appeal tribunal; see Chapter 57 for details.

**Exceptions** – There is no right of appeal to a tribunal about:

■ most administrative decisions about housing benefit claims and payments, although you can appeal to a tribunal about when the benefit should begin and about backdating;

■ whether the authority should run a disregard scheme for a war pension (see Chapter 22(7)) under 'Benefits that are partly disregarded');

■ the level of local housing allowance (see 9 above);

■ your maximum rent, if the rent officer or Northern Ireland Housing Executive fixed one (see 10 above); *or*

■ discretionary housing payments (see 16 above).
HB&CTB(D&A) Regs, reg 16 and Sch

### The dispute period

Whether you are asking the local authority to revise a decision or asking for an appeal, your letter should reach the authority within one calendar month of the day it sent the decision notice. If you are asking for a revision of the decision and have asked for a written statement (see above), the time the authority took to deal with that is ignored when calculating the month. If you are appealing the decision, you have 14 days from the date the written statement is sent out to ask for an appeal.

Your local authority (or the tribunal, in the case of an appeal) can agree to extend the 1-month time limit if the delay was caused by special circumstances (or, if you are appealing, the tribunal agrees; see Chapter 57(8)). In this case, explain what your special circumstances are when you request the revision/appeal, as otherwise they may not be taken into account. In all cases, 13 months is the absolute limit for asking for the decision to be changed.
HB&CTB(D&A) Regs, regs 4(1), 5, & 19; TP(FTT)SEC Rules, rule 23

### The Ombudsman

You can make a complaint to the Ombudsman if you feel the local authority or Northern Ireland Housing Executive administered your claim unfairly or caused unreasonable delays. See Chapter 59(5).

## D. CALCULATING HOUSING BENEFIT

### 20. How much do you get?

Follow the steps below to work out your entitlement to housing benefit. We first give the steps if you are on a means-tested benefit (income support, income-based jobseeker's allowance, income-related employment and support allowance or the guarantee credit of pension credit), then the steps if you are not.

### If you (or your partner) are on a means-tested benefit
**Step 1: Work out your eligible rent**
Housing benefit is worked out on your weekly eligible rent; this can be less than your actual rent (see 8 above).
**Step 2: Deduct amounts for non-dependants**
If you have one or more non-dependants in your home, your housing benefit is reduced by flat-rate amounts (though there are exceptions to this). For who counts as a non-dependant and other details, see 21 below.
**Step 3: Amount of benefit per week**
Housing benefit equals your weekly eligible rent minus any amounts for non-dependants.

*Example:* If your weekly eligible rent is £90 and you have no non-dependants, the weekly amount of your housing benefit is £90. But if you have one non-dependant, and a flat-rate deduction of £78.65 applies, the weekly amount of your housing benefit is £11.35.

### If you (and your partner) are not on a means-tested benefit
**Step 1: Your capital**
If your capital (including your partner's) is more than £16,000, you cannot get housing benefit. Not all capital counts. For how to work out your capital, see 22 and 25 below.
**Step 2: Your eligible rent**
Housing benefit is worked out on your weekly eligible rent; this can be less than your actual rent (see 8 above).
**Step 3: Deduct amounts for non-dependants**
If you have one or more non-dependants in your home, your housing benefit is reduced by flat-rate amounts (though there

are exceptions to this). For who counts as a non-dependant and other details, see 21 below.
**Step 4: Work out your weekly income**
This includes your (and your partner's) income from some, but not all, sources. For how to work out your weekly income, see 23 and 25 below.
**Step 5: Work out your applicable amount**
This figure represents your weekly living needs. For how to work out your applicable amount, see 24 and 25 below and Chapter 21.
**Step 6: Do you have 'excess income'?**
If your income is *less* than, or equal to, your applicable amount, you do not have *'excess income'*. Go to Step 7. If your income is *greater* than your applicable amount, you have excess income. The amount of the excess income is the difference between your income and your applicable amount. Go to Step 8.
**Step 7: Amount of benefit if you do not have 'excess income'**
Housing benefit equals your weekly eligible rent less amounts for non-dependants. This is exactly the same as for people who are on a means-tested benefit. For an example, see above.
**Step 8: Amount of benefit if you have 'excess income'**
Housing benefit equals your weekly eligible rent less amounts for non-dependants and less 65% of your excess income. If the result is less than 50p, you will not be awarded benefit. See below.

*Example if you have excess income:* If your weekly eligible rent is £90, you have no non-dependants and you have excess income of £20, the weekly amount of your housing benefit is:

| | |
|---|---|
| Eligible rent | £90.00 |
| Less 65% of the £20 excess income | £13.00 |
| *Weekly housing benefit* | *£77.00* |

But if you have one non-dependant and a flat-rate deduction of £15.25 applies, the weekly amount of your housing benefit is:

| | |
|---|---|
| Eligible rent | £90.00 |
| Less non-dependant deduction | £15.25 |
| Less 65% of the £20 excess income | £13.00 |
| *Weekly housing benefit* | *£61.75* |

The 65% figure is also called a *'taper'*: as your excess income goes up, your benefit goes down. You can have so much excess income that you do not qualify for any benefit. The amount(s) of your non-dependant deduction(s) can also mean you do not qualify for any benefit.
HB Regs, reg 71

If the calculation comes out at less than 50p (the minimum housing benefit award), you will not get any benefit.
HB Regs, Reg 75

### 21. Non-dependants

Deductions are made from your housing benefit if you have one or more non-dependants, even if you are on income-related employment and support allowance (ESA), income support, income-based jobseeker's allowance (JSA) or the guarantee credit of pension credit. It is assumed that they will contribute towards your rent, whether they do or not. A deduction cannot be cancelled on the grounds that your non-dependant pays you nothing. But there are cases when no deduction can be made.
HB Regs, reg 74

### Who is a non-dependant?

A non-dependant is someone who normally lives in your home on a non-commercial basis – usually an adult son, daughter, friend or relative. None of the following are your non-dependants (so there is no deduction for any of them):

- your *'family'* (see 24 below). For example, an 18-year-old who is included in your family is not your non-dependant;
- foster children or a child or qualifying young person (see Chapter 41(1)) placed with you for adoption;
- someone with whom you share just a bathroom, toilet or communal area (or in sheltered accommodation, a communal room);
- joint occupier(s), tenant(s) or sub-tenant(s), resident landlord (and their partner); *or*
- your or your partner's carer if they are provided by a charity or voluntary organisation that charges you for this (even if someone else pays the charge for you).

Almost anyone else who lives with you is your non-dependant.

HB Regs, reg 3

### No non-dependant deduction

**Your (or your partner's) circumstances** – There is no deduction for your non-dependants (no matter how many you have) if you or your partner:

- are certified by a consultant ophthalmologist as severely sight impaired or blind, or have ceased to be so certified in the past 28 weeks; *or*
- get the care component of disability living allowance (DLA; any rate), the daily living component of personal independence payment (PIP; any rate), armed forces independence payment, attendance allowance or constant attendance allowance.

**Your non-dependant's circumstances** – There is no deduction for a non-dependant if they:

- are aged under 18;
- are aged under 25 and on income support, income-based JSA or assessment-phase income-related ESA;
- are aged under 25 and entitled to universal credit (unless they have any earnings);
- are on pension credit;
- get a Work-Based Learning for Young People training allowance;
- have been in an NHS hospital for over 52 weeks;
- are detained in prison or a similar institution;
- have their normal home elsewhere;
- are not living with you because they are a member of the armed forces away on operations; *or*
- are a full-time student (see Chapter 32(2)); there is a deduction in the summer vacation if they take up remunerative work (see below), unless they (or their partner) are aged 65 or over.

HB Regs, reg 74(1), (6)-(8) & (10)

### The amounts of the deductions

❏ **Non-dependants aged 25 or over on income-related ESA, income support or income-based JSA** – The weekly amount is £15.25.

❏ **Non-dependants on pension credit** – No deduction.

❏ **Other non-dependants not in remunerative work** – Regardless of your non-dependant's income, the weekly amount is £15.25.

❏ **Non-dependants in remunerative work (excluding those on pension credit)** – The weekly amount depends on your non-dependant's weekly gross income.

| Weekly gross income | Weekly deduction |
| --- | --- |
| £439 or more | £98.30 |
| £354 to £438.99 | £89.55 |
| £265 to £353.99 | £78.65 |
| £204 to £264.99 | £48.05 |
| £139 to £203.99 | £35.00 |
| Under £139 | £15.25 |

HB Regs, reg 74(1)-(2)

If you cannot provide evidence of your non-dependant's gross income (and they are in remunerative work and not receiving pension credit), your local authority must consider all the circumstances of the case before making the highest of the above deductions. If you later provide evidence showing the deduction should have been lower, the authority should award you arrears of housing benefit, as you will have been underpaid (see 14 above).

### Which non-dependants are in remunerative work?

*'Remunerative work'* means work that averages 16 or more hours a week. If your non-dependant is on maternity, paternity, shared parental, adoption or sick leave, they do not count as being in remunerative work (even if paid full pay or statutory maternity, paternity, shared parental, adoption or sick pay). If your non-dependant gets income-related ESA, income support or income-based JSA for more than three days in any benefit week (Monday to Sunday), they do not count as being in remunerative work.

HB Regs, reg 6

### Your non-dependant's gross income

Your non-dependant's income is relevant if they are in remunerative work. It is assessed gross, which, in the case of earnings, means before tax, national insurance and other deductions are made. All other income is counted, except DLA, PIP, armed forces independence payment, attendance allowance, constant attendance allowance and payments from the Macfarlane Trusts, the Eileen Trust, the Skipton Fund, the Caxton Foundation, the Scottish Infected Blood Support scheme, an approved blood scheme, MFET Ltd, the Independent Living Fund, the Fund and an approved Thalidomide relief and assistance trust. If your non-dependant has capital, only the interest is counted as gross income. If your non-dependant is in a couple, add their partner's gross income (but see below).

HB Regs, reg 74(9)

### Other points about non-dependants

You usually get a deduction for each non-dependant (apart from those for whom no deduction applies). But if you have non-dependants who are a couple, you get only one deduction for the two of them. This is the higher figure of the two amounts that would have applied to them if each was single and each had the income of both.

If you are a joint occupier (see 5 above), and your non-dependant is also a non-dependant of the other joint occupier(s), the deduction is shared between you and the other joint occupier(s).

HB Regs, reg 74(3)-(5)

### Concession if you are aged 65 or over

If you or your partner are aged 65 or over, special non-dependant deduction rules apply. If a non-dependant comes to live with you, their income will be disregarded for 26 weeks. If you already have a non-dependant living with you and their circumstances or income change (meaning a higher deduction applies), the local authority will not increase the amount of the deduction for a 26-week period. If changes occur more than once, the 26-week period runs from the date of the first change. If your non-dependant's income decreases, the authority should reduce the deduction immediately if appropriate.

HB(SPC) Regs, reg 59(10)-(12)

## 22. Capital

Your local authority needs to assess your capital if you are not on income-related employment and support allowance, income support, income-based jobseeker's allowance, the guarantee credit of pension credit or universal credit. If you are one of a couple, your partner's capital is included with yours. For how capital is assessed, see Chapter 22(22)-(37). There are different capital rules for claimants who have reached pension credit qualifying age (see 25 below).

If your capital is over £16,000, you cannot get housing benefit. If your capital is £6,000 or less (£10,000 or less for people who have reached pension credit qualifying age), it is disregarded. If it is more than £6,000 but no more than £16,000, you are treated as having income – known as 'tariff income' (see Chapter 22(25)). In rare cases, some people in care homes are entitled to housing benefit (see Chapter 38(3)), and the first £10,000 (instead of £6,000) of their capital is disregarded.

If a child in your family owns capital, this is disregarded.

## 23. Income

Your local authority needs to assess your income if you are not on income-related employment and support allowance, income support, income-based jobseeker's allowance, the guarantee credit of pension credit or universal credit. If you are one of a couple, your partner's income is included with yours. For how income is assessed, see Chapter 22(2)-(21). There are different income rules for claimants who have reached pension credit qualifying age (see 25 below).

If your income is greater than your applicable amount, this affects the amount of housing benefit you get (see 20 above).

## 24. Applicable amounts

Your local authority needs to assess your applicable amount if you are not on income-related employment and support allowance (ESA), income support, income-based jobseeker's allowance (JSA), the guarantee credit of pension credit or universal credit. The *'applicable amount'* is a figure that is intended to reflect your weekly living needs and those of your family. If you (or your partner) have reached pension credit qualifying age, see 25 below. If you are under pension credit qualifying age, your applicable amount is made up of:

■ **personal allowances** – you get one or more of these for various members of your family, including children; *plus*
■ **premiums** – many people, but not all, get one or more premiums to take account of family responsibilities, disabilities and responsibilities as a carer; *plus*
■ **additional components** – apply only if you are entitled to main-phase ESA.

HB Regs, reg 22

You must meet conditions for each part of the applicable amount. You can ask for a written statement from the authority about what premiums you have been awarded and why. If you think any have been missed, you can challenge the decision (see 19 above).

### Your family

Applicable amounts are based on the circumstances of your family. *'Family'* is used in a technical sense and means:

■ you (the claimant); *and*
■ your partner. This can be your spouse or civil partner, as

long as you are living in the same household. It can also include your partner if you are unmarried and you are effectively living together as a married couple; *and*
■ dependent child(ren) or young people who are members of your household and under the age of 16 (or under the age of 20 if they are a 'qualifying young person' – see Chapter 41(1)). If you have a child(ren) born on or after 6.4.17, you may not receive an amount for them if you receive an amount for two children already (the rules reflect those of child tax credit – see Chapter 23(4)). The definition of a dependent child includes your natural or adopted children and others you are responsible for (eg a grandchild). Foster children are not usually included. If a child who is normally in local authority care spends time with you at home, the authority can include that child or not as a member of your family for the benefit week(s) (Monday to Sunday) when the child stays with you. This is an 'all or nothing' rule: the authority cannot give you just part of a personal allowance or family premium.

SSCBA, S.137(1); HB Regs, regs 19-21

### Personal allowances

Lower personal allowances can apply to people aged under 25, unless the claimant is entitled to main-phase ESA.

| Personal allowances | | per week |
|---|---|---|
| Single person | aged 25 or over | £73.10 |
| | aged 16-24 | £57.90 |
| | entitled to main-phase ESA* | £73.10 |
| Lone parent | aged 18 or over | £73.10 |
| | aged under 18 | £57.90 |
| | entitled to main-phase ESA* | £73.10 |
| Couple | one or both aged 18 or over | £114.85 |
| | both under 18 | £87.50 |
| | both under 18 but claimant entitled to main-phase ESA* | £114.85 |
| Dependent child** | | £66.90 |

HB Regs, Sch 3, Part 1

\* includes claimants receiving national insurance credits for limited capability for work (see Box D.3, Chapter 11)
\*\* an additional dependent child allowance will not usually be paid for a third or subsequent child born on or after 6.4.17; exceptions apply (they reflect those of child tax credit – see Chapter 23(4))

### Premiums

There are six premiums, each with specific qualifying conditions (see Chapter 21). Unless otherwise specified in that chapter, each premium to which you are entitled is added to the total of your applicable amount.

| Premiums | | per week |
|---|---|---|
| Family* | ordinary rate | £17.45 |
| | lone parent rate** | £22.20 |
| Disability*** | single | £33.55 |
| | couple | £47.80 |
| Disabled child | | £62.86 |
| Severe disability | single | £64.30 |
| | couple (one qualifies) | £64.30 |
| | couple (both qualify) | £128.60 |
| Enhanced disability | single | £16.40 |
| | couple | £23.55 |
| | child | £25.48 |
| Carer | | £36.00 |

\* will not be included in new claims made on or after 1.5.16 or those of existing claimants who have a child or become responsible for a child (or qualifying young person) for the first time on or after 1.5.16

** applies in limited circumstances (see Chapter 21(7))
*** does not apply if there is an entitlement to main-phase ESA

### Additional components
If you are entitled to main-phase ESA (or national insurance credits for limited capability for work), you may be entitled to an additional component depending on whether you are placed in the work-related activity group or the support group (see Chapter 11(6)):
■ work-related activity component (applies in limited circumstances): £29.05 a week;
■ support component: £37.65 a week.

## 25. Rules for people who have reached pension credit qualifying age
The rules for claimants who have reached pension credit qualifying age (see Chapter 44(2)) are different (unless you or your partner receive income support, income-based jobseeker's allowance, income-related employment and support allowance or universal credit). The main differences are listed below.

### Applicable amount
Your personal allowance is based on the pension credit *'standard minimum guarantee'* (see Chapter 44(3)) and, if you or your partner are aged 65 or over, the maximum *'savings credit'* (see Chapter 44(4)). For a single claimant, the personal allowance is £163, or £176.40 if you are aged 65 or over. For a couple it is £248.80, or £263.80 if either of you is aged 65 or over.

The following extra sums can be included in your applicable amount following the usual housing benefit rules:
■ personal allowances for dependent children and young people (see 24 above);
■ family premium (see Chapter 21(7));
■ severe disability premium (see Chapter 21(3));
■ enhanced disability premium (for any qualifying dependent child or young person, but not for yourself or your partner) (see Chapter 21(4));
■ disabled child premium (see Chapter 21(8)); *and*
■ carer premium (see Chapter 21(6)).

### Income and capital
There are different rules about how income and capital affect the amount of housing benefit you get, depending on whether you receive pension credit and, if so, which elements are in payment.
**Guarantee credit** – If you or your partner receive the guarantee credit of pension credit, all of your capital and income will be disregarded and you will receive full housing benefit. This applies even if your capital exceeds the usual housing benefit limit of £16,000. Since there is no capital limit for pension credit, it is possible to receive the guarantee credit even though your savings would exceed the housing benefit limit.
HB(SPC) Regs, reg 26

**Savings credit only** – If you or your partner are aged 65 or over and receive the savings credit but not the guarantee credit of pension credit and do not have more than £16,000 capital, the local authority will use the assessment of your income and capital that the Pension Service used to calculate your savings credit (see Chapter 44(4)). The authority will then adjust this figure by adding:
■ any of your partner's income or capital that was not taken into account in the pension credit calculation;
■ in very limited circumstances, any income of a non-dependant that is treated as yours under housing benefit rules; *and*
■ any pension credit savings credit.

They will then subtract (if applicable):
■ the higher housing benefit disregard of lone parent's earnings and the 'additional earnings disregard' (see Chapter 22(6));
■ the normal housing benefit disregard of childcare costs (see Chapter 22(6));
■ earnings from permitted work (see Chapter 33(3)); *and*
■ any discretionary disregard of war pensions allowed by your local authority.
HB(SPC) Regs, reg 27(4)

**No pension credit payable** – If you or your partner have reached pension credit qualifying age but do not receive pension credit, your income and capital will be assessed by the local authority in much the same way as it is for pension credit (see Chapter 44(5) and (6)).
HB(SPC) Regs, reg 28

# 26 Support for mortgage interest loans

| | | |
|---|---|---|
| 1 | Introduction | 190 |
| 2 | What loans are covered? | 191 |
| 3 | Loans for repairs and improvements (legacy benefits and pension credit) | 191 |
| 4 | Loans taken out while on benefits or between claims (legacy benefits and pension credit) | 191 |
| 5 | Liability to make owner-occupier payments | 192 |
| 6 | Your home | 192 |
| 7 | Loan conditions | 193 |
| 8 | Calculating the SMI loan | 193 |
| 9 | Calculation for loan interest payments | 194 |
| 10 | Calculation for alternative finance payments | 194 |
| 11 | The standard rate | 194 |
| 12 | Deductions | 195 |
| 13 | How SMI loans are made | 195 |
| 14 | How long can SMI loans continue? | 195 |
| 15 | Interest on SMI loans | 195 |
| 16 | Repayment | 196 |

## 1. Introduction
You may be able to get help to cover the interest payments on your mortgage or eligible home improvement loans if you are getting one of the following *'qualifying'* means-tested benefits:
■ income-based jobseeker's allowance*;
■ income-related employment and support allowance*;
■ income support*;
■ pension credit; *or*
■ universal credit.
This help will come in the form of loan payments from the DWP: *'support for mortgage interest'* (SMI) loans. These must be repaid with interest once your property has been sold. The SMI loans may be secured by a charge on your property (see 7 below). You do not need to accept an offer of these loans; the scheme is voluntary.
* these are referred to as *'legacy benefits'*

### What happens if you already get help with your housing costs?
SMI loans were introduced on 6.4.18. Before this date, you could get help towards the interest payments on your mortgage and on home improvement loans as part of your means-tested benefit; you did not need to pay this back. If you were receiving such support by 6.4.18, the DWP should have contacted you to offer the SMI loans; you will not be able to stay on the old system of support (except during a transitional period while the SMI loans are being set up; note that if a

person cannot act for themselves in respect of the loans, the period can be extended until someone has been appointed to act on their behalf – see 7 below).
LMIR Regs, regs 19-20

For details of the old system, see *Disability Rights Handbook* 42nd edition, Chapters 24 and 26.

### When can an offer of SMI loans be made to you?
The DWP may offer you SMI loans to cover any eligible interest on *'owner-occupier payments'* (see 2 below) that you are liable to make (see 5 below) on the accommodation that you occupy as your home (see 6 below).

If you are claiming universal credit, you are not eligible for an offer of SMI loans if you or your partner have any earnings. This is irrespective of the nature of the work, how much you earn or how long you work for.
LMIR Regs, reg 3

See 7 below for the conditions that must be met before SMI loans can be made.

You can accept the offer of SMI loans at any time, as long as you are still getting a qualifying benefit.

## 2. What loans are covered?
SMI loans can cover *'owner-occupier payments'*. These are usually *'loan interest payments'*. For universal credit and pension credit only, they can also be *'alternative finance payments'*.
LMIR Regs, Sch 1, paras 2(1) & 5(1)

### Loan interest payments
**Universal credit** – These are interest payments on any loan secured on the accommodation that you occupy (or are treated as occupying) as your home (see 6 below).
LMIR Regs, Sch 1, para 5(2)

**Legacy benefits and pension credit** – These are interest payments on a loan that was taken out:
■ to buy the accommodation that you occupy (or are treated as occupying) as your home (see 6 below);
■ for certain repairs and improvements (see 3 below); *or*
■ to pay off an earlier loan, but only to the extent that the earlier loan would have qualified if it had not been paid off. For example, if your outstanding mortgage was £10,000 and you borrow £12,000 to repay it, only the interest on the £10,000 used to repay the original loan is covered.

If part of a loan is taken out for a different purpose (eg a business loan), that part of the loan will not be covered.
LMIR Regs, Sch 1, para 2

A loan will not be covered if it was taken out to buy a home while you or your partner were entitled to certain benefits or between claims (see 4 below).

### Alternative finance payments
These are payments made under alternative finance arrangements (such as sharia-compliant loans) set up to enable you to buy the accommodation that you occupy (or are treated as occupying) as your home (see 6 below).
LMIR Regs, Sch 1, para 5(3)

## 3. Loans for repairs and improvements (legacy benefits and pension credit)
The interest on loans taken out and used within six months (or longer if reasonable) to pay for repairs and improvements to your home is covered by the SMI loans. The works must be *'undertaken with a view to maintaining the fitness of the [home] for human habitation'* and be for one of the following:
■ adapting your home for *'the special needs of a disabled person'* (see below);
■ providing a bath, shower, wash basin, sink or lavatory (and associated plumbing, including providing hot water not connected to a central heating system);

■ providing ventilation, natural lighting, insulation or electric lighting and sockets;
■ providing facilities for preparing and cooking food, storing fuel or refuse, or for drainage;
■ providing separate bedrooms for children (or young people aged under 20) of different sexes aged 10 or over who live with you and who you are responsible for;
■ repairs to existing heating systems or of unsafe structural defects; *or*
■ damp proofing.

Loans to pay service charges for any of these works are covered, as are loans used to pay off an existing loan for repairs, but only to the extent that the existing loan would have qualified if it had not been paid off.
LMIR Regs, Sch 1, para 2(4)-(5)

### Who counts as a disabled person?
Someone is considered to be *'a disabled person'* if, on the date the loan for repairs and improvements is taken out:
■ they meet the conditions for a disability premium, disabled child premium, enhanced or higher pensioner premium (for income support and income-based jobseeker's allowance (JSA), although they don't have to be receiving any of those premiums or be entitled to income support or JSA);
■ they are being paid main-phase employment and support allowance (ESA), or would be paid it but for the contributory ESA time limit (see Chapter 11(20)) or have been disqualified from receiving it in certain circumstances (see Chapter 11(17));
■ they are entitled to universal credit and have a limited capability for work (see Chapter 12(2)) or a limited capability for work-related activity (see Chapter 12(5));
■ had they been entitled to income support, they would have qualified for the disability premium (for ESA);
■ they would qualify for the disabled child element of child tax credit (for income support, JSA and ESA);
■ they are aged 75 or over (for pension credit and ESA);
■ had they been entitled to income support, they would have qualified for the higher pensioner or disability premium (for pension credit); *or*
■ (for pension credit) they are aged under 20, you or your partner are responsible for them and they:
  – get disability living allowance, personal independence payment (or, if they are 18 or 19, would get one of these were they not in hospital) or armed forces independence payment;
  – are certified by a consultant ophthalmologist as severely sight impaired or blind (or have ceased to be so certified in the past 28 weeks); *or*
  – meet the conditions for the second or third bullets above.

The disabled person can be you, a member of your family or someone else who lives with you or will be living with you.
LMIR Regs, reg 2

## 4. Loans taken out while on benefits or between claims (legacy benefits and pension credit)
The interest on loans taken out during the following *'relevant periods'* is not normally covered:
■ while you or a member of your family were entitled to any of the legacy benefits or pension credit;
■ within a break in entitlement to a legacy benefit or pension credit of 26 weeks or less; *or*
■ while you or your partner were taking part in an employment programme and your income from this prevented you claiming a legacy benefit or pension credit.
LMIR Regs, Sch 1, para 3(1)-(3)

Even if you took on the loan during a relevant period, you may be entitled to a restricted amount of help towards the interest if you were already receiving some form of housing support. The intention in the following two cases is to restrict the help to the level you were already receiving when you took on the loan.

**Replacement or additional loans** – If you already had a mortgage and you increased it or took out an additional loan during a relevant period, the additional amount is not met. You can replace one mortgage with another but if the new one is larger, you will only get help up to the level available on the old mortgage. If your new mortgage is used to buy a home and you pay off all or part of the mortgage on your old home from the sale of that property, help for the new mortgage is restricted to the level of help that applied to the old mortgage.
LMIR Regs, Sch 1, para 3(4)

**Previously getting housing benefit** – If you took on a mortgage during a relevant period, help with loan interest is restricted to the level of housing benefit payable in the week before the week you bought the home. If you were getting both housing benefit and housing costs (in the award of the legacy benefit or pension credit) in that week, the restriction is applied to the total of housing benefit payable plus the housing costs. The restricted amount can only then be increased if the standard rate (see 11 below) goes up.
LMIR Regs, Sch 1, para 3(6)&(7)

### Exemptions
If you took on a loan during a relevant period, you can get help towards the interest without the above restrictions if:
- the loan was taken out, or increased, to buy *'alternative accommodation more suited to the needs of a disabled person'* (see 3 above for who counts as a disabled person); *or*
- an additional or increased loan was taken out because you sold your home to buy another solely to provide separate bedrooms for children (or young people aged under 20) of different sexes aged 10 or over who live with you and you are responsible for.
LMIR Regs, Sch 1, para 3(8)&(9)

### 5. Liability to make owner-occupier payments
You must be liable to make owner-occupier payments. You are also liable to make such payments if your partner (including if you are one of a couple but claiming as a single person – see Chapter 14(3)) has a liability to make them.
LMIR Regs, Sch 2, paras 2(1) & 5(1)

If you share the liability to make payments with someone other than your partner, you will be treated as liable to the proportion of those payments that you are responsible for.
LMIR Regs, reg 3(3)

### Treated as liable to make payments
**A child or young person is liable** – You will be treated as liable to make payments if the person who is actually liable is a child or qualifying young person (see Chapter 16(4)) you are responsible for (universal credit only).
LMIR Regs, Sch 2, para 5(2)(a)

**If you take over paying from someone else** – If the person liable to make payments on your home stops making them, you can be treated as liable to make them in the following circumstances:
- you have to make the payments to continue living in your home;
- it would be unreasonable to expect you to make other arrangements (universal credit only); *and*
- it is reasonable to treat you as liable to make the payments.
LMIR Regs, Sch 2, paras 2(2)(a) & 5(2)(b)

**You share responsibility for the payments** – You will be treated as liable to make payments if you share responsibility for the payments with other members of the household, none of whom are close relatives of you or your partner (legacy benefits and pension credit only). A *'close relative'* is a parent, parent-in-law, step-parent, son, daughter, son/daughter-in-law, stepson/daughter, sister, brother or the partner of any of those.
LMIR Regs, reg 2(1) & Sch 2, para 2(2)(b)

**Repairs to your home** – If the liability for payments on your home is waived in return for you doing reasonable repairs or redecoration to your home, you can be treated as liable to make them (universal credit only).
LMIR Regs, Sch 2, para 5(2)(c)

**On strike** – If one or more members of your family are on strike and you are not, you will be treated as liable to make all the payments (legacy benefits and pension credit only).
LMIR Regs, Sch 2, para 2(3)

### Treated as not liable to make payments
**To a member of your household** – You are treated as not liable to make payments if you are liable to pay them to anyone living in your household.
LMIR Regs, Sch 2, paras 3 & 6(a)

While the term *'household'* is not defined in legislation, it should be given its normal everyday meaning, ie a domestic establishment containing the essentials of home life.
R(SB)4/83

'Household' should not be confused with 'dwelling'. A single dwelling or property may have several different households within it, each containing independent living arrangements.

**Arrears of payment (universal credit only)** – You are treated as not liable to make any payment that is more than you usually pay, which has been set up to cover:
- outstanding arrears of any payment or charge for your current or previous accommodation; *or*
- any other unpaid liabilities to make a payment or charge.
LMIR Regs, Sch 2, para 6(b)

**Contrived liability** – Even if neither of the conditions above applies, you can still be treated as not liable to make payments if the DWP considers that the liability was contrived in order to secure the offer of SMI loans or an increase to such loans (universal credit only).
LMIR Regs, Sch 2, para 6(c)

### 6. Your home
You cannot generally be treated as occupying more than one home. Exceptions apply, depending on which benefit you are claiming.

If you are claiming universal credit, the circumstances in which you can be treated as occupying more than one home, or treated as occupying a home that you are not currently living in, are similar to those that apply to the universal credit housing costs amount (with the exception of the condition that applies to large families). See Box G.2 in Chapter 24 for details.
LMIR Regs, Sch 3, paras 11-18

If you are claiming one of the legacy benefits or pension credit, the circumstances in which you can be treated as occupying a home you are temporarily absent from are

similar to those that apply to housing benefit (see Chapter 25(6)). If you are occupying more than one home, have been delayed in moving into your new home, are living elsewhere during essential repairs or are studying full-time, see below.
LMIR Regs, Sch 3, paras 4-10

**Croft land** – If your home is on a croft, the croft land used for your home is treated as part of your accommodation (universal credit only).
LMIR Regs, Sch 3, para 12(3)

### Treated as occupying more than one home
If you are claiming one of the legacy benefits or pension credit, you can be treated as occupying two homes and can therefore get SMI loans for both in any of the following circumstances.

**Moving home** – You move to a new home and the liability to make payments on both your new home and your old home is unavoidable; you can get SMI loans on both homes for up to four weeks (unless you are living elsewhere due to essential repairs, in which case – see below).

**Fear of violence** – You move because of fear that violence may occur in your old home (regardless of who might cause the violence) or in the locality (in which case, only if the violence would be caused by a close relative or former partner) and it is reasonable to cover the interest payments for both homes. A *'close relative'* is a parent, parent-in-law, step-parent, son, daughter, son/daughter-in-law, stepson/daughter, sister, brother or the partner of any of those.

**Students** – You or your partner are a full-time student or are on a training course, it is unavoidable that you need to maintain two homes and it is reasonable to cover the interest payments for each home.
LMIR Regs, reg 2(1) & Sch 3, para 6

### Delays in moving into your new home
If you are claiming one of the legacy benefits or pension credit and are delayed in moving into your new home, you can be treated as occupying the new home for up to four weeks and may therefore get SMI loans for it. The delay must be reasonable and be due to one of the following circumstances:

**Waiting for your new home to be adapted** – Your new home is being adapted to meet your disablement needs or those of a member of your family.

**Waiting for a loan or grant before moving** – You are waiting for a local authority loan or grant to help with the move or with setting up home. However, this rule only applies if:
■ there is a child under the age of 6 in your family;
■ you qualify for a disability premium or pensioner premium (see Chapter 21(2) and (5)); or
■ you receive child tax credit with a disabled child element (see Chapter 23(4)).

**Waiting to leave hospital or a care home** – You become liable to make payments for the new home while waiting to leave hospital or a care home.
LMIR Regs, Sch 3, para 7

### You are living elsewhere during essential repairs
If you are claiming one of the legacy benefits or pension credit, you have to move into temporary accommodation so that essential repairs can be carried out to your home and you:
■ intend to return to your home following the repairs; *and*
■ are liable to pay for either the temporary accommodation or your home (but not both),
you can be treated as normally living in the property for which you are liable to make payments and may therefore get SMI loans for it.
LMIR Regs, Sch 3, para 5

### Full-time study
If you are claiming one of the legacy benefits or pension credit, are a full-time student or are on a training course, and you are liable to make owner occupier payments for either (but not both):
■ the home you occupy when attending the course; *or*
■ the home you occupy during breaks from the course,
you can be treated as normally living in that home and may therefore get SMI loans for it. If you are a full-time student, you will not be treated as occupying the home while you are absent from it outside the period of study, unless you are being treated in hospital.
LMIR Regs, Sch 3, para 4

## 7. Loan conditions
Before the SMI loans can be made, you (and your partner, if you have one) must sign and return a loan agreement. The DWP must provide you (and your partner) with the following information in the six-month period that ends on the day you accept the offer:
■ the terms and conditions of the loan agreement;
■ an explanation of the legal charge or standard security, if one is going to be set up (see below); *and*
■ where you can get further information and independent legal and financial advice on SMI loans.
LMIR Regs, regs 4-6

### Appointees
If a person cannot act for themselves and needs someone to accept the loan agreement on their behalf (eg an appointee – see Chapter 56(4)), that person will need to have power of attorney status or be appointed as a deputy by the Court of Protection (for details, go to: www.gov.uk/power-of-attorney and www.gov.uk/become-deputy; for details of the Scottish equivalents, go to www.publicguardian-scotland.gov.uk/power-of-attorney/power-of-attorney/what-is-a-power-of-attorney).

### The legal charge
To ensure that the SMI loans are recoverable from you, the DWP can place a *'legal charge'* (or in Scotland, a standard security) on your property. This will be registered at your regional Land Registry in England and Wales, or the Registers of Scotland if you live there.

The legal charge will give the DWP the right to recover the total of any SMI loans made to you, plus interest (see 15 below), from any equity available once your home has been sold (or the ownership otherwise transferred) – see 16 below.

If you have a partner who does not share ownership of the property with you, they will need to give their written consent to the setting up of the legal charge or standard security.

**Jointly-owned property** – In England and Wales, if you own your property jointly with one or more others (other than your partner), the DWP can place an *'equitable charge'* on your beneficial interest in the property instead, in which case the DWP will only be able to recover SMI loans from that interest.

In Scotland, this situation is also covered by the standard security.
LMIR Regs, reg 5(2)&(3)

## 8. Calculating the SMI loan
There are different calculations for loan interest payments and for alternative finance payments. If you pay both, each calculation is made separately, then the results are added together.
LMIR Regs, reg 10

See 9 below for the calculation for loan interest payments and 10 below for the calculation for alternative finance payments.

You cannot take out a partial loan; any SMI loan offered will be for the full amount as calculated.

The DWP will not charge administration fees for setting up the SMI loans.

## 9. Calculation for loan interest payments

To calculate how much is to be included in your SMI loan, the following steps are taken:

**Step 1:** The amount of capital you currently owe in connection with a qualifying loan or loans (see 2 above) is worked out. If the total is higher than a ceiling figure (see below), that ceiling figure is used instead (unless the loan was taken out for the purposes of adapting the property to meet the needs of a disabled person; see below).

**Step 2:** The result of Step 1 is multiplied by the standard rate (see 11 below) and the resulting figure is divided by 52 to give a weekly figure (or, in the case of universal credit, by 12 to give a monthly figure).

**Step 3:** Your income is worked out. This will be your weekly income taken into account in the assessment of your means-tested benefit (see Chapters 22(2)-(21) and 44(5)) or your monthly income taken into account in the assessment of your universal credit (see Chapter 17(7)-(15)). If your income is no more than the applicable amount of your means-tested benefit (see Chapters 18(6), 19(7) and 20(6)) or the universal credit or pension credit equivalents (see Chapters 16(2) and 44(3)), your SMI loan will be the result from Step 2. If your income is greater than the applicable amount of your means-tested benefit or the universal credit or pension credit equivalents, calculate the difference between the two.

**Step 4:** The result of Step 3 is deducted from the result of Step 2. The resulting figure is your SMI loan.

LMIR Regs, reg 11(1)

### The ceiling

If your loan (or the total of your loans) is above a certain set level or *'ceiling'*, your SMI loan is worked out only on the part of the loan up to the ceiling. The ceiling is set at one of two levels: £100,000 or £200,000.

The higher ceiling of £200,000 applies if you are claiming universal credit. The higher ceiling also applies if you have an award of a legacy benefit made on or after 5.1.09 (and which does not link to a previous award made before 5.1.09). The higher ceiling applies if you were already entitled to one of these benefits on 5.1.09, but were serving a waiting period. The higher ceiling continues to apply if you move onto pension credit as long as no more than 12 weeks separate the last day of your award of the legacy benefit and the first day of your award of pension credit.

---

If the £200,000 ceiling does not apply, a £100,000 ceiling will apply instead.

LMIR Regs, regs 2 & 11(2)

**Loans taken out for adaptations** – Any loan (or part of a loan) that was taken out to pay for necessary adaptations to the home to meet the needs of a disabled person will be disregarded when working out whether your loan(s) exceed the ceiling.

If you are claiming a legacy benefit or pension credit, see 3 above for who counts as a disabled person.

If you are claiming universal credit, the disabled person can be you, your partner, or a child or qualifying young person (see Chapter 16(4)) you (or your partner) are responsible for, if you (or they) receive:

- the care component of disability living allowance at the middle or highest rate;
- attendance allowance, constant attendance allowance or exceptionally severe disablement allowance;
- the daily living component of personal independence payment (PIP); *or*
- armed forces independence payment.

LMIR Regs, regs 2 & 11(3)

*Example:* Amanda currently owes £190,000 on her mortgage. She has rheumatoid arthritis and receives the daily living component of PIP and universal credit. She has recently taken out a loan of £25,000 to have a downstairs toilet built because of her reduced mobility. She does not have income that is greater than her universal credit maximum amount, so only the first two steps in the calculation are needed here:

**Step 1:** The £190,000 mortgage is a qualifying loan. The loan of £25,000 is not subject to the ceiling. Consequently, the total of her loans that can be covered are £190,000 plus £25,000, giving £215,000.

**Step 2:** The result of Step 1, £215,000, is multiplied by 2.61% (the standard rate, see 11 below), giving £5,611.50. This figure is divided by 12, giving £467.63. This figure is her SMI loan.

### Changes in the amount owed

Any change in the amount of capital you owe on a loan is recalculated annually, on the anniversary of the date when the SMI loans started (or, if you have been moved onto SMI loans after previously receiving such support from universal credit, a legacy benefit or pension credit, on the anniversary of the date when housing costs were first included in the benefit award).

LMIR Regs, reg 11(4)&(5)

## 10. Calculation for alternative finance payments

The calculation for alternative finance payments is similar to that for loan interest payments (see 9 above), but in this case for Step 1, the purchase price of your home is worked out instead. The *'purchase price'* is the amount needed to buy your home, less the amount of any initial payment you made to buy it and any subsequent alternative finance payments you (or your partner) made before the SMI loans started (or, if you have been moved onto SMI loans after previously receiving such support from universal credit, a legacy benefit or pension credit, before housing costs were first included in the benefit award). If the purchase price is higher than a ceiling figure (see 9 above), that ceiling figure is used instead. All the other steps in the calculation are the same as for loan interest payments.

LMIR Regs, reg 12

## 11. The standard rate

The DWP uses a standard interest rate in the SMI loan calculation. This is based on the Bank of England's published monthly average mortgage rate. It will only change when

the Bank of England average mortgage rate differs from the standard rate by 0.5% or more. When that happens, the new Bank of England average mortgage rate becomes the new standard rate. At the time of writing, the rate is 2.61%.
LMIR Regs, reg 13

## 12. Deductions
### Non-dependant deductions
If you are claiming one of the legacy benefits or pension credit, in calculating the SMI loan a deduction is made for each non-dependant living in your home. A *'non-dependant'* is someone who normally lives in your home on a non-commercial basis – usually an adult son, daughter, friend or relative. It is assumed that the non-dependant will contribute towards your housing costs, whether they do or not. In some circumstances, the deduction will not be made; the rules are the same as for housing benefit (see Chapter 25(21)).
**Calculating the deduction** – The non-dependant deduction is normally worked out in the same way as the non-dependant deduction for housing benefit (see Chapter 25(21)). However, if you are also getting other housing costs covered by your means-tested benefit (see Chapter 27), the calculation is more complicated:
**Step 1:** The non-dependant deduction is determined (as it would apply to housing benefit – see Chapter 25(21)).
**Step 2:** The SMI loan is calculated (see 9 above).
**Step 3:** The SMI loan figure (from Step 2) is added to the amount of the other housing costs (see Chapter 27).
**Step 4:** The result of Step 2 is divided by the result of Step 3.
**Step 5:** The result of Step 1 is multiplied by the result of Step 4. The resulting figure is your non-dependant deduction.
LMIR Regs, reg 14

*Example:* Victor lives with his grown up son, Adam. Victor has a mortgage, and is entitled to a SMI loan towards the interest; the SMI loan has been worked out at £48 a week. Adam earns £185 a week. Victor gets income-related employment and support allowance, which includes an amount towards other housing costs of £16 a week.
**Step 1:** A non-dependant deduction of £35 a week applies to Adam, based on his weekly gross income (see Chapter 25(21).
**Step 2:** The SMI loan is £48 a week.
**Step 3:** Adding £48 to £16 gives £64.
**Step 4:** Dividing the result from Step 2, £48, by the result from Step 3, £64, gives 0.75.
**Step 5:** Multiplying the result from Step 1, £35, by the result from Step 4, 0.75, gives £26.25. This will be the non-dependant deduction that will be made from Victor's SMI loan.

### Insurance payment deductions
If you are claiming one of the legacy benefits or pension credit, in calculating the SMI loan a deduction is made if you (or your partner) receive payments under a mortgage protection policy used to meet repayments on a mortgage or on a loan for eligible repairs or improvements. The deduction will be equal to the mortgage protection payment; if the mortgage protection payment is the same as or more than the SMI loan, as calculated so far, the SMI loan will not be made.
LMIR Regs, reg 14A

## 13. How SMI loans are made
You will be sent a letter confirming when the SMI loans will start. The SMI loans will go straight to the mortgage lender.
LMIR Regs, reg 17

In the case of universal credit, the SMI loans are paid monthly, in arrears. In the case of legacy benefits and pension credit, they are paid 4-weekly in arrears.
LMIR Regs, reg 7

### Qualifying period
In the case of universal credit and legacy benefits, there is normally a *'qualifying period'* before SMI loans can be paid.
If you are claiming universal credit, you are not eligible for SMI loans until you have been entitled to universal credit for nine consecutive monthly assessment periods (see Chapter 16(1)).
If you are claiming one of the legacy benefits, you are not normally eligible for SMI loans until you have been entitled, or treated as entitled, to the legacy benefit for 39 consecutive weeks. For the circumstances in which you can be treated as entitled to the legacy benefit, see Chapter 27(4); the rules that apply to the waiting periods for housing costs also apply to SMI loan qualifying periods.
The qualifying period will not apply if you are claiming pension credit.
LMIR Regs, regs 2 & 8

**Linking rule** – If you stop claiming a legacy benefit for any reason, and reclaim it within 52 weeks, you will not need to serve the qualifying period again to be eligible for SMI loans.
LMIR Regs, reg 9(7)

If you (or your former partner) were entitled (or treated as entitled) to a legacy benefit at any time in the month before claiming universal credit, and the legacy benefit covered interest payments or allowed a claim for SMI loans, you will not have to serve the qualifying period again to be eligible for SMI loans via your universal credit award. If you were part way through the qualifying period when the legacy benefit stopped, you will only have to serve the remaining weeks of that qualifying period.
LMIR Regs, reg 21

## 14. How long can SMI loans continue?
Once SMI loans have been set up, they can continue indefinitely. They will stop, however, in the following circumstances:
■ you are no longer entitled, or treated as entitled, to a qualifying benefit (see 1 above) – see below for an exception if you or your partner start work;
■ you are no longer liable, or treated as liable, to make owner occupier payments (see 2 and 5 above);
■ you are no longer occupying, and cannot be treated as occupying, the accommodation (see 6 above);
■ the loan agreement is terminated, in accordance with its terms; *or*
■ in the case of universal credit, you or your partner start earning.
LMIR Regs, reg 9

If you want to stop getting SMI loans, you can do this at any time. You will still have to repay the SMI loans, plus the interest, that you have received so far (see 16 below).

### Starting work
If you or your partner start work, and consequently are no longer entitled to a qualifying benefit, you may continue to get SMI loans for the first four weeks (see Chapter 33(4)).
LMIR Regs, reg 9(4)-(6)

## 15. Interest on SMI loans
The DWP will charge interest on the SMI loans that you have borrowed. This will build up daily and will be added to the total at the end of each month. The interest is compound, ie it will be based on the total amount of SMI loans plus any earlier interest that has already been added to that total. The interest will continue to build up until you have paid off the SMI loans (and interest) in full.

The interest rate can be revised twice a year, with any changes being made on the 1 January or 1 July.
LMIR Regs, reg 15

### 16. Repayment

You do not need to pay back the DWP until your property has been sold, or the ownership of it otherwise transferred to someone else*. If there is enough equity from the sale or transfer, the full amount of SMI loans plus the interest must be repaid. However, if the equity does not cover the total you owe, the remainder will be written off.

Repayment is also required when you die; if you have a partner and you are both legal owners of the property, repayment is required when you are both dead. In either case, repayment of the SMI loans can be made from your (or their) estate.

Once the SMI loans have been repaid in full, any charge that was placed on your property (see 7 above) will be removed.

You can voluntarily pay off some or all of the amount owed at any time before the sale (eg if you return to work). The minimum amount you can repay at any one time is normally £100. However, if the full amount of the SMI loans you owe is less than £100, you can pay this off in one go. There are no early-repayment fees.

If your property is sold for less than its market value, it will be treated as having been sold at its full market value for repayment purposes.

* this does not apply if the property is transferred to your partner in the event of your death and they continue to live there, or to you from a former spouse or civil partner under a court order or maintenance undertaking and you continue to live there

LMIR Regs, reg 16

# 27 Housing costs

| 1 | Introduction | 196 |
|---|---|---|
| 2 | Housing costs you can get help with | 196 |
| 3 | Waiting periods | 196 |
| 4 | If you are not entitled to the means-tested benefit during the waiting period | 197 |
| 5 | Once you have qualified for housing costs | 197 |

### 1. Introduction

The following means-tested benefits can help with certain housing costs:
- income-related employment and support allowance (ESA),
- income support;
- income-based jobseeker's allowance (JSA); *and*
- pension credit.

This chapter focuses on the help towards housing costs available through these benefits. If you are eligible for universal credit (see Box E.1, Chapter 14), your award of that benefit may include an amount to cover housing costs, the 'housing costs amount'. See Chapter 24(18) for details.

There is no longer any assistance through means-tested benefits towards the interest on mortgages or home improvement loans. Instead there is a new loans scheme to provide such help: *'support for mortgage interest loans'* – see Chapter 26 for details.

For the sake of simplicity, we generally confine the legal references to those applicable to income-related ESA and income support.

### When can housing costs be included?

Housing costs can be included in your award if you or your partner are liable for housing costs at the home you normally live in and the type of housing cost is covered. See 2 below for details.

ESA Regs, Sch 6, para 1(1); IS Regs, Sch 3, para 1(1)

You must normally have been entitled to the means-tested benefit for a number of weeks, the 'waiting period', before housing costs can be included in your award (see 3 below).

### Non-dependants

The amount towards your housing costs is reduced if you have any *'non-dependants'* living with you (eg adult son or daughter, friend or relative). It is assumed they will contribute towards your housing costs, whether they do or not. In some cases, your or your non-dependant's circumstances exempt you from the deduction; the rules are almost the same as for housing benefit (see Chapter 25(21)).

No deduction is made if a deduction for that non-dependant is already being made from your housing benefit. If a non-dependant deduction is also being made from your support for mortgage interest loans (see Chapter 26), the non-dependant deduction on your housing costs will be reduced by an equivalent amount.

ESA Regs, reg 71 & Sch 6, para 19; IS Regs; reg 3 & Sch 3, para 18

### Absence from home

Generally, you can get help on only one home at a time and this must be the home you occupy. In some situations, you are treated as occupying your home when you are not actually there – eg during a temporary absence or when moving home; the rules are almost the same as for housing benefit (see Chapter 25(6) and (7)).

ESA Regs, Sch 6, para 5; IS Regs, Sch 3, para 3

### 2. Housing costs you can get help with
### Liability for housing costs

You (or your partner) must be liable for housing costs for the home you live in. You will not get help with housing costs if the person you pay is a member of your household. If you share liability with someone else, you are normally treated as liable for your share only. If it is reasonable to do so, you can be treated as liable for the costs if the person normally liable is not paying them and you must pay them to carry on living in your home.

If someone living with you is liable for the housing costs and that person is not a close relative of you or your partner, you can be treated as sharing the costs if it is reasonable to do so. A *'close relative'* is a parent, parent-in-law, son, daughter, son-in-law or daughter-in-law, step-parent, stepson or stepdaughter, brother, sister or the partner of any of those.

ESA Regs, reg 2 & Sch 6, para 4; IS Regs, reg 2 & Sch 3, para 2

### Housing costs covered

The following housing costs can be included in your award:
- some service charges payable as a condition of your occupancy (eg under a lease) relating to the provision of adequate accommodation (CIS/1460/1995). House insurance can be included if payments are made under the terms of the lease, rather than as a condition of the mortgage (R(IS)4/92). Service charges for repairs and improvements are not met. Service charges are not met if they would be ineligible under the housing benefit rules (see Chapter 25(12));
- ground rent or other rent payable under a long lease of over 21 years;
- payments under a co-ownership scheme;
- rent if you are a Crown tenant;
- payments for a tent and site fees; *and*
- rent charges (sometimes due as a condition of a freehold).

ESA Regs, Sch 6, para 18; IS Regs, Sch 3, para 17

### 3. Waiting periods

From April 2016, there is generally a 39-week waiting period at the start of your entitlement to a means-tested benefit before housing costs are included in your award. This replaced a

13-week waiting period introduced on 5.1.09. Before 5.1.09 longer waiting periods were in place; for details, see *Disability Rights Handbook* 33rd edition, page 22.

The 39-week waiting period can sometimes start to run even if the means-tested benefit is not actually in payment. This would apply if, without the inclusion of housing costs, your income would exceed your applicable amount. Once you have claimed the benefit, you can be 'treated as entitled' to it and the waiting period will proceed. After 39 weeks, if you make a new claim for the benefit, the housing costs can be included in your award, and payment of the benefit may begin. See 4 below for details of when you can be treated as entitled to means-tested benefits.

The waiting period begins at the start of your benefit entitlement even if you have no housing costs at the time. So, if you incur eligible housing costs while on benefit, having already served the waiting period, housing costs can be included in your award immediately.

ESA Regs, Sch 6, para 9(1); IS Regs, Sch 3, para 8(1); JSA Regs, Sch 2, paras 7(1); HCSA(A&M) Regs; HCA Regs, reg 8

### No waiting period
The waiting period does not apply to claims for pension credit. For income-related employment and support allowance and income support, if your partner has reached pension credit qualifying age (see Chapter 44(2)), or, for income-based jobseeker's allowance, you or your partner have reached that age, housing costs are included in your award from the start of your benefit entitlement, or from the day they reach the qualifying age if this happens when you are part-way through the waiting period. There is no waiting period for help with payments under a co-ownership scheme, rent for a Crown tenant or tent payments.

ESA Regs, Sch 6, para 10; IS Regs, Sch 3, para 9; JSA Regs, Sch 2, para 8; HCSA(A&M) Regs

## 4. If you are not entitled to the means-tested benefit during the waiting period
Throughout the waiting period, you must usually be entitled to the means-tested benefit, although breaks in entitlement of up to 12 weeks are ignored. In the following circumstances you can be treated as entitled to the means-tested benefit.

### During a break in claims, or if there is a change of claimant
You are treated as entitled to the means-tested benefit:
■ during a gap in entitlement of 12 weeks or less;
■ during a gap between claims of up to 52 weeks if you are protected under the back-to-work linking rule, or up to 104 weeks if you are a *'work or training beneficiary'* (see 5 below);
■ for any period in which it is decided retrospectively that you were entitled to the benefit (eg following an appeal);
■ during any time your partner was getting (or treated as getting) the benefit for both of you if you swap to become the claimant instead;
■ during a gap between claims while you or your partner were on certain government training schemes;
■ for any period in which your ex-partner was getting (or treated as getting) the benefit for both of you, if you claim within 12 weeks of separating;
■ for any period in which someone was claiming the benefit for you as their dependent child, if you claim within 12 weeks of the end of the claim and your claim includes a child who was also their dependant; *or*
■ for any period in which your new partner was getting (or treated as getting) the benefit as a single person or lone parent, if you claim within 12 weeks of becoming a couple.
In the last three cases, the 12-week linking period is extended to 52 weeks if the back-to-work linking rule applies, or to 104

weeks if you (or, in the last case, your partner) are a *'work or training beneficiary'* (see 5 below).

ESA Regs, Sch 6, para 15; IS Regs, Sch 3, para 14; JSA Regs, Sch 2, para 13

You are treated as entitled to and receiving income-related employment and support allowance (ESA) during any time you have received income support, income-based jobseeker's allowance (JSA) or pension credit, or during any break in entitlement to those benefits (as listed above). You are treated as entitled to and receiving income-based JSA during any time you have received income support or income-related ESA (including entitlement breaks listed above). You are treated as entitled to and receiving income support during any time you have received income-based JSA or income-related ESA (including entitlement breaks listed above).

ESA Regs, Sch 6, para 20(1)(c); JSA Regs, Sch 2, para 18(1)(c); Income Support (Jobseeker's Allowance Consequential Amendments) Regs 1996, reg 32

### If your income or capital is over the limit
If you cannot get the means-tested benefit only because your income is equal to or higher than your applicable amount (including, in the case of income-related ESA or income-based JSA, if you have contributory ESA or contribution-based JSA equal to or higher than your applicable amount) and/or your capital is over £16,000, you are treated as entitled to the benefit for up to 39 weeks if you meet one of the following conditions on each day (but gaps of up to 12 weeks are allowed):
■ you are entitled to contributory ESA, contribution-based JSA, statutory sick pay or incapacity benefit; *or*
■ you are entitled to national insurance credits for incapacity for work, limited capability for work or unemployment; *or*
■ you are treated as entitled to the benefit during a break in claims, or a change of claimant (see above); *or*
■ you are a single parent or eligible for income support as a carer – provided:
  – you are not working 16 hours or more a week; *and*
  – your partner (if you are a carer) is not working 24 hours or more a week; *and*
  – you are not a full-time student excluded from income support or JSA (or, in the case of income-related ESA, receiving disability living allowance, personal independence payment or armed forces independence payment); *and*
  – you are not absent from the UK other than in the circumstances described in Chapter 54(8).
You must have claimed and been refused benefit and then reclaim after the waiting period. The 39 weeks run from when your unsuccessful claim is made, so don't delay claiming.
If you have an insurance policy taken out to cover against the risk of being unable to meet the housing costs, the 39 weeks is extended to cover the period that payments are made under the policy, provided your capital is within the limit of £16,000 throughout.

ESA Regs, Sch 6, para 15(8)-(12); IS Regs, Sch 3, para 14(4)-(6); JSA Regs, Sch 2, para 13(5)-(9)

## 5. Once you have qualified for housing costs
You will not have to serve the waiting period again if you have a break in your claim of 12 weeks or less, or longer if you are still treated as entitled to benefit (see 4 above).
**Back-to-work linking rule** – If your means-tested benefit stops because you or your partner start work (employed or self-employed) or because your working hours or earnings increase, you do not have to serve the waiting period again on a new claim if the break in claims is no more than 52 weeks. Housing costs can be included from the start of your new claim. You will get similar protection if you take part in certain government training schemes that take you off the benefit.

ESA Regs, Sch 6, para 15(16)-(17); IS Regs, Sch 3, para 14(11)-(12); JSA Regs, Sch 2, para 13(13)-(14)

**Work or training beneficiary** – If you are moving into work or training from employment and support allowance (ESA), you may be covered by a more generous 104-week linking rule if you are a *'work or training beneficiary'*. This applies if you had a limited capability for work for more than 13 weeks in your previous ESA claim and you started work or training within one month of ceasing to be entitled to ESA. This rule does not apply if the reason for your previous ESA award ending was that you were found not to have a limited capability for work.
ESA Regs, Sch 6, paras 1(3A)-(3C) & 15(15)

**Starting work** – When you start work, or increase your hours or earnings, and so lose entitlement to income-related ESA, income-based jobseeker's allowance or income support, you may continue to get housing costs, payable as income support, for the first four weeks (see Chapter 33(4)).

**Insurance payments** – If you have a break in your claim of 26 weeks or less and payments from an insurance policy for unemployment have run out, your two claims are linked and the period in between, when you were receiving the insurance payments, is ignored. Consequently, housing costs will resume from the start of your linked claim.
ESA Regs, Sch 6, paras 15(13)-(14); IS Regs, Sch 3, para 14(8)-(9); JSA Regs, Sch 2, para 13(10)-(11)

# 28 Council tax

| | | |
|---|---|---|
| 1 | What is council tax? | 198 |
| 2 | Your dwelling | 198 |
| 3 | How much council tax? | 198 |
| 4 | Exempt dwellings | 198 |
| 5 | Who is liable to pay? | 198 |
| | Summary of council tax exemptions for dwellings – Box G.10 | 199 |
| | People who are disregarded for council tax discount purposes – Box G.11 | 200 |
| 6 | Who is a resident of a dwelling? | 199 |
| 7 | How to pay less council tax | 199 |
| 8 | Disability Reduction scheme | 200 |
| 9 | Discount scheme | 201 |
| 10 | Second homes and long-term empty properties | 201 |
| 11 | Appeals | 201 |
| 12 | Council tax reduction scheme | 201 |
| | For more information – Box G.12 | 201 |

## 1. What is council tax?
Council tax is a domestic property-based tax paid to the local authority to help pay for the services it provides. It applies only in England, Scotland and Wales. Domestic rates are payable in Northern Ireland.

## 2. Your dwelling
Council tax is only charged on domestic properties or 'dwellings'. A *'dwelling'* is a self-contained unit of living accommodation, such as a house, flat, bungalow, houseboat or mobile home. It does not matter whether the dwelling is owned or rented. One council tax bill is due on each dwelling, unless it is exempt (see 4 below). If a property is divided into self-contained units (eg flats), each unit is a separate dwelling and gets a separate bill (unless exempt). If a property contains units that are not self-contained (eg a house with a number of rooms with different people in each, but they all share some accommodation) the property is one dwelling and gets one bill (unless exempt). A self-contained unit is defined as *'a building or part of a building which has been constructed or adapted for use as separate living accommodation'*. If a property contains living and business accommodation, council tax is due for the domestic part (unless exempt) and the business part is subject to non-domestic rates.
LGFA, Ss.4(2) & 72(2); Council Tax (Chargeable Dwellings) Order

## 3. How much council tax?
### Council tax valuation bands
Every property in a local authority area is placed in a valuation band, labelled from A (the lowest) to H (the highest) (or A to I in Wales), depending on its value. The higher the band, the more council tax you are liable to pay.

The value of a dwelling does not relate to its current market value. In England and Scotland, it is based on 1991 property values; in Wales, 2003 property values.

In England and Wales, dwellings are valued by the Valuation Office Agency (VOA), and in Scotland by the local assessor. These bodies also decide what counts as a dwelling and how many dwellings there are in a property.
LGFA, Ss.5(2)-(3) & 74(2)

### Challenges and appeals
You have the right to challenge the valuation of your dwelling if, within six months, you have become newly liable for council tax there (eg through moving) or if there has been a material reduction in its value (eg through partial demolition or its adaptation for use by a disabled person). You can also ask for a change if part of the property begins to be used for business purposes.

In England and Wales, if the VOA does not agree to the change, you can appeal to the independent Valuation Tribunal. An appeal must be made within three months of receiving the decision. In Scotland, if the local assessor does not agree to the change, they will refer the proposal to the Valuation Appeal Committee.

If the property is rebranded to a lower council tax band, you will be entitled to a refund of any 'overpaid' council tax, back to the date when you became liable to pay council tax on the dwelling.
*Holdsworth v Bradford MBC* [2015] RA 559

You can also appeal within six months of a successful challenge on a comparable dwelling (eg another property on the same street or on a new estate), if this suggests that the value of your own property should be changed.

In other circumstances, you can ask the VOA or local assessor to reconsider the band for your dwelling and, if it is wrong, they may alter it. But if they do not agree, you do not have the right of appeal.

## 4. Exempt dwellings
If a home is an exempt dwelling, no council tax is due on it. Most exemptions are for unoccupied dwellings. The main conditions for exemptions are given in Box G.10.

If your local authority has not awarded an exemption, you can ask for one. An exemption can be backdated to the date it should have first applied. There is no time limit and no need to show 'good cause' for applying late but you will need to produce evidence that the exemption has applied throughout the period. You can appeal against a decision on exemption (see 11 below).

## 5. Who is liable to pay?
Unless a dwelling is exempt, someone will be liable to pay council tax on it. This usually depends on who is resident there (see 6 below). The rules for the dwelling in which you are resident are given below. If you own or rent a dwelling that has no residents, you are usually liable for council tax there (whether or not you are also liable on the dwelling in which you are resident).

**Backdating** – If you were liable for council tax in the past but were not billed, a bill can be backdated. There is no time limit, but local authorities must issue bills as soon as is reasonably practicable.

**Appeals** – See 11 below.

## General rules for the dwelling in which you reside

The following rules apply to the dwelling in which you are resident (see 6 below). A partner, as referred to below, includes a partner of the same sex.

If you own the dwelling, you are liable for council tax. Your partner, if they live with you, is jointly liable with you (even if not a joint owner). Any other joint owners who live with you are also jointly liable.

If you rent the dwelling and do not have a resident landlord, you are liable for council tax. Your partner, if they live with you, is jointly liable with you (even if they are not included on the letting agreement). Any other residents who rent the dwelling on the same letting agreement are also jointly liable.

A tenant who abandons a property without ending the tenancy by lawful notice can still be held liable for council tax for the period afterwards.

*Leeds City Council v Broadley* [2016] EWCA Civ 1213

The landlord is liable in the following cases:

- if you rent from a resident landlord;
- if it is a care home, or (in most cases) a hostel;
- if you rent accommodation that is not self-contained and/ or any others who rent it have separate letting agreements (even if the landlord does not live there); *or*
- if you are an asylum seeker receiving asylum support (other than temporary support) from either the government or the local authority.

LGFA, Ss.6, 8, 75 & 76

### Special cases

If you and all other occupiers are *'severely mentally impaired'* (see Box G.11) or are students, the dwelling in which you live is exempt (see Box G.10). If anyone else lives with you, including carers, the property will not be exempt, but you may be eligible for a discount (see 9 below).

If you are aged under 18, you are not liable for council tax on any dwelling in which you live. Other resident(s) aged 18 or over are liable instead. If there are none, the dwelling is exempt (see Box G.10).

## 6. Who is a resident of a dwelling?

You are a *'resident'* of a dwelling if it is your *'sole or main residence'*. You can only be a resident of one dwelling at a time. Deciding where you are resident is usually straightforward. In difficult cases, the local authority should take into account how much time you spend at different addresses, where you work, where your children go to school, how much security of tenure you have at different addresses, and other relevant information. You can appeal against a decision about where you are resident (see 11 below).

LGFA, Ss.6(5) & 99(1)

## 7. How to pay less council tax

There are three schemes for reducing council tax bills. You can get help through all three at the same time if you meet the

---

## G.10 Summary of council tax exemptions for dwellings

*Note:* Local authorities have to take reasonable steps to check whether any discounts apply before deciding on the amount to charge.

❑ **An unoccupied dwelling (whether furnished or not) can be exempt if it is:**
- left empty by someone in prison or a similar institution;
- left empty by someone now living in a hospital, a care home or a hostel where personal care is provided;
- left empty by someone now living elsewhere so they can receive or provide personal care due to old age, disablement, illness, past or present alcohol or drug dependence, or past or present mental illness or disorder;
- left empty by someone who has died, where probate or letters of administration have not been granted, or less than six months have passed since the granting of probate or letters of administration;
- left empty by a student owner;
- the responsibility of a bankrupt's trustees;
- to be occupied by ministers of religion; *or*
- a pitch or mooring that is not occupied by a caravan or boat.

❑ **A dwelling is also exempt if it is:**
- wholly occupied by a person (or persons) who is *'severely mentally impaired'* (see Box G.11) and no one else could be liable. You do not lose the exemption if a student or students also occupy the dwelling;
- wholly occupied by people under the age of 18;
- unoccupied, and is part of a single property containing another dwelling where someone lives, and letting it separately would be a breach of planning control (or, in Scotland, the dwelling would be difficult to let separately);
- in Scotland and is a housing association trial flat for pensioners or for people with disabilities;

- unoccupied and occupation is legally prohibited (eg it is unfit for habitation or subject to a compulsory purchase order);
- unoccupied and a planning condition prevents occupancy;
- under charitable ownership and has been unoccupied for less than six months;
- an armed forces barracks or married quarters or used as visiting forces accommodation;
- a repossessed property where the property is unoccupied;
- a student hall of residence; *or*
- currently wholly occupied by students (including students temporarily absent from their course).

❑ **In Wales and Scotland only**
**A substantially unfurnished, unoccupied dwelling is exempt if:**
- structural or major repair works are needed, are in hand, or have been completed recently (for up to 12 months in total); *or*
- it is unoccupied for any other reason (which could be that it has just been built) and has been for less than six months.

❑ **In England and Wales only**
An exemption applies where there are at least two dwellings (ie two self-contained units) within a single property and one occupant is a *'dependent relative'* of someone who lives in another part of the property. The exemption applies only to the part of the property where the dependent relative lives. The definition of 'relative' is quite straightforward and includes quite distant relatives (eg great-great-grandchild) and common-law relations. If there is a dispute about your status as a relative, seek advice. The dependent relative must be:
- aged 65 or over; *or*
- *'severely mentally impaired'* (see Box G.11); *or*
- *'substantially and permanently disabled'*, the definition of which is open to wide interpretation.

*Council Tax (Exempt Dwellings) Order 1992 (as amended); &*
*Council Tax (Exempt Dwellings)(Scotland) Order 1997, Sch 1*

conditions for all of them. The schemes are:

- the Disability Reduction scheme (see 8 below);
- the discount scheme (see 9 below);
- the council tax reduction scheme (see 12 below).

Some dwellings are exempt from council tax (see 4 above).

## 8. Disability Reduction scheme

You can get a disability reduction if you or any other *'resident'* (see 6 above) in your dwelling is *'substantially and permanently disabled'*. This can be an adult or a child of any age, whether or not they are related to you.

At least one of the following three conditions must also be met:

- you have an additional bathroom or kitchen needed by the disabled person; *or*
- you have a room (other than a bathroom, kitchen or toilet) needed by and predominantly used by that person; *or*
- you have enough space in your dwelling for that person to use a wheelchair indoors.

Disability reductions are available in all types of dwellings, including care homes and hostels.

In Scotland, water charges (collected with the council tax) can also be reduced under this scheme.

Council Tax (Reductions for Disabilities) Regulations

There is no general test of who counts as *'substantially and permanently disabled'*, although it is clear that it includes

---

### G.11 People who are disregarded for council tax discount purposes

#### People who are 'severely mentally impaired'

This means anyone who:

- *'has a severe impairment of intelligence and social functioning (however caused) which appears to be permanent'; and*
- has a certificate from a registered medical practitioner confirming this (which may cover a past, present or future period); *and*
- is entitled to one of the following benefits:
  - disability living allowance (DLA) middle or highest rate care component;
  - personal independence payment (PIP) daily living component (either rate) or armed forces independence payment (AFIP);
  - attendance allowance, constant attendance allowance (or an equivalent benefit);
  - employment and support allowance (ESA) in Scotland, but see below for England and Wales;
  - incapacity benefit;
  - severe disablement allowance;
  - income support including a disability premium due to incapacity, or whose partner has a disability premium for them included in their income-based jobseeker's allowance;
  - universal credit including the work capability amount;
  - the disabled worker element of working tax credit; *or*
- is over state pension age and would have been entitled to one of the above benefits if under state pension age.

*Note:* When ESA was introduced in 2008, the DWP stated that ESA would be a qualifying benefit. Although council tax legislation has not been amended, your local authority may still treat ESA as a qualifying benefit – if it doesn't, you can appeal the decision (see 11 in this chapter).

#### Carers

A carer is disregarded if they meet all the following conditions; they:

- provide care for at least 35 hours a week on average. The law refers to *'care'*, not *'support'*;
- are 'resident' (see 6 in this chapter) in the same dwelling as the person cared for;
- are not the partner of the person cared for;
- are not the parent of the person cared for, if the person cared for is aged under 18; *and*
- care for a person who is entitled to one of the following:
  - middle or highest rate DLA care component (only the highest rate in Scotland);
  - either rate of the PIP daily living component (only the enhanced rate in Scotland) or AFIP; *or*
  - either rate of attendance allowance (only the higher rate in Scotland) or constant attendance allowance.

#### People in hospital, a care home or certain kinds of hostel

People whose sole or main residence is a hospital or care home are disregarded (ie a short stay does not count). People in hostels who have no residence elsewhere are also disregarded; this includes bail or probation hostels along with night shelters and other similar accommodation.

#### Anyone whose 'sole or main residence' is elsewhere

Anyone whose sole or main residence is with someone else or who is living in another institute (not a hospital or care home) to receive care is disregarded. For where someone is 'resident', see 6 in this chapter.

#### Young people, students, student nurses, youth trainees, apprentices and others

The following individuals or groups are ignored:

- everyone aged 17 or under;
- 18-19-year-olds for whom child benefit is payable (see Chapter 41(1));
- education-leavers aged under 20 (but only if they left on or after 1 May, and then only until 31 October inclusive that year);
- school or college-level students aged under 20, if their term-time study normally amounts to 12 or more hours a week;
- students, if their study amounts to at least an average of 21 hours a week for periods of at least 24 weeks a year;
- student nurses whose academic course means they count as a 'student', or who are studying for their first nursing registration;
- foreign language assistants;
- trainees under the age of 25 on training funded by the Skills Funding Agency or Education Funding Agency;
- apprentices undertaking training that leads to an accredited qualification (eg an NVQ), subject to limitations on pay;
- people in prison or similar institutions;
- members of a religious community that provides for all the individuals' needs;
- members of some international organisations or visiting forces;
- foreign spouses and dependants of students;
- diplomats and their spouses.

*Council Tax (Discount Disregards) Order 1992;*
*Council Tax (Additional Provisions for Discount Disregards) Regs 1992;*
*Council Tax (Discounts)(Scotland) Order 1992;*
*Council Tax (Disregards)(Scotland) Regs 1992 – each as amended*

people who have been disabled for life and also those who have become disabled later in life. There is also no general test of what it means for the disabled person to 'need' the room or the wheelchair, except that they must be *essential or of major importance to [his or her] well-being by reason of the nature and extent of [his or her] disability'*.

However, it is clear that disability reductions are not limited to dwellings specially constructed or adapted to provide a room or wheelchair space.

The Sandwell High Court judgment has been misinterpreted by many authorities as denying a reduction to disabled people who use another room instead of a dedicated bedroom. In fact, the judgment simply emphasised that there must be an *'appropriative causative link between the disability and the requirement of the use of the room, because the use has to be essential or of major importance, because of the nature and extent of the disability'*. This has been further clarified in a more recent decision, which states that the room must be extra or additional, in the sense that it would not be required for the relevant purpose if the person were not disabled.
*R (Sandwell MDC) v Perks* [2003] EWHC 1749 (Admin); *South Gloucestershire Council v Titley & Clothier* [2006] EWHC 3117 (Admin)

**How much is it worth?** – If you qualify for a disability reduction, your council tax bill is reduced to the amount payable for a dwelling in the valuation band below yours. If your dwelling is in band A, your bill is reduced by one-sixth.

**Getting a reduction and backdating** – The person liable for council tax (not necessarily the disabled person) has to make an application. The local authority may have a standard form for this (and in some areas you may have to make a separate application for each financial year). If you should have been given a disability reduction in the past, but were not, it should be backdated, but backdating may be limited to six years.
Council Tax (Reductions for Disabilities) Regulations, reg 3(1)(b); *Arca v Carlisle City Council* [2013] RA 248

You can appeal against a decision on disability reductions (see 11 below).

## 9. Discount scheme
The council tax discount scheme is applied to dwellings where fewer than two adults are resident (see 6 above). You can get a discount if:
■ there is only one resident in your dwelling: in this case your discount equals 25% of your council tax liability; *or*
■ there are no residents in your dwelling: in this case your discount may be up to 50% of your council tax liability (but see 10 below). If your home is empty, you may qualify for exemption instead of a discount (see 4 above).
LGFA, Ss.11 & 79

**Counting the residents** – Several groups of people are 'disregarded' when counting the number of residents in your dwelling; they are sometimes called 'invisible'. See Box G.11.

**The second adult rebate** – A discount (known as the *'second adult rebate'*) is also available if the gross income of the other resident is low enough. If the other person is on income-based jobseeker's allowance, income-related employment and support allowance or income support, the discount is 25%; if their gross income is under £193 a week, the discount is 15% and if their gross income is between £193 and £249 (inclusive), the discount is 7½ %.
Council Tax Reduction Schemes (Prescribed Requirements) (England) Regulations 2012, Sch 3

**Getting a discount and backdating** – Your local authority may automatically grant a discount, but you can also apply for one. They may have a standard form. A discount can normally be backdated to the date it should have first applied. There is no time limit within which you can apply for the discount, but backdating may be limited to six years.
*Arca v Carlisle City Council* [2013] RA 248

You can appeal against a decision on discounts (see 11 below).

## 10. Second homes and long-term empty properties
In Scotland, local authorities have the power to reduce the discount offered on furnished second homes from 50% to just 10%. In England and Wales, authorities have discretion to reduce the discount below 50% or to offer no discount at all. People who need to live elsewhere because of their (or their partner's) job, including armed forces personnel who have to live in alternative accommodation provided by the Ministry of Defence, receive an automatic discount of at least 50% on their home.

Properties that have been unoccupied and substantially unfurnished for more than two years may not qualify for a discount and the council tax may be increased by up to 50%.
LGFA, S.11B; The Council Tax (Prescribed Classes of Dwellings) Regs; The Council Tax (Discount for Unoccupied Dwellings) (Scotland) Regs 2005

## 11. Appeals
You have the right to appeal against decisions on:
■ whether a dwelling is exempt from council tax;
■ who is liable to pay council tax;
■ where you are resident;
■ whether a disability reduction applies; *and*
■ whether a discount applies.

The appeal should first go to the local authority. There is no time limit for lodging the appeal. If it is refused, you can appeal to the Valuation Tribunal for England or the Valuation Tribunal for Wales (within two months of receiving the decision, or within four months of your original appeal if the authority has not responded) or Valuation Appeal Committee in Scotland (within four months of your original appeal).

## 12. Council tax reduction scheme
From April 2013 a new *'council tax reduction scheme'* was introduced. This replaced council tax benefit (see *Disability Rights Handbook 37th edition*, Chapter 20). Since the new scheme came with a UK-wide 10% drop in funding, many claimants are substantially worse off; others, in particular those over pension credit qualifying age, are protected (see below). There are different arrangements in England, Scotland and Wales.

### England and Wales
In England and Wales, each local authority must have a council tax reduction scheme in place, subject to certain conditions. Because each authority has a different scheme, we cannot describe each one in detail. Below, we describe the general requirements of local schemes, but you should contact your local authority, your local Citizens Advice or other advice agency, for details of the scheme in your area. You can also use the Law Society online tool: http://counciltaxhelp.net/
The Council Tax Reduction Schemes (Default Scheme)(England) Regs 2012; The Council Tax Reduction Schemes (Default Scheme)(Wales) Regs 2013

**How do the schemes operate?** – Local schemes operate either by allowing a percentage discount or by calculating an amount of money to be allowed as a discount. The discount

---

### G.12 For more information

Your local Citizens Advice has information on housing benefit and council tax reduction schemes and should be able to advise you. If you want to look at the law, see CPAG's *Housing Benefit and Council Tax Reduction Legislation*. For further information, see the publications listed in Chapter 60.

can be for the full amount of the council tax or for a lower amount.

In England, most authorities have chosen to require all liable people under pension credit qualifying age (see Chapter 44(2)) to pay something.

In Wales, authorities are able to be more generous, as the Welsh government is making up for the 10% drop in funding.

More generous rules apply if you have reached pension credit qualifying age (see below).

If you have capital over £16,000, you are not eligible for council tax reduction. Nor are you eligible if you are subject to immigration control, are not habitually resident or do not have the right to reside in the UK (see Chapter 53).

Some local schemes have reduced the upper capital limit to below £16,000, increased non-dependant deductions, set a minimum income floor for the self-employed, applied a two-child limit, limited or removed entitlement to backdating and the second adult rebate or set their own rates for some or all of the allowances and premiums in the calculation.

The reduction scheme applies after any reductions have been applied under the Disability Reduction scheme (see 8 above) or the discount scheme (see 9 above).

**If you are over pension credit qualifying age** – The government has set out detailed rules which English and Welsh local authorities must follow. These are similar to the rules for housing benefit. A maximum council tax reduction is calculated, based on the council tax you are liable for, minus any deductions for non-dependants (see Chapter 25(21); although lower figures are used than for housing benefit). An applicable amount is calculated and your income and capital assessed (see Chapter 25(25)). If your income is less than the applicable amount, you are entitled to maximum council tax reduction. If your income is greater than your applicable amount, you are entitled to a reduction equal to your maximum council tax reduction minus 20% of your excess income.

The Council Tax Reduction Schemes (Prescribed Requirements) (England) Regs 2012; The Council Tax Reduction Schemes & Prescribed Requirements (Wales) Regs 2013

**Claims, reviews and appeals** – Local authorities must accept claims in writing, and can accept them online or by phone. All decisions on council tax reduction must be put in writing. If you are unhappy with a decision, you can ask the authority to review it. If you are not satisfied with the outcome of the review, you can appeal to the Valuation Tribunal for England or the Valuation Tribunal for Wales.

You cannot appeal a decision to recover an overpayment of council tax reduction to a Valuation Tribunal. You can, however, apply for a discretionary reduction to reduce the liability for the same period (see below). If this is refused, you have a right of appeal to the Valuation Tribunal.
*DG v Liverpool City Council* [VTE, 4310M140277/CTR, 11 January 2016]

**Discretionary reduction scheme** – Your local authority can make a discretionary reduction to further reduce your council tax bill if you would otherwise suffer hardship. If you have a disability which means it is unlikely that you could return to work, this could be a *'strong case'* to be awarded 100% support. If you are refused a discretionary reduction, you can appeal to a Valuation Tribunal.

LGFA, S.13A(1)(c); *SC v East Riding of Yorks Council* [2014] EW Misc B46 (VT); Practice Statement VTE/PS/A11 (11.8.15), paras 25-30; *R(Logan) v LB Havering* [2015] EWHC 3193 (Admin), para 43

### Scotland

The Scottish government has sought to protect claimants from the UK-wide 10% drop in funding by making up the difference. Hence, a single system replicates the old council tax benefit system. It is similar to housing benefit.

A maximum council tax reduction is calculated based on the council tax you are liable for, minus deductions for non-dependants (see Chapter 25(21), although lower figures are used than for housing benefit). An applicable amount is calculated (see Chapter 25(24), although the two-child limit will not apply) and your income and capital assessed (see Chapter 25(22) and (23)). If you receive universal credit and your income frequently fluctuates, an estimate can be made of your income and the universal credit payable.

There is similar provision if you are over pension credit qualifying age (see Chapter 25(25)).

If your income is less than the applicable amount, you are entitled to maximum council tax reduction. If your income is greater than your applicable amount, you are entitled to a reduction equal to your maximum council tax reduction minus 20% of your excess income.

Awards can be backdated for up to six months.
The Council Tax Reduction (Scotland) Regulations 2012

**Reviews** – If you are unhappy with a decision, you can ask the local authority to review it within two months. If you are not satisfied with the outcome of the review, you can request a further review within 42 days, to be heard by an independent Council Tax Reduction Review Panel.
The Council Tax Reduction (Scotland) Amendment (No.2) Regulations 2013

---

This section of the handbook looks at:

| | |
|---|---|
| The social fund | Chapter **29** |
| Housing grants | Chapter **30** |
| Other loans and grants | Chapter **31** |

# Grants and loans

# 29 The social fund

| | | |
|---|---|---|
| 1 | What is the social fund? | 203 |
| 2 | Sure Start maternity grants | 203 |
| 3 | Funeral payments | 203 |
| 4 | Cold weather payments | 204 |
| 5 | Winter fuel payment | 204 |

## 1. What is the social fund?

The social fund makes payments to cover specific costs, eg Sure Start maternity grants and funeral, cold weather and winter fuel payments. You are legally entitled to a payment if you are eligible for one. If you disagree with a decision, you can ask for a mandatory reconsideration and, if you are unhappy with the result of this, you can appeal to a tribunal (see Chapter 57).

## 2. Sure Start maternity grants

You are entitled to a *'Sure Start maternity grant'* of £500 if:
- you:
  - (or a member of your family) are pregnant or have given birth in the last three months (including stillbirth after 24 weeks of pregnancy);
  - (or your partner) have had a child under the age of 1 placed with you for adoption;
  - (or your partner) have been appointed a guardian of, or have adopted (including a recognised adoption outside the UK), or been granted a child arrangements order for, a child under the age of 1;
  - (or your partner) have been granted a parental order for a child born to a surrogate mother; *or*
  - are the parent (but not the mother or her partner) of a child under the age of 1, and are responsible for the child; *and*
- there is no other member of your family who is under the age of 16 (excluding any you have adopted or become responsible for as a foster or kinship carer, provided that the child(ren) was over the age of 1 when you became responsible for them), although a grant can be awarded for each child of a multiple birth where there is no other child under 16. If you have a multiple birth and you have another child under 16, a grant can be awarded for each child in that multiple birth less the number of children born to a single pregnancy already in your household: eg if you give birth to triplets but already have twins under 16 you can be awarded just one grant. If you are claiming for someone under the age of 20 who is the parent of the child, the grant is payable provided the parent has no other children under 16; *and*
- you or your partner are receiving one of the following *'qualifying benefits'* on the day you claim the maternity grant:
  - income support;*
  - pension credit;*
  - income-based jobseeker's allowance;*
  - income-related employment and support allowance;*
  - child tax credit that includes a child element or disabled child element;

  - working tax credit that includes the disabled worker element or severe disability element; *or*
  - universal credit; *and*
- you have received health and welfare advice about child health matters and, if applying before the birth, advice about maternal health; *and*
- you claim within the time limits (see below).

\* you are treated as receiving one of these benefits if you are entitled to support for mortgage interest loans
SFM&FE Regs, regs 5 and 5A

Claim on form SF100, available from the DWP or your antenatal clinic. You must claim in the 11 weeks before the week your baby is due, or in the three months following the date of the birth or adoption, guardianship, child arrangements order or parental order. In the case of adoption, guardianship and child arrangements orders, the child must be under the age of 1 at the date of claim. If you are waiting for a decision on a qualifying benefit, you must still claim within the time limit and if your claim is refused because you are not yet getting the qualifying benefit, you should re-claim within three months of it being awarded.
C&P Regs, Sch 4, para 8

In Scotland, the Sure Start maternity grant is due to be replaced from summer 2019 by a new, expanded *'Best Start grant'*.

## 3. Funeral payments

You are entitled to a funeral payment if:
- you or your partner accept responsibility for the costs of a funeral (ie you have paid or are liable to pay them) that takes place in the UK (or in another European Economic Area country – see Chapter 53(1) or Switzerland if you or a member of your family are classified as a 'worker' or have the right to reside in the UK under European Community law – see Chapter 53(5)); *and*
- you or your partner are receiving a 'qualifying benefit' on the day you claim a funeral payment. These are the same as for Sure Start maternity grants (see 2 above) but also include housing benefit; *and*
- the deceased was ordinarily resident in the UK when they died; *and*
- you claim within the time limits (see below); *and*
- you fall into one of the groups of people who are eligible to claim (see below).

SFM&FE Regs, reg 7

### Who can claim?

You must fall into one of the following groups.
- ❏ You were the partner of the deceased when they died or immediately before either of you moved permanently into a care home. 'Partner' includes opposite and same-sex couples whether or not you were married or in a civil partnership.
- ❏ The deceased was a child you were responsible for and there is no 'absent parent' (unless they were getting one of the above qualifying benefits when the child died), or the deceased was a stillborn child.
- ❏ You were a close relative or close friend of the deceased and it is reasonable for you to accept responsibility for the

funeral costs, given the nature and extent of your contact with the deceased. *'Close relative'* means parent (or parent-in-law), son (-in-law), daughter (-in-law), brother (-in-law), sister (-in-law), stepson/daughter (-in-law) or step-parent.

You cannot get a payment as a close relative or friend of the deceased if:

- the deceased had a partner when they died; *or*
- there is a parent, son or daughter of the deceased who is not:
  - getting a qualifying benefit (see above); *or*
  - in prison or hospital immediately following a period on a qualifying benefit; *or*
  - a person resident in a care home whose costs are met in whole or in part by a local authority; *or*
  - aged under 18, or 18-19 and a qualifying young person (see Chapter 41(1)); *or*
  - aged 18 or over and in full-time education; *or*
  - a fully maintained member of a religious order; *or*
  - someone who was estranged from the deceased; *or*
  - receiving asylum support; *or*
  - ordinarily resident outside the UK; *or*
- there is a close relative (see above) of the deceased, other than a person who falls into one of the groups above, who was in closer contact with the deceased than you were, or had equally close contact and is not getting a qualifying benefit.

SFM&FE Regs, reg 7 & 8

### How much do you get?
The following costs can be met (in each case, if necessary):

- the costs of obtaining a new burial plot plus burial fees or the costs of cremation including medical fees, and the costs of obtaining documentation in connection with the disposal of the body;
- the cost of documentation needed to release the deceased's assets;
- the reasonable costs of transport for the portion of journeys in excess of 80 kilometres undertaken to transport the body within the UK to a funeral directors or a place of rest and to transport the coffin, bearers and mourners in two vehicles to the funeral;
- the costs of one return journey from your home for you or your partner to arrange or attend the funeral if you are responsible for the funeral costs; *and*
- up to £700 for other funeral expenses (or £120 if you have a pre-paid funeral plan that doesn't cover these expenses).

The following amounts are deducted from an award of a funeral payment (note that a funeral payment is recoverable from the deceased's estate):

- any of the deceased's assets that are available to you without probate or letters of administration (arrears of most benefits and tax credits are ignored here), although if you have a joint account with the deceased, the assets become yours at the point of death and cannot be deducted;
- any lump sum due to you or a member of your family on the death of the deceased from an insurance policy, occupational or war pension, burial club or similar scheme; *and*
- any amount from a pre-paid funeral plan or similar scheme.

SFM&FE Regs, regs 9 & 10

### How and when to claim
You must claim within six months of the funeral. Use form SF200, available from a Jobcentre Plus office or the DWP Bereavement Service (0800 731 0469; textphone 0800 731 0464; Northern Ireland: 0800 085 2463). If you are waiting for a decision on a qualifying benefit, the rules are the same as for Sure Start maternity grants (see 2 above).

C&P Regs, Sch 4, para 9

In Scotland, funeral payments are due to be replaced by a new *'funeral expense assistance'* from summer 2019.

## 4. Cold weather payments
These are automatic payments (you do not need to claim) of £25 for each qualifying week made by the DWP if:

- the average temperature recorded or forecast over seven consecutive days at the designated weather station for your area is 0°C (freezing) or less; *and*
- you have been awarded income support\*, income-based jobseeker's allowance\* (JSA) or income-related employment and support allowance\* (ESA) for at least one of those days and you are responsible for a child under the age of 5, or you are getting child tax credit that includes the disabled child element, or your income support, JSA or ESA includes one of the disability or pensioner premiums; *or*
- you have been awarded universal credit and have a child under the age of 5, or your award includes a disabled child addition in the child amount, or you have been assessed as having (or treated as having) a limited capability for work or limited capability for work-related activity, and you are not in employment or gainful self-employment during the qualifying week (although this does not apply if your award includes the disabled child addition); *or*
- you have been awarded pension credit; *or*
- you have been awarded income-related ESA and you have been assessed as having (or treated as having) a limited capability for work or limited capability for work-related activity for at least one of those days; *and*
- you are not resident in a care home.

\* you are treated as receiving one of these benefits if you are entitled to support for mortgage interest loans

Social Fund Cold Weather Payments Regs

## 5. Winter fuel payment
This is a lump sum paid if you have reached pension credit qualifying age (see Chapter 44(2)) in the *'qualifying week'* (the week beginning 17.9.18 for winter 2018/19).

You are not entitled to a payment if during that week you:

- are subject to immigration control (see Chapter 53(2)) or not ordinarily resident in Great Britain (see Chapter 53(3)), although you may be entitled if you reside in another European Economic Area country\* (see Chapter 53(1)) or in Switzerland, provided you have a genuine and sufficient link to the UK social security system; *or*
- have been receiving free inpatient treatment in hospital (or a similar institution) for more than 52 weeks; *or*
- are in custody serving a sentence imposed by a court; *or*
- are getting pension credit, income-based jobseeker's allowance (JSA) or income-related employment and support allowance (ESA) and you have been living in a care home for 13 weeks or more at the end of the qualifying week (disregarding temporary absences).

\* excluding Cyprus, France, Gibraltar, Greece, Malta, Portugal and Spain

Social Fund Winter Fuel Payment Regs

### How much do you get?
If you or your partner do not receive pension credit, income-based JSA or income-related ESA and you are:

- aged under 80 (but over pension credit qualifying age), you will get £200 if you are the only person in the household entitled to a payment, or £100 if you share a household with one or more other people entitled to a payment;
- aged 80 or over, you will get £300 if you are the only person in the household aged 80 or over, or £150 each if there are more people aged 80 or over entitled to a payment. If one of you is 80 or over and the other under

80 (but over pension credit qualifying age) you will get £200 and £100 respectively.

If you are receiving pension credit, income-based JSA or income-related ESA, you will get £200 (or £300 if you or your partner are aged 80 or over) regardless of who else is in the household. If you are one of a couple and your partner receives pension credit, income-based JSA or income-related ESA, they will receive the payment instead.

If you have been living in a care home for 13 weeks or more at the end of the qualifying week and are not getting pension credit, income-based JSA or income-related ESA, you will get £100 if you are aged under 80 (but over pension credit qualifying age), or £150 if you are aged 80 or over.

### How do you claim?
You should automatically receive a payment without making a claim if you received a payment last year and your circumstances have not changed, or you are getting a state pension or another social security benefit (excluding child benefit or housing benefit) in the qualifying week. Otherwise, you must make a claim (ring 0800 731 0160 for a claim-form), which must be received by the Winter Fuel Payment Centre by 31.3.19.

# 30 Housing grants

| | | |
|---|---|---|
| 1 | Housing renewal grants system | 205 |
| 2 | Disabled facilities grants | 205 |
| | Disabled facilities grants: personal allowances and premiums – Box H.1 | 206 |
| | Grant system in Scotland – Box H.2 | 206 |
| 3 | Discretionary power to assist with housing repairs, adaptations and improvements | 208 |
| 4 | Alternative housing | 208 |
| | For more information – Box H.3 | 208 |

## 1. Housing renewal grants system
Mandatory disabled facilities grants are available from local authorities in England, Wales and Northern Ireland (see 2 below and Box H.1). Local authorities in England and Wales also have a discretionary power to help with adaptation or improvement of living conditions by providing grants, loans, materials or other forms of assistance (see 3 below).

Community equipment, aids and minor adaptations that help people to live at home or with daily living, and which cost less than £1,000, should be provided free of charge in England. In Wales, the Rapid Response Adaptations Programme aims to provide adaptations costing up to £350 within 15 days of a referral by a local authority or health worker.
The Care & Support (Preventing Needs for Care & Support) Regs 2014, reg 4 & CS(CAR) Regs, reg 3

In Scotland, the housing grants system is different (see Box H.2).

## 2. Disabled facilities grants
A mandatory disabled facilities grant can help with the cost of adapting a property for the needs of a disabled person.
  To be eligible, you must be:
■ an owner-occupier;
■ a private tenant;
■ a landlord with a disabled tenant;
■ a local authority tenant; *or*
■ a housing association tenant.
Occupiers of caravans and some houseboats are also eligible.
HGCRA, S.19

### Treated as disabled
You are treated as disabled if:
■ your sight, hearing or speech is substantially impaired;
■ you have a mental disorder or impairment of any kind;
■ you are physically substantially disabled by an illness, injury, impairment present since birth, or otherwise; *or*
■ you are registered (or could be registered) disabled with the social care department.
HGCRA, S.100

### What can a grant be awarded for?
A grant can be awarded for:
■ facilitating a disabled occupant's access to and from the home;
■ making the home safe for the disabled occupant and others living with them;
■ facilitating a disabled occupant's access to a living room;
■ facilitating a disabled occupant's access to, or providing, a bedroom;
■ facilitating a disabled occupant's access to, or providing, a room in which there is a lavatory, bath or shower and wash-hand basin, or facilitating the use of any of these;
■ facilitating the preparation and cooking of food by the disabled occupant;
■ improving the heating system to meet the disabled occupant's needs, or providing a suitable heating system;
■ facilitating a disabled occupant's use of a source of power, light or heat;
■ facilitating access and movement around the home to enable the disabled occupant to care for someone dependent on them, who also lives there;
■ facilitating access to and from a garden by a disabled occupant; *or*
■ making access to a garden safe for a disabled occupant.
HGCRA, S.23(1)

### The test of resources
Disabled facilities grants for adults are means tested, but there is no means test if an application is made for the benefit of a disabled child or qualifying young person (see Chapter 41(1)).
**The relevant person** – A test of resources is applied to the person with disabilities and their partner, if they have one. This is the case even if the disabled person is not the grant applicant. For example, a disabled person lives with his brother, who has sole ownership of the property. The brother who owns the property can make the application for a disabled facilities grant to carry out adaptations for the benefit of his disabled brother. The test of resources applies only to the disabled brother (known as the '*relevant person*'), not to the brother who has applied.
HRG Regs, reg 5

**The test of resources** – The test is similar, but not identical, to the housing benefit calculation (see Chapter 25(20)), but there are a number of important differences.
❑ There are no non-dependant deductions.
❑ There is an extra premium (the '*housing allowance*', sometimes called the 'grant premium') designed to reflect housing costs, currently £61.30. This is added to the total applicable amount for every grant application.
❑ If the relevant person receives:
  – income-related employment and support allowance (ESA);
  – income support;
  – income-based jobseeker's allowance;
  – the guarantee credit of pension credit;
  – housing benefit;
  – universal credit;
  – working tax credit or child tax credit (where annual income is less than £15,050); *or*

– (in Wales only) help from the council tax reduction scheme,

the applicable amount is automatically £1 and all their income and capital are disregarded, giving a zero contribution (see below).

❏ There is no capital cut-off point. The first £6,000 of capital is disregarded. Weekly tariff income is assumed on capital over £6,000, at £1 for each £250 (or part of £250) for those under 60, and at £1 for each £500 (or part of £500) where the disabled person or their partner is aged 60 or over.

❏ Some regulations, including those relating to the disability premium and the rate of tariff income, refer specifically to the relevant person being 60 years old rather than 'pension credit qualifying age'.

❏ A relevant person aged 60 or over but not yet of pension credit qualifying age can qualify for a pensioner premium of £63.55 for a single person or £94.40 for a couple.

❏ There is a system of stepped tapers on 'excess income' (see below).

---

## H.1  Disabled facilities grants: personal allowances and premiums

The personal allowances and premiums used in the test of resources (see 2 in this chapter) are as follows.

### Personal allowances
**Single person**

| | |
|---|---|
| Main-phase employment and support allowance | £64.30 |
| Aged under 25 | £47.95 |
| Aged 25 or over but under pension credit age | £60.50 |
| Pension credit age but under 65 | £124.05 |
| Aged 65 or over | £143.80 |

**Lone parent**

| | |
|---|---|
| Main-phase employment and support allowance | £64.30 |
| Aged under 18 | £47.95 |
| Aged 18 or over | £60.50 |

**Couple**

| | |
|---|---|
| Both aged under 18 | £72.35 |
| One or both aged 18 or over but under pension credit age | £94.95 |
| One or both pension credit age but under 65 | £189.35 |
| One or both aged 65 or over | £215.50 |
| **Dependent child** | £52.59 |

### Premiums
**Family**

| | |
|---|---|
| Ordinary rate | £6.75 |
| Lone parent rate | £22.30 |
| Increase for child aged under 1 | £10.50 |

**Disability**

| | |
|---|---|
| Single | £25.85 |
| Couple | £36.85 |

**Enhanced disability**

| | |
|---|---|
| Single | £12.60 |
| Couple | £18.15 |
| Child | £19.60 |

**Severe disability**

| | |
|---|---|
| Single | £50.35 |
| Couple (one qualifies) | £50.35 |
| Couple (both qualify) | £100.70 |
| **Disabled child** | £48.72 |
| **Carer** | £27.75 |

**Pensioner**

| | |
|---|---|
| Single | £63.55 |
| Couple | £94.40 |

---

❏ Personal allowances and premiums have been frozen for a number of years. Most are in line with the housing benefit rates used in 2008/09. See Box H.1 for the rates.

❏ Working tax credit and child tax credit are disregarded as income.

❏ There are no ESA additional components included in the applicable amount, but main-phase contributory ESA is a qualifying benefit for the disability premium.

❏ War Pensions scheme payments for those with a disablement of 80% or higher and getting constant attendance allowance are disregarded.

❏ Armed Forces Compensation scheme payments (tariff 1-6) are disregarded.

### Working out your contribution
The test of resources is set up to calculate how much, if anything, you can afford to contribute towards the cost of the works. It is done by calculating the value of a notional standard repayment loan you could afford to take out using a proportion of your 'excess income' (see below) to repay the loan. If you have no excess income, your contribution will be zero. The higher the amount of excess income, the higher the proportion expected to be used towards repaying the notional loan. The calculation is as follows:

### Step 1: Work out your capital
Your capital, together with your partner's, is taken into account. Certain types of capital are disregarded. The rules are similar to those for means-tested benefits (see Chapter 22(22)-(37)). However, the capital value of the home to

---

## H.2  Grant system in Scotland

In Scotland, local authorities are allowed to provide grants, loans, subsidised loans, practical assistance and information or advice to home owners for repairs, improvements, adaptations and the buying or selling of a house.
*HSA, S.71*

### Grants and loans
Assistance *must* be by way of a grant if the adaptations are essential to the disabled person's assessed needs and the work is structural or involves permanent changes to the house (except extensions for living accommodation in the existing structure or any other structure). A grant must also be given for work to provide a standard amenity to meet the needs of a disabled person, ie a fixed bath or shower, wash-hand basin or sink (in each case with a hot and cold water supply) or a toilet.

The grant will be for 100% of approved costs if the applicant or a member of their household receives income-related employment and support allowance, income-based jobseeker's allowance, income support, universal credit or the guarantee credit of pension credit. In other cases, the minimum grant will be for 80% of approved costs.
*Housing (Scotland) Act 2006 (Scheme of Assistance) Regs 3 & 4*

A guide for disabled people living in private housing is available at www.gov.scot/Publications/2011/03/29090945/1.

### Tenants
Tenants are eligible for a grant or loan if the work the grant or loan relates to:
■ has, for a period of two years before the tenant's application, been the tenant's responsibility under the tenancy; or
■ is for the adaptation of a disabled person's house to make it suitable for their accommodation, welfare or employment, or for the reinstatement of any house adapted; or

which your application relates is disregarded whether or not you live there. The first £6,000 of your capital is disregarded. Tariff income of £1 per £250 (or part of £250) over £6,000 is assumed if the relevant person is aged under 60, and £1 per £500 (or part of £500) if the relevant person is 60 or over.

HRG Regs, reg 40

### Step 2: Work out your income

Your average earnings and other income are based on your income over the 12 months before your application or a shorter period if that gives a more accurate figure. The earnings and income disregards are similar to those for housing benefit (see Chapter 22(6)-(20)).

HRG Regs, regs 20, 21 & 22

### Step 3: Work out your applicable amount

This represents your weekly living needs and those of your family (see Chapter 25(24) and (25) and Box H.1). Add the housing allowance (see above).

HRG Regs, reg 14

### Step 4: Work out your excess income

If your income is less than or equal to your applicable amount, you have no excess income. Your contribution is zero. If your income is greater than your applicable amount, the excess income is the difference between the two figures.

### Step 5: Work out your contribution

Excess income is apportioned into four bands and multiplied by the relevant *'loan generation factor(s)'*. The bands and multipliers are shown below.

HRG Regs, reg 12

---

■ is required as a matter of urgency for the health, safety or security of the occupants of a house, including, in particular, work to repair it or to provide a means of escape from fire or other fire precautions.

*HSA, S.92*

For further information go to www.scotland.gov.uk/ Resource/Doc/348026/0115913.pdf.

### Applications

A grant or loan application must include full details of the proposed work, including plans, specifications, the location of the work, an estimate of the cost and other information the authority may reasonably require. An authority may ask for information to support the accuracy of such details.

*HSA, S.74*

### Decisions on applications

The local authority has discretion to approve or refuse an application for a grant or loan. If one is approved, the authority must calculate the approved expense and, where the application is made for a grant or subsidised loan, the applicant's contribution. The authority may only approve a grant or loan application if it considers that:

■ the owners of all the land on which the work is to be carried out have given written consent to the application and to being bound by the conditions of the grant or loan (if the premises to which adaptations are to be made are in a tenement and the adaptations are to the common area, then the consent of all co-owners is required);

■ the house will provide satisfactory accommodation for a reasonable time and meet reasonable standards of physical condition and amenities; *and*

■ the work will not prevent the improvement of any other house in the same building. The authority must not approve an application if the work has already begun, unless there were good reasons for starting the work early.

*HSA, S.75*

---

| Loan generation factors | owner-occupiers | tenants |
|---|---|---|
| Band 1: First £47.95 | 18.85 | 11.04 |
| Band 2: £47.96 to £95.90 | 37.69 | 22.09 |
| Band 3: £95.91 to £191.80 | 150.77 | 88.34 |
| Band 4: £191.81 or more | 376.93 | 220.86 |

The sum total of Bands 1-4 is the value of the notional loan the relevant person is expected to contribute towards the cost of the works.

*Example:* The contribution of an owner-occupier with an excess income of £100 is calculated as follows:

| | | |
|---|---|---|
| Band 1: £47.95 | x 18.85 = | £903.86 |
| Band 2: £47.95 | x 37.69 = | £1,807.24 |
| Band 3: £4.10 | x 150.77 = | £618.16 |
| *Applicant's contribution* | | £3,329.26 |

If the works cost £11,000, the grant is calculated as follows:

| | |
|---|---|
| Total cost of works | £11,000.00 |
| Less applicant's contribution | £3,329.26 |
| *Grant amount* | £7,670.74 |

### Subsequent grants

If a relevant person has had to make a contribution to a previous grant on the same dwelling (in the last 10 years for owner-occupiers or five years for tenants), the value of that contribution is deducted from the assessed contribution on a subsequent grant application. The works under the first grant must have been carried out to the satisfaction of the local authority for this offsetting to apply. If the contribution on the earlier grant was more than the cost of the works, leading to a 'nil-grant approval', the value of the works properly carried out can be offset against a subsequent grant contribution.

HRG Regs, reg 13

### Applying for a disabled facilities grant

Disabled facilities grants are administered by the local housing authority rather than the social care department (if these are different). An application form should be available from the housing authority. It must be supported by a certificate stating that the disabled occupant intends to live in the property for at least five years after the works are completed, or for a shorter period if there are health or other special reasons.

HGCRA, Ss.21 & 22

It is important to make a formal application for a grant because the 6-month time limit for the local authority to make a decision only begins from the date of the formal application. The authority cannot refuse to allow you to make a formal application or refuse to give you an application form.

HGCRA, Ss.2 & 34

**Delays** – If you do not get a decision within six months of submitting a formal application, write and ask why and request that a decision be made. Seek legal advice if you still do not get a decision or if you have been prevented from applying. You can make a complaint of maladministration to the relevant Ombudsman if you are dissatisfied with the way the local authority has dealt with your grant/application and it has not responded adequately to your complaint (see Chapter 59(5)).

### Approval of a disabled facilities grant

The maximum grant payable under a mandatory disabled facilities grant is £30,000 in England, £25,000 in Northern Ireland and £36,000 in Wales. Local authorities can provide further assistance for extra costs under their discretionary power (see 3 below).

The Disabled Facilities Grants (Maximum Amounts & Additional Purposes) (England) Order 2008, Reg 2

In order to approve an application for a disabled facilities

grant, the housing authority must be satisfied that the works are both necessary and appropriate for the needs of the disabled person, and reasonable and practicable in relation to the property. In determining whether the works are necessary and appropriate, the housing authority must consult with social care. This is why housing authorities often direct people to the social care department first for an assessment (normally undertaken by an occupational therapist).
HGCRA, S.24

In addition to the cost of the adaptation work, a grant can cover other fees and costs, including applications for building regulations approval, applications for planning permission, and assistance provided by a home improvement agency. It may be possible to complete some works without planning permission under permitted development rights, but always check with your local authority.
Housing Renewal Grants (Services & Charges) Order 1996

## H.3 For more information

Guidance on assistance with repairs, improvements and adaptations is in:
■ Circular 05/2003, *Housing Renewal* (Office of the Deputy Prime Minister, 17.6.03, http://webarchive.nationalarchives.gov.uk/20120919132719/www.communities.gov.uk/documents/corporate/pdf/145088.pdf); *and*
■ *Home Adaptations for Disabled People* (Home Adaptations Consortium, October 2013, updated 2015, https://homeadaptationsconsortium.files.wordpress.com/2013/09/dfg-good-practice-guide-10-september.pdf).
Equivalent guidance for Wales:
■ National Assembly for Wales Circular 20/02 Annex D, (disabled facilities grants) revised April 2007, http://gov.wales/about/foi/publications-catalogue/circular/circulars2002/NAFWC202002?lang=en
A leaflet on disabled facilities grants (available in alternative formats) can be found at:
■ www.gov.uk/government/publications/disabled-facilities-grant

**Home improvement agencies** – Independent home improvement agencies offer advice about grants and can help people to apply for grants, obtain other sources of finance to help pay for works, find good builders, and ensure works are properly carried out. Ask your local authority if there is one in your area, or contact: Foundations (0300 124 0315; www.foundations.uk.com), Care & Repair Scotland (0141 221 9879; www.careandrepairscotland.co.uk) or Care & Repair Cymru (0300 111 3333; www.careandrepair.org.uk).
**VAT relief** – For information about VAT relief on building works, see leaflet 701/7, *VAT reliefs for people with disabilities,* available from HMRC (0300 123 1073; www.gov.uk/government/publications/vat-notice-7017-vat-reliefs-for-disabled-people).

### Energy efficiency schemes
The following schemes can provide help with energy-efficiency improvements to your home:
❏ Affordable Warmth grant scheme in Northern Ireland: 0300 200 7874; www.nidirect.gov.uk/articles/affordable-warmth-grant-scheme
❏ Warmer Homes Scotland Scheme: 0808 808 2282; http://www.energysavingtrust.org.uk/scotland/grants-loans/heeps/heeps-warmer-homes-scotland-scheme
❏ Welsh Government Warm Homes Nest scheme: 0808 808 2244; www.nestwales.org.uk/home

If approved, the adaptations should usually be completed within one year by one of the contractors who supplied an estimate for the application. The housing authority has the discretion to approve a mandatory grant but to stipulate that it will not be paid for up to 12 months from the date of application.
HGCRA, Ss.36, 37 & 38

If, after the application has been approved, the disabled person's circumstances change before the works are completed, the local housing authority has the discretion as to whether to proceed with paying for all, part or none of the works. It must take into account all the circumstances of the case before deciding how to proceed.
HGCRA, S.41

**Placing a charge** – Local authorities may place a charge against a property if a disabled facilities grant exceeds £5,000 and the application is from an owner. In deciding whether to place a charge on a property, authorities should consider the circumstances of the applicant. The charge would apply for 10 years, which means the value of the charge could be repayable if the ownership of the adapted property changes within 10 years. In England, the maximum charge is £10,000. In Wales, the size of the charge is determined by the local authority. Before requiring any repayment, the authority must consider in each case whether it is reasonable to collect the charge, having regard to the financial and other circumstances of the grant recipient and the reasons for the sale of the property.
Disabled Facilities Grant (Conditions relating to approval for payment of Grant) General Consent 2008 (England); Disabled Facilities Grant (Conditions relating to approval for payment of Grant) General Consent 2008 (Wales)

### 3. Discretionary power to assist with housing repairs, adaptations and improvements
**England and Wales** – Local housing authorities in England and Wales have a discretionary power to provide financial and other assistance for repairs, improvements and adaptations. Local authorities can set their own conditions for assistance, such as whether to carry out a means test and the circumstances under which financial assistance should be repaid.

Assistance may be in the form of grants, loans, labour, materials, advice or any combination of these. Accommodation may be acquired, adapted, improved or repaired, demolished or replaced (if it has been demolished). Authorities may take security, including a charge on a person's home. People in all tenures may be helped, including owner-occupiers, tenants and landlords (including companies and registered social landlords). To find out what is available in your area, contact your local housing authority.
Regulatory Reform (Housing Assistance)(England & Wales) Order 2002, art 3

When providing assistance, the local authority must set out in writing the terms and conditions that apply and must take into account your ability to afford any repayment or contribution towards the costs. If you are refused assistance, ask for a written decision and ask what system of review or appeal the authority operates. If you are still not happy with the decision, you should seek advice and/or consider making a complaint to the relevant Ombudsman (see Chapter 59(5)).
**Northern Ireland** – In Northern Ireland, discretionary grants are different. For details, contact the Northern Ireland Housing Executive, The Housing Centre, 2 Adelaide Street, Belfast BT2 8PB (03448 920 900; www.nihe.gov.uk/index/benefits/home_improvement_grants.htm).

### 4. Alternative housing
Many people prefer to move to a property designed to be accessible for a disabled person rather than undertaking major adaptations to their current home. However, even an accessible property may need some adaptations to suit your particular needs.

If you are seeking social housing (ie council or housing association properties), contact your local authority and make sure you are put on the housing register. It is important to stress your housing requirements. Most housing association properties are allocated via local authorities but some associations operate their own waiting lists, particularly for wheelchair users, so it is worthwhile contacting housing associations directly.

# 31 Other loans and grants

| | | |
|---|---|---|
| 1 | Introduction | 209 |
| 2 | Budgeting loans | 209 |
| 3 | Budgeting advances | 210 |
| 4 | Discretionary Assistance Fund in Wales | 210 |
| 5 | Scottish Welfare Fund | 211 |
| 6 | Discretionary Support Payments in Northern Ireland | 211 |

## 1. Introduction

**Budgeting loans and advances** – Budgeting loans are administered by the DWP. They are interest-free loans for people who have been on a qualifying benefit for at least 26 weeks. They are intended to meet intermittent expenses for specified items which it may be difficult to budget for, enabling the cost to be spread over time. See 2 below for details. Budgeting loans have been replaced by budgeting advances (see 3 below) for those who come under the universal credit system (see Box E.1, Chapter 14).

**Local welfare assistance schemes** – Since April 2013, local authorities have had responsibility for grants and loans to help with independent living or in crisis situations. In England, each authority may manage its own scheme; many no longer do so however. To find out what help, if any, is available in your area, contact your local authority or county council (or use the CPAG online service www.cpag.org.uk/lwas). The Welsh, Scottish and Northern Irish governments have developed their own national schemes (see 4, 5 and 6 below).

## 2. Budgeting loans

To be eligible for a budgeting loan you must meet all the following conditions.

❏ You must be receiving one of the following *'qualifying benefits'* when your application for a budgeting loan is decided:
  – income-related employment and support allowance (ESA);
  – income support;
  – income-based jobseeker's allowance (JSA);
  – pension credit; *or*
  – universal credit (pension credit only),
  and you and/or your partner must have been receiving a qualifying benefit throughout the 26 weeks before the decision (ignoring breaks of 28 days or less). Waiting days at the start of a JSA or ESA claim do not count. You do not count as being in receipt of a benefit if none is paid due to a sanction. However, hardship payments (see Chapter 13(15)) are classed as payments of income-based JSA. For joint-claim couples (see Chapter 13(2)), only the partner who is paid JSA is eligible for a budgeting loan.

❏ You or your partner must not be involved in a trade dispute.

❏ Your application must be for one of the following:
  – furniture and household equipment;
  – clothing and footwear;
  – maternity expenses;
  – funeral expenses;
  – rent in advance and/or removal expenses to secure new accommodation;
  – improvement, maintenance and security of the home;

  – travelling expenses;
  – expenses associated with seeking or re-entering work; *or*
  – HP and other debts for expenses associated with any of the above.
Budgeting Loan Guide, directions 2 & 8

### How much do you get?
The minimum award that can be made is £100.

### Maximum amounts payable

| | |
|---|---|
| Single person* | £348 |
| Couple* | £464 |
| Lone parent or couple responsible for a child/ qualifying young person | £812 |

* and not responsible for a child or qualifying young person

The highest award that can be made is the lesser of: the amount you apply for, or the maximum amount (as above) less any budgeting loan debt owed by you and your partner. The amount of your award will be reduced on a pound-for-pound basis by any savings you or your partner have over £1,000 (or £2,000 if you or your partner are aged 63 or over). Capital is worked out in the same way as for the qualifying benefit, depending on which benefit you are getting (except that Family Fund payments and refugee integration loans are disregarded).

Additionally, if you have other budgeting or crisis loans outstanding, you are not allowed to owe more than £1,500 to the social fund in total.
Budgeting Loan Guide, directions 9, 52 & 53

### Repayment of budgeting loans
A decision maker can only award an amount you are likely to be able to repay. The loan will be scheduled for repayment within 104 weeks at a standard rate. If you have asked for a loan (within your maximum amount) that cannot be repaid within 104 weeks at standard repayment rates, the decision maker may give you alternative options with higher repayment rates. However, they cannot ask you to pay more than 20% of your available income (ie your income-related ESA, income support or income-based JSA applicable amount or pension credit appropriate minimum guarantee plus any child tax credit or child benefit, but excluding housing costs).

Decisions about repayment terms are not subject to review, but if you have difficulty repaying the loan, you can ask for the repayment rate to be reduced. Write to the DWP giving details of your financial situation and how much you can afford to repay.

Loans are normally repaid by deductions from your or your partner's income-related ESA, income support, pension credit or income-based JSA. If you don't get enough benefit, or your benefit stops, deductions can be made from most other social security benefits, but not from disability living allowance, personal independence payment, attendance allowance or child benefit.
The Social Fund (Recovery by Deductions from Benefits) Regs 1988, reg 3

### Applying for a budgeting loan
Apply on form SF500 (available from your local Jobcentre Plus office or www.gov.uk/budgeting-help-benefits/how-to-claim), giving full details of your circumstances.

### Reviews
You can ask for a budgeting loan decision to be reviewed by a *'reviewing officer'* based in the office that made the decision. The reviewing officer will only look at your circumstances at the time of the original decision and is bound by the same rules as the original decision maker. You must request the review in writing within 28 days of the date the decision

was issued to you. The time limit can be extended if there are *'special reasons'*; this is not defined in law, so each case should be considered on its merits. Your application must explain why you disagree with the decision. If a late review is not accepted or your circumstances have changed, it may be better to make a new claim instead.

If you are not happy with the review decision, you can ask for a further review by the Independent Case Examiner (see Chapter 59(1)). You should ask for this in writing within 28 days of the date of the review decision (although there is discretion to accept the request outside the 28 days if it is within six months).

## 3. Budgeting advances

To be eligible for a budgeting advance, you must meet all the following conditions.

❑ You, or your partner, must be receiving universal credit.
❑ You make an application for a budgeting advance.
❑ For a continuous period of at least six months at the time you apply, you or your partner must have been receiving one of the following *'qualifying benefits'*:*
   – universal credit;
   – income-related employment and support allowance;
   – income support;
   – income-based jobseeker's allowance; *or*
   – pension credit.
❑ Neither you nor your partner earn too much (see below).
❑ Neither you nor your partner owe any repayments to the DWP for an earlier budgeting advance.
❑ The DWP is satisfied that they will reasonably be able to recover the payment from you.

* This does not apply, however, if the budgeting advance is for an expense related to you or your partner getting or keeping a job.

PAB Regs, regs 12 & 14

### Earnings

You normally cannot get a budgeting advance if, in the six complete monthly assessment periods (see Chapter 16(1)) before your application:

■ you are single and your earnings exceeded £2,600; *or*
■ you are in a couple and your joint earnings exceeded £3,600.

However, if the budgeting advance is for an expense related to you or your partner getting or keeping a job (and you have not been receiving a qualifying benefit for six months), you cannot get an advance if:

■ you are single and your earnings exceeded £433.33 multiplied by the number of complete monthly assessment periods since the start of your claim; *or*
■ you are in a couple and your earnings exceeded £600 multiplied by the number of complete monthly assessment periods since the start of your claim.

See Chapter 17(1)-(6) for how earnings are assessed.

PAB Regs, reg 13

### How much do you get?

The minimum award that can be made is £100.

### Maximum amounts payable

| | |
|---|---|
| Single person* | £348 |
| Couple* | £464 |
| Lone parent or couple responsible for a child/ qualifying young person | £812 |
| * and not responsible for a child or qualifying young person | |

The amount of your award will be reduced on a £1-for-£1 basis by any savings you or your partner have over £1,000.

PAB Regs, regs 15 & 16

### Payment and repayment

A budgeting advance will normally be paid by direct credit transfer into your bank or building society account. Repayment will normally be made over 12 months (or 18 months in exceptional circumstances) from your ongoing universal credit award. The DWP will write to you and tell you how much they will be deducting from you. If payments cannot be made from your ongoing award (eg if you come off universal credit), you will still be liable to pay back any remaining debt.

PAB Regs, regs 17 & 18

## 4. Discretionary Assistance Fund in Wales

The Discretionary Assistance Fund provides two types of support through the award of grants: *'individual assistance payments'* and *'emergency assistance payments'*.

### Individual assistance payments

An individual assistance payment (IAP) may be made to help you:

■ establish yourself in the community following a stay in an institution or care home where you have received significant and substantial care for a minimum of three months;
■ remain living independently in the community rather than enter an institution or care home;
■ ease exceptional pressures on you and your family over and above the pressure of living on a low income;
■ set up home in the community as part of a planned resettlement programme or independently secure accommodation following a period of homelessness;
■ care for a prisoner or young offender on release on temporary licence; *or*
■ with one-off or short-term travel expenses, if deemed essential in support of independent living or in connection with a crisis.

**Are you eligible?** – To be eligible for an IAP, you must meet all the following conditions.

❑ You must be receiving income-related employment and support allowance, income support, income-based jobseeker's allowance, universal credit or pension credit when your application for an IAP is decided (or are due to leave an institution or care home in the next six weeks and be likely to receive one of these benefits on leaving).
❑ You must not be:
   – resident in a care home, unless there are plans to discharge you within six weeks;
   – an inpatient in hospital or other medical establishment, unless there are plans to discharge you within six weeks;
   – under a DWP sanction;
   – excluded from the Discretionary Assistance Fund because of fraud or misspend of award;
   – lawfully detained, unless there are plans to release you within six weeks, or on a temporary release licence; *or*
   – a member of a religious order who is fully maintained by that order.
❑ You must not have savings of more than £500 (£1,000 for pensioners).

### Emergency assistance payments

An emergency assistance payment (EAP) can be awarded to help with expenses that have arisen as a result of an emergency or disaster. To be eligible for an EAP, you must be aged 16 or over and meet all the following conditions.

❑ You have not applied for an EAP in the last 28 days, unless there is a different reason for your application.
❑ You have not had more than two EAP awards in the last 12 months.

❑ You are not:
- resident in a care home or a hospital inpatient, unless there are plans to discharge you within two weeks;
- in prison or on bail pending a court hearing;
- a student supported by student income streams;
- excluded from the Discretionary Assistance Fund because of fraud or misspend of award; *or*
- a member of a religious order who is fully maintained by that order.

❑ You have no other resources to see you through the crisis.

❑ You are not waiting for a first benefit payment from a new claim or been sanctioned. In these situations, you should be referred for a short-term advance or universal credit advance (see Chapter 56(6)) or a hardship payment (see Chapters 11(16) and 13(15)).

### How to apply

You can claim an IAP or EAP by telephone (0800 859 5924 or 033 0101 5000), online (https://moneymadeclear. wales/discretionary-assistance-fund/) or by post (on the form available from the website). Most EAP awards are paid through PayPoint, for which you will need a working mobile phone. However, they can also be paid directly into your bank account.

If you are unhappy with a decision, you can ask for a review.

## 5. Scottish Welfare Fund

The Scottish Welfare Fund is grant-based and provides two types of support: *'community care grants'* and *'crisis grants'*.

### Community care grants

A community care grant may be paid to help you:
- establish or maintain a settled home if you are leaving care or imprisonment, where, without a grant, there is a risk that you will not be able to do so (this can include help with housing costs if you are aged 18-21 and making a new claim for universal credit in a full service area and are not eligible for help with these through that benefit);
- maintain a settled home, where, without a grant, there is a risk of you needing to go into a care institution;
- establish or maintain a settled home after being homeless, or otherwise living an unsettled way of life;
- maintain a settled home in a situation where you, or someone in your household, is facing exceptional pressure; *or*
- care for a prisoner or young offender on release on temporary licence.

### Crisis grants

A crisis grant can be awarded to meet expenses that have arisen as a result of an emergency or disaster in order to avoid serious damage or serious risk to the health and safety of you or your family.

### How to apply

Applications are made to your local authority. The underlying test of eligibility for both community care grants and crisis grants is severity of need. Qualifying benefits (see 2 above) may be used to help decide if you are eligible but they are not a requirement.

Crisis grants are generally awarded as cash or cash equivalent, whereas community care grants may be awarded as cash, cash equivalent or in kind (for example white goods or travel vouchers).

### Reviews

If you are unhappy with a decision, you can ask for a review. You should do this by writing to your local authority within 20 working days. If you are still unhappy with the decision

following this review, you can ask the Scottish Public Services Ombudsman (SPSO) to carry out an independent review. You can apply for the review online, in writing or by phone (www.spso.org.uk/ or 0800 014 7299), and should do so within one month of receiving the initial review decision. If the earlier decision has resulted in some grant or loan being awarded, this cannot be removed by the SPSO.

## 6. Discretionary Support Payments in Northern Ireland

*'Discretionary Support Payments'* (DSPs) may be provided in the form of loans or grants. To qualify for a DSP:
- you must be aged at least 18, or at least 16 and without parental support;
- you must be resident and present in Northern Ireland and the DSP must be for a need in Northern Ireland; *and*
- your annual income must be below a set threshold, currently £16,286.

You cannot get a DSP if you are:
- a prisoner;
- in a care home or hospital, unless there are plans to discharge you within two weeks;
- a member of a religious order who is fully maintained by that order;
- in (or treated as being in) full-time third-level education;*
- subject to a trade dispute;* *or*
- under a DWP sanction.*

\* unless the need arises as a consequence of a disaster

### Loans

A DSP may be provided in the form of a loan for the provision of:
- immediate help with short-term living expenses;
- household items, or help with their repair or replacement;
- travel expenses in order to: visit a close relative who is ill, attend a close relative's funeral, ease a domestic crisis, visit a child who is with the other parent pending a family court decision or move to suitable accommodation; *or*
- rent in advance to a landlord (other than the Northern Ireland Housing Executive).

Only three loans may be awarded in a rolling 12-month period and the total debt cannot exceed £1,000.

### Grants

A DSP may be awarded as a grant where:
- the grant is to provide help for you, or your immediate family, to remain or begin living independently in the community;
- you, or your immediate family, are prevented from remaining in your home;
- the grant is to provide help in the form of living expenses where your total DSP debt exceeds £1,000; *or*
- you are eligible for a loan for living expenses but cannot afford to repay it.

Only one grant may be awarded in a rolling 12 month-period (unless it is for one of the first two conditions above and in the event of a disaster).

### How to apply

Claims can be made by phoning 0800 587 2750 (textphone: 0800 587 2751). If you are unhappy with a decision, you can ask for a review to be carried out by a discretionary support officer. If you are unhappy with the review decision, you can ask for a further review to be carried out by a discretionary support commissioner.

### Repayment

The maximum period for repaying a loan is normally 52 weeks, although it may be extended to 78 weeks in exceptional circumstances.

# Education and work

This section of the handbook looks at:

| | |
|---|---|
| Financing studies | Chapter **32** |
| Benefits and work | Chapter **33** |
| Employment and training | Chapter **34** |
| Income tax | Chapter **35** |

# 32 Financing studies

| | | |
|---|---|---|
| 1 | Loans, grants and bursaries | 212 |
| | Rates of grants and loans (2018/19) – Box I.1 | 213 |
| 2 | Students and means-tested benefits | 214 |
| 3 | Effect of a loan, grant or bursary | 215 |
| | Student support and means-tested benefits (pre-universal credit) – Box I.2 | 216 |
| | Student support and universal credit – Box I.3 | 217 |
| 4 | Other benefits | 217 |
| | For more information – Box I.4 | 217 |

## 1. Loans, grants and bursaries

Financial support for new students in higher education comes in the form of tuition fee loans, means-tested loans for living expenses, and supplementary grants and institutional bursaries and scholarships for students in particular circumstances.

Entitlement to student support depends on where you are studying and where you are from. Contact:
■ Student Finance England, if you live in England;
■ Student Finance NI, if you live in Northern Ireland;
■ Student Awards Agency for Scotland (SAAS), if you live in Scotland; *and*
■ Student Finance Wales, if you live in Wales.
See Box I.4 for contact details.

**Fees** – Universities and colleges across the UK can charge up to £9,250 a year for full-time undergraduate courses. Institutions in Northern Ireland charge up to £4,160 a year for students from Northern Ireland. The standard tuition fee in Scotland is £1,820 but SAAS will pay your fees if you meet the residency conditions. Students from Scotland who study elsewhere follow the same rules as those from other parts of the UK, but support will be different.

**Full-time loan**

Eligible students can apply for student loans for living costs and tuition fees. You begin to pay back the loan once you reach a certain salary level. If you receive a maintenance grant (see below), the maximum loan for living costs you can receive will be reduced. For further information, go to www.gov.uk/student-finance or the website of the equivalent funding body in Northern Ireland, Scotland or Wales (see Box I.4).

**Grants and bursaries**

**Maintenance grant** – In England, students who started their course before September 2016 are eligible for grants of up to £3,593, depending on household income. Students eligible for means-tested benefits may get a *'special support grant'* instead, which is disregarded in the assessments of those benefits. For new students, grants have been replaced by increased maintenance loans (see Box I.1). All Welsh students can get a £1,000 annual maintenance grant and those from low income households may be eligible for an additional grant. In Northern Ireland, a maximum grant of £3,475 is payable.

**Institutional bursaries and scholarships** – Universities and colleges in England charging more than £6,000 must have measures in place to recruit students from poorer backgrounds and support them when they are studying. Each university has its own scheme, but they generally include means-tested bursaries and scholarships. Students in Northern Ireland and Wales should ask universities and colleges directly about extra bursaries for students receiving the full maintenance grant.

**Part-time students**

Part-time students from England who started courses from September 2012 who are studying at least 25% of the intensity of the equivalent full-time course can apply for tuition fee loans on the same basis as full-time students. (From August 2018, part-time students in England can apply for loans for living costs; the amount will depend on the intensity of study.)

Welsh part-time students who started their courses from September 2014 can also apply for fee loans on a similar basis, as well as for help with the costs of study if the intensity of the course is at least 50%.

Part-time students from Northern Ireland on courses involving at least half the hours of a full-time course and who are on low incomes can apply for a means-tested fee grant and course grant to help with course expenses, books and travel.

Part-time students from Scotland studying in Scotland can apply for a grant from SAAS towards fees and other study costs.

**Supplementary grants**

If you are on a designated course and funded by Student Finance in England, Northern Ireland or Wales, and meet the residency criteria, you may be eligible for supplementary grants including:
■ disabled students' allowances (DSAs) – see below;
■ parents' learning allowance and childcare grant – for full-time students (and part-time students in Wales) with dependent children;
■ adult dependants' grant; *and*
■ travel costs, if you attend a clinical placement in the UK as part of your full-time course in medicine or dentistry or a college or university outside the UK.
With the exception of DSAs, these are means tested. Previous study may prevent you getting maintenance grants and

---

help with tuition fees but does not affect entitlement to supplementary grants. In Scotland, similar grants are available for single parents and students with adult dependants; contact the SAAS for details.

**Disabled students' allowances** – DSAs are not means tested. They are for additional disability-related costs of study, covering specialist equipment, non-medical helpers and general or other expenditure. Full- or part-time postgraduates in the UK can get DSAs if they do not receive an equivalent award from their Research Council (or similar organisation). For rates, see Box I.1. To receive a DSA, you will require a needs assessment to identify your extra study-related needs. Your awarding authority will advise on the process. For more information, see Box I.4 and ask the Student Finance body for the leaflet *Bridging the gap*.

### Other financial support

Other sources of financial support include:

**Hardship funds** – There are similar schemes in each UK country but they may have different names. Each institution administers the funds, which are available to support students experiencing financial hardship. Contact the student support officer responsible for financial advice at your educational institution.

**Education maintenance allowance (EMA)** – This is a term-time payment of £30 a week for eligible students, depending on household income. Students must attend school or college from Year 12 and follow a course up to level 3. EMA is not available to students in England.

**16-19 bursary fund (England)** – This scheme is made up of two elements. The first element is a bursary of £1,200 a year payable to students who are:

■ in care or have left care;
■ getting income support or universal credit; *or*
■ getting employment and support allowance and either disability living allowance or personal independence payment.

The second element is a discretionary fund for students who need help with the costs of transport, food or equipment. The school or college decides how much to pay and when to pay it. Payments may be in kind, eg a transport pass, and can be linked to behaviour or attendance.

**Advanced learner loans** – Tuition fee loans are available to all learners aged 19 and over for qualifications at levels 3 and 4. Loans are also available for courses at levels 5 and 6 which provide a clear route to developing high-level technical and professional skills.

**NHS bursaries** – These are for NHS-funded places on health professional courses in England and Wales. Equivalents are available in Scotland from local funders.

**Teacher training bursaries** – Support for teaching training, including postgraduate study, is available. In England and Wales, there can be substantial incentives for shortage subjects.

**Postgraduate courses** – Students from England starting postgraduate master's courses in 2018/19 can apply for a loan of £10,609. Other financial support may be available from Research Councils, your university or charitable trusts, depending on your subject.

---

## I.1 Rates of grants and loans (2018/19)

### Student grants (England)
**Maintenance grant**
**English students enrolled for academic years 2012/13 to 2015/16** – Up to £3,593 payable with full grant below £25,000 income, reducing to nil above £42,620. Students enrolled before 2012 should contact Student Finance England for information on grant rates. From September 2016, maintenance grants were replaced by increased maintenance loans for new students (see below).
*Note:* For the grants elsewhere in the UK, contact the relevant funding body.

### Disabled students' allowances (DSAs)
The figures shown are English rates and are the maximum in each case for disability-related costs of study. For rates elsewhere in the UK, contact the relevant funding body (see Box I.4).

**Major items**

| | |
|---|---|
| Specialist equipment | £5,529 per course |

**Non-medical helper**

| | |
|---|---|
| Full-time course | £21,987 a year |
| Part-time course up to 75% | £16,489 a year |

**General/other expenditure**

| | |
|---|---|
| Full-time course | £1,847 a year |
| Part-time course up to 75% | £1,385 a year |

| | |
|---|---|
| **Postgraduate (maximum DSA)** | £10,993 a year |

For postgraduate courses in England and Wales there is one allowance for all costs. PGCE/ITT courses are eligible for DSAs at undergraduate rates. DSAs for postgraduate study in Scotland and for most Research Council-funded study are the same as undergraduate rates.

**Travel:** Extra travel costs incurred because of disability, not normally for everyday travel costs: no maximum amount.

### Student loans
**Tuition fees**
Tuition fees vary according to the country in which you study. Universities and colleges can charge up to £9,250 a year for full-time undergraduate courses. Tuition fee loans are available to cover the costs; they are paid direct to the institution. You must start repaying the loan in instalments after you finish the course and are earning over a certain amount. Institutions in Northern Ireland charge a maximum of £4,160 a year to students from Northern Ireland. Most Scottish students studying in Scotland do not pay tuition fees for full-time courses.

**Maintenance loans**
The loan rates below are for English students who enrolled on their course in the academic years 2012/13 to 2015/16.

| Place of residence | Full year | Final year |
|---|---|---|
| Parental home | £4,960 | £4,557 |
| London | £8,702 | £7,925 |
| Elsewhere | £6,236 | £5,800 |

The loan rates below are the maximum amounts for English students on new courses from September 2016, depending on whether they are eligible for certain benefits.

| Place of residence | Not eligible | Eligible |
|---|---|---|
| Parental home | £7,324 | £8,640 |
| London | £11,354 | £12,382 |
| Elsewhere | £8,700 | £9,916 |

*Note:* For the rates elsewhere in the UK, contact the relevant funding body.

**Professional and Career Development Loans** – These are for vocational courses, sponsored by the government and offered by banks. You can borrow £300 to £10,000, but if you have a poor credit rating you may not receive this support.

**Charities and trusts** – Trusts will not usually provide your main source of finance, but may give top-ups or pay for a special need. Some trusts give small grants or loans to students with disabilities who are in particular difficulty. See Box I.4.

## 2. Students and means-tested benefits

This section covers the position of disabled students aged under 20 on advanced courses and those aged 20 or over in full-time advanced or non-advanced education. See Chapter 42 for the position of disabled students aged under 20 on non-advanced courses. Advanced education includes a course leading to a first or postgraduate degree, a higher education diploma, teaching courses, BTEC, HND, HNC, Certificate of Higher Education or any other course of a standard above advanced GNVQ, A level or equivalent.

When claiming means-tested benefits, you are treated as a full-time student from the date your course starts through to the last day of the course, or earlier if you completely abandon or are dismissed from the course. The *'last day of the course'* is the date on which the last day of the final academic year is officially scheduled to fall.

**Is the course full time or part time?** – If you are on a course of advanced education, whether it is full time or part time usually depends on how it is classed by the institution you study at. If the institution classes it as full time, you will need to provide convincing evidence to persuade the DWP otherwise, bearing in mind that what matters is the course itself rather than the hours you attend.

If you are on a course of non-advanced further education in England or Wales, it is full time if it involves more than 16 hours of guided learning a week. Guided learning hours refer to contact teaching hours, one-to-one or group tutorials, teaching sessions and facilitated workshops. They do not include private study or time spent taking an assessment. In Scotland, a course is full time if structured learning packages make up the hours to over 16 and up to 21 a week. The DWP usually asks to see your 'learning agreement', which should set out your guided learning hours.
ESA regs, reg 131; IS Regs, reg 61

If you are claiming universal credit, the rules are different – see below.

**Part-time students** – If you are eligible for income-related employment and support allowance (ESA), income support or universal credit, you can study part time (unless, in the case of universal credit, it is not compatible with your work-related requirements – see below). For ESA and universal credit, if you undergo a work capability assessment (see Chapter 12), your ability to perform tasks will be considered in the context of what you do on a typical day, including studying – for example, your ability to get around campus, how long you can comfortably sit and your ability to hold a pen and take notes.

**Couples** – If your partner is not a student, they may be able to claim means-tested benefits in the normal way.

### Income-related ESA

Chapter 18 deals with the rules for claiming income-related ESA. Full-time students can claim only if they are entitled to disability living allowance, personal independence payment or armed forces independence payment.
ESA regs, reg 18

If you qualify for income-related ESA as a full-time student and are not a 'qualifying young person' (see Chapter 41(1)), you will be treated as having a limited capability for work without having to pass the work capability assessment. You may be sent a capability for work questionnaire or invited to attend a face-to-face assessment, so that it can be decided whether you should be placed in the work-related activity group or the support group (see Chapter 11(4)-(5)).
ESA regs, reg 33(2)

You will not be treated as being in full-time education while you are on any course that you have to attend as part of your work-related activity (see Chapter 11(14)) or while you are on a traineeship programme (see Chapter 34(4)).
ESA regs, reg 14(2A)&(2B)

### Income support

Chapter 19 deals with the main rules for income support. You are eligible for income support during term time and all the vacations if you fit into one of the following categories:
- you have been receiving income support on the grounds of disability or incapacity since before 27.10.08 and have not yet been transferred to ESA (See Chapter 11(28)); *and*
  - your applicable amount includes a disability or severe disability premium; *or*
  - you have been incapable of work (or entitled to statutory sick pay) for 28 weeks; *or*
  - you are claiming disabled students' allowance (DSA) because of deafness;
- you are a lone parent with a child aged under 5; *or*
- you are a refugee on a course learning English.

If you are single or a student couple (ie both full-time students) and you have responsibility for a child or young person, you can claim income support during the summer vacation if you are eligible under the usual rules (see Box F.1, Chapter 19). Alternatively, you could claim jobseeker's allowance (JSA) if you are available for work (see 4 below).
IS Regs reg 4ZA & Sch 1B

### Pension credit

Pension credit is not affected by any type of study you do. Student loans and grants are disregarded as income.

### Housing benefit

Most students on full-time courses are excluded from housing benefit until their course ends. However, you can claim housing benefit if you:
- get income-related ESA, income support or income-based JSA as a full-time student;
- get universal credit as a full-time student (unless your universal credit award includes a housing costs amount);

■ have (or are treated as having) a limited capability for work under ESA rules for a continuous period of 28 weeks (two or more periods of limited capability can be added together if they are no more than 12 weeks apart). You should claim ESA to have your limited capability for work acknowledged. You will need to take part in work capability assessments (see Chapter 12). You do not, however, have to be actually receiving ESA to qualify;

■ qualify for a disability premium or severe disability premium, or you have been incapable of work for 28 weeks or you qualify for a DSA because of deafness;

■ are a lone parent with a dependent child or qualifying young person (see Chapter 41(1));

■ are a lone foster parent and a local authority or voluntary organisation has placed the child with you;

■ are one of a couple, your partner is also a student and you have a dependent child or qualifying young person. You will be eligible for housing benefit throughout the course (not just in the summer vacation as for JSA and income support);

■ are waiting to return to your course after an agreed break because you were ill or had to care for someone. You can get housing benefit once you have recovered or your caring responsibilities have ended until either the date you return to your course or the date your education establishment has agreed you can return to your course, whichever is earlier, but only for a maximum period of one year and providing you are not eligible for a student loan or grant during this time; *or*

■ are aged under 21 and a full-time student on a non-advanced course (the age limit can be extended to under 22 if you turned 21 while on the course), or you are a 'qualifying young person' (see Chapter 41(1)).

HB Regs, reg 56

If you are one of a couple and your partner is not a student, your partner can claim housing benefit. In this case, the student rules will apply to your income.

HB Regs, reg 8(1)(e)

**Living in student accommodation** – If you are eligible for housing benefit, you can claim if you are renting accommodation provided by the educational establishment.

HB Regs, reg 57

**Two homes** – If you have a partner and have to live in two separate homes while you are on your course, you can get housing benefit for both homes only if you are eligible for housing benefit as a student and the local authority decides this is reasonable. The assessment of housing benefit for each home will be based on your applicable amount as a couple and your joint income.

HB Regs, regs 7(6)(b)

**Non-dependant deductions** – If you are a full-time student living in someone else's home as a non-dependant, no deduction is made from the householder's housing benefit during your period of study, including, normally, summer vacations. However, if you get a job (for 16 or more hours a week) during the summer vacation, a non-dependant deduction will be applied.

HB Regs, reg 74(7)(c)-(d)

**Size criteria restriction** – If you are a full-time student living away from your normal home, for the purpose of calculating the householder's housing benefit you will still count as occupying a room for up to 52 weeks' absence.

**Universal credit**

You are not normally able to claim universal credit if you are *'receiving education'*, which means you are undertaking:

■ a course of full-time advanced education;

■ any other full-time course of study or training and are supported by a loan, grant or bursary (but not a traineeship or a course of education or training to improve your skills

that your work coach has referred you on as part of a work preparation requirement – see Chapter 15(4))); *or*

■ any other course of study or training that is not compatible with any work-related requirements that have been placed on you by your work coach (see Chapter 15(1)).

WRA 2012, S.4(1)(d); UC Regs, reg 12

However, you are able to claim universal credit even if you are receiving education if you:

■ are in non-advanced education, are under the age of 21 (or are 21 and reached that age while undertaking the course) and have no parental support (see Chapter 14(4));

■ are entitled to attendance allowance, disability living allowance or personal independence payment *and* you have a limited capability for work (see Chapter 12(2)). This is more restrictive than income-related ESA (see above) and will potentially act as a disincentive for prospective students to move to 'full service areas' (see Box E.1, Chapter 14) to study;

■ are responsible for a child or 'qualifying young person' (see Chapter 16(4));

■ are a single foster parent;

■ are one of a couple, your partner is also a student and they are responsible for a child or qualifying young person (including as a foster parent);

■ have reached pension credit qualifying age (see Chapter 44(2)) and have a partner who has not reached that age;

■ are waiting to return to your course after taking time out because of illness or caring responsibilities (the rules are the same as for housing benefit above); *or*

■ have a partner who is not a student (or who is able to claim universal credit as a student themselves).

UC Regs; regs 3(2)(b), 13(4) & 14

## 3. Effect of a loan, grant or bursary

**Income-related ESA, income support, income-based JSA and housing benefit**

The way in which loans, grants or bursaries affect income-related employment and support allowance (ESA), income support, income-based jobseeker's allowance (JSA) and housing benefit normally depends on whether the income is intended for living costs or course costs, and on the period of time it is intended to cover. In general, loans, grants or bursaries specifically intended to cover course costs are disregarded. Course costs include tuition fees, exam fees, travel, books and equipment. Amounts intended to cover the maintenance of a dependent child or childcare costs are disregarded.

If you are entitled to a student loan, it is treated as income regardless of whether you actually take it or not. This rule will not apply to any income-related ESA you claim if you have to suspend your course because of illness.

**Period of study** – In general, loans, grants and bursaries that cannot be disregarded are taken into account over the period for which they are payable. How your loan counts as income depends on what year of the course you are in.

❏ In your first year, the loan income will be disregarded until the first day of the first term.

❏ Between your first and final year, the loan is usually taken into account from the start of the first benefit week in September until the end of the last benefit week in June (42 or 43 weeks).

❏ In your final year, the loan is divided by the number of weeks from the start of the first benefit week in September until the benefit week that coincides with the last day of your course.

ESA Regs, reg 137; IS Regs, reg 66A

Box I.2 lists the types of student support and how they count as income for assessing income-related ESA, income support, income-based JSA and housing benefit.

## Universal credit

Student income is taken into account in the monthly assessment period (see Chapter 16(1)) in which the course begins (including for the second or subsequent years) and each further monthly assessment period during which you are undertaking the course. It is disregarded in the assessment period in which the last week of the course or the start of the long (usually summer) vacation falls. It continues to be disregarded during any assessment periods that fall completely in the long vacation.

UC Regs, reg 68(1)

The maximum student loan to which you are entitled will be taken into account as student income, regardless of whether you actually take it or not. Any grant paid during the loan period will be disregarded unless it is paid to maintain someone who is included in your universal credit award or to cover rent included in your housing costs amount (see Chapter 24).

UC Regs, regs 68(2)-(3) & 69(1)

If you do not get a loan, any grant for your maintenance is taken fully into account, including hardship fund payments. Extra grants to cover the following are disregarded:

■ tuition or examination fees;
■ expenses paid for a disability;
■ extra costs due to term-time residential study away from your college or university;
■ housing costs for a home other than where you live while attending your course (unless you already get the housing costs amount for this home);
■ living expenses for another person, but only if you are not getting universal credit for that person;
■ books, equipment and travel expenses for attending the course; *and*
■ childcare costs.

UC regs, regs 68(4) & 70

Box I.3 lists the types of student support and how they count as income for assessing universal credit.

## Other payments

**Hardship funds** – Rules differ according to how the funds will be used and whether they are paid as a single lump-sum payment, as instalments or as interim payments. For income-related ESA, income support, income-based JSA and housing benefit, the following rules apply.

❏ A payment intended to cover one-off costs counts as capital and will be disregarded for 52 weeks unless it is intended for daily living expenses, in which case it will be taken into account immediately. *'Daily living expenses'* can include food, ordinary clothing, rent eligible for housing benefit, fuel, council tax and water charges.

❏ Payments made in instalments count as income and will be disregarded in full unless they are for daily living expenses, in which case £20 a week will be disregarded. Regular payments intended and used for anything else, such as childcare expenses, are disregarded.

❏ Interim payments intended to bridge the gap before starting a course or receiving the student loan are disregarded even if they are intended to cover daily living expenses.

ESA regs, regs 138 & 142, IS Regs, regs 66B & 68

---

## I.2 Student support and means-tested benefits (pre-universal credit)

| Type of student support | Counted as income |
|---|---|
| **Full-time student maintenance loan** <br> The maximum loan you are entitled to is treated as income, whatever amount you actually borrow. If you don't apply for a loan, the decision maker will still take into account the maximum loan you could have got if you had applied. | Yes |
| **Loan disregards** <br> When your benefit is worked out, £10 a week of your loan is disregarded. In addition, disregard the following: <br> a) £303 a year for travel costs from a loan (academic year 2017/18); *and* <br> b) £390 a year for books and equipment from a loan (academic year 2017/18). | |
| **Tuition fees loan** <br> The loan is paid direct to the university. | No |
| **Disabled students' allowance and travel expenses grant** | No |
| **Childcare grant and parents' learning allowance** | No |
| **Special support grant** | No |
| **Maintenance grant** <br> If you are not eligible for a student loan, the equivalent disregard for travel and books applies. | Yes |
| **Adult dependants' grant** <br> This counts in full as income. | Yes |
| **Institutional bursaries and scholarships** <br> If the bursary is to help with course costs <br> If the payments are for living costs | <br> No <br> Yes |
| **NHS and social work bursaries and grants** <br> Amounts for travel expenses, course costs and childcare are disregarded. <br> NHS bursary dependants' grant | Yes <br><br><br> Yes |
| **Social work incentive bursary (studying in Northern Ireland)** <br> Amounts intended to cover course and travel costs | <br><br> No |
| **Postgraduate awards** <br> Research Council tuition fees <br> Research Council maintenance grant <br> Teacher training bursary | <br> No <br> Yes <br> Yes |
| **Postgraduate loan** <br> 30% of the maximum loan you are entitled to is treated as income, whatever amount you actually borrow. If you don't apply for a loan, the decision maker will still take into account the maximum loan you could have got if you had applied. | Yes |
| **Loan disregards** <br> After your income is calculated, apply the same disregards as for student maintenance loan above. | |
| **Advanced learner loan** | No |
| **Professional and Career Development Loans** <br> The part intended to cover fees/examination costs <br> Amounts intended for everyday living expenses | <br> No <br> Yes |

**Voluntary or charitable payments** – One-off or irregular payments are treated as capital. Regular payments are disregarded as income (see Chapter 22(8)).

**Leaving early?** – If you leave before the end of your course, a loan may continue to be taken into account but without any disregard, whether or not you repay all or part of it. Grants that must be repaid continue to be taken into account as income until you've repaid them or until the end of the term or vacation when you left the course.

ESA regs, reg 91(4) & 104(4)-(7), IS Regs, reg 29(2B) & 40(3A)-(3AB)

For universal credit, your student income is disregarded in the monthly assessment period in which you completely leave or abandon your course.

UC regs, regs 13 & 68(1)(c)(ii)

**Professional and Career Development Loans** – These are always treated as income rather than capital, no matter how they are paid. The loan is taken into account if it is intended for daily living expenses.

## 4. Other benefits

### Jobseeker's allowance (JSA)

Students on full-time courses are normally excluded from JSA until the end of their course, or until they abandon it or are dismissed from it. However, if you are single or have a partner who is also a student and you are responsible for a child or qualifying young person (see Chapter 41(1)), you can get JSA during the summer vacation if you are available for work.

You can get JSA temporarily while waiting to return to your course after an agreed break because you were ill or had to care for someone. The rules are the same as for housing benefit (see 2 above). For details on JSA, see Chapter 13.

JSA Regs, reg 1(3D); JSA Regs 2013, reg 45(6)

**Contributory employment and support allowance (ESA)**
In general, you can get contributory ESA during vacations and term time and it is not paid at a reduced rate because of any

---

## I.3 Student support and universal credit

| Type of student support | Counted as income |
| --- | --- |
| **Full-time student maintenance loan** <br> The maximum loan you are entitled to is treated as income, whatever amount you actually borrow. If you don't apply for a loan, the decision maker will still take into account the maximum loan you could have got if you had applied; £110 a month is disregarded. <br><br> If you are not entitled to a loan but receive a grant, the grant income is taken into account as income, subject to the disregards in (3) in this chapter. | Yes |
| **Postgraduate loan** <br> 30% of the maximum loan you are entitled to is treated as income, whatever amount you actually borrow. If you don't apply for a loan, the decision maker will still take into account the maximum loan you could have got if you had applied; £110 a month is disregarded. | Yes |
| **Tuition fees loan** | No |
| **Maintenance grant** | No |
| **Special support grant** | No |
| **Disabled students' allowance and travel expenses grant** | No |
| **Childcare grant and parents' learning allowance** | No |
| **Adult dependants' grant** | Yes |
| **NHS and social work bursaries and grants** <br> NHS bursary dependants' grant | No <br> Yes |
| **Professional and Career Development Loans** <br> Counts as capital | |
| **Advanced learner loan** | No |

---

## I.4 For more information

### Careers help
**England** – Schools have a duty to provide careers advice to all pupils from year 8 to year 13. Face-to-face guidance is limited and schools instead provide web, email and phone support. You can also get help from your local Information and Advice Support Service, which has a duty to provide information and advice to disabled young people up to the age of 25 (councilfordisabledchildren.org.uk/information-advice-and-support-services-network/find-your-local-ias-service).

The National Careers Service provides advice online and through a helpline and webchat to those aged 13 or over. A face-to-face service is available to those aged 19 or over (18 or over if you are a Jobcentre Plus customer). Contact 0800 100 900 (nationalcareersservice.direct.gov.uk).

**Scotland, Wales and Northern Ireland** – For advice in Scotland, contact Skills Development Scotland (www.skillsdevelopmentscotland.co.uk). For Wales, contact Careers Wales (www.careerswales.com). For Northern Ireland, see www.nidirect.gov.uk/campaigns/careers.

**Post-graduation** – If you have left higher education, you can use the careers service where you studied or at your nearest university; you should be able to use it for up to three years after graduation. Prospects has an extensive graduate careers website (www.prospects.ac.uk/careers-advice).

### Student grants and loans
For information on student grants, loans and entitlement, contact the relevant funding body:
- **England**: Student Finance England (0300 100 0607; www.gov.uk/student-finance)
- **Northern Ireland**: Student Finance NI (0300 100 0077; www.studentfinanceni.co.uk)
- **Scotland**: Student Awards Agency for Scotland (0300 555 0505; www.saas.gov.uk)
- **Wales**: Student Finance Wales (0300 200 4050; www.studentfinancewales.co.uk)

For information on:
- repayment of student loans, contact: The Student Loans Company (0300 100 0609; www.slc.co.uk)
- Professional and Career Development Loans, contact: the National Careers Service (0800 100 900; www.gov.uk/career-development-loans)
- Hardship funds: ask your student union, personal tutor or welfare office

### Charities and trusts
An information booklet for disabled students, *Funding from charitable trusts*, is available to download free at www.disabilityrightsuk.org/funding-charitable-trusts.

grant or loan you get. If your contributory ESA ends after 12 months of claiming, you may be able to claim income-related ESA (see Chapter 18) if you are entitled to disability living allowance (DLA), personal independence payment (PIP) or armed forces independence payment.

*Note:* To be entitled to ESA you must go undergo the work capability assessment (see Chapter 12). In considering your ability to carry out the activities in this assessment, the DWP will look at how you manage in your daily life, including studying (eg your ability to get around campus and how long you can comfortably sit).

### DLA and PIP

DLA (see Chapter 4) and PIP (see Chapter 5) are not means tested, so grant or loan income will not affect the amount of your benefit. There are no rules that restrict the hours or type of study you can do. Starting an education course does not usually result in the DWP re-assessing your award. However, they will need to re-assess your award if your care or mobility needs have changed in such a way that you may now qualify for a different rate or have ceased to qualify. If you still get DLA and report a change in your care or mobility needs, you will be re-assessed under PIP (see Box B.6 in Chapter 5).

**DLA, PIP and student support** – If your college or university provides you with care and assistance, it may claim some, or all, of your DLA care component or PIP daily living component towards its costs. The care component or daily living component will stop if you are living in a residential college that counts as a 'care home' (see Chapter 5(8) for the definition; the rules are the same for DLA).

If you are a higher education student and need help with personal care, you can apply for assistance from your local adult social care department. If you already receive such support, your needs can be re-assessed if there is a change in your circumstances, such as leaving home to attend a course or a change in your health. See Chapter 36 for details. You can apply for disabled students' allowances to cover the extra disability-related costs or expenses you have while studying (see 1 above and Box I.1).

# 33 Benefits and work

| | | |
|---|---|---|
| 1 | Going back to work | 218 |
| 2 | Can you work while claiming ESA or benefits for incapacity? | 218 |
| 3 | Permitted work | 219 |
| 4 | Can you still get help towards rent, council tax or other housing costs? | 219 |
| 5 | Carer's allowance | 220 |
| 6 | Income support | 220 |
| | Going back to work – a checklist – Box I.5 | 221 |
| 7 | Jobseeker's allowance | 220 |
| 8 | Tax credits | 220 |
| 9 | Universal credit | 220 |
| 10 | Starting self-employment | 222 |
| 11 | Benefit cap | 222 |
| 12 | Health benefits | 222 |
| 13 | Industrial injuries benefit | 222 |
| 14 | Voluntary work | 222 |
| 15 | Stopping work again | 222 |

## 1. Going back to work

This chapter looks at the effect on benefit entitlement of doing paid or voluntary work and the linking rules that can help you return to benefit without losing out.

**What happens to your disability benefits?** – Disability living allowance (DLA), personal independence payment (PIP) and attendance allowance are payable whether or not you are working. They are not means tested, so earnings do not affect the amount of your benefit.

*Note:* Starting a job may suggest that your care or mobility needs have changed, so your benefit entitlement could be reconsidered. It is possible that your care needs may actually increase if you move into work. The DWP views starting or leaving work as a potential 'change of circumstances' for DLA and PIP.

## 2. Can you work while claiming ESA or benefits for incapacity?

Generally, if you do any work, whether or not you expect to be paid, you are treated as capable of work for the week in which you do the work (Sunday to Saturday) and so are not entitled to the following benefits:
- employment and support allowance (ESA);
- incapacity benefit or severe disablement allowance (SDA);
- income support based on incapacity for work (see Box F.1 in Chapter 19);
- disability premium under the 'incapacity condition' (see Chapter 21(2)); *and*
- national insurance credits for limited capability or incapacity for work (see Box D.3 in Chapter 11).

IW Regs, reg 16(1); ESA Regs, reg 40(1); ESA Regs 2013, reg 37(1)

If you come off ESA to start paid work, you can protect your right to return to the benefit for up to 12 weeks (see 15 below).

### Exempt work

You are allowed to do the kinds of work described below while remaining on benefit, although that work might not be ignored completely. The sort of activities or tasks you can do, whether connected with the work or not, could be taken into account when deciding whether you pass the work capability assessment (see Chapter 12) for ESA. When you start work, your case may be referred to a DWP healthcare professional for an opinion and you may be subject to a face-to-face assessment (see Chapter 12(14)) if the activities you carry out in your work suggest that your limited capability for work may have changed. If there is an assessment due anyway during a period of exempt work, it will also go ahead.

The following kinds of work are exempt:
- *'permitted work'* – see 3 below;
- work as a councillor. If you receive a councillor's allowance of more than £125.50 a week (excluding expenses), the excess will be deducted from your contributory ESA, incapacity benefit or SDA;
- care of a relative or domestic tasks carried out in your own home. A *'relative'* is a parent (or in-law or step-parent), son/daughter (in-law/step), brother, sister, or the partner of any of them, or grandparent, grandchild, uncle, aunt, nephew or niece;
- any activity carried out during an emergency to protect another person or to prevent serious damage to property or livestock;
- (for ESA only) fostering a child, if you receive payment from a local authority or voluntary organisation;
- (for ESA only) caring for a young person in Scotland who is provided with continuing care by a local authority that pays you for this;
- (for ESA only) looking after someone who is not normally a member of your household but temporarily in your care (ie a respite care arrangement), if you receive payment from a health body, voluntary organisation or local authority (or from the person placed with you by the local authority);
- a DWP-approved unpaid work trial or work placement;

IW Regs, reg 16(3)(a)-(d); ESA Regs, regs 40(2)(a),(c)-(e) & 45(7); ESA Regs 2013, regs 37(2)(a),(c)-(e) & 39(1)(f)

- self-employed work done while you are 'test trading' for up to 26 weeks with help from a self-employment provider arranged by the DWP;

- voluntary work (not for a relative) – see 14 below;
- duties undertaken as a disability member of a First-tier Tribunal – but only one full day or two half days a week is allowed;

IW Regs, reg 17(5),(6)&(7), ESA Regs, regs 45(5)-(6) & 40(2)(b); ESA Regs 2013, regs 39(1)(d)&(e) & 37(2)(b)

- work which is so minimal that it can be regarded as trivial or negligible – eg someone who occasionally does small jobs for a business (eg signing cheques).

Decision Makers Guide, Vol 3, Chap 13, para 13857

### Dialysis, radiotherapy and other treatments

If you receive certain specified types of treatment for two or more days in a week, you can work on the other days and continue to receive incapacity benefit or SDA for the days of treatment (including days of preparation and recuperation specified as part of the treatment).

If you receive such treatment and can thus be treated as having a limited capability for work for the week (see Chapter 12(3)), you can work on the other days and continue to receive contributory ESA for that week.

IW Regs, reg 13, ESA Regs, reg 46; ESA Regs 2013, reg 40

### If your partner works

Your partner's earnings do not affect the basic amount of contributory ESA, incapacity benefit or SDA you get, but for incapacity benefit and SDA they can affect an adult dependant's addition. Your partner's earnings affect income support, income-related ESA and income-based jobseeker's allowance (see Chapter 22(4)-(6)).

## 3. Permitted work

Permitted work allows you to try out work within certain limits and remain entitled to the benefits listed in 2 above. Providing you work within the stated limits, any earnings from permitted work will not generally affect other benefits you are receiving (see below). There are three types of permitted work. You must inform the DWP that you are due to start permitted work; call 0800 169 0310.

### Permitted work lower limit

You can earn up to £20 a week. This limit means such work should not interfere with your income support award if you qualify for the disability premium.

### Permitted work higher limit

You can earn up to £125.50 a week. You must work less than 16 hours a week; your hours are averaged over the current week and the four preceding weeks, or over the period of a *'recognisable cycle'* of work. Before 3.4.17, there was a 52-week limit on this type of permitted work in some circumstances; this limit no longer applies.

### Supported permitted work

You can earn up to £125.50 a week. Supported permitted work is work that is:

- carried out as part of your treatment programme under medical supervision while you are an inpatient or a regular outpatient of a hospital or similar institution; *or*
- done under the supervision of a person employed by a public or local authority or voluntary or community-interest organisation that provides or arranges work opportunities for disabled people.

In the latter case, you do not need the person to be working alongside you. The support must be ongoing and regular, but the frequency of contact can vary depending on your needs. The means of contact can vary and be face to face or by phone. The work can be in the community or a sheltered workshop.

IW Regs, reg 17(2)-(4) & (8); ESA Regs, reg 45(2)-(4) & (8); ESA Regs 2013, reg 39(1) (a)-(c) & (2)

### Effect of earnings

For employment and support allowance (ESA), earnings from permitted work are calculated in the same way as they are under the income assessment for income-related ESA (see Chapter 22(4)-(5)). For benefits paid for incapacity, earnings from permitted work are calculated in the same way as they are for the carer's allowance dependant's addition (see Chapter 8(5)).

ESA Regs, reg 88; ESA Regs 2013, regs 76-84, R(IB)1/06 (CoA: 'Doyle') & CE Regs

If your earnings from permitted work are no higher than the £20 or £125.50 limit (whichever is appropriate), your ESA, incapacity benefit or severe disablement allowance will not be affected. If you get housing benefit while claiming one of these benefits (or national insurance credits for limited capability or incapacity for work), your earnings from permitted work will be disregarded. If you get income support, only £20 of your earnings can be disregarded. See Chapter 22(6) for more on earnings disregards.

## 4. Can you still get help towards rent, council tax or other housing costs?

### Housing benefit

You can claim housing benefit whether or not you are in work (see Chapter 25). It is means tested, so the amount you get depends on the level of your (and your partner's) income and savings. See Chapter 22(4)-(6) for the way earnings are assessed.

If someone you live with claims housing benefit, they may be liable for non-dependant deductions from their housing benefit, depending on how much you earn (see Chapter 25(21)).

**Extended payments** – If your income-related employment and support allowance (ESA), income-based jobseeker's allowance (JSA) or income support stops because you (or your partner) start work or increase your hours or earnings, your housing benefit may carry on for an extra four weeks at the existing rate. To qualify, you must have been on income-related ESA, income-based JSA or income support (or a combination of these) for at least 26 weeks immediately before starting work (or increasing your hours or earnings). Time spent on contribution-based JSA will count towards the 26 weeks but if you were receiving only contribution-based JSA immediately before starting work, you will not qualify for this run-on. The work, or increased hours or earnings, must be expected to last at least five weeks.

An extended payment of housing benefit can also be made if you have received contributory ESA, incapacity benefit or severe disablement allowance (or a combination of these benefits) for at least 26 weeks before you start work or increase your hours or earnings.

In either case, you do not have to make a separate claim. Simply inform the DWP or the local authority within four weeks that you or your partner have started or are about to start work or that your earnings or hours have increased.

HB Regs, reg 72-73

Once the extended payments end, housing benefit is based on your new circumstances. You do not have to make a new claim. Your benefit entitlement will be continuous.

### Support for mortgage interest loans run-on and housing costs run-on

If your income-related ESA, income-based JSA or income support stops because you or your partner start work or increase your weekly hours or earnings, any support for mortgage interest loans (see Chapter 26) or housing costs (see Chapter 27) you were getting may be paid for an extra four weeks at the existing rate, whatever your earnings. The job (or increased hours or earnings) must be expected to last at least five weeks. You can get this help if you or your partner were getting benefit continuously for at least 26 weeks and you

received support for mortgage interest loans or housing costs immediately before starting (or extending) the work. You do not have to make a separate claim. Simply inform the DWP that you are starting work or increasing your hours/earnings.
LMIR Regs, reg 9(4)-(6); IS Regs, reg 6(5)-(8)

### Council tax reduction

The extended payments rule that applies to housing benefit when you return to work (see above) may also apply to any council tax reduction you are receiving. Check with your local authority for details. See Chapter 28(12) for more on the council tax reduction scheme.

### Universal credit housing costs amount

If you move into work, your universal credit can continue to help with your rent through the *'housing costs amount for renters'* (see Chapter 24(7)-(17)). Unfortunately, support for mortgage interest loans will stop when you do any paid work (see Chapter 26(1)).

## 5. Carer's allowance

You can work and claim carer's allowance at the same time as long as your earnings (less any allowable deductions) are no more than £120 a week. There is no limit on the number of hours you can work, although you must continue to provide care for at least 35 hours a week. Work during breaks from caring (see Chapter 8(11)) does not affect carer's allowance.

Carer's allowance is not means tested. Provided your earnings do not exceed the above limit, the full amount of carer's allowance is payable. Caring costs of up to half your net earnings can be disregarded if you pay someone other than a close relative to look after the disabled person you care for or a child aged under 16 (for whom you get child benefit). Your partner's earnings do not affect the basic amount of carer's allowance you get, but can affect an adult dependant or child dependant's addition. See Chapter 8(5) for details.

Income support to top up your carer's allowance is affected in a different way. For carers, there is no limit on the number of hours you work, but only £20 of your net earnings can be disregarded (see Chapter 22(6)).

## 6. Income support

If you get income support on the grounds of incapacity for work, you may do permitted work of less than 16 hours a week (see 3 above) or other exempt work (see 2 above). If you get income support on any other grounds (eg because you are a carer), you can work for less than 16 hours in any job.

If you are the claimant and your partner works, they must work less than 24 hours a week, although there are some exceptions (see Chapter 19(3)).

In each case, you can only keep a maximum of £20 of your earnings or joint earnings for a couple (see Chapter 22(6)).

If your income support stops because you or your partner start work or increase your hours or earnings, you may continue to get support for mortgage interest loans or housing costs paid for up to four weeks (see 'Support for mortgage interest loans run-on and housing costs run-on' in 4 above).

## 7. Jobseeker's allowance

If you are working less than 16 hours a week, you are eligible for jobseeker's allowance (JSA). If your partner works and you get income-based JSA, they must work less than 24 hours a week. You must still sign on for work and actively look for, and be available to take up, a full-time job. Earnings above the earnings disregard affect the amount you get (see Chapter 13(19)). For income-based JSA only, your partner's earnings also affect the amount of your benefit (see Chapter 22(4)-(6)).

If your income-based JSA stops because you or your partner start work or increase your hours or earnings, you

may continue to get support for mortgage interest loans or housing costs paid for up to four weeks (see 'Support for mortgage interest loans run-on and housing costs run-on' in 4 above).

## 8. Tax credits

You may qualify for tax credits if you are in work (employed or self-employed) or have dependent children and a low income (see Chapter 23). If you qualify for tax credits, you are unlikely to be worse off in work, but it is worth getting advice before taking a job so you know just how your income would be affected. Although tax credits include elements that reflect individual and family needs, including disabilities, they do not allow access to help with mortgage interest.

For all working tax credit (WTC) awards, if you stop work or your normal working hours fall below the minimum required for a WTC claim, which is either 16 or 30 hours a week (or 24 hours a week for some couples with children), you will be treated as being in work for a further four weeks, allowing for a 4-week run-on of WTC. You must report your change of circumstances to HMRC within one month to receive the run-on.
WTC(E&MR) Regs, reg 7D

In order to initially qualify for WTC, your job must be expected to last for at least four weeks.

If you are claiming WTC to top up earnings from self-employment, the employment needs to be on a commercial basis with a view to the realisation of profits and it must be organised and regular. If your income from self-employment falls below the hours you declare that you work, multiplied by the national living wage or national minimum wage that applies in your case (see Box I.5), then you may be asked for evidence that you meet this test.

## 9. Universal credit

Universal credit is replacing several means-tested benefits for people of working age. It is being introduced over several years; see Box E.1 in Chapter 14. For details of universal credit, see Chapters 14 to 17.

Universal credit does not provide for *'permitted work'* (as described in 3 above), even if you are also entitled to employment and support allowance (which does provide for permitted work). However, you are encouraged to do some work, even if only for a few hours a week, if you can.

If you are working, you can continue to claim universal credit as long as your earnings and any other income you have are less than a certain amount, calculated using the *'maximum amount'* that applies in your case (see Chapter 16(1) for details). A *'childcare costs amount'* is included in your maximum amount if you pay for certain types of childcare to stay in work (see Chapter 16(8)). When your earnings are calculated, some may be disregarded using the *'work allowance'* (see Chapter 16(9)).

Universal credit can include help towards some housing costs; see 4 above.

### Work capability amount

If your disability or health condition limits your ability to work, additional support may be provided in universal credit through the *'work capability amount'* (see Chapter 16(6)). This may not be payable if you move into full-time work (ie where your earnings are greater than your *'earnings exemption threshold'* – see Chapter 16(12)), depending on whether or not you have had a work capability assessment (WCA; see Chapter 12).

❏ If you have been found to have a limited capability for work at a WCA before you start the full-time work and are already getting the work capability amount, you can continue to receive it. You will lose it only if at a future WCA you are found not to qualify.

## I.5 Going back to work – a checklist

This is a guide to the main help available if you are in work or looking for work. Where there is more information in this or other chapters, we refer you to the right place in this handbook. For information about other kinds of help, ask at your Jobcentre Plus office.

The benefits marked with an asterisk (*) are being replaced with universal credit over time; see Box E.1 in Chapter 14 for details.

### Working 16 hours a week or more

**Tax credits*** – Top up earnings if you are in low-paid work. See Chapter 23.

**Income support*** – You can stay on income support in some circumstances – eg, you are a carer. Keep up to £20 a week of earnings. Income support gives access to support for mortgage interest loans (see Chapter 26); tax credits do not. See Chapter 19.

**Housing benefit*** – Help with rent. See Chapter 25.

**Council tax reduction** – Help with council tax. See Chapter 28(12).

**Universal credit** – Top up earnings if you are in low paid work. See Chapters 14 to 17.

### Working under 16 hours a week

**Permitted work** – Employment and support allowance (ESA), incapacity benefit and severe disablement allowance (SDA) can be paid in addition to permitted work earnings of up to a maximum of £125.50 a week (see Chapter 33(3)).

**Income support*** – You can stay on income support if work is permitted or you are eligible for a reason other than incapacity for work. Keep up to £20 a week of earnings. See Chapter 33(6).

**Jobseeker's allowance (JSA)** – Keep up to £20 a week of earnings. You must still look for full-time work. See Chapter 33(7).

**Housing benefit*** – Help with rent. See Chapter 25.

**Council tax reduction** – Help with council tax. See Chapter 28(12).

**Universal credit** – Top up earnings if you are in low paid work. See Chapters 14 to 17.

### When you start work

**Housing benefit extended payments** – Existing rate paid for the first four weeks after coming off ESA, incapacity benefit, income-based JSA, income support or SDA. See Chapter 33(4).

**Support for mortgage interest loans run-on** – Existing support for mortgage interest loans paid for the first four weeks after coming off income-related ESA, income-based JSA or income support. See Chapter 33(4).

**Housing costs run-on** – Existing housing costs paid for the first four weeks after coming off income-related ESA, income-based JSA or income support. See Chapter 33(4).

**Benefit linking rules** – Various linking rules help you reclaim benefit on the same terms as before if you have to stop work again. See Chapter 33(15).

### Equipment and support at work

**Access to Work** – Can help pay for equipment and adaptations at work and can cover extra disability-related costs such as travel to work and support workers. See Chapter 34(3).

**Work and Health Programme** – Helps you find and keep a job if you're out of work. See Chapter 34(2).

### Trying out a job

**Benefit linking rules** – Various linking rules help you reclaim benefit without losing out after a trial period at work. See Chapter 33(15).

**Work trials** – Allow you to stay on benefit and receive travel and meal allowances for up to 30 working days while you and the employer decide if you will be suitable for a job.

**Employment on Trial** – Your JSA will not be sanctioned if you leave a job voluntarily during the trial period. See Chapter 13(14).

### Starting a business

Contact: Business Support in England (helpline: 0300 456 3565; textphone 0191 581 0052), Business Gateway in Scotland (helpline: 0300 013 4753; textphone: 0800 023 2071; www.bgateway.com/) or Business Wales (helpline: 0300 060 3000; https://businesswales.gov.wales/).

There is useful information on starting a business at www.gov.uk/browse/business.

**New Enterprise Allowance** – Financial help for people out of work and entering self-employment. See Chapter 33(10).

**Enterprise clubs** – Local clubs you can attend if you want to start self-employment. They are attended by local businesses, advisers and other people looking to start self-employment.

### Looking for work

**JSA** – Weekly benefit providing a basic income if you are looking for work. See Chapter 13.

**Access to Work** – Help with the cost of travel, support workers and communication support at interviews paid through the Access to Work scheme. See Chapter 34(3).

**Budgeting loan** – A budgeting loan can help with the expenses of looking for work or starting work if you have been getting income-related ESA, income-based JSA or income support for at least 26 weeks. See Chapter 31(2).

**Work clubs** – Local support groups you can attend to share experiences, gain contacts and develop skills to help re-engage in the workplace.

**Flexible support fund** – A discretionary fund that Jobcentre Plus can tap into to help you with financial barriers into employment, eg buying a suit. Speak to your work coach for more information.

### Childcare costs

**Working tax credit*** – Includes a childcare element covering up to 70% of eligible childcare costs. See Chapter 23(7).

**Housing benefit*** – Certain childcare costs can be disregarded from your earnings in the benefit assessment. See Chapter 22(6).

**Universal credit** – Includes a childcare costs amount covering up to 85% of eligible childcare costs. See Chapter 16(8).

### Employment rights

**Equality Act** – See Chapter 3.

**National minimum wage** – £7.38 an hour for workers aged 21-24, £5.90 if aged 18-20 and £4.20 if aged 16/17. The apprentice minimum wage is £3.70 an hour for apprentices under 19 and for those aged 19 or over in their first year of an apprenticeship.

**National living wage** – £7.83 an hour for workers aged 25 or over.

**Other rights at work** – Contact your trade union or ACAS (Advisory, Conciliation and Arbitration Service): 0300 123 1100, Text Relay service 18001 0300 123 1100.

❑ If you have not had a WCA before you start the full-time work, you will not be referred to a WCA to assess whether you are entitled to the work capability amount unless you are also entitled to attendance allowance, disability living allowance, personal independence payment or armed forces independence payment.
UC Regs, reg 41

## 10. Starting self-employment
### New Enterprise Allowance scheme
You may get help under the *'New Enterprise Allowance scheme'* if you are aged 18 or over and want to start a business, and you receive:
■ (or your partner receives) jobseeker's allowance or employment and support allowance;
■ income support as a lone parent or on the basis of incapacity (see Box F.1 in Chapter 19); *or*
■ universal credit (if any of the work-related requirements apply to you; see Box E.3 in Chapter 15).
The scheme includes help from a business mentor to develop a business idea and write a business plan. You can get ongoing support from a business mentor in the early months of trading. You might also be able to get a loan to help with start-up costs. To apply for a start-up loan go to www.gov.uk/apply-start-up-loan. The New Enterprise Allowance scheme can provide a weekly allowance for up to 26 weeks of your business venture. For details, contact your work coach at the local Jobcentre Plus office.

### Self-employment and universal credit
If you are self-employed and claiming universal credit, you will be asked at the work search interview (see Chapter 14(5)) about the hours you work and the earnings you receive in your business to find out if you can be treated as being in *'gainful self-employment'*.

If your earnings from the self-employment (plus any earnings from other employment) are less than a set minimum amount, the *'minimum income floor'*, you may be treated as having earnings equal to that amount and your universal credit will be calculated using this higher figure. This will not apply, however, during a 12-month start-up period. See Chapter 17(5) for details.

See Chapter 17(3) for how self-employed earnings are worked out in the universal credit calculation and Chapter 17(4) for which business-related expenses can be deducted.

You will be offered help from a business mentor to develop your business and write a business plan. This support will last for 12 weeks, and can be extended for a further year if the business plan is viable.

## 11. Benefit cap
The benefit cap places a restriction on the total amount of benefits you can claim, based on your situation. See Box G.6 in Chapter 25 for details, and Chapter 16(10)-(12) for the similar cap in universal credit.

If you return to work and receive working tax credit, you are exempt from the cap (the government has said this will also apply if you work enough hours to qualify for working tax credit but are not paid it because your income is too high). In the case of universal credit, you are exempt from the cap if you have net monthly earnings (or combined earnings if you are one of a couple) at or above the *'earnings exemption threshold'* (see Chapter 16(12)).

The benefit cap is not applied during a 39-week *'grace period'* if you were previously working for 50 weeks out of the last 52 weeks, were not claiming income support, employment and support allowance or jobseeker's allowance while you were working, and you lost your job through no fault of your own. A similar 9-month grace period applies to universal credit (see Chapter 16(12)).

If you have reached pension credit qualifying age (see Chapter 44(2)), the cap will not apply.

## 12. Health benefits
You may qualify for help with prescription charges, hospital travel costs, dental treatment, sight tests and glasses. If your income and savings are low, claim on form HC1, available from the doctor, dentist or optician or by ringing 0300 123 0849. You qualify automatically if you get income-related employment and support allowance, income-based jobseeker's allowance or income support. If you get tax credits or universal credit you may qualify, depending on the level of your earnings. See Chapter 52.

## 13. Industrial injuries benefit
Industrial injuries disablement benefit is not affected by your work or earnings. If you claim housing benefit, any industrial injuries benefit is taken into account in full. However, it is disregarded for tax credits.
TC(DCI) Regs, reg 7

## 14. Voluntary work
If you get incapacity benefit or severe disablement allowance you are allowed to do voluntary work for anyone other than a close relative (parent (or in-law or step-parent), son/daughter (in-law/step), brother, sister or the partner of any of these). If you get employment and support allowance or income support, you are allowed to do voluntary work for anyone other than a relative (see 2 above). You must not be paid for your work, other than expenses *'reasonably incurred by [you] in connection with that work'*. Permitted expenses could include travel, meals, childminding, the costs of caring for a dependant, equipment needed for work and use of a telephone. There is no limit on the number of hours you can volunteer.
IW Regs, regs 2 & 17(6); IS Regs, reg 6(1)(c); ESA Regs, regs 2 & 45(6)&(10); ESA Regs 2013, reg 39(1)(e)&(6)

See Chapter 19(3) for more on income support and voluntary work.

## 15. Stopping work again
If you stop claiming benefits to begin work, but then stop working and re-claim benefit, there are linking rules that may allow you to go back to your previous benefit on the same terms as before.
**Rapid re-claim** – You can make a rapid re-claim if you were claiming jobseeker's allowance (JSA) or income support before starting work, the job ended within 26 weeks and your circumstances are broadly the same as when you made the previous claim. In the case of JSA, you can re-open your JSA claim online; in the case of income support, you can complete a rapid re-claim form. Both should speed up the processing of your new claim. Rapid re-claim also applies to housing benefit if you are making a rapid re-claim for JSA or income support.

### Incapacity-related benefits
New claims for incapacity benefit, income support paid on the grounds of incapacity or severe disablement allowance can normally no longer be made. Consequently, the linking rules that allowed you to re-claim these benefits after a break in entitlement have been abolished. You will have to make a new claim for employment and support allowance (ESA) instead.

### Employment and support allowance
**12-week linking rule** – Any two periods of limited capability for work (ie days when you have a limited capability for work) separated by no more than 12 weeks are treated as a single period (see Chapter 11(11)). So if you re-claim ESA within 12 weeks of a previous award, you will not have to serve any waiting days (see Chapter 11(10)). If you had

served the 13-week assessment phase in the previous award, you can go back onto the rate of payment of the earlier ESA award straightaway (as long as the previous award was not terminated because you were found not to have a limited capability for work; see Chapter 12(2)).

ESA Regs, regs 7, 35A & 145(1); ESA Regs 2013, regs 7, 32 & 86

### Other linking rules
**Housing costs** – For linking rules and other help, see Chapter 27(5).
**Housing benefit** – If you have been claiming housing benefit continuously since before 1996, you are exempt from the rent restrictions described in Chapter 25(8). To keep the exemption, any break in claim must be no longer than four weeks. See Chapter 25(11) for details.

# 34 Employment and training

| | | |
|---|---|---|
| 1 | Introduction | 223 |
| 2 | Work and Health Programme | 223 |
| 3 | Access to Work | 223 |
| | Access to Work: examples – Box I.6 | 224 |
| 4 | Training | 225 |
| 5 | Benefits and training | 225 |

## 1. Introduction
This chapter covers some of the services and programmes designed to help you get and remain in work. Some schemes pay allowances or provide services to make finding work easier, others seek to compel you to find work by cutting or removing your benefit if you do not take particular actions recommended to you.
**Jobcentre Plus** – Jobcentre Plus is the DWP organisation providing benefits and services for people of working age (ie between the ages of 16 and pension credit qualifying age – see Chapter 44(2)). Most people who claim benefits from Jobcentre Plus have a *'work coach'* allocated to them to deal with claims and provide information on work and training opportunities.
**Disability employment advisers** (DEAs) – DEAs provide specialist advice and information on Jobcentre Plus programmes for disabled people. The work coach and DEA roles are complementary. There are a limited number of DEAs and they are predominantly being used to support work coaches, rather than dealing with claimants directly.
**Universal credit: Youth Obligation** – The *'Youth Obligation'* will apply to you if you are aged 18-21, live in a 'full service area' (see Box E.1 in Chapter 15) and need to meet all the universal credit work-related requirements (see Box E.3 in Chapter 15). After an initial three-week intensive support period, you will be encouraged to take up an apprenticeship or traineeship or gain work-based skills; if you are still claiming universal credit after six months, you will have to take up such activity.

## 2. Work and Health Programme
The new *'Work and Health Programme'* is being set up in England and Wales to provide work support to people with a health condition or disability, as well as those who have been unemployed for over two years. The programme is voluntary, unless you have been claiming jobseeker's allowance or universal credit (and need to meet all the work-related requirements – see Box E.3 in Chapter 15) for two years.

The programme should provide you with personal support to help you find sustained employment. This may include:
■ identifying your employment needs;
■ matching your skills to available work;
■ putting you in touch with employers; *and*
■ managing your health problems to reduce their impact on work.
For details, contact your work coach.

### Fair Start Scotland
Employment support has been devolved to the Scottish government. From April 2018, the *'Fair Start Scotland'* service has replaced two existing schemes: 'Work First Scotland' and 'Work Able Scotland'. The new service, which is voluntary, has been set up to help people find employment, including those facing barriers moving into work. It aims to provide tailored and personalised support for all those who take part.

The service offers pre-work support for 12 to 18 months. If you move into work, you should receive in-work support for a further 12 months. If you need intensive support due to your disability, you may be offered supported employment.

For details, contact your work coach.

## 3. Access to Work
If you have a disability or health condition, a grant from *'Access to Work'* can pay for practical support to help you start work, stay in work or move into self-employment. An Access to Work grant can cover such costs as:
■ special aids, equipment or software for employment;
■ adaptations to the equipment you already use;
■ adaptations to existing (but not to new) premises;
■ adaptations to your vehicle so you can get to work;
■ help with travel to work if you can't use public transport because you are disabled (a medical opinion is needed before this support is granted), or support with travel training or 'buddying' to help you adapt to using public transport if you have recently become disabled;
■ a support worker to provide help in the workplace (eg support with training on the job if you have a learning disability, or a reader);
■ disability awareness training for your colleagues;
■ the cost of moving equipment if you change location or job;
■ a communicator for support at job interviews; *and*
■ an interpreter or lip speaker when you need to be meeting or communicating with others.

### Excluded expenditure
Certain types of expenditure might not be covered, such as expenditure on standard equipment, and it is important to get clarification on this during the application process (see below). See Box I.6 for examples of situations where Access to Work can help.

Access to Work will not cover costs that should be met by your employer as a *'reasonable adjustment'* under the Equality Act (see Chapter 3(4)). In such cases, the Access to Work adviser may discuss this with you and your employer.
**Repairs and maintenance** – Repairs and maintenance of equipment are not covered by Access to Work. You could check whether your employer has a duty to cover them under the Equality Act as a reasonable adjustment. Even if this duty does not apply, you could ask the employer if they would share maintenance and insurance costs, and agree that you can take the equipment if you move to another job. If you are self-employed, contact the Business Support helpline (see Box I.5) to see if there are other resources available.

### Who can get help?
You may be eligible if you are employed (including as an apprentice), self-employed or unemployed and have a job to start or a job interview, and you are disabled. Access to Work defines disability as in the Equality Act (see Chapter 3(2)) but

extends it to include impairments and health conditions that are only apparent in the workplace.

Access to Work can provide help to take part in government work placements (such as Jobcentre Plus work trials) or work placements under the government-supported internship or traineeship programmes (for the period of the work placement). Some self-arranged work placements may also be covered.

Access to Work is available if you are setting up your own business and enrolled on the New Enterprise Allowance scheme (see Chapter 33(10)).

*Note:* Access to Work does not cover Northern Ireland, which has its own version.

**Help for people with mental health conditions** – The Workplace Mental Health Support Service is provided by Remploy. The service provides a range of support, including:
■ work-focused mental health support for six months;
■ an assessment of your needs to identify coping strategies;
■ a personalised support plan, detailing the steps needed for you to remain in, or return to, work; *and*
■ identifying reasonable adjustments within the workplace or of working practice.

For details, call 0300 456 8114.

**Exclusions** – You might not qualify for Access to Work if you are claiming certain benefits while working. Check this with an Access to Work adviser.

**How much support can you get?**
If you are working for an employer and have been in a job for less than six weeks, are self-employed or are about to start work, Access to Work will cover 100% of approved costs. If you have been working for an employer for six weeks or more when you apply for help, Access to Work may pay only some of the costs of certain types of support; this is called *'cost sharing'*. Whether cost sharing applies, and the exact share of the costs, will depend on the number of employees in the organisation you work for. See our Access to Work factsheet for further information (www.disabilityrightsuk.org/access-work).

Access to Work funding agreements can cover up to three years. However, reviews usually take place at least once a year to assess whether funding will continue.

**Annual cap** – There is an annual cap on the total amount of support that can be provided under Access to Work; this is currently set at £57,200. In exceptional cases, this can be averaged over a period of two or more years.

**Applications**
Contact Access to Work by phone (0800 121 7479; textphone 0800 121 7579) or apply online (www.gov.uk/access-to-work/apply). General details will first be obtained, such as your national insurance number, the employer's contact details, a brief description of the job, details of your disability or health

---

# I.6   Access to Work: examples

### Danielle
Danielle works for the local hospital as an assistant in medical records. Her job involves tracking hospital notes, filing, merging and moving data and records, and using standard office equipment. Danielle has Asperger's syndrome and needs intensive support to learn to do tasks. She also experiences difficulties with travel to and from work.

Access to Work has provided funding for a support worker to help Danielle learn tasks and then allow her to work independently. Danielle's role has been analysed and broken down into bite-sized chunks so she can use them as a prompt. She also gets help with travel to and from work.

### Fiona
Fiona works for a care inspectorate. Her job involves meetings, site visits and compiling intensive reports on care homes.

Fiona is dyslexic and this was affecting her work. Although she uses assistive technology – Dragon and a Dictaphone – she was still experiencing difficulties. During her assessment with her adviser it was established that Fiona was off with work-related stress and had been for six months. The absence was not linked to her dyslexia, but stemmed from a number of personal issues. Fiona wanted to return to work but was very anxious and stressed about going back and was experiencing fatigue, disturbed sleep and dizziness.

Fiona was referred to the Workplace Mental Health Support Service. A support plan was agreed to provide her with a range of coping strategies to equip her with the tools and resources to effectively manage workplace stress and anxiety. She returned to work and was assigned a new line manager. Access to Work also funded training to help with the dyslexia. Fiona now has regular reviews with her new manager and has a far healthier work-life balance. She feels she has regained her productivity and stamina and is much more supported in her role. Consequently she has had no further absence from work in the past six months.

### Ryan
Ryan is profoundly deaf. He is employed as a part-time British Sign Language (BSL) teacher. He is also a self-employed plasterer. In his teaching job, Ryan experiences communication difficulties in meetings, as none of the other team members are hearing impaired. Access to Work has provided funding for a BSL interpreter to provide communication support for Ryan when he attends meetings.

As a plasterer, Ryan has the appropriate skills and equipment to undertake the work; his only difficulty is communication. Access to Work has provided funding for a BSL interpreter who helps Ryan overcome the communication difficulties encountered in the job, eg on site dealing with customers or contractors, and then at home accessing answer machine messages and making telephone calls (when texting, emails or Minicom is not appropriate). Ryan has also been provided with special aids and equipment such as a Ubi Duo communication device for short conversations (face-to-face only) when it would be impractical to call out an interpreter.

### Anne
Anne is registered blind, and has had bilateral congenital cataracts and undeveloped retinas since birth. She has some residual vision but is unable to read printed documents or see her computer screen. She works as a rehabilitation officer, working two days a week in the office and three days visiting service users in their homes. Access to Work provides Anne with funding for:
■ a support worker;
■ specialist software to enhance the content of her computer screen; *and*
■ a large computer screen to afford the best opportunity of viewing her work.

The support worker acts as her driver, her facilitator when she is teaching orientation and mobility, and her assistant when she has lengthy reports and departmental documents to read. Anne uses Zoomtext, specialist software that enables her to use a computer in the same way as her sighted peers. The large computer screen complements the software being used, allowing her to see as much as possible.

condition and how this will affect your work. Before you apply, think about the tasks involved in the job and the impact your disability may have on them.

This will usually be followed up with a telephone interview by an Access to Work adviser to assess your eligibility. In the meantime, if you think you may get help from the scheme, you can download an Access to Work eligibility letter to take to your employer or the job interview (www.gov.uk/government/publications/access-to-work-eligibility-letter-for-employees-and-employers).

**Delays** – If there is a delay in the application, ask the Access to Work adviser to explore temporary alternatives. If you are employed, speak to your employer to see if they can help.

### Challenging decisions
Although there is no formal appeal procedure, you can ask for a decision to be reconsidered by a different Access to Work adviser.

## 4. Training
There are many government training programmes and new initiatives are often launched, which you can find out about at your local Jobcentre Plus office. If you have a disability, various types of help are available to enable you to take part in government training programmes, including individually tailored programmes, aids, equipment, adaptations to premises and equipment, a readership service for blind people and an interpreter service for deaf people. Contact your work coach (see 1 above) or ring the National Careers Service helpline (0800 100 900) or Skills Development Scotland (0800 917 8000).

### Work-based learning
Work-based learning (WBL) is the name generally used for government-funded schemes that allow you to achieve recognised vocational qualifications at the same time as gaining relevant, practical experience in work situations. WBL covers a number of programmes and courses, such as apprenticeships or combining a job with study towards a vocational qualification. In WBL, you can be an employed or unemployed trainee. If you are not employed while training, a training allowance might be available.

### Traineeships
These are for people aged 16 to 24, who are looking for work and who need help securing an apprenticeship or other job. A traineeship lasts for up to six months, and is made up of a work experience placement, work preparation and training, and help with English and maths (if you need it).

For information, speak to your work coach at Jobcentre Plus, contact the National Careers Service or Skills Development Scotland (see above) or go to www.gov.uk/government/collections/traineeships-programme.

### Supported internships
This is a study programme for 16-24-year-olds with a statement of special educational needs, learning difficulty assessment or an education, health and care plan. It is for those who want to move from education into work and who need extra support to do so. It includes on-the-job training by job coaches and the chance to study for qualifications where appropriate. It lasts for a minimum of six months. For information, ring the National Careers Service or Skills Development Scotland (see above) or go to www.preparingforadulthood.org.uk/downloads/supported-internships.

### Apprenticeships
An apprenticeship is a real job with training. Apprentices work alongside experienced staff to gain job-specific skills. Off the job, usually on a day-release basis, apprentices receive training

to work towards a nationally recognised qualification. This training is sometimes funded by the government.

If you are employed on an apprenticeship scheme, you must be paid at least the national minimum wage for apprentices (see Box I.5). If you are aged 19 or over and have completed the first year of an apprenticeship, the full national minimum wage/living wage for your age must be paid. For information, including vacancy and registration details, go to www.gov.uk/topic/further-education-skills/apprenticeships or www.skillsdevelopmentscotland.co.uk.

### Time to Train
If you work in an organisation with 250 or more employees, you have the right to request time off for study or training. To qualify, you must have worked for your employer continuously for at least 26 weeks. The training must help you to do your job better. Your employer does not have to pay for the training, but if they recognise the benefit of the training to their business they may choose to pay for it. Your employer may pay you for the training time but they do not have to.

### Specialist Employability Support
This provides mentoring and training to help you into work if you have a disability and are not able to use other employment programmes, such as Access to Work and the Work and Health Programme. To apply, contact your local Jobcentre Plus office.

## 5. Benefits and training
### Disability living allowance (DLA) and personal independence payment (PIP)
DLA and PIP are not usually affected if you take part in training or if you get a training allowance. Your ability to start a training programme may suggest a lessening in your care or mobility needs, so your benefit may be reconsidered. However, starting training is not a relevant change of circumstances that must be reported to the DWP in relation to DLA or PIP. (Examples of relevant changes for the purposes of DLA or PIP would be a significant increase or decrease in your care or supervision needs or a deterioration or improvement in your ability to get around outdoors.)

### Income support
If you are aged under 25, not a 'qualifying young person' (see Chapter 41(1)) and taking part in training provided by the DWP, Skills Funding, the Welsh government or, in Scotland, a local enterprise company, you may be able to claim income support to top up your training allowance. See Chapter 22(12) for how a government training allowance is treated in the income support calculation.
IS Regs, Sch 1B, para 28

Once you leave the programme, you are no longer eligible for income support unless you are covered by one of the other situations listed in Box F.1 in Chapter 19. You may be able to claim jobseeker's allowance instead, although sanctions may apply if you do not have a *'good reason'* for not completing a programme – see Chapter 13(11).

**Disability premium** – If you were getting a disability premium before beginning the programme, it will not be withdrawn even though you may no longer be receiving the qualifying benefit. At the end of the programme, you will continue to receive the disability premium only if you meet the qualifying conditions (see Chapter 21(2)).
IS Regs, Sch 2, para 7(1)(b)

### Jobseeker's allowance
You may be able to get jobseeker's allowance (JSA) on some training courses, depending on the type of course and your individual circumstances. In some cases, you may be regarded as a student; most full-time students are excluded from JSA (see Chapter 32(4)).

Some of those on a traineeship (see 4 above) can get JSA even if the training is full time. Check with Jobcentre Plus if this could apply to you.

### Employment and support allowance (ESA)
You may get ESA on certain training courses. This depends on the course and your individual circumstances.

In some cases, you may be regarded as a student; most full-time students are excluded from income-related ESA (see Chapter 32(2) for exceptions). There are no rules to prevent you from studying or training and receiving contributory ESA. However, the assessment of your ability to complete the activities in the work capability assessment will take into account how you manage on your course. Starting a course may lead to a re-assessment of your limited capability for work.

If your course is funded by the European Social Fund, seek advice.

You cannot usually get ESA if you are on an apprenticeship, as you would normally be doing employed work of over 16 hours a week.

**Training allowances** – A day when you receive a government training allowance (other than just travel and meals expenses) cannot count as a day of limited capability for work. This means that when you start a programme that includes such an allowance, you will cease to be entitled to ESA.

ESA Regs, reg 32(2)&(3)(b); ESA Regs 2013, reg 27(2)&(3)(b)

### Universal credit
You may be able to get universal credit on some training courses, depending on the course and your circumstances; see Chapter 32(2).

### Non-government training courses
If you get a training allowance on a non-government course, it is treated differently from a government training allowance. It will be taken into account in full as income for income support and other means-tested benefits unless some or all of it can be disregarded under the normal rules.

# 35 Income tax

| | | |
|---|---|---|
| 1 | Introduction | 226 |
| 2 | Income | 226 |
| 3 | Tax allowances | 226 |
| 4 | Income tax rates (non-savings income) | 227 |
| 5 | Working out your tax | 227 |
| 6 | Notice of coding | 227 |
| 7 | Tax on savings income and dividends | 227 |
| 8 | Tax refunds | 228 |
| 9 | Arrears of tax | 228 |
| 10 | Self-assessment | 228 |
| 11 | Self-employment | 228 |
| 12 | Personal tax accounts | 228 |

## 1. Introduction
This chapter briefly outlines income tax, but applies only to incomes up to £100,000, above which allowances may be withdrawn. Contact details for HMRC are at www.gov.uk/contact-hmrc. Alternatively, HMRC has a tax helpline (0300 200 3300, textphone 0300 200 3319) and a self-assessment helpline (0300 200 3310, textphone 0300 200 3319). For independent advice, contact TaxAid (0345 120 3779 or www.taxaid.org.uk) and for the over-60s, Tax Help for Older People (0845 601 3321 and 01308 488 066 or www.taxvol.org.uk).

To check if you are paying the right amount of tax, you need to know what income is taxable (see 2 below), what allowances you are entitled to (see 3 below) and the appropriate rate of tax (see 4 below). Allowances and tax rates change each year (from 6 April). The figures and allowances in this chapter are for 6.4.18 to 5.4.19.

## 2. Income
Many types of income (eg earnings and state benefits) are taxable, but some are exempt (eg interest on an Individual Savings Account or 'ISA') and so are ignored for tax. Tax relief is allowed on certain outgoings (eg pension contributions).

The following are the only taxable state benefits:
- adult dependants' additions paid with certain benefits (but not additions for children);
- bereavement allowance, widowed mother's/parent's allowance and widow's pension;
- carer's allowance;
- contributory employment and support allowance;
- long-term incapacity benefit (but not if you transferred from invalidity benefit – see Box D.6 in Chapter 11);
- income support (if you are directly involved in a trade dispute);
- invalidity allowance (paid with a state pension);
- industrial death benefit;
- jobseeker's allowance;
- state pension; *and*
- statutory adoption pay, statutory maternity pay, statutory paternity pay, statutory shared parental pay and statutory sick pay.

## 3. Tax allowances
Tax allowances are amounts of annual income on which you do not have to pay tax. You are entitled to a *'personal allowance'*; you may also be entitled to a *'blind person's allowance'* or *'married couple's allowance'*, or if you are married or in a civil partnership you may benefit from transferring some allowances between you. If you think you have not had the correct allowances, a refund may be due (see 8 below).

**Personal allowance** – Everyone has a personal allowance that can be set against all taxable income – for the tax year 6.4.18 to 5.4.19 it is £11,850. Spouses and civil partners each have their own income limit.

In some limited circumstances, the full amount of personal allowance is not available (eg if your income is over £100,000 or you do not meet certain residence conditions).

**Marriage allowance** – If you do not use your full personal allowance, and are not entitled to married couple's allowance, you can apply to transfer £1,185 of your personal allowance to your spouse or civil partner: the *'marriage allowance'*. Otherwise, you cannot transfer it or carry it forward to a future year. The marriage allowance has to be claimed, either online at www.gov.uk/apply-marriage-allowance, by phoning HMRC on 0300 200 3300, or via your personal tax account (see 12 below). Tax relief on marriage allowance is restricted to 20% and this amount is taken off tax due for the year. To see how it works, see the example in 5 below.

**Blind person's allowance** – You get an extra allowance of £2,390 if you are registered blind (but not if registered as partially sighted). In Scotland and Northern Ireland, you must be unable to do any work for which eyesight is essential. Spouses or civil partners can transfer surplus allowance from one to the other. If both spouses/civil partners are registered blind, one of them can get both their own blind person's allowance and the other's surplus allowance. You can receive the allowance for the tax year before the one in which you are registered as blind if you had obtained the evidence for registration (eg an ophthalmologist's certificate) before the end of that tax year.

**Married couple's allowance** – This is for married couples or civil partners who live together if at least one of them was born before 6.4.35; the allowance for 2018/19 is £8,695. Tax relief on married couple's allowance is restricted to 10% and this amount is taken off tax due for the year.

The married couple's allowance may be reduced if the income of the higher-earning partner is above £28,900 (by £1 for every £2 over this limit). The married couple's allowance can be reduced to a minimum of £3,360.

## 4. Income tax rates (non-savings income)

| Taxable income | rate for tax year 2018/19 |
| --- | --- |

**UK rates and bands**

| | |
| --- | --- |
| The first £34,500 | 20% (basic rate) |
| From £34,501 to £150,000 | 40% (higher rate) |
| Over £150,000 | 45% (additional rate) |

**Scottish rates and bands***

| | |
| --- | --- |
| The first £2,000 | 19% (starter rate) |
| From £2,001 to £12,150 | 20% (basic rate) |
| From £12,151 to £32,423 | 21% (intermediate rate) |
| From £32,424 to £150,000 | 41% (higher rate) |
| Over £150,000 | 46% (top rate) |

* Rates and bands if you are a Scottish taxpayer. You will normally be a Scottish taxpayer if you live in Scotland for most of the tax year – see www.litrg.org.uk/tax-guides/tax-basics/what-scottish-rate-income-tax/do-i-have-pay-scottish-income-tax for details.

For more information on rates and allowances, see https://www.gov.uk/government/publications/rates-and-allowances-income-tax/income-tax-rates-and-allowances-current-and-past

## 5. Working out your tax
### Step 1: Work out your taxable income
Add up income from all sources for the tax year (6 April to 5 April). Include taxable state benefits, but not exempt income (see www.litrg.org.uk/tax-guides/tax-basics/what-income-taxable).
### Step 2: Deduct personal allowances
Deduct your personal allowance (plus the blind person's allowance if you qualify) from your taxable income in Step 1. If your taxable income exceeds £100,000, the basic personal allowance is reduced by £1 for every £2 of income over £100,000 until it is reduced to nil (for 2018/19, this will be the case for incomes over £123,700). Blind person's allowance is not reduced whatever your income level.
### Step 3: Work out your tax
a) Work out the tax on the result from Step 2 using the income limits and tax rates in the table in 4 above (use the Scottish rate band, if you are a Scottish taxpayer). Different tax rates may apply on savings income from banks and building societies and on dividend income (see 7 below).

b) If you get married couple's allowance, work out 10% of it and deduct the result from the tax payable in (a), or if you get marriage allowance, work out 20% of that and deduct the result from the tax payable in (a). This is the tax you are due to pay (before taking off any tax already paid at source).

*Example:* James, aged 68, is married to Annie, 58. James is registered blind. He gets a private pension of £11,514 for this tax year and state pension of £7,035. Annie has a part-time job and earns £5,000. As Annie's income is less than her personal allowance, they can benefit from the marriage allowance and Annie can transfer £1,185 to James.

**Step 1: James's taxable income**

| | |
| --- | --- |
| Private pension | £11,514 |
| State pension | £7,035 |
| *All taxable income* | *£18,549* |

**Step 2: Deduct personal allowances**

| | |
| --- | --- |
| Personal allowance | £11,850 |
| Blind person's allowance | £2,390 |
| *Total personal allowances* | *£14,240* |
| Subtract allowances from income | |
| *Taxable income* | *£4,309* |

**Step 3: James's tax**

| | |
| --- | --- |
| a) 20% of £4,309 | £861.80 |
| b) Less 20% of £1,185 marriage allowance | £237.00 |
| *Tax due to be paid* | *£624.80* |

James will know if he is due to pay tax or due a refund by checking his P60 (issued by the pension company after the tax year end) to see how much tax he paid on his private pension through PAYE (see 6 below) against tax due of £624.80.

## 6. Notice of coding
If you have earnings or private pension income, tax will generally be deducted under PAYE (Pay As You Earn). HMRC should send you a notice of coding (form P2), setting out your allowances and any necessary deductions and how these are to be allocated against different sources of income. Contact HMRC if you think it is incorrect; the contact details will be on the coding notice.

For example, a single person who is registered blind would get allowances of £14,240 (personal allowance £11,850 plus blind person's allowance £2,390). Their code would be 1424L; the final digit of the allowance is replaced by the letter L if the basic personal allowance applies. Other letters (N, M or T) may be used; N and M are used for the giver or receiver of the marriage allowance (see 3 above); T is used in most other cases. In some cases, a code BR will be used instead; this is a basic rate of 20% on earnings with no personal allowances.

If you are a Scottish taxpayer, your tax code will start with the letter S. So, if you have the basic personal allowance, your tax code will be S1185L.

If HMRC think you have not paid enough tax under PAYE, or have paid too much tax, they will send you a tax calculation after the end of the tax year. This will either be a *'P800'* tax calculation or a *'simple assessment letter'* (PA302). You should check the calculation carefully to make sure it is correct.

## 7. Tax on savings income and dividends
**Savings income from banks and building societies** – Until April 2016, tax of 20% was deducted by banks, building societies, etc from most interest on savings. However, from 6.4.16, interest is paid in full (gross) and income tax is *not* deducted at source before you receive it. Interest on savings is only taxable if it exceeds the *'personal savings allowance'*. This is £1,000 if your taxable income is less than £46,350 in the tax year; and £500 if your taxable income is between £46,350 and £150,000.

The tax rate on savings income depends on the level of your income. If all your taxable income is less than your personal allowances, no tax is due. If your taxable income (including interest but after deducting personal allowances) is less than £5,000, you are not liable for tax on the interest. If you are a basic-rate taxpayer and your taxable income is over £5,000, tax is due at 20% on savings income that exceeds your personal savings allowance. Higher-rate taxpayers pay 40% tax on interest that exceeds their personal savings allowance. Tax due on savings income may be paid through your PAYE coding or self-assessment (see 10 below). Additional-rate taxpayers pay tax at 45% on savings income.

If your savings income is more than your personal savings allowance and your total taxable income is more than £17,850, you must tell HMRC. If you pay tax under PAYE, you can telephone HMRC on 0300 200 3300; textphone 0300 200 3319 – HMRC may try to collect the tax due through your tax code. If you are in self-assessment, you can do this on your tax return.

**Dividends** – Until April 2016, the basic tax rate on dividends was 10%. The tax deducted at source (the *'tax credit'*) covered tax due at 10%, but was not refundable. From 6.4.16, dividends are no longer paid with a tax credit, but are paid in full (gross) to you, and a *'dividend allowance'* of £2,000 is available. If you receive dividend income of more than £2,000, then the excess is taxable at the *'dividend rate'*, which is 7.5% if the excess falls into the basic tax rate band (see 4 above), 32.5% if it falls into the higher rate band and 38.1% if it falls into the additional rate band.

## 8. Tax refunds
The time limit for claiming a refund of overpaid tax is four years following the end of the relevant tax year (eg a claim for the 2014/15 tax year expires on 5.4.19). The time limit can be extended if tax was overpaid due to HMRC or other government department error and there is no dispute or doubt as to the facts (extra-statutory concession B41). To claim a refund, sign in to your personal tax account (see 12 below), write to HMRC with the details or, for savings tax refunds, ask for form R40.

If you become unemployed part way through the tax year (and do not expect to go back to work) or you retire permanently (and do not get a pension from your old employer) or return to full-time study, a tax refund can be claimed on form P50. You can do this four weeks or more after leaving work/retiring/returning to study; send your P45 (which your former employer should give you when you leave) with the completed P50 to HMRC. You need to estimate your income for the rest of the tax year. If you leave work and claim jobseeker's allowance, you cannot get a tax refund until the end of the tax year.

## 9. Arrears of tax
If you have not paid enough tax, HMRC can claim it from you, usually within four years. In some circumstances (eg deliberate tax evasion) the time limit is 20 years. HMRC could charge penalties if you are at fault.

Arrears of tax may be wholly or partly waived if they have arisen because HMRC failed to take account of information they have about you and you reasonably believed your affairs were in order. This concession may be given if you are notified of the arrears after the end of the tax year following that in which HMRC received information indicating you had underpaid tax or if HMRC failed repeatedly and arrears have built up over two or more tax years. If you believe this applies to you, write to HMRC claiming a waiver under extra statutory concession A19 (see www.litrg.org.uk/tax-guides/employed/what-if-i-do-not-pay-enough-tax for more information).

## 10. Self-assessment
You may be asked to complete a tax return if you have income that is not taxed at source (eg savings interest in excess of the personal savings allowance, dividend income in excess of the dividend allowance, or rents) or if your circumstances have changed. Some taxpayers (eg self-employed people) are asked to do this annually. If in any tax year you receive taxable income or taxable capital gains which HMRC do not know about, you must notify them within six months of the end of the tax year (eg by 5.10.19 for 2018/19).

Keep records of your income and capital gains to enable you to complete a tax return; these should usually be kept for 22 months after the end of the relevant tax year. If you are self-employed or have rental income, that period is extended by four years.

If you regularly file a tax return, you will be sent a notice to complete a tax return shortly after the end of the tax year. Paper returns must be filed by 31 October. HMRC will calculate your tax and let you know by 31 January how much to pay. Tax returns filed online are due by 31 January. If you want HMRC to collect tax due through your PAYE code for the following year, complete and file paper returns by 31 October or online returns by 31 December. Tax should be paid in full by 31 January or you may be charged interest or a penalty. There is also an immediate penalty if the return is filed late and further penalties can arise, depending on how late you file the return or pay the tax due. In some circumstances, you may be able to claim you had a reasonable excuse for late filing or payment, or otherwise be able to appeal against penalties.

Some people who have had to complete self-assessment tax returns in the past, but who do not receive a notification from HMRC that they need to complete a return for the 2017/18 tax year, should receive a simple assessment letter instead (see 6 above). If you do not receive a notice to complete a tax return or a simple assessment letter by September 2018 and you usually complete a tax return, you should contact HMRC on 0300 200 3310 (textphone 0300 200 3319) to check what they want you to do.

## 11. Self-employment
Register with HMRC as soon as possible after you become self-employed. A penalty may be charged if you fail to do so by 5 October (for tax purposes) or 31 January (for national insurance contributions) after the end of the tax year in which you started the business. To register, fill out the online registration form (www.gov.uk/log-in-file-self-assessment-tax-return/register-if-youre-self-employed) or ring the newly self-employed helpline (0300 200 3500; textphone 0300 200 3519). You will be asked to complete a tax return each year. You can find more information at www.gov.uk/working-for-yourself.

## 12. Personal tax accounts
HMRC launched the *'personal tax account'* at the end of 2015 (see www.gov.uk/personal-tax-account). Everyone has a personal tax account. You can use your personal tax account to do various things, including checking your PAYE tax code, completing and submitting a tax return, claiming a tax refund, managing your tax credits, checking your state pension and telling HMRC about a change in your address.

To access your account, you need to prove your identity, by using your Government Gateway account (see www.gov.uk/government-gateway), if you have one, or by using GOV.UK Verify (see www.gov.uk/government/publications/introducing-govuk-verify/introducing-govuk-verify). You also need a national insurance number (see Chapter 56(1)).

This section of the handbook looks at:

| | |
|---|---|
| Care and support services | Chapter **36** |
| Paying for care and support | Chapter **37** |
| Benefits in care homes | Chapter **38** |

# Care and support

# **36** Care and support services

| | |
|---|---|
| **A** | **Care and support** |
| 1 | What is care and support? | 229 |
| | Glossary: Care and support – Box J.1 | 230 |
| | Care and support legislation – Box J.2 | 232 |
| | Directions, guidance and circulars – Box J.3 | 234 |
| 2 | Healthcare and social care | 229 |
| 3 | The needs assessment | 231 |
| 4 | Personal budgets | 232 |
| 5 | Direct payments | 233 |
| **B** | **Care and support in care homes** |
| 6 | What is a care home? | 235 |
| | Healthcare and nursing care: England and Wales – Box J.4 | 236 |
| 7 | How to apply for help | 235 |
| 8 | Choice of home | 235 |
| 9 | More expensive care homes | 237 |
| **C** | **Common rules** |
| 10 | Continuity of care and cross-border placements | 237 |
| | Adult social care: Scotland – Box J.5 | 238 |
| | Community care and residential care: Northern Ireland – Box J.6 | 240 |
| 11 | If you are not satisfied with your care services | 241 |

## A. CARE AND SUPPORT

### 1. What is care and support?

*'Care and support'* is a combination of practical, financial and emotional support for adults who need extra help to manage their lives and be independent – including older people, people with a disability or long-term illness, people with mental health problems, and carers. The stated purpose of *'care and support'* is *'to help people achieve the outcomes that matter to them in their life'*. Underpinning it is the need to ensure that the focus is on *'the needs and goals of the person concerned'*.

Care & Support Statutory Guidance, Chapter 1.1; Part 2 Code of Practice (General Functions), Chapter 1, para 30

Care and support includes an assessment of your needs and the drafting of a care and support plan (see 3 below) that includes a personal budget (see 4 below), the provision of services and/or the allocation of funds to enable you to buy your own care and support (see 5 below), subject to a means test. The support could include home care, personal assistants, day services, or the provision of aids and adaptations. It could also include care and support in a care home (see 6 to 9 below).

Local authorities may charge for care and support services (see Chapter 37).

Care and support applies in England (since April 2015) and Wales (since April 2016). For the adult support system in Scotland, see Box J.5; for that in Northern Ireland, see Box J.6. **Law and guidance** – Care and support was introduced in England through the Care Act 2014 and in Wales through the Social Services and Well-being (Wales) Act 2014. See Box J.2 for details.

In England, regulations and statutory guidance issued under the Care Act 2014 by the Department of Health set out how local authorities should undertake their care and support responsibilities. Similar regulations and guidance set out in codes of practice apply in Wales. See Box J.3 for details.

### 2. Healthcare and social care

There is no obvious dividing line between a social care need and a healthcare need. Legislation allows adult social care and health bodies to work together using pooled budgets and joint commissioning of services. Health bodies might not provide services they consider are not reasonably required, taking into account their own resources.

It is important to know if your care needs are considered to be healthcare needs under the NHS, as most healthcare is free at the point of delivery but there are charges for most social care. Local authorities can only provide or arrange social care packages. The NHS is responsible for meeting the cost of registered nursing care in care homes that provide it, as well as all other reasonably required healthcare. See Box J.4 for details.

In England, the *National Framework for NHS Continuing Healthcare and NHS-funded Nursing Care,* and in Wales, *Continuing NHS Health Care: The National Framework for Implementation in Wales* (see Box J.3), outline the criteria under which the NHS should fully fund care, including social care (and in care homes, including the accommodation costs). The criteria were developed as a result of the *Coughlan* and *Grogan* cases, which established that where a person's primary need is a health need, the NHS should fully fund the care.

*Coughlan* [1999] Civ 1871 (EWCA); *Grogan v Bexley NHS care trust* [2006] 44 (Admin) (EWHC)

**Intermediate care services (including re-ablement)**
**England** – *'Intermediate care services'* should help you to either leave hospital earlier or avoid admission to hospital or a care home. They should last no longer than six weeks. There are four types:

- crisis response – services providing short-term care of up to 48 hours;
- home-based intermediate care – intensive services provided in your own home, mainly by health professionals such as nurses and therapists;
- bed-based intermediate care – services delivered away from home (eg in a community hospital); *and*
- re-ablement – services to help you live independently, provided in your own home mainly by care and support professionals.

Although intermediate care services cover both health and social care, they should be free. When they end, you should be assessed to see if you need ongoing health services and/or care and support.

The Care & Support (Preventing Needs for Care & Support) Regs 2014; Care & Support Statutory Guidance, Chapter 2.12

## J.1 Glossary: Care and support

**Adult** – Any person aged 18 or over.

**Adult social care** – The local authority section that has responsibility for the care and support needs of adults.

**Care and support** – A combination of practical, financial and emotional support for adults who need extra help to manage their lives and be independent. It includes both care in your own home and in a care home. See Chapter 36(1).

**Care and support plan** – A plan drawn up after your needs assessment (see below), setting out what your care and support needs are, how they will be met and what services you will receive. See Chapter 36(3).

**Care package** – The range of services offered to you by your local authority following a needs assessment. It may include day services, aids and adaptations for your home, and personal care.

**Carer** – Someone who provides support or who looks after a family member, partner or friend who needs help because of their age, physical or mental illness, or disability. It would not usually include anyone employed to carry out that role, or a volunteer.

**Continuity of care** – This ensures that your care and support needs continue to be met if you move to another local authority area. See Chapter 36(10).

**Deferred payment agreement** – You can use such an agreement to defer or delay paying the costs of care and support in a care home until a later date. This means you can put off selling your home. See Chapter 37(12).

**Direct payments** – If you have been assessed as needing care and support services, you can be given your personal budget (see below) as a cash payment so that you can arrange and buy these services directly rather than getting them from your local authority. See Chapter 36(5).

**Duty** – If a local authority has a 'duty' to do something, it must do it and can be legally challenged if it fails to do so.

**Free personal care** – Care that can be provided without charge in your home if you are aged 65 or over. It only applies in Scotland. See Box J.7.

**Indicative budget** – An amount that the local authority estimates would be sufficient to meet your care and support needs. See Chapter 36(4).

**Individual budget** – The Scottish equivalent to the personal budget. See Box J.5.

**Individual service fund** – One version of a personal budget under which the budget is held by a care provider, although you can choose how some or all of it is spent. See Chapter 36(4).

**Intermediate care services** – A range of services to help you leave hospital earlier or avoid admission to hospital or a care home. They should be free. See Chapter 36(2).

**Needs assessment** – The process of finding out what care and support you need. It is carried out by your local authority. See Chapter 36(3).

**NHS continuing healthcare** – A package of healthcare arranged and funded solely by the NHS. See Box J.4.

**NHS-funded nursing care** – Nursing, provided by a registered nurse, that must be funded by the NHS. See Box J.4.

**Non-residential care and support** – This is care and support provided in your own home or in the community.

**Personal budget** – A statement that sets out the cost to the local authority of meeting your care and support needs. It includes the amount that you must pay towards that cost yourself (on the basis of a financial assessment), as well as any amount that the authority must pay. See Chapter 36(4).

**Personal care** – The physical assistance, prompting or supervision that you need in connection with your bodily functions (such as feeding, bathing and toileting). See Chapter 36(6).

**Personal expenses allowance** – If you are in a care home and using all your income to pay for your care, the 'personal expenses allowance' is the amount you are allowed to keep to cover your personal needs. See Chapter 37(10).

**Portability** – Another name for 'continuity of care'. See above.

**Preferred accommodation** – If you tell your local authority you want to enter a particular care home, that home is your 'preferred accommodation'. See Chapter 36(8).

**Residential care** – This is care in a care home, with or without nursing, for older people or people with disabilities who need 24-hour care.

**Resource allocation scheme** – The system some local authorities use to calculate your personal budget. See Chapter 36(4).

**Respite care** – A service giving carers a break, by providing short-term care for the person with care needs in their own home or in a residential setting.

**Self-directed support** – The system used in Scotland that allows you to choose how support is provided to you. See Box J.5.

**Self-funder** – This is where you arrange and pay for your care and support services (including care home fees) without financial help from the local authority. See Chapter 37(1) and (7).

**Self top-up** – In limited circumstances, you can use your own money to pay for a more expensive care home: the 'self top-up'. See Chapter 36(9).

**Support plan** – A plan drawn up for carers, setting out their support needs, how they will be met and what services they will receive. See Chapter 36(3).

**Third-party top-up** – If you have chosen a care home that costs more than you have been allowed in your personal budget (see above), a third party can agree to meet the difference: the 'third-party top-up'. See Chapter 36(9).

Think Local Act Personal has produced a simple guide to the most commonly used social care words and phrases. It can be found at: www.thinklocalactpersonal.org.uk/Browse/Informationandadvice/CareandSupportJargonBuster.

**Wales** – From April 2017, the *'Integrated Care Fund'* has been introduced. While local areas may take different approaches to organising their intermediate care services, the following should always take place:

❏ **Assessing the need for intermediate care** – this includes gathering information about you and deciding what sort of intermediate care is best for you. If you are in hospital, your assessment may include developing goals to include in the referral to the intermediate care team. If you are at home, the assessment may be completed by a social worker, community nurse, crisis response team, or community social care occupational therapist.

❏ **Acceptance by the intermediate care service** – an *'individual plan'* is then developed by the intermediate care team, based on your assessment. Goals are agreed with you, which are reviewed regularly. The plan should contain enough information for visiting staff to know what needs to be done.

❏ **Delivery of the service** – this should always be based on the agreed plan. If problems arise, support staff should be able to contact the assessor in the intermediate care team.

❏ **A formal review** – this should take place when you are near to achieving your goals, with a clear plan for transition from the intermediate care service. If you have ongoing support needs, there may be a handover to a new homecare provider or day service. If you have achieved your desired level of independence, the plan may include information about how to refer yourself back into the service if you need to, and links to community services that can support you.

Integrated Care Fund Guidance 2017-18

## Delayed discharges

Discharge from hospital should not be delayed if you are fit for discharge. In England, if the delay is due to care and support services not being in place – a delayed transfer of care – the local authority must reimburse the health body financially. You should not be pressured into leaving hospital until suitable care and support arrangements are in place.

Care & Support (Discharge of Hospital Patients) Regs 2014; Care & Support Statutory Guidance, Annex G

## 3. The needs assessment

If you have difficulty managing at home because of age, illness or disability, you can ask your local authority for an assessment of your needs. If it is apparent to the authority that you might have a need for care and support, you should not have to ask for an assessment. Even if the authority thinks you may not have eligible needs or may be able to pay for care and support yourself, you should not be denied an assessment. See Box J.2 for the law on assessments.

You may have a face-to-face assessment, a supported self-assessment or an online or phone assessment. The assessment must find out the total extent of your needs before your eligibility for care and support is considered. The financial assessment process (see Chapter 37) must not influence the assessment of your needs.

If you need assistance urgently, your local authority can temporarily provide or arrange care and support services before an assessment is carried out. Once temporary services are in place, the authority is required to assess you as soon as practicable.

**Delays** – There are no national rules about how quickly assessments must take place, although guidance states that they should be carried out over an appropriate and reasonable timescale. If you experience unreasonable delay, use the complaints procedure first and then the appropriate Ombudsman (see 11 below).

CA, S.9; The Care & Support (Assessment) Regs 2014; Care & Support Statutory Guidance, Chapter 6; SSWB(W)A, Ss.19 & 24; Part 3 Code of Practice (Assessing the needs of individuals), Chapter 1, paras 32 & 33

**No recourse to public funds?** – If you have care and support needs but you have no recourse to public funds (see Chapter 53(2)), an assessment should be carried out first to determine whether not providing support would be in potential breach of your human rights or European Community treaty rights. In most cases, unless this can be established, the local authority will be prevented from providing support. Seek expert advice if you are in this situation (see Chapter 58).

Nationality, Immigration & Asylum Act 2002, Sch 3; No Recourse to Public Fund Network's *Practice Guidance for Local Authorities* (England) 6 April 2016

## Assessments for carers

Carers have similar rights to an assessment, where it appears they may have some need for support. Carers are defined as those who provide care or intend to do so, but not those providing care under a contract. Carers' assessments must identify not only the carer's needs for support, but also the sustainability of the caring role itself. Local authorities can charge carers for services provided directly to them, but some provide them free.

CA, S.10; Care & Support (Assessment) Regs 2014; Care & Support Statutory Guidance, Chapter 6.16-6.19; SSWB(W)A, S.24; Part 3 Code of Practice (Assessing the needs of individuals), Chapter 1, para 15

## Eligibility criteria

There are national eligibility criteria setting minimum thresholds for adult care and support needs which all local authorities must meet. Authorities can decide to meet other ineligible needs if they choose to do so. Care and support needs are only eligible if:

■ they arise from, or are related to, a physical or mental impairment or illness;

■ as a result of the needs, you are unable to achieve two or more of the specified outcomes (see below); *and*

■ there is likely to be a significant impact on your wellbeing as a consequence of being unable to achieve these outcomes.

**The specified outcomes** – Local authorities must consider whether you are unable to achieve two or more of the following outcomes:

■ managing and maintaining nutrition;

■ maintaining personal hygiene;

■ managing toilet needs;

■ being appropriately clothed;

■ being able to make use of your home safely;

■ maintaining a habitable home environment;

■ developing and maintaining family or other personal relationships;

■ accessing and engaging in work, training, education or volunteering;

■ making use of necessary facilities or services in the local community (including public transport and recreational facilities or services); *or*

■ carrying out any caring responsibilities you have for a child.

If you are unable to achieve at least two of the outcomes, the local authority does not need to consider the impact of each individually, but should consider whether the combined effect has a significant impact on your wellbeing.

**Carer support needs** – Carers may be eligible for support in their own right. The national eligibility threshold for carers is based on the impact their needs for support have on their wellbeing, in a similar way to that for adults with care needs.

**The decision** – After making the eligibility decision, the local authority must provide you with a copy of their decision, agree with you which needs you would like them to meet, consider how those needs may be met, and establish that you are ordinarily resident in their area.

CA, S.13; Care & Support (Eligibility Criteria) Regs 2014; Care & Support Statutory Guidance, Chapter 6.100-6.134; SSWB(W)A, Ss.32 & 33; Part 4 Code of Practice (Meeting Needs), Chapter 1

## The care and support plan

Following the needs and carer assessments and determination of eligibility, if the local authority decides to meet your needs, a *'care and support plan'* must be drawn up. You should be involved in the development of this.

The plan should detail:

- the needs identified by the assessment;
- whether the needs are eligible needs;
- the needs that the authority is going to meet and how it intends to do so;
- the personal budget (see 4 below); *and*
- information and advice on what you can do to reduce the needs and prevent or delay the development of needs in the future.

In developing the plan, the authority must inform you which, if any, of your needs may be met by a direct payment (see 5 below). You should be given a copy of the final plan.

For carers, a similar *'support plan'* must be drawn up.

CA, S.25; Care & Support Statutory Guidance, Chapter 10; SSWB(W)A, Ss.54 & 55; Part 4 Code of Practice (Meeting Needs), Chapter 2

**Reviews** – Local authorities should review your care and support plan (or the support plan for carers) six to eight weeks after it is put in place (the 'initial review'). Annual reviews should take place thereafter. You have the right to request a review at any time if you feel your needs warrant it, eg if your circumstances have changed.

CA, S.27; Care & Support Statutory Guidance, Chapter 13; Part 3 Code of Practice (Assessing the needs of individuals), Chapter 1, paras 92-100

### Restrictions

Local authorities have been reluctant, in some cases, to provide expensive packages of care for people to remain in their own homes. It is often cheaper to arrange for people to go into a care home. Case law has established that it may be lawful to provide care in a care home rather than meet 24-hour needs at home. However, the Local Government Ombudsman found maladministration causing injustice when a local authority failed to consider a man's wishes when placing him in a residential home, and said, *'Councils have no right to disregard a client's wishes in this manner.'*

London Borough of Hillingdon (07A01436) September 2008

### Unhappy with the result?

If you are refused an assessment or feel it has not taken account of your needs, or there is a delay in carrying it out, you can use the complaints procedure (or seek legal advice if it is urgent) – see 11 below.

## 4. Personal budgets

A *'personal budget'* is a statement that sets out the cost to the local authority of meeting your care needs (including those met by care in a care home). It includes the amount that you must pay towards that cost yourself (on the basis of a financial assessment, see Chapter 37), and any amount the authority must pay. A personal budget can be set up as:

- a managed account held by the local authority;
- a managed account held by a third party, often called an *'individual service fund'*;
- a direct payment (see 5 below); *or*
- a 'mixed package' that includes elements of some or all of the approaches above.

Local authorities must ensure that however the personal budget is set up, the decision is recorded in your plan and you are given as much flexibility and choice as is reasonably practicable in how your needs are met.

If an individual service fund is available, the local authority should provide you with information and advice on how the arrangement will work, including any contractual requirements, how the provider will manage the budget on your behalf, and advice on what to do if a dispute arises.

**The indicative budget** – You should first be given an *'indicative budget'*, which is the amount that adult social care considers is sufficient to meet your eligible needs as identified in your care and support plan (see 3 above). It is important that your care and support plan and the indicative budget are detailed so you can see which of your needs have been taken into account, how much they are likely to cost, what services, if any, will be provided and who will provide them. If the indicative budget does not meet all the needs in your care and support plan that are to be paid for, it should be adjusted to ensure it does. The final amount to meet your eligible care and support needs is your personal budget.

CA, S.26; Care & Support Statutory Guidance, Chapter 11

### Resource allocation schemes

These are used widely in calculating personal budgets. Courts have been critical of the lack of transparency in these schemes, holding that a scheme should only be a starting point. There remains an absolute duty to meet eligible

## J.2 Care and support legislation

The law set out in this box applies to residential and non-residential care and support in England and Wales. The duties and powers of statutory authorities come from Acts, Regulations and Orders, as interpreted by case law. In following the law, authorities must act in accordance with directions and statutory guidance, and take account of other guidance (see Box J.3).

The Care Act 2014 created a single law relating to care and support, replacing the various pieces of legislation that previously related to adult social care in England. The Social Services and Well-being (Wales) Act 2014 made similar provisions in Wales.

The law in Scotland is covered in Box J.5; that in Northern Ireland in Box J.6.

### Assessment of need for care and support

S.9(1) of the **Care Act 2014** (England) and s.19(1) of the **Social Services & Well-being (Wales) Act 2014** states: *'... where it appears to a local authority that an adult may have needs for care and support, the authority must assess (a) whether the adult does have needs for care and support, and (b) if the adult does, what those needs are.'*

S.10(1) and s.24(1) of these two Acts provide for an assessment of a carer's needs for support in similar terms. 'Carer' is stated as meaning *'an adult who provides or intends to provide care for another adult (an 'adult needing care')'* but usually excludes carers providing care under a contract or as voluntary work.

### Meeting care and support needs

S.8 of the **Care Act 2014** gives local authorities examples of what may be provided to meet needs:

- accommodation in a care home or in premises of some other type;
- care and support at home or in the community;
- counselling and other types of social work;
- goods and facilities; *and*
- information, advice and advocacy,

and the way it could be provided:

- by arranging for someone who does not work for the authority to provide a service;
- by providing a service itself; *or*
- by making direct payments.

S.34 of the **Social Services & Well-being (Wales) Act 2014** has similar provisions.

needs, and local authorities have a duty to explain how an individual's personal budget has been arrived at.

*R(Savva) v Kensington and Chelsea* [2010] 414 (Admin) (EWCH) (13 CCLR 227); *R(KM) v Cambridge CC* [2012] (SC)

### Your needs and local authority resources

Once your personal budget is awarded, the local authority may not withdraw or reduce it without conducting a re-assessment of your care and support needs.

Seek advice (see Chapter 58) if you are not getting the personal budget or services you need because of local authority resources problems. Courts have been consistent in finding that authorities cannot take resources into account once you have been assessed as having an eligible need.

### 5. Direct payments

*'Direct payments'* allow a person who has been assessed as having eligible needs to receive cash to arrange and pay for services themselves. Therefore, direct payments can give you more control over the way your care needs are met. You can have a combination of some services provided directly by adult social care and others arranged by yourself with direct payments.

**Who can have a direct payment?** – Local authorities have a duty to offer direct payments to people who fall within the following rules. To get a direct payment, you must:
- be aged at least 16;
- be a disabled person, carer or someone with parental responsibility for a disabled child; *and*
- have been assessed as having eligible care and support needs or eligible carer needs and the authority is satisfied that giving you a direct payment is an appropriate way to meet these needs.

You may nominate a person to receive a direct payment on your behalf if the local authority is satisfied that you have capacity to make this decision and that the nominated person is capable of managing direct payments and agrees to receive the payments.

---

S.13(1) of the Care Act 2014 provides for a local authority to determine whether any of the needs meet the eligibility criteria. S.32 of the Social Services & Well-being (Wales) Act 2014 has similar provisions.

S.18(1)&(5) of the Care Act 2014 confers a duty on a local authority to meet eligible needs for care and support if the adult is ordinarily resident in the authority's area or is present in its area but of no settled residence. S.19 of the Care Act 2014 confers a power on a local authority to meet other non-eligible needs for care and support, and provides for the meeting of urgent needs prior to a needs assessment for all adults (whether or not they are ordinarily resident in its area). Ss.35 and 36 of the Social Services & Well-being (Wales) Act 2014 have similar provisions.

There are similar provisions for carers under s.20 of the Care Act 2014 and s.40 of the Social Services & Well-being (Wales) Act 2014.

### Care and support plans and personal budgets

Following an assessment, if the local authority is required to meet your needs, it must prepare a 'care and support plan' or a 'support plan' (for carers) and help you decide how to have your needs met. It must also tell you which (if any) needs may be met by direct payments. (Ss.24 & 25 of the **Care Act 2014**; ss.54 & 55 of the **Social Services & Well-being (Wales) Act 2014**.)

In England, everyone whose needs are met by a local authority must receive a personal budget as part of the care and support plan or support plan (s.26 of the Care Act 2014).

### Mental health services

Local authorities and health bodies have a joint responsibility for people who have been detained or admitted to hospital under ss.3, 37, 47 or 48 of the **Mental Health Act 1983**. S.117 of the 1983 Act (as amended by the Care Act 2014) also places a duty to provide aftercare services.

### Nursing care

S.22 of the **Care Act 2014** (s.47 of the **Social Services & Well-being (Wales) Act 2014**) provides that a local authority may not meet needs that are required to be provided under the NHS Act 2006 unless they are merely incidental and ancillary to meeting other needs and they are of a nature that a local authority could be expected to provide.

### Charges

Local authorities can charge for non-residential and residential care and support (eg domiciliary and day care services or care in a care home) under s.14 of the **Care Act 2014** (or under s.59 of the **Social Services & Well-being (Wales) Act 2014**).

The Care & Support (Charging & Assessment of Resources) Regulations 2014 make provision for financial assessments and charging (or the Care & Support (Charging) (Wales) Regulations 2015 and Care & Support (Financial Assessment) (Wales) Regulations 2015).

Those who have care and support provided under s.117 of the Mental Health Act 1983 cannot be charged.

### Promoting individual well-being

Local authorities must promote well-being when carrying out any of their care and support functions in respect of any individual. The well-being principle (or 'duty' in Wales) applies in all cases where an authority is carrying out a care and support function or making a decision (s.1 of the **Care Act 2014** or ss.2 & 4 of the **Social Services & Well-being (Wales) Act 2014**).

### Providing information and advice

Local authorities *'must establish and maintain a service for providing people in its area with information and advice relating to care and support for adults and support for carers'* (s.4 of the **Care Act 2014**).

In Wales, *'A local authority must secure the provision of a service for providing people with (a) information and advice relating to care and support, and (b) assistance in accessing care and support'* (s.17 of the **Social Services & Well-being (Wales) Act 2014**).

### Useful publications and websites

If you are challenging a decision about the help you get or need at home or about care in a care home, the following may be useful:
- *Community Care Law Reports* (Legal Action Group) – a quarterly digest of case law
- *Care Act Manual* by Tim Spencer-Lane (2015, Sweet and Maxwell)
- *Community Care and the Law* – The Pauline Thompson memorial edition (6th Edition, March 2017, Legal Action Group)
- *Schwehr on Care* website – www.schwehroncare.co.uk
- *Centre for Adults' Social Care – Advice, Information and Dispute Resolution* website – www.cascaidr.org.uk

## J.3 Directions, guidance and circulars

Local authorities and health bodies should follow directions, guidance and circulars, which are usually available on the internet. Guidance should be read in conjunction with the relevant legislation (see Box J.2).
**England:** Health Service Directions, Guidance and Circulars (HSGs and HSCs); Local Authority Circulars (LACs and LAC(DH)s).
**Scotland:** Community Care Circulars (CCDs); Chief Executive Letters (CELs).
**Wales:** Welsh Government Circulars (WGCs), previously Welsh Assembly Government Circulars (WAGCs); National Assembly for Wales Circulars (NAfWCs) and Welsh Office Circulars (WOCs); Welsh Health Circulars (WHCs).
**Northern Ireland:** Bills and statutory rules plus Office of Social Services Circulars/Guidance; Health Service Circulars (HSS); Letters and Urgent Communications.

### Challenging decisions

Useful directions/guidance/circulars:

❑ **Charging and financial assessments** – England: *Care and Support Statutory Guidance* (Department for Health) – regularly updated; last update 12.2.18 – Chapter 8 and Annexes B to F; LAC(DHSC)(2018)(1). Scotland: *Charging for Residential Accommodation Guide (CRAG)* – a new version is usually issued each April and updates when required: CCD 2/2018. Wales: *Social Services & Well-being (Wales) Act 2014 Part 4 and 5 Code of Practice (Charging and Financial Assessment)*. Northern Ireland: HSC(ECCU) 1/2018.

❑ **Ordinary residence** – England: *Care and Support Statutory Guidance* – Chapters 19 to 21 and Annex H. Scotland: CCD 1/2016. Wales: *Social Services & Well-being (Wales) Act 2014 Part 11 Code of Practice (Miscellaneous and General)*, Chapter 2.

❑ **Choice of Accommodation** – England: *Care and Support Statutory Guidance* – Chapter 1 and Annex A. Scotland: CEL 32(2013). Wales: *Social Services & Well-being (Wales) Act 2014 Part 4 and 5 Code of Practice (Charging and Financial Assessment)*, Chapter 10.

❑ **NHS continuing healthcare and NHS-funded nursing care** – England: *The NHS Continuing Healthcare (Responsibilities of social services authorities) Directions* (2013); *The National Framework for NHS Continuing Healthcare and NHS-funded Nursing Care* (revised November 2012 with Decision Support Tool revised June 2016). Scotland: *Hospital Based Complex Clinical Care*, DL(2015)11. Wales: *Continuing NHS Healthcare: The National Framework for Implementation in Wales* (June 2014).

❑ **Deferred payments** – England: *Care and Support Statutory Guidance* – Chapter 9. Scotland: CCD 13/2004. Wales: *Social Services & Well-being (Wales) Act 2014 Part 4 and 5 Code of Practice (Charging and Financial Assessment)*, Annex D.

❑ **Free personal and nursing care** – Scotland: CCD 5/2003; CCD 1/2010.

**Intermediate care** – England: *Intermediate Care – Halfway Home* (July 2009); LAC(DH)(2010)6; *National Institute for Health & Care Excellence guideline [NG74]* – September 2017; *Understanding Intermediate Care including reablement* (Social Care Institute for Excellence – October 2017); *Care and Support Statutory Guidance* – Chapter 2. Wales: *Integrated Care Fund Guidance* (2017/18).

Direct payments can be available to people who lack the mental capacity to agree to and manage the payments themselves; payments can be made to a willing and appropriate person (an *'authorised person'*) on the disabled person's behalf.
CA, Ss.31 & 32; Care & Support (Direct Payments) Regs 2014; Care & Support Statutory Guidance, Chapter 12; SSWB(W)A, Ss.50-53; Care & Support (Direct Payments)(Wales) Regs 2015; Part 4 Code of Practice (Meeting Needs), Chapter 3

### What can direct payments be used for?

Direct payments can be used to arrange services (including equipment) to meet your assessed needs. Local authorities should allow you to choose how best to meet your assessed needs. Guidance states that a *'direct payment is designed to be used flexibly and innovatively and there should be no unreasonable restriction placed on the use of the payment, as long as it is being used to meet eligible care and support needs'*. You cannot usually use a direct payment to purchase services from the local authority.
Care & Support Statutory Guidance, Chapter 12.35

**Care homes** – Direct payments can usually only be used to purchase respite care in a care home for periods of up to four weeks (120 days for children) in any one year. Separate periods in a care home of less than four weeks are added together towards the maximum only if you are at home for 28 days or less in between. In November 2013, several English local authorities became 'development sites' for the use of direct payments for care in a care home, whatever the duration of the stay. The aim was to introduce direct payments for long-term care in a care home nationally from April 2016, but it is anticipated that this will now be considered as part of a Green Paper on social care due to be published in summer 2018.

**Partners and relatives** – Direct payments cannot normally be used to pay for services from your spouse, partner or a close relative (or their spouse or partner) living in your household unless the local authority considers that it is necessary. You can use your direct payment to employ a close relative if they are not living with you. You can pay a close relative in the same household to provide management or administrative support for your direct payment.

**Your responsibilities** – Guidance states that local authorities should give clear advice as to your employment responsibilities and signpost you to organisations that provide support for users of direct payments. Authorities must check that the money you have been given is spent on the care you have been assessed as needing. If not, they could ask for it to be paid back.

**Getting advice** – The Disability Rights UK Personal Budgets helpline gives advice on direct payments, as well as general advice and information about independent living organisations (0330 995 0404 : Tues and Thurs 9.30am-1.30pm; email personalbudgets@disabilityrightsuk.org).

### How much are you paid?

Local authorities determine the direct payment rate. They must make direct payments equal to their estimate of the reasonable cost of the service to meet your assessed needs and fulfil your legal obligations if you employ your carer/s as *'personal assistant/s'* (eg training, national insurance contributions, employers' liability insurance, holiday and sick pay). If you choose a more expensive way to meet your assessed needs than is *'reasonable'*, you will have to pay the extra cost yourself.

Payments made will not affect your benefits but may affect the benefits received by the person you pay. If you claim benefit as a couple, any direct payment you pay to your partner for care you receive will be taken into account as income in your couple benefit calculation.

You may be asked to contribute towards the cost of your care. The amount of your contribution will be calculated using the same charging rules as for care arranged by the local authority (see Chapter 37). You will be paid your direct payment either net (with the charge taken off) or gross (where you pay the amount you are assessed to pay in the same way as if you were getting a service).

If you are unhappy with the amount you are offered or any other aspect of the direct payment, you should use the complaints procedure (see 11 below).

## B. CARE AND SUPPORT IN CARE HOMES

### 6. What is a care home?

We use the term 'care home' to describe homes that provide personal care or nursing care. The homes must be registered and have evidence that they meet outcomes specified in regulations. Care homes are run by a range of providers. Health bodies as well as local authorities can arrange care in homes that provide nursing.

In England, the Care Quality Commission registers and inspects homes; reports are available on its website (www.cqc.org.uk). Care homes in Wales are registered and regulated by the Care and Social Services Inspectorate Wales (www.cssiw.org.uk).

Care homes are required to provide service users with appropriate information and support in relation to their care or treatment.

**Homes providing personal care** – These can be run by private or voluntary organisations or private individuals. *'Personal care'* means: physical assistance, prompting or supervision given to a person in connection with bodily functions such as feeding, bathing, toileting, etc. The need for personal care triggers the requirement for care home registration.
Health & Social Care Act 2008 (Regulated Activities) Regs 2014, reg 2

There is no requirement for homes to provide board as well as personal care, although most do. If healthcare is needed, it should be provided by community health services in the same way as for a person in their own home.

**Homes providing nursing care** – These may be run by NHS bodies or independent organisations. They provide nursing care as well as personal care, and as part of their registration criteria must have a suitably qualified registered nurse working at the home at all times. Health services such as continence advice, stoma care, physiotherapy, chiropody, specialist feeding equipment, etc, as well as free continence products, should be provided to residents by the NHS.

### 7. How to apply for help

If you think you might need care in a care home, either on a temporary or permanent basis, ask your local authority for a needs assessment (see 3 above). Guidance advises that *'local authorities must undertake an assessment for any adult with an appearance of need for care and support, regardless of whether or not it thinks the individual has eligible needs or of their financial situation'* (eg because you have capital above the capital limit).
Care & Support Statutory Guidance, Chapter 6.13; Part 3 Code of Practice (Assessing the needs of individuals), Chapter 1, para 15

**The contract** – If it is agreed you need care in a care home and you need help with the funding because you cannot afford the fees, the local authority enters into a contract with the home and is liable for the full cost of your care home. It will usually recover from you any contribution you are assessed as having to pay (see Chapter 37). Even if you agree to pay an assessed contribution directly to the care home, the authority remains liable for the full cost. Nursing care costs are the responsibility of the NHS, as described in Box J.4.

Even if you can pay the fees yourself, this does not mean the local authority should not arrange your care. If you are too frail physically or mentally to make your own contract with the home, and others are not willing or able, the authority must make the arrangements and charge the full cost.
CA, S.18(4)

Chapter 38 covers the benefits you can receive in a care home.

**Urgent cases** – If your need is urgent, the local authority can arrange for care in a care home without carrying out a formal needs assessment. The assessment should then be done as soon as possible following admission.
CA, S.19(3)

### 8. Choice of home

If the local authority decides, after the needs assessment, to offer you a place in a care home, it may suggest a particular home or give you advice on homes to choose from. In all cases where a local authority is making the arrangements, you have the right to choose your own care home: 'preferred accommodation' (see below).

However, if a health body places you in a home providing nursing care and pays the full fee, you do not have the same right to choose a particular home, although Department of Health guidance states that *'[health bodies] should commission services using models that maximise personalisation and individual control and that reflect the individual's preferences, as far as possible'*.
The National Framework for NHS Continuing Healthcare & NHS-funded Nursing Care, para 169

#### Preferred accommodation

If you tell your local authority you want to enter a particular care home, that home is called *'preferred accommodation'*. There are legally binding regulations and guidance intended to ensure you have a genuine choice over where you live. In reality, this choice may be restricted, as described below.

Guidance states that if you require a particular type of accommodation to ensure that your assessed needs are met, you have the right to choose between different providers as long as:

■ the accommodation is suitable in relation to your assessed needs. It must meet the identified outcomes established as part of your care and support plan (see 3 above);

■ to do so would not cost the local authority more than the amount specified in your personal budget (see 4 above) for accommodation of that type;

■ the accommodation is available. If a place is not available in your preferred accommodation, you may have to wait. The authority should ensure that adequate and suitable care is available while you wait, taking account of your needs and wishes. If you unreasonably refuse to move to a suitable interim arrangement, the authority can decide it has reasonably met its statutory duties and may ask you to make your own arrangements. Seek advice if this happens; *and*

■ the provider of the accommodation is willing to enter into a contract with the local authority to provide the care at the rate identified in your personal budget on the authority's terms and conditions.

If you choose accommodation outside your local authority area, the authority should take into account the cost of care in that area when setting your personal budget.
CA, S.30; Care & Support & After-care (Choice of Accommodation) Regs 2014; Care & Support Statutory Guidance, Annex A, paras 5-16; SSWB(W)A, S.57; The Care & Support (Choice of Accommodation)(Wales) Regs 2015; Part 4 & 5 Code of Practice (Charging & Financial Assessment), Chapter 10

There is also guidance on cross-border placements in the different countries of the UK (see 10 below).

#### Local authority refusals

A series of challenges have been brought by care home providers to local authority decisions on the usual rates to be paid for placements. All except one have been successful,

## J.4 Healthcare and nursing care: England and Wales

Most people who need help to pay for their care get it from the local authority. However, if someone has a primary healthcare need, the NHS will be responsible for the full cost of their fees in a care home (most often in a nursing home but sometimes in a residential care home) or the cost of their care in the community. Even if someone gets help from the local authority to pay for care in a home that provides nursing care, the NHS will still be responsible for paying for care they receive from a registered nurse (see below). Healthcare in Scotland is covered in Box J.5, that in Northern Ireland in Box J.6.

### NHS continuing healthcare

*'NHS continuing healthcare'* means a package of care arranged and funded solely by the NHS for a person aged 18 or over to meet physical or mental health needs that have arisen as the result of illness. Clinical Commissioning Groups and the NHS Commissioning Board are responsible for NHS continuing healthcare.

Individuals with complex, intense or unpredictable healthcare needs whose primary need for care arises from their health needs and who are assessed as meeting the eligibility criteria for NHS continuing healthcare should be funded by the NHS. Care home residents fully funded by the NHS do not contribute towards their care home fees but are usually treated as hospital inpatients for benefits purposes (see Chapter 55). The overriding test for NHS continuing healthcare is whether a person's primary need is for healthcare. You can request an assessment for NHS continuing healthcare wherever you are – whether at home, in hospital or in a care home.

### England

Eligibility for NHS continuing healthcare is established using the directions (see Box J.3) and guidance: *The National Framework for NHS Continuing Healthcare and NHS-funded Nursing Care* (revised November 2012 with Decision Support Tool revised June 2016). The guidance lays out the principles and processes that should be followed when deciding whether someone has a 'primary health need' and is therefore eligible for NHS continuing healthcare funding. The guidance states that the assessment should be person-centred and understandable, and that your carers and other agencies should be involved. The guidance advises that the following factors should be considered when making a decision as to whether your primary need is for healthcare:

■ the nature of the needs, including the type of interventions and help required;
■ intensity – the extent and severity of needs, including the need for sustained care;
■ complexity – how the needs arise, whether they are stable or require monitoring;
■ unpredictability – the degree to which needs fluctuate and the level of risk if adequate and timely care is not provided.

If it is decided that you have a primary need for healthcare, the NHS will be responsible for providing for your health and social care needs. The guidance advises that the decision should generally be made within 28 days.

If you think you are eligible for NHS continuing healthcare, ask your GP or local authority adult social care service.
**Personal health budgets** – If you are eligible for NHS continuing healthcare, you can request a *'personal health budget'* from your local Clinical Commissioning Group. Similar to adult social care personal budgets (see 4 in this chapter), they allow you to manage your healthcare and support needs in a way that suits you.

In some areas, the Clinical Commissioning Group and the local authority work together so that transfers from a social care personal budget to a personal health budget (or vice versa) are seamless.

### Wales

*Continuing NHS healthcare: The National Framework for Implementation in Wales* (revised June 2014) sets out the principles and processes that should be followed when deciding whether someone has a 'primary health need' and is therefore eligible for continuing NHS healthcare. It also states that if someone has health needs that are beyond the powers of a local authority, that does not of itself mean the individual is eligible for continuing NHS healthcare; in these circumstances joint packages of health and social care are appropriate.

### Problems with NHS continuing healthcare

If you feel your need for care is primarily due to health needs, but you have been refused NHS continuing healthcare, there is a process you can use to challenge the decision. The decision notice you receive should set out the basis on which the decision was made and should explain the arrangements and timescales for dealing with a review of the eligibility decision at local level and further, if necessary, at an NHS Independent Review Panel.

If, after that process, you still disagree with a decision, you can ask for the case to be considered by the Parliamentary and Health Service Ombudsman or the Public Services Ombudsman for Wales (see Chapter 59(5)).

If you are already receiving NHS continuing healthcare, your case should be reviewed after three months and each year following that. If a decision is made that you no longer satisfy the criteria for NHS continuing healthcare, you have the right to challenge the decision as above.

If you disagree with the type and location of the NHS care offered or the treatment received, you should complain using the normal adult social care and NHS complaints procedure (see Chapter 36(11)).

*Beacon* is working in partnership with NHS England to provide a service for people in England who need independent expert advice in relation to NHS continuing healthcare (0345 548 0300; www.beaconchc.co.uk/).

### NHS-funded nursing care

Even if you do not qualify for fully funded NHS continuing healthcare, the NHS is responsible for funding the cost of nursing provided by a registered nurse in a nursing home. This *'NHS-funded nursing care'* (FNC) is determined by a framework that is part of the NHS continuing healthcare assessment.

In England, from April 2018, the standard FNC rate is £158.16 a week (for people on the earlier 'high band' rate, there is a transitional rate of £217.59 a week). In Wales, nursing rates are set by local health boards; the standard weekly rate agreed from April 2017 is £148.01 a week.

Payment is made either to the care home (which must pass it on to you or reduce your fees by that amount or explain how the amount has been taken into account in calculating your fees) or to the local authority if it is arranging, or arranging and funding, your care and accommodation.

If you are funded by the local authority, the FNC payment does not affect the level of charges unless your income is such that the authority charges meant you were paying for part of your nursing costs.

with the common grounds of challenge being a failure by the authority to undertake lawful consultation with the care providers and/or a failure to have due regard to the actual costs of care in accordance with statutory guidance. If your choice of accommodation is refused (or you are asked to pay a top-up – see 9 below) on the grounds that the rate payable is greater than the usual cost adopted by the authority, then the decision may be challengeable if the figure was set unlawfully in the first place.

Judgments: EWHC 2676 (Admin); EWHC 3096 (Admin), EWHC 3371 (Admin); 2012 Judgments: EWHC 1867 (Admin); EWHC 236 (Admin) (unsuccessful); EWHC 2655 (Admin)

## 9. More expensive care homes

If you have chosen a home that costs more than the amount specified in your personal budget (see 4 above), the local authority can make arrangements for your preferred accommodation (given that it satisfies the other conditions in 8 above) if a third party or, in limited circumstances, you will meet the additional cost and continue doing so for as long as you are likely to be in that home. These are usually known as *'third-party top-ups'* or *'self top-ups'*.

Care & Support Statutory Guidance, Annex A; Part 4 & 5 Code of Practice (Charging & Financial Assessment), Annex C

There are specific duties placed on local authorities to ensure that there are enough local care homes for you not to be left waiting for your assessed needs to be met. The local authority must ensure that at least one option is available that is within your personal budget amount (and should ensure that there is more than one). If there is no suitable accommodation available within your personal budget, the authority must arrange care in a more expensive home and increase your personal budget accordingly. In these circumstances, the authority must not ask for the payment of a top-up.

Care & Support Statutory Guidance, Annex A, para 12; Local Government Ombudsman decision 16 008 387

### Third-party top-ups

Local authorities must ensure that any third party is reasonably able to pay top-up fees for the time you are in the home. If the third party is unable to keep up payments, you may have to move to a cheaper home; seek advice if this is likely to happen.

Care & Support Statutory Guidance, Annex A, paras 23-25; Part 4 & 5 Code of Practice (Charging & Financial Assessment), Annex C, paras 8.3-8.8

Guidance is clear that the local authority remains responsible for the care home's full fees even if a third party is making a contribution. Third parties may have to meet the greater share of any subsequent fee increases.

Care & Support Statutory Guidance, Annex A, paras 28 & 35-37; Part 4 & 5 Code of Practice (Charging & Financial Assessment), Annex C, para 8.9

### Self top-ups

As a resident, you are not usually allowed to make your own top-up payment, eg by using your personal allowance, disregarded income or capital.

R v E Sussex ex p Ward [2000] (3 CCLR 132)

However, if you are either within the period of the 12-week disregard of your property or using the provisions for a 'deferred payment agreement' (see Chapter 37(12)), you can use your own money to pay a self top-up for a more expensive home.

A self top-up is also allowed where your accommodation is provided for mental health aftercare.

Care & Support Statutory Guidance, Annex A, para 39

In other circumstances, you are allowed to pay for 'extras' that are outside of the care package. As long as you do not feel pressured by the home owner or the local authority, there is no reason why you should not enter into a contract with the home owner for extra services.

### Top-ups and healthcare

If you are receiving NHS continuing healthcare (see Box J.4) in a care home, the full cost of care to meet your needs will be provided. However, there may be other charges levied by the care home for non-care services you may wish to buy. Unless it is possible to separately identify and deliver the NHS-funded elements of the service, you will not usually be allowed to pay for higher-cost services and/or accommodation (as distinct from purchasing additional services). There may be circumstances where the health body should consider the case for paying a higher-than-usual cost, for example if an individual with challenging behaviour wants a larger room and the behaviour is linked to feeling confined.

The National Framework for NHS Continuing Healthcare & NHS-funded Nursing Care, part 2, para 99.2; Continuing NHS Healthcare: The National Framework for Implementation in Wales, para 4.26-4.35

A health body may restrict the amount it is willing to pay for care in a care home to the standard rate for basic accommodation as long as it meets your assessed needs. It may therefore be necessary for you to pay a top-up for NHS continuing healthcare packages at more expensive care homes.

R(Southall) v Dudley PCT [2009] 1780 (Admin) (EWHC)

## C. COMMON RULES

### 10. Continuity of care and cross-border placements
**Continuity of care**
*'Continuity of care'* (also known as portability) ensures that your needs continue to be met if you move to another local authority area to live. The authority in the area you are moving to must, when you advise them of your proposed move, carry out an assessment before you move and take into account your current care and support plan (see 3 above). It must also provide a written explanation if it assesses you as having different needs to those identified in your current care and support plan.

If the local authority in the area you are moving to has not carried out the assessment before you move, it must continue to meet the care and support needs that were being met by the original authority until it has carried out its own assessment.

CA, Ss.37-38; Care & Support (Continuity of Care) Regs 2014; Care & Support Statutory Guidance, Chapter 20; SSWB(W)A, S.56; Part 4 Code of Practice (Meeting Needs), Chapter 2, paras 109-112

## J.5 Adult social care: Scotland

### Healthcare and social care

Local authority social work departments have duties to provide help to *'persons in need'* and are responsible for the provision of a range of care services. Social work departments and health boards have set up pooled budget arrangements and community healthcare partnerships with single shared assessments. There is free nursing and personal care for people aged 65 or over and free nursing care to those under 65 (see below).

**Intermediate care services** – People aged 65 or over can have free home care for up to four weeks following some types of hospital treatment, including surgery as a day patient and overnight stays. Home care is wider in definition than 'personal care' and includes aids and equipment, meals on wheels, laundry and shopping needed during a period of recovery.

*CCD 2/2001; CCD 5/2003; Maximising Recovery, Promoting Independence: An Intermediate Care Framework for Scotland (2012)*

### Self-directed support

**The needs assessment**

If you have difficulty managing at home because of age, illness or disability, you can ask your local authority adult social work department for an assessment of your needs. See below for the law on assessments. If you are assessed as having eligible care needs, you will be allocated funding to provide that support: an *'individual budget'*.

**Assessments for carers** – If you are an adult carer (but not a paid carer), you have the right to have your needs assessed. A *'carer support plan'* will be drawn up, identifying your needs and detailing how they are to be met. The local authority cannot charge for services it provides in support of your caring role. Young carers aged 16 to 18 can have their needs assessed too, in which case a similar *'young carer statement'* will be drawn up.

*Carers (Scotland) Act 2016; Carers (Waiving of Charges for Support) (Scotland) Regs 2014*

### What is self-directed support?

*'Self-directed support'* allows you to choose how support is provided by giving you control over your individual budget. There are four options to choose from:

- you take a direct payment (see below);
- you allocate funds to a provider of your choice. The local authority holds the budget but you are in charge of how it is spent (an *'individual service fund'*);
- the local authority arranges a service directly for you; *or*
- you choose a mix of these options for different types of support.

For more information, see: www.selfdirectedsupportscotland.org.uk.

*Social Care (Self-directed Support)(Scotland) Act 2013*

### Direct payments

With a small number of exceptions, anyone, regardless of age, who is assessed as needing an eligible care service will be eligible for *'direct payments'* as part of self-directed support. You can use direct payments to buy a wide range of services, eg help with shopping, support in employment or accessing college. You can employ a close relative, provided the authority is *'satisfied that securing the service from such a person is necessary to meet the beneficiary's need for that service or, subject to an exception, is necessary to safeguard or promote the welfare of a child in need'*.

With a direct payment, you receive funding to cover the costs of the eligible care service and you decide how the money should be spent. The amount of funding being made available should be made clear to you and the transfers of funding by you will be monitored by the local authority.

Local direct payment support organisations can give advice and practical help. For details, ring your local authority or Disability Information Scotland (0300 323 9961).

*Self-directed Support (Direct Payments) (Scotland) Regs 2014*

### Care in care homes

**Who can get help with care home fees?**

If you need help with care home accommodation and fees, you need to approach your local authority adult social work department. If your primary need is for healthcare rather than social care, you will be entitled to fully funded NHS continuing healthcare instead (see below).

If you get help from your local authority, the amount you pay normally depends on an assessment of your means (see Chapter 37). Chapter 38 covers the benefits you can receive in a care home.

If you are aged 65 or over, you should only be asked to contribute towards accommodation and living costs; the local authority will pay a set amount for both nursing and personal care. If you are under 65, the authority will pay a fixed amount towards nursing care only. See below for details.

**Mental health aftercare services** – In most cases, local authorities can charge for the provision of aftercare and other services. Any charge should be means tested and offset against entitlement to free personal or nursing care if you are aged 65 or over, or for nursing care only if you are under 65.

*The Mental Health (Care & Treatment) (Scotland) Act 2003, Ss.25-27*

### NHS continuing healthcare

*'NHS continuing healthcare'* means a package of care arranged and funded solely by the NHS for a person aged 18 or over to meet physical or mental health needs that have arisen as the result of illness (see Box J.4 for details).

*Hospital Based Complex Clinical Care DL(2015)(11)*

**Problems with NHS continuing healthcare** – If you feel your need for nursing home care is primarily due to health needs, but you have been refused NHS continuing healthcare, there are a number of steps you can take. First, request a review by your health board. This will lead to a second assessment/review by another medical practitioner. Such reviews should normally be heard within two weeks. If you remain dissatisfied, you can follow the NHS Scotland complaints procedure within six months of the initial decision (www.healthscotland.scot/contact-us/comments-and-complaints). If you still disagree with the health board's decision, you can ask to have your case considered by the Scottish Public Services Ombudsman (0800 377 7330).

### Free personal and nursing care

If you are aged 65 or over and assessed as needing personal care (see Box J.7), you will receive a fixed payment of £174 a week from your local authority, with a further payment of £79 if you need nursing care (£253 in total). If you are under 65, you can only be considered for the nursing care payment. These payments are made regardless of your income and capital and are issued by the authority direct to the care home.

*CCH(S)A; CCD 5/2003*

You can choose whether or not to take these payments.

If you take the payments, you can decide whether you want the local authority to contract with the home for any payments it is making (with you contracting separately with the home for your accommodation and living expenses) or for the authority to make the contract with the home on your behalf for all of the costs. There may be advantages in this arrangement, since the authority's standard contract may restrict increases in the care home fees and may also include provisions for monitoring the quality of care.

If you choose not to take the payments, you can continue to make your own arrangements direct with the home. However, this may preclude your eligibility for free personal and nursing care: a Court of Session judgment stated that a local authority is only obliged to provide free personal care if it has arranged the service. This decision was confirmed and supplemented by further guidance and directions from the government.

*Argyll & Bute Council – Judicial review of Decision of Scottish Public Services Ombudsman [2007] CSOH 168; CCD 1/2010*

**Hospital admissions** – If you are admitted to hospital, your local authority will continue to make payments (including direct payments) at the full flat rate for two weeks after your admission and at 80% for a subsequent month, or until your future placement arrangements are confirmed. You will still need to pay for accommodation and living costs; you may get help with these but that will depend on a financial assessment carried out by the authority (see Chapter 37).

*CCD 5/2003*

### The contract

The local authority will enter into a contract with the care home if it is agreed you need a placement and help with paying the fees. The authority is liable for the full cost of the placement to the care home. It will usually recover from you any contribution you are assessed as having to pay (see Chapter 37) or you can pay this directly to the care home.

### Choice of home

If the local authority decides, after the needs assessment, to offer you a place in a care home, it may suggest a particular home or give you advice on homes to choose from. In all cases where a local authority is making the arrangements, you have the right to choose your own care home: 'preferred accommodation'.

**Preferred accommodation** – If you tell your local authority you want to enter a particular care home, that home is called *'preferred accommodation'*. You can choose to move into a preferred home if:

- there is a place available;
- the social work department has decided the home is suitable for your needs;
- the social work department and the owner of the home can agree a contract;
- the home you have chosen will not cost the social work department more than it usually expects to pay for a home providing the sort of care you need; *and*
- the home is willing to accept you.

If there is no place available in the home you have chosen, you can ask social work staff to provide you with help to stay in your own home until there is a suitable vacancy.

*Social Work (Scotland) Act 1968, Ss.12 & 59; SWSG5/93; CEL 32(2013)*

### More expensive homes

If you have chosen a home that costs more than the amount specified in your individual budget (see above) and the local authority agrees, they can make arrangements for this preferred accommodation. Any shortfall in the funding then needs to be paid by a third party (for example a friend or family member) or, in limited circumstances, you. The additional cost will need to be paid for as long as you are likely to be in that home.

**Third-party top ups** – Guidance states that the local authority has discretion to collect top-up payments and contract with the care home, or to leave the third party to make top-up payments direct to the home. If a home's fees rise above the level of the third-party agreement, the authority should consider the impact of moving you to a cheaper room or home and take steps, where possible, to enable you to remain in your current home.

*CCD 6/2002 and CCD 5/2003, CCD 2/2018 (contains CRAG)*

**Self top-ups** – People who are better off as a result of receiving free personal or nursing care can use some of their money to pay for a more expensive care home.

*Additional Payments (Scotland) Regs 2002 & CCD 7/2002*

## If you are not satisfied with your care services

The complaints procedure has two stages. With the first stage, *'frontline resolution'*, the local authority will offer to discuss the complaint with you to try to resolve the matter. This should normally happen within five working days. If the matter is not resolved, it should move to the next stage: *'investigation'*; this should be completed in 20 working days. If you are still not satisfied, you can take your case to the Scottish Public Services Ombudsman (see Chapter 59(5)).

Alternatively, you can complain directly to the Care Inspectorate (www.careinspectorate.com/; 0345 600 9527).

## The legislation

S.12 of the Social Work (Scotland) Act 1968 sets out local authorities' *'general duty'* to promote social welfare by making available advice, guidance and assistance to *'persons in need'*. Local authorities have a duty to undertake an assessment of need under s.12A of the 1968 Act. S.2 of the Chronically Sick & Disabled Persons (Scotland) Act 1970 sets out local authorities' duty to provide disabled people with the services they have been assessed as needing.

The Social Care (Self-directed Support) (Scotland) Act 2013 gives people a range of options for how their social care is delivered, beyond just direct payments, empowering people to decide how much control they want over their own support arrangements.

The Public Bodies (Joint Working)(Scotland) Act 2014 seeks to integrate all planning and service provision for adult health and social care services either to a lead local authority or lead health board or to a joint board. It is up to each health and local authority to determine service provision for their area.

**Direct payments** – S.7 of the Community Care & Health (Scotland) Act 2002 gives authorities powers to make direct payments to people to arrange and buy community care. The Social Care (Self-directed Support) (Scotland) Act 2013 expands on these powers.

**Mental health services** – Under ss.25-27 of the Mental Health (Care & Treatment) (Scotland) Act 2003, local authorities have a duty to provide services for people with a mental disorder regardless of whether they have been in hospital.

**Free personal and nursing care** – The Community Care & Health (Scotland) Act 2002 provides for free personal care (as defined in s.2(28) of the Regulation of Care (Scotland) Act 2001) and nursing care.

**Charges** – Local authorities can charge for non-residential and residential services in accordance with the Social Work (Scotland) Act 1968.

## Cross-border placements

If your care and support plan (see 3 above) states that your wellbeing is best achieved by a placement in a care home in a different country in the UK (England, Wales, Scotland or Northern Ireland), there is co-operation between the countries based on agreed principles.

The four administrations of the UK have set out steps which the 'first' local authority* (ie the placing authority)

## J.6 Community care and residential care: Northern Ireland

### Community care

*'Community care'* aims to keep people living in their own home or in the community with appropriate help and support. The Department of Health is responsible for community care and delivering these services. It is run by the five Health and Social Care Trusts (HSCTs), which provide integrated health and social care services across Northern Ireland.

### The needs assessment

If you have difficulty managing at home because of age, illness or disability, ask your local HSCT for an assessment of your needs. The assessment will look at your individual circumstances and needs. Before you undergo the assessment, make a list of things that are difficult or that you cannot do because of your illness or disability. The services that can be provided include home help, aids and equipment, respite care and day centre care. The services can be provided just for a short time in some circumstances, eg following hospital discharge.

**Assessments for carers** – Carers have the right to an assessment of their needs. HSCTs can then supply services directly to carers to help them in their caring role. A carer can request an assessment even if the person they are caring for does not want an assessment for themselves.

*Carers & Direct Payments (Northern Ireland) Act 2002; Ss.1-7*

The Department of Health has produced an A-Z guide for carers (www.nidirect.gov.uk/publications/a-to-z-guide-carers).

**Self-directed support** – Self-directed support aims to offer you choice and greater control of how your care is delivered if you have been assessed as needing services. You can choose to have your services delivered by the HSCT, by direct payment (see below) or have a combination of both.

### Direct payments

If you are assessed as needing personal social services (eg a home help or a place in a daycare centre) you may be able to get a cash payment from your local HSCT so that you can arrange the service for yourself. If you have such an assessed need, you are eligible to receive direct payments if you are in one of the following groups:

■ a disabled person aged 16 or over;
■ a carer; *or*
■ someone with parental responsibility for a disabled child.

*Carers & Direct Payments (Northern Ireland) Act 2002; Ss.8-9*

A guide to direct payments has been produced by the Department of Health (www.health-ni.gov.uk/publications/guidance-receiving-direct-payments). The Centre for Independent Living NI (http://cilni.org) provides information on direct payments and how to manage them.

### Residential care

#### Who can get help with care home fees?

If you need help with care home accommodation and fees, you need to approach your local HSCT. Help will be provided only if you been assessed as having eligible care needs (see above).

If you get help from the HSCT, the amount you pay normally depends on an assessment of your means – see Chapter 37. Chapter 38 covers the benefits you can receive in a care home.

#### Nursing care

HSCTs are responsible for paying for the nursing care of residents who otherwise pay the full cost of their nursing home care: *'funded nursing care'*. In each case, the HSCT will pay the nursing home a flat-rate payment of £100 a week for anyone who is either self-funding or otherwise assessed to pay the nursing home fees at the full rate.

If you are entering a nursing home and wish to receive funded nursing care, you will be asked to take part in a nursing needs assessment as part of the overall needs assessment. This will determine your nursing needs and the most appropriate way to meet them. You should be fully involved in this process and can request a copy of the assessment, which will explain what your nursing needs are and how they will be met. A future date will also be set to review your nursing needs.

*HSS(ECCU) 1/2006*

### Complaints
#### Community care

If you have a complaint about services that are provided to you in the community, there is a single-tier local resolution process. Make your complaint direct to your HSCT; you can do this verbally, in writing or by email. You should do it as soon as you can; complaints about incidents that occurred more than 12 months ago will only be accepted if there is good reason for the delay.

Your complaint should be acknowledged within two to three working days of receipt and you should receive a full response within 20 working days; the HSCT should let you know if they need more time.

Once the HSCT has investigated the complaint, they will write a report and let you know whether or not they will take any action to resolve the matter. If you are not happy with the response you receive, you can refer your complaint to the Northern Ireland Public Services Ombudsman (0800 343 424; https://nipso.org.uk).

*The Health & Social Care Complaints Procedure Directions (Northern Ireland) 2009*

#### Residential care

If your complaint relates to a placement in a nursing or residential home, you can complain to the manager of the home, which should have its own complaints procedure. If you are not happy with their response, you can raise your concerns with the HSCT that placed you there.

The Patient and Client Council gives guidance on making complaints about health and personal social services in Northern Ireland (www.patientclientcouncil.hscni.net).

### The Legislation

The Chronically Sick & Disabled Persons (NI) Act 1978, Health & Personal Social Services (NI) Act 1972, Health & Personal Social Services & Public Health (NI) Order 1986, Disabled Person's (NI) Act 1989, Health & Personal Social Services Act (NI) 2001, Carers & Direct Payments (NI) Act 2002, Health & Social Services (NI) Act 2002 and Health & Social Care (Reform) Act (NI) 2009 contain the relevant legislation.

and the 'second' local authority* (ie the authority in whose area you are placed) should follow regardless of whether the placement is paid for by the authority or by you:

**Step 1:** Care and support planning

**Step 2:** Initial liaison between the first and second authorities

**Step 3:** Arrangements for ongoing management of the placement

**Step 4:** Confirmation of the placement

As a general rule, responsibility for you if you are placed in cross-border residential care remains with the first authority.

* or Health and Social Care Trust in Northern Ireland

**NHS-funded nursing care** – The four administrations of the UK have also reached separate bilateral agreements as to which administration shall be responsible for the costs of any NHS-funded nursing care (see Box J.4) you may require if you are placed cross-border into a care home:

■ between England and Scotland or between England and Northern Ireland (in either direction), the health service of the country of the first authority will be responsible. In England, therefore, your responsible Clinical Commissioning Group will pay the costs;

■ between England and Wales (in either direction), the second authority's health service will be responsible; *and*

■ between Wales and Scotland, Wales and Northern Ireland, and Scotland and Northern Ireland, the first authority's health service will retain responsibility.

CA, S.39 & Sch.1; The Care & Support (Cross-border Placements & Business Failure: Temporary Duty) (Dispute Resolution) Regs 2014; Care & Support Statutory Guidance, Chapter 21; Part 11 Code of Practice (Miscellaneous & General), Annex 2

## 11. If you are not satisfied with your care services
### Complaints

**England** – There is a two-stage combined health and adult social care complaints procedure. Complaints should normally be made within 12 months of the incident/issue, unless there are special circumstances. You can complain in writing, verbally or by email, and your complaint should be acknowledged within three working days. The local authority or health body should then contact you and offer to discuss the complaint and the way it will be handled and explain the possible results. The complaint should then be investigated speedily and efficiently. When the investigation is finished (which should be in a maximum of six months), you should be given a written explanation of how it was considered and the conclusion. If you are not satisfied with the resolution, you can take the matter to the appropriate Ombudsman (see Chapter 59(5)).

Local Authority Social Services Complaints (England) Regs 2006; Local Authority Social Services & NHS Complaints (England) Regs 2009

**Wales** – The complaints procedure has two stages: local resolution and formal investigation. With the local resolution, the local authority will offer to discuss the complaint with you to try to resolve the matter. This should normally happen within 10 days. If the matter is not resolved, it should move to the next stage, formal investigation. An independent investigator will be appointed to assist with this. The investigation should be completed in 25 days. If you are still not satisfied, you can take your case to the Public Services Ombudsman for Wales (see Chapter 59(5)).

The Social Services Complaints Procedures (Wales) Regs 2014

### Complaints to care homes

All care homes must have a complaints procedure that is accessible and explained to you. Initially, you should complain to the manager of the home. The complaints procedure for the home should also make it clear how to complain to the appropriate registration body (see 6 above). If you make your own arrangements and fund your own care, you can complain to the relevant Ombudsman (see Chapter

59(5)) if your complaint has not been resolved by the care home provider.

Local Government Act 1974, Part IIIA (as amended by the Health Act 2009)

If the NHS or local authority is involved in any way with your care, you can use the adult social care and NHS complaints procedures (see above and Chapter 59(4)). If you are not satisfied with the outcome of your complaint, you have the right to request that the relevant Ombudsman considers your complaint (see Chapter 59(5)).

### Further steps

You may wish to take your complaint to local councillors or your MP (or Assembly Member in Wales) if you feel it would be helpful for them to know the system is not working for you. If you have exhausted the complaints procedure, you can contact the relevant Ombudsman (see Chapter 59(5)). The Ombudsman can investigate complaints against local authorities if there has been maladministration.

Local Authority Social Services Act 1970

If it is not possible to resolve your dispute via the complaints procedure, you may wish to consider a legal remedy such as judicial review. You can also complain to the local authority's Monitoring Officer (usually the Chief Executive or Chief Legal Officer), who is responsible for ensuring that decisions are lawful and procedures correctly followed. It is also possible to ask the Secretary of State to use her/his default powers, but these extend only to statutory duties, not to discretionary powers – ie if you feel the authority has withdrawn or failed to provide a service that it has a duty under law to provide.

It may be useful to contact a national organisation or seek legal advice to discuss ways of pursuing your case. You must act quickly. Contact a law centre (see Chapter 58(2)) or the Disability Law Service (020 7791 9800; http://dls.org.uk).

# 37 Paying for care and support

| A | Common rules | |
|---|---|---|
| 1 | Charging for care and support | 241 |
| 2 | Couples and maintenance | 243 |
| 3 | When can charges not be made? | 243 |
| 4 | If you cannot afford to pay the charge | 243 |
| | Charging in Scotland, Wales and Northern Ireland – Box J.7 | 242 |
| B | **Paying for non-residential care and support** | |
| 5 | Introduction | 243 |
| 6 | Disability-related benefits and expenditure | 244 |
| C | **Paying for care homes** | |
| 7 | Introduction | 244 |
| 8 | Capital and income | 244 |
| | Capital and income – Box J.8 | 246 |
| 9 | Key points of the financial assessment | 245 |
| 10 | Personal expenses allowance | 245 |
| 11 | Treating your home as capital | 248 |
| 12 | Deferred payment agreements | 248 |
| 13 | Deprivation of capital | 249 |
| 14 | Meeting the costs of your own home | 249 |
| 15 | What happens if you move out? | 249 |

## A. COMMON RULES

### 1. Charging for care and support

The Care Act 2014 provides a statutory framework in England for charging and financial assessments for both non-residential and residential care and support. The first part, introduced in April 2015 is not significantly different from the previous legal provisions. The second part, with more fundamental reform, was due to be implemented in April 2016, then delayed until April 2020, and finally shelved in November 2017, when it was announced that a new Green Paper on social care will be published in summer 2018 instead. Charging in Scotland, Wales and Northern Ireland is covered in Box J.7.

**Guidance** – The Care Act rules are explained in the *Care and Support Statutory Guidance* (see Box J.3 in Chapter 36). This guidance must be followed by local authorities; this chapter largely reflects that guidance.

### The financial assessment

The financial assessment is based on your income and capital.

Importantly, earnings are disregarded. If the local authority takes your capital into account, the minimum limit above which you can be charged the full cost of your care and support should be the same for both non-residential and residential care and support, and the authority can use the same tariff income; see Box J.8. Disability-related benefits may be taken into account as income where they are payable, but see 6 below.

---

## J.7 Charging in Scotland, Wales and Northern Ireland

### Charging in Scotland

The charge will be determined by your local authority, subject to an assessment of your needs and means to pay. Guidance on charging for non-personal non-residential care services provides minimum charging thresholds, which are uprated annually: the proposed rates for 2018/19 are £134 a week for a single person (£204 for a couple) for those under state pension age, and £204 a week for a single person (£311 for a couple) for those over state pension age.

*CoSLA: National Strategy & Guidance for Charges Applying to Non-residential Social Care Services (2018/19)*

### Free personal care

People aged 65 or over are not charged for personal care. If you live at home, the amount of personal care you will receive is determined by a local authority assessment, with no limit set on the amount authorities can provide. Limits apply if you live in a care home (see Box J.5). Free personal care services may be arranged by the authority, or you can ask for a direct payment (see Box J.5). Receipt of free personal care while you live at home will not adversely affect entitlement to attendance allowance, disability living allowance, personal independence payment or any other state benefit. *'Free personal care'* includes:

■ help with personal assistance;
■ personal hygiene;
■ continence management;
■ dealing with problems arising from immobility;
■ simple treatments;
■ counselling and psychological support, including behaviour management;
■ the provision of reminding and safety devices; *and*
■ broad provision for food and diet.

The definition of free personal care covers physical assistance with care and help with the mental processes related to that care – eg helping someone to remember to wash.

*CCH(S)A*

Free personal care payments start from the date the assessed service is provided and cannot be backdated (eg to the date of referral or date of assessment). If you are assessed as needing free personal care but told you will have to wait before it can be provided, seek advice. You may be charged for shopping, domestic chores or other forms of non-personal care.

A Court of Session judgment has ruled that a local authority is only obliged to provide free personal care if it provided or arranged the service; it is at the authority's discretion whether to provide the payment to a private care provider if the care is arranged without their involvement.

*CCD 1/2008; Argyll & Bute Council – Judicial review of Decision of Scottish Public Services Ombudsman [2007] CSOH 168; CCD 1/2010*

From April 2019, free personal care will also be available to people aged under 65.

### Charging in Wales

Local authorities have the discretion to charge and can be more generous than the legislation requires. The way that your income and capital are treated in the assessment is broadly similar to that in England (see Box J.8).

Local authorities are required (if they decide to charge) to include certain financial safeguards so that non-residential service users keep a minimum amount of their income. This includes a financial buffer of 35% (and a further 10% flat-rate disability-related expenditure disregard) above the basic levels of income support, employment and support allowance or pension credit. There is a weekly maximum charge of £80 for non-residential care and support. For those in residential care, you should be left with at least the 'minimum income amount' (see Chapter 37(10)) of £28.50 a week.

*The Care & Support (Charging)(Wales) Regs 2015; The Care & Support (Financial Assessment)(Wales) Regs 2015*

### Charging in Northern Ireland

Health and Social Care Trusts (HSCTs) provide integrated health and social care services across Northern Ireland. When services are being provided, an HSCT may carry out a financial assessment to determine what your contribution to the cost should be and whether the HSCT should make a contribution. The way that your income and capital are treated in the assessment is broadly similar to that in England (see Box J.8). The HSCT should financially assess only the person who needs the service; no other person is required to contribute.

HSCTs can choose when to charge for care services delivered in a person's home (domiciliary care). HSCTs have generally chosen not to charge for services provided in the home setting, except for the home help scheme and the meals on wheels service. People over 75 are not charged. A standard charge that is not means tested is applied to meals on wheels. If an HSCT decides to charge you for a domiciliary care service, it must first carry out a financial assessment. In its financial assessment, the HSCT should not take into account any disability-related benefit that you are receiving.

For those in residential care, you should be left with at least the personal expenses allowance (see Chapter 37(10)) of £25.27 a week.

Any charges must be *'reasonable'*, and if you feel they are excessive, you have the right to complain.

*Health & Personal Social Services (Assessment of Resources) Regs 1993; HSS(SS)1/80*

Local authorities can decide not to charge at all or can have policies that are more generous than the guidance. But if an authority has decided to charge, it must carry out a financial assessment of what you can afford to pay and explain how the assessment has been carried out (except where a 'light touch assessment' is allowed – see below).

The local authority, as part of your care and support plan (Chapter 36(3)), should give you written details of how much you will be charged, a breakdown of how the charge has been worked out and details of what to do if you think you cannot afford the charge. The authority will be treated as having carried out a financial assessment if you refuse an assessment or do not co-operate with an assessment.

CA, S.14; CS(CAR) Regs; Care & Support Statutory Guidance, Chapter 8 & Annexes B, C & E

### Self-funders
If you ask them to, your local authority must make arrangements to meet your eligible need for non-residential care and support, even if you are self-funding (although you may need to pay an additional arrangement fee for this service). This is called the 'right to request'. For care and support in a care home, authorities have the power to make arrangements if you are self-funding but cannot charge you an additional fee for making those arrangements.

CA, Ss.13 & 18(3); Care & Support Statutory Guidance, Chapter 8.56

### 'Light-touch' financial assessments
A financial assessment will not have to be carried out if the local authority is satisfied, on the basis of evidence, that you can, and will continue to be able to, afford any charges due. Guidance gives some circumstances where a light-touch assessment is appropriate, such as where:
- you have significant financial resources;
- there is only a small charge for a particular service and it is clearly affordable within the relevant minimum income guarantee (see 5 below); *or*
- it is clear that, due to your level of income, you would not be able to afford the charge.

CA, S.14(8); CS(CAR) Regs, regs 10(2)&(3); Care & Support Statutory Guidance, Chapter 8.22-8.26

## 2. Couples and maintenance
Only your own income and capital is taken into account in the financial assessment, as the local authority has no power to assess couples according to their joint resources. This means a local authority cannot normally approach your partner for any contribution towards the cost of care and support. However, an exception applies if you have gone into a care home temporarily and your partner is still being paid benefit for both of you as a couple; see 9 below.

Care & Support Statutory Guidance, Chapter 8.8

## 3. When can charges not be made?
Local authorities cannot charge or demand a contribution from anyone (family, carer or friend) other than the person using the service, nor can they charge for needs assessments and care planning.

Local authorities cannot charge for certain types of care and support that must be arranged free of charge. These are:
- intermediate care, which must be provided free of charge for up to six weeks (see Chapter 36(2)). Authorities have the discretion to offer this free of charge for longer than six weeks where there are clear preventive benefits in doing so;
- community equipment (aids and minor adaptations). Aids must be provided free of charge whether they are provided to meet, prevent or delay needs. A minor adaptation is one costing £1,000 or less;
- care and support provided to people with Creutzfeldt-Jakob disease;

- aftercare services or support provided under s.117 of the Mental Health Act 1983 for people who have previously been detained in hospital;
- any service or part of a service that the NHS is under a duty to provide, including NHS continuing healthcare and NHS-funded nursing care (see Box J.4 in Chapter 36); *and*
- any service that the local authority is under a duty to provide through other legislation.

CA, S.14(7); Care & Support Statutory Guidance, Chapter 8.14

## 4. If you cannot afford to pay the charge
If it charges for services, the local authority has a duty to decide how much you can afford to pay and can reduce the charge, or not charge you, if it is not reasonable for you to pay the charge. It may not withdraw a service or a personal budget because you fail to pay the charge. This is because the decision to meet a need for care and support is separate from, and comes before, any decision to charge.

### Complaints
You can complain about the amount you are being charged using the procedure described in Chapter 36(11). Some authorities have a charges complaints or appeals procedure that is shorter than the standard complaints procedure, but you can insist on using the standard complaints procedure.

## B. PAYING FOR NON-RESIDENTIAL CARE AND SUPPORT

## 5. Introduction
A local authority may charge for non-residential care and support that it either provides or arranges, including for services provided at home and other services in the community (eg day care and outreach). Carers may also be charged for direct services they receive, although, in practice, very few authorities have exercised this power, recognising the significant value and cost effectiveness of supporting carers.

Guidance instructs local authorities on the minimum level of income that you should be left with following charging – the *'minimum income guarantee'*. Rates for this are set as follows:

| Basic allowances | | per week |
|---|---|---|
| Single person | 18-24 | £72.40 |
| | 25 to pension credit age | £91.40 |
| | pension credit age | £189.00 |
| Lone parent | 18 or over | £91.40 |
| Member of couple | one or both 18 or over | £71.80 |
| | one or both pension credit age | £144.30 |
| Child dependant | | £83.65 |

| Premiums | | per week |
|---|---|---|
| Disability | single | £40.35 |
| | member of couple | £28.75 |
| Enhanced disability | single | £19.70 |
| | member of couple | £14.15 |
| Carer | | £43.25 |

The qualifying conditions for the premiums are based on those for income support (see Chapter 21(2), (4) and (6)). The disability and enhanced disability premiums do not apply if you, or your partner, have reached pension credit qualifying age (see Chapter 44(2)).

CS(CAR) Regs, reg 7; Care & Support Statutory Guidance, Chapter 8.35 & 8.42 & Annex C para 48; LAC(DHSC)(2018)1

## 6. Disability-related benefits and expenditure
### Disability-related benefits

These may be taken into account as income and are defined as:

■ disability living allowance (DLA) care component;
■ personal independence payment (PIP) daily living component;
■ attendance allowance;
■ constant attendance allowance; *and*
■ exceptionally severe disablement allowance.

The DLA or PIP mobility component, the war pensioner's mobility supplement and armed forces independence payment are disregarded.

CS(CAR) Regs, Sch 1, paras 4, 8, 9 & 10

### Disability-related expenditure

If disability-related benefits are taken into account, the local authority should assess your *'disability-related expenditure'* (DRE); guidance gives examples of the main types, including expenditure on special clothing or footwear, additional bedding costs, or special dietary needs. Guidance also states that the care and support plan (see Chapter 36(3)) may be a good starting point for considering what is necessary disability-related expenditure, but that it should not be limited to what is necessary for care and support, for example above-average heating costs should be considered.

CS(CAR) Regs, Sch 1, para 4; Care & Support Statutory Guidance, Chapter 8.42, Annex C, paras 39-41

The High Court has held that a local authority should have carried out a home visit to gather the information needed to assess the amount of DRE. It also found that the authority was wrong to deny that costs related to a service user's holiday, eg paying a carer to accompany them, could be DRE. The court held that such costs are capable of being DRE if they can be considered *'reasonable expenditure needed for independent living'*.

R(B) v Cornwall CC [2009] 491 (Admin) (EWHC)

Some local authorities have decided to allow a set amount for normal disability-related costs to avoid intrusive questions; the amount varies from authority to authority. Authorities have their own lists of DRE but these might not be comprehensive and you can ask for a review so that other expenditure can be taken into account. Payments to relatives might be disallowed as DRE, but authorities should look at each case on its merits.

R on the application of *Stephenson v Stockton on Tees BC* [2005] Civ 960 (CoA) (7CCLR 459)

### Only daytime care services provided

If you get higher rate attendance allowance or highest rate DLA care component (ie for both daytime and night-time care needs) but you receive only day services, the local authority should not take all of your benefit into account, just the part for daytime care.

R v Coventry City Council ex p Carton [2001] (4CCLR 41);

However, in calculating entitlement to PIP, no distinction is made between day and night care. If your local authority charges against PIP, it should take account of the reality of your day and night care needs and the care it is providing. Authorities are expected to *'take steps to ensure that adults in receipt of care and support before the implementation of the Care Act are not made worse off as a result of any changes to the charging rules'*.

Department of Health 'Frequently asked questions – Charging for Care'

In addition, guidance states that day or night care that is not being arranged by the local authority should be included in your DRE. Authorities should undertake an assessment of your DRE and allow you to keep enough benefit to meet any needs not being met by the authority.

Care & Support Statutory Guidance, Annex C, paras 39 & 40(c)(i)

## C. PAYING FOR CARE HOMES

## 7. Introduction

If you need help with care home accommodation and fees, you need to approach your local authority adult social care department. Help will be provided only if you have assessed eligible needs (see Chapter 36(3)).

The system of assessing eligible needs, providing a personal budget and charging is the same whether your accommodation is provided in a home managed or owned by a local authority, or in a home managed or owned by a voluntary or private organisation (sometimes described as the 'independent sector').

Local authorities can charge for providing residential care and support. The amount you pay normally depends on an assessment of your means (see 8 to 11 below). Authorities can also make arrangements for the care and support of someone who is paying the care home fees themselves because they have sufficient income or more than the capital threshold (ie they are *'self-funding'* – see below).

If you are moving to a care home and you do not want to sell your home, it may be possible to enter into a 'deferred payment agreement' (see 12 below). If you have given away assets, the local authority may still take their value into account in the financial assessment (see 13 below).

CA, Ss.9 -17

**Healthcare and nursing care** – If your primary need is for healthcare rather than social care, you will be entitled to fully funded NHS continuing healthcare. Even if it is decided that the NHS is not responsible for the full fees of the care home under NHS continuing healthcare, it is still responsible for your registered nursing care costs in a nursing home. See Box J.4 in Chapter 36 for details.

**Hospices** – Care in hospices is free at the point of use.

### Paying your own fees: 'self-funders'

If you enter a care home and don't want or need help with the fees (ie you are a 'self-funder'), you should still ask for an assessment of your needs; the local authority has a duty to carry out such an assessment if it appears to them that you may have care and support needs. The authority can then help you with a care and support plan to meet your eligible needs. It may suggest other options to meet your care needs or advise whether the type of home you plan to go into is suitable for your needs and whether, once your capital is below the capital limit (see Box J.8), it will agree to help with the funding.

CA, S.9

## 8. Capital and income
### Capital

If you are in a care home (on either a permanent or temporary basis) and your savings are above the upper capital limit (see Box J.8), you will have to pay the full cost of your accommodation until your capital drops to this limit. Some capital is ignored or disregarded in the assessment. If you have capital between the lower and upper capital limits, a *'tariff income'* is assumed. Capital under the lower capital limit is disregarded. Capital is either *'actual'*, ie you own it and it is available to you, or *'notional'*, ie you are treated as owning the asset even if it is unclaimed or transferred to another person in an effort to avoid care home charges. See Box J.8 and 11 to 13 below for details (including about how your property is treated).

Care & Support Statutory Guidance, Annex B

### In a care home and capital reaching the upper capital limit

If you are already in a care home but have not needed help because your capital is above the upper capital limit and you are self-funding (see 7 above), you will need to contact the adult social care department to ask for help when your capital nears the upper capital limit. They will then undertake an assessment of your care and support needs to determine your eligibility for help (see Chapter 36(3)). You should contact the adult social care department where the care home is situated; this applies even if you moved to a care home in a new local authority area from that which you were in when you lived in your home in the community.

**Couples with joint capital** – If you have a joint account in excess of £46,500, it may be worth splitting your account so that you don't have to wait until your joint account is down to this figure to get help with funding. For example, if you have £55,000 in a joint account, your partner will only get help after £8,500 has been paid in fees and your account is down to £46,500. If you split the account so you each have £27,500, help will be available after spending only £4,250 in fees.

### Income
In general, assume all income counts unless all or part of it is specifically disregarded. The 'income disregards' are similar to those for income support (see Chapter 22(3)). However, income support, income-based jobseeker's allowance, income-related employment and support allowance, universal credit and pension credit are taken into account as income by local authorities (except for payments towards housing costs and the savings disregard applied to the savings credit element of pension credit). See Box J.8 for details.
CA, Ss.14 & 17; Care & Support Statutory Guidance, Annex C

## 9. Key points of the financial assessment
The assessment is based largely on income support rules but there are important differences, and the local authority has some discretion (see Box J.8). Whatever your source(s) of income, you will generally be left with no less than the personal expenses allowance (see 10 below). Except for any income disregarded in the assessment (see Box J.8), the rest of your income goes towards meeting the costs for your accommodation.

Any difference between what you have to pay and the amount agreed in your personal budget (see Chapter 36(4)) is met by the local authority, which is liable for the full cost of the fees (but see Chapter 36(9) if you have chosen more expensive accommodation than the authority thinks you need).

If the application of the law affects you unfairly, urge the local authority to use its discretion to correct that unfairness by letting you keep more of your income than your personal expenses allowance.

### Temporary residents
If you are a temporary resident in the care home, the charging assessment is slightly different to allow for your costs at home (see 14 below).

The local authority may choose to charge short-term residents based on its non-residential charging policy for the first eight weeks.
Care & Support Statutory Guidance, Chapter 8.34

### Lacking capacity
At the time of the financial assessment, the local authority must establish whether the person has capacity to take part in the assessment. Where a person lacks such capacity, the authority should involve the appropriate legal representative or, if there is no such representative, consideration should be given as to whether the appointment of a Property and Affairs Deputyship is required.
Care & Support Statutory Guidance, Chapter 8.18-19

### Couples
If you are one of a couple, the law does not allow a joint charging assessment; only the resident's own income and capital affects the assessment. However, if you are one of a couple going temporarily into a care home and your partner is the claimant of income support or pension credit for both of you, guidance states that *'where the cared-for person receives income as one of a couple, the starting presumption is that the cared-for person has an equal share of the income'*.
Care & Support Statutory Guidance, Annex C, para 5

### Mental health aftercare
If your accommodation is provided as part of an aftercare package under s.117 of the Mental Health Act 1983, you should not be charged for your accommodation.
CA, S.14(6); Care & Support Statutory Guidance, Chapter 8.14

You should seek advice if you are being charged or have been charged in the past and have not received a refund. If you receive aftercare under s.117, you will be entitled to benefits (including income support, income-based jobseeker's allowance, income-related employment and support allowance, universal credit and pension credit) in the normal way. However, disability living allowance (DLA) care component, attendance allowance and personal independence payment (PIP) daily living component will not be payable, as s.117 is an *'enactment relating to persons under disability'* for the purposes of defining those people *'resident in a care home'* for whom DLA care component, attendance allowance or PIP daily living component is not payable.
CDLA/870/04; Decision Makers Guide, Chapter 61, Appendix 1; PIP Regs, reg 28(2)

An independent review of the Mental Health Act 1983 was announced in October 2017, with a report due in autumn 2018.

## 10. Personal expenses allowance
You receive the same *'personal expenses allowance'* (PEA) whether you are in a local authority or an independent care home and whether it is on a temporary or permanent basis. In England it is set at £24.90 a week; in Wales it is called the *'minimum income amount'* and is set at £28.50 a week.

Your PEA can be spent as you wish on personal items. Neither the care home nor the local authority can demand that you spend your PEA in any particular way.

The PEA should not be used for care that has been contracted for by the local authority and/or assessed as necessary by the authority or the NHS. Needs for continence supplies or chiropody should be reflected in the care plan and there should be no pressure from local authorities or care home providers to spend your PEA on them. Your PEA can be used to buy extra services from the care home if they are genuinely additional to services that have been contracted for by the authority and/or assessed as necessary by the authority or the NHS.
Care & Support Statutory Guidance, Annex C, para 45

## J.8 Capital and income

Local authority assessments of capital and income are similar to those for income support. In this box, we outline how local authority assessments of capital and income differ from those for means-tested benefits (including income support, income-related employment and support allowance (ESA), income-based jobseeker's allowance (JSA), pension credit and universal credit – see Chapters 17, 22 and 44(5)-(6)).

### Capital limits
**Local authority charging** – For local authority charging purposes, for both temporary and permanent residents, these are: in England and Northern Ireland, £23,250 upper limit and £14,250 lower limit (for tariff income purposes); in Scotland, £27,250 upper limit and £17,000 lower limit.

In Wales, there are different capital limits for residential care and non-residential care. In each case, there is a single limit, so no tariff income assessment is needed. The capital limit for residential care is £40,000; the capital limit for non-residential care is £24,000.

**Means-tested benefits** – For income-related ESA/income support/income-based JSA, the capital limits are:
■ £16,000 upper limit and £6,000 lower limit (for tariff income) for temporary residents; *and*
■ £16,000 upper limit and £10,000 lower limit (for tariff income) for permanent residents.

For universal credit, there is a £16,000 upper limit and £6,000 lower limit for both temporary and permanent residents.

For pension credit, there is no capital upper limit. A £10,000 limit for tariff income purposes applies to both temporary and permanent residents.

### Tariff income
The tariff income for local authority charging purposes and for income-related ESA, income support and income-based JSA purposes is calculated using £1 a week for every £250 (or part of £250) in excess of the lower limits. For universal credit, the tariff income (or 'assumed income') is £4.35 a month for each £250 (or part of £250) in excess of £6,000. For pension credit, the tariff income (or 'deemed income') is £1 a week for every £500 (or part of £500) in excess of £10,000.

### Arrears of benefits
There is a 52-week limit on the disregard of arrears of some benefits for charging assessments and for universal credit. For income-related ESA, income support, income-based JSA and pension credit, this period is extended in certain circumstances (see Chapters 22(27) and 44(6)).

### Your home
See also Chapter 37(11). If you are a temporary resident, the value of your main or only home is disregarded if:
■ you intend to return to live in it as your home; *and*
■ it is still available to you; *or*
■ your property is up for sale and you intend to use the proceeds to buy a more suitable property to return to.
*CS(CAR) Regs, Sch 2, para 1*

### Temporary resident
You count as a *'temporary resident'* if your stay is unlikely to last more than 52 weeks or *'in exceptional circumstances (is) unlikely substantially to exceed that period'*.
*CS(CAR) Regs, reg 2(1); Care & Support Statutory Guidance, Annex F, para 4*

If you are unsure of your long-term plans, it is usually best to say you intend to return to your own home. However, if you are one of a couple going into a care home on a trial basis with a view to a permanent stay, you will still be treated as a couple for pension credit purposes, whereas if you are one of a couple going permanently into a care home, you will be treated as two single people and any pension credit entitlement will be paid to each of you based on your individual resources (see Chapter 38(6)). Therefore, it may be financially beneficial in these circumstances to be permanent from the day of entering the care home.

### Permanent resident
You count as a *'permanent resident'* if you are not a temporary or short-term resident and the agreed intention is for you to remain in a care home.
*CS(CAR) Regs, reg 2(1)*

The local authority must disregard the value of your property for the first 12 weeks that you are a permanent resident in a care home (see Chapter 37(11)). In addition to the statutory property disregards listed in Chapter 37(11), the authority has discretion, not found in means-tested benefits, to apply a property disregard in other circumstances. In guidance, examples are given where a carer has given up their own home in order to care, or the person remaining is an elderly companion of the resident, particularly if they have given up their own home. These examples are not exhaustive. If you think a disregard should apply to your property, and it has not been, use the complaints procedure (see Chapter 36(11)).
*CS(CAR) Regs, Sch 2, para 2; Care & Support Statutory Guidance, Annex B, paras 34 - 46*

### While your home is up for sale
Unlike for means-tested benefits, if you are a permanent resident when your old home is up for sale, the local authority does not disregard the value for 26 weeks or longer where reasonable. It counts as capital from the 13th week after you have become a permanent resident. See also Chapter 37(11).

Although the local authority may help towards your care home fees while your home is up for sale, you will have to pay back the full amount once the home is sold. See also Chapter 37(12) for information about deferred payment agreements.

### Joint capital
If you jointly own capital (other than property) with your partner (or any other person), the local authority, to avoid administrative difficulties, will divide it into equal shares in the charging assessment regardless of what your actual share is. Once you are in sole possession of your actual share, you will be treated as owning that actual amount.
*CS(CAR) Regs, reg 24*

This applies whether you are a temporary or permanent resident, unlike the means-tested benefit rules for couples, which count your capital together until you become a permanent resident, when the local authority divides your capital.

See Chapter 37(11) if you jointly own property.

### Personal possessions
The value of these is disregarded unless you bought them with the intention of reducing your capital in order to avoid or lessen charges.
*CS(CAR) Regs, Sch 2, para 13*

## Income

**Disability benefits** – Attendance allowance, disability living allowance (DLA) care component and personal independence payment (PIP) daily living component are taken fully into account while you still get them, unless you are a temporary resident. However, for the purposes of non-residential care, local authorities must ensure that in addition to the minimum income guarantee (see Chapter 37(5)) or personal expenses allowance (see Chapter 37(10)), you get to keep enough of your benefits to pay for things to meet those needs not being met by the local authority (see Chapter 37(6)). DLA and PIP mobility components are disregarded.

**Means-tested benefits** – Income support, income-related ESA, income-based JSA, pension credit and universal credit are taken fully into account but payments in these benefits made towards housing costs are disregarded. See below for the savings disregard applied to the savings credit element of pension credit.

*CS(CAR) Regs, Sch1, paras 8 & 11; Care & Support Statutory Guidance, Annex C, para 16*

**Payments for your home** – Housing benefit or housing costs and council tax reduction being paid in relation to your usual home are disregarded. The local authority can disregard any payments you are making towards your housing costs as a temporary resident (see Chapter 37(14)).

*CS(CAR) Regs, Sch1, para 3*

**Tax credits and child benefit** – Working tax credit is taken fully into account. Child tax credit is disregarded. Child benefit (unless the child is in the accommodation with you) and guardian's allowance are disregarded.

*CS(CAR) Regs, Sch1, paras 33, 38 & 39; Care & Support Statutory Guidance, Annex C, para 17*

**Earnings** – Earnings from employment (including self-employment) are disregarded.

*CS(CAR) Regs, reg 14*

**Occupational and personal pensions** – If you do not live with your spouse/civil partner, half your personal or occupational pension or payment from a retirement annuity contract will be disregarded if you pass at least this amount to your spouse/civil partner. If you pass nothing or less than half, there is no disregard. The disregard is for both temporary and permanent residents. (The means-tested benefit rules do not have a similar disregard.)

*CS(CAR) Regs, Sch 1, para 16*

## Savings disregard

The Department of Health and devolved governments apply a savings disregard for residents aged 65 or over. The amounts below are for 2018/19.

❏ If you are a resident receiving qualifying income of less than £133.82 a week (or less than £212.97 for couples), you will not have a savings disregard.

❏ If you are a resident receiving qualifying income between £133.82 and £155.60 a week (or between £212.97 and £237.55 for couples), you will have a savings disregard of an amount equal to the savings credit award or £5.75 a week (£8.60 for couples), whichever is less. Where your income is in excess of £155.60 (or £237.55 for couples), your savings disregard will be £5.75 (£8.60 for couples), or £6.30 (£9.45 for couples) in Scotland.

❏ If you are a resident receiving qualifying income above the limit for receiving savings credit (£190 a week or £278 for couples), you will have a disregard of £5.75 a week (£8.60 for couples), or £6.30 (£9.45 for couples) in Scotland.

Note that the income limits could be higher if you are entitled to additional amounts, eg for severe disability or for carers.

*CS(CAR) Regs, Sch 1, para 40; Care & Support Statutory Guidance, Annex C, para 33*

## Third-party payments

Third-party top-ups to meet the additional cost of more expensive accommodation (see Chapter 36(9)) are taken fully into account as your notional income by the local authority. This is not the case for means-tested benefits.

Third-party payments made for the purpose of discharging any arrears of payments for accommodation are not taken into account as income.

*CS(CAR) Regs, reg 17(3)&(4)*

## Deprivation of assets

Local authorities have powers that may be used to treat you as having notional capital, ie as possessing capital that you have given away, or as having notional income, ie as possessing income that you have given away or sold the rights to. Chapter 37(13) explains the deprivation of capital rules. There is also an additional power, the 'transfer of assets to avoid charges rules', which has different conditions (see below).

*CS(CAR) Regs. regs 17 & 22; Care & Support Statutory Guidance, Annex C, paras 34-38 & Annex E*

## Transfer of assets to avoid charges

The *'transfer of assets to avoid charges'* rules may be applied if you have needs that have been or are being met by a local authority and you:

■ transferred cash or any other asset, which would have affected the charging assessment, to someone else; *and*

■ did this 'with the intention of avoiding charges'; *and*

■ were not paid anything, or given anything, in return for the transfer; *or*

■ were paid, or given something, less than the value of the asset in return for the transfer.

If these circumstances apply, the person or persons to whom you transferred the asset is *'liable to pay … the difference between the amount the authority would have charged were it not for the transfer of the asset, and the amount it did in fact charge…'.*

*CA, S.70; Care & Support Statutory Guidance, Annex E, paras 21-23*

Some people mistakenly think that if they have given away assets before entering a care home, it cannot affect the amount they would have to pay for a care home. However, if they have deliberately deprived themselves of assets in order to avoid or reduce a charge for care and support, the deprivation rules may be applied – even if the transfer took place before entering the care home (see Chapter 37(13)).

Obviously, if you have given away something that would not have affected the charging assessment at all, the deprivation rule cannot apply, nor can the 'transfer of assets to avoid charges' rules. If the local authority refuses to arrange a place for you in a care home because the asset you gave away, together with other savings, was worth more than the capital limit in your country (see above), seek urgent advice.

*See Robertson v Fife Council [2002] UKHL 35 (HoL)*

### Increasing the PEA

Local authorities have discretion to allow more PEA in *'some circumstances where it would not be appropriate for a local authority to leave a person only with the PEA'*. Guidance provides examples, but they are not exhaustive. If you need to keep more of your income to lead a more independent life or pursue an activity that is important to you, you should let the local authority know and ask it to increase your PEA.

If you are one of a couple, the PEA may be increased so that you can help support your partner at home, perhaps because you are not married or registered as civil partners and so cannot have half of your personal or occupational pension disregarded (see Box J.8), or because, as the care home resident, you are getting a means-tested benefit (eg pension credit) paid for both of you.

Care & Support Statutory Guidance, Annex C, para 46

The local authority should not demand a charge that would leave your partner without enough money to live on. However, the authority could consider being on a means-tested benefit as having enough to live on. If the amount allowed for your partner leaves them without enough money to live on, you should seek advice with a view to using the complaints procedure (see Chapter 36(11)).

Care & Support Statutory Guidance, Annex C, para 5

## 11. Treating your home as capital

The value of your previous home will have a mandatory disregard applied when the local authority assesses your resources:

■ if you are temporarily resident in a care home; *or*
■ for the first 12 weeks of being a permanent resident in a care home.

The value of your previous home will also be disregarded if it is occupied, and has been continuously occupied since before you went into the care home, by:

■ your partner or former partner (unless you are estranged or divorced from them);
■ your estranged or divorced partner and they are a lone parent; *or*
■ a family member or relative who is:
  – aged 60 or over;
  – incapacitated (see below); *or*
  – aged under 18 and you are liable to maintain them.

The value of your previous home may be disregarded for 12 weeks following the ending of one of the above disregards if the relative dies or moves into a care home themselves. Local authorities also have discretion to disregard the value of the property if anyone else lives there (see Box J.8).

**Relative** – A *'relative'* is your parent, parent-in-law, son, daughter, son/daughter-in-law, step-parent, stepson/daughter, brother, sister, or the partner (including civil partner) of any of the above, grandparent, grandchild, uncle, aunt, nephew or niece.

**Incapacitated** – This is not defined, but guidance says you count as incapacitated if you get:

■ armed forces independence payment;
■ attendance allowance or constant attendance allowance;
■ disability living allowance;
■ incapacity benefit;
■ personal independence payment; *or*
■ severe disablement allowance,

or you would meet the incapacity conditions for any of these.

CS(CAR) Regs, Sch.2, paras 3, 4 & 5; Care & Support Statutory Guidance, Annex B, paras 34-45

### Selling your home

If your home is taken into account, its value will be based on the current selling price, less any debts (such as a mortgage) charged on it, and less 10% to cover the expenses that would be involved in selling it. Its value should be reassessed

periodically. The capital value of your home is assessed in this way until it is sold, and added to any other capital you have. The local authority may help towards your fees while your home is being sold (see 12 below). Once your home is sold, the capital realised from the sale, less any debts and the expenses involved in the sale, is taken into account.

CS(CAR) Regs, reg 20; Care & Support Statutory Guidance, Annex B, para 14

The local authority cannot make you sell your home to pay the assessed charge for your accommodation, other than through the courts. However, the authority can place a legal charge on the property so that it can recover outstanding debts when the property is eventually sold.

### If you jointly own property

If you are a joint owner of a property, it is your 'beneficial interest' in the property that should be valued as capital, not the property itself. The value of this interest is determined by your ability to re-assign the interest to someone else and there being a willing buyer for it, which will depend on the conditions in which the joint interest has arisen. Seek advice if you disagree with how your share is valued.

If you jointly own a property with your spouse or civil partner who decides to sell in order to move (eg to a smaller house), you can give them some of your share of the proceeds to help buy the new home. The local authority should not consider this as deprivation of capital.

## 12. Deferred payment agreements

By entering into a *'deferred payment agreement'* you can defer or delay paying the costs of care and support until a later date. This means that you can put off selling your home (or other capital asset) while you settle into care. The local authority has to offer you a deferred payment agreement if you meet the following criteria:

■ your eligible care and support needs are to be met in a care home;
■ your capital is less than (or equal to) a set limit (see Box J.8), excluding the value of your home; *and*
■ the value of your home is not disregarded (see 11 above).

**How do deferred payment agreements work?** – The scheme allows the local authority to enter into a written agreement with you whereby:

■ the authority places a first legal mortgage charge on your property;
■ the authority contracts to pay the full fees of the placement in the home;
■ you are assessed to pay a weekly charge to the authority based on your weekly income (less the 'disposable income allowance' – see below); *and*
■ payment of the balance of the weekly cost of the placement is deferred until you die or the property is sold.

**Loan style agreements** – An alternative to a deferred payment agreement is a *'loan style agreement'*. This allows you to borrow the costs for your accommodation and care without the local authority making arrangements or requiring a weekly charge. Note that you would be entering into a contract with the care home as a self-funder, which is likely to mean that a higher fee would be required.

CA, S.34; The Care & Support (Deferred Payment) Regs 2014; Care & Support Statutory Guidance, Chapter 9

### The disposable income allowance

The local authority may demand that you make a contribution towards care costs from your income, but you have a right to keep a proportion of it: the *'disposable income allowance'*. This is a fixed amount of up to £144 per week, which the authority must allow you to keep if you wish (either in full or in part). The authority can require you to contribute the rest of your income towards the care costs.

Care & Support Statutory Guidance, Chapter 9.44

## Local authority refusals

The local authority can refuse a deferred payment agreement even though you meet the criteria (above) if they are unable to secure a charge on your property or if you do not agree to the terms and conditions of the agreement (such as a requirement to insure and maintain the property). The authority may also limit the amount of the deferred payment to exclude a top-up (see Chapter 36(9)) which they believe to be unsustainable. Use the complaints procedure, if you wish to challenge the decision (see Chapter 36(11)).

Care & Support Statutory Guidance, Chapter 9.11 & 9.12

## Costs

If you enter into a deferred payment agreement, you must pay for land registry searches and other legal and administrative expenses relating to placing a legal charge on your property. The local authority may charge interest on the deferred payment to recoup the costs associated with deferring payments. The agreement must make clear all the fees deferred and any interest and administrative charges.

Care & Support Statutory Guidance, Chapter 9.65

## Deferred payment agreements and benefits

If you are under pension credit qualifying age, you will not be entitled to income support or income-related employment and support allowance (ESA) while the property is not for sale if your interest in the property is worth more than £16,000. If you have reached pension credit qualifying age, it is also unlikely that you will be entitled to pension credit while the property is not for sale, as the 'deemed income' applied on capital above £10,000 is likely to mean your income will exceed your 'appropriate minimum guarantee' (see Chapter 44(3)). This means the total debt repayable to the local authority at the end will be greater.

You will retain your entitlement to attendance allowance, disability living allowance care component or personal independence payment daily living component during a deferred payment agreement because you will be treated as a 'self-funder', if it is clear you will eventually pay back the local authority in full. This is the case even if you get income support, income-related ESA or pension credit with the severe disability premium (or pension credit equivalent) during this period.

It is important to ensure you receive all the benefits you are entitled to during the period of the deferred payment agreement to help reduce the debt to the local authority.

## 13. Deprivation of capital

If you have given away assets, eg your former home, or sold them for less than they are worth to avoid or lessen the charge, or converted them into a form that is disregarded to take advantage of the disregard, the local authority may take their value into account in the charging assessment. These 'notional capital' rules are not mandatory and authorities have discretion not to apply them. If they do apply them, they are similar to the notional capital rules for means-tested benefits (see Chapter 22(36)).

CS(CAR) Regs, para 22; Care & Support Statutory Guidance, Annex E

The local authority can decide that you have disposed of property to reduce the residential charge, without having to consider whether you knew of the capital limit or anticipated the need to enter a care home.

*Yule v South Lanarkshire Council* [2000] (SLT1249)

The local authority must take account of your 'subjective purpose' in disposing of the property and give reasons for accepting or rejecting any evidence you provide.

*R (on the application of Beeson) & Dorset CC & SoS for Health* [2002] HRLR15 (EWCA)

The local authority *'diminishing notional capital'* rule reduces any notional capital on a weekly basis. It is reduced by the difference between the charge you are currently paying and the charge you would have paid if the authority had not taken notional capital into account.

CS(CAR) Regs, para 23

**The 'transfer of assets to avoid charges' rules** – In certain circumstances, a local authority may charge a person you have transferred resources to for the difference between the amount assessed as due to be paid for the care home and the amount you are paying (see Box J.8).

## 14. Meeting the costs of your own home

If you are a *'temporary resident'* (see Box J.8), the local authority can disregard payments you are making towards *'any housing-related costs which [you are] liable to meet in respect of [your] main or only home'*.

CS(CAR) Regs, Sch 1, para 2

Housing-related costs can include ground rent, service charges, water rates and insurance premiums.

Care & Support Statutory Guidance, Annex F, para 12

If no one is living in your home and you have entered a care home for a short period, see Chapter 38(3) for information about housing benefit and the universal credit housing costs amount.

After 52 weeks in a care home, or 13 weeks in the case of a trial period (see Chapter 25(6)), you will no longer be able to get housing benefit, means-tested benefit* housing costs or support for mortgage interest loans (via the means-tested benefit). After six months as a temporary resident, you will no longer be able to get the universal credit housing costs amount or support for mortgage interest loans (via universal credit). However, your liability to pay rent and/or a mortgage for your former home continues until you have terminated your tenancy or sold your home. If you have given notice on your tenancy, you will be able to continue to claim housing benefit for up to four weeks (see Chapter 38(3)).

If your former home is vacant and you are permanently in a care home, you should not have to pay council tax.

If your partner, children or relatives continue to live in your home, the help they can receive for housing costs depends on their circumstances. If they are paying the housing costs, even though you are the person liable for them, they can claim housing benefit, means-tested benefit* housing costs, the universal credit housing costs amount or support for mortgage interest loans instead of you.

* ie income support, income-based jobseeker's allowance, income-related employment and support allowance or pension credit

## 15. What happens if you move out?

When you move out of a care home, you will be entitled to benefits in the usual way. Your local adult social care department can advise you on local authority benefits and services available in your area.

If you leave the care home temporarily, the local authority can use its discretion to vary the personal expenses allowance to enable you to have more money while away (see 10 above).

You may be able to claim personal independence payment daily living component or attendance allowance for periods away from the care home. Chapter 38 covers the effect on benefits of stays in, and absences from, care homes.

# **38** Benefits in care homes

| | | |
|---|---|---|
| 1 | What benefits are you entitled to? | 250 |
| 2 | Disability benefits | 250 |
| 3 | Housing benefit and universal credit housing costs amount | 251 |
| 4 | Income support, income-based JSA and income-related ESA | 251 |
| 5 | Universal credit | 252 |
| 6 | Pension credit | 253 |
| 7 | Special help for war pensioners | 253 |

## 1. What benefits are you entitled to?

If you have moved into a care home (either temporarily or permanently), with or without help from the local authority, the only social security benefits that may be affected are:

- attendance allowance;
- disability living allowance care component;
- personal independence payment daily living component;
- constant attendance allowance and exceptionally severe disablement allowance;
- income-related employment and support allowance, income-based jobseeker's allowance and income support;
- universal credit;
- pension credit;
- housing benefit; *and*
- council tax reduction.

All other social security benefits can be claimed and paid in the normal way, subject to the standard rules outlined in the rest of this handbook. It normally makes no difference whether the care home you are in is owned or managed by a local authority or by a private or voluntary organisation.

## 2. Disability benefits

Normally, you cannot be paid the following benefits after the first 28 days in a care home:

- attendance allowance – see Chapter 6(7);
- disability living allowance (DLA) care component – see Chapter 4(8); *or*
- personal independence payment (PIP) daily living component – see Chapter 5(8).

However, if you pay the fees for the care home without funding (or only with interim funding – see Chapter 37(12)) from the local authority, you will be able to keep your attendance allowance, DLA care component or PIP daily living component (see below).

The armed forces independence payment can continue to be paid indefinitely if you are in a care home.

### Resident in a care home

You are considered to be *'resident'* in a care home, and therefore cannot be paid attendance allowance, DLA care component or PIP daily living component, if the costs of any *'qualifying services'* (accommodation, board and personal care) provided for you are paid for out of public or local funds under specified legislation (see Chapters 5(8) and 6(7) under 'What is a care home'). Qualifying services do not include domiciliary services, including personal care, provided to you in your own home. If you go into a care home from the community, the days you enter and leave are counted as days in the community.

AA Regs, reg 7; DLA Regs reg 9; PIP Regs regs 28 & 32(2)

### Mobility component

DLA and PIP mobility components are not affected by stays in a care home. They are only affected if your stay is in hospital or a similar institution (but see below).

### NHS continuing healthcare

A Court of Appeal judgment held that if you are receiving fully funded NHS continuing healthcare in a residential care home (see Box J.4 in Chapter 36), you should continue to receive the DLA mobility component, as you cannot be considered to be an inpatient. This does not apply, however, if you are in a nursing home or a residential care home where you receive medical or other treatment from (or under the direct supervision of) a qualified doctor or nurse employed by the home.

The judgment also applies to the PIP mobility component.

The DLA care component and PIP daily living component are not payable if you are receiving NHS continuing healthcare in a nursing home or a residential care home.

*Sec. of State for Work & Pensions v Alexander Slavin* [2011] Civ 1515 (EWCA); Decision Makers Guide, Vol 10, Chap 61, paras 61821-22; Advice for Decision Making, Chapter P3, para P3062 & Appendix 1

### Paying your own fees

If you are paying your own fees, you are a *'self-funder'* and can receive attendance allowance, DLA care component or PIP daily living component as long as you:

- do not get any funding from the local authority; *or*
- are only getting funding on an interim basis from the local authority and will be paying it back in full; ie you are a *'retrospective self-funder'*. This is most likely to apply if you are in the process of selling your home and/or you have a 'deferred payment agreement' with the authority (see Chapter 37(12)).

AA Regs, reg 8(6); DLA Regs, reg 10(8); PIP Regs, reg 30(5); R(A)1/02; Decision Makers Guide, Vol 10, Chap 61, paras 61749-51; Advice for Decision Making, Chapter P3, paras P3047-49

If you become a funded care home resident, payment of attendance allowance, DLA care component or PIP daily living component should be simply suspended if there is a possibility that you will become a retrospective self-funder (thus making it easier to backdate payment of the benefit where appropriate).

CA/2364/2009; Decision Makers Guide, Vol 10, Chap 61, para 61751; Advice for Decision Making, Chapter P3, para P3049

As *'qualifying services borne out of public or local funds'* do not include NHS-funded nursing care (see Box J.4 in Chapter 36), you can receive attendance allowance, DLA care component or PIP daily living component if you are in a nursing home receiving NHS-funded nursing care only (and not NHS continuing healthcare; see above) and the above two bullet points apply.

SSCBA, Ss.67(4) & 72(8); PIP Regs, reg 28

**Scotland** – If you are aged 65 or over, you will not be entitled to attendance allowance, DLA care component or PIP daily living component (after 28 days in the care home) if you are receiving local authority help with the cost of your care under the 'free personal care' arrangements (see Box J.7 in Chapter 37). If you are under 65, you will continue to be paid DLA care component or PIP daily living component if the only help you get is for 'free nursing care'.

### Direct payments

Local authorities can give you direct payments, as part of your personal budget (or individual budget in Scotland), so that you can arrange your own care at home or buy up to four weeks respite care in any one year (see Chapter 36(5)). Although attendance allowance, DLA care component and PIP daily living component are not normally affected in these circumstances, they could be affected if you need another period of care or hospital treatment within the 'linking period' (see Chapters 5(8) and 6(7)).

*Example:* You receive the PIP daily living component. You use your direct payment to buy four weeks in a care home, then two weeks later your carer falls ill, so you return to the care home. This time your stay is funded by the local authority under a contract with the home. Your PIP daily living component is affected immediately as it links with a period when your care was funded by local authority money because you were using the payment from the authority to buy your respite care.

**Long-term care in a care home** – The government is currently testing the use of direct payments in care homes in designated areas. It is anticipated that any further implementation will be considered as part of a Green Paper on social care due in summer 2018. Guidance states that where such payments are made for an indefinite period, attendance allowance, DLA care component and PIP daily living component are not payable.

DMG Memo 26/13; Advice for Decision Making Memo 10/13

## 3. Housing benefit and universal credit housing costs amount
### Registered care homes
You cannot usually get housing benefit or the universal credit housing costs amount to cover the costs of a registered care home (see below for help with meeting the costs of your own home). For housing benefit purposes, *'residential accommodation'* is defined as accommodation provided in a care home or an independent hospital. For universal credit housing costs amount purposes, *'care home'* is defined in the same way. Care homes, including local authority care homes, are required to be registered with the appropriate body (see Chapter 36(6)).

HB Regs, reg 9(1)(k)&(4); UC Regs, reg 25(2)(a) & Sch 1, paras 1 & 3(d)

Some care homes have de-registered and become 'Supported Living' accommodation. In this situation, you will usually be able to claim housing benefit.

**Shared Lives** – If you live in a Shared Lives household, you are eligible to claim housing benefit or the universal credit housing costs amount as such a household is not defined as 'residential accommodation' or a 'care home'.

HB/CTB Circular A20/2005, para 12

### Help with meeting the costs of your own home
**Housing benefit or support for mortgage interest loans** – If you go into a care home for a temporary stay or for respite care, you can continue to receive housing benefit – or (if you are getting income-related employment and support allowance, income-based jobseeker's allowance, income support or pension credit) help to cover mortgage interest payments with 'support for mortgage interest loans' – for up to 52 weeks, as long as:

- your stay is not likely to last longer, or in exceptional circumstances substantially longer, than this;
- you intend to return to your own home; *and*
- you have not rented your normal home to someone else.

HB Regs, reg 7(16)&(17); LMIR Regs, Sch 3, para 10

However, if you go into a care home for a trial period with a view to a permanent admission but you intend to return to your home if the care home does not suit you, then housing benefit (or support for mortgage interest loans) is paid only for up to 13 weeks (see Chapter 25(6)). If the care home suits you and you are not going to return home, then, if the other conditions continue to be met, you will continue to be eligible for housing benefit (or support for mortgage interest loans) for the whole 13-week period.

HB Regs, reg 7(11)&(12); LMIR Regs, Sch 3, para 8; R(H)4/06

If you become a permanent resident at the end of the 13-week trial period or if you move directly from your former home to a care home on a permanent basis, and you remain liable for the rent on your former home (because a notice period for the termination of the tenancy is being served), you can be treated as occupying your former home for up to four weeks, as long as that liability could not reasonably have been

avoided. Hence, housing benefit can be paid on your former home for that period.

HB Regs, reg 7(7)

**Universal credit** – If you come under the universal credit system and go into a care home for a temporary stay or for respite care, you can continue to receive the universal credit housing costs amount (or help to cover mortgage interest payments with 'support for mortgage interest loans') for up to six months as long as your absence from home does not exceed, or is not expected to exceed, six months.

UC Regs, reg 25(4) & Sch 3, para 9; LMIR Regs, Sch 3, para 18

## 4. Income support, income-based JSA and income-related ESA
If you are a resident in a care home under pension credit qualifying age (see Chapter 44(2)) and are not eligible to claim universal credit (see Box E.1 in Chapter 14), you may be able to claim income support, income-based jobseeker's allowance (JSA) or, more likely, income-related employment and support allowance (ESA).

If you are eligible to claim universal credit, see 5 below. If you have reached pension credit qualifying age, see 6 below.

### Capital limits in care homes
You must have no more than £16,000 capital. Tariff income of £1 for every £250 (or part of £250) starts at £10,000 for permanent residents and £6,000 for temporary residents. See Chapter 22(25).

**Is the stay temporary or permanent?** – If you know you want to stay in a care home, your admission can be permanent from the start. Most local authorities, however, prefer you to have a trial period to see if you like it. During a trial period (and for temporary stays), the lower capital limit for income support, income-based JSA and income-related ESA is £6,000. This goes up to £10,000 only when your stay is permanent. The upper capital limit is £16,000 for both temporary and permanent residents. You are still considered to be a permanent resident if you are temporarily absent from the care home.

### Calculation of income support, income-based JSA or income-related ESA in care homes
If you are resident in a care home, your income support, income-based JSA or income-related ESA is worked out in the standard way (see Chapters 19(6), 20(5) and 18(5))). In each case, your award will consist of:

- your personal allowance; *and*
- any premiums to which you are entitled (which can include the severe disability premium (SDP) while you are getting disability living allowance (DLA) care component or personal independence payment (PIP) daily living component). See Chapter 21; *and*
- for income-related ESA, any additional component (see Chapter 18(7)).

Even if you are not entitled to income support, income-based JSA or income-related ESA in your own home, you may be entitled when you go into a care home.

**Temporary admission (single person)** – If you go into a care home for a temporary period (less than 52 weeks), the amount of income support, income-based JSA or income-related ESA you get will usually not change because you will be treated as living in your own home (but see note below).

**Temporary admission (couple)** – If one of you goes into a care home (or if you go into different rooms in the same care home or into different care homes) for a temporary period, for income support, income-based JSA or income-related ESA purposes you will still be assessed as a couple, but you will each get the appropriate single person rate in your award if this amount is more than the couple rate. If the appropriate single person rate is greater, the person at home (or in a different room in the same care home or in a different care home) will get a single rate personal allowance plus any appropriate premiums and any housing costs (and any additional component for income-related ESA), and the person in care will get a single rate personal allowance plus appropriate premiums (and any additional component for income-related ESA). These are then added together and your combined income is subtracted from this figure to give the amount of income support, income-based JSA or income-related ESA to be paid to the claimant.

If you go into the same room in the care home, you will get the couple rate of income support, income-based JSA or income-related ESA plus appropriate premiums (and any additional component for income-related ESA). Housing benefit will continue to be paid for your rent at home.
IS Regs, Sch 7, para 9; JSA Regs, Sch 5, para 5; ESA Regs, Sch 5, para 4

*Note:* If SDP and, for income support and income-based JSA only, the enhanced disability premium are included in your award, they will no longer be included if payment of DLA care component or PIP daily living component ceases. The enhanced disability premium will continue to be included in your award of income-related ESA if you receive the support component.

**SDP and temporary admissions** – There is often confusion about the payment of SDP if one of a couple goes into a care home for a temporary period. If carer's allowance is paid to a carer, SDP will not be paid. However, in other circumstances, a Commissioner's Decision held that SDP should be included in the award of income support, income-based JSA or income-related ESA for each qualifying person, even where a partner in the community may have prevented its inclusion previously.
R(IS)9/02 & Decision Makers Guide, Vol 4, Chap 23, paras 23231-33

In practice, SDP is often left out of the award for both temporary and permanent admissions, and if you are being assessed by the local authority you do not see any benefit from the extra money anyway. In this case, you should check that the authority is not assuming you are getting SDP and therefore including it in the calculation of your charge, even if you are not being paid it.

Some local authorities do not assess for a residential charge for the first eight weeks of a temporary stay but continue to charge at the non-residential rate instead. Where this is the case, if no one receives carer's allowance for caring for you and SDP was not previously included in your award, you may now become eligible for SDP, which will not be taken away in local authority charges.

**Permanent admission (single person)** – If you go into a care home on a permanent basis, the amount of any income support, income-based JSA or income-related ESA will usually only change in the following circumstances (but see note below).

❑ If you have capital between £6,000 and £10,000, income support, income-based JSA or income-related ESA will increase, as there will no longer be a tariff income applied because of the increased lower capital limit from £6,000 to £10,000 (see above).

❑ If you have capital between £10,000 and £16,000, a reduction in tariff income will be applied (and therefore income support, income-based JSA or income-related ESA will increase), due to the increased lower capital limit.

❑ If you are a single person and have a carer who receives carer's allowance, or you are living with a non-dependant in the community, you may become entitled to, or there may be an increase in, income support, income-based JSA or income-related ESA when you enter a care home permanently. This is because carer's allowance will no longer be payable to your carer and your non-dependant will no longer count as a non-dependant. Therefore, SDP will be included in your income support, income-based

JSA or income-related ESA award for any period in which attendance allowance, DLA care component or PIP daily living component remains in payment.
IS Regs, Sch 2, para 13(2)(a); JSA Regs, Sch 1, para 15(1); ESA Regs, Sch 4, para 6(2)(a)

If you are retrospectively self-funding (see 2 above), you will still be entitled to income support, income-based JSA or income-related ESA if you are selling your property.

**Permanent admission (couple)** – If you are permanently in a care home, each of you will be treated as separate single claimants.
IS Regs, reg 16(1) & (3)(e); JSA Regs, reg 78(1) & 3(d); ESA Regs, reg 156(1) & 4(d)

Jointly owned capital will be split and the income support, income-based JSA or income-related ESA calculation should be based solely on each of your individual capital and income. See Chapter 22(26) for information about joint capital. If you both enter the same care home, you may still be assessed by the DWP as a couple, although case law has established that most people should be assessed as separate individuals even if they share a room. Seek advice if you are treated as a couple in this situation.
R(IS)1/99

*Note:* If SDP and, for income support and income-based JSA only, the enhanced disability premium are included in your award, they will no longer be included if payment of DLA care component or PIP daily living component ceases. The enhanced disability premium will continue to be included in your income-related ESA award if you receive the support component.

### Maintenance and liable relatives
The income and capital of the non-resident spouse or civil partner cannot be taken into account in considering a permanent resident's claim to income support, income-based JSA or income-related ESA. However, spouses or civil partners are each liable to maintain the other and the non-resident spouse/civil partner can be asked to make a contribution. The non-resident should not feel pressured into paying more than they can reasonably afford given their resources and expenses; unless the DWP obtains a court order, payment is voluntary. In practice, legal proceedings are rarely undertaken, although the DWP may put pressure on the non-resident spouse/civil partner to make 'voluntary' payments.

Normally, payments made by the non-resident spouse/civil partner are taken into account as the resident spouse's/civil partner's income. But if you are receiving payments to help meet the cost of more expensive 'preferred' accommodation (see Chapter 36(9)), they are disregarded for income support, income-based JSA and income-related ESA.

## 5. Universal credit
If you are eligible to claim universal credit (see Box E.1 in Chapter 14) and are resident in a care home, you may be able to claim that benefit. You must be under pension credit qualifying age (see Chapter 44(2)) and meet the *'basic conditions'* and *'financial conditions'* (see Chapter 14(2)).

### Capital limits in care homes
You must not have more than £16,000 capital. Capital in excess of £6,000 is treated as generating a monthly income of £4.35 for each £250 (or part of £250) in excess of £6,000 (see Chapter 17(17)).

### Calculation of universal credit in care homes
If you are resident in a care home, your universal credit is worked out in the standard way (see Chapter 16(1)).

**Temporary admission (single person)** – If you go into a care home for a temporary period (less than six months), your universal credit will not usually change because you will be treated as still living in your own home.

**Temporary admission (couple)** – Couples are not treated as two single people if one is going into a care home on a temporary basis. This means your universal credit will usually be the same amount as when you were both living at home.

**Permanent admission (single person)** – If you go into a care home on a permanent basis, your universal credit will not usually change. If you are retrospectively self-funding (see 2 above), you will still be entitled to universal credit if you are selling your property.

UC Regs, Sch 10, para 6

**Permanent admission (couple)** – If you are permanently in a care home, each of you will usually be treated as separate single claimants. Joint capital will be split, and the universal credit calculation should be based solely on each of your individual capital and income (see Chapter 17(19) for information about joint capital). If you both enter the same care home, you may still be assessed by the DWP as a couple, although case law has established that most people should be assessed as individuals even if they share a room.

R(IS)1/99

Guidance to decision makers on what would be useful to consider when deciding whether a couple who are permanently in a care home are members of the same household include:

- the structure of days – do they decide (even by default) at what time to get up, have meals, go to bed, etc;
- how the accommodation they live in is to be arranged – do they decide which room is to be the dining room, the living room, etc;
- can they decide who can come and stay with them, and for how long;
- can they insist that other people do not enter their accommodation without permission;
- can they decide the decor and furnishing of their accommodation;
- do they have facilities for preparing food and making tea, coffee and other hot drinks; *and*
- do they have responsibility for running the household – are they responsible for getting repairs done, replacing domestic appliances or buying food.

Seek advice if you are treated as a couple in this situation.

Advice for Decision Making, Chapter E2, para E2071

## 6. Pension credit

If you are a resident in any type of registered care home and have reached pension credit qualifying age (see Chapter 44(2)), you may be able to claim pension credit.

### Capital limits in care homes

There is no upper capital limit for pension credit. Capital under £10,000 does not result in any 'deemed' income (see Chapter 44(6)). Deemed income from capital above £10,000 is £1 a week for every £500 (or part of £500). (The similar 'tariff income' is calculated differently by local authorities when assessing your charges – see Box J.8 in Chapter 37.)

### Calculation of pension credit in care homes

If you are a resident in a care home, your pension credit guarantee credit element is worked out in the usual way by adding your 'standard minimum guarantee' to any additional amounts you are entitled to, which can include the *additional amount for severe disability* while a qualifying benefit is payable. The *'qualifying benefits'* are: attendance allowance, disability living allowance care component at the middle or highest rate, personal independence payment daily living component and armed forces independence payment. See Chapter 44(3). The pension credit savings credit element is also worked out in the usual way (see Chapter 44(4)).

**Temporary admission (single person)** – There will usually be no change in your pension credit during a temporary stay (less than 52 weeks) because you will be treated as living in your own home (but see note below).

**Temporary admission (couple)** – Couples are not treated as two single people if one is going into a care home on a temporary basis. This means your pension credit will usually be the same amount as when you were both living at home. However, if the additional amount for severe disability (see above) is included in your award, it will no longer be included if the qualifying benefit (see above) in payment to the resident has been suspended. This is the case even if your partner is living at home in the community and receiving a qualifying benefit themselves. This is because you, as the resident, are treated as still being in the household and are not disregarded for the purposes of qualifying for the additional amount for severe disability. A similar situation occurs when one of a couple is temporarily in hospital, but the pension credit regulations provide for this by allowing a single additional amount for severe disability to continue in payment for the partner at home. In practice, however, the DWP also appears to apply this hospital provision to a care home situation.

SPC Regs, reg 6(5) & Sch 1, para 1(2)(b)

**Permanent admission (single person)** – If you go into a care home on a permanent basis, your pension credit will usually change only if you were living with a non-dependant in the community or you had a carer receiving carer's allowance. This is because you may become entitled to pension credit (or there may be an increase in your pension credit) due to the additional amount for severe disability being included in your award for any period that a qualifying benefit (see above) remains in payment.

SPC Regs, reg 5(1)(b) & Sch 1, para 1(1)(a)

As there is no upper capital limit for pension credit, you may be entitled to it while living in a care home even if your capital is more than the local authority charging capital limit and you are therefore self-funding.

You will also be entitled to pension credit if you are retrospectively self-funding (see 2 above) because you are selling your property.

**Permanent admission (couple)** – If you are permanently in a care home, each of you will usually be treated as separate single claimants. Joint capital will be split, and the pension credit calculation should be based solely on each of your individual capital and income (see Chapter 44(6) for information about joint capital). If you both enter the same care home, you may still be assessed by the DWP as a couple, although case law has established that most people should be assessed as individuals even if they share a room. Seek advice if you are treated as a couple in this situation.

SPC Regs, reg 5(1)(b); R(IS)1/99

*Note:* If the additional amount for severe disability is included in your pension credit award, it will no longer be included if payment of the qualifying benefit (see above) ceases.

## 7. Special help for war pensioners

If you get a war disablement pension or have had a gratuity for your disability, you may qualify for help with your care home fees from Veterans UK. It can cover medical treatment, nursing home fees and respite breaks that you need wholly or mainly because of that disability. These services are not means tested, but you must apply before arranging them. For details, ring the Veterans Helpline (0808 191 4218), email veterans-uk@mod.uk or visit www.gov.uk/government/organisations/veterans-uk.

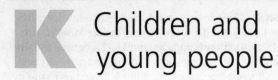

# Children and young people

This section of the handbook looks at:

| | |
|---|---|
| Maternity and parental rights | Chapter **39** |
| Disabled children | Chapter **40** |
| Child benefit | Chapter **41** |
| Young disabled people | Chapter **42** |

# **39** Maternity and parental rights

| | | |
|---|---|---|
| 1 | Help with health costs | 254 |
| 2 | Maternity and parental leave | 254 |
| 3 | Statutory maternity pay | 254 |
| 4 | Maternity allowance | 255 |
| 5 | Paternity leave | 255 |
| 6 | Statutory paternity pay | 255 |
| 7 | Statutory shared parental pay | 255 |
| 8 | Rights for adoptive parents | 255 |
| 9 | Unable to work due to sickness or disability? | 256 |
| 10 | When your baby is born | 256 |
| | For more information – Box K.1 | 256 |

## 1. Help with health costs

You are entitled to free prescriptions and dental treatment if you are pregnant or have had a baby in the past 12 months and have a valid maternity exemption certificate. Ask your doctor, midwife or health visitor for form FW8.

Vouchers to buy milk (including infant formula milk), fruit and vegetables are available under the Healthy Start scheme. They are for pregnant women and for families with children under the age of 4, and who are on certain means-tested benefits. For details, see Chapter 52(6).

## 2. Maternity and parental leave

**Maternity leave** – Employed women are entitled to 52 weeks' statutory maternity leave. You must meet strict notice conditions, including letting your employer know you are pregnant and telling them, by the end of the 15th week before your baby is due, when you want to take your maternity leave.
Maternity & Parental Leave etc Regs 1999, regs 4-12A

**Parental leave** – Parents who have worked for the same employer for at least one year are entitled to 18 weeks' unpaid parental leave for each child, which can be taken up until the child's 18th birthday. You cannot take more than four weeks' parental leave for any one child in a year, unless otherwise agreed with your employer.
Maternity & Parental Leave etc Regs 1999, regs 13-16

**Shared parental leave** – Mothers can choose to end their maternity leave early (after an initial 2-week recovery period, or 4-week period if they work in a factory) and hand over their unused leave to their partner. This is called *'shared parental leave'* and can last for up to 50 weeks. The mother can switch back to receiving maternity leave if she chooses. Shared parental leave is also available to couples who have adopted a child.

Shared parental leave can only be taken in the first year of your child's life (or within one year of their adoption). You can take up to three separate blocks of shared parental leave. You must give your employer at least eight weeks' notice that you want to take a block of leave.

To qualify, you must have worked for the same employer for at least 26 weeks by the 15th week before your baby is due (or by the week you are matched with your adopted

child). In turn, your partner must have been employed or self-employed for at least 26 weeks in the 66 weeks before the week in which your baby is due (or matched) and earned an average of at least £30 a week for any 13 weeks in this period.
The Shared Parental Leave Regs 2014

**Time off for antenatal care** – Every pregnant employee is entitled to time off with pay to keep antenatal appointments made on the advice of a doctor, midwife or health visitor.

## 3. Statutory maternity pay

If you are an employee, you may be able to get *'statutory maternity pay'* (SMP) from your employer when you stop work to have your baby. You will not have to repay it if you do not return to work. If you have more than one employer, you may be eligible for SMP from each employer. You qualify if:

- you have been employed by the same employer continuously for at least 26 weeks into the 15th week (the *'qualifying week'*) before the week your baby is due (a 'week' starts on Sunday and runs to the end of the following Saturday);
- you are employed in the qualifying week (it doesn't matter if you are off work sick or on holiday);
- your average gross weekly earnings are at least £116; *and*
- you give your employer the right notice (see below).
SSCBA, Ss.164 & SMP Regs, reg 11(1)

**How much do you get?** – SMP is paid by your employer for up to 39 weeks. For the first six weeks you get 90% of your average weekly earnings (with no upper limit). The average is calculated from your gross earnings in the eight weeks, if paid weekly, or two months, if paid monthly, before the end of the 15th week before the week your baby is due. The remaining 33 weeks are paid at the standard rate of £145.18, or 90% of your average weekly earnings (whichever is less).
SSCBA, S.166 & SMP Regs, reg 21

SMP is treated as earnings, so deductions such as income tax and national insurance contributions will be made.

**When is it paid?** – SMP can start from the 11th week before the week in which your baby is due. You decide when you stop work and start your maternity pay period; you can work up until your baby's birth. If your baby is born early (ie before the 11th week before the week it is due), SMP will start the day after the birth. See 9 below if you are off work with a pregnancy-related illness.
SSCBA, S.165 & SMP Regs, reg 2

You can work during your maternity pay period for the employer who pays you SMP for up to 10 days ('keeping in touch' days) without losing any SMP.
SMP Regs, reg 9A

**How do you claim?** – You must tell your employer at least 28 days before the date you want to start your SMP, or if this is not possible, as soon as is reasonably practicable. Your employer may ask you to inform them in writing. You must also give them your maternity certificate (form MAT B1), which your doctor or midwife will normally give you 20 weeks before your baby is due. Tell your employer as soon as is reasonably practicable if your baby is born early.
SSCBA, S.164(4)&(5)

**If you can't get SMP** – If you are not eligible for SMP, your employer must give you form SMP1 within seven days of their decision and must also return your maternity certificate. You may be eligible for maternity allowance (see 4 below).

**Challenging a decision** – You can ask your employer for a written statement about your SMP position. If you disagree, you can refer your case to the HMRC Statutory Payments Disputes Team (see Chapter 10(10)) for a decision. If HMRC decides against you, you can appeal to a First-tier Tribunal (Tax). Your employer can also appeal.

## 4. Maternity allowance

If you cannot get statutory maternity pay, you may qualify for tax-free *'maternity allowance'*. To qualify, you must have been employed or self-employed for at least 26 weeks in the 66 weeks before the week in which your baby is due (the *'test period'*), and earned an average of at least £30 a week for any 13 weeks in this test period.
SSCBA, S.35

**How much do you get?** – Maternity allowance is £145.18 a week, or 90% of your average weekly earnings (whichever is less). The DWP will add up your gross earnings in the 13 weeks during the 66-week test period in which you earned the most, then divide by 13 to work out your average weekly earnings. Earnings in different jobs and from a mixture of employed and self-employed work can be added together. If you are self-employed and have paid 13 Class 2 national insurance contributions in the test period, you will be treated as having earnings sufficient to result in the full rate of maternity allowance.
SSCBA, S.35A

**When is it paid?** – Maternity allowance is paid for up to 39 weeks and can start from 11 weeks before the week in which your baby is due. If you are employed or self-employed, you may delay the start of your maternity allowance until the baby's birth (but see 9 below if you are off work with a pregnancy-related illness). If you are not employed, your maternity allowance will start from the 11th week before the week your baby is due.

Once you are on maternity allowance, you can work for your employer (or as a self-employed person) for up to ten 'keeping in touch' days and continue to receive it.
SSCBA, S.35(2)

**How do you claim?** – Fill in claim-form MA1 and send it to the DWP together with your maternity certificate (MAT B1), proof of your income (eg payslips) and form SMP1 (if you did not qualify for SMP from your employer). If you have more than one employer, you must get an SMP1 from each employer. MA1 forms are available from the Jobcentre Plus claim-line (0800 055 6688; textphone 0800 023 4888), your antenatal clinic or the website (www.gov.uk/maternity-allowance/how-to-claim).

Send in form MA1 as soon as you can once you are 26 weeks pregnant. Maternity allowance can only be backdated for up to three months, so don't delay claiming because you are still working or waiting for the MAT B1 or SMP1 – you can send them later. If you are not entitled to maternity allowance, the DWP should check whether you could get employment and support allowance instead (see 9 below).

**The benefit cap** – Maternity allowance is included in the list of benefits to which the 'benefit cap' applies. The cap limits the total weekly benefits that can be claimed; see Chapter 16(10) and Box G.6 in Chapter 25 for details (including exemptions).

**Helping in your spouse/civil partner's business** – If you are expecting a baby, a reduced rate maternity allowance of £27 a week can be paid for up to 14 weeks if you are helping without pay in your spouse or civil partner's business. It will not apply if you are a partner in their business.
SSCBA, S.35B; Social Security (Maternity Allowance)(Participating Wife or Civil Partner of Self-employed Earner) Regs 2014

## 5. Paternity leave

*'Paternity leave'* is one or two consecutive weeks' leave to support the mother or care for the child. To qualify, you must be the:
■ father of the child;
■ mother's husband or partner;*
■ child's adopter;
■ husband or partner* of the child's adopter; *or*
■ intended parent (if you are having a baby through a surrogacy arrangement).
\* including same-sex partners

You must have worked for the same employer for at least 26 weeks by the 15th week before the week the baby is due (or by the week you are matched with your adopted child). You must meet strict notice conditions. Paternity leave must be taken within 56 days of the birth or adoption placement. Use form SC3 to notify your employer (available from: www.gov.uk/paternity-pay-leave/how-to-claim).
The Paternity & Adoption Leave Regs 2002, regs 4-14

## 6. Statutory paternity pay

If you are taking time off work to care for a child, you may be entitled to *'statutory paternity pay'* (SPP). This is payable for one or two consecutive weeks. It must be taken within eight weeks of the birth or adoption placement. To be eligible, you must have worked for the same employer for at least 26 weeks by the 15th week before the week the baby is due (or by the week you are matched with your adopted child). You must have average gross weekly earnings of at least £116. SPP is £145.18 a week, or 90% of your average earnings (whichever is less). You must meet strict notice conditions; if you have already given your employer notice that you plan to take paternity leave, this can serve for SPP as well.
SSCBA, S.171ZA-E

**If you can't get SPP** – If you are not eligible for SPP, your employer must give you form SPP1 explaining why you don't qualify. You may be able to claim income support while you are on paternity leave (see Box F.1 in Chapter 19).

## 7. Statutory shared parental pay

Mothers can choose to give up their statutory maternity allowance, maternity allowance or statutory adoption pay early, in which case the remaining pay will then be available to their partner as *'statutory shared parental pay'* (SSPP). The conditions when this are possible are the same as for shared parental leave (see 2 above).

**How much do you get?** – SSPP is £145.18 a week, or 90% of your average weekly earnings (whichever is less).
The Statutory Shared Parental Pay (General) Regs 2014

## 8. Rights for adoptive parents

You have a right to 52 weeks' adoption leave if you have worked for the same employer for at least 26 weeks by the week in which you are notified of being matched with a child for adoption. A couple adopting jointly can choose who takes adoption leave and who takes paternity leave.
The Paternity & Adoption Leave Regs 2002, regs 15-27

To qualify for *'statutory adoption pay'* (SAP), you must have worked for the same employer for at least 26 weeks by the end of the week in which you are notified of being matched with a child for adoption and have average gross weekly earnings of at least £116. SAP can be paid for up to 39 weeks. It is paid at 90% of your average weekly earnings (with no upper limit) for the first six weeks. The remaining 33 weeks are paid at the standard rate of £145.18 a week, or 90% of your average earnings (whichever is less). You can continue to be paid SAP if you work for your employer for up to 10 days during your adoption pay period.

Adoptive parents can also get parental leave (see 2 above) and statutory shared parental pay (see 7 above).
SSCBA, S.171ZL-ZN

### 9. Unable to work due to sickness or disability?

If you are employed, you may be able to get statutory sick pay (SSP) – see Chapter 10. If you can't get SSP, you may be able to get employment and support allowance (ESA) – see Chapter 11.

**If you are entitled to SMP or maternity allowance**

You can stay on SSP up until the date of the baby's birth, or the date you are due to start your maternity leave. But if you are off work with a pregnancy-related illness in the last four weeks before the week your baby is due, your statutory maternity pay (SMP) or maternity allowance starts automatically.
SMP Regs, reg 2(4)

**SMP** – Once your SMP begins, any SSP stops. You can continue to receive ESA while you are on SMP if you continue to meet the basic qualifying conditions (see Chapter 11(7)). Contributory ESA and SMP overlap, so you are paid whichever is higher. SMP is treated as income with respect to income-related ESA, less Class 1 national insurance contributions, tax and half of any contributions you make towards an occupational or personal pension scheme.
ESA Regs, regs 80 & 95(2)(b) & Sch 8, paras 1 & 4

**Maternity allowance** – You can claim or continue to receive ESA while receiving maternity allowance if you continue to meet the basic qualifying conditions (see Chapter 11(7)). Contributory ESA and maternity allowance overlap, so you are paid whichever is higher. Maternity allowance is treated in full as income with respect to income-related ESA. You are automatically treated as having a limited capability for work while you are entitled to maternity allowance.
ESA Regs, reg 20(1)(e)

**If you are not entitled to SMP or maternity allowance**

You may be entitled to ESA from six weeks before the week the baby is due and up to two weeks after the birth if you meet the basic qualifying conditions (see Chapter 11(7)). You need your maternity certificate, but not medical certificates, and will be treated as having a limited capability for work (see Chapter 12(3)).

---

### K.1 For more information

#### Pregnancy and parenthood

Disabled parents can get information from Disability, Pregnancy and Parenthood (disabledparent.org.uk). Advice on maternity and parental leave is available from Working Families (0300 012 0312; www.workingfamilies. org.uk), whose free guide, *From Child to Adult*, on disability, transition and family finances, can be downloaded from their website.

#### Education

The organisations Contact and Independent Parental Special Education Advice (IPSEA) can offer advice on special educational needs and education, health and care plans (Contact: 0808 808 3555 or https://contact.org.uk/; IPSEA: www.ipsea.org.uk).

The Advisory Centre for Education Adviceline provides independent advice on a wide range of education issues (0300 011 5142 – Monday to Wednesday, 10am to 1pm, term time only; www.ace-ed.org.uk).

**Scotland** – For advice and the *Parent's guide to additional support for learning*, contact Enquire (0345 123 2303; http://enquire.org.uk/publications/).

---

You may be able to get ESA outside of these weeks, but must usually pass the limited capability for work assessment and meet the basic qualifying conditions. You will be treated as having a limited capability for work during your pregnancy if there would be a serious risk to the health of you or your unborn child if you did not refrain from work (see Chapter 12(3)).
ESA Regs, reg 20(1)(d)&(f)

### 10. When your baby is born

Claim child benefit (see Chapter 41).

A new baby may entitle you to child tax credit for the first time. If you already get this, your entitlement may increase from the date of birth if you notify HMRC within one month. See Chapter 23.

A new baby may mean you can get more help or qualify for the first time for housing benefit (see Chapter 25). Tell your local authority housing benefit section.

Your baby automatically qualifies for free prescriptions.

You have six weeks (21 days in Scotland) to register your baby's birth. When you register the birth, the registrar will give you form GMS1 (EC58 in Scotland). You need to complete this and send it to your GP so your baby can get an NHS number.

See Chapter 29(2) for details of the Sure Start maternity grant.

# 40 Disabled children

| 1 | What help can you claim? | 256 |
|---|---|---|
| 2 | Disability living allowance | 258 |
| 3 | Carer's allowance | 258 |
| 4 | Low income benefits | 258 |
| 5 | Tax credits | 259 |
| 6 | Help with housing costs | 259 |
| 7 | Child support | 259 |
| 8 | Family Fund | 259 |

### 1. What help can you claim?

If your child is disabled, you may be entitled to benefits or services described elsewhere in this handbook. Your right to some benefits or services will depend only on the effects of your child's disability; your right to others will depend on your own financial or other circumstances. The benefits checklist on pages 4-5 is a quick guide to the help available. In this chapter we highlight some of the specific help for disabled children. For further information, ring the Contact Helpline (0808 808 3555).

#### From birth

**Needs assessments** – You can apply to the local authority social care department for an assessment of your child's special needs (see Chapter 36(3)).

**Education, health and care plans** – In England, your child will be eligible for an *'education, health and care plan'* (EHC plan). These have replaced special educational needs (SEN) assessments and learning difficulty assessments. EHC plans cover your child's educational needs as well as the help your child may need from health services and social care.

Each plan is drawn up by the local authority following an assessment of your child's needs. Ask your local authority to assess your child if you think they will need a plan. Once the assessment has taken place, the authority will send you a draft of the plan. You will have 15 days to comment on it (eg if you think that your child should go to a specialist needs school). The authority must give you the final EHC plan within 20 weeks of the assessment.

You can challenge a decision:

- not to carry out an assessment;
- not to create an EHC plan;
- on the special educational support in the plan; *and*
- on the school named in the plan.

Contact your local authority first to let them know why you disagree with the decision. Include evidence to support your case, such as a letter from your child's doctor, health visitor or nursery worker. If you can't resolve the matter with the authority, you can appeal to the First-tier Tribunal (Special Educational Needs and Disability). See Box K.1 for organisations that can provide support with such appeals.

You may be able to get a personal budget for your child if they have an EHC plan (see Chapter 36(4)).

The EHC plan must be reviewed once a year and can remain in place until your daughter or son is 25.

Children & Families Act 2014, Ss.37-50

SEN assessments remain in place in Scotland, Wales (where they are also known as additional learning needs assessments) and Northern Ireland. Following the initial assessment, these too should be reviewed annually.

**Family Fund** – You may get help from the Family Fund with some of the extra costs arising from your child's disability (see 8 below).

**Loans and grants** – If you have been getting income support, income-related employment and support allowance (ESA), income-based jobseeker's allowance (JSA) or pension credit for at least 26 weeks, you may be eligible for a budgeting loan to help meet one-off costs (see Chapter 31(2)); if you have been getting universal credit for at least six months, you may be eligible for a budgeting allowance instead (see Chapter 31(3)). Grants to meet one-off costs are now administered by local authorities under 'local welfare assistance schemes' (see Chapter 31(1)).

**Home adaptations** – You may get help with adaptations in the home (see Chapter 30).

**Healthy Start vouchers** – You can get vouchers towards milk, fruit and vegetables if you are pregnant or have a child aged under 4 and get certain means-tested benefits. Pregnant women aged under 18 qualify regardless of whether they get one of those benefits. See Chapter 52(6) for details.

## From age 13 weeks

**Disability living allowance (DLA) care component** – You can be awarded the care component of DLA for your baby from when they are 3 months old; claim any time beforehand. See 2 below and Chapter 4(14). If your baby is terminally ill (Box B.8 in Chapter 5 explains the legal definition), they qualify automatically for the highest rate care component and payment can begin as soon as you claim DLA after the birth.

If your baby is awarded DLA, a disabled child premium is included in the award of your housing benefit and health benefits (see Chapter 21(8)).

If your baby is awarded DLA care component at the lowest or middle rate, the disabled child rate of the disabled child element is included in your child tax credit award (see Chapter 23(4)). Alternatively, if you claim universal credit, you will get the lower rate of the disabled child addition included in the award (see Chapter 16(4)).

If your baby is awarded DLA highest rate care component, an enhanced disability premium is included in the award of your housing benefit and health benefits (see Chapters 21(4)) and the severely disabled child rate of the disabled child element is included in your child tax credit award (see Chapter 23(4)). Alternatively, if you claim universal credit, you will get the higher rate of the disabled child addition included in the award (see Chapter 16(4)).

If your baby is awarded DLA middle or highest rate care component, you may be eligible for carer's allowance (see Chapter 8).

The benefit cap (which limits the total weekly benefits that can be claimed – see Chapter 16(10) and Box G.6 in Chapter 25) will not apply to your household if your child is awarded DLA.

## From 2 years

**Vaccine damage payment** – You can claim a vaccine damage payment (see Chapter 49).

**Blue Badge** – You may be able to apply for a Blue Badge for parking concessions once your child is 2 years old. It is possible to apply for a child under the age of 2 if they have a condition that means they must always have bulky equipment out of doors or be near a vehicle in case they need treatment (see Chapter 7(1)).

**Free early education and childcare** – In England, you can get up to 570 hours free early education and childcare a year for your 2-year-old if you receive one of the following benefits:

- income-related ESA, income support, income-based JSA or pension credit guarantee credit;
- universal credit (if your annual net earnings are less than £15,400);
- child tax credit or working tax credit and your taxable income is below £16,190;
- working tax credit run-on (see Chapter 23(6)); *or*
- support under the Immigration and Asylum Act.

This is usually taken as 15 hours each week for 38 weeks of the year. Your 2-year-old can also get such free education and childcare if they:

- are looked after by a local authority;
- have a current EHC plan or SEN assessment;
- get DLA; *or*
- have left care under a special guardianship, child arrangements or adoption order.

In Scotland there is a similar scheme; see www.earlylearningandchildcare.scot/who-qualifies.

## From 3 years

**DLA higher rate mobility component** – A disabled child can be awarded DLA higher rate mobility component (see 2 below and Chapter 4(9)). Claim from three months beforehand. The higher rate mobility component gives access to leasing a car through the Motability scheme (see Box B.16 in Chapter 7) and leads to automatic entitlement to a Blue Badge for parking (see Chapter 7(1)).

Your car can be exempt from vehicle tax if your child gets higher rate mobility component (see Chapter 7(2)).

**Free early education or childcare** – All 3-4-year-olds in England can get up to 570 hours of free early education or childcare a year. This is usually taken as 15 hours each week*. In some circumstances, you may be able to get 1,140 hours free childcare a year, usually taken as 30 hours each week*. For instance, this may apply if you (and your partner, if you have one), are in work and for at least 16 hours a week earn at least the national minimum or living wage that applies in your case (see Box I.5 in Chapter 33). You need to apply for the extra hours online (www.gov.uk/help-with-childcare-costs/free-childcare-and-education-for-2-to-4-year-olds).

In Scotland, 3-4-year-olds can get up to 600 hours of free early learning and childcare a year. In Wales, 3-4-year-olds can get 10 hours a week* free early education. In Northern Ireland, children can get free pre-school education in the year before they start primary school. In each case, contact your local authority for details.

* for 38 weeks of the year

## From 5 years

**DLA lower rate mobility component** – A disabled child can be awarded DLA lower rate mobility component. Claim from three months beforehand. It is often awarded to children with a learning disability or sensory impairment, but any disabled child who needs extra supervision or guidance outdoors on unfamiliar routes may qualify (see Chapter 4(13)).

**School meals** – In England and Wales, all children in Reception, Year 1 and Year 2 at state schools automatically get free school meals. In Scotland, free school meals are available to all children in the first three years of primary school.

If you get income support, income-related ESA, income-based JSA, the guarantee credit of pension credit or support under the Immigration and Asylum Act, you are entitled to free school meals for each child attending school. You also qualify if you get child tax credit (but are not eligible for working tax credit) and your taxable income is below £16,190 (£16,105 in Scotland) or working tax credit run-on (see Chapter 23(6)). In Scotland and Northern Ireland, you can qualify if you get working tax credit alongside child tax credit (in Scotland this applies if your taxable income is less than £6,420; in Northern Ireland if it is less than £16,190).

If you get universal credit, you may be entitled to free school meals for each child attending school, but earnings limits apply. In England, from 1.4.18, you cannot have annual net earnings (or combined earnings, if you are one of a couple) of over £7,400; this is assessed in up to three of your most recent assessment periods. There is protection for those already getting free school meals. In Scotland, you cannot have net earnings (or combined earnings, if you are one of a couple) of over £610 in the month before your application. In Northern Ireland, you cannot have annual net earnings (or combined earnings, if you are one of a couple) of over £14,000

**School clothing grants** – In some cases you can get a discretionary school clothing grant from the local authority.

**Travel to school** – If your child has to travel more than two miles to their nearest suitable school, the travel is free. For a disabled child, you may get help even if travel to school is less than two miles. Local authorities also have discretion to help meet a parent's travel costs if a child boards in a residential special school that is some distance from the family home.

### From 8 years
**Travel to school** – In England and Scotland, if your child has to travel more than three miles to their nearest suitable school, travel is free. In Wales and Northern Ireland this only applies once they are in secondary school. For a disabled child, you may get help even if travel to school is less than three miles.

### From 16 years
At 16, a disabled young person has the option of claiming social security benefits in their own right (see Chapter 42).

**DLA and personal independence payment (PIP)** – Young people aged 16 or over who do not have an existing award of DLA cannot claim DLA and need to apply for PIP instead (see Chapter 5). Young people already receiving DLA before their 16th birthday will be invited to claim PIP on reaching that age; see Chapter 42(2) for details.

## 2. Disability living allowance
Disability living allowance (DLA) provides help towards the extra costs of bringing up a disabled child. It is paid in addition to almost any other income you have and gives you access to other kinds of help. DLA has two parts:
- **a care component** – for children needing a lot of extra personal care, supervision or watching over because of their disability. This is paid at three different rates. It can be paid from the age of 3 months, or from birth for a terminally ill baby;
- **a mobility component** – a higher rate for children aged 3 years or over who cannot walk or have severe walking difficulties and a lower rate for children aged 5 or over who can walk but who need extra guidance or supervision

on unfamiliar routes outdoors. The higher rate may also be paid to children getting the highest rate care component who are severely mentally impaired with extremely disruptive behaviour, and to children who are deaf-blind or who have a severe visual impairment.
See Chapter 4 for details.

## 3. Carer's allowance
If your child gets the middle or highest rate of the care component of disability living allowance or either rate of the daily living component of personal independence payment, you may get carer's allowance for looking after them (see Chapter 8). Carer's allowance is not means tested, but if you are working, you cannot earn more than £116 a week (after deductions for certain allowable expenses) – see Chapter 8(5).

If you are on a low income and entitled to carer's allowance (even if it cannot be paid because you receive another benefit), a carer premium is included in the award of your income support, income-related employment and support allowance, income-based jobseeker's allowance or housing benefit (see 4 below and Chapter 21(6)), or an 'additional amount for carers' is included in your pension credit award.

If you receive universal credit and you meet the qualifying conditions for carer's allowance (or would do so but for the fact that your earnings are too high), a carer amount is included in your universal credit award (see Chapter 16(7)).

## 4. Low income benefits
If your income is low and you do not have savings of more than £16,000, you may be able to claim one of the following means-tested benefits to top up your income: income support, income-based jobseeker's allowance (JSA), income-related employment and support allowance (ESA), pension credit or universal credit. Which one you can claim will depend on your circumstances.

You may be able to claim income support if you are under pension credit qualifying age (see Chapter 44(2)) and care for a child who gets the middle or highest rate of the care component of disability living allowance (DLA) or either rate of the daily living component of personal independence payment (PIP). If your child does not get DLA/PIP at one of these rates, you may be able to claim income support on some other basis (see Box F.1 in Chapter 19); for instance, you may be able to claim income support as a lone parent if you are responsible for a child under the age of 5. Normally, you cannot claim income support if you work 16 hours or more a week, but this restriction does not apply if you are eligible for income support as a carer. However, your partner must not be working 24 hours or more a week (unless they too can be treated as a carer for income support). See Chapter 19 for more on income support.

If you are not eligible for income support, you may be able to claim income-based JSA (see Chapter 20). Alternatively, if you have a limited capability for work because of ill health or disability, you may be able to claim income-related ESA (see Chapter 18).

If you are eligible for universal credit (see Box E.1 in Chapter 14), you will need to claim universal credit instead of one of the above three benefits. See Chapters 14 to 17.

If you have reached pension credit qualifying age, you will need to claim pension credit (see Chapter 44).

### Carer premium and carer amount
If you or your partner are entitled to carer's allowance, a carer premium is included in the award of your income support, income-based JSA or income-related ESA (see Chapter 21(6)); an equivalent 'additional amount for carers' can be included in your pension credit award.

If you receive universal credit and you meet the qualifying conditions for carer's allowance (or would do so but for the fact that your earnings are too high), a carer amount is included in your universal credit award (see Chapter 16(7)).

## 5. Tax credits

**Child tax credit (CTC)** – This is an income-related payment for people (whether in or out of work) who are responsible for children. A disabled child element at the severely disabled child rate is included in your CTC award for each child who gets the highest rate of the disability living allowance (DLA) care component or the enhanced rate of the personal independence payment (PIP) daily living component; a disabled child element at the disabled child rate is included for each child who is certified as severely sight impaired or blind or gets any other rate of DLA or PIP. See Chapter 23(2).

**Working tax credit (WTC)** – This provides financial support for people in (relatively) low-paid work. Only certain groups of people can claim, including lone parents working 16 hours or more a week. Couples with a dependent child normally need to work at least 24 hours a week, although there are some exceptions (including where one parent works at least 16 hours and their partner is entitled to carer's allowance). These hours can be worked by one parent or shared between the couple, as long as one partner works at least 16 hours. See Chapter 23(5).

## 6. Help with housing costs

**Rent** – If you rent your home, you may get housing benefit, whether or not you are working. You cannot have savings of more than £16,000 (unless you or your partner receive the guarantee credit of pension credit). See Chapter 25 for details.

Your housing benefit award will include:
- a disabled child premium for each child who is certified as severely sight impaired or blind or who gets disability living allowance (DLA) or personal independence payment (PIP);
- an enhanced disability premium for each child who gets the highest rate of the DLA care component or the enhanced rate of the PIP daily living component;
- a carer premium if you or your partner are entitled to carer's allowance.

If you are eligible for universal credit (see Box E.1 in Chapter 14), you will normally receive help with rent from that benefit rather than housing benefit (see Chapter 24).

If you have a child who gets the middle or highest rate of the DLA care component and your local authority accepts that they cannot share a bedroom due to their disability, they should be allowed an individual bedroom under the 'size criteria' used to cap rent costs in both housing benefit (see Chapter 25(9) and Box G.9) and universal credit (see Chapter 24(9)).

**Council tax** – For details of the help available towards council tax, see Chapter 28. You may get a reduction in your council tax through the Disability Reduction scheme if your child uses a wheelchair indoors or needs an extra room because of their disability (see Chapter 28(8)).

**Support for mortgage interest loans** – If you are getting income support, income-based jobseeker's allowance, income-related employment and support allowance, the guarantee credit of pension credit or universal credit, you may be able to get loans to cover the interest on your mortgage and on loans used to adapt your home for the special needs of your disabled child (see Chapter 26).

**Home adaptations** – If you need adaptations in the home, see if you can get help from social care (see Chapter 36) or a disabled facilities grant from your local housing authority (see Chapter 30) or a housing grant in Scotland (see Box H.1 in Chapter 30). A disabled facilities grant to meet the needs of a disabled child in England, Wales or Northern Ireland is not means tested.

## 7. Child support

Most forms of child support maintenance from an ex-partner are fully disregarded as income for all means-tested benefits (see Chapter 22(9)), universal credit and tax credits.

## 8. Family Fund

The purpose of the Family Fund is to ease the stress on families arising from the day-to-day care of a disabled or seriously ill child by providing grants and information. It is an independent charity financed by the government.

**Do you qualify?** – You can apply for help from the Fund if you are caring at home for a disabled or seriously ill child under the age of 18 and you are entitled to tax credits or certain benefits. The Fund is discretionary but works within general guidelines agreed with the government. You cannot get help for a child who is in local authority care.

**What kind of help is there?** – The Family Fund cannot help with items that should be available from the NHS or your local authority but can complement that support. It can help with:
- holidays or leisure activities for the whole family;
- a washing machine or tumble dryer if you need to do extra washing because of your child's disability;
- bedding and clothing if there is extra wear and tear;
- a computer for your child;
- play equipment related to your child's special needs.

The Fund will also consider other items related to the care of your child.

**Applying to the Family Fund** – You can get an application form from the Family Fund, 4 Alpha Court, Monks Cross Drive, York YO32 9WN (01904 550 055), download one from their website or apply online (www.familyfund.org.uk). The Fund may ask one of their visitors to arrange to see you if it is the first time you have applied. If you wish to appeal against a decision or make a complaint, you can write to the Chief Executive.

# 41 Child benefit

| 1 | Do you qualify? | 259 |
|---|---|---|
| 2 | How much do you get? | 260 |
| 3 | Who should claim it? | 260 |
| 4 | How do you claim? | 260 |
| 5 | What happens after you claim? | 260 |
| 6 | Guardian's allowance | 261 |

## 1. Do you qualify?

You can get child benefit if you are responsible for a child or qualifying young person, you are not subject to immigration control (see Chapter 53(2)) and you pass the residence and presence tests (see Chapter 53(3)). There is no lower age limit for the child. You do not have to be the parent or stay at home with the child. Child benefit is administered by HMRC.

**Child** – This is a child under the age of 16.

**Qualifying young person** – This is a young person under the age of 20 who is in full-time, non-advanced education (ie more than 12 hours a week at school or college) or approved, unwaged training. The training must not be provided under a contract of employment. Nineteen-year-olds can only be included if they started such education or training before their 19th birthday (or were accepted or enrolled to undertake it).

You cannot count homework, private study, unsupervised study or meal breaks towards the 12 hours and the education can only be up to and including A-level, Scottish Highers, NVQ Level 3 or equivalent. In England, traineeships as part of the 16-19 study programmes are considered to be full-time, non-advanced education.

Once your child has turned 16, you must inform HMRC by 31 August that they are going into qualifying full-time education or training, otherwise the child benefit for them will stop.

If the young person becomes entitled to employment and support allowance, income support, income-based jobseeker's allowance, universal credit or any tax credit, you cannot get child benefit for them.

SSCBA, S.142 & CB Regs, regs 1, 3 & 8

### What happens when the young person leaves school?

When the young person leaves school, college or approved training, you can continue to get child benefit for them until the first Sunday after the *'terminal date'*. This is the first of the following days after the young person's education or approved training ends: the last day in February, May, August or November. If the young person has entered for an exam before leaving school or college, they can be treated as still in education until the date of that exam.

CB Regs, reg 7(2)

**Child benefit extension period** – When a 16-17-year-old ceases education or approved training, you may continue to get child benefit during the *'child benefit extension period'*. This period lasts for 20 weeks starting from the Monday following the week in which the young person left the education or training. To get child benefit during the extension period you must:

■ write and ask for benefit to continue within three months of the education or training finishing; *and*
■ have been entitled to child benefit immediately before the extension period began.

The young person must:

■ be under 18 and not be in education or training; *and*
■ be registered for work, education or training, as directed by the DWP; *and*
■ not be working for 24 hours or more a week.

CB Regs, reg 5

### Other conditions

You cannot get child benefit if:

■ the child or young person is in local authority care (but see below) or in detention for more than eight weeks unless they regularly stay with you for at least one day each week (midnight to midnight: effectively also including two nights). But if you are excluded from child benefit this way, you can get it again if the child or young person is home for at least seven consecutive days;
■ you get an allowance as the foster carer or prospective adopter of a child or young person placed with you by a local authority;
■ the young person is married, in a civil partnership or cohabiting (unless their spouse or partner is in full-time non-advanced education or approved unwaged training themselves – and the spouse or partner cannot be the child benefit claimant).

SSCBA, Sch 9, paras 1 & 3; CB Regs, regs 12, 13 & 16

**Local authority care** – Even if the child or young person is in local authority care, you may still get child benefit for them if they are in residential accommodation provided solely:

■ because of their disability; *or*
■ because it is likely that their health would be significantly impaired, or would worsen, were they not in this accommodation.

CB Regs, regs 9 & 18(b)

### 2. How much do you get?

For an only or eldest child (or qualifying young person), you will receive £20.70 a week. For each other child or qualifying young person, you will receive £13.70 a week.

**Does child benefit affect means-tested benefits?** – Child benefit is disregarded when working out working tax credit, child tax credit, income-related employment and support allowance, housing benefit, universal credit, income support and income-based jobseeker's allowance (unless your claim for one of the latter two benefits began before April 2004 and you continue to receive support for your children through it).

**Child dependant's additions** – If you are still entitled to a child dependant's addition with another benefit, the addition is reduced to £8 if you get the higher £20.70 rate of child benefit for that child or young person.

### The income tax charge

The value of your child benefit is reduced through a tapered income tax charge if you, or your partner, have an *'adjusted net income'* (ie your income less certain tax reliefs such as pension contributions, etc) of over £50,000 for the tax year. If both you and your partner have an adjusted net income of over £50,000, the one with the higher income is liable for the charge (regardless of who receives the child benefit).

The charge is equal to 100% of child benefit received if your income is £60,000 or more, or a sliding scale from 0% to 99% of child benefit received if your income is between £50,000 and £60,000.

You must fill in a self-assessment tax return each tax year to pay the charge (see Chapter 35(10)). You can choose not to receive child benefit if you or your partner do not wish to pay the charge. You may subsequently decide to withdraw that choice if you or your partner are no longer liable to pay the charge.

### 3. Who should claim it?

The person responsible for the child or young person must make the claim and must be living with the child or young person or be contributing at least the rate of child benefit for their support.

SSCBA, S.143(1)

If you get child benefit for a child under the age of 12, you are entitled to national insurance 'credits for parents and foster parents' (see Box D.3 in Chapter 11). These can protect the amount of state pension you may get. So if your national insurance contribution record is affected because you are bringing up children, it is important to claim child benefit.

More than one person can be eligible for child benefit for the same child, but only one person can be paid.

### 4. How do you claim?

Just after your baby is born you should receive an information pack containing a child benefit claim-pack. If you don't receive one, you can get a CH2 claim-form by ringing HMRC (see below) or downloading one from www.gov.uk/child-benefit/how-to-claim.

You will be asked to send the birth or adoption certificate with the form. Send everything to the Child Benefit Office, Washington, Newcastle upon Tyne NE88 1ZD. Don't delay making your claim; it can only be backdated for three months from the date HMRC receives it.

For more information, contact HMRC on 0300 200 3100 or textphone 0300 200 3103.

### 5. What happens after you claim?

The birth or adoption certificate will be returned to you and you will be sent a written decision. If your claim is not successful or is stopped later, you can challenge the decision (see Chapter 57).

Benefit is normally paid every four weeks unless this would cause hardship, in which case you must write to HMRC saying why you want weekly payments. You can choose to be paid into a bank, building society or Post Office card account (see Chapter 56(5)).

**The benefit cap** – Child benefit is included in the list of benefits to which the 'benefit cap' applies. The cap limits the total weekly benefits that can be claimed; see Chapter 16(10) and Box G.6 in Chapter 25 for details (including exemptions).

## 6. Guardian's allowance

This is a tax-free benefit for anyone looking after a child who is effectively an orphan. You can get guardian's allowance if you are responsible for a child who is not your birth or adopted child and both parents of the child are dead, or one is dead and the other is:

■ missing; *or*
■ divorced or had their civil partnership dissolved and liable for neither custody or maintenance of the child; *or*
■ serving a prison sentence of more than two years from the date the other parent dies; *or*
■ detained in a hospital under certain sections of the Mental Health Act 1983 (or equivalent legislation).

SSCBA, S.77(2) & Guardian's Allowance (Gen.) Regs, regs 6 & 7

Guardian's allowance is £17.20 a week and does not depend on your income or savings or whether you have paid national insurance contributions. It can be paid in addition to child benefit. If you receive guardian's allowance, your household will be exempt from the benefit cap (see 5 above). Claim on form BG1 (call 0300 200 3101 or textphone 0300 200 3103 or download it from www.gov.uk/government/publications/guardians-allowance-claim-form-bg1) and send it to the Guardian's Allowance Unit at the Child Benefit Office (see 4 above).

# 42 Young disabled people

| 1 | Becoming a claimant | 261 |
| 2 | From disability living allowance to personal independence payment | 261 |
| 3 | Employment and support allowance | 261 |
| 4 | Income support | 261 |
| 5 | Universal credit | 261 |

## 1. Becoming a claimant

At the age of 16 you can claim benefits in your own right, even if you are still at school. If your parents are still entitled to child benefit and child tax credit for you as a 'qualifying young person' (see Chapter 41(1)), these payments will stop if you claim employment and support allowance, jobseeker's allowance, income support, tax credits or universal credit.

## 2. From disability living allowance to personal independence payment

Personal independence payment (PIP) replaces disability living allowance (DLA) for people aged 16 or over. DLA remains in place for children until their 16th birthday. When you turn 16, you will be re-assessed under PIP (unless your existing DLA award was made under the special rules for terminal illness – see Boxes B.6 and B.8 in Chapter 5).

**The PIP re-assessment** – If you are getting DLA when you are approaching your 16th birthday, the DWP will write to your parents or guardian to explain about claiming PIP. The letter will also ask whether you will need an appointee to act on your behalf (see Chapter 56(4)). Shortly after you turn 16, the DWP will write to you (or your appointee) inviting you to claim PIP. Contact the PIP helpline (see Chapter 61(2)) if this letter does not arrive. Your DLA will continue to be paid until a decision on your PIP entitlement is made. See Chapter 5 for more on PIP, and Box B.6 in that chapter for more on the re-assessment process.

## 3. Employment and support allowance

Employment and support allowance (ESA) can be paid from your 16th birthday. To stay on it, you need to get through the work capability assessment (see Chapter 12). ESA has two separate elements: contributory ESA and income-related ESA (see below).

**Late claims** – If you miss claiming ESA from your 16th birthday, your award can be backdated for up to three months (see Chapter 11(9)).

**ESA rates** – If you are aged under 25, in the first 13 weeks of your claim (the 'assessment phase') the basic allowance of ESA is paid at a lower rate of £57.90 a week. Following this, in the main phase of your claim, you will continue to get the lower rate of the basic allowance only if you are placed in the 'work-related activity group'; otherwise you will receive the full rate. For details, see Chapter 11(6).

### Contributory ESA

To be entitled to contributory ESA, you must normally meet the national insurance contribution conditions (see Chapter 11(23)). Before 1.5.12, you did not need to meet these conditions if your limited capability for work began before the age of 20 (or 25 in some cases). This would enable you to receive *'contributory ESA in youth'* (CESA(Y)). For details on CESA(Y), see *Disability Rights Handbook* 36th edition, page 63.

### Income-related ESA

This is the means-tested element of ESA. It can be paid on its own or as a top-up to contributory ESA. See Chapter 18.

If you are in full-time education, you must get disability living allowance, personal independence payment or armed forces independence payment to be eligible for income-related ESA. In this case, you will also be treated as having a limited capability for work without having to pass the work capability assessment. You may be sent a 'capability for work questionnaire' (see Chapter 12(9)) to assess whether you meet the conditions for the work-related activity group (see Chapter 11(4)) or the support group (see Chapter 11(5)). If you are placed in the work-related activity group, you will have to attend work-focused interviews and take part in work-related activity.

ESA Regs, reg 18

## 4. Income support

You can claim income support instead of ESA if you fit into one of the categories listed in Box F.1 in Chapter 19.

**In education** – If you are an orphan or are living away from your parents for one of the reasons listed in Chapter 19(5), you can claim income support if you are aged under 21 and have enrolled on, been accepted for or are studying on a course of full-time non-advanced education. You can still claim if you are aged 21 if you were already on the course when you reached that age.

IS Regs, Sch 1B, para 15A

## 5. Universal credit

Universal credit is replacing means-tested benefits (including income-related ESA and income support). See Box E.1 in Chapter 14 for details of its introduction. You will not be eligible for universal credit if you are aged 16-17 unless you:

■ have a limited capability for work under the work capability assessment (see Chapter 12(2)) or are still waiting to be assessed and are covered by a fit note (see Chapter 10(9));
■ have regular and substantial caring responsibilities for a severely disabled person (see Chapter 16(7));
■ are responsible for a child;
■ are one of a couple and your partner is responsible for a child or qualifying young person (see Chapter 41(1));
■ are pregnant, and it is 11 weeks or less before the week the baby is due;
■ have had a baby within the last 15 weeks; *or*
■ are without parental support (see Chapter 14(4)).

UC Regs, reg 8

For more on universal credit, see Chapters 14 to 17.

# Retirement

This section of the handbook looks at:

| | |
|---|---|
| Benefits in retirement | Chapter **43** |
| Pension credit | Chapter **44** |
| State pension | Chapter **45** |

# **43** Benefits in retirement

| | | |
|---|---|---|
| 1 | What benefits can you get? | 262 |
| 2 | What if you go on working? | 262 |
| 3 | Employment and support allowance and incapacity benefit | 262 |
| 4 | Carer's allowance | 262 |
| 5 | Severe disablement allowance | 262 |
| 6 | Care and mobility | 263 |
| 7 | Housing benefit | 263 |
| 8 | Other benefits | 263 |

## 1. What benefits can you get?

You can claim state pension once you reach *'state pension age'* – currently 65 for men, and rising from 60 to 65 for women; see Chapter 45(2) for details. Pension credit is a means-tested benefit for people who have reached the qualifying age (see Chapter 44 for details).

This chapter looks at other benefits you may be able to get at state pension age. Sometimes you need to decide whether to draw state pension or receive another benefit instead. Some benefits, such as attendance allowance, can be paid in addition to state pension.

## 2. What if you go on working?

You can claim state pension at state pension age whether or not you go on working. If you put off claiming state pension, you may be able to earn extra state pension or receive a one-off taxable lump-sum payment (see Chapter 45(8)).

If you work after state pension age, you will not have to pay national insurance contributions. You will need to give your employer proof of your age (such as a passport or birth certificate).

SSCBA, Ss.6(3) & 11(2)

**Statutory sick pay** – If you are employed, are earning £116 a week or more, and have been sick for four or more days in a row, claim statutory sick pay from your employer. There is no age limit.

## 3. Employment and support allowance and incapacity benefit

If you get employment and support allowance or incapacity benefit, it will stop when you reach state pension age. You should claim state pension instead.

WRA 2007, S.1(3)(c); SSCBA, S.30A(5)

## 4. Carer's allowance

There is no upper age limit for claiming carer's allowance but you must meet the usual qualifying conditions (see Chapter 8(2)).

If you are entitled to carer's allowance after state pension age, you may not appear to be better off due to the overlapping benefits rule. Carer's allowance overlaps with state pension, so once you reach state pension age and draw your pension, carer's allowance can only continue to be paid if your state pension is less than £64.60 a week (the rate of carer's allowance). However, even if your carer's allowance is overlapped, it is often still worth claiming because it can increase your income from pension credit or housing benefit through the 'additional amount for carers' or 'carer premium' (see below).

OB Regs, reg 4(1)&(5)

If you were aged 65 or over and entitled to invalid care allowance on 27.10.02, your carer's allowance continues even if you no longer care for a disabled person or you start earning over £120 a week. Otherwise, you must continue to meet the qualifying conditions for carer's allowance to get it after the age of 65.

**Additional amount for carers and the carer premium** – If you get carer's allowance, or would get it but for the overlapping benefits rule, your pension credit award will include an *'additional amount for carers'* of £36 a week, and your housing benefit award will include a *'carer premium'* of the same amount. This means you may start getting higher levels of these benefits when you are awarded carer's allowance, or you may become entitled to benefit for the first time.

As explained above, if you were aged 65 or over and entitled to invalid care allowance on 27.10.02, you can continue to be entitled to carer's allowance – and thus the additional amount for carers or carer premium – even if you are no longer caring for the disabled person.

The additional amount for carers or carer premium continues for up to eight weeks after your entitlement to carer's allowance ceases – eg if the disabled person's qualifying benefit (see Chapter 8(2)) stops after 28 days in hospital. If the disabled person regains the qualifying benefit, your additional amount for carers or carer premium should resume.

SPC Regs, Sch 1, para 4

## 5. Severe disablement allowance

Severe disablement allowance (SDA) was abolished for new claimants from 6.4.01 onwards, so the information here applies only to people entitled to it before that date.

SDA overlaps with state pension. If your state pension is lower than SDA, your state pension can be topped up to your full SDA entitlement, including any age-related addition. On the other hand, you can put off claiming state pension and keep your tax-free SDA; if you would be due to pay tax on your state pension, you may be better off doing that in some situations even if your pension is a bit higher than your SDA.

OB Regs, reg 4(1)&(5)

Once you reach the age of 65 you continue to get SDA even if you are no longer incapable of work or 80% disabled, provided you were entitled to SDA immediately before your 65th birthday. You no longer need to send in medical certificates.

Social Security (Severe Disablement Allowance) Regs 1984, reg 5

There is more information about SDA in Chapter 15, *Disability Rights Handbook*, 25th edition. If you don't have a copy, send us an A4 stamped addressed envelope and we'll send you a photocopy of the SDA information.

### 6. Care and mobility

**Attendance allowance** – This is a benefit for ill or disabled people aged 65 or over who have care or supervision needs. There is no upper age limit. Many older people fail to claim attendance allowance. Some people do not realise that it is tax free, is not means tested, and can be paid in addition to state pension or pension credit. Others put their problems down to old age rather than disability. See Chapter 6 for full details.

**Personal independence payment** – If you are aged 65 or over, you cannot claim personal independence payment for the first time. However, if you were getting personal independence payment before you reached 65, you can retain your entitlement as long as you continue to meet the other qualifying conditions. See Chapter 5(3).

### 7. Housing benefit

You may be entitled to help with all or part of your rent through housing benefit. If you apply for pension credit you will be asked if you want to claim housing benefit. If you are not entitled to pension credit, you may still be eligible; in this case, claim directly from the local authority, not the DWP. See Chapter 25 for details.

### 8. Other benefits

For information about help towards your council tax, see Chapter 28. Chapter 29(5) covers the winter fuel payment. For information on grants from local authorities for other one-off expenses, see Chapter 31. For help towards NHS health costs, see Chapter 52.

# 44 Pension credit

| 1 | What is pension credit? | 263 |
|---|---|---|
| 2 | Who can claim pension credit? | 263 |
| 3 | Guarantee credit | 263 |
| 4 | Savings credit | 264 |
| 5 | Income | 264 |
| 6 | Capital | 265 |
| 7 | How to claim | 267 |
| 8 | Backdating and advance claims | 267 |
| 9 | How pension credit is paid | 267 |
| 10 | Challenging decisions | 267 |
| 11 | Passporting to other benefits | 267 |

### 1. What is pension credit?

Pension credit is the commonly used name for state pension credit, a means-tested benefit for people who have reached the qualifying age (see 2 below). Pension credit has two elements: guarantee credit (see 3 below) and savings credit (see 4 below).

**Future changes** – As universal credit replaces means-tested benefits for people of working age (see Box E.1 in Chapter 14), the support currently available for rent and dependent children through two of those benefits (housing benefit and child tax credit) will no longer be available. To replace these benefits for claimants who have reached pension credit qualifying age, two new elements will be introduced for pension credit: a 'housing credit' (to cover eligible rent) and additional amounts for children (which will be similar to those available under universal credit).

### 2. Who can claim pension credit?

To claim pension credit, you must have reached the 'qualifying age', which is being raised from 60 to 66 between April 2010 and October 2020, alongside the rise in women's state pension age. To check the qualifying age at the time you want to claim, contact the Pension Service

(0800 991 234) or use the state pension age calculator at www.gov.uk/state-pension-age.
SPCA, S.1(2)(b)&(6)

Only one of a couple can claim. You are considered to be one of a couple if you are married, in a civil partnership, or cohabiting (whether with someone of the opposite or the same sex).
SPCA, S.4(1); SPC Regs 1(2)

You must be present in Great Britain (GB), habitually resident and not subject to immigration control (see Chapter 53(2)-(4)). Pension credit can be paid for the first four weeks of a temporary absence from GB (see Chapter 54(9)). There is no limit on the number of hours you can work, but most earnings are taken into account (see 5 below). There is no capital limit for pension credit, but capital over £10,000 will be counted as generating income (see 6 below).

### 3. Guarantee credit

Guarantee credit is worked out by comparing your 'appropriate minimum guarantee' with your income (see 5 below for how income is assessed). Your appropriate minimum guarantee always includes a 'standard minimum guarantee', which is:

■ for a single claimant: £163 a week;
■ for couples: £248.80 a week.

Your appropriate minimum guarantee can also include:

■ an additional amount for severe disability: £64.30 a week for a single person or couple if one partner qualifies (or £128.60 for a couple if both qualify), based on the same qualifying conditions as the severe disability premium (see Chapter 21(3));
■ an additional amount for carers: £36 a week, based on the same qualifying conditions as the carer premium (see Chapter 21(6));
■ an amount for eligible housing costs (see Chapter 27);
■ a 'transitional' extra amount if you were getting income support, income-based jobseeker's allowance or income-related employment and support allowance immediately before you started to get pension credit that was payable at a higher rate than the pension credit.
SPC Regs, reg 6 & Sch 1

Pension credit does not include any amounts for children. If you have children, claim child tax credit (see Chapter 23).

Your income, as calculated in 5 below, is compared to your appropriate minimum guarantee. If your income is less, the difference is paid as your guarantee credit.
SPCA, S.2(2)

*Example:* Rashida is single and her only income is state pension of £125.95 a week. Her guarantee credit is worked out as follows:

| | |
|---|---|
| Appropriate minimum guarantee | £163.00 |
| Less income | £125.95 |
| *Guarantee credit* | *£37.05* |

## 4. Savings credit

Savings credit is being phased out. It may still be paid, however, if you (and your partner, if you have one):

- are aged 65 or over; *and*
- had reached state pension age (see Chapter 45(2)) by 6.4.16; *and*
- have *'qualifying income'* above your *'savings credit threshold'*.

Before 6.4.16, savings credit could be paid if you were 65 or over, but your partner had not reached that age; if you qualified this way, you can continue to receive savings credit as long as you continue to meet the other qualifying conditions.
SPC Regs, reg 7A

| Savings credit thresholds | per week |
|---|---|
| Single person | £140.67 |
| Couple | £223.82 |

Some people will receive savings credit and guarantee credit; others will receive only savings credit. The maximum amount of savings credit payable is £13.40 a week for a single person and £14.99 for a couple. The calculation is as follows:

**Step 1: Work out your total income**
This is the same figure used in the guarantee credit calculation (see 5 below for how income is assessed).

**Step 2: Work out your appropriate minimum guarantee**
Again, this is the figure used for guarantee credit (see 3 above).

**Step 3: Work out your qualifying income**
This is your total income used to calculate guarantee credit but excluding working tax credit, incapacity benefit, contributory employment and support allowance, contribution-based jobseeker's allowance, severe disablement allowance, maternity allowance or maintenance payments made by a spouse/civil partner or former spouse/civil partner.

**Step 4: Compare the savings credit threshold with your qualifying income**
If your qualifying income is the same as or less than the savings credit threshold (see above), you will not be entitled to savings credit. If your qualifying income is more than the threshold, make a note of the difference and go to Step 5.

**Step 5: Calculate 60% of the difference from Step 4**
Work out 60% of the difference between the savings credit threshold and your qualifying income. If the result is more than the maximum savings credit figure of £13.40 for a single person (or £14.99 for a couple), use the relevant maximum savings credit figure instead.

**Step 6: Calculate the savings credit**
If your total income is the same as or less than your appropriate minimum guarantee, your savings credit will be the figure you arrived at in Step 5.

If your total income is more than your appropriate minimum guarantee, you must work out 40% of the difference between your total income and your appropriate minimum guarantee. You then deduct this 40% figure from the amount you arrived at in Step 5.
SPCA, S.3 & SPC Regs, regs 7 & 9

*Example:* Paul is a single claimant with a state pension (basic and additional) of £130 a week and an occupational pension of £52.20 a week. The calculation is as follows:

**Step 1:** Paul's total income is:

| | |
|---|---|
| State pension | £130.00 |
| Plus occupational pension | £52.20 |
| *Total income* | *£182.20* |

**Step 2:** His appropriate minimum guarantee is £163 – he does not qualify for any of the additional amounts. His income is above this amount, so he does not qualify for guarantee credit.

**Step 3:** All his income is qualifying income, so his qualifying income is also £182.20.

**Step 4:** He compares his qualifying income with the savings credit threshold (£140.67 for a single person). It is higher, so he works out the amount by which his qualifying income is above the threshold:

| | |
|---|---|
| Qualifying income | £182.20 |
| Less Paul's savings credit threshold | £140.67 |
| *Difference equals* | *£41.53* |

**Step 5:** He works out 60% of the difference:

| | |
|---|---|
| £41.53 x 60% = | £24.92 |

This is more than the maximum savings credit of £13.40 for a single claimant, so for the next step he uses that figure of £13.40.

**Step 6:** His total income is more than his appropriate minimum guarantee – the difference is:

| | |
|---|---|
| Paul's total income | £182.20 |
| Less appropriate minimum guarantee | £163.00 |
| *Difference equals* | *£19.20* |

He works out 40% of this difference, which comes to £7.68. He takes this figure from the maximum savings credit (the result of Step 5):

| | |
|---|---|
| Maximum savings credit | £13.40 |
| Less | £7.68 |
| *Savings credit* | *£5.72* |

**Not sure if you are entitled to savings credit?**
The calculation for savings credit is complicated. If you are not sure whether you qualify, you should apply anyway. For more information about your likely entitlement, see www.gov.uk/pension-credit-calculator.

## 5. Income

When your pension credit is worked out, some types of income, including state and private pensions, are counted in full; some types of income are fully disregarded; others are partially disregarded. If you have a source of income not covered below, check with the Pension Service to see how it is treated.

Income is assessed after the deduction of income tax and, if you have earnings, after the deduction of national insurance contributions and half of any contribution you make to a private pension. Income is assessed on a weekly basis, so if

you have income paid for other periods, it is calculated as a weekly equivalent. For a couple, the income of both partners is added together.
SPC Regs, regs 14, 17 & 17A(4A)

**Income generally counted in full** – The following types of income are counted in full:

- earnings (which can include any statutory sick/maternity/paternity/adoption/shared parental pay) but see below for partial disregards;
- working tax credit;
- state, occupational and private pensions;
- income from annuities and retirement annuity contracts;
- most social security benefits (except those listed below);
- war disablement or war widow's/widower's pension (but see below for disregards);
- regular payments from an equity release scheme;
- income from the Financial Assistance Scheme;
SPCA, S. 15(1) & 16(1); SPC Regs, reg 17A(2)(h)-(j)

- guaranteed income payment and survivor's guaranteed income payment made under the Armed Forces Compensation scheme (but see below for partial disregards);
- pension paid to victims of Nazi persecution (but see below for partial disregards);
- payments under the Pneumoconiosis, etc (Worker's Compensation) Act 1979;
- maintenance payments from a spouse/civil partner or former spouse/civil partner;
- payments from boarders, lodgers or sub-tenants (but see below for partial disregards);
- income from the Pension Protection Fund;
- 'deemed income' from capital over £10,000 (see 6 below).
SPC Regs, regs 15(5)-(6)

**Disregarded income** – Forms of income that are fully disregarded include:

- attendance allowance, disability living allowance, personal independence payment, constant attendance allowance, armed forces independence payment and war pensioner's mobility supplement;
- housing benefit;
- Christmas bonus;
- social fund payments including the winter fuel payment;
- bereavement support payment;
- child benefit, child tax credit, guardian's allowance and child special allowance;
- increases for dependent children paid with certain other benefits;
- exceptionally severe disablement allowance (paid in the War Pensions and Industrial Injuries schemes) and war pensions' severe disablement occupational allowance;
SPC Regs, reg 15(1) & Sch 4, paras 2 & 3

- war widow's, widower's or surviving civil partner's supplementary pension;
- payments, other than social security benefits or war pensions, paid as a result of a personal injury that you or your partner receive;
- income abroad while transfer to the UK is prohibited;
- charges for currency conversion if income is not paid in sterling;
- actual income from capital;
SPC Regs, Sch 4, paras 4-6, 13-14, 15, 16 & 18

- payments from your local authority social care department for personal care;
- charitable and voluntary payments (except for voluntary payments from a spouse/civil partner or former spouse/civil partner, which are counted in full); *and*
- any other type of income not specified in the legislation as being counted.

**Partially disregarded income** – Forms of weekly income that are partially disregarded include:

- £5 of your earnings from work if you are single or £10 if you are a couple. A higher £20 disregard applies in some situations, eg for some disabled people or carers. The rules are similar to those for other means-tested benefits (see Chapter 22(6)), but there are minor differences; for details contact the Pension Service;
SPC Regs, Sch 6

- £10 of the total of any income from a war widow's or widower's pension, war disablement pension, a guaranteed income payment or survivor's guaranteed income payment made under the Armed Forces Compensation scheme (if this has been reduced to less than £10 by another armed forces pension, the remainder can be disregarded from that pension instead), pension paid for victims of Nazi persecution or widowed parent's/mother's allowance;
- £20 payment from a tenant, sub-tenant or boarder. In the case of a boarder, half of any payment above £20 is also disregarded. The disregard applies to each tenant and/or boarder making payments;
- if you have used the equity in your home to buy an annuity, any part of the income that is being used to pay the interest on the loan is disregarded.
SPC Regs, Sch 4, paras 1, 7-7A, 8-9 & 10

**Income from trust funds**
This will be disregarded if the trust fund was set up from a lump sum received for a personal injury. In other situations, trust fund income is generally taken into account. Discretionary payments made by trustees are disregarded, unless they are for everyday living expenses (see Chapter 22(10)), in which case up to £20 can be disregarded.
SPC Regs, Sch 4, paras 11 & 13

**Notional income**
In some cases, you can be treated as having 'notional' income that you are not actually receiving. This will apply if there is income available that you have chosen not to take – eg if you have not claimed your state pension or not drawn a personal or occupational pension that you are entitled to. You may also be assessed as having notional income if you have given up the right to an income you could have received.

**Deferring your state pension** – If you defer drawing your state pension (see Chapter 45(8)), you will be treated as having the state pension that you would have been entitled to had you claimed it, less any overlapping benefit, such as carer's allowance (see Chapter 8(6)).

**Pension pots** – If you have a defined contribution occupational or personal pension and choose to leave the resultant *'pension pot'* alone, you will be treated as having the income that you would have received had you bought an annuity with the pension pot. If you take out a lump sum from the pension pot, this will be treated as capital (see 6 below).
SPC Regs, reg 18

## 6. Capital
Capital includes any savings, investments, land and property you own. If you have capital of £10,000 or less, this will not affect your pension credit. There is currently no upper capital limit for pension credit* but if you have capital of more than £10,000, you will be counted as having an extra £1 a week income for every £500 (or part of £500) over this limit. In pension credit this is called *'deemed income'*, while for other benefits the term is 'tariff income' (or 'assumed income' for universal credit). For example, if you have savings of £11,050, you will be deemed to have an income of £3 a week from that capital; if you have savings of £19,300, you will have a deemed income of £19 a week. If you have a partner, your capital is assessed together, but the amount that is disregarded (see below) is still the same.
SPCA, Ss.5 & 15(2) & SPC Regs, regs 14 & 15(6)

Most forms of capital are taken into account, including: cash, bank and building society savings, National Savings accounts and certificates, stocks and shares, premium bonds, income bonds and property (other than your home). However, some types of capital are disregarded (see below).

\* An upper capital limit will be introduced when the housing credit is introduced (see 1 above). At the time of writing, further details are not known.

**How capital is valued** – Your capital is generally valued at its current market or surrender value, less 10% if there would be costs involved in selling and less any debt secured on it.

SPC Regs, reg 19

**Joint capital** – If you own capital jointly with other people, you would normally all be assessed as having an equal share. See Chapter 22(26) for more about valuation of joint property for other means-tested benefits; the position is similar for pension credit.

## Disregarded capital

In working out your deemed income from capital, the following types of capital are disregarded indefinitely or, where stated, for a certain period of time.

❑ **Your home and property**

■ the value of your home;

■ the value of a property occupied by someone who is a parent, parent-in-law, son, daughter, son-in-law, daughter-in-law, step-parent, stepson, stepdaughter, brother, sister (or partner of any of these), grandparent, grandchild, uncle, aunt, nephew or niece of yourself or your partner, if they have reached pension credit qualifying age or are *'incapacitated'*. The value will be disregarded if your partner or former partner lives there and you are not estranged but are living apart due to circumstances (eg if you have moved to a care home);

■ the value of a property for up to 26 weeks if: you have bought it and plan to live there; you are trying to sell it; you are carrying out essential repairs or alterations in order to live there; or, you are taking legal action so you can live there. In each case, more time is allowed if that is reasonable in the circumstances to enable you to conclude the matter;

■ the value of your former home if you left because of a breakdown in the relationship with your partner – for up to 26 weeks (or indefinitely if your former partner lives there and is a lone parent);

■ any future interest in property other than land or premises that you have let out;

SPC Regs, Sch 5, paras 1-7

■ the following types of capital received for specific purposes are disregarded for up to a year (or until an assessed income period ends if that is longer – see 9 below): money received, eg from the sale of a property, that is earmarked to buy a new home; money from an insurance policy that is to be used for repair or replacement; or money, such as a loan or grant, to pay for essential repairs or improvements.

SPC Regs, Sch 5, paras 17-19

❑ **Other disregards**

■ personal possessions;

■ business assets while you are self-employed. If sickness or disability means you cannot work, the assets will be disregarded if you intend to start or resume work in your business as soon as you are able to or as soon as you recover. If the self-employment ends, the assets will be disregarded for as long as is reasonable in the circumstances to allow you to sell them;

■ the surrender value of a life insurance policy (although if this matures or is cashed in, the money you receive will count as part of your capital);

■ the value of a pre-paid funeral;

SPC Regs, Sch 5, paras 8, 9, 9A, 10 & 11

■ the £10,000 ex-gratia payment made to Far East Prisoners of War or their widows, widowers or surviving civil partners;

■ Second World War compensation payments – eg for forced labour or lost property;

■ any charge for currency conversion if your capital is not held in sterling;

■ the value of the right to receive income from an occupational pension, personal pension or retirement annuity contract (although you may still be treated as possessing notional income – see 5 above);

■ a lump-sum payment received because you deferred drawing your state pension (see Chapter 45(8));

■ any social care or NHS direct payments; *and*

■ the initial larger payment of bereavement support payment (for 52 weeks after you receive it).

SPC Regs, Sch 5, paras 12, 14, 21, 22-23, 23A, 23C & 23E

## Personal injury payments and trust funds

If you or your partner received a lump-sum payment due to a personal injury, this will be disregarded. If you used the money to set up a trust fund, the value of this trust will be disregarded. Payments from special trusts, eg the Macfarlane or Eileen Trusts are also disregarded indefinitely or for a certain period. The rules are the same as for other means-tested benefits (see Chapter 22(29)).

SPC Regs, Sch 5, paras 13, 15, 16 & 28

## Arrears of benefits

Arrears (or ex-gratia payments) of the following benefits are disregarded for one year after you get them or until the end of your assessed income period (if you have one and it is longer – see 9 below):

■ attendance allowance, disability living allowance and personal independence payment;

■ housing benefit and council tax benefit;

■ armed forces independence payment;

■ income support;

■ income-related employment and support allowance;

■ income-based jobseeker's allowance;

■ pension credit;

■ universal credit;

■ supplementary pensions (paid to war widows, widowers or surviving civil partners);

■ constant attendance allowance and exceptionally severe disablement allowance (paid under the War Pensions or Industrial Injuries schemes);

■ child tax credit and child benefit;

■ bereavement support payment; *and*

■ social fund or local welfare assistance payments.

If the amount of arrears or compensation is £5,000 or more and it is paid because of official error, and you receive the payments in full while you are getting pension credit, it will be disregarded for as long as you continue to receive pension credit. Payments under Supporting People services are treated in the same way as arrears of benefits.

SPC Regs, Sch 5, paras 17, 20, 20A & 20B

## Notional capital

If you have 'deprived' yourself of capital in order to get pension credit or to increase the amount you receive, you will be treated as still having that capital; this is known as *'notional capital'*. This might occur if you gave money to a relative in order to get more pension credit. However, you will not be assessed as having notional capital if you used your savings to repay or reduce a debt or to buy goods or services that are 'reasonable' given your circumstances – eg a decision maker might consider replacing a car to be reasonable but not buying a luxury car. Notional capital you are treated as having will reduce over time in line with the rules for other means-tested benefits (see Chapter 22(37)).

SPC Regs, regs 21-22; DWP guide to Pension Credit: PC10S

## 7. How to claim

Ring 0800 991 234 (textphone 0800 169 0133) to make a claim over the phone or get a form sent to you. If you are making the claim over the phone, you should have the following handy:

- your national insurance number;
- details of your income, savings or investments;
- your bank account details (if you have one); *and*
- information on any housing costs (eg service charges).

## 8. Backdating and advance claims

Normally, your pension credit will run from the date that your completed claim is received at the relevant office, or the date that you provide all the required details of your circumstances if you claim by phone (see also Chapter 56(2)). Your claim can be backdated for up to three months if you met the qualifying conditions throughout that period.
C&P Regs, regs 4F & 19(2)-(3)

If you will become eligible for pension credit in the future, for instance because you are coming up to the qualifying age or you are about to have a drop in income, you can make a claim up to four months in advance of this change.
C&P Regs, regs 4E & 13D

## 9. How pension credit is paid

For people who started claiming pension credit before 6.4.10, it is normally paid weekly in advance on a Monday. If you reach the qualifying age from 6.4.10 onwards, it is normally paid weekly, fortnightly or four weekly in arrears, with the payday determined by your national insurance number.

If your pension credit payment is less than £1 a week, it may be paid at 13-week intervals in arrears. If the weekly amount is less than 10p, no pension credit will be paid unless it can be paid with another benefit. See Chapter 56(5) for more about benefit payments.
C&P Regs, regs 26B & 26BA; SPC Regs, reg 13

**Assessed income periods** – Before 6.4.16, if you or your partner were aged 65 or over and the other was at least 60, the decision maker could set an *'assessed income period'* for your pension credit award. This would normally be set for five years, or for an indefinite period if you were aged 75 or over.

During the assessed income period, you do not have to inform the Pension Service of any changes in your retirement provision (eg occupational and personal pensions, regular payments from an equity release scheme, income from annuities and payments from the Financial Assistance Scheme and Pension Protection Fund). You must, however, report other changes that may affect your benefit, including a change in earnings, moving home, a change in family circumstances or a period in hospital (see Chapter 55(3)).

Assessed income periods were abolished for new claims from 6.4.16, but if you were already on one at that date, it should continue to run its course for the time being. Unless your assessed income period ends for some other reason (eg you marry or get a new partner, you stop being treated as a couple, or you or your partner reach the age of 65), it will end on a fixed date between 14.7.16 and 28.3.19.
SPCA, SS.6-10; SPC Regs, regs 10-12

Further details on assessed income periods can be found in Chapter 45, *Disability Rights Handbook*, 40th edition. If you don't have a copy, send us an A4-sized, stamped addressed envelope and we'll send a photocopy.

## 10. Challenging decisions

Decisions on your pension credit claim are made by DWP decision makers based at the Pension Service (see Chapter 2(1)). The rules for decisions, mandatory reconsiderations and appeals are the same as for other DWP benefits (see Chapter 57).

## 11. Passporting to other benefits

Pension credit can help meet certain housing costs (see Chapter 27). You may get housing benefit to help with rent (see Chapter 25) and help from your local authority towards your council tax (see Chapter 28). If you get the guarantee credit, you will be passported to full housing benefit and council tax support, and may be entitled to help with health costs, such as free dental treatment (see Chapter 52), and with hospital travel fares (see Chapter 55(2)). If you receive either element, you may get help from the social fund (see Chapter 29), budgeting loans (Chapter 31(2)) and support for mortgage interest loans (see Chapter 26).

# 45 State pension

| 1 | Introduction | 267 |
|---|---|---|
| 2 | When can you get a state pension? | 267 |
| | State pension – the qualifying conditions – Box L.1 | 268 |
| 3 | Working and the state pension | 268 |
| 4 | New state pension | 269 |
| 5 | Category A state pension | 269 |
| 6 | Category B state pension | 270 |
| | Home responsibilities protection – Box L.2 | 270 |
| 7 | Additional state pension | 271 |
| 8 | Other state pension payments | 271 |
| 9 | Non-contributory state pension | 271 |
| | Private pensions and further information – Box L.3 | 272 |
| 10 | How do you claim state pension? | 272 |
| 11 | How is state pension paid? | 272 |

## 1. Introduction

The Pensions Act 2014 introduced a new state pension. This will only apply to you if you reach state pension age (see 2 below) on or after 6.4.16. See 4 below for details.

If you reached state pension age before 6.4.16, you will get a state pension based on the pre-April 2016 rules: a Category A, Category B or Category D pension – see 5, 6 and 9 below. Your existing state pension will not be affected by the new rules.

State pension is taxable.

## 2. When can you get a state pension?

You can get a state pension if you have reached state pension age, you meet the national insurance contribution conditions (see Box L.1) and, where necessary, have made a claim. If you do not draw your state pension at state pension age, you may get extra state pension or a one-off taxable lump-sum payment when you do start to claim (see 8 below).

**State pension age** – For men, state pension age is currently 65; for women born on or before 5.4.50, it is 60. The Pensions Act 1995 introduced an equal state pension age of 65 for both men and women; this is being phased in over a number of years. Once that phase is complete in November 2018, retirement ages for both men and women who have not yet reached state pension age will rise to 66 by October 2020 and to 67 by 6.4.28. To find out your state pension age, contact the Pension Service or check the state pension calculator at www.gov.uk/state-pension-age.

## 3. Working and the state pension

Earnings you receive after reaching state pension age do not affect your state pension and you do not have to pay national insurance contributions on them. If you carry on working and do not draw your pension, you may earn extra state pension or a one-off lump sum (see 8 below). If you have already claimed your state pension, you can give up your claim in order to earn extra state pension or receive a lump sum. You can only give up a state pension once, and cannot backdate that choice.
*WBRP Regs, reg 2(1) & (2)*

There is an earnings limit for an increase for an adult dependant (see 5 below).

## L.1  State pension – the qualifying conditions

This box explains the contribution conditions for the basic state pension and new state pension. Your contribution record is built up through paid national insurance (NI) contributions and NI credits. The rules that apply to you will depend on when you reach or reached state pension age. Your contribution record may be protected by *'home responsibilities protection'* (HRP) for years from 1978/79 to 2009/10 if you were looking after a child or caring for someone and you do not have sufficient contributions or credits to count towards your basic state pension (see Box L.2).

### If you reached state pension age before 6.4.10

If you reached state pension age before 6.4.10, you must have met two contribution conditions to qualify for the basic state pension.

**The first condition** – In at least one tax year since 6.4.75 you paid enough NI contributions for this to be a 'qualifying year' (see below for what is meant by a qualifying year) or you paid 50 flat-rate contributions at any time before 6.4.75. You are treated as meeting this condition if you were entitled to long-term incapacity benefit or main-phase employment and support allowance in the year you reached state pension age, or the preceding year.

**The second condition** – To receive a full basic state pension, about nine out of every ten years of your 'working life' would need to be qualifying years. If you do not have enough qualifying years for a full basic state pension, you may get a partial pension, but at least a quarter of the years in your 'working life' must count as qualifying years, otherwise no pension is payable.
*SSCBA, Sch 3, para 5(2),(3)&(6); WBRP Regs, reg 6*

**Working life** – Your *'working life'* is the period on which your contribution record is based. This is normally from the start of the tax year in which you became 16 to the last full tax year before you reached state pension age.

Women who reached state pension age before 6.4.10 normally have a working life of 44 years, so will need to have 39 qualifying years for a full basic state pension and at least ten qualifying years to receive any basic state pension.

Men who reached state pension age before 6.4.10 normally have a working life of 49 years, so will need at least 44 qualifying years for a full basic state pension and at least 11 qualifying years to receive any basic state pension.
*SSCBA, Sch 3, paras 5(5)&(8)*

### If you reached state pension age on or after 6.4.10 and before 6.4.16

If you reached state pension age on or after 6.4.10 and before 6.4.16, you can receive a basic state pension as long as you have at least one qualifying year during your working life (which runs from the year you reached 16 to the last full tax year before you reached state pension age).

To receive a full basic state pension, you will need at least 30 qualifying years. If you have at least one qualifying year, but less than 30, you will receive a partial basic state pension. The qualifying years can be based on paid NI contributions, NI credits or a combination of the two. As explained in Box L.2, any years of HRP you have built up will be converted into qualifying years of credits.

### If you reach state pension age on or after 6.4.16

If you reach state pension age on or after 6.4.16, you must have paid NI contributions for a minimum qualifying period of ten years to be entitled to any state pension. If you have not paid or been credited with NI contributions before 6.4.16, you will need 35 qualifying years to get the full rate of the new state pension.

If you have paid or been credited with NI contributions under the earlier state pension, those years will count as qualifying years towards the minimum period in the new state pension. If you pay contributions as a self-employed person, or you are credited with NI contributions, you will still be able to build up your state pension in this way.

**Protecting the pension you have already built up** – Your NI contribution record at 5.4.16 is used to calculate a *'starting amount'* in the new state pension.

If your starting amount is higher than the full new state pension, for example because you have a lot of additional state pension, then you will get this higher amount when you reach state pension age.

If your starting amount is lower than the full new state pension, each qualifying year you add to your NI contribution record after 5.4.16 will add a fixed amount on top, until you get to the full level of the new state pension or reach state pension age, whichever occurs first.

### NI contributions and credits

**NI Contributions** – From 1948 until 1975, NI contributions were paid at a flat rate. Between 1961 and 1975 there was also a system of graduated contributions, giving entitlement to graduated retirement benefit.

Since 1975, employees pay Class 1 NI contributions as a percentage of gross earnings, collected with income tax. Class 2 NI contributions (self-employed) also count towards state pension and it is sometimes possible to pay Class 3 (voluntary) NI contributions to make up gaps in your NI contribution record. However, years in which you were paying married woman's reduced rate NI contributions do not count towards your state pension.

For more on NI contributions, see Chapter 11(21).

**NI Credits** – In certain circumstances you can be credited with NI contributions that will count towards state pension. For example, you will normally be credited with an NI contribution for any week in which you have a limited capability for work due to illness or disability. Since 6.4.10 'carer's credit' has replaced HRP. For more on NI credits, see Box D.3 in Chapter 11.

## 4. New state pension

*'New state pension'* is based on your own national insurance (NI) contribution record. See Box L.1 for the contribution conditions. You will not build up any additional state pension (see 7 below) under the new state pension; from 6.4.16 your NI contributions or credits go towards a single-tier pension.

If you only pay into the new state pension and meet the contribution conditions in full, you will receive a pension of £164.35 a week (which will be uprated for inflation).

If you paid or were credited with NI contributions before 6.4.16, you may get more or less than £164.35 a week depending on how much basic state pension and additional state pension you had built up by 6.4.16. But as long as you meet the minimum qualifying period, the amount of new state pension you will get for those contributions will be no less than what you would have received from the state pension under the pre-April 2016 rules (see Box L.1). If the state pension you have already built up is higher than £164.35 a week, the difference is called your *'protected payment'*. Your protected payment is paid on top of your new state pension and increases each year in line with inflation.

If you put off drawing your new state pension for at least nine weeks, it is increased by 1% for every nine weeks you put off drawing it. This is called deferring your state pension. The extra amount will be paid with your regular state pension payments once you start drawing them. You cannot claim the extra amount as a lump sum.

### Spouses and civil partners

If you reach state pension age on or after 6.4.16, your state pension will be based on your NI record alone. You cannot derive a higher pension from the NI record of your spouse or civil partner, unless you are a woman who opted to pay reduced-rate NI contributions.

### Widows, widowers and surviving civil partners

If your spouse or civil partner reached state pension age before 6.4.16, or died before 6.4.16 but would have reached state pension age on or after that date, you may be able to inherit part of their additional state pension.

If your spouse or civil partner reaches state pension age, or dies under state pension age, on or after 6.4.16, you may be able to inherit half of their protected payment.

## 5. Category A state pension

This is normally based on your own national insurance (NI) contribution record. However, widows, widowers, surviving civil partners, divorced people and those whose civil partnership has been dissolved may be able to use the contribution record of their former spouse/civil partner to help them qualify.
SSCBA, S.44(1) & 48 and WBRP Regs, reg 8

If you meet the NI contribution conditions in full, you can receive a basic state pension of £125.95 a week. You may receive less if you do not have a full NI contribution record. It is no longer possible to make a new claim for an increase for a dependent adult or child. However, if you are already receiving an increase, then the weekly amounts are:

| Dependant's increase | per week |
|---|---|
| For an adult dependant | £68.35 |
| For the first dependent child (tax free) | £8.00 |
| For each other dependent child (tax free) | £11.35 |

SSCBA, S.44(4) & Sch 4(Part IV)

### Adult dependency increase

Since 6.4.10 it has not been possible to claim this. However, if you are already receiving it, you can continue to receive it until you no longer meet the qualifying conditions or until 5.4.20, whichever is earlier.
PA, S.4

Before 6.4.10, claims could be made for a dependent wife or someone looking after your dependent child, or in limited circumstances, a husband.
SSCBA, Ss.83-85

If your dependant is working, the increase will not be paid if they earn more in any week than their earnings limit (occupational and personal pensions count as earnings here). The earnings limit for an adult dependant is £73.10 if they live with you, and £68.35 if you do not live together (except

### Your qualifying years

A *'qualifying year'* is a tax year in which you have paid, been treated as having paid, or been credited with, enough NI contributions for a basic state pension.

Before 1975, qualifying years were calculated by adding up all your stamps and dividing them by 50.

Since 1975, a qualifying year is one in which you have paid, been treated as having paid, or been credited with, NI contributions on earnings equivalent to 52 times the *'lower earnings limit'* for that year.

In the year April 2018 to April 2019, the lower earnings limit is £116 a week. However, people will only start to pay NI contributions on earnings above a higher level of £162 a week, the *'primary threshold'*. Although they will not be paying NI contributions, people with earnings between £116 and £162 will still be building up entitlement to a state pension and other contributory benefits. When we refer in this handbook to people who have 'paid NI contributions', we are including those in this position who are treated in the same way as those paying NI contributions.

For self-employed people and those paying voluntary NI contributions, the test is the number of flat-rate contributions, as it was before 1975, but divided by 52.

A qualifying year can also be made up of a combination of NI credits and paid NI contributions.

### Working out your state pension

If, when you receive information about your state pension, you think it is not correct, you can ask for more information about your NI contribution record and question any gaps in your record that you think should have been covered by NI contributions, credits or HRP. If you disagree with the information you are given, you may want to get advice to challenge this.

**State pension statement** – To check your NI contribution record, you can ask for a state pension statement if you are more than 30 days away from your state pension age. The statement will show your current entitlement based on records held by HMRC. It should allow you (with some help if necessary) to make the right decisions about your future NI contribution position.

If you have contracted out of the additional state pension (see Box L.3), statements issued from November 2015 will also include an estimate of the equivalent amount you will receive from your employer's pension or personal pension.

To get a statement, contact the Future Pension Centre (part of the Pension Service) (0800 731 0175; textphone 0800 731 0176; www.gov.uk/government/publications/application-for-a-state-pension-statement). To obtain a forecast online, go to www.gov.uk/check-state-pension.

in the case of a person who looks after your children but does not live with you, where there is no earnings limit).
Social Security Benefit (Dependency) Regs, reg 8

If your adult dependant receives an income maintenance benefit (eg contributory employment and support allowance), that benefit will reduce or cancel out a dependant's increase to your state pension.
OB Regs, reg 10

### Child dependency increase
This is not payable on new claims for state pension from 6.4.03. If you have dependent children, claim child tax credit when you claim state pension (see Chapter 23).

### 6. Category B state pension
This is a pension based on the national insurance (NI) contribution record of your spouse/civil partner or late spouse/civil partner. If they had not fully met the NI contribution conditions, you will receive a reduced-rate state pension.

Category A and Category B pensions overlap. So if, for example, you are a married woman with a basic state pension of £30 based on your own NI contributions, you cannot receive this in addition to a £75.50 Category B pension based on your husband's NI contributions. Instead, your state pension will be topped up to £75.50 using your husband's NI contributions.
SSCBA, Ss.51A & 52

### Married women
If you have no basic state pension, or a basic state pension of less than £75.50 a week based on your own NI contributions, you can claim a Category B pension of up to this amount based on your husband's NI contribution record once both of you have reached state pension age.

Before 6.4.10, your husband had to have claimed his own state pension before you could claim a Category B pension based on his NI contributions. However, the rules have changed so you can now claim this even if your husband is deferring his pension.

If he has a reduced NI contribution record, you will receive a proportionally reduced state pension. Any earnings you receive after you reach state pension age do not affect your state pension.
SSCBA, S.48A; PA, S.2

### Married men, same-sex spouses and civil partners
If you are entitled to a basic state pension of less than £75.50 a week, you may be able to claim a Category B pension based on your spouse's or civil partner's NI contribution record as long as they were born on or after 6.4.50 and you have both reached state pension age.

### Widows, widowers and surviving civil partners
If you qualify for a full Category B pension, you could get £125.95 a week basic state pension, and, if applicable, a

---

## L.2 Home responsibilities protection

Home responsibilities protection (HRP) can protect your basic state pension rights for tax years 1978/79 to 2009/10 if you had a child or you were looking after someone who was sick or disabled and you did not have enough national insurance (NI) contributions or credits in the tax year. From 2002/03 to 2009/10 it can also help you build up state second pension in certain cases.

On 6.4.10, HRP was replaced by 'carer's credit' and 'credits for parents and foster parents', as explained in Box D.3 in Chapter 11. If you reach state pension age on or after that date, any years of HRP will be converted into a qualifying year of NI credits.

For people who reached state pension age before 6.4.10, HRP can help meet the second contribution condition for the full basic state pension (see Box L.1). The number of years in which you were awarded HRP will be deducted from the number of qualifying years you normally need for a full basic state pension. HRP cannot reduce the required number of qualifying years to less than 20 for a full pension.
SSCBA, Sch 3, para 5(7)

### Do you qualify?
You qualify for HRP if, throughout a complete tax year between 1978/79 and 2009/10, you:
- spent at least 35 hours a week looking after someone who got attendance allowance, disability living allowance middle or highest rate care component or constant attendance allowance, for 48 or more weeks in the year (52 weeks for tax years before 6.4.94); or
- received income support and were substantially engaged in looking after a sick or disabled person; or
- were paid child benefit for a child under 16; or
- were a registered foster carer (for tax years 2003/04 onwards).

HR Regs, reg 2(1)-(4)

### Does anything affect HRP?
**Work** – Work makes no practical difference. If you qualify for HRP, you will get it if you have not paid or been treated as having paid enough NI contributions that tax year to count for state pension.

**Change of circumstances** – If you were a foster carer or getting child benefit or income support for only part of the tax year but you were caring for a disabled person for the rest of the same year, you can apply for HRP for the basic state pension. But if you met the qualifying conditions for only part of that year, you will not get HRP for that year.
HR Regs, reg 2(1)(c)

**Married women and widows** – You cannot get HRP for any tax year in which you paid or were liable to pay reduced-rate NI contributions.

### How do you apply?
If you are entitled to HRP for years when you were receiving child benefit or income support, you do not have to apply. Your HRP should be recorded automatically.

If you reach state pension age on or after 6.4.08 and you discover you were not the child benefit claimant, although you were the one staying at home to look after a child, you may be able to have HRP put on your account if your partner you were living with cannot make use of it because they already have a qualifying year through paid NI contributions.
HR Regs, reg 2(2)(aa) & (5)(aza)

If you qualify for HRP in any of the other ways, or if you were covered partly by one of the conditions and partly by another, you will have to apply for each tax year you need HRP.

If you have not been awarded HRP automatically, you can only apply retrospectively for the tax years up to and including 2001/02; you can apply at any time until you reach state pension age.

To apply, complete form CF411, available from your local Jobcentre Plus office, from www.gov.uk/government/publications/national-insurance-application-form-for-home-responsibilities-protection-cf411, or by ringing HMRC (0300 200 3500; textphone 0300 200 3519).
HR Regs, reg 2(5)(b)-(c)

proportion of the additional state pension built up by your late spouse or civil partner.
SSCBA, S.48B

## 7. Additional state pension

You will not build up any additional state pension under the new state pension. If you receive a state pension based wholly or partly on the pension rules before 6.4.16, your pension may include an amount derived from the additional state pension.

From 1978 to April 2002 this was built up under the *'state earnings-related pension scheme'* (SERPS). From April 2002 to 5.4.16 the *'state second pension'* (S2P) replaced SERPS. If you were an employee with annual earnings above the level needed to qualify for the basic state pension, you will have contributed to the additional state pension unless you were contracted out through an employer's pension scheme or a personal pension scheme (see Box L.3). Between 2002 and 5.4.16, some people who did not have earnings were credited with earnings for S2P purposes (see below). Details of the calculation of SERPS and S2P can be found in Chapter 46, *Disability Rights Handbook*, 40th edition. If you don't have a copy, send us an A4-sized, stamped addressed envelope and we'll send a photocopy.

### Credited with earnings for S2P

Some disabled people, carers and people with low earnings will have been credited with earnings into S2P. If you had annual qualifying earnings of at least the lower earnings limit (£5,824 in 2015/16) but less than the *'low earnings threshold'*, you were treated as though you had earnings at that level (£15,300 in 2015/16). You could also be treated as having earnings at the low earnings threshold if, throughout the year, you were:

■ paid carer's allowance, or would have been paid it but for overlapping benefits rule (see Chapter 8(6)); *or*
■ entitled to 'carer's credit' or 'credits for parents and foster parents' (from 6.4.10; see Box D.3 in Chapter 11) or got home responsibilities protection because you were caring for a disabled person or a child under the age of 6 (before 6.4.10; see Box L.2); *or*
■ paid the long-term rate of incapacity benefit, or would have been paid it but for the overlapping benefits rule or because you did not meet the contribution conditions; *or*
■ paid contributory employment and support allowance that:
  – had been payable for a continuous period of 52 weeks; *or*
  – included a support component; *or*
  – (for a man born between 6.4.44 and 5.4.47 or a woman born between 6.4.49 and 5.4.51) had been payable for a continuous period of 13 weeks following a period on statutory sick pay,
  or would have been paid it but for the overlapping benefits rule or because you did not meet the contribution conditions; *or*
■ paid severe disablement allowance.

From 2010/11 onwards it was possible to combine periods when you paid national insurance contributions with periods when any of the above conditions (or a combination of these conditions) applied. Before April 2010 you had to meet just one of these conditions throughout the year and periods when you had actually paid national insurance contributions could not be included.
PA S.9(2) & Sch 1, Part 6, para 34(4)

## 8. Other state pension payments

A Category A or B pension may include the following additional payments.

### Graduated retirement benefit

This is based on graduated contributions made between April 1961 and April 1975. Levels of payment are low – typically less than £1 a week. Graduated retirement benefit can be paid on its own.

### Invalidity addition

This may be paid if, within eight weeks before reaching state pension age, you were receiving:
■ an invalidity allowance with your invalidity benefit; *or*
■ incapacity benefit transitional invalidity allowance; *or*
■ an age addition with long-term incapacity benefit.
Provided you get some additional state pension, you can get the invalidity addition even if you do not get any basic state pension. It is paid at the same rate as your invalidity allowance or age addition but is offset against additional state pension or contracted-out deduction.
SSCBA, S.47

### Extra state pension for deferring retirement

If you do not draw your Category A or Category B state pension at state pension age, you may get a higher pension or a lump sum when you start to draw it at a later date. This is called *'deferment'*.

For periods of deferment after 6.4.05, your state pension (including any additional state pension and graduated retirement benefit) is increased by 1% for each five weeks that you put off drawing your state pension, as long as you defer it for at least five weeks. Alternatively, if you defer your state pension for at least 12 consecutive months, instead of an increased state pension you can receive a one-off taxable lump sum based on the amount of pension you would have received plus interest. (This lump sum will be disregarded for income-related benefits such as pension credit or housing benefit.) If you defer for less than a year, you will not receive interest payments but you can have your backdated pension paid as a lump sum. You can defer your state pension for as long as you want to and receive extra pension or a lump sum in this way.

For periods of deferment of at least seven weeks before April 2005, your state pension (including any additional state pension and graduated retirement benefit) is increased by 1% for each seven weeks that you deferred drawing your state pension.
SSCBA, Sch 5

You cannot clock up extra state pension by keeping another income replacement benefit (such as widow's pension) or pension credit after state pension age. An increase for an adult dependant will not be made if you defer claiming state pension. However, a married woman who has deferred her Category B pension may receive an increase to this as long as she does not receive certain other state pensions or benefits in the meantime. Since April 2006 you can draw graduated retirement benefit without this affecting any increase for deferring a Category B pension.
WBRP Regs, reg 4(1)

### Age addition

This is 25p a week for people aged 80 or over.
SSCBA, S.79

## 9. Non-contributory state pension

Category D pension is non-contributory and paid at a rate of £75.50 a week to people who do not have a contributory state pension. To qualify, you must be aged 80 or over, meet certain residency conditions and have reached state pension age by 6.4.16. If you have a contributory state pension of less than £75.50, you can receive a Category D pension to top up your state pension to a total of £75.50. To claim, ask the Pension Service for a claim-form for the Category D pension.
SSCBA, S.78

## 10. How do you claim state pension?

Normally, the Pension Service contacts you with details about claiming your pension about four months before you reach state pension age. However, this does not always happen; the Pension Service may not have your current address, especially if you have not worked for some time.

Ring 0800 731 7898 (textphone 0800 731 7339) to make a claim over the phone or to ask for a claim-form, download the claim-form (www.gov.uk/government/publications/the-basic-state-pension) or claim online (www.gov.uk/claim-state-pension-online). If you live in Northern Ireland, ring 0808 100 2658 or claim online (www.nidirect.gov.uk/services/claim-your-state-pension-online).

You do not need to make a claim for Category A or B state pension in certain circumstances, eg if you were getting employment and support allowance, income support, jobseeker's allowance, incapacity benefit or pension credit at some point in the eight weeks leading up to your state pension age. However, there are exceptions. If you qualify and so do not need to make a claim for state pension, you will be notified two weeks before state pension age.

If you have decided to defer drawing your state pension at state pension age, you should contact the Pension Service up to four months before you do wish to draw it. If you have already started to draw your state pension but now wish to defer it, contact the Pension Service. You can only defer your state pension once and you cannot backdate this choice.
C&P Regs, Sch 4, para 13

## 11. How is state pension paid?

State pension is normally paid into a Post Office, bank or building society account. See Chapter 56(5) for more on payments.

If you reached state pension age before 6.4.10, you could choose to receive it weekly in advance or in arrears every four or 13 weeks. If you reach state pension age on or after 6.4.10, payments are normally made in arrears every four weeks. However, if you were previously receiving a working age benefit that was paid fortnightly in arrears, your state pension will usually continue to be paid in that way.

Payday for people claiming their state pension before 6.4.10 is generally Monday (or Thursday if you claimed in 1984 or earlier) but it can now be any weekday. If your state pension is £5 or less a week, it is normally paid in a lump sum with your Christmas bonus.

---

## L.3 Private pensions and further information

### Pension options

In addition to building up a basic state pension, employees earning more than the lower earnings limit (currently £116 a week) will normally have built up additional pension through the state second pension (S2P) (see Chapter 45(7)) unless they 'contracted out' and joined their employers' occupational pension scheme or a personal pension instead. From 6.4.16, under the new state pension, you cannot build up any more S2P.

If you contracted out of the state scheme through your employer's occupational pension, both you and your employer paid a lower rate of national insurance (NI).

If you contracted out with an appropriate personal pension or a stakeholder pension (a type of personal pension which meets certain conditions), HMRC paid a rebate of your NI contributions to your scheme provider. Not all private pension schemes were contracted out of S2P, so it was possible to build up entitlement to both types of pension at the same time.

From 6.4.12, contracting out of S2P for employers' money purchase pension schemes and personal pension schemes has been abolished, so no more rebates were paid for years after the 2011/12 tax year. Instead, you will have paid full-rate NI and built up S2P from April 2012. The funds you built up in an existing scheme will stay invested in it and if you or your employer also put money into the scheme, you can continue to do so.

From 6.4.16, contracting out of the S2P for employers' salary-related pension schemes has ended. If you are a member of one of those schemes, you pay the full rate of NI contributions from that date.

If you were self-employed, you were not able to build up S2P or join an occupational pension, but you could pay into a personal pension.

Often, the best way of building up a second pension for your retirement is to join an occupational pension scheme if your employer runs one. Your employer will provide details of the terms and conditions of the scheme.

All employers now need to automatically enrol eligible workers into a pension scheme. This duty was phased in between October 2012 and February 2018.

### Private pensions and social security benefits

A private pension will be counted as income for means-tested benefits, such as income-related employment and support allowance (ESA – see Chapter 22(7)) and universal credit (see Chapter 17(10)). It is also counted as income for pension credit, although it may help you qualify for the savings credit element of that benefit (see Chapter 44(4)).

A private pension will not normally affect your entitlement to non-means-tested benefits. However, an occupational or personal pension over certain levels may affect contributory ESA, incapacity benefit or contribution-based jobseeker's allowance. A private pension counts as earnings if your partner is claiming an increase for you as an adult dependant or if they are claiming an increase for a child dependant. More information is given in the appropriate sections of this handbook.

### Problems with occupational, personal and stakeholder pensions

If you are a member of an occupational pension scheme or have a personal or stakeholder pension and you have a problem with your pension, ask your pension provider for details of their complaints procedure.

If you are not satisfied with the response or need further help or advice, you can contact the Pensions Advisory Service (Helpline 0300 123 1047; www.pensionsadvisoryservice.org.uk/contacting-us). They can give general information or individual advice about pension problems.

If you have a complaint about the running of your pension plan, and you have been unable to resolve it directly with the people running the plan, you can contact the Pensions Ombudsman, an independent body set up to resolve pension complaints (www.pensions-ombudsman.org.uk/contact-us). The Pensions Regulator, which regulates pension schemes, is based at Napier House, Trafalgar Place, Brighton BN1 4DW (0345 600 7060; www.thepensionsregulator.gov.uk/individuals.aspx).

The Pension Tracing Service provides a free tracing service for people who want to contact a scheme in which they may have pension rights but do not know the contact address: The Pension Tracing Service (0800 731 0193; textphone 0800 731 0176; www.gov.uk/find-pension-contact-details).

This section of the handbook looks at:

| | |
|---|---|
| Industrial Injuries scheme | Chapter **46** |
| Armed Forces Compensation scheme | Chapter **47** |
| Criminal injuries compensation | Chapter **48** |
| Vaccine damage payments | Chapter **49** |
| Compensation recovery | Chapter **50** |

# Compensation schemes

# 46 Industrial Injuries scheme

| | | |
|---|---|---|
| 1 | Who is covered by the scheme? | 273 |
| 2 | Industrial accidents | 273 |
| | Accidents at work – principles of entitlement – Box M.1 | 274 |
| 3 | Prescribed industrial diseases | 273 |
| 4 | Common law compensation | 275 |
| 5 | What benefits can you claim? | 275 |
| 6 | How do you claim IIDB? | 275 |
| 7 | How is your claim decided? | 276 |
| | How is disablement assessed? – Box M.2 | 276 |
| | Prescribed degrees of disablement – Box M.3 | 278 |
| 8 | How much do you get? | 279 |
| 9 | Challenging the decision | 279 |
| 10 | If your condition gets worse | 279 |
| 11 | Extra allowances | 280 |
| 12 | Constant attendance allowance | 280 |
| 13 | Exceptionally severe disablement allowance | 280 |
| 14 | Reduced earnings allowance | 280 |
| | For more information – Box M.4 | 280 |
| 15 | Retirement allowance | 281 |

## 1. Who is covered by the scheme?
The Industrial Injuries scheme provides no-fault tax-free benefits for an employee who has a personal injury caused by an accident at work, or who contracts a prescribed disease while working.

*SSCBA, S.94 for accidents & Ss.108-110 for prescribed diseases*

You are covered by the Industrial Injuries scheme if you are an *'employed earner'*, ie you are working for an employer. It doesn't matter if you do not earn enough to pay national insurance (NI) contributions, or if you are too old or too young to pay them. Nor does it matter if the accident happens on your first day at work. What counts is that you are gainfully employed under a contract of service or as an office-holder with taxable earnings.

You will not be covered if you are genuinely self-employed or you are a volunteer, unless the accident happens while you are doing specified types of voluntary work, eg as a special constable. There is a discretion to treat someone who is illegally employed as an employed earner.

*SSCBA 1992, Ss.2(1) & 96-97; Social Security (Employed Earners' Employment for Industrial Injuries Purposes) Regs 1975, Sch 1, Part 1 & Sch 3*

**Working outside the UK** – You are covered by the scheme if your accident occurred, or you contracted a prescribed disease, in the UK. Some people are covered even though they were working outside the UK when the accident happened or when they contracted the disease – eg mariners, airmen and women, people paying Class 1 or Class 2 NI contributions as volunteer development workers, continental shelf workers, and certain people working in other European Economic Area countries.

*SSCBA, Ss.117–120*

**Appeals** – If there is any doubt over your status as an employed earner, your case is decided by an HMRC officer; you have the right to appeal to a First-tier Tribunal (Tax).

It may be possible to show that you are an employee for benefit purposes (despite the tax and NI arrangements) if the real relationship between you and the contractor is that of an employee and employer. This applies in particular to building workers, who are very often categorised as self-employed. Your trade union may be able to advise you.

**Pre-1948 cases** – Before 5.12.12, there were separate benefit schemes for diseases, conditions and accidents that occurred or arose before 5.7.48. Since 5.12.12, awards of benefit under these old schemes have been transferred to the Industrial Injuries scheme described in this chapter. A claim relating to this earlier period will be treated as a claim for industrial injuries benefit.

## 2. Industrial accidents
If you have an accident at work, you should report the details as soon as possible to your employer. Do this even if things don't seem serious at first. A cut can turn septic. A pain in the stomach can turn out to be a hernia. An accident book or an equivalent electronic record must be kept at any workplace where 10 or more people usually work.

In most cases it will be clear that an 'accident' has happened and that it was 'industrial', but case law has expanded these concepts to include less obvious situations. For example, a conversation or verbal harassment could constitute an accident. Box M.1 looks at these issues in more detail and at some of the problems that can arise.

If you are in any doubt about whether you are covered by the Industrial Injuries scheme, you should seek advice and claim benefit anyway. Case law is complex so always get advice if you are turned down.

## 3. Prescribed industrial diseases
Benefit can be paid for over 80 different diseases or conditions that are prescribed as being risks of particular jobs and not risks common to the general population. These are listed in DWP guide DB1 (see Box M.4) along with the types of job you must have worked in to qualify for benefit.

For some diseases, there are rules about the length of time you must have worked in the job. For example:

❑ **Occupational deafness** – See 6 below.
❑ **Chronic obstructive pulmonary disease** – To qualify, you must have worked underground in a coal mine for a total of 20 years or more (this includes periods off sick) and have a defined reduction in lung capacity. In April 1997 the medical conditions were modified, so if your claim was refused under the old rules, you should re-apply. In July 2008 coverage was extended so that each two years of work as a screen worker on the surface of a coal mine before 1.1.83 is equivalent to one year working underground.

*IIPD Regs, Sch 1*

❑ **Cataract** – To qualify, you must have worked in a listed job for at least five years.

*IIPD Regs, reg 2(e)*

❑ **Osteoarthritis of the hip** – To qualify, you must have worked in agriculture as a farmer or farm worker for a total of 10 years or more.

*IIPD Regs, Sch 1*

## M.1 Accidents at work: principles of entitlement

### What is an 'accident'?

You must first show that an 'accident' has occurred. While this is usually clear-cut, there are situations where it may not be immediately obvious. In CI/2414/98, for example, a conversation with a colleague causing the claimant to suffer stress and depression was accepted as an accident and the opinion given that words alone such as *'verbal sexual harassment at work [could] amount to an accident or series of accidents as might misinformation designed to shock or causing shock'*.

In most cases an accident will involve an unexpected event. But what if an expected event causes an unexpected injury? In *CAO v Faulds* (R(I)1/00), the claimant was a fireman suffering post-traumatic stress disorder after attending a series of horrific incidents. The House of Lords rejected the argument that attending such incidents was the job for which he had been trained and so could not constitute 'accidents' to him, and decided that an accident need not be an unexpected event but that the sustaining of an *unexpected* personal injury caused by an *expected* event or incident may itself amount to an accident.

### Accident or process?

Problems can arise if the injury developed relatively slowly through the normal course of work. This is called injury by *'process'*. If your injury developed as a result of a continuous process at work, you will not be entitled to industrial injuries benefits, unless your injury is listed as one of the prescribed industrial diseases.

However, the cumulative effect of a series of small incidents, each of which is separate and identifiable, that were slightly out of the ordinary can count as an accident. But each one must have led to some physiological or pathological change for the worse. For example, in R(I)43/55 the claimant developed a psychoneurotic condition and skin disorder. He had been working near a machine that irregularly produced loud explosive reports. Any one of them could have been the start of a major explosion. It was held that each explosion was an 'accident' with a cumulative effect on his condition.

If a process has been going on for only a short time, or you have just started a new job or have had a change in working conditions, it may be easier to show you have suffered injury by accident, but each case will be a matter of fact and degree.

### What about other causes of injury?

If you have a condition that predisposes you to certain injuries, you can still be covered by the scheme but some aspect of your employment must have caused the injury in question. For example, an asthma sufferer had an acute asthma attack due to fumes from a fire at work. He was covered, as it was probable that he would not have had that attack if it had not been for the fire at work.

Your claim will fail if it was pure coincidence that you had the heart attack, strain, fit, etc at work rather than somewhere else, although this is not always clear-cut. In R(I)6/82, it was confirmed that even if an accident happens out of the blue it will count as an 'industrial' one if the activity you are doing represents a special danger to you because of something in yourself or you are injured because of coming into contact with the employer's plant or premises (eg by falling onto the floor).

### Is it an 'industrial' accident?

To count as an 'industrial' accident, it must have arisen *out of* and *in the course of* employment. The difference between these phrases is clearly shown in *CAO v Rhodes* (R(I)1/99). Here, a Benefits Agency worker was assaulted by a neighbour whom she had reported for undeclared earnings. As the worker was at home on sick leave, she was found to have had an accident out of her employment but not in the course of it. Had she been working at home on the day, the outcome might have been different.

If your accident happens during an early arrival, late stay or permitted break on the employer's premises, you would probably be covered. But if you had got in early or overstayed the break purely for your own purposes (eg to have a game of snooker), you would have taken yourself outside the course of your employment.

### Travelling to and from work

In the main, you are not covered if you have an accident while travelling to or from your regular workplace but you may be covered while travelling in the employer's time to an irregular workplace so that your journey can be accepted as having formed part of the work you were employed to do (see R(I)7/85). One important (but not conclusive) factor is whether you were being paid for the time spent on the journey or were able to claim overtime or time off in lieu for it. You will usually be covered if you are in transport provided by your employer. You will not be covered if your journey is for your own purposes, unconnected with your work (unless it is reasonably incidental to it).

Peripatetic workers, such as home helps, are normally accepted as covered when travelling between jobs but not when travelling to the first or from the last job.

### Emergencies

If you have an accident while responding to an emergency, you will be covered if what you did was reasonably incidental to your normal duties and was a sensible reaction to the emergency. Besides the obvious emergencies of fire and flood, unexpected occurrences can also count. In one case, a lorry driver delivering bricks helped move a concrete mixer out of the way and was injured. He was covered as, even though that was not a normal part of his duties, it was reasonably incidental to his work and it was in his employer's interests for him to complete his delivery quickly.

### Accidents treated as 'industrial'

Some accidents can be 'treated as' arising out of work. If you have broken any rules but what you have done is for the purposes of, and in connection with, your employer's business, you will be covered if you have an accident. You may have problems if what you have done is not part of your job, but if you can show that your employer would not automatically have stopped you doing the activity in question, you might succeed. You must also show that it was in your employer's interests.

You will be covered for an injury during the course of your work caused by someone else's misconduct, negligence or skylarking, by an animal or by being struck by an object or by lightning, provided you did not contribute directly or indirectly to the accident.

*SSCBA 1992, Ss.98–101*

It is up to you to claim benefit for a prescribed disease. If you have any reason to suspect that your illness is related to your work, ask the DWP and your doctor for advice. If you do not, you may lose benefit. For example, employees whose work involves regular use of a computer keyboard or mouse may not realise that they may be covered by prescribed disease A4 (task-specific focal dystonia) if they experience cramp of the hand or forearm. Similarly, welders or hairdressers with hay fever symptoms may have a claim for prescribed disease D4, allergic rhinitis.

If your disability arises from a non-listed condition that was contracted at work, you may still be able to claim under the 'accident' provisions. Case law has shown that the 'catching' of the condition can be accepted as an industrial accident; such cases include a nursery nurse who contracted poliomyelitis from an infected child (CI/159/50) and a tinner whose frequent burns on the hands caused cysts (R(I)24/54).

## 4. Common law compensation
As well as a claim for benefits under the Industrial Injuries scheme, you may have a civil claim for personal injury against your employer. With industrial diseases, this could apply even if you did the job years ago or the employer has ceased trading. In some cases an award can be significantly more than can be claimed in benefits. You may also claim for non-listed conditions. Normally, your employer has to be partly at fault, but for some industrial diseases (eg deafness) there are no-fault compensation schemes that have been negotiated between unions and employers. The time limit for filing civil claims is three years from the date of the accident. For diseases, the three years start from the date you became aware that your disease or condition was caused by work.

You will need a solicitor. While many solicitors deal with personal injury claims, it is important to choose a solicitor who specialises in your specific condition, particularly if you have an asbestos-related disease. If you are in a union, they may be able to help. See Chapter 58(2).

For information about the way in which benefits and compensation payments affect each other, see Chapters 17(22), 22(29), 48 and 50.

For certain dust diseases, including mesothelioma, byssinosis and pneumoconiosis, when a civil compensation claim may not be possible because the employer is no longer in business, a lump-sum payment can be claimed under the Pneumoconiosis etc (Workers' Compensation) Act 1979. Negligence need not be proved. You should make a claim under the Act at the same time as you claim industrial injuries disablement benefit (IIDB – see 5 below). Any payment made will be based on your age and the IIDB percentage assessment of your disablement, but do not wait for an assessment before claiming under the Act. Posthumous claims can be made by dependants but any payment made is substantially less than is paid if the person with the disease makes the initial claim. For claim-forms and more information, ring 0800 279 2322. If you have mesothelioma, you can make a claim under the Mesothelioma Scheme 2008 even if your illness was not caused by work.

There are special schemes in particular industries, eg mining and the NHS. Trade unions should be able to advise members on these and on benefits and other types of compensation.

## 5. What benefits can you claim?
### Industrial injuries disablement benefit
Industrial injuries disablement benefit (IIDB) is the main industrial injuries benefit and is paid to compensate those who have suffered disablement from a *'loss of physical or mental faculty'* caused by an industrial accident or prescribed disease (see Box M.2). Your employer does not have to be at fault in any way for you to get benefit.

You can claim whether or not you are incapable of work or have had any drop in earnings. IIDB is tax free and paid in addition to earnings or other non-means-tested benefits. As long as your disablement is assessed at 14% or more, benefit is normally payable from 15 weeks from the date of the accident or onset of the disease. For some prescribed chest diseases, you can get benefit if the assessment is from 1% to 13%. For occupational deafness, you can get benefit only if your disablement is 20% or more.

If you are claiming for a prescribed disease (PD), the date of onset should be the date the disease started, not the date of claim. As benefit is only payable 15 weeks after this date, you should check this and challenge it if necessary. However, for occupational deafness, the date of onset must be the date a successful claim was made, and payment can start from that day. There is no 15-week waiting period for PD D3 (diffuse mesothelioma) or PD D8 and PD D8A (primary carcinoma of the lung); these diseases are paid at the 100% rate from the date of claim.
SSCBA 1992, S.103; IIPD Regs, regs 20(4) & 28

### Reduced earnings allowance
Reduced earnings allowance (which replaced special hardship allowance from 1.10.86) was abolished on 1.10.90 for accidents or diseases occurring after that date. If your accident or the onset of a prescribed disease (which must be listed before 10.10.94) occurred before 1.10.90, you can still claim reduced earnings allowance. It is tax free and paid in addition to any earnings or other non-means-tested benefits you receive. See 14 below for more details.

### Retirement allowance
Retirement allowance replaces reduced earnings allowance if you are already getting at least £2 a week reduced earnings allowance and are not in regular employment when you reach state pension age. See 15 below for more details. Retirement allowance is tax free and paid in addition to any earnings or other non-means-tested benefits you receive.

### Industrial death benefit
Industrial death benefit was payable if the death occurred before 11.4.88. It was abolished on 5.12.12. Those widowed on or after 11.4.88 as a result of an industrial accident or prescribed disease are entitled to widows' benefits, bereavement benefits or bereavement support payment (depending on when the death occurred) without having to meet any contribution conditions (see Chapter 51).

## 6. How do you claim industrial injuries disablement benefit (IIDB)?
To claim IIDB, ring the Barnsley IIDB Centre (0800 121 8379, textphone 0800 169 0314) or go to www.gov.uk/industrial-injuries-disablement-benefit/how-to-claim. You need form BI100A for an accident or BI100PD for any of the prescribed industrial diseases.

Benefit cannot be backdated more than three months even if you have a good reason for not claiming earlier.

There are special time limits for these prescribed diseases:
❑ **Occupational deafness** – To qualify, you must have worked in one or more of the listed jobs as an employed earner for a total of at least 10 years, and have a hearing loss of at least 50db in each ear, due, in the case of at least one ear, to occupational noise. If you qualify, you will be paid from the date your claim is received in the IIDB Centre – and that date must be within five years of the last day you worked in one of the jobs listed. There is no backdating of claims.
IIPD Regs, regs 2(c), 25 & 34

❑ **Occupational asthma** – You cannot get IIDB for occupational asthma if you last worked as an employed earner in the listed job more than 10 years before your date of claim. But this 10-year limit does not apply if you have asthma because of an industrial accident and have been awarded IIDB for life or for a period which includes your date of claim. If you are outside these time limits, a return to a listed job for just one day would start the period running again.

IIPD Regs, reg 36

## 7. How is your claim decided?

All decisions are made by a DWP decision maker acting on behalf of the Secretary of State.

### Accident cases

The decision maker first decides whether you have had an industrial accident and, if so, whether it arose out of and in the course of your work. If the decision is in your favour, you will be asked to go for a medical examination.

You will be examined by one (or possibly two) DWP healthcare professionals. They will provide the decision maker with a report giving an opinion on whether you have a loss of faculty as a result of the accident and, if so, the extent to which that loss of faculty leads to disablement and the period over which it is likely to last. The percentage assessment of your disablement can cover a past period as well as a forward one.

The decision maker will then decide your claim based on this report and on any other available evidence, such as a letter from your GP or hospital consultant. In practice, they will normally adopt the DWP healthcare professional's opinion.

### Prescribed industrial diseases

The decision maker will decide if you have worked in one of the jobs listed for your particular disease or condition and whether the disease was caused by that job. For many prescribed diseases, there is a presumption in law that, unless

## M.2 How is disablement assessed?

The legislation uses three different terms when considering disablement questions. These are:
- loss of faculty;
- disability; *and*
- disablement.

They are each used as different concepts and must not be confused. They are not defined in law but have been considered by the Social Security Commissioners, particularly in R(I)1/81.

### Loss of faculty

A *'loss of faculty'* is any pathological condition or any loss (including a reduction) of the normal physical or mental function of an organ or part of the body. This does include disfigurement, even though there may not actually be any loss of faculty. For industrial injuries disablement benefit (IIDB), the loss of faculty must be caused by an industrial accident or prescribed disease.

A loss of faculty is not itself a disability. It is the starting point for the assessment of disablement. It is a condition that is either an actual cause of one or more disabilities or a potential cause of disability. For example, the loss of one kidney is a 'loss of faculty'. If the other kidney works normally, you may not notice any problems. But you will have lost your back-up kidney, so this is a potential cause of disability in the future. Appeal tribunals have assessed the loss of one kidney (the other functioning properly) at between 5% and 10%.

### Disability

A *'disability'* means an inability to perform a bodily or mental process. This can be a complete inability to do something (eg walking), or it can be a partial inability to do something (eg you can lift light weights but not heavy ones). The disability must result from the relevant 'loss of faculty' to count for IIDB. Note that the availability of artificial aids may reduce the actual disability; the only reported Commissioners' decisions on this, R(1)7/67 and R(1)7/63, concerned spectacles.

### Disablement

*'Disablement'* is the sum total of all the separate disabilities you may experience. It represents your overall inability to perform the 'normal' activities of life – the loss of your health, strength and power to enjoy a 'normal' life. There is a complete scale of assessment from 1-100% disablement. Every case is decided individually, so it is possible to give only general guidelines. Some types of disability have a fixed percentage, which can be increased or decreased

depending on the circumstances of the case. These 'scheduled assessments' are listed in Box M.3. Other disabilities are assessed in relation to this list.

### What is taken into account?

The assessment is done by comparing your condition (all your disabilities due to the relevant loss of faculty) with that of a person of the same age and sex whose physical and mental condition is 'normal'. The decision maker, or in practice the DWP healthcare professional who assesses you, also has to make judgments about what is normal for someone of your age and sex. For example, how much hearing loss is normal for a man of 50? At what age does it become normal to lose teeth and wear false teeth?

SSCBA, Sch 6, paras 1–3

If your condition differed from normal prior to the accident and therefore the industrial injury is more disabling than it would otherwise be, the assessment may be increased to take account of this. For example, decision makers *'are entitled to increase the disablement percentage to take account of the fact that, when disaster struck, he was blind. They are not entitled to compensate him for the blindness itself, but they are entitled to take account of the fact that a particular happening to a blind man, or somebody suffering from some other disability, may be more serious of itself than it would be in the case of a man who suffered from no disability'* (Murrell v Secretary of State for Social Security (appendix to R(I)3/84)).

The decision maker must also consider how your condition affects you, rather than just considering what is generally true of people with your condition or taking the same drugs. Inconvenience, genuine embarrassment, anxiety or depression can all increase the assessment.

If your disablement also has a mental element, R(I)4/94 provides a useful summary of the ways in which that might affect the assessment of disablement. R(I)13/75 discusses what is meant by the terms 'hysteria', 'malingering' and 'functional overlay'. See also CSI/1180/01 and CI/1756/02.

There have been a number of cases involving stress-related conditions, which are particularly difficult to assess in relation to the schedule. CI/1307/99 is useful in this respect, the Commissioner using the tariffs for facial disfigurement and loss of sight as bearing the closest comparison in that they interfere with interpersonal communications.

The fact of your loss of earning power or incapacity for work cannot be taken into account in the assessment. Nor can the fact that your disabilities may lead to extra expenses. But the disabilities that lead to incapacity for work (or extra expenses) are taken into account, along with disabilities that do not affect your working capacity at all.

the contrary can be proved, the condition was caused by your job if you were working in the listed job on the date of onset or within one month of that date. For some prescribed diseases, the date you were last working in the listed job is irrelevant.

If it is decided you do not meet these employment conditions, your claim will be refused. You have one month to ask for a mandatory reconsideration of the decision (see 9 below).

If the decision maker decides you meet the employment conditions, you will be asked to go for an examination by one (or possibly two) DWP healthcare professionals. They will send a report to the decision maker giving their opinion on whether you have the prescribed disease, any resulting loss of faculty, the level and period of your disablement, the date of onset and whether your disease is due to your employment. The healthcare professional(s) can obtain reports from your hospital consultant and GP if necessary. Although in deciding

your claim the decision maker has to take into account all the available evidence, they will normally adopt the DWP healthcare professional's opinion.

If you are terminally ill, or claiming for certain asbestos-related diseases or some prescribed cancers, your claim will be fast-tracked and you will be sent for an examination while the employment questions are being considered. If you have diffuse mesothelioma (PD D3) or primary carcinoma of the lung (PD D8 and D8A), an examination may not be necessary if your diagnosis is confirmed by your consultant, GP or specialist nurse. This is because, provided you meet the employment conditions, you are automatically assessed as 100% disabled once diagnosis is confirmed.

For some prescribed diseases you may be asked to have a particular test before being sent for an examination – for example, for occupational deafness, a hearing test, and for chronic obstructive pulmonary disease, a breathing test. If the results of those tests show that you meet the particular criteria

The assessment does not depend only on your condition on the day (or time of day) you are examined. If your condition varies, the healthcare professional must work out an average assessment taking into account your good and bad spells. It is arguable that any loss of life expectancy should also be taken into account, as well as the effect of your knowledge of the nature of your disability on your life.

### Scheduled and non-scheduled assessments
The scheduled assessments, listed in Box M.3, are fixed on the assumption that your condition has stabilised and there are no added complications.

If your disability is not in the schedule, the decision maker *'may have such regard as may be appropriate to the prescribed degrees of disablement'*. They should try to assess your disabilities so that your percentage assessment looks right in relation to the scheduled assessments. R(I)2/06 sets out the approach to be taken by appeal tribunals to questions of assessment.
*GB Regs, reg 11(8)*

Note that 100% is not total and absolute disablement; it is just the legal maximum assessment. If the scale could go higher, some people would be assessed as 200% disabled or more.

If you have had either arm amputated just below the shoulder, you will be assessed at 80% – even if you cope perfectly well. If the amputation has not yet stabilised, or there are other complications with it, a higher assessment can be made.

If you cannot use one arm at all, you may well be assessed at 80% – as if you had actually lost your arm. CI/1199/02 illustrates this point in relation to vibration white finger (PD A11).

### Several conditions
Four different disabilities due to the same accident or prescribed disease may each be assessed as causing 10% disablement, but the assessment will not always be the total of 40%. This is because the interaction of different conditions in one person may be far more disabling – so the final assessment could well be higher. If you have several of the minor scheduled conditions, the total percentage assessment could be less or more than the actual total of the percentages for each of the scheduled conditions. The healthcare professional will give their opinion on what is the appropriate assessment for you – given your age, sex and physical and mental condition as a whole. So even for the scheduled assessments, the healthcare professional may increase (or decrease) the percentage(s) if that is reasonable in a particular case. The formula for assessing

disablement that has more than one cause is set out in CI/2183/2011, which notes that it is essential to establish accurately the dates of each accident and the onset of each disease.

### Pre-existing condition
If your disability has some other cause, you may have problems – eg where a previous back injury is followed by an industrial injury to your back. However, your percentage assessment should only be cut, or offset, if there is evidence that a pre-existing condition would have led to a degree of disablement even if the accident had not happened. If there is no evidence for this, the offset should not be made. R(I)1/81 explains the concepts fully.

If an offset is justified, the net assessment (ie after the offset) should reflect any greater disablement because of the interaction between the two (or more) causes of the same disability. Note that a pre-existing condition may cause disablement later. Although the disablement you would have had from that pre-existing condition alone cannot be taken into account, its interaction with the effects of the industrial injury may lead to greater disablement. This could justify a request for a supersession on the grounds of a change of circumstances (see 10 in this chapter).
*GB Regs, reg 11(3)*

### Conditions arising afterwards
If a condition is 'directly attributable' to the industrial accident or disease, it is assessable in the normal way. If it is not 'directly attributable', but is also a cause of the same disability, then whether or not any greater disablement can be taken into account depends on the percentage assessment for the industrial accident or disease. If the disablement resulting from the industrial accident is assessed at 11% or more, that assessment can be increased to reflect the extent to which the industrial injury is worsened because of the later condition. This can be done at the time of the assessment, or later on an application for a supersession.

Note that in reaching the 11% benchmark, account is taken of any greater disablement due to the interaction with a pre-existing condition that is also an effective cause of the disability.

The 11% rule does not apply where one is considering the interaction between two or more industrial accidents or diseases (see R(I)3/91).
*GB Regs, reg 11(4)*

for those conditions, you will be sent for an examination. If not, your claim will be disallowed. You have one month to ask for a mandatory reconsideration of the decision (see 9 below).

If you receive (or have received) industrial injuries disablement benefit for the same disease, the decision maker may need to decide whether there has been a worsening of your condition or whether you have contracted the disease afresh. This is known as the recrudescence question.

As the questions to be decided on your claim are often complex, try to get advice if your claim is turned down. See Chapter 58.

## How disablement is assessed

The DWP examining healthcare professionals(s) will give an opinion on the extent and likely duration of your disablement and must consider all the disabilities resulting from the accident or disease, including the worsening of pre-existing conditions. They will assess the disablement resulting from

## M.3 Prescribed degrees of disablement

| Description of injury | Degree |
|---|---|
| ■ Loss of both hands or amputation at higher sites | 100% |
| ■ Loss of a hand and a foot | 100% |
| ■ Double amputation through leg or thigh, or amputation through leg or thigh on one side and loss of other foot | 100% |
| ■ Loss of sight to such an extent as to render the claimant unable to perform any work for which eyesight is essential | 100% |
| ■ Very severe facial disfiguration | 100% |
| ■ Absolute deafness | 100% |
| ■ Forequarter or hindquarter amputation | 100% |

### Amputation cases – upper limbs (either arm)

| | |
|---|---|
| ■ Amputation through shoulder joint | 90% |
| ■ Amputation below shoulder with stump less than 20.5 centimetres from tip of acromion | 80% |
| ■ Amputation from 20.5 centimetres from tip of acromion to less than 11.5 centimetres below tip of olecranon | 70% |
| ■ Loss of a hand or of the thumb and four fingers of one hand or amputation from 11.5 centimetres below tip of olecranon | 60% |
| ■ Loss of thumb | 30% |
| ■ Loss of thumb and its metacarpal bone | 40% |
| ■ Loss of four fingers of one hand | 50% |
| ■ Loss of three fingers of one hand | 30% |
| ■ Loss of two fingers of one hand | 20% |
| ■ Loss of terminal phalanx of thumb | 20% |

### Amputation cases – lower limbs

| | |
|---|---|
| ■ Amputation of both feet resulting in end-bearing stumps | 90% |
| ■ Amputation through both feet proximal to the metatarso-phalangeal joint | 80% |
| ■ Loss of all toes of both feet through the metatarso-phalangeal joint | 40% |
| ■ Loss of all toes of both feet proximal to the proximal inter-phalangeal joint | 30% |
| ■ Loss of all toes of both feet distal to the proximal inter-phalangeal joint | 20% |
| ■ Amputation at hip | 90% |
| ■ Amputation below hip with stump not exceeding 13 centimetres in length measured from tip of great trochanter | 80% |
| ■ Amputation below hip and above knee with stump exceeding 13 centimetres in length measured from tip of great trochanter, or at knee not resulting in end-bearing stump | 70% |
| ■ Amputation at knee resulting in end-bearing stump or below knee with stump not exceeding 9 centimetres | 60% |
| ■ Amputation below knee with stump exceeding 9 centimetres but not exceeding 13 centimetres | 50% |

| | |
|---|---|
| ■ Amputation below knee with stump exceeding 13 centimetres | 40% |
| ■ Amputation of one foot resulting in end-bearing stump | 30% |
| ■ Amputation through one foot proximal to the metatarso-phalangeal joint | 30% |
| ■ Loss of all toes of one foot through the metatarso-phalangeal joint | 20% |

### Other injuries

| | |
|---|---|
| ■ Loss of one eye, without complications, the other being normal | 40% |
| ■ Loss of vision of one eye, without complications or disfigurement of the eyeball, the other being normal | 30% |

### Loss of fingers of right or left hand
❏ **Index finger:**

| | |
|---|---|
| ■ Whole | 14% |
| ■ Two phalanges | 11% |
| ■ One phalanx | 9% |
| ■ Guillotine amputation of tip without loss of bone | 5% |

❏ **Middle finger:**

| | |
|---|---|
| ■ Whole | 12% |
| ■ Two phalanges | 9% |
| ■ One phalanx | 7% |
| ■ Guillotine amputation of tip without loss of bone | 4% |

❏ **Ring or little finger:**

| | |
|---|---|
| ■ Whole | 7% |
| ■ Two phalanges | 6% |
| ■ One phalanx | 5% |
| ■ Guillotine amputation of tip without loss of bone | 2% |

### Loss of toes of right or left foot
❏ **Great toe:**

| | |
|---|---|
| ■ Through metatarso-phalangeal joint | 14% |
| ■ Part, with some loss of bone | 3% |

❏ **Any other toe:**

| | |
|---|---|
| ■ Through metatarso-phalangeal joint | 3% |
| ■ Part, with some loss of bone | 1% |

❏ **Two toes of one foot, excluding great toe:**

| | |
|---|---|
| ■ Through metatarso-phalangeal joint | 5% |
| ■ Part, with some loss of bone | 2% |

❏ **Three toes of one foot, excluding great toe:**

| | |
|---|---|
| ■ Through metatarso-phalangeal joint | 6% |
| ■ Part, with some loss of bone | 3% |

❏ **Four toes of one foot, excluding great toe:**

| | |
|---|---|
| ■ Through metatarso-phalangeal joint | 9% |
| ■ Part, with some loss of bone | 3% |

*GB Regs, Sch 2*

any *'loss of faculty'* by comparing your condition with that of a healthy person of the same age and sex. For this purpose, your job and other personal circumstances do not matter. See Box M.2 for details on the principles of assessment.

The decision maker can make a *'provisional'* or a *'final'* assessment. A provisional assessment is reviewed towards the end of a set period and reassessed, so if your condition is taking time to stabilise, you may have a series of provisional assessments. If your disablement is less than 14% and it seems unlikely the current assessment can be added to any other assessments to reach the 14% minimum for payment, a final assessment will be made. A final assessment may be for life if your disablement is considered permanent and unlikely to change appreciably, or it may be for a fixed period. In the latter case, the decision maker is effectively saying you will no longer be affected by the accident or disease after a specified date. This is not the same as saying there is no longer any disablement but rather that the causative link has been broken.
SSCBA, Sch 6, para 6

Reduced earnings allowance is payable only during the period of a disablement assessment of at least 1%. If your assessment is a final one for a limited period, it cannot be paid beyond that period. To safeguard your award of reduced earnings allowance, you can either challenge the decision on the period of the assessment (see 9 below) or you can wait until near the end of the assessment period and ask for the decision to be superseded on the grounds of a change of circumstances (see 10 below). As either option could result in a nil assessment, you might decide to wait. But, to be safe, you should apply for a supersession before your final assessment ends because if there is a break of even one day between assessment periods, you could permanently lose the reduced earnings allowance (see 14 below).

## 8. How much do you get?
### Lump-sum gratuities – pre-1.10.86 claims
If you claimed industrial injuries disablement benefit (IIDB) before 1.10.86 and your disablement was assessed at 1-19%, you were paid a lump-sum gratuity (unless you were claiming for certain chest diseases for which a pension was paid). The amount of gratuity paid depended on the percentage and duration of your assessment; if it was 20% or over, you were paid a weekly pension as now.

If you were entitled to special hardship allowance, you could choose to have the IIDB paid as a weekly pension on top, instead of as a lump sum. This is no longer possible, but an existing pension in lieu of a gratuity can continue (if you remain entitled to reduced earnings allowance, which replaced special hardship allowance) until the end of the period of your assessment.
Social Security (Industrial Injuries & Diseases) Miscellaneous Provisions Regs 1986, reg 12

A gratuity for a final life assessment lasts for seven years (R(I)11/67) when deciding if any offset is appropriate against a further award for a subsequent accident or disease or an increase in the original assessment. (For an example of how this works in practice, see *Disability Rights Handbook* 23rd edition, page 151.)

### Weekly pension – claims from 1.10.86
Since 1.10.86, you can get benefit only if your total disablement is assessed at 14% or more, or at least 1% for pneumoconiosis and byssinosis.

Benefit is paid as a weekly pension. Assessments of 14-19% disablement are paid at the 20% rate. Assessments of 24% (or 44%, etc) are rounded down and paid at the 20% rate (or 40%, etc). Assessments of 25% (or 45%, etc) are rounded up and paid at the 30% rate (or 50%, etc). For pneumoconiosis and byssinosis, assessments of 1-10% are

paid at the 10% rate (ie £17.48) and assessments of 11-24% are paid at the 20% rate.
SSCBA, S.103(3); IIPD Regs, regs 15B & 20(1A)

Anyone diagnosed as having pneumoconiosis (PD D1) is automatically treated as at least 1% disabled and therefore entitled to benefit. It appears (from R(I)1/96) the DWP may have treated such claims incorrectly in the past, so you should contact them if you had a claim for pneumoconiosis rejected. Benefit can be paid back to 25.8.94 if appropriate and compensation paid for official error.

### Percentages and amounts

| 20% | £ 34.96 | 50% | £ 87.40 | 80% | £139.84 |
|-----|---------|-----|---------|-----|---------|
| 30% | £ 52.44 | 60% | £104.88 | 90% | £157.32 |
| 40% | £ 69.92 | 70% | £122.36 | 100% | £174.80 |

### Aggregation of assessments
Disablement assessments for more than one industrial injury or disease can be added together, or *'aggregated'*, if the assessment periods overlap. This can help you reach the minimum payment figure of 14% during the period of the overlap, so it is worth claiming IIDB for even 'minor' injuries.

An assessment on a claim made on or after 1.10.86 can be aggregated with any assessment(s) on claim(s) for accidents or diseases before that date. Case law has established that this includes pre-1986 life awards for which a gratuity has been paid. Decision makers will aggregate only if you have at least one assessment that has been made on or after 1.10.86. So, for example, they would refuse to aggregate two pre-1.10.86 life awards of 11% and 9% but would aggregate them if either award was increased on or after 1.10.86, or a successful claim for a further accident/disease was made on or after 1.10.86, even if the accident/disease occurred before this date. See R(I)4/03.

If you have had a gratuity in the past and think this percentage assessment is not being aggregated with any further assessment(s), you should ask the DWP to supersede any previous decision and award you a weekly pension, if this brings you to at least 14%, or to increase your existing pension to take account of the earlier assessment. Decision makers are advised to revise on the grounds of official error or to supersede if the decision was made after 24.7.95 (the date of CI/522/93 (see R(I)1/03)); arrears cannot be paid back to a date earlier than 24.7.95. Decision makers should also consider compensation (see Chapter 59(2)) but may need to be prompted. Assessments of under 20% for occupational deafness cannot be aggregated. Aggregation of assessments is carried out only if it is to your advantage.
SSCBA, S.103(2); IIPD Regs, regs 15A, 15B & 20

## 9. Challenging the decision
If you disagree with the Secretary of State's decision on your claim, you can ask for a mandatory reconsideration of the decision. You have one month from the date of the decision in which to do this. If you are not satisfied with the reconsidered decision, you have the right of appeal to an appeal tribunal. When you appeal, provide as much detail as possible as to why you disagree with the decision. As industrial injuries benefits are complex, you may need expert advice; your trade union or an advice centre may help (see Chapter 58). For details of the process for challenging decisions, see Chapter 57.

## 10. If your condition gets worse
To increase your assessment or extend the period it covers, you must ask for the decision to be superseded on the grounds of a change in circumstances. Any new assessment could be lower rather than higher. It could even be reduced to nil, which could then also involve a loss of reduced earnings allowance. Retirement allowance is not affected because it is awarded for

life and not linked to any disablement assessment.

Try to get advice before applying. You should be particularly careful if you have now developed arthritis or spondylosis, as this can often lead to your disability being assessed as 'constitutional' and not due to the effects of your injury or prescribed disease.

### Payment and aggregation of assessments following a supersession

If your request for an increased assessment is successful and the new percentage is 14% or more, you will get a pension. If you had been paid a gratuity for that injury in the past, as this will have been more than seven years ago, no offset will be appropriate (see 8 above).

If your assessment is increased but remains under 14%, you will not get benefit unless you can aggregate that percentage with another current assessment(s). In this case, the whole percentage assessment becomes available for aggregation, not just the actual increase in percentage gained. This can be added to any current assessments you have, including final life assessments for which you received a lump-sum gratuity.

However, the position is slightly different if you are currently getting a pension in lieu of a gratuity for the original assessment. In this case, your right to a pension in lieu will end and you will receive the balance (if any) of the original gratuity, plus the appropriate gratuity for the increase in the percentage assessment or period. Or, if your disablement is assessed at 14% or more, you will receive a pension at the appropriate rate.

Social Security (Industrial Injuries & Diseases) Miscellaneous Provisions Regs 1986, reg 12(3)

### 11. Extra allowances

The following additional allowances can be paid:

| Additional allowances | per week |
| --- | --- |
| Constant attendance allowance | |
| – part time | £34.95 |
| – normal maximum | £69.90 |
| – intermediate rate | £104.85 |
| – exceptional rate | £139.80 |
| Exceptionally severe disablement allowance | £69.90 |
| Unemployability supplement* | |
| (earnings limit £6,526 per year) | £108.05 |

* abolished from 6.4.87: payable to existing claimants only

### 12. Constant attendance allowance

Constant attendance allowance is automatically considered when your disablement assessment totals 95% or more. Your need for care and attention must be the result of an industrial accident/disease. If you think this has been missed, contact the Barnsley IIDB Centre (see 6 above). If you receive disability living allowance care component, personal independence payment daily living component or attendance allowance, it will be reduced by the amount of constant attendance allowance you receive.

SSCBA 1992, S.104

There is no right of appeal if your claim is refused, but you can ask for the decision to be looked at again if you feel some facts were not taken into account.

### 13. Exceptionally severe disablement allowance

This is automatically considered if you qualify for one of the two higher rates of constant attendance allowance. However, your need for that level of attendance must be likely to be permanent. Again, there is no right of appeal if your claim is refused. For more details of this and constant attendance allowance, read DWP guide DB1 (see Box M.4).

SSCBA 1992, S.105

### 14. Reduced earnings allowance

You can claim reduced earnings allowance (REA) if your accident happened before 1.10.90 or your disease started before 1.10.90 (provided the disease, or the extension to the prescribed disease category, was added to the prescribed list before 10.10.94). REA will not be paid for newly prescribed diseases or extensions to those already listed.

You must claim REA separately from industrial injuries disablement benefit (IIDB). To claim REA, ring 0800 121 8379. A claim for REA cannot be backdated for more than three months. It is possible to have more than one award of REA if you have had more than one industrial accident or disease (R(I)2/02). However, you cannot be paid more than 140% of the maximum rate of disablement benefit when your IIDB and REA awards are added together.

Once you have made a successful claim for REA, you can make renewal claims, subject to the usual rules. But if you were entitled to REA on 30.9.90, a break in entitlement of just one day may mean you lose REA for good.

If you are getting REA when you reach state pension age and are not in regular employment, your REA will be replaced by retirement allowance, paid at a lower rate (see 15 below). However, there appears to be a loophole in the law that allows anyone claiming REA for the first time after state pension age to be paid REA, provided they are not in regular employment at the time of claim, without ever having this converted to retirement allowance. So, if you are nearing state pension age and considering claiming REA, it may be worth seeking advice about the possibility of delaying your claim. If your REA award ends after retirement, when you are not in regular employment, you cannot re-qualify for another award: you have lost the benefit permanently.

SSCBA, Sch 7, para 11; CI/402/2012

### Who qualifies for REA?

To qualify for REA, you must have a current assessment of at least 1% in respect of an accident or disease that occurred before 1.10.90 (see above). You must also be unable to return to your regular job or do work of an equivalent standard because of the effects of the disablement caused by your accident or disease.

The broad aim is to make up the difference between what you are capable of earning, as a result of the injury or disease, in any suitable alternative employment and what you would have been likely to earn now in your regular job if you had not had the accident or disease and were still in your regular job. There are two ways of qualifying for REA.

❑ **Under the continuous condition** – You must have been incapable of following both your *'regular occupation'* and any *'employment of an equivalent standard which is suitable in [your] case'* ever since 90 days after your accident happened or your disease began.

❑ **Under the permanent condition** – It is enough if you

are now *'incapable, and likely to remain permanently incapable, of following [your] regular occupation'* and also incapable of any *'employment of an equivalent standard ...'*

SSCBA, Sch 7, para 11(1)

### Earnings

On a first claim, your pre- and post-accident earnings are individually assessed. On subsequent claims for the same accident or disease, revisions may be linked to the general movement in earnings of broad occupational groups, depending on how the law applies to your situation.

Social Security (Industrial Injuries) (Reduced Earnings Allowance & Transitional) Regs 1987, reg 2

Broadly, if your post-accident earnings are less than your pre-accident earnings would be now, the difference is made up by REA, subject to a maximum payment of £69.92. This comparison may be totally hypothetical, eg if your regular job no longer exists or disabilities that cannot be taken into account in the REA assessment make you incapable of any work. If you are unable to do any work because of the accident or disease, you should get maximum REA.

### Challenging decisions

Case law on REA, much of which originally applied to the earlier special hardship allowance, is complex and extensive. If your claim is turned down or you do not get maximum REA, do not give up without first getting expert advice. As well as depending on case law, your claim may rest on many detailed facts as well as medical evidence. There may be arguments over what your 'regular' occupation is, particularly if your accident happened during lower-paid 'stop gap' work; or you may argue that your reasonable prospects of advancement should be taken into account.

You have a right of appeal against the refusal of REA or the amount awarded, as long as you have previously asked for a mandatory reconsideration of the decision. See Chapter 57 for more on challenging decisions.

### No percentage assessment?

To get REA, you must have a current disablement assessment of at least 1%. You also need to be sure that the loss of faculty identified by the DWP healthcare professional(s) in their report covers all the disabilities caused by the industrial accident/disease and is sufficient to contribute materially to your being incapable of following your regular occupation. The DWP healthcare professional(s) gives their opinion on the link between the accepted loss of faculty and your inability to follow your regular occupation. The decision maker is not bound to accept this but in practice usually does.

If you do not have a current percentage assessment or the loss of faculty needs to be more broadly identified, you have to tackle that side of things first, by asking for a mandatory reconsideration and, if this is unsuccessful, appealing (see 9 above). If the decision on your disablement assessment is revised or changed at appeal, the decision maker can revise the decision on your REA, if this is to your advantage. This precludes the need for a separate appeal on the REA question.

### 15. Retirement allowance

Retirement allowance can range from a minimum of £2 a week to a maximum of £17.48 a week. It is the lower of 10% of the maximum rate of disablement benefit or 25% of the reduced earnings allowance (REA) you received immediately before reaching state pension age (see Chapter 45(2)) or ceasing regular employment, if that was later. In practice, if you had maximum REA, your retirement allowance would be £17.48. If you had retired and claimed your state pension before 10.4.89, you do not get retirement

allowance, but your REA is frozen for life.

Retirement allowance is payable for life and is not linked with any percentage assessment of disability. It is only payable if you are transferring from REA. If you want to stay on REA when you reach state pension age, you can only do so while you remain in regular employment (see below). However, if you are approaching state pension age and have not yet claimed REA, you should consider delaying your claim in order to keep it indefinitely (see 14 above).

Retirement allowance replaces REA if, when you have reached state pension age, you give up regular employment and on the day before you give up that employment your award(s) of REA adds up to at least £2 a week. If you stopped work before reaching state pension age, you are treated as giving up regular employment in the week you reach state pension age. If you continue regular employment after state pension age, your REA will be replaced by retirement allowance when you stop work.

SSCBA, Sch 7, paras 12 & 13

**Regular employment** – This is defined as gainful employment under a contract of service that requires you to work for an average of at least 10 hours a week over any 5-week period (not counting any week of permitted absence such as leave or sickness), or gainful employment (which may be self-employment) that you undertake for an average of at least 10 hours a week over any 5-week period.

Social Security (Industrial Injuries) (Regular Employment) Regs 1990

# 47 Armed Forces Compensation scheme

| 1 | Armed Forces Compensation scheme | 281 |
|---|---|---|
| | War Pensions scheme – Box M.5 | 282 |
| 2 | Who can claim? | 282 |
| | Far East prisoners of war – Box M.6 | 284 |
| 3 | How much can you get? | 282 |
| 4 | Survivor's benefits | 283 |
| 5 | Does anything affect what you get? | 284 |
| 6 | How do you claim? | 284 |
| 7 | Appeals | 284 |
| 8 | Extra help you can get | 285 |
| | For more information – Box M.7 | 284 |

## 1. Armed Forces Compensation scheme

The Armed Forces Compensation scheme (AFCS) provides compensation for injuries, illnesses or death caused by service on or after 6.4.05. The War Pensions scheme provides compensation for injuries, illnesses or death caused by service before this date – see Box M.5 for details.

As the AFCS is a 'no fault' scheme, an award would not stop you from making a civil claim for negligence against the Ministry of Defence. However, any award made by the AFCS would be taken into consideration by the courts when assessing damages.

If your AFCS claim is successful, you will receive a tax-free lump sum, assessed under a 15-level tariff system. The most serious injuries are graded as Level 1 and attract the highest payments, and the least severe injuries graded as Level 15. It is possible to receive the lump sum while still in service.

If your illness or injury is likely to cause a significant decrease in earning capacity, you will also receive a tax-free 'guaranteed income payment' (see 3 below). A 'survivor's guaranteed income payment' will be made to a surviving partner (including same-sex partners) where the service person's death was due to service. See 4 below.

## 2. Who can claim?

All members of HM armed forces (including Ghurkhas) are covered by the Armed Forces Compensation scheme (AFCS), even if they have chosen to remain in the 1975 Armed Forces Pension scheme. You can claim under the AFCS if you are a member of the reserve forces. Serving personnel are also covered.

You can get compensation for disablement or death due to incidents which were the direct consequence of your duties in the armed forces, including terrorism and warlike activities, or negligence by the Ministry of Defence as an employer.

You or your dependants can claim compensation for an attributable:

- death in service;
- injury or illness in service (whether or not resulting in a medical discharge);
- illness or death occurring within seven years of leaving service; *or*
- condition(s) or death that develop at a later date (eg some cancers), with no time limit. For details of the exceptions list of illnesses, ring the Veterans UK Helpline (0808 1914 218).

You can also claim for a pre-existing condition that is made significantly worse by service.

Generally, your injury, illness, death or disablement must occur while you are on duty. This can include injuries caused by service-related physical activities, including physical education, exercise and sport approved by the relevant service authorities.

You can get compensation in certain exceptional circumstances when you are off duty, eg if you were a victim of a terrorist attack and were targeted because of being a service person.

ARF(CS) Order, arts 7-13

## 3. How much can you get?

The level of an award is based on a tariff that lists the injuries for which compensation may be paid. The 15 tariff levels are graduated according to the seriousness of the condition.

### Lump-sum payments

A lump sum may be paid for pain and suffering, paid according to which of the 15 tariff levels applies to you. It can be awarded while you are still in service.

### Guaranteed income payment

A *'guaranteed income payment'* (GIP) for life, to compensate for loss of earnings, is payable to those whose injuries are assessed at tariff levels 1-11. It is calculated by multiplying your basic salary (excluding allowances) by a figure determined by your age. A younger claimant's pay would be multiplied by a higher figure, as they would have had longer until their retirement and their potential loss of earnings is therefore greater.

Once the GIP has been calculated, you will receive a percentage of the full GIP payment, depending on the tariff level of your illness or injury. The percentages fall into four bands:

| Tariffs | percentage of the GIP calculation |
| --- | --- |
| 1-4 (Band A) | 100% |
| 5-6 (Band B) | 75% |
| 7-8 (Band C) | 50% |
| 9-11 (Band D) | 30% |
| 12-15 | No GIP payable |

You cannot receive a GIP while in service, but it will be payable on discharge.

ARF(CS) Order, art 24

### Length of GIP awards

There is no regular review mechanism once a decision has been made and awards are intended to be full and final, taking into account the expected development of the illness or injury. However, if the long-term effect of an illness or injury is unclear, an interim award will be made, based on the appropriate tariff level at that time. This can be paid for up to two years before the condition is re-assessed, at which time the award can be confirmed, increased or lowered. Awards can be reviewed in exceptional circumstances, eg if the condition becomes worse than expected.

ARF(CS) Order, art 52

## M.5 War Pensions scheme

The War Pensions scheme remains in place for those with existing awards on 6.4.05, and for new claimants whose injury, ill health or bereavement was caused by service before 6.4.05. You do not need to have been on active service when the injury or illness was caused, providing it is linked to your time in service. You can also claim for illnesses suffered during service which have caused permanent damage, or pre-existing conditions which have worsened through service.

### Who can claim?

You can claim for any present disablement resulting from:

- an injury or condition caused or worsened by service in HM armed forces at any time including service in the Home Guard, Nursing and Auxiliary Services, the Ulster Defence Regiment from 1970 and the Territorial Army;
- a physical injury or disease sustained as a civilian during World War 2 as a result of enemy action;
- a physical injury or disease sustained while carrying out duties as a Civil Defence Volunteer in World War 2;
- an injury or condition caused or worsened by service during World War 2 in the Polish Forces under British Command or while serving in the Polish Resettlement Forces;
- certain injuries or illnesses sustained while serving in the Naval Auxiliary Services, Coastguard or Merchant Navy in World War 2, or conflicts in the Gulf, Falklands, Suez or Korea, or while being held prisoner.

### How much can you get?

The amount of your basic war pension depends on your degree of disability, assessed on a percentage basis as in the Industrial Injuries scheme (see Box M.2 in Chapter 46). If your assessment is 20% or more, a weekly pension is paid.

The maximum pension at the 100% rate is £185.40. If your assessment is less than 20%, you will receive a one-off lump-sum gratuity, unless the claim is for noise-induced sensorineural hearing loss. No payment can be made for sensorineural hearing loss alone, but if your assessment is 20% or more for the hearing loss, this can be added to your assessment for any other disability to increase the percentage you are awarded.

### Supplementary allowances

Tax-free supplementary allowances can be paid on top of your basic war pension or gratuity. Some allowances you have to claim, others are paid automatically. You need to make a claim for the following allowances:

- ❑ **War pensioners' mobility supplement**\* – This is paid if your pensioned disablement is assessed at 40% or more and is the sole or main cause of your walking difficulties.

## 4. Survivor's benefits

If your death is due to service, your surviving spouse, civil partner or any partner (including same-sex partners) who was in a *'substantial and exclusive relationship'* with you will be entitled to make a claim for survivor's benefits under the Armed Forces Pension scheme (AFPS). There are three types of such payment under the scheme: the survivor's guaranteed income payment, the bereavement grant and child payments.

ARF(CS)Order, art 30

### Survivor's guaranteed income payment

Your surviving partner will receive a *'survivor's guaranteed income payment'*, payable for life. This is calculated by multiplying your salary at the time of your death by a factor based on your age at the time of death; 60% of this figure is paid as the survivor's guaranteed income payment.

ARF(CS) Order, arts 29(1)(a) & 34

### Bereavement grant

Your surviving partner may also receive a tax-free *'bereavement grant'*, which will vary depending on the pension scheme you were in (AFPS 75, AFPS 05 or AFPS 15) and whether you were in service at the time of your death.

❏ If you die in service and were a member of AFPS 75, your partner will receive a grant of £25,000.

❏ If you die in service and were a member of AFPS 05 or AFPS 15, your partner will receive no grant if your salary was above £25,000. If your salary was below £25,000,

---

You will have an automatic entitlement if you have had a leg amputated and your pensioned disablement is assessed at 40% or more.

❏ **Constant attendance allowance**\* – This is paid if your pensioned disablement is assessed at 80% or more and causes you to need a lot of care, attention or supervision. It is paid at four different rates, which depend on the level of care you need.

❏ **Unemployability supplement**\* – This is paid if your pensioned disablement is assessed at 60% or more and consequently you are likely to be permanently unable to work. You must be under 65 when you first claim, but once awarded, it can continue to be paid after the age of 65. If you have reached the age of 65, you should receive a top-up from the DWP of the difference between the basic state pension and the unemployability supplement and comforts allowance (see below).

❏ **Allowance for lowered standard of occupation**\* – This is paid if your pensioned disablement is assessed at 40% or more and consequently you are unable to do your regular job or work of an equivalent standard.

❏ **Clothing allowance** – This is £239 a year, paid if your pensioned disablement is 20% or more and causes exceptional wear and tear to your clothing.

❏ **Treatment allowance** – This is paid if you have lost earnings due to having treatment at home or in hospital as a result of the pensioned disablement.

❏ **Rent allowance** – This can be paid to a surviving spouse or civil partner towards their accommodation costs if they are claiming a war widow's/widower's pension *and* a child allowance.

The following allowances are paid automatically:

❏ **Exceptionally severe disablement allowance** – This is paid if you receive constant attendance allowance at one of the two highest rates.

❏ **Severe disablement occupational allowance**\* – This is paid if you receive one of the two highest rates of constant attendance allowance, but you are normally in employment.

❏ **Comforts allowance** – This is paid if you receive unemployability supplement and/or constant attendance allowance.

❏ **Age allowance** – This is paid when you turn 65 if your disablement is assessed at 40% or more.

\* These allowances overlap with state benefits of a similar nature, so you will not be paid both at the same time.

### War widow's or widower's pension

A pension can be paid if your spouse/civil partner's death was due to, or substantially hastened by, an illness or injury for which they were either receiving a war pension or to which they would have been entitled had they claimed. You can also claim if your spouse/civil partner was receiving constant attendance allowance at any rate (or would have been had they not been in hospital) or if they were receiving unemployability supplement and their pensionable disablement was assessed at 80% or more.

You cannot be paid a war widow's/widower's pension as well as a national insurance bereavement benefit or widow's pension, but a war widow's/widower's pension is tax free and normally paid at a higher rate. You can also get benefits based on your own national insurance contributions, eg state pension or contributory employment and support allowance.

### The benefit cap and universal credit

The benefit cap (which limits the total weekly benefits that can be claimed; see Chapter 16(10) and Box G.6 in Chapter 25) does not apply to households in which someone is receiving a war pension or a war widow's/widower's pension.

Under universal credit, war pensions and war widow's/widower's pensions are not taken into account as income.

### How do you claim?

To make a claim, contact Veterans UK (see Chapter 47(6)). There is no time limit for claiming and you can claim for any illness or injury, providing you can show a link between that illness or injury and your service. However, you will usually only receive an award from the date of your claim and, if your claim is made more than seven years after leaving the forces, the burden of proof will be on you to show that the illness or injury was caused by service. You cannot make a claim while still serving in the forces.

For illness or injury caused by service on or after 6.4.05, you need to claim under the Armed Forces Compensation scheme instead (see Chapter 47).

### Challenging the decision

Decisions on war pensions can be reviewed at any time, which means that if your condition deteriorates, you can request a review of your assessment. However, the assessment could be reduced as well as increased, so you could end up with a smaller payment.

If you are not happy with the level of award, the date from which the award will run, the refusal of an award, or any changes to the amount or period of the award, you can appeal to a War Pensions and Armed Forces Compensation Tribunal in England and Wales. In Scotland and Northern Ireland, the appeal is made to the Pensions Appeal Tribunal of that country. See 7 in this chapter for details of the appeal process.

It is important that you get help with a reconsideration or appeal. Some ex-service organisations like The Royal British Legion can help prepare your case and represent you at the tribunal (0808 802 8080). Alternatively, an advice centre may be able to help.

your partner will receive a grant for the difference between your salary and £25,000.

❏ If your service ended before your death, your partner will receive a grant of £37,500, regardless of your pension scheme.

A bereavement grant can be paid to an eligible child if you do not leave a surviving partner. Where there is more than one eligible child, the grant will be divided equally between them.
ARF(CS)Order, arts 29(1)(b)&(6) and 35

### Child payments
Dependent children will qualify for *'child payments'*, which will stop when they reach the age of 18. They may continue to qualify for child payments after that age if they are in full-time education or vocational training and are aged under 23. They may also continue to qualify if they are unable to engage in paid work due to a mental or physical impairment and were dependent on you at the time of your death.
ARF(CS) Order, arts 29(1)(c), 31, 32 & 36

### 5. Does anything affect what you get?
The level of your award is not affected by state benefits, capital or income (other than your salary, insofar as it is used to calculate guaranteed income payment (GIP)). If you have already received compensation for the injury or illness through the civil courts, this will be taken into account when assessing your award. Payments received under the Armed Forces Pension scheme will also affect the amount of GIP.

### Social security benefits and tax credits
If you are receiving a GIP, other state benefits may be affected. For means-tested benefits (income support, income-based jobseeker's allowance, income-related employment and support allowance and pension credit), the first £10 of your GIP is disregarded, but the rest is treated as income. The same disregard applies to housing benefit, although local authorities have the discretion to apply a 100% disregard, which means that none of the GIP is treated as income. Most authorities apply a 100% disregard, but this varies as the matter is under constant review and revised from time to time.

For tax credits, the entire GIP is normally disregarded as income. However, a survivor's GIP only attracts a disregard of £300 a year and the remaining amount is treated as income.

A lump sum paid under the AFCS is treated as capital for means-tested benefits and no disregard is applied.

Under universal credit, a GIP or a survivor's GIP is completely disregarded.

If you are receiving a GIP, your household will normally be exempt from the benefit cap (see Chapter 16(10) and Box G.6 in Chapter 25). However, if you are living with parents or friends, the exemption will not apply to them (as the exemption only applies to you, your partner or your children).

### 6. How do you claim?
To get a claim-form, ring the Veterans UK Helpline (0808 1914 218), write to Veterans UK, Norcross, Thornton-Cleveleys FY5 3WP or go to www.gov.uk/government/organisations/veterans-uk.

You must complete a claim form within seven years of:
■ the incident that caused or worsened your injury; *or*
■ the date you sought medical advice for an illness; *or*
■ leaving the service, if the illness or injury was not due to a particular incident.

There are exceptions to these time limits if you have a late-onset condition. The scheme also allows for some discretion when dealing with exceptional circumstances.

Dependants' benefits are not normally awarded if your death occurs more than seven years after leaving service. If you die in service or within seven years of leaving service, the normal rule is that a claim must be made within three years of your death.
ARF(CS) Order, arts 46-49

### What happens after you claim?
Veterans UK will check your service records, if appropriate, to decide if you come within the scheme. If you do, the cause and the degree of your disability will be decided by Veterans UK doctors after medical evidence has been obtained. The cause of the illness or injury is decided using the 'balance of probabilities' standard of proof, meaning the claim will be successful if it is more likely than not that it was due to service.
ARF(CS) Order, art 61

### 7. Appeals
The Armed Forces Compensation scheme (AFCS) has a 3-stage appeal process.
**Reconsideration** – Apply for a reconsideration in writing within 12 months of your AFCS decision, giving reasons why you think the decision is wrong. You can provide further information or evidence relating to your injury or illness to back up your case.
**Appeal to an independent tribunal** – Apply within 12 months of your AFCS decision or the date of a reconsidered decision. Use the appeal form, which is available at www.gov.uk/government/publications/war-pension-and-afcs-notice-of-appeal or by ringing 0808 1914 218.

Once they receive your appeal, Veterans UK may reconsider the decision and amend the award, or may refer it to the tribunal. In England and Wales, your appeal will be heard by the War Pensions and Armed Forces Compensation Tribunal; Scotland and Northern Ireland have separate Pensions Appeal Tribunals. These are independent of Veterans UK.

If the case goes to the tribunal, The Royal British Legion can provide representation and assistance (see Box M.7). Some decisions do not carry a right of appeal and, in such

---

### M.6 Far East prisoners of war

Tax-free lump-sum payments of £10,000 can be claimed by former prisoners of the Japanese during World War 2, or by their widows or widowers. Former members of the forces, civilians and some members of the colonial forces are included. The payment is disregarded indefinitely for means-tested benefits (including universal credit) and there is no time limit for claiming. For details and claim-forms ring the Veterans UK Helpline (0808 191 4218) or go to www.gov.uk/guidance/pensions-and-compensation-for-veterans.

---

### M.7 For more information

#### Veterans UK Helpline
Ring the Veterans UK Helpline (0808 191 4218) to enquire about the Armed Forces Compensation scheme or the War Pensions scheme and to get claim-forms and leaflets. Information is also available at www.gov.uk/government/organisations/veterans-uk.

#### The Royal British Legion
The Royal British Legion provides advice and support on a number of matters including the Armed Forces Compensation scheme, war pensions, benefits, debt advice, care homes, resettlement, training, employment and remembrance travel. Contact them on 0808 802 8080 or www.britishlegion.org.uk.

cases, the tribunal will decide the appeal cannot be heard. There is no further right of appeal.

**Appeal to an Upper Tribunal** – A further appeal can be made to an Upper Tribunal on a point of law (in Northern Ireland appeals will go to the Pensions Appeal Commissioners). It is not sufficient that you think the tribunal made the wrong decision – you must be able to show there was a legal error in the way the decision was reached (see Box O.11, Chapter 57).

To appeal to the Upper Tribunal, contact the tribunal's office in writing within six weeks of the decision, explaining why you disagree with their decision. The tribunal can review the original decision, place the matter for appeal before the Upper Tribunal, or refuse your application to appeal further. If the tribunal turns down your application, you can apply directly to the Upper Tribunal. See Chapter 57(18) for more on appeals to the Upper Tribunal.

### 8. Extra help you can get
**State benefits**
Unlike the old War Pensions scheme, the Armed Forces Compensation scheme does not carry supplementary allowances. However, this allows you to claim the corresponding social security benefits (see the benefits checklist on pages 4 and 5).

A guaranteed income payment will not affect contributory benefits. Therefore, if you are unable to work because of a service-related injury, you could claim contributory employment and support allowance (see Chapter 11(18)-(27)).

**Armed forces independence payment**
The armed forces independence payment (AFIP) is an alternative to personal independence payment (PIP). If you are not eligible for AFIP, you can claim PIP instead (see Chapter 5).

You are eligible for the AFIP if you receive a guaranteed income payment of 50% or more (see 3 above). If you are eligible, you will not need an additional medical assessment to receive the AFIP and you will not need to undergo regular re-assessments to keep getting it.

The amount payable is £145.35 a week, which is equivalent to the enhanced rates of the mobility and daily living components of PIP.

The AFIP is tax free and can be paid anywhere in the world. It is not stopped if you are in hospital (excepting the Royal Chelsea Hospital), a care home or prison.

Contact the Veterans UK Helpline (0808 1914 218) for more on the AFIP.
ARF(CS) Order, arts 24A-24F

# 48 Criminal injuries compensation

| | | |
|---|---|---|
| 1 | Who can claim? | 285 |
| 2 | How do you claim? | 286 |
| 3 | How much do you get? | 286 |
| 4 | How is your claim decided? | 286 |
| 5 | If you don't agree with the decision | 287 |
| 6 | If your condition changes | 287 |
| | For more information – Box M.8 | 286 |

## 1. Who can claim?
You may be eligible for a payment from the Criminal Injuries Compensation Authority if you sustain an injury directly attributable to you being a direct victim of a crime of violence in Great Britain or in certain listed offshore situations.
Criminal Injuries Compensation Scheme, para 8 & Annex C

A crime of violence includes:
■ a physical attack;
■ any other violent act or omission which causes physical injury to you;
■ a threat against you that would make a person of reasonable firmness fear immediate violence;
■ a sexual assault; *or*
■ arson.
Criminal Injuries Compensation Scheme, para 4 & Annex B, para 2

You can claim compensation if you are injured when trying to stop someone from committing a crime, or trying to stop a suspected criminal, or helping the police to do so. In such cases, the injury must be directly attributable to your taking an exceptional and justified risk; the risk will not be considered exceptional if it would normally be expected of you in the course of your work.
Criminal Injuries Compensation Scheme, para 5

You may be eligible to make a claim for a mental injury if you were present at and witnessed an incident in which a loved one sustained a criminal injury or if you were involved in the immediate aftermath of such an incident.
Criminal Injuries Compensation Scheme, para 6

You can claim compensation even if your assailant has not been convicted.
Criminal Injuries Compensation Scheme, para 9

You will be eligible for a payment only if you were 'ordinarily resident' in the UK on the date of the incident or you meet certain nationality requirements, such as being a British citizen or EU national or a member of the armed forces or an accompanying close relative.
Criminal Injuries Compensation Scheme, paras 10-16

Compensation will be reduced or withheld unless the Authority is satisfied that you:
■ reported the incident to the police as soon as reasonably practicable, taking into consideration your age, capacity and the effect of the incident on you;
■ co-operated as far as reasonably practicable in bringing the assailant to justice;
■ took all reasonable steps to assist with the application; *and*
■ are of good character and have no unspent convictions.
Compensation may be reduced or withheld if your conduct before, during or after the incident makes it inappropriate to make an award or a full award. In this case, conduct does not include intoxication through alcohol or drugs to the extent that such intoxication made you more vulnerable to becoming a victim of a crime of violence.
Criminal Injuries Compensation Scheme, paras 22-27 & Annex D

**Violence within the family** – If you and your assailant were living together as members of the same family, you can apply for compensation provided that:
■ you were injured on or after 1.10.79; *and*
■ where you and the assailant were both adults, you no longer live together and are unlikely to do so again.
Compensation will not be payable unless the Authority is satisfied that the assailant will not benefit from the award.
Criminal Injuries Compensation Scheme, paras 19, 20 & 21

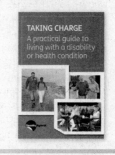

## 2. How do you claim?

You can apply online (www.gov.uk/claim-compensation-criminal-injury) or on the helpline (0300 003 3601). You can apply for compensation even if your assailant is unknown or has not yet been arrested.

Applications should be made as soon as possible after the incident and must normally be received by the Criminal Injuries Compensation Authority within two years of the date of the incident. This time limit may be extended only in exceptional circumstances and where it is clear that the application can be determined without further extensive enquiries; reasons for any delay should be provided with the application.
Criminal Injuries Compensation Scheme, paras 87-89

Responsibility for making a case for compensation lies with you, which means that you need to provide the Authority with the evidence necessary to decide your case. Where appropriate, the Authority will ask you to provide medical evidence. If there are costs involved in obtaining the evidence, you may be expected to meet them. The cost of obtaining medical evidence will vary, but you will not be expected to pay more than £50 in total.
Criminal Injuries Compensation Scheme, paras 92-97

## 3. How much do you get?

Compensation is made up of several possible elements.

❏ **For the injury itself** – A fixed sum assessed by reference to a tariff that groups together injuries of comparable severity and allocates a sum of compensation to them. The Criminal Injuries Compensation Authority will consider the medical information on your injury and decide where in the tariff your injury features.
Criminal Injuries Compensation Scheme, paras 32-41 & Annex E

❏ **Loss of earnings** – No compensation is paid for the first 28 weeks of lost earnings. Beyond that, loss of earnings and/or earning potential incurred as a direct consequence of the injury will be compensated at the rate of statutory sick pay (see Chapter 10(6)), subject to certain rules – eg you must have no or very limited capacity for paid work as a direct result of the injury.
Criminal Injuries Compensation Scheme, paras 42-49 & Annex F

❏ **Special expenses** – Examples of these include care and supervision costs, the cost of equipment such as a wheelchair, and costs towards medical, dental or optical treatment. To qualify, you must have lost earnings or earnings capacity (or if not normally employed, be incapacitated to a similar extent) for more than 28 weeks. The award will be calculated from the date of injury. You must also be able to prove that the goods or services are not available free of charge from another source.
Criminal Injuries Compensation Scheme, paras 50-56

### Compensation if the victim has died

If someone has died as a result of a criminal injury, compensation may be made to a qualifying relative in the form of a *'bereavement payment'*, a *'child's payment'* or a *'dependency payment'*. A *'qualifying relative'* is a person who, at the time of the deceased's death, was their:

■ spouse or civil partner, living with them in the same household;*

■ partner (other than a spouse or civil partner), living with them in the same household and had done so for a continuous period of at least two years immediately before the date of the death;*

■ spouse or civil partner, or a former spouse or civil partner, who was financially dependent on them;

■ parent; *or*

■ child.

\* or who did not live with the deceased because of either person's ill-health or infirmity
Criminal Injuries Compensation Scheme, paras 57 & 59

**Bereavement payment** – If you are a qualifying relative and were not divorced or estranged from the deceased at the time of death, you may be eligible for a bereavement payment. This is a fixed sum of £11,000 if you are the only qualifying relative, or £5,500 for each person who qualifies.
Criminal Injuries Compensation Scheme, paras 61-62

**Child's payment** – You may be eligible for a child's payment if the child is a qualifying relative who was under 18 at the time of the deceased's death and dependent on them for parental services. The amount of a child's payment is £2,000 for each year, proportionally reduced for part years, up to the child's 18th birthday. The Authority may also pay an additional amount for such 'reasonable' expenses incurred by the child as a direct result of the loss of parental services.
Criminal Injuries Compensation Scheme, paras 63-66 & Annex F

**Dependency payment** – A dependency payment may be made to a qualifying relative who, at the time of the deceased's death, was financially or physically dependent on them. The amount payable is based on the rate of statutory sick pay and depends on various factors, including the number of dependants.
Criminal Injuries Compensation Scheme, paras 67-74 & Annex F

### Funeral expenses

If a person has died as a result of a criminal injury, a funeral payment may be made towards their funeral expenses for the benefit of their estate. This is normally set at £2,500 but may be increased to cover *'expenses reasonably incurred'*, up to a further £2,500.
Criminal Injuries Compensation Scheme, paras 75-77

### Compensation from the courts

The full amount of a compensation payment for personal injury or damages made by a civil or criminal court for the same injury (less any amount of 'recoverable' benefit – see Chapter 50) is deducted from an award under the scheme.
Criminal Injuries Compensation Scheme, para 85

## 4. How is your claim decided?

The Criminal Injuries Compensation Authority's staff will look at your application to check that the information you have given is correct. When you apply, you are asked to

---

## M.8 For more information

The Criminal Injuries Compensation Authority publishes a digital guide (www.gov.uk/guidance/criminal-injuries-compensation-a-guide) to the Criminal Injuries Compensation scheme.

Victim Support is an independent national charity for people affected by crime. Contact your local Victim Support scheme for help (0808 168 9111).

### Traffic accidents

If you are the victim of an uninsured or untraced motorist, there is a different scheme for compensation for personal injuries. This is run by the Motor Insurers' Bureau (MIB), established by motor insurers, which has agreements with the government to provide that compensation. Compensation is worked out in the same way as for common law damages. If the driver cannot be traced, you should report the accident to the police within 14 days for personal injury or five days for damage to personal property. You must apply to the MIB within three years of the accident for personal injury or six years (five years in Scotland) if the claim is just for property or vehicle damage. For details, ring 0190 883 0001 (www.mib.org.uk).

consent to the Authority contacting the police, your doctor, your employer or any other relevant person, to obtain confirmation of the incident, your injuries, loss of earnings, etc. They may ask you for other details. In some cases, you might be asked to undergo a medical examination by a health professional chosen by the Authority.

The Authority's staff will decide if you come within the scheme, and, if so, will assess the amount of compensation. You will be sent a written decision. You must reply in writing within 56 days and accept the decision before any payment is made. If the award has been reduced or disallowed, you will be given reasons.

### 5. If you don't agree with the decision

If you are unhappy with the decision, you can apply, in writing, for a review. The Authority must receive your request within 56 days of the date of the letter notifying you of the decision. The 56-day time limit can be extended if you can show there are exceptional circumstances that justify the granting of an extension; the request must be made in writing.

Your review application must be supported by reasons, together with any additional evidence. Reviews involve a full reconsideration of eligibility and the amount of the award, which could result in your award being increased, unchanged, reduced or withdrawn.

After the review, if you are still dissatisfied with the decision, you can appeal to a First-tier Tribunal (see Chapter 57).

Criminal Injuries Compensation Scheme, paras 117-134

### 6. If your condition changes

The Criminal Injuries Compensation Authority can re-open your case if you received an award but your medical condition has deteriorated to the extent that the original assessment is unjust given your present condition. It can also re-open a case where a person has since died as a result of the injury. If you apply more than two years after the original decision, it is important to give as much information and medical evidence as you can with your application; the Authority will only consider the application if it has enough evidence without needing to make further extensive enquiries.

Criminal Injuries Compensation Scheme, paras 114-116

# 49 Vaccine damage payments

| 1 | What is the Vaccine Damage scheme? | 287 |
|---|---|---|
| 2 | Who qualifies? | 287 |
| 3 | What is 'severe disablement'? | 287 |
| 4 | How do you claim? | 287 |
| 5 | What if you are refused? | 288 |
| 6 | Does it affect other benefits? | 288 |

### 1. What is the Vaccine Damage scheme?

The Vaccine Damage scheme provides a tax-free lump sum of £120,000 for someone who is (or was immediately before death) severely disabled as a result of vaccination against specific diseases.

### 2. Who qualifies?

A payment can be made to someone who has been severely disabled as a result of vaccination against:

- diphtheria;
- haemophilus influenzae-type B (HIB);
- human papillomavirus;
- influenza (except for influenza caused by a pandemic influenza virus);
- measles;
- meningococcal groups B, C and W (meningitis B, C and W);
- mumps;
- pandemic influenza A (H1N1) 2009 virus (swine flu; vaccination up to 31.8.10);
- pertussis (whooping cough);
- pneumococcal infection;
- poliomyelitis;
- rotavirus;
- rubella (German measles);
- smallpox (vaccination up to 1.8.71);
- tetanus; *or*
- tuberculosis.

Claims can be made on the basis of combination vaccines, eg diphtheria, tetanus and pertussis (DTP), measles and rubella (MR), measles, mumps and rubella (MMR), and the five-in-one vaccine.

People damaged before birth as a result of vaccinations given to their mothers during pregnancy are included in the scheme, as are those who have contracted polio through contact with someone who was vaccinated against it using an oral vaccine.

The claimant must also meet the following conditions.

- ❑ The vaccination must have been given in the UK or Isle of Man (except for serving members of the armed forces and their immediate families vaccinated outside the UK as part of service medical facilities).
- ❑ The vaccination must have been given either when the claimant was aged under 18 (except for rubella, poliomyelitis, meningococcal group C, meningococcal group W*, pandemic influenza A (H1N1) 2009 virus and human papillomavirus) or at a time of an outbreak of the disease within the UK or Isle of Man.
- ❑ The claimant must be over the age of 2 on the date of the claim, or, if they have died, they must have been over the age of 2 when they died.
- ❑ The claim can be made at any time up to and including the claimant's 21st birthday, or, if they have died, the date on which they would have attained that age, or up to six years after the date of the vaccination, whichever date is later.
- ❑ In the case of someone who contracted poliomyelitis through contact with someone who was vaccinated against it, they must have been *'in close physical contact'* with the other person during the period of 60 days that began on the 4th day after the vaccination. They must also have been looking after the vaccinated person or been looked after jointly with them.

* in this case, the claimant must have been aged under 26

VDPA, Ss.1-3 & VDP Regs, regs 5-5A

### 3. What is 'severe disablement'?

A person is considered severely disabled if the disablement due to vaccination damage is assessed at 60% or more. Disablement is assessed in the same way as for industrial injuries disablement benefit (see Box M.2 in Chapter 46).

VDPA, S.1(4)

### 4. How do you claim?

You can claim using claim-form VAD1A, which you can get by ringing 01772 899 944 (textphone: 0345 604 5312) or by downloading it from: www.gov.uk/vaccine-damage-payment/how-to-claim. Send your completed form to: Vaccine Damage Payments Unit, Palatine House, Lancaster Road, Preston, Lancashire PR1 1HB.

Don't delay claiming. If you have supporting medical evidence, send a copy with the claim, otherwise the Vaccine Damage Payments Unit will obtain medical evidence on your behalf. If the disabled person is aged under 18, the claim should be made by the parents or guardian.

## 5. What if you are refused?

If your claim is refused, you will be sent a written decision with reasons. If you disagree with this decision, you can ask the DWP to reconsider it.

**Reconsiderations** – If you want a reconsideration of a DWP decision (technically called a 'reversal'), write to the Vaccine Damage Payments Unit (see 4 above) requesting a reconsideration and giving reasons why you think the decision is wrong. You may do this at any time. You can provide new evidence in support of your request.

If you want a reconsideration of a tribunal decision, you may only do this within six years of the date you were notified of the original decision or within two years of the date you were notified of the tribunal decision, if that is later.

In either case, if you disagree with the reconsidered decision, you can appeal to a First-tier Tribunal (see below).

If the DWP has made a payment, they can reconsider the decision at any time if they have reason to believe there was a misrepresentation or non-disclosure of relevant information.

**Appeals** – You can appeal to a First-tier Tribunal, but only if you have already requested a reconsideration of the decision (as above) and have received notification of the reconsidered decision. The appeals process is described in Chapter 57.

VDPA, Ss.3A-5 & VDP Regs, regs 11 & 11A

## 6. Does it affect other benefits?

The capital value of a vaccine damage payment held in a trust fund is disregarded for income-related employment and support allowance (ESA), income support, income-based jobseeker's allowance (JSA), housing benefit and universal credit. If the payment is not held in a trust fund, its capital value can be disregarded for up to 52 weeks from the date you receive it, to allow you time to set up a trust. After that it will be taken fully into account.

Any regular payments made from the trust fund to or for the disabled person are disregarded for income-related ESA, income support, income-based JSA, housing benefit and universal credit. Other lump-sum payments will be treated as capital and will reduce benefit if the payments bring the total capital above the lower capital limit (see Chapters 17(17) and 22(25)).

# 50 Compensation recovery

| | | |
|---|---|---|
| 1 | Compensation recovery | 288 |
| 2 | Benefits that can be recovered | 288 |
| 3 | Exempted payments | 289 |
| 4 | Lump-sum payments | 289 |
| 5 | Challenging decisions | 289 |
| | For more information – Box M.9 | 289 |

## 1. Compensation recovery

If, as a result of an accident, injury or disease, you claim compensation, the person or organisation that pays the compensation (the *'compensator'*) is liable to pay damages to you and repay benefits to the DWP via the Compensation Recovery Unit (CRU). The compensator can deduct some or all of the amount they have to pay to you from the gross compensation award, a practice known as *'offsetting'*.

It is not the actual benefits that are recovered, but an amount equivalent to the total amount of *'recoverable'* benefits paid as a result of your accident, injury or disease. Not all social security benefits are recoverable, as some are paid for reasons that have no connection to the compensation claim. Recoverable benefits are listed in 2 below.

Social security benefits are not paid in respect of pain, suffering, personal inconvenience and so on, and therefore no offsetting can be made against the general damages element of your compensation award.

Social Security (Recovery of Benefits) Act 1997

**The period of recovery** – In cases involving accidents and injuries, benefits are recoverable from the day following the accident or injury for a period of five years, or up to the date the claim is settled, whichever is earlier. In disease cases, the 5-year recovery period begins on the date on which a recoverable benefit is first claimed as a consequence of the disease.

Social Security (Recovery of Benefits) Act 1997, S.3

### The certificate

Before a compensation payment is made, the compensator must request a certificate from the CRU. This certificate lists the recoverable benefits that have been paid. The CRU will issue a certificate to the compensator and send a copy to you (or your solicitor), so that both parties can estimate the extent of any potential offsetting. Since offsetting can greatly affect the size of the net compensation award, both sides should take it into account when conducting negotiations.

Social Security (Recovery of Benefits) Act 1997, S.4

**Reviews** – You and the compensator have the right to request a review of a certificate at any time if either of you believe that the calculation shown on the certificate is incorrect or that benefits have been included which were not paid as a consequence of the accident, injury or disease. However, the next stages in challenging a certificate (mandatory reconsideration and appeal) can be made only after the final compensation payment has been made and the total amount of recoverable benefit has been repaid to the CRU. See 5 below for details on mandatory reconsiderations and appeals.

Social Security (Recovery of Benefits) Act 1997, S.10; D&A Regs, reg 9

## 2. Benefits that can be recovered

Compensation can be reduced to take account of benefits paid for the following:

- **loss of earnings** – employment and support allowance (ESA), industrial injuries disablement benefit, incapacity benefit, income support, invalidity benefit, jobseeker's allowance, reduced earnings allowance, severe disablement allowance, sickness benefit, statutory sick pay (paid before 6.4.94), unemployment benefit, unemployability supplement, universal credit;
- **cost of care** – attendance allowance, disability living allowance (DLA) care component, personal independence payment (PIP) daily living component, constant attendance allowance, exceptionally severe disablement allowance;
- **loss of mobility** – DLA and PIP mobility component, mobility allowance.

In making an order for a compensation payment, the court must specify how much is to be awarded under each of these three headings.

Social Security (Recovery of Benefits) Act 1997, Sch 2

*Example: offsetting*
A compensation award is agreed.

The award consists of:

| | |
|---|---|
| General damages | £40,000 |
| Loss of earnings | £30,000 |
| Loss of mobility | £30,000 |
| *Compensation award:* | *£100,000* |

The CRU certificate lists the following recoverable benefits:

| | |
|---|---|
| ESA totalling | £15,000 |
| PIP mobility component totalling | £10,000 |
| *Recoverable benefits:* | *£25,000* |

The compensator cannot offset against the general damages element of the award, but may offset the ESA paid against the loss of earnings heading. They therefore deduct £15,000 from this, leaving £15,000 to be paid to the injured person. Similarly, the compensator may offset the £10,000 of PIP paid against the loss of mobility heading, leaving £20,000 to be paid to the injured person. The injured person has settled their claim for a total of £100,000. Following offsetting, they receive £75,000 from the compensator, having already received £25,000 in recoverable benefits from the DWP.

## 3. Exempted payments

Some compensation payments are exempt from the recovery rules. They are:
- vaccine damage payments;
- Criminal Injuries Compensation scheme payments (but see Chapter 48(3));
- payments from the Macfarlane and Eileen Trusts, MFET Ltd, the Caxton Foundation and the Skipton Fund;
- payments from an approved blood scheme;
- payments from an approved Thalidomide relief and assistance trust;
- payments from the UK Asbestos and EL Scheme Trusts;
- payments from the government-funded trust for people with variant Creutzfeldt-Jakob disease;
- payments from the London Bombings Relief Charitable Fund;
- payments under the Fatal Accidents Act 1976;
- contractual sick pay from an employer;
- payments made under the NHS Industrial Injuries scheme;
- payments made to the injured person by an insurer under the terms of an insurance contract agreed before:
  - the date on which the injured person first claims a recoverable benefit in consequence of the disease in question; or
  - the occurrence of the accident or injury in question;
- payments under the NCB Pneumoconiosis Compensation scheme; and
- payments for sensorineural hearing loss of less than 50dB in one or both ears.

Social Security (Recovery of Benefits) Act 1997, Sch 1(5); The Social Security (Recovery of Benefits) Regs, reg 2

## 4. Lump-sum payments

The compensator can reduce any part of your compensation award (including damages paid for pain and suffering) if you have had a lump-sum payment under:
- the Pneumoconiosis etc. (Workers' Compensation) Act 1979 (including any extra-statutory payments made following the rejection of a claim under that Act);
- the 2008 Diffuse Mesothelioma scheme; or
- the 2014 Diffuse Mesothelioma Payment scheme.

The Social Security (Recovery of Benefits)(Lump Sum Payments) Regs 2008

## 5. Challenging decisions

### Mandatory reconsiderations

If your compensation payment has been reduced to take account of benefit recovery and you think the certificate is wrong, you can contact the Compensation Recovery Unit (CRU) and ask them for a mandatory reconsideration of the decision. You should send them copies of letters you have received from the compensator telling you the compensation payment has been reduced. You should request the mandatory reconsideration within one month of the date the compensator makes the final payment to the CRU. You will receive notification of the result of the reconsideration: the *'mandatory reconsideration notice'*.

Social Security (Recovery of Benefits) Act 1997, S.10

### Appeals

If you disagree with the reconsidered decision, you can appeal to a First-tier Tribunal. You cannot appeal unless you have received the mandatory reconsideration notice. You must appeal within one month of being sent the notice; if you apply late you must show that there are special reasons for the delay. Use appeal form SSCS3 (http://hmctsformfinder.justice.gov.uk/HMCTS/GetForm.do?court_forms_id=4395). You must explain which of the four following reasons apply in your case:
- an amount, rate or period specified in the certificate is wrong; or
- the certificate shows benefits or lump sums that were not paid as a result of the accident, injury or disease for which compensation was paid; or
- benefits or lump sums listed have been included that have not been, and are not likely to be, paid to you; or
- the compensation payment made was not due to the accident, injury or disease.

You need to include a copy of the mandatory reconsideration notice with your appeal.

Social Security (Recovery of Benefits) Act 1997, Ss.11&12; D&A Regs, reg 9ZB

***Warning:*** A tribunal dealing with an appeal against recovery is entitled to decide whether or not the benefits recovered were in fact paid because of the accident, injury or disease. Both the tribunal's decision and the evidence on which it is based can potentially raise doubts about entitlement to those benefits. Consequently, it would be wise to seek advice before lodging an appeal.

R(CR)2/02

## M.9 For more information

Further information can be found in the guide CRU27, *Compensation, social security benefits and lump sum payments*, which can be downloaded from the Compensation Recovery Unit (CRU) website (www.gov.uk/government/publications/compensation-social-security-benefits-and-lump-sum-payments-technical-guide).

Technical guidance can be found at: www.gov.uk/government/publications/recovery-of-benefits-and-or-lump-sum-payments-and-nhs-charges-technical-guidance/recovery-of-benefits-and-lump-sum-payments-and-nhs-charges-technical-guidance

## Disability Rights UK training

### Disability Confidence

We provide a range of training and consultancy opportunities that can bring about measurable change for your organisation through inclusive culture and practices. Our courses can help you to improve disability equality within your organisation as well as enhance the experience of customers and service users.

We offer bespoke training and consultancy to the public, private and voluntary sectors. This can range from tailored versions of our disability awareness courses, to consultancy around web accessibility testing, policy review and recommendations for focus group recruitment and leadership.

All of our courses are delivered by people with lived experience of disability or health conditions.

To find out more or get details of our next course, visit **www.disabilityrightsuk.org/how-we-can-help**

# Other matters

This section of the handbook looks at:

After a death     Chapter **51**

Health benefits     Chapter **52**

# 51 After a death

| | | |
|---|---|---|
| 1 | What to do after a death | 290 |
| 2 | Income-related benefits | 290 |
| 3 | Bereavement support payment | 290 |
| 4 | Bereavement benefits before 6.4.17 | 291 |
| 5 | Widowed before 9.4.01 | 291 |
| 6 | What happens to other benefits? | 291 |
| 7 | Death of a child | 292 |

## 1. What to do after a death

Following a death there can be many practical issues to deal with. This process, combined with the emotional effects of bereavement, can be difficult to cope with. You can get practical help and advice from a funeral director, GP, solicitor, religious organisation, social care department or Citizens Advice. A health visitor or district nurse may help if the death was at home. If the death was in hospital, the ward sister or hospital chaplain might help. One of the first things you may need to do is transfer insurance policies (eg car and home insurance) into your name.

If you need support and comfort, there are organisations that can help – for example, Cruse Bereavement Care (helpline: 0808 808 1677; www.cruse.org.uk), Cruse Bereavement Care Scotland (helpline: 0845 600 2227; www.crusescotland.org.uk) and Winston's Wish, which offers a service to bereaved children and their families (0808 802 0021; www.winstonswish.org.uk).

**Social fund funeral expenses** – If you receive income-related employment and support allowance, income support, income-based jobseeker's allowance, housing benefit, pension credit, working tax credit (that includes the disabled worker or severe disability element), child tax credit (that includes a child element or disabled child element) or universal credit, you may be able to get a payment from the social fund for funeral expenses (see Chapter 29(3)).

## 2. Income-related benefits

If you are below pension credit qualifying age (see Chapter 44(2)) and on a low income, you may be able to get income-related employment and support allowance (ESA), income support or income-based jobseeker's allowance (JSA), depending on your circumstances. See Chapters 18, 19 and 20 respectively. For each of these benefits, £10 a week of widowed parent's or widowed mother's allowance is disregarded in the assessment of your income. In some areas, you may need to claim universal credit instead (see Box E.1 in Chapter 14). If you have reached pension credit qualifying age, see Chapter 44 for details of that benefit.

**Late claims** – If your claim for income support or JSA is late and it was not reasonable to expect you to claim earlier because of the death of your partner, parent, son, daughter, brother or sister, your claim can be backdated for up to one month (see Chapter 56(3)).

**Carers** – If you are getting carer's allowance or income support because you have been caring for the person who has died, your benefit can continue for up to eight weeks following their death (see Chapter 9(8)). The carer premium

in other means-tested benefits may also continue for up to eight weeks (see Chapter 21(6)). The carer amount in universal credit can continue for the remainder of the monthly assessment period in which the person you cared for died, and for the following two assessment periods (see Chapter 16(7)).

**Housing costs** – If you have a mortgage and are claiming income-related ESA, income support, income-based JSA, pension credit or universal credit, you may be entitled to help towards the mortgage with 'support for mortgage interest loans'. If you are eligible for pension credit, you can get this help straightaway; for other benefits, there is a 39-week qualifying period (or nine monthly assessment periods for universal credit) before the loans can be paid. See Chapter 26.

**Rent and council tax** – Housing benefit helps towards rent if you are on a low income. In the assessment of your income, £15 a week of widowed parent's or widowed mother's allowance is disregarded. See Chapter 25. For help towards rent if you are claiming universal credit, see Chapter 24. For help towards council tax, see Chapter 28.

**Pension arrears** – If your spouse or civil partner was receiving pension credit or state pension (or any other benefit combined for payment with these), arrears of these benefits can automatically be paid to you on their death without the need for a claim.

## 3. Bereavement support payment

*'Bereavement support payment'* is a benefit available to people whose spouse or civil partner dies on or after 6.4.17. It replaced three earlier bereavement benefits: 'bereavement payment', 'bereavement allowance' and 'widowed parent's allowance'. Widowed parent's allowance remains in place if your spouse or civil partner died before 6.4.17 (see 4 below). For women widowed before 9.4.01, 'widow's pension' and 'widowed mother's allowance' remain in place (see 5 below).

### Do you qualify?

To qualify for bereavement support payment, your spouse or civil partner must have paid Class 1 or 2 national insurance contributions on earnings in any one tax year equal to 25 times the lower earnings limit for that year (see Chapter 11(24)). If your spouse or civil partner died as a result of an industrial accident or prescribed industrial disease, the contribution conditions are treated as satisfied. You must have been ordinarily resident in Great Britain when your spouse or civil partner died (with exceptions). Bereavement support payment is not payable beyond state pension age (see Chapter 45(2)).

Pensions Act 2014, Ss.30-31

### How much do you get?

Bereavement support payment consists of two components: an initial larger payment followed by up to 18 monthly instalments. Each is set at *'standard rate'* and a *'higher rate'*. The standard rate of the initial payment is £2,500; the higher rate is £3,500. The standard rate of the monthly instalment is £100; the higher rate is £350. In either case, the higher rate is payable if:

- you were pregnant when your spouse or civil partner died;

- you were entitled to child benefit when your spouse or civil partner died; *or*
- you became entitled to child benefit after your spouse or civil partner died – for a child or qualifying young person (see Chapter 41(1)) who was living with you or your late spouse or civil partner immediately before the death. The higher rate will continue to apply even if your entitlement to child benefit ceases later.

The standard rate is payable in all other cases.

Bereavement Support Payment Regulations 2017, regs 3-5

Bereavement support payment is tax free.

**Other benefits** – The initial payment is treated as capital for means-tested benefits (including universal credit) but can be disregarded for up to 52 weeks from the date of payment; the monthly instalments are disregarded as income.

Bereavement support payment is not taken into account when calculating the benefit cap (which limits the total weekly benefits that can be claimed – see Chapter 16(10) and Box G.6 in Chapter 25). It is not affected by the 'overlapping benefits rule' (see 6 below).

### Claims and payment periods
To claim bereavement support payment in England, Scotland or Wales, ring the DWP Bereavement Service (0800 731 0469; textphone 0800 731 0464) or download a claim-form from: www.gov.uk/bereavement-support-payment/how-to-claim. In Northern Ireland, ring 0800 085 2463 or download a claim-form from: www.nidirect.gov.uk/publications/bereavement-support-payment-application-form.

Claim bereavement support payment as soon as you can. To get the initial payment, you must claim bereavement support payment within 12 months of your spouse or civil partner's death. The monthly instalments can be paid for up to 18 months following your spouse or civil partner's death. The 18-month period cannot be extended if you delay claiming; it can, however, be backdated for up to three months (though no further back than the date of your spouse or civil partner's death).

Bereavement Support Payment Regulations 2017, reg 2

Bereavement support payment is not affected if you remarry or otherwise enter into a new relationship.

## 4. Bereavement benefits before 6.4.17
Bereavement benefits were available to people whose spouse died on or after 9.4.01 (or whose registered civil partner died on or after 5.12.05) and before 6.4.17. (A woman whose husband died before 9.4.01 can continue to get widow's benefits – see 5 below.)

There were three bereavement benefits before 6.4.17: bereavement payment, bereavement allowance and widowed parent's allowance. Although bereavement payment and bereavement allowance can no longer be claimed, you can continue to get widowed parent's allowance for as long as you meet the qualifying conditions.

**Bereavement payment** – This was a tax-free, lump-sum payment of £2,000.

SSCBA, S.36

**Bereavement allowance** – This was available if you were aged 45 or over when your spouse/civil partner died and was payable for up to 52 weeks following their death.

SSCBA, S.39B

**Widowed parent's allowance** – Widowed parent's allowance (WPA) is a regular payment for men and women bereaved on or after 9.4.01 (5.12.05 for civil partners) and before 6.4.17, who have at least one dependent child or 'qualifying young person' under 20 (see Chapter 41(1)). Men widowed before 9.4.01 who have dependent children can also qualify. Women pregnant by their late husband can qualify, including those who became pregnant following certain fertility treatments, including the donation of eggs, sperm or embryos. This rule also applies to a woman whose late partner was a registered civil partner. A woman whose husband died before 9.4.01 can continue to claim widowed mother's allowance (see 5 below). WPA cannot be paid beyond state pension age (see 6 below).

SSCBA, S.39A

The contribution conditions for WPA are the same as those for the basic state pension for people who reached state pension age before 6.4.10 (see Box L.1 in Chapter 45).

SSCBA, Sch 3, para 5(2)&(3)

If your spouse or civil partner met the contribution conditions, you will get the full rate of £117.10 a week. If your spouse or civil partner's contribution record was incomplete, you will get a proportionately reduced amount of WPA, unless they died as a result of an industrial accident or prescribed industrial disease.

WBRP Regs, reg 6 & SSCBA, S.60(2)&(3)

WPA is suspended for any period when you are cohabiting with a same/opposite-sex partner. If you remarry or form a civil partnership, the benefit ceases.

SSCBA, S.39A(4)-(5)

You may get an additional state pension (SERPS, or state second pension – see Chapter 45(7)) based on your spouse/civil partner's earnings. The maximum amount of additional pension that you can inherit is restricted. You may only inherit a maximum of 50% of your partner's state second pension. You may be able to inherit a greater percentage of your partner's SERPS, depending on their date of birth.

WPA for yourself is taxable. Increases for children payable on claims made before 6.4.03 are tax free. WPA is included in the list of benefits to which the 'benefit cap' applies (see Chapter 16(10) and Box G.6 in Chapter 25).

## 5. Widowed before 9.4.01
The following benefits are for women widowed before 9.4.01:
**Widow's pension** – This is payable if you were aged 45 or over when your husband died. The amount you are paid is related to your age when your husband died; payments range from £35.13 a week if you were aged 45, to £117.10 if you were aged 55 or over. An additional state pension (see Chapter 45(7)) may be payable with widow's pension.

SSCBA, Ss.38 & 39

**Widowed mother's allowance** – This is usually payable if you have dependent children. The amounts and qualifying conditions are the same as those for widowed parent's allowance (see 4 above).

SSCBA, Ss.37 & 39

Widow's pension and widowed mother's allowance are suspended for any period when you are cohabiting with a same/opposite-sex partner. If you remarry or form a civil partnership, the benefit ceases.

SSCBA, Ss.37(3)-(4) & 38(2)-(3)

Widow's pension and widowed mother's allowance are both included in the list of benefits to which the 'benefit cap' applies (see Chapter 16(10) and Box G.6, Chapter 25).

## 6. What happens to other benefits?
**Overlapping benefits** – Widowed parent's allowance and widows' benefits overlap with contributory employment and support allowance, incapacity benefit, carer's allowance, severe disablement allowance, contribution-based jobseeker's allowance, maternity allowance, unemployability supplement and state pension. You cannot receive two overlapping benefits at the same time; you'll receive the higher of the overlapped benefits. Bereavement support payment is not affected by this rule.

OB Regs, reg 4

**Industrial death benefit** – If your husband died before 11.4.88 and you get industrial death benefit, it is paid in full on top of any state pension you are entitled to based on your own national insurance contributions.

### When you reach state pension age
Bereavement support payment, widowed parent's allowance and widow's pension cannot be paid beyond state pension age (see Chapter 45(2)). Widowed mother's allowance can be paid indefinitely if you have dependent children (but it overlaps with state pension – see above). See Chapter 45 for details of the state pension, including how it works for widows, widowers and surviving civil partners.

SSCBA, Ss.39A(4)(b), 39B(4)(a), 38(2) & 37(3)

### 7. Death of a child
Benefits will be affected by the death of your child, but dealing with different agencies after such a loss may be unbearable. Since the agencies concerned do need to be informed quickly, you could ask someone to make the calls on your behalf, perhaps an advice worker or a good friend.

Some benefits will continue to be paid for eight weeks after the death of your child. These include carer's allowance, child benefit, child tax credit and any carer premium, disabled child premium, enhanced disability premium and child allowances paid in means-tested benefits.

The child amount and childcare costs amount in universal credit can continue to be included in your award for the remainder of the monthly assessment period in which your child's death occurred and for the following two assessment periods.

The Child Death Helpline (0800 282 986) and the Compassionate Friends Helpline (0345 123 2304) provide support and comfort to bereaved parents and families.

# 52 Health benefits

| | | |
|---|---|---|
| 1 | Who qualifies for help? | 292 |
| 2 | Prescription charges | 292 |
| 3 | Sight tests and glasses | 293 |
| 4 | Free NHS dental treatment | 293 |
| 5 | Low Income scheme | 293 |
| 6 | Healthy Start vouchers and vitamins | 294 |

### 1. Who qualifies for help?
Some people qualify for help with NHS charges, vouchers for glasses or contact lenses and hospital travel fares because of their circumstances. You qualify automatically if you or a member of your family receive:
- income-related employment and support allowance, income support, income-based jobseeker's allowance or pension credit guarantee credit; or
- child tax credit or working tax credit and child tax credit or working tax credit with a disabled worker element or severe disability element, and your relevant income for tax credit purposes is £15,276 or less, and you are named on a valid NHS tax credit exemption certificate.

You qualify automatically if you are awarded universal credit (either as a single claimant or as a joint claimant) and:
- the award does not include a child amount, you (or your partner) do not have a limited capability for work and, if you (or your partner) work, your monthly earnings (or combined earnings) are no more than £435;
- the award includes the child amount and, if you (or your partner) work, your monthly earnings (or combined earnings) are no more than £935; or
- you (or your partner) have a limited capability for work and, if you (or your partner) work, your monthly earnings (or combined earnings) are no more than £935,

in which case, a child or qualifying young person (see Chapter 16(4)) you are responsible for will also qualify.

If you qualify for a tax credit exemption certificate, the NHS Business Services Authority will send it to you when your award has been confirmed by HMRC. This may take several weeks, so if you need chargeable treatment while waiting, you may be able to use your tax credit award notice as evidence of entitlement. If you have to pay, get a receipt from the pharmacist, dentist, optician or hospital and claim a refund later. Your exemption certificate is valid until the date specified on the certificate, regardless of changes to your tax credit entitlement.

Some people qualify for an HC2 (full) or HC3 (partial) certificate for help with NHS charges, hospital travel costs and vouchers for glasses on the basis of low income. If you qualify on low-income grounds, your partner and dependent children also qualify. See 5 below.

Young care leavers maintained by an English or Welsh local authority and people living permanently in a care home funded wholly or partly by a local authority are entitled to an HC2 certificate by making a claim under the Low Income scheme (see 5 below) without having to satisfy a further means test.

Asylum seekers (and their dependants) supported by the government should automatically be issued with HC2 certificates; those not supported by the government need to apply under the Low Income scheme (see 5 below).

The NHS Business Services Authority manages the health benefits scheme. For details, see NHS leaflets HC11 and HC12 (and the Welsh equivalents), available from the NHS forms-line (0300 123 0849) or website (www.nhsbsa.nhs.uk/nhs-low-income-scheme). See Chapter 55(2) for details of the Healthcare Travel Costs scheme.

NHS(TERC) Regs, reg 5

### 2. Prescription charges
Prescriptions are free in Northern Ireland, Scotland and Wales but cost £8.80 in England (2018/19) for each item, so you should take advantage of exemptions and prepayment certificates that save money on frequent prescriptions. If you are a hospital outpatient, exemptions from charges made by hospitals for prescribed drugs are the same as those listed below. Patients living in Scotland or Wales but registered with a GP in England can apply for a free 'entitlement card' that confirms their entitlement to free prescriptions.

**Exemptions**
**Who is automatically exempt?** – Your prescriptions are free if you are in any of the groups listed in 1 above or are:
- aged under 16, or under 19 and in full-time education; or
- aged 60 or over.

**Who can get an exemption certificate?** – You can get an exemption certificate for free NHS prescriptions if you:
- are pregnant or have given birth in the last 12 months. Get form FW8 from your doctor, midwife or health visitor;
- are a war pensioner (the treatment needed must be due to your accepted war disablement);
- are undergoing treatment for cancer, the effects of cancer or the effects of cancer treatment; or
- have a specified condition (see below).

NHS(CDA) Regs, reg 7

**What are the specified conditions?** – If you have one of the conditions listed below, you are entitled to an exemption certificate:
- a continuing physical disability that prevents you leaving home without help from another person (a temporary disability is excluded even if it is likely to last a few months);
- a permanent fistula (eg caecostomy, colostomy, laryngostomy or ileostomy) which needs continuous surgical dressing or an appliance;
- diabetes mellitus (except where treatment is by diet alone), myxoedema, hypoparathyroidism, diabetes insipidus or other forms of hypopituitarism, forms of hypoadrenalism

(including Addison's disease) for which specific substitution therapy is essential, and myasthenia gravis;

■ epilepsy which needs continuous anticonvulsive therapy.

Claim on form FP92A, available from your doctor.

NHS(CDA) Regs, reg 7(1)(e)

### How to claim

Complete the declaration on the back of the prescription form. The pharmacist will ask for evidence that you are eligible for free prescriptions. When you collect your prescription take your exemption certificate, prepayment certificate or benefit award notice. You should not be refused the prescription if you do not have the evidence but your entitlement may be checked later and if you were not exempt you will be asked to pay the prescription charge. You may also be charged a penalty of up to five times the cost of the prescription, subject to a £100 maximum.

**Refunds** – You can claim a refund within three months (later if you have good cause) of the date you paid for the prescription if you should have been entitled to help. When you pay, ask your pharmacist for receipt form FP57 and follow the instructions on the form.

NHS(CDA) Regs, reg 10

### What is a prescription prepayment certificate?

If you are not exempt from charges, or your income is too high to get the HC2 certificate (see 5 below), a prepayment certificate saves money if you need four or more items in three months or 13 or more items in a year. A 3-month certificate costs £29.10, a year's certificate £104 (2018/19). Apply on form FP95, available from pharmacists, the NHS Business Services Authority (0300 330 1341), or online (https://apps. nhsbsa.nhs.uk/ppcwebsales/patient.do).

NHS(CDA) Regs, reg 9

### 3. Sight tests and glasses

You qualify for free NHS eyesight tests and vouchers for glasses or contact lenses if you:

■ are in any of the groups listed in 1 above;

■ are aged under 16, or under 19 and in full-time education;

■ (in England) are a prisoner on release from prison; *or*

■ need complex or powerful lenses.

NHS eyesight tests or examinations are also free if you are:

■ aged 60 or over;

■ living in Scotland;

■ registered blind, severely sight-impaired, sight-impaired or partially sighted; *or*

■ diagnosed as having diabetes or glaucoma (or have been advised by an ophthalmologist that you are at risk of glaucoma) or aged 40 or over and the parent, brother, sister, son or daughter of a person with glaucoma.

NHS (Optical Charges & Payments) Regs 1997, regs 3 & 8

You may qualify for vouchers for glasses or contact lenses and help towards the cost of sight tests if your income is low (see 5 below). Ask for a voucher when you have your eyes tested. The value of the voucher depends on the strength of the lenses you need, with additions for clinically necessary prisms or tints. You will usually be asked for evidence that you qualify. When you buy the glasses, give the supplier the voucher. If the glasses cost more, you must pay the extra.

**Refunds** – You can claim a refund within three months (later if you have good cause) of the date you paid for the items if you should have been entitled to help. When you pay, ask your optician for a receipt. Ring 0300 123 0849 to get an HC5 refund claim-form.

### 4. Free NHS dental treatment

You qualify for free NHS dental treatment if you:

■ are in any of the groups listed in 1 above;

■ are aged under 18, or under 19 and in full-time education;

■ are pregnant – if you were pregnant when the dentist accepted you for treatment;

■ have given birth in the past year – if you start a course of dental treatment before your child's first birthday;

■ are an NHS inpatient and the treatment is carried out by a hospital dentist; *or*

■ are an NHS Hospital Dental Service outpatient (but there may be a charge for dentures and bridges).

NHS (Dental Charges) Regs 2005, regs 3(2) & 7; Sch 5

For information on the Low Income scheme, see 5 below.

In Scotland, oral health and dental examinations are free for everyone, and in Wales are free for those aged under 25 or over 60.

Tell your dentist you qualify (you will usually be asked for evidence) and fill in the declaration on the form they give you.

**Refunds** – You can claim a refund within three months (later if you have good cause) of the date you paid for treatment if you should have been entitled to help. When you pay, ask your dentist for a receipt. Ring 0300 123 0849 to get an HC5 refund claim-form.

### 5. Low Income scheme

The NHS Low Income scheme for help with NHS charges, travel costs and optical vouchers is operated by the NHS Business Services Authority (NHSBSA). If your capital is £16,000 or less, you may be eligible for help. For the Low Income scheme, a comparison is made between your income and your requirements (see below).

If your income is less than or equal to your requirements (plus 50% of the current cost of an English prescription), you are entitled to full help with NHS charges, travel costs, vouchers towards the cost of glasses and free eye tests. The NHSBSA will send you an HC2 certificate.

NHS(TERC) Regs, reg 5(2)(e)&(f)

If your income is higher than your requirements by more than 50% of the prescription charge (the difference is called your *'excess income'*), you cannot get help with the cost of NHS prescriptions but may get help with travel costs (see Chapter 55(2)) and other NHS charges. The NHSBSA will send you an HC3 certificate (partial help) to show how much you have to contribute towards the charges.

For sight tests, your maximum contribution is the excess income figure. For glasses or lenses, the maximum voucher value is reduced by twice your excess income. For dental charges, your maximum contribution is three times your excess income.

NHS(TERC) Regs, reg 6

## The income assessment

**Income and capital** – The assessment of income and capital is broadly the same as for income support (see Chapter 22) but there are differences.

❑ Assumed tariff income is £1 a week for every £250 (or part of £250) of capital in excess of £6,000, up to the upper capital limit of £16,000. This applies even if you or your partner are aged 60 or over.

❑ If you live permanently in a care home, the upper capital limit is £23,250 (£24,000 in Wales).

❑ If you receive employment and support allowance (ESA), earnings from exempt work (see Chapter 33(2)) are disregarded.

❑ If you are on strike, your pre-strike earnings are taken into account.

❑ If you are receiving contributory ESA that is being sanctioned (see Chapter 11(15)), this is taken into account as if the sanction had not been applied (unless you come under the universal credit system).

❑ The savings credit element of pension credit is disregarded.

❑ Some Scottish student maintenance loans are disregarded in England and Wales. The £10 disregard for other student loans only applies if your assessment includes any premiums, or you or your partner get a disabled students' allowance because of deafness. Loans are calculated over 52 weeks, unless it is the final year of study or a 1-year or sandwich course. Student maintenance grants in excess of the normal maximum are disregarded.

❑ If you have a lodger (without board), the standard disregard in rental income is £20.

**Requirements** – Your *'requirements'* are worked out in the same way as the income support applicable amount (see Chapter 19(7)), with significant differences.

❑ A disability premium is included if you receive ESA with a support/work-related activity component or you have been continuously incapable of work for 28 weeks; the premium is not included if you (and your partner) are aged 60 or over. If you are single or a lone parent and receive ESA with a support component (or have been receiving ESA or been incapable of work for at least 28 weeks, and are also receiving personal independence payment daily living component, disability living allowance care component at the middle or highest rate or armed forces independence payment), the disability premium will be paid at a higher rate of £37.65.

❑ If you are aged under 25, you are entitled to the same personal allowance as someone aged 25 or over if you receive ESA with a support/work-related activity component or you have been continuously incapable of work for 28 weeks.

---

## Disability Rights UK publications

### Taking Charge

Do you have a physical or mental health condition?
Have you just been given a life-changing diagnosis?
Is your health starting to worsen in later life?

This guide covers the services and support that can help you lead an independent life. It covers:

■ what you have a right to expect
■ resources and equipment
■ protection from discrimination
■ your rights in practice

To order our publications, visit
**www.disabilityrightsuk.org**

---

❑ Generally, net weekly housing costs are taken into account including: mortgage capital repayments; payments on an endowment policy or hire purchase agreement in connection with buying your home; repayments of interest and capital on a loan to adapt your home for the special needs of a disabled person; rent and council tax less housing benefit and council tax reduction. Amounts for non-dependants are deducted (see Chapter 25(21)).

❑ If you live permanently in a care home, your requirements are the total amount of weekly charge for the accommodation (including all meals and services provided) plus the amount for personal expenses (see Chapter 37(10)).

NHS(TERC) Regs, regs 16 & 17 & Sch 1

### How do you claim?

Claim on form HC1, available from the NHSBSA (www.nhs.uk/NHSEngland/Healthcosts/Documents/2016/HC1-April-2016.pdf; 0300 123 0849). Hospitals, GPs, dentists, opticians and advice agencies may also have the form. If you are unable to act for yourself, someone else can claim for you. Claim on form HC1(SC) if you live in a care home and the local authority helps with the fees, or if you are a 16-17-year-old care leaver and a local authority supports you.

The NHSBSA will send its decision to you. If you are entitled to full help, they will send an HC2 certificate. If you are entitled to partial help, they will send an HC3 certificate. HC2 and HC3 certificates are usually valid for periods of between six months and five years, depending on your circumstances.

**If you are not happy with the decision** – There is no right of appeal but you can write and ask the NHSBSA to reconsider its decision (Service Improvement Team, Help with Health Costs, Bridge House, 152 Pilgrim Street, Newcastle upon Tyne NE1 6SN).

## 6. Healthy Start vouchers and vitamins

Healthy Start provides vouchers for fresh milk, infant formula milk and plain fresh or frozen fruit and vegetables. It also provides coupons for claiming free vitamin supplements locally without a prescription. You are eligible if:

■ you are at least 10 weeks pregnant, aged under 18 and not subject to immigration control (see Chapter 53(2)); *or*

■ you are at least 10 weeks pregnant or have a child aged under 4 and you or a member of your family get:
  – income-related employment and support allowance;
  – income support;
  – income-based jobseeker's allowance;
  – child tax credit (but not working tax credit, unless paid during the 4-week run-on period – see Chapter 23(6)) and your relevant income is less than £16,190 (2018/19); *or*
  – universal credit and, if you (or your partner) work, your monthly earnings (or combined earnings) are no more than £408;

You can get more information and an application leaflet (HS01) from the website (www.healthystart.nhs.uk) or the Healthy Start helpline (0345 607 6823). You might also get an application leaflet from a GP surgery or baby clinic. Applications to the scheme must be supported by a midwife, health visitor or other registered health professional.

Healthy Start Scheme and Welfare Food (Amendment) Regs 2005

**Nursery Milk scheme** – Children aged under 5 who attend approved daycare facilities (including registered childminders) for two hours or more a day, and some 4-year-olds in Reception classes, are eligible for free milk. Babies under 1 year may be given infant formula instead. For more information, see www.nurserymilk.co.uk.

This section of the handbook looks at:

| | |
|---|---|
| Coming to the UK | Chapter **53** |
| Leaving the UK | Chapter **54** |
| Benefits in hospital | Chapter **55** |
| Claims and payments | Chapter **56** |
| Challenging decisions | Chapter **57** |

# Common rules to benefits

# 53 Coming to the UK

| | | |
|---|---|---|
| 1 | Introduction | 295 |
| 2 | Immigration status | 295 |
| 3 | Residence and presence tests | 296 |
| 4 | Habitual residence test | 297 |
| 5 | Right to reside requirement | 298 |
| 6 | Other forms of support | 300 |

## 1. Introduction

To qualify for most benefits you must satisfy the rules about immigration status and the rules about residence and presence in Great Britain (GB), the United Kingdom (UK) or the Common Travel Area. GB means England, Scotland and Wales. UK means GB plus Northern Ireland. Common Travel Area means UK, the Channel Islands, the Isle of Man and the Republic of Ireland.

In Northern Ireland, the Channel Islands and the Isle of Man, social security benefits come under separate legislation from that of GB, but reciprocal agreements can help if you move between these places and GB.

**EEA countries** – The European Economic Area (EEA) consists of the EU member states: Austria, Belgium, Bulgaria, Croatia, Cyprus, *Czech Republic, Denmark, *Estonia, Finland, France, Germany, Greece, *Hungary, Italy, *Latvia, *Lithuania, Luxembourg, Malta, Netherlands, *Poland, Portugal, Republic of Ireland, Romania, *Slovakia, *Slovenia, Spain, Sweden, UK (including Gibraltar, but not the Channel Islands or Isle of Man), together with Iceland, Norway and Liechtenstein. Rules applying to EEA nationals also generally apply to Swiss nationals.

**A8** – This term refers to the eight countries marked * above.
**A2** – This term refers to Bulgaria and Romania.

### EEA co-ordination rules
If you (or a family member) have moved between EEA states, are an EEA or Swiss national (or a refugee or stateless person resident in an EEA state) *and* have been employed, self-employed, studying or claiming certain benefits in one or more EEA states, you may be covered by the EEA social security co-ordination rules. In most cases, these rules are more favourable and can override UK rules regarding residence and presence requirements. They can enable you to use periods of residence, and employment and national insurance contributions completed or paid, in another EEA country to satisfy the requirements for UK benefits. However, being covered by these rules can mean you are not entitled to disability and carer's benefits (see 3 below).
EU Reg 883/04; EU Reg 987/2009

### European law
The European law referred to in this chapter (and Chapter 54) has not changed as a result of the 2016 UK referendum result to leave the EU. It will remain in force until the UK formally leaves the EU. However if you, or your family member, are an EEA national, your *future* residence rights in the UK may be affected by the residence rights you have *before* the UK formally leaves the EU and you should obtain specialist immigration advice if this could affect you.

### Reciprocal agreements
Reciprocal social security agreements with some countries* may help you receive benefits. Non-EEA countries covered by reciprocal agreements are Barbados, Bermuda, Canada, Chile, Isle of Man, Israel, Jamaica, Jersey & Guernsey, Mauritius, New Zealand, Philippines, Turkey, USA and former Yugoslavia. Agreements differ, some contain rules similar to EEA co-ordination rules, and not all benefits are covered. There are 'association' and 'co-operation' agreements with Algeria, Morocco, San Marino, Slovenia, Tunisia and Turkey.
* including Switzerland and all EEA countries except A8 (unless part of former Yugoslavia) and A2 countries, Greece and Liechtenstein – the reciprocal agreement applies if you are not covered by EEA rules

## 2. Immigration status
Your immigration status will exclude you from specific benefits only if you are defined as a 'person subject to immigration control' and you do not come under one of the exemptions below.

### Person subject to immigration control
You are defined as a *'person subject to immigration control'* (PSIC) if you are *not* an EEA national (see 1 above) and you:
- require leave to enter/remain in the UK but do not have it; *or*
- have leave to enter/remain in the UK subject to a condition that you do not have recourse to public funds (see below); *or*
- have been given leave to enter or remain as a result of a *'maintenance undertaking'* (a written undertaking given by someone else in pursuance of the immigration rules, to be responsible for your maintenance and accommodation).

If you do not come within this definition then you are *not* excluded from benefit entitlement, eg if you have refugee status, humanitarian protection or indefinite leave to enter/remain (unless the latter is given as the result of a maintenance undertaking) or are a family member of an EEA national who has a right to reside in the UK (eg as a 'worker' – see 5 below).

### Benefits you are excluded from
If you *are* defined as a PSIC, unless you come under one of the exemptions below, you are excluded from the following benefits:
- attendance allowance, disability living allowance (DLA) and personal independence payment (PIP);
- carer's allowance;
- child benefit;
- child tax credit and working tax credit;
- contributory employment and support allowance 'in youth' (CESA(Y)) and incapacity benefit 'in youth' (IB(Y));
- housing benefit and council tax reduction;
- income-based jobseeker's allowance (JSA);
- income-related employment and support allowance (ESA);
- income support;

- pension credit;
- severe disablement allowance (SDA);
- social fund; *and*
- universal credit.

Immigration and Asylum Act 1999, S.115; ESA Regs, reg 11; ESA Regs 2013, reg 12; Social Security (Incapacity Benefit) Regs 1994, reg 16; TCA, S.42; TC(I) Regs, reg 3

### Public funds

All the benefits listed above (except CESA(Y) and IB(Y)), as well as local welfare assistance payments (except the Discretionary Assistance Fund in Wales), council tax reduction, homelessness assistance and housing provided under specific provisions, are classed as *'public funds'*. This is only relevant if you have time-limited leave that is subject to a *'no recourse to public funds'* condition, in which case receiving one of these benefits (or someone being paid it on your behalf) may jeopardise your right to stay in the UK, now or in the future. However, the Home Office does *not* regard you as having 'recourse to public funds' if benefit is paid because you come under one of the exemptions below.

Immigration Rules, paras 6, 6A, 6B & 6C

Get expert advice (see Box O.1) before making a claim if you, or someone that could be included in your claim, is subject to a 'no recourse to public funds' condition, or does not have leave to enter/remain, has overstayed leave or if you are unsure about your or their immigration status. Note that information is exchanged between the benefit authorities and the Home Office.

### Exemptions (1): means-tested benefits

You are not excluded from housing benefit, income-related ESA, income-based JSA, income support, pension credit or universal credit if you:

- are a national of Macedonia or Turkey and are lawfully present in the UK; *or*
- have leave as a result of a maintenance undertaking (see above) and either you have been resident in the UK for at least five years (beginning on the date of your entry to the UK or the signing of the maintenance undertaking, if later) or your sponsor has died (or, if more than one, they all have).

Social Security (Immigration & Asylum) Consequential Amendments Regs 2000, regs 2(1)-(1A) & Sch, Part 1

**If your partner is a PSIC** – If your partner is a PSIC and you are entitled to income-based JSA*, income-related ESA* or income support*, your personal allowance will be that of a single person. If your partner is a PSIC and you are entitled to universal credit* or pension credit, you must claim as a single person.

Except for pension credit, your partner's income and capital will still affect your claim.

* unless they are in one of the exempt groups above

IS Regs, reg 21(3) & Sch 7, para 16A; JSA Regs, reg 85(4) & Sch 5, para 13A; ESA Regs, reg 69 & Sch 5, para 10; SPC Regs, reg 5; UC Regs, regs 3(3), 18(2), 22(3) & 36(3)

### Exemptions (2): tax credits

You are not excluded from tax credits if you:

- have leave as a result of a maintenance undertaking (see above) and either you have been resident in the UK for at least five years (beginning on the date of your entry to the UK or the signing of the maintenance undertaking, if later) or your sponsor has died (or, if more than one, they all have); *or*
- (child tax credit only) are a national of Algeria, Morocco, San Marino, Tunisia or Turkey and are lawfully working (or have lawfully worked) in the UK; *or*
- (working tax credit only) are a national of Macedonia or Turkey and are lawfully present in the UK; *or*
- (child tax credit only) claim child tax credit immediately following an award of income support or income-based

JSA for a child while you are a lawfully present national of Turkey.

TC(I) Regs, reg 3

**If your partner is a PSIC** – and you are not (or you are but are in one of the exempt groups above), your joint claim will be treated as if your partner were not a PSIC (except that the couple element of working tax credit is not paid unless you or your partner have a child or your partner is a national of Macedonia or Turkey and they are lawfully present in the UK).

WTC(E&MR) Regs, reg 11(4) & (5)

### Exemptions (3): disability and carer's benefits and child benefit

You are not excluded from attendance allowance, DLA, PIP, carer's allowance, child benefit, CESA(Y), IB(Y) or SDA if:

- you are the family member of an EEA (including UK) national; *or*
- either you, or a member of your family who you are living with, are a national of Algeria, Morocco, San Marino, Tunisia or Turkey and are lawfully working (or have lawfully worked) in GB; *or*
- you have leave as a result of a maintenance undertaking; *or*
- (for child benefit and, for Guernsey, Jersey and the Isle of Man, attendance allowance, PIP and DLA only) you are covered by a reciprocal agreement (see 1 above)

Social Security (Immigration & Asylum) Consequential Amendments Regs 2000, reg 2(2),(3)&(4)(b) & Sch, Part 2

### Exemptions (4): social fund

You are not excluded from social fund payments if you are in any of the groups listed in Exemptions (1) or Exemptions (3) above.

### If you get a positive decision on your asylum claim

If you are granted refugee status, you may be able to claim tax credits and child benefit backdated to the date of your asylum application. You must claim tax credits within one month, and child benefit within three months, of receiving the letter notifying you of your refugee status. However, the amount of tax credits paid will be net of any subsistence payments of asylum support you have received.

TC(I) Regs, reg 3(4)-(9); Child Benefit & Guardian's Allowance (Admin) Regs 2003, reg 6(2)(d)

If you are aged 18 or over and have (or someone you are a dependant of has) been granted refugee status or humanitarian protection, you can apply for an 'integration loan'. Details and application forms are available at www.gov.uk/refugee-integration-loan.

Once you are granted refugee status, humanitarian protection or (provided it is not subject to a 'no recourse to public funds' condition) discretionary leave, you are no longer a PSIC while you have that leave, and you can claim all benefits. You are also exempt from the 'habitual residence test' and from the requirement to have lived in the UK for the past three months for child benefit and child tax credit, and if you (or the family member that you have joined in the UK under the family reunion provisions) have been granted refugee status or humanitarian protection you are exempt from the 'past presence test' for disability and carer's benefits (see 3 below).

### 3. Residence and presence tests

Entitlement to many benefits depends on satisfying residence and presence tests for that benefit.

### Meaning of terms

**Present** – This means physically present in GB throughout the whole day. (See Chapter 54 for when you can be treated as present in GB while you are abroad.)

**Resident** – You are usually 'resident' in the country where you have your home for the time being.

**Ordinarily resident** – This term is not defined in regulations. You should be *'ordinarily resident'* in the place where you normally live for the time being if there is a degree of continuity about your stay such that it can be described as settled. In practice, claims are usually refused for reasons other than you not being ordinarily resident.

**Habitually resident** – This term is not defined in regulations. See 4 below for how this test is applied.

**Right to reside** – This term does not have a single statutory definition. See 5 below for how this test is applied.

### Disability and carers benefits

**Attendance allowance, carer's allowance, disability living allowance and personal independence payment** – You must be habitually resident in the Common Travel Area (see 1 above), be present in GB, and satisfy the *'past presence test'* – ie: have been present in GB for not less than 104 weeks in the last 156 weeks.

**Exceptions** – For attendance allowance, carer's allowance, disability living allowance (DLA) and personal independence payment (PIP), the past presence test does not apply if:

■ you are terminally ill;
■ you have been granted refugee leave or humanitarian protection, or you have been granted leave as the dependent family member of someone with either one of these types of leave; *or*
■ you are covered by the EEA co-ordination rules (see Note below), you are habitually resident in GB or another EEA country (see 1 above) and you can demonstrate a genuine and sufficient link to the UK.

If DLA is claimed for a baby under six months old, a 13-week presence test applies until their 1st birthday. If DLA is claimed for a baby aged 6-36 months, the test is 26 weeks in the last 156 weeks.

AA Regs, regs 2-2C; DLA Regs, regs 2-2C; ICA Regs, regs 9-9C; PIP Regs, regs16 & 21-23A

*Note:* If you are covered by the EEA co-ordination rules (see 1 above), you are not entitled to attendance allowance, carer's allowance, the care component of DLA or the daily living component of PIP unless the UK is your *'competent state'* (ie the state responsible) for paying these benefits. The UK may not be your competent state if you, or the member of your family that brings you within the co-ordination rules, receive a pension from another EEA state – seek advice if this applies.

SSCBA, Ss.65(7), 70(4A) & 72(7B); WRA 2012, S.84; EU Regulation 883/04

**Employment and support allowance 'in youth', incapacity benefit 'in youth' and severe disablement allowance** – For contributory employment and support allowance 'in youth' (CESA(Y)), incapacity benefit 'in youth' and severe disablement allowance, you must be present and ordinarily resident in GB, and have been present for not less than 26 weeks in the last 52 weeks. Once you satisfy these requirements, you do not need to do so again during the same period of limited capability for work or incapacity for work.

ESA Regs, reg 11; ESA Regs 2013, reg 12; Social Security (Severe Disablement Allowance) Regs 1984, reg 3; Social Security (Incapacity Benefit) Regs 1994, reg 16

### Funeral and winter fuel payments

For a funeral payment, the deceased must have been ordinarily resident, and the funeral must normally take place, in the UK. However, it can take place in any EEA state if you or your partner are (or are the family member of) an EEA national with 'worker' or 'self-employed' status (including if either status is retained) or with a permanent right of residence acquired in less than five years.

SFM&FE Regs, reg 7(9)&(10)

For a winter fuel payment you must, in the 'qualifying week' (see Chapter 29(5)) be either:

■ ordinarily resident in GB; *or*
■ covered by the EEA co-ordination rules (see 1 above), demonstrate a genuine and sufficient link to the UK, and be habitually resident in Switzerland or an EEA country (other than Cyprus, France, Gibraltar, Greece, Malta, Portugal, Spain or the UK).

Social Fund Winter Fuel Payment Regs, reg 2

### Tax credits and child benefit

**Tax credits** – For working tax credit and child tax credit, you (and your partner if you claim jointly) must be present and ordinarily resident in the UK. For child tax credit only, you (and your partner if you claim jointly) must also have:

■ a right to reside in the UK (see 5 below) – unless you have been receiving child tax credit since 30.4.04; *and*
■ been living in the UK for the three months before your claim, unless in an exempt group (see below).

TCA, S.3(3); TC(R) Regs, reg 3

**Child benefit** – To be entitled to child benefit, you *and* the child must be present in GB (or Northern Ireland if claiming there). In addition, you must:

■ be ordinarily resident in the UK;
■ have a right to reside in the UK (see 5 below), unless you have been receiving child benefit since 30.4.04; *and*
■ have been living in the UK for the three months before your claim, unless you are in an exempt group (see below).

SSCBA, S.146; CB Regs, regs 23 & 27

**Exempt groups** – The exempt groups for child tax credit and child benefit are the same as the first three groups exempt from the habitual residence test (see 4 below) plus if you are:

■ (or are the family member of) a non-EEA national who would otherwise count as a 'worker' or 'self-employed'; *or*
■ returning to the UK either having worked abroad while paying UK national insurance contributions or after an absence of less than a year if either you were ordinarily resident in the UK for three months before departure or you satisfied the temporary absence rules (see Chapter 54(11)).

**Child in another EEA state** – You may be able to claim child benefit for a child in education in another EEA state and, if you are covered by the EEA co-ordination rules (see 1 above), you may be able to claim child benefit and child tax credit for a child living in another EEA state regardless of whether they are in education.

CB Regs, regs 21 & 25; EU Regulation 883/04

### Means-tested benefits

For housing benefit, income-related employment and support allowance, income-based jobseeker's allowance, income support, pension credit, universal credit and council tax reduction, you must satisfy the habitual residence test (see 4 below) and (except for housing benefit – see Chapter 54(10)) be present in GB.

**Partner abroad** – If you used to live in GB or abroad with your partner who is now abroad, they will be treated as your partner (with their income and capital affecting your entitlement to benefit) unless you do not intend to resume living together or the absence is likely to exceed 52 weeks (or six months for universal credit).

IS Regs, reg 16(2); ESA Regs, reg 156(3); JSA Regs, reg 78(2); SPC Regs, reg 5(1) (a); HB Regs, reg 21(2); UC Regs, regs 3(6) & 10

### 4. Habitual residence test

For means-tested and disability benefits, unless you are exempt (see below), you must be *'habitually resident'* in the Common Travel Area (see 1 above). For means-tested benefits, this includes having a right to reside (see 5 below) in the Common Travel Area. For income-based jobseeker's allowance (JSA) only, it also includes the requirement to have been living in the Common Travel Area for the past three months, unless you have been working abroad and paying Class 1 or Class 2 national insurance contributions.

Only the claimant is subject to the habitual residence test (HRT). For universal credit, couples generally have to make a joint claim, so both partners are subject to the HRT; if your partner fails the HRT, you can claim universal credit as a single person, with a single person's maximum amount, but your partner's income and capital is taken into account.

If you are not accepted as habitually resident by the DWP, the housing benefit office must make its own decision, not simply follow the DWP decision.

### Exemptions

For means-tested benefits, you are exempt from the HRT if you:

- have refugee status, humanitarian protection, discretionary leave, leave granted under the 'destitution domestic violence concession' or temporary protection granted under the displaced persons provisions; *or*
- are an EEA national (see 1 above) with *'worker status'* or *'self-employed status'* – including if you have *'retained'* either status (see 5 below); *or*
- are a family member (ie spouse, civil partner or (grand) child (who is either under 21 or a dependant)) or dependent (grand)parent of someone in the group above; *or*
- have a *'permanent right to reside acquired in less than five years'* (see 5 below); *or*
- are not a *'person subject to immigration control'* (see 2 above) and have been legally removed from another country; *or*
- (housing benefit only) are getting income-based JSA (and either have been getting *both* housing benefit and income-based JSA since 31.3.14 or have a right to reside other than as a jobseeker), income-related employment and support allowance (ESA), income support or pension credit; *or*
- (income-related ESA only) are being transferred from an award of income support that is part of a continuous period of entitlement to means-tested benefits since 30.4.04.

There are no exemptions from the HRT for attendance allowance, carer's allowance, disability living allowance (DLA) and personal independence payment (PIP) other than for serving members of the armed forces and their families.

### Satisfying the habitual residence test

If you are not exempt, you must show you are habitually resident (including, for means-tested benefits, that you have a right to reside – see 5 below). There is no definitive list of factors that determine habitual residence, but you must show a *'settled intention'* to live here. In most cases, you also need to be actually resident for an *'appreciable period'* of time, which is not a fixed period of time and will depend on your circumstances. However, you can, depending on your circumstances, be accepted as habitually resident after a shorter period, or even from your first day of residence, if you are:

- returning to the Common Travel Area (see 1 above) and you were previously habitually resident here; *or*
- (for income-based JSA, income-related ESA, pension credit or the mobility component of DLA or PIP only) covered by the EEA co-ordination rules – see 1 above.

Seek specialist advice if you have concerns about satisfying, or being exempt from, the HRT or if you need to challenge a decision that you are not habitually resident.

IS Regs, regs 21-21AA; ESA Regs, regs 69-70; JSA Regs, regs 85-85A; SPC Regs, reg 2; HB Regs, reg 10; UC Regs, regs 3(3), 9, 18(2), 22(3) and 36(3); PIP Regs, regs 16(c) & 20; *Swaddling v Adjudication Officer, C-90/97* [1999] (ECJ)

## 5. Right to reside requirement

For child tax credit and child benefit, you need to have a *'right to reside'* in the UK. For each of the means-tested benefits (as part of satisfying the habitual residence test (HRT) – see 4 above), you need to have a right to reside in the Common Travel Area (see 1 above).

However, you do not need a right to reside for:

- child tax credit or child benefit if your claim was made before 1.5.04; *or*
- housing benefit, income-based jobseeker's allowance (JSA), income support, pension credit or, since 31.10.11, income-related employment and support allowance (ESA), if it is part of a *continuous* period of entitlement to one or more of these benefits (or council tax benefit) that included 30.4.04. Note that this rule does not apply to universal credit.

The Social Security (Habitual Residence) Amendment Regs 2004, reg 6

### Who has a right to reside

The main circumstances in which you have a right to reside are if you are:

- a British citizen;
- an Irish citizen – for means tested benefits (because Ireland is part of the Common Travel Area);
- someone with leave to enter/remain in the UK;
- an EEA national with *'worker status'*. This means you are employed in the UK providing services that you are paid for, which involve activities that are *'genuine and effective'* (see below). If you are a Croatian/A2/A8 national, see warning below;
- an EEA national who has *'retained worker status'* (see below). If you are a Croatian/A2/A8 national, see warning below;
- an EEA national with *'self-employed status'*. This means you are established in the UK in order to pursue self-employed activity which is *'genuine and effective'* (see below);
- an EEA national who has *'retained self-employed status'* (see below);
- an EEA national and you are *'self-sufficient'* (including while enrolled as a student). This requires you to have sufficient resources and comprehensive sickness insurance cover;
- an EEA national and you have a *'permanent right to reside acquired in less than five years'* (eg if you had worker or self-employed status but it ended due to permanent incapacity and either you had resided in the UK continuously for two years or the incapacity was due to an accident at work or an occupational disease that entitles you to a benefit such as industrial injuries benefit; or because you retired after working in the UK for at least the last year and you had resided in the UK continuously for three years);
- an EEA national and you are a *'jobseeker'* in the UK. After three months, the DWP will apply the *'genuine prospects of work test'* (see below). Having a right to reside as a jobseeker will only satisfy the right to reside requirement for child benefit, child tax credit and income-based JSA. If you are a Croatian/A2/A8 national, see warning below;
- a *'family member'* (see below) of an EEA national (in most cases, other than a British citizen) in one of the seven bullet points immediately above or in the bullet point immediately below;
- someone who has acquired a *'permanent right to reside'* after five years of 'residing legally' in the UK (this includes having a right to reside as defined in one of the eight bullet points immediately above, but excludes a derivative right to reside – see below); *and*
- someone with a *'derivative right to reside'*. The main examples are if you are the primary carer of a child in

education in the UK, whose (step)parent has been an EEA 'worker' (see above) in the UK while that child was also in the UK, or you are the primary carer of a child who is an EEA national and is self-sufficient (see above) in the UK. Others can have a right to reside, depending on their circumstances.

*The Immigration (EEA) Regs 2016; Directive 2004/38/EC*

### 'Genuine and effective' activities
For your work to give you worker or self-employed status, it must entail activities that are *'genuine and effective'* as opposed to activities that are on such as small scale as to be *'marginal and ancillary'*. Factors to be taken into account include: the duration of the work, the number of hours you work each week, the regularity of your work and the level of your earnings. There is no fixed amount of any of these factors that is conclusive, and all the circumstances of your employment or self-employment must be taken into account.

### Retained worker status
You have *'retained worker status'* as an EEA national if you were previously a 'worker' (see above), and since then one or more of the following have applied:
- you are temporarily unable to work due to an illness or accident. *'Temporary'* simply means not permanent – there is no time limit to how long this can be. It is your inability to work that must be temporary, even if your health condition is permanent. You do not need to claim any benefit (eg ESA) in connection with your health condition to retain your status on this basis;
- you are involuntarily unemployed and registered as a jobseeker with Jobcentre Plus. If you were employed less than one year, you only retain worker status for six months. If you were employed more than one year, you retain worker status for as long as you remain in the labour market, but after six months the DWP will apply the *'genuine prospects of work test'* (see below);
- you stopped work (or stopped looking for work while retaining worker status as in the bullet point above) due to late pregnancy or childbirth; *or*
- you are in vocational training (connected to your former work, if you are voluntarily unemployed).

***Note:*** If you are not working but still under a contract of employment (eg you are on sick leave), whether or not you are paid, you are still a worker, so do not need to *retain* that status. If you are a Croatian/A2/A8 national, see warning below.

### Retained self-employed status
You have *'retained self-employed status'* as an EEA national if you were previously self-employed (see above) and since then:
- you are temporarily unable to work due to an illness or accident (see the first bullet point in 'retained worker status' above); *or*
- you are involuntarily unemployed and registered as a jobseeker (see the second bullet point in 'retained worker status'); *or*
- you are in vocational training (see the fourth bullet point in 'retained worker status') – it is strongly arguable that you should be able to retain self-employed status in this situation.

*Gusa v Minister for Social Protection, C-442/16 [2017]*

***Note:*** You can continue to be self-employed if you are in a maternity period and intend to resume your self-employment at the end of this period.

### 'Genuine prospects of work test'
After three months with a right to reside as a jobseeker, or six months if you have retained your worker status while involuntarily unemployed and registered as a jobseeker, you are likely to be asked to provide *'compelling'* evidence that you are seeking employment and have a genuine chance of being engaged. The DWP calls this the *'genuine prospects of work test'*. It does not apply if you have any alternative right to reside. Seek advice if your evidence is not accepted as compelling, and/or if an alternative residence right is not accepted.

### 'Family member'
You are a family member of an EEA national if you are their spouse, civil partner, or their (or their spouse/civil partner's) (grand)child (who is either aged under 21 or a dependant) or dependent (grand)parent. You can be treated as the family member of an EEA national if you hold a valid residence document and are their *'extended family member'*. This will be the case if you are their:
- partner (not married or in a civil partnership) in a durable relationship; *or*
- family member, and you need their personal care on serious health grounds, or you continue to be dependent on them or a member of their household and were dependent or a member of their household in the country you previously lived in.

If you are the family member of a British citizen, this will not generally give you a right to reside. However, in limited circumstances if the British citizen previously lived with a right to reside (eg as a worker) in another EEA country, and you lived there with them before you both moved to the UK, you may have a right to reside as their family member. Get advice if you need to rely on this.

If you are the family member of a jobseeker, this will only satisfy the right to reside requirement for child benefit, child tax credit and income-based JSA.

In some circumstances, you can retain your right to reside as a family member if the EEA national dies, leaves the UK or your marriage or civil partnership to them is ended with divorce or dissolution.

### Warning: Croatian/A2/A8 nationals
If you are (or your family member is) a Croatian, A2 or A8 national (see 1 above), restrictions during the period after your country joined the EU may affect whether you have a right to reside today if you need to rely on periods when the restrictions applied (eg if you need to show you have a permanent right to reside).

**Croatian nationals** – At the time of writing, the restrictions applying to Croatian nationals were due to end on 30.6.18, but could be extended for a further two years. During the period of restrictions, most Croatian nationals can only take employment if they hold, and work in accordance with, an *'accession worker authorisation document'*. Limited categories of Croatian nationals are exempt from this requirement, including those who have completed a year of authorised work. While subject to restrictions, a Croatian national:
- has no right to reside as a jobseeker;
- is only defined as a 'worker' (see above) if their work is authorised; *and*
- cannot retain their 'worker' status in the ways listed above.

**A2 nationals** were subject to similar restrictions (and exemptions) between 1.1.07 and 31.12.13.

**A8 nationals** were subject to similar restrictions on their residence rights and were required to work for an *'authorised employer'* (this included employment either during the first month or registered under the Worker's Registration scheme) between 1.5.04 and 30.4.11. However, the last two years of the restrictions on A8 nationals were held by the Court of Appeal to be unlawful in a decision that the DWP is seeking to appeal against. Seek up-to-date advice if your (or your family member's) residence rights during the period 1.5.09 to 30.4.11 affect your current residence rights.

The Accession (Immigration & Worker Registration) Regs 2004; The Accession (Immigration & Worker Authorisation) Regs 2006; The Accession of Croatia (Immigration & Worker Authorisation) Regs 2013; *SSWP v Gubeladze [2017] EWCA Civ 1751*

### 6. Other forms of support

**Asylum support** – If you (or someone you are a dependant of) are aged 18 or over, have an outstanding asylum claim or appeal (or, in limited circumstances, if these have been refused) and are destitute, you may be able to get asylum support (accommodation and/or subsistence payments). Seek advice for details (see Box O.1).

**Help from social care** – You may be eligible for assistance from your local authority social care department (see Chapter 36). You may be entitled to accommodation and/or other assistance from the authority, particularly if you are an unaccompanied child aged under 18 or you have a dependent child, or you have needs beyond destitution (eg due to your age or disability). Remember that information is exchanged between social care departments and the Home Office. Seek independent advice before you apply and if you are refused assistance.

# 54 Leaving the UK

| | | |
|---|---|---|
| 1 | Introduction | 300 |
| 2 | Disability benefits | 300 |
| 3 | Carer's allowance | 300 |
| 4 | Incapacity and maternity benefits | 301 |
| 5 | Employment and support allowance | 301 |
| 6 | Jobseeker's allowance | 301 |
| 7 | Universal credit | 301 |
| 8 | Income support | 302 |
| 9 | Pension credit | 302 |
| 10 | Housing benefit | 302 |
| 11 | Tax credits | 302 |
| 12 | Child benefit | 303 |
| 13 | Employer-paid benefits | 303 |
| 14 | Industrial injuries disablement benefit | 303 |
| 15 | Retirement, widows' and bereavement benefits | 303 |
| | For more information – Box O.1 | 302 |

### 1. Introduction

You may be able to receive benefits while you are abroad. Some benefits (eg state pension) can be paid no matter how long you are away, while rules for others are more complex and vary depending on the country you go to. You may benefit from European Economic Area (EEA) co-ordination rules if you go to an EEA country, or from a reciprocal agreement – see Chapter 53(1). If you are not covered by EEA co-ordination rules or a reciprocal agreement, the general rules on payment of benefits abroad apply. Some rules treat you as being in Great Britain (GB) for the purposes of certain benefits if you (or a family member you live with) are a member of the armed forces serving abroad, a crown servant posted overseas (or your partner is) or one of certain categories of airmen, mariners and continental-shelf workers.

This chapter covers general rules and indicates benefits payable in EEA countries. EEA co-ordination rules and reciprocal agreements are too varied to cover here, so if you plan to go abroad get specialist advice. Contact the International Pension Centre (see Chapter 61) for information about receiving state pension abroad. For other benefits, contact the office that pays them. In each case, they will need to know the purpose, destination and intended length of your visit.

**Temporary absence** – For many benefits, one condition for payment while abroad is that your absence is temporary. For some benefits, *'temporary absence'* is defined as an absence that is, at the beginning of the absence, unlikely to exceed 52 weeks. For benefits where the term is not defined, in deciding whether your absence is temporary, the DWP should consider all the circumstances, including your intentions and the purpose and length of your absence. If the decision maker decides your absence is not temporary, you have a right of appeal, as long as you have previously asked for a mandatory reconsideration of the decision (see Chapter 57).

### 2. Disability benefits

You continue to be entitled to personal independence payment (PIP), attendance allowance and disability living allowance (DLA) during a temporary absence (defined as unlikely to exceed 52 weeks) abroad for:
- the first 13 weeks; *or*
- the first 26 weeks, if the absence is solely in connection with medical treatment for your illness or disability that began before you left GB.

AA Regs, reg 2; DLA Regs, reg 2; PIP Regs, regs 17 & 18

**EEA** – You can continue to be paid attendance allowance or DLA in another EEA country if your entitlement to the benefit began before 1.6.92 and you (or a family member) were last employed or self-employed in the UK.

If, on or after 8.4.13, you move to another EEA country, you can continue to be paid, or make a new claim for, attendance allowance, DLA care component or PIP daily living component if you:
- are habitually resident in another EEA state or Switzerland; *and*
- are covered by the EEA co-ordination rules (see Chapter 53(1)); *and*
- can demonstrate a genuine and sufficient link to the UK social security system.

You will be paid as long as the UK remains the 'competent state' (ie the state responsible for paying your benefits).

SSCBA, Ss.65(7), 70(4A) & 72(7B); WRA 2012, S.84; AA Regs, reg 2B; DLA Regs, reg 2B; PIP Regs, reg 23

For periods before 8.4.13, if your attendance allowance or DLA care component was stopped because you went to another EEA country, you may be paid arrears back to when the benefit stopped if the UK continued to be responsible for paying your benefits (but seek specialist advice if the period was before 18.10.07). For details, write to: Exportability Co-ordinator, Room B201, DCS, Warbreck House, Warbreck Hill Road, Blackpool FY2 0YE (0125 333 1044).

C&P Regs, reg 6(35-37); D&A Regs, Reg 7(9A)

DLA and PIP mobility components cannot be exported to another EEA country.

European Court of Justice, Case C-537/09 Bartlett

**PIP rapid re-claim**

If you need to re-claim PIP after a temporary absence abroad, you may be able make a rapid re-claim. This will use the information from your previous award and should be much quicker to process. You can make a rapid re-claim if you:
- were receiving PIP before you left GB;
- were abroad for more than 13 weeks but less than 12 months;
- have not reached the award review date of your previous claim (see Chapter 5(20)); *and*
- can confirm that your daily living and mobility needs have not changed since before you went abroad.

### 3. Carer's allowance

**General rules** – This will be paid during a temporary absence abroad for up to four weeks (this could be without the disabled person if it is during a 'break in care' – see Chapter 8(11)). If you go abroad temporarily specifically to care for that person, you will receive carer's allowance for as long as they continue to receive a qualifying benefit (see Chapter 8(2)).

ICA Regs, reg 9

**EEA** – The rules are the same as for attendance allowance/ personal independence payment daily living component/ disability living allowance care component (see 2 above).

## 4. Incapacity and maternity benefits

**General rules** – If you are temporarily absent from GB, you can continue to be paid incapacity benefit, severe disablement allowance (SDA) or maternity allowance for the first 26 weeks of the absence if the DWP agrees. There is no right of appeal if they refuse; your only recourse is judicial review. You are not subject to the 26-week limit and do not require DWP agreement if you are receiving attendance allowance, disability living allowance, personal independence payment or armed forces independence payment. However, in all cases you must satisfy one of the following conditions:

- at the time you go abroad you have been continuously incapable of work for at least six months and remain continuously incapable while abroad; *or*
- you have gone abroad *'for the specific purpose of being treated'* by another person for an illness or disability that began before you left. The treatment does not need to be your only reason for going abroad, but going abroad to convalesce or for a change of air, even on your doctor's advice, is not enough. It does not matter whether the treatment is available in the UK or not. In some cases claimants did not receive any treatment, but went abroad specifically to try to get it.

PA Regs, reg 2

**EEA** – You may be able to get maternity allowance if you go to another EEA country. Long-term incapacity benefit and SDA can continue to be paid in another EEA country.

## 5. Employment and support allowance

**4-week rule** – You can continue to be entitled to employment and support allowance (ESA) for the first four weeks of a temporary absence from GB if the period of absence is unlikely to exceed 52 weeks and you continue to meet the other qualifying conditions for the benefit.

ESA Regs, reg 152; ESA Regs 2013, reg 89

**26-week rule** – You can continue to be entitled to ESA during the first 26 weeks of a temporary absence from GB if the absence is solely:

- in connection with arrangements made for treatment for a condition directly related to your limited capability for work, which began before you left GB; *or*
- because you are accompanying a dependent child in connection with arrangements made for treatment of their condition.

In either case, the period of absence must be unlikely to exceed 52 weeks and you must continue to meet the other qualifying conditions for the benefit. The treatment must take place outside GB and must be by, or under the supervision of, a person appropriately qualified to carry out that treatment.

ESA Regs, reg 153; ESA Regs 2013, reg 90

**NHS treatment abroad** – You can continue to be entitled to ESA during a temporary absence from GB if you continue to meet the other qualifying conditions for the benefit and your absence is for the purpose of receiving NHS treatment outside GB.

ESA Regs, reg 154; ESA Regs 2013, reg 91

**Partner abroad** – If you are claiming income-related ESA and you stay in GB, you will get benefit for your partner for the first four weeks. If they are accompanying a dependent child abroad for treatment (as under the 26-week rule above), you will get benefit for them for the first 26 weeks. After this, benefit will be reduced. Your partner's income and capital will

affect your award unless you do not intend to resume living together or the absence is likely to exceed 52 weeks.

ESA Regs, reg 156(1)&(3) & Sch 5, paras 6-7

**EEA** – Contributory ESA can continue to be paid in another EEA country.

SPC Regs, reg 5

## 6. Jobseeker's allowance

**General rules** – If you are entitled immediately before you leave, you can continue receiving jobseeker's allowance (JSA) during a temporary absence abroad if you are receiving NHS treatment outside GB or if the absence is unlikely to exceed 52 weeks and you satisfy one of the following rules – you can be paid for:

- the first **four weeks** if:
  - you are in Northern Ireland and continue to meet the qualifying conditions for the benefit;
  - (unless you come under the universal credit system) you are abroad with your partner and a disability premium, severe disability premium or pensioner premium is payable for your partner; *or*
  - (unless you come under the universal credit system) you are under 25 and receive a government training allowance but are not receiving training (although certain training courses are excluded);
- the first **eight weeks** if you are taking your dependent child abroad for medical treatment by an appropriately qualified person;
- up to **seven days** if you are abroad for a job interview for no longer than that and you give notice (written, if required) to the Jobcentre Plus office and on your return you satisfy the employment officer that you attended the interview; *or*
- the first **15 days** if you go abroad to take part in annual continuous training as a member of a reserve force.

JSA Regs, regs 50 & 170; JSA Regs 2013, reg 41

**Partner abroad** – If you are the claimant and you stay in GB, your income-based JSA will include benefit for your partner for the first four weeks (or eight weeks, if they meet the conditions of the 8-week rule above) of their absence abroad. However, if you are claiming as a joint-claim couple and on the date you make your claim your partner is abroad, you will only be paid for them for the first four weeks if they are in Northern Ireland (and the absence is unlikely to exceed 52 weeks) or they are receiving a training allowance (as above) or for up to seven days if they are attending a job interview. If you are already claiming JSA as a joint-claim couple and your partner goes abroad for NHS treatment at a hospital (or similar institution) outside GB, you continue to be paid as a couple for up to four weeks. Otherwise, or at the end of the period, your applicable amount will be paid as if you are single, but your partner's work, income and capital will affect your award unless you do not intend to resume living together or the absence is likely to exceed 52 weeks.

JSA Regs, regs 3E, 50, 78(1)-(3), 86C, 170, Sch 5, paras 10-11 and Sch 5A, para 7

**EEA** – For contribution-based JSA, if you go to an EEA country to look for work, have been registered with the Jobcentre Plus office for (normally) four weeks and meet the qualifying conditions up to the date you leave the UK, you can usually get benefit in the EEA country for up to three months. You must register as unemployed in the country where you are seeking work within seven days and comply with their procedures.

## 7. Universal credit

If you are entitled immediately before you leave, you can continue receiving universal credit during a temporary absence abroad for:

- **one month**, if the absence is not expected to exceed, and does not exceed, one month; *or*

- **two months**, if the absence is in connection with the death of your partner or child (or qualifying young person; see Chapter 16(4)) or a close relative of you, your partner or child (or qualifying young person) and it would be unreasonable for you to return to GB within the first month; *or*
- **six months**, if the absence is not expected to exceed, and does not exceed, six months and is solely in connection with medically approved care, convalescence or treatment of you, your partner or your child (or qualifying young person).

If you have a joint claim for universal credit, the rules above must apply to both you and your partner.

**Partner or child abroad** – If you stay in GB while your partner is abroad, your entitlement will not be affected while one of the groups above applies to them. If none of these apply, you will cease to be entitled to universal credit as joint claimants; you must claim as a single person. In this case, the 'standard allowance' in your award will be that for a single person (see Chapter 16(3)) but your partner's income and capital will still affect your award until your partner has been, or is expected to be, apart from you for six months, when you will cease to be treated as a couple (see Chapter 14(3)).

If your child (or qualifying young person) is abroad, they can be included in your award while one of the groups above applies to them.

UC Regs, reg 3(6), 4(7) & 11

## 8. Income support

If you are entitled immediately before you leave, you can continue receiving income support during a temporary absence abroad if:

- you are receiving NHS treatment outside GB; *or*
- the absence is unlikely to exceed 52 weeks, you continue to meet the other qualifying conditions for the benefit and you satisfy the 4- or 8-week rule below.

**4-week rule** – You can be paid income support for the first four weeks if:

- you are in Northern Ireland; *or*
- you and your partner are both abroad and a disability premium, severe disability premium or pensioner premium applies to the partner of the claimant; *or*
- you have been continuously incapable of work during the 364 days before the day you leave GB, or 196 days if you are terminally ill or entitled to personal independence payment enhanced rate daily living component, disability living allowance highest rate care component or armed forces independence payment (two or more periods of incapacity are treated as continuous if the break between them is not more than 56 days each time); *or*
- you are incapable of work and your absence is *'for the sole purpose of receiving treatment from an appropriately qualified person for the incapacity by reason of which'* you are eligible for income support; *or*

---

### 0.1 For more information

For further information on benefits for people entering and leaving the UK, see *Welfare Benefits and Tax Credits Handbook* (2018/19), Part 11 and *Benefits for Migrants Handbook* (9th Ed) (both published by Child Poverty Action Group).

For immigration advice, contact a law centre (see Chapter 58(2)).

DWP and HMRC leaflets (including some in languages other than English) for countries covered by a reciprocal agreement with the UK are available from the International Pension Centre (see Chapter 61).

---

- you are in one of the groups that can claim income support (see Box F.1 in Chapter 19) other than if you are entitled to statutory sick pay, or are incapable of work (unless you are covered by one of the last two bullet points), or are a 'person subject to immigration control', or are in full-time education, or involved in a trade dispute.

**8-week rule** – You can get income support for the first eight weeks abroad if you are taking your dependent child abroad for medical treatment by an appropriately qualified person.

IS Regs, reg 4

**Partner abroad** – If you are the claimant and you stay in GB, your income support will include benefit for your partner for the first four weeks (or eight weeks, if they meet the conditions of the 8-week rule above) of their absence abroad. After this, your applicable amount will be paid as if you were single, but your partner's work, income and capital will affect your award unless you do not intend to resume living together or the absence is likely to exceed 52 weeks.

IS Regs, reg 16(1)&(2) and Sch 7, paras 11 & 11A

## 9. Pension credit

You continue to be entitled to pension credit during a temporary absence from GB for up to:

- **4 weeks**, if the absence is not expected to exceed that. The four weeks can be extended by up to four further weeks if the absence is in connection with the death of a close relative and the DWP considers it would be unreasonable for you to return within the first four weeks; *or*
- **26 weeks**, if the absence is not expected to exceed that and you are receiving medical treatment, or medically approved convalescence, due to a condition that began before leaving GB.

**Partner abroad** – If one of the above circumstances applies to your partner, your pension credit will include benefit for them for the relevant period of their temporary absence. After this, they cease to be treated as your partner and your benefit will be reduced.

SPC Regs, reg 5

## 10. Housing benefit

The rules on whether you are entitled to housing benefit during a temporary absence from GB are part of the general 'temporary absence' rules (in which you can be treated as occupying your home while absent from it in certain circumstances – see Chapter 25(6)). You are entitled to housing benefit, if you intend to return to your home, and have not let or sub-let it, for up to:

- **4 weeks**, if your absence is unlikely to exceed four weeks or you are covered by the any of the groups listed under the 52-week rule in Chapter 25(6) (other than those in the bullet point below). The four weeks can be extended by up to four further weeks if the absence is in connection with the death of a close relative and the local authority considers it would be unreasonable for you to return within the first four weeks; *or*
- **26 weeks**, if your absence from GB is unlikely to exceed (or in exceptional circumstances, substantially exceed) 26 weeks and you:
  - are an inpatient in hospital or similar institution; *or*
  - (or your partner or dependent child) are undergoing medically approved treatment, care or convalescence in non-residential accommodation.

## 11. Tax credits

If you are ordinarily resident in, but temporarily absent* from, the UK, you are treated as present and can therefore either claim, or continue to be entitled to, tax credits for the first eight weeks, or for the first 12 weeks if the absence is in connection with:

- your treatment for a disability; *or*

■ the treatment (for a disability) or death of your partner, the sibling, parent, (great)grandparent, child (including a child you are responsible for) or (great)grandchild of you or your partner.

\* defined as unlikely to exceed 52 weeks

TC(R) Regs, reg 4

**EEA** – If you are in the UK, child tax credit can be paid for family members living in another EEA country. It can also be paid if you go to another EEA country.

## 12. Child benefit

If you are ordinarily resident in, but temporarily absent\* from, the UK, you continue to be entitled to child benefit for the first eight weeks, or for the first 12 weeks if the absence is in connection with:

■ your treatment for a disability or illness; *or*
■ the treatment (for a disability or illness) or death of your partner, or the sibling, parent, (great)grandparent, child (including a child you are responsible for), or (great) grandchild of you or your partner.

\* defined as unlikely to exceed 52 weeks

If a woman gives birth while outside the UK and one of the two bullet points above applies, the baby will be treated as being in the UK for up to 12 weeks from the start of the mother's absence.

Child benefit can be paid for the first 12 weeks of your child's temporary absence abroad. It may be paid for longer if your child goes abroad:

■ for the specific purpose of being treated for an illness or disability that began before they left the UK; *or*
■ solely to receive full-time education in another EEA country (or Switzerland) or on an educational exchange or visit.

CB Regs, Part 6

The same rules apply to guardian's allowance.

**EEA** – You may be paid benefit for a child resident in another EEA country and also if you go to another EEA country.

## 13. Employer-paid benefits

You can receive statutory sick, maternity, paternity, adoption and shared parental pay while abroad, unless your employer is not required to pay Class 1 national insurance contributions for you – eg because they are not present or resident, and do not have a place of business, in the UK.

## 14. Industrial injuries disablement benefit

Basic disablement pension and retirement allowance are both payable while you are abroad. However, there are time limits for other industrial injuries benefits.

**Reduced earnings allowance (REA)** – REA is payable for the first three months of a temporary absence abroad if you were entitled before you left and your absence is not connected with work, or for longer if the DWP agrees. If you lose REA for one day, you may lose it for good.

**Constant attendance allowance and exceptionally severe disablement allowance** – These are payable for the first six months of a temporary absence abroad, or longer if the DWP agrees.

PA Regs, reg 9

**EEA** – Any industrial injuries benefit (including those above) can be paid without time limit in an EEA country.

## 15. Retirement, widows' and bereavement benefits

These are payable no matter how long you are away. If you intend to go for longer than six months, inform the DWP so arrangements can be made for paying your benefit abroad. If you are living permanently in a country outside the EEA, you can only receive annual upratings if that country has a reciprocal agreement with the UK covering the payment of annual increases or you are covered by a co-operation and association agreement.

You will not be entitled to bereavement support payment unless at the date of your spouse/civil partner's death you were ordinarily resident in GB.

PA Regs, reg 4; Pensions Act 2014, S.30(1)(c)

**EEA** – If you are living in another EEA country, you can get annual benefit increases as if you were in the UK. For bereavement support payment, the requirement to be ordinarily resident in GB when your spouse or civil partner dies does not apply if you are living in another EEA country on that date.

# 55 Benefits in hospital

| | | |
|---|---|---|
| 1 | What should you do beforehand? | 303 |
| 2 | Hospital travel fares | 303 |
| 3 | What happens to means-tested benefits? | 304 |
| | Means-tested benefits: hospital-stay timeline – Box O.2 | 305 |
| 4 | What happens to non-means-tested benefits? | 305 |
| 5 | Long-term stays | 306 |
| 6 | What about when you leave hospital? | 306 |
| 7 | Discharged before you're ready? | 307 |
| | For more information – Box O.3 | 306 |

## 1. What should you do beforehand?

Stays in hospital (or a similar institution – see below) as an inpatient can affect benefits. Four of the main disability benefits – attendance allowance, disability living allowance (DLA), personal independence payment (PIP) and carer's allowance – can be stopped after just a few weeks in hospital, as can child benefit (see 4 below). In turn, this can affect your entitlement to income-related employment and support allowance, income support, housing benefit and pension credit (see 3 below and Box O.2). Universal credit can be affected by the stopping of carer's allowance (see 3 below). Consequently, you must let the DWP know if you or a dependant are admitted to hospital. If you get carer's allowance, you must tell the DWP if the person you are caring for is admitted.

If you get housing benefit and a spell in hospital results in attendance allowance, DLA, PIP, carer's allowance or child benefit being stopped, you also need to tell the local authority.

Write to the office(s) dealing with your benefits to let them know the date you expect to be admitted to hospital and how long you are likely to stay. You should still report your actual admission or tell the office(s) if it is cancelled or postponed.

**Fit notes** – If you need fit notes to get benefit when in hospital, ask the ward sister or charge nurse for them.

**Hospital or similar institution** – Benefits are affected by a stay in a *'similar institution'* in the same way as a stay in hospital. 'Similar institution' is not defined in legislation, although you must receive inpatient medical treatment or professional nursing care in the home under specified NHS legislation. What matters is not so much the nature of the accommodation, but whether your assessed needs for care are such that the NHS is under a duty to fund the accommodation free of charge, in which case you will still be treated as an inpatient.

Social Security (Hospital In-Patients) Regs 2005, reg 2(4); R(DLA)2/06

**Private patients** – If you are a private patient paying the whole cost of accommodation and non-medical services in hospital, you are not considered to be an inpatient and therefore the normal rules of benefit entitlement apply, not those described in this chapter.

## 2. Hospital travel fares

**Healthcare Travel Costs scheme** – You may be able to get help with fares or other travel expenses for yourself (and for someone who has to go with you, where it is considered medically necessary) if you are either exempt from NHS charges or qualify for full help with them (see Chapter 52(1)). Help is also available if you are covered by the Low Income scheme (see Chapter 52(5)). If your income is above the low-income level but would fall below it if you paid the fares, you may still be eligible for help with part of the cost. Help with fares or other travel expenses is also available if you:

- live in the Isles of Scilly and need to travel to a mainland hospital; *or*
- live in the Scottish Islands or Highlands and need to travel more than five miles by sea or 30 miles by land to get to hospital; *or*
- are getting NHS treatment abroad. Costs can be met up to the embarkation point as per normal travel expenses (see below); however, the overseas travel is part of the treatment costs and must be agreed beforehand by the health authority.

NHS(TERC) Regs, regs 3, 5, 5B, 6 & 9

**Parents** – If your child (aged under 16) has to go into hospital or attend on a regular basis, you may claim help with travel expenses to accompany your child to and from the hospital.

NHS(TERC) Regs, regs 3(3)(a)

**Inpatients sent home on short leave** – If you are sent home temporarily as part of your treatment or for the hospital's convenience, your fares are regarded as part of your treatment costs and should be met by the hospital and not under the Healthcare Travel Costs scheme.

### What travel expenses can be covered?

You can get help with the cost of travelling by the cheapest means of transport that is reasonable in your circumstances, including your age and condition. This is normally the cost of standard-class public transport. If public transport is available but you choose to go by car, your fuel costs would normally only be covered up to the amount of the standard-class fare. However, if there is a valid reason why you cannot use public transport (eg you are unable to use it because of a physical disability or it is not available) and you go by car or taxi, your fuel costs or fares will be covered. You must get agreement from the hospital first for the use of taxis. The travel costs of an escort can also be met if you need to be accompanied for medical reasons.

NHS(TERC) Regs, regs 3(3)(b) & (5)

### How to claim the cost of fares

The hospital will refund your fares if you show them proof of your entitlement (eg your benefit award letter or tax credit exemption certificate) and your travel receipts. If you have already claimed on low-income grounds, show your HC2 certificate (full entitlement) or your HC3 certificate (partial entitlement).

If you haven't yet claimed on low-income grounds, use form HC5 to claim a refund, and form HC1 to establish your entitlement to full or partial help. You can get the forms by ringing the NHS Forms-line (0300 123 0849). The HC5 must be returned within three months of paying your fares.

**Partial help with fares** – The amount shown on an HC3 certificate for partial help is the amount you are expected to be able to pay for travel expenses in any one week (from Sunday to the following Saturday). If your actual hospital travel expenses in any particular week covered by that HC3 certificate are higher, the excess is refunded. This helps if you have to travel long distances to hospital or if you have to make several visits to the same, or to different, hospitals within the same week.

### Other sources of help

Other possible sources of help with travel expenses for patients and visitors include hospital endowment funds, education departments, adult social care departments, the Family Fund (see Chapter 40(8)) and various charities. For advice about these, contact a hospital social worker or an advice centre.

**War pensioners** – If you attend hospital for treatment for a war disablement, you can claim for expenses regardless of your income. Contact Veterans UK (see Chapter 47(6)).

## 3. What happens to means-tested benefits?

### Income-related employment and support allowance, income support and pension credit

If you go into hospital, income-related employment and support allowance (ESA), income support and pension credit can sometimes continue to be paid indefinitely without being reduced. However, the disability, enhanced disability and higher pensioner premiums in income support (and any premiums and additional components in income-related ESA) are stopped after 52 weeks. Also, if benefits such as disability living allowance, attendance allowance, personal independence payment or carer's allowance are stopped, this will affect the amount of benefit you receive. See Box O.2 for details.

Income-related ESA, income support and pension credit can continue to be paid for a temporary period while you are receiving NHS hospital treatment abroad (see Chapter 54(5) and (8)-(9)).

### Jobseeker's allowance

You cannot normally claim jobseeker's allowance (JSA) while you are in hospital because you will not be considered to be capable of work or able to meet the labour market conditions. However, if you are already receiving JSA when you go into hospital, you can be treated as not having a limited capability for work for up to 13 weeks, during which time you can also be treated as being available for work and actively seeking work. Consequently, your JSA can continue to be paid. See Chapter 13(4)) for details.

When your JSA stops, you should claim ESA.

JSA can continue to be paid for a temporary period while you are receiving NHS hospital treatment abroad (see Chapter 54(6)).

### Housing benefit

If you get housing benefit, it will be reduced during a spell in hospital if benefits such as attendance allowance, disability living allowance, personal independence payment or carer's allowance are stopped. See Box O.2 for details.

### Tax credits

Child tax credit and working tax credit are not automatically affected by a stay in hospital. However, if you stop being treated as employed because of a stay in hospital, you no longer qualify for working tax credit (see Chapter 23(6)).

### Universal credit

If you go into hospital, universal credit is normally paid indefinitely without being reduced. However, if your partner is in hospital and their stay is expected to last, or has lasted, for more than six months, your joint claim will end and you will need to claim as a single person. See 5 below for how the housing costs amount can be affected by a stay in hospital.

UC Regs, reg 3(6)

If a child or qualifying young person you are responsible for (see Chapter 16(4)) is in hospital, you will still get a child amount in your universal credit award if their stay is temporary. However, the child amount will stop if their stay is expected to last, or has lasted, for more than six months.

UC Regs, reg 4(7)(a)

**The carer amount** – If the person you are caring for goes into hospital, the carer amount will no longer be included in your universal credit award once you no longer meet the qualifying conditions for carer's allowance (see Chapter 8(2)).

UC Regs, regs 29(1) & 30(1)

### 4. What happens to non-means-tested benefits?

Most non-means-tested benefits continue to be paid indefinitely. The exceptions are attendance allowance, disability living allowance (DLA), personal independence payment (PIP) and carer's allowance, as well as child benefit, guardian's allowance and any child dependant's addition that may still be payable with other benefits. They are treated in the following way.

### During the first 28 days

If you are aged under 18 on the day you go into hospital, DLA and PIP can be paid indefinitely. Otherwise, these benefits, along with attendance allowance, can only be paid for the first 28 days of a hospital stay. Once you have been in hospital for more than 28 days, they stop.

AA Regs, regs 6 & 8(1)(a); DLA Regs, regs 8, 10(1) & 12A-12B(1); PIP Regs, regs 29 & 30(1)

Attendance allowance, DLA care component and PIP daily living component will stop before the 28 days are up if you had been in hospital or a care home in the 28 days before the current hospital stay. The number of days during each hospital (or care home) stay are added together and payment of the benefit will stop after a total of 28 days.

AA Regs, regs 8(2); DLA Regs, reg 10(5); PIP Regs, reg 32(4)

The mobility component of both DLA and PIP will stop before the 28 days are up only if you had been in hospital in

---

## O.2 Means-tested benefits: hospital-stay timeline

This box relates to:
- income-related employment and support allowance (ESA);
- income support;
- housing benefit; *and*
- pension credit.

These benefits can continue to be paid throughout your stay in hospital, but may be reduced depending on your circumstances. In particular, your benefit may be cut when the following *'qualifying benefits'* are withdrawn:
- attendance allowance;
- disability living allowance (DLA) care component at the middle or highest rate; *and*
- personal independence payment (PIP) daily living component.

### Stage 1 – from day one

There is normally no cut in your benefit during your first 28 days in hospital, unless you had been in hospital or a care home in the 28 days before the current hospital stay and your qualifying benefit stops as a result, in which case, see Stage 2 below.

**Extra benefit** – You may qualify for the severe disability premium (or equivalent pension credit additional amount) temporarily while your carer or another non-dependant is in hospital. See Chapter 21(3).

### Stage 2 – after 28 days

After 28 days in hospital, attendance allowance stops; if you were aged 18 or over on the day you went into hospital, DLA and PIP stop. These benefits may stop earlier if you had been in hospital or a care home in the 28 days before the current hospital stay; see 4 in this chapter. Once one of these qualifying benefits stop, any severe disability premium (or equivalent pension credit additional amount) in your means-tested benefit normally also stops. However, if you have a partner and both of you had been getting a qualifying benefit, you keep the premium even after your qualifying benefit stops, but at the single rate of £64.30.

ESA Regs, Sch 4, paras 6(5) & 11(2)(b)(i); IS Regs, Sch 2, paras 13(3A) & 15(5)(b)(i); PC Regs, reg 6(5) & Sch 1, para 1(2)(b)

If you are entitled to income-related ESA or income support only because a severe disability premium is included in the award, when the premium stops at the 28-day stage you will lose the income-related ESA or income support. The same applies if an additional amount for severe disability in the guarantee credit of pension credit stops. If you are getting housing benefit, you should tell your local authority about the loss of income-related ESA, income support or pension credit so that they can reassess your award.

A carer premium (or equivalent pension credit additional amount) is withdrawn eight weeks after carer's allowance stops (see Chapter 8(11)) or, if your carer's allowance is overlapped by another benefit, after the qualifying benefit stops (see Chapter 21(6)).

### Stage 3 – after 52 weeks

You can continue to receive income-related ESA, income support and pension credit for the duration of your stay in hospital. However, for income support, any disability premium, enhanced disability premium or higher pensioner premium will stop after you have been in hospital for 52 weeks (unless you have a partner who remains at home and satisfies the condition for the premium themselves).

IS Regs, reg 2(1) & Sch 2, paras 10(6), 11(2) & 13A(2)

Similarly, any premiums and the work-related activity or support components in income-related ESA will stop after you have been in hospital for 52 weeks if you are single or, if you are one of a couple, if you have both been in hospital for 52 weeks.

ESA Regs, Sch 5, para 13

If non-dependant deductions are being made from your income-related ESA, income support, pension credit or housing benefit, they will stop after your non-dependant has been in hospital for 52 weeks (ignoring absences from hospital of up to 28 days).

ESA Regs, Sch 6, para 19(7)(g); IS Regs, Sch 3, para 18(7)(g)

**Housing costs** – Once you have been away from your home continuously for 52 weeks, you can no longer be treated as occupying it. You would therefore no longer be entitled to housing benefit, support for mortgage interest loans or income-related ESA, income support or pension credit housing costs, though someone still living in your home could possibly claim these benefits if they were treated as liable to pay the rent, mortgage or housing costs themselves.

**Child** – Once a child has been in hospital for 52 weeks, you continue to have an allowance for them included in your income support award (if it is still included) for as long as you keep visiting the child.

**Treatment abroad** – Special rules apply for patients receiving NHS hospital treatment abroad (see Chapter 54(5) and (8)-(9)).

### Pension credit

The guarantee credit of pension credit is reduced in a similar fashion to income-related ESA and income support. The savings credit element is not reduced directly, but the amount may still change once the additional amounts in the 'appropriate minimum guarantee' of the guarantee credit are withdrawn or when you are no longer treated as a couple.

the 28 days before the current hospital stay.
DLA Regs, reg 12B(3); PIP Regs, reg 32(4)

You count days in hospital from the day after you are admitted to the day before you go home. Neither the day you go in nor the day that you leave count as days in hospital.
AA Regs, reg 6(2A); DLA Regs, reg 8(2A) & 12A(2A); PIP Regs, reg 32(2)

### After 28 days
Attendance allowance stops. If you were aged 18 or over on the day you went into hospital, DLA and PIP stop. Your carer's allowance will stop if the person you are caring for has been in hospital for more than 28 days and their attendance allowance, DLA care component or PIP daily living component has stopped.

If you claim attendance allowance when you are already in hospital, it cannot be paid until you leave. If you were aged 18 or over on the day you went into hospital and claim DLA or PIP during the stay, it cannot be paid until you leave.

Constant attendance allowance (payable in the War Pensions and Industrial Injuries schemes) and war pensioners' severe disablement occupational allowance stop.
Naval, Military and Air Forces Etc. (Disablement & Death) Service Pensions Order 2006, art 53

**Motability** – If you have a Motability agreement in force when you go into hospital, once payment of the mobility component has stopped, Motability should not seek to recover your vehicle for up to 28 days. They can defer the return of your vehicle for longer than this, at their discretion. Once the vehicle is returned, any advance payment outstanding will be returned to you on a pro rata basis.

### After 12 weeks
**Child in hospital** – Child benefit or guardian's allowance is paid for the first 12 weeks if your child or a child you care for goes into hospital. After 12 weeks, you can continue to get these benefits for a child in hospital only if you are regularly spending money on the child's behalf (eg on clothing, pocket money, magazines). If you continue to get child benefit, you will continue to get any child dependant's addition that may still be payable with other benefits (such as carer's allowance), but otherwise this will also end.
SSCBA, S.143(4) & CB Regs, reg 10

**If you or your partner are in hospital** – Child benefit normally continues to be paid. Carer's allowance stops after the carer has been in hospital for 12 weeks (but it may stop sooner – see Chapter 8(11)).

### Employer-paid benefits
Going into hospital does not affect entitlement to statutory sick pay, statutory maternity pay, statutory shared parental pay, statutory adoption pay or statutory paternity pay.

## 5. Long-term stays
If you have to stay in hospital for a long-term period, state pension can continue to be paid indefinitely.

If you are in the support group (see Chapter 11(5)), you

may continue to receive contributory employment and support allowance (ESA) indefinitely, although the support component is stopped after you have been in hospital for 52 weeks.
ESA Regs, Sch 5, para 13; ESA Regs 2013, reg 63(1)(b)

Income-related ESA, income support and pension credit can also be paid indefinitely (as long as the other qualifying conditions continue to be met), although the rate may be affected by the withdrawal of benefits such as personal independence payment (see Box O.2). Also, the disability, enhanced disability and higher pensioner premiums in income support stop after 52 weeks (unless you have a partner at home who meets the conditions for the premium themselves). Similarly, any premiums and the work-related activity or support components in income-related ESA stop after you have been in hospital for 52 weeks if you are single; if you are one of a couple, these stop after both of you have been in hospital for 52 weeks.
IS Regs, reg 2(1) & Sch 2, paras 10(6), 11(2) & 13A(2); ESA Regs, Sch 5, para 13

### Housing costs
Once you have been in hospital for a continuous period of 52 weeks, if you have no dependants living in your home, you can no longer receive housing benefit, support for mortgage interest loans or income-related ESA, income support or pension credit housing costs. The maximum period of absence in one stretch during which housing benefit, support for mortgage interest loans or housing costs can be paid is 52 weeks (see Chapter 25(6) for the housing benefit rules; those for the other benefits are similar). If you have dependants or other people living in your home, their right to benefit depends on their own circumstances. If you are one of a couple and have been in hospital for 52 weeks, you and your partner are treated as separate claimants.

**Universal credit** – In the case of universal credit, if your hospital stay exceeds, or is expected to exceed, six months and you have no dependants living in your home, you will be treated as not occupying the home, and therefore will not be entitled to the housing costs amount. If you have a partner living in your home, and your hospital stay exceeds, or is expected to exceed, six months, they will need to claim universal credit as a single person.

## 6. What about when you leave hospital?
Whether or not any benefit has been changed or stopped while you or a dependant have been in hospital, make sure you inform the office that administers each benefit as soon as you know the date you or your dependant are coming home.

You should still report your actual date of discharge, or tell the appropriate office if it is cancelled or postponed.

### Temporary absence from hospital
If you, or a dependant, spend a few days at home – perhaps for a trial run, or if you are in and out of hospital on a regular pattern – tell the office that administers each benefit and ask them to pay the full amount of benefit for the days at home. Get a note from the hospital to say how many days you have at home. For all benefits except attendance allowance, disability living allowance (DLA) and personal independence payment (PIP), the day you are admitted is treated as a day *out* of hospital and the day you are discharged is treated as a day *in* hospital. For attendance allowance, DLA and PIP, see below.
Social Security (Hospital In-Patients) Regs 2005, reg 2(5)

**Can your carer get carer's allowance?** – If you go home regularly each weekend and receive attendance allowance, DLA care component (at the middle or highest rate) or PIP daily living component, your carer might qualify for the full rate of carer's allowance. This is because carer's allowance is a weekly benefit and is never paid on a daily basis. See

---

### O.3 For more information

■ More information on help with hospital travel fares is available at: www.nhsbsa.nhs.uk/help-travel-eye-care-wigs-and-fabric-support-costs/travel-receive-nhs-treatment; or ring the NHS Helpline for advice (0300 330 1343)

■ Leaflet 2 *Notes for people getting a war pension living in the United Kingdom*, is available at: www.gov.uk/government/publications/war-pension-scheme; or ring the Veterans UK Helpline for advice (0808 1914 218)

Chapter 8(2) to check whether your carer can meet the 35 hours a week caring test.

**Attendance allowance, DLA and PIP** – These are adjusted to be paid at a daily rate if you are expected to return to hospital within 28 days. Attendance allowance, DLA care component and PIP daily living component are also paid at a daily rate if you are expected to return to a care home within 28 days. This rule ceases to apply once you have been out of hospital for 28 days.

The daily rate rule does not apply if, on the day of discharge, you are not expected to return to hospital within 28 days, even if you do return to hospital within that period. If you are not expected to return to hospital within 28 days (and when you are finally discharged from hospital) full benefit resumes from the first payday.

C&P Regs, reg 25; UCPIP(C&P) Regs, reg 50

Both the day you are admitted or return to hospital and the day you are discharged or leave hospital count as days out of hospital. You can be paid for both of those days as well as whole days out of hospital.

AA Regs, reg 6(2A); DLA Regs, regs 8(2A) & 12A(2A); PIP Regs, reg 32(2)

### Permanently out of hospital

In general, you should get the benefit you were receiving before you went into hospital at the normal rate. If you go from hospital into a care home, see Chapter 38.

If you did not draw any benefit before you went into hospital, see Chapter 11 on employment and support allowance or, if you have reached pension credit qualifying age, Chapter 44. Once you leave hospital, all the normal rules for these benefits will apply to you.

### 7. Discharged before you're ready?

If acute nursing care in hospital is no longer essential for you, the hospital will clearly wish to discharge you. It may be impossible for you to return home without support services in place. Before being discharged, your care needs should have been assessed. Don't agree to a discharge unless you are happy with the arrangements for continuing care and support as set out in your care and support plan (see Chapter 36(3)). Don't agree to move to a care home unless you are absolutely clear about how, and for how long, the full cost will be met.

# **56** Claims and payments

| | | |
|---|---|---|
| 1 | Making a claim | 307 |
| 2 | Date of claim | 307 |
| | Work-focused interviews – Box O.4 | 308 |
| 3 | Backdating delayed claims | 308 |
| | Interchange of claims – Box O.5 | 309 |
| | Can your claim for benefit be backdated? – Box O.6 | 310 |
| 4 | Appointees | 310 |
| 5 | Payments | 310 |
| 6 | Short-term advances and universal credit advances | 311 |
| 7 | Overpayments | 311 |
| 8 | Civil penalties and fraud | 312 |

### 1. Making a claim

For most benefits, you are encouraged to make first contact by telephone. Details of your claim can be taken on the phone; a statement may then be sent to you to check the details are correct. Claims for many benefits can also be made online; for universal credit, this is the standard way to claim.

For details about how to claim each benefit, see the relevant chapter in this handbook. Here we look at some of the common rules about, and problems with, claiming.

**Who should claim?** – You should claim (or ask the DWP for advice) as soon as you think you might qualify. If you cannot make enquiries or claim yourself, get someone else to do so; the DWP can accept a claim made by someone else on your behalf as long as you have signed it. The DWP can appoint someone to act on behalf of anyone who cannot act for themselves (see 4 below).

**Defective claims** – If you make a *'defective'* claim (ie one not completed in accordance with DWP instructions, eg you don't use the correct form), the claim should be referred back to you. If it is referred back, and you correct the defect within one month (eg you return the properly completed claim-form), or longer if an extension is agreed, your claim must be treated as though the original claim had been properly made. See 2 below for the rules on income support and jobseeker's allowance. You can challenge a decision to disallow benefit on the basis that the claim was defective through the normal reconsiderations and appeals process (see Chapter 57).

C&P Regs, regs 4(7), 4G(3)-(5) & 4H(6)-(7); UCPIP(C&P) Regs, regs 8(5)-(6), 11(5)-(6), 13(4)-(5), 15(3)-(4), 21(4)-(5) & 23(3)-(4); *Novitskaya V London Borough of Brent & Anon* [2009] EWCA Civ 1260

**National insurance (NI) numbers** – For most benefits, you must give your NI number when you claim (and your partner's if you are claiming for them) and enough information to confirm the number is yours. If you don't know your number, give the DWP sufficient information to allow them to trace it or go to www.gov.uk/lost-national-insurance-number. If you don't have an NI number, you are still entitled to benefit if you apply for a number and provide enough information and evidence for one to be allocated to you. To apply for an NI number, contact 0800 141 2075 (textphone 0800 141 2438).

SSAA, S.1(1A) & (1B)

### 2. Date of claim

The date your claim is *'made'* is usually the day it is received, properly completed, in a DWP office, DWP-approved office or (for tax credits) HMRC office. Sometimes your claim can be treated as though it were made on an earlier date.

❏ For disability living allowance and attendance allowance, your date of claim is the date you requested a claim-form from the DWP as long as you return the completed claim-form within six weeks.*

C&P Regs, reg 6(8)&(9)

❏ For personal independence payment (PIP), your date of claim is normally the date you telephoned the PIP claim-line. If you asked for a paper claim, your date of claim is the date that the DWP received your request, as long as you return the completed form within one month.*

UCPIP(C&P) Regs, reg 12(1)(b)&(c)

❏ For employment and support allowance telephone claims, your date of claim is normally the date you telephoned the claim-line. For written claims, your date of claim is the date you informed the DWP of your intention to claim, as long as they receive a properly completed claim-form from you within a month of your first contact*. For details, see Chapter 11(9).

C&P Regs, reg 6(1F) & UCPIP(C&P) Regs, regs 14 & 16

❏ For pension credit, your date of claim is the date you informed the DWP or local authority office of your intention to claim, as long as you provide all the information and evidence they require within one month.*

C&P Regs, reg 4F(3)

* or a longer period if the DWP agrees to an extension

### Claims for income support

Your date of claim for income support is the date you first told the DWP you wanted to claim, as long as you return the claim-form (or signed statement if the claim was made over the phone) fully completed with the required information and evidence within one month. Until you do this, you have not made your claim, unless you can show that one of the following situations applies:

# O.4 Work-focused interviews

You have to take part in one or more 'work-focused interviews' if you are claiming employment and support allowance (ESA), incapacity benefit, income support or severe disablement allowance (SDA). You also have to take part in a work-focused interview if your partner is claiming extra for you in incapacity benefit, income support or SDA.

In the work-focused interview, a work coach will discuss your work prospects. We describe what happens at a work-focused interview in Chapter 11(13); the process is similar for each benefit.

An interview for one benefit counts for all others, so you don't have to go through interviews for each benefit you claim.

You also have to take part in work-focused interviews if you are claiming universal credit (unless none of the work-related requirements apply to you – see Box E.3 in Chapter 15; see Chapter 15(3) for details of these. See Chapter 13(5) and (7) for details of the work-focused interviews as they apply to jobseeker's allowance.

You do not have to attend a work-focused interview if you have reached pension credit qualifying age (see Chapter 44(2)).

## What if you don't attend or take part ?

The 'sanctions' for not taking part in an ESA work-focused interview are described in Chapter 11(15). If you are claiming incapacity benefit, SDA or income support on the grounds of incapacity, sanctions are applied as follows: for the first four weeks £14.52 is deducted from your benefit, thereafter £29.05 is deducted.
*Social Security (Incapacity Benefit Work-focused Interviews) Regs 2008, reg 9*

For other benefits, the rules are as follows.

**New claims** – Unless you can show you had good cause for not attending or taking part in a work-focused interview, your claim will not proceed. If the interview had been deferred, with the result that benefit was already in payment, then entitlement will stop. In either case, you should claim again, and challenge the decision if you think it is wrong (see below).
*JPI Regs, reg 12(2)(a)&(b) & (13)*

**Benefit in payment** – If you are already claiming benefit and you fail to attend or take part in a work-focused interview without good cause, a deduction of £14.62 a week is made from your benefit. The deduction continues until you do take part in a work-focused interview or reach pension credit qualifying age.
*JPI Regs, regs 12(2)(c), 12(9), (13) & 13*

If your partner fails to attend or take part in a work-focused interview when required to do so without good cause, £14.62 a week is deducted from your benefit. This deduction continues until they do take part in a work-focused interview.
*Social Security (Jobcentre Plus Interviews for Partners) Regs 2003, reg 11*

## Challenging sanction decisions

When the decision maker informs you that you have failed to take part in an interview, you have five working days in which to show 'good cause' for that failure. If you are not able to do so and the decision maker imposes the sanction, you can ask for a mandatory reconsideration (see Chapter 57(3)) and then, if this is unsuccessful, appeal (see Chapter 57(7)).
*ESA Regs, reg 61(1); JPI Regs, reg 11(4)*

If you are successful and the sanction is overturned, any arrears due are paid back in full.

❑ You have a 'physical, learning, mental or communication difficulty' and it is not reasonably practicable for you to get help with your claim or get the required information or evidence.
❑ The information or evidence required:
  – does not exist; *or*
  – can only be obtained at serious risk of physical or mental harm to you and it is not reasonably practicable for you to get it by other means; *or*
  – can only be obtained from a third party and it is not reasonably practicable for you to get it from them.
*C&P Regs, regs 4(1B) & 6(1A)*

Send in your claim-form or signed statement explaining your difficulties, or ring the DWP (or get someone else to contact them for you). If you do this within one month and they accept your reasons, your date of claim will be the date you first told the DWP you wanted to claim.

If there is other evidence needed to decide your claim but it is not specified in the claim-form, it does not affect your date of claim if you can't provide it with your claim.

## Claims for jobseeker's allowance (JSA)

Your date of claim is the date you first contacted the DWP, as long as you provide all the required evidence before or at your 'work-focused interview'. If you fail to attend the interview, or provide the required evidence, your date of claim will be the date that you eventually do so. In the case of a joint claim (see Chapter 13(2)) where you are both required to attend an interview, and fail to do so, the date of claim will be the date that one of you does attend. However, you will only be paid the single person rate of JSA until you both attend an interview.
*C&P Regs, reg 6(4ZB)&(4A); JSA Regs, Sch 5, para 17A*

If you cannot get all the evidence for one of the reasons outlined above for income support, contact the DWP to explain your difficulties. If you do this within one month and they accept your reasons, your date of claim will be the date you first told the DWP you wanted to claim.
*C&P Regs, regs 4(1B) & 6(4AB)*

If you are claiming JSA under the universal credit system, your date of claim is the date you informed the DWP of your intention to claim, as long as the appropriate office receives a properly completed claim-form from you, or the required information and evidence if the claim is made over the phone, within one month (or a longer period if the DWP agrees to an extension) of your first contact.
*UCPIP(C&P) Regs, regs 20 & 24*

## 3. Backdating delayed claims

If you could have qualified for a benefit for a period before you actually claimed it, you may be able to get your claim backdated. If you want your claim backdated, you should state this when you claim. Backdating time limits are given in Box O.6. and below.

**Income support and jobseeker's allowance (JSA)** – These can be backdated for up to one month or three months in the limited circumstances described below.

**Housing benefit** – If you are below the qualifying age for pension credit (see Chapter 44(2)), housing benefit can be backdated for up to one month if you ask for it and have continuous 'good cause' for the delay in claiming (see Chapter 25(16)). If you have reached pension credit qualifying age (and are not claiming income support, income-related employment and support allowance (ESA) or income-based JSA), housing benefit can normally be backdated for up to three months without you having to ask for it or show good cause.

**Universal credit** – This can be backdated for up to one month in limited circumstances; see Chapter 14(7) for details.

### Delays in qualifying benefits

Entitlement to some benefits may depend on you, a member of your family or someone else getting another benefit, known as a *'qualifying'* benefit. For example, carer's allowance depends on the person you care for receiving the appropriate rate of personal independence payment (PIP), disability living allowance (DLA) or attendance allowance (see Chapter 8(2)).

**Claiming the benefit** – Claim straight away; do not wait for a decision on the qualifying benefit. Once you have made this claim, if you have not already claimed the qualifying benefit, you have another 10 days to do so. If the first claim is refused because the qualifying benefit has not yet been awarded, claim again once you get a decision awarding the qualifying benefit. If you do this within three months of the decision awarding the qualifying benefit (which might be after a reconsideration or appeal if the qualifying benefit is at first refused), the second claim can be backdated to the date of the first claim, or to the date from which the qualifying benefit is awarded, if that is later.
C&P Regs, reg 6(16)-(18)

**Qualifying benefit reinstatements** – Where entitlement to one benefit depends on another, if one stops the other stops too. If you challenge the decision on the qualifying benefit and it is reinstated, make a fresh claim for the other benefit within three months of the date of the decision to reinstate the qualifying benefit – the other benefit will then be fully backdated. For example, if your PIP is stopped, you may lose entitlement to income-related ESA. If you get back your PIP after a successful appeal, make a fresh claim for income-related ESA and it will be paid again from the date it was stopped.
C&P Regs, reg 6(19)-(21)

**Income support/income-based JSA additional rule** – When you are getting income support or income-based JSA and make a claim for a benefit that could provide access to a premium, eg carer's allowance, it is possible that while you are waiting for the carer's allowance to be awarded the income support/JSA might be stopped for some other reason, eg a small increase in your income. In this case, when the carer's allowance is eventually awarded, make a fresh claim for income support/JSA within three months of the date of this award and the income support/JSA can be paid from the time the previous claim for it ended.
C&P Regs, reg 6(30)

**Carer's allowance** – If you have been waiting for the person you are caring for to be awarded a qualifying benefit (see Chapter 8(2)), and you claim carer's allowance within three months of the date of a decision to award the qualifying benefit, your claim for carer's allowance can be treated as having been made on the first day of the benefit week in which the qualifying benefit became payable.
C&P Regs, reg 6(33)

### Backdating income support and JSA

**Administrative reasons: one-month backdating** – Income support and JSA can be backdated for up to one month if any one or more of the following administrative reasons apply, as a result of which you could not reasonably have been expected to make the claim earlier.

❑ You couldn't attend the Jobcentre Plus office to make your claim because it was closed or because of transport difficulties, and there were no alternative arrangements available.

❑ You tried to ring the DWP to let them know of your intention to claim, but could not get through because their lines were busy or inoperable.

❑ You tried to claim JSA online under the universal credit system but their computers were down.

❑ There were adverse postal conditions.

❑ You were not informed of the end of entitlement to a previous benefit (under the universal credit system, just ESA) until after it actually ended.

❑ You stopped being one of a couple in the month before you claimed.

❑ You claimed JSA after your partner failed to attend a work-focused interview.

❑ Your partner, parent, son, daughter, brother or sister died in the month before you claimed.
C&P Regs, reg 19(6)&(7), UCPIP(C&P) Regs, reg 29(4)&(5)

**Special reasons: 3-month backdating** – Income support and JSA can be backdated for up to three months if one or more of the special reasons below apply, as a result of which you could not reasonably have been expected to claim earlier.

❑ You were given information by a DWP official that led you to believe your claim would not succeed – especially if what you understood was affected by your disability or communication difficulties.

❑ You were given written advice by a solicitor or other professional adviser, a medical practitioner, a local authority, or a person working in Citizens Advice or a similar advice agency, which led you to believe your claim would not succeed.

❑ You or your partner were given written information about your income or capital by an employer or ex-employer, or a bank or building society, which led you to believe your claim would not succeed (this does not apply if you are claiming JSA under the universal credit system).

❑ You were prevented by bad weather from attending the Jobcentre Plus office.

❑ You have difficulty communicating because you are deaf or blind, or you have learning, language or literacy difficulties.

## O.5 Interchange of claims

If you make a claim for one benefit, then find you should have claimed a different benefit instead, or you were also entitled to another benefit, the rules on interchanging benefit claims may help you get arrears of benefit beyond the usual limits. Your original claim may be treated as a claim for another benefit, either as an alternative to the original claim or in addition. But not all benefits can count as a claim for any other. Within each group below, the benefits listed are interchangeable with each other:

■ employment and support allowance and maternity allowance;

■ state pension and bereavement benefit;

■ disability living allowance, attendance allowance, industrial injuries constant attendance allowance and personal independence payment;

■ child benefit, guardian's allowance and maternity allowance claimed after your baby has been born;

■ bereavement benefit and bereavement support payment.

A claim for income support can be treated as a claim for carer's allowance, but not the other way round.
C&P Regs, reg 9 & Sch 1; UCPIP(C&P) Regs, reg 25

If the decision maker treats one claim as another, then the date of the original claim counts as the date of claim for the alternative benefit cland arrears may be payable from then. However, the overlapping benefits rule could prevent some or all of the arrears being payable (see Chapter 8(6)).

You cannot appeal against a decision on whether to treat a claim for one benefit as a claim for another but you can ask the decision maker to look at the decision again (see 'Ground 9' in Box O.8).

❏ You are ill or disabled (this is not accepted as a special reason for JSA). There is no definition of 'ill' or 'disabled' in the regulations.

❏ You were caring for someone who is ill or disabled. You do not have to live with the person or be related to them.

❏ You had to deal with a domestic emergency affecting you.

In the last four cases, you will also need to show it was not reasonably practicable for you to get help to make your claim. The test is about your ability to get help, not whether someone should have offered it (CIS/2057/1998).

C&P Regs, reg 19(4)&(5), UCPIP(C&P) Regs, reg 29(2)&(3)

You should give full details of your reasons for claiming late on your claim-form (or when you make the call if the claim is made over the phone). You can challenge a decision on backdating through the mandatory reconsideration and appeals process (see Chapter 57).

**Test cases**
If you are claiming following a test case, any backdating that might apply under the normal rules is generally limited to the date the test case decision was given. See Chapter 57(6).

## 4. Appointees

If a person is or might be entitled to benefit and cannot act for themselves, the decision maker can appoint someone aged 18 or over, an *'appointee'*, to act on their behalf. An appointee is usually a relative or friend, but can also be a body of people such as a firm of solicitors or a housing association. An appointment may be appropriate, for example, if the claimant is unable to act for themselves because of a severe learning disability, mental illness or dementia. Contact the office dealing with the claim and they will make the arrangements.

If you are the appointee, it is your responsibility to deal with the claim, including, for example, notifying changes of circumstances. The appointee is responsible for claiming on time and their own circumstances will be relevant in deciding whether there are special reasons for backdating a delayed claim, or for not providing all the evidence needed for a claim.

If you are appointed to act for the claimant in relation to one benefit, that appointment can cover all social security benefits, including tax credits, universal credit and payments from the social fund. A separate appointment must be made for housing benefit.

C&P Regs, reg 33; UCPIP(C&P) Regs, reg 57; Universal Credit (Transitional Provisions) Regs 2014, reg 16

The DWP reviews individual appointments to ensure they are still appropriate. Appointments for working-age claimants are reviewed every eight years, and for pension-age claimants every five years.

## 5. Payments

Benefit payments are normally paid into a bank, building society or credit union account. They can also be paid into a Post Office card account, which accepts payment of benefits or tax credits but only allows cash withdrawals at Post Office counters or cash machines situated at some Post Office branches (as listed at www.postoffice.co.uk/atm-locator). You can nominate someone else to withdraw your money for you and they will be issued with the card.

If for some reason you are unable to open or use any of the above accounts, you will be paid by the Government Payment Service instead. You'll be issued with a card that can be used (with proof of identity) to collect payments at PayPoint outlets.

The following benefits are paid through wages: statutory sick pay, statutory maternity pay, statutory paternity pay, statutory adoption pay and statutory shared parental pay.

**Compensation for delays** – You may be due compensation if payments are delayed (see Chapter 59(2)).

**Forgotten PIN** – If you have forgotten your PIN, ask for a replacement. Contact the bank or building society into which your benefit is paid. If your benefit is paid into a Post Office card account, ring their helpline (0345 7223 344; textphone 0345 7223 355).

---

## O.6 Can your claim for benefit be backdated?

If you could have qualified for a benefit for a period before you actually claimed it, you may be able to get your claim backdated. There are time limits for how far back each benefit can be backdated.

| Benefit | Backdating limit |
|---|---|
| **Disability living allowance, personal independence payment, attendance allowance** | initial or renewal claim – no backdating |
| **Income support, jobseeker's allowance** | generally no backdating; possibly 1 or 3 months – see 3 in this chapter |
| **Universal credit** | generally no backdating; possibly 1 month – see Chapter 14(7) |
| **Carer's allowance** | 3 months |
| **Employment and support allowance** | 3 months |
| **Housing benefit** | 3 months if you have reached pension credit qualifying age, otherwise possibly 1 month – see 3 in this chapter and Chapter 25(16) |
| **State pension** | 12 months |
| **Pension credit** | 3 months |
| **Tax credits** | 1 month |
| **Child benefit, guardian's allowance, maternity allowance** | 3 months |
| **Bereavement support payment** | 3 months |
| **Widowed parents' allowance** | 3 months (or 12 months if death has been difficult to establish) |
| **Industrial injuries disablement benefit** | 3 months from the first day you were entitled to benefit (15 weeks after date of accident/accepted date of onset of disease) |

*C&P Regs, reg 19 & Sch 4; UCPIP(C&P) Regs, regs 26-29; HB Regs, reg 83(12)&(12A); HB(SPC) Regs, reg 64(1); TC(C&N) Regs, regs 7 & 8*

## 6. Short-term advances and universal credit advances

*'Short-term advances'* of benefit are payable to claimants of any contributory benefit or income-related benefit except housing benefit. They provide an advance of your future benefit award, which will then be recovered from later payments of benefit. For universal credit, they are called *'universal credit advances'*. If you need the equivalent of a short-term advance while on housing benefit, you may be able to get a 'payment on account' – see Chapter 25(15).

The advances are intended to help you:

■ if you are waiting for your first payment;
■ if there has been a change of circumstances that will increase your benefit and you are waiting for this to be paid;
■ where you have just received your first payment of benefit and it covers a shorter period than the following payments (eg your first payment was for one week and your next payment is due in two weeks' time); *or*
■ if it is impractical for benefit to be paid on time (eg because of a technical problem in processing the claim).

To be eligible for an advance, you must be able to show that you are in financial need. This means that due to one of the above circumstances there is a serious risk to the health or safety of you, your partner or your children.

PAB Regs, regs 3-10

You cannot appeal against a decision not to award an advance but you can ask the decision maker to look at the decision again (see 'Ground 9' in Box O.8).

D&A Regs, Sch 2, para 20A

### How do you apply?

To apply for a short-term advance of income support, employment and support allowance or jobseeker's allowance, call 0800 169 0310 (textphone 0800 169 0314). For a short-term advance of carer's allowance, call 0800 731 0297 (textphone 0800 731 0317). For a short-term advance of pension credit or state pension, call 0800 731 0469 (textphone 0800 731 0464). For a universal credit advance, call 0800 328 5644 (textphone 0800 328 1344). In each case, you must tell the adviser about your circumstances and how much you think you need to borrow.

### Repayment

There is a maximum repayment period for short-term advances of 12 weeks, which may be extended to 24 weeks in exceptional circumstances (eg if you are escaping domestic violence). In the case of universal credit advances, there is a maximum repayment period of 12 months.

For short-term advances, the repayment rate is limited to 25% of your weekly benefit. For universal credit advances, the repayment rate is limited to 15% of your standard allowance (see Chapter 16(2)) or 25% if you have earnings.

O&R Regs, reg 11; Short Term Benefit Advances: Guidance for Benefit Centres

## 7. Overpayments

Overpayments are amounts of benefit you have been paid which you were not entitled to. Whether or not they are recoverable, depends on the benefit concerned and the circumstances of the case.

Overpayments of tax credits are always recoverable (although HMRC can decide not to recover an overpayment in the case of official error) – see Chapter 23(21). Overpayments of universal credit are always recoverable and, if you come under the universal credit system, so are overpayments of contributory employment and support allowance (ESA) and contribution-based jobseeker's allowance (JSA).

SSAA, Ss.71ZB-71ZF

Overpayments of housing benefit are almost always recoverable – see Chapter 25(18).

**The general rule** – The general rule common to most other benefits (both means-tested and non-means-tested) is that an overpayment of benefit is recoverable if it was overpaid because you misrepresented, or failed to disclose, a *'material fact'*, even if you acted in all innocence. A 'material' fact is one that would have affected the amount of your benefit. A 'fact' is not the same as a conclusion drawn from fact. For example, the conclusion that you have a 'limited capability for work' is drawn from the facts of your case.

SSAA, S.71(1); R(SB)2/92

Once a fact is 'known' to you and the duty to report it has been made clear to you, you have no excuse for not disclosing the fact – even if you have a mental disability.

European Court of Human Rights: 'B' v the UK

When a decision is made on one benefit that could affect entitlement to another, you have a duty to inform the office dealing with the benefit that might be affected – even if both benefits are dealt with by the same government department.

House of Lords: 'Hinchy'

**The recovery decision** – In deciding whether there has been a recoverable overpayment, the decision maker must first revise or supersede your entitlement to benefit and decide how much you should have been paid. Then they must identify the material fact that you failed to disclose or misrepresented. Finally, they need to decide how much of the overpayment is recoverable.

SSAA, S.71

Neither the DWP nor local authorities (for housing benefit) have the right to recover overpayments if you are subject to a bankruptcy or debt relief order.

SC: 'Payne & Anor'

### If the overpayment is not recoverable

If an overpayment is not recoverable under legislation, you do not normally need to pay back the overpayment. Nevertheless, the DWP may ask you to pay it back; you should not feel under pressure to do so. The DWP is not allowed to take you to court to recover overpayments arising from their official error.

CPAG v Secretary of State [2010] UKSC 54

### Overpayments of benefit when your health improves

There is a helpful principle that applies to benefits related to your health condition, eg disability living allowance, personal independence payment, attendance allowance and employment and support allowance. If there has been an improvement in your health condition and you did not know you should have reported it, you should not be left with an overpayment. Similarly, if your health condition turns out not to be as severe as originally believed, and you did not know you should have reported the mistake in the original information, you should not be left with an overpayment. Any reduction in your benefit in either case should thus not be backdated. For details, see Chapter 57(5) under 'What if your benefit goes down?'.

## Appointees and others

Overpayments can be recovered from someone other than the claimant if it is they who have misrepresented or failed to disclose a material fact. If that person is an appointee acting on behalf of the claimant (see 4 above), the decision maker may decide that the overpayment is recoverable from either the claimant or the appointee or both. In general, if the appointee has retained the benefit instead of paying it to, or applying it for the benefit of, the claimant, only the appointee is liable. If the appointee has acted with due care and diligence, only the claimant is liable.

R(IS)5/03

## Appeals

If you want to challenge a decision that you were paid the wrong amount of benefit, you can ask for a mandatory reconsideration (see Chapter 57(3)) and then, if this is unsuccessful, appeal (see Chapter 57(7)). In the same way, you can challenge a decision that the overpayment is recoverable and decisions relating to the period of the overpayment, from whom it is recoverable and the amount owed.

## Amount of the overpayment

The recoverable overpayment is the difference between the amount of benefit you actually received and the amount you should have received, if the decision maker had known the correct facts from the beginning of the period of overpayment. The overpayment amount is reduced by:

- any amount that is taken out of a later award of a different benefit ('offsetting');
- any extra income support, income-related ESA, income-based JSA, universal credit or pension credit you (or your partner) should have been paid had benefit been paid correctly, not necessarily for the same period as the overpayment (R(IS)5/92, CSIS/8/95).

PAOR Regs, regs 5 & 13; O&R Regs, regs 8 &16

For more details about overpayments, read the notes to section 71 of the Social Security Administration Act 1992 in *Social Security: Legislation Volume III* (see *Legal references* at the front of this handbook).

## Diminution of capital

If you have been overpaid income support, income-related ESA, income-based JSA or pension credit because you did not tell the DWP about all your capital or savings, or you misrepresented the nature of your capital, allowance is made for the capital you would have spent if you had not been paid benefit. Similar allowance is made if you have been overpaid universal credit because of an error relating to your capital and the period of the overpayment is at least three months.

At the end of each 13-week period (or 3-month period for universal credit), starting with the first day of the overpayment, your capital is treated as having been reduced by the amount of benefit you were overpaid during that period. At the same time, any assumed income (see Chapter 17(17)) or tariff income (see Chapter 22(25)) will be recalculated.

Your capital cannot be treated as diminished in this way over any period shorter than 13 weeks/three months. However, if you spent any of that capital during the overpayment period, the overpayment would end on the day your capital reached the appropriate limit, assuming the notional capital rules do not apply (see Chapters 17(27) and 22(36)). The treatment of diminution of capital under this rule would also apply to the reduced amount.

PAOR Regs, reg 14; O&R Regs, reg 7

A similar diminution of capital principle applies to housing benefit.

HB Regs, reg 103

The diminution of capital principle is different from the diminishing notional capital rule explained in Chapter 22(37).

## 8. Civil penalties and fraud

### Civil penalties

A decision maker may impose a civil penalty of £50 if they consider that you have negligently made an incorrect statement or representation or given incorrect information or evidence that has resulted in a benefit overpayment and you have not taken reasonable steps to correct the error.

A civil penalty can also be imposed if you failed, without reasonable excuse, to provide information or evidence, as required to do so, or failed to notify a relevant change of circumstances, in connection with a claim or award of benefit, that has resulted in an overpayment. The DWP interprets *'reasonable excuse'* as meaning *'a credible reason or justification for [you] failing to do what was required of [you], or for doing it late'*.

In each case, the decision maker cannot impose a penalty if, in respect of the overpayment, you have been charged with an offence, cautioned or given a legal notice about a penalty.

WRA 2012, S.116; The Social Security (Civil Penalties) Regulations 2012; Decision Makers' Guide, Vol 3, Chap 9, para 09436

The civil penalty will be added to the overpayment amount and will be recovered in the same manner. If you wish to challenge a decision to impose a civil penalty, you can ask for a mandatory reconsideration (see Chapter 57(3)) and then, if this is unsuccessful, appeal (see Chapter 57(7)).

### Fraud

Fraud is dishonestly or knowingly making a false statement or providing a false document or information to get benefit or more benefit. It is also fraud if:

- there has been a change of circumstances affecting entitlement to your or another person's benefit; *and*
- the change is one you are required to notify; *and*
- you know the change affects your own or the other person's entitlement; *and*
- you fail to give a prompt notification of the change in *'the prescribed manner to the prescribed person'* (eg giving notice in writing to the relevant authority).

These rules apply to appointees or to anyone else with a right to receive benefit on behalf of another person. They also apply to third parties such as landlords if they know, or would be expected to know, of changes in a tenant's occupation of a dwelling or liability to pay rent.

SSAA, S.112

**Fraud interviews** – If fraud is suspected, the DWP may ask you to attend an interview with a fraud officer. Seek advice beforehand and if possible take a friend with you who is not involved in the matter. Following the interview, the DWP may decide it is more appropriate to offer an administrative penalty or a formal caution as an alternative to prosecution, even if it believes you have committed fraud. If you are prosecuted and found guilty of fraud, the court can fine you or imprison you, or both.

**Alternatives to prosecution** – If the DWP believes they have enough evidence to successfully prosecute, they may give you the option of paying an administrative penalty as an alternative to prosecution. The administrative penalty is a minimum of £350, which rises to an equivalent of 50% of the overpayment (whichever is greater); the maximum is £5,000. You also have to repay the overpayment. You have 14 days to change your mind after you have agreed to pay an administrative penalty.

SSAA, S.115A; WRA 2012, S.114

A formal caution may be offered as an alternative to prosecution. This is a DWP administrative practice, not a criminal procedure. But if you are later found guilty of another offence, the formal caution may be used in court when you are sentenced (in England and Wales, but not in Scotland).

Different rules apply to tax credits, which have a penalty

system in place (see Chapter 23(12)). If HMRC believes fraud is involved, it may prosecute in the courts.

If you are accused of fraud, get legal advice as soon as you can (see Chapter 58).

# 57 Challenging decisions

| | | |
|---|---|---|
| 1 | Who makes decisions? | 313 |
| 2 | Ways of changing decisions | 313 |
| 3 | Mandatory reconsiderations | 313 |
| 4 | 'Any time' revisions and supersessions | 314 |
| 5 | Backdating after a change of circumstances | 315 |
| | Backdating supersessions – Box O.7 | 315 |
| | Grounds for revising or superseding a decision – Box O.8 | 316 |
| 6 | When a 'test case' is pending | 317 |
| 7 | Appeals | 317 |
| 8 | Making an appeal | 318 |
| 9 | What happens when you appeal? | 318 |
| 10 | Appeals without a hearing | 318 |
| 11 | Withdrawing an appeal | 318 |
| 12 | Striking out an appeal | 318 |
| | Human Rights Act – Box O.9 | 319 |
| 13 | Preparing your case | 319 |
| | Upper Tribunal and Commissioners' decisions – Box O.10 | 320 |
| 14 | If your circumstances change before the appeal | 320 |
| 15 | Special needs, access to the hearing and expenses | 321 |
| 16 | At the hearing | 321 |
| 17 | The appeal decision | 322 |
| | Errors of law – Box O.11 | 322 |
| 18 | Appeals to the Upper Tribunal | 323 |

## 1. Who makes decisions?

The Secretary of State for Work and Pensions is responsible for decision-making for most social security benefits, but in practice decisions are made on their behalf by an officer called a decision maker. Decisions on appeal are made by a Social Security and Child Support First-tier Tribunal (a tribunal) in the Social Entitlement Chamber within the Ministry of Justice. Appeals against decisions of tribunals are made to the Upper Tribunal in the Administrative Appeals Chamber. Administration for both of these tribunals is carried out by HM Courts & Tribunals Service.

Housing benefit has a similar decisions and appeals system. Decisions are made by a local authority officer. The ways of changing decisions described in this chapter apply equally to housing benefit decisions unless otherwise stated. Decisions on appeal are made by a Social Security and Child Support tribunal.

Some HMRC decisions use the same appeal system:

❑ **Working tax credit, child tax credit, child benefit and guardian's allowance** – Decisions are made by an officer of HMRC. The tax credits decision-making process is different from that for social security benefits (see Chapter 23(13)). Decisions on appeal are made by a Social Security and Child Support tribunal.

❑ **National insurance credits** – Decisions are made by HMRC officers based in the National Insurance Contributions and Employer Office. The decision-making and appeal process is the same as for social security benefits.

Decisions on national insurance contributions and employed earner status are made by HMRC. Appeals are usually made to a tribunal in the Tax Chamber.

There are separate systems for statutory sick pay (Chapter 10(10)), statutory maternity, paternity, shared parental and adoption pay (Chapter 39) and the Armed Forces

Compensation scheme (Chapter 47(7)). There are modified rules for vaccine damage payments (Chapter 49(5)).

Council tax reductions and discounts are administered by local authorities. Decisions are made by a local authority officer. Each authority has its own procedure to consider disputes. Appeals are made to a Valuation Tribunal (see Chapter 28(11)).

## 2. Ways of changing decisions

Once a decision is made, it stands and is binding until it is changed by one of the methods listed below. The two main ways in which the DWP changes decisions are by *'revising'* them or *'superseding'* them.

When they revise a decision, they replace it with a new decision that takes effect from the date the original decision was made. It is as if the original decision had never been made. On the other hand, when they supersede a decision, they replace it with a new decision that takes effect from that moment onwards.

Revisions, supersessions and appeals are covered in 3 to 16 below.

### Changing a decision made by a decision maker

There are four ways of changing a decision made by a decision maker on behalf of the Secretary of State:

■ revise the decision;
■ supersede the decision;
■ appeal against the decision;
■ correct an accidental error – arithmetic or clerical errors can be corrected by a decision maker at any time but this is discretionary and there is no right of appeal against a refusal to correct.

D&A Regs, reg 9A; UCPIP(D&A) Regs, reg 38

### Changing a decision made by a tribunal

There are four ways to change a decision made by a tribunal:

■ correct an accidental error;
■ set aside the decision;
■ supersede the decision;
■ appeal against the decision.

These are covered in more detail in 17 and 18 below.

## 3. Mandatory reconsiderations

**Dispute period** – There is a *'dispute period'*, which is normally one month from the date a decision maker's decision is sent to you, during which you can ask for the decision to be looked at again: the *'mandatory reconsideration'*. When you do this, a decision maker will consider your reconsideration request and, if they agree with it, they will *'revise'* the decision.

A decision can be revised on *'any grounds'* (ie for any reason) other than for a change of circumstances that occurred after the decision was made (in which case, you must make a fresh claim or ask for the award to be superseded – see Box O.8). The time limit can be extended in special circumstances (see below). Outside the dispute period, a decision can be revised only if certain grounds are satisfied (see 4 below and Box O.8).

D&A Regs, reg 3(1); UCPIP(D&A) Regs, reg 5(1); TP(FTT)SEC Rules, Sch 1

**Appeal rights** – A decision cannot be appealed unless the decision has first been reconsidered by a decision maker (unless it is a housing benefit decision). The process is called the mandatory reconsideration because it is a required step on the way to appeal. For more about appeals, see 7 below.

SSA S.12(3A); D&A Regs, reg 3ZA; UCPIP(D&A) Regs, reg 7

### Mandatory reconsideration time limit

Your request for a mandatory reconsideration must normally be received no later than one calendar month from the day after the decision was posted to you. The exceptions to this are either if you haven't had a written statement of reasons and you request one, which gives you at least an extra 14 days (see below), or if the first option listed below under 'Extending the time limit for revision' applies.

D&A Regs, reg 3(1)(b); UCPIP(D&A) Regs, reg 5(1)(b) & TP(FTT)SEC Rules, Sch 1

The date the decision is posted is taken to be the date on the decision letter. For example, if the decision letter is dated 10 October 2018, your mandatory reconsideration request must be received on or before 10 November 2018. If there is no corresponding date in the next month, your request must be received by the last day of that month. Keep a record of the date you make your request.

DWP guidance says that decision makers should accept requests received one day late unless they are certain the decision letter was actually posted on the day it is dated.

Decision Makers Guide, Vol 1, Chap 3, para 03063

### How do you ask for a mandatory reconsideration?

It is important to act within the one-month time limit, otherwise you could lose arrears of benefit or even find you cannot challenge the decision at all. You can normally ask for a mandatory reconsideration over the phone, but you should confirm your request in writing to the office address on the decision letter and keep a copy of it. For DWP-administered benefits, you can also complete and return a CRMR1 mandatory reconsideration request form (available at: www.gov.uk/mandatory-reconsideration/how-to-ask-for-mandatory-reconsideration). If you are near the deadline for requesting a mandatory reconsideration, phone to register the reconsideration and say you will write with more details (or return the CRMR1), otherwise a postal delay could result in your request being too late. For housing benefit, your request *must* be in writing to the local authority. A few days after posting your mandatory reconsideration request, phone the office you sent it to, to make sure they have received it.

When you request a mandatory reconsideration, you should explain why you think the decision is wrong. If you can, get evidence to back up your argument. If you cannot send this straight away, let them know how long it is likely to take to obtain.

### Written statement of reasons for the decision

If the decision letter did not include reasons, you can ask for a *'written statement of reasons'*. You must do this within one month of the date of the decision. If you ask for the written statement within one month and it is provided within that time, the 1-month dispute period is extended by 14 days; if it is provided after one month, the dispute period is extended to 14 days from the date it is provided. Unfortunately, you cannot always tell from the decision letter whether reasons are included, and the written statement you are sent might not explain the decision fully; so try to ask for a mandatory reconsideration within the 1-month time limit, even if you are also asking for written reasons.

D&A Regs, reg 3(1)(b)(ii)-(iii); UCPIP(D&A) Regs, reg 5(1)(b)(ii)-(iii) & TP(FTT)SEC Rules, Sch 1

### Extending the time limit for revision

If you have missed the normal 1-month deadline, there are two options.

❏ Ask for a late revision; the dispute period can be extended if strict conditions are met (see below). If the application is accepted, the decision can still be revised for any reason – you are not limited to certain grounds – and benefit can be fully backdated.

❏ Look for grounds to revise or supersede the decision outside the dispute period. Grounds are limited and, for a supersession, arrears of benefit are normally paid only from the date you apply. See 4 and 5 below and Box O.8.

**Late revision** – An application for a late revision may be accepted if:

■ the decision maker thinks it is reasonable to grant the application;

■ the application has merit;* *and*

■ there are special circumstances for the delay – you must show that it was not practicable for you to apply in time. The longer the delay, the better the reason must be.

The decision maker cannot take into account the fact that you did not know the time limits or the law, nor that an Upper Tribunal or court has reinterpreted the law.*

Apply for a late revision in writing; include the name of the benefit, the date of the decision, why you think it should be revised and your reasons for the delay. If you are refused a late revision once, you cannot apply again.

* This does not apply to revisions over personal independence payment, universal credit, and contribution-based jobseeker's allowance and contributory employment and support allowance under the universal credit system.

D&A Regs, reg 4; UCPIP(D&A) Regs, reg 6

**How long is the extended time limit?** – You cannot get a late revision more than 13 months after the date the decision was sent to you (plus any extension because you asked for a written statement of reasons – see above).

D&A Regs, reg 4(3)(b); UCPIP(D&A) Regs, reg 6(3)(c)

### The mandatory reconsideration notice

Once a decision has been reconsidered, the decision maker will send you two copies of a *'mandatory reconsideration notice'* to let you know the outcome. You will need the extra copy of the notice if you wish to appeal.

If the decision has been revised as a consequence of the reconsideration, the revised decision takes effect from the date of the earlier decision, so benefit can be backdated to that date.

SSA, S.9(3)

**Appeals** – If the decision has not been changed wholly in your favour, you normally have one month in which to appeal against it.

TP(FTT)SEC Rules, rule 22(2)(d)(i)

Even if you have requested the mandatory reconsideration outside the normal 1-month dispute period and do not meet the conditions for a late revision, you can still appeal against a decision provided the mandatory reconsideration request was made within 13 months of the decision.

CE/766/2016

For more about appeals, see 7 below.

## 4. 'Any time' revisions and supersessions

It is best to challenge a decision within the dispute period if you can. However, this may not always be possible: your circumstances might change later or you might only realise later that the decision was wrong. You can ask the decision maker at any time to reconsider a decision, however long ago it was made, but only if certain grounds are satisfied (see Box O.8). If the grounds are satisfied, the decision maker will revise or supersede the decision as appropriate.

**The difference between revising and superseding a decision** – A decision can be revised only if it was wrong at the time it was made. A revised decision replaces the original decision, so its effect is fully backdated. Generally, a decision is superseded if there is a later change. A supersession creates a new decision that takes effect from a later date and leaves the original decision unchanged; backdating is usually limited to that later date. Box O.7 summarises the backdating rules.

SSA, Ss.9 & 10

Whether a decision is revised or superseded depends on which grounds (listed in Box O.8) apply. If you are not sure what to ask for, just explain why you think the decision is wrong. The decision maker can treat a request to supersede as one to revise, and a request to revise as one to supersede. If there are grounds to both revise and supersede, the decision should be revised.

D&A Regs, regs 3(10) & 6(5); UCPIP(D&A) Regs, regs 20(1) & 33(1)

### Applying for a decision to be revised or superseded

It is best to ask in writing for a decision to be revised or superseded. For housing benefit this is the only option, but with other benefits you can ring or go to the appropriate office in person. However, if you do this, you should confirm your request in writing. Explain which one or more of the grounds (listed in Box O.8) apply and why. The decision maker need not take into account anything not raised in your application. If you can, provide evidence to back up your argument. If you cannot send this straightaway, say that you are sending it soon. Keep a copy of your letter and any evidence you send.

### Appeal rights

If one of the grounds in Box O.8 is satisfied, the decision maker can do any of the following: revise the original decision, supersede it, or decide not to supersede but confirm the original decision as correct. In any of these cases, you have a right of appeal, although you will first need to request a mandatory reconsideration of the new decision (see 3 above).

If the decision maker refuses to revise, you do not have a right of appeal. Rarely, if the application to supersede is obviously hopeless and could not alter the benefit award, the decision maker can refuse to make a decision. As no decision is made, there is no right of appeal. For more about appeals, see 7 below.
R(DLA)1/03

### 5. Backdating after a change of circumstances

Whether benefit can be backdated following a change of circumstances depends on the precise nature of the change. Tell the DWP or local authority about the change as soon as you can. For most benefits, if you tell them about the change within one month, benefit is fully backdated to the date of the change.
D&A Regs, reg 7(2)(a); UCPIP(D&A) Regs, Sch 1, paras 1, 6, 12 & 15

For universal credit, a change that is favourable to you will usually take effect from the first day of the monthly assessment period (see Chapter 16(1)) in which you told the DWP of the change.
UCPIP(D&A) Regs, Sch 1, paras 20 & 21

For personal independence payment (PIP), disability living allowance (DLA) and attendance allowance, an increase can be paid from the day on which you first satisfy the 3- or 6-month qualifying period (see Chapters 4(4), 5(4) and 6(3)) if you tell the DWP about the change within one month of completing the qualifying period. If you can only give the month and not the day that you would have first satisfied the disability test, the decision maker must assume that you satisfied it on the last day of that month.
D&A Regs, reg 7(9)(b); UCPIP(D&A) Regs, Sch 1, para 15; Decision Makers Guide, Vol 1, Chap 4, para 04400

**Late notification** – If the change of circumstances happened more than a month ago, you may still be able to get benefit backdated to the date of the change if you apply within 13 months of the change (or, in the case of PIP, DLA or attendance allowance, within 13 months of the end of your 3- or 6-month qualifying period – see Chapters 4(4), 5(4) and 6(3)).

Write to the appropriate office, giving details of the change of circumstances and the reasons for not telling them earlier. To backdate benefit, the decision maker must be satisfied that:
■ it is reasonable to grant the application; *and*
■ the change is relevant to the decision that is to be superseded (see 'Ground 1' in Box O.8); *and*
■ there are special circumstances that are relevant to the application (eg a serious illness); *and*
■ because of the special circumstances it was not practicable for you to notify the change of circumstances within one month of the date of change.
The longer the delay, the better the reason must be. The decision maker will not take account of the fact that you did

not know the time limits or the law, nor that an Upper Tribunal or court has reinterpreted the law.
D&A Regs, reg 8; UCPIP(D&A) Regs, reg 36

### What if your benefit goes down?

If your circumstances changed, and as a result your benefit should have gone down or stopped, the general rule is that the new decision takes effect from the date of the change, no matter how late you reported it. If the DWP or local authority decides you have been paid too much benefit, they may try to recover the overpayment (see Chapter 56(7)). There are exceptions, however, for the following:
■ the disability tests for PIP, DLA or attendance allowance;
■ limited capability for work for employment and support allowance (ESA) or universal credit; *and*

---

## O.7 Backdating supersessions

A *revised* decision takes effect from the date the original decision took effect, so benefit is fully backdated.

A *superseded* decision generally takes effect from the date you apply for the decision to be superseded, so benefit can only be backdated to this date. Exceptions to the rule are listed below.

| Event | Date change takes effect |
|---|---|
| **Award of a qualifying benefit** | full backdating to the start of existing award or, if later, date qualifying benefit starts |
| **Following a reinterpretation of the law in a test case** | the date of the test case decision |
| **Change of circumstances** | |
| ■ notified within 1 month | the date of change |
| ■ for universal credit – notified during a monthly assessment period (see Chapter 16(1)) | the start of the assessment period |
| ■ for disability living allowance, personal independence payment or attendance allowance – notified within 1 month of completing 3- or 6-month qualifying period for new rate or component | the end of the qualifying period |
| ■ notified after 1 month | the date notified – no backdating |
| ■ notified after 1 month (but within 13 months) and there are special circumstances for the delay (see Chapter 57(5) under 'Late notification') | the date of change or, for universal credit, the start of the monthly assessment period in which the change occurred |
| **Official error** | |
| ■ all benefits | generally full backdating to the date of the original decision |

## O.8 Grounds for revising or superseding a decision

Outside the dispute period (see Chapter 57(3)), a decision can only be reconsidered for specific reasons, or *'grounds'*. If at least one of the grounds outlined in this box is met, a decision can be either revised or superseded. We have called them 'Ground 1', 'Ground 2', etc for convenience, but these numbers are not used officially, so in your application you must clearly state which of the grounds applies to you. We include only the main grounds here; the full list is contained within the appropriate regulations: D&A Regs, regs 3 & 6; UCPIP(D&A) Regs, parts 2 & 3; HB&CTB(D&A) Regs, regs 4 & 7; Child Benefit & Guardian's Allowance (D&A) Regs, regs 5-13. In the footnotes we refer only to the first two sets of these regulations, which cover most social security benefits.

If you ask for a decision to be looked at again, you must show that one of the grounds is met. Similarly, if the decision maker decides for themselves to revise or supersede the decision, they must show that a ground is met. If no ground is met, the decision cannot be changed no matter how wrong it may be (CDLA/3875/2001).

*Note:* A decision made by a First-tier or Upper Tribunal cannot be revised on any grounds and cannot be superseded because of an 'error of law'; so Grounds 2 and 4 cannot be used.

### Ground 1: Change of circumstances

Any decision can be *superseded* if there has been a *'relevant change of circumstances since [it] had effect'*, or such a change is anticipated.

*D&A Regs, reg 6(2)(a); UCPIP(D&A) Regs, reg 23(1)*

**What changes are 'relevant'?** – A change of circumstances is *'relevant'* if it calls for serious consideration by the decision maker and could (but not necessarily would) change some aspect of the award, such as the amount or length of the award. For example, if you receive the standard rate of the daily living component of personal independence payment (PIP) and your condition deteriorates so that your care needs increase, this is a relevant change of circumstances because it could lead to entitlement to the enhanced rate.

Note the following points:

❑ A decision to refuse benefit cannot be superseded due to a later change of circumstances. You must make a fresh benefit claim.

❑ For work capability assessment and PIP decisions, a new report from a DWP-approved healthcare professional enables a decision to be superseded (see Ground 3 below). For other benefits, such as disability living allowance, a different medical opinion is not in itself a relevant change of circumstances. However, a new medical report may provide evidence of a change of circumstances – eg the report may indicate that your condition has deteriorated (R(DLA)6/01).

❑ A change in legislation is a relevant change of circumstances and a supersession can take effect from the date on which the law changes. However, new case law (a decision of a court or Upper Tribunal) does not count as a relevant change of circumstances (R(I)2/94) – but it can instead lead to a supersession for error of law: see 'Ground 2'.

The backdating rules following a change of circumstances are described in Chapter 57(5).

### Ground 2: Error of law

A decision can be *superseded* if it was based on a mistake about the law (eg the decision maker misinterpreted the relevant law). In practice, supersession of a decision maker's decision generally only happens where the legal error comes to light because of an Upper Tribunal or court decision on another claim – a test case (see Chapter 57(6)). When this happens, arrears of benefit can only go back as far as the date of the test case decision. For any other error of law, the decision should be *revised* as an official error, in which case arrears of benefit can go back as far as the date of the original decision (see 'Ground 4').

*D&A Regs, reg 6(2)(b)(i); UCPIP(D&A) Regs, reg 24(a)*

*Note:* A decision of a First-tier or Upper Tribunal cannot be superseded because of an error of law. You may, however, be able to appeal further (see Chapter 57(17)).

### Ground 3: New medical report

A new medical report from a DWP-approved healthcare professional is grounds for a decision maker to *supersede* a decision (including a tribunal decision):

■ awarding personal independence payment; *or*

■ that you have (or are treated as having) a limited capability for work or limited capability for work-related activity for employment and support allowance (ESA), universal credit or national insurance credits for limited capability for work.

The decision maker must look at all the relevant evidence, including the medical evidence used for earlier decisions (CIB/3985/2001).

*D&A Regs, reg 6(2)(r); UCPIP(D&A) Regs, reg 26*

### Ground 4: Official error

A decision can be *revised* if it arose from an official error by the DWP, HMRC or a local authority (or a body designated to act on their behalf), as long as no one outside the department or authority caused or materially contributed to the error.

*D&A Regs, regs 1 & 3(5)(a); UCPIP(D&A) Regs, regs 2 & 9(a)*

The revised decision takes effect from the same date as the original decision, which means that arrears of benefit can go back as far as the date of the original decision – no matter how long ago that was made.

### Ground 5: Award of a qualifying benefit

Entitlement to some benefits may depend on you, a member of your family or someone else getting another benefit. This is called a *'qualifying'* benefit. If you or someone else become entitled to a qualifying benefit, or to an increase in such a benefit, and as a result your existing award should be increased, your award can be *revised* or *superseded*.

You will get arrears of benefit back to the start of the existing award (by revision) or to the start of the award of the qualifying benefit (by supersession), if that is later. For example, if you apply for income-related ESA and PIP daily living component at the same time, but PIP is awarded only after a delay, your income-related ESA award can be revised to include the severe disability premium back to the start of the ESA award, with arrears paid from that date.

For universal credit, any extra benefit is payable from the start of the monthly assessment period (see Chapter 16(1)) in which the award of the qualifying benefit was made.

*D&A Regs, regs 3(7), 6(2)(e) & 7(7); UCPIP(D&A) Regs, regs 12 & 23 & Sch 1, para 31*

This rule can increase entitlement only to a benefit you already have. If you don't have an existing award, see Chapter 56(3) for rules on backdating claims.

### Ground 6: Incorrect facts

Any decision (including a First-tier or Upper Tribunal decision) can be *superseded* if it was made in ignorance of, or was based on a mistake about, a material fact. For example, when you filled in your PIP 'How your disability affects you' form, you may have underestimated the help you need carrying out daily living activities. If you give the DWP this information now, they can supersede the decision.

*D&A Regs, reg 6(2)(b)(i) & (c); UCPIP(D&A) Regs, regs 24(a) & 31*

A decision favourable to you (eg to increase your benefit) can only take effect from the day you apply for the original decision to be superseded. There is generally no backdating (see Box O.7).

*SSA, S.10(5)*

If you think the DWP, HMRC or local authority made a mistake and neither you nor anyone else outside the department or authority contributed to the mistake, this may be an official error, which generally means you can get full arrears (see 'Ground 4' above).

**Mistakes in your favour** – The general rule is that if you were paid more benefit than you were entitled to because a decision was made in ignorance of a relevant fact, or was based on a mistake about a fact, a decision maker can *revise* the decision at any time (but only *supersede* the decision if it was made by a First-tier or Upper Tribunal).

*D&A Regs, regs 3(5)(b) & 6(2)(c); UCPIP(D&A) Regs, regs 9(b) & 31*

The new decision generally takes effect from the same date as the original decision took effect. (See Chapter 57(5) under 'What if your benefit goes down?' for an important exception.) If there is an overpayment, the decision maker must consider whether it is recoverable under the normal overpayment rules (see Chapter 56(7)).

*SSA, S.9(3); D&A Regs, reg 7(5); UCPIP(D&A) Regs, regs 35 & 37*

### Ground 7: Revision during the appeal process

If you appeal, a decision maker can *revise* the decision under appeal at any time before the appeal is decided. This means, for example, if an appeal tribunal is adjourned for further evidence, the decision maker can revise the original decision once that evidence is produced, making a further hearing unnecessary.

*D&A Regs, reg 3(4A); UCPIP(D&A) Regs, reg 11(1)*

### Ground 8: Following the outcome of an earlier appeal

A decision can be *revised* at any time following a successful appeal against an earlier, related decision. For example: you appeal against a decision that you do not satisfy one of the disability tests for PIP. You also make a second claim for PIP, which is unsuccessful. If the appeal against the first decision is successful, benefit is paid up to the date of the decision refusing the new claim. The decision maker can now *revise* the second decision so that payment of the benefit can continue.

*D&A Regs, reg 3(5A); UCPIP(D&A) Regs, reg 11(2)*

### Ground 9: No appeal rights

A decision that carries no right of appeal can be either *revised* or *superseded* at any time, without needing specific grounds. These decisions include most administrative decisions about claims and payment of benefit (see Chapter 57(7)).

*D&A Regs, regs 3(8) & 6(2)(d); UCPIP(D&A) Regs, regs 10 & 25*

### Ground 10: Sanctions

If a decision maker wishes to impose a benefit sanction, any decision that ESA, jobseeker's allowance or universal credit is payable can be *superseded*, including one made by a First-tier or Upper Tribunal. A decision to apply a sanction to these benefits can, in turn, be *revised* at any time. So if you are outside the dispute period, you can still challenge a sanction. The new decision takes effect from the same date as the original decision. If the sanction is lifted, you should get arrears of benefit for the entire period of the sanction (less any hardship payments, etc that you received in the meantime).

*D&A Regs, regs 3(5C) & (6) & 6(2)(f); UCPIP(D&A) Regs, regs 14 & 27*

■ disablement for severe disablement allowance or industrial injuries benefits.

For these benefits, the reduction is backdated only as far as the date when you knew or could *'reasonably have been expected to know'* that you should have reported the change.

*D&A Regs, reg 7(2)(c); UCPIP(D&A) Regs, Sch 1, paras 7-8, 16-17 & 23-24*

The same applies to a decision made on another benefit as a result of one of the above disability or limited capability for work decisions. For example, if DLA stops following a routine check, any severe disability premium included in income-related ESA will stop only from the date the DLA decision takes effect if you could not *'reasonably have been expected to know'* about a reduction in your care needs earlier and reported it then.

*D&A Regs, reg 7A(2); UCPIP(D&A) Regs, Sch 1, para 31*

In deciding whether you could *'reasonably have been expected to know'* earlier, the decision maker should take into account:

■ how much you knew about the reasons for awarding you benefit;

■ what information was given to you about reporting changes of circumstances; *and*

■ your ability to recognise when a gradual improvement results in a relevant change of circumstances. A slight change in your care or mobility needs, or your ability to carry out activities in the ESA work capability assessment, would not normally be a change that you could reasonably be expected to report.

*Decision Makers Guide, Vol 1, Chap 4, paras 04240 to 04241*

## 6. When a 'test case' is pending

A decision on your claim may be affected by a matter of law that is under appeal in another case – this is called a *'test case'*. A decision maker can postpone making a decision in your case until the test case has been decided. Alternatively, they can make the decision in your case as though the test case has been decided in a way that is unfavourable to you. If the test case turns out to be favourable, the decision maker must then go back and revise the decision.

*SSA, S.25 & 27(2); D&A Regs, reg 21; UCPIP(D&A) Regs, reg 44(2)(c)*

When the decision maker decides your case following the test case, your arrears of benefit (if any) can only go back as far as the date the test case was decided.

*SSA, S.27(3)*

## 7. Appeals

You have the right to appeal to a tribunal against any decision on a claim for benefit or against any decision that revises or supersedes another decision, unless it is specifically listed in law as one with no right of appeal. When a decision is made about your benefit, you must be given a written decision notice that says whether you have a right to appeal.

### No right of appeal

There is no right of appeal against:

■ any decision that has not first been reconsidered by a decision maker (unless it is a housing benefit decision): the *'mandatory reconsideration'* (see 3 above);

*D&A Regs, reg 3ZA(2); UCPIP(D&A) Regs, reg 7(2)*

■ most administrative decisions about the way you claim or are paid benefit;

■ any part of a housing benefit decision that adopts a rent officer's determination (see Chapter 25(10)); *or*

■ decisions to postpone when a test case is pending (see 6 above).

*The full list is in SSA, Sch 2; D&A Regs, reg 27 & Sch 2; HB&CTB(D&A) Regs, Sch; UCPIP(D&A) Regs, Sch 3*

If you do not have a right to appeal, you can ask for the decision to be revised or superseded (see 'Ground 9' in Box O.8). Alternatively, you can ask for a judicial review; you should get specialist advice from a law centre or solicitor before doing this.

### Tribunal rules

Tribunals must act within a set of rules whose stated overriding objective is to deal with appeals *'fairly and justly'*. You and the DWP and/or any other parties to the appeal must co-operate with the tribunal and help it meet this objective.

A tribunal can overlook a failure to comply with the rules or ask you to remedy a failure to comply. The tribunal cannot overlook a failure to appeal within 12 months of the end of the normal appeal time limit.

TP(FTT)SEC Rules, rules 2, 5, 7 & 22(8)(b)

## 8. Making an appeal

Appeals for DWP-administered benefits and HMRC-administered benefits and tax credits in England, Scotland and Wales are made direct to HM Courts and Tribunals Service (HMCTS). Appeals for the equivalent benefits in Northern Ireland are made direct to The Appeals Service. Housing benefit appeals are made to the local authority or, in Northern Ireland, to the Northern Ireland Housing Executive.

Although you can appeal by letter, it is best to use an approved form so that you supply all the required information to make a valid appeal. If you are sent a mandatory reconsideration notice (see 3 above), this will provide details of what form to use and where to get it.

Appeals for DWP-administered benefits can be made on appeal form SSCS1, available from HMCTS or from www.gov.uk/social-security-child-support-tribunal/appeal-tribunal. Appeals for social security benefits in Northern Ireland can be made on appeal form NOA1(SS), available from: www.nidirect.gov.uk/publications/appeals-form-noa1ss. For housing benefit, your local authority will provide its own appeal form.

Your appeal must give your name and address and that of your representative if you have one. You must give an address where documents can be sent to you if your own address is inappropriate. You must give details of the decision being appealed (date, name of the benefit, what the decision is about) and grounds for your appeal.

In appealing a decision relating to a DWP/HMRC-administered benefit, your appeal must also include a copy of:
- the mandatory reconsideration notice (see 3 above); *and*
- any written statement of reasons for the decision you may have (see 3 above).

TP(FTT)SEC Rules, rule 22(3)&(4)

### Choosing to attend your appeal hearing

The SSCS1 form will ask whether you want to attend a hearing of your appeal. It is better to attend a hearing, especially if your case involves medical or disability questions (eg decisions about the work capability assessment or personal independence payment). See 10 below for details of appeals without hearings.

### Time limits for appeals

Your appeal request must normally be received by HMCTS within one calendar month of the date that the mandatory reconsideration notice was sent to you (see 3 above).

TP(FTT)SEC Rules, rule 22(2)(d)(i)

**Late appeal** – If you miss the deadline, the tribunal will decide whether to accept it. You should explain in the appeal form why it has been delayed. The tribunal can accept the late appeal as long as it is made within 12 months of the end of the normal 1-month time limit.

TP(FTT)SEC Rules, rule 22(8)

## 9. What happens when you appeal?

In the case of DWP-administered benefits, HM Courts & Tribunals Service (HMCTS) will send a copy of your appeal to the DWP. The DWP will write a *'response'* and return it to HMCTS together with the documents relevant to the decision. The DWP will send copies of these to you (and your representative, if you have one). The DWP must provide HMCTS with a response within 28 days. A similar process takes place with appeals for HMRC-administered benefits, with HMRC preparing the response and returning it to HMCTS.

If you are appealing against a housing benefit decision, the local authority will send your appeal to HMCTS, together with a copy of their response to the appeal and all the documents they have that are relevant to the decision. You will be sent copies of these.

TP(FTT)SEC Rules, rule 24

### Pre-appeal revisions

When the DWP is preparing its response, a decision maker may decide to revise it at this stage. If they do, your appeal comes to an end if the new decision is *'more advantageous'* to you (see below) – even if it does not give you everything you want. If you wish to continue, you must appeal again.

If the decision is revised but the new decision is not more advantageous to you, your appeal will go ahead against the revised decision.

The decision maker can decide to revise the decision again at any time until the appeal is decided (see 'Ground 7' in Box O.8).

SSA, S.9(6); D&A Regs, reg 30(3)-(5); UCPIP(D&A) Regs, reg 52(4)

### When is a decision 'more advantageous'?

A decision is more advantageous to you if:
- more benefit is paid (or would be but for a restriction, suspension or disqualification);
- the award is for a longer period;
- a sanction or disqualification of benefit is lifted wholly or partly;
- an overpayment of benefit is reduced or cancelled; *or*
- you will get some financial gain.

*Note:* This is not a complete list.

D&A Regs, reg 30(2); UCPIP(D&A) Regs, reg 52(5)

## 10. Appeals without a hearing

An appeal is decided without a hearing only if all parties consent and the tribunal agrees that a hearing is unnecessary.

TP(FTT)SEC Rules, rule 27(1)

If there is no hearing, the tribunal will study all the appeal papers and come to a decision based on these papers alone. The tribunal will be made up in the same way as for a hearing (see 16 below). You can send comments or extra evidence to the tribunal to consider at any time before they make their decision. You will not be told when the decision is due to be made, so send your evidence or comments as soon as possible. If you need time to prepare your information, contact the tribunal clerk. Say when you expect to send the information and ask for the decision to be delayed until you have sent it.

## 11. Withdrawing an appeal

You can withdraw your appeal at any time before the hearing. You do not need to give a reason and do not need the agreement of the DWP, local authority or tribunal (unless the tribunal has specifically directed that its consent is required). You must write to HM Courts & Tribunals Service stating that you wish to withdraw the appeal. You can withdraw the appeal at the hearing itself, but only with the consent of the tribunal.

TP(FTT)SEC Rules, rule 17

## 12. Striking out an appeal

Your appeal, or any part of it, can be struck out if:
- the tribunal does not have jurisdiction (ie the power and authority) to deal with the appeal (eg it is about a decision

that does not carry a right of appeal);

■ you have failed to comply with a direction given to you (eg to provide additional evidence);

■ you have failed to co-operate with the tribunal to the extent that it feels it can no longer deal with your appeal fairly or justly; *or*

■ the tribunal feels that your appeal, or part of it, has no reasonable prospects of success.

If a decision maker thinks the tribunal does not have jurisdiction or your appeal has no prospects of success, they can write to HM Courts & Tribunals Service (HMCTS) asking for the appeal to be struck out. If the tribunal is considering striking out the appeal, they will ask you to comment before deciding whether to do so.

The tribunal may give you a direction, which you must comply with, otherwise your appeal will be struck out. A time limit will be provided. If you do not comply with the direction within the given time limit, the tribunal can strike out your appeal automatically. It can decide any of the questions under appeal against you and bar you from further proceedings. HMCTS will write to you if your appeal has been struck out.

**Reinstatement** – If your appeal is struck out because of a failure to comply with a direction, you can write and ask for your appeal to be reinstated and any decision made to be set aside. HMCTS must receive your request within one month of the date of the letter notifying you that your appeal has been struck out.

TP(FTT)SEC Rules, rule 8

If the tribunal decides that another type of court or tribunal has jurisdiction to deal with your appeal, it can transfer your appeal instead of striking it out.

TP(FTT)SEC Rules, rule 5(3)(k)

## 13. Preparing your case

Read the decision maker's response to the appeal to see where you disagree with it. Find out if there is a local advice centre that can advise you and maybe support you at the hearing itself (see Chapter 58).

The tribunal need not consider any issue not raised by the appeal. It is important to give as much detail as you can about why and how you think the decision is wrong. If you are happy with part of your award, you should say so and ask the tribunal not to look at it.

The tribunal 'stands in the shoes of the decision maker' and can only look at circumstances existing at the time of the decision you are appealing against, so if your circumstances change while you are waiting for the appeal to be heard, you should consider making another claim or asking for a supersession (see 14 below).

SSA, S.12(8)

### Check the law

Tribunals must make decisions by applying the particular facts of your case to relevant legislation and case law.

**Legislation** – Legislation is made up of Acts of Parliament and Regulations. The appeal papers should refer to the parts of the legislation relevant to your appeal. You can also look these up in *The Law Relating to Social Security* (see *Legal references* at the front of this handbook).

**Case law** – This consists of decisions of the Upper Tribunal (see Box O.10) and the courts. The appeal papers may refer you to some relevant decisions, but other decisions may be helpful too. We produce up-to-date case law summaries covering the principle disability benefits (www.disabilityrightsuk.org/how-we-can-help/benefits-information/law-pages/case-law-summaries). Our factsheet *Finding the Law* provides general advice on finding the relevant law to support your appeal (www.disabilityrightsuk.org/finding-law).

### Sort out the facts and evidence

After looking at the legislation and case law, you may have a clearer idea of which facts are important for your appeal and what extra evidence you need. Most appeals concern a dispute about facts or different interpretations of the same facts. If you do not understand the law, just concentrate on the facts. Read the chapter in this handbook on the benefit you are appealing about to get an idea of what facts will be important.

You do not have to prove your facts 'beyond reasonable doubt'. You just have to prove they are true 'on a balance of probabilities', which means showing they are more likely than not to be true. Your word is just as much 'evidence' as any document. However, try to get as much other evidence as you can to back up what you are saying, as this helps tip the balance of probabilities your way.

You may need to call witnesses and, if so, you should get their agreement beforehand. Try to ensure their account will back up your case. If a witness cannot attend the hearing, ask them to give you a written statement for the tribunal.

If you can, send further evidence or comments on the appeal to HM Courts & Tribunals Service well before the hearing. Make a copy of your evidence and take it with you to the hearing.

### Getting medical evidence

If your appeal involves a disability question, try to get supporting medical evidence. The tribunal can only consider your circumstances up to the date of the decision you are appealing against (see 14 below), so medical evidence obtained later only helps if it relates back to the time covered by the decision under appeal.

The evidence can come from medical professionals such as your GP, specialist nurse, physiotherapist or hospital consultant. When you request a letter or statement from them, ask specific questions. Try to get information directly relevant to the case, rather than general comments about your condition. Make sure they are aware of your condition and how it relates to the question(s) under appeal; if you have kept a diary of your care needs, give them a copy.

If the appeal papers contain a report from a DWP-approved healthcare professional, read it carefully to see where you might need to get your own medical evidence to counter what is said in the report. Make sure you ask for comments specifically on the points in dispute. For example, if you disagree with a healthcare professional's report that says you can walk 100 metres without severe discomfort, ask your GP or physiotherapist for an opinion about how far you can walk without severe discomfort.

The tribunal should not automatically treat a report from a DWP-approved healthcare professional as more reliable or accurate than that of any other medical professional, eg your GP. The tribunal should consider all the evidence in a case and decide which it accepts and which it rejects.

R(DLA)3/99; see also R(M)1/93 & CIB/3074/2003

---

## O.9  Human Rights Act

The Human Rights Act 1998 incorporates into UK law the rights guaranteed under the European Convention on Human Rights. Arguments based on Convention rights can be made in social security appeals. Decision makers and tribunals must interpret the law in a way that is consistent with the Act as far as they are able. You should seek legal advice if you think it may apply in your case.

You can find the Human Rights Act and detailed commentary on its provisions in *Social Security: Legislation 2017/18 Volume III* (see *Legal references* at the front of this handbook).

**Difficulties obtaining evidence?** – If you think you will be unable to get supporting medical evidence by the time of the hearing, you can ask for a postponement to allow you more time to get it (see 16 below). If you do not think you can get the evidence you need (eg because you cannot afford it), you can ask the tribunal to request a copy of your medical records or refer you for a medical examination and report. It will do this if it thinks it cannot decide the appeal without further medical evidence. If it does so, it will cover the costs of obtaining the records or arranging the examination and report.
SSA, S.20 & TP(FTT)SEC Rules, rule 25(3)

If you are only able to provide evidence to the tribunal after the hearing, but before they have sent their decision to you, the tribunal can still consider the evidence.
CI/3837/2016

**Going ahead without further evidence** – There is no rule that says you must have medical or other evidence to confirm or endorse what you say. You can go ahead with your appeal even if you cannot get supporting evidence.

## 14. If your circumstances change before the appeal
It can take some months for your appeal to be heard and your circumstances may change in the meantime. The tribunal can only look at your situation as it was up to the time of the decision you are appealing against. It decides whether the decision was correct at the time it was made, based on your circumstances at that time. If your situation has changed between the decision and the tribunal hearing, it cannot take that into account.
SSA, S.12(8)(b)

For disability living allowance renewals, this is the case even if a change takes place after a renewal decision is made but before it takes effect. The only exception is if the change is one that is almost certain to occur, such as a child reaching a particular age (eg 3, when the mobility component becomes payable).
R(DLA)4/05 & CDLA/4331/2002

If you are appealing against an outright refusal of your claim, your circumstances change while your appeal is pending and you think it is now clearer that you qualify for the benefit concerned, you should make a fresh claim.

If you are already getting the benefit (but, for example, not at the rate you want), ask the DWP or local authority to supersede the award decision because your circumstances have changed. If you don't, you could lose out because of the time limits on backdating.

If the new claim or request to supersede is unsuccessful, it is important to put in a second appeal (after going through the mandatory reconsideration process – see 3 above) because your first appeal cannot take into account the period covered by the second decision. The benefit may be put into payment by a successful outcome in the first appeal then stopped from the date of the unfavourable second decision. The decision maker can revise the second decision following a successful appeal against the first decision (see 'Ground 8' in Box O.8), but there is no guarantee this will happen. To be safe, put in a second appeal. Ask for a single tribunal to hear the appeals together. For appeals on limited capability for work, see also Chapter 12(18).

**Tax credits** – Tax credit appeals have similar rules. If your

---

## O.10 Upper Tribunal and Commissioners' decisions

Decisions of the Upper Tribunal are binding on First-tier Tribunals and decision makers. In 2008 the Upper Tribunal replaced the Social Security Commissioners (the Commissioners). Decisions of the Commissioners are also binding on First-tier Tribunals and decision makers. In this box, we explain the reference systems used.

### Decisions of the Upper Tribunal
Some Upper Tribunal decisions carry more legal weight than others. Most decisions are made by a single judge. If an appeal is thought to be particularly complex or likely to affect a large number of other claims, a tribunal of three judges decides the appeal. Decisions made by three judges carry more weight than those made by a single judge.

**Unreported decisions** – When an appeal is made to the Upper Tribunal, it is given a reference number in the form CJSA/2280/2009, where: 'C' indicates the decision is unreported; the initials following indicate the benefit claimed (in this case, jobseeker's allowance); the first set of numbers is a specific reference for the case; and 2009 is the year that the appeal was made. The decision will keep this reference unless it is published on the HM Courts & Tribunals Service (HMCTS) website or is 'reported' (see below). For the sake of brevity, we use this reference in the handbook for all Upper Tribunal decisions, even after they have been published or reported.

**Published on the website** – If a decision is thought to be of importance it is published on the HMCTS website. The decision then acquires a reference in the form *Secretary of State for Work and Pensions v JB (JSA)* [2010] UKUT 4 (AAC), where: the Secretary of State for Work and Pensions and JB (the initials of the person who claimed the benefit) are the parties to the appeal and JSA indicates the benefit claimed (in this case, jobseeker's allowance); [2010] UKUT

indicates a decision published on the website in 2010 and made by the UK Upper Tribunal; 4 is the reference number; and AAC means the Administrative Appeals Chamber. Decisions published on the website carry no more legal weight than any other decision.

**Reported decisions** – A *'reported'* decision is one that is published in printed form (as well as on the internet) after having been selected for its importance by a board of Upper Tribunal judges. These judges must broadly agree with the decision's reasoning before it can be reported. A reported decision therefore generally carries more weight than an unreported decision (although an unreported one may be preferred if it is more recent).

When a decision is reported, an additional reference is added: our example would become *Secretary of State for Work and Pensions v JB (JSA)* [2010] UKUT 4 (AAC); [2010] AACR 25. The reference [2010] AACR 25 indicates it is the 25th decision reported in the Administrative Appeals Chamber Reports of 2010.

### Decisions of the Commissioners
Decisions of the Commissioners are still binding on decision makers and First-tier Tribunals. As with decisions of the Upper Tribunal, a decision made by three Commissioners carries more weight than that made by a single Commissioner and a reported decision generally carries more weight than an unreported decision.

When an appeal was first registered with the Commissioners' office it was given a reference number in the form CDLA/1234/2002 – the same form as for unreported decisions of the Upper Tribunal (see above). This reference has remained unless the decision was reported.

On reporting, the decision was given a new reference in the form R(DLA)5/06 – the fifth DLA decision reported in 2006.

Slightly different reference systems were used by the Scottish and Northern Irish Commissioners (see *Disability Rights Handbook* 34th edition, page 260).

circumstances change after the date of the decision you are appealing against, you should tell HMRC, who may then issue a new decision reflecting your new circumstances. If you are not satisfied with that decision, request a mandatory reconsideration and, if this is unsuccessful, put in a further appeal. If you have more than one appeal ongoing, ask for a single tribunal to hear all the appeals together.

## 15. Special needs, access to the hearing and expenses

If you have any special needs, check with the tribunal clerk beforehand about accessibility, what facilities are available and how your needs can be met to enable you to be present at your hearing and get home again within a reasonable time. You should ask for whatever you need. If HM Courts & Tribunals Service (HMCTS) refuse to provide it, seek advice.

For example, if it is too far for you to walk easily to the tribunal room from the nearest point at which a car can set you down, ask for a wheelchair to be waiting for you. If you need breaks during a hearing (eg to go to the toilet, take food or medication, stretch your legs or change position), ask for them. It helps if you tell the tribunal clerk before the hearing what you might need.

### Out-of-centre and domiciliary tribunals

HMCTS can arrange for the tribunal hearing to take place nearer to you than their usual venues (at an 'out-of-centre' venue) or in your home (a 'domiciliary hearing'). You should provide medical evidence of your need for an alternative venue.

The tribunal may hold a preliminary hearing to decide whether to adjourn for an alternative venue – you can send a representative to this hearing. If the tribunal refuses your request for an alternative venue and decides to deal with your appeal in your absence, it must be satisfied that it already has enough evidence to make a decision. Otherwise, it must adjourn and make arrangements to get further evidence (eg by referring you for a medical report or arranging a video link to your home).
CIB/2751/2002

A local disability group may know of a suitable and fully accessible venue near your home that could be used instead of an HMCTS venue.

### Claiming expenses

You can claim travel expenses for yourself and a travelling companion if you need one. If you cannot travel by public transport, you can claim for taxi fares or a private ambulance. You can get compensation for loss of earnings and for childminding expenses up to set maximums. You can claim for a basic meal if you are away from home or work for more than a specified time. If you are not sure what you, or someone with you, can claim, ask the tribunal clerk: ring the number on the hearing notice. If you need anything more than travel expenses for yourself by public transport, agree the expenses with the clerk well before the hearing.

## 16. At the hearing

You must be given at least 14 days' notice of the time and place of a hearing, starting from the day the hearing notice is sent to you. In practice, you are usually given much more notice than this. You can be given shorter notice if you consent, or in urgent or exceptional circumstances.
TP(FTT)SEC Rules, rule 29

**Asking for a postponement** – If the date is inconvenient or it does not give you enough time to prepare your case, write to the tribunal clerk and ask if the hearing can be postponed. If time is short, you can ring the clerk (the phone number will be at the top of the hearing notice) but you should also write to confirm your request. The same applies if you are ill on the day or have a domestic emergency. The tribunal will decide whether to grant a postponement. If you have not had the postponement confirmed, it is best to go along to the hearing if you can in case your request is refused and the appeal is decided in your absence.
TP(FTT)SEC Rules, rule 5(3)(h)

### Who is at the hearing?

**You and your representative** – It is always best to attend the hearing yourself; see 15 above if there is a problem with access. You are entitled to have someone with you to represent you (see Chapter 58) and you can also bring a companion for support. Both you and your representative have the right to speak, and you can call witnesses.
TP(FTT)SEC Rules, rules 11 & 28

**Tribunal members** – The tribunal is made up of a legally qualified tribunal judge and possibly one or two other people, depending on the type of appeal:
- for personal independence payment, disability living allowance and attendance allowance – a judge, a doctor and a *'disability member'* (see below);
- for the work capability assessment – a judge and a doctor;
- for severe disablement allowance and industrial injuries benefit – a judge and a doctor;
- for difficult financial matters about trust funds or business accounts – a judge and an accountant; *and*
- for any other matter (including a declaration of industrial accident) – a judge alone.

The hearing cannot go ahead unless all the tribunal members are present (except in exceptional circumstances and only if you and/or your representative agree). Members are drawn from a panel appointed by the Judicial Appointments Commission.

To avoid a conflict of interest, the tribunal must not include a doctor who has ever provided advice or prepared a report about you, or has ever been your regular doctor.

Where the tribunal would normally consist of a judge and one doctor, a second doctor can be appointed if the complexity of the medical issues demands it.

Although an additional member may be appointed to a particular tribunal, there can never be more than three tribunal members. The appeal tribunal can ask an expert to attend the hearing or give a written report, but the expert cannot take part in the decision making.

**The disability member** – The disability member is a person who is *'experienced in dealing with the physical or mental needs of disabled persons because they work with disabled persons in a professional or voluntary capacity or are themselves disabled'*. They cannot be a medical practitioner but can be a paramedic, physiotherapist or nurse.
TCEA, S.4 & Sch 2; Qualifications for Appointment of Members to the First-tier Tribunal & Upper Tribunal Order 2008; First-tier & Upper Tribunal (Composition of Tribunal) Order 2008

**Others** – Apart from tribunal members, there may be a *'presenting officer'* to put the decision maker's case. The presenting officer is there to help the tribunal and so may also identify any points in your favour. A clerk is present to deal with the administration of the hearing. They may have an assistant.

If the tribunal agrees, any other person can be present during the hearing. The hearing will be open to the public unless the tribunal decides otherwise. You can ask for a private hearing. The decision is made at the discretion of the tribunal. In practice, the only members of the public who are likely to be present are other claimants (to see what happens before their own appeal is heard) or advisers (to help them in their work).
TP(FTT)SEC Rules, rule 30

## What happens at the hearing?

The hearing itself should be fairly informal. The tribunal is *'inquisitorial'*: its job is to enquire and investigate and ask questions (in contrast to the *'adversarial'* courts, where the judges or magistrates mainly hear arguments).

There is no set procedure, so the tribunal judge decides which procedure will most effectively determine each appeal. The judge will begin by introducing the members of the tribunal and explaining its role. Often, the judge then clarifies what they understand to be the issues before them to make sure that everyone understands what the appeal is about.

If there is a presenting officer, the judge often asks them to present the decision maker's case first. Other tribunals may begin by asking you direct factual questions. A common procedure for disability-related appeals is to ask you to describe what you do on an average day.

At some point in the hearing, you will be asked to explain your case. Have a written note of your main points so you don't forget anything. If you are interrupted, you can ask tactfully to make all your points before answering questions. Where possible, back up your argument with documentary evidence (eg bills, bank statements, doctor's letters). At the end of your statement, repeat the decision you want the tribunal to make. You can question the presenting officer, if there is one, and any witnesses. Listen carefully, and ask questions if you think anything is being misunderstood or misrepresented.

---

## O.11 Errors of law

### Can you understand the tribunal decision?

The tribunal's statement of reasons (see Chapter 57(17)) must set out clearly what it decided and why. If you had put forward specific arguments, the statement must show clearly how the tribunal dealt with them. It must also show that the tribunal understood and correctly applied the relevant law. If the statement is not clear on any of the above, this may amount to an error of law.

### Identifying errors of law

Identifying an error of law is essential if you wish to appeal to an Upper Tribunal from a First-tier Tribunal decision. It will also be helpful if you want to challenge other decisions on grounds of error of law or official error ('Ground 2' and 'Ground 4' in Box O.8).

Several Commissioners' decisions, including R(A)1/72, R(IS)11/99 and R(I)2/06, set out what might constitute an error of law. A decision might be wrong in law if any of the following apply:

❏ The tribunal did not understand, or correctly apply, the relevant law (including not taking into account relevant case law).
❏ There has been a breach of the rules of natural justice (ie the procedures followed were incorrect, unfair or biased or you were not given a proper chance to make your case).
❏ The tribunal did not make the findings of fact needed to apply the law correctly.
❏ The evidence does not support the decision.
❏ The tribunal did not give adequate reasons for the decision (including failing to explain clearly how it resolved disputes about relevant facts or evidence or interpretation of the law).
❏ The tribunal took irrelevant matters into account.
❏ The decision is perverse: there is such a clear inconsistency between the law, the facts of the case and the decision, that no tribunal acting reasonably could have made the decision.

---

Once the tribunal is satisfied that each party has had the opportunity to present its case, the judge will ask everyone (except the clerk) to leave the tribunal room while the tribunal makes its decision.

**Medical examinations** – For severe disablement allowance or industrial injuries appeals involving an assessment of the extent of your disability, the doctor on the tribunal will examine you in private, usually towards the end of the hearing. After the examination, the hearing may start again to discuss the doctor's findings.

The tribunal cannot carry out a physical examination for any other benefit. It cannot ask you to undergo a walking test for the mobility component of personal independence payment or disability living allowance. It will, however, watch how you walk into and out of the room and how you cope with what might be a lengthy hearing. The tribunal can also refer you for a medical examination and report (see 13 above).

TP(FTT)SEC Rules, rule 25

## 17. The appeal decision

You will get a decision notice on the day of the hearing or soon after. A copy of the decision notice is sent to the department that made the original decision so they can put the tribunal decision into effect and pay you any benefit owed.

**Statement of reasons** – If the appeal is unsuccessful, you can ask for a more detailed explanation, the *'statement of reasons'* for the decision. If you want to appeal to the Upper Tribunal, you need this statement. Make sure you write and ask for it within the normal 1-month time limit (see 18 below). Once you have read the statement of reasons, it should be clear to you how and why you have been unsuccessful. If it is not, this may be an error of law (see Box O.11) and it may be possible to appeal further to the Upper Tribunal.

### If you disagree with the decision

A decision of an appeal tribunal can be changed in the following ways:

■ apply to the tribunal to correct an accidental error (see below);
■ apply for the decision to be set aside (see below);
■ appeal to the Upper Tribunal if there is an error of law – see 18 below (if you cannot appeal, see below for some ideas of what to do);
■ apply to the DWP or local authority to supersede the decision if there has been a relevant change of circumstances or such a change is anticipated (see 'Ground 1' in Box O.8). This can include a change of circumstances that occurred after the decision under appeal was made but which only came to light during the appeal process (the tribunal itself would have been prevented from taking the change into account); *or*
■ apply to the DWP or local authority to supersede the decision if it was made in ignorance of, or was based on a mistake about, a material fact (see 'Ground 6' in Box O.8).

**Correcting an accidental error** – An accidental error in the decision of an appeal tribunal can be corrected at any time. Arithmetic or clerical errors can be corrected in this way (eg if it is clear the tribunal accidentally gave the wrong starting date for an award of benefit). Write to HM Courts & Tribunals Service. There is no right to appeal against a refusal to correct the decision.

TP(FTT)SEC Rules, rule 36

**Setting aside for procedural reasons** – A decision may be set aside by a tribunal if it considers it is in the interests of justice to do so because:

■ a document relevant to the appeal wasn't sent to, or wasn't received in sufficient time by, any party to the proceedings, their representative or the tribunal; *or*

- a party to the proceedings or a representative wasn't present at the hearing; *or*
- there has been some other procedural irregularity.

You must apply in writing to have the decision set aside within one month of the date the decision was given or sent to you. The tribunal can extend the time limit.
TP(FTT)SEC Rules, rules 5(3)(a) & 37

Setting aside wipes out all or part of the tribunal's decision. There must be a fresh hearing before a new appeal tribunal. You cannot appeal against a refusal to set aside. A refusal to set aside starts afresh the time limits for asking for permission to appeal to the Upper Tribunal. This does not apply, however, if the application to set aside was made late (unless the tribunal granted an extension to the time limit).
TCEA, S.11(5)(d)(iii); TP(FTT)SEC Rules, rule 38(3)(c)&(4)

**If you cannot appeal to the Upper Tribunal** – If you think there is an error of law in the decision but you are out of time for appealing, are refused permission (or leave) to appeal or your appeal fails, you may want to try one of the following:
- ❏ **Fresh claim** – If no benefit is being paid, make a fresh claim. Normal backdating rules will apply.
- ❏ **Supersession for incorrect fact** – If some benefit is being paid, the tribunal decision can be superseded if it was made in ignorance of, or was based on a mistake about, a material fact (see 'Ground 6' in Box O.8). If you think an error of law has been made, it is possible for the decision maker to correct it when they supersede the decision. This is because the supersession must reconsider all aspects of the decision.
- ❏ **Supersession for change of circumstances** – If some benefit is being paid, the tribunal decision can be superseded due to a change of circumstances later on. If you think an error of law has been made, it is possible for the decision maker to correct it when they supersede the decision.

## 18. Appeals to the Upper Tribunal

You can appeal to the Upper Tribunal only if there is an error of law in the First-tier Tribunal decision (see Box O.11). You cannot appeal about the facts. As it is sometimes hard to separate the law from the facts, ask an experienced adviser to check the decision. Do not delay, as strict deadlines must be met. To appeal, you must take the following steps.

**Step 1:** Ask the tribunal for a *'statement of reasons'* for its decision (see 17 above) within one month of the date it gave or sent you the decision notice. The tribunal can extend the time limit.
TP(FTT)SEC Rules, rules 5(3)(a) & 34

**Step 2:** Apply for permission (or, in Scotland, leave) to appeal to the tribunal within one month of being sent:
- the statement of reasons; *or*
- notification of amended or corrected reasons following a review (see below); *or*
- notification that an application to set aside is unsuccessful.

Write a letter stating why you think the decision was legally wrong and what result you seek. Head it *'Application for permission to appeal to the Upper Tribunal'*. Make a copy, and send it to the tribunal clerk with copies of the tribunal decision notice and its statement of reasons. If there is no statement of reasons, the tribunal may treat the application as a request for one. An application can only be allowed without a statement of reasons if the tribunal thinks it is in the interests of justice to do so.
TP(FTT)SEC Rules, rule 38

**Reviewing the decision** – On receiving your application for permission to appeal, the tribunal can review its decision. In particular, the tribunal can:
- correct an accidental error in the decision;
- amend the reasons for the decision; *or*
- set aside the decision.

If it sets aside the decision, it must make a new decision or refer the appeal to the Upper Tribunal. You must be sent a notification of any new or amended decision.

You may be given the opportunity to comment before the review takes place. If you are not, the notification must state that you can ask for the new decision to be set aside and a further review made.

If you think the new or amended First-tier Tribunal decision contains an error of law, you have one month from the date the notification is sent to ask again for permission to appeal to the Upper Tribunal (repeating Step 2).
TCEA, S.9; TP(FTT)SEC Rules, rules 39 & 40

**Step 3:** If the tribunal refuses permission to appeal, you can apply for permission direct to the Upper Tribunal. You must normally do so within one month of being sent the notice refusing permission. Use form UT1, available from the Upper Tribunal offices (see Chapter 61) or from: http://hmctsformfinder.justice.gov.uk/HMCTS/FormFinder.do. Enclose a copy of the tribunal decision notice, the tribunal's statement of reasons and the notice refusing permission to appeal. Send these to the Upper Tribunal office. If you are posting them and you are close to the time limit, send them by recorded delivery.
TCEA, S.11; TP(UT) Rules, rule 21

**Step 4:** If permission to appeal is granted by the tribunal, you must make a formal appeal to the Upper Tribunal normally within one month of being sent the notice granting permission. You will be sent a form on which to do this.

If permission is granted by the Upper Tribunal, you will not have to appeal formally unless the Upper Tribunal specifically asks you to do so, as your application for permission will be treated as the appeal.
TCEA, S.11; TP(UT) Rules, rule 23

If you miss any of the normal 1-month deadlines, the Upper Tribunal can allow your application if it thinks it is fair and just to do so. Your late application must contain details of why it was late.
TP(UT) Rules, rules 5(3)(a), 7 & 21(6)

The decision maker has the same rights of appeal as you. If the decision maker asks for permission to appeal, you will be sent a copy of their application and asked to comment.

### Payment pending appeal

If you appeal to the Upper Tribunal, then the DWP, HMRC or local authority will put the decision of the tribunal into effect until your appeal is settled. If the decision maker appeals (or intends to appeal), the tribunal's decision may be suspended and you will not be paid until the appeal is finally decided. If this causes hardship, ask the relevant office to consider lifting the suspension.

### The Upper Tribunal's decision

If the Upper Tribunal finds that a First-tier Tribunal's decision is wrong in law (see Box O.11):
- it can give the decision that the tribunal should have given if it can do so without making fresh or further findings of fact; *or*
- if it thinks it appropriate, it can make fresh or further findings of fact and then give a decision.

If there are not enough findings of fact, and the Upper Tribunal does not make new findings, the case is referred to a new First-tier Tribunal. The Upper Tribunal may give directions to the new tribunal to make sure the error of law is not repeated.
TCEA, S.12

There is a quicker procedure: if both you and the decision maker agree on an outcome, the Upper Tribunal can set aside the First-tier tribunal's decision by consent, making the provisions necessary to put into effect what has been agreed.
TP(UT) Rules, rule 39

# Help and information

This section of the handbook looks at:

| | |
|---|---|
| Getting advice | Chapter **58** |
| Making a complaint | Chapter **59** |
| Useful publications | Chapter **60** |
| Government addresses | Chapter **61** |

# 58 Getting advice

| | | |
|---|---|---|
| 1 | Who can help you? | 324 |
| 2 | Free legal help | 324 |

## 1. Who can help you?

Your local Citizens Advice can help with benefits advice and many other matters. Citizens Advice may be able to represent you if you have a problem or are making an appeal. If not, they may be able to tell you if another local organisation could help; other independent advice centres may provide similar services.

Your local authority might have a welfare rights service or a list of local advice centres. Contact your town hall for information.

A local DIAL (Disability Information and Advice Line) group or other disablement advice centre may be able to offer advice and, in some cases, might be willing to represent you.

## 2. Free legal help

Most solicitors will not be familiar with the social security system, so you should normally first seek advice from your local Citizens Advice, DIAL or other advice agency. Some firms of solicitors, however, employ welfare rights specialists.

If you live or work in the catchment area of a law centre, contact them to see if they can help. Law centres can sometimes give benefits advice as well as help in other areas of the law such as housing, employment and immigration. For details of your nearest law centre, contact the Law Centres Network (www.lawcentres.org.uk).

Your Citizens Advice may have volunteer lawyers and can possibly refer you to one at a special advice session. Many trade unions offer free legal advice to their members. Free legal advice in England and Wales is available from the Civil Legal Advice (CLA) helpline (0345 345 4345; textphone 0345 609 6677).

---

### Disability Rights UK

**Visit our website**
Our website contains a wealth of information about benefits and disability rights news. You can also find out about our strategic priorities, news about our current campaigns and nationwide projects as well as information about training opportunities.

Visit our shop to buy Radar NKS keys, our publications, and download some of our guides free of charge.

**Join Disability Rights UK**
Membership is open to individuals (from £7.50 a year) and organisations (from £52 a year). Become a member and take advantage of our new online forums.

To find out more about what we do, visit
**www.disabilityrightsuk.org**

---

### Legal Aid

**England and Wales** – In England and Wales, free legal advice or 'Legal Aid' is not available for most types of welfare benefits advice. It is only available for benefit appeals to the Upper Tribunal (see Chapter 57(18)) and higher courts and for First-tier Tribunals where the tribunal itself has identified an error of law in its own decision (see Box O.11 in Chapter 57).

Advice and assistance through participating solicitors and advice agencies in such cases are available if you pass an income test and you (and your partner) do not have capital of more than £8,000 (including any equity on your home). You will automatically pass the income test if you receive income-related employment and support allowance, income support, income-based jobseeker's allowance, pension credit (guarantee credit) or universal credit. In other circumstances, you may pass the test, whether or not you are in or out of work, if your income is low enough. Use website www.gov.uk/check-legal-aid to see if you qualify.

Not all solicitors are part of the scheme; ring the CLA helpline (see above) for details of participating solicitors and advice agencies.

**Scotland** – The Scottish Legal Aid Board manages a Legal Aid scheme that covers a broad range of welfare benefits advice. Ring 0845 122 8686 or look at the website (www.slab.org.uk) for details of participating solicitors.

**Northern Ireland** – Contact the Legal Services Agency (028 9040 8888; www.justice-ni.gov.uk/topics/legal-aid) for details of the scheme in Northern Ireland.

# 59 Making a complaint

| | | |
|---|---|---|
| 1 | Complaints about the DWP | 324 |
| 2 | Financial redress for maladministration: the Special Payment scheme | 325 |
| 3 | Complaints about medical assessments | 325 |
| 4 | Health and social care | 325 |
| 5 | Complaining to the Ombudsman | 326 |

## 1. Complaints about the DWP

When the DWP has made a mistake, you can expect them to explain what went wrong and why, and to apologise. They should not treat you any differently just because you have complained. To make a complaint, take the following steps.

❏ Contact the office dealing with your claim; contact details will be on any of the letters you have been sent. You can contact the office by phone, in person or in writing. Give them your national insurance number, name and contact details. Let them know what happened, when it happened, how it has affected you and what you want to happen to put things right.

❏ If you are not satisfied with the initial response, you can ask for your complaint to go to a Complaint Resolution Manager. They will contact you, usually by phone, to discuss your complaint and agree how to deal with it. They should contact you again within 15 working days to tell you the outcome or when you can expect a response, if it will take longer.

❑ If you are not satisfied with the response from the Complaint Resolution Manager, you should be asked if you want your complaint to be sent to a senior manager. If you agree, the senior manager will ask for an independent internal review of your complaint. They should contact you within 15 working days to tell you the outcome or when you can expect a response, if it will take longer.

❑ If you are not satisfied with the result of this final response, you can ask the Independent Case Examiner (PO Box 209, Bootle L20 7WA; 0345 606 0777) to look into your complaint. You must contact them within six months of getting the final response and send them a copy of it. The Independent Case Examiner can only look at your complaint if it concerns maladministration; they cannot look at disputes concerning legislation (you should challenge these through the normal reconsiderations and appeals process – see Chapter 57).

❑ If you are not satisfied with the Independent Case Examiner's response, contact your MP, who can, if the complaint is on the grounds of maladministration, refer your case to the Ombudsman (see 5 below).

If your complaint is about a medical assessment, see 3 below. If your complaint is with a company providing services to the DWP, you should go through their complaints procedure first. If you are not satisfied with the result of this, the case should be referred to the Independent Case Examiner (see above).

## 2. Financial redress for maladministration: the Special Payment scheme

You can claim compensation or *'financial redress'* through the Special Payment scheme if you have lost money due to DWP maladministration (be it a mistake or a delay) or because you have received wrong or misleading advice from them. The scheme has three types of payment: *'loss of statutory entitlement'*, *'actual financial loss or costs'* and *'consolatory payments'*.

Guidance on the scheme is in DWP guide *Financial Redress for Maladministration*, available via our website (www.disabilityrightsuk.org/links-government-departments).

### Loss of statutory entitlement

If DWP maladministration has resulted in you losing entitlement to a benefit, and the normal ways for dealing with this are not available to you (ie backdating, reconsideration or appeal), the DWP should consider awarding a special payment to cover the loss.

### Actual financial loss or costs

Where DWP maladministration has resulted in you having additional costs or losses, the DWP should consider awarding a special payment to cover these. If you have had to pay professional fees to try to sort the matter out, these will usually be met only if you can show that:

■ you made all reasonable attempts to use the complaint resolution process before seeking professional help;

■ the issue would not have been resolved within a reasonable timescale if you had not sought the help; *and*

■ the fees are reasonable.

**Interest for delay** – An additional element can be included in the special payment if there has been a significant delay in paying benefit arrears. The additional element will be calculated as if it were simple interest (generally using the HMRC standard interest rate).

### Consolatory payments

If you have suffered an injustice or hardship because of DWP maladministration, the DWP should consider awarding a consolatory payment. In making such a payment, the DWP should consider your circumstances and the impact on you of any maladministration (eg the impact if you have a health condition may be more severe than if you have no health problems). Consolatory payments normally range between £25 and £500, although higher amounts can be considered, depending on your circumstances.

### Claiming special payments

Write to the office handling your claim to ask for a special payment. You should explain fully the circumstances of the case and provide copies of any evidence you have showing that you have suffered losses or expenses due to the maladministration.

## 3. Complaints about medical assessments

If you disagree with a benefit decision that was based on medical advice provided by a healthcare professional from a *'provider'* company (Independent Assessment Services, Capita or Maximus) who carried out a medical assessment on behalf of the DWP, you should challenge this through the normal DWP reconsiderations and appeals process (see Chapter 57).

However, if you wish to make a complaint about the conduct or professionalism of such a person, or about the appointment arrangements or facilities at the assessment, you will need to contact the provider directly and follow their complaints procedure. Use the contact details on the letters they have sent to you. If you have been through the provider's complaints process and the problem remains unresolved and involves maladministration, you can complain to the Independent Case Examiner (PO Box 209, Bootle L20 7WA; 0345 606 0777). The Independent Case Examiner cannot concern itself with a healthcare professional's clinical findings, but can examine complaints about the way a medical assessment was conducted – eg if the healthcare professional was rude or insensitive.

If you are not satisfied with the Independent Case Examiner's response, contact your MP, who can, if the complaint is on the grounds of maladministration, refer your case to the Ombudsman (see 5 below).

## 4. Health and social care

In England, there is a standard complaints procedure to use if you are not happy with care services provided by local authorities or with health services provided by the NHS. See Chapter 36(11) for details.

For complaints in the rest of the UK about hospitals, GPs and NHS services, the best starting point is your local Community Health Council in Wales, the Patient Advice and Support Service (provided by Citizens Advice) in Scotland, or the Patient and Client Council in Northern Ireland. They can advise you on the correct procedure and might be able to help you make your complaint.

Patients detained in hospitals or care homes under the Mental Health Act can contact the Care Quality Commission (0300 061 6161; www.cqc.org.uk), who will look into the complaint. In Scotland, contact the Mental Welfare Commission for Scotland (0800 389 6809; www.mwcscot.org.uk).

## 5. Complaining to the Ombudsman

Complaining to an Ombudsman is not an alternative to the normal appeals process, nor an extension of that process. You complain to an Ombudsman about the way a decision was taken or the way you were treated, rather than the decision itself. Before you can complain to an Ombudsman, you should first go through the normal complaints procedure and, where appropriate, contact the Independent Case Examiner (see 1 above). Keep a copy of your complaint letter and anything connected with it. There is no fee for making a complaint to an Ombudsman.

An Ombudsman investigates whether maladministration has caused injustice. Ombudsmen do not generally investigate personnel matters, although the Northern Ireland Ombudsman does so in some cases.

❑ **Maladministration** – This includes matters such as bias, prejudice, incorrect action, unreasonable delay and failure to follow (or have) proper procedures and rules.

❑ **Injustice** – This covers not only financial and other material or tangible loss but also inconvenience, anxiety or stress, and even a sense of outrage about the way in which something has been done.

Ombudsmen have powers similar to those of the High Court (Court of Session in Scotland) for obtaining evidence.

If an Ombudsman upholds your complaint, they will expect the body that you have complained against to provide you with some remedy. This may be an apology, a change in procedures, financial compensation, or any combination of these or similar measures.

### Which Ombudsman?

In England you complain to:

■ the Parliamentary and Health Service Ombudsman (PHSO; 0345 015 4033; www.ombudsman.org.uk) about central government (eg the DWP), health bodies, doctors, dentists, opticians, etc. The PHSO can also investigate health-related cases where maladministration has caused hardship, complaints about clinical judgment, and refusal of access to official information;

■ the Local Government and Social Care Ombudsman (0300 061 0614; www.lgo.org.uk) about local government, eg local authority housing benefit offices or social care departments (but not complaints about the internal management of schools).

---

### Disability Rights UK publications

#### Factsheets

Factsheets on a range of disability-related issues can be found in the *How we can help* section of our website.

#### Guides

We produce a range of guides to promote independent living. Some are available as printed copies to buy and others as PDFs to download free of charge.

#### Next year's handbook

The 44th edition of *Disability Rights Handbook* (2019-2020) will be published in April 2019.

To order our publications, visit
**www.disabilityrightsuk.org**

---

In Scotland and Wales, you complain to the PHSO about central government. For devolved matters, the Scottish Public Services Ombudsman (0800 377 7330; www.spso.org.uk) deals with complaints about the Scottish Government and its agencies, and the Public Services Ombudsman for Wales (0300 790 0203; www.ombudsman-wales.org.uk) deals with complaints about the Welsh Government. Each also deals with complaints about other public bodies in Scotland and Wales, including health, housing and social care. In Northern Ireland, contact the Northern Ireland Public Services Ombudsman (NIPSO: 0800 343 424; https://nipso.org.uk) to complain about any public services.

You can ask your local Citizens Advice to check with the Ombudsman first to make sure that it can investigate a complaint against a particular government body, such as a quango.

### How to complain

You can complain directly to any of the Ombudsmen except the PHSO (if it is about a government department or agency) and, in cases concerning central government, the NIPSO. Only an MP can refer a complaint to the PHSO if it is about a government department or agency. You should normally approach your own MP; approach an MP for another constituency only if yours refuses to refer your complaint. If you approach another MP, they will usually contact your own MP before deciding whether to refer your complaint.

### Other Ombudsmen

As well as the government Ombudsmen, there are several others, including the Financial Ombudsman, Housing Ombudsman and Legal Ombudsman. For details, check the website (www.ombudsmanassociation.org) or ask your local Citizens Advice. For information about the Pensions Ombudsman, see Box L.3 in Chapter 45.

# 60 Useful publications

| | | |
|---|---|---|
| 1 | Benefits guides | 326 |
| 2 | DWP leaflets and guidance | 326 |
| 3 | Disability Rights UK publications | 327 |
| 4 | The Equality Act | 327 |

## 1. Benefits guides

In several chapters in this handbook we suggest other sources of information, including guidance and reference books. Look in boxes called 'For more information'.

Listed below is a selection of other guides, the publishers and the prices.

❑ *Help with Housing Costs Vol 1: Guide to Universal Credit and Council Tax Rebates 2018/2019*, Chartered Institute of Housing and Shelter, £41

❑ *Help with Housing Costs Vol 2: Guide to Housing Benefit 2018-2019*, Chartered Institute of Housing and Shelter, £41

❑ *Welfare Benefits and Tax Credits Handbook 2018/2019, 20th edition*, Child Poverty Action Group (CPAG), £61 (£15 for unwaged benefit claimants)

❑ *Child Support Handbook 2018/2019, 26th edition*, CPAG, £36 (£10 for unwaged benefit claimants)

❑ *Council Tax Handbook 2018, 12th edition*, CPAG, £26

❑ *Fuel Rights Handbook 2016, 18th edition*, CPAG, £26

❑ *Benefits for Migrants Handbook 2017/18, 9th edition*, CPAG, £36

## 2. DWP leaflets and guidance

DWP leaflets and official guidance should be available from your local Jobcentre Plus office. You can download official

DWP guidance, such as the *Decision Makers Guide*, from our website (www.disabilityrightsuk.org/links-government-departments).

### 3. Disability Rights UK publications
We produce a range of guides and publications to promote independent living. They can be ordered from our website (www.disabilityrightsuk.org), and include the following.
- *Taking Charge* (a practical guide to living with a disability or health condition), £13.99
- *Holidays in the British Isles* (a guide to accessible holidays in the British Isles), £12.99

The following guides can be downloaded free from our website.
- *Into Higher Education* (a guide for disabled people thinking about studying in higher education)
- *Into Apprenticeships* (a guide for disabled people, parents and key advisers about applying for apprenticeships in England)
- *Doing Life Differently* (set of two: Sport and Transport)

### Factsheets
We produce over 60 factsheets covering a range of benefits and care issues. They are free to download from www.disabilityrightsuk.org/how-we-can-help/benefits-information/factsheets.

### 4. The Equality Act
There is information on the Equality Act in a number of publications, including the following.
- *Blackstone's Guide to the Equality Act 2010* edited by Wadham, Ruebain, Robinson and Uppal
- *Equality and Discrimination – The New Law* by Brian J Doyle (Jordans)
- *Discrimination in Employment* edited by O'Dempsey, Casserley, Robertson and Beale (Legal Action Group)
- *Employment Law: An Adviser's Handbook* by Tamara Lewis (Legal Action Group)
- *Employment Tribunal Claims* by Naomi Cunningham and Michael Reed (Legal Action Group)

# 61 Government addresses

| | | |
|---|---|---|
| 1 | Introduction | 327 |
| 2 | Central offices for benefits, pensions and tax credit enquiries | 327 |
| 3 | Upper Tribunal (Administrative Appeals) | 327 |
| 4 | Government departments | 327 |

## 1. Introduction
This chapter provides contact details for central offices that administer various benefits and tax credits. It also provides contact details for the three national offices of the Upper Tribunal (Administrative Appeals) and the three key government departments.

## 2. Central offices for benefits, pensions and tax credit enquiries
### Attendance Allowance Unit
Mail Handling Site A, Wolverhampton WV98 2AD (Helpline 0800 731 0122; textphone 0800 731 0317 – Mon-Fri, 8am-6pm)

### Carer's Allowance Unit
Mail Handling Site A, Wolverhampton WV98 2AB (0800 731 0297; textphone 0800 731 0317 – Mon-Thurs 8.30am-5pm, Fri 8.30am-4.30pm)

### Child Benefit Office
PO Box 1, Newcastle upon Tyne NE88 1AA (0300 200 3100; textphone 0300 200 3103 – Mon-Fri 8am-8pm, Sat 8am-4pm)

### Disability Living Allowance
**If you are aged under 16** – Disability Benefit Centre 4, Post Handling Site B, Wolverhampton WV99 1BY (0800 121 4600; textphone 0800 121 4523 – Mon-Fri 8am-6pm)
**If you are aged 16 or over (and were born after 8.4.48)** – (0800 121 4600; textphone 0800 121 4523 – Mon-Fri 8am-6pm)
**If you were born on or before 8.4.48** – Disability Living Allowance DLA65+, Mail Handling Site A, Wolverhampton WV98 2AH (0800 731 0122; textphone 0800 731 0317 – Mon-Fri 8am-6pm)

### Future Pension Centre
The Pension Service 9, Mail Handling Site A, Wolverhampton WV98 1LU (0800 731 0175; textphone 0800 731 0176)

### HM Revenue & Customs
Tax Credit Office, Preston PR1 4AT (0345 300 3900; textphone 0345 300 3909 – Mon-Fri 8am-8pm, Sat 8am-4pm, Sun 9am-5pm)

### International Pension Centre
The Pension Service 11, Mail Handling Site A, Wolverhampton WV98 1LW (state pension enquiries: 0191 218 7777; textphone 0191 218 7280 – Mon-Fri 8am-6pm GMT; enquiries about other benefits, see: www.gov.uk/international-pension-centre)

### Personal Independence Payment
Helpline: 0800 121 4433; textphone 0800 121 4493 – Mon-Fri, 8am-6pm

### Vaccine Damage Payments Unit
Palatine House, Lancaster Road, Preston, Lancashire PR1 1HB (01772 899 944; textphone 0345 604 5312 – Mon-Thurs 8:30am-5pm, Friday 8:30am-4:30pm)

## 3. Upper Tribunal (Administrative Appeals)
### England and Wales
Upper Tribunal (Administrative Appeals Chamber), 5th Floor, 7 Rolls Buildings, Fetter Lane, London EC4A 1NL (020 7071 5662)

### Northern Ireland
Tribunal Hearing Centre, 2nd floor, Royal Courts of Justice, Chichester Street, Belfast BT1 3JF (028 9072 4883)

### Scotland
Upper Tribunal (Administrative Appeals Chamber), George House, 126 George Street, Edinburgh EH2 4HH (0131 271 4310)

## 4. Government departments
### Department for Education
Piccadilly Gate, Store Street, Manchester M1 2WD (0370 000 2288) www.gov.uk/government/organisations/department-for-education

### Department of Health
Richmond House, 79 Whitehall, London SW1A 2NS (020 7210 4850; textphone 020 7451 7965) www.gov.uk/government/organisations/department-of-health

### Department for Transport
Great Minster House, 33 Horseferry Road, London SW1P 4DR (Enquiries 0300 330 3000) www.gov.uk/government/organisations/department-for-transport

# Index

## A

**abroad, benefits payable 300-3**
*see also – person from abroad*
**absence from home**
 carers 60
 housing benefit 177-79
 jobseeker's allowance 100
 universal credit 168
**Access to Work 223-25**
**accidents at work** – *see Industrial Injuries*
 *scheme*
**action plan 73**
**actively seeking work 101**
**adaptations**
 housing benefit 179
 housing grants 205-9
**additional components 69, 77, 133**
**additional state pension 271**
**adoption leave 255**
**advance payments** – *see short-term*
 *advances*
**age**
 addition with incapacity benefit 81
 state pension age 268
**agent** – *see appointees*
**alcohol problems 49**
**alternative claims 309**
**alternative housing 208-9**
**amounts, universal credit 122-26**
**appeals 313, 317-23**
 access to hearing 321
 Armed Forces Compensation scheme
  284-85
 domiciliary hearing 321
 housing benefit 186-87
 Industrial Injuries scheme 279
 late appeal 318
 limited capability for work 94-96
 – deterioration pending appeal 96
 – tactics 95
 limited capability for work-related activity
  96
 medical evidence 319-20
 medical examination 322
 no appeal rights 317-18
 postponing 321
 recovery of benefits from compensation
  288-89
 setting aside 322-23
 social care 241
 special needs 321
 statement of reasons 322, 323
 striking out 318-19
 suspending payment 323
 tax credits 161
 time limits 318
 tribunal decision 322-23
 tribunal members 321
 – and exempt work 219
 universal credit 120

 Upper Tribunal 323
 withdrawing 318
**applicable amounts**
 housing benefit 189-90, 190
 income support 137
 income-based jobseeker's allowance 139
 income-related employment and support
  allowance 133
**appointees 45, 55, 310**
**apprenticeships 225**
**Armed Forces Compensation scheme**
**281-85**
 appeals 284-85
 bereavement grant 283-84
 claims 284
 guaranteed income payment 282
 lump-sum payments 282
 other benefits 284
 survivor's guaranteed income payment
  283
**armed forces independence payment**
**285**
**arrears of benefit**
 carer's allowance 141
 ignored as capital 131, 151, 266
 *see also – backdating*
**artificial aids 19, 35-36, 89-90**
**asbestos-related diseases 275, 277**
**assessment periods 121**
**assessment phase 69**
**assistance dogs 14, 40**
**asthma, occupational 275-76**
**asylum support 300**
**attendance allowance 46-55**
 abroad 300
 age limits 46
 appeals 317-23
 assessment 53-54
 attention 49-50, 51
 – bodily function 49
 – frequent 50
 – night attention 50
 – overlap with supervision 51
 – prolonged 50
 – reasonably required 50
 – repeated 50
 – simpler methods 51
 care and support services 244
 care homes 47-48, 247, 250-51
 claims 51-54
 – backdating 54
 – completing the claim-form 52-53
 – date of claim 51-52
 – linked 46
 – terminal illness 46
 dialysis 46, 51
 diary 52-53, 54
 domestic duties 49-50
 falls 50-51
 habitual residence test 297-98
 hospital 47, 48, 51, 305-6, 307

 ignored as income for benefits 146
 immigration control, subject to 295-96
 other benefits 46-47
 payment 55
 – at daily rate 307
 prison 47
 qualifying conditions 46
 qualifying period 46
 rates 46
 reconsiderations 54-55
 residence and presence tests 296-300
 respite care 48
 supervision 50-51
 tax 46
 terminal illness 34-35, 46
 watching over 51
**autistic 20**
**available for work**
 jobseeker's allowance 99-101
 universal credit 114

## B

**backdating**
 change of circumstances 315-17
 claims 308-10, 310
 on receipt of a qualifying benefit
  160-61, 309, 315, 316
 revisions 316-17
 supersessions 315
 universal credit 108
**bedroom tax 180-81**
**benefit cap 222**
 earnings exemption theshold 125
 universal credit 125-26
**benefit penalty** – *see sanctions*
**benefit week 58-59, 184**
**benefit year 76**
**benefits checklist 4-5**
*see also – under name of benefit*
**bereavement allowance 291**
**bereavement payment 291**
**bereavement support payment 290-91**
**blind**
 attendance allowance 49
 Blue Badge scheme 56
 child tax credit, child element, disabled
  child rate 156
 communication support 223, 224
 disability living allowance 18
 disability premium 140
 disabled child premium 143
 disablement percentage assessments
  278
 income support eligibility 135
 limited capability for work assessment
  85, 91
 non-dependant deduction 188
 severe disability premium 141
 sight tests 293

tax allowance 226
working tax credit, disabled worker
  element 159
**Blue Badge scheme 55-57**
**boarders 59, 129, 149, 265**
**budgeting advances 210**
**budgeting loans 209-10**
**bursaries for students 212-14, 215-17,
216, 217**
**byssinosis 275, 279**

# C

**Capita 10, 35, 44, 325**
**capital or savings**
assumed income 130
budgeting loans 209
capital limits for benefit 129-30, 150-51
care homes
  – income support 251
  – local authority funding and charging
    242, 244-45, 246-47, 248-49
  – pension credit 253
  – universal credit 252
child tax credit 159
dependent child 130, 150
deprivation of capital 131, 153-54, 247,
  249
diminishing capital 153-54
housing benefit 189, 190
income support 134, 150-54
income-based jobseeker's allowance
  138, 150-54
income-related employment and support
  allowance 132, 150-54
jointly owned 130, 151, 246, 248, 266
notional capital 131, 153-54, 247, 249,
  266
pension credit 265-66
saving benefit payments 146
tariff income 151, 265
trust fund 131, 151-52, 266
universal credit 106, 129-31
working tax credit 159
**care and support 229-53**
care and support plan 232
care homes 235-41, 244-53
  – direct payments 234
charging
  – care homes 241-43, 244-49
  – disability-related expenditure 244
  – non-residential services 243-44
complaints 241, 243
continuity of care 237
cross-border placements 240-41
direct payments 233-35
health or social care 229
help with the cost of care 232-35
intermediate care 230-31
needs assessments 231-32
personal budgets 232-33
services 229-41
**care component** – *see disability living
  allowance care component*
**care homes**
benefit entitlement 18, 33-35, 47-48,
  250-53
benefits and charges 245, 247
charging assessment 241-43, 244-49
choice of home 235-37, 239
complaints 239, 240, 241
contracts 235, 239

couples and maintenance 243, 245, 252
couples in care homes 251-52, 252, 253
cross-border placements 240-41
deferred payment agreements 248-49
help with fees 235, 238, 244-49
hospices 18, 33, 47, 244
hospital 35, 48, 307
local authority needs assessment 231-32
personal expenses allowance 245-48
preferred accommodation 235, 239
respite/temporary care 48, 246, 249,
  251-52, 252-53, 253
top-up payments 237, 239
treatment of former home 130, 246,
  248
trial period in a care home 179, 246
types of care home 235
**Care Quality Commission 235**
**care services** – *see care and support*
**Career Development Loans 214, 216,
217**
**careers 217**
**carer amount, universal credit 123-24**
**carer premium 143**
over pension credit qualifying age 262
**carers**
absence from home 60
after a death 58, 63
contribution credits 63, 78
help from social care 231
home responsibilities protection 270
hospital 61-62, 306
income support 62
  – carer premium 143
  – eligibility 135
  – remunerative work 136
jobseeker's allowance 62
limited capability for work 63
universal credit 62-63
*see also* – *carer's allowance*
**carer's allowance 58-62**
abroad 300-1
additional amount for carers, pension
  credit 263
amount 59
backdating 59
benefit cap 58
carer amount, universal credit 123-24
carer premium 143
claims 59
contribution credits 63, 78
earnings 59-60
education 59
employment and support allowance 63
habitual residence test 297-98
hospital 61-62, 306-7
immigration control, subject to 58,
  295-96
income support 61, 62
jobseeker's allowance 62
over state pension age 63
overlapping benefits 61
qualifying benefits 58
qualifying conditions 58-59
residence and presence tests 296-300
severe disability premium 58, 141
state pension 61
tax 58
time off from caring 61
universal credit 61, 62-63
**carer's credit 63, 78, 271**
**cars 55-57**
**case law 319, 320**

**change of circumstances 315-17, 316,
320-21**
housing benefit 184
tax credits 162
universal credit 109
**charging**
for care homes 241-43, 244-49
for non-residential services 241-43, 242,
  243-44
for services under the Mental Health Act
  243, 245
**charitable payments 129, 147**
**chemotherapy 83, 87**
**child amount, universal credit 122**
**child benefit 259-61**
abroad 303
extension period 260
immigration control, subject to 295-96
in hospital 306
qualifying young person 259-60
residence and presence tests 296-300
**child elements, child tax credit 155-56**
**child support 147-48, 259**
**child tax credit 154-56, 159-64**
abroad 302-3
age limit 154
appeals 161, 313, 317-23
backdating 160-61
'better off', 154
calculation 161-64
change of circumstances 162
claims 160-61
  – joint claims 155, 156
  – renewal claims 161
complaints 161
elements 155-56
  – rates 162
habitual residence test 297-98
hospital 304
immigration control, subject to 295-96
income 159-60
mandatory reconsiderations 161
overpayments 164
payment 161
penalties 161
qualifying conditions 154-55
residence and presence tests 296-300
underpayments 164
**childcare costs**
carer's allowance 60
housing benefit earnings disregard
  145-46
universal credit 124
working tax credit 157-58
**childcare costs amount, universal
credit 124**
**childcare, free 257**
**children 256-59**
*see also* – *young people*
**chronic obstructive pulmonary
disease, miners 273**
**civil penalties 312**
**claimant commitment 101-2, 110**
**claims 307-10**
alternative 309
backdating 108, 308-10, 310
couples, changing claimants 137-38
couples, joint claim
  – child tax credit 155
  – jobseeker's allowance 97-98
  – universal credit 106-7
  – working tax credit 156
date of claim 108, 307-8

defective 108, 307
delays in payment 325
late claims 108, 308-10
national insurance number 307
work-focused interviews 308
*see also – under name of benefit*
**close relative**
claimant in a care home 248
housing benefit 178
severe disability premium 142
social fund funeral payment 203-4
**clothing**
budgeting loans 209
help from the Family Fund 259
school clothing grant 258
**cold weather payments 204**
**Commissioners' decisions 320**
*see also – appeals*
**Community Care and Health
(Scotland) Act (2002) 239**
**community care, Northern Ireland 240**
**compensation**
Armed Forces Compensation scheme
281-85
criminal injuries compensation 285-87
delays in benefit payment 325
industrial injury 275
maladministration 325
recovery of benefit from compensation
288-89
**complaints 241, 324-26**
**congestion charging exemption 57**
**constant attendance allowance 140,
280, 283**
abroad 303
in hospital 306
**continuing healthcare, NHS, 236, 238**
**continuity of care 237**
**contribution-based jobseeker's
allowance 97, 104-5**
contribution conditions 104-5
*see also – jobseeker's allowance*
**contributions** – *see national insurance*
**contributory benefits 10**
**contributory employment and support
allowance 68, 75-77**
abroad 301
contribution conditions 76-77
contribution credits 76, 78-79
councillors 77
education, full-time 217-18, 261
employer-paid benefits 77
hospital 77, 306
immigration control, subject to 295-96
linking rule 76
occupational and personal pensions 77
period of limited capability for work 76
prison 77
qualifying conditions 75
rates 69, 77
residence and presence tests 296-300
students 217
tax 75
time limits 75
**cooking test 28-29**
**council tax 198-202**
appeals 198, 201
Disability Reduction scheme 200-201
discount scheme 201
exempt dwellings 198
liability 198-99
reduction scheme 201-2
second adult rebate 201

second homes 201
severe mental impairment 200
**councillors 77, 218**
**couple 97-98, 106-7, 132, 133, 137-38,
155, 243, 245, 251-52, 252, 253**
**credits, national insurance
contribution 63, 76, 78-79**
**criminal injuries compensation 285-87**
**cross-border placements, care and
support 240-41**

**D**

**date of claim 307-8**
**deaf**
and blind 18-19
attendance allowance 49
disability living allowance 18-19, 20
disablement percentage assessments
278
limited capability for work assessment
85, 91
occupational deafness 275
**death**
bereavement benefits 290-92
carers' benefits 63
child's death 292
criminal injuries compensation 286
funeral expenses 203-4
service widows, widowers and surviving
civil partners 283-84
universal credit 122, 124
**decision maker 11**
**decisions 313**
written statement of reasons 314
**deferred payment agreements 248-49**
**delayed discharges 231**
**delays**
compensation for 25
in claiming 308-10
in payment 325
in qualifying benefit 160-61, 309, 315
personal independence payment 44
**dental treatment 293**
**Department for Work and Pensions
9-10**
**dependants' additions 59, 60, 81,
269-70**
**descriptors** – *see employment and
support allowance*
**dialysis** – *see kidney dialysis*
**direct payments for care 233-35, 238,
240, 250-51**
**disability, definition 9, 11-12**
**disability employment adviser 223**
**disability living allowance 16-30**
abroad 300
adults 28-30
age limits 16
appeals 317-23
appointees 310
assessment 24-25
awards 25
care and support services 244
care component 22-24, 29-30
care homes 18, 247, 250-51
claims 24
– backdating 25
– completing the claim-form 26-27
– date of claim 24
– linked 17
– renewal (from age 65) 29-30

– terminal illness 34-35
diary 24
disability tests 18-19, 22-23
habitual residence test 297-98
hospital 17, 305-6, 307
ignored as income for benefits 17, 128,
146, 160, 265
immigration control, subject to 295-96
mobility component 18-22
other benefits 17
payment 25
payment at daily rate 307
qualifying conditions 16
qualifying periods 17
reconsiderations 25
residence and presence tests 296-300
– presence test for babies 297
students 218
supersessions 314-15
– change of circumstances 315-17
– grounds for supersession 316-17
terminal illness 17, 19, 22, 34-35
*see also – disability living allowance care
component*
*see also – disability living allowance
mobility component*
**disability living allowance care
component**
attention 22
– bodily function 22
– frequent 22
– prolonged 22
– repeated 22
– significant portion 22
care and support services 244
care homes 18, 247, 250-51
cooking test 28-29
development 23, 27
dialysis 24
disability tests 22-23
extra care and supervision needs 23
fits 23, 27
hearing 20, 23, 26
hospital 305
infants 23
learning skills 27
night needs 22, 23, 27
other benefits 257
play 27
rates 17
respite care 48
seeing 22, 23, 26
social skills 27
speech 22, 26
supervision 22, 23
terminal illness 22, 34-35
watching over 23
*see also – disability living allowance*
**disability living allowance mobility
component**
amputations 19
artificial aids 19
behavioural problems 21
coma 19
deaf/blind 18-19
disability tests 18-19
exemption from vehicle tax 17, 57
exertion 18
guidance 21
higher rate 18, 20
hospital 305-6
ignored as income, care and support
244

intermittent abilities 19-20
learning disabilities 20, 21
lower rate 18, 20-22
Motability 56
rates 17
severe discomfort 19
severe mental impairment 20
severe visual impairment 18
supervision 21-22
terminal illness 19, 34-35
virtually unable to walk 19-20, 21
walking test 21, 26
*see also – disability living allowance*
**disability premium 140**
**Disability Reduction scheme 200-1**
**disabled child premium 143**
**disabled facilities grants 205-8**
**disabled students' allowance 213, 216, 217**
**disabled worker element, working tax credit 158**
**disablement benefit, industrial injuries 275-80**
**discount scheme, council tax 201**
**Discretionary Assistance Fund (Wales) 210-11**
**discretionary housing payments 185**
**Discretionary Support Payments 211**
**discrimination, disability** – *see Equality Act (2010)*
**dismissal**
jobseeker's allowance 103
universal credit 117-18
**dispute period 313**

# E

**earnings**
adult dependant limit 59
carer's allowance 59-60
child dependant limit 59
child tax credit 159-60
councillors 77, 218
earnings disregards 145-46, 265
effect on means-tested benefits 126-28, 144-46, 265
jobseeker's allowance 105
pension credit 265
permitted 219
state pension 268, 271
universal credit 126-28
working tax credit 159-60
**education**
contribution credits 79
discrimination 14
education, health and care plans 256-57
full-time education
– child benefit 259-60
– housing benefit 214-15
– income support 136, 214, 261
– income-related employment and support allowance 132, 214, 261
– universal credit 215
grants and loans 212-14, 215-17, 217
part-time education 212, 214
special educational needs 256
**education, health and care plans 256-57**
**education maintenance allowance 213**
**EEA (European Economic Area) 295**
**Eileen Trust 129, 131, 147, 151, 289**
**elements, tax credits 155-56, 157-58**

**employment and support allowance 68-82, 132-34**
abroad 301
appeals 74, 94-96, 317-23
assessment phase 68, 69
claims 70-71
– date of claim 70-71
– health and work conversation 72
– late claims 71
– terminal illness 70
contributory employment and support allowance 68, 75-77
descriptors 83, 84-85, 86, 87, 88-89
disqualification 74-75
hardship payments 74-75
income-related employment and support allowance 68, 132-34
limited capability for work assessment 68, 83-86
limited capability for work-related activity assessment 68, 87, 88-89
linking rule 72
main phase 69
payments 72
presence conditions 70
qualifying conditions 69-70, 75, 132
rates 69, 77, 133-34
residence and presence tests 296-300
sanctions 73-74
support goup 69
terminal illness 70
training 226
waiting days 72
work 70, 132, 218-19
work capability assessment 68-69, 82-97
work-focused interviews 72-73
work-related activity 73
work-related activity group 69
*see also – contributory employment and support allowance*
*see also – income-related employment and support allowance*
**Employment on Trial 103**
**Employment Tribunal 15, 103**
**energy efficiency schemes 208**
**enhanced disability premium 142**
**enhanced pensioner premium 142**
**epilepsy (attendance allowance) 50**
**Equality Act (2010) 11-15**
disability, definition 11-12
discrimination 12
– justification 12
education 14, 15
employment rights 13, 15
enforcement 15
goods and services 13-14, 15
harassment 12
housing 14
prohibited conduct 12
reasonable adjustments 12, 13, 14
transport 13-14, 14-15
victimisation 12
**Equality & Human Rights Commission 13, 15**
**errors of law 316, 322**
**ex-gratia payments 146, 151, 185**
**eyesight tests 293**

# F

**face-to-face assessment 93**
**face-to-face consultation 44**
**family element, child tax credit 155**
**Family Fund 259**
**family premium 143**
**Far East prisoners of war 153, 266, 284**
**fares**
to hospital 292, 303-4
to school 258
to tribunal 321
to work, Access to Work 223
**financial redress for maladministration 325**
**First-tier Tribunal 313**
**fit notes 66, 70, 303**
**flexible support fund 221**
**fluctuating conditions 36**
**foster carers 78-79, 135, 270**
**foster parents 78-79, 111, 112, 113, 119, 122**
**fostering allowances 129, 149**
**fraud 312-13**
**full-time education** – *see education*
**full-time work 218-23**
income support 134-36
income-related employment and support allowance 132
jobseeker's allowance 98, 139
**funded nursing care 236**
**funeral payments 203-4**

# G

**glasses 293**
**good cause for late claim 185**
**graduated retirement benefit 271**
**grants**
housing grants 205-9
student 212-14, 215-17, 217
Sure Start maternity grants 203
**guardian's allowance 261**
**guide dogs 101**

# H

**habitual residence test 297-98**
**hardship payments**
employment and support allowance 74
jobseeker's allowance 103-4
universal credit 119-20
**harmful information 35**
**health and work conversation 70, 72**
**health benefits 292-94**
**healthcare 229-31, 236, 238**
**Healthy Start food and vitamins 294**
**heating costs, help with 204-5, 208**
**higher pensioner premium 142-43**
**HM Revenue & Customs 11, 313**
**home responsibilities protection 270**
**hospices 18, 33, 47**
**hospital 303-7**
after one year (long-term stays) 305, 306
attendance allowance 47, 48, 305-6, 307
children 17, 306
day in hospital 307
disability living allowance 17, 305-6, 307
fares 303-4
linking rule 35, 47, 48

payment at daily rate 307
personal independence payment 33, 35, 305-6, 307
similar institution 303
temporary absence 306-7
universal credit 304-5
**housing benefit 175-90**
abroad 302
absence from home 177-79
appeals 186-87, 317-23
applicable amount 189-90, 190
backdating 185, 308
bedroom tax 179, 180-81
benefit cap 175, 176
calculation 187-90
capital 150-54, 189, 190
care homes 179, 251
change of circumstances 184
childcare costs 145-46
claims 184
– backdating 308
complaints, Ombudsman 187
discretionary housing payments 185
ex-gratia payments 185
extended payments 219
fuel charges 183
habitual residence test 297-98
hospital 178, 179, 303, 304, 305, 306
immigration control, subject to 295-96
income 144-50, 189, 190
joint occupiers 177
local housing allowance 180-82, 185
meal deductions 183
moving home 179
non-dependant deductions 187-89
overpayments 185-86
payments 184-85
personal allowances 189, 190
premiums 139-43, 189-90, 190
rent 177
– eligible rent 179-80
– liability 177
rent officers' determinations 182
rent restrictions 179-83
– exceptions 182-83
– local housing allowance 180-82
– rent officers' determinations 182
renting from a relative 178
residence and presence tests 296-300
revisions 186, 314-15, 316-17
service charges 183
students 214-15, 215, 216
supersessions 314-15, 316-17
two homes 179
underpayments 185
water charges 183
**housing costs, means-tested benefits 196-98**
liability 196
moving house 179, 196
non-dependant deductions 187-89, 196
run-on 219-20
service charges 183, 196
temporary absences 177-79, 196
waiting periods 196-98
**housing costs, universal credit 123, 165-75**
amount for owner-occupiers 123, 174-75
– qualifying period 175
amount for renters 123, 167-74
– cap rent 173
– care homes 167, 169

– core rent 172-73
– excessive payments 174
– joint tenants 172-73, 174
– local housing allowance 173
– non-dependant deductions 171-72
– payment periods 169
– size criteria 169-71, 173
– Tenant Incentive scheme 174
– two homes 172, 173
arrears of payment 166
calculation
– joint tenants 174
– private sector 172
– social rented sector 174
– two homes 172
care homes 251
conditions 165-66
– liability 165-66, 166
– occupation 166
– payment 165
moving home 168
service charges 166, 167, 170, 174, 175
temporary absences 168
two homes 168, 172, 173
**housing for disabled people 208-9**
**housing grants 205-9**
**Human Rights Act (1998) 319**


**I**

**immigration status 295-96**
**improvement grants 205-9**
**incapacity benefit 80-82**
abroad 301
amount 81
contribution credits 78
dependant's additions 81
occupational or personal pension 81
transferred from invalidity benefit 82
work 81, 218-19
*see also – incapacity for work*
**incapacity for work**
contribution credits 78
councillors 218
disability premium 140
income support eligibility 135
permitted work 219
tribunal members 219
voluntary work 222
*see also – incapacity benefit*
*see also – statutory sick pay*
**income**
housing benefit 189, 190
means-tested benefits 144-50
pension credit 264-65
tax credits 159-60
universal credit 128-29
**income support 134-38**
abroad 302
appeals 317-23
applicable amount 137
capital 150-54
care homes 251-52
– local authority charging 247
– payments disregarded as income 149
carer premium 143
carers 135, 136, 141, 143
claims 137-38
– backdating 137, 309-10
– date of claim 307-8
disability premium 140
education, full-time 136

enhanced disability premium 142
habitual residence test 297-98
hospital 303, 304, 305, 306
housing costs 196-98
immigration control, subject to 295-96
income 144-50
maintenance 147-48
passport to other benefits 138
pensioner premium 142-43
personal allowances 137
premiums 137, 139-43
qualifying conditions 134
residence and presence tests 296-300
severe disability premium 141-42
students 135, 136, 214, 215, 216
tax 226
work 134-36
young people 136, 261
**income tax 226-28**
**income-based jobseeker's allowance 138-39**
capital 150-54
care homes 251-52
habitual residence test 297-98
housing costs 196-98
income 144-50
residence and presence tests 296-300
students 215, 216, 217
*see also – jobseeker's allowance*
**income-related employment and support allowance 132-34**
abroad 301
additional component 69, 133
applicable amount 133
capital 150-54
care homes 251-52
– local authority charging 247
carer premium 143
couples 132, 133
education, full-time 132, 214, 261
enhanced disability premium 142
habitual residence test 297-98
hospital 303, 304, 305, 306
housing costs 196-98
immigration control, subject to 295-96
income 144-50
pensioner premium 142-43
personal allowances 133
premiums 133, 139-43
prison 134
qualifying conditions 132
rates 132-34
residence and presence tests 296-300
severe disability premium 141-42
students 132, 214, 215, 216
work 132
**incontinence 37, 38, 85, 89, 91**
**Independent Assessment Services 10, 35, 325**
**indicative budget, care and support 232**
**industrial death benefit 275**
**Industrial Injuries scheme 273-81**
accidents at work 273, 274, 276
aggregating assessments 279, 280
appeals 273, 279, 281
assessment of disablement 276-77, 278-79
backdating 275
claims 275-76
constant attendance allowance 280
deteriorating condition 279-80
disablement benefit 275-80

exceptionally severe disablement
allowance 280
prescribed diseases 273-75, 276-78
reduced earnings allowance 280-81
retirement allowance 281
**intermediate care services 230-31**
**internships, supported 225**
**invalid care allowance** – *see carer's*
*allowance*
**invalidity benefit 82**

**J**

**Jobcentre Plus 10, 223**
**jobseeker's allowance 97-105, 138-39**
abroad 301
actively seeking work 101
aged 16 or 17 years 139
appeals 317-23
available for work 99-101
benefit cap 97
carers 99-100, 105
claimant commitment 101-2
claims 98-99
– backdating 309-10
– date of claim 308
– waiting days 98
contribution-based jobseeker's allowance
104-5
couples 97-98
disability-related restrictions 100
earnings 105
hardship payments 103-4
holidays 101
hospital 304
housing costs 139, 196-98
immigration control, subject to 295-96
income-based jobseeker's allowance
138-39
jobseeker's direction 99
jobseeking period 105
joint-claim couples 97-98
limited capability for work 98
linking rules 105
misconduct 103
occupational or personal pension 105
qualifying conditions 97-98, 104-5,
138-39
rates 105, 139
remunerative work 98
sanctions 102-3
signing on 99
students 217
trial period 103
voluntarily leaving work 103
work-focused interviews 98-99
**jury service 79, 135, 150, 152**

**K**

**kidney dialysis**
attendance allowance 46, 51
disability living allowance
– care component 24
– qualifying period 17
treated as having a limited capability for
work 83

**L**

**late appeals 318**
**late claims 308-10**
**late revisions 314**
**laundry**
attendance allowance 49
Family Fund 259
**learning difficulties**
limited capability for work-related activity
assessment 89
**learning disabilities**
appointees 310
backdating benefit 309
disability living allowance 20
limited capability for work assessment 86
**leaving hospital 306-7**
**Legal Aid 324**
**liable relatives 252**
**limited capability for work assessment**
**83-86**
appeals 94-96
artificial aids 89-90
exceptional circumstances 93-94
mandatory reconsiderations 94
mental, cognitive and intellectual
function descriptors 83, 86, 91-92
physical descriptors 83, 84-85, 88-91
'specific' disease or disablement 83
**limited capability for work-related**
**activity assessment 87, 88-89**
appeals 96
descriptors 88-89
mandatory reconsiderations 94
**linking rules**
attendance allowance 46
disability living allowance 17
employment and support allowance 72,
76, 198, 222-23
hospital 35, 47, 48
housing costs 197-98
jobseeker's allowance 105
limited capability for work 72, 76, 222-23
personal independence payment 32
respite care 48
support for mortgage interest loans 195
work or training beneficiary 198
**living wage, national 221**
**loans for repairs 191**
**loans, budgeting 209-10**
**loans, student 212-14, 215-17, 217**
**local authority, help for disabled**
**people 229-41**
**local authority accommodation** – *see*
*care homes*
**local housing allowance**
housing benefit 180-82, 185
universal credit 173
**local welfare assistance schemes 209**
**lone parent**
child support 259
earnings disregard 145
family premium 143
**lower earnings limit 75, 76**

**M**

**Macfarlane Trusts 129, 131, 147, 151,**
**289**
**maintenance grant 212, 213, 216, 217**
**maintenance payments 147-48, 160,**
**243, 252**

**mandatory reconsiderations 313-14**
attendance allowance 54
disability living allowance 25
personal independence payment 44-45
tax credits 161
time limits 313-14
work capability assessment 94
**maternity 254-55, 256**
**maternity allowance 255, 256**
**maternity grant, Sure Start 203**
**maternity leave 254**
**maximum amount, universal credit**
**122**
**means-tested benefits 10**
**medical evidence**
appeals 319-20
fit note 66, 70
**medical examinations**
appeals 322
attendance allowance 54
complaints 325
disability living allowance 25
industrial injuries disablement benefit
276, 277
personal independence payment 44
work capability assessment 93
**medical treatment**
absent from home 178
going abroad 300, 301, 302, 303
limited capability for work 83
limited capability for work-related activity
87
refusing treatment 50
**mental health**
work capability assessment 83, 86, 91-92
**Mental Health Act (1983) 233, 245**
**milk vouchers 294**
**minimum income floor, universal**
**credit 127-28**
**minimum wage, national 221**
**Ministry of Justice 11**
**mobility checklist 56**
**mobility component** – *see disability*
*living allowance mobility component*
**mortgage interest** – *see support for*
*mortgage interest loans*
**Motability scheme 56**
**Motor Insurers' Bureau 286**

**N**

**national insurance**
benefit year and tax year 76
contribution amounts 75-76
contribution conditions 76-77, 104-5,
268-69
contribution credits 76, 78-79
**national insurance number 307**
**needs assessment, care and support**
**231-32**
**New Enterprise Allowance 222**
**new state pension 269**
**NHS benefits 292-94**
**NHS continuing healthcare 236, 238,**
**250**
**NHS Low Income scheme 293-94**
**NHS-funded nursing care 236**
**non-contributory benefits 10**
**non-contributory state pension 271**
**non-dependants 171-72, 187-89, 195,**
**196**
**non-means-tested benefits 10**

**notional capital 153-54, 249, 266**
universal credit 131
**notional income 150, 265**
pension pots 265
universal credit 129
**Nursery Milk scheme 294**
**nursing care, charging for 236, 238-39, 240**
**nursing homes** – see care homes

## O

**occupational pensions 272**
care homes 247
carer's allowance 59
contribution-based jobseeker's allowance 105
contributory employment and support allowance 77
incapacity benefit 81
means-tested benefits 147
pension credit 265
universal credit 129
**occupational sick pay 65-66, 144**
**Ombudsman 272, 326**
**overlapping benefits 61, 77**
**overpayments of benefits 164, 185-86, 311-12, 315-17**

## P

**parental leave 135, 254**
**parking concessions 55-57**
**partially sighted**
industrial injuries 278
sight tests 293
working tax credit, disabled worker element 159
**partner** – see couple
**part-time student 212, 214**
**part-time work 98, 132, 134-36, 219, 221**
**passport or gateway to other benefits 17, 32, 47, 134, 138, 139, 267**
**paternity leave 255**
**payments, benefit 310**
**pension** – see state pension
**pension credit 263-67**
abroad 302
advance claims 267
appeals 317-23
appropriate mimimum guarantee 263-64
arrears of benefits 266
assessed income period 267
backdating 267
capital 265-66
care homes 253
– local authority charging 247
claims 267
guarantee credit 263-64
habitual residence test 297-98
hospital 303, 304, 305, 306
housing benefit 190
housing costs 196-98, 263
immigration control, subject to 295-96
income 264-65
notional capital 266
notional income 265
passport to other benefits 267
payment 267
qualifying conditions 263

residence and presence tests 296-300
savings credit 264
standard minimum guarantee 263
students 214
trust funds 265, 266
**Pension Service, the 10**
**pensioner premium 142-43**
**Pensions Advisory Service 272**
**Pensions Ombudsman 272**
**Pensions Regulator 272**
**period of incapacity for work (statutory sick pay) 64**
**period of limited capability for work 76**
**permitted work 219**
**person from abroad 295-300**
**personal allowances 133, 137, 139, 189**
**personal budget, care and support 232-33**
**personal care, free 238-39, 242**
**personal expenses allowance 245-48**
**personal health budget 236**
**personal independence payment 30-46**
abroad 300
age limits 30-32
aids or appliances 35-36
appeals 317-23
appointees 45, 310
assessment, the PIP 35-41, 44
assistance 35
care and support services 244
care homes 33-35, 247, 250-51
claims 41-44
– completing the form 42-43
– date of claim 41
– linked 32
– terminal illness 32, 34-35
daily living activities 36-39
daily living component 36
decisions 44-45
diary 41-44
earnings 33
face-to-face consultation 44
fluctuating conditions 36
habitual residence test 297-98
hospital 33, 305-6, 307
ignored as income for benefits 146
immigration control, subject to 295-96
mandatory reconsiderations 44-45
mobility activities 40-41
mobility component 40
other benefits 32, 33
payment 45
– at daily rate 307
prison 33
prompting 35
qualifying conditions 30
qualifying period 32
rates 32-33
repeatedly 36
required period condition 32
residence and presence tests 296-300
respite care 48
reviews 45
students 218
supersessions 314-15
– change of circumstances 45, 315-17
– grounds for supersession 316-17
supervision 35
tax 30
terminal illness 32, 34-35
**personal injury**
common law compensation (industrial

injuries) 275
**compensation recovery 288-89**
criminal injuries compensation 285-87
traffic accidents 286
trust funds 129, 131, 147, 151, 265, 266
**personal pensions 59, 77, 81, 105, 147, 247, 272**
see also – occupational pensions
**personal tax accounts 228**
**PIN, forgotten 310**
**plasmapheresis 83**
**pneumoconiosis 118, 275, 279**
**preferred accommodation 235**
**pregnancy 254-55, 256**
babies and benefits 256-57
employment and support allowance 83, 84, 87
health benefits 254, 292, 293, 294
income support 135
limited capability for work 83, 84, 256
maternity allowance 255, 256
maternity grant, Sure Start 203
statutory maternity pay 254-55, 256
statutory sick pay 64-65, 256
universal credit 107, 112, 119
**premiums 139-43**
**prescribed industrial diseases 273-75, 276-78**
**prescription charges 292-93**
**presence conditions 296-300**
**primary threshold 75**
**prison**
armed forces independence payment 285
attendance allowance 47
contribution credits 79
council tax 199, 200
employment and support allowance 77, 134
housing benefit 188
income support housing costs 135
jobseeker's allowance 99, 101
personal independence payment 33
statutory sick pay 65
universal credit 109, 113
**public funds 296**
**public transport concessions 56**

## Q

**qualifying young person 122, 155, 259-60**

## R

**radiotherapy 83, 87**
**Railcard 56**
**rapid re-claim 222**
**reconsiderations** – see mandatory reconsiderations
**reduced earnings allowance 280-81**
**refugees 296, 298, 300**
**relative** – see close relative
**remunerative work 98, 132, 134-36, 139, 156-57, 188**
**renal failure** – see kidney dialysis
**renovation grants 205-8**
**rent**
housing benefit 175-90
universal credit 167-74

residence and presence tests 296-300
residential care homes – *see care homes*
resource allocation schemes, care and
  support 232-33
respite care 48, 61, 234
retirement
  deferring retirement 271
  state pension age 268
retirement allowance 281
retirement pension – *see state pension*
reviews (budgeting loans) 209-10
revisions
  'any grounds' 313
  'any time' 314-15
  appealing a revised decision 315
  backdating 315-17
  mandatory reconsiderations 313-14
  time limit 314
right to reside 297, 298-300
  worker status 298
road tax exemption – *see vehicle tax,*
  *exemption from*

## S

sanctions
  employment and support allowance
    73-74
  jobseeker's allowance 102-3
  universal credit 114-19
savings – *see capital or savings*
school meals 258
Scottish Welfare Fund 211
Secretary of State 11, 313
self top-ups, care homes 237, 239
self-directed support (care services)
  238, 240
self-employment
  earnings 126-28, 144-45
  income tax 228
  national insurance contributions 76
  universal credit 126-28
  working tax credit 156-57, 160
self-funder, care and support 243, 244,
  250
SERPS, 271
service charges
  housing benefit 183
  housing costs 196
  universal credit 166, 167, 170, 174,
    174-75
setting aside decisions 322-23
severe disability element, working tax
  credit 157
severe disability premium 141-42
  care homes 252
severe disablement allowance 81
  abroad 301
  immigration control, subject to 295-96
  over pension age 262
  permitted work 219
  rates 81
  re-assessment 80-82
  volunteers 222
severe mental impairment
  council tax 200
  disability living allowance 20
shared parental leave 254
short-term advances 311
sight tests 293
signing on 99
Skipton Fund 129, 131, 147, 151, 289

social fund, the 203-5
  cold weather payments 204
  funeral payments 203-4
  Sure Start maternity grants 203
  winter fuel payment 204-5
Social Work (Scotland) Act (1968) 239
special educational needs 256-57
specialist employability support 225
stakeholder pension 272
standard allowance, universal credit
  122
state pension 267-72
  abroad 303
  additional state pension 271
  carer's allowance 262
  claims 272
  deferring claims 265, 269, 271
  new state pension 269
  non-contributory state pension 271
  payment 272
  qualifying conditions 268-69
  severe disablement allowance 262
  state pension age 268
  work 268
state pension credit – *see pension*
  *credit*
state second pension 271
statutory adoption pay 255-56
statutory maternity leave – *see*
  *maternity leave*
statutory maternity pay 254-55, 256
statutory paternity leave – *see*
  *paternity leave*
statutory paternity pay 255
statutory shared parental leave – *see*
  *shared parental leave*
statutory shared parental pay 255
statutory sick pay 64-67
  abroad 65, 303
  appeals 66
  evidence of sickness 66
  hospital 66
  period of entitlement 64-65
  period of incapacity for work 64
  pregnancy 64, 256
  qualifying conditions 64
  qualifying days 65
  rate 65
  *see also – employment and support*
    *allowance*
strikers
  contribution credits 78
  income support 135, 136
  statutory sick pay 65
  universal credit 116, 117, 126
students 212-18
  benefits 214-18
  Career Development Loans 214, 216,
    217
  disabled students' allowance 213, 216,
    217
  equipment 213
  grants and loans 212-14, 215-17, 217
  hardship funds 213, 216
  part-time study 212, 214
  postgraduate 213, 216, 217
supersessions 314-15, 316-17
  appeal rights 315
  backdating 315-17
  change of circumstances 315-17
  grounds for 316-17
  revise or supersede 314
supplementary grants (students) 212-13

supplementary payments (Northern
  Ireland) 31, 58
support for mortgage interest loans
  190-96
  alternative finance payments 191
  appointees 193
  calculation 193-94
  – alternative finance payments 194
  – loan interest payments 194
  ceiling 194
  – adaptations 194
  interest on loan payments 195
  legacy benefits 190
  legal charge 193
  – jointly-owned property 193
  liability 192
  loan conditions 193
  loan interest payments 191
  loans for repairs 191
  non-dependant deductions 195
  occupying accommodation 192-93
  – full-time study 193
  – moving home 193
  owner-occupier payments 191
  power of attorney 191, 193
  qualifying period 195
  – linking rule 195
  repayment 196
  replacement loans 192
  run-on 219-20
  standard rate 194-95
  starting work 195, 219-20
support group 69
support plan, carers 232

## T

tax 226-28
tax credits 154-64
Tenant Incentive schemes 174, 177
terminal illness
  attendance allowance 34-35, 46
  disability living allowance 17, 19, 34-35
  disability premium 140
  employment and support allowance 70,
    83, 87
  personal independence payment 32,
    34-35
  universal credit 123
test cases 310, 315, 317
third-party top ups, care homes 237,
  239
time limits
  appeals 318
  mandatory reconsiderations 313-14
  revisions 314
Time to Train 225
trade dispute – *see strikers*
traffic accidents 286
traineeships 225
training credits 79
training schemes 148, 152, 225
transport schemes 56
*see also – fares*
tribunals – *see appeals*
trust funds
  means-tested benefits 147, 151-52
  pension credit 265, 266
  universal credit 129, 131
  vaccine damage payments 288

## U

**unemployability supplement 283**
**universal credit 62-63, 106-31, 165-75**
abroad 301-2
advance payments 109, 311
aged 16-17, 107, 261
amounts 122-26
appeals 120, 317-23
assessment periods 121
benefit cap 125-26
calculation 121-26
capital 129-31
– limits 129-30
– notional capital 131
care homes 109, 252-53
– local authority charging 247
carer amount 123-24
carers 111, 112, 114, 118, 123-24
change of circumstances 109, 315-17
child amounts 122
childcare costs amount 124
claimant commitment 110
claims 107-8
– backdating 108, 315-17
– date of claim 108
– interviews 108
– joint claims 106
– late claims 108
decisions 108
earnings 126-28
– benefit cap 125
– change of circumstances 109
– minimum income floor 127-28
– notional 128
– self-employed 126-28
– threshold 112
education, full-time 215, 217
habitual residence test 297-98
hardship payments 119-20
hospital 109, 303, 304-5
housing costs amount 123, 165-75, 251
– amount for owner-occupiers 123, 174-75
– amount for renters 123, 167-74
immigration control, subject to 295-96
income 128-29
– notional 129
– student 217
interviews 110-11
mandatory reconsiderations 120, 313-14
maximum amount 122
passport to other benefits 106
payment 108-9
prisoners 109
qualifying conditions 106
qualifying young person 122
rates 121
residence and presence tests 296-300
sanctions 114-19
– good reason 118
– higher-level 116-17
– lowest-level 115
– low-level 115-16
– medium-level 116
– misconduct 117-18
– reduction period 116, 117
– sanction calculation 118-19
– sanction period 115
– voluntary redundancy 117
standard allowance 122
students 215, 216, 217

taper 121
volunteering 111, 114
work
– childcare costs 124
– earnings 126-28
– paid 111
– trial period 117
work allowance 124-25
work capability amount 123, 220-22
– limited capability for work 83-85
– limited capability for work-related
activity 87, 123
– waiting periods 123
work capability assessment 82-97
work-related requirements 110-14
– caring responsibilities 111, 112, 114
– childcare responsibilities 111, 114
– disability 111, 112, 113
– domestic violence 113
– work availability requirement 114
– work preparation requirement 111
– work search requirement 111-14
– work-focused interview requirement
110-11
**Upper Tribunal 323**
decisions 320

## V

**vaccine damage payments 287-88**
**variant Creutzfeldt-Jakob disease 131,
151, 289**
**vehicle tax, exemption from 57**
**Veterans UK Helpline 284**
**vitamins 294**
**voluntary work, effect on benefits
111, 114, 136, 149, 150, 222**
**vouchers for glasses 293**

## W

**War Pensions scheme 282**
**water charges 183**
**welfare supplementary payments
(Northern Ireland) 157**
**widowed mother's allowance 291**
**widowed parent's allowance 291**
**widows, widowers and surviving civil
partners 290-92**
abroad 303
carer's allowance 63
contribution credits 79
funeral expenses 203-4
**winter fuel payment 204-5**
**work 218-23**
**work allowance, universal credit
124-25**
**Work and Health Programme 223**
**work capability amount, universal
credit 123, 220-22**
**work capability assessment 82-97**
appeals 94-96, 317-23
exceptional circumstances 93-94
face-to-face assessment 93
limited capability for work assessment
83-86
limited capability for work-related activity
assessment 87, 88-89
mandatory reconsiderations 94
questionnaire 88-93

re-assessments 96-97
**work coach 72, 110, 223, 308**
**work or training beneficiary 198**
**work search interview 108, 110**
**work search reviews 111**
**work trial 221**
**work-based learning 225**
**work-focused interviews 72-73, 98-99,
110-11, 308**
**work-related activity group 69**
**work-related requirements, universal
credit 110-14**
**working tax credit 156-64**
abroad 302-3
age limit 156
appeals 161, 313, 317-23
backdating 160-61
'better off' 154
calculation 161-64
change of circumstances 162
childcare element 157-58
claims 160-61
– renewal claims 161
complaints 161
disabled worker element 158
elements 157-58
– rates 162
habitual residence test 297-98
hospital 304
immigration control, subject to 295-96
income 159-60
mandatory reconsiderations 161
maternity leave 157
off sick 157
overpayments 164
payment 161
penalties 161
qualifying benefits, disabled worker
element 158
qualifying conditions 156
remunerative work 156-57
residence and presence tests 296-300
severe disability element 157
test, disability 159
underpayments 164

## Y

**young people 261**
education grants 212-14
employment and support allowance 132,
261
income support 136, 261
jobseeker's allowance 139
personal independence payment 261
universal credit 107, 261
**Youth Obligation 223**